TENTH EDITION

Elementary and Middle School Mathematics

Teaching Developmentally

John A. Van de Walle
Late of Virginia Commonwealth University

Karen S. Karp
Johns Hopkins University

Jennifer M. Bay-Williams
University of Louisville

With contributions by
Jonathan Wray
Howard County Public Schools

Elizabeth Todd Brown
University of Louisville (Emeritus)

 Pearson

330 Hudson Street, NY NY 10013

Vice President and Editor in Chief: Kevin M. Davis
Portfolio Manager: Drew Bennett
Managing Content Producer: Megan Moffo
Content Producer: Yagnesh Jani
Portfolio Management Assistant: Maria Feliberty
Executive Product Marketing Manager: Christopher Barry
Executive Field Marketing Manager: Krista Clark
Development Editor: Kim Norbuta
Digital Studio Producer: Lauren Carlson
Senior Digital Producer: Allison Longley
Procurement Specialist: Deidra Smith
Cover Designer: Studio Montage
Cover Art: shutterstock.com/Petr Vaclavek
Editorial Production and Composition Services: SPi-Global
Full-Service and Editorial Project Manager: Jason Hammond/Kelly Murphy, SPi-Global
Text Font: Janson Text LT Pro 9.75/12

Credits and acknowledgments for materials borrowed from other sources and reproduced, with permission, in this textbook appear on the appropriate page within the text or on page 697.

Every effort has been made to provide accurate and current Internet information in this book. However, the Internet and information posted on it are constantly changing, so it is inevitable that some of the Internet addresses listed in this textbook will change.

Library of Congress Cataloging-in-Publication Data

Names: Van de Walle, John A. | Karp, Karen, 1951- author. | Bay-Williams,
    Jennifer M., author. | Wray, Jonathan A., author.
Title: Elementary and middle school mathematics : teaching developmentally.
Description: Tenth edition / John A. Van de Walle, late of Virginia
    Commonwealth University, Karen S. Karp, University of Louisville, Jennifer M.
    Bay-Williams, University of Louisville ; with contributions by Jonathan
    Wray, Howard County Public Schools. | Boston : Pearson, [2019] | Includes
    bibliographical references and index.
Identifiers: LCCN 2017037185 | ISBN 9780134802084
Subjects: LCSH: Mathematics--Study and teaching (Elementary) |
    Mathematics--Study and teaching (Middle school)
Classification: LCC QA135.6 .V36 2019 | DDC 510.71/2--dc23
LC record available at https://lccn.loc.gov/2017037185

10 9 8 7 6 5 4 3 2 1

ISBN 10: 0-13-480208-X
ISBN 13: 978-0-13-480208-4

John A. Van de Walle

The late John A. Van de Walle was a professor emeritus at Virginia Commonw
He was a leader in mathematics education who regularly gave professional developme
shops for K–8 teachers in the United States and Canada focused on mathematics instructio
that engaged students in mathematical reasoning and problem solving. He visited and taught
in many classrooms and worked with teachers to implement student-centered mathematics
lessons. He co-authored the *Scott Foresman-Addison Wesley Mathematics K–6* series and contributed to the original Pearson School mathematics program *enVisionMATH*. Additionally,
John was very active in the National Council of Teachers of Mathematics (NCTM), writing
book chapters and journal articles, serving on the board of directors, chairing the educational
materials committee, and speaking at national and regional meetings.

Karen S. Karp

Karen S. Karp is a visiting professor at Johns Hopkins University (Maryland). Previously, she
was a professor of mathematics education at the University of Louisville for more than twenty
years. Prior to entering the field of teacher education, she was an elementary school teacher in
New York. She is the coauthor of *Developing Essential Understanding of Addition and Subtraction
for Teaching Mathematics in PreK–Grade 2, Discovering Lessons for the Common Core State Standards
in Grades K–5* and *Putting Essential Understanding of Addition and Subtraction into Practice
PreK–Grade 2*. She is a former member of the board of directors for the National Council of
Teachers of Mathematics (NCTM) and a former president of the Association of Mathematics
Teacher Educators. She continues to work in classrooms to support teachers in ways to instruct
students with disabilities.

Jennifer M. Bay-Williams

Dr. Jennifer Bay-Williams is a professor at the University of Louisville. She has written many
articles and books around K–12 mathematics education, including the three book series related
to this book—*Teaching Student Centered Mathematics*—and various other books, including
*Everything You Need for Mathematics Coaching, Developing Essential Understanding of Addition and
Subtraction in Prekindergarten–Grade 2, On the Money* (financial literacy book series), and *Math
and Literature: Grades 6–8*. Jennifer taught elementary, middle, and high school in Missouri
and in Peru, and continues to learn and work in K–8 classrooms in rural and urban settings.
Jennifer has been a member of the NCTM board of directors, AMTE secretary, president,
and lead writer for *Standards for the Preparation of Teachers of Mathematics* (AMTE, 2017), and
is currently on the TODOS: Mathematics for All Board of Directors.

Jonathan Wray is the technology contributor to *Elementary and Middle School Mathematics, Teaching Developmentally* (sixth–tenth editions). He is the acting coordinator of secondary mathematics curricular programs in the Howard County public school system. He has served as the president of the Association of Maryland Mathematics Teacher Educators (AMMTE) and the Maryland Council of Teachers of Mathematics (MCTM) and currently is manager of the Elementary Mathematics Specialists and Teacher Leaders (ems&tl) Project. Jon also served on the NCTM Board of Directors (2012–2015). He has been recognized for his expertise in infusing technology in mathematics teaching and was named an outstanding technology leader in education by the Maryland Society for Educational Technology (MSET). He was a primary and intermediate grades classroom teacher, gifted and talented resource teacher, elementary mathematics specialist, curriculum and assessment developer, grant project manager, and educational consultant.

Elizabeth Todd Brown is the assessment and media contributor to *Elementary and Middle School Mathematics, Teaching Developmentally* (tenth edition). She is a professor emeritus from the University of Louisville. She was also an elementary and middle school teacher in Iowa, Missouri, and Kentucky and continues to volunteer weekly at a local elementary school in Louisville. Todd coauthored the book, *Feisty Females*, and has written articles on the importance of early mathematics learning. She served as president of the local NCTM affiliate Greater Louisville Council of the Teachers of Mathematics and was the chair of the volunteers for the NCTM Regional in Louisville in 1998 and 2013. Todd was the 1998 Kentucky Presidential Awardee for Excellence in Teaching Mathematics and Science.

Brief Contents

Contents

PART I   Teaching Mathematics: Foundations and Perspectives

The fundamental core of effective teaching of mathematics combines an understanding of how students learn, how to promote that learning by teaching through problem solving, and how to plan for and assess that learning daily. That is the focus of these first six chapters, providing discussion, examples, and activities that develop the core ideas of learning, teaching, planning, and assessment for each and every student.

PART II   Teaching Student-Centered Mathematics

Each of these chapters *applies* the core ideas of Part I to the content taught in K–8 mathematics. Clear discussions are provided for how to teach the topic, what a learning progression for that topic might be, and what worthwhile tasks look like. Hundreds of problem-based, engaging tasks and activities are provided to show how the concepts can be developed with students. These chapters are designed to help you develop pedagogical strategies now, and serve as a resource and reference for your teaching now and in the future.

CHAPTER 19
**Developing Geometric Thinking
and Geometric Concepts   500**

CHAPTER 20
Developing Concepts of Data and Statistics   543

Preface

All students can learn mathematics with understanding. It is through the teacher's actions that every student can have this experience. We believe that teachers must create a classroom environment in which students are given opportunities to solve problems and work together, using their ideas and strategies, to solve them. Effective mathematics instruction involves posing tasks that engage students in the mathematics they are expected to learn. Then, by allowing students to interact with and productively struggle with *their own mathematical ideas* and *their own strategies*, they will learn to see the connections among mathematical topics and the real world. Students value mathematics and feel empowered to use it.

Creating a classroom in which students design solution pathways, engage in productive struggle, and connect one mathematical idea to another, is complex. Questions arise, such as, "How do I get students to wrestle with problems if they just want me to show them how to do it? What kinds of tasks lend themselves to this type of engagement? Where can I learn the mathematics content I need to be able to teach in this way?" With these and other questions firmly in mind, we have several objectives in the tenth edition of this textbook:

1. Illustrate what it means to teach mathematics using a problem-based approach.
2. Serve as a go-to reference for all of the mathematics content suggested for grades preK–8 as recommended in the Common Core State Standards (NGA Center & CCSSO, 2010) and in standards used in other states, and for the research-based strategies that illustrate how students best learn this content.
3. Present a practical resource of robust, problem-based activities and tasks that can engage students in the use of significant mathematical concepts and skills.
4. Focus attention on student thinking, including the ways students might reason about numbers, and possible challenges and misconceptions they might have.

We are hopeful that you will find that this book is a valuable resource for teaching and learning mathematics!

New to this Edition

The following are highlights of the most significant changes in the tenth edition.

Common Challenges and Misconceptions

Every chapter in Part II offers at least one table that summarizes common challenges students encounter in learning that topic (Chapter 15, Fraction Operations has three). The table includes the challenge, provides an example of what that might look like in either a sample of student work or a statement, and then offers some brief ideas of what you might do to help. Knowing common student challenges and misconceptions is a critical part of planning and can greatly influence how a lesson is structured and what problems you use. The research from many sources has been merged into these practical references.

Routines

More and more classrooms are using innovative lesson designs and short discussion routines to help students develop number sense, flexibility, and the mathematical practices. In Chapter 4, we have added se new sections on: 3-Act Tasks, Number Talks, and Worked Examples. For example, worked examples are mentioned in some of the tables identifying student challenges, because there is research to suggest that analyzing worked examples is effective in helping students learn.

Mathematical Modeling

Since the ninth edition, there has been significant national dialogue about the importance of mathematical modeling and what this might look like across the grades. The *Guidelines for Assessment & Instruction in Mathematical Modeling Education* (GAIMME) Report (COMAP & SIAM, 2016) provides excellent guidance. Therefore, the section in Chapter 13 on mathematical modeling was completely rewritten to reflect the GAIMME report, as well as to showcase a number of excellent books and articles that have emerged recently.

Infusion of Technology

You may notice that Chapter 7 (Technology) from the previous edition is gone. Readers and reviewers have commented that this chapter is not needed in part because using technology is much more commonly understood and used, and in part because it makes far more sense to talk about technology *as it relates to the mathematics*. We have heard you and we have integrated technology discussions, tools, and ideas throughout the book.

MyLab Education

Digital learning and assessment resources have been expanded significantly via MyLab Education. The following resources have been designed to help you develop the pedagogical knowledge *and* content knowledge needed to be a successful teacher of mathematics:

- **Video examples:** Embedded throughout all chapters, these examples allow you to see key concepts in action through authentic classroom video, as well as clips of children solving math problems. Additional videos feature your authors and other experts introducing and briefly explaining strategies for teaching important topics.
- **Self-checks:** Designed for self-study, these multiple-choice items are tied to each chapter learning outcome, and help you assess how well you have mastered the concepts covered in the reading. These exercises are self-grading and provide a rationale for the correct answer.
- **Application exercises:** Video and scenario-based exercises appear throughout the chapters and provide an opportunity for you to apply what you have learned to real classroom situations. There are also ten exercises on *observing and responding to student thinking* that include video clips of children talking through and solving problems on a whiteboard app; accompanying questions ask you to analyze and child's reasoning, identify any misconceptions, and explain any actions or prompts you might use as the teacher to guide the student's learning. Expert feedback is provided after submitting your response.
- **Math practice:** Located at the end of most content chapters, these sets of questions provide an opportunity to practice or refresh your own mathematics skills through solving exercises associated with the content from that chapter. These questions are also self-grading.
- **Blackline masters, activity pages, and expanded lessons:** These documents are linked throughout each chapter and make it easy for instructors and students to download and print classroom-ready handouts that can be used in a methods class or school settings.

Major Changes to Specific Chapters

Every chapter in the tenth edition has been revised to reflect the most current research, standards, and exemplars. This is evident in the approximately *300 new references* in the tenth edition! This represents our ongoing commitment to synthesize and present the most current evidence of effective mathematics teaching. Here we share changes to what we consider the most significant (and that have not already been mentioned above).

Teaching Mathematics in the 21st Century (Chapter 1)

The new Association of Mathematics Teacher Educators (AMTE) Standards for Preparing Teachers of Mathematics (AMTE, 2017) are described in Chapter 1. We added a section on how to create a whole school agreement with a cohesive mathematics message.

Exploring What It Means to Know and Do Mathematics (Chapter 2)

Chapter 2 was revised in several significant ways, including revisions to the exemplar tasks (one in each content domain) to each have a common format, and to each have a stronger focus on multiple strategies. The discussions on theory were condensed, and making connections between theory and teaching were revised to be more succinct and explicit.

Teaching through Problem Solving (Chapter 3)

The NCTM Teaching Practices (2014) have been integrated into Chapter 3. A completely revamped section, now titled Developing Procedural Fluency, focuses on the importance of connecting conceptual and procedural knowledge, and includes a new list of ways to adapt drill-related tasks to emphasize understanding and connections (Boaler, 2016). Talk moves in the Discourse section have been revised to include eight talk moves (Chapin, O'Conner, & Anderson, 2013).

Teaching through Problem Solving (Chapter 4)

Beyond the new routines section (described above), the families section was heavily revised and the lesson plan steps condensed and formatted for easier readability.

Teaching Mathematics Equitably to All Students (Chapter 6)

We expanded our emphasis on using an asset-based approach, focusing on students' strengths rather than deficits. We emphasize a focus on using students' prior knowledge and experiences to drive instructional decisions. There is also a revamping of the section on gifted and talented students including attention to an excellence gap (students who may be overlooked).

Basic Facts (Chapter 9)

Recent research (e.g., Baroody et al., 2016) has uncovered a new and effective addition reasoning strategy—Use 10, which has been added to this chapter, along with new visuals and insights on teaching subtraction facts effectively.

Developing Strategies for Multiplication and Division (Chapter 12)

In new updates in this chapter, there are expanded examinations of the written records of computing multiplication and division problems including lattice multiplication, open arrays, and partial quotients. There is also a new section of the use of the break apart or decomposition strategy for division. A conversation about the selection of numbers for computational estimation problems is also shared.

Algebraic Thinking, Equations, and Functions (Chapter 13)

In addition to the new section on mathematical modeling, there are several new ideas and strategies for supporting algebraic thinking, including adapting the hundreds chart to explore patterns and options for creating tables with more structure to help students notice relationships.

Developing Fraction Concepts (Chapters 14)

Fraction concepts has an expanded focus on the fundamental ideas of sharing and iterating. This chapter also has been reorganized, has more contexts for comparing fractions, and more attention to student challenges in understanding fractions.

Ratios, Proportions, and Proportional Reasoning (Chapter 17)

The sections on additive and multiplicative reasoning have been significantly revised, including a new discussion on social justice mathematics. Additionally, significantly more literature connections are provided in this chapter and new activities.

Developing Concepts of Data Analysis (Chapter 20)

This chapter had numerous enhancements and changes! In addition to four new figures and completely updated technology options, the discussion of variability is woven throughout the chapter (including more attention to measures that are resistant to outlier), and sections on boxplots, histograms, and bivariate data were expanded and revised (see new subsection on bivariate categorical data).

An Introduction to *Teaching Developmentally*

If you look at the table of contents, you will see that the chapters are separated into two distinct sections. The first section consists of six chapters and covers important ideas that cross the boundaries of specific areas of content. The second section, consisting of 16 chapters, offers teaching suggestions and activities for every major mathematics topic in the preK–8 curriculum. Chapters in Part I offer perspectives on the challenging task of helping students learn mathematics. Having a feel for the discipline of mathematics— that is, to know what it means to "do mathematics"—is critical to learning how to teach mathematics well. In addition, understanding constructivist and sociocultural perspectives on learning mathematics and how they are applied to teaching through problem solving provides a foundation and rationale for how to teach and assess preK–8 students. You will be teaching diverse students including students who are English learners, are gifted, or have disabilities. In this text, you will learn how to apply instructional strategies in ways that support and challenge *all* learners. Formative assessment strategies and strategies for diverse learners are addressed in specific chapters in Part I (Chapters 5, and 6, respectively), and throughout Part II chapters.

Each chapter of Part II focuses on one of the major content areas in preK–8 mathematics curriculum. It begins with identifying the big ideas for that content, and provides guidance on how students best learn that content through many problem-based activities to engage them in understanding mathematics, as well as considering what challenges they may encounter and how you might help them.

Hundreds of tasks and activities are embedded in the text. Take out pencil and paper, or use technology, and try the problems, thinking about how you might solve them *and* how students at the intended grades might solve them. This is one way to actively engage in *your learning* about *students learning* mathematics. In so doing, this book will increase your own understanding of mathematics, the students you teach, and how to teach them effectively.

Some Special Features of This Text

By flipping through the book, you will notice many section headings, a large number of figures, and various special features. All are designed to make the book more useful as a long-term resource. Here are a few things to look for.

CHAPTER

14

Developing Fraction Concepts

LEARNER OUTCOMES

After reading this chapter and engaging in the embedded activities and reflections, you should be able to:

14.1 Describe and give examples for fractions constructs and fraction models.

14.2 Explain foundational concepts of fractional parts, including iteration and partitioning.

14.3 Illustrate the concept of equivalence across fraction models.

14.4 Describe strategies for comparing fractions and ways to teach this topic conceptually.

Fractions are one of the most important topics students need to understand to be successful in algebra and beyond, yet it is an area in which U.S. students, as well as students in many countries, struggle (OECD, 2014). National Assessment of Educational Progress (NAEP) results have consistently shown that students have a weak understanding of fraction concepts (Sowder & Wearne, 2006; Wearne & Kouba, 2000). This lack of understanding is then translated into difficulties with fraction computation, decimal and percent concepts, and algebra (Bailey, Hoard, Nugent, & Geary, 2012; Booth & Newton, 2012; Brown & Quinn, 2007; National Mathematics Advisory Panel, 2008; Siegler, Fazio, Bailey, & Zhou, 2013). Therefore, it is critical that you teach fractions well, present fractions as interesting and important, and commit to helping students understand the meaning of fractions.

BIG IDEAS

♦ Fractions can and should be represented across different interpretations (e.g., part-whole and division) and different models: area (e.g., $\frac{1}{3}$ of a garden), length (e.g., $\frac{3}{4}$ of an inch), and set (e.g., $\frac{1}{2}$ of the marbles).

♦ Fractions are equal shares of a whole or a unit. Therefore, equal sharing activities (e.g., 2 sandwiches shared with 4 friends) build on whole-number knowledge to introduce fractional quantities.

♦ Partitioning and iterating are ways students to understand the meaning of fractions. Partitioning can be thought of as splitting the whole equally (e.g., splitting a whole into fourths), and iterating can be thought of as making a copy of each piece and counting them (e.g., one-fourth, two-fourths, etc.).

♦ Equivalent fractions are ways of describing the same amount by using different-sized fractional parts.

♦ Fractions can be compared by reasoning about the relative size of the fractions. Estimation and reasoning are important in teaching understanding of fractions.

337

◄ **Learning Outcomes**

To help readers know what they should expect to learn, each chapter begins with learning outcomes. Self-checks are numbered to cover and thus align with each learning outcome.

◄ **Big Ideas**

Much of the research and literature espousing a student-centered approach suggests that teachers plan their instruction around big ideas rather than isolated skills or concepts. At the beginning of each chapter in Part II, you will find a list of the big mathematical ideas associated with the chapter. Teachers find these lists helpful to quickly envision the mathematics they are to teach.

Activity 21.9   CCSS-M: 7.G.B.4; 7.SP.C.6; 7.SP.C.7b

Chance of Hitting the Target?

Project a target such as the one illustrated here with concentric circles having radii of 2 inches, 6 inches, 8 inches, and 10 inches, each region shaded a different color. Ask students to determine the fraction and percent of each colored region in the circle.

Ask students to discuss what the probability for landing on the center (assuming all throws land on the circle and are thrown randomly). Ask students to discuss why data may or may not match the percent of the area that is covered (e.g., people with good aim will be able to hit the smaller areas more often). Then, have students propose what point values they would assign to each region. Students may assign values in various ways. For example, they may think the skinny outer circle is harder to land on and give it more points than other sections, even though the area of that region may be more. Allow them time to share their reasoning and to critique others' ways of assigning points.

◄ Activities

The numerous activities found in every chapter of Part II have always been rated by readers as one of the most valuable parts of the book. Some activity ideas are described directly in the text and in the illustrations. Others are presented in the numbered Activity boxes. Every activity is a problem-based task (as described in Chapter 3) and is designed to engage students in doing mathematics.

Adaptations for Students with Special Needs and English Learners ►

Chapter 6 provides detailed background and strategies for how to support students with special needs and English learners (ELs). But, many adaptations are specific to a activity or task. Therefore, Part II chapters offer adaptations and instructions within activities (look for the icon) that can meet the needs of students with special needs and ELs.

Activity 9.2   CCSS-M: 1.OA.A.1; 1.OA.C.6; 2.OA.B.2

How Many Feet in the Bed?

Read *How Many Feet in the Bed?* by Diane Johnston Hamm. On the second time through the book, ask students how many more feet are in the bed when a new person gets in. Ask students to record the equation (e.g., 6 + 2) and tell how many. Two less can be considered as family members get out of the bed. Find opportunities to make the connection between counting on and adding using a number line. For ELs, be sure that they know what the phrases "two more" and "two less" mean (and clarify the meaning of foot, which is also used for measuring). Acting out with students in the classroom can be a great illustration for both ELs and students with disabilities.

ENGLISH LEARNERS

STUDENTS with SPECIAL NEEDS

📄 *FORMATIVE ASSESSMENT* Notes. To assess understanding of division algorithms, call on different students to explain individual steps using the appropriate terminology that connects to the concept of division. Use an Observation Checklist to record students' responses, indicating how well they understand the algorithm. For students who are having difficulty, you may want to conduct a short diagnostic interview to explore their level of understanding in more detail. Begin by having the student complete 115 ÷ 9 and ask them to talk about what they are thinking as they carry out specific steps in the process. If there is difficulty explaining, have the student use base-ten materials to directly model the problem and attempt to link the actions to the procedure. Then ask them to discuss verbally the connections between what was done with the models and what was written symbolically. ■

◄ Formative Assessment Notes

Assessment is an integral process within instruction. Similarly, it makes sense to think about what to be listening for (assessing) as you read about different areas of content development. Throughout the content chapters, there are formative assessment notes with brief descriptions of ways to assess the topic in that section. Reading these assessment notes as you read the text can help you understand how best to assist students who struggle.

Technology Notes ►

Infusing technological tools is important in learning mathematics. We have infused technology notes throughout Part II. A technology icon is used to identify places within the text or activity where a technology idea or resource is discussed. Descriptions include open-source (free) software, applets, and other Web-based resources, as well as ideas for calculator use.

🖱 *TECHNOLOGY* Note. An amazing computer tool for drawing two-dimensional views of block buildings is the Isometric Drawing Tool, available at the NCTM Illuminations website. Using mouse clicks students can draw either whole cubes, faces, or just lines. The drawings, however, are actually "buildings" and can be viewed as three-dimensional objects that when rotated can be seen from any vantage point. Prepared investigations lead students through the features of the tool. ■

Standards for
Mathematical
Practice

MP1. Make sense of
problems and persevere
in solving them.

◀ Standards for Mathematical Practice Margin Notes

Connections to the eight Standards of Mathematical Practice from the *Common Core State Standards* are highlighted in the margins. The location of the note indicates an example of the identified practice in the nearby text.

---

372 **Chapter 14** Developing Fraction Concepts

 RESOURCES FOR CHAPTER 14

LITERATURE CONNECTIONS
The Doorbell Rang
Hutchins (1986)
Often used to investigate whole-number operations of multiplication and division, this book is also an excellent early introduction to fractions. The story is a simple tale of two children preparing to share a plate of 12 cookies. Just as they have figured out how to share the cookies, the doorbell rings and more children arrive. You can change the number of children to create a sharing situation that requires fractions (e.g., 8 children).

The Man Who Counted: A Collection of Mathematical Adventures
Tahan (1993)
This book contains a story, "Beasts of Burden," about a wise mathematician, Beremiz, and the narrator, who are traveling together on one camel. They are asked by three brothers to solve an argument: *Their father has left them 35 camels to divide among them: half to one brother, one-third to another, and one-ninth to the third brother.* The story is an excellent context for fractional parts of sets (and adding fractions). Changing the number of camels to 36 or 34, does not solve the challenge because the sum of $\frac{1}{2}$, $\frac{1}{3}$, and $\frac{1}{9}$ will never be one whole, no matter how many camels are involved. See Bresser (1995) for three days of activities with this book.

Apple Fractions
Pallotta (2002)
This book offers interesting facts about apples while introducing fractions as fair shares (of apples, a healthier option than books that focus on chocolate and cookies!). In addition, the words for fractions are used and connected to fraction symbols, making it a good connection for fractions in grades 1–3.

RECOMMENDED READINGS
Articles
Clarke, D. M., Roche, A., & Mitchell, A. (2008). Ten practical tips for making fractions come alive and make sense. *Mathematics Teaching in the Middle School, 13*(7), 373–380.

Ten excellent tips for teaching fractions are discussed and favorite activities are shared. An excellent overview of teaching fractions.

Lewis, R. M., Gibbons, L. K., Kazemi, E., & Lind T. (2015). Unwrapping students ideas about fractions. *Teaching Children Mathematics, 22*(3), 158–168.

This excellent read provides a how-to for implementing sharing tasks, including sequencing of tasks, questions to pose, and formatives assessment tool to monitor student understanding.

Freeman, D. W., & Jorgensen, T. A. (2015). Moving beyond brownies and pizzas. *Teaching Children Mathematics, 21*(7), 412–420.

This article describes student thinking as they compare fractions. In the more4U pages, they offer excellent sets of tasks with a range of contexts, each set focusing on a different reasoning strategy for comparing fractions.

Books
Lamon, S. (2012). *Teaching fractions and ratios for understanding: Essential content knowledge and instructional strategies.* New York, NY: Taylor & Francis Group.

As the title implies, this book has a wealth of information to help with better understanding fractions and teaching fractions well. Many rich tasks and student work are provided throughout.

McNamara, J., & Shaughnessy, M. M. (2010). *Beyond pizzas and pies: 10 essential strategies for supporting fraction sense (grades 3–5).* Sausalito, CA: Math Solutions Publications.

This book has it all—classroom vignettes, discussion of research on teaching fractions, and many activities, including student work.

Websites
Rational Number Project (http://www.cehd.umn.edu/ci/rationalnumberproject/rnp1-09.html).

This project offers excellent lessons and other materials for teaching fraction concepts effectively.

◀ End of Chapter Resources

The end of each chapter there are *Resources*, which include "Literature Connections" (found in all Part II chapters) and "Recommended Readings."

Literature Connections. Here you will find examples of great children's literature for launching into the mathematics concepts in the chapter just read. For each title suggested, there is a brief description of how the mathematics concepts in the chapter can be connected to the story. These literature-based mathematics activities will help you engage students in interesting contexts for doing mathematics.

Recommended Readings. In this section, you will find an annotated list of articles and books to augment the information found in the chapter. These recommendations include NCTM articles and books, and other professional resources designed for the classroom teacher.

Supplements for Instructors

Qualified college adopters can contact their Pearson sales representatives for information on ordering any of the supplements described below. These instructor supplements are all posted and available for download (click on Educators) from the Pearson Instructor Resource Center at www.pearsonhighered.com/irc. The IRC houses the following:

- **Instructor's resource manual:** The Instructor's Resource Manual for the tenth edition includes a wealth of resources designed to help instructors teach the course, including chapter notes, activity suggestions, and suggested assessment and test questions.
- **Electronic test bank:** An electronic test bank (TB) contains hundreds of challenging questions as multiple-choice or short-answer questions. Instructors can choose from these questions and create their own customized exams.
- **PowerPoint™ presentation:** Ideal for instructors to use for lecture presentations or student handouts, the PowerPoint presentation provides ready-to-use graphics and text images tied to the individual chapters and content development of the text.

Acknowledgments

Many talented people have contributed to the success of this book and we are deeply grateful to all those who have assisted over the years. Without the success of the first edition, there would certainly not have been a second, much less ten editions. The following people worked closely with John on the first edition, and he was sincerely indebted to Warren Crown, John Dossey, Bob Gilbert, and Steven Willoughby, who gave time and great care in offering detailed comments on the original manuscript.

In preparing this tenth edition, we have received thoughtful input from the following mathematics teacher educators who offered comments on the ninth edition. Each reviewer challenged us to think through important issues. Many specific suggestions have found their way into this book, and their feedback helped us focus on important ideas. Thank you to Jessica Cohen, Western Washington University; Shea Mosely Culpepper, University of Houston; Shirley Dissler, High Point University; Cynthia Gautreau, California State University in Fullerton; Kevin LoPresto, Radford University; Ryan Nivens, East Tennessee State University; Adrienne Redmond-Sanogo, Oklahoma State University; and Douglas Roebuck, Ball State University. We are indebted to you for your dedicated and professional insight.

Additionally, we are very grateful for the ideas and reviews as we developed the tenth edition. Graham Fletcher, mathematics specialist, Atlanta, Georgia, provided strong support in the development of high leverage routines, including, of course, the new section on 3-Act Tasks. Susan Peters, mathematics teacher educator, University of Louisville, provided critical feedback and helpful ideas for developing concepts of data analysis. Their input resulted in significant improvements to those chapters. We continue to seek suggestions from teachers who use this book so please email us at teachingdevelopmentally@gmail.com with any advice, ideas, or insights you would like to share.

We are extremely grateful to our Pearson team of editors! Each of them has worked hard to turn our ideas (and yours) into a reality. And that is why we have been able to continue to evolve this book in a way to make it accessible online and via hard copy. Drew Bennett, our editor, has helped us define the direction of this edition and make important decisions that would make the book a better product for pre-service and in-service teachers. Our development editor, Kim Norbuta, has been supportive and positive, keeping us on target, even with the tightest of deadlines. Our content producer Yagnesh Jani was always available with the missing resources and answers we needed. Finally, we are very grateful to Jason Hammond and his editing team at SPi-Global, who carefully and conscientiously assisted in preparing this edition for publication. It has been a pleasure to interact with each of them and they have given us peace of mind to have knowledgeable, strong support.

We would each like to thank our families for their many contributions and support. On behalf of John, we thank his wife, Sharon, who was John's biggest supporter and a sounding board as he wrote the first six editions of this book. We also recognize his daughters, Bridget (a fifth-grade teacher in Chesterfield County, Virginia) and Gretchen (an Associate Professor of psychology at Rutgers University–Newark). They were John's first students, and he tested many ideas that are in this book by their sides. We can't forget those who called John "Math Grandpa": his granddaughters, Maggie, Aidan, and Grace.

From Karen Karp: I would like to express thanks to my husband, Bob Ronau, who as a mathematics educator graciously helped me think about decisions while offering insights and encouragement. In addition, I thank my children, Matthew, Tammy, Joshua, Misty, Matt, Christine, Jeffrey, and Pamela for their kind support and inspiration. I also am grateful for my wonderful grandchildren, Jessica, Zane, Madeline, Jack and Emma, who have helped deepen my understanding about how children think.

From Jennifer Bay-Williams: I would like to begin by saying thank you to the many mathematics teachers and teacher educators whose presentations at conferences, blogs, tweets, articles and classroom lessons have challenged and inspired me. I am forever grateful to my husband, Mitch Williams, whose background in English/Language Arts and great listening skills have been an amazing support. Finally, thank you to my children, MacKenna (14 years) and Nicolas (11 years), along with their peers and teachers, who continue to help me think more deeply about mathematics teaching and learning.

CHAPTER 1

Teaching Mathematics in the 21st Century

LEARNER OUTCOMES

After reading this chapter and engaging in the embedded activities and reflections, you should be able to:

1.1 Summarize the factors that influence the effective teaching of mathematics.

1.2 Describe the importance of content standards, process standards and standards of mathematical practice.

1.3 Explore the qualities needed to learn and grow as a professional teacher of mathematics.

Some of you will soon find yourself in front of a class of students; others of you may already be teaching. What general ideas will guide the way you will teach mathematics as you grow in the teaching profession? This book will help you become comfortable with the mathematics content of the preK–8 curriculum. You will also learn about research-based strategies that help students come to know mathematics and be confident in their ability to do mathematics. These two things—your knowledge of mathematics and how students learn mathematics—are the most important tools you can acquire to be successful.

 ## Becoming an Effective Teacher of Mathematics

As part of your personal desire to build successful learners of mathematics, you might recognize the challenge that mathematics is sometimes seen as the subject that people love to hate. At social events of all kinds—even at parent–teacher conferences—other adults may respond to the fact that you are a teacher of mathematics with comments such as "I could never do math," or "I can't calculate the tip at a restaurant–I just hope they include suggestions for tips at the bottom of my receipt." Instead of dismissing or ignoring these disclosures, consider what positive action you can take. Would people confide that they don't read and hadn't read a book in years—not likely. Families' and teachers' attitudes toward mathematics may enhance or detract from students' ability to do math. It is important for you and for students' families to know that mathematics ability is not inherited—anyone can learn mathematics. Moreover, learning mathematics is an essential life skill (OECD, 2016). So, you need to find ways of countering negative statements about mathematics, especially if they are declared in the presence of students. Point out that it is a myth that only some people can be successful in learning mathematics. Only in that way can the chain of passing apprehension from family member to child, or in rare cases from teacher to student, be broken. There is much joy to be had in solving mathematical problems, and it is essential that you model an excitement for learning and nurture a passion for mathematics in your students.

Ultimately, your students need to think of themselves as mathematicians in the same way as they think of themselves as readers. As students interact with our increasingly mathematical and technological world, they need to construct, modify, communicate or integrate new information in many forms. Solving novel problems and approaching new situations with a mathematical perspective should come as naturally as using reading to comprehend facts, insights, or news. Particularly because this century is a quantitative one (Hacker, 2016), we must prepare students to interpret the language and power of numeracy. Hacker states that "decimals and ratios are now as crucial as nouns and verbs" (p. 2). So, for your students' sake, consider how important mathematics is to interpreting and successfully surviving in our complex economy and in our changing environment. Learning mathematics opens up a world of important ideas to students.

The goal of this book is to help you understand the mathematics methods that will make you an effective teacher. We also base this book on the collective wisdom of an organization of mathematics educators and mathematicians who developed a set of standards for what knowledge, skills and dispositions are important in cultivating a well-prepared beginning teacher of mathematics (Association of Mathematics Teacher Educators, 2017). This book infuses those standards for developing elementary and middle school teachers of mathematics using the suggestions of what best supports teacher candidates in methods courses. Because the authors of this book were also engaged in the creation and writing of the *Standards for Preparing Teachers of Mathematics*, the book is aligned with the AMTE standards. As you dig into the information in the chapters ahead, your vision of what is possible for all students and your confidence to explore and teach mathematics will grow.

 ## A Changing World

In *The World Is Flat* (2007), Thomas Friedman discusses how globalization has created the need for people to have skills that are long lasting and will survive the ever-changing landscape of available jobs. He names categories of workers who regardless of the shifting terrain of job options—will always be successful in finding employment. One of these "untouchable" categories is—math lover. Friedman emphasizes that in a world that is digitized and surrounded by algorithms, math lovers will always have career opportunities and choices. Yet, there is a skills gap of qualified people as science, technology, engineering, and mathematics (STEM) jobs take more than twice as long to fill as other jobs in the marketplace (Rothwell, 2014).

Now every teacher of mathematics has the job to prepare students with career skills while developing a "love of math" in students. Lynn Arthur Steen, a well-known mathematician and educator, stated, "As information becomes ever more quantitative and as society relies increasingly on computers and the data they produce, an innumerate citizen today is as vulnerable as the illiterate peasant of Gutenberg's time" (1997, p. xv). So, as you see there are an array of powerful reasons why children will benefit from the study of mathematics and the instructional approaches you will learn in this book. Your students need to acquire the mental tools to make sense of mathematics—in some cases for mathematical applications that might not yet be known! This knowledge serves as a lens for interpreting the world.

Our changing world influences what should be taught in preK–8 mathematics classrooms as there is a relationship between early mathematics performance and success in middle school (Bailey, Siegler, & Geary, 2014) and high school mathematics (Watts, Duncan, Siegler, & Davis-Kean, 2014). As we prepare preK–8 students for jobs that possibly do not currently exist, we can predict that there will be few jobs where just knowing simple computation is enough to be successful. We can also predict that many jobs will require interpreting complex data, designing algorithms to make predictions, and using multiple strategies to approach new problems.

As you prepare to help students learn mathematics for the future, you will need some perspective on the forces that effect change in the mathematics classroom. This chapter addresses the leadership that you, the teacher, will develop as you shape the mathematics experience for your students. Your beliefs about what it means to know and do mathematics and about how students make sense of mathematics will affect how you approach instruction and the understandings and skills your students take from the classroom. The enthusiasm you demonstrate about mathematical ideas will translate into your students' interest in this amazing and beautiful discipline.

Factors to Consider

Over the years, there have been significant reforms in mathematics education that reflect the technological and informational needs of our society, research on how students learn mathematics, the importance of providing opportunities to learn for all students, and ideas on how and what to teach from an international perspective. Just as we would not expect doctors to be using the exact same techniques and medicines that were prevalent when you were a child, teachers' methods are evolving and transforming via a powerful collection of expert knowledge about how the mind functions and how to design effective instruction (Wiggins, 2013).

There are several significant factors in this transformation. One factor is the public or political pressure for change in mathematics education due largely to information about student performance in national and international studies. These large-scale comparisons of student performance continue to make headlines, provoke public opinion, and pressure legislatures to call for tougher standards backed by testing. This research is important because international and national assessments provide strong evidence that mathematics teaching *must* change if students are to be competitive in the global market and able to understand the complex issues they will confront as responsible citizens of the world (Green, 2014).

National Assessment of Education Progress (NAEP). Since the 1960s, the United States regularly gathers data on how fourth-, eighth-, and twelfth-grade students are doing in mathematics on the NAEP (https://nces.ed.gov/nationsreportcard). These data provide a tool for policy makers and educators to measure the overall improvement of U.S. students over time in what is called the "Nation's Report Card." NAEP uses four achievement levels: below basic, basic, proficient, and advanced, with proficient and advanced representing substantial grade-level achievement. The criterion-referenced test is designed to reflect the current curriculum but keeps a few stable items for purposes of long-term comparison. In the most recent NAEP mathematics assessment in 2015, less than half of all U.S. students in grades 4 and 8 performed at the desirable levels of proficient and advanced (40 percent in fourth grade and 33 percent in eighth grade) (National Center for Education Statistics, 2015). Despite encouraging gains in the NAEP scores over the last 30 years due to important shifts in instructional practices (particularly at the elementary level) (Kloosterman, Rutledge, & Kenney, 2009b), students' performance in 2015 still reveals disappointing levels of competency. For the first time in 25 years the number of students performing at proficient and advanced dropped two points at fourth grade and three points at eighth grade (Toppo, 2015). We still have work to do!

Trends in International Mathematics and Science Study (TIMSS). In 2015, 49 nations participated in the third International Mathematics and Science Study (https://timssandpirls.bc.edu), the largest international comparative study of students' mathematics and science achievement—given regularly since 1995. Data are gathered in grades 4, and 8 from a randomly selected group of students resulting in a sample of more than 600,000 with approximately 20,000 of the students from the United States. The results revealed that U.S. students performed above the international average of the TIMSS countries at both the fourth grade and the eighth grade but were outperformed at the fourth-grade level by education systems in Singapore, Hong Kong, Republic of Korea, Chinese Taipei, Japan, Northern Ireland, Russian Federation, Norway, Ireland, England, Belgium, Kazakhstan, and Portugal and outperformed at the eighth-grade level by education systems in Singapore, Republic of Korea, Chinese Taipei, Hong Kong, Japan, Russian Federation, Kazakhstan, Canada, and Ireland. These data provide valuable benchmarks that allow the United States to reflect on our teaching practices and our overall competitiveness in preparing students for a global economy. If you've heard people talk about how mathematics is taught in Singapore—these rankings are why. But these data do not suggest that we should use the curriculum from other higher performing countries as there are many variables to consider. However we can learn a common theme from these examples: a teaching focus in these nations that emphasizes conceptual understanding and procedural fluency. Both of which are critically important to the long-term growth of problem solving skills (OECD, 2016; Rittle-Johnson, Schenider, & Star, 2015). In fact, teaching in the high-achieving countries more closely resembles the long-standing recommendations of the National Council of Teachers of Mathematics, the major professional organization for mathematics teachers, discussed next.

National Council of Teachers of Mathematics (NCTM). One transformative factor in the teaching of mathematics is the leadership of the National Council of Teachers of Mathematics (NCTM). The NCTM, with more than 60,000 members, is the world's largest mathematics education organization. This group holds an influential role in the support of teachers and an emphasis on what is best for learners. Their guidance in the creation and dissemination of standards for curriculum, assessment, and teaching led the way for other disciplines to create standards and for the eventual creation of the CCSS-M. For an array of resources, including the web-based Illuminations component which consists of a set of exciting instructional experiences for your students, visit the NCTM website (www.nctm.org).

MyLab Education   Self-Check 1.1

The Movement toward Shared Standards

We share the history of the standards here so you have a sense of how mathematics instruction has changed over time and how external factors and emerging research play a role in that process. These important ideas are all connected to your future as a teacher of elementary or middle school mathematics.

The momentum for reform in mathematics education began in earnest in the early 1980s. The main impetus was a response to a need for more problem solving as well as the research of developmental psychologists who identified how students can best learn mathematics. Then in 1989, NCTM published the first set of standards for a subject area in the *Curriculum and Evaluation Standards for School Mathematics*. Many believe that no other document has had such an enormous effect on school mathematics or on any other area of the curriculum.

NCTM followed in 1991 with a set of standards for teaching that articulated a vision of teaching mathematics for all students, not just a few. In 1995, NCTM added to the collection the *Assessment Standards for School Mathematics*, which focused on the importance of integrating assessment with instruction and indicated the key role that assessment plays in implementing change (see Chapter 5). In 2000, NCTM released *Principles and Standards for School Mathematics* as an update of its original standards document. Combined, these documents prompted a revolutionary reform movement in mathematics education throughout the world.

As these documents influenced teacher practice, ongoing debate about the mathematics curriculum continued with many arguing that instead of hurrying through numerous topics every year, the curriculum needed to address content more deeply. Guidance was needed in deciding what mathematics content should be taught at each grade level and, in 2006, NCTM released *Curriculum Focal Points*, a little publication with a big message—the mathematics taught at each grade level needs to be focused, provide depth, and explicitly show connections. The goal of the Focal Points was to support a coherent curriculum and give clarity to teachers and students as to what should be taught at each grade. The resulting sequence of key concepts provided a "structural fiber" that helped students understand mathematics (Dossey, McCrone, & Halvorsen, 2016, p. 18).

In 2010, the National Governors Association (NGA) Center for Best Practices and Council of Chief State School Officers (CCSSO) presented the *Common Core State Standards*, which are grade-level specific standards which incorporate ideas from *Curriculum*

Focal Points as well as international curriculum documents. A large majority of U.S. states adopted these as their standards and other states were stimulated to create new standards of their own. In less than 25 years, the standards movement transformed the country from having little to no coherent vision on what mathematics should be taught and when, to a more widely shared idea of what students should know and be able to do at each grade level.

In the following sections, we discuss three significant components of the standards that are critical to your work as a highly effective teacher of mathematics.

Mathematics Content Standards

As noted earlier, the dialogue on improving mathematics teaching and learning extends beyond mathematics educators. Policymakers and elected officials considered previous NCTM standards documents, international assessments, and research on the best way to prepare students to be "college and career ready." The National Governors Association Center for Best Practices and the Council of Chief State School Officers (CCSSO) collaborated with other professional groups and entities to develop shared expectations for K–12 students across states, a focused set of mathematics content standards and practices, and efficiency of material and assessment development (Porter, McMaken, Hwang, & Yang, 2011). As a result, they developed *Common Core State Standards for Mathematics* (CCSS-M) which can be downloaded at http://www.corestandards.org/math.

The CCSS-M articulates an overview of *critical areas* of mathematics content that are expectations for each grade from K–8 to provide a coherent curriculum built around big mathematical ideas. These larger groups of related standards are called *domains*, and there are eleven that relate to grades K–8 (see Figure 1.1). At this time, approximately 37 states, Washington, D.C., four territories, and Department of Defense Schools have adopted the CCSS-M. A few states chose not to adopt the standards from the start, some created their own versions, and others are still deciding their level of participation or reevaluating their own standards compared to CCSS-M. This change represents the largest shift of mathematics content in the United States in more than 100 years.

MyLab Education   **Video Example 1.1**

Watch this video (https://www.youtube.com/watch?v=5pBOnvzC_Yw&list=PLD7F4C7DE7CB3D2E6&index=15) by one of the authors of the CCSS-M to hear more about the shifts made in these standards.

The *Common Core State Standards* were developed with strong consideration given to the research on what is known about the development of students' understanding of mathematics over time (Cobb & Jackson, 2011). The selection of topics at particular grades reflects not only rigorous mathematics, but also what is known from research and practice about learning progressions which are sometimes referred to as *learning trajectories* (Clements & Sarama, 2014; Confrey, Maloney, & Corley, 2014). These progressions can help teachers know the sequence of what came before a particular concept as well as what to expect next as students reach key points

Kindergarten	Grade 1	Grade 2	Grade 3	Grade 4	Grade 5	Grade 6	Grade 7	Grade 8
Counting and Cardinality								
Operations and Algebraic Thinking						**Expressions and Equations**		
Number and Operations in Base-Ten						**The Number System**		
Measurement and Data						**Statistics and Probability**		
Geometry								
			Number and Operations—Fractions			**Ratios and Proportional Relationships**		**Functions**

FIGURE 1.1 *Common Core State Standards* domains by grade level.

along a pathway to desired learning targets (Corcoran, Mosher, & Rogat, 2009). Although these paths are not identical for all students, they can inform the order of instructional experiences which will support movement toward understanding and application of mathematics concepts. There is a website for the "Progressions Documents for the Common Core Math Standards" (http://ime.math.arizona.edu/progressions) where progressions for the domains in the Common Core State Standards can be found.

Although you may have heard people suggest that they are not in favor of the *Common Core State Standards*, many of those comments reflect people's concern with the testing that is associated with the standards, not the content standards or the mathematical practices which are described next.

The Process Standards and Standards for Mathematical Practice

To prepare students for college and career readiness and a lifetime of enjoying mathematical ideas, there are additional standards that emphasize the important processes in doing mathematics. The process standards refer to the mathematical methods and strategies which preK–12 students acquire to enhance their use of mathematical content knowledge. NCTM developed these standards as part of the *Principles and Standards* document (2000) and stated that the process standards should not be regarded as separate content or strands in the mathematics curriculum, rather, they are central and integral components of all mathematics learning and teaching. The five process standards and ways you can develop these elements in your students can be found in Table 1.1. Members of NCTM have free access to the *Principles and Standards* and nonmembers can sign up for 120 days of free access to the full document on the NCTM website (www.nctm.org) under the tab *Standards and Focal Points*.

The *Common Core State Standards* also go beyond specifying mathematics content expectations to also include Standards for Mathematical Practice. These are "'processes and proficiencies'

TABLE 1.1   THE FIVE PROCESS STANDARDS FROM *PRINCIPLES AND STANDARDS FOR SCHOOL MATHEMATICS*

Process Standard	How Can You Develop These Processes in Your Students?
Problem Solving	• Start instruction with a problem to solve—as problem solving is the vehicle for developing mathematical ideas. • Select meaningful mathematical tasks. • Set problems in a situation to which students can relate. • Use a variety of strategies to solve problems. • Have students self-assess their understanding of the problem and their strategy use.
Reasoning and Proof	• Have students consider evidence of why something is true or not. • Create opportunities for students to evaluate conjectures—do they hold true? • Encourage students to use logical reasoning to see if something always works or their answers make sense. • Demonstrate a variety of ways for students to justify their thinking through finding examples and counter-examples to use in a logical argument.
Communication	• Invite students to talk about, write about, describe, and explain their mathematical ideas as a way to examine their thinking. • Give students opportunities to share ideas so that others can understand and actively discuss their reasoning. • Share examples of student work, so students can compare and assess others' thinking. • Present precise mathematical language and notation so that the word usage and definitions can act as a foundation for students' future learning.
Connections	• Emphasize how mathematical ideas explicitly connect to students' prior mathematical knowledge and future learning. • Assist students in developing the relationships between the mathematics being learned and real-world contexts and in other subject areas.
Representation	• Encourage students to use multiple representations to explore relationships and communicate their thinking. • Create opportunities for students to move from one representation of a mathematical concept or idea to another to add depth of understanding. • Provide problems where students can use mathematical models to clarify or represent a situation.

Source: Adapted with permission from NCTM (National Council of Teachers of Mathematics). (2000). *Principles and standards for school mathematics.* Reston, VA: NCTM. Copyright 2000 by the National Council of Teachers of Mathematics. All rights reserved.

with longstanding importance in mathematics education" (NGA Center & CCSSO, 2010, p. 6) that are based on the underlying frameworks of the NCTM process standards (Koestler, Felton, Bieda, & Otten, 2013). Teachers must develop these mathematical practices in each and every student (NGA Center & CCSSO, 2010, pp. 7–8) as described briefly in Table 1.2 to help them reach proficiency. A more detailed description of the Standards for Mathematical Practice can be found in Appendix A and you may find versions of these practices that spell out explanations and examples by individual grade level either through your state documents or on the web or in publications such as the Koestler, Felton, Bieda, and Otten (2013) book described in the resources section at the end of the chapter.

Regardless of the standards used in your state it is your job to support the parents and families of your students to educate them about the research behind the standards used. Incorporate your classroom website, newsletters, back to school night, family math events to share examples of how concepts are being built in very purposeful ways—even if they differ from the "way the parents were taught" when they were in school (Walkowiak, 2015). There is a nonprofit website called YouCubed (www.youcubed.org) that offers a parent section where videos and resources are available to help you support parents' understanding of these ideas and approaches.

TABLE 1.2   THE STANDARDS FOR MATHEMATICAL PRACTICE FROM THE CCSS-M

Mathematical Practice	K–8 Students Should Be Able to:
Make sense of problems and persevere in solving them.	• Explain what the problem is asking. • Describe possible approaches to a solution. • Consider similar problems to gain insights. • Use concrete objects or drawings to think about and solve problems. • Monitor and evaluate their progress and change strategies if needed. • Check their answers using a different method. • Try again with another approach if one attempt is not successful or when they feel "stuck."
Reason abstractly and quantitatively.	• Explain the relationship between quantities in problem situations. • Represent situations using symbols (e.g., writing expressions or equations). • Create representations that fit the word problem. • Use flexibly the different properties of operations and objects.
Construct viable arguments and critique the reasoning of others.	• Understand and use assumptions, definitions, and previous results to explain or justify solutions. • Make conjectures by building a logical set of statements. • Analyze situations and use examples and counterexamples. • Explain their thinking and justify conclusions in ways that are understandable to teachers and peers. • Compare two possible arguments for strengths and weaknesses to enhance the final argument.
Model with mathematics.	• Apply mathematics to solve problems in everyday life. • Make assumptions and approximations to simplify a problem. • Identify important quantities and use tools or representations to connect their relationships. • Reflect on the reasonableness of their answer based on the context of the problem.
Use appropriate tools strategically.	• Consider a variety of tools, choose the most appropriate tool, and use the tool correctly (e.g., manipulative, ruler, technology) to support their problem solving. • Use estimation to detect possible errors and establish a reasonable range of answers. • Use technology to help visualize, explore, and compare information.
Attend to precision.	• Communicate precisely using clear definitions and appropriate mathematical language. • State accurately the meanings of symbols. • Specify appropriate units of measure and labels of axes. • Use a level of precision suitable for the problem context.
Look for and make use of structure.	• Identify and explain mathematical patterns or structures. • Shift viewpoints and see things as single objects or as comprised of multiple objects or see expressions in many equivalent forms. • Explain why and when properties of operations are true in a particular context.
Look for and express regularity in repeated reasoning.	• Notice if patterns in calculations are repeated and use that information to solve other problems. • Use and justify the use of general methods or shortcuts by identifying generalizations. • Self-assess as they work to see whether a strategy makes sense, checking for reasonableness prior to finalizing their answer.

Source: Based on Council of Chief State School Officers. (2010). *Common Core State Standards.* Copyright © 2010 National Governors Association Center for Best Practices and Council of Chief State School Officers. All rights reserved.

TABLE 1.3   THE SIX GUIDING PRINCIPLES FROM THE *PRINCIPLES TO ACTIONS*

Guiding Principle	Suggestions for Classroom Actions That Align with the Principles
Teaching and learning	• Select focused mathematics goals. • Use meaningful instructional tasks that develop reasoning, sense making, and problem-solving strategies. • Present and encourage a variety of mathematical representations that connect the same ideas or concepts. • Facilitate student discussions and conversations about important mathematical ideas. • Ask essential questions that are planned to be a catalyst for deeper levels of thinking. • Use a strong foundation of conceptual understanding as a foundation for procedural fluency. • Encourage productive struggle—as it is a way to deepen understanding and move toward student application of their learning. • Generate ways for students to provide evidence of their thinking through discussions, illustrations, and written responses.
Access and equity	• Establish high expectations for all students. • Provide supports targeted to student needs (equity not equality). • Provide instructional opportunities for students to demonstrate their competence in different ways—creating tasks with easy entry points for students who struggle and extension options for those who finish quickly. • Identify obstacles to students' success and find ways to bridge or eliminate those barriers. • Develop all students' confidence that they can do mathematics. • Enhance the learning of all by celebrating students' diversity.
Curriculum	• Build connections across mathematics topics to capitalize on broad themes and big ideas. • Look for both horizontal and vertical alignment to build coherence. • Avoid thinking of a curriculum as a checklist or disconnected set of daily lessons.
Tools and technology	• Include an array of technological tools and manipulatives to support the exploration of mathematical concepts, structures, and relationships. • Think beyond computation when considering the integration of technology. • Explore connections to how technology use for problem solving links to career readiness.
Assessment	• Incorporate a continuous assessment plan to follow how students are performing and how instruction can be modified and thereby improved. • Move beyond test results that just look at overall increases and decreases to pinpoint specific student needs. • Consider the use of multiple assessments to capture a variety of student performance. • Encourage students to self-assess sometimes by evaluating the work of others to enhance their own performance. • Teach students how to check their work.
Professionalism	• Develop a long-term plan for building your expertise. • Build collaborations that will enhance the work of the group of collaborators as you enhance the performance of the students in the school. • Take advantage of all coaching, mentoring and professional development opportunities and be a life-long learner. • Structure in time to reflect on and analyze your instructional practices.

How to Effectively Teach the Standards

NCTM also developed a publication that capitalizes on the timing of the adoption of the new standards across many states to explore the specific learning conditions, school structures, and teaching practices which will be important for a high-quality education for all students. The book *Principles to Actions* (2014) uses detailed classroom stories and student work samples to illustrate the careful, reflective work required of effective teachers of mathematics through 6 guiding principles (see Table 1.3 and Appendix B). A series of presentations (webcasts), led by the authors of the publication, explore several of the guiding principles and are available on the *Principles to Actions* portion of NCTM's website (www .nctm.org).

 Pause & Reflect

Take a moment now to select one or two of the six guiding principles that seem especially significant to you and are areas in which you wish to develop more expertise. Why do you think these are the most important to your teaching? •

VIDEO EXAMPLE

An Invitation to Learn and Grow

Think back to when you were a student in preK–8 classrooms. What are your remembrances of learning mathematics? Here are some thoughts from in-service and pre-service teachers of whom we asked the same question. Which description do you resonate with?

> I was really good at math in lower elementary grades, but because I never understood why math works, it made it very difficult to embrace the concepts as I moved into higher grades. I started believing I wasn't good at math so I didn't get too upset when my grades reflected that. *Kathryn*

> As a student, I always felt lost during mathematics instruction. It was as if everyone around me had a magic key or code that I missed out on getting. *Tracy*

> I remember math being very challenging, intimidating, and capable of making me literally sick to my stomach. Math was a bunch of rules and formulas I was expected to memorize, but not to understand. *Mary Rebekah*

> I consider myself to be really good at math and I enjoy mathematics-related activities, but I often wonder if I would have been GREAT at math and had a completely different career if I cared about math as much as I do now. Sometimes I feel robbed. *April*

> Math went from engaging, interactive instruction that I excelled at and loved, to lecture-style instruction that I struggled with. I could not seek outside help, even though I tried, because the teacher's way was so different from the way of the people trying to help me. I went from getting all As to getting low Bs and Cs without knowing how the change happened. *Janelle*

> Math class was full of elimination games where students were pitted against each other to see who could answer a math fact the fastest. Because I have a good memory I did well, but I hated every moment. It was such a nerve-wracking experience and for the longest time that is what I thought math was. *Lawrence*

> Math was never a problem because it was logical, everything made sense. *Tova*

As you can see these memories run the gamut with an array of emotions and experiences. The question now becomes, what do you hope your former students will say as they think back to your mathematics instruction? The challenge is to get each and every student to learn mathematics with understanding and enthusiasm. Would you relish hearing your students, 15 years after leaving your classroom, state that you encouraged them to be mathematically minded, curious about solving new problems, self-motivated, able to critically think about both correct and incorrect strategies, and that you nurtured them to be risk takers willing to try and persevere on challenging tasks? What will your legacy be?

The mathematics education described in this book may not be the same as the mathematics content and the mathematics teaching you experienced in grades K–8. As a practicing or prospective teacher facing the challenge of teaching mathematics from a problem-solving approach, this book may require you to confront some of your personal beliefs—beliefs about what it means to *do mathematics*, how one goes about *learning mathematics*, how to *teach mathematics*, and what it means to *assess mathematics*. Success in mathematics isn't merely about speed or the notion that there is "one right answer." Thinking and talking about mathematics as a means to sense making is a strategy that will serve us well in becoming a society where all citizens are confident in their ability to do math.

Becoming a Teacher of Mathematics

This book and this course of study are critical to your professional teaching career. The mathematics education course you are taking now as a pre-service teacher or the professional development you are experiencing as an in-service teacher will be the foundation for much of the mathematics instruction you do in your classroom for the next decade. The authors of this book take that seriously, as we know you do. Remember like a workout to benefit fully from this book you can't just go and watch others exercise (or do mathematics), you must participate with enthusiasm, energy, and effort. You bring many strengths to the teaching of mathematics including your willingness to try new things, a fresh perspective on how technology can be integrated into instruction and your stance as a lifelong learner. Therefore, this section lists and describes the characteristics, habits of thought, skills, and dispositions you will continue to cultivate to reach success as an effective teacher of mathematics.

Knowledge of Mathematics.
You will need to have a profound, flexible, and adaptive knowledge of mathematics content (Ma, 1999). This statement is not intended to scare you if you feel that mathematics is not your strong suit, but it is meant to help you prepare for a serious semester of learning about mathematics and how to teach it. You cannot teach what you do not know. Additionally, the "school effects" for mathematics are great, meaning that unlike other subject areas, where students have frequent interactions with their family or others outside of school on topics such as reading books, exploring nature, or discussing current events, in the area of mathematics what we do in school is often "it" for many students. An absence of in-school opportunities to gain mathematics knowledge can result in students forever being economically disadvantaged and without the potential for social mobility (OECD, 2016). This is not merely about time spent but instead on how that time is used; the quality of instruction. These findings add to the gravity of your responsibility, because a student's learning for the year in mathematics will likely come from you. If you are not sure of a fractional concept or other aspect of mathematics content knowledge, now is the time to make changes in your depth of understanding and flexibility with mathematical ideas to best prepare for your role as an instructional leader. You will need to be able to "translate confusion into understanding" (Green, 2014, p. 105). You don't want to work on the brink of your knowledge base—instead you need to soak up the knowledge so you will feel more confident and can speak with added passion and enthusiasm. This book and your professor or instructor will help you in that process.

Persistence.
You need the ability to stave off frustration and demonstrate persistence. Dweck (2007) has described the brain as similar to a muscle—one that can be strengthened with a good workout! People are not just "wired" for learning mathematics they must perform hard work and persevere to understand new ideas. As you move through this book and work the problems yourself, you will learn methods and strategies that will help you anticipate the barriers to students' learning and identify strategies to get them past these stumbling blocks. It is likely that what works for you as a learner will work for your students. As you conduct these mental "workouts," if you ponder, struggle, talk about your thinking, and reflect on how these new ideas fit or don't fit with your prior knowledge, then you will enhance your repertoire as a teacher. Remember as you model these characteristics for your students, they too will value perseverance more than speed. In fact, Einstein did not describe himself as intelligent—instead he suggested he was just someone who continued to work on problems longer than others. Creating opportunities for your students to productively struggle is part of the learning process (Stigler & Hiebert, 2009; Warshauer, 2015).

Positive Disposition.
Prepare yourself by developing a positive attitude toward the subject of mathematics. Research shows that teachers with positive attitudes teach math in more successful ways that result in their students liking math more (Karp, 1991) and performing at higher levels (Palardy & Rumberger, 2008). If in your heart you say, "I never liked math," that mindset will be evident in your instruction (Maloney, Gunderson, Ramirez, Levin, & Beilock, 2014). The good news is that research shows that changing attitudes toward mathematics is relatively easy (Tobias, 1995) and that attitude changes are long-lasting (Dweck, 2006). Additionally, math

methods courses have been found to be effective in increasing positive attitudes, more so than student teaching experiences (Jong & Hodges, 2015). Also, teachers who studied key concepts in math methods classes were more effective in and attentive to planning lessons on those big ideas—even years after taking the course (Morris & Hiebert, 2017). By expanding your knowledge of the subject and trying new ways to approach problems you can learn to enjoy doing activities in class and presenting mathematics instruction in schools. Not only can you acquire a positive attitude toward mathematics, as a professional educator it is essential that you do.

To explore your students' attitudes toward mathematics consider using this interview protocol. Here you can explore how the classroom environment may affect their attitudes.

MyLab Education   **Teacher Resource: Interview Protocol**

Readiness for Change. Demonstrate a readiness for change, even for change so radical that it may cause you disequilibrium. You may find that what is familiar will become unfamiliar and, conversely, what is unfamiliar will become familiar. For example, you may have always referred to "reducing fractions" as the process of changing $\frac{2}{4}$ to $\frac{1}{2}$, but this language is misleading as the fractions are not getting smaller. Such terminology can lead to mistaken connections. Did the reduced fraction go on a diet? A careful look will point out that *reducing* is not the term to use; rather, you are writing an equivalent fraction that is *simplified* or in *lowest terms*. Even though you have used the language *reducing* for years, you need to become familiar with more precise language such as "simplifying fractions."

On the other hand, what is unfamiliar will become more comfortable. It may feel uncomfortable for you to be asking students, "Did anyone solve it differently?" especially if you are worried that you might not understand their approach. Yet this question is essential to effective teaching. As you bravely use this strategy, it will become comfortable (and you will learn new strategies!).

Another potentially difficult shift in practice is toward an emphasis on concepts as well as procedures. What happens in a procedure-focused classroom when a student doesn't understand division of fractions? A teacher with only procedural knowledge is often left to repeat the procedure louder and slower, "Just change the division sign to multiplication, flip over the second fraction, and multiply." We know the use of a memorized approach doesn't work well if we want students to fully understand the process of dividing fractions, so let's consider an example using $3\frac{1}{2} \div \frac{1}{2} =$ _____. You might start by relating this division problem to prior knowledge of a whole number division problem such as $25 \div 5 =$ _____. A corresponding story problem might be, "How many orders of 5 pizzas are there in a group of 25 pizzas?" Then ask students to put words around the fraction division problem, such as "You plan to serve each guest $\frac{1}{2}$ a pizza. If you have $3\frac{1}{2}$ pizzas, how many guests can you serve?" Yes, there are seven halves in $3\frac{1}{2}$ and therefore 7 guests can be served. Are you surprised that you can do this division of fractions problem in your head?

To respond to students' challenges, uncertainties, and frustrations you may need to unlearn and relearn mathematical concepts, developing comprehensive conceptual understanding and a variety of representations along the way. Supporting your mathematics content knowledge on solid, well-supported terrain is your best hope of making a lasting difference in your students' learning of mathematics—so be ready for change. What you already understand will provide you with many "Aha" moments as you read this book and connect new information to your current mathematics knowledge.

Willingness to Be a Team Player. Your school must work as a unit where all teachers are supporting children not just for the one grade they teach but in a coherent manner across the grades. When this idea of a team is implemented, then teachers agree to use the same language, symbols, models and notation to give students a familiar thread that ties the concepts and procedures together year after year. This established understanding is called a Whole School Agreement (Karp, Bush, & Dougherty, 2016) and your eager collaboration is essential in making this approach work well.

Lifelong Learning, Make Time to Be Self-Aware and Reflective. As Leinwand wrote, "If you don't feel inadequate, you're probably not doing the job" (2007, p. 583). No matter whether you are a preservice teacher or an experienced teacher, there is always more to learn about the content and methodology of teaching mathematics. The ability to examine oneself for areas that need improvement or to reflect on successes and challenges is critical for growth and development. The best teachers are always trying to improve their practice through the reading latest article, reading the newest book, attending the most recent conference, or signing up for the next series of professional development opportunities. These teachers don't say, "Oh, that's what I am already doing"; instead, they identify and celebrate each new insight. Highly effective teachers never "finish" learning nor exhaust the number of new mental connections that they make and, as a result, they never see teaching as stale or stagnant. An ancient Chinese proverb states, "The best time to plant a tree is twenty years ago; the second best time is today." Explore this self-reflection chart on professional growth to list your strengths and indicate areas for continued growth.

Think back to the quotations from the teachers at the beginning of this section. Again, what memories will you create for your students?

As you begin this adventure let's be reminded of what John Van de Walle said with every new edition, "Enjoy the journey!"

MyLab Education **Teacher Resource: Professional Growth Chart**

MyLab Education **Video Example 1.2**

Watch this video of John Van de Walle as he speaks to teachers about the challenges of teaching in ways focused on a problem-solving approach.

MyLab Education **Self-Check 1.3**

RESOURCES FOR CHAPTER 1

RECOMMENDED READINGS

Articles

Buckheister, K., Jackson, C., & Taylor, C. (2015). An inside track: Fostering mathematical practices. *Teaching Children Mathematics, 22*(1), 28–35.

The authors share a game used with early elementary students and through teacher-student dialogue they describe how the several mathematical practices can be developed.

Hoffman, L., & Brahier, D. (2008). Improving the planning and teaching of mathematics by reflecting on research. *Mathematics Teaching in the Middle School, 13*(7), 412–417.

This article addresses how teachers' beliefs influence their mathematics instruction. The authors discuss how to pose higher-level problems, ask thought-provoking questions, face students' frustration, and use students' mistakes to enhance their understanding of concepts.

Books

Bush, S., & Karp, K. (2015) *Discovering lessons for the Common Core State Standards in grades K–5.* Reston, VA: NCTM.

Bush, S., & Karp, K. (2014) *Discovering lessons for the Common Core State Standards in grades 6–8.* Reston, VA: NCTM.

These two books align lessons in articles from the past 15 years of NCTM journals with the Common Core State Standards and the Standards for Mathematical Practices. The books provide a way to see how the standards play out in instructional tasks for classroom use.

Koestler, C. Felton, M., Bieda, K. & Otten, S. (2013). *Connecting the NCTM process standards and the CCSSM practices.* Reston, VA: NCTM.

Expanding on the brief description of the Standards for Mathematical Practice in the CCSSM document, this book integrates those processes into the content with specific examples.

Exploring What It Means to Know and Do Mathematics

LEARNER OUTCOMES

After reading this chapter and engaging in the embedded activities and reflections, you should be able to:

2.1 Investigate what it means to do mathematics.

2.2 Describe essential components of mathematical proficiency, including the importance of a relational understanding.

2.3 Connect learning theories to effective teaching practices.

This chapter explains how to help students learn mathematics. To get at how to help students learn, however, we must first consider what is important *to* learn. Let's look at a poorly understood topic, division of fractions, as an opening example. If a student has learned this topic well, what will they know and what should they be able to do? The answer is more than being able to successfully implement a procedure (e.g., commonly called the "invert and multiply" procedure). There is much more to know and understand about division of fractions:

- What does $3 \div \frac{1}{4}$ mean conceptually?
- What situation might this expression represent?
- Will the result be greater than or less than 3 and why?
- What strategies can we employ to solve this problem?
- What illustration or manipulative might illustrate this problem?
- How does this expression relate to subtraction? To multiplication?

All of these questions can be answered by a student who fully understands a topic such as division of fractions. We must help students reach this level of procedural fluency and conceptual understanding.

This chapter focuses on the "what" and "how" of teaching mathematics. First, *what* does doing mathematics look like (be ready to experience this yourself through four great tasks!) and what is important to know about mathematics? Second, *how* do we help students develop a strong understanding of mathematics?

What Does It Mean to Do Mathematics?

Doing mathematics means generating strategies for solving a problem, applying that strategy, and checking to see whether an answer makes sense. Doing mathematics means demonstrating mathematical process (see Table 1.1), which in the CCSS-M are effectively described in eight Mathematical Practices (see Table 1.2 and Appendix A). Doing mathematics begins with establishing goals for students that reflect these practices and then posing worthwhile tasks that open up the opportunity for such processes to develop (NCTM, 2014).

Goals for Students

One way to determine if your goals for students focus on doing mathematics is to consider the verbs in lesson and unit plans. Objectives or instructions that ask students to listen, copy, memorize, drill, and compute are lower-level thinking tasks and do not adequately prepare students for the real act of doing mathematics. In contrast, the following verbs engage students in doing higher-level mathematics:

analyze	design	justify
apply	develop	model
compare	explain	predict
connect	explore	represent
construct	formulate	solve
critique	generalize	use
describe	investigate	verify

These verbs may look familiar to you, as they are on the higher level of Bloom's (revised) Taxonomy (Anderson & Krathwohl, 2001) (see Figure 2.1).

In observing a third-grade classroom where the teacher focused on doing mathematics (i.e., focusing on the process standards), researchers found that students began to (1) connect to previous material, (2) respond with information beyond the required response, and (3) conjecture or predict (Fillingim & Barlow, 2010). When students engage in mathematical processes and practices a daily basis, they receive an empowering message: "You are capable of making sense of this—you are capable of doing mathematics!"

An Invitation to Do Mathematics

As noted above, after selecting goals that focus on mathematical processes and practices, the next step is to pose worthwhile tasks. The purpose of this section is to provide *you* with opportunities to engage with such tasks—four different problems across the mathematical strands and across K–8. None requires mathematics beyond elementary school mathematics, but they do require higher-level thinking. For each, stop and solve first. Then read the "Explore" section. Continue to engage with the task. Then, you will be doing mathematics and seeing how others may think about the problem differently (or the same). Have fun!

Task 1. Pattern Search: Start and Jump Numbers.

Begin with a number (start) and add (jump) a fixed amount. For example, start with 3 and jump by 5s. Use the Start and Jump Numbers Activity Page or write the list on a piece of paper. Examine the list and record as many patterns as you see.

MyLab Education   **Activity Page: Start and Jump Numbers**

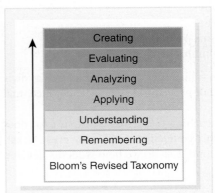

FIGURE 2.1 Bloom's (Revised) Taxonomy (Anderson & Krathwohl, 2001).

Source: Anderson, L.W., & Krathwohl, D. R. (Eds.). (2001). *A taxonomy for learning, teaching, and assessing: A revision of Bloom's Taxonomy of educational objectives: Complete Edition*. New York, NY: Addison Wesley, Longman.

Explore. Here are some questions to guide your pattern search:

- Do you see at least one alternating pattern?
- Have you noticed an odd/even pattern? Why is this pattern true?
- What do you notice about the numbers in the tens place?
- Do the patterns change when the numbers are greater than 100?

Have you thought about what happens to your patterns after the numbers are more than 100, for example 113? One way is as 1 hundred, 1 ten, and 3 ones. But, of course, it could also be "eleventy-three," where the tens digit has gone from 9 to 10 to 11. How do these different perspectives affect your patterns? What would happen after 999?

Extend. Sometimes when you have discovered some patterns in mathematics, it is a good idea to make some changes and see how the changes affect the patterns. What changes might you make in this problem? Your changes may be even more interesting than the following suggestions. But here are some ideas:

- Change the start number but keep the jump number equal to 5. What is the same and what is different?
- Keep the same start number and explore with different jump numbers.
- What patterns do different jump numbers make? For example, when the jump number was 5, the ones-digit pattern repeated every two numbers—it had a "pattern length" of 2. But when the jump number is 3, the length of the ones-digit pattern is 10! Do other jump numbers create different pattern lengths?
  - For a jump number of 3, how does the ones-digit pattern relate to the circle of numbers in Figure 2.2? Are there similar circles of numbers for other jump numbers?
  - Using the circle of numbers for 3, find the pattern for jumps of multiples of 3, that is, jumps of 6, 9, or 12.

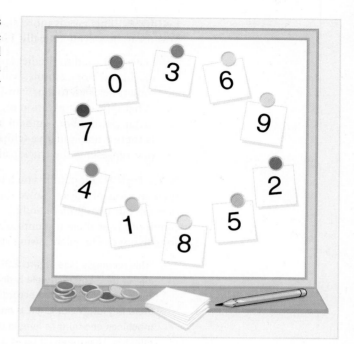

FIGURE 2.2   For jumps of 3, this cycle of digits will occur in the ones place. The start number determines where the cycle begins.

Calculators facilitate exploration of this problem. Using calculators make the list generation accessible for young children who can't skip count yet, and they make it possible to readily explore bigger jump numbers like 25 or 36. Most simple calculators have an automatic constant feature that will add the same number successively. For example, if you press 3 + 5 = and then keep pressing =, the calculator will keep counting by fives from the previous answer. Consider demonstrating this with an online calculator (http://calculator-1.com) or app for the white board so the class can observe and discuss the counting.

Task 2. Analyzing a Situation: Two Machines, One Job.

Ron's recycle shop started when Ron bought a used paper-shredding machine. Business was good, so Ron bought a new shredding machine. The old machine could shred a truckload of paper in 4 hours. The new machine could shred the same truckload in only 2 hours. How long will it take to shred a truckload of paper if Ron runs both shredders at the same time?

MyLab Education   **Application Exercise 2.1: Observing and Responding to Student Thinking** Click the link to access this exercise, then watch the video and answer the accompanying questions.

VIDEO EXAMPLE

Use the Two Machines, One Job Activity Page to record your solution to this problem. Do not read on until you have an answer or are stuck. Can you check that you are correct? Can you approach the problem using a picture?

MyLab Education   **Activity Page: Two Machines, One Job**

Explore. This task is more challenging than the last one, though you might be surprised at how it can be solved logically. Here are some things to consider:

- Have you tried to predict approximately how much time you think it should take the two machines? For example, will it be closer to 1 hour or closer to 4 hours? Estimating can sometimes lead to a new insight.
- What type of illustration might help solve this problem? For example, could you draw a rectangle or a line segment to stand for the truckload of paper?
- Is there a manipulative (chips, plastic cubes, pennies) you might use to make a collection that represents the truckload?

Strategies. Hopefully you have solved this problem in some way that makes sense to you—there are lots of ways to solve this particular task! Understanding other people's strategies can develop our own understanding. And, teachers are always in a position where they must try to figure out how their students are thinking about a problem. The following is one explanation for solving the problem, using strips (based on Schifter & Fosnot, 1993):

> "This rectangle [see Figure 2.3] stands for the whole truckload. In 1 hour, the new machine will do half of this." The rectangle is divided in half. "In 1 hour, the old machine could shred $\frac{1}{4}$ of the paper." The rectangle is divided accordingly. "So in 1 hour, the two machines have done $\frac{3}{4}$ of the truck, and there is $\frac{1}{4}$ left. What is left is one-third as much as what they already did, so it should take the two machines one-third as long to do that part as it took to do the first part. One-third of an hour is 20 minutes. That means it takes 1 hour and 20 minutes to do it all.

As with the teachers in these examples, it is important to decide whether your solution is correct through justifying why you did what you did; this reflects real problem solving rather than checking with an answer key. After you have justified that you have solved the problem in a correct manner, try to find other ways that students might solve the problem—in considering multiple ways, you are making mathematical connections.

Task 3. Generalizing Relationships: One Up, One Down. This problem has two parts, addition and multiplication. For your use, or to use with students, download One Up, One Down: Addition Activity Page or One Up, One Down: Multiplication Activity Page.

MyLab Education   **Activity Page: One Up, One Down: Addition**

MyLab Education   **Activity Page: One Up, One Down: Multiplication**

Addition. When you add 7 + 7, you get 14. When you make the first number 1 more and the second number 1 less, you get the same answer:

$$\begin{array}{ccccc} \uparrow & & \downarrow & & \\ 7 & + & 7 & = & 14 \\ 8 & + & 6 & = & 14 \end{array}$$

Does it work for 5 + 5? For what other problems is this pattern true? What else do you notice about this pattern? Why is this pattern true?

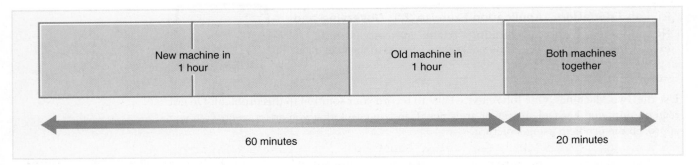

FIGURE 2.3   Cora's solution to the paper-shredding problem.

Multiplication. When you multiply 7 × 7 you get 14. When you make the first number 1 more and the second number 1 less, you get one less:

$$\uparrow \qquad \downarrow$$
$$7 \quad \times \quad 7 \quad = 49$$
$$8 \quad \times \quad 6 \quad = 48$$

Does this work for 5 × 5? For what other problems is this pattern true? What else do you notice about this pattern? Why is this pattern true?

Explore. If you explored both of these, you may have noticed that there are many more patterns or generalizations in the addition situation than in the multiplication situation. Consider:

- What manipulative or picture might illustrate the patterns?
- How is the pattern altered if the sums/products begin as two consecutive numbers (e.g., 8 × 7)? If they differed by 2 or by 3?
- What if you instead go "Two up, two down"? (e.g., 7 + 7 to 9 + 5 OR 7 × 7 to 9 × 5)?
- What if both factors increase (i.e., one up, one up)?
- What manipulative or picture might illustrate why the patterns work?
- In what ways is the addition situation similar to and different than the multiplication situation?

Strategies. Let's look at the multiplication pattern using illustrations. To compare the before and after products, draw rectangles (or arrays) with a length and height of each of the factors (see Figure 2.4[a]), then draw the new rectangle (e.g., 8-by-6-unit rectangle). You may prefer to think of multiplication as equal sets. For example, using stacks of chips, 7 × 7 is seven stacks with seven chips in each stack (set) (see Figure 2.4[b]). The expression 8 × 6 is represented by eight stacks of six (though six stacks of eight is a possible interpretation). See how the stacks for each expression compare.

Have you made some mathematical connections and conjectures in exploring this problem? In doing so you have hopefully felt a sense of accomplishment and excitement—one of the benefits of *doing* mathematics.

Task 4. Experimenting and Justifying: The Best Chance of Purple.

Samuel, Susan, and Sandu are playing a game. The first one to spin "purple" wins! Purple means that one spin lands on red and one spins lands on blue (see Figure 2.5). Each person chooses to spin each spinner once or one of the spinners twice. Samuel chooses to spin spinner A twice; Susan chooses to spin spinner B twice; and Sandu chooses to spin each spinner once. Who has the best chance of purple? (based on Lappan & Even, 1989).

Think about the problem and what you know. Experiment. Use the Best Chance of Purple Activity Page to explore this problem.

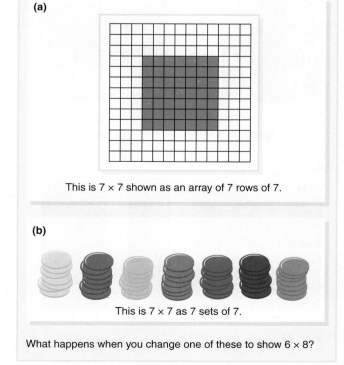

(a)

This is 7 × 7 shown as an array of 7 rows of 7.

(b)

This is 7 × 7 as 7 sets of 7.

What happens when you change one of these to show 6 × 8?

MyLab Education   **Activity Page: Best Chance of Purple**

FIGURE 2.4 Two physical ways to think about multiplication that might help in the exploration.

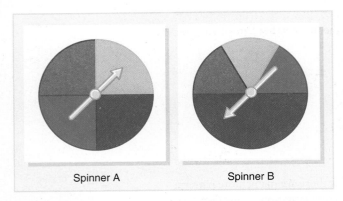

FIGURE 2.5 You may spin A twice, B twice, or A then B. Which choice gives you the best chance of spinning a red and a blue (purple)?

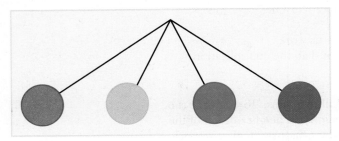

FIGURE 2.6 A tree diagram for spinner A in Figure 2.5.

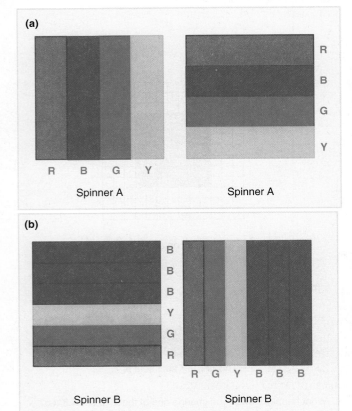

FIGURE 2.7 Grids can illustrate the chance of spinning purple with two spins.

Explore. A good strategy for learning is to first explore a problem concretely, then analyze it abstractly. This is particularly helpful in situations involving chance or probability. Use a paper clip with the spinners on your Activity Page, or use a virtual spinner. Consider the following as you explore:

• Who is most likely to win and why?
• For Sandu's turn (spinner A, then spinner B), would it matter if he spun B first and then A? Why or why not?
• How might you change one spinner so that Susan has the best chance at purple?

Strategies. Just like the earlier tasks, there are multiple strategies for approaching this task.

Strategy 1: Tree Diagrams. On spinner A, the four colors each have the same chance of coming up. You could make a tree diagram for A with four branches and all the branches would have the same chance (see Figure 2.6). Spinner B has different-sized sections, leading to the following questions:

• What is the relationship between the blue region and each of the others?
• How could you make a tree diagram for B with each branch having the same chance?
• How can you add to the diagram for spinner A so that it represents spinning A twice in succession?
• Which branches on your diagram represent getting purple?
• How could you make tree diagrams for each player's choices?
• How do the tree diagrams relate to the spinners?

Tree diagrams are only one way to approach this. If the strategy makes sense to you, stop reading and solve the problem. If tree diagrams do not seem like a strategy you want to use, read on.

Strategy 2: Grids. Partition squares to represent all the possible outcomes for spinner A and spinner B. Although there are many ways to divide a square into four equal parts, if you use lines going all in the same direction, you can make comparisons of all the outcomes of one event (one whole square) with the outcomes of another event (drawn on a different square). For two independent events, you can then create lines going the other direction for the second event. Samuel's two spins are represented in Figure 2.7(a). If these two squares are overlapped, you can visually see that two parts (two-sixteenths) are "blue on red" or "red on blue." Susan's probability can be determined by layering the squares in Figure 2.7(b); and Sandu's from layering one square from Figure 2.7(a) with one from Figure 2.7(b).

Why are there four parts for spinner A and 6 parts for spinner B? How is the grid strategy alike and different from the tree diagram? One strategy may make more sense to you, and one may make more sense to another. Hearing other students' explanations and reasoning for both strategies are important in building a strong understanding of mathematics.

Interesting mathematics problems such as the four presented here are plentiful. The Math Forum, for example, has a large collection of classic problems along with discussion, solutions, and extensions. NCTM teacher journals include monthly problems, and readers submit student solutions for these tasks, which appear in an issue a few months later.

Where Are the Answers?

Did you notice that no answers were shared for these four rich tasks? You may be wondering if your answer is correct, or if there are other answers. But, one aspect of being mathematically proficient is to rely on one's own justification and reasoning to determine if an answer is correct. Consider the message students receive when the textbook or the teacher is the source of whether an answer is correct: "Your job is to find the answers that the teacher already has." In the real world of problem solving and doing mathematics, there are no answer books. A person must be able to make sure they have used an appropriate strategy and reached a reasonable conclusion— we hope you feel this is the case for the tasks you solved in this section.

MyLab Education   **Self-Check 2.1**

What Does It Mean to Know Mathematics?

In setting learning objectives for students, we often ask, "What will students know and be able to do?" The previous section focused on what students need to be able to do; this section focused on what students need to know. *Procedural knowledge* refers to *how* to complete an algorithm or procedure. *Conceptual knowledge* refers to *connected* knowledge: "mental connections among mathematical facts, procedures, and ideas" (Hiebert and Grouws 2007, p. 380). Both procedural and conceptual knowledge are foundational to procedural fluency and conceptual understanding, discussed later.

As an example, consider what is important for a student to know about a fraction such as $\frac{6}{8}$? At what point do they know enough that they can claim they "understand" fractions? It is more complicated than it might first appear. Here is a partial list of what they might know or be able to do:

- Read the fraction.
- Identify the 6 and 8 as the numerator and denominator, respectively.
- Recognize it is equivalent to $\frac{3}{4}$.
- Know it is more than $\frac{1}{2}$ (recognize relative size).
- Draw a region that is shaded in a way to show $\frac{6}{8}$.
- Locate $\frac{6}{8}$ on a number line.
- Illustrate $\frac{6}{8}$ of a set of 48 pennies or counters.
- Know that there are infinitely many equivalencies to $\frac{6}{8}$.
- Recognize $\frac{6}{8}$ as a rationale number.
- Realize $\frac{6}{8}$ might also be describing a ratio (girls to boys, for example).
- Be able to represent $\frac{6}{8}$ as a decimal fraction.

A number of items on this list refer to procedural knowledge (e.g., being able to find an equivalent fraction) and others refer to conceptual knowledge (e.g., recognizing $\frac{6}{8}$ is greater than $\frac{1}{2}$ by analyzing the relationship between the numerator and denominator). A student may know that $\frac{6}{8}$ can be simplified to $\frac{3}{4}$ but not recognize that $\frac{3}{4}$ and $\frac{6}{8}$ are equivalent (having procedural knowledge without conceptual knowledge). A student may be able to find one fraction between $\frac{1}{2}$ and $\frac{6}{8}$, but not be able to find others, meaning that while they have some procedural knowledge to find a common denominator, they do not have enough conceptual knowledge to recognize they could also change to denominators of sixteenths to find more in-between fractions (and recognize there are infinitely many options).

Understanding is hard to define, but it can be explained as a measure of the quality and quantity of connections that an idea has with existing ideas. The extent that a student understands why an algorithm works or understands relationships is their depth of understanding.

Relational Understanding

Understanding exists along a continuum from an *instrumental understanding*—doing something without understanding (see Figure 2.8) to a *relational understanding*—knowing what to do and why. These two terms were introduced by Richard Skemp in 1978 and continue to be a useful way to think about the depth of a student's mathematical understanding.

In the $\frac{6}{8}$ example, a student who only knows a procedure for simplifying $\frac{6}{8}$ to $\frac{3}{4}$ has an understanding near the instrumental end of the continuum, while a student who can draw diagrams, give examples, and find numerous equivalencies, has an understanding toward the relational end of the continuum. Here we briefly share two (interrelated) important ways to nurture a relational understanding.

 Explore with Tools. A *tool* is any object, picture, or drawing that can be used to explore a concept. *Manipulatives* are physical objects that students and teachers can use to illustrate and discover mathematical concepts, whether made specifically for mathematics (e.g., connecting cubes) or for other purposes (e.g., buttons). Choices for manipulatives (including virtual manipulatives) abound—from common objects such as lima beans to commercially produced materials such as Pattern Blocks. Figure 2.9 shows six examples, each representing a different concept, just to give a glimpse (Part II of this book is full of more options). More and more of these interactives and others (e.g., algebra tiles, geometric solids, number lines, adjustable spinners) are available in a digital format, for example, on NCTM's Illuminations website (http://illuminations.nctm.org) and on the National Library of Virtual Manipulatives (NLVM) website (http://nlvm.usu.edu).

A tool does not "illustrate" a concept. The tool is used to visualize a mathematical concept and only your mind can impose the mathematical relationship on the object (Suh, 2007b; Thompson, 1994). As noted in *Task 4: Experimenting and Justifying: The Best Chance of Purple*, manipulatives can be a testing ground for emerging ideas. They are more concrete and provide insights into new and abstract relationships. Consider each of the concepts and the corresponding model in Figure 2.9. Try to separate the physical tool from the relationship that you must impose on the tool in order to *see* the concept.

The examples in Figure 2.9 are models that can show the following concepts:

a. The concept of "6" is a relationship between sets that can be matched to the words *one, two, three, four, five,* or *six*. Changing a set of counters by adding one changes the relationship. The difference between the set of 6 and the set of 7 is the relationship "one more than."

b. The concept of "measure of length" is a comparison. The length measure of an object is a comparison relationship of the length of the object to the length of the unit.

c. The concept of "rectangle" includes both spatial and length relationships. The opposite sides are of equal length and parallel and the adjacent sides meet at right angles.

d. The concept of "hundred" is not in the larger square but in the relationship of that square to the strip ("ten") and to the little square ("one").

e. "Chance" is a relationship between the frequency of an event happening compared with all possible outcomes. The spinner can be used to create relative frequencies. These can be predicted by observing relationships of sections of the spinner.

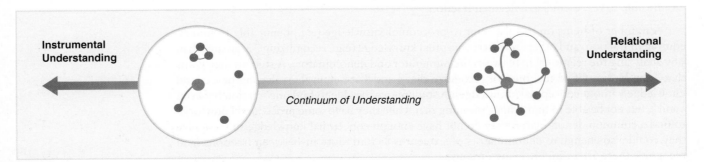

FIGURE 2.8 Understanding is a measure of the quality and quantity of connections that a new idea has with existing ideas. The greater the number of connections to a network of ideas, the better the understanding.

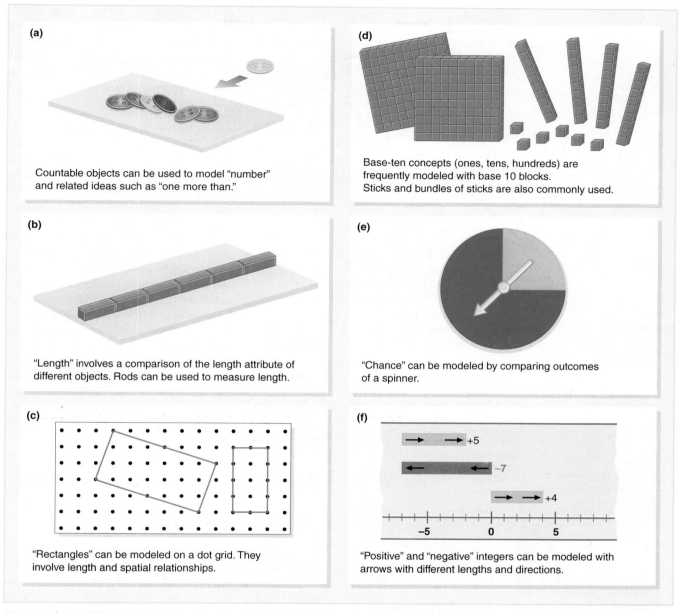

FIGURE 2.9 Examples of tools to illustrate mathematics concepts.

f. The concept of a "negative integer" is based on the relationships of "magnitude" and "is the opposite of." Negative quantities exist only in relation to positive quantities. Arrows on the number line model the opposite of relationship in terms of direction and size or magnitude relationship in terms of length.

A variety of tools (including calculators) should be accessible for students to select and use appropriately as they engage in doing mathematics.

While tools can be used to support relational understanding, they can be used ineffectively and not accomplish this goal. One of the most widespread misuses of tools occurs when the teacher tells students, "Do as I do." There is a natural temptation to get out the materials and show students how to use them to "show" the concept. It is just as possible to move blocks around mindlessly as it is to "invert and multiply" mindlessly. Neither promotes thinking or aids in the development of concepts (Ball, 1992; Clements & Battista, 1990; Stein & Bovalino, 2001). On the other extreme, it is ineffective to provide no focus or purpose for using the tools. This will result in nonproductive

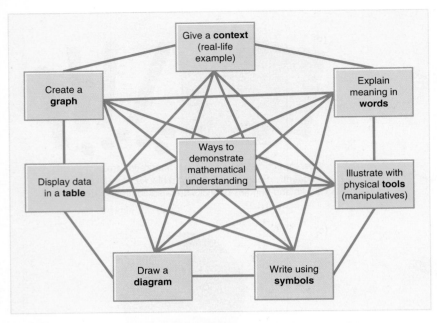

FIGURE 2.10 Web of Representations. Translations between and within each representation of a mathematical idea can help students build a relation understanding of a mathematical concept.

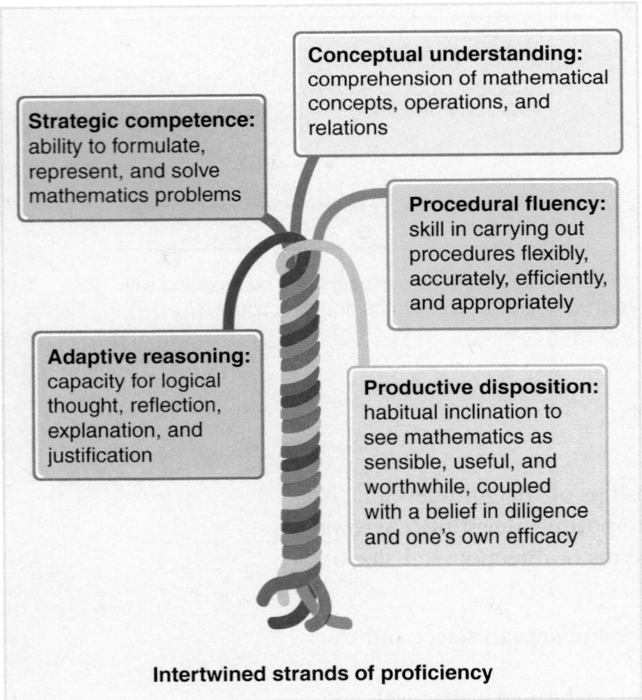

FIGURE 2.11 *Adding It Up* describes five strands of mathematical proficiency.

Source: National Research Council. (2001). *Adding It Up: Helping Children Learn Mathematics*, p. 5. Reprinted with permission from the National Academy of Sciences, courtesy of the National Academies Press, Washington, DC.

Diagram labels:
- Conceptual understanding: comprehension of mathematical concepts, operations, and relations
- Strategic competence: ability to formulate, represent, and solve mathematics problems
- Procedural fluency: skill in carrying out procedures flexibly, accurately, efficiently, and appropriately
- Adaptive reasoning: capacity for logical thought, reflection, explanation, and justification
- Productive disposition: habitual inclination to see mathematics as sensible, useful, and worthwhile, coupled with a belief in diligence and one's own efficacy

Intertwined strands of proficiency

and unsystematic investigation (Stein & Bovalino, 2001). The goal is to set up tasks with the tools so that students notice important mathematical relationships that can be discussed, connecting the concrete representations to abstract concepts.

Connect Representations. In order for students to build connections among ideas, different representations must be included in instruction, and opportunities must be provided for students to make connections among the representations. Figure 2.10 illustrates a Web of Representations showing ways to demonstrate understanding. Students who have difficulty translating a concept from one representation to another also have difficulty solving problems and understanding computations (Lesh, Cramer, Doerr, Post, & Zawojewski, 2003). Therefore, strengthening students' ability to move between and among these representations improves their understanding. For example, give students the Translation Task Activity Page to complete for a topic they are learning. You can fill out one box and ask them to insert the other representations, or you can invite a group to work on all four representations for a given topic (e.g., multiplication of whole numbers).

> **MyLab Education** Activity Page: Translation Task

Mathematical Proficiency

This chapter started with an invitation to do mathematics, engaging you in the mathematical processes or practices (See Tables 1.1, 1.2, and Appendix A). Students who are able to demonstrate these practices are mathematically proficient. In other words, proficiency isn't only knowing the list of content from your grade, it is being able to demonstrate the practices *as it applies to that content*. The mathematical practices are based on research on how students learn as described in the National Research Council (NRC) report *Adding It Up* (NRC, 2001), which can be read for free at https://www.nap.edu/read/9822. Figure 2.11 illustrates these interrelated and interwoven strands.

Conceptual Understanding. Conceptual understanding is a flexible web of connections and relationships within and between ideas, interpretations and images of mathematical concepts—a relational understanding. Consider the web of associations for ratio as shown in Figure 2.12. Students with a conceptual understanding will connect what they know about division and numbers to make sense of scaling, unit prices, and so on. Note how much is involved in having a relational understanding of ratio.

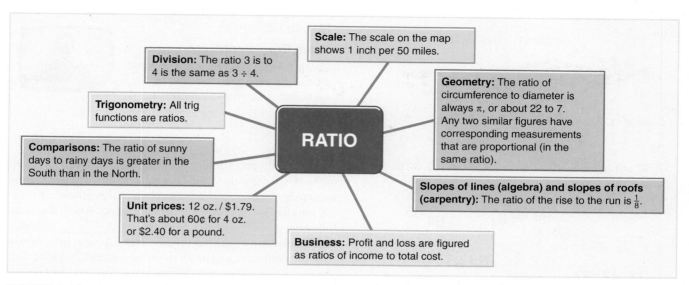

FIGURE 2.12   Potential web of ideas that could contribute to the understanding of "ratio."

Conceptual understanding includes the network of representations and interpretations of a concepts through the use of pictures, manipulatives, tables, graphs, words, and so on (see Figure 2.10). An illustration for ratios across these representations is provided in Figure 2.13.

Procedural Fluency. Procedural fluency is sometimes confused with being able to do standard algorithms correctly and quickly, but it is much bigger than that. Look at the four descriptors of procedural fluency in Figure 2.11. Recall that procedural knowledge is a foundation (knowing how to do an algorithm). Also important is procedural understanding (knowing why an algorithm works). But, procedural fluency is more than procedural understanding. Fluency includes four components: efficiency, accuracy, flexibility and appropriate strategy selection. Let's look at the problem 37+28. Figure 2.14 illustrates four approaches. Which ones represent a student who is has procedural fluency with two-digit addition? A fluent student does not automatically stack the numbers and apply the standard algorithm (though they know how to do this); the fluent student looks at the problem and considers which strategy will be *efficient* given the numbers in the problem and *selects an appropriate strategy*. In this case, a student might move two from the 37 to the 28 to adapt the equation to 35+30 (If this reminds you of One Up, One Down, good for you!). Or a student might add 2 onto 28, add 37+30, and then take 2 away from the answer (see Figure 2.14[c]). Given a different problem, like 54+37, the student might opt for a different strategy, such as adding the tens (80) and the ones (11) and combing them (91), showing *flexibility* in which strategies they use.

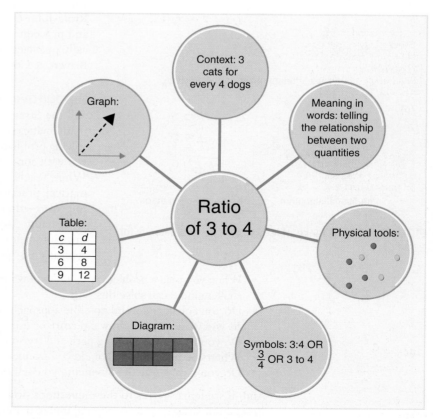

FIGURE 2.13   Multiple representations for ratio of 3 to 4.

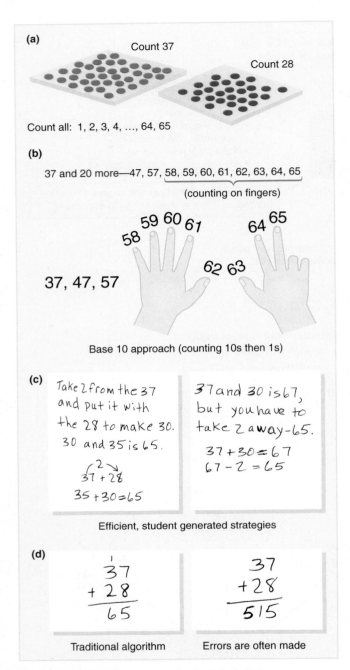

FIGURE 2.14 A range of levels of procedural fluency for 37 + 28.

Ironically, procedural fluency is often mistaken for learning standard algorithms and being able to do them quickly and accurately. An overemphasis on standard algorithms can actually interfere with the development of fluency. Think about the following problem: $40{,}005 - 39{,}996 = \underline{\hspace{2cm}}$. Applying the standard algorithm involves regrouping across zeros, a tedious, inefficient, and prone-to-error method. Noticing that the numbers are close together, and therefore lend to a counting up strategy, efficiently leads to a result of 9. Number lines are an important representation in building fluency:

	4	5
Efficient Strategy:	39,996 40,000	40,005

Procedures support concepts (and vice versa) and both conceptual and procedural knowledge contributed to student development of procedural flexibility (Schneider, Rittle-Johnson, & Star, 2011). Both conceptual understanding and procedural fluency are crucial to becoming mathematically proficient (Baroody, Feil, & Johnson, 2007; Bransford, Brown, & Cocking, 2000).

Productive Disposition. As the Mathematical Practices and the Strands of Proficiency describe, being proficient at mathematics is not just what you know, but how you go about solving problems. Mathematical practices need to be interwoven with conceptual development (Kobiela & Lehrer, 2015). When teachers are intentional and explicit about mathematical practices, students' participation and confidence improves—they develop a productive disposition (Wilburne, Wildmann, Morret, & Stipanovic, 2014). For which of the questions below might a student with a productive disposition typically say "yes"?

- When you read a problem you don't know how to solve, do you think, "Great, something challenging. I can solve this."?
- Do you consider several possible approaches before diving in to solve?
- As you work, do you draw a picture or use a manipulative?
- Do you recognize a wrong path and try something else?
- When you finish a problem, do you wonder whether it is right? If there are other answers?
- Do you have a way of convincing yourself or a peer that your answer is correct?

And, if students say yes to these questions, which mathematical practices are they accessing? Procedural fluency and conceptual understanding are supported by and support a productive disposition.

MyLab Education   Self-Check 2.2

How Do Students Learn Mathematics?

Now that you have had the chance to experience doing mathematics, you may have a series of questions: Why take the time to solve these problems—isn't it better to do a lot of shorter practice problems? Can students solve such challenging tasks? In other words, how does "doing mathematics" relate to learning mathematics? The answer lies in learning theory and research on how people learn.

Learning theories such as constructivism and sociocultural theory have influenced the way in which mathematics is taught. Your teaching practices will be influenced by how you believe people learn, which may be informed by one of these learning theories and from your own pragmatic experiences. It is important for you to attend to your own beliefs and how they relate to your teaching practice (Davis & Sumara, 2012). Here we briefly describe two theories that are important to understanding how students learn mathematics. These theories are not competing and are compatible (Norton & D'Ambrosio, 2008).

Constructivism

Constructivism is rooted in Jean Piaget's work, developed in the 1930s and translated to English in the 1950s. At the heart of constructivism is the notion that learners are not blank slates but rather creators or constructors of their own learning (Cobb, 1988; Fosnot, 1996; von Glasersfeld, 1996). Integrated *networks*, or *cognitive schemas*, are formed by constructing knowledge and they are used to build new knowledge. Through *reflective thought*—the effort to connect existing ideas to new information—people modify their existing schemas to incorporate new ideas (Fosnot, 1996). All people construct or give meaning to things they perceive or think about. As you read these words you are giving meaning to them. Whether listening passively to a lecture or actively engaging in synthesizing findings in a project, your brain is applying prior knowledge in your existing schemas to make sense of the new information.

To connect to the metaphor of building construction, the *tools* we use to build understanding are our existing ideas and knowledge. The *materials* we use are things we see, hear, or touch, as well as our own thoughts and ideas. In Figure 2.15, blue and red dots are used as symbols for ideas. Consider the picture to be a small section of our cognitive makeup. The blue dots represent existing ideas. The lines joining the ideas represent our logical connections or relationships that have developed between and among ideas. The red dot is an emerging idea, one that is being constructed. Whatever existing ideas, blue dots, are used in the construction will be connected to the new idea, red dot, because those were the ideas that gave meaning to it. If a potentially relevant idea, blue dot, is not accessed by the learner when learning a new concept, red dot, then that potential connection will not be made.

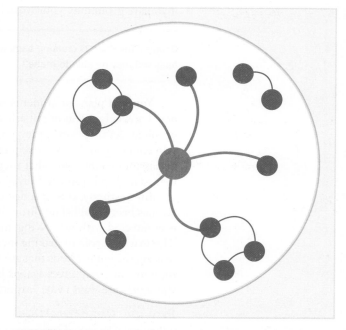

FIGURE 2.15 We use the ideas we already have (blue dots) to construct a new idea (red dot), in the process developing a network of connections between ideas. The more ideas used and the more connections made, the better we understand.

Sociocultural Theory

In the 1920s and 1930s, Lev Vygotsky, a Russian psychologist, began developing what is now called sociocultural theory. Like constructivism, this theory assumes active meaning-seeking on the part of the learner. An important aspect of sociocultural theory is that the way in which information is internalized, or learned, depends on whether it was within a learner's zone of proximal development (ZPD) (Vygotsky, 1978). Simply put, the ZPD refers to a range of knowledge that may be out of reach for a person to learn on his or her own, but is accessible if the learner has support from peers or more knowledgeable others. In a true mathematical community of learners there is something of a common ZPD that emerges across learners as well as the individual ZPDs of each person (Cobb, 1994; Goos, 2004). Social interaction is essential for learning to occur. And, a community of learners is affected not only by culture the teacher creates, but by the broader social and historical culture of the members of the classroom (Forman, 2003).

Implications for Teaching Mathematics

Learning theories are not teaching strategies—theory *informs* teaching. This section outlines teaching strategies that are informed by constructivist and sociocultural perspectives. You will see these strategies revisited in more detail in Chapters 3 and 4, where a problem-based model for instruction is discussed, and in Part II of this book, where you learn how to apply these ideas to specific areas of mathematics.

Importantly, if these strategies are grounded in how people learn, it means *all* people learn this way—students with special needs, English language learners, students who struggle, and students who are gifted. Too often, when teachers make adaptations and modifications for particular learners, they trade in strategies that align with learning theories and research for methods that seem "easier" for students. These strategies, however, provide fewer opportunities for students to connect ideas and build knowledge—thereby impeding, not supporting, learning.

Build New Knowledge from Prior Knowledge. If you are teaching a new concept, like division, it must be developed using what students already know about equal subtraction and sharing. Consider the following task and how you might introduce it to third graders and if you are grounding your work in constructivist or sociocultural learning theories.

Goodies Toy Store is creating bags with 3 squishy balls in each. If they have 24 squishy balls, how many bags will they be able to make?

You will plan for students to access their prior knowledge, use cultural tools, and build new knowledge. You might ask students to use manipulatives or to draw pictures to solve this problem. As they work, they might have different ways of thinking about the problem (e.g., skip counting up by 3s, or skip counting down by 3s). These ideas become part of a classroom discussion, connecting what they know about equal subtraction and addition, and connecting that to multiplication and division.

Interestingly, this practice of connecting ideas is not only grounded in learning theory, but has been established through research studies. Making mathematical relationships explicit is connected with improving student conceptual understanding (Hiebert & Grouws, 2007). The teacher's role in making mathematical relationships explicit is to be sure that students are making the connections that are implied in a task. For example, asking students to relate today's topic to one they investigated last week, or by asking "How is Laila's strategy like Marco's strategy?" are ways to be "explicit" about mathematical relationships.

Provide Opportunities to Communicate about Mathematics. Learning is enhanced when the learner is engaged with others working on the same ideas. The interaction in such a classroom allows students to engage in reflective thinking and to internalize concepts that may be out of reach without the interaction and input from peers and their teacher. In discussions with peers, students will be adapting and expanding on their existing networks of concepts.

Create Opportunities for Reflective Thought. Classrooms need to provide structures and supports to help students make sense of mathematics in light of what they know. For a new idea to be interconnected in a rich web of interrelated ideas, children must be mentally engaged. They must find the relevant ideas they possess and bring them to bear on the development of the new idea. In terms of the dots in Figure 2.15 we want to activate every blue dot students have that is related to the new red dot we want them to learn. It is through student thinking, talking, and writing, that we can help them reflect on how mathematical ideas are connected to each other.

Encourage Multiple Strategies. Encourage students to use strategies that make sense to them. The student whose work is presented in Figure 2.16 may not understand the algorithm she used. If instead she were asked to use her own approach to find the difference, she might be able to get to a correct solution and build on her understanding of place value and subtraction.

Even learning a basic fact, like 7×8, can have better results if a teacher promotes multiple strategies. Imagine a class where students discuss and share ways to figure out the product. One student might think of 5 eights (40) and then 2 more eights (16) to equal 56. Another may have learned 7×7 (49) and add on 7 more to get 56. Still another might think "8 sevens" and take half of the sevens (4×7) to get 28 and double 28 to get 56. A class discussion sharing these ideas brings to the fore a wide range of useful mathematical "dots" relating addition and multiplication concepts.

Engage Students in Productive Struggle. Have you ever just wanted to think through something yourself without being interrupted or told how to do it? Yet, how often in mathematics class does this happen? As soon as a student pauses in solving a problem the teacher steps in to show or explain. While this may initially get the student to an answer faster, it does not help the student learn mathematics—engaging in productive struggle is what helps students learn mathematics. As Piaget describes, learners are going to experience disequilibrium in developing new ideas. Let students know this disequilibrium is part of the process.

Productive struggle is critical to developing conceptual understanding (Hiebert & Grouws, 2007). Notice the importance of both words in "productive struggle." Students must have the tools and prior knowledge to solve a problem, and not be given a problem that is out of reach, or they will struggle without being productive; yet students should not be given tasks that are straightforward and easy or they will not be struggling with mathematical ideas. When students, even very young students, know that struggle is expected as part of the process of doing mathematics, they embrace the struggle and feel success when they reach a solution (Carter, 2008). We must redefine what it means to "help" students. Rather than showing students how to do something, we must employ strategies, like asking probing questions, that keep students engaged in productive struggle.

Treat Errors as Opportunities for Learning. When students make errors, it can mean a misapplication of their prior knowledge in a new situation. Remember that from a constructivist perspective, the mind is sifting through what it knows in order to find useful approaches for the new situation. Students rarely give random responses, so their errors are insight into limited or misconceptions they might have. For example, students comparing decimals may incorrectly

$$\begin{array}{r} \overset{5}{\cancel{6}}\overset{13}{0}\overset{}{\cancel{3}} \\ -\ 2\ 5\ 7 \\ \hline 6 \end{array}$$

There is nothing in this next column, so I'll borrow from the 6.

FIGURE 2.16 This student's work indicates that she has a misconception about place value and regrouping.

apply "rules" of whole numbers, such as "the more digits, the bigger the number" (Martinie, 2014). Often one student's misconception is shared by others in the class and discussing the problem publicly can help other students understand (Hoffman, Breyfogle, & Dressler, 2009). You can introduce errors and ask students to imagine what might have led to that answer (Rathouz, 2011). This public negotiation of meaning allows students to construct deeper meaning for the mathematics they are learning.

Scaffold New Content. The practice of *scaffolding*, often associated with sociocultural theory, is based on the idea that a task otherwise outside of a student's ZPD can become accessible if it is carefully structured. For concepts completely new to students, the learning requires more structure or assistance, including the use of tools (e.g., manipulatives) or more assistance from peers. As students become more comfortable with the content, the scaffolds are removed and the student becomes more independent. Scaffolding can provide support for those students who may not have a robust collection of "blue dots."

Honor Diversity. Finally, and importantly, these theories emphasize that each learner is unique, with a different collection of prior knowledge and cultural experiences. Since new knowledge is built on existing knowledge and experience, effective teaching incorporates and builds on what the students bring to the classroom, honoring those experiences. Thus, lesson contexts are selected based on students' interests, knowledge and experiences. Classroom culture influences the individual learning of your students. Support a range of approaches and strategies for doing mathematics. Each students' ideas should be valued and included in classroom discussions of the mathematics. (See also the discussion of Culturally Responsive Mathematics Instruction in Chapter 6.)

MyLab Education **Self-Check 2.3**

MyLab Education **Application Exercise 2.2:**

How Do Students Learn Mathematics? Click the link to access this exercise, then watch the video and answer the accompanying questions.

Connecting the Dots

It seems appropriate to close this chapter by connecting some dots, especially because the ideas represented here are the foundation for the approach to each topic in the content chapters. This chapter began with discussing what *doing* mathematics is and challenging you to do some mathematics. Each of these tasks offered opportunities to make connections between mathematics concepts—connecting the blue dots.

Second, you read about what is important to know about mathematics—that having relational knowledge (knowledge in which blue dots are well connected) requires conceptual and procedural understanding as well as other proficiencies. The problems that you solved in the first section emphasized concepts and procedures while placing you in a position to use strategic competence, adaptive reasoning, and a productive disposition.

Finally, you read how learning theory—the importance of having opportunities to connect the dots—connects to mathematics learning. The best learning opportunities, according to constructivism and sociocultural theories, are those that engage learners in using their own knowledge and experience to solve problems through social interactions and reflection. This is what you were asked to do in the four tasks. Did you learn something new about mathematics? Did you connect an idea that you had not previously connected?

This chapter focused on connecting the dots between theory and practice—building a case that your teaching must focus on opportunities for students to develop their own networks of blue dots. As you plan and design instruction, you should constantly reflect on how to elicit prior knowledge by designing tasks that reflect the social and cultural backgrounds of students, to challenge students to think critically and creatively, and to include a comprehensive treatment of mathematics.

 # RESOURCES FOR CHAPTER 2

RECOMMENDED READINGS

Articles

Carter, S. (2008). Disequilibrium & questioning in the primary classroom: Establishing routines that help students learn. *Teaching Children Mathematics, 15*(3), 134–137.

This is a wonderful teacher's story of how she infused the constructivist notion of disequilibrium and the related idea of productive struggle to support learning in her first-grade class.

Whitacre, I., Schoen, R. C., Champagne, Z., & Goddard, A. (2016). Relational thinking: What's the difference? *Teaching Children Mathematics, 23*(5), 303–309.

These authors illustrate the importance of relational thinking sharing interesting results from students related to subtraction, and offering strategies for developing procedural flexibility.

Wilburne, J. M., Wildmann, T., Morret, M., & Stipanovic, J. (2014). Classroom strategies to make sense and persevere. *Mathematics Teaching in the Middle School, 20*(3), 144–151.

Four strategies are shared that not only help build perseverance, but also develop the other mathematical practices and ultimately develop students' productive dispositions.

Books

Boaler, J. (2016). *Mathematical mindsets: Unleashing student potential through creative math, inspiring messaging, and innovative teaching.* San Francisco, CA: Jossey Bass.

Full of excellent tasks and strategies for engaging students, this very popular book is a great resource for K–12 teachers. Research and examples build a strong case for engaging students in doing mathematics to help them become mathematically proficient.

Mason, J., Burton, L., & Stacey, K. (2010). *Thinking mathematically* (2nd ed.). Harlow, England: Pearson Education.

This classic book is about doing mathematics. There are excellent problems to explore along the way, with strategy suggestions. It is an engaging book that will help you learn more about your own problem solving and become a better teacher of mathematics.

CHAPTER 3

Teaching through Problem Solving

LEARNER OUTCOMES

After reading this chapter and engaging in the embedded activities and reflections, you should be able to:

3.1 Contrast and describe approaches to problem solving.

3.2 Describe teaching practices that support student learning for all students

3.3 Critique mathematical tasks to determine if they promote problem solving and procedural fluency.

3.4 Explain ways to engage students in classroom discourse.

Imagine yourself in a mathematics classroom. What are students working on? What are they talking about? If that classroom embodies the ideas in Chapter 2 of doing mathematics, then you will see students working on a task carefully selected by the teacher that allows them to add to their prior knowledge, connect mathematical ideas, and learn important conceptual and procedural knowledge related to the topic. *Principles to Actions* (NCTM, 2014) includes reasoning and problem solving as one of eight mathematics teaching practices, explaining that effective teachers engage students in solving and talking about tasks that can be solved in different ways by different students. The first of the eight mathematical practices in CCSS-M explains that mathematically proficient students are able to make sense of a situation, select solution paths, consider alternative strategies, and monitor their progress—problem solve (NGA Center & CCSSO, 2010). In this chapter, we focus on how to teach through problem solving, including how to select worthwhile tasks and facilitate student engagement (e.g., talking and writing) with those tasks.

 Problem Solving

The world in which we live and work has changed, and will continue to change, dramatically. In particular the mathematics we need for careers and for personal finance is completely different now than it was 25 years or 50 years ago. Yet, mathematics lessons in many classrooms may look the same as a generation or two generations ago. What do you remember about the types of problems or tasks that you were expected to do in school? Were you given instructions and then asked to follow them to get to a correct solution? Were you given encouragement to solve the problem differently? To come up with your own way to solve the problem? To consider if a particular strategy was efficient? Were you asked to determine when a particular strategy was useful (and when it was not)?

Skills needed in the 21st-century workplace are less about being able to compute and more about being able to design solution strategies. Priorities for students today include critical thinking, communication, collaboration, and creativity, as well as being able to use technology (Partnership for 21st Century Skills, n.d.). Students engaged in these inquiry-based or problem-based practices are encouraged to ask: Why? What would happen if? What is another way? How does this way compare to that way? Will this always work? Inquiry is a disposition of openness, curiosity, and wonder (Clifford & Marinucci, 2008). This disposition comes naturally to young students—our goal as teachers is to nurture it, not squelch it.

Too often mathematics teaching still follows the pattern of the teacher showing one way to do a skill, and students practicing that skill using the same procedure. Unfortunately, this approach to mathematics teaching has not been successful for many students and it does not prepare students for their 21st-century lives. Here are a few shortcomings of a teach-by-telling approach:

- It communicates that there is only one way to solve the problem, misrepresenting the field of mathematics and disempowering students who naturally may want to try to do it their own way.
- It positions the student as a passive learner, dependent on the teacher to present ideas, rather than as an independent thinker with the capability and responsibility for solving the problem.
- It assumes that all students have the necessary prior knowledge to understand the teacher's explanations—which is rarely, if ever, the case.
- It decreases the likelihood a student will attempt a novel problem without explicit instructions on how to solve it. But that's what doing mathematics is—figuring out an approach to solve the problem at hand.

Are you thinking that showing students is the helpful, preventing students from struggling while also saving time? If so, you are in good company. But, there is strong research showing that engaging students in productive struggle (i.e., allowing time and opportunity for them to grapple with a task and figure out mathematical strategies) leads to increased conceptual understanding (Hiebert & Grouws, 2007; NCTM, 2014). To be effective in preparing students to do mathematics, you have to consider alternatives to teaching by telling, and find ways to engage students in productive struggle (while not frustrating them).

Schroeder and Lester (1989) describe three approaches to problem solving that are used in classrooms. The distinctions between these ways are important because, as you will read, only attending to one of these approaches, will not lead to your students becoming mathematically proficient. Spoiler alert: the approaches are sequenced with the most important coming last!

Teaching *for* Problem Solving

Teaching *for* problem solving starts with learning the abstract concept and then moving to solving problems as a way to apply the learned skills (explain-practice-apply). For example, students learn the algorithm for adding fractions and, once that is mastered, solve story problems that involve adding fractions. This is the most common approach, and is often the way textbooks are written (practice first, then solve story problems). The major shortcoming of this approach is that students learn very early in school that the stories they encounter are going to be solved using the skill they just learned. Therefore, there is no point in reading the story to see what is happening and what needs solved, the numbers can be lifted out and the skill applied. This habit has resulted in students having difficulties with story problems, multistep problems, and solving high-level tasks. In other words, the pattern of explain-practice-apply works against preparing students to *do mathematics*. Yet, solving application problems after a skill is learned *is* important. The key is to be sure that the application problem is complex enough that reading and making sense of the situation is necessary to solving it.

Teaching *about* Problem Solving

Students need guidance on *how* to problem solve. This includes the process of problem solving and learning strategies that can help in solving problems—for example, "draw a picture."

Four-Step Problem Solving Process. George Pólya, a famous mathematician, wrote a classic book, *How to Solve It* (1945), which outlined four steps for problem solving. These steps for problem solving continue to be widely used today. For example, they are reflected in the first mathematical practice, "Making sense of problems and persevere in solving them" (NGA Center & CCSSO, 2010, p. 6). The four steps are summarized here:

1. *Understand the problem.* First, you must figure out what the problem is about and identify what question or problem is being posed.
2. *Devise a plan.* Next, you think about how to solve the problem. Will you want to write an equation? Will you want to model the problem with a manipulative? (See the next section, "Problem-Solving Strategies.")
3. *Carry out the plan.* This step is the implementation of your selected plan.
4. *Look back.* This final step, arguably the most important as well as most often skipped, is when you determine whether your answer from step 3 answers the problem as originally understood in step 1. Does your answer make sense? If not, loop back to step 2 and select a different strategy to solve the problem, or loop back to step 3 to fix something within your strategy.

The beauty of Pólya's framework is its generalizability; it can and should be applied to many different types of problems, from simple computational exercises to authentic and worthwhile multistep problems. Explicitly teaching these four steps to students can improve their ability to think mathematically.

Problem-Solving Strategies. Strategies for solving problems are identifiable methods for approaching a task. These strategies are "habits of mind" associated with thinking mathematically (Levasseur & Cuoco, 2003; Mark, Cuoco, Glodenberg, & Sword, 2010). Students select or design a strategy as they devise a plan (Pólya's step 2). The following labeled strategies are commonly encountered in grades K–8, though not all of them are used at every grade level.

- *Visualize.* Seeing is not only believing—it is also a means for understanding! Using manipulatives, acting it out, drawing a picture, or using dynamic software are ways to help represent, understand, and communicate mathematical concepts.
- *Look for patterns.* Searching for patterns, including regularity and repetition in everyday, spatial, symbolic, or imaginary contexts, is an important entry point into thinking mathematically. Patterns in number and operations play a huge role in helping students learn and master basic skills starting at the earliest levels and continuing into middle and high school.
- *Predict and check for reasonableness.* This is sometimes called "Guess and Check," but students are predicting more than they are guessing. This is not as easy as it may sound, as it involves making a strategic attempt, reflecting, and adjusting if necessary. The quantitative analysis (the answer is too small or too big) supports student sense making and is a bridge to algebra (Guerrero, 2010).
- *Formulate conjectures and justify claims.* As students interpret a problem, making conjectures and then testing them can help students solve the problem and deepen their understanding of the mathematical relationships. This reasoning is central to doing mathematics (Lannin, Ellis, & Elliott, 2011).
- *Create a list, table, or chart.* Systematically accounting for possible outcomes in a situation can provide insights into its solution. Students may make an organized list, a table or t-chart, or chart information on a graph. The list, table, or chart is used to search for patterns in order to solve the problem.
- *Simplify or change the problem.* Simplifying the quantities in a problem can make a situation easier to understand and analyze. This can lead to insights that can be applied to the original, more complex quantities in a problem. One way to simplify the problem is to test specific examples. The results of testing examples can provide insights into the structure of the task.
- *Write an equation.* Using or inventing symbols, numbers, notations, and equations are compact ways of modeling a situation. Writing an equation can provide insights into the structure of the problem and be used in solving the task.

Mathematical problem solving is founded in curiosity. The ways of thinking described here become the tools by which students can enter into unfamiliar and novel tasks. These strategies are not distinct, but interrelated. For example, creating a list is a way of looking for patterns. When students employ one of these strategies, it should be identified, highlighted, and discussed. Labeling a strategy provides a useful means for students to talk about their methods, which can help students make connections between and among strategies and representations. Over time, these mathematical ways of thinking will become habits.

It is important not to "proceduralize" problem solving. In other words, don't take the problem solving out of problem solving by telling students the strategy they should pick and how to do it. Instead, pose a problem that lends itself to different strategies, and ask students to approach the problem in a way that makes the most sense to them,

MyLab Education   Video Example 3.1

Watch the third-grade teacher in this video describe a problem-solving approach.

The classic handshake problem (see also the Handshake Problem Activity Page) is an example of a task that lends to many strategies:

Eight friends met for a skating party. Each friend shook hands once with everyone else. How many handshakes occurred?

MyLab Education   Activity Page: Handshakes

Without suggesting any strategy, ask students to explore this problem, design a solution strategy, implement it, and be ready to share. The following are common solution strategies:

Visualize by acting it out or drawing a picture:

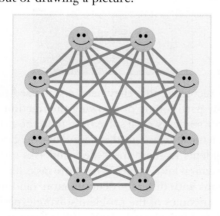

Create a smaller problem and record in a table:

Number of friends	2	3	4	5	6	7	8
Number of handshakes	1	3	6	10	15	21	28

Write an equation:

$$7 + 6 + 5 + 4 + 3 + 2 + 1 + 0 = 28$$

Note: The first friend can shake 7 hands, the next friend only has 6 hands to shake (she already shook hands with the first friend), and so on down to 0 handshakes for the last person.

During the sharing of results, you can help students understand the strategies other students used and see connections among the strategies. Additionally, you can highlight a particular strategy so that more students are able to use that strategy on a future task.

Similar problems can be posed to support the development of these problem solving strategies for example:

---

1. If six softball teams play each other once in a round-robin tournament, how many games will be needed?

2. How many blocks are needed for the 10th staircase?

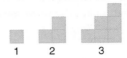

Teaching *through* Problem Solving

This approach means that students learn mathematics through inquiry. They explore real contexts, problems, situations, and models, and from those explorations they learn mathematics. So, teaching *through* problem solving might be described as upside down from teaching *for* problem solving—with the problem or task presented at the beginning of a lesson and related knowledge or skills emerging from exploring the problem. Consider the following task, given to students who have not learned the algorithm for adding fractions with different denominators:

What fraction of this flag is blue?

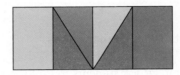

By partitioning, students might label each section with their fraction of the whole, labeling the blue parts as illustrated here:

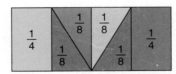

As students work, they recognize that they need equal-sized pieces in order to combine. They change $\frac{1}{4}$ to $\frac{2}{8}$ (either by partitioning or knowing the fraction equivalency) and then add the blue pieces to get $\frac{3}{8}$. After students have solved the task, the teacher convenes the class to highlight important mathematical ideas—in this case that you can only combine same-sized pieces. The teacher asks students to share their ideas and asks questions that help build and connect conceptual *and* procedural knowledge. With more tasks like this one, students learn the procedure for adding fractions with different denominators (and understand it!). Notice that mathematical ideas are the outcomes of the problem solving experience rather than elements taught before problem solving (Hiebert et al., 1996, 1997). Importantly, the process of solving problems is completely interwoven with the learning; children are *learning* mathematics by *doing* mathematics and by doing mathematics they are learning mathematics (Cai, 2010).

Teaching through problem solving acknowledges what we now know about what it means to learn and do mathematics (see Chapter 2). Our understanding is always changing, incomplete, situated in context, and interconnected. What we learn becomes part of our expanding and evolving network of ideas—a network without endpoints. What we learn through problem solving and inquiry can change what we thought we knew before, and can be the basis for asking new questions that can lead to new learning (Thomas & Brown, 2011). Teaching through problem solving positions students to engage in inquiry and has a positive impact on students

(Boaler & Sengupta-Irving, 2016; Cobb, Gresalfi, & Hodge, 2009; Langer-Osuna, 2011). In these more effective classrooms, students:

- Ask questions
- Determine solution paths
- Use mathematical tools
- Make conjectures
- Seek out patterns
- Communicate findings
- Make connections to other content
- Make generalizations
- Reflect on results

Hopefully this sounds familiar. This list reflects the Standards for Mathematical Practice (CCSS-M) and reflects the strands of mathematical proficiency.

MyLab Education   Self-Check 3.1

Teaching Practices for Teaching through Problem Solving

Classrooms where students are learning through problem solving do not happen by accident—they happen because the teacher uses practices and establishes expectations that encourage risk taking, reasoning, the generation and sharing of ideas, and so forth. Teaching *through* problem solving involves more than just tweaking a few things; it is a paradigm shift from traditional mathematics teaching where students repeat what the teacher demonstrates. At first glance, it may seem that the teacher's role is less demanding because the students are doing the mathematics, but the teacher's role is actually more demanding in such classrooms. Table 3.1 lists eight research-informed teaching practices from NCTM's (2014) *Principles to Actions*, along with the teacher actions that relate to that practice. All eight are addressed throughout this book and all are important to teaching mathematics *through* problem solving. In this chapter, we address tasks, building procedural fluency, and orchestrating discourse (three of the teaching practices).

Ensuring Success for Every Student

The NCTM Teaching Practices were designed to address issues related to access and equity—in other words, they are intended to ensure that all students have access to learning important mathematics. Teaching through problem solving provides opportunities for all students to become mathematically proficient (Boaler, 2008; Diversity in Mathematics Education, 2007; Silver & Stein, 1996). Teaching through problem solving:

- *Focuses students' attention on ideas and sense making.* When solving problems, students are necessarily reflecting on the concepts inherent in the problems. Emerging concepts are more likely to be integrated with existing ones, thereby improving understanding. This approach honors the different knowledge students bring to the classroom.
- *Develops mathematical practices and processes.* By definition, teaching through problem solving positions students to be the "doers," and as they are doing the mathematics, they are developing mathematical practices that are essential to becoming mathematically proficient.
- *Develops student confidence and identities.* As students engage in learning through problem solving, they begin to identify themselves as doers of mathematics (Boaler, 2008, Cobb, Gresalfi, & Hodge, 2009; Leatham & Hill, 2010). When students' peers and teachers listen to and respect their ideas, it impacts students' emerging mathematical identities (Aguirre, Mayfield-Ingram, & Martin, 2013) and later pursuit of careers that lead to higher socioeconomic status (Boaler & Selling, 2017).

TABLE 3.1 EIGHT MATHEMATICAL TEACHING PRACTICES THAT SUPPORT STUDENT LEARNING.

Teaching Practice	To Enact the Mathematics Teaching Practice, a Teacher:
1. Establish mathematics goals to focus learning	• Articulates clear learning goals that identify the mathematics students will learn in a lesson or lessons. • Identifies how the learning goals relate to a mathematics learning progression. • Helps students understand how the work they are doing relates to the learning goals. • Uses the articulated goals to inform instructional decisions involved in planning and implementation.

2. Implement tasks that promote reasoning and problem solving	• Selects tasks that:
	  • Have maximum potential to build and extend students' current mathematical understanding.
	  • Have multiple entry points.
	  • Require a high level of cognitive demand.
	• Supports students to make sense of and solve tasks using multiple strategies and representations, without doing the thinking for the students.

3. Use and connect mathematical representations	• Supports students to use and make connections between various representations. • Introduces representations when appropriate. • Expects students to use various representations to support their reasoning and explanations. • Allows students to choose which representations to use in their work. • Helps students attend to the essential features of a mathematical idea represented in a variety of ways.
4. Facilitate meaningful mathematical discourse	• Facilitates productive discussions among students by focusing on reasoning and justification. • Strategically selects and sequences students' strategies for whole class discussion. • Makes explicit connections between students' strategies and ideas.

5. Pose purposeful questions	• Asks questions that
	  • Probe students' thinking and that require explanation and justification.
	  • Build on students' ideas and avoids funneling (i.e., directing to one right answer or idea).
	  • Make students' ideas and the mathematics more visible so learners can examine the ideas more closely.
	• Provides appropriate amounts of wait time to allow students to organize their thoughts.

6. Build procedural fluency from conceptual understanding	• Encourages students to make sense of, use, and explain their own reasoning and strategies to solve tasks. • Makes explicit connections between strategies produced by students and conventional strategies and procedures.
7. Support productive struggle in learning mathematics	• Helps students see mistakes, misconceptions, naïve conceptions, and struggles as opportunities for learning. • Anticipates potential difficulties and prepares questions that will help scaffold and support students' thinking. • Allows students time to struggle with problems. • Praises students for their efforts and perseverance in problem solving.
8. Elicit and use evidence of student thinking	• Decides what will count as evidence of students' understanding. • Gathers evidence of students' understanding at key points during lesson. • Interprets students' thinking to gauge understanding and progress toward learning goals. • Decides during the lesson how to respond to students to probe, scaffold, and extend their thinking. • Uses evidence of students' learning to guide subsequent instruction.

Source: Based on Principles to Actions: Ensuring Mathematical Success For All (NCTM), © 2014.

- *Builds on students' strengths.* Because good problems have multiple paths to the solution, students can apply strategies that they understand and that lend to their learning preferences. Students may solve 42−26 by applying various mental strategies, using a manipulative such as base-ten blocks, by counting forward (or backward) on a hundreds chart, or by applying an algorithm. Furthermore, students expand on these ideas and grow in their understanding as they hear and reflect on the solution strategies of others.
- *Allows for extensions and elaborations.* Extensions and "what if" questions can motivate and challenge all students, as well as provide enrichment for advanced learners or quick finishers. For example, students can generate their own questions related to the problem they solved.
- *Engages students so that there are fewer discipline problems.* Many discipline issues in a classroom are the result of boredom, not understanding directions or an algorithm, or simply finding little relevance in the task. Most students like to be challenged and enjoy being permitted to solve problems in ways that make sense to them, giving them less reason to act out or cause trouble.

- *Provides formative assessment data.* As students discuss ideas, draw pictures or use manipulatives, defend their solutions and evaluate those of others, and write reports or explanations, they provide the teacher with a steady stream of valuable information. These products provide rich evidence of how students are solving problems, what misconceptions they might have, and how they are connecting and applying new concepts. With a better understanding of what students know, a teacher can plan more effectively and accommodate each student's learning needs.
- *Invites creativity* Students enjoy the creative process of problem solving, searching for patterns, and showing how they figured something out. Teachers find it exciting to see the surprising and inventive ways students think. Teachers know more about their students and appreciate the diversity within their classrooms when they focus on problem solving.

When students have confidence, show perseverance, and enjoy mathematics, it makes sense that they will achieve at a higher level and want to continue learning about mathematics, opening many doors to them in the future.

MyLab Education   **Self-Check 3.2**

Tasks That Promote Problem Solving

In order to create classroom experiences for students where they develop the mathematical practices, you must select tasks that promote problem solving. Such a worthwhile task may take on many different forms. It might be clearly defined or open-ended; it may involve problem solving or problem posing; it may include words or be purely symbols; it may take only a few minutes to solve or may take weeks to investigate; it may be real-life or abstract. Also, a task can be problematic initially, but then become routine as a student's knowledge and experience grows, or be problematic for some students, but not for others, based on their previous experiences. For a task to lend to problem-solving, in other words be *problematic*, it must pose a question for which (1) there is no prescribed rules or methods to solve and (2) there is not a perception that there is one "correct" solution method (Hiebert et al., 1997).

Here is a task for you to try (see also the Missing Numbers Activity Page):

$10 + \blacksquare = 4 + (3 + \blacktriangle)$.

Find a number to replace the square and a number to replace the triangle so that the equation is true.

Find more pairs of numbers that will make the equation true.

What do you notice about the numbers for any correct solution?

MyLab Education   **Activity Page: Missing Numbers**

Is this a worthwhile task? It does not have a prescribed approach and there are numerous ways to approach the problem—so it meets the first criteria of being problematic. This task has other features that also make it worthwhile, which include: high-level cognitive demand, multiple entry and exit points, and relevant contexts.

High-Level Cognitive Demand

Tasks that promote problem solving are cognitively demanding, meaning they involve high-level thinking. Low cognitive demand tasks (also called *routine problems* or *lower-level tasks*) involve stating facts, following known procedures (computation), and solving routine problems. On Bloom's Taxonomy, they are at the remembering level–the lowest level.

> **MyLab Education** Video Example 3.2
>
> As described in How Thinking Works TED Talk (https://www.youtube.com/watch?v=dUqRTWCdXt4), schools must focus on teaching students to *think* (rather than follow instructions and remember facts).

VIDEO EXAMPLE

High-level cognitive demand tasks, on the other hand, involve understanding, analyzing information and applying it, and evaluating strategies,, as indicated by the other levels of Bloom's Taxonomy (see Chapter 2, Figure 2.1). Table 3.2 provides descriptors for the low-level and high-level cognitive demand descriptors (Smith & Stein, 1998). The Missing Numbers task above and the tasks in Chapter 2 each involve high-level cognitive demand. And, the task does not need to have a context or take days to solve to have a high level of cognitive demand—but it must provide students an opportunity to reason and make sense of the mathematics (NCTM, 2014).

Multiple Entry and Exit Points

Because your students will likely have a wide range of experiences in mathematics, it is important to use problems that have *multiple entry points*, meaning that the task can be approached in a variety of ways and has varying degrees of challenge within it. Having multiple entry points can accommodate the diversity of learners in your classroom because students are encouraged to use a variety of strategies that are supported by their prior experiences. Having a choice of strategies can lower the anxiety of students, particularly English learners (Murrey, 2008). Students are encouraged to engage with the task in a way that makes sense to them, rather than trying to recall or replicate a procedure shown to them.

Tasks should also have *multiple exit points*, or various ways to express solutions that reveal a range of mathematical sophistication and have the potential to generate new questions. As

---

TABLE 3.2   LEVELS OF COGNITIVE DEMAND

Low-Level Cognitive Demand	High-Level Cognitive Demand
Memorization Tasks • Involve either producing previously learned facts, rules, formulas, or definitions or memorizing • Are routine—involving exact reproduction of previously learned procedure • Have no connection to related concepts	**Procedures with Connections Tasks** • Focus students' attention on the use of procedures for the purpose of developing deeper levels of understanding of mathematical concepts and ideas • Suggest general procedures that have close connections to underlying conceptual ideas • Are usually represented in multiple ways (e.g., visuals, manipulatives, symbols, problem situations) • Require that students engage with the conceptual ideas that underlie the procedures in order to successfully complete the task
Procedures without Connections Tasks • Specifically call for use of the procedure • Require little cognitive demand, with little ambiguity about what needs to be done and how to do it • Have no connection to related concepts • Are focused on producing correct answers rather than developing mathematical understanding • Require no explanations, or explanations focus solely on the procedure that was used	**Doing Mathematics Tasks** • Require complex and nonalgorithmic thinking (i.e., nonroutine—there is not a predictable, known approach) • Require students to explore and understand the nature of mathematical concepts, processes, or relationships • Demand self-monitoring or self-regulation of one's own cognitive processes • Require students to access relevant knowledge in working through the task • Require students to analyze the task and actively examine task constraints that may limit possible solution strategies and solutions • Require considerable cognitive effort

Source: Adapted from Smith, M. S., & Stein, M. K. (1998). Selecting and creating mathematical tasks: From research to practice. *Mathematics Teaching in the Middle School, 3*(5), 344–350. Reprinted with permission.

students employ their multiple approaches and varied displays of their solutions (e.g., various pictures, demonstrations with manipulatives, acting out a problem, using a table or a graph, etc.), opportunities emerge for students to defend their strategy, critique the reasoning of others, learn new approaches, all the while thinking at a high level about mathematics.

Consider the opportunities for multiple entry and exit points in the following kindergarten or first-grade tasks.

TASK 1: [The teacher places a bowl of objects (e.g., toy cars) on the table.] Do we have enough [toy cars] for everyone in the class?

TASK 2: [The teacher gives each student a page with pictures of cars copied in rows (see Do We Have Enough? Activity Page). Do we have enough cars for everyone in the class?

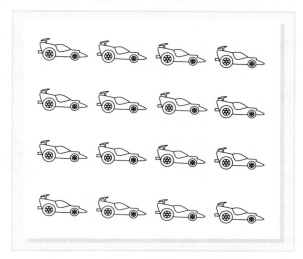

MyLab Education   Activity Page: Do We Have Enough?

At first glance, the first task might seem the more engaging because it includes actual manipulatives. But, in the particular case, having toy cars (or a cube representing a car) available, might lead to one (low-level) strategy: passing the cars out to see if there are enough for each child. The second task is more problematic. Students might count the cars. As they count, you can observe their thinking: Do they start at the top and count across the rows? Or do they haphazardly count and miss or double-count? Do they count by ones? By twos? By fours? Instead of counting cars, students might count their friends in the class first. Or, students might "assign" a car to each friend, writing names on each car. Counting the cars is just one aspect of the task; students must also decide how that number compares to the number of students in the class. Does a student just know that the number of cars is greater or less than the number of students? Do they represent each child in the class with a counter, and match a counter with a pictured car? Do they look for the two numbers on a hundreds chart or number line to compare? Because the second task is more problematic, it offers many more options for how to begin the task (entry) and how to show a solution for the task (exit), making it a worthwhile task for the class.

Figure 3.1(a) provides a high level task that has multiple entry and exit points.

⏸ Pause & Reflect

Before studying the solutions in Figure 3.1(b), read the problem, select a strategy and solve it. ●

Figure 3.1(b) illustrates a range of solutions. Student (b) used percentages as a way to compare; student (d) found simplified fractions to compare quantities; student (g) used part-part

(a)

Ms. Rhee's mathematics class was studying statistics. She brought in three bags containing red and blue marbles. The three bags were labeled as shown below:

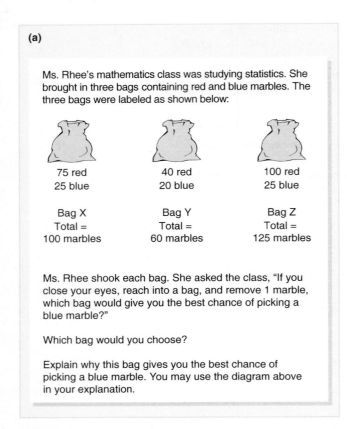

75 red	40 red	100 red
25 blue	20 blue	25 blue
Bag X	Bag Y	Bag Z
Total =	Total =	Total =
100 marbles	60 marbles	125 marbles

Ms. Rhee shook each bag. She asked the class, "If you close your eyes, reach into a bag, and remove 1 marble, which bag would give you the best chance of picking a blue marble?"

Which bag would you choose?

Explain why this bag gives you the best chance of picking a blue marble. You may use the diagram above in your explanation.

(b)

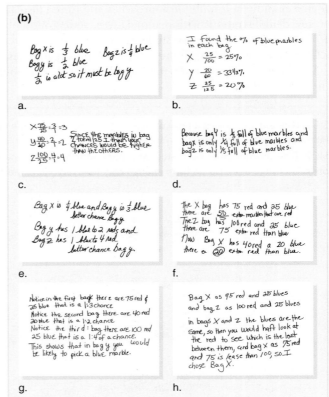

FIGURE 3.1 A task with multiple entry and exit points, as illustrated by the range of student solutions.

Source: Smith, M. S., Bill, V., & Hughes, E. K. (2008). Thinking Through a Lesson: Successfully Implementing High-Level Tasks. *Mathematics Teaching in the Middle School, 14*(3), 132–138. Reprinted with permission.

ratios to reason about the quantities. In addition, several solutions reveal student misconceptions. Notice that in solution (a), the student has recorded part-part ratios, but then is comparing the values as though they are fractions (part-whole) and in solution (f) the student is comparing differences, rather than attending to the multiplicative relationships. During a classroom discussion, the teacher's role is to ensure that the strategies are strategically shared (perhaps sharing some less advanced strategies first or related strategies together). In doing this, students can clear up misconceptions, make connections among the strategies and among mathematical ideas (i.e., ratio, fractions, percents, and probability), and thereby advance their understanding of mathematics (Smith, Bill, & Hughes, 2008).

Relevant Contexts

Certainly one of the most powerful features of a worthwhile task is that the problem that begins the lesson can get students excited about learning mathematics. Compare the following introductory tasks on multiplying 2 two-digit numbers. Which one do you think would more exciting to fourth-grade students?

Classroom A: "Today we are going to use grid paper to show the sub-products when we multiply 2 two-digit numbers."

Classroom B: "The school is planning a fall festival and class is selling water. The principal said we have 14 cases of bottled water in the storage closet. I looked in the storage closet and could see that a case had 7 rows, with 5 bottles in each row. How can we use the information about one case to figure out how many bottles of water we have?" If we sell each one for $2.00, how much money might we make?.

Contexts must reflect the cultures and interests of the students in your classroom (this is a critical component of Culturally Responsive Mathematics Instruction in Chapter 5). Using everyday situations can increase student participation, increase student use of different problem strategies, and help students develop a productive disposition (Tomaz & David, 2015). Here we share two strategies for incorporating relevant contexts—using literature and connecting to other subjects.

Use Literature. Children's literature and adolescent literature are rich sources of problems. Picture books, poems, media, and chapter books can be used to create high cognitive demand tasks with multiple entry points. An example of literature lending itself to mathematical problems is the very popular children's picture book *Two of Everything* (Hong, 1993). In this magical Chinese folktale, a couple finds a pot that doubles whatever is put into it. (Imagine where the story goes when Mrs. Haktak falls in the pot!). Students can explore the following problem: How many students would be in our class if our whole class fell in the Magic Pot? Figure 3.2 illustrates different ways that students in second grade approached the problem (multiple entry points) and different ways they explained and illustrated how they figured it out (multiple exit points). Notice that the student using the hundreds chart is incorrect. The teacher will need to follow up to determine whether this was a copy error or a misconception.

In *Harry Potter and the Sorcerer's Stone* (Rowling, 1998), various lessons can be built on the description of Hagrid as twice as tall and five times as wide as the average man. Students in grades 2–3 can cut strips of paper that are as tall as they are and as wide as their shoulders are (you can cut strips from cash register rolls). Then they can figure out how big Hagrid would be if he were twice as tall and five times as wide as they are. In grades 4–5, students can create a table that shows each student's height and width and look for a pattern (it turns out to be about 3 to 1). Then they can figure out Hagrid's height and width and see whether they keep the same ratio (it is 5 to 2). In grades 6–8, students can create a scatter plot of their widths and heights and see where Hagrid's data would be plotted on the graph. Measurement, number, and algebra content are all embedded in this example. Whether students are 5 or 13, literature resonates with their experiences and imaginations, making them more enthusiastic about solving the related mathematics problems and more likely to learn and to see mathematics as a useful tool for exploring the world.

Nonfiction literature (picture books, chapter books, newspapers, magazines, and the web) have the added benefit of students learning about the *real* world around them. There are books of lists (e.g., Scholastic Book of Lists (Buckley & Stremme, 2006)) and world record books, for example, which provide many great contexts for exploring the world, and comparing world data to your class (see Bay-Williams & Martinie, 2009; Petersen, 2004; Sheffield

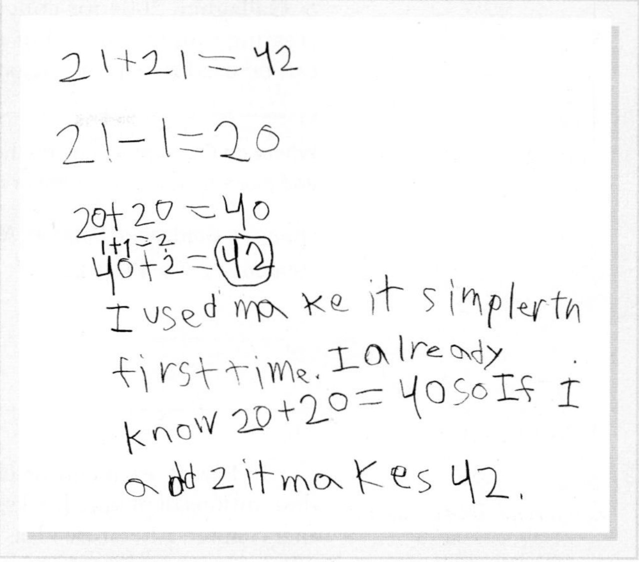

Robbie adds tens and ones to solve.

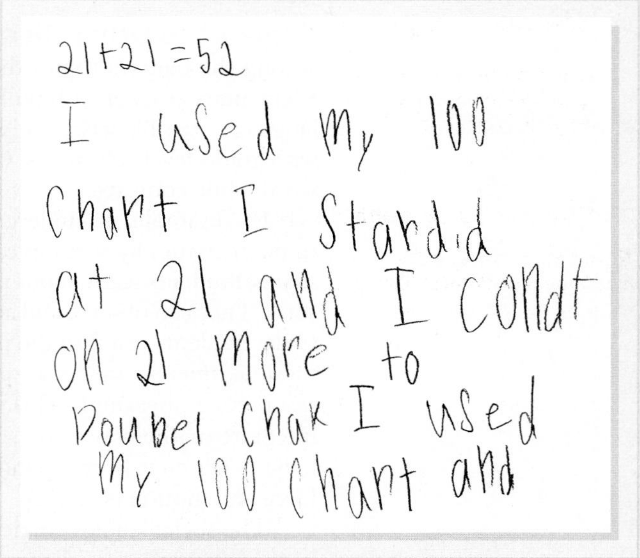

Kylee uses a hundreds chart and counts on.

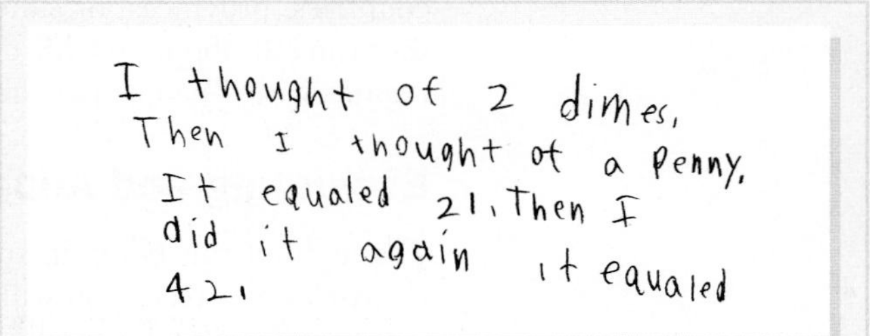

Benjamin uses the context of money to combine.

FIGURE 3.2 Second-grade students use different problem-solving strategies to figure out how many students there would be if their class of 21 were doubled.

& Gallagher, 2004 for collections of mathematics lessons using nonfiction). Dates lend to creating number lines. For example, the dates for the seven wonders of the ancient world can be used to explore negative numbers.

Where on the number line do these wonders of the ancient world go? Can you find the other wonders and place them on the number line?

Hanging Gardens of Babylon: About 600 B.C.　　　Great Pyramids: About 2500 B.C.

Statue of Zeus: 435 B.C.　　　Lighthouse of Alexandria: About 250 B.C.

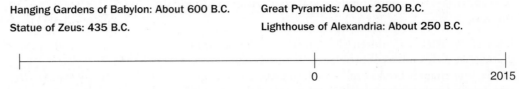

In Part II, each end-of-chapter resource section includes "Literature Connections," quick descriptions of picture books, poetry, and novels that can be used to explore the mathematics of that chapter. Literature ideas are also found in articles in journal articles (e.g., *Teaching Children Mathematics*) and teacher books (e.g., *Math & Literature Series, Using Children's Literature to Teach Problem Solving in Math* (White, 2014)).

Connect to Other Disciplines. Interdisciplinary lessons help students see connections among the courses/topics they are studying, which often feel completely separate to them. Elementary teachers can pull ideas from the topics being taught in social studies, science, and language arts; likewise, middle school teachers can link to these subjects as they collaborate with grade-level colleagues. Other familiar contexts such as art, sports, and pop culture are also worthwhile contexts.

For example, in kindergarten, students can link their study of natural systems in science to mathematics by sorting leaves based on color, smooth or jagged edges, feel of the leaf, and shape. Students learn about rules for sorting and can use Venn diagrams to keep track of their sorts. They can observe and analyze what is common and different in leaves from different trees. Older students can find the perimeter and area of various types of leaves and learn about why these perimeters and areas differ. Like with literature, there are high quality print and online resources. For example AIMS (Activities in Mathematics and Science) has numerous books that integrate mathematics and science. In *Looking at Lines* (AIMS, 2005), middle school students hang paper clips from a handmade balance to learn about linear equations (mathematics) and force and motion (science).

The social studies curriculum is rich with opportunities to do mathematics. Timelines of historic events are excellent opportunities for students to work on the relative sizes of numbers and to make better sense of history. Students can explore the areas and populations of various countries, provinces, or states and compare the population densities, while in social studies they can talk about how life differs between regions with 200 people living in a square mile and regions with 5 people per square mile.

Evaluating and Adapting Tasks

Throughout this book, in student textbooks, on the Internet, at workshops you attend, and in articles you read, you will find suggestions for tasks that *someone* believes are effective for teaching a particular mathematics concept. Yet a large quantity of what is readily available falls short when measured against the standards of being (1) high level and (2) promoting problem solving. This is particularly true with the plethora of worksheets that pop up on web searches and sites for teachers. Beware of the low-level cognitive demand tasks cloaked in clever artwork—they may look fun, but if the mathematics is not problematic, those graphics are not going to help your students think at a high level. Make sure it is the mathematics itself that is clever and engaging.

	Task Evaluation and Selection Guide
Task Potential	Try it and ask . . . ❑ What is problematic about the task? ❑ Is the mathematics interesting? ❑ What mathematical goals does the task address (and are they aligned to what you are seeking)? ❑ What strategies might students use? ❑ What key concepts and/or misconceptions might this task elicit?
Problem-Solving Strategies	Will the task elicit more than one problem-solving strategy? Which strategies are possible? ❑ Visualize ❑ Look for patterns ❑ Predict and check for reasonableness ❑ Formulate conjectures and justify claims ❑ Create a list, table, or chart ❑ Simplify or change the problem ❑ Write an equation
Features	To what extent does the task have these key features? ❑ High cognitive demand ❑ Multiple entry and exit points ❑ Relevant contexts
Assessment	In what ways does the task provide opportunities for you to gain insights into student understanding through? ❑ Using tools or models to represent mathematics ❑ Student reflection, justification, and explanation ❑ Multiple ways to demonstrate understanding

FIGURE 3.3 Use these reflective questions in selecting tasks that promote problem solving.

An intentional selection process can help with selecting high quality tasks (Barlow, 2010; Breyfogle & Williams, 2008–2009). The Task Evaluation and Selection Guide in Figure 3.3 provides reflective questions to help you evaluate whether a task you are considering has the maximum potential to help your children learn relevant mathematics. These questions are meant to help you consider to what extent the task meets these criteria, so all boxes do not need to be checked off. A task could rate very high on the number of problem solving strategies, but miss the mark in terms of being relevant for students, hence you decide to trade out the context for something more interesting. Or, the task is complete with the features and problem solving strategies, but it does not match your mathematical goals for the lesson. You may choose to alter the task to focus on the mathematics you have selected or save it for when it is a better match.

Certainly, teaching the operations has often been devoid of the features described in this chapter. You may be wondering how you will be able to teach all the operations by teaching through problem solving. Boaler (2016) offers ideas for adapting tasks are particularly applicable to the operations, but applies to all content areas.

1. *Allow multiple ways:* Explicitly ask students to use multiple methods, strategies, and representations to solve.
2. *Make it an exploration:* Change the task so there is more to it than a single computation. For example, rather than ask kindergartners to add 3+5, ask them to find numbers they can add to get the number 8.

3. *Postpone teaching a standard method:* Begin with students' intuition about how to solve a problem type before learning about conventional methods.
4. *Add a visual requirement:* Visualization enhances understanding. Students can use two different manipulatives to justify their solution, or show how an equation fits a drawing of a story situation.
5. *Increase the number of entry points:* You can increase the entry points by asking students to write down everything they know about the problem, or listing any possible ideas for how they might solve the problem.
6. *Reason and convince:* Require students to create convincing mathematical arguments and to expect the same from their peers. Ask them to be skeptics and to ask clarifying questions of each other. (Modeling argument and questioning is important to be sure it focuses on supporting each other's thinking.)

Just as students become adept at problem solving strategies, with time and commitment you will become adept at evaluating and adapting tasks to better support student learning. Imagine that you are teaching fourth grade and are seeking a worthwhile task for this goal:

4.G.A.2: Classify two-dimensional figures based on the presence or absence of parallel or perpendicular lines, or the presence or absence of angles of a specified size. Recognize right triangles as a category, and identify right triangles. (NGA Center & CCSSO, 2010, p. 32)

You type "classify triangles" into a web search. Hundreds of links and worksheet images appear, like the one in Figure 3.4.

⏸ Pause *&* Reflect

How does this task measure up on the Task Evaluation and Selection Guide? How might you adapt the task so that it rates higher on some of these measures of a worthwhile task? ●

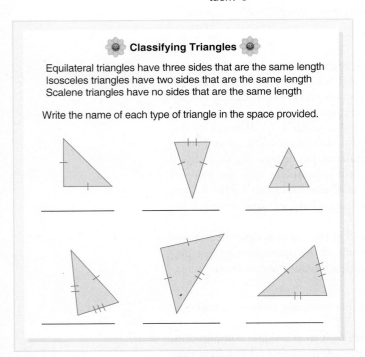

FIGURE 3.4 Example of a categorizing triangles worksheet.

This worksheet appears to match the learning goals, but it does not include high-level cognitive demand, multiple entry points, or relevant contexts. Here are some ways you might adapt it:

1. Remove the tick marks telling which sides are the same, distribute just the grid of triangles, letter them, and ask students to write similarities and differences between pairs of triangles. This provides multiple entry points and a high level of cognitive demand.
2. Only use the list of terms at the top and ask students to identify examples of each in the room or in a picture book.
3. Cut out the triangles, ask students to create piles of what they consider the "same" triangles and to put names on their groups. In a later discussion, different possible ways to sort triangles can be discussed and appropriate terminology can be reinforced.

Extensions might be added to make this task a stronger task. These might include asking students, "Can you build two triangles of different sizes that are both isosceles?" "Can you create a triangle with three obtuse angles? Why or why not?" "If a triangle is classified as [right], then which classifications for sides are possible or impossible?" Each of these adaptations takes very little time, and greatly increases the tasks potential to develop a deep understanding of geometry concepts.

Developing Procedural Fluency

In Chapter 2, we discussed the importance of developing mathematical proficiency through conceptual understanding and procedural proficiency. In Chapter 3 we have focused on problem solving and the features of a tasks that support problem solving. In this section, we focus on teaching concepts *and* procedures *through* problem solving, using five examples.

Example Tasks

Developing procedural fluency involves developing conceptual understanding and making connections among mathematical ideas (Bay-Williams & Stokes Levine, 2017; NCTM, 2014.

As you read, consider how each task opens up opportunities to make such connections between concepts and procedures.

Topic 1: Partitioning   Grades: K–1

Six bowls of cereal are placed at two different tables. Draw a picture to show a way that six bowls might be placed at two tables. Can you find more than one way? How many ways do you think there are?

MyLab Education **Application Exercise 3.1: Observing and Responding to Student Thinking** Click the link to access this exercise, then watch the video and answer the accompanying questions.

In kindergarten or grade 1, students may determine one or two ways to decompose 6 or may find all the ways (multiple entry points). Students can share how they thought about it and what patterns they noticed as they found new ways. For example, a student might note that as one table gets a bowl, the other table loses a bowl, so 1 bowl moves over. They may notice that there are then 7 possible ways. The task can be extended to other totals and other contexts, such as "How many ways can you put 10 toys into 2 baskets? Students begin to notice that numbers can be taken apart and put back together in different ways. They also begin to learn about addition, perhaps recording number sentences such as $1+5=6$, discussing the meaning of the symbols and how the numbers represent to the situation.

Topic 2: Adding Two-Digit Whole Numbers   Grades: 1–2

What is the sum of 48 and 25? How did you figure it out?

Even though there is no story or situation to resolve, this task is problematic because students must figure out how they are going to approach the task. (They have not been taught the standard algorithm at this point.) Students might work on the problem using manipulatives, pictures, or mental strategies. This following list contains just some of the approaches created by students in one second-grade classroom:

4$\boxed{8}$ + 2$\boxed{5}$ (Boxed digits "help" them.)
40 + 20 = 60
8 + 2 = 10 $\boxed{3}$ (The 3 is left from the 5.)
60 + 10 = 70
70 + 3 = 73

---

40 + 20 = 60
60 + 8 = 68
68 + 5 = 73

---

48 + 20 = 68
68 + 2 ("from the 5") = 70
"Then I still have that 3 from the 5."
70 + 3 = 73

---

25 + 25 = 50 $\boxed{23}$
50 + 23 = 73
Teacher: Where does the 23 come from?
"It's sort of from the 48."
How did you split up the 48?
"20 and 20 and I split the 8 into 5 and 3."

---

48 − 3 = 45 $\boxed{3}$
45 + 25 = 70
70 + 3 = 73

As students share their ways, they are deepening their conceptual understanding of place value, they are learning place value strategies for solving addition tasks, and they are developing a foundation for learning the standard algorithm, which is also based on place value. Note: Operations for whole numbers, decimals, fractions, and integers can be explored in a similar manner.

Topic 3: Area of a Rectangle   **Grades: 3–4**
Find the area of the cover of your math book by covering it with color tiles. Repeat for the areas of books of various sizes. What patterns do you notice in covering the book? Is this pattern or rule for covering any rectangle?

As students begin to cover surfaces, they may run out of tiles, or they may just get tired of placing tiles. They notice that each row has the same number of tiles, so they just need to know how many rows will cover the book and they can skip count or multiply to find the total number of tiles. This develops the concept of area, strengthens understanding of multiplication as repeated addition, and leads to the procedure for area of a rectangle. Most measurement formulas can be developed through problem solving, as you will read in Chapter 18.

Topic 4: Division of Fractions   **Grades: 5–7**
Anthony is knitting scarves for gifts for his sisters. Each scarf is one yard long and he can knit $\frac{1}{4}$ of a scarf each day. How long will it take him to make 3 scarves?

When students explore this task without the label "division of fractions," they can approach the problem in multiples ways. Leah, Kelly, Jaden, and MacKenna solved the task applying what they knew, including skip counting by fourths (Leah), measurement equivalencies (Kelly), ratios of yards to days (Jaden), and rates of days per yards (MacKenna). To extend their thinking about scarf-making, they were asked, "What would happen if Anthony decided to make $\frac{3}{4}$ of a scarf in one day?" A review of their second task shows that they used both their strategies and their answers from the first task in interesting ways. With more experiences with scarf-making with other rates, students can begin to connect to the concept of division and to generalize how solve such problems. Series of related tasks can help students connect concepts and procedures. The scarf length and the amount completed per day can vary to help students look for patterns across the problem set.

MyLab Education	Leah's Solution
MyLab Education	Kelly's Solution
MyLab Education	Jaden's Solution
MyLab Education	MacKenna's Solution

Topic 5: Ratios and Proportions   **Grades: 6–8**
Jack and Jill were at the same spot at the bottom of a hill, hoping to fetch a pail of water. They both begin walking up the hill, Jack walking 5 yards every 25 seconds and Jill walking 3 yards every 10 seconds. Assuming constant walking rate, who will get to the pail of water first?

Students can engage in this task in a variety of ways. They can represent the problem visually with jumps on a number line or symbolically using a rate approach (determining the number of yards per second for each person). This task focuses on how students are able to compare ratios. By specializing and considering several examples, either in this context or another, students will begin to generalize a procedure for comparing ratios, which is the essence of proportional reasoning. See It's a Matter of Rates Expanded Lesson for a full lesson on this task.

MyLab Education	Expanded Lesson: It's a Matter of Rates

Teaching mathematical concepts and procedures through problem solving helps students go beyond acquiring isolated ideas toward developing a connected and increasingly complex network of mathematical understanding (Cai, 2010; Carpenter, Franke, Jacobs, Fennema, & Empson, 1998; Fuson, Kalchman, & Bransford 2005; Lesh & Zawojewski, 2007; Schneider, Rittle-Johnson, & Star, 2011).

What about Drill and Practice?

The phrase "drill and practice" slips off the tongue so rapidly that the two words *drill* and *practice* appear to be synonyms—and, for the most part, they have been. In the interest of developing a new perspective on drill and practice, consider definitions that differentiate between these terms as different types of activities.

> *Practice* refers to varied tasks or experiences focused on a particular concept or procedure.
>
> *Drill* refers to repetitive exercises designed to replicate a procedure or algorithm.

Practice. Practice, as defined here, has numerous benefits, as this chapter has described. Students have an increased opportunity to develop conceptual ideas, alternative and flexible strategies for solving, and making connections between concepts and procedures. Importantly, using worthwhile tasks as practice sends a clear message that mathematics is about figuring things out.

Drill. Most textbooks include sets of exercises with every lesson. There is a seemingly endless amount of downloaded worksheets that focus on drill. What has all of this drill accomplished over the years? It has worked against developing mathematical practices, and created generations of people who don't remember the skills they learned, do not like mathematics, and do not pursue professions that involve mathematics.

What Does Appropriate Drill Look Like? In a review of research, Franke, Kazemi, and Battey (2007) report that drill improves procedural knowledge, but not conceptual understanding. But when the number of problems is reduced and time is then spent discussing problems, both procedural and conceptual knowledge are supported. The key is to keep drill short and to connect procedures to the related concepts. And, use the ideas listed above for adapting tasks to make drill more effective.

Technology makes possible differentiated drill. For example, *First in Math®* a subscription-based online game, offers students a self-paced approach to practicing basic math skills and complex problem-solving tasks. Programs such as this provide students with the opportunity to earn electronic incentives and move on to more difficult exercises based on their readiness.

Drill and Student Errors. As discussed earlier, the range of background experiences that students bring means that students will develop understanding in different ways and at different rates. For students who do not pick up new concepts quickly, there is a temptation to give in and "just drill 'em." In reality, when a student is making errors on a procedure, it is often a mis*concept*ion. Using a medical metaphor, students' computational errors are a symptom, not the problem. Therefore remediation should include activities that strengthen the student's conceptual knowledge and connecting that concept to the procedure.

MyLab Education **Self-Check 3.3**

Orchestrating Classroom Discourse

While tasks that promote problem solving are a necessary component to an effective mathematics lesson, for the problem solving to occur requires skill at orchestrating classroom discourse. To help students become productive mathematical thinkers, teachers must be comfortable with uncertainty, ask key questions, be able to respond to students, probe student thinking, prompt students to reflect on their thinking, and know the difference between productive and nonproductive struggle (Heaton & Lewis, 2011; Kazemi & Hintz, 2014; Towers, 2010). Teachers, themselves, must display productive dispositions, showing students they are willing to explore, experiment and make conjectures, recognize multiple solution paths, make connections among strategies, and monitor and reflect on their work. The goal of productive discourse is to keep the cognitive demand high while students are learning and formalizing mathematical concepts (Breyfogle & Williams, 2008–2009; Kilic et al., 2010; Smith, Hughes, Engle, & Stein, 2009). Note that the purpose is not for students to tell their answers and get validation from the teacher. The aspects involved in orchestrating classroom discourse are so important, they directly involve three out of the eight teaching practices from *Principles to Actions* (NCTM, 2014): facilitate meaningful mathematical discourse; pose purposeful questions; and elicit and use evidence of student thinking.

Classroom Discussions

The value of student talk in mathematics lessons cannot be overemphasized. As students describe and evaluate solutions to tasks, share approaches, and make conjectures, learning will occur in ways that are otherwise unlikely to take place. Students—in particular English learners, other students with more limited language skills, and students with learning disabilities—need to use mathematical vocabulary and articulate mathematics concepts in order to learn both the language and the concepts of mathematics. Students begin to take ownership of ideas (strategic competence) and develop a sense of power in making sense of mathematics (productive disposition). As they listen to other students' ideas, they come to see the varied approaches in how mathematics can be solved and see mathematics as something that they can do.

Smith and Stein (2011) identified five teacher actions for orchestrating productive mathematics discussions: anticipating, monitoring, selecting, sequencing, and connecting. The first action, *anticipating* responses to the selected worthwhile task, takes place before the lesson even begins. As students are working, the teacher *monitors*, observing strategies students are using and asking questions, such as:

- How did you decide what to do? Did you use more than one strategy?
- What did you do that helped you make sense of the problem?
- Did you find any numbers or information you didn't need? How did you know that the information was not important?
- Did you try something that didn't work? How did you figure out it was not going to work?

These and similar questions are designed to help students reflect on their own strategies and help the teacher determine which strategies to *select* for a public discussion after the lesson. Having selected a range of strategies to be shared, the teacher strategically *sequences* the presentations so that particular mathematical ideas can be emphasized. Perhaps most importantly, the teacher designs questions and strategies that *connect* strategies and mathematical concepts. These tend to be questions that are specific to the task, but some general questions include:

- How did [Leslie] represent her solution? What mathematical terms, symbols, or tools did she use? How is this like/different from [Colin's] strategy?
- Was there something in the task that reminded you of another problem we've done?
- What might you do the same or differently the next time you encounter a similar problem?

Notice these questions focus on the problem solving process as well as the answer, and what worked as well as what didn't work.

Because of the benefits of talking about mathematics, it is critical to make sure that everyone participates in the classroom discussion. You may need to explicitly discuss with students why discussions are important and what it means to actively listen and respond to others' ideas. For example, children can demonstrate they are listening by making eye contact with the speaker and through nonverbal cues (e.g., nodding); letting the speaker finish before sharing questions or ideas; and responding appropriately and respectfully by asking questions or summarizing the speaker's ideas (Wagganer, 2015). Wait time is also critical to ensuring participation and thinking (Roake, 2013). Chapin, O'Conner, and Anderson (2013) describe specific *talk moves*, strategic ways to ask questions and invite participation in classroom discussions. These moves are briefly described in Table 3.3, including example question prompts.

The following exchange illustrates an example of discourse with a small group of students discussing how to solve $27 - 19 = $ _____ . The teacher is asking two students (Tyler and Aleah) to think about their different answers.

Tyler: Well, I added one to nineteen to get twenty. So then I did twenty-seven take away twenty and got seven. But I added one, so I needed to take one away from the seven, and I got six.

Teacher: What do you think of that, Aleah?

Aleah: That is not what I got.

Teacher: Yes, I know that, but what do you think of Tyler's explanation?

Aleah: Well, it can't be right, because I just counted up. I added one to nineteen to get twenty and then added seven more to get twenty-seven. So, I counted eight altogether. Six can't be right.

Teacher: Tyler, what do you think of Aleah's explanation?

Tyler: That makes sense, too. I should have counted.

Teacher: So, do you think both answers are right?

Tyler: No.

Aleah: No. If it was twenty-seven minus twenty, the answer would be seven, because you count up seven. So, if it is nineteen, it has to be eight.

Tyler: Oh, wait. I see something. I did get the seven . . . . ? See, I got the twenty-seven take away twenty is seven. But then . . . ? I see . . . ? it's twenty-seven take away nineteen. I took away twenty! I took away too many so I have to add one to the seven. I get eight, just like Aleah! (Kline, 2008 , p. 148)

TABLE 3.3   TALK MOVES FOR SUPPORTING CLASSROOM DISCUSSIONS

Talk Moves	What It Means	Example Prompts
UNDERSTANDING IDEAS		
1. Wait time	Ironically, one "talk move" is to not talk. Quiet time should not feel uncomfortable, but should feel like thinking time. High-level thinking requires processing time. Give students time to think before responding.	"This question is important. Let's take some time to think about it." "In one minute I am going to ask you the answer to this question: . . . "
2. Partner talk	This moves gives students a chance to verbalize and refine their ideas before sharing with the whole class. It also gives students a chance to hear someone else's ideas to both inform their own thinking and to support the thinking of their partner.	"Is the answer going to be greater than or less than 1? Turn and talk to your partner for 30 seconds." "Rosa proposes that we can use the hundreds chart. Talk to your elbow partner about how the hundreds chart can help us solve this problem."
3. Revoicing	This move involves restating a students statement as a question in order to clarify what a student said, apply appropriate language to a student's idea, and involve more students in hearing a student's idea.	"So, you were saying . . . " "You used the hundreds chart and counted on?"
4. Say more	Sometimes students (especially young ones or ones new to talking about mathematics) give 2- to 3-word responses. This move involves eliciting more information to get to their thinking.	"You said you added these two numbers. How did you add them?" "Can you say more about why you used _____ strategy?"
5. Who can repeat?	Asking students to restate someone else's ideas in their own words will ensure that ideas are stated in a variety of ways and encourage students to listen to each other.	"Who can repeat what Ricardo just said?" "Who can explain Emma's strategy but in your own words?"
DEEPENING STUDENT REASONING AND UNDERSTANDING		
6. "Why . . . "& "When . . . "	This move us designed to deepen a student's understanding of a strategy or idea. The teacher presses students to tell *why* a strategy works and *when* it works.	"Why do you think that is true?" "When will that strategy work?"
7. What do you think?	Rather than restate, as in revoicing, this move asks the student to critique the idea proposed by another student.	"What do you think about Amalia's approach?" "Do you agree or disagree with Johanna? Why?"
8. Tell me more . . .	This is a request for students to add on to someone's idea, along with inviting students to give examples and make connections. It is intended to get more participation from students and deepen student understanding.	"What might we add to Jerod's explanation?" "Can you give an example?" "Do you see a connection between Julio and Briana's strategies?"

Adapted from: Based on Chapin, S., O'Conner, C., & Anderson, N. (2013). *Classroom Discussions: Using Math Talk to Help Students Learn* (3rd ed.). Sausalito, CA: Math Solutions. Reprinted with permission.

 Pause & Reflect

What "talk moves" do you notice in the previous vignette? See if you can identify two. •

Considerable research into how mathematical communities develop and operate provides us with additional insight for developing effective classroom discourse (e.g., Kazemi & Hintz, 2014; Rasmussen, Yackel, & King, 2003; Stephan & Whitenack, 2003; Wood, Williams, & McNeal, 2006; Yackel & Cobb, 1996). Suggestions from this collection of research include the following recommendations:

- Encourage student—student dialogue rather than student—teacher conversations that exclude the rest of the class. When students have differing solutions, have students work these ideas out as a class. "George, I noticed that you got a different answer than Tomeka. What do you think about her explanation?"
- Encourage students to ask questions. "Pete, did you understand how they did that? Do you want to ask Antonio a question?"
- Ask follow-up questions whether the answer is right or wrong. Your role is to understand student thinking, not to lead students to the correct answer. So follow up with probes to learn more about their answers. Sometimes you will find that what you assumed they were thinking is not accurate. And if you only follow up on wrong answers, students quickly figure this out and get nervous when you ask them to explain their thinking.

- Call on students in such a way that, over time, all students are able to participate. Use time when students are working in small groups to identify interesting solutions that you will highlight during the sharing time. Be intentional about the order in which the solutions are shared; for example, select two that you would like to compare presented back-to-back. All students should be prepared to share their strategies.
- Demonstrate to students that it is okay to be confused and that asking clarifying questions is appropriate. This confusion, or disequilibrium, just means they are engaged in doing real mathematics and is an indication they are learning.
- Move students to more conceptually based explanations when appropriate. For example, if a student says that he knows 4.17 is more than 4.1638, you can ask him (or another student) to explain why this is so. Say, "I see *what* you did but I think some of us are confused about *why* you did it that way."
- Be sure *all* students are involved in the discussion. ELs, in particular, need more than vocabulary support; they need support with mathematical discussions (Moschkovich, 1998). For example, you can use sentence starters or examples to help students know what kind of responses you are hoping to hear and to reduce the language demands. Sentence starters can also be helpful for students with disabilities because it adds structure. You can have students practice their explanations with a peer. You can invite students to use illustrations and actual objects to support their explanations. These strategies benefit not just the ELs and other students in the class who struggle with language, but all students.

Orchestrating productive discourse is difficult, especially if you are used to teaching through a teacher-directed approach. Remember the purpose is to unveil student thinking and to help students understand each others' thinking. Warning signs that you are taking over children's thinking include interrupting a child's strategy or explanation, manipulating the tools instead of allowing the child to do so, and asking a string of closed questions (Jacobs, Martin, Ambrose, & Philipp, 2014). Taking over children's thinking sends the message that you do not believe they are capable and can inhibit the discourse you are trying to encourage.

Questioning Considerations

Questions are important in learning about student thinking, challenging conclusions, and extending the inquiry to help generalize patterns. Questioning is very complex and something that effective teachers continue to improve on throughout their careers. Here are some major considerations in questioning that influence student learning.

1. *The "level" of the question.* Questions are leveled in various models. For example, Bloom's Taxonomy (revised) includes six levels, with remembering considered to be low level, and each of the others one more cognitively demanding than the previous ones (Anderson & Krathwohl, 2001). Smith and Stein's (1998) *Levels of Cognitive Demand* include two low-level demand categories and two high-level demand categories. The key is to ask high level questions (see Table 3.2). This is critical if students are to think at high levels about mathematics.
2. *The type of understanding that is targeted.* Both procedural and conceptual knowledge are important, and questions must target both and connect the two. If questions are limited to questions, such as "How did you solve this?" or "What are the steps?" then students will be thinking about procedures, but not about related concepts. Questions focused on conceptual knowledge and making connections include, "Will this rule always work? (Why?)" "When will this strategy work?" "How does the equation you wrote connect to the picture?" and "Why use common denominators to add fractions?"
3. *The pattern of questioning.* Some patterns of questioning are not as effective as others in encourage student reasoning and problem solving (Herbel-Eisenmann & Breyfogle, 2005). One common pattern goes like this: teacher asks a question, student answers the question, teacher confirms or challenges answer. This "initiation-response-feedback" or "IRF" pattern does not lead to classroom discussions that encourage all students to think. Another pattern is "funneling," when a teacher continues to probe students in order to get them to a particular answer. This is different than a "focusing" pattern, which uses probing questions to help students understand the mathematics. The talk moves described previously are intended for a focusing pattern of questioning.

4. *Who is doing the thinking.* You must be sure your questions engage all students! When you ask a great question, and only one student responds, then students will quickly figure out they don't need to think about the answer and all your effort to ask a great question is wasted. Instead, use strategies to be sure everyone is accountable to think about the question you posed. Ask students to first write their ideas on a notecard or individual white board, then talk to a partner about the question, and finally ask for contributions as a whole class. This think-pair-share strategy maximizes student participation.

5. *How you respond to an answer.* When you confirm a correct solution rather than use one of the talk moves, you lose an opportunity to engage students in meaningful discussions about mathematics and thereby limit the learning opportunities. Use student answers to find out if other students think the conclusions made are correct, whether they can justify why, and if there are other strategies or solutions to the problem.

How Much to Tell and Not to Tell

One of the most perplexing dilemmas for teachers is how much information and direction to provide to students during mathematical inquiry. On one hand, telling can diminish what is learned and lower the level of cognitive demand in a lesson by eliminating the productive struggle that is key to conceptual understanding. On the other hand, to tell too little can sometimes leave students floundering. Three things that teachers need to tell students are (Hiebert et al., 1997):

- *Mathematical conventions.* Symbols such as + and =, terminology, and labels are conventions. As a rule of thumb, symbolism and terminology should be introduced *after* concepts have been developed as a means of expressing or labeling ideas.
- *Alternative methods.* When an important strategy does not emerge naturally from students, then the teacher needs to introduce the strategy, being careful to introduce it as "another" way, not the only or the best way.
- *Clarification or formalization of students' methods.* It is appropriate and necessary to help students clarify or interpret their ideas and point out related ideas. A student may add 38 and 5 by noting that 38 and 2 more is 40 with 3 more making 43. This strategy can be related to the Make 10 strategy used to add 8 + 5. Drawing everyone's attention to this connection can help other students see the strategy, while also building the confidence of the student(s) who originally proposed the strategy.

Writing

Classroom discourse includes oral and written language. Writing improves student learning and understanding (Pugalee, 2005; Steele, 2007). The act of writing is a reflective process and involves students in metacognition, which is connected to learning (Bransford, Brown, & Cocking, 2000). Metacognition refers to conscious monitoring (being aware of how and why you are doing something) and regulation (choosing to do something or deciding to make changes) of your own thought process.

Writing plays a critical role in classroom discourse. Writing can serve as a rehearsal for a classroom discussion. It can be difficult for students to remember how they solved a problem. A written record or a predrawn picture can be used for reference during discussions. Writing helps students focus on the need for precise language in mathematics and understand that illustrations can support a good explanation. Posting different written solutions, just like hearing about solutions, engages students in reflecting on which strategy makes sense. And, a written product provides evidence for you to further analyze student understandings after the lesson. For example, the student work in Figure 3.5

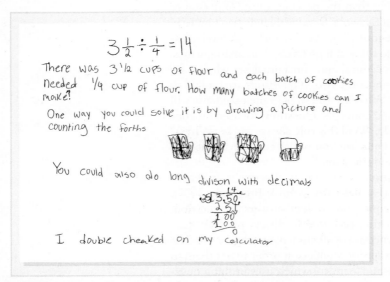

FIGURE 3.5 A student gives an example and explains how to solve. $3\frac{1}{2} \div \frac{1}{4}$.

illustrates how a fifth-grade student is thinking about division by the fraction $\frac{1}{4}$. Writing for different audiences can also be valuable. First-grade students writing to third-grade students, such as in a pen pal structure, can lead students to explain more and enjoy the process (Lampe & Uselmann, 2008). To help elicit better explanations, consider using sentence frames, such as "I (We) think the answer is ____. We think this because ____."

Graphic Organizers. Graphic organizers can be used to help students connect representations, as in the template illustrated here.

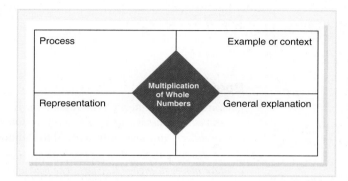

In each box, students record the problem, explanation, illustration, and the general math concept (Wu, An, King, Ramirez, & Evans, 2009; Zollman, 2009). The requirements for each box can be adapted as needed for the content area; for example, in geometry you may have boxes for characteristics, illustrations, examples and nonexamples.

The I-THINK framework supports the problem solving process and metacognitive skills (Lynch, Lynch, & Bolyard, 2013; Thomas, 2006):

Individually think about the task

Talk about the problem.

How can it be solved?

Identify a strategy to solve the problem.

Notice how your strategy helped you solve the problem.

Keep thinking about the problem. Does it make sense? Is there another way to solve it?

Using organizers like I-THINK can help students be more aware of their mathematical thinking and better at communicating that thinking to you, which provides you with better formative assessment data.

Technology Tools in Writing. There are many free programs that allow students to write, edit, and submit work to you electronically, including text editing tools (e.g., Google Docs), wikis (e.g., Wikispaces), and blogging tools (e.g., WordPress). Web-based tools such as these can be used on a variety of devices in the mathematics classroom, the computer lab, the library, and at home to allow students and teachers to collaboratively draft, read, and edit one another's mathematical ideas.

Mobile apps can function as digital whiteboards with audio capture capabilities. Students can record and capture their mathematical representations on the screen while sharing their verbal reasoning. These files can be archived and shared electronically. Doceri, Educreations, Explain Everything, and Show Me are just a few of these powerful, free or low-cost apps. The Smartpen (available from Livescribe) allows students and teachers to easily capture written representations and audio recordings and make them accessible to others in digital format. Users need the Livescribe Smartpen, dot paper, and a computer or tablet with which to sync pencasts.

MyLab Education **Self-Check 3.4**

MyLab Education **Application Exercise 3.2: Orchestrating Classroom Discourse** Click the link to access this exercise, then watch the video and answer the accompanying questions.

RESOURCES FOR CHAPTER 3

RECOMMENDED READINGS

Articles

Jacobs, V. R., Martin, H. A., Ambrose, R. C., & Philipp, R. A. (2014). Warning signs! *Teaching Children Mathematics, 21*(2), 107–113.

This article shares three common teaching moves that tend to take over students thinking. The vignettes and illustrations are very helpful in thinking about what not *to do, along with helpful alternatives to support student thinking.*

Reinhart, S. C. (2000). Never say anything a kid can say! *Mathematics Teaching in the Middle School, 5*(8), 478–483.

This timeless article tells the experience of a middle school teacher who questioned his own "masterpiece" lessons after realizing that his students were often confused and therefore started moving towards a teaching through problem solving approach. Reinhart's suggestions for questioning techniques and involving students are superb.

Rigelman, N. R. (2007). Fostering mathematical thinking and problem solving: The teacher's role. *Teaching Children Mathematics, 13*(6), 308–314.

This is a wonderful article for illustrating the subtle (and not so subtle) differences between true problem solving and "proceduralizing" problem solving. Because two contrasting vignettes are offered, it gives an excellent opportunity for discussing how the two teachers differ philosophically and in practice.

Roake, J. (2013). Planning for processing time yields deeper learning. *Education Update, 55*(8), 1, 6–7.

This article provides a brief description of 10 tips for building think time into discussions, with connections to brain research. A quick read with important ideas!

Books

Chapin, S., O'Conner, C., & Anderson, N. C. (2013). *Talk moves: A teacher's guide for using classroom discussions in math* (3rd ed.). Sausalito, CA: Math Solutions.

As described in this chapter, this book provides specific, strategic talk moves to engage learners. The book includes a plethora of examples, videos, and other resources to support your professional learning.

Kazemi, E., & Hintz, A. (2014). *Intentional talk: How to structure and lead productive mathematical discussions.* Portland, ME: Stenhouse Publishers.

Through wonderful classroom vignettes and illustrations, these authors describe how to facilitate a meaningful classroom discussion with various purposes, such as comparing, justifying, clarifying, and troubleshooting.

Thiessen, D. (Ed.) (2017). *Exploring math through literature.* Reston, VA: NCTM.

This e-book has dozens and dozens of great literature-based lesson ideas, including student activity pages. You can search by content and by grade. Related articles provide descriptions of how to use the activities and photos and illustrations of how they were used in classrooms.

White, J. (2014). *Using children's literature to teach problem solving in math: Addressing the Common Core in Grade K–2.* New York, NY: Taylor & Francis.

This book is organized around the eight Mathematical Practices (NGA Center & CCSSO, 2010) and offers suggested books and lessons addressing various content topics. Each lesson provides excellent insights into engaging students in learning through problem solving.

Planning in the Problem-Based Classroom

LEARNER OUTCOMES

After reading this chapter and engaging in the embedded activities and reflections, you should be able to:

4.1 Explain the features of a three-phase lesson plan format for problem-based lessons.

4.2 Design lessons using a planning process focused on mathematical inquiry.

4.3 Describe specific lesson design ideas, including ways to differentiate instruction.

4.4 Explain strategies for working with families, including effective homework practices.

Designing a lesson that engages students in problem solving looks quite different from a traditional "explain, then practice" style. The mathematical practices such as modeling mathematics, reasoning quantitatively, and looking for generalizations and structure are rarely developed in a tell-students-how lesson design (Munter, Stein, & Smith, 2015). In contrast, a problem-solving lesson approaches learning as a complex process, builds on each student's prior knowledge, and prioritizes making connections among mathematical ideas, and thereby also incorporates the mathematical practices. Preparing a lesson shifts from preparing an agenda of *what will happen* to creating a "thought experiment" to consider *what might happen* (Davis, Sumara, & Luce-Kapler, 2008). The three-phase lesson format and the process for preparing such a lesson discussed in this chapter are intended to support the creation of lessons that support mathematical inquiry.

 ## A Three-Phase Lesson Format

A three-phase lesson format provides a structure for lessons where students focus on a topic of inquiry, engage in action, and follow up with discussion, reflection, and connections. We refer to these three phases as *before*, *during*, and *after*, referring to students' engagement in a worthwhile task—what happens to set up that inquiry, what happens as they explore, and what happens after the task is solved (see Figure 4.1). In this section, we describe each phase's goals, along with appropriate teacher actions and specific examples across the mathematics curriculum.

The *Before* Lesson Phase

The *before* phase is the first 5 to 10 minutes of a lesson and is intended to get students ready for a focus task or exploration that engages them in higher-level thinking and using the mathematical practices. In the *before* phase, you must find the right balance of giving enough structure and

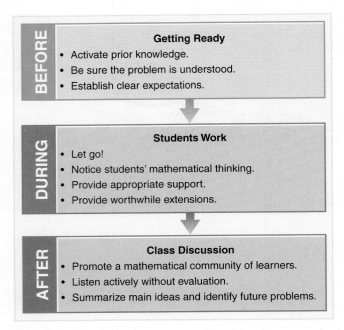

FIGURE 4.1 Teaching through problem solving lends itself to a three-phase structure for lessons.

guidance so that students the focus task is accessible, without giving so much structure and guidance that you have lowered the cognitive demand of the focus task. There are three goals in the *before* phase of a lesson.

Activate Prior Knowledge. This means both to remind students what they have previously learned and connect to their personal experiences, as it relates to the day's mathematical learning goal(s). What form this might take will vary with the topic, as shown in the following three options and examples.

The following problem (for *during* phase) is designed to help students use a "think addition" strategy to solve a subtraction problem.

Concept: Subtraction	**Grades: 2–3**

Dad says it is 503 miles to the beach. When we stopped for gas, we had gone 267 miles. How much farther do we have to drive?

Before presenting this problem, you can elicit prior knowledge by asking the class to supply the missing part of 100 after you give one part. Try numbers like 80 or 30 at first; then try 47 or 62. When you present the actual task, you might ask students if the answer to the problem is more or less than 300 miles. A second way to activate prior knowledge is connect to the students' life experiences. If the problem does not begin with a context you can add one. This helps students see mathematics as relevant and helps them make sense of the mathematics in the problem.

Sometimes activating prior knowledge involves vocabulary and possible tools that might be used for the focus task. Consider the following open-ended task exploring perimeter (based on Lappan & Even, 1989).

Concept: Perimeter	**Grades: 4–6**

Assume that the edge of a square is 1 unit. Add square tiles to this shape so that it has a perimeter of 18 units.

Instead of beginning your lesson with this problem, you might consider activating prior knowledge in one of the following ways:

- Draw a 3-by-5 rectangle of squares on the board and ask students what they know about the shape. (It's a rectangle. It has squares. There are 15 squares. There are three rows of five.) If no one mentions the words *area* and *perimeter*, you could write them on the board and ask if those words can be used in talking about this figure.
- Provide students with some square tiles or grid paper and say, "I want everyone to make a shape that has a perimeter of 12 units. After you make your shape, find out what its area is." After a short time, have several students share their shapes. Students can also use a virtual geoboard, like the one found at the Math Playground.

Each of these warm-ups uses the vocabulary needed for the lesson. The second activity suggests the tiles as a model students may elect to use and introduces the idea that there are different figures with the same perimeter.

Be Sure the Task Is Understood. You must be sure that students understand the problem before setting them to work. This does not mean to explain *how* to solve it, just that they understand the task. To be effective in doing this, you must analyze the problem and anticipate student approaches and possible misinterpretations or misconceptions (Wallace, 2007). Time spent building understanding of the task is critical to the rest of the lesson. Ask questions such as, "What are we trying to figure out? Do we have enough information?" and "What do you already know that can help you get started?" The more questions raised and addressed prior to the task, the more engaged students will be in the *during* phase.

As you will read in the chapter on basic facts, a strategy approach is more effective than drill or memorization. The most difficult facts can each be connected or related to a fact already learned, called a *foundational fact* or *known fact*, the goal of the lesson with the following focus task:

Concept: Multiplication Facts   **Grades: 3–4**

Use a known fact to help you solve each of these facts: 4×6, 6×8, 7×6, 3×8.

For this lesson, students must understand what it means to use a known fact. They have most likely used foundational facts in addition. Ask, "When you learned addition facts, how could knowing $6 + 6$ help you find the answer to $6 + 7$" and follow up with asking, "What might a known fact be in multiplication?"

In the case of story problems it is important to help students understand the meaning of the sentences without giving away how to solve the problem. This is particularly important for ELs and students who are struggling readers.

Concept: Multiplication and Division   **Grades: 3–5**

The local candy store purchased candy in cartons holding 12 boxes per carton. The price paid for one carton was $42.50. Each box contained 8 candy bars that the store planned to sell individually. What was the candy store's cost for each candy bar?

Questions to ensure understanding include: "What is the problem asking? How does the candy store buy candy? What is a carton? What is in a box? What does that mean when it says 'each box'?" The last question here is to identify vocabulary that may be misunderstood. Asking students to reread a problem does little good, but asking students to restate the problem or tell what question is being asked helps students be better readers and problem solvers.

Establish Clear Expectations. There are two components to establishing expectations: (1) how students are to work and (2) what products they are to prepare for the discussion.

It is always a good idea for students to have some opportunity to discuss their ideas with classmates prior to sharing their thoughts in the *after* phase of the lesson. When students work in groups, though, there is the possibility of some students not contributing or learning. On the other hand, when students work alone, they have no one to look to for an idea and no chance to talk about the mathematics and practice what they might later share with the whole group. So it is essential to have students be individually accountable and also work together.

One way to address both individual accountability and sharing with other students is a think-write-pair-share approach (Buschman, 2003b). The first two steps are done individually, and then students are paired for continued work on the problem. With independent written work to share, students have something to talk about.

Because teaching through problem solving focuses on processes (strategies) and solutions, it is important to model and explain what a final product might be. One expectation could be a written explanation and/or illustration of the problem. As noted earlier, writing supports student learning in mathematics, and having multiple ways to demonstrate knowledge is important for providing access to all learners (multiple exit points). One effective strategy is to have each student write and illustrate their solution independently, then present the team's solution as a group, with each person sharing a part of the presentation.

These *before* phase goals may occur in any order. For example, for some lessons you might do a short activity to activate students' prior knowledge for the problem and then present the problem and clarify expectations. Other times, you might first explain expectations and then pose an opening task that will revisit relevant, previously learned content.

The *During* Lesson Phase

Once curiosity has been piqued, students engage in mathematical activity alone, with partners, or in small groups to explore, gather and record information, make and test conjectures, and solve the mathematical task. In this *during* phase, students need to have access to tools, such as models, images, diagrams, and notation. In making instructional decisions in the *during* phase you must ask yourself, "Does my action lead to deeper thinking or is it taking away the thinking?" These decisions are based on carefully listening to students and knowing the content goals of the lesson. There are four goals in this phase (see Figure 4.1).

Let Go! Once students understand what the problem is asking, it is time to *let go*. Encourage students to embrace the struggle. Doing mathematics takes time, and solutions are not always obvious. It is important to communicate to students that spending time on a task, trying different approaches, and consulting each other are important to learning and understanding mathematics. Although it is tempting to rescue students who are feeling frustrated and uncertain in the *during* phase, they will learn more if you provide support without just showing/telling them how. Avoid these three teaching moves, which often result in you (the teacher) taking over a student's thinking: (1) interrupting a student's strategy, (2) manipulating the tools, and (3) asking a series of closed questions (Jacobs, Martin, Ambrose, & Philipp, 2014). Instead try to understand the student and focus on helping them navigate the problem. Ask questions like:

"What is this problem asking you to do?"

"How have you organized the information?"

"What about this problem is difficult?" and

"Is there a different strategy (or manipulative) that you might try?"

These questions support student thinking, yet do not tell them how to solve the problem.

Students will look to you for approval of their results or ideas. Avoid being the source of right and wrong, and instead have students' mathematical reasoning be the source. To respond to questions like, "Is this right?", ask, "How can you decide?" or "Why do you think that might be right?" or "Can you check that somehow?" Such questions reminds students that the correctness of an answer lies in the justification, not in the teacher's brain or answer key.

Letting go also means allowing students to make mistakes. When students make mistakes (*and* when they are correct), ask them to explain their process or approach to you. They may catch their mistake. In addition, in the *after* portion of the lesson, students will have an opportunity to explain, justify, defend, and challenge solutions and strategies. This process of uncovering misconceptions or computational errors nurtures the important notion that mistakes are opportunities for learning (Boaler & Humphreys, 2005) and a natural part of doing mathematics.

Notice Students' Mathematical Thinking. Take this time to find out what different students are thinking, what ideas they are using, and how they are approaching the problem. This is a time for observing, listening, and interacting with students. "Professional noticing" means that you are trying to understand a student's approach to a problem and decide an appropriate response to extend that student's thinking in the moment (Jacobs, Lamb, & Philipp, 2010). Consequently, your questions must be based on the students' work and responses to you. This is very different from listening for or leading students toward an answer or approach that you have pre-selected or assumed. As you notice the range of strategies, consider how they are related and in what order you might sequence the sharing of solutions in the *after* phase (Smith & Stein, 2011).

The *during* phase is a great opportunity to find out what your students know, how they think, and how they are approaching the task you have given them. As students are working, any of the following prompts can help you notice what they know and are thinking:

- Tell me what you are doing.
- I see you have started to [multiply/subtract/etc.] these numbers. Can you tell me why?
- Can you tell me more about . . . ?
- Why did you . . . ?
- How did you solve it?
- How does your picture connect to your equation?
- I am not clear on what you have done here. Will you explain it so I can understand?

Don't be afraid to say you don't understand their strategy. When you are open to learning, you help students feel more comfortable with engaging in the mathematics.

Be aware that your actions can inadvertently shut down student thinking and damage self-esteem. "It's easy" and "Let me help you" are two such statements. Think about the message each one sends. If a student is stuck and you say, "It's easy," then you inadvertently say, "You are not very smart or you wouldn't be stuck." Similarly, saying "Let me help you" communicates that you think the student cannot solve the problem without help. The probing questions offered here, in contrast, communicate to students the real messages you want to send: "Doing mathematics takes time and thinking. You can do it—let's see what you know and go from there."

Provide Appropriate Support. Consider ways to support student thinking without taking away their responsibility of designing a solution strategy and solving the problem in a way that makes sense to them.

If a group or a student is searching for a place to begin, first be sure they understand the task. Then, ask students what they have tried: "What have you tried so far?" "Where did you get stuck?" Third, you can suggest general strategies, for example, "Have you thought about drawing a picture?" "What if you used cubes to act out this problem?" These teacher moves support student thinking (Jacobs & Ambrose, 2008). Consider the following high quality task.

Concept: Percent Increase and Decrease   **Grades: 6–8**

In Fern's Furniture Store, Fern has priced all of her furniture at 20 percent over wholesale. In preparation for a sale, she tells her staff to cut all prices by 10 percent. Will Fern be making a 10 percent profit, less than a 10 percent profit, or more than a 10 percent profit? Explain your answer.

Imagine a pair of students is stuck and you stop by their group to help. They communicate they don't know what to do. How will you respond? Consider the following suggestions—they provide a start, but don't take away the challenge:

- "Try drawing a picture or a diagram that shows what 10 percent off and 20 percent more means."
- "Have you tried picking a price and seeing what happens when you increase the price by 20 percent and then reduce the price by 10 percent?"

Notice that these suggestions are not directive, but rather serve as starters. After offering a tip or suggestion, walk away—this keeps you from helping too much and the students from relying on you too much.

Provide Worthwhile Extensions. Students solve problems at different rates. Anticipate how you might extend a task in an interesting way for those that finish early without it seeming like extra work. For example, look back at the area and perimeter task earlier in this chapter. If a student finds one solution quickly, say, "I see you found one way to do this. Do you think there other solutions?" This may be enough to send the students into a flurry of efforts to find different ways. Then, you can continue to push their thinking by asking questions like, "Are any of the solutions different or more interesting than others? Which of the shapes with a perimeter of 18 has the largest area and which has the smallest area? Does the perimeter always change when you add another tile?" Questions that begin "What if . . . ?" or "Would that same idea work for . . . ?" are ways to extend student thinking in a motivating way. As another example, consider the following task.

Concept: Percent Increase and Decrease   **Grades: 6–8**

The dress was originally priced at $90. If the sale price is 25 percent off, how much will it cost on sale?

> **MyLab Education** **Application Exercise 4.1: Observing and Responding to Student Thinking** Click the link to access this exercise, then watch the video and answer the accompanying questions.
>
>
> ▶ VIDEO EXAMPLE

This is an example of a straightforward problem with a single answer. Many students will solve it by multiplying by 0.25 and subtracting the result from $90. Ask students, "Could you find another way? Rico solved it by finding 75 percent of 90—does this work? Will it work in all situations? Why?" Or you can extend the use of different representations by asking, "How would you solve it using fractions instead of decimals? Draw me a diagram that explains what you did."

Second graders will frequently solve the next problem by counting or using addition.

Concept: Addition and Subtraction   **Grades: K–2**

Maxine had saved up $9. The next day she received her allowance. Now she has $12. How much allowance did she get?

To extend student thinking, ask, "How would you do that on a calculator?" and "Can you write two equations that represent this situation?" These are ways of encouraging children to connect $9 + ? = 12$ with $12 - 9 = ?$.

The *After* Lesson Phase

In the *after* phase of the lesson, you facilitate a classroom discussion (see Chapter 3 section with this title). Your students will share, justify, challenge, and compare various solutions to the task they have solved. Ideas generated in the *during* phase must have a chance to "bump against each other" so that mathematical ideas can emerge (Davis & Simmt, 2006, p. 312). The *after* phase is an important time to make drawings, notations, and writing visible to others; to make connections between the ideas that have emerged; and to create spaces for students to take up, try on, and expand on the ideas of others. It is in the *after* phase where much of the learning will occur, as students reflect individually and collectively on the ideas they have explored. The expectations for the *after* phase require careful consideration of possible student responses, recognition of the responses generated in the *during* phase, and a willingness to be open to unanticipated responses.

It is challenging but critical to plan sufficient time for a discussion. Twenty minutes is not at all unreasonable for a class discussion. It is not necessary for every student to have finished, but all students need to have something to share. This is not a time to check answers, but time for the class to share and compare ideas.

Promote a Mathematical Community of Learners. Engage the class in productive discussion, helping students work together as a community of learners. In a community of learners, students feel comfortable taking risks and sharing ideas, students respect one another's ideas even when they disagree, and ideas are defended and challenged respectfully, and logical or mathematical reasoning is valued. You must teach your students about your expectations for this time!

Listen Actively without Evaluation. As in the *during* phase, the goal here is noticing students' mathematical thinking and, in addition, making that thinking visible to other students. When you serve as a member of the classroom community and not as the sole evaluator, students will be more willing to share their ideas during discussions. Resist the temptation to judge the correctness of an answer. When you say, "That's correct, Dewain," there is no longer a reason for students to think about and evaluate the response. Had students disagreed with Dewain's response or had a question about it, they will not challenge or question it because you've said it was correct. Consequently, you will not have the chance to hear and learn from them and notice how they are thinking about the problem. You can support student thinking without evaluation: "What do others think about what Dewain just said?" (See Orchestrating Classroom Discourse in Chapter 3 for elaboration of these ideas.)

Relatedly, use praise cautiously. Praise offered for correct solutions or excitement over interesting ideas suggests that the students did something unusual or unexpected. This can be negative feedback for those who do not get praise. Comments such as "Good job!" and "Super work!" roll off the tongue easily, but do nothing to help the student or those listening to know what was good about the work, statement, and idea. In place of praise that is judgmental, Schwartz (1996) suggests comments of interest and extension: "I wonder what would happen if you tried . . ." or "Please tell me how you figured that out." Notice that these phrases express interest and value the student's thinking. For example, if Ethan is sharing his work (see Figure 4.2) to show how many different ways five people could be on the two stories of a house, you can ask Ethan to explain his thinking and ask Ethan and his classmates such things as, "Are all of these ways different?" and "I wonder if there are other ways?" These prompts engage all students in thinking about Ethan's solution thereby valuing his thinking and extending everyone else's thinking as well.

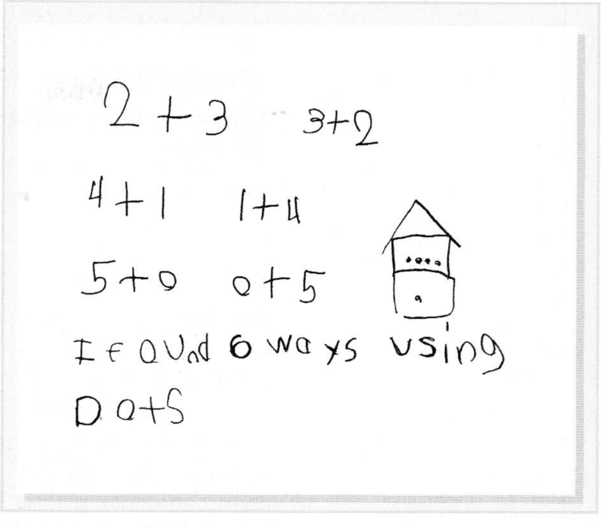

FIGURE 4.2 Ethan shows his thinking about "How many ways 5 people might be on two floors of a house."

There will be times when a student will get stuck in the middle of an explanation. Be sensitive about calling on someone else to "help out." You may be communicating that the student is not capable on his or her own. Allow think time. You can offer to give the student time and come back to them after hearing another strategy. Remember that the *after* phase is your window into student thinking (i.e., formative assessment); listening actively will provide insights for planning tomorrow's lesson and beyond.

Summarize Main Ideas and Identify Future Tasks. A major goal of the *after* phase is to formalize the main ideas of the lesson, making connections between strategies or different mathematical ideas. It is also a time to reinforce appropriate terminology, definitions, or symbols.

If a task involves multiple methods of computing, list the different strategies on the board. These can be labeled with the student's name and an example. Ask students questions that help them understand the strategies, comparing and making connections among them.

There are numerous ways to share verbally, such as a partner exchange, where one partner tells one key idea and the other partner gives an example. Following oral summaries with individual written summaries is important to ensure that you know what each child has learned from the lesson. For example, exit slips (handouts with one or two prompts that ask students to explain the main ideas of the lesson) can be used as an "exit" from the math instruction. Or be creative—ask students to write a newspaper headline to describe the day's activity and a brief column to summarize it. Many engaging templates and writing starters are available online.

Finally, challenge students to think beyond the current task. Each task is just a specific example of a general category of tasks (Goldenberg & Mason, 2008). Ask students to make conjectures and look for generalizations for addressing related tasks. For example, when comparing fractions, suppose that a group makes this generalization and you display it: *When deciding which fraction is larger, the fraction in which the bottom number is closer to the top number is the larger fraction. Example: $\frac{4}{7}$ is not as big as $\frac{7}{8}$ because 7 is only 1 from 8 but 4 is 3 away from 7.* This is an interesting hypothesis, but it is not correct in all instances. The conjecture needs to discussed in this *after* phase, as a homework activity, or in a subsequent lesson to determine whether it is always right or to find fractions for which it does not work (counterexamples).

MyLab Education   Self-Check 4.1

MyLab Education   Application Exercise 4.2: A Three-Phase Lesson Format

Click the link to access this exercise, then read the scenario and answer the accompanying questions.

 ## Process for Preparing a Lesson

In this section, we look more closely at the *decision-making* that goes into designing a three-phase lesson. The first column (green) in Figure 4.3 illustrates the multitude of decisions to make prior to planning the actual three-phase lesson. None of these decisions is made in isolation. You might decide to adapt the task based on the mathematics of the task or because of your students' needs. The assessment decisions may relate to the task, the students, or the content goals. Once the content and task decisions are made, the three-phase lesson is ready to be designed (see purple-shaded steps in Figure 4.3). Finally, it is important to review and finalize the plan, taking into consideration the flow of the lesson, anticipated student responses and possible challenges. Here we describe each planning step, including an example lesson titled "Fixed Areas Expanded Lesson" is to illustrate the decision-making process.

MyLab Education   Expanded Lesson: Fixed Areas

Step 1: Determine the Learning Goals

How do you decide what mathematics your students need to learn? Every state has mathematics curriculum standards. Many U.S. states have adopted the *Common Core State Standards* (NGA Center & CCSSO, 2010), which identifies mathematics content by grade level or have slightly modified these standards as their own state's standards. It is important to ask:

• What should my students be able to *do* when this lesson is over?"

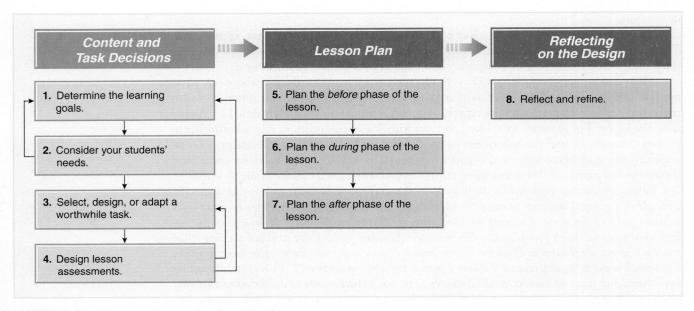

FIGURE 4.3   Eight-step process for planning a lesson.

- What content (conceptual and procedural) is important?
- What mathematical practices/processes will be developed?

Content Goals: Fixed Areas. A big idea in developing measurement concepts is that area and perimeter are related. In looking at the standards for fourth grade, you read, "Apply the area and perimeter formulas for rectangles in real world and mathematical problems" (NGA Center & CCSSO, 2010, p. 25). A possible goal for one lesson on this topic is for students to explore the relationship between area and perimeter, specifically that one can change while the other stays the same.

This goal leads to the development of observable and measurable *objectives*. There are numerous formats for lesson objectives, but the key is that they tell the things you want your students to *do* or *say* to demonstrate what they know.

In our perimeter example, the objectives might be:

1. Students will be able to draw a variety of rectangles with a given area and accurately determine the perimeter of each.
2. Students will be able to explain relationships between area and perimeter.
3. Students will describe a process (their own algorithm) for finding perimeter of a rectangle.

As a counterexample, "Students will understand that the perimeter can change and the area can stay the same" is not a well-designed objective because "understanding" is not observable or measurable.

Step 2: Consider Your Students' Needs

What do your students already know or understand about the selected mathematics concepts? Perhaps they already have some prior knowledge of the content you have been working on, which this lesson is aimed at expanding or refining. Examine the relevant learning expectations from previous grades and for the next grade. Be sure that the mathematics you identified in step 1 includes something new or at least slightly unfamiliar to your students. At the same time, be certain that your objectives are not out of reach.

Questions to consider include:

- What context might be engaging to this range of learners?
- What might students already know about this topic that can serve as a launching point?
- What misconceptions might need to be addressed?
- What visuals or models might support student understanding?
- What vocabulary support might be needed?

Student Considerations: Fixed Areas. By grade 4, many students will have prior experiences with perimeter and area. Some students may think that for a given area, there is only one perimeter (this lesson challenges this idea). Also, though students may notice generalizations on how to find area and perimeter, the focus of the lesson should not be on measurement formulas, but on the relationship between area and perimeter.

Step 3: Select, Design, or Adapt a Worthwhile Task

With your goals and students in mind, you are ready to consider what task, activity, or exercise you might use. Chapter 3 provided extensive discussion on what to consider for this step (see Tasks that Promote Problem Solving), so here we simply offer reflective questions:

- Does the task I am considering address the content goals (step 1) and the needs of my students (step 2)?
- Does the task have potential to engage my students in the Mathematical Practices?
- Will the task require students to apply problem solving strategies?

If the answers to these questions are yes, the task can become the basis for your lesson. You may still decide on minor adaptations, like adding in a children's book or changing the context, to better connect to your students. If you find the task does not fit your content and student needs, then you will need to either make substantial modifications or find a new task.

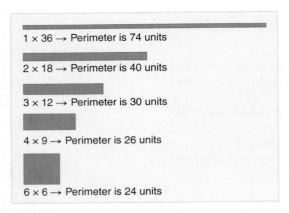

1 × 36 → Perimeter is 74 units

2 × 18 → Perimeter is 40 units

3 × 12 → Perimeter is 30 units

4 × 9 → Perimeter is 26 units

6 × 6 → Perimeter is 24 units

FIGURE 4.4 Possible rectangles with whole number sides and total area of 36 square units.

It is absolutely essential that you do the task yourself. It is only in exploring the task that you can identify possible challenges, anticipate student approaches, and determine the strategies you want to high-light. Teachers who consider ways students might solve the task are better able to facilitate the lesson in ways that support student learning (Matthews, Hlas, & Finken, 2009; Stein, Remillard, & Smith, 2007).

Task Considerations: Fixed Areas. A valuable focus of inquiry is, "What happens to the perimeter when we fix the area, but allow the shape to change?" You might challenge fourth graders to figure out how many rectangles they can create with a given area. This exploration might become the basis for asking, "What rectangles of the same area result in the largest or the smallest perimeter?" You will need to decide what fixed area to use. After exploring, you might decide that 36 square units is a good choice because it results in five different choices, including a square (see Figure 4.4). Students might wonder whether they should consider 1×36 the same as 36×1 and whether a square is considered a rectangle. And, you also might want to attend to the fact that as shape becomes more square, the perimeter decreases.

Several contexts are possible for this task. For example, the square tiles could be tables and the perimeter contextualized as how many people can sit around the tables when arranged in different ways. Or, the task could focus on fencing in an area for a pet or a playground.

Step 4: Design Lesson Assessments

Thinking about what you want students to experience and how they are going to demonstrate their understanding of the content goals is an important consideration that occurs early in the planning process, not at the end. It is important to assess in a variety of ways (see Chapter 5). *Formative assessment* allows you to gather information that can be used for adjusting the direction of the lesson midstream or making changes for the next day, as well as informing the questions you pose in the discussion of the task for the *after* phase of the lesson. *Summative assessment* captures whether students have learned the objectives you have listed for the lesson.

Assessment Considerations: Fixed Areas. Three objectives are listed in step 1, each of which needs to be assessed. Here we share some possibilities:

Objective	Assessments
1. Students will be able to draw a variety of rectangles with a given area and accurately determine the perimeter of each.	• In the *during* phase, use a checklist to observe if each student is able to create at least three different rectangles and accurately find the perimeter. • In the *during* phase, ask each student, "How did you figure out the perimeter of that [pick one] rectangle?"
2. Students will be able to explain relationships between area and perimeter.	• In the *during* phase, ask, "What have you noticed about the relationship between area and perimeter of these rectangles?" • At the end of lesson, ask students to complete an exit slip (written summary) to explain the relationship between area and perimeter of a rectangle using illustrations to support their explanation.
3. Students will describe a process (their own algorithm) for finding perimeter of a rectangle.	• In the *during* phase, ask, "How are you finding perimeter? Are you seeing any patterns or shortcuts? Explain it to me." • In the *after* phase, discuss different strategies students used to find the perimeter.

Step 5: Plan the *Before* Phase

As discussed earlier, the *before* phase should elicit students' prior knowledge, provide context, and establish expectations. Questions to guide your thinking include:

• Would a simpler version of the task activate prior knowledge, introduce vocabulary, and/ or clarify expectations?

- In what ways can you connect the task with previous mathematical experiences, other disciplines, or an interesting current event?
- What presentation strategies and questions will minimize misinterpretations and clarify expectations?

Options available for presenting tasks include having it written on paper, using their texts, using the document camera on a projection device; or posting on an interactive whiteboard, chalkboard, or chart paper. Students need to know (1) the resources or tools they might use; (2) whether they will work independently or in groups; (3) if in groups, how groups will be organized, including assigned roles; and (4) how their work will be presented (e.g., completing a handout, writing in a journal, preparing a team poster) (Smith, Bill, & Hughes, 2008).

Planning *Before* Phase: Fixed Areas. Plan to begin by distributing square tiles to students and asking them to build a rectangle using 12 tiles (a simpler version of the task). Clarify vocabulary (perimeter and area) and expectations (that 3×4 is the same as 4×3).

Decide on a context. For example, with a school play on the horizon, you might use the context of a stage, asking students to think about building a stage that has an area of 36 square meters. Consider questions to raise curiosity like, "Does it matter what the length and width are for the stage floor in terms of how much space we have for doing our play? Would one shape of rectangle be better or worse than another? Find different possibilities and then pick one that will best serve the performers."

Step 6: Plan the *During* Phase

The *during* phase is an opportunity for students to fully engage in the task and for you to notice what students are thinking, and provide support and challenges when needed. Carefully prepare prompts that can help students who may be stuck or who may need accommodations that will give them a start without taking away the challenge of the task. Have options of other materials such as geoboards or grid paper. Prepare extensions or challenges you can pose to students. This phase is also a time for you to think about which groups might share their work, and in what order, in the *after* phase of the lesson.

During Phase: Fixed Areas. You might make one trip around the room to see that students are actually building a rectangle and recording its dimensions. In the second round, ask the questions you prepared in step 4 for each objective. If students finish early, ask them to consider applying their conjecture of the best dimensions for a stage that is 48 square meters.

Step 7: Plan the *After* Phase

The *after* phase is when you connect the task to the learning goals. Even if the mathematics is obvious to you, students may complete the activity without making the intended connections. That means careful planning of the *after* phase is critical. The following questions should be taken into consideration (Smith, Bill, & Hughes, 2008):

1. How you will organize the discussion to accomplish the mathematical goals (e.g., which solutions will be shared and in what order)?
2. What questions you will ask to help students make sense of the mathematics, make connections to other mathematics, see patterns, and make generalizations?
3. How will you involve all students (over time, not in every lesson)?
4. What evidence are you seeking that will tell you the students understand?

Importantly, the point of the *after* phase is not just to hear student solutions, but to compare and analyze those tasks, making connections among the strategies and generalizations about the mathematics. Plan an adequate amount of time for your discussion. A worthwhile problem can take 15 to 20 minutes to discuss.

After Phase: Fixed Areas. First, ask different groups to draw one of their rectangles, with its measurements, on the interactive whiteboard. Second, ask the following questions:

- What strategies did you use to find the rectangles?
- What do you notice about these possible rectangles?
- How did you find the perimeters of these rectangles?
- If you were the stage architect, which of the rectangles would you pick and why?

Ask students to complete their exit slip (see assessment table).

Step 8: Reflect and Refine

A well-prepared lesson that maximizes the opportunity for students to learn must be focused and aligned. Steps 5, 6, and 7 result in a tentative lesson plan. The final step is to review this tentative plan in light of the lesson considerations determined in steps 1–4, making changes or additions as needed. There is often a temptation to do a series of "fun" activities that seem to relate to a topic but that have different learning goals. Look to see that objectives, assessments, and questions are aligned. If the questions all target only one objective, add questions to address each objective or remove the objective that is not addressed.

Questioning is critically important to the potential learning (see discussion in Chapter 3). Using your objectives as the focus, review the lesson to see that in the *before* phase you are posing questions that capture students' attention and raise curiosity about how to solve the problem. In the *during* and *after* phases, you are using questions based on the objectives to focus students' thinking on the critical features of the task and what you want them to learn. Research on questioning indicates that teachers rarely ask high-level questions—this is your chance to review and be sure that you have included some challenging questions that ask students to extend, analyze, compare, generalize, and synthesize. And, be sure you have a plan to make sure each student is thinking about and responding to each of these high-level questions.

Reflect and Refine: Fixed Areas. This lesson is well-aligned, with a worthwhile task (e.g., multiple entry and exit points), a lesson plan that increases in challenge and engages students in mathematical reasoning, and formative assessments aligned to each objective. Higher-level questions based on the objectives are posed to students in the *during* and *after* phases. Some additional questions to have prepared for early finishers or advanced students include the following:

Is there a number of tiles for which there is only one option for building a rectangle? What is its area and perimeter? Are there other examples?

For what number of tiles (less than 100) are there the most possible rectangles?

MyLab Education   **Self-Check 4.2**

 ## High-Leverage Routines

The basic lesson structure we have been discussing assumes that a class will be given a task or problem, allowed to work on it, and end with a discussion. Here we share high-leverage routines that fit within this structure. High-leverage routines are routines designed around developing student numeracy and engaging students in actively engaging in doing mathematics (McCoy, Barnett, & Combs, 2013; Shumway, 2011). There are many open education resources that provide high-leverage routines. For example, Estimation 180 (www.Estimation180.com), Open Middle (www.openmiddle.com), and Which One Doesn't Belong (http://wodb.ca/) are very well-used because of mathematical growth teachers see in their students. Here we share several high-leverage lesson designs, routines, and ideas.

3-Act Math Tasks

There are many good examples of three-phase problem-based lessons, though searches by content often lead to practice worksheets rather than quality lessons. An excellent model of a three-phase lesson is 3-Act Math Tasks. The concept of a 3-Act Math Task originated from high school teacher/leader, Dan Meyer. In Act-1, the teacher shares a visual context (e.g., a video) that peaks student interest and fosters curiosity. Unlike traditional problems, the questions and conflicts that arise from the context are student generated. It is here where students buy into the problem by making assumptions, predictions and estimations. In Act-2, students identify the variables (unknown quantities) needed to solve their problem and define a solution path. Act-3 concludes with a reveal through digital media, which is followed by sharing out and discussing the mathematics. For elementary examples, see Graham Fletcher's posts (https://gfletchy.com/3-act-lessons/) and for middle (and high) school go to Dan Meyer's Three-Act Math Tasks or go to Dane Elhert's blog post, "Promoting Growth Mindset with 3-Act Math" on NCTM's website (www.nctm.org) where more links to 3-Act Math Tasks are provided (Elhert, 2015).

Number Talks

Like the name implies, this is a brief (5–15 minutes) time in which students are talking about a particular problem and how it might be solved, with the intent to develop procedural fluency (efficiency, flexibility, accuracy, and efficiency) (Parrish, 2014; Parrish & Dominick, 2016). Here are two whole number examples:

CONCEPT: ADDING STRATEGIES GRADE: 1	
Talk 1:	**Talk 2:**
1. **8 + 2 =**	1. **12 + 8 =**
2. **10 + 5 =**	2. **12 + 19 + 8 =**
3. **8 + 7 =**	3. **39 + 9 + 11 =**

Students solve these problems using mental math and then they share how they thought about it. The point of number talks is the talk. The teacher facilitates the discussion asking questions to hear how students thought about the problems, seeking different strategies and focusing students' attention on the possible ways to solve the problems. In the two examples above, the teacher might ask, "How are these equations alike or different?" Notice in the first talk, the first two equations are known facts that can be used to solve the third problem. In the second talk, the problems are set up to help students notice they can add numbers in different orders, and they can select a way that seems more manageable.

Number talks are also important for rational numbers beyond whole numbers. Students must also develop flexibility with fractions and decimals (positive and negative). Consider a (rational) number talk for this problem: $3\frac{1}{2} - 2\frac{5}{8} = $ _____. How might students solve it? One way might be to think of one-half as four-eighths and then subtract with regrouping. But, mentally, there are more efficient strategies. For example, a student might notice that $2\frac{1}{2}$ and $3\frac{1}{2}$ are one apart (e.g., one inch), but the difference is $\frac{1}{8}$ less than one whole, so $\frac{7}{8}$. Another student might count up three-eighths to 3 and then four more eighths to $3\frac{1}{2}$. Students may be using a number line to visualize or solve the task (concrete or mentally), or picturing circles or other manipulatives.

Worked Examples

Like it sounds, a worked example is an already-solved task that students analyze, including tasks solved correctly, partially, and incorrectly. Using worked examples has been found to improve student procedural and conceptual knowledge (Booth, Lange, Koedinger, & Newton, 2013; Star & Verschaffel, 2016). And, using incorrect worked examples is particularly beneficial for students with disabilities or who struggle with mathematics (Booth, Cooper, Donovan, Huyghe, Kodeinger, & Paré-Blagoev, 2015). Worked examples can bring to light alternatives solution strategies, common errors/misconceptions, or introduce new content (Barlow, Gerstenschlager, & Harmon, 2016; McGinn, Lange, & Booth, 2015). A worked example could be used in a number talk, a full lesson, or homework. For example, a homework problem could be a worked example in which students are asked to identify the error and then solve the problem correctly (Walk & Lassak, 2017). To design an effective worked example:

- Analyze the topic you are teaching, anticipate important strategies and common misconceptions,
- Write or find a problem that highlights that strategy or concept,
- Complete the problem (as an anonymous student) in a way that brings attention to the strategy or misconception, and
- Construct a question that requires students to explain the misconception, error, or concept.

After students have had an opportunity to complete and/or discuss the worked example, give students related problems to solve. Examples of worked examples are provided in Figure 4.5.

Warm-ups and Short Tasks

Beyond number talks and worked examples, other short tasks (5–10 minutes) can be incorporated using other formats (e.g., in writing, working alone or in small groups). The three-phase lesson can be applied in as few as 10 minutes. You might plan two or three cycles in a single lesson, have a morning problem, or have these on hand for when there are extra minutes between transitions. Review these short tasks and think about how you might implement a *before*, *during* and *after* design.

Kindergarten	Ms. Joy's class has three fish in their fish tank and Ms. Lo's class has five fish in their fish tank. If we combined the fish, how many would we have?
Grade 2	If you have forgotten the answer to the addition fact 9 + 8, how might you figure it out in your head?
Grade 4	On your virtual geoboard, make a figure that has only one line of symmetry. Make a second figure that has at least two lines of symmetry.
Grade 6	After playing the game "Race" four times, you notice that it took 30 minutes. If this rate is constant, how many games can you play in 45 minutes? In 2 hours?
Grade 8	Write a situation that fits each equation below: $y = 12x$ $y = 30x + 5$

Pose the task to students (*before*). Then, ask students to *think-pair-share*. Students first spend time developing their own thoughts and ideas on how to approach the task (*think*). Then they pair with a classmate and discuss each other's strategies (*pair*). This can occur as a brief *during* phase. After partners have shared, small groups or the whole class can share and compare

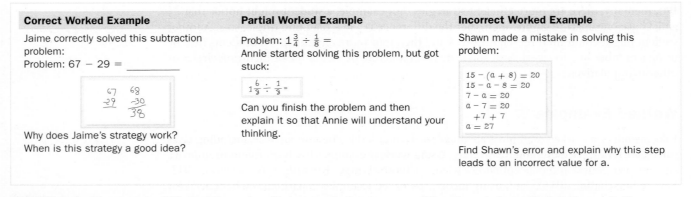

Correct Worked Example	Partial Worked Example	Incorrect Worked Example
Jaime correctly solved this subtraction problem: Problem: 67 − 29 = _____ $\begin{array}{cc} 67 & 68 \\ -29 & -30 \\ \hline & 38 \end{array}$ Why does Jaime's strategy work? When is this strategy a good idea?	Problem: $1\frac{3}{4} \div \frac{1}{8} =$ Annie started solving this problem, but got stuck: $1\frac{6}{8} \div \frac{1}{8} =$ Can you finish the problem and then explain it so that Annie will understand your thinking.	Shawn made a mistake in solving this problem: $15 - (a + 8) = 20$ $15 - a - 8 = 20$ $7 - a = 20$ $a - 7 = 20$ $\quad +7 + 7$ $a = 27$ Find Shawn's error and explain why this step leads to an incorrect value for a.

FIGURE 4.5 Three types of Worked Examples. Each example focuses on a different grade band (K–2, 3–5, and 6–8).

strategies (*share*). Think-pair-share provides an opportunity to test out ideas and to practice articulating them. For ELs, students with learning disabilities, and students who tend not to participate, this offers both a nonthreatening chance to speak and an opportunity to practice what they might later say to the whole class.

Learning Centers

A particular topic may lend itself to having students work at different tasks at various classroom locations. Each learning center can emphasize the curriculum goal using different manipulatives, situations, or technology. For example, knowing that a number can be decomposed into two other numbers is an important relationship for young children to understand. To develop this understanding, students need opportunities to create part-part-whole relationships using different objects. A lesson might focus on the number 6 and include four stations, one with counters in two piles, one with cubes creating two towers, one with finding dominoes that equal 6, and one with paper and pencil asking students to find ways two friends can share 6 plums.

The *before* phase is important when using learning centers, as it is still important to elicit prior knowledge, ensure the task is understood, and establish clear expectations. It may include modeling what happens at each center. The *during* phase is still the time where students engage in the task, but they are stopping and rotating to new centers within this phase of the lesson. It is still important to ask questions and keep track of strategies students are using to later highlight. In the *after* phase, you may decide to focus on one particular center, or you may begin with the center that was the least challenging for students and progress to the one that was most challenging. Or, you may not discuss what was done at each center, but instead ask students to talk about what they learned about the number 6, for example.

Learning centers can also be used for independent work. Even in this case, the three-phase model can be implemented by placing a series of reflective questions for students to use as they participate in the task at the center. A good task for this type of center is one that can be repeated. For example, students might play a game where one student covers part of a known number of counters and the other student names the amount in the covered part. Good technology-supported tasks, especially Internet applications, can be the focus of a learning center. Lessons such as "Fraction Game" on the NCTM Illuminations website are engaging and can played over and over again.

Planning three-phase inquiry lessons using worthwhile tasks and ensuring that the lesson meets the needs of all students requires intentional and ongoing effort. Questions are likely to surface. Frequently Asked Questions on this instructional design may help you as you contemplate how to plan for your students, or consider ways to advocate for teaching through problem solving with other teachers, families, and administrators.

MyLab Education   **Teacher Resource: Frequently Asked Questions**

 ## Differentiating Instruction

Every classroom contains a range of student abilities and backgrounds. Perhaps the most important work of a teacher is to be able to plan (and teach) lessons that support and challenge *all* students to learn important mathematics. The three-phase lesson plan is highly effective in meeting the needs of a range of learners. Students are asked to make sense of the task (*before*), bring their own skills and ideas to the problem to solve it in their own way (*during*), and then articulate their thinking, as well as hear the thinking of others (*after*). In contrast, in a traditional highly directed lesson, the assumption is made that all students will understand one approach. Students not ready to understand the ideas presented must focus their attention on following rules or directions in an instrumental manner (i.e., without a conceptual understanding). In addition to using a problem-based approach, there are specific adaptations that can meet the needs of the diverse learners in your classroom; this is the focus of Chapter 6.

Differentiating instruction means that a teacher's lesson plan includes strategies to support the range of different academic backgrounds found in classrooms that are academically, culturally, and linguistically diverse (Tomlinson, 1999). When considering what to differentiate, first consider the learning profile of each student. Second, consider what can be differentiated across three critical elements:

- *Content* (what you want each student to know)
- *Process* (how you will engage them in thinking about that content)
- *Product* (what they will show, write, or tell to demonstrate what they have learned)

Third, consider how the physical learning environment might be adapted. This might include the seating arrangement, specific grouping strategies, and access to materials.

Content can be differentiated in many ways, including resources or manipulatives used, mathematics vocabulary developed, examples and nonexamples used to develop a concept, and teacher-directed groups used to provide foundations for a new concept (Cassone, 2009).

Process can also be differentiated in various ways. Tomlinson and McTighe (2006) suggest that in thinking about process, teachers think about selecting strategies that build on students' readiness, interests, and learning preferences. In addition, the process should help students learn effective strategies and reflect on which strategies work best for them. Open questions and tiered lessons are two ways to differentiate the process. (Products are discussed in Chapter 5.)

Open Questions

Many questions in textbooks are closed, meaning there is one answer, and often only one way to get there. Such a task cannot meet the needs of range of learners in the classroom. *Open questions* are broad-based questions that invite meaningful responses from students at many developmental levels (Small, 2017).

One number is about one-half of another. Their product is close to 100. What might the numbers be?

You can take a closed task and make it open—for example, rather than ask students to add 8+12, say, "The answer is 20, what is the equation?" You can give "clues" and ask students to write an equation that fits the clues. Note that once a problem is turned into an open task, it could be used as a Number Talk!

Open questions are particularly useful in taking low cognitive demand tasks and turning them into high cognitive demand tasks. Compare these two tasks:

Task A: Write 35,045,011 in scientific notation.

Task B: Write two numbers that are more easily compared when in scientific notation. Write two numbers that are difficult to compare when in scientific notation.

The *after* phase of lessons that include open questions can be rich with debate as students critique the solutions and ideas of their peers.

Tiered Lessons

Tiered lessons include a set of similar problems focused on the same mathematical goals, but adapted to meet the range of learners, with different groups of students working on different tasks. For example, students might all be working on decomposing numbers, but some students are finding ways to decompose 5 into two numbers, some are working on decomposing 8 into two numbers, and some are working on decomposing 8 and also considering more than two addends. An adaptation may not be about the *content*; it may be any of the following (Kingore, 2006):

1. *The degree of assistance.* This might include providing examples or partnering students.
2. *How structured the task is.* Students with special needs, for example, benefit from highly structured tasks, but gifted students often benefit from a more open-ended task.

3. *The complexity of the task given.* This can include making a task more concrete or more abstract or including more difficult problems or applications.
4. *The complexity of process.* This includes how quickly paced the lesson is, how many instructions you give at one time, and how many higher-level thinking questions are included as part of the task.

Consider the following:

Original Task

Eduardo had 9 toy cars. Erica came over to play and brought 8 cars. Can you figure out how many cars Eduardo and Erica have together? Explain how you know.

The teacher distributes cubes to students to model the problem and paper and pencil to illustrate and record how they solved the problem. He asks students to be ready to explain their solution.

Adapted Task

Eduardo had some toy cars. Erica came over to play and brought her cars. Can you figure out how many cars Eduardo and Erica have together? Explain how you know.

The teacher asks students what is happening in this problem and what they are going to be doing. Then he distributes task cards that tell how many cars Eduardo and Erica have. He has varied how hard the numbers are, giving the students who are struggling numbers less than 10 and the more advanced students open-ended cards with multiple solutions.

- Card 1 (easier)

Eduardo has 6 cars and
Erica has 8 cars.

- Card 2 (moderate)

Eduardo has 13 cars and
Erica has 16 cars.

- Card 3 (advanced)

> Eduardo has _ cars and
> Erica has _ cars. Together
> they have 25 cars. How many
> cars might Eduardo have and
> how many might Erica have?

In each case, students must use words, pictures, models, or numbers to show how they figured out the solution. Various tools are provided (connecting cubes, counters, and hundreds chart) for their use.

There are (at least) three options for how to organize the use of the task cards:

1. Give everyone the cards in order.
2. Give students only one card, based on their current academic readiness (e.g., easy cards to those who have not yet mastered addition of single-digit numbers).
3. Give out cards 1 and 2 based on readiness and use card 3 as an extension for those who have successfully completed card 1 or 2.

Notice that this tiered lesson addresses both the complexity of the task and complexity of the process (instructions are broken down by first starting with a no-numbers scenario).

The following example illustrates how to tier a lesson based on how much *structure* is provided (some are more open-ended than others), yet all tasks focus on the same learning goal of identifying properties of parallelograms.

Topic: Properties of Parallelograms   **Grade: 5–6**

Students are given a collection of parallelograms, including squares and rectangles as well as nonrectangular parallelograms. The following tasks are distributed to different groups based on their learning needs and prior knowledge of quadrilaterals:

- Group A, open ended: Explore the set of parallelograms. Measure angles and sides using your ruler and protractor. Make a list of the properties that you think are true for every parallelogram.
- Group B, slightly structured: Use your ruler and protractor to measure the parallelograms. Record any patterns that are true for all of the parallelograms related to sides, angles, and diagonals.
- Group C, highly structured: Explore the parallelograms to find patterns and rules that define the shapes as parallelograms. Use a ruler to measure the sides and a protractor to measure the angles. First, sort the parallelograms into rectangles and nonrectangles.

  1. What pattern do you notice about the measures of the *sides* of all the parallelograms in the *nonrectangle* set?
     What pattern do you notice about the measures of the *sides* of all the parallelograms in the *rectangle* set?
  2. What pattern do you notice about the measures of the *angles* of all the parallelograms in the *nonrectangle* set?
     What pattern do you notice about the measures of the *angles* of all the parallelograms in the *rectangle* set?

Parallel Tasks

Parallel tasks, like tiered lessons, involve students working on different tasks all focused on the same learning goal. With parallel tasks, the focus is on choice (Small, 2017). Giving a choice increases student motivation and helps students become more self-directed learners (Bray, 2009; Gilbert & Musu, 2008).

Topic: Scientific Notation   **Grade: 8**

Select one of the numbers below and represent it at least four different ways.

3,500,000,000   0.0035

Choices can be embedded within stories:

Topic: Subtraction   **Grades: 2–3**

Eduardo had {12, 60, 121} marbles. He gave Erica {5, 15, 46} marbles. How many marbles does Eduardo have now?

An adaptation for fractions can include pairing the choices, with option (a) being less challenging than option (b) (Phelps, 2012).

Topic: Addition   **Grades: 5–6**

Camila is making trail mix. She puts in some raisins and ___ cups of nuts. In total she has ___ cups of trail mix. How many cups of raisins did she put in the trail mix?

a. $\frac{3}{4}$, $1\frac{1}{2}$ b. $\frac{5}{8}$, $2\frac{1}{4}$

Parallel tasks provide choice, and students tend to choose the numbers that provide the greatest challenge without being too difficult. What they choose, therefore, also provides useful formative assessment data.

Flexible Grouping

Allowing students to collaborate on tasks provides support and challenges, increasing their chance to communicate about mathematics and build understanding. Collaboration is also an important life skill. Students feel that working in groups improves their confidence, engagement, and understanding (Nebesniak & Heaton, 2010). *Flexible grouping* means that the size and makeup of small groups vary in a purposeful and strategic manner. In other words, sometimes students are working in partners because the nature of the task best suits two people; other times they are in groups of four because the task has enough tasks or roles to warrant a larger team.

Groups can be selected based on the students' academic abilities, language needs, social dynamics, and behavior. Avoid ability grouping! As opposed to differentiation, ability grouping means that groups are formed and those needing more support in the low group are meeting different (lesser) learning goals than students in the high group. Although this may be well-intentioned, it only puts the students in the low group further behind, increasing the gap between more and less dependent students and significantly damaging students' self-esteem.

MyLab Education   Video Example 4.1

Watch this video (https://www.youtube.com/watch?v=R4iAwShVIBE) that details some of the negative effects of ability grouping.

The first key to successful grouping is *individual accountability*. That means that while the group is working together on a product, individuals must be able to explain the process, the content, and the product. Although this may sound easy, it is not. Second, and equally important, is building a sense of *shared responsibility* within a group. At the start of the year, it is important to do team building activities and to set the standard that all members contribute to the group understanding. Resources for team building activities (though there are many) include *Team Building Games on a Shoestring* (a free downloadable collection, all done with shoestrings) (Heck, 2006), *Team Building Activities for Every Group* (Jones, 1999), and *Feeding the Zircon Gorilla and Other Team Building Activities* (Sikes, 1995).

Beyond individual accountability and shared responsibility, teachers must teach students how to engage in productive discussions. This can be modeled before having students work in groups, for example, a teacher might say, "What might you say to a partner if they don't get the right answer?" and then model various responses (Ghousseini, Lord, & Cardon, 2017). As groups are working, you can support their interdependence in various ways. When someone asks you a question, for example, rather than answer, pose it to the rest of the group. When observing groups, rather than ask Angela what she is doing, you can ask Bernard to explain what Angela is doing. Other ways to build individual accountability and shared responsibility include: have all students participate in the oral report to the whole class; tell students you may call on any member to explain what their group did; and have each student write and record their group's strategies. The more you use these strategies and others like them, the more effectively groups will function and the more students will learn.

MyLab Education   **Self-Check 4.3**

 ## Planning for Family Engagement

Teaching mathematics developmentally, addressing the increased content demands articulated in the Common Core State Standards Initiative (NGA Center & CCSSO, 2010), and ensuring that students are mathematically proficient requires everyone's commitment. Parental involvement at school results in higher levels of student academic achievement (Barnard, 2004; Lee & Bowen, 2006). Parents know the importance of mathematics for their child's future. They participate in their child's learning by doing such things as supporting homework, volunteering at the school, and meeting with teachers, even if they may recall unpleasant experiences or difficulties with mathematics from their own schooling. Understanding that memories of mathematics classes are not always pleasant for parents and appreciating their support prepares us to suitably identify for parents the mathematics goals that students should be experiencing in the 21st century. This is important because research has found that positive parent emotions lead to positive student emotions, and positive student emotions are connected to better performance (Else-Quest, Hyde, & Hejmadi, 2008).

Communicating Mathematics Goals

Every year parents need opportunities to get information directly from the leaders and teachers in the school about their child's mathematics program, including the kind of instruction that might differ from what they experienced in their own schooling. For example, even if your school has been engaged for several years in implementing a mathematics program that reflects the NCTM *Principles to Actions* or the Common Core State Standards, the curriculum will still be new to the parents of your students. Without such opportunities for communication, parents may draw their own conclusions about the effectiveness of the mathematics curriculum, develop frustrations and negative opinions about what is happening in their child's classroom or school, and communicate this apprehension to other parents. Table 4.1 highlights common questions parents ask about problem-based mathematics programs.

TABLE 4.1   PARENT QUESTIONS RELATED TO MATHEMATICS TEACHING AND LEARNING

Category	Types of Questions
Pedagogy	• Why isn't the teacher teaching? (And what is the point of reinventing the wheel?) • Are children doing their own work when they are in groups? Is my child having to do the work of other students? • Are calculators and other technology interfering with my child's fluency?
Content	• Is my child learning the basic skills? • Why is my child learning different algorithms (strategies) (than I learned) for doing the operations? • Why are there less skills and more story problems?
Student Learning and Outcomes	• Will these standards prepare my child for middle school, high school, college, and beyond (e.g., ready for ACT, SAT, Algebra in eighth or ninth grade)? • Why is my child struggling more than in previous year?

Source: From Bay-Williams, J. M., & Meyer, M. R. (2003). What Parents Want to Know about Standards-Based Mathematics Curricula. *Principal Leadership, 3*(7), 54–60. Copyright 2003 National Association of Secondary School Principals. www.principals.org. Reprinted with permission.

Be proactive! Don't wait for concerns or questions to percolate. Strategies include engaging parents in family math nights, using positive homework practices, and sharing where to find mathematics-related resources for their children.

Invite Parents/Guardians to Your Math Lessons. Invite parents into your mathematics lessons. If parents can witness firsthand your questioning and the many ways that problems can be solved, they will have a vision of how they can support learning at home. For example, they may notice that you encourage students to select their own strategy and explain how they know it works. Parents will also pick up on the language that you are using and will be able to reinforce that language at home. A number talk can be an excellent example of good mathematical thinking, and something parents can repeat at home.

Family Math Nights

There are many ways to conduct a family or community mathematics event, such as including a math component in a back-to-school night, discussing it in a PTA meeting, or hosting a showcase for a new mathematics program. One idea is to host a Math Orientation Workshop (Ernst & Ryan, 2014). The purpose of this even is to develop consistency between the way math is taught in school and the way parent's help at home. Beyond a focus on the content, parents can learn about *dispositions* of effective problem solvers, including the importance of asking questions; developing persistence; using multiple ways to solve problems; learning from mistakes; and reflecting on whether solutions make sense (see Ernst & Ryan (2014) for more details on designing and implementing this event). Providing opportunities to parents to learn about the mathematics prior to their children learning it can lead to increased relationships with parents and increased student achievement (Knapp, Jefferson, & Landers, 2013).

Engage in Doing Mathematics. The heart of a Family Math Night is having positive experiences doing mathematics! When choosing mathematical tasks to use with parents, be sure the tasks focus on content that really matters to them and relates to what they already know is a part of the mathematics curriculum. Figure 4.6 contrasts two problems focused on decomposing numbers with connections to supporting basic fact mastery. Tasks and activities throughout this book are also ideal for a Family Math Night.

 Pause *&* Reflect

What distinctions do you notice between the two tasks in Figure 4.6? What is valued as "doing mathematics" in both of the problems? ●

The potential each of these problems has to support and challenge children in making sense of mathematics should be made explicit during a discussion with parents. After giving parents time to do both tasks and discussing solution strategies (as you would with students), ask

---

TASK 1:

Find the answer to these equations. Use counters or draw pictures to show your work.

$1 + 5 =$ _____ $0 + 6 =$ _____

$3 + 3 =$ _____ $2 + 4 =$ _____

TASK 2:

The parking lot has only blue and red cars. There are 6 cars parked. How many blue and how many red cars might be in the parking lot? Find as many ways as you can. Draw a picture and write an equation for each answer.

Extensions: Can you find all of the ways to have 6 red and blue cars in the parking lot? How many ways can you find to have a total of 5 cars? How many ways can you find to have a total of 7 cars? Do you see a pattern?

FIGURE 4.6 Two tasks to explore at a kindergarten or first-grade Family Math Night.

participants to consider the learning opportunities in the two contrasting tasks. Ask questions such as these:

> What skills are being developed in each problem?
>
> Which problem gives more opportunity to make connections between mathematics and the real world?
>
> Which task would your child be most motivated to solve? Why?

Help parents identify the depth of the mathematics in the worthwhile task. For example, in grades K–2 children are building important foundations of number and operations through algebraic reasoning—looking for patterns, reasoning, and generalizing. Share the CCSS Mathematical Practices or your state's list of mathematical practices/processes. Focus on the goal of having students becoming mathematically proficient as described in those standards. Ask parents "Where do you see these proficiencies being supported in the two tasks we did?"

Talk about Learning through Inquiry. When parents ask questions that point to their belief that mathematics is best learned through direct instruction—just as they learned it—remind them of the experience parents had in *doing* mathematics with the parking lot task. Point to the difference between being *shown* how to do something (e.g., this is how you add, now practice this) and *developing* an understanding of something (e.g., How many different ways can you partition 6? How do you know if you have found all the ways?). You can help parents identify the skills and concepts that are developed through these two experiences. Ask, "In what ways are children learning about addition? About subtraction? How do the different ways support eventual mastery of the basic facts?" Point out that skills are still important, and children benefit by generating their own procedures. Encourage families to engage in inquiry at home. Give them a task to take home. The Family Math Take-Home Planning Guide can help you prepare such a task.

MyLab Education   **Teacher Resource: Family Math Take-Home Planning Guide**

Describe Your Role. In an inquiry-based classroom, parents may not think the teacher is "teaching." Explain your role in *organizing* (selecting a worthwhile task), *facilitating* (setting up and monitoring the task and student engagement with the task), and *questioning* (asking questions in each lesson phase to help students make connections or to deepen their understanding).

Justify the Use of Cooperative Groups. Parents may wonder about their child working in cooperative groups because this may differ from their own mathematics learning experiences. You can justify the use of cooperative groups in a variety of ways:

1. *Share the one-page parent overview from the NCTM Families Ask department titled "Cooperative Learning" (Coates & Mayfield, 2009).* Families Ask, a feature posted on the NCTM website and published in *Mathematics Teaching in the Middle School*, provides more than 20 excellent discussions on a range of topics appropriate for parents in elementary and middle school.

2. *Include a feature in your parent newsletter.* Early in the year, you can feature cooperative learning, addressing its importance across content areas. In mathematics, this can include the following benefits: hearing different strategies, building meaning, designing solution strategies, and justifying approaches, all of which are essential to building a strong understanding of mathematics and important life skills.

3. *Send home letters introducing math units.* If you are about to teach a unit on adding and subtracting fractions, a letter can help parents know the important aspects of the content. This is a great time to mention that students will work in groups so that they can see different ways to solve tasks.

4. *Do a cooperative learning mathematics activity at a Family Math Night.* Use a task that lends itself to assigning roles to different members of the group and won't take long to solve. Have parents work with two or three others to solve the task.

5. *Invite parents to assist in a mathematics group assignment.* Seeing firsthand the dialogue and thinking that happens in cooperative groups can go a long way in illustrating how valuable cooperative groups can be!

Advocate for Use of Technology. Parents may be avid users of technology, yet still have concerns about their child using calculators and computers if they have not mastered their basic facts. Even though research overwhelmingly finds that students using calculators achieve at least as much as those not using calculators, calculators are widely blamed for students' lack of reasoning and sense making. Reassure parents that students will learn the basic facts and procedures and that a calculator can support that learning. The calculator is used when it is *appropriate* to support the mathematical goals of the day. For example, students can use calculators when the goal is learning volume, not when the goal is learning how to multiply. Mastery of basic facts should *not* be a prerequisite to using a calculator. Instead, you must be make good decisions about whether a calculator supports or detracts from solving a particular problem (and learning the intended mathematics).

Provide Support for Problem Solving. Teaching parents how to help their children has been found to make a difference in supporting student achievement (Cooper, 2007). Parents value school mathematics, but they associate mathematics with skills and seatwork (Remillard & Jackson, 2006). It is your job to help them understand the broader goals of mathematics. Real mathematics involves more word problems and far fewer "naked number" skill problems. Skills that can be executed on a $1 calculator are less necessary in the 21st-century workplace, but number sense, reasoning, and being able to solve real problems is absolutely essential. Provide parents with a card that includes reading strategies for helping their child interpret story problems, such as the one featured in Figure 4.7.

Parents may worry when they see their child struggle with a single mathematics problem because they may believe that fast means successful. But faster isn't smarter. Cathy Seeley's book with this same title (2009) is a great read on this topic written for families, educators, and policymakers.

Solving Math Story Problems—Try These Strategies:

- Read problem aloud.
- Paraphrase what the story is about.
- Discuss math vocabulary.
- Find and write the question.
- Draw a picture of the problem.
- Act out the problem (have fun!).
- Use household items to illustrate the problem.

FIGURE 4.7 A note card for parents to help their child solve story problems.

Seeley offers 41 brief messages, many of which can address parent questions about mathematics (e.g., "A Math Message to Families: Helping Students Prepare for the Future"). Explain that engaging in productive struggle is one of the two most effective ways teachers can develop conceptual understanding in students (the other is making connections between mathematical ideas) (Hiebert & Grouws, 2007).

Address Concerns about Procedures. Students should be using strategies that make sense to them, and this applies to the procedures such as dividing whole numbers. Yet, parents may think that they are not learning the standard algorithms. Point out that the skills are still there, they just look different because they are presented in a way based on understanding, not just memorization. Second, explain that standard algorithms are one technique, but mathematically proficient students must have access to multiple strategies so that they can select the most efficient strategy in any given situation. Pose examples, such as these:

$$69 + 47 = \underline{\hspace{1cm}}$$

$$309 - 288 = \underline{\hspace{1cm}}$$

$$487 + 345 = \underline{\hspace{1cm}} + 355$$

Ask for volunteers to share the ways that they thought about the problems. For the subtraction problem, for example, the following might be shared:

- 300 take away 288 is 12, then add the 9 back on to get 21
- 288 up to 300 is 12 and up 9 more is 21
- 309 to 300 is 9, then down to 290 is 10 more (19), and then to 288 is 2 more (21)

These reasoning strategies, over numerous problems, reinforce place-value concepts and the relationship between addition and subtraction. Noticing that these values are both near 300 helps select a strategy. Point out that this bird's-eye view of the problem (looking at it holistically first, then deciding how to solve it) is important in being "good" at mathematics.

Homework Practices

You may have heard parents say, "I am not good at math" or "I don't like solving math problems." Parents may feel this way and, given the research just described, it is particularly important to redirect parents to portray mathematics in a positive light. For example, "Even though math can be hard, stick with it and you will figure it out." Teaching parents how to help their children has also been found to make a difference in supporting student achievement (Cooper, 2007).

Homework can and should be a positive experience for students and their families! Be strategic and creative in what you send home. Rather than a long collection of low cognitive demand tasks, shorten the number of tasks and be sure they require higher-level thinking. Select homework that will be comprehensible to parents. It is a mistake to require students use a new approach, unfamiliar to most parents (e.g., using arrays to multiply) on a homework assignment . Rather than require a single method, give students choice of approach (Bay-Williams, Duffett, & Griffith, 2016; Larson, 2016). This not only removes parent frustration, it provides opportunities for comparing approaches the next day. Consider projects that engage families in gathering data about their home or community. For example, Muir (2016) describes a "Counting with the Count" assignment. Each week, a student takes home the Count (Sesame Street character) and the family selects a numeracy project (e.g., How much milk does my family drink in a week?). The student determines how the data will be gathered, and a week later shares their findings and passes the Count to the next student. Here we share some strategies for making homework effective.

Mimic the Three-Phase Lesson Model. Complete a brief version of the *before* phase of a lesson to be sure the students understand the homework before they go home. At home, students complete the *during* phase. When they return with the work completed, apply the sharing techniques of the *after* phase of the homework. This is different than just checking answers, it can be a time to engage students in rich learning opportunities, if the focus is on comparing across problems (rather than on individual problems) and focusing on errors and difficulties (rather than on correct answers) (Otten, Cirillo, & Herbel-Eisenmann, 2015). An example of looking across problems is to ask students to sort a set based on common characteristics (Walk & Lassak, 2017). You can ask students what difficulties they had as part of the discussion and/or use worked examples from your students or that you created (see above). Students can even practice the *after* phase with their family if you encourage this through parent or guardian communications.

Use a Distributed-Content Approach. Homework can address content that has been taught earlier in the year as practice, that day's content as reinforcement, or upcoming content as groundwork. Interestingly, research has found that distributed homework that combines all three components is more effective in supporting student learning (Cooper, 2007). The exception is students with learning disabilities, who perform better when homework focuses on reinforcement of skills and current class lessons.

Promote an "Ask-Before-Tell" Approach with Parents. Parents may not know how best to support their child when he or she is stuck or has gotten a wrong answer. One important thing you can do is to ask parents to implement an "ask-before-tell" approach (Kliman, 1999). This means that before parents explain something, they should ask their child to explain how he or she did it. The child may self-correct (a life skill), and if not, at least the parent can use what they heard from their child to provide targeted assistance. Teach successful homework strategies to students, and share these strategies with parents. For example, the following ideas, suggested by Wieman & Arbaugh (2014), can be posted in your classroom and sent home:

Math Thinking Bookmark
When stuck on a math problem, ask: ● What do you need to figure out? ● What is the problem about? ● What words are confusing? What words are familiar? ● Did you have similar problems to look at? ● What math words or steps do you use in class? ● Where do you think you should begin? ● What have you tried so far? What else can you try? ● Can you describe where you are stuck or what is confusing? ● Can you make a drawing, table, or diagram to help you think about the problem? ● Does your answer make sense? ● Is there more than one answer? ● How might you check your answer?

- Look for examples in our notes or daily work. Try those problems again.
- If you are stuck, take a break, then come back and try again.
- If you are confused, write a statement or question describing what is confusing.
- Ask for help using specific questions (from parents, peers, or online support sites)

Provide Good Questioning Prompts for Parents. Providing guiding questions for parents or guardians supports a problem-based approach to instruction as they help their children. Figure 4.8 provides a teacher-made bookmark with guiding questions that can be emailed to parents, used as a bookmark in their text, or taped into homework journals.

Resources for Families

Parents will be a better able to help to their child if they know where to find resources. The Internet can provide a wealth of information, but it can also be an overwhelming distraction. Help families locate good places to find math support. First, check whether your textbook provides websites

FIGURE 4.8 Sample bookmark with questions for parents to help their children with homework.

with online resources for homework. These resources can include tutorials, video tutoring, connections to careers and real-world applications, multilingual glossaries, podcasts, and more. Second, post websites that are good general resources. Here are some examples:

- *Math Forum.* Under the tab "For Parents and Concerned Citizens" are many resources. For example, "Ask Dr. Math" is a great homework resource with an enormous archive of explanations. See also Math Discussion Groups, Key Issues in Math, and high quality math tasks.
- *Figure This! Math Challenges for Families.* This NCTM upper elementary and middle school resource has a teacher corner and a family corner. It offers outstanding resources to help families engage in *doing* mathematics together. It is also available in Spanish.
- *National Library of Virtual Manipulatives* (http://nlvm.usu.edu/en/nav/vlibrary.html) This site has numerous applets and virtual tools for learning about many mathematics topics.

There are also great websites for specific content. For example, Conceptua Math has excellent digital tools for exploring fraction operations. Share these sites with families as you introduce new units. Finally, print books can be important resources for teachers (see Resources at end of chapter).

Seeing Mathematics in the Home. In the same way that families support literacy by reading books with their children or pointing out letters of the alphabet when they encounter them, families can and should support numeracy. Because this has not been the practice in many homes, it means you have the responsibility to help parents see the connection between numeracy and everyday life. Consider asking families to make the *Math Promise* (Legnard & Austin, 2014). Family members make this promise to one another, which means they explicitly agree they will do math together—get to know each other's mathematical reasoning, play math games, and notice mathematics in their daily lives. Kliman (1999) offers some excellent suggestions, which include asking parents to share anecdotes and find mathematics in the books they read, have scavenger hunts, and create opportunities during household chores. Prepare an engaging letter to families that shares suggestions, such as the examples in the Math-at-Home Letter for Pre-K–2, the Math-at-Home Letter for Grades 3–5, and the Math-at-Home Letter for Grades 6–8.

MyLab Education   **Teacher Resource: Math-at-Home Letter for Pre-K–2**

MyLab Education   **Teacher Resource: Math-at-Home Letter for Grades 3–5**

MyLab Education   **Teacher Resource: Math-at-Home Letter for Grades 6–8**

Trips in the car can include informal and fun mathematics explorations. For example, license plates can be noted and family members can try to use the numbers on the plate to create a true mathematics equation or someone can select a target number, and the values from the plate are used to try to reach that target number (Hildebrandt, Biglan, & Budd, 2013). Today's Date (Mistretta, 2013) is another activity that can be a part of informal family discussions. Today's Date involves taking the date (e.g., 18) and thinking of different expressions, ways to write it, and connections to personal interests (e.g., a favorite athletes number or the age of a cousin). These tasks have many possible solutions and can be used repeatedly at any time of the year.

Involving *All* Families

Some families are at all school events and conferences, whereas others rarely participate. However, all families want their children to be successful in school. Parents who do not come to school events may have anxiety related to their own school experiences, or they may feel complete confidence that the school and its teachers are doing well by their child and that they do not need to participate. In some cultures, questioning a teacher may be perceived as disrespectful. Rodríguez-Brown, a researcher on Hispanic families, writes, "It is not that Latino parents do not want to support their children's learning. . . . [They] believe that it is disrespectful to usurp the teachers' role" (2010, p. 352).

Try to find ways to build a strong rapport with all families. Some strategies to consider include the following:

1. *Honor different strategies for doing mathematics.* Although this is a recommendation in standards documents, it is particularly important for children from other countries because they may have learned different ways to do the operations (Civil & Planas, 2010).

2. *Communicate with positive notes and phone calls.* Be sure to find a way to compliment each student's mathematical thinking (not just a good score on quiz) at some point early in the school year.

3. *Host informal gatherings to discuss mathematics teaching and learning.* Having regular opportunities to meet with the parents allows for the development of rapport and trust. Consider hosting events in out-of-school facilities. Schools in high-poverty communities have found that having parent events at a community center or religious institution brings in families that are reluctant to come into a school.

4. *Incorporate homework that involves the family.* When a student brings in homework that tells about his or her family and you provide positive feedback or a personal comment, then you are establishing a two-way communication with the family via homework.

5. *Translate letters that are sent home.* If you are doing a class newsletter for families or a letter describing the next mathematics unit, make an effort to translate the letter into the native language of the families represented in your class. Or ask students write a letter to their parents about what they are learning using their parents' first language, including visuals to support their writing. Ask parents to respond (in their language of choice). This is a great practice for helping students know what they need to learn, and it communicate the importance of family involvement.

6. *Post homework on your web page.* For parents that are not native speakers of English, posting problems on your site makes it easier for them to take advantage of online translations. Although these translations may not be perfectly accurate, they can aid in helping parents and students understand the language in the problems.

For more suggestions, see Chapter 6 and read the NCTM research brief titled "Involving Latino and Latina Parents in Their Children's Mathematics Education" (Civil & Menéndez, 2010).

MyLab Education   **Self-Check 4.4**

 **RESOURCES** FOR CHAPTER 4

RECOMMENDED READINGS

Articles

Barlow, A., Gerstenschlager, N. E., & Harmon, S. E. (2016). Learning from the unknown student. *Teaching Children Mathematics, 23*(2), 75–81.

This article shares ideas and examples for using worked examples (both correct and incorrect) to improve student understanding, as well as their ability to critique each other's reasoning.

Williams, L. (2008). Tiering and scaffolding: Two strategies for providing access to important mathematics. *Teaching Children Mathematics, 14*(6), 324–330.

Using a second-grade fraction lesson and a third-grade geometry lesson as examples, Williams shares how they were tiered, and then how scaffolds, or supports, were built into the lesson. A very worthwhile article.

Focus Issue: Differentiation (October 2012). *Teaching Children Mathematics.*

This issue has a wonderful collection of articles with pragmatic suggestions for differentiating instruction.

Books

Boaler, J. (2009). *What's math got to do with it?: How parents and teachers can help children learn to love their least favorite subject.* New York, NY: Penguin Books.

Jo Boaler luminously describes how math can be understandable and fun, how children can excel in math, and how parents and schools can help.

Shumway, J. M. (2011). *Number sense routines: Building numerical literacy every day in grades K–3.* Portland, ME: Stenhouse.

Jessica Shumway provides excellent descriptions and illustrations of many high leverage routines for developing number sense including counting and data routines. A great resource for early elementary teachers!

Small, M. (2017). *Good questions: Great ways to differentiate math instruction in the standards-based classroom.* (3rd Edition). Reston, VA: National Council of Teachers of Mathematics and New York, NY: Teachers College Press.

Each chapter focuses on mathematics strands and offers open tasks and parallel tasks, followed by purposeful questions. A great resource to find worthwhile tasks and have ideas for implementing them effectively.

Whitenack, J. W., Cavey, L. O., & Henney, C. (2015). *It's elementary: A parent's guide to K–5 Mathematics.* Reston, VA: NCTM

In an engaging, parent-friendly manner, these authors explain current teaching practices and fundamental math concepts, with many examples and student work.

Creating Assessments *for* Learning

LEARNER OUTCOMES

After reading this chapter and engaging in the embedded activities and reflections, you should be able to:

5.1 Differentiate between formative and summative assessment.

5.2 Describe four important methods for assessing students' mathematics understanding.

5.3 Analyze types of rubrics and their uses.

5.4 Explain the value of having students self-assess.

5.5 Identify ways that tests can be used in the classroom to enhance learning.

5.6 Explore ways to show evidence of and communicate about student learning that result in grades and more targeted instructional decisions.

What ideas about assessment come to mind from your personal experiences? Tests? Quizzes? Grades? Studying? Anxiety? All of these are common shared memories. Now suppose that you are told that the assessments you use should be designed to help students learn and to help you teach mathematics. How can assessment do those things?

Integrating Assessment into Instruction

When using a problem-based approach, you might ask, "How do I assess? A joint position statement on the formative assessment process from the Association of Mathematics Teacher Educators (AMTE) and the National Council of Supervisors of Mathematics (NCSM) (n.d.) stress three important ideas: (1) Assessment should enhance students' learning, (2) assessment is a valuable tool for making instructional decisions, and (3) feedback should help learners progress. These ideas align with the distinction between assessment *of* learning, where students are only evaluated on what they know at a given moment in an effort to home in on what they don't know, and assessment *for* learning (AFL), where students are continually evaluated so that instruction can be targeted to gaps and their learning is improved over time (Hattie, 2015; Wiliam & Leahy, 2015).

Assessment is not separate from instruction and in fact should include an alignment with your standards as well as the critical CCSS mathematical practices and NCTM processes that occur in the course of effective problem-based instructional approaches (Fennell, Kobett, & Wray, 2017). The typical end-of-chapter or end-of-year test of skills may have value, but it rarely reveals the type of data that can fine-tune instruction so that it is tailored to improve individual students' performance. In fact, Daro, Mosher, and Corcoran (2011) state that "the starting point is the mathematics and thinking the student brings to the lesson, not the deficit of mathematics they do not bring" (p. 48). NCTM's *Principles to Actions* (2014) urges teachers in their mathematical teaching practices to incorporate evidence of student thinking into an ongoing refinement of their instruction.

What Are the Main Assessment Types?

Assessments usually fall into two major categories: summative or formative. *Summative assessments* are cumulative evaluations that take place usually after instruction is completed (assessment *of* learning). They commonly generate a single score that measures overall progress towards content and practice/process standards, such as an end-of-unit test or a state standardized test. Although the scores from these assessments are important for schools and teachers, used individually they often do not shape day-to-day teaching decisions.

On the other hand, the *formative assessment process* (assessment *for* learning) includes tools that check the status of students' development during instructional activities, preassess, or attempt to identify students' naïve understandings or misconceptions related to the standards they are learning (Duckor, Holmberg, & Rossi Becker, 2017; Hattie, 2009; Popham, 2008; Wiliam & Leahy, 2015). When implemented well, the process of formative assessment is one of the most powerful influences on achievement (Hattie, 2009). It dramatically increases the speed and amount of student learning (Nyquist, 2003; Wiliam, 2007; Wilson & Kenney, 2003) by providing targeted feedback to the student and using the results and evidence collected to inform decision making about next steps in the learning progression. As Wiliam states, "To be formative, assessment must include a recipe for future action" (2010, slide 41).

Wiliam notes three key components of the formative assessment process: (1) Identify where learners are; (2) identify the goal for the learners; and (3) identify paths to reach the goal. Let's look a case of this process in action. For example, an assessment for a third-grade class might have students solve this word problem: "If Lindy has 34 shells in her collection and Jesse has 47, how many shells are in both collections?" Immediately the teacher observes one student quickly jotting down a straight line on the paper, making a tick mark with a 34 underneath and using small arcs to jump up four times to 74, then making one jump of six and another jump of one and indicating 81 with a tick mark (see Figure 5.1). Another student selects from a collection of base-ten materials in the center of the table, models each number, groups the tens together, then combines the ones and trades 10 of the ones for an additional ten piece, getting 81 as an answer. Observing a different student, the teacher notes he is using counters but is counting by ones. First, he counts out the 34, then the 47, and then recounts them all to reach 78 (miscounting along the way). The evidence gathered from observing these three students reveals the need for very different instructional paths. This teacher is at the first step in Wiliam's three key processes, noting where students are in their learning. Moving into the second step, the teacher notes that one student should move to more challenging tasks, whereas the other two students need to move closer to the CCSS standard of representing and solving addition and subtraction problems within 100 through more targeted instruction. In the third step, targeted lessons are designed that will reach each student's need.

If summative assessment could be described as a digital snapshot, formative assessment is like streaming video. One is a picture of what a student knows captured in a single moment of time; the other is a moving picture that demonstrates active student thinking and reasoning.

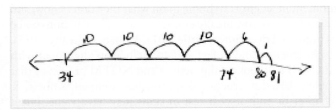

FIGURE 5.1   A student uses an empty number line to add 34 + 47.

MyLab Education
Video Example 5.1

In this video (https://www.youtube.com/watch?v=kPf0nQFfv50), Dylan Wiliam discusses strategies that support formative assessment.

VIDEO EXAMPLE

In this chapter and throughout Part II of this book in Formative Assessment Notes, we will focus on several tools in the formative assessment process that can be used for evaluating students' understanding.

What Should Be Assessed?

Appropriate assessment of students' mathematical proficiency (National Research Council, 2001) should reflect the full range of mathematics: concepts and procedures, mathematical processes and practices, and even students' disposition to mathematics.

Conceptual Understanding and Procedural Fluency. Assessments can provide students with opportunities to demonstrate how they understand essential concepts in more than one way. For example, you can assess students as they complete an activity, observing as students discuss and justify—in short, while students are doing mathematics—and gain information that provides insight into the nature of the students' understanding of that idea. You can also ask for more detail, something often not possible on tests.

Procedural fluency should also be assessed. This fluency includes understanding the procedure—if a student can compute with fractions yet has no idea of why he needs a common denominator for addition but not for multiplication, then the procedure has not been "mastered" to the extent it must be for a student to have procedural fluency.

Competence and Adaptive Reasoning. Truly understanding mathematics is more than just assessing content knowledge. The skills represented in the five process standards of *Principles and Standards* and the eight Standards for Mathematical Practice from the *Common Core State Standards* should also be assessed. One way to communicate to students that the processes and practices are important is to craft a corresponding list of rubric statements about doing mathematics that your students can understand so they recognize what you expect. Here are several examples for use with individual work, group work, or discussions:

Problem Solving

- Works to make sense of and fully understand problems before beginning
- Perseveres to demonstrate a variety of strategies
- Evaluates the reasonableness of answers

Reasoning

- Justifies solution methods and results
- Recognizes and uses counterexamples
- Makes conjectures and/or constructs logical progressions of statements based on reasoning

Communication

- Explains ideas in writing using words, pictures, numbers/equations, graphs, and tables (depending on grade level)
- Analyzes the thinking of others
- Uses precise language, units, and labeling to clearly communicate ideas

Connections

- Makes connections between mathematics and real contexts
- Makes connections between mathematical ideas

Representations

- Uses representations such as drawings, graphs, symbols, and models to help think about and solve problems
- Moves between models
- Explains how different representations are connected

Examples of rubric statements should be discussed and explicitly modeled with your students to help them understand these valuable behaviors. Share weak and strong examples of anonymous student work with the class to help all students identify ways to improve (Barlow, Gerstenschlager & Harmon, 2016).

Productive Disposition. Collecting data on students' ability to persevere, as well as their confidence and belief in their own mathematical abilities, is also important. This evidence is most often obtained with observation, students' self-reports, interviews, and writing. Information on perseverance and willingness to attempt problems is available to you every day when you use a problem-solving approach.

> **MyLab Education** **Self-Check 5.1**

 ## Assessment Methods

There are four basic approaches in the formative assessment process that can be used to evaluate students' understanding: observations, questions, interviews, and tasks. Here we will discuss each approach in depth.

Observations

All teachers learn useful bits of information about their students every day. When the three-phase lesson format suggested in Chapter 3 is used, the flow of evidence about student performance increases dramatically, especially in the *during* and *after* portions of lessons. If you have an organized plan for gathering this evidence while observing and listening to students during regular classroom instruction, at least two very valuable results occur. First, information that may have gone unnoticed is suddenly visible and important. Second, observation data gathered systematically can be combined with other data and used in planning lessons, providing feedback to students, conducting parent conferences, and determining grades.

Depending on what evidence you may be trying to gather, several days to two weeks may be required to complete observations on how each student is progressing on a standard. Shorter periods of observation will focus on a particular cluster of concepts or skills or on particular students. Over longer periods, you can note growth in mathematical processes or practices, such as problem solving, modeling, or reasoning. To use observation effectively, you should take seriously the following maxim: *Only try to collect data on a reasonable number of students in a single class period.*

For example, first graders may be playing a game in which each child draws a domino, adds the dots on the two halves and compares their total to the other child's. As students play, the teacher observes the way in which students are adding the two parts of the domino and how they use numbers. Some students count every dot on the domino. Others use a counting-on strategy (the student sees four dots on one half and counts on from four to tally the total number). Some will recognize certain dot patterns without counting. Others may be unsure whether 12 is greater than 11. Data gathered from asking questions about and listening to a pair of students work on an activity or an extended project provide significant insights into students' thinking (Petit & Zawojewski, 2010).

Anecdotal Notes. The act of *professional noticing* is a process where you observe learners through a focus on three phases: (1) attending, (2) interpreting, and (3) deciding (Jacobs, Lamb, & Philipp, 2010). You want to collect anecdotal notes to help understand learners' strategies and interpret their thinking as you plan next steps. That means you *attend* to everything such as if the child is nodding his head, using fingers to count, creating appropriate models or using strategies that are clearly described and defended. Then you *interpret* those gestures, comments, drawings and actions by making notes of students' strengths and the level of sophistication of their conceptual understanding. The last step is noting *decisions* for subsequent instructional actions.

One system for recording observations is to write these anecdotal notes on an electronic tablet and store them in a spreadsheet or in a multicolumn table that documents such things as students' use of mathematical practices. Focus your observations on about five students a day. The students selected may be members of one or two cooperative groups or a group identified as needing additional support.

MyLab Education	Teacher Resource: Multicolumn Table

Checklists. To focus your attention, a checklist with several specific processes, mathematical practices, or content objectives can be devised (see Figure 5.2). As you can see, there is a place for comments that should concentrate on students' achievement of big ideas and conceptual understandings. For example, you will probably find a note such as "is recognizing how multiplication facts can be related, such as using 10×7 to think about 9×7" more helpful than "knows the easy multiplication facts but not the hard ones." Or, for older students "is estimating answers to multiplication of decimals to locate the proper placement of the decimal" more useful than "cannot accurately multiply decimals."

Another Observation Checklist involves listing all students in a class on one to three pages (see Figure 5.3). Across the top of the page are specific abilities or common misconceptions to look for possibly based on learning progressions. Symbols such as pluses and minuses, checks, or codes can be entered in the grid and used to identify patterns of student performance (Accardo & Kuder, 2017). A full-class checklist is more likely to be used for long-term objectives such as problem solving strategies, strategic use of representations or tools, and such skill areas as basic fact fluency or computational estimation. Dating entries or noting specifics about observed performance is also helpful.

MyLab Education	Blackline Master: Observation Checklist

NAME: Sharon V.

PLACE VALUE	NOT THERE YET	ON TARGET	ABOVE AND BEYOND	COMMENTS
Understands numerator/ denominator		✓		
Area models		✓		Used pattern blocks to show $\frac{2}{3}$ and $\frac{3}{6}$
Set models	✓			
Uses fractions in real contexts	✓			
Estimates fraction quantities		✓		Showing greater reasonableness
MATHEMATICAL PRACTICES				
Makes sense of problems and perseveres		✓		Stated problem in own words
Models with mathematics	✓			Reluctant to use abstract models
Uses appropriate tools		✓		

FIGURE 5.2 A focused checklist and rubric can be made for each student.

Topic: Mental Computation Adding 2-digit numbers Names	Not There Yet *Can't do mentally*	On Target *Has at least one strategy*	Above and Beyond *Uses different methods with different numbers*	Comments
Lalie		✓ 3-18-2017 3-21-2017		
Pete	✓ 3-20-2017	✓ 3-24-2017		Difficulty with problems using 8 and 9
Sid			✓+ 3-20-2017	Flexible approaches used
Lakeshia		✓		Counts by tens, then adds ones
George		✓		
Pam	✓			Beginning to add the group of tens first
Maria		✓ 3-24-2017		Using a posted hundreds chart

FIGURE 5.3 A class observation checklist.

TABLE 5.1   QUESTION TYPES BASED ON THE NCTM *PRINCIPLES TO ACTIONS*

Type of Question	Sample Questions
Information gathering	What does the equal sign mean? Share an example. What are the properties of a trapezoid?
Student thinking	How does the model you drew relate to this fraction equivalence problem? How does your equation fit the story in the word problem?
Mathematical structures, connections, and relationships	Are both of these expressions equivalent? How do you know? What is the maximum number of digits you can get in a sum when you add two 3-digit numbers? Why?
Reflection and justification	How are the two solutions strategies you used to solve the problem today alike? Different? When would you choose to use each one? What does it mean that multiplication and division are inverse operations?

Questions

There are four main types of questions used in mathematics instruction (NCTM, 2014). Students should be asked a variety of these questions and different lessons may require a specific focus on one type over another. Here in Table 5.1 are the four question types and sample questions that fit each category.

Probing student thinking through questioning can provide useful data and insights that could inform instruction. Also, your use of questions helps students get past being "stuck" and promotes their ability to think for themselves. As you circulate around the classroom to observe and evaluate students' understanding, your use of questions is one of the most important ways to formatively assess in each lesson phase. Have these Question Probes on a tablet or in print as you move about the classroom to prompt and probe students' thinking. Remember, by challenging students who are secure with their answers or thinking helps them focus on their reasoning. "Formative" (http://goformative.com) is a digital tool where teachers create or select multiple choice, short answer, true/false or question probes, allowing students quick access from any digital device, where they can generate solutions using a digital whiteboard interface.

MyLab Education   **Teacher Resource: Question Probes**

To ensure you are asking questions that have potential for assessing students' understanding, consider videotaping yourself teaching mathematics and have a colleague score how many high level or how many recall questions you are asking. Use a matrix such as the Cognitive Rigor Matrix (Simpson, Mokalled, Ellenburg, & Che, 2014/2015) which is a blend of Bloom's Taxonomy and Webb's Depth of Knowledge (2002) to enhance the analysis of your questions.

Interviews

"An assessment system designed to help steer the instruction system must give good information about direction as well as distance to travel. A system that keeps telling us we are not there yet is like a kid in the back seat whining 'are we there yet?'" (Daros et al., 2011, p. 51). Interviews, particularly diagnostic interviews, are a means of getting in-depth information about an individual student's knowledge of concepts and strategy use to provide needed navigation. Interviews are a blending of observations with questioning.

The diagnostic interview is a one-on-one investigation of a student's thinking about a particular concept, procedure, process, or mathematical practice that lasts from 3 to 10 minutes. The challenge of diagnostic interviews is that they are assessment opportunities, not teaching opportunities, making it hard to watch or listen to students make errors and not respond immediately. Instead, use the interviews to listen to students' descriptions of their strategies and probe their understanding with the purpose of discovering both strengths and gaps.

To start, select a problem that matches an essential understanding your students are studying and have paper, pencils, and a variety of materials available (particularly those models and materials used during previous instruction). Also, prepare notes about what you anticipate would be emerging understandings, common methods, or common misunderstandings. Ask the student to solve the problem making sure the student verbalizes his or her reasoning at several points during the interview. Encourage multiple representations by asking the student to demonstrate their thinking using materials or drawings. Fennell, Kobett, and Wray (2015) called this method the "show me" approach.

MyLab Education   **Video Example 5.2**

Watch this video of Brooke in a diagnostic interview about subtraction of decimals. What do you learn from her use of drawings to explain her thinking? For example, why doesn't she draw the tenths on each whole? What does that tell you about her strengths?

Examples of diagnostic interviews depend on the student's needs and could include the following starting points:

- Which is greater, $\frac{7}{8}$ or $\frac{7}{7}$?
- Are the two numbers circled the same?

- What is the unit rate (cost per cap) if we paid $102.00 for 17 caps?
- Solve $6\frac{1}{4} \times 2\frac{3}{4} = $ _____. Draw a picture to illustrate the solution.

In each case, the initial problem should be aligned to recent work or your attempts to pinpoint underlying foundational gaps in understanding. Also, see some sample interview options, including a Sample Interview for Primary Grades, a Sample Interview for Intermediate Grades, a Sample Interview for Middle Grades, and Student Observation and Interview: Learning through Problems.

MyLab Education   Teacher Resource: Sample Interview for Primary Grades

MyLab Education   Teacher Resource: Sample Interview for Intermediate Grades

MyLab Education   Teacher Resource: Sample Interview for Middle Grades

MyLab Education   Teacher Resource: Student Observation and Interview: Learning through Problems

---

Sometimes students self-correct a mistake during an interview but, more frequently, teachers unearth a student's misunderstanding or reveal what strategies students have mastered. When you focus on exploring errors and identify common pitfalls, you can use the assessment results to build greater sophistication in students' conceptual understanding (Bray & Santagata, 2014).

Interviews can be time intensive, but they have the potential to provide evidence that you simply cannot get any other way. So, how can you accomplish these interviews? Think of them as tools to be used for only a few students at a time, not for every student in the class. Briefly interview a single student while others work on a task or are in learning centers. You can also work with one student using a digital tablet and screencasting app (e.g., Explain Everything, www.explaineverything.com) to record the whole conversation and written work.

After examining hundreds of research studies, Hattie (2009) found that the feedback that teachers received from students on what they knew and did not know was critical in improving students' performance. That is precisely what diagnostic interviews are designed to do! For example, are you certain that your students have a good understanding of place value, or are they just completing exercises according to rote procedures? Instruction will be more successful if you can pinpoint why a student is having difficulty before you try to fix the problem.

Let's look at an actual example of a diagnostic interview.

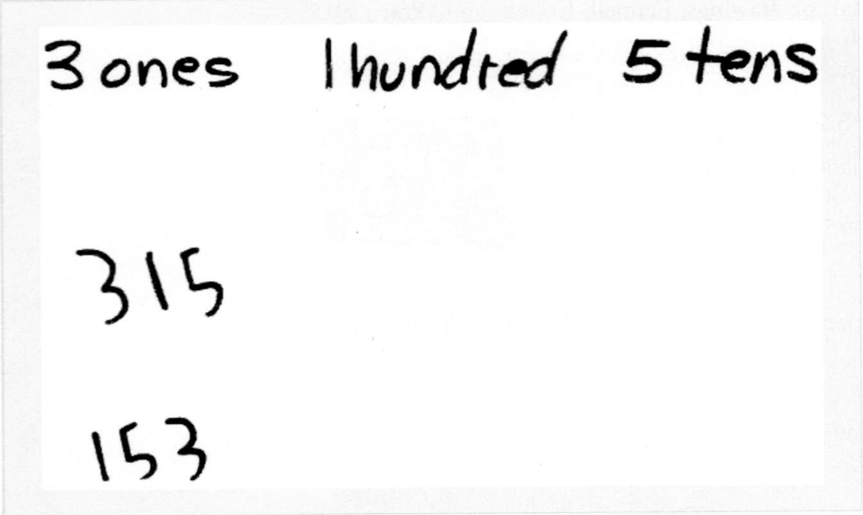

3 ones   1 hundred   5 tens

315

153

FIGURE 5.4 Student work on a diagnostic interview task.

Ms. Marsal was working with George, a student with disabilities who was displaying difficulty with calculating multidigit numbers. George also made unreasonable estimates to computation problems, in some cases thinking the answer would result in a number in the tens when it was actually in the hundreds. To get feedback from George that could reveal what he understood and where any gaps might be, Ms. Marsal adapted a task (Griffin & Lavelle, 2010) for the interview. She asked George to write the number that goes with 3 ones, 1 hundred, and 5 tens (see the top of Figure 5.4). Although base-ten materials were available, they went untouched. George wrote 315 (writing the number in the left-to-right order he saw the numerals, without attention to place value) in response. As is necessary in diagnostic interviews, Ms. Marsal resisted the temptation to immediately correct him, and instead probed further by asking George to take out the amount shown (3 ones, 1 hundred, and 5 tens) using base-ten materials. Showing fluency with the values of base-ten materials, George took out the correct amounts and placed them on the table, in the order given in the problem, not in place value order. Then when offered a place value mat, George said, "I get it," and placed the materials in the correct positions on the mat. When asked to write the number that corresponded with the materials, George wrote 153 as seen in Figure 5.4. Ms. Marsal asked why he got two different numbers and which number he thought was correct. George quietly pondered and then pointed to the second number and said, "This one is right; I think you were trying to trick me."

Although this interview revealed that the student had a good grasp of the value of the base-ten materials, it also revealed that there were lingering gaps in his understanding of the place-value concepts. Yet, this case is one in which the diagnostic interview was an actual learning experience. Notice that the teacher linked the assessment to previous classroom instruction through the use of concrete materials and the structured semiconcrete support of the place-value mat. This connection provided a way for George to think about the actual size of the number rather than just the individual digits. In addition, the cognitive dissonance caused by the getting two different numerical outcomes, one responding to just the written numbers and words and the other using corresponding concrete materials, enabled more connected ideas to emerge. Planning could then begin for future instruction for the student based on actual evidence.

There is no one right way to plan or structure a diagnostic interview. In fact, flexibility is a key ingredient. You should, however, have an overall plan that includes an easier task and a more challenging task in case you have misjudged the starting point. Also, did you notice that the teacher in the vignette had instructional materials ready for the student to use? Be sure you have materials available that have the potential to provide insights into students' understanding. Also, be prepared to probe students' thinking with questions like these:

* Can you explain what you just did?
* How would you explain this idea to a second grader (or your younger sister)?
* Can you draw a picture to help you think about this problem?
* What does this [point to something on the paper] stand for?
* Why did you solve it that way?
* Can you show me what you are thinking with the [materials such as fraction pieces, counters, hundreds chart, and so on]?
* Why do you think you got two different answers? Which one do you think is correct?
* If you tried to do this problem again, which approach would you try first?

In each case, it is important to explore whether students (1) understand what he or she did, and (2) can use models to connect actions to what he or she wrote or explained earlier.

Consider these suggestions as you implement diagnostic interviews:

- *Avoid revealing whether a student's answer is right or wrong.* Often facial expressions, tone of voice, or body language can give students an idea as to whether their answer is correct or incorrect. Instead, use a response such as "Can you tell me more?"
- *Wait silently for the student to answer.* Give ample time to allow the student to think and respond. Only then should you move to rephrasing the question or probing for a better understanding of the student's thoughts. After the student gives a response (whether it is accurate or not), wait again! This second wait time is even more important because it encourages the student to elaborate on his or her initial thought and provide more information.
- *Avoid interjecting clues or teaching.* The temptation to help is sometimes overwhelming. Watch and listen. Your goal is to use the interview not to teach but to find out where the student is in terms of conceptual understanding and procedural fluency.
- *Give opportunities for students to share their thinking without interruption.* Encourage students to use their own words and ways of writing things down. Correcting language or spelling can sidetrack the flow of students' explanations.

The benefits of the diagnostic interview become evident as you plan instruction that capitalizes on students' strengths while recognizing possible weaknesses and confusion. Also, unlike summative tests, you can always ask another question to find out why a student is taking an incorrect or unexpected path. You may also discuss results of interviews with colleagues to gain shared insights (Stephan, McManus, & Dehlinger, 2014).

Tasks

Tasks refer to products, including problem-based tasks, writing, and students' self-assessments. Good assessment tasks for either instructional or formative assessment purposes should permit every student in the class, regardless of mathematical ability, to demonstrate his or her knowledge, skill, or understanding.

Problem-Based Tasks. *Problem-based tasks* are tasks that are connected to actual problem-solving activities used in instruction. High quality tasks permit every student to demonstrate their abilities (Rigelman & Petrick, 2014; Smith & Stein, 2011). They also include real-world or authentic contexts that interest students or relate to recent classroom events. Of course, be mindful that English language learners may need support with contexts, as challenges with language should not overshadow the attention to their mathematical ability.

Problem-based tasks have several critical components that make them suitable components of the formative assessment process. They:

- Focus on an important mathematics concept or skill aligned to valued learning targets.
- Stimulate the connection of students' previous knowledge to new content.
- Allow multiple solution methods or approaches with a variety of tools.
- Offer opportunities for students to correct themselves along the way.
- Provide occasions for students to confront common misconceptions.
- Encourage students to use reasoning and explain their thinking.
- Create opportunities to observe students' use of mathematical processes and practices.
- Generate data for instructional decision making as you listen to your students' thinking.

Notice that the following examples of problem-based tasks are not elaborate, yet when followed by a discussion, each can engage students for most of a class session (see Problem-Based Tasks for other tasks). What mathematical ideas and practices are required to successfully respond to each of these tasks? Will the task help you determine how well students understand the ideas?

MyLab Education   **Teacher Resource: Problem-Based Tasks**

Shares (Grades K–2)

Learning Targets: (1) Solve multistep problems involving the operations. (2) Use manipulatives and words to describe a solution.

Leila has 6 gumdrops, Darlene has 2, and Melissa has 4. They want to share them equally. How will they do it? Draw a picture to help explain your answer.

At second grade, the numbers in the "Shares" task should be larger. What additional concepts would be involved if the task were about sharing cookies and the total number of cookies was 34?

The Whole Set (Grades 3–4)

Learning Targets: (1) Determine a whole, given a fractional part (using a set model). (2) Make sense of quantities and their relationships in a context.

Mary counted 15 cupcakes left from the whole batch that her mother made for the picnic. "We've already eaten two-fifths," she noticed. How many cupcakes did her mother bake?

In the following task, students are asked to think about the thinking of other students. Analysis of "other" students' performances is a good way to create tasks.

Decimals (Grades 4–5)

Learning Targets: (1) Compare two decimals by reasoning about their size. (2) Analyze and critique the reasoning of others.

Alan tried to make a decimal number as close to 50 as he could using the digits 1, 4, 5, and 9. He arranged them in this order: 51.49. Jerry thinks he can arrange the same digits to get a number that is even closer to 50. Do you agree or disagree? Explain.

This next task is a good example of an open-ended assessment. Consider how much more valuable this task is than asking for the angle measure in the triangle.

Two Triangles (Grades 7–8)

Learning Targets: (1) Classify two-dimensional shapes into categories based on their properties. (2) Attend to precision by applying definitions to define categories.

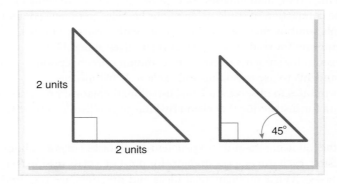

Tell everything you can about these two triangles. Given what you wrote about the two triangles, determine which of the following statements are true: The large triangle is an isosceles triangle; the small triangle is an isosceles triangle; the large triangle has an area of 2 square units; the small triangle has an area of 1 square unit; the large triangle has at least one angle that measures 45 degrees; the small triangle has at least one angle that measures 30 degrees; the two triangles are similar. Explain your thinking.

Algebra: Graphing Functions (Grade 8)

Learning Targets: (1) Compare and analyze quadratic functions. (2) Build a logical argument for a conjecture using reasoning.

Does the graph of $y = x^2$ ever intersect the graph of $y = x^2 + 2$? What are some ways that you could test your conjecture? Would your conjecture hold true for other equations in the form of $y = x^2 + b$? Within all quadratic functions of the form $y = ax^2 + b$, when would your conjecture hold true?

Much can be learned about students' understanding in a discussion that follows students solving these tasks individually. You can even collect their answers and share the most interesting incorrect answers to develop a conversation about mathematics as in the "My Favorite No" video at TeachingChannel www.teachingchannel.org. Students must develop the habit of sharing, writing, and listening to justifications. Students should compare and make connections between strategies and debate ideas in order to assist them in organizing their thoughts, thinking about their position, and analyzing the positions of others. This habit can be developed by forcing students to take a position (e.g., Does the order of factors affect the answer in a multiplication problem?). The resulting discussions will often reveal students' naïve conceptions while serving as connections to ideas learned in previous lessons.

Equation/Written Symbols	Word Problem/Real-World Situation
36 + 49 =	
Manipulatives/Illustration	Explain Your Thinking

FIGURE 5.5 Translation task template with example task.

Translation Tasks. One important assessment option is what we refer to as a *translation task*. Using four possible representations for concepts, students are asked, for example, to demonstrate understanding using words, models, numbers and word problems. As students flexibly move between these representations, there is a better chance that a concept will be integrated into a rich web of ideas.

So, what is a good way of structuring a translation task? With use of template based on a format for assessing concept mastery from Frayer, Fredrick, and Klausmeier (1969) (see Figure 5.5) and a Translation Task Activity Page, you can give students a computational equation and ask them to:

- Tell a story or write a word problem that matches the equation.
- Illustrate the equation with materials, models, or drawings.
- Explain their thinking about the process of arriving at an answer or describe the meaning of the operation.

MyLab Education	Activity Page: Translation Task for Grades K–2
MyLab Education	Activity Page: Translation Task for Grades 3–5
MyLab Education	Activity Page: Translation Task for Grades 6–8

A students' ability to communicate how they solved a problem is critical for open-response questions on many summative assessments (Parker & Breyfogle, 2011).

Translation tasks can be used for whole-class lessons or for individual or small-group diagnosis. For example, second-grade children may be given an equation such as 36 + 49 = ? The task could be to draw a model, say, of base-ten materials in the "Model/Illustration" area (younger children can use manipulatives), describe a story problem or real-world situation in the upper right corner and explain to another person in writing (or scripted or audio recorded for younger children) how they solved the addition in the fourth area marked "Explain Your Thinking/Describe the Meaning of the Operation." Think about using translation tasks when you want to find out more about a student's ability to represent ideas in various forms and explain how these representations are connected. Depending on the age of the student and the concept, the translation task can start in any section of the template. For example, in the "Word Problem" area, write "One side of the rectangle is 6 cm. The area is 48 cm². How long is the other side?"

In small groups, with a grade-level partner, or a math coach you can share effective tasks, analyze samples of students' work to try to decipher common errors, categorize student strategy use and engage in discussions to better understand each student and to best respond with targeted instruction (Kazemi, Gibbons, Lomax & Franke, 2016; Morrow-Leong, 2016). Working as a team to create, implement, and analyze assessments will enrich your ability to select and administer meaningful performance-based questions or tasks and enhance your professional judgment by questioning or confirming your thinking.

Writing. As an assessment tool, writing in journals, exit slips, or other formats about tasks provides a unique window to students' perceptions and ways that they are thinking about an idea. Students' writing can make sense of problems, express early ideas about concepts, unearth confusion, connect representations, or even clarify strategy use (Casa et al., 2016). When students explain their thinking about their solutions to a task in writing prior to class discussions, the written record can serve as a rehearsal for the class conversation. Students who otherwise have difficulty thinking on their feet now have a script to support their contributions. Call on more reluctant talkers first so that their ideas are heard and valued.

Students can summarize a response to a task through such prompts as:

Concepts and Processes

- "I think the answer is . . . I think this because . . ."
- Write an explanation for a new or younger student of why the answer to 4×7 is the same as 7×4 and whether this relationship works for 6×49 and 49×6. If so, why?
- Write an explanation for a new or younger student of when does the ratio of 3:6 mean the same thing as 4:8 and when do they mean something different?
- Explain to a student in class (or an absent student) what you learned about decimals.
- If you got stuck today in solving a problem, where in the problem did you have trouble?
- After you got the answer the problem, what did you do so that you were convinced your answer was reasonable? How sure are you that you got the correct answer?
- Write a story/word problem that goes with this (equation, graph, diagram, picture, model).

MyLab Education   **Video Example 5.3**

Watch this video of students who are writing a letter to another student about how to decide how large an area to house shopping carts is needed in a fictitious store.

If you are working with preK–1 students, these writing prompts may sound too advanced as it may be difficult for prewriters and beginning writers to express ideas. To begin the development of the writing-in-mathematics process in these early grades, use a language experience approach. After an activity or task, write the words "Giant Journal" and a topic or prompt on a large flipchart or interactive whiteboard. As students respond verbally, write down their thoughts, including the contributor's name and even drawings when appropriate, as in Figure 5.6.

Mathematically proficient children are able to "justify their conclusions, communicate them to others, and respond to the arguments of others" (NGA, 2010, pp. 6–7). Helping children pull evidence to show how they answered a problem often requires showing them the work of other children. By showing exemplars and counterexamples from real or "created" peers, children begin to identify elements of a sound argument and cohesive communication

(Lepak, 2014). Focusing on the analysis of other students' errors can increase understanding and expand learning opportunities (Bray, 2011; Pace & Ortiz, 2016).

Finally, student writing is an excellent form of communication with parents during conferences. Student writing shows evidence of their thinking, telling parents much more than any grade or test score.

MyLab Education   Self-Check 5.2

MyLab Education
Application Exercise 5.1:
Integrating Assessments into
Instruction Click the link to access
this exercise, then watch the video and
answer the accompanying questions

Rubrics and Their Uses

Problem-based tasks may tell us a great deal about what students know, but how do we analyze and use this information? These assessments yield an enormous amount of evidence that must be evaluated by examining more than just a simple count of correct answers. One step in the process of moving from teaching tasks to assessment tasks involves the addition of a rubric. A *rubric* is a scale based on predetermined criteria with two important functions: (1) It permits students to see what is central to excellent performance, and (2) it provides the teacher with scoring guidelines that support the equitable analysis of students' work. The evidence collected from rubrics helps teachers target follow-up instruction building on students' strengths and responding to any gaps and misunderstandings.

In a teaching-through-problem-solving approach, you will often include criteria and performance indicators on your rubrics such as the following:

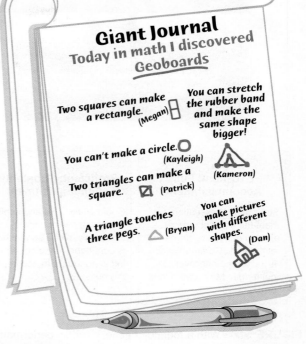

FIGURE 5.6   Writing in preK or kindergarten may be a class product on a chart or white board.

- Solved the problem(s) accurately and effectively
- Persevered and demonstrated resilience when facing a challenging problem
- Explained strategies used or justified their answer
- Used logical reasoning
- Expressed a grasp of numerical relationships and/or mathematical structure
- Incorporated multiple representations and/or multiple strategies
- Demonstrated an ability to appropriately select and use tools and manipulatives (including virtual manipulatives)
- Communicated with precise language and accurate units
- Identified general patterns of ideas that repeat, making connections from one big idea to another

Generic Rubrics

Generic rubrics identify broad categories of performance and therefore can be used for multiple assignments. The generic rubric allows a teacher to score performances by first sorting into two broad categories, as illustrated in the four-point rubric shown in Figure 5.7. Then student work is separates into two additional levels as shown. A rating of 0 is given for no response, no effort, or for answers that are off task. The advantage of the four-point scale is the relatively easy initial sort into "Got It" or "Not There Yet."

Another possibility is to use your three- or four-point generic rubric as in Figure 5.7 on a reusable form (see Four-Point Rubric). This method is especially useful for planning

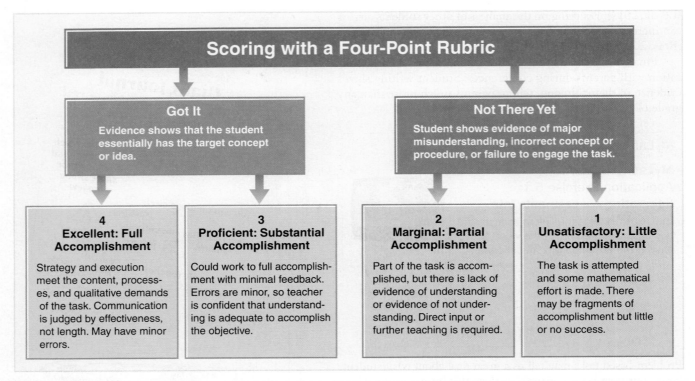

FIGURE 5.7 With a four-point generic rubric, performances are first sorted into two categories. Each performance is then considered again and assigned to a point on the scale.

Observation Rubric

Partition Regions into Equal Shares (3/19)

Above and Beyond Clear understanding. Communicates concept in multiple representations. Shows evidence of using idea without prompting. Can partition rectangles and circles into two, four, and eight equal shares. Explains that partitioning the same wholes into more shares makes smaller shares.	Sally Latania Greg	Zal
On Target Understands or is developing well. Uses designated models. Can partition regions into equal shares and describes as "halves" and "fourths." May need prompt to compare halves and fourths.	Lavant Julie George Maria	Tanisha Lee J.B. John H.
Not There Yet Some confusion or misunderstanding. Only models idea with help. Needs help to do activity. No confidence.	John S.	Mary

FIGURE 5.8 Record names in a rubric during an activity or for a single topic over several days.

purposes. But there are times when the generic rubrics do not give enough definition of the specific criteria for a particular task. For those instances, try a task-specific rubric.

Task-Specific Rubrics

Task-specific rubrics include specific statements, also known as *performance indicators*, that describe what students' work should look like at each rubric level and, in so doing, establish criteria for acceptable performance on that particular task (see Figure 5.8 and Anecdotal Note Rubric). Initially, it may be difficult to predict what student performance at different levels should look like, but your criteria depend on your knowledge and experience with students at that grade level and your insights about the task or mathematical concept. One important part of setting performance levels is predicting students' common misconceptions or the expected approaches to similar problems.

To facilitate developing performance levels, write out indicators of "proficient" or "on target" performances before using the task. This self-check ensures that the task is likely to accomplish your purpose. If you find you are writing performance indicators in terms of the number of correct responses, you are most likely looking at drill or practice exercises, not the problem-based tasks for which a task-specific rubric is appropriate. Like athletes who continually strive for better performances rather than "good enough," students should always recognize opportunities to excel. When you take into account the total performance (processes, practices, answers, justifications, extension, and so on), it is always possible to "go above and beyond."

Early in the year, discuss your rubric (such as Figure 5.8) with the class and post it prominently. Make it a habit to discuss students' performance on tasks in terms of the rubric. For example, if you are using the anecdotal note rubric, rubric language can be used informally: "Tanisha, the rubric states to get an 'Above and Beyond' you need to solve the problem with two different representations and explain your thinking. Is that what you did?" This approach lets students know how well they are doing and encourages them to persevere by giving specific areas for improvement.

 Pause *&* Reflect

Consider the task titled "The Whole Set" on page 92. Assume you are creating a task-specific four-point rubric to share with fourth graders. What indicators would you use for level 3 and level 4 performances? Start with a level 3 performance, then think about level 4. Try this exercise before reading further. ●

Determining performance indicators is always a subjective process based on professional judgment. Here is one possible set of indicators for the "The Whole Set" task:

3. Determines the correct answer or uses an approach that would yield a correct answer if not for minor errors. The drawing or the explanation does not fully describe the sharing process. Giving a correct result and reasoning for the number eaten but an incorrect result for the total baked would also be a level 3 performance.
4. Determines the total number of cupcakes baked and the amount of each equal share using words, pictures, and numbers to explain and justify the result and how it was obtained. Demonstrates a knowledge of fractional parts and the relation to the whole.

What about level 1 and level 2 performances? Here are suggestions for the same task:

2. Uses some aspect of fractions appropriately (e.g., divides the 15 into 5 groups instead of 3) but fails to illustrate an understanding of how to determine the whole. Shows evidence that they don't understand a fraction is a number (students may suggest a fraction is two whole numbers.)
1. Shows some effort but little or no understanding of what makes the whole set of cupcakes or how to make equal shares.

Unexpected methods and solutions that you didn't predict will happen. Don't limit students into demonstrating their understanding only as you thought they would when there is evidence that they are accomplishing your objectives in different ways. Such occurrences can help you revise or refine your rubric for future use.

Indicators such as these should be shared ahead of time with students. Sharing indicators before working on a task clearly conveys what is valued and expected. In addition, when you return papers, review the indicators with students, including examples of correct answers and successful explanations. This debriefing will help students understand how they may have done better.

 Pause *&* Reflect

How can having students assess peers' work (both strong and weak responses) support their ability to generate more in-depth answers? ●

Often it is useful to show anonymous students' work and discuss it as a group (including responses that would get full credit). Have students share what score they would give and the reasoning behind their choice. You might also have students use the rubric to evaluate a peer's work, having them discuss whether the classmate is clearly communicating. Such rubric rating activities of peers have helped middle schoolers reap long-term benefits in effectively expressing mathematical ideas (Lepak, 2014).

 ## Student Self-Assessment

Wiliam and Leahy (2015) stress that a key strategy in effectively incorporating the formative assessment process into instruction is the activation of students as "owners of their own learning" (p. 169). Students' abilities to self-regulate as active participants in their own learning process has shown to be a predictor of mathematics achievement in the intermediate elementary grades (Ocak & Yamac, 2013; Yüksel, 2013). Student self-assessments should not be the only measure of students' learning or dispositions, but rather a record of how students perceive their strengths and weaknesses as they begin to take responsibility for their learning. This assessment of their own progress and growth is an important lifelong learning skill.

You can gather student self-assessment data in several ways, including preassessments that catch areas of confusion or naïve conceptions prior to formally assessing students on particular content or by using exit slips (paper slips or a web application with a quick question or two) when students are concluding the instructional period (Wieser, 2008). Younger students can put a sticky note with their name on it on a chart with "Got It" or "Not There Yet" as a way to have them describe where they are in the learning process. Watch the "Stoplight Method" video at Teaching Channel (www.teachingchannel.org) for another quick and useful approach that can be used at any grade. Other formative assessment tools and technology include Google Forms (www.google.com/forms/about), Kahoot (getkahoot.com), Padlet (padlet.com/my/dashboard), Plickers (www.plickers.com), Today's Meet (todaysmeet.com), and Formative (goformative.com).

As you plan for student self-assessment, consider what you need to know to help you find better instructional strategies and revised learning targets. Convey to your students why you are having them do this activity—they need to grasp that they must play a role in their mastery of mathematics rather than just focus on completing a task. Encourage them to be honest and candid. Use open-ended prompts such as:

- How well do you think you understand the work we have been doing on fractions during the last few days? What is still causing you difficulty?
- Write two of the important things you learned in class today (or this week).
- Which problem(s) on the activity sheet/quiz did you find the most challenging? Which were the easiest?
- What are your strengths in learning mathematics this week? What did you feel you understood well?

Discussions of how students can improve can start when they analyze their own mistakes or have discussions with other students about which answers they think are correct. When students get back a test—make sure they use the feedback and revisit any errors and confirm that they understand what they need to learn next or how to revise. This attention to using feedback and mistakes to improve one's understanding moves students from a performance orientation to a mastery orientation (Pintrich, 2003).

Although in general, it takes additional time to infuse students' self-assessments into the daily schedule, allowing students to take part in the formative assessment process is motivating and encourages them to monitor and adapt their approaches to learning. Remember, start the process of incorporating ideas in this chapter over time building strategy by strategy (Petit & Bouck, 2015) and growing your ability to effectively assess students.

Tests

Tests will always be a part of assessment and evaluation, and like all other forms of assessment, they should match the goals of your instruction. Tests can be designed to find out what concepts students understand and how their ideas are connected. Tests should go beyond just knowing how to perform an algorithm and instead require the student to demonstrate a conceptual basis for the process. Additionally, tests should explore how students have internalized concepts by requiring explanation of students' thinking, application of ideas to new situations and flexibility by permitting multiple correct answers. The following examples of open response items will illustrate these ideas.

1. Write a multiplication problem that has an answer that falls between the answers to these two problems:

$$\begin{array}{cc} 49 & 45 \\ \times\,25 & \times\,30 \end{array}$$

2. **a.** In this division exercise, what number tells how many tens were shared among the 6 sets?
   b. Instead of writing the remainder as "R2," Elaine writes "$\frac{1}{3}$." Explain the difference between these two ways of recording the leftover part.

$$\begin{array}{cc} 49\ \text{R2} & 49\frac{1}{3} \\ 6)\overline{296} & 6)\overline{296} \end{array}$$

3. Draw two figures on a grid that have the same area but different perimeters. List the area and perimeter of each.
4. For each subtraction fact, write an addition fact that helps you think of the answer to the subtraction fact.

$$\begin{array}{cccc} 12 & \mathbf{9} & 9 & 14 \\ \underline{-3} & \underline{+3} & \underline{-4} & \underline{-7} \\ 9 & 12 & & \end{array}$$

5. On a number line, draw pictures using arrows to show why $^-3 + {}^-4$ is the same as $^-3 - {}^+4$.

Expanding the Usefulness of Tests

If a test is well constructed, much more information can be gathered than simply the number of correct or incorrect answers. The following considerations can help maximize the value of your tests:

1. *Encourage students to use models, manipulatives and drawings.* Students can use models to work on test questions when those same models have been used during instruction to develop concepts. Simple drawings can be used to represent counters, base-ten pieces, fraction pieces, and the like (see Figure 5.9). Provide examples in class of how to draw the models before you ask students to draw on a test.
2. *Include opportunities for explanations.* Give students the time and space to describe their thinking and their use of strategies. This component also can reveal strong or faulty reasoning (Fagan, Tobey & Brodesky, 2016).

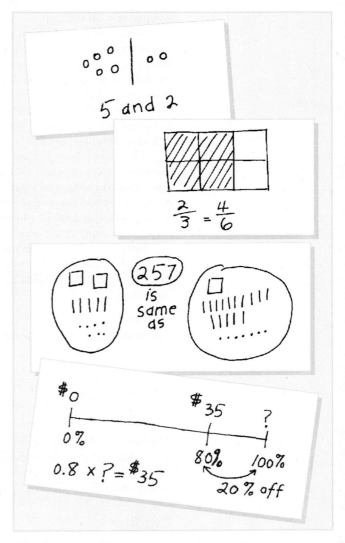

FIGURE 5.9 Students can use drawings to illustrate concepts on tests.

3. *Use open-ended questions.* Tests in which questions have only one correct answer tend to limit what you can learn about what the student knows and can do and what they are ready to know and do!

4. *Permit students to use technology when appropriate.* For example, except for tests of computational skills, calculators can allow students to focus on what you really want to test.

Another option is to consider quizzes done in collaboration with a peer. These "partner quizzes" (Danielson & Luke, 2006) allow for more complex problems, so that students can benefit from a group effort. Although some partners will work individually first and then discuss the problems, others will discuss ideas along the way. Once they have a partner for a quiz, they will not get that partner again (and no talking to others—only your partner). The teacher comments on and evaluates only one of the team's quizzes and then partners are able to revise and resubmit. The increased student dialogue and discussion of answers links well to the goal of analyzing the reasoning of others!

Improving Performance on High-Stakes Tests

Many school systems have mandated summative tests in mathematics at every grade from 3 through 8. but the method of testing and even the objectives to be tested remain up to individual states. These assessments will likely include performance items with open responses and not just rely on multiple-choice questions (Sawchuk, 2010).

Whatever the specifics of the testing program in your particular state, these external tests can impose significant pressures on school districts, which in turn put pressure on principals, teachers, students and parents. External evaluation that has such consequences is typically referred to as *high-stakes* testing. High stakes tests make the pressures of testing significant for both students (Will I pass? Will my parents be upset with my score?) and teachers (Will my class meet proficiency levels?). The pressures certainly have an effect on instruction. Because you will likely not be able to avoid the pressures of high-stakes testing, the question becomes, "How will you respond?"

The best advice for succeeding on high-stakes tests is to teach the big ideas in the mathematics curriculum that are aligned with your required state standards. Students who have learned conceptual ideas in a manner focused on relational understanding and who have learned the processes and practices of doing mathematics will perform well on tests, regardless of the format or specific objectives. In short, a problem-based approach is the best course of action for raising test scores.

Remember students' grades should be measured by valid and reliable data collected from a variety of formative and summative assessments (NCTM, 2016). When using multiple sources of data important decisions can be made about ways to improve instruction, curriculum and assessment.

MyLab Education **Self-Check 5.5**

Communicating Grades and Shaping Instruction

Assessment and evaluation go hand in hand. Although we've described the process of using tools to identify students' strengths and gaps to provide targeting supports for learning or additional challenges, assessment is also used as a way to assign grades and communicate important results to stakeholders, particularly parents.

Grading

A grade is a statistic used to communicate to others the achievement level that a student has attained in a particular area of study. The accuracy or validity of the grade is dependent on the evidence used in generating the grade, the teacher's professional judgment, and the alignment of the assessments with standards. Determining a grade requires using results of formal assessments along with other evidence about a student's work—it is not merely averaging available scores.

For effective use of the assessment information gathered from problems, tasks, and other appropriate methods to assign grades, some hard decisions are inevitable. Some are philosophical, some depend on school policies about grades, and all require us to examine what we value and the objectives we communicate to students and parents.

Among the many components of the grading process, one truth is undeniable: *What gets graded by teachers is what gets valued by students*. Using observations, interviews, exit slips, journals, and rubric scores to provide feedback and encourage a pursuit of excellence must also relate to grades (NCTM, 2014). However, mistakenly converting four out of five on a rubric score to a percentage or suggesting a three out of four on a rubric is a grade of C can focus the attention away from an emphasis on learning and striving for excellence (Kulm, 1994). Instead, grading must be based on the performances for which you assigned rubric ratings; otherwise, students will soon realize that these are not important scores. The grade at the end of the marking period should reflect a holistic view of where the student is relative to grade-level goals.

Shaping Instruction

For assessments to be useful, teachers must know how to act on the evidence revealed in an assessment or set of assessments to address the learning needs of students (Heritage, Kim, Vendlinski, & Herman, 2009). This process includes shifting from one approach or strategy development to another, pointing out examples or counterexamples to students, or using different materials and prompts. Knowing how to shape the next steps in instruction for an individual when the content is not learned is critical if you are going to avoid "covering" topics and move toward student growth and progress. If instead you just move on without some students grasping the learning objectives, "students accumulate debts of knowledge (knowledge owed to them)" (Daro, Mosher, & Corcoran, 2011, p. 48). Summative assessment scores on high-stakes tests are often of little utility in creating instructional next steps to help students progress (Daro, Mosher, & Corcoran, 2011). But the formative assessment process described throughout this book can help. Interspersed in Part II of this book are Formative Assessment Notes that suggest ways to assess areas where students may struggle; including in some cases specific activities as follow-up lessons. As you learn more about your students through assessment, you will be able to target instruction that will address their naïve understandings and capitalize on their strengths through the learning supports provided in each chapter.

MyLab Education   Self-Check 5.6

**MyLab Education   Application Exercise 5.2:
Communicating Grades and Shaping Instruction** Click the link to access this exercise, then watch the video and answer the accompanying questions

VIDEO EXAMPLE

RESOURCES FOR CHAPTER 5

RECOMMENDED READINGS

Articles

Duker, B., Holmberg, C., & Rossi Becker, J. (2017). Making moves: Formative assessment in mathematics. *Mathematics Teaching in the Middle School, 22*(6), 334–342.

The authors describe a framework of seven moves that increase students' higher-level thinking through engaging class discussions. Tasks, examples of the moves, and insights about student learning are shared.

Kling, G., & Bay-Williams, J. (2014). Assessing basic fact fluency. *Teaching Children Mathematics, 20*(8), 488–497.

A variety of ideas are shared including observations, interviews, journaling, and quizzes on the road to fact fluency. The limitations and risks of using timed tests are discussed.

Books

Fennell, F., Kobett, B., & Wray, J. (2017). *The formative 5: Everyday assessment techniques for every math classroom.* Thousand Oaks, CA: Corwin Press.

The focus is on formative assessments for use in every grade for every learner. Emphasizing the strategies of observations, interviews, show me, hinge questions and exit tasks, this valuable guide includes actual stories from classrooms.

Wright, R., Martland, J., & Stafford, A. (2006). *Early numeracy: Assessment for teaching and intervention.* London, UK: Paul Chapman Educational Publishers.

This book includes diagnostic interviews for assessing young students' knowledge and strategy use related to number and addition and subtraction. Using frameworks, teachers can pinpoint students' misconceptions and identify appropriate interventions.

CHAPTER

6

Teaching Mathematics Equitably to All Students

LEARNER OUTCOMES

After reading this chapter and engaging in the embedded activities and reflections, you should be able to:

6.1 Differentiate between a modification and an accommodation.

6.2 Describe the components of a multitiered system of support for struggling students and identify successful components of interventions for students with disabilities.

6.3 Explain characteristics of culturally responsive instruction, including how to focus on developing academic vocabulary during mathematics instruction and attending to students' mathematical identities.

6.4 Apply knowledge of working with students who are gifted and talented mathematically.

6.5 Illustrate approaches that are used to develop students' resilience and reduce resistance in learning mathematics.

The NCTM position statement on Access and Equity in Mathematics Education states that we should hold the expectation that all children can reach mathematics proficiency and that high levels performance must be attained regardless of race, ethnicity, gender, socioeconomic status, ability, or linguistic background and including student in special education and gifted education (NCTM, 2014). Students need opportunities to advance their knowledge supported by teaching that gives attention to their individual learning needs. Students' backgrounds are not only an important part of who they are as people, but who they are as learners—and this background enriches the classroom.

Many *achievement* gaps are actually *instructional* gaps or *expectation* gaps. For example, when teachers say, "I just cannot put this class into groups to work; they are too unruly" or "My students can't solve word problems—they don't have the reading skills" they are setting low expectations for students. Operating under the belief that some students cannot do mathematics ensures that they won't have ample opportunities to prove otherwise. Instead we suggest you consider Storeygard's (2010) mantra for teachers, which proclaims, "My kids can!"

There is also another perspective of an *opportunity* gap that considers the inputs into students' education, rather than just students' outputs. This perspective focuses on the *performance* of individual students and thereby asks teachers to ponder over the disparities between available *opportunities* to learn (Carter & Welner, 2013; OECD, 2016; NCTM, 2012). In other words, what are we, as teachers, doing to support students' success? The spirit of the work described in this chapter is perhaps more aligned with the efforts to address the opportunity gap. How can we design instruction in advance of finding weak student performance?

Mathematics for Each and Every Student

Teaching for equity is much more than providing students with an equal opportunity to learn mathematics, instead it attempts to attain equal outcomes for all students by being sensitive to individual differences. How you will maintain equal outcomes and high expectations and yet provide for individual differences with strong support can be challenging. Equipping yourself with an ever-growing collection of instructional strategies for a variety of students is critical. A strategy that works for one student may be completely ineffective with another, even for a student with the same exceptionality. Addressing the needs of *each and every student* means providing access and opportunity for:

- Students who are identified as struggling or having a disability
- Students from different cultural backgrounds
- Students who are English learners (ELs)
- Students who are mathematically gifted
- Students who are unmotivated or need to build resilience

You may think, "I do not need to read the section on mathematically gifted students because they will be pulled out for math enrichment." Students who are mathematically talented need to be challenged in the daily core instruction, and their abilities and passion need to be encouraged and expanded (Plucker & Peters, 2016).

Although the goal of equity is to offer each and every student access to important mathematics inequities exist, even if unintentionally. For example, if teachers do not build in opportunities for student-to-student interaction in a lesson, they may not be addressing the needs of ELs, who need opportunities to speak, listen, and write in small-group situations. It takes more than a desire to be fair or equitable; it takes knowing the strategies that support each learner and making every effort to incorporate those strategies into your teaching.

As you work with students' areas of strength, identify opportunities to stretch students' thinking in ways that change unfamiliar experiences to more familiar ones. For example, if you are teaching area and you are discussing plots of land or gardens with students who live in an urban setting, reading a story such as *City Green* (Disalvo-Ryan, 1994) can help make the unknown known. Students can see how a land plot in an urban community can be divided and shared among neighbors. With this approach in mind, all students can experience the background context needed for the task.

Essential in making decisions about how you can adapt instruction to meet individual learner's needs is the use of *accommodations* and *modifications*. An *accommodation* is a response to the needs of the environment or the learner; it does not alter the task. For example, you might write down directions for a student instead of just saying them or printing the task in a larger font. On the other hand, a *modification* changes the task, making it more accessible to the student. For example, suppose the task begins with finding the area of a compound shape, as shown here.

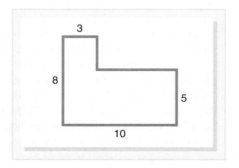

You may decide instead to decompose the shape into two rectangles and ask the student to find the area of each shape and combine. Then have the student attempt the next shape without the modification—you should always lead back to the original task. However, if you decide to begin with rectangular regions and build to compound shapes composed of rectangles, you have *scaffolded* the lesson in a way to ramp up to the original task. In planning accommodations and modifications, the goal is to enable each student to successfully reach your learning objectives, not to change the objectives. This approach is how equity is achieved—by reaching equal *outcomes*, not by equal treatment. Treating students the same when they each learn differently does not make sense.

Complete an Accommodation or Modification Needs table to reflect on how you will plan for students in your classroom. Record evidence that you are adapting the learning situation.

MyLab Education	Teacher Resource: Accommodation or Modification Needs Table
MyLab Education	Self-Check 6.1

Providing for Students Who Struggle and Those with Special Needs

Mathematics learning disabilities are best thought of as cognitive differences, not cognitive deficits (Lewis, 2014). Students with disabilities often have mandated individualized education programs (IEPs) that guarantee access to grade-level mathematics content—preferably in a general education classroom. This legislation also implies that educators consider individual learning needs not only in terms of *what* mathematics is taught but also *how* it is taught.

Multitiered System of Support: Response to Intervention

In many schools, a systematic process for achieving higher levels performance for all students includes a multitiered system of support frequently called Response to Intervention (RtI). This approach emphasizes ways for struggling students to get immediate assistance and support rather than waiting for them to fail on a high stakes test before they receive help. Multitiered models are centered on three interwoven elements: high-quality curriculum, instructional support (interventions), and formative assessments that capture students' strengths and weaknesses. These models were initially designed to determine whether low achievement was due to a lack of high-quality mathematics (i.e., "teacher-disabled students") (Baroody, 2011; Ysseldyke, 2002) or due to an actual learning disability. This model can also determine instructional options for gifted students who may need to have advanced mathematical challenges beyond what other students study. RtI is a multitiered student support system that is often represented in a triangular format. As you might guess, there are a variety of RtI models developed by school systems as they structure unique approaches to responding to students' needs.

As you move up the tiers, the number of students involved decreases, the teacher–student ratio decreases, and the intensity of the intervention increases. Each tier in the triangle represents a level of instruction with corresponding monitoring of results and outcomes, as shown in Figure 6.1. The foundational and largest portion of the triangle (tier 1) represents the core instruction that is used with all students based on a high-quality mathematics grade level curriculum, research-based instructional practices and ongoing progress monitoring.

Tier 2 represents students who did not reach the level of achievement expected during tier 1 instruction. Students moved to tier 2 should receive supplemental targeted instruction using interventions that incorporate explicit strategies with systematic teaching of critical skills and concepts, more frequent instructional opportunities, and more supportive and precise prompts (Torgesen, 2002). The NCTM Position Statement on Interventions (2011) endorses the use of interventions that increase in intensity as students demonstrate continuing struggles with learning mathematics.

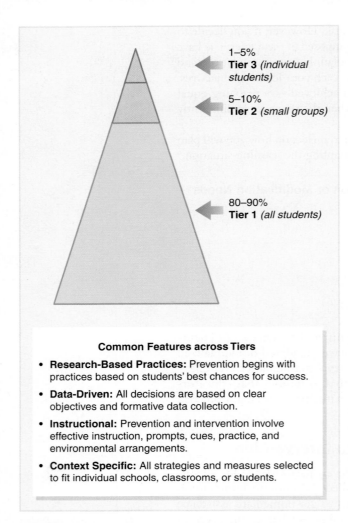

1–5%
Tier 3 *(individual students)*

5–10%
Tier 2 *(small groups)*

80–90%
Tier 1 *(all students)*

Common Features across Tiers

- **Research-Based Practices:** Prevention begins with practices based on students' best chances for success.
- **Data-Driven:** All decisions are based on clear objectives and formative data collection.
- **Instructional:** Prevention and intervention involve effective instruction, prompts, cues, practice, and environmental arrangements.
- **Context Specific:** All strategies and measures selected to fit individual schools, classrooms, or students.

FIGURE 6.1 Multitiered systems of support

Source: Based on Scott, Terence, and Lane, Holly. (2001). *Multi-Tiered Interventions in Academic and Social Contexts.* Unpublished manuscript, University of Florida, Gainesville.

If further assessment after tier 2 interventions reveals students have made favorable progress, interventions are faded and discontinued. But, if difficulties and struggles remain, interventions can be adjusted in intensity, and in rare cases, students are referred to tier 3 for more intensive assistance. Tier 3 may include comprehensive mathematics instruction or a referral for special education evaluation or special education services. Strategies for the three tiers are outlined in Table 6.1.

An important part of the RtI model is the guiding of students' movement within tiers which includes the examination of their growth and development through *progress monitoring*. One way to collect evidence of student knowledge of concepts and skills is through the use of diagnostic interviews. Diagnostic interviews are described in Chapter 5 and examples are shared throughout the book in Formative Assessment Notes. Another approach is to assess students' growth toward fluency in basic facts, an area that is a well-documented barrier for students with learning disabilities (Mazzocco, Devlin, & McKenney, 2008). Combining instruction with short daily assessments of basic facts proved to be a way to help students not only better remember facts but also generalize to other facts (Woodward, 2006). The collection of information gathered from these assessments reveals whether students are making the progress expected or if more intensive instructional approaches need to be put into place.

Implementing Interventions

NCTM suggests a set of effective, research-based strategies (NCTM, 2007) for teaching the subset of students for whom the initial core instruction (tier 1) was not effective. These approaches include explicit strategy instruction, think-alouds, concrete and visual representations of problems, peer-assisted learning activities, and gathering formative assessment data.

Explicit Strategy Instruction. Explicit instruction is characterized by highly structured, teacher-led instruction on a specific strategy. When engaging in explicit instruction you do not merely demonstrate the strategy and have students practice it; instead, you try to illuminate the decision making along the way—a process that may be troublesome for some learners without this level of support. After you assess students so you know what to target, use a tightly organized sequence, from modeling the concept or strategy, to prompting students through the model, to practice. Your instruction uses these teacher-led explanations of concepts and strategies to build meaning, including pointing out critical connections between new knowledge and concepts they already know. Let's look at a classroom teacher using explicit instruction:

As you enter Mr. Logan's classroom, you see a small group of students seated at a table listening to the teacher's detailed explanation and watching his demonstration of equivalent fraction concepts. The students are using manipulatives, as suggested by Mr. Logan, and moving through carefully selected and sequenced tasks. He tells the students to take out the red "one-fourth" pieces and asks them to check how many "one-fourths" will exactly cover the blue "one-half" piece. Mr. Logan asks, "Is equivalent a word you know?" Then, to make sure students don't allow for any gaps or overlaps in the pieces, he asks them to talk about their reasoning process by asking the question, "What are some things you need to keep in mind as you cover the half with fourths?" Mr. Logan writes their responses on the adjacent white board as $\frac{2}{4} = \frac{1}{2}$ and also as "two-fourths is the same as one-half" to connect the ideas that they

TABLE 6.1   INTERVENTIONS FOR TEACHING MATHEMATICS

Tiers	Intervention
Tier 1	**A highly qualified regular classroom teacher:** • Incorporates high-quality grade-level curriculum and has expectations for all students to be challenged • Builds in CCSSO *Standards for Mathematical Practice* and/or NCTM process standards • Commits to teaching the curriculum as defined • Uses multiple representations such as manipulatives, visual models, and symbols • Monitors progress to identify struggling students and students who excel • Uses flexible student grouping • Fosters active student engagement in "doing math" • Communicates high expectations
Tier 2	**A highly qualified regular classroom teacher, with collaboration from other highly qualified educators (i.e., special education teacher):** • Works with students in small groups in supplemental sessions to the core instruction • Conducts diagnostic interviews to target a student's strengths and weaknesses (identify the abilities rather than focusing on the disabilities) • Collaborates with special education, gifted, and EL specialists • Creates lessons that emphasize the big ideas or themes • Incorporates CSA (concrete, semi-concrete, abstract) approach • Shares a *think-aloud* to demonstrate how to make problem solving decisions • Incorporates explicit strategy instruction (i.e., summarizes key points and reviews key vocabulary or concepts) • Models specific behaviors and strategies, such as how to handle measuring tools or geoboards • Uses prompts or self-questions written on cards or posters to help students follow, for example, the stages of solving multistep word problems (Hord & Marita, 2014) • Uses peer-assisted learning, in which another student can provide help • Supplies families with additional instructional support materials to use at home • Encourages student use of self-regulation and self-instructional strategies such as revising notes, writing summaries, and identifying main ideas • Teaches test-taking strategies and allows the students to use a highlighter on the test to emphasize important information • Revisits content from a previous grade to ramp back up to grade-level curriculum
Tier 3	**A highly qualified special education teacher:** • Works one-on-one with students • Uses tailored instruction based on specific areas of weakness • Modifies instructional methods, motivates students, and adapts curricula • Uses explicit contextualization of skills-based instruction

are looking for how many fourth pieces cover the one-half piece. Then he asks them to compare the brown "eighths" and the yellow "sixths" to the piece representing one-half and records their responses. The students take turns answering these questions aloud. During the lesson, Mr. Logan frequently stops, asks for points of clarification, and directly highlights components of the task. For example, he asks, "Are you surprised that it takes more eighths to cover the half than fourths?" Vocabulary words, such as whole, numerator, denominator, and equivalent, are written on the "math wall" nearby and the definitions of these terms are written and reinforced throughout the lesson. At the completion of the lesson, students try some similar examples and then they come back together for a whole class discussion.

A number of aspects of explicit instruction can be seen in Mr. Logan's approach to teaching fractions. He employs a teacher-directed teaching format, carefully describes the use of manipulatives, and incorporates a model-prompt-practice sequence. This sequence starts with verbal discussions and demonstrations with concrete models, followed by prompting, questioning, and then independent practice. The students derive mathematical knowledge from the teacher's oral, written, and visual clues.

Concrete models support explicit strategy instruction. For example, a teacher demonstrating a multiplication array with one-inch squares might say, "Watch me. Now make a rectangle with the squares that looks just like mine. Let's point out the groups—one group of five, two groups of five, three groups of five, and four groups of five" to show 4 × 5. In contrast, a teacher with a more inquiry-oriented approach might say, "Using these squares, how can you show me a representation for four groups of five?" Although initially more structured, the use of concrete models in this fashion provides students with disabilities greater access to abstract concepts.

The use of self-instructive prompts, or self-questions, can help students structure the entire learning process from beginning to end. Consider these options: read and restate the problem; draw a picture, link this problem to previous problems that are similar; write the problem in a mathematical sentence; act the problem out; carry out operations; and check answers using another approach (i.e., hundreds chart, number line, equation). Unlike more inquiry-based instruction, the teacher may initially model these steps and explain components using terminology that is easily understood by students who did not discover these ideas independently. Yet, consistent with what we know about how all students learn, students are still doing problem solving (not just skill development).

Using strategy discussion for students with disabilities has an advantage in that it makes more explicit the covert thinking that others use in mathematical problem solving. Although students with disabilities hear other students' thinking strategies in the *after* phase of each lesson, they frequently cannot keep up with the rapid pace of the sharing. Without extra time to reprocess the conversation, students with disabilities may not have access to these helpful strategies. Students can begin to understand when they have an opportunity to learn. Students who are never given opportunities to engage in self-directed learning (based on the assumption that that is not an area of strength) will be deprived of the opportunity to develop skills in this area. In fact, the best explicit instruction is scaffolded, meaning it moves from a highly structured, single-strategy approach to multiple models, including examples and nonexamples. But don't unintentionally over-scaffold as you want to move students to independence. To be effective, make mathematical relationships explicit so that students, rather than only learning how to do that day's mathematics, make connections to other mathematical ideas.

Concrete, Semi-Concrete, Abstract Approach. The concrete, semi-concrete, abstract (CSA) approach has been used in mathematics education in a variety of forms for years (Dobbins, Gagnon, & Ulrich, 2014; Griffin, Jossi, & van Garderen, 2014; Heddens, 1964; Hunter, Bush, & Karp, 2014). Based on Bruner and Kennedy's stages of representation (1965), this model reflects concrete representations that encourage learning through movement or action with manipulative materials to semi-concrete representations of drawings or pictures and learning through abstract symbols. Built into this approach is the return to visual models and concrete representations as needed or as students begin to explore new concepts or extensions of concepts previously learned. This is not to say that CSA is a rigid approach where you only move to abstraction after the other phases. Instead, it is an integrated model where there is parallel modeling of number symbols throughout to explicitly relate concrete models and visual representations to corresponding numerals and equations (see Figure 6.2). CSA also includes modeling the mental conversations that go on in your mind to help students articulate their thinking. Used in a combination with explicit strategy instruction, this approach met with high levels of success for students with disabilities (Flores, Hinton, & Strozier, 2014; Mancl, Miller, & Kennedy, 2012; Miller & Kaffar, 2011).

Peer-Assisted Learning. Students with special needs benefit from other students' modeling and support (McMaster & Fuchs, 2016). The basic notion is that students learn best when take on the role of an apprentice working with a more skilled peer or "expert." Although the peer-assisted learning approach shares some characteristics of the explicit strategy instruction model, it is distinct because knowledge is presented on an "as-needed" basis as opposed to a predetermined sequence. Students can be paired with older students or peers who have more sophisticated understandings of a concept. At other times during tasks, tutors and tutees can reverse roles. Having students with disabilities "teach" others is an important part of the learning process, so giving them a chance to explain to a peer or younger student is a valuable learning tool.

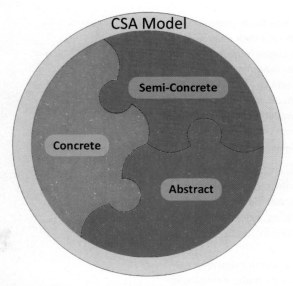

FIGURE 6.2 Integrated CSA model

Think-Aloud. When you use a "think-aloud" you demonstrate how you might accomplish a task while verbalizing the thinking and reasoning that accompany the actions. Remember, don't start where your thinking is; assess and start where the student's thinking is. Let's look at an example. Consider a problem in which fourth-grade students are asked to determine how much paint is needed to cover the walls of their classroom. Rather than merely demonstrating, for example, how to use a ruler to measure the distance across a wall, the think-aloud strategy involves talking through the process and identifying the reasons for each action while measuring the space. As you place a tick mark on the wall to indicate where the ruler ended in the first measurement, you might state, "I used this line to mark off where the ruler ends. How should I use this line as I measure the next section of the wall? I know I have to move the ruler, but should I repeat what I did the first time?" All of this dialogue occurs prior to placing the ruler for a second measurement.

Often, teachers share with students alternatives for another way they could have carried out the task. When you use this metacognitive strategy, talk about and model possible approaches (and the reasons behind these approaches) to make your invisible thinking processes visible to students.

Although you will choose any of these strategies as needed for interventions, your goal is always to work toward high student responsibility for learning. Movement to higher levels of understanding of content can be likened to the need to move to a higher level on a hill. For some, formal stair steps with support along the way is necessary (explicit strategy instruction); for others, ramps with encouragement at the top of the hill will work (peer-assisted learning). Other students can find a path up the hill on their own with some guidance from visual representations (CSA approach). All people can relate to the need to have different support during different times of their lives or under different circumstances, and it is no different for students with special needs (see Table 6.2). Yet, students with special needs must eventually learn to create

TABLE 6.2   COMMON STUMBLING BLOCKS FOR STUDENTS WITH DISABILITIES

Stumbling Blocks for Students	What Will I Notice?	What Should I Do?
Trouble forming mental representations of mathematical concepts	• Can't interpret a number line • Has difficulty going from a problem about a garden plot (finding area) to graph or dot paper representation	• Explicitly teach the representation—for example, exactly how to draw a diagram (e.g., partition a number line) • Use larger versions of the representation (e.g., number line or grid paper) so that students can move on or interact with the model
Difficulty accessing numerical meanings from symbols or issues with number sense	• Has difficulty with basic facts; for example, doesn't recognize that $3 + 5$ is the same as $5 + 3$ • Does not understand the meaning of the equal sign • Can't interpret whether an answer is reasonable	• Explicitly teach multiple ways of representing a number showing the variations at the same time • Use a number balance to support understanding of the equal sign • Use multiple representations for a single problem (base-ten blocks, illustrations, and numbers) rather than using multiple problems
Difficulty keeping numbers and information in working memory	• Loses counts of objects • Gets confused when other students share multiple strategies during the *after* portion of the lesson • Forgets how to start the problem-solving process	• Use ten-frames to help students organize counts • Explicitly model how to use skip counting • Record in writing the ideas of other students during discussions • Incorporate a chart that lists main steps in problem solving as an independent guide or make bookmarks with questions students can ask themselves as self-prompts
Lacks organizational skills and the ability to self-regulate	• Misses steps in a process • Writes computations in a way that is random and hard to follow	• Use routines as often as possible or provide self-monitoring checklists to prompt steps along the way • Use graph paper to record problems or numbers • Create math walls as a reference
Misapplies rules or overgeneralizes	• Applies rules such as "Always subtract the smaller from the larger" too literally, resulting in errors such as $35 - 9 = 34$ • Mechanically applies poorly understood algorithms—for example, adds $\frac{7}{8}$ and $\frac{12}{13}$ and generates the answer $\frac{19}{21}$.	• Give examples as well as counterexamples to show how and when "rules" should be used and when they should not • Tie rules to conceptual understanding; don't emphasize memorizing rote procedures

a path to new learning on their own, as that is what will be required in the real world after formal education ends. Leaving students only knowing how to climb steps with support and then having them face hills without constant assistance from others will not help them attain their life goals.

Teaching and Assessing Students with Learning Disabilities

Students with learning disabilities often have difficulties with perceptual or cognitive processing that may affect memory; general strategy use; attention; the ability to speak or express ideas in writing; the ability to perceive auditory, visual, or written information; or the ability to integrate abstract ideas. Although specific learning needs and strategies that work for one student may not work for another, here are four questions that can guide your planning:

1. What organizational, behavioral, and cognitive skills are necessary for students with special needs to derive meaning from this activity?
2. Which students have significant weaknesses in any of these skills or concepts?
3. What are the students' strengths?
4. How can I provide use students' areas of strength to help them focus on the conceptual task in the activity? (Karp & Howell, 2004, p. 119).*

Each phase of the lesson evokes specific planning considerations for students with disabilities. Some strategies apply throughout a lesson. The following discussion is based on Karp and Howell (2004) and provides some specific suggestions for support while maintaining the challenge.

Structure the Environment.

- *Centralize attention.* Move the student close to the board or teacher. Face students when you speak to them and use gestures. Remove competing stimuli.
- *Avoid confusion.* Word directions carefully and specifically and ask the student to repeat them. Give one direction at a time. Use the same language for consistency. For example, talk about base-ten materials as ones, tens and hundreds rather that saying "flats," "rods," and other labels referring to their shape rather than their value.
- *Create smooth transitions.* Ensure that transitions between activities have clear directions and that there are limited chances for students to get off task.

Identify and Remove Potential Barriers.

- *Help students remember.* Memory is often not a strong suit for students with disabilities, so, develop mnemonics (memory aids) for familiar steps or write directions that can be referred to throughout the lesson. For example, STAR is a mnemonic for solving word problems: **S**earch the problem for important information; **T**ranslate words into models, pictures, symbols or actions; **A**nswer the problem; **R**eview your solution for reasonableness (Gagnon & Maccini, 2001).
- *Provide vocabulary and concept support.* Explicit attention to vocabulary and symbols is critical throughout the lesson. When appropriate, preview essential terms and related prior knowledge/concepts, creating a "math wall" of words and symbols to provide visual cues and definitions.
- *Use "friendly" numbers.* Instead of using $6.13, use $6.00 to emphasize conceptual understanding rather than mixing computation and conceptual goals. Incorporate this technique when computation and operation skills are *not* the lesson objective.
- *Vary task size.* Assign students with disabilities fewer problems to solve. Some students can become frustrated by the enormity of a very large task.
- *Adjust the visual display.* The density of words, illustrations, and numbers on a page can overload students. Find ways to put one problem on a page or increase font size.

---

*Adapted list reprinted with permission from Karp, K., & Howell, P. (2004). Building Responsibility for Learning in Students with Special Needs. *Teaching Children Mathematics, 11*(3), pp. 118–126. Copyright © 2004 by the National Council of Teachers of Mathematics. All rights reserved.

Provide Clarity.

- *Repeat the timeframe.* Support students in time management by giving them additional reminders about the time left for exploring the materials, completing tasks, or finishing assessments.
- *Ask students to share their thinking.* Use the think-aloud method or the think-pair-share strategy.
- *Emphasize connections.* Provide concrete representations, pictorial representations, and numerical representations. Pose carefully phrased questions to help students connect representations such as visuals, materials, and words. For example, as you fold a strip of paper into fourths, point out the part-whole relationship with gestures as you pose a question about the relationship between $\frac{2}{4}$ and $\frac{1}{2}$.
- *Adapt delivery modes.* Incorporate a variety of visual materials: images, examples, and models. Read problems or assessments or generate audio for text with voice creation software. Provide written instructions in addition to oral instructions.
- *Emphasize the relevant points.* Some students with disabilities may inappropriately focus on the color of a cube instead of the quantity of cubes when filling a prism to measure volume.
- *Support the organization of written work.* Provide tools and templates so students can focus on the mathematics rather than the organization of a table or chart. Use graphic organizers, picture-based models, and paper with columns or grids.
- *Provide examples and nonexamples.* Show examples of acute angles as well as angles that are not acute. Help students focus on the characteristics that differentiate the examples from those that are not examples.

Consider Alternative Assessments.

- *Propose alternative products.* Provide students with options for how to demonstrate understanding (e.g., a verbal response that is scripted by another person, audio recorded, or modeled with a manipulative). Use voice recognition software or word prediction software that can generate a whole menu of word choices when students type a few letters.
- *Encourage self-monitoring and self-assessment.* Students with disabilities often lack skills in self-reflection. Ask them to review an assignment or assessment to explain what was difficult and what they think they got right can help them be more independent and take greater responsibility for their learning.
- *Consider feedback charts.* Help students monitor their growth by charting progress over time.

Emphasize Practice and Summary.

- *Consolidate ideas.* Create or have students create study guides that summarize key mathematics concepts and allow for review.
- *Provide extra practice.* Use carefully selected problems (not a large number) and allow the use of familiar models.*

Not all of these strategies will apply to every lesson or every student with special needs, but as you think about a particular lesson and individual students in your class, you will find that many of these ideas will allow a student to engage in the task and accomplish the learning goals. Explore Strategies for Making Math Accessible for a handy collection of cards that you can use to think about planning instruction for individual students. The Center for Applied Special Technology (CAST) also has a website contains resources and tools to support students' learning, especially those with disabilities, through universal design for learning (UDL).

MyLab Education   **Teacher Resource: Strategies for Making Math Accessible**

---

*Adapted list reprinted with permission from Karp, K., & Howell, P. (2004). Building Responsibility for Learning in Students with Special Needs. *Teaching Children Mathematics, 11*(3), pp. 118–126. Copyright © 2004 by the National Council of Teachers of Mathematics. All rights reserved.

Adapting for Students with Moderate/Severe Disabilities

Students with moderate/severe disabilities (MSD) often need extensive modifications and individualized supports to learn mathematics. This population of students may include those with severe autism, sensory disorders, limitations affecting movement, cerebral palsy, and combinations of multiple disabilities.

Originally, the mathematics curriculum for students with moderate or severe disabilities was called "functional," in that it often focused on life-related skills such as managing money, telling time, using a calculator, measuring, and matching numbers to complete such tasks as entering a telephone number or identifying a house number. Now directives and assessments have broadened the curriculum to address grade-level expectations.

When possible, the mathematics content should be connected to life skills and features of jobs. Shopping skills and food preparation are both options for mathematical problem solving activities. At other times, link mathematical learning objectives to everyday events. For example, when the operation of division is studied, figuring how cookies can be equally shared at a party or how game cards can be dealt would be appropriate. Students can also undertake a small project such as constructing a box to store different items as a way to explore shapes and both length and volume measurements.

Do not believe that all basic facts must be mastered before students with moderate or severe disabilities can move forward in the curriculum; students can learn geometric or measuring concepts. Geometry for students with moderate and severe disabilities is more than merely identifying shapes, but is in fact critical for orienting in the real world. Concepts such as parallel and perpendicular lines and curves and straight sides become helpful for interpreting maps of the local area. Students who learn to count bus stops and judge time can be helped to successfully navigate their world.

The handout Math Activities for Students with Moderate or Severe Disabilities offers ideas across the curriculum and Additional Strategies for Supporting Students with Moderate or Severe Disabilities offers strategies to modify grade-level instruction.

MyLab Education   **Teacher Resource: Math Activities for Students with Moderate or Severe Disabilities**

MyLab Education   **Teacher Resource: Additional Strategies for Supporting Students with Moderate or Severe Disabilities**

MyLab Education   **Self-Check 6.2**

MyLab Education   **Application Exercise 6.1: Providing for Students Who Struggle and Those with Special Needs** Click the link to access this exercise, then watch the video and answer the accompanying questions.

Culturally and Linguistically Diverse Students

We are lucky to live in a country with rich diversity in cultural practices and languages. Students' native languages are not only an important part of their cultural heritage, but of how they think, communicate, and learn. From 1980 to 2015, the number of school-aged children who speak a language other than English at home rose from 4.7 million to approximately 11.9 million (22 percent) of school-aged children (National KIDS COUNT, 2015) with 4.5 million participating in EL programs in 2013–2014 (NCES, 2017).

Funds of Knowledge

Students from different countries, regions, or experiences, including those who speak different languages, should be seen as a resource in teaching (Gutierrez, 2009). Valuing a person's cultural background is a set of intentional actions that communicates to the student, "I want to know about you, I want you to see mathematics as part of your life, and I expect that you can do high-level mathematics." In getting to know students, we access their funds of knowledge-the essential knowledge or information students use to survive and thrive (Chao, Murray, & Gutiérrez, 2014).

Instead of teaching ELs from a deficit model that focuses on a lack of knowledge and experience, we can connect their experiences at home and with family to those of the mathematics classroom. Family and community activities, such as playing games, cooking, and story-telling, can serve as cultural and linguistic resources in learning mathematics.

MyLab Education   **Video Example 6.1**

Watch this video of a teacher who is talking about how to use the diversity of the students in her classroom to enhance instruction and develop community. How does she use gestures to teach mathematics ideas to English Learners?

Mathematics as a Language

Mathematics is commonly referred to as a "universal language," but that is not the case. Conceptual knowledge (e.g., what multiplication is) is universal. But procedures and symbols are culturally determined. In the United States, for example, 3×4 is interpreted as three groups of four. In other countries that expression is interpreted as three taken four times. As you will also read in Chapters 11 and 12, there are many algorithms for whole-number operations.

How we do mathematics is also culturally determined. For example, mental mathematics is highly valued in other countries, whereas in the United States, recording every step is valued. Compare the following two division problems from a fourth-grade classroom (Midobuche, 2001):

$$
\begin{array}{r}
495 \\
3\overline{)1485} \\
-12 \\
\hline
28 \\
-27 \\
\hline
15 \\
-15 \\
\hline
0
\end{array}
\qquad
\begin{array}{r}
495 \\
3\overline{)1485} \\
28 \\
15 \\
0
\end{array}
$$

Can you understand the thinking of the first student? If you learned division in the United States, that is likely easy to follow. But, if you learned division in another country, you may wonder why the first solution has so many numbers recorded. Can you follow the second example? It is, in effect, the same thinking process, but the multiplication and related subtraction are done mentally. The critical equity question, though, is not whether you can follow an alternative approach, but how you will respond when you encounter a student using a different approach:

- Will you require the student show their steps, disregarding the way they learned it?
- Will you ask the student to elaborate on how they did it?
- Will you have the student show other students their way of thinking?

The latter two responses communicate to students that you are interested in their way of knowing mathematics and that your support for a range of algorithms shows that you value their culturally influenced strategies (Gutiérrez, 2015).

Culturally Responsive Mathematics Instruction

Culturally responsive mathematics instruction includes attention to mathematical thinking, language and culture and it is not just for recent immigrants; it is for *all* students, including students from different ethnic groups, socioeconomic status, and so on. It includes consideration for content, relationships, cultural knowledge, flexibility in approaches, use of familiar or interesting learning contexts, a responsive learning community, and working in cross-cultural partnerships (Aguirre & del Rosario Zavala, 2013). Culturally responsive mathematics instruction can improve the performance of all students, as well as narrow the academic performance gap and increase students mathematics course taking (Boaler, 2008; Kisker et al., 2012; Thompson, 2017). Table 6.3 lists four Aspects of Culturally Responsive Mathematics Instruction, along with questions to guide planning, teaching and assessing. Also, see Reflection Questions to Guide Teaching and Assessing Culturally Relevant Instruction. If these reflective questions become internalized and are part of what you naturally think about as you plan, teach, and assess, then you are likely to lead a classroom where all students are challenged and supported.

> **MyLab Education**   **Teacher Resource: Reflection Questions to Guide Teaching and Assessing Culturally Relevant Instruction**

Communicate High Expectations. Too often, our first attempt to help students, in particular ELs, is to simplify the mathematics and/or remove the language from the lesson which can instead limit opportunities to learn. Culturally responsive instruction stays focused on the big ideas of mathematics (i.e., is based on state standards) and helps students engage in and stay focused on those critical areas. In addition to focusing on the big ideas, using tasks worthy of groupwork, emphasizing multiple representations, incorporating student justifications and presentations are features of classrooms that support equitable opportunities to learn mathematics (Cabana, Shreve, & Woodbury, 2014; Dunleavy, 2015). For example, in a lesson on perimeter and area of nonstandard shapes, a recording sheet might begin with definitions of each term and then a drawing or photograph added to illustrate the situation (Murrey,

TABLE 6.3   ASPECTS OF CULTURALLY RESPONSIVE MATHEMATICS INSTRUCTION

Aspect of Culturally Responsive Instruction	Teacher Reflection Questions
Communicate high expectations	• Does teaching focus on understanding big ideas in mathematics? • Are students expected to engage in problem solving and generate their own approaches to problems? • Are connections made among mathematical representations? • Are students justifying their strategies and answers, and are they presenting their work?
Make content relevant	• In what ways is the content related to familiar aspects of students' lives? • In what ways is prior knowledge elicited/reviewed so that all students can participate in the lesson? • To what extent are students asked to make connections between school mathematics and mathematics in their own lives? • How are student interests (events, issues, literature, or pop culture) used to build interest and mathematical meaning?
Attend to students' mathematical identities	• In what ways are students invited to include their own experiences within a lesson? • Are story problems generated from students and teachers? Do stories reflect the real experiences of students? • Are individual student approaches presented and showcased so that each student sees his or her ideas as important to the teacher and peers? • Are alternative algorithms shared as a point of excitement and pride (as appropriate)? • Are multiple modes used to demonstrate knowledge (e.g., visuals, explanations, models) valued?
Ensure shared power	• Are students (rather than just the teacher) justifying the correctness of solutions? • Are students invited (expected) to engage in whole-class discussions in which they share ideas and respond to one another's ideas? • In what ways are roles assigned so that every student feels that he or she is contributing to and learning from other members of the class? • Are students given a choice in how they solve a problem? In how they demonstrate knowledge of the concept?

2008). The teacher can incorporate opportunities for students to share their definitions and to discuss the meaning of the task prior to engaging in solving it. In this way, ELs are able to use appropriate mathematical language and focus on finding a solution.

Make Content Relevant.
There are really two components for making content relevant. One is to think about the *mathematics*: Is the mathematics presented meaningfully and is it connected to other content? The second is to select relevant contexts. Is the mathematics presented so that it connects to authentic situations in students' lives?

Mathematical Connections

Helping students see that mathematical ideas are interrelated will fill in or deepen their understanding of and connections to previously taught content. For example, consider the following problem:

Melisa is making braided bracelets. To prepare one she needs six strands of colored rope, each of them $1\frac{1}{4}$ feet long. She wants to make eight, one for each of her friends who are coming to her party. How much rope does she need to have?

Although the mathematics here is presented in a conceptual and meaningful manner, it is important to connect whole number and fraction operations. For example, to find how much rope is needed for eight people ($6 \times 1\frac{1}{4}$ feet, or $7\frac{1}{2}$ feet per person, then $8 \times 7\frac{1}{2}$ to find the total amount of rope), a student may use addition (because they are unsure how to handle the fraction), not recognizing that multiplication can be used. Asking questions such as, "How did you decide to [add/multiply]?" and "Are these ways equivalent?" helps students make meaningful connections between whole numbers and fractions and between addition and multiplication.

Context Connections

Making content relevant includes using contexts like braiding friendship bracelets in the problem above. If students are considering something familiar they can focus on the mathematics! For example, sometimes data provided in textbook tasks can be replaced with data from your students' community, or their families making it much more interesting to students, while teaching students important mathematical applications (Bartell et al., 2017; Simic-Muller, 2015; Turner, Sugimoto, Stoehr, & Kurz, 2016). Using everyday situations can increase student participation, enhance the use of different problem strategies, and help students develop a productive disposition (Tomaz & David, 2015).

Attend to Students' Mathematical Identities.
A focus on student's mathematical identities overlaps with the previous section, but merits its own discussion. A student's *mathematical identity* includes his or her disposition toward mathematics and sense of competence as learner and contributor in the mathematics classroom (Cobb, Gresalfi, & Hodge, 2009). Attending to a student's identity has a powerful impact on your development of equitable teaching practices (Aguirre, Mayfield-Ingram & Martin, 2013). Whether intentional or not, all teaching is identity work, as students are constantly adapting and redefining themselves based on their experiences (Gutiérrez, 2015). Our goal is to develop productive dispositions in each and every student (i.e., the tendency to believe that steady effort in learning mathematics pays off and to see oneself as an effective learner and doer of mathematics [NRC, 2001]). There are a number of ways that teachers can shape students' mathematical identities. One way to do that is "assigning competence" (Boaler & Staples, 2014, p. 27). As the teacher listens to students' contributions during small group work, during later discussion, the teacher can attribute ideas to individuals, saying, "That relates to the strategy Nicolas used." This approach recognizes Nicolas as capable in mathematics, influencing how he perceives himself, as well as how other classmates might perceive him.

Seeing mathematics from various cultures also provides opportunities for students to put faces on mathematical contributions (Remillard et al., 2014). Both researchers and teachers have found that telling stories about their own lives, or asking students to tell stories, makes the mathematics relevant to students and can raise student achievement (Turner et al., 2009). The Where to Find Mathematics in Homes and Communities handout provides ideas for finding mathematics relevant to things at home or in the community.

MyLab Education   **Teacher Resource: Where to Find Mathematics in Homes and Communities**

The following teacher's story illustrates one way to incorporate family history and culture by reading *The Hundred Penny Box* (Mathis, 2006). The story describes a 100-year-old woman who remembers an important event in her life for every one of her 100 pennies she collected each year. Each penny is more than just money; it is a "memory trigger" for her life.

Taking a cue from the book, I asked students to collect one penny from each year they were alive starting from the year of their birth and not missing a year. Students were encouraged to bring in additional pennies their classmates might need. Then the children consulted with family members to create a penny timeline of important events in their lives. Using information gathered at home, they started with the year they were born, listing their birthday and then recording first steps, accidents, vacations, pets, births of siblings, and so on. Then I asked them to find how many years between certain events or to calculate their age when they adopted a pet or learned to ride a bicycle. I also used these events in the weeks and months to come as subjects of story problems and other mathematics investigations on number lines.

Ensure Shared Power. When we think about creating a positive classroom environment, one in which all students feel as if they can participate and learn, we address considerations related to power. The teacher plays a major role in establishing and distributing power, whether it is intentional or not by telling students whether answers are right or wrong (rather than having students determine correctness through reasoning), demonstrating processes for solving problems (rather than give choices for how students will engage in the problem), and determining who will solve which problems (rather than allowing students flexibility and choice). Effective teachers establish a classroom environment where everyone feels their ideas are worth consideration. The way that you assign groups, seat students, and call on students sends clear messages about who has power in the classroom. Distributing power among students leads to empowered students. Visit https://www.youtube.com/watch?v=EjLOuUhN6xY to see an excellent TedxTalk on culturally relevant pedagogy in mathematics.

Teaching Strategies That Support Culturally and Linguistically Diverse Students

Creating effective learning opportunities for ELs involves integrating the principles of bilingual education with those of effective mathematics instruction. That leads to a double challenge as when learning about mathematics, students may be learning content in English for which they do not know the words in their native language such as *numerator* and *denominator*.

Story problems may also be difficult for ELs not just because of the language but also because the sentence structure in story problems is different from sentences in conversational English (Janzen, 2008). ELs need to use both English and their native language to read, write, listen, and speak as they learn content—a position similarly addressed in the NCTM position statement on Teaching Mathematics to ELs (NCTM, 2013). The strategies discussed here are the ones that appear most frequently in the literature as critical to increasing the mathematics achievement of ELs (e.g., Celedón-Pattichis & Ramirez, 2012; Echevarria, Vogt, & Short, 2012). See handout Reflective Questions for Planning and Teaching Mathematics Lessons for ELs in an "at-a-glance" set of questions useful for instructional planning and teaching of ELs.

> **MyLab Education**   **Teacher Resource: Reflective Questions for Planning and Teaching Mathematics Lessons for ELs**

Focus on Academic Vocabulary

Although a person might develop conversational English language skills in a few years, it takes as many as seven years to learn *academic language*, which is the language specific to a content area such as mathematics (Cummins, 1994). Academic language is harder to learn because it is not used in a student's everyday world.

Honor Use of Native Language. Valuing a student's language is one of the ways you value his or her cultural heritage. In a mathematics classroom, students can communicate in their native language while continuing their English language development (Haas & Gort, 2009; Moschkovich, 2009). For example, a good strategy for students working in small groups is having students discuss the problem in their preferred language. If a student knows enough English, then the presentation in the *after* phase of the lesson can be shared in English. If the student knows little or no English and does not have access to a peer who shares his or her native language, then visuals or pictures, a translator, Web-based mathematics glossary, or self-made dictionary can be components of a support system. ELs will often *code-switch*—moving between two languages. Research indicates that this practice supports mathematical reasoning because the student is selecting the language from which they can best express their ideas (Moschkovich, 2009).

Certain native languages can support learning mathematical words. Because several languages have their roots in Latin, many mathematics words are similar across languages (Celedón-Pattichis, 2009; Gómez, 2010). For example, *aequus* (Latin), *equal* (English), and *igual* (Spanish) are cognates. See if you can figure out the English mathematics terms for the following Spanish words: *división, hexágano, ángulo, triángulo, álgebra, circunferencia*, and *cubo*. Students may not make this connection if you do not point it out, so explicitly teaching students to look for cognates is important.

MyLab Education   **Video Example 6.2**

Watch this video of a teacher who speaks both Spanish and English shows how she is able to capitalize on her fluency to support some of her ELs. Notice how she uses cognates as a bridge that benefits all students.

Use Content and Language Objectives. If students know the purpose of a lesson, they are better able to make sense of the details when they may be challenged by some of the oral or written explanations. Students should know the language goals they will be developing alongside the mathematical goals. Here are two examples of dual objectives:

1. Students will analyze properties and attributes of three-dimensional solids. (mathematics)
2. Students will describe in writing and orally a similarity and a difference between two different solids. (language and mathematics)

Explicitly Teach Vocabulary. Intentional vocabulary instruction must be part of mathematics instruction for all students. There is strong evidence that teaching a set of academic vocabulary words intensively across several days using a variety of instructional activities supports ELs (Baker et al., 2014). Vocabulary support can happen throughout a lesson, as well as reinforced before or after a lesson.

MyLab Education   **Video Example 6.3**

Watch this video where the teacher discusses her strategy for building vocabulary through consistent use across multiple lessons.

These additional opportunities to learn reinforce understanding as they help students learn the terminology. Here are other examples to consider:

* Personal math dictionaries that link concepts and terms with drawings or clip art (Kersaint, Thompson, & Petkova, 2009)
* Graphic organizers that look at multiple ways to define a term (see Figure 6.3 and the Vocabulary Reference Card Template Activity Page)

MyLab Education   **Activity Page: Vocabulary Reference Card Template**

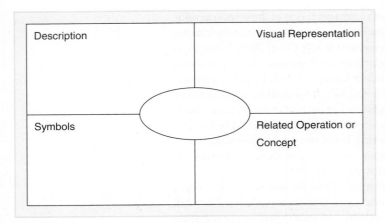

FIGURE 6.3 Vocabulary reference card—place the target word in the center and fill in the other sections.

- Games focused on vocabulary development (e.g., Charades, "$10,000 Pyramid," "Concentration")
- Mathematics word walls, including visuals and translations
- Skits, poems, or songs to address the everyday and the mathematical meanings of words (Seidel & McNamee, 2005)
- Foldables of key words for a topic (i.e., Dinah Zike's Teaching Mathematics with Foldables (Zike, 2003)

All students benefit from an increased focus on language; however, too much emphasis on language can diminish the focus on the mathematics. Importantly the language support should be *connected* to the selected mathematics task or activity (Bay-Williams & Livers, 2009).

As you analyze a lesson, identify terms related to the mathematics and to the context that may need explicit attention. Consider the following task, released from the 2009 National Assessment of Educational Progress (NAEP) (National Center for Education Statistics, 2011):

Sam did the following problems.

$$2 + 1 = 3$$
$$6 + 1 = 7$$

Sam concluded that when he adds 1 to any whole number, his answer will always be odd.

    Is Sam correct? _____

    Explain your answer.

In order for students to engage in this task, the terms *even* and *odd* must be understood. Both terms may be known for other meanings beyond the mathematics classroom (*even* can mean level and *odd* can mean strange). "Concluded" is not a math word but must be understood if an EL is to understand the meaning of the problem. Finally, you must give guidance on how students will explain their answers—must it be in words, or can they use pictures or diagrams? Offering multimodal communication options is valuable (Moffett, Malzahn, & Driscoll, 2014).

 Pause & Reflect

Odd and *even* are among hundreds of words that take on different meanings in mathematics from everyday usage. Others include *product, mean, sum, factor, acute, foot, division, difference, similar,* and *angle.* Can you name at least five others? ●

Foster Student Participation during Instruction

Student participation is important to learning and is especially critical for ELs (Tomaz & David, 2015; Wager, 2014). Teachers need to consider (1) efforts to ensure ELs understand and have the background for engaging in the focus tasks and (2) building structures for student participation throughout the lesson.

Build Background Knowledge. Similar to building on prior knowledge, building background takes into consideration native language and culture as well as content (Echevarria, Vogt, & Short, 2012). If possible, use a context and appropriate visuals to help students understand the task you want them to solve. For example, Pugalee, Harbaugh, and Quach (2009) spray-painted a coordinate axis in a field, so that students could build background related to linear equations. Students were given various equations and contexts and had to physically find (and walk to) points on the giant axis, creating human graphs of lines. This nonthreatening, engaging activity helped students make connections between what they had learned and what they needed to learn.

Some aspects of English and mathematics are particularly challenging to ELs (Whiteford, 2009/2010). Examples include the following:

- The names of teen numbers in English sound like their decade number—if you say *sixteen* and *sixty*, you can hear how similar they are. Emphasizing the *n* helps ELs hear the difference.
- Teen numbers also don't correspond to place value. For example, the Spanish word for 16 is an amalgamation of "ten and six" (as opposed to the English reversal of "six ten").
- Decimal places are hard to distinguish from other place values. Emphasizing the *th* sound helps students differentiate between hundreds and hundredths.
- U.S. measurement systems have unrelated terminology for every new unit and are not organized by base 10. Although this system is hard for all learners, having no life experiences with cups, pints, inches, miles, and other customary units adds to the challenge for ELs.

When encountering content that may be unfamiliar or difficult for ELs, devote additional time to building background so students can engage successfully in the tasks.

Use Comprehensible Input. *Comprehensible input* means that the message you are communicating is understandable. Modifications include simplifying sentence structures and limiting the use of nonessential or confusing vocabulary. Note that these modifications do not lower expectations for the lesson. Sometimes unnecessary words and phrases in questions make them less clear to nonnative speakers. Compare the following sets of teachers' directions:

Not Modified: You have an activity sheet in front of you that I just gave out. For every situation, I want you to determine the total area for the shapes. You will be working with your partner, but each of you needs to record your answers on your own paper and explain how you got your answer. If you get stuck on a problem, raise your hand.

Modified: Please look at your paper. [Holds paper and points to the first picture.] You will find the area of each shape. What does *area* mean? [Allows wait time.] How can you calculate area? [*Calculate* is more like the Spanish word *calculary,* so it is more accessible to Spanish speakers.] Talk to your partner. [Points to mouth and then to a pair of students as she says this.] Write your answers. [Makes a writing motion over paper.] If you get stuck [shrugs shoulders and looks confused], raise your hand [demonstrates].

Notice that three things were done: sentences were shortened, confusing words were removed, and related gestures and motions were added to the oral directions. Also, notice the wait time the teacher gives. It is very important to provide extra time after posing a question or giving instructions to allow ELs time to translate, make sense of the request, and then participate.

Another way to provide comprehensible input is to use a variety of tools to help students visualize and understand what is verbalized. In the preceding example, the teacher is modeling the instructions. Effective tools include manipulatives, pictures, real objects, multimedia, demonstrations, and diagrams. For example, if teaching volume of rectangular solids, show a cube and a rectangular container and ask, "How many same-sized cubes will fill this container?" As you ask, physically start to move cubes into the container to illustrate. Review relevant terms such as base, length, width, and height by having students help label a container.

Engage Students in Discourse That Reflects Language Needs. Discourse, or the use of classroom discussion as a means to make sense of the mathematics, is essential for the learning (Banse, Palacios, Merritt, & Rimm-Kaufman, 2016; Cirillo et al., 2014), but it is particularly important for ELs who need to engage in productive language (writing and speaking) as well as receptive language (listening and reading) (Baker et al., 2014).

There are strategies you can use in classroom discourse that help ELs understand and participate in discussions. Practicing an explanation first with a partner can increase participation. *Revoicing* is a research-based strategy that supports student participation, using gestures and visuals, inviting students to share and justify and asking other students to respond to ELs' ideas (Turner, Dominguez, Maldonado, & Empson, 2013). Because ELs cannot always explain their ideas fully, rather than just calling on another student, *pressing* for details is important. This pressing, sometimes known as expansion moves (Choppin, 2014), is not just so the teacher can decide whether the idea makes sense; it is so that other students can make sense of the idea (Maldonado, Turner, Dominguez, & Empson, 2009).

Plan Cooperative/Interdependent Groups to Support Language Development. The use of cooperative groups is a valuable way to support ELs (Baker et al., 2014). Group work provides an opportunity for students to use language, but only if the groups are formed in ways that consider students' language skills. Placing an EL with two English-speaking students may result in the EL being left out. On the other hand, grouping all Spanish speakers together prevents the students from having opportunities to participate in the mathematics lesson in English. Consider placing a bilingual student in a group with a student with limited English, or place students that have the same first language together with English speakers so that they can help each other understand and participate (Garrison, 1997; Khisty, 1997).

Implementing Strategies for English Learners

ELs' needs must be considered at each step of the instructional planning process. Explore the Guide for Planning and Teaching Mathematics to English Learners. In the following example, the teacher uses several techniques mentioned in the guide and described above to provide support for ELs while keeping expectations high.

MyLab Education   **Teacher Resource: Guide for Planning and Teaching Mathematics to English Learners**

Ms. Steimer is teaching a third-grade lesson that involves the concepts of estimating length (in inches) and measuring to the nearest half-inch. Students are asked to use estimation to find three objects that are about 6 inches long, three objects that are about 1 foot long, and three objects that are about 2 feet long. Once identified, students are to measure the nine objects to the nearest half-inch and compare the measurements with their estimates.

Ms. Steimer has several ELs in her class including a student from Korea who knows very little English and a student from Mexico who speaks English well but is new to U.S. schools. These two students are not familiar with the measurement units of feet or inches. She takes time to address the language and the increments on the ruler to the entire class. Because the word *foot* has two meanings, Ms. Steimer decides to address that explicitly before launching into the lesson. She begins by asking students what a "foot" is. She allows time for students to discuss the word with a partner and then share their answers with the class. She explains that today they are going to be using the measuring unit of a foot (while holding up the foot ruler). She asks students what other units can be used to measure length. In particular, she asks her ELs to share what units they use in their countries of origin, having metric rulers to show the class. She asks students to study the ruler and compare the centimeter to the inch by posing these questions: "Can you estimate about how many centimeters are in an inch? In 6 inches? In a foot?"

Moving to the lesson objectives, Ms. Steimer uses a ruler on the document camera and enlarges the image so all students can see the demarcations. Below the ruler she has a paper snake whose length ends at the $8\frac{1}{2}$ inch mark. Then, she asks students how long the snake is and writes their reply of $8\frac{1}{2}$ inches. Next, she asks students to tear a paper strip that they estimate is 6 inches long. Students then measure their paper strips with rulers to the nearest half inch. Now she has them ready to begin estimating and measuring.

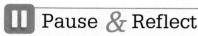

Pause & Reflect

What specific strategies did Ms. Steimer use to support ELs? •

There are several strategies in this example that provide support for ELs: Discussion of the word *foot* using the think-pair-share technique recognized the potential language confusion and allowed students the chance to talk about it prior to the task. The efforts to use concrete models (the ruler and the torn paper strip) and to build on students' prior experience (use of the metric system) provided support so that the ELs could succeed in this task. Most important, Ms. Steimer did not diminish the challenge of the task with these strategies. If she had altered the task, for example, by not expecting the ELs to estimate because they didn't know the inch very well, she would have lowered her expectations. Conversely, if she had simply posed the problem without taking time to have students study the ruler or to provide visuals, she may have kept her expectations high but failed to provide the support that would enable her students to succeed. Finally, by making a connection for all students to the metric system, she showed respect for the students' cultures and broadened the horizons of other students to measurement in other countries.

Consider a particular lesson you are planning and use the Sheltering a Lesson for English Learners planning sheet to record adaptations and instructional strategies that need to be included.

MyLab Education	**Teacher Resource: Sheltering a Lesson for English Learners**
MyLab Education	**Self-Check 6.3**

Providing for Students Who Are Mathematically Gifted

Students who we are describing as mathematically gifted include those who have high ability, high interest, advanced learning capabilities, exceptional promise (NCTM, 2016) or talent. Like the tiered model in RtI, "giftedness" is not a permanent trait but instead fluctuates with academic topic and student needs (Plucker & Peters, 2016). These students need interventions too.

Some students may have an intuitive knowledge of mathematical concepts, whereas others have a passion for the subject even though they may have to work hard to learn it. But many students can be nurtured to enjoy expanding opportunities that allow them to grow beyond "proficiency." Right now, fewer than 10 percent of U.S. students are performing at advanced levels in mathematics (NCES, 2017); which is just not enough.

Students' abilities may become apparent to parents and teachers when they grasp and articulate mathematics concepts at an age earlier than expected. They are often found to easily make connections between topics of study but are frequently unable to explain how they quickly got an answer (Rotigel & Fello, 2005). Many teachers have a keen ability to spot talent when they note students who have strong number sense or visual/spatial sense (Gavin & Sheffield, 2010). Note that these teachers are not pointing to students who are speedy with their basic facts, but those who have the ability to reason and make sense of mathematics.

Using tests to identify high ability learners can perpetuate inequities (Plucker & Peters, 2016). Another option is to "use different tests" or to "use tests differently" (Matthew & Peters, 2017). Instead, do not wait for students to demonstrate their mathematical talent; screen everyone and do not only use a teacher nomination approach. Another option is to "cultivate your own" and develop such skills as tenacity and a growth mindset for higher level performance in advanced programs through challenging tasks and inquiry-based instruction. The curriculum should be adapted to consider level, complexity, breadth, depth, and pace (Assouline & Lupkowski-Shoplik, 2011; Johnsen & Sheffield, 2014; Renzulli, Gubbins, McMillen, Eckert, & Little, 2009; Saul, Assouline, & Sheffield, 2010).

There are four basic categories for adapting mathematics content for gifted mathematics students: (1) acceleration and pacing, (2) enrichment (depth), (3) sophistication (complexity), and (4) creativity (Johnsen, Ryser, & Assouline, 2014). In each category, your students should apply, rather than just acquire, information. The emphasis on using, implementing, and extending ideas must overshadow the mental collection of facts and concepts.

Acceleration and Pacing

Acceleration recognizes that your students may already understand the mathematics content that you plan to teach. Some teachers use "curriculum compacting" (Reis & Renzulli, 2005) to give a short overview of the content and assess students' ability to respond to mathematics tasks that would demonstrate their proficiency. Allowing students to increase the pace of their own learning can give access to curriculum different from grade level content while demanding more independent study. But, moving students to higher mathematics (by moving them up a grade, for example) will not alone succeed in engaging them if the learning remains at a slow pace. Research reveals that when gifted students are accelerated through the curriculum they become more likely to explore STEM (science, technology, engineering, and mathematics) fields (Sadler & Tai, 2007).

Depth

Enrichment activities go in a depth beyond the topic of study to content that is not specifically a part of your grade-level curriculum but is an extension of the original mathematics. For example, while studying place value both using very large numbers or decimals, students can stretch their knowledge to study other bases such as base five, base eight, or base twelve. This extension provides a view of how our base-ten numeration system fits within the broader system of number theory. Other times the format of enrichment can involve studying the same topic as the rest of the class while differing on the means and outcomes of the work. Examples include group investigations, solving real problems in the community, writing data-based letters to outside audiences, or identifying applications of the mathematics learned.

Complexity

Another strategy is to increase the sophistication of a topic by raising the level of complexity or pursuing greater rigor of content, possibly outside the regular curriculum or by connecting mathematics to other subject areas. For example, while studying a unit on place value, students can deepen their knowledge to study other numeration systems such as Roman, Mayan, Egyptian, Babylonian, Chinese, and Zulu. This approach provides a multicultural view of how our numeration system fits within historical number systems (Mack, 2011). In the algebra strand, when studying sequences or patterns of numbers, students can learn about Fibonacci sequences and their appearances in the natural world in shells and plant life. See the Mathematics Integration Plan that can be used to help plan ways to integrate core content or create independent explorations or research projects. Using this approach, students can think about a mathematics topic through another perspective or through an historic or futuristic viewpoint.

MyLab Education   Teacher Resource: Mathematics Integration Plan

Creativity

By presenting open-ended problems and investigations students can use divergent thinking to examine mathematical ideas—often in collaboration with others. These collaborative experiences could include students from a variety of grades and classes volunteering for special mathematics projects, with a classroom teacher, principal, or resource teacher taking the lead. Their creativity can be stimulated through the exploration of mathematical "tricks" using binary numbers to guess classmates' birthdays (Karp & Ronau, 2009) or design large-scale investigations of the amount of food thrown away at lunchtime (Ronau & Karp, 2012). A group might find mathematics in art (Bush, Karp, Lenz, & Nadler, 2017; Bush, Karp, Nadler, & Gibbons, 2016). Another aspect of creativity provides different options for students in culminating performances of their understanding, such as demonstrating their knowledge through inventions, experiments, simulations, dramatizations, visual displays, and oral presentations.

Noted researcher on mathematically gifted students, Benbow states that acceleration combined with depth through enrichment is best practice (Read, 2014). Then learning is not only sped up but the learning is deeper and at more complex levels.

Strategies to Avoid

There are a number of ineffective approaches for gifted students, including the following:

1. *Assigning more of the same work.* This approach is the least appropriate way to respond and the most likely to result in students' hiding their ability.
2. *Giving free time to early finishers.* Although students may find this opportunity rewarding, it does not maximize their intellectual growth to "go beyond" and can lead to students hurrying to finish a task.
3. *Assigning gifted students to help struggling learners.* Routinely assigning gifted students to teach students who are not meeting expectations does not stimulate their intellectual growth and can place them in socially uncomfortable situations.
4. *Providing pull-out opportunities.* Unfortunately, generalized gifted programs are often unrelated to the regular mathematics curriculum (Assouline & Lupkowski-Shoplik, 2011). Disconnected, add-on experiences are not enough to build more complex and sophisticated understandings of mathematics.
5. *Offering independent enrichment on the computer.* Although there are excellent enrichment opportunities to be found on the Internet and terrific apps, the practice of having gifted students use a computer program that focuses on skills does not engage them in a way that will enhance conceptual understanding and support their ability to justify their thinking.

Sheffield writes that gifted students should be introduced to the "joys and frustrations of thinking deeply about a wide range of original, open-ended, or complex problems that encourage them to respond creatively in ways that are original, fluent, flexible and elegant" (1999, p. 46). Accommodations, modifications, and interventions for mathematically gifted students must strive for this goal.

MyLab Education   **Self-Check 6.4**

Reducing Resistance and Building Resilience

There are students who may decide that they won't be able to learn mathematics, so why try? Teachers need to "reach beyond the resistance" and find ways to listen to students, affirm their abilities, and motivate them. Here are a few strategies for getting there.

Give Students Choices That Capitalize on Their Unique Strengths

Students often need to have power over events by having a stake and a say in what is happening. Therefore, focus on creating inviting and familiar instruction as you connect students' interests to the content. Setting up situations where these students feel success with mathematics tasks can bring them closer to becoming excited about learning mathematics.

Nurture Traits of Resilience

Benard (1991) suggests there are four traits found in resilient individuals—social competence, problem solving skills, autonomy, and a sense of purpose and future. Use these characteristics to motivate students and help them reach success. Encourage students to persevere despite occasionally facing frustration or confusion. Thinking critically and flexibly helps students develop strategies that will serve students in all aspects of their lives. Also, nurture high levels of student responsibility and autonomy, intentionally fostering a disposition that students can and will be able to master mathematical concepts.

Make Mathematics Irresistible

Motivation is based on what students expect they can do and what they value (Wigfield & Cambria, 2010). The use of games, brainteasers, mysteries that can be solved through mathematics, and counterintuitive problems that leave students asking, "How is that possible?" help generate excitement. But the main thrust of the motivation emerges from you as you enthusiastically communicate a passion for the content.

Give Students Leadership in Their Own Learning

High-achieving students tend to suggest their failures were from lack of effort and see the failure as a temporary condition that can be resolved with hard work. On the other hand, students with a history of academic failure can attribute their failures to lack of ability. This internal attribution is more difficult to counteract, as students think their innate lack of mathematical ability prevents them from succeeding no matter what they do. So, help students develop achievable personal learning goals by asking them to reflect on their performance on a unit assessment, write personal goals for the next unit, or set weekly targets for mastery of basic facts.

MyLab Education **Self-Check 6.5**

 **RESOURCES** FOR CHAPTER 6

RECOMMENDED READINGS

Articles

Bay-Williams, J., & Livers, S. (2009). Supporting math vocabulary acquisition. *Teaching Children Mathematics, 16*(4), 238–246.

Looking at words used in the mathematics classroom that have multiple meanings (i.e., mean, table), the authors show ways to support ELs in the classroom.

Hodges, R., Rose, R., & Hicks, A. (2012). Interviews as RtI tools. *Teaching Children Mathematics, 19*(1), 30–36.

This article emphasizes ways to identify the strengths and weaknesses of students with disabilities and the implication for instruction within an RtI framework.

Iliev, N., & D'Angelo, F. (2014). Teaching mathematics through multicultural literature. *Teaching Children Mathematics, 20*(7), 452–457.

The authors blend strategies for teaching reading and mathematics for young learners.

Books

Johnsen, S. K., & Sheffield, L. J. (Eds.). (2013). *Using the common core state standards for mathematics with gifted and advanced learners.* Reston, VA: NCTM.

This book, in collaboration with the National Association for Gifted Children, provides examples and strategies for practitioners. Trajectories for talent development are detailed, as are ideas for encouraging creativity and critical thinking.

Civil, M., & Turner, E. (2014). Common core state standards in mathematics for English language learners: Grades K–8. Alexandria, VA: TESOL Press.

Through a collection of classroom based vignettes, the authors share teaching practices that support ELs with the Standards for Mathematical Practices.

CHAPTER 7

Developing Early Number Concepts and Number Sense

LEARNER OUTCOMES

After reading this chapter and engaging in the embedded activities and reflections, you should be able to:

7.1 Recognize that teaching mathematics to very young children involves providing high quality number activities using a developmental approach.

7.2 Demonstrate how to develop children's counting skills, including subitizing (immediately recognizing a total number of objects in an organized collection) to three or five without counting each object.

7.3 Plan ways to teach children to compare quantities and describe relationships between numbers.

7.4 Develop ways to connect mathematical ideas to the real-world activities of young learners.

Young children enter school with many ideas about number and these ideas should be built upon using a variety of experience to develop new relationships and advanced mathematics understandings. This chapter emphasizes the development of numbers up to 20, but also considers the number names and counting sequences up to 100 by ones and tens. These foundational ideas can be extended to content that enhances the development of number (measurement, data, operations) and content directly affected by how well early number concepts have been developed (basic facts, place value, and computation). We begin by introducing critical big ideas about counting and comparing number quantities to nurture and build young children's number concepts and number sense.

BIG IDEAS

* Counting tells how many things are in a set. When counting a set of objects, the last word stated in the counting sequence names the quantity for that set (*cardinality*).

* Numbers relate through comparisons of quantities, including greater-than, less-than, and equal-to relationships. These comparisons are made through one-to-one correspondence of objects in sets. For example, the number 7 is 3 more than 4; 2 less than 9; composed of 3 and 4, as well as 2 and 5; is 3 less than 10; and can be quickly recognized in several patterned arrangements of dots. These ideas about the number 7 extend to composing and decomposing larger numbers, such as 17, 57, and 370.

- Number concepts are intimately tied to operations with numbers based on situations in the world around us. Application of number relationships to problem solving marks the beginning of making sense of the world in a mathematical manner.

- *Number sense* means that you can think about different sized quantities and use numbers and relationships in multiple ways to estimate and solve problems. This idea includes understanding the magnitude (or size) of numbers.

 ## Promoting Good Beginnings

Research indicates that preschoolers' early mathematical performance establishes a foundation for their future academic success more so than other cognitive measures including reading ability, memory skills or spatial sense (Frye et al., 2013; Levine et al., 2010; Watts, Greg, Duncan, Siegler, & Davis-Kean, 2014). Surprisingly, the National Research Council (2009) noted that what a 5- or 6-year-old child knows about mathematics can predict not only their future mathematics achievement, but also their future reading achievement. Attention to early mathematical ideas is critical!

The National Council of Teachers of Mathematics' (NCTM's) position statement on Early Childhood Learning emphasizes that all children need an early foundation of challenging mathematics (2013). This document provides the following research-based recommendations:

1. Enhance children's natural interest in mathematics and assist them in using mathematics to make sense of their world.
2. Build on children's experience and knowledge using familiar contexts.
3. Base mathematics curriculum and teaching practices on a solid understanding of both mathematics and child development.
4. Use formal and informal experiences to strengthen children's problem solving and reasoning processes.
5. Provide opportunities for children to explain their thinking about mathematical ideas.
6. Assess children's mathematical knowledge, skills, and strategies through a variety of formative assessment approaches.

 ## Pause & Reflect

Although all of these recommendations are critical, which two do you think are most important for your own professional growth? ●

The *Curriculum Focal Points* (2006) suggests that preschoolers start to develop whole number understanding through counting, one-to-one correspondence, cardinality, comparing and ordering quantities. In kindergarten children count to 100 by ones and tens, count from numbers other than one, write numbers up to 20 and make comparisons between two groups as to whether one group of objects is greater than, less than, or equal the other. In first grade children count, read and write numbers to 120, including counting from numbers other than one. Then first graders move to place value concepts and relating counting to the operations of addition and subtraction (NGA Center & CCSSO, 2010).

In 2009, the NCR Committee on Early Childhood Mathematics identified three foundational areas in mathematics content for early learners: the number core, the relations core, and the operations core. This chapter focuses on the first two core areas; Chapter 8 addresses the third core in examining the meaning of the operations. Note that as you develop children's abilities in counting, the conversations about number relationships begin. Therefore, the activities and concepts in this chapter are not sequential but coexist in a rich environment of mathematical experiences where children see connections between numbers.

MyLab Education **Self-Check 7.1**

The Number Core: Quantity, Counting, and Cardinality

Even 2- and 3-year-old children count their fingers, toys, people at the table, and other small sets of objects. Questions such as "Who has more?" or "Are there enough?" are part of children's daily lives. Evidence indicates that when children have such experiences, they begin to develop understanding of the concepts of number and counting (Baroody, Li, & Lai, 2008; Clements & Sarama, 2014).

Quantity and the Ability to Subitize

Children explore quantity before they can count. They can identify which cup is bigger or which plate of blueberries has more berries. Soon they need to attach an amount to the quantities to explore them in greater depth. When you look at an number of objects, sometimes you are able to just "see" how many are there, particularly for a small group of items. For example, when you roll a die and immediately know that it is five without counting the dots, that ability to "just see it" is called *subitizing*. There are times when you are able to subitize for even larger amounts, when you decompose a group of dots shown in a pattern of ten by seeing five in one row and mentally doubling it to get ten. "Subitizing is a fundamental skill in the development of children's understanding of number" (Baroody, 1987, p. 115) and can be developed and practiced through experiences with patterned sets.

Many children easily recognize patterned sets of dots on dice due to the many games they have played. Similar instant recognition (subitizing) can be developed for other patterns (see Figure 7.1). Naming these amounts immediately without counting moves students away from an overuse of counting by ones and toward the use of number patterns. This shift facilitates "counting on" (from a known patterned set) or learning combinations of numbers (seeing a patterned set of two known smaller patterns). To support beginning learners in subitizing use three objects organized in patterns that are symmetric before moving to numbers such as five or more challenging images. Children can try Okta's Rescue at NCTM's Illumination website (http://illuminations.nctm.org) to subitize a variety of different sets. Encourage students to move beyond counting by ones as soon as possible and instead have them focus on patterns. Good materials to use in pattern recognition activities include a set of dot plates made with paper plates and the sticky dots commonly available in office supply stores (see Figure 7.2). Note that some patterns are combinations of two smaller patterns or a pattern with one or two additional dots. These should be made in two colors to highlight the patterns. Keep the patterns compact and organized because if the dots are too spread out, the patterns are hard to identify. Seeing a number as a combination of parts is critical understanding for students as they will need to flexibly compose and decompose numbers as they learn to calculate.

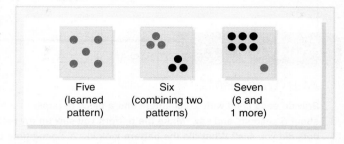

FIGURE 7.1 Recognizing a patterned set.

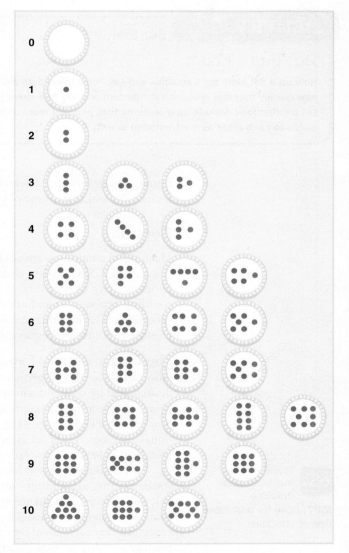

FIGURE 7.2 A collection of patterns for dot plates.

TECHNOLOGY Note. Explore interactive web-based activities such as #Flash from "Fuel the Brain." Base-ten blocks or ten-frames flash on the screen for a set time limit. The student is then asked to input what number was shown. Children can practice subitizing and basic addition using flashed images of ten frames and base-ten materials. ■

Activity 7.1

CCSS-M: K.CC.B.4

Learning Patterns

STUDENTS with SPECIAL NEEDS

Provide each child with 10 counters and a piece of paper or a paper plate as a mat. Hold up a dot plate for about 5 seconds and say, "Make the pattern you saw on my plate using the counters on your plate. How many dots did you see? What did the pattern look like?" Spend time discussing the configuration of the pattern and the number of dots. Then show the plate again so children can self-check. Do this activity with a few new patterns each day. To modify for children with disabilities, you may need to give the child a small selection of premade dot plates. Then instead of creating the pattern with counters, the child finds the matching dot plate.

Activity 7.2

CCSS-M: K.CC.B.4a; K.CC.B.4b

Dot Plate Flash

Hold up a dot plate for 3 seconds and say, "How many dots did you see? What did the pattern look like?" Children like to see how quickly they can recognize the pattern and say how many dots. When needed, show a plate a second time so children can get another look. Include easy patterns first, and add more dots as children's confidence builds. Children can also flash dot plates to each other as a workstation activity.

Instant-recognition activities with dot plates are exciting and can be done in 5 minutes at any time of day and at any time of year.

Counting

Meaningful counting activities begin with 3-year-olds, but by the end of kindergarten (NGA Center & CCSSO, 2010), children should be able to count to 100. For children to have an understanding of counting, they must construct this idea by working through a variety of counting experiences and activities. Only the counting sequence of number words is a rote procedure. The meaning attached to counting is the key conceptual idea on which all other number concepts are developed.

The Development of Verbal Counting Skills. Research-based learning trajectories (also called *learning progressions*) can help you design instruction that moves children to the desired goal by using information about the path on which these ideas typically develop. The counting trajectory (Clements & Sarama, 2014) identifies the overarching goals of counting and how to help a child progress to more sophisticated levels of thinking through specific instructional activities. Table 7.1 is based on this research and is a selection of levels and sublevels identified as benchmarks (pp. 36–46) in the trajectory.

Verbal counting has at least two separate skills. First, a child must be able to produce the standard string of counting words in order: "One, two, three, four . . . ." Second, a child must be able to connect this sequence in a one-to-one correspondence with the objects in the set being counted. Each object must get one and only one count. As part of these skills, children should recognize that each counting number identifies a quantity that is one more than the previous number and that the new quantity is embedded in the previous quantity (see Figure 7.3). This knowledge will be helpful later in decomposing numbers (breaking them apart).

CCSS **Standards for Mathematical Practice**
MP7. Look for and make use of structure.

TABLE 7.1   LEARNING TRAJECTORY FOR COUNTING

Levels of Thinking	Characteristics
Precounter	Here the child has no verbal counting ability. A young child looking at three balls will answer "ball" when asked how many. The child does not associate a number word with a quantity.
Reciter	The child verbally counts using number words, but not always in the right order. Sometimes they say more numbers than they have objects to count, skip objects, or repeat the same number.
Corresponder	A child at this level can make a one-to-one correspondence with numbers and objects, stating one number per object. If asked "How many?" at the end of the count, they may have to recount to answer.
Counter	This child can accurately count objects in an organized display (in a line, for example) and can answer "How many?" accurately by giving the last number counted (called *cardinality*). They may be able to write the matching numeral and may be able to say the number just after or before a number by counting up from 1.
Producer	A child at this level can count out objects to a certain number. If asked to give you five blocks, they can show you that amount.
Counter and Producer	A child who combines the two previous levels can count out objects, tell how many are in a group, remember which objects are counted and which are not, and respond to random arrangements. They begin to separate tens and ones, like 23 is 20 and 3 more.
Counter Backwards	A child at this level can count backward by removing objects one by one or just verbally as in a "countdown."
Counter from Any Number	This child can count up starting from numbers other than one. They are also able to immediately state the number before and after a given number.
Skip Counter	Here the child can skip-count with understanding by a group of a given number—tens, fives, twos, and so on.

Source: Based on Clements and Sarama (2014).

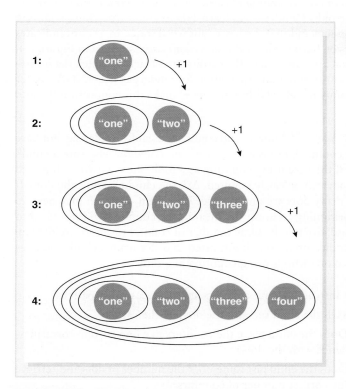

FIGURE 7.3   In counting, each number is one more than the previous number.

Source: National Research Council. (2009). *Mathematics learning in early childhood: Paths toward excellence and equity*, p. 27. Reprinted with permission from the National Academy of Sciences, courtesy of the National Academies Press, Washington, DC.

Activity 7.3   CCSS-M: K.CC.A.1; K.CC.A.2

Up and Back Counting

ENGLISH LEARNERS

Counting up to and back from a target number in a rhythmic fashion is an important counting exercise. Line up five children and five chairs. As the whole class counts from 1 to 5, the children sit down one at a time. When the target number, 5, is reached, it is repeated; then the child who sat on 5 now stands, and the count goes back to 1 with the children standing up one at a time, and so on, "1, 2, 3, 4, 5, 5, 4, 3, 2, 1, 1, 2 . . . ." Start at numbers other than one. To modify this activity for English learners, give each child who is in front of the class one card from a set of cards with the target numerals (e.g., 1 to 5, 15 to 20, or 55 to 65) and the corresponding number word. These cards will provide a visual to help children connect the written numeral and number word to the number being said.

Experience and guidance are major factors in children's development of counting skills. While many children come to kindergarten able to count sets of 10 or beyond, some children may have less background knowledge and may require additional practice. In some cases, use counterexamples to help clarify a number. For example, you can label four blocks as "four" but also consider labeling six blocks as "not four," stating, "That's six blocks, not four blocks." This precision will help children grasp the meaning of a number (Frye et al., 2013).

Children's literature with repeated phrases, such as the classic *Goodnight Moon* (Brown, 1947), provides an opportunity for students to count. Students can press the equal sign on a calculator each time the little rabbit says goodnight in his bedtime routine. At the completion of the book they can compare how many "goodnights" were recorded. Follow-up activities include using the same automatic-constant feature on the calculator with different stories or books to skip-count by twos (e.g., pairs of animals or people), fives (e.g., fingers on one hand or people in a car), or tens (e.g., dimes, "ten in a bed," apples in a tree).

The size and arrangement of the set are also factors related to success in counting. Obviously, longer number strings require more practice to learn. The first 12 counting words involve no pattern or repetition, and many children do not easily recognize a pattern in the teen numbers. Children learning the skills of counting—that is, matching oral number words with objects—should initially be given sets of blocks or counters that they can move. For many children, especially children with disabilities, it is important to have an organized plan for counting. The children should count objects from left to right, move the objects as they count, or point and touch them as they orally say each number word in sequence. Consistently ask, "How many do you have in all?" at the end of each count.

Cardinality

Fosnot and Dolk (2001) state that an understanding of cardinality and its connection to counting is not a simple task for 4-year-olds. Children will learn *how* to count (matching counting words with objects) before they understand that the last count word stated in a count indicates the amount of the set (how many you have in all) or the set's *cardinality* as shown in Figure 7.4. Children who make this connection are said to have the cardinality principle, which is a refinement of their early ideas about quantity and is an expectation for kindergartners (NGA Center & CCSSO, 2010). Most, but certainly not all, children by age $4\frac{1}{2}$ make this connection (Fosnot & Dolk, 2001).

FORMATIVE ASSESSMENT Notes. Children who count successfully orally may not have attached meaning to their counts. Here is a diagnostic interview for assessing a child's understanding of cardinality and if they are using counting as a tool. Show a card with five to nine large dots in a row so that they can be easily counted. Ask the child to count the dots. If the count is accurate, ask, "How many dots are on the card?" Early on, children may need to count again, but a child who is beginning to grasp the meaning of counting will not need to recount. Now ask the child, "Please give me the same number of counters as there are dots on the card." Here is a sequence of indicators to watch for, listed in order from a child who does not attach meaning to the count to one who is using counting as a tool:

Does the child not count but instead take out counters and make a similar pattern?

Will the child recount the dots on the card?

Does the child place the counters in a one-to-one correspondence with the dots?

Does the child just remember the number of dots and retrieve the correct number of counters?

Can the child show that there are the same number of counters as dots?

As the child shows competence with patterned sets, move to using random dot patterns. ■

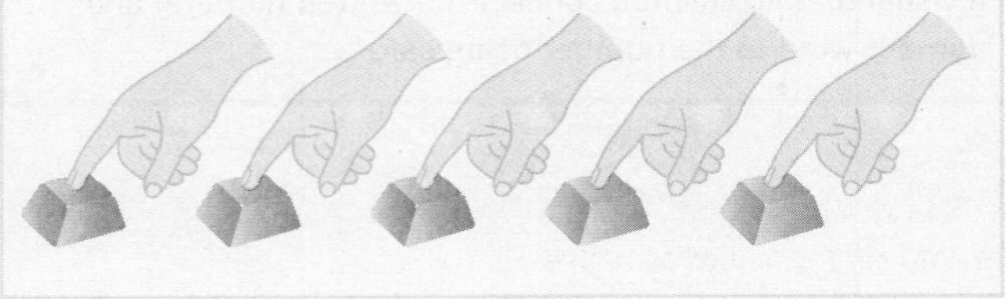

FIGURE 7.4 The child has learned cardinality if, after counting five objects, he or she answers the question "How many do you have in all?" with "Five."

To develop the full understanding of counting, engage children in games or activities that involve counts and comparisons, such as Activity 7.4.

Activity 7.4

CCSS-M: K.CC.B.5

Fill the Tower

Children take turns rolling a die and collecting the indicated number of counters. They place these counters on one of the towers on their Fill the Tower Game Board. The object is to fill all towers with counters. As an option, require that the towers be filled exactly so that a roll of 5 cannot be used to fill four empty squares. To modify this activity for children with disabilities, use a die with only 2 or 3 (dots or numerals) on the sides. You can increase the number choices on the die when you have evidence that the child is counting accurately. A modification for children who need a challenge is to have them use a die with higher numbers and a game board with larger towers.

STUDENTS with SPECIAL NEEDS

MyLab Education Activity Page: Fill the Tower Game Board

Playing Fill the Tower provides opportunities for you to talk with children about number and assess their thinking. Observe how they count the dots on the die. Ask, "How do you know you have the right number of counters?" and "How many counters did you put in the tower? How many more do you need to fill the tower?"

Regular classroom routines, such as counting how many napkins or snacks are needed at snack time, how many materials are needed for an activity, how many children plan to eat the school lunch, or even simply taking attendance, are additional opportunities for children to engage in purposeful counting. Have students count groups of children as in the video "Mingle and Count," which can be found at Teaching Channel (www.teachingchannel.org). Look for ways to make these situations into real problems and discuss children's strategies. Explore The Find Activity Page for another opportunity to build children's counting strategies.

MyLab Education Activity Page: The Find

Thinking about Zero

Children need to discover the number zero (Clements & Sarama, 2014), particularly as understanding its value is a required standard of kindergartners (NGA Center & CCSSO, 2010). Surprisingly, it is not a concept that is easily grasped without intentionally building understanding. Three- and four-year-old children can begin to use the word *zero* and the numeral 0 to symbolize that there are no objects in the set. With the dot plates discussed previously (see Figure 7.2), use the zero plate to discuss what it means when there is no dot on the plate. We find that because early counting often involves touching an object, zero is sometimes not included in the count. Zero is one of the most important digits in the base-ten system, and purposeful conversations about it and its position on the number line are essential. Activities 7.1, 7.2, and 7.12 are useful in exploring the number zero.

Numeral Writing and Recognition

Kindergartners are expected to write numbers from 0 to 20 (NGA Center & CCSSO, 2010). Helping children read and write the 10 single-digit numerals is similar to teaching them to read and write letters of the alphabet. Neither has anything to do with number concepts. Numeral writing can be engaging. For example, ask children to trace over pages of numerals, make numerals from clay, trace them in shaving cream on their desks, press the numeral on a calculator, write them on the interactive whiteboard or in the air, and so on.

Activity 7.5

CCSS-M: K.CC.A.3

Number Necklaces

Place a necklace (a card with a yarn string) that has a numeral (use Numeral Cards) on each (you can also show the corresponding amount with objects). Initially, display a number and ask children who are wearing that number to step forward. Now is a good time to show numbers written backwards to highlight how those images do not match anyone in the room. Call out different numbers or show different amounts, and children should either step forward or find a peer with the same amount. This game can progress to calling out a number, and then two children who add to that number pair up or having children separate into groups of odd or even numbers.

MyLab Education   Activity Page: **Numeral Cards**

Activity 7.6

CCSS-M: K.CC.B.4; K.CC.B.5

Number Tubs

Give each child four to six closed margarine tubs, each containing a different number of pennies or counters. Ask the child to find a tub with a particular number of counters. First, they can estimate. Then after the child looks inside and counts to find the correct tub, add a new twist. Allow the child to label the tubs with sticky notes to show the amount inside. At first, the child may make four dots to represent four counters, but eventually, with encouragement, the numeral can be written. Discuss the value of writing the numbers in a form that all can understand and that helps avoid recounting.

Activity 7.7

CCSS-M K.CC.B.4c; K.CC.A.2

Line Them Up!

STUDENTS
with
SPECIAL NEEDS

Use painters' tape on the floor or a clothesline as a number line and print the Numeral Cards or use the sequence of numbers you want the children to investigate (such as 0 through 20). Mix the cards and place them face down in a pile. Ask a child to take the top card from the pile and place/attach the card on the number line in the appropriate position. Have a second child take the next card off the pile and so on. As children place their numeral cards, ask, "How did you know where to place your number?" "Is your number before or after . . . " and "Does your number go on the left or the right of . . . ?" Continue placing the cards until all the cards are correctly positioned on the number line in the conventional sequence. Have the children read the sequence forward as well as backward and discuss the need for even units on the number line. You can modify this activity by using smaller sets of easier numbers, longer sequences of larger numbers, placing the numbers out of sequence or improperly spaced or by using number sequences that start at a number other than zero or one. Also, try the Line 'Em Up! Activity Page to order any ten numbers of your choice.

MyLab Education   Activity Page: **Numeral Cards**
MyLab Education   Activity Page: **Line 'Em Up!**

Common preK and kindergarten exercises have children match sets of objects with numerals. Children are given pictured sets (e.g., frogs) and asked to write or match the number that tells how many. Alternatively, they may be given a number and told to make a set with that many objects. The NCTM Illuminations website offers activities in the "Let's Count to 5" unit, such as Focus on Two, Three in a Set, and Finding Four, where children make sets (0–5 objects) and connect number words or numerals to the sets. Songs, rhymes, and activities that appeal to visual, auditory, and kinesthetic learners are included. Also, try the Button Counts Activity Page where children can roll a die and place buttons on a shirt. When children are successful with these matching-numeral-to-sets activities, it is time to move on to more advanced concepts, such as counting on and counting back.

MyLab Education   Activity Page: **Button Counts**

Counting On and Counting Back

Counting on is the ability to start counting from a given number other than one and it is considered a landmark on a child's path to number sense (Fosnot & Dolk, 2001). For example, if a child is given a group of five cubes and then given two more and asked how many in all, if the child does not recount the five cubes but just uses the counting sequence and states six, seven, they are counting on. Counting on from a particular number and counting back are often difficult skills. In particular, for English learners, counting back is more difficult (try counting back in a second language you have learned). A strategy is to allow students to bob their head as they must keep track of several things: the counting sequence, the number they are starting at and how many they need to count beyond that number (Betts, 2015). Because this "double-counting" process (Voutsina, 2016) is not easily kept in working memory, teachers can model the actions and use a *think-aloud* to orally share their thinking as they pull these multiple components together.

Eventually, first-graders should be able to start from any number less than 120 and count on from there (NGA Center & CCSSO, 2010). Children will later realize that counting on is adding and counting back is subtracting. Frequent use of Activities 7.7, 7.8, and 7.9 is recommended.

Activity 7.8   CCSS-M: K.CC.A.2; K.CC.B.5

Counting On with Counters

Have children set 10 or 12 counters lined up left to right on their desk. Tell them to count four counters and push them under their left hands or place them out of sight in a cup (see Figure 7.5). Then, pointing to the hidden counters in the hand or cup, ask "How many are there?" (Four.) "So, let's count like this: fooour . . . (pronouncing the first number slowly and pointing to their hand), five, six . . . ." Repeat with other numbers of hidden counters.

Activity 7.9   CCSS-M: K.OA.A.1; 1.OA.B.5

Real Counting On

This game for two requires a deck of cards (numbers 1 to 7), a die, a paper cup, and counters. The first player turns over a number card and places the indicated number of counters in the cup. Place the card next to the cup as a reminder of how many are inside. The second player rolls the die and places that many counters next to the cup (see Figure 7.6). Together they decide how many counters in all. Give children the Real Counting on Recording Sheet with columns for "In the Cup," "On the Side," and "In All" to support their organization. Increase to higher numbers when children master the smaller numbers. For children with disabilities, keep the number of counters in the cup constant (such as 5) and have them count on from that number until they are fluent. Then move on to the full game.

STUDENTS with SPECIAL NEEDS

MyLab Education   Activity Page: Real Counting on Recording Sheet

---

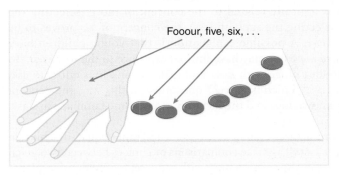

FIGURE 7.5   Counting on: "Hide four. Count, starting from the number of hidden counters."

FIGURE 7.6   How many in all? How do children count to tell the total?

Observe how children determine the total amounts in Activity 7.9. Children who are not yet counting on may empty the counters from the cup or will count up from one without emptying the counters. As children continue to play, they will eventually use counting on as that strategy becomes meaningful and useful.

Activity 7.10   CCSS-M: K.CC.B.4.A

Counting Moose Tracks

Before this activity, read *Moose Tracks!* (Wilson, 2006) a delightful story about a moose that thinks someone has been in his house because of all the footprints he keeps finding. In the end, he is the one creating all the footprints! Give pairs of children a Moose Tracks Game Board, one die, and two game pieces, such as different colored centimeter cubes. Children take turns rolling the die and moving their game piece along the game board. Play continues until both children have traveled the length of their tracks. Because the board has separate spaces for each "moose track," children work on one-to-one correspondence as they move their game piece along the path on the board.

Alternatively, rather than moving one game piece along the board, have children place the number of centimeter cubes along their track that corresponds to the number on the die. For example, if the child rolls a 4, he places 4 cubes along his track in 4 separate spaces on his gameboard. For his next turn, he places 3 cubes for a 3 on the die. By using several of the cubes, as opposed to moving just one cube along the board, the child has a visual record of the one-to-one correspondence as they use numbers in the counting sequence.

MyLab Education   Activity Page: Moose Tracks Game Board

Board games have been shown to support students from low SES in expanding their ability to sense the size or magnitude of numbers which expands their early numerical developing (Siegler, 2010).

MyLab Education   Self-Check 7.2

The Relations Core: More Than, Less Than, and Equal To

The concepts of "more," "less," and "same" are basic relationships contributing to children's overall understanding of number. Almost any kindergartener can choose the set that is *more* if presented with two sets that are obviously different in number. In fact, Baroody (1987) states, "A child unable to use 'more' in this intuitive manner is at considerable educational risk" (p. 29). Classroom activities should help children build on and refine this basic notion.

Though the concept of less is logically related to the concept of more (selecting the set with more is the same as *not* selecting the set with less), the concept of *less* proves to be more difficult for children than *more*. A possible explanation is that young children have many opportunities to use the word *more* but may have limited exposure to the word *less*. To help children, frequently pair the idea of *less* with *more* and make a conscious effort to ask, "Which is less?" questions as well as "Which is more?" questions. In this way, the concept can be connected with the better-known idea and the term *less* can become familiar. Also ask, "Which has fewer?"

For all three relationships (more/greater than, less/less than, and same/equal to), children should construct sets using counters as well as make comparisons or choices between two given sets. Conduct the following activities in a spirit of inquiry with requests for children's explanations, such as "Can you show me how you know this group has less?"

Activity 7.11
CCSS-M: K.CC.C.6

Make Sets of More/Less/Same

Provide about eight cards with pictures of sets of 4 to 12 objects (or use Dot Cards), a set of counters, word cards labeled *More*, *Less*, and *Same* (see the More-Less-Same Activity Page), and paper plates or low boxes that can define the work space, to support children with disabilities. Next to each picture card, have children make three collections of counters: a set that is more than the amount in the picture, one that is less, and one that is the same (see Figure 7.7). Have children who struggle begin by creating a collection of items that matches the picture. For children who are ready to use symbols >, <, = between the quantities, use the Relationship Cards Activity Page.

STUDENTS
with
SPECIAL
NEEDS

MyLab Education   Activity Page: Dot Cards
MyLab Education   Activity Page: More-Less-Same
MyLab Education   Activity Page: Relationship Cards

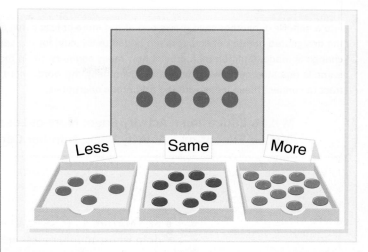

FIGURE 7.7   Making sets that are more, less, and the same.

Activity 7.12
CCSS-M: K.CC.A.3; K.CC.C.6

Find the Same Amount

Give children a collection of cards with pictures of sets on them, such as Dot Cards. Have children pick any card in the collection and then find another card with the same amount to form a pair. Continue finding other pairs. This activity can be altered to have children find dot cards that are "less" or "more." Some children with disabilities may need a set of counters with a blank ten-frame to help them "make" a pair instead of finding a pair.

STUDENTS
with
SPECIAL
NEEDS

MyLab Education   Activity Page: Dot Cards

FIGURE 7.8   Materials to play "More, Less, or the Same."

Activity 7.13
CCSS-M: K.CC.A.3; K.CC.C.6; K.O.A.A.1

More, Less, or the Same

This activity is for partners or a small group. Make four to five sets of the cards from the More-or-Less Cards and two sets of Number Cards (see Figure 7.8). To play, one child draws a number card, places it face-up, and puts that number of counters into a cup. Next, another child draws one of the more-or-less cards and places it next to the number card. For the More cards, the designated number of counters are added to the cup; for the Less cards, counters are removed; and, for Zero cards, no change is made. Children then predict how many counters are in the cup. The counters are emptied and counted and then the game is repeated by drawing new cards. Eventually, the words *more* and *less* can be paired or substituted with *add* and *subtract* to connect these ideas with the arithmetic operations.

MyLab Education   **Activity Page: More-or-Less Cards**
MyLab Education   **Activity Page: Number Cards**

 FORMATIVE ASSESSMENT **Notes.** Observe children as they do these activities. Children whose number ideas are completely tied to counting and nothing more will select cards at random and count each dot. Others will begin by estimating and selecting a card that appears to have about the same number of dots. This performance demonstrates a significantly higher level of understanding. Also, observe how the dots are counted. Are the counts made accurately? Is each dot counted only once? Does the child touch the dot? A significant milestone (subitizing) occurs when children recognize small patterned sets without counting. ■

Developing Number Sense by Building Number Relationships

Howden (1989) described *number sense* as a "good intuition about numbers and their relationships. It develops gradually as a result of exploring numbers, visualizing them in a variety of contexts, and relating them in ways that are not limited by traditional algorithms" (p. 11). *Principles and Standards for School Mathematics* suggests that the ability to think flexibly about numbers including various ways to represent and use numbers is an indication of number sense.

❚❚ Pause & Reflect

You already have seen some of the early foundational ideas about number. Stop now and make a list of all of the important ideas that you think children should *know about* the number 8. Put your list aside, and we will revisit your ideas later. ●

The discussion of number sense begins as we look at the relationships and connections children should make about numbers up to 20. But "good intuition about numbers" does not end with these smaller whole numbers. Children continue to develop number sense competencies as they use numbers in operations, build place-value understanding, and devise flexible methods of computing and making estimates involving large numbers.

Relationships between Numbers 1 through 10

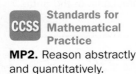
Standards for Mathematical Practice
MP2. Reason abstractly and quantitatively.

Once children acquire cardinality and can meaningfully use their counting skills, they need to expand their collection of ideas about number sense to develop the knowledge needed to meaningfully work with operations. We want children to move away from counting by ones to solve simple story problems and have the strategies for mastering basic facts by emphasizing the development of number relationships such as those in Figure 7.9:

- *One and two more, one and two less.* The two-more-than and two-less-than relationships involve more than just the ability to count on two or count back two. Children should know that 7, for example, is 1 more than 6 and 2 less than 9.

- *Benchmarks numbers of 5 and 10.* Because the number 10 plays such a large role in our numeration system and because two fives equals 10, it is very useful to develop relationships for the numbers 1 to 10 connected to the benchmarks of 5 and 10.
- *Part-part-whole relationships.* To conceptualize a number as being composed of two or more parts is the most important relationship that can be developed about numbers. For example, 7 can be thought of as a set of 3 and a set of 4 or a set of 2 and a set of 5.

The principal tool young children will use as they construct these relationships is the one number tool they possess: counting. Initially, you will notice a lot of counting by ones, and you may wonder if you are making progress. Have patience! As children construct new relationships and begin to use more powerful ideas, counting by ones will become less and less necessary.

One and Two More; One and Two Less. When children count, they don't automatically think about the way one number is related to another. Their goal is only to match number words with objects until they reach the end of the count. To learn that 6 and 8 are related by the corresponding relationships of "two more than" and "two less than" requires reflection on these ideas. Counting on (or back) one or two counts is a useful tool in constructing these ideas. Begin with Activity 7.14, which focuses on the two-more-than relationship.

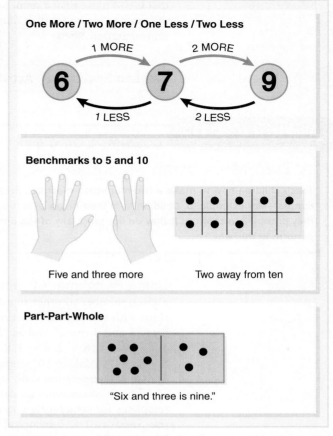

FIGURE 7.9   Three number relationships for children to develop.

Excerpt from *Principles and Standards* reprinted by permission of the National Council of Teachers of Mathematics. Copyright 2000.

Activity 7.14   CCSS-M: K.OA.A.2; 1.OA.C.5

Make a Two-More-Than Set

Provide children with six Dot Cards. For each card, children should display a set of counters that is two more than the set shown on the card. Similarly, spread out eight to ten dot cards, and for each card, find a card that is two less than it. (Omit the 1 and 2 cards for two less than, and so on.) Also, see the Expanded Lesson Two More Than/Two Less Than and the Two More Than and Two Less Than Activity Pages.

MyLab Education	Activity Page: Dot Cards
MyLab Education	Activity Page: Two More Than and Two Less Than
MyLab Education	Expanded Lesson: Two More Than/Two Less Than

In activities where children find a set or make a set, they can also select the matching Number Cards that identify the quantity in the set. Children can be encouraged to take turns reading the associated number sentence to their partner. If, for example, a set has been made that is two more than a set of four, the child can say, "Two more than four equals six" or "Six is the same as two more than four." The next activity combines the relationships into a symbolic representation.

> **MyLab Education**   Activity Page: **Number Cards**

Activity 7.15

CCSS-M: 1.OA.C.5

A Two-More-Than Machine

Teach children how to make a two-more-than machine. Press 0 $\boxed{+}$ 2 $\boxed{=}$ on a calculator. Now have them press any number—for example, 5. Children hold their finger over the $\boxed{=}$ key and predict the number that is two more than 5. Then they press $\boxed{=}$ to confirm. If they do not press any of the operation keys ($\boxed{+}$, $\boxed{-}$, $\boxed{\times}$, $\boxed{\div}$), the "machine" will continue to perform in this way.

Using Benchmark Numbers 5 and 10. Here again, we want to help children relate a given number to other numbers, specifically 5 and 10 to support thinking about relationships with various combinations of numbers. For example, consider how the knowledge of 8 as "5 and 3 more" and as "2 away from 10" can play a role in how a child thinks about $5 + 3, 8 + 6, 8 - 2, 8 - 3, 8 - 4$, and $13 - 8$. For example, $8 + 6$ may be thought of as $8 + 2 + 4$ ("Making 10" strategy). Later, similar relationships can be used in the development of mental computation skills with larger numbers, such as $68 + 7$.

The most common models for exploring the *benchmark* numbers 5 and 10 (and effective templates for structuring counting of manipulatives) are Five-Frames and Ten-Frames. The *five-frame* is a 1×5 array and the *ten-frame* is simply a 2×5 array, both positioned horizontally, in which counters or dots are placed to illustrate numbers (see Figure 7.10).

> **MyLab Education**   Blackline Master: **Five-Frames**
>
> **MyLab Education**   Blackline Master: **Ten-Frames**

CCSS Standards for Mathematical Practice

MP3. Construct viable arguments and critique the reasoning of others.

For preK or kindergarten children who have not yet explored a ten-frame, it is a good idea to begin with a five-frame. Provide about 10 counters that will fit in the five-frame sections and try Activity 7.16.

Activity 7.16

CCSS-M: K.CC.C.7; K.OA.A.5

Five-Frame Tell-About

Explain that only one counter is permitted in each section of the Five-Frame. Have children show three on their five-frame, as seen in Figure 7.11(a). "What can you tell us about 3 from looking at your five-frame?" After hearing from several children, try other numbers from 0 to 5. Children may initially place their counters on the five-frame in any manner. For example, with four counters, a child may place two on each end and say, "It has a space in the middle" or "It's two and two." There are no wrong answers with the initial placements. Focus attention on how many more counters are needed to make five. Next, try numbers between 5 and 10. As shown in Figure 7.11(b), numbers greater than 5 are shown with a full five-frame plus additional counters on the mat but not in the frame. In discussion, focus attention on these larger numbers as 5 and some more: "Seven is the same as five and two more."

> **MyLab Education**   Blackline Master: **Five-Frame**

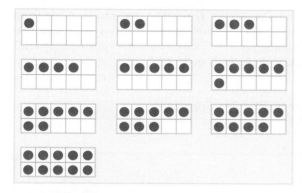

FIGURE 7.10   Ten-frames.

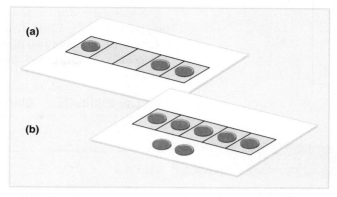

FIGURE 7.11   A five-frame focuses on five as the benchmark.

When five-frames have been used for a week or so, consider introducing ten-frames. Play a ten-frame version of a "Five-Frame Tell-About," but soon introduce the following convention for showing numbers on the ten-frame: Always fill the top row first, starting on the left, the same way you read. When the top row is full, place counters in the bottom row, also from left to right. This approach will provide structure for seeing a full row in the ten-frame as five without counting, as in Figure 7.10. At first, children may continue to count every counter by ones. But then ask questions such as "What are you looking at in the ten-frame to help you find how many?" and "How does knowing you have a full row help you find how many you have?"

 **Standards for Mathematical Practice**
MP7. Look for and make use of structure.

Move children to a problem-solving situation by having them create different numbers, as suggested in Activity 7.17.

Activity 7.17   CCSS-M: K.CC.C.6; K.CC.C.7

Number Medley

ENGLISH LEARNERS

Begin by having all children make the same number on their Ten-Frame. Then call out or hold up random numbers between 0 and 10. After each number, the children change their ten-frames to show the new number. Ask, "How do you decide to change your ten-frame?" If working with ELs, consider saying the number in their native language or writing the number. Children can play this game independently by using a prepared list of about 15 random numbers. One child plays "teacher" and the rest use the ten-frames.

MyLab Education   **Blackline Master: Ten-Frame**

How children use the ten-frame can provide you with insights into children's number concept development; therefore, activities like this one can be used as a diagnostic interview. Observe that some children doing Activity 7.17 will take all counters off and begin each new number from a blank frame. Others will have learned what each number looks like. And others will soon learn to adjust numbers by adding on or taking off only what is required, often subitizing a row of five. These strategies of moving from one number to another number more efficiently need to come from the children. Look for opportunities to draw children's attention to how others are making these changes by having children share strategies. To add another dimension to the activity, have the children tell, *before* changing their ten-frames, how many more counters need to be added (addition) or removed (subtraction). For example, if the frame showed 6, and the teacher called out "4," the children would respond, "Subtract two!" and then change their ten-frames accordingly. A discussion of how they know what to do is valuable.

Small ten-frame cards are an important variation of ten-frames and can be made from cardstock. Use the Little Ten- Frames Activity Page, with a set of 20 cards that consists of a 0 card, a 10 card, and two of each of the numbers 1 to 9. The cards allow for simple practice activities to reinforce the 5 and 10 as benchmarks, as in Activity 7.18.

> **MyLab Education**   Blackline Master: Little Ten-Frames

Activity 7.18   CCSS-M: K.CC.B.5

ENGLISH LEARNERS

Ten-Frame Flash

Flash Little Ten-Frame Cards to the class or a small group and see how quickly the children can tell how many dots are shown. This activity is fast-paced, takes only a few minutes, can be done at any time, and is highly engaging. For ELs, producing the English word for the number may take more time, so either make pairs with similar language skills, or encourage children to use their preferred language.

> **MyLab Education**   Activity Page: Little Ten-Frame Cards

Important variations of "Ten-Frame Flash" include:

CCSS Standards for Mathematical Practice

MP7. Look for and make use of structure.

- Saying the number of empty spaces on the card instead of the number of dots
- Saying one more than the number of dots (or two more, one less, or two less/fewer)
- Saying the "10 fact"—for example, "Six and four equals ten"
- Saying the sum by adding the flashed card to a card they have at their desk

Ten-frame tasks are surprisingly challenging for children, as there is a lot to keep in their working memory. Children must reflect on the two rows of five, the empty spaces, how a particular number is more or less than 5 and how far away it is from 10.

> **MyLab Education**   Video Example 7.2
>
> Watch this video on working memory to see how much young children have to keep all of these ideas in their working memory.

How well children can respond to "Ten-Frame Flash" is a quick diagnostic assessment of their current number concept level. Because the distance to 10 is so important, another assessment is to point to a numeral less than 10 and ask, "If this many dots were on a ten-frame, how many empty spaces would there be?" Or, you can also simply ask, "If I have seven, how many more do I need to equal ten?" There are virtual activities with five-frames and ten-frames on the NCTM Illuminations webpage with associated games that develop counting and basic computation skills. These activities can be used with individual learners as there is a voice-over option that will ask children questions about the tasks.

> **MyLab Education**   Video Example 7.3
>
> Watch this video to see how a teacher partners students to explore combinations of ten and some more using a quick flash approach.

❚❚ Pause & Reflect

Before reading on, gather eight counters. Count out the set of counters in front of you as if you were a 4- or 5-year-old. ●

Part-Part-Whole Relationships. Any child who has learned how to count meaningfully can count out eight objects as you just did. What is significant about the experience is what it did *not* cause you to think about. Nothing in counting a set of eight objects will cause a child to focus on the fact that it could be made of two parts. For example, separate the counters you just counted into two piles and reflect on the combination. It might be 2 and 6, 7 and 1, or 4 and 4. Make a change in your two piles of counters and say the new combination to yourself. Focusing on a quantity in terms of its parts (*decomposing numbers*) has important implications for developing number sense. Of the three number relationships (Figure 7.9), *part-whole* ideas are easily the most important, and the ability to think about numbers in terms of the *part-part-whole* relationship is a major milestone in the development of number sense.

Most part-part-whole activities focus on a single number for the entire activity. For example, a pair of children might work on breaking apart or building the number 7 throughout the activity. They can either build (*compose*) the designated quantity in two or more parts, or else they start with the full amount and separate it into two or more parts (*decompose*). This situation is known as a "both addends unknown" problem which should be developed in kindergarten possibly starting by working on the number 4 or 5. As concepts develop, children extend to numbers 6 to 12.

When children do these activities, have them say or "read" the parts aloud and then write them down on some form of recording sheet (or do both). Reading and writing the combinations serve as a means of encouraging reflective thought focused on the part-part-whole relationship. Writing can be in the form of drawings, numbers written in blanks (a group of _____ cubes and a group of _____ cubes), or addition equations ($3 + 5 = 8$ or $8 = 2 + 6$). There is a clear connection between part-part-whole concepts and addition and subtraction ideas.

Activity 7.19 and its variations may be considered the "basic" part-part-whole task.

Activity 7.19   CCSS-M: K.OA.A.3; 1.OA.C.6

Build It in Parts

ENGLISH LEARNERS

Provide children with one type of material in different colors, such as connecting cubes or squares of colored paper. Ask children, "How many different combinations for a particular number can you make using two parts?" (If you wish, you can allow for more than two parts.) Use a familiar every day context, or consider a situation from a piece of children's literature. For example, ask how many different combinations of six hats the peddler in the picture book *Caps for Sale* (Slobodkina, 1938) can wear, limiting the color choices to two and keeping the colors clustered together (i.e., 3 red and 3 blue caps, 4 red and 2 blue, etc.). (Note that the book is also available in Spanish for some ELs) Each different combination can be displayed on a small mat. Here are just a few ideas, each of which is illustrated in Figure 7.12.

- Use two counters, such as lima beans spray-painted on one side (available commercially in plastic).
- Make two different colored bars of connecting cubes. Keep the same colors together on the bar.
- Make combinations of two Dot Strips.
- Make combinations of Two-Column Cards. All pieces except the single squares are cut from two columns of the cardstock.
- Make combinations of two Cuisenaire rods connected as a train to match a given amount.
- Use beads on a pipe cleaner or use an arithmetic rack that has 10 beads in two rows.

MyLab Education   Blackline Master: Dot Strips
MyLab Education   Blackline Master: Two-Column Cards

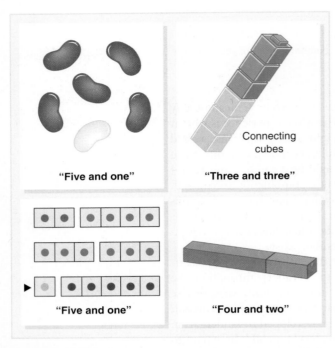

FIGURE 7.12 Assorted materials for building parts of six.

As you observe children working on the "Build It in Parts" activity, ask them to "read" a number sentence that matches the representation to their partner. Two or three children working together may have quite a large number of combinations, including repeats. Encourage them to look for patterns by asking, "Do you have all possible combinations? How do you know?"

Missing-Part Activities. An important variation of part-part-whole activities is referred to as *missing-part* activities. In a missing-part activity, children are given the whole amount and part of the whole. They then use their already developed knowledge of the part-part-whole relationship to tell what the covered or hidden part is. If they are unsure, they simply uncover the unknown part and say the full combination. Missing-part activities can be challenging because the missing part increases the difficulty level because they encourage children to reflect on the combinations for a number. They also serve as the forerunner to subtraction. With a whole amount of 8 but with only 3 showing, the child can later learn to say and write "8 − 3 = 5."

The next three activities illustrate variations of this important idea of a missing part. For any of these activities, you can use a context from familiar classroom events or from a children's book, such as the disappearing treats in *Pete the Cat and the Missing Cupcakes* (Dean & Dean, 2016).

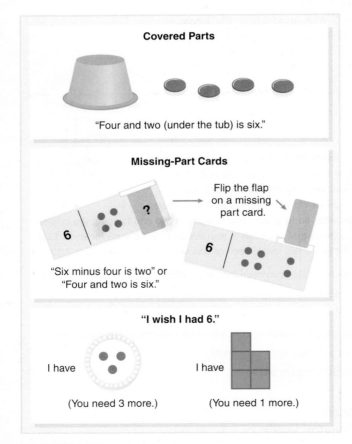

FIGURE 7.13 Missing part activities.

Activity 7.20 CCSS-M: K.OA.A.2

Covered Parts

A set of counters equal to the target amount is counted out, and the rest are put aside. One child places the counters under a margarine tub or piece of cardstock. The child then pulls some counters out into view. (This amount could be none, all, or any amount in between.) For example, if 6 is the whole and 4 are showing, the other child says, "Four and *two* equals six." If there is hesitation or if the hidden part is unknown, the hidden part is immediately shown (see Figure 7.13).

Activity 7.21 CCSS-M: K.OA.A.4

Missing-Part Cards

For each number from 4 to 10, make Missing-Part Cards. Each card has a numeral for the whole and two dot sets with one set covered by a flap. For the number 8, you need nine cards with the visible part ranging from 0 to 8 dots. Children use the cards as in "Covered Parts," saying, "Four and two equals six" for a card showing 6, four dots showing and two dots hiding under the flap.

MyLab Education   **Activity Page: Missing-Part Cards**

Activity 7.22   CCSS-M: K.OA.A.1; K.OA.A.2

STUDENTS
with
SPECIAL
NEEDS

I Wish I Had

Hold out a bar of connecting cubes, a Dot Strip, a dot plate or a Two-Column Cards, showing six or less and say, "I wish I had six." The children respond with the part that is needed to equal 6. Counting on can be used to check. The game can focus on a single number (especially as a starting point for children with disabilities), or the "I wish I had" number can change each time (see Figure 7.13). Consider adding a familiar context, like "I wish I had six books to read." See the corresponding Expanded Lesson: I Wish I Had.

MyLab Education   **Blackline Master: Dot Strip**
MyLab Education   **Blackline Master: Two-Column Cards**
MyLab Education   **Expanded Lesson: I Wish I Had**

TECHNOLOGY Note. There are lots of ways you can use online tools to create part-part-whole activities. All that is needed is a program that permits children to create sets of objects on the screen. Look at Pearson's Tools4Math (http://www.pearsonsuccessnet.com/snp_swf/tools/math/en/player.html) and choose "Counters." Children can stamp different counters. The tabulator shows how many in word or numeral form. This program offers an opportunity to solve problems involving part-part-whole and missing-part situations. ∎

❚❚ Pause & Reflect

Remember the list you made previously about what children should know about the number 8? Let's refer to it and see if you would add to it or revise it based on what you have read to this point. Look at the list before reading on. ●

Here is a possible list of the kinds of things that children should learn about the number 8 (or any number up to about 20) while they are in preK and kindergarten:

- Count to 8 (know the number words and their sequence)
- Count 8 objects and know that the last number word tells how many
- Recognize, read, and write the numeral 8 and pair it with an accurate amount of objects or units
- State more and less by 1 and 2—8 is one more than 7, one less than 9, two more than 6, and two less than 10
- Recognize *patterned sets* for 8 such as

- Relate to the *benchmark numbers* of 5 and 10: 8 is 3 more than 5 and 2 away from 10
- State part-part-whole relationships: 8 is the same 5 and 3, 2 and 6, 7 and 1, and so on (including knowing the missing part of 8 when some quantities are hidden)
- Identify doubles: double 4 equals 8
- State relationships to the real world: my brother is 8 years old; my reading book is 8 inches wide

Then extend these ideas to numbers beyond ten and further refine children's understanding of number.

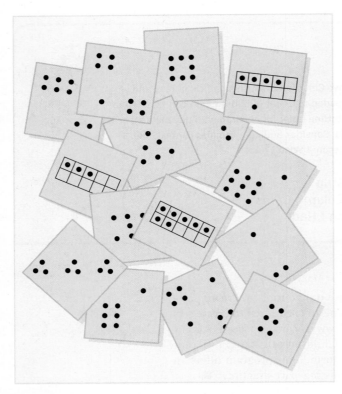

FIGURE 7.14 Dot cards.

As children learn about ten-frames, patterned sets, and other relationships, the Dot Cards provide a wealth of activities (see Figure 7.14) and help them think flexibly about numbers. The full set of cards contains dot patterns, patterns that require counting, combinations of two and three simple patterns, and ten-frames with "standard" as well as unusual dot placements. These dot cards add another dimension to many of the previous activities and can be used effectively in Activities 7.23, 7.24, and 7.25.

MyLab Education   Activity Page: Dot Cards

Activity 7.23   CCSS-M: K.CC.C.6

Double War

The game of "Double War" (Kamii, 1985) is played like the War card game, but on each play, both players turn up two Dot Cards instead of one. The winner is the player with the larger total number. Children can and should use many different number relationships to determine the winner without actually finding the total number of dots. A modification of this activity for children with disabilities would have the teacher (or another child) do a "think-aloud" and describe her thinking about the dots using relationships as she figures who wins the round. This modeling is critical for children who struggle.

MyLab Education   Activity Page: Dot Cards

Activity 7.24   CCSS-M: K.CC.C.6; K.OA.A.2

Difference War

Deal out the Dot Cards to two players, and prepare a collection of about 40 counters. On each play, players turn over one card from the top of the stack. The player with the greater number of dots wins as many counters as the difference between the two cards. Used cards are put aside. The game is over when the cards or counters run out. The player with the most counters wins the game. This game can also be played so the person with "less" wins the number of counters in the difference. Modify the game for children who need a challenge by having them turn two cards, find the sums, and make the comparisons.

MyLab Education   Activity Page: Dot Cards

Activity 7.25   CCSS-M: K.OA.A.2; 1.OA.C.6

Number Sandwiches

Select a number between 5 and 12, and have children find combinations of two Dot Cards that total that number. Children make a sandwich with the two cards by placing them back to back with the dot sides facing out. When they have found at least 10 pairs, the next challenge is for the partner to name the number on the other side. The cards are flipped over to confirm. The same pairs can be used again to name the other hidden part.

MyLab Education   Activity Page: Dot Cards

FORMATIVE ASSESSMENT Notes. To assess part-part-whole relationships, use a missing-part diagnostic interview (similar to Activity 7.20). Begin with a number you believe the child has "mastered," say, 5. Have the children count out that many counters into your open hand. Close your hand around the counters and confirm that the child knows how many are hidden. Then remove some and show them in the open palm of your other hand (see Figure 7.15). Ask the child, "How many are hidden?" "How do you know?" Repeat with different amounts removed, trying three or four missing parts for each number. If the child responds quickly and correctly and is clearly not counting in any way, call that a "mastered number" and check it off on the child's assessment record. Repeat the process with the next higher number. Continue until the child begins to struggle. In early kindergarten, you will find a range of mastered numbers from 4 to 8. By the end of kindergarten, children should master numbers through 10 (NGA Center & CCSSO, 2010). ■

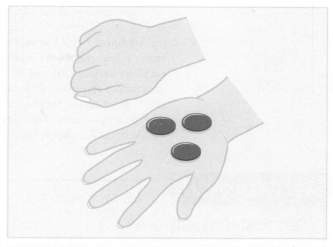

FIGURE 7.15 A missing-part assessment. "There are eight in all. How many are hidden?"

Relationships for Numbers 10 through 20 and Beyond

Although preK, kindergarten, and first-grade children experience numbers up to 20 and beyond daily, it should not be assumed that they will automatically extend the set of relationships they developed with smaller numbers to numbers beyond 10. And yet these larger numbers play a big part in many counting activities, in basic facts, and in much of what we do with mental computation. In fact, several researchers suggest the movement to number instruction beyond 10 and even beyond 20 as soon as possible sets the stage for developing initial place-value knowledge (Fosnot & Dolk, 2001; Wright, Stranger, Stafford, and Martland, 2006).

Pre–Place-Value Concepts. Recognizing a set of ten plays a major role in children's early understanding of numbers between 10 and 20. When children see a set of six together with a set of ten, they should know without counting that the total is 16. This work with composing and decomposing numbers from 11 through 19 in kindergarten is seen as an essential foundation for place value (NGA Center & CCSSO, 2010).

❚❚ Pause & Reflect

Say to yourself, "One ten." Now think about that idea from the perspective of a child just learning to count to 20! What could "one ten" possibly mean when ten tells me how many fingers I have and is the number that comes after nine? How can it be one of something? ●

Wright and colleagues (2006) outlined a three-level progression of children's understanding of ten:

1. *An initial concept of ten.* The child understands ten as ten ones and does not see the ten as a unit. When children work on a task involving tens, they will count by ones.
2. *An intermediate concept of ten.* The child understands ten as a unit composed of ten ones but relies on materials or representations to help complete tasks involving tens.
3. *A facile concept of ten.* The child solves tasks involving tens and ones without using materials or representations. Children mentally think about two-digit numbers as groups of tens and ones.

First-graders should know that "10 can be thought of as a bundle of ten ones—called a 'ten'" (NGA Center & CCSSO, 2010, p. 15). The difficulty in children discussing "one ten and six ones" (what's a one?) does not mean that a set of ten should not figure prominently in the discussion of the teen numbers. Initially, children do not see a numeric pattern in the numbers between 10 and 20. Rather, these number names are simply ten additional words in the number sequence. In some languages, the teens are actually stated as 10 and 1, 10 and 2, 10 and 3. But because this logical pattern is not the case in English, for many children, the teens provide a significant challenge.

Activity 7.26 helps children visualize the idea of ten and "some more."

Activity 7.26   CCSS-M: K.NBT.A.1

Ten and Some More

Use a simple two-part mat and a story that links to whatever counters you are using. Then have children count out ten coffee stirrers onto the left side of the mat. Next, have them put five stirrers on the other side. Together, count all of the stirrers by ones. Chorus the combination: "Ten and five equals fifteen." Turn the mat around: "Five and ten equals fifteen." Repeat with other numbers in a random order, but then always keep 10 on the left side of the mat. After playing the game for a while, bundle the 10 stirrers with a rubber band.

Following this activity, explore numbers through 20 in a more open-ended manner. Provide each child with a Double Ten-Frame mat. In random order, have children show numbers up to 20 on the frames and have them discuss how counters can be arranged on the mat so that it is easy to see how many are there. At first, not every child will create a full set of 10, but as this idea becomes more popular, they will develop the notion that teens are 10 and some more. Then challenge children to find ways to show 26 counters or even more.

MyLab Education   **Blackline Master: Double Ten-Frame**

Extending More-Than and Less-Than Relationships. The relationships of one more than, two more than, one less than, and two less than are important for all numbers and are built from children's knowledge of the same concepts for numbers less than 10. The fact that 17 is one less than 18 is connected to the idea that 7 is one less than 8. Children may need explicit support in making this connection.

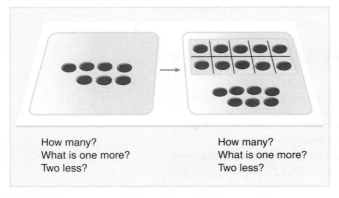

How many?
What is one more?
Two less?

How many?
What is one more?
Two less?

FIGURE 7.16 Extending relationships to the teens.

Activity 7.27   CCSS-M: K.CC.C.6; K.NBT.A.1

More and Less Extended

Project an image of seven counters and ask what is two more, or one less, and so on. Now add a filled ten-frame to the display (or 10 in any pattern) and repeat the questions. Pair up questions by covering and uncovering the ten-frame as in Figure 7.16.

Numbers to 100: Early Introductions. By the end of the school year, kindergartners are expected to be able to count to 100 (NGA Center & CCSSO, 2010). Therefore, early exposure to numbers to 100 is important. Although it is unlikely that children in kindergarten or first grade will initially have a facile understanding of tens and ones related to place value, they should learn much about the sequence of numbers and the counting patterns to 100, if not beyond.

The Hundreds Chart (Figure 7.17) is an essential tool for every K–2 classroom. A useful version of the chart is made of transparent pockets into which each of the 100 numeral cards can be inserted. You can hide a number by inserting a blank card in front of a number in the pocket. You can insert colored pieces of paper in the slots to highlight various number patterns. And you can remove some or all of the number cards and have children replace them in their correct location (see Chapter 10 for more ideas and activities). A digital version of a hundreds chart called "One Hundred Boxes" can be found at Fuel the Brain (http://www.fuelthebrain.com). Random expressions are generated and students must find the correct box to color. A variety of boards chosen at random or the student can specify.

1	2	3	4	5	6	7	8	9	10
11	12	13	14	15	16	17	18	19	20
21	22	23	24	25	26	27	28	29	30
31	32	33	34	35	36	37	38	39	40
41	42	43	44	45	46	47	48	49	50
51	52	53	54	55	56	57	58	59	60
61	62	63	64	65	66	67	68	69	70
71	72	73	74	75	76	77	78	79	80
81	82	83	84	85	86	87	88	89	90
91	92	93	94	95	96	97	98	99	100

FIGURE 7.17   A hundreds chart.

MyLab Education   **Blackline Master: Hundreds Chart**

FORMATIVE ASSESSMENT Notes. Replacing the number cards from a Blank Hundreds Chart is a good learning center activity for two children. By listening to how they go about finding the correct locations for numbers, you can learn a lot about how well they have constructed an understanding of the 1-to-100 sequence. ■

MyLab Education   **Blackline Master: Blank Hundreds Chart**
MyLab Education   **Self-Check 7.3**

Number Sense in Their World

Here we examine ways to broaden early knowledge of numbers. Relationships of numbers to real-world quantities and measures and the use of numbers in simple estimations can help children develop flexible, intuitive ideas about numbers.

Calendar Activities

Although 90 percent of the classrooms surveyed in a study reported using calendar-related activities (Hamre, Downer, Kilday, & McGuire, 2008), these activities are not considered the kind of mathematics instruction that will support young learners in reaching mathematical literacy. The NRC Committee (2009) stated that "using the calendar does not emphasize foundational mathematics" (p. 241). In particular, they say that although the calendar may be helpful in developing a sense of time, it does not align with the need to develop mathematical relationships related to the number 10 because the calendar is based on groups of seven. The NRC concludes, "Doing the calendar is not a substitute for teaching foundational mathematics" (p. 241). Ethridge and King (2005) suggest that children learn to parrot the response for the predictable questions and they didn't always understand some of the concepts presented. Clements, Baroody, and Sarama (2013) suggest avoiding the inappropriate use of the calendar, as it engages only a few children. The key message is that doing calendar math should be thought of as an "add on" and not take time away from essential preK–2 mathematics concepts.

Estimation and Measurement

One of the best ways for children to think of real quantities is to associate numbers with measures of things. Measures of length, weight, and time are good places to begin. Just measuring and recording results will not be very effective unless there is a reason for children to be interested in or think about the result. To help children think about what number might tell how long the desk is or how heavy the book is, it important if they could first write down or tell you an estimate. To produce an estimate is, however, a very difficult task for young children. They do not easily grasp the concept of "estimate" or "about." For example, suppose that you have cut out a set of very large footprints, each about 18 inches long. You would ask, "About how many of the giant's footprints will it take to measure across the rug in our reading corner?" The key word here is *about*, and it is one that you will need to spend a lot of time helping your children understand. To this end, the request of an estimate can be made in ways that help with the concept of "about." For example, the following questions can be used with early estimation activities:

- *More or less than* _____? Will the rug be more or less than 10 footprints long? Will the apple weigh more or less than 20 blocks? Are there more or less than 15 connecting cubes in this long bar?
- *Closer to* _____ *or to* _____? Will the rug be closer to 5 footprints or closer to 20 footprints long? Will the apple weigh closer to 10 blocks or closer to 30 blocks? Does this bar have closer to 10 cubes or closer to 50 cubes?
- *About* _____? (You can even suggest possible numbers as options.) About how many footprints long is the rug? About how many blocks will the apple weigh? About how many cubes are in this bar?

Asking for estimates using these formats helps children learn what you mean by *about*. Every child can make a close estimate with some supportive questions and examples. However, rewarding children for the closest estimate in a competitive fashion will often result in their trying to seek precision and not actually estimate. Instead, discuss all answers that fall into a reasonable range. One of the best approaches is to give children ranges as their possible answers: "Does your estimate fall between 10 and 30? Between 50 and 70? Or 100 and 130?" Of course, you can make the choices more divergent until they grasp the idea.

Here are some activities that can help children connect numbers to real situations.

CCSS **Standards for Mathematical Practice**
MP2. Reason abstractly and quantitatively.

Activity 7.28   CCSS-M: K.MD.A.1

Add a Unit to Your Number

Write a number on the board. Now suggest some units to go with it and ask the children what they can think of that fits. For example, suppose the number is 9. "What do you think of when I say 9 *dollars*? 9 *hours*? 9 *cars*? 9 *kids*? 9 *meters*? 9 *o'clock*? 9 *hand spans*? 9 *gallons*?" Spend time discussing and exploring each unit. Let children suggest other appropriate units. Children from different cultures and ELs may be able to share different units used in their culture.

ENGLISH LEARNERS

Activity 7.29   CCSS-M: K.MD.A.1

Is It Reasonable?

Select a number and a unit—for example, 15 feet. Could the teacher be 15 feet tall? Could a house be 15 feet wide? Can a man jump 15 feet high? Could three children together stretch their arms 15 feet? Pick any number, large or small, and a unit with which children are familiar. Then make up a series of these questions. Also ask, "How can we find out if it is reasonable or not? Who has an idea about what we can do?" When children are familiar with this activity, have them select the number and unit and create the questions.

These activities are problem based in the truest sense. Not only are there no clear answers, but children can easily begin to pose their own questions and explore the numbers and units most interesting to them.

Represent and Interpret Data

Graphing activities are good ways to connect children's worlds with number and relationships. Graphs can be quickly made from any data gathered with children, such as favorites (ice cream flavors, sports teams, pets), number of sisters and brothers, and transportation modes to school. Once children classify and count the number of objects in each category (a kindergarten standard in the CCSS-M), graphs can be used to share the information. Here are some other options for graphs that are linked to children's literature:

- *Chrysanthemum* (Henkes, 2008): create a graph of the length of children's first names (i.e., use categories 3, 4, 5 letters and so on).
- *This Is the Way We Go to School* (Baer, 1990): make a graph of the way children come to school
- *We're Going on a Leaf Hunt* (Metzger, 2008): have children collect a leaf from around their home or around the school, create a graph of different types of leaves.
- *3 Little Firefighters* (Murphy, 2003): use children's career aspirations to make a graph (i.e., sort jobs into public service, entertainment, education, etc.)

In the early stages of number development, the use of graphs is primarily for developing number relationships and for connecting numbers to real quantities in the children's environment. The graphs focus attention on tallies and counts of realistic things. Once a simple bar graph is made, it is very important to take the time to ask questions (e.g., "What do you notice about our class and our ice cream choices?"). Equally important, graphs clearly exhibit comparisons between numbers that are rarely made when only one number or quantity is considered at a time. See Figure 7.18 for an example of a graph and corresponding questions. At first, children may be challenged with questions involving differences, but these comparison concepts add considerably to children's understanding of number.

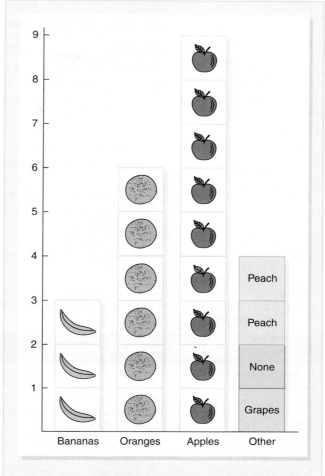

Class graph showing fruit brought for snack. Paper cutouts for bananas, oranges, apples, and cards for "others."

- Which snack (or refer to what the graph represents) is most, least?
- Which are more (less) than 7 (or some other number)?
- Which is one less (more) than this snack (or use fruit name)?
- How much more is _____ than _____ ? (Follow this question immediately by reversing the order and asking how much less.)
- How much less is _____ than _____ ? (Reverse this question after receiving an answer.)
- How much difference is there between _____ and _____ ?
- Which two bars together are the same as _____ ?

FIGURE 7.18   Relationships and number sense in a bar graph.

MyLab Education   Self-Check 7.4

MyLab Education   **Application Exercise 7.1: Number Sense in Their World** Click the link to access this exercise, then watch the video and answer the accompanying questions.

VIDEO EXAMPLE

In Part II of the book, and starting here you will find each chapter contains a table of common challenges and misconceptions (see Table 7.2). We suggest that students acquire these naïve conceptual understandings or "glitches" in how they perform a procedure in a variety of ways including previously taught "rules" that have gone beyond their range of usefulness. Using a constructivist approach, we point out these systematic patterns—not to highlight students' flaws—but as an anticipatory framework to support your knowledge of the potential ideas students might bring to your classroom. Then we offer ways to develop next instructional steps to help in the continuous reconstruction of students' prior knowledge through discussion and further experiences.

TABLE 7.2   COMMON CHALLENGES AND MISCONCEPTIONS ABOUT EARLY NUMBER CONCEPTS AND HOW TO HELP

Common Challenge or Misconception	What It Looks Like	How to Help
1. The child does not know the counting sequence	The child might skip numbers or go out of order saying "one, two, four, nine, three, five. Child may be able to orally count to a certain point (e.g., from 1 to 10) but then uses student generated number words (e.g., ten, one teen, two-teen, three-teen, . . .).	• Use a puppet that makes a variety of counting errors having students correct the mistakes made. • Practice counting together out loud (forward and backward). • Read counting books. • Prepare cards with numerals and have children place them in order on a number line (see Activity 7.7). • Match the written numeral with the written number word.
2. The child counts without using a one-to-one correspondence	Child does not attach one number word to each object. He either double counts, saying two number words for one object or touches more than one object as he says one number word. For example, he may touch two objects as he says two syllable counting words such as "se-ven" or "thir-teen."	• As the child counts objects, have him place one object in each space of an egg carton or ten-frame. • Make a plan for counting: arrange objects in a row, count objects from left to right, touch one object and say each number word out loud, move each object as it is counted across a line on a work mat or place into a bag or box. • If a child splits the count across two-syllable counting words, have the child work on matching the written numeral with the written number word. • Have children use a pointer to touch each object as they count.
3. The child does not count on	Child counts out one set and then when given more objects, recounts the first set, starting back at one. The child when counting on 3 more from 7 counts 1, 2, 3 rather than 8, 9, and 10.	• After child counts out one set and states how many, cover the collection with a sheet of paper or put the collection in a cup. The idea is to remove the objects from sight, forcing the child to create a mental image of the objects. Let the child peek at the hidden collection if needed but, encourage the child to think about how many before peeking. Use Activities 7.8 or 7.9. • Use quick images to work on child's subitizing skills such as in Activities 7.2 or 7.18.
4. The child is confused by perceptual cues such as spacing or size of counters	Child uses a visual cue and think that a smaller set of larger counters is greater than a larger set of smaller counters. Child thinks the top row has more circles because the row is longer. ● ● ● ● ● ○ ○ ○ ○ ○	• Students lack the ability to conserve which develops through more experiences and activities with counting. Pose situations that ask students to use one to one correspondence to "prove" the two amounts are equal. • Use matching to compare sets. For example, stack counters on top of images to match the sets.

Common Challenge or Misconception	What It Looks Like	How to Help
5. Child does not understand the cardinality principle	When asked "How many?" the child recounts all of the objects or points to the last object counted.	• Play board games that have a linear path and instead of moving one marker along the path, leave one counter in each space. For example, if the child rolls a 4 on the die, she places 4 counters, one in each space on the board. Ask, "How many spaces did you travel?" • Provide lots of counting opportunities, followed by asking "How many?" • When counting collections together, say, "1, 2, 3, 4, 5. We have 5 pencils."
6. Child has difficulty counting the "teen" numbers or decade numbers	The child may say one-teen, two-teen and so on The child may say twenty-ten or forty-ten	• Play numerous games with counting or count as children line up to leave the room. Consistent practice will provide familiarity with the "teen" numbers. • Play a game that "crosses the decade" where one child in a pair has the numbers ending in 9 up to 100 such as 29, the other has the decade number such as 30. One student holds up a card the other must find in their set of cards either the number that comes before or after.
7. Child writes the numeral backwards or reverses the digits in the "teen numbers"	The child hears nineteen and writes 91. Writes the following for 3. 	• Use a vertical number line to show the pattern in writing the teen numbers • Give children a sheet of numerals and ask them to circle the numerals that are not written correctly. It is important for students to see counterexamples of numerals written backwards to sort between the visual appearance of correctly written numerals and incorrectly written ones.
8. Child is not sure of the magnitude of numbers from 1–20	Student consistently is unsure or incorrect when asked to show which number is greater than or less than another.	• Use a walk on number line to have the students count the number of units (placing down cardstock pieces of the length as the unit) from the start (or zero) of the number line. Show how the lengths of the two row of units compares.

RESOURCES FOR CHAPTER 7

LITERATURE CONNECTIONS

Children's literature abounds with wonderful counting books and visually stimulating number-related picture books. Have children talk about the mathematics in the story. Begin by talking about the book's birthday (copyright date) and how old the book is. Here are a few ideas for making literature connections to concepts for early learners.

10 Little Hot Dogs

Himmelman (2010)

This predictable-progression counting book highlights 10 dachshund puppies climbing on and off a chair. Children can create their own stories using a mat illustrated with a Chair and move counters representing the puppies on or off. Two children can compare the numbers of dogs on their chairs. Who has more puppies? How many more? How many different ways can you put 6 puppies on the two chairs?

MyLab Education   **Activity Page: Chair Mat**

Pete the Cat and His Four Groovy Buttons

Litwin (2012)

Pete is one cool cat who never gets flustered. He starts with four groovy buttons on his shirt, but one by one they pop off and he ends up with zero—or does he? As he counts down, the numeral is shown, along with the written word and the recording of a related subtraction equation. The story is a perfect lead-in to counting objects and counting backwards. Using a five-frame with buttons can help children model Pete's situation.

RECOMMENDED READINGS

Articles

Dyson, N., Jordan, N., & Hassinger-Das, B. (2015). The story of Kyle. *Teaching Children Mathematics, 21*(6), 354–361.

This useful article presents evidence-based interventions that support children's number sense. Suggestions are shared for interventions developing counting and cardinality as well as for using contexts for thinking about operations.

Books

Dougherty, B., Flores, A., Louis, E., & Sophian, C. (2010). *Developing essential understanding of number and numeration for teaching mathematics in prekindergarten—grade 2.* Reston, VA: NCTM.

This book describes what big mathematical ideas a teacher needs to know about number, how number connects to other mathematical ideas, and how to teach and assess this pivotal topic.

Richardson, K. (2003). *Assessing math concepts: The hiding assessment.* Bellingham, WA: Mathematical Perspectives.

This book is part a series of nine assessment books with diagnostic interviews covering number topics from counting through two-digit numbers. Extensive explanations and examples are provided.

CHAPTER 8

Developing Meanings for the Operations

LEARNER OUTCOMES

After reading this chapter and engaging in the embedded activities and reflections, you should be able to:

8.1 Demonstrate how to develop children's skills in generalizing the problem structures with additive situations involving joining, separating, part-part-whole, and comparison where the unknown can be in any position.

8.2 Explain how students can apply the properties of the operations as strategies to either add, or subtract.

8.3 Demonstrate how to develop children's skills in generalizing the problem structures with multiplicative situations involving equal groups, comparison, area, and arrays where the unknown can be in any position.

8.4 Explain how students can apply the properties of the operations as strategies to either multiply, or divide.

8.5 Describe strategies for teaching students how to solve contextual problems.

Helping students learn to connect different meanings, interpretations, and relationships to the four operations of addition, subtraction, multiplication, and division can assist them in accurately and fluently applying these operations in real-world settings. This is the goal of this chapter—in which students learn to see mathematical situations in their day-to-day lives or in story problems and begin to make models of these situations in words, pictures, models, and/or numbers (e.g. equations). The Operations Core builds and expands on the National Research Council's (NRC, 2009) Number Core and Relations Core discussed in Chapter 7 and will be extended in the discussion of place value in Chapter 10. As children learn to connect the big ideas listed below, they can and should simultaneously be developing more sophisticated ideas about number, recognizing ways to think about basic fact combinations, and accurately and fluently applying these operations in real-world situations. This reasoning develops *operation sense*.

In the *Common Core State Standards* (NGA Center & CCSSO, 2010), children in K–2 are expected to be able to think about addition and subtraction situations that involve adding to, taking from, putting together, and taking apart using increasingly sophisticated strategies. In second grade, solving compare situations is added to the expectations as is the exploration of multiplication as equal groups, using rectangular arrays to model problems. In third grade, students solve problems (including two-step problems) using all four operations and they develop an understanding of the relationship between multiplication and division including applying the properties of multiplication. In fourth grade, students expand the interpretation of multiplicative situations as a comparison with a reference unit, continue to solve multistep word problems, interpret remainders and learn the algorithm for adding and subtracting multi-digit numbers. In fifth grade, students are expected to perform fluently with all operations using multi-digit whole numbers using strategies that consider place value and the application of the properties of the operations as well as the algorithm for multiplication.

BIG IDEAS

◆ Addition and subtraction are connected. Addition names the whole in terms of the parts, and subtraction names a missing part.

◆ Multiplication involves counting groups of equal size and determining how many are in all (multiplicative thinking) or using a reference set as a unit in a multiplicative comparison.

◆ Multiplication and division are related. Division names a missing factor in terms of the known factor and the product.

◆ Models can be used to solve contextual problems for all operations and to figure out what operation is involved in a problem regardless of the size of the numbers. Models also can be used to give meaning to number sentences. Representing contextual situations with equations is at the heart of algebraic thinking.

Developing Addition and Subtraction Operation Sense

Contextual problems are the primary teaching tool that you should use to help children activate problem-solving strategies (Jong & Magruder, 2014; Schwartz, 2013) and gain a rich understanding of the operations. What might a good lesson that is built around contextual problems look like? The answer comes more easily if you think about children not just solving the problems but also using multiple representations to explain how they went about solving the problem; why they think they are correct; and how it makes sense within the context the situation. If they are recording their ideas on paper, whatever they put on their paper, whether a written explanation or a drawing they used to help them solve the problem, it should explain what they did well enough to allow someone else to understand it. With the emphasis on children explaining their ideas and reasoning, lessons should focus on two or three problems and the related discussions of strategies.

From an adult's perspective, the ideas of addition and subtraction seem quite simple. For example, think about how you would solve the following problem.

Standards for Mathematical Practice

MP2. Reason abstractly and quantitatively.

Zoe had 7 beads. After she bought some more beads, she had 15 beads. How many beads did Zoe buy?

Most adults and older students solve this problem by subtracting 15 − 7. But young children do not initially view this situation as subtraction because 15 − 7 is the "opposite" operation or action implied in the problem. Instead, they will model the action in the problem solving it by adding on or counting up from 7 to 15. Their approach may seem less efficient than simply subtracting, but it makes sense to young children because it mirrors the situation in the problem.

MyLab Education   **Video Example 8.1**

Watch Arriel solve a similar problem by counting on.

VIDEO EXAMPLE

Eventually, after having experience making sense of story problems, working with different combinations of numbers, and examining the results of doing addition and subtraction, students will begin to generalize that they get the same result by subtracting and will eventually use subtraction for these kinds of problems. This example illustrates how children's initial conceptions differ from adults—even with something we consider so basic as addition and subtraction. Children's conceptions are the best foundation on which to build future learning. Therefore, the perspective on addition and subtraction taken in this chapter is based on what has been learned from numerous research studies about children's understanding of operations. Through this research, we are aware that children can solve contextual or story problems by reasoning through the relationships in the problems. We also know that different problems have different structures that can affect the difficulty level of the problem. When teachers are familiar with these structures, they are better able to plan and differentiate instruction. These structures support the learning of additive situations and don't expire (Karp, Bush, & Dougherty, 2014) as these same structures can support students' thinking about addition and subtraction with larger whole numbers as well as with fractions and decimals.

CCSS Standards for Mathematical Practice
MP1. Make sense of problems and persevere in solving them.

Addition and Subtraction Problem Structures

Let's begin with a look at four categories of problem structures for additive situations (which include both addition and subtraction) that help children develop a schema to separate important information and to structure their thinking. Researchers have separated addition and subtraction problems into structures based on the kinds of relationships involved (Verschaffel, Greer, & DeCorte, 2007). These include *change* problems (*join* and *separate*), *part-part-whole* problems, and *compare* problems (Carpenter, Fennema, Franke, Levi, & Empson, 2014). The basic structure for each of these three categories of problems is illustrated in Figure 8.1.

CCSS Standards for Mathematical Practice
MP7. Look for and make use of structure.

Each of the problem structures is illustrated with the story problems that follow using the number family 4, 8, and 12. Depending on which of the three quantities is unknown, a different problem type results. Note that the problems are described in terms of their structure and interpretation and not as addition or subtraction problems. Contrary to what you may have thought, a joining action does not always mean addition, nor does separate or remove always mean subtraction.

Change Problems—Join and Add To. For the action of joining, there are three quantities involved: an initial or *start amount*, a *change amount* (the part being added or joined), and the *resulting amount* (the total amount after a change takes place). In Figure 8.1(a), this action is illustrated by the change being "added to" the start amount. Provide students with the Join Story Activity Page where they work with counters and model the problem on the story situation graphic organizer.

CCSS Standards for Mathematical Practice
MP2. Reason abstractly and quantitatively.

MyLab Education   Activity Page: Join Story

MyLab Education   Video Example 8.2

Watch this video of Jocelyn solving a change unknown addition problem. You will see how she reasons to get the answer using doubles facts she already knows.

VIDEO EXAMPLE

Change Problems—Separate and Take From. *Separate* problems are commonly thought of *take away* or *take from* problems in which part of a quantity is physically being removed from the start amount (see Figure 8.1[b]). Notice that in *separate* problems the start amount is the whole or the largest amount, whereas in the *join* problems, the result is the largest amount (whole). Have students use the Separate Story Activity Page as a graphic organizer.

MyLab Education   Activity Page: Separate Story

Problem Type and Structure with Physical Action Involved: **Change Problems**			
	Result Unknown	**Change Unknown**	**Start Unknown**
Join (add to) **(a)**	Sandra had 8 pennies. George gave her 4 more. How many pennies does Sandra have altogether? 8 + 4 = □	Sandra had 8 pennies. George gave her some more. Now Sandra has 12 pennies. How many did George give her? 8 + □ = 12	Sandra had some pennies. George gave her 4 more. Now Sandra has 12 pennies. How many pennies did Sandra have to begin with? □ + 4 = 12
Separate (take from) **(b)**	Sandra had 12 pennies. She gave 4 pennies to George. How many pennies does Sandra have now? 12 − 4 = □	Sandra had 12 pennies. She gave some to George. Now she has 8 pennies. How many did she give to George? 12 − □ = 8	Sandra had some pennies. She gave 4 to George. Now Sandra has 8 pennies left. How many pennies did Sandra have to begin with? □ − 4 = 8

Problem Type and Structure with No Physical Action Involved: **Part-Part-Whole** and **Compare Problems**			
	Whole Unknown	One Part Unknown	Both Parts Unknown
Part-Part-Whole **(c)**	George has 4 pennies and 8 nickels. How many coins does he have? 4 + 8 =	George has 12 coins. Eight of his coins are pennies, and the rest are nickels. How many nickels does George have? 12 = 4 + □ or 12 − 4 = □	George has 12 coins. Some are pennies and some are nickels. How many of each coin could he have? 12 = □ + □
	Difference Unknown	Larger Quantity Unknown	Smaller Quantity Unknown
	Situations of How many more?		
Compare **(d)**	George has 12 pennies, and Sandra has 8 pennies. How many more pennies does George have than Sandra? 8 + □ = 12	George has 4 more pennies than Sandra. Sandra has 8 pennies. How many pennies does George have? 8 + 4 = □	George has 4 more pennies than Sandra. George has 12 pennies. How many pennies does Sandra have? □ + 4 = 12
	Situations of How many fewer?		
	George has 12 pennies. Sandra has 8 pennies. How many fewer pennies does Sandra have than George? 12 − 8 = □	Sandra has 4 fewer pennies than George. Sandra has 8 pennies. How many pennies does George have? □ − 4 = 8	Sandra has 4 fewer pennies than George. George has 12 pennies. How many pennies does Sandra have? 12 − 4 = □

FIGURE 8.1 Basic structures for addition and subtraction story problem types. Each structure has three numbers. Any one or more of the three numbers can be the unknown in a story problem.

Part-Part-Whole Problems. *Part-part-whole* problems also known as *put together and take apart* problems in the *Common Core State Standards* (NGA Center & CCSSO, 2010), involve two parts that are conceptually or mentally combined into one collection or whole, as in Figure 8.1(c). These problems are different from change problems in that there is no action of physically joining or separating the quantities. In these situations, either the missing whole (total unknown), one of the missing parts (one addend unknown), or both parts (two addends unknown) must be found. There is no meaningful distinction between the two parts in a part-part-whole situation, so there is no need to have a different problem for each part as the unknown. The third situation in which the whole or total is known and the two parts are unknown creates opportunities to think about all the possible decompositions of the whole as instead of having one answer, this situation usually produces a set of correct answers (Caldwell, Kobett & Karp, 2014; Champagne, Schoen, & Riddell, 2014). This structure links directly to the idea that numbers are embedded in other numbers. For example, students can break apart 7 into 5 and 2, where each of the addends (or parts) is embedded in the 7 (whole). See the Part-Part-Whole Story Activity Page for the corresponding graphic organizer.

MyLab Education   Activity Page: Part-Part-Whole Story

Compare Problems. *Compare* problems involve the comparison of two quantities. The third amount in these problems does not actually exist but is the *difference* between the two quantities (see Figure 8.1[d]). Like part-part-whole problems, comparison problems do not typically involve a physical action. The corresponding Compare Story Activity Page can help students model the situation. The unknown quantity in compare problems can be one of three quantities: the smaller amount, the larger amount, or the difference. For each of these situations, two examples are provided: one problem in which the difference is stated in terms of "how many more?" and another in terms of "how much less?" (or how many fewer). Note that initially the language of "more," "less," and "fewer" may confuse students and may present a challenge in interpreting the relationships between the quantities.

You can find more examples of compare problems as well as the other problem types in the *Common Core State Standards* (Table 1 in the CCSS Mathematics Standards Glossary; NGA Center & CCSSO, 2010, p. 88).

MyLab Education   Activity Page: Compare Story

⏸ Pause & Reflect

Go back through the example story problems in Figure 8.1 and match the numbers in the problems with the components of the structures. For each problem, first print off the corresponding graphic organizer, and second, use a set of counters to model (solve) the problem as you think children might do. Then, for example, which numbers in the Join Problems match to start, change, or result spaces on your graphic organizer (and which space represents the unknown)? Write either an addition or subtraction equation that you think best represents the problem as you did it with counters and then compare your equation to the ones in Figure 8.1. ●

As you look back at the equations for each of the problems, you may have written some equations where the unknown quantity is not isolated on the right side of the equal sign. For example, the equation for the join problem with start part unknown is □ + 4 = 12. This equation is referred to as the *semantic* equation for the problem because the numbers are written in the order that follows the meaning of the story problem (see Figure 8.2). When an equation does not isolate the unknown on one side of the equal sign, an equivalent equation can be written for the same problem, in this case, for □ + 4 = 12, we can write 12 − 4 = □. This equation is referred to as the *computational* form of the equation, which isolates the unknown quantity and would be used if you were to solve this equation with a calculator. Children typically begin to think about and model the situation based on the sequence played out in the problem, which is modeled more appropriately by the semantic equation. Help students see how these equations are equivalent and that there are several ways to represent a given situation in an equation.

 Standards for Mathematical Practice
MP4. Model with Mathematics.

Presenting the variety of problem types in Figure 8.1 supports students in developing schema to structure their thinking and understand the meaning of the operations. Researchers suggest that students (particularly those with disabilities) should be explicitly taught these underlying structures so that they can identify important characteristics of the situations and determine when to add or subtract (Fagnant & Vlassis, 2013; Xin, Jitendra, & Deatline-Buchman, 2005). Over time "concreteness fading" (Goldstone & Son, 2005) occurs when each time students incrementally move from the modeling of the physical situation to a more abstract mental representation. When children are then exposed to new problems, the familiar characteristics will assist them in generalizing from similar problems on which they have practiced the actual action.

Quantity Unknown	Join Problems	Separate Problems
Result Unknown	$8 + 4 = \square$	$12 - 4 = \square$
Change Unknown	$8 + \square = 12$ (semantic) $12 - 8 = \square$ (computational)	$12 - \square = 8$ (semantic) $12 - 8 = \square$ (computational)
Start Unknown	$\square + 4 = 12$ (semantic) $12 - 4 = \square$ (computational)	$\square - 4 = 8$ (semantic) $4 + 8 = \square$ (computational)

FIGURE 8.2 The semantic and computational equations for the six join and separate problems.

Problem Difficulty. The structure of some problem types is more difficult than others. For example, problems in which a physical action is taking place, as in join and separate problems with result-unknown or the both-parts unknown problems are easier because children can directly model the physical action or act out the situation. That is why these types start being presented in kindergarten. However, the join or separate problems in which the start is unknown (e.g., Sandra had some pennies) are often the most difficult, probably because students attempting to model the problems directly do not know how many counters to put down to begin. Instead, they often use trial and error (Carpenter, Fennema, Franke, Levi, & Empson, 2014) to determine the unknown start amount. Problems in which the change amounts are unknown can also be difficult.

Part-part-whole problems can be difficult for children for two reasons: (1) There is no action to model because the situation describes a conceptual bringing together of quantities, and (2) it is a challenge for children to grasp that a quantity can represent two things at once. For example, if the problem describes three cars and four trucks in a parking lot and asks how many vehicles are in the lot, children have to understand that the cars and trucks are also part of the larger category of vehicles.

Children often have more experiences with the relationships of more and greater than, so you need to ensure they have opportunities to think about relationships described using the language fewer and less than. Even so, some children misinterpret the language of "how many more?" as meaning "to add" instead of "find the difference." Note that when the larger amount is unknown, stating the problem using the term *more* is easier for children because the relationships between the quantities and the operation more readily correspond to each other. In the smaller unknown situation, stating the problem using the term *fewer* is easier for children for the same reason. Similar to the part-part-whole problems, the lack of a physical action in these situations makes it difficult for children to model or act out these kinds of problems. As a result, many children will solve compare problems as part-part-whole problems without making separate sets of counters for the two amounts. The whole is used as the large amount, one part for the small amount and the second part for the difference.

MyLab Education **Video Example 8.3**

Take a look at this video of a diagnostic interview of a second-grader named Richard. Note that Richard struggles with both the addition and subtraction problems he is given. What surprised you in Richard's interview? How might this student struggle to solve problems in a whole class setting? What might be some next steps in Richard's instruction?

VIDEO EXAMPLE

Now let's look at ideas for supporting the teaching of addition and subtraction.

Teaching Addition and Subtraction

Combining the use of situations and models (counters, drawings, number lines, bar diagrams) is important in helping students construct a deep understanding of addition and subtraction. Building the understanding of these operations now will support these operations with larger numbers, fractions, and decimals later on. Note that addition and subtraction are taught at the same time to reinforce their inverse relationship.

Contextual Problems. There is more to think about than simply giving students problems to solve. In contrast to the rather straightforward and brief problems given in the previous section, you also need to set more complex problems in meaningful contexts.

Fosnot and Dolk (2001) point out that in story problems, students tend to focus on getting the answer. "Context problems, on the other hand, are connected as closely as possible to children's lives, rather than to 'school mathematics.' They are designed to anticipate and to develop children's mathematical modeling of the real world" (p. 24). They have potential to provide "memorable imagery that can act as a touchstone for teacher and learners in building and discussing abstract concepts" (Gerofsky, 2009, p. 36). Contextual problems might derive from recent experiences in the classroom; a field trip; a discussion in art, science, or social studies; or from children's literature.

Because contextual problems connect to life experiences, they are important for ELs, too, even though it may seem that the language presents a challenge to them. Some strategies to support comprehension of contextual problems include using a noun-verb word order, replacing terms such as "his/her" and "it" with a name, and removing unnecessary vocabulary words. A visual aid, or actual students modeling the story, would also be effective strategies for ELs and students with disabilities.

For example, the here is a contextual problem written to support comprehension:

Yesterday, we measured how long you were using cubes. Dion and Rosa asked how many cubes long they are when they lie down head to foot. Rosa was $49\frac{1}{2}$ cubes long, and Dion was 59 cubes long. How long are Rosa and Dion when lying head to foot? (See Figure 8.3.)

Lessons Built on Context or Story Problems. What might a good lesson built around word problems look like? The answer comes more naturally if you think about students not just solving the problems but also using words, pictures, and numbers to explain how they solved the problems and justify why they are correct. In a single lesson, focus on a few problems with in-depth discussions rather than multiple problems with little elaboration. Students should use whatever physical materials or drawings they feel will help them. Whatever they record should explain what they did well enough to allow someone else to understand their thinking.

A particularly effective approach is having students correct each others' written solutions. By using anonymous work, students can analyze the reasoning used, assess the selection of the operation, find the mistakes in computation and identify errors in copying numbers from the problem.

Choosing Numbers for Problems. The structure of the problem will change the challenge of the task, but you can also vary the problem's complexity by the numbers you choose to use. In general, the numbers in the problems should align with the students' number development. But, if at first a student struggles with a problem, use smaller numbers to see if it is the size of the numbers causing the obstacle. You can also intensify the challenge by increasing the size of the numbers.

Rather than wait until students develop techniques for computing numbers, use word problems as an opportunity for them to learn about number and computation simultaneously. For example, a problem involving the combination of 30 and 42 has the potential to help first- and second-graders

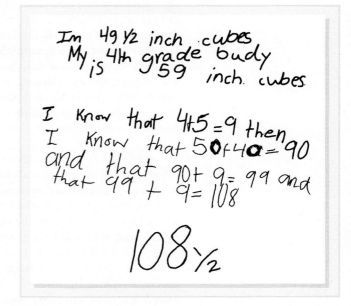

FIGURE 8.3 Student work shows a child's thinking about the total measurement of Rosa's and Dion's heights.

focus on sets of 10. As they decompose 42 into 40 and 2, it is not at all unreasonable to think that they will add 30 and 40 and then add 2 more. The structure of a word problem can strongly influence the type of strategy a student uses to solve multidigit problems. This thinking is especially true for students who have not been taught the standard algorithms for addition and subtraction which are not required until fourth grade (NGA Center & CCSSO, 2010).

Introducing Symbolism. Preschoolers initially have little need for the symbols $+$, $-$, and $=$ as they listen and respond orally to addition and subtraction situations, however, by kindergarten and first grade these symbolic conventions are required. Therefore, whenever young children are engaged in solving story problems, introduce symbols as a way to record what they did as they share their thinking. Say, "You had the whole number of 12 in your problem, and the number 8 was one of the parts of 12. You found out that the unknown part was 4. Here is a way we write that: $12 - 8 = 4$." The minus sign should be read as "minus" or "subtract" but *not* as "take away." The addition sign is easier because it is typically a substitute for "and." Some children may describe a counting-up strategy to find the solution of 4, so also record the equivalent equation as $8 + 4 = 12$.

Some care should be taken with the equal sign, as it is a relational symbol meaning "is the same as" and is not an operations symbol. However, many children think of it as a symbol that signals that the "answer is coming up next" which is an obstacle to understanding equations (Byrd, McNeil, Chesney, & Matthews, 2015). In fact, children often interpret the equal sign in much the same way as pressing the $=$ on a calculator: "give me the answer."

MyLab Education   Video Example 8.4

Watch this video (https://www.youtube.com/watch?v=eO3OQI9Jwts) illustrate some misinterpretations of the equal sign.

An equation such as $4 + 8 = 3 + 9$ has no "answer" and is still true because both sides represent the same quantity. As you record and read the equal sign in equations, use the phrase "is the same as" in place of or in conjunction with "equals." Avoid reading the equation as $2 + 2$ "makes" 4. Using a variety of *nonstandard equations* such as $9 = 5 + 4$, $6 = 6$, and $3 + 3 = 2 + 4$, and relational thinking can help students understand the meaning of the equal sign (Knuth & Stephens, 2016; Powell, Kearns, & Driver, 2016), as this knowledge is expected in first grade. Sharing a variety of equation formats with students is essential for students' development of algebraic thinking.

Another approach is to think of the equal sign as a balance; whatever is on one side of the equation "balances" or equals the other side (also see Chapter 13). This concept of the equal sign will support algebraic thinking in future grades if developed early (Knuth, Stephens, McNeil, & Alibali, 2006; Powell, Kerns & Driver, 2016). But, it is important for students in all grades beyond grade 2 to be assessed as to their knowledge of the meaning of the equal sign as teachers have been shown to overestimate their students' understanding of this symbol (Miller-Bennett, 2017).

FORMATIVE ASSESSMENT Notes. Observing how students solve story problems will provide information about their understanding of number, strategies they may be using to answer basic facts, and methods they are using for multidigit computation. Look beyond the answers they get on a worksheet. For example, a child who uses counters and counts each addend and then recounts the entire set for a join-result-unknown problem (this approach is called *count all*) needs to develop more sophisticated strategies. With more practice, they will count on from the first set. This strategy will be modified to count on from the larger set; that is, for $4 + 7$, the child will begin with 7 and count on, even though 4 is the start amount in the problem. Eventually, students use facts retrieved from memory, and their use of counters fades completely or counters are used only when necessary. Observations of children solving problems can inform what numbers to use in problems and what questions to ask that will focus students' attention on more efficient strategies. ■

Standards for Mathematical Practice

MP5. Use appropriate tools strategically.

Model-Based Problems. Many students will use counters, bar diagrams, or number lines to solve story problems. These models are thinking tools that help them understand what is happening in the problem and keep track of the numbers and steps in solving the problem. Problems can also be posed using models when there is no context involved.

Addition. When the parts of a set are known, addition is used to name the whole in terms of the parts. This simple definition of addition serves both *action situations* (join and separate) and static or *no-action situations* (part-part-whole).

Each part-part-whole model shown in Figure 8.4 represents $5 + 3 = 8$. Some of these are the result of a definite put-together or joining action, and some are not. Notice that in every example, both parts are distinct, even after the parts are combined. For children to see the relationship between the two parts and the whole, the image of the five and three must be kept as two separate sets. Therefore, the two parts should be in different piles, on different sections of a mat, or (in the case of counters) in different colors. This structure helps children reflect on the action after it has occurred. "These red chips are the ones I started with. Then I added these three blue chips, and now I have eight chips altogether."

The use of *bar diagrams* (also called *strip* or *tape diagrams*) as semiconcrete visual representations is a central fixture many international curricula and are increasingly found in U.S. classrooms. As with other tools, these diagrams support students' mathematical thinking by generating "meaning-making space" (Murata, 2008, p. 399) and are a precursor to the use of number lines. Murata states, "Tape diagrams are designed to bring forward the relational meanings of the quantities in a problem by showing the connections in context" (p. 396). Here is an example. Notice how the corresponding bar diagram (see Figure 8.5) visually connects to the part-part-whole diagram students have been using since kindergarten.

Peyton had 686 boxes of Girl Scout cookies to sell. She sold some of them. If 298 boxes were left over, how many boxes of cookies did she sell?

You can find online bar diagram tools called "Thinking Blocks" at Math Playground's website and as a free app in the iTunes Store. Thinking Blocks can be used to help students model and solve contextual problems involving operations with whole numbers and fractions.

A *number line* is an essential model, but it can initially present conceptual difficulties for children below second grade and students with disabilities (National Research Council, 2009). This initial confusion is partially due to their difficulty in seeing the unit, which is a challenge when it appears in a continuous line. A number line is also a shift from counting a number of individual objects in a collection to counting continuous length units. There are, however, ways to support young learners as you introduce and model number lines (see Figure 8.6).

A number line measures distances from zero the same way a ruler does. If you don't emphasize the unit (length), children may focus on the tick marks or numerals instead of the spaces (a misunderstanding that becomes apparent when

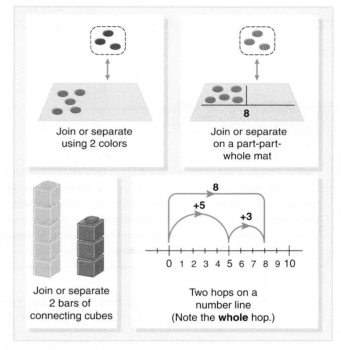

FIGURE 8.4 Part-part-whole models for $5 + 3 = 8$ and $8 - 3 = 5$.

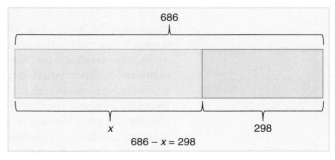

FIGURE 8.5 A bar diagram that supports students' thinking about the problem.

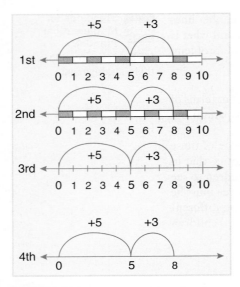

FIGURE 8.6   Sequence of number lines.

their answers are consistently off by one). At first, children can build a number path by using a given length, such as a set of Cuisenaire rods of the same color. This path will show that each length unit is "one unit," and that same unit is repeated over and over (iterated) to form the number line (Dougherty, Flores, Louis, & Sophian, 2010). Also, playing board games with number paths helped students develop a better concept of number magnitude and helped them estimate more accurately on a number line (Siegler & Ramani, 2009). In each version of the number line sequence, arrows (hops) are drawn for each number in an expression to illustrate the length concept more clearly. To model the part-part-whole concept of 5 + 3, start by drawing an arrow from 0 to 5, indicating, "This much is five." Do *not* point to the tick mark for 5, saying, "This is five." Then show the three hops and count "six, seven, eight" (not "one, two, three") to demonstrate the counting-on model and reinforce the mental process. Eventually, the use of a ruler or a scale in a bar graph or coordinate grid will reinforce this model.

There's an interactive number line at the Math Learning Center that helps students visualize number sequences and model strategies for addition, subtraction, multiplication, and division. It can be used to represent sequences of numbers, including whole numbers and multiples of a variety of numbers.

CCSS-M: K.OA.A.2; 1.OA.A.1; 1.OA.A.2; 2.OA.A.1

Up and Down the Number Line

Create a large number line on the floor of your classroom, or display one in the front of the room. (Make sure your line starts with a tick mark at zero and has arrows at each end of the line.) Use a stuffed animal for hopping, or if the number line is large enough, ask a student to walk the number line. Pose a variety of problem situations and talk about the movement required for each. Start with a context that requires moving a distance, such as the frog hopping away from the lily pad to emphasize the spaces (units of length) on the number line. This activity supports students' development of a mental image for thinking about the meaning of addition and subtraction.

Experiences with using number lines are essential because they will be used with third graders to locate fractions and add and subtract time intervals, fourth-graders will locate decimals and use them for measurement, and fifth-graders will use perpendicular number lines in coordinate grids (NGA Center & CCSSO, 2010).

Subtraction. In a part-part-whole model, when the whole and one of the parts are known, subtraction can be used to name the missing part. If you start with a whole set of 8 and remove a set of 3, the 2 sets that you know are the sets of 8 and 3. The expression 8 − 3, read "eight minus three," names the set of 5 that remains (note that we didn't say "take away"). Notice that the models in Figure 8.4 are models for subtraction as well as addition (except for the action). Helping children see that they are using the same models or pictures connects the two operations through their inverse relationship. Unfortunately, many times this relationship is presented solely through the use of fact families and often students just observe that they are using the same numbers and do not see the central structure of part + part = whole and whole − part = part (Ding, 2016). Ding (2016) additionally suggests the use of real-world contexts via word problems to help students make meaning of this relationship. Also, there is a need to explicitly point to the usefulness of using the inverse to check answers as in, 61 − 43 = 18 because 43 + 18 = 61 (Ding & Auxter, 2017).

Activity 8.2

CCSS-M: K.OA.A.2; 1.OA.A.1; 1.OA.A.2; 2.OA.A.1

Missing-Part Subtraction

Use a context or story about something that is hiding, as in the "lift-the-flap" book *What's Hiding in There?* (Drescher, 2008), where animals are concealed in various locations in the woods. Explain to the children that they can model the animals by using a fixed number of tiles placed on a mat. One child separates the tiles into two parts while another covers his or her eyes. The first child covers one of the two parts with a sheet of paper, revealing only the other part (see Figure 8.7[b]). The second child says the subtraction sentence. For example, "Nine minus four [the visible part] is five [the hidden part]." The hidden part can be revealed for the child to self-check. Have children record both the subtraction equation and the addition equation. ELs may need sentence prompts such as "____ minus ____ equals ____."

ENGLISH LEARNERS

Activity 8.3

CCSS-M: K.OA.A.3; 1.OA.A.1; 1.OA.B.4

Guinea Pigs in Cages

Use the book *Guinea Pigs Add Up* (Cuyler, 2010) to think about a growing and changing population of class pets—guinea pigs! There are many options for using this story, such as starting with two addends unknown: "How many ways can you place 10 guinea pigs in two cages?" Use the Activity Page Both Addends Unknown. Another idea is to use the book as a context for missing-part thinking for subtraction. Use the Guinea Pig Problem Activity Page to pose questions to the students about the numbers of pigs in the cage, numbers adopted, and how many are left. Students can use the Cage Mat and the little Guinea Pig Counters Activity Pages and model the problem. Encourage children to pose their own questions and record the appropriate number sentences.

MyLab Education   **Activity Page: Both Addends Unknown**
MyLab Education   **Activity Page: Guinea Pig Problem**
MyLab Education   **Activity Page: Cage Mat**
MyLab Education   **Activity Page: Guinea Pig Counters**

Note that in Activities 8.2 and 8.3, the situations end with two distinct parts, even when there is a remove action. The removed part remains on the mat as a model for an addition equation to be written after writing the subtraction equation. A discussion of how two equations can be written for the same situation is an important opportunity to connect the operations of addition and subtraction.

Subtraction as Think-Addition. Thinking about subtraction as "think-addition" rather than "take-away" is significant for mastering subtraction facts. Because the tiles for the remaining part or unknown addend are left hidden under the cover for Activity 8.2, when children do such activities they are encouraged to think: "What goes with the part I see to make the whole?" For example, if the total or whole number of tiles is 9, and 6 tiles are removed from under the cover, the child can think in terms of "6 and what amount add to 9?" or "What goes with 6 to equal 9?" The mental activity is "think-addition" instead of "count what's left." Later, when working on subtraction facts, a subtraction fact such as $9 - 6 = \square$ should trigger the same thought pattern: "6 and what equals 9?"

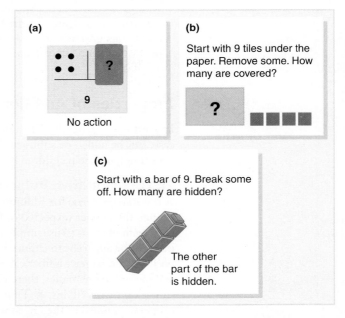

(a)

9

No action

(b)

Start with 9 tiles under the paper. Remove some. How many are covered?

?

(c)

Start with a bar of 9. Break some off. How many are hidden?

The other part of the bar is hidden.

FIGURE 8.7   Models for $9 - 4$ as a missing-part problem.

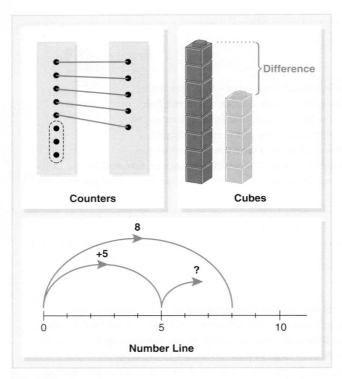

Counters   Cubes

Number Line

FIGURE 8.8 Models for the difference between 8 and 5.

Comparison Models. *Comparison situations* involve two distinct sets or quantities and the difference between them. Several ways of modeling the difference relationship are shown in Figure 8.8. The same model can be used whether the difference or one of the two quantities is unknown.

Note that it is not immediately clear to students how to associate either the addition or subtraction operations with a comparison situation. From an adult vantage point, you can see that if you match part of the larger amount with the smaller amount, the large set can now be thought of as the whole in a part-part-whole model. In fact, many children do model compare problems in just this manner. But it is a challenge to show students this idea if they do not construct it themselves.

Have students make two amounts (perhaps with two bars of connecting cubes) to show how many pencils are in their backpacks. Discuss the difference between the two bars to generate the third number. For example, if the students make a bar of 10 and a bar of 6, ask, "How many more do we need to match the bar of 10?" The unmatched cubes in the larger bar show that the difference is 4. "What equations can we make with these three numbers?" Have children make up other story problems that involve the two amounts of 10 and 6. Discuss which equations go with the problems that are created.

Properties of Addition and Subtraction

Properties are generalized algebraic rules that support the understanding of how numbers, in this case, can be added or subtracted. Explicit attention to these properties, (build the terminology over time), will help children become more flexible and efficient in how they combine numbers.

The Commutative Property for Addition. The *commutative property* (sometimes known as the *order property*) for addition means you can change the order of the addends and it does not change the answer (expected of first graders in CCSS-M). Although the commutative property may seem obvious to us (simply reverse the two piles of counters on the part-part-whole mat), it may not be apparent to children. Because this property is essential in problem solving (counting on from the larger number), mastery of basic facts (if you know 3 + 9, you also know 9 + 3), and mental mathematics, there is value in spending time helping children construct the relationship (Baroody, Wilkins, & Tiilikainen, 2003). First-graders do not need to be able to name the property as much as they need to understand and visualize the property, know why it applies to addition but not subtraction, and apply it. But, always name the property accurately and never use a "nickname" that will later confuse the student (and subsequent teachers), such as saying the "ring around the Rosie" or "flip flop" property for the commutative property. Those arbitrary names are confusing as students progress (Karp, Bush, & Dougherty, 2016). Use the precise terminology.

Schifter (2001) describes students who discovered the commutative property while examining sums to ten but later when they were asked whether they thought it would always work many were unsure if it worked with large numbers. The point is that children may see and accept the commutative property for sums they've experienced but not be able to explain or even believe that this property works for all addition combinations. Asking students to think about when properties do (and don't) apply is the heart of mathematics, addressing numeration, reasoning, generalizing, and algebraic thinking.

CCSS Standards for Mathematical Practice

MP7. Look for and make use of structure.

To help children focus on the commutative property, pair problems that have the same addends but in different orders. Using different contexts helps children focus on the significant similarities in the problems. The following problems are examples.

Tania is on page 32 in her book. Tomorrow she hopes to read 15 more pages. What page will she be on if she reads that many pages?

The milk tray in the cafeteria had 15 cartons. The delivery person filled the tray with 32 more milk cartons. How many milk cartons are now on the tray?

Ask if anyone notices how these problems are alike. When done as a pair, some children will notice that when they have solved one, they have essentially solved the other problem. Note that students may attempt to overgeneralize the commutative property to subtraction. Use contextual situations or story problems to help them confront this misconception.

The Associative Property for Addition. The *associative property* for addition states that when adding three or more numbers, it does not matter whether the first pair is added first or if you start with any other pair of addends (expected of first graders in CCSS-M). This property allows for a great deal of flexibility so students can change the order in which they group numbers to work with combinations they know. For example, knowing this property can help students identify "combinations of ten" from the numbers they are adding by mentally grouping numbers differently from just reading the expression from left to right.

Activity 8.4   CCSS-M: 1.OA.B.2

More Than Two Addends

Give students six sums to find involving three or four addends as in this More Than Two Addends Activity Page. Within each problem, include at least one pair with a sum of 10 or perhaps a double: $4 + 7 + 6, 5 + 9 + 9$, or $3 + 4 + 3 + 7$. Students should show how they added the numbers (see Figure 8.9). For students with disabilities, you may need to initially support them in their decision making, suggesting that they look for a 10 or a double and have them underline or circle those numbers as a starting point.

STUDENTS with SPECIAL NEEDS

MyLab Education   **Activity Page: More Than Two Addends**

As students share their solutions, there will be some who added using different pairs and in a different order but got the same result. From this discussion, you can help them conclude that they can add numbers in any order by using both the associative property and the commutative property. Learning to adjust strategies to fit the numbers puts learners on the beginning of the road to computational fluency.

The Zero Property. Story problems involving zero and using zeros in the three-addend sums (e.g., $4 + 0 + 3$) are good opportunities to help children understand zero as an identity element in addition or subtraction (see Table 3 in the CCSS Mathematics Glossary, p. 90). Occasionally, children

FIGURE 8.9   A student shows how she used check marks to keep track of numbers added.

believe that $6 + 0$ must be more than 6 because "adding makes numbers bigger," or that $12 - 0$ must be 11 because "subtracting makes numbers smaller." Instead of making meaningless rules about adding and subtracting zero, create opportunities for discussing adding and subtracting zero using contextual situations.

MyLab Education Self-Check 8.2

Developing Multiplication and Division Operation Sense

Standards for Mathematical Practice
MP8. Look for and express regularity in repeated reasoning.

A key component of the third-grade curriculum is to help students develop *operation sense* with respect to multiplication and division. This sense making means facilitating students' connecting the different meanings of multiplication and division to each other, as well as connecting to addition and subtraction. Operation sense supports students' effective application of these operations in real-world settings.

Multiplication and Division Problem Structures

As with addition and subtraction, there are problem structures that will help you in formulating and discussing multiplication and division tasks. These structures will also benefit your students in generalizing as a way to identify familiar situations.

Most researchers identify four different classes of multiplicative structures: equal groups, comparison, area (CCSS includes arrays with area), and combinations (see Figure 8.10). Of these, the two structures *equal groups* (the focus in CCSS third-grade standards) and *multiplicative comparison* (the focus in CCSS fourth-grade standards), are by far the most prevalent in elementary school. Arrays begin to be considered in second grade with addition situations with equal groups, and area problems are introduced in the third grade as a component of the topic of measurement. Problems with combinations are found in seventh grade when students identify all of the possible outcomes in situations exploring probability.

Equal-Group Problems. Equal group problems involve three quantities: the number of groups (sets or parts of equal size), the size of each group (set or part) and the total of all the groups (whole or product). The parts and wholes terminology is useful in making the connection to addition. When the number of groups and size of groups are known, the problem is a *multiplication* situation with an unknown product (How many in all?). When either the group size is unknown (How many in each group?) or the number of groups is unknown (How many groups?), then the problem is a *division* situation. But note that these division situations are not alike. Problems in which the size of the group is unknown are called fair-sharing or *partition division* problems. The whole is shared or distributed among a known number of groups to determine the size of each. If the number of groups is unknown but the size of the equal group is known, the problems are called *measurement division* or sometimes *repeated-subtraction* problems. The whole is "measured off" in groups the given size. Use the illustration in Figure 8.10(a) as a reference.

MyLab Education Video Example 8.6

Watch this video to see Andrew demonstrating measurement division as he uses information of the total and the size of each group to find the number of groups (unknown).

Older students tend to prefer the partition model to the measurement models saying they find it easier (Kinda, 2013), but it is important to emphasize both as the context of the problem leads to the corresponding structure!

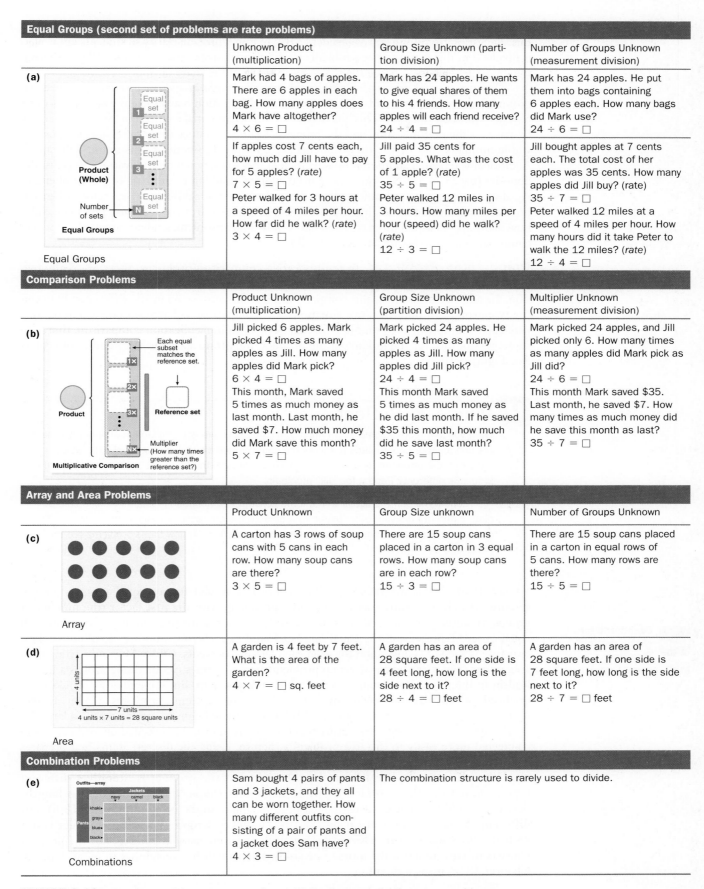

Equal Groups (second set of problems are rate problems)			
	Unknown Product (multiplication)	Group Size Unknown (partition division)	Number of Groups Unknown (measurement division)
(a) Equal Groups	Mark had 4 bags of apples. There are 6 apples in each bag. How many apples does Mark have altogether? $4 \times 6 = \square$	Mark has 24 apples. He wants to give equal shares of them to his 4 friends. How many apples will each friend receive? $24 \div 4 = \square$	Mark has 24 apples. He put them into bags containing 6 apples each. How many bags did Mark use? $24 \div 6 = \square$
	If apples cost 7 cents each, how much did Jill have to pay for 5 apples? (*rate*) $7 \times 5 = \square$ Peter walked for 3 hours at a speed of 4 miles per hour. How far did he walk? (*rate*) $3 \times 4 = \square$	Jill paid 35 cents for 5 apples. What was the cost of 1 apple? (*rate*) $35 \div 5 = \square$ Peter walked 12 miles in 3 hours. How many miles per hour (speed) did he walk? (*rate*) $12 \div 3 = \square$	Jill bought apples at 7 cents each. The total cost of her apples was 35 cents. How many apples did Jill buy? (rate) $35 \div 7 = \square$ Peter walked 12 miles at a speed of 4 miles per hour. How many hours did it take Peter to walk the 12 miles? (*rate*) $12 \div 4 = \square$

Comparison Problems			
	Product Unknown (multiplication)	Group Size Unknown (partition division)	Multiplier Unknown (measurement division)
(b) Multiplicative Comparison	Jill picked 6 apples. Mark picked 4 times as many apples as Jill. How many apples did Mark pick? $6 \times 4 = \square$ This month, Mark saved 5 times as much money as last month. Last month, he saved $7. How much money did Mark save this month? $5 \times 7 = \square$	Mark picked 24 apples. He picked 4 times as many apples as Jill. How many apples did Jill pick? $24 \div 4 = \square$ This month Mark saved 5 times as much money as he did last month. If he saved $35 this month, how much did he save last month? $35 \div 5 = \square$	Mark picked 24 apples, and Jill picked only 6. How many times as many apples did Mark pick as Jill did? $24 \div 6 = \square$ This month Mark saved $35. Last month, he saved $7. How many times as much money did he save this month as last? $35 \div 7 = \square$

Array and Area Problems			
	Product Unknown	Group Size unknown	Number of Groups Unknown
(c) Array	A carton has 3 rows of soup cans with 5 cans in each row. How many soup cans are there? $3 \times 5 = \square$	There are 15 soup cans placed in a carton in 3 equal rows. How many soup cans are in each row? $15 \div 3 = \square$	There are 15 soup cans placed in a carton in equal rows of 5 cans. How many rows are there? $15 \div 5 = \square$
(d) Area	A garden is 4 feet by 7 feet. What is the area of the garden? $4 \times 7 = \square$ sq. feet	A garden has an area of 28 square feet. If one side is 4 feet long, how long is the side next to it? $28 \div 4 = \square$ feet	A garden has an area of 28 square feet. If one side is 7 feet long, how long is the side next to it? $28 \div 7 = \square$ feet

Combination Problems		
(e) Combinations	Sam bought 4 pairs of pants and 3 jackets, and they all can be worn together. How many different outfits consisting of a pair of pants and a jacket does Sam have? $4 \times 3 = \square$	The combination structure is rarely used to divide.

FIGURE 8.10 The four problem structures for multiplication and division story problems.

As students explore word problems and if you choose to create your own problems keep this suggestion from Jong and Magruder (2014) in mind: provide clarity so students know who is involved in the sharing. The problem should plainly answer this question: Who is sharing the items? Is the person doing the sharing also a part of the share or not?

Sometimes equal-group problems have been called *repeated-addition* problems, as the equal group is being added over and over. And in fact, multiplication is an efficient way to carry out a repeated-addition situation. This link may be an important initial connection for young learners to make, as the multiplication and the repeated addition produce the same results for positive whole numbers. But by the time students are multiplying fractions, this notion falls apart. Additionally, repeated addition is not an efficient way to carry out multiplication—it is just the opposite (try 23 × 57). So, move away from additive thinking to thinking of a multiplier and equal sets as soon as you are able to do so. There is also a subtle difference between equal-group problems and those that might be termed *rate* problems ("If there are four apples per child, how many apples would three children have?"). In a rate problem, students are working with a composed unit (in this case, apples per child).

Comparison Problems. In multiplicative comparison problems, there are really two different sets or groups, as there were with comparison situations for addition and subtraction. In additive situations, the comparison is an amount or quantity difference between the two groups. In multiplicative situations, the comparison is based on one group being a particular multiple of the other (a reference set). With multiplication comparison, there are three possibilities for the unknown: the product, the group size, and the number of groups (see Figure 8.10[b]).

❚❚ Pause & Reflect

What you just read is complex yet important. Stop now and get a collection of about 35 counters and a set of paper plates to model the equal-groups examples starring "Mark." Match the story with the structure model in Figure 8.10(a). How are the problems alike and how are the problems different? Repeat for "Jill" problems.

Repeat the same process with the multiplicative comparison problems using a colored plate different from your other plates to represent the reference set. Again, start with the first problem in each set and then the second problem. Reflect on how these problems are the same and different. ●

Array and Area Problems. The *array* is a model for an equal-group situation (Figure 8.10[c]). It is shown as a rectangular grouping, with the first factor (the number of groups) representing the number of rows and the second factor (the number of items in each equal group) representing the equal number found in each row (number of columns). This structure is the U.S. convention for what each factor represents. CCSS-M groups arrays with area rather than with the equal-group problems because arrays can be thought of as a logical lead-in to the row-and-column structure of an area problem. But remember an array can be modeled with circular counters or any items as you see in the sample problems in Figure 8.10(c) (also using dots [Matney & Daugherty, 2013]). Yet, if you begin to use the small square tiles for the array and move the tiles tightly together, the result can be recorded on grid paper and connected more easily to the area problem structure. Using the discrete items first prepares students for the more sophisticated use of continuous units with measuring area.

Standards for Mathematical Practice

MP6. Attend to precision.

What distinguishes *area* from the others is that the product is literally a different type of unit from the two factors. In a rectangular shape, the product of two lengths (length × width) is an area, usually measured in square units. Note in Figure 8.10(d) how different the square units are from the two factors of length: 4 feet times 7 feet is not 28 feet but 28 square feet. The factors are each one-dimensional entities, but the product consists of two-dimensional units. The study of area will be considered in great depth in Chapter 18 on measurement.

Combination Problems. *Combination* problems involve counting the number of possible pairings that can be made between two or more sets (things or events). This structure is more complex and therefore not a good introductory point for multiplication, but it is important that you recognize it as another category of multiplicative problem structures. Students often start by using the model shown in Figure 8.10(e) where one set is the row (pants) and the other the column (jackets) in a matrix format. Counting how many combinations of two or more things or events are possible is important in determining probabilities—a seventh grade standard.

Teaching Multiplication and Division

Multiplication and division are often taught separately, with multiplication preceding division. It is important, however, to combine multiplication and division soon after multiplication has been introduced in order to help children see how these operations have an inverse relationship. In most curricula, these topics are first presented in second grade, become a major focus in third grade, with continued development in the fourth and fifth grades.

A major conceptual hurdle in working with multiplicative structures is understanding that while a group contains a given number of objects these groups can also be considered as single entities (Blote, Lieffering, & Ouewhand, 2006; Clark & Kamii, 1996). Children can solve the problem, "How many apples in 4 baskets of 8 apples each?" without thinking multiplicatively simply by counting out 4 sets of 8 counters and then counting all. To think multiplicatively about this problem as *four sets of eight* requires children to conceptualize each group of eight as a single entity to be counted four times. Experiences with making and counting equal groups, especially in contextual situations, are extremely useful.

Contextual Problems. When teaching multiplication and division, it is essential to use interesting contextual problems instead of more sterile story problems (or "naked numbers")—and yes, assessments focus on these contextual problems! Consider the following problem.

Yesterday, we discovered that it took 7 yards of paper to cover the bulletin board in the school's lobby. There are 25 more bulletin boards of the same size in the school's hallways. How many yards of paper will we need if we cover all the bulletin boards in the school hallways?

This problem is based on students' experiences and builds on a known context that students can access. When a familiar and relevant context is used, students are more likely to demonstrate a spontaneous and meaningful approach to solve the problem, as they are connected to it.

The tendency in the United States is to have students solve many problems in a single lesson with a focus on getting the answers. But if you change the focus to sense making, solving only a few problems using multiple representations strategically such as physical materials, drawings, as well as equations can be a better approach. Whatever students write on paper, they should explain it in enough detail for another person to follow their thinking. Leave enough space on an activity sheet to encourage multiple strategies—it is amazing how leaving only a small space will just prompt an answer and nothing more. Look at Teaching Channel (www.teachingchannel.org) to watch a video of students solving problems in "Choose 3 Ways."

Introducing Symbolism. When students solve simple multiplication story problems before learning about multiplication symbolism, they will most likely begin by writing repeated addition equations to represent what they did. This moment is your opportunity to introduce the multiplication sign and explain what the two factors mean.

The U.S. convention is that 4×8 refers to 4 sets of 8, not 8 sets of 4. There is no reason to be so rigid about this convention that you would mark a student as incorrect (particularly because the convention is just the opposite in some countries where they say 4 taken 8 times). The important thing is that the students can tell you what each factor in their equations represents and that their equations match the context. These conventions allow

Standards for Mathematical Practice
MP5. Use appropriate tools strategically.

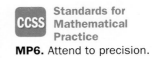

Standards for Mathematical Practice
MP6. Attend to precision.

us to communicate clearly about the problem with each other. The quotient 24 divided by 6 is represented in three different ways: $24 \div 6$, $6\overline{)24}$, and $\frac{24}{6}$. Students should understand that these representations are equivalent. The fraction notation becomes important at the middle school level. Students often mistakenly read $6\overline{)24}$ as "6 divided by 24" due to the left-to-right order of the numerals. Generally, this error does not match what they are thinking.

CCSS Standards for Mathematical Practice

MP6. Attend to precision.

Compounding the difficulty of division notation is the unfortunate phrase "goes in to," as in "6 goes into 24." This phrase carries little meaning about division, especially in connection with a fair-sharing or partitioning context. The "goes in to" terminology is simply ingrained in adult parlance; it has not been in textbooks for years. Instead of this phrase, use appropriate terminology with students, such as "How many groups of 6 are in 24?"

Choosing Numbers for Problems. When selecting numbers for multiplicative story problems or activities, there is a tendency to think that large numbers pose a burden to students or that 3×4 is somehow easier to understand than 4×17. An understanding of products or quotients is not affected by the size of numbers as long as the numbers are within your students' grasp. A contextual problem involving 14×8 is appropriate for third-graders. When given the challenge of using larger numbers, children are likely to invent computational strategies (e.g., ten 8s and then four more 8s) or model the problem with manipulatives.

Remainders. More often than not in real-world situations, division does not result in a whole number. For example, problems with 6 as a divisor will result in a whole number only one time out of six. In the absence of a context, a remainder can be dealt with in only two ways: it can either remain a quantity left over or be partitioned into fractions (including decimal fractions). In Figure 8.11, the problem $11 \div 4$ is modeled to show the remainder as a fraction.

In real contexts, remainders must be interpreted (grade four standard). Besides "left over" or "partitioned as a fraction," remainders can have three additional effects on answers:

- The remainder is discarded, leaving a smaller whole-number answer.
- The remainder can "force" the answer to the next highest whole number.
- The answer is rounded to the nearest whole number for an approximate result.

These problems illustrate all five possibilities.

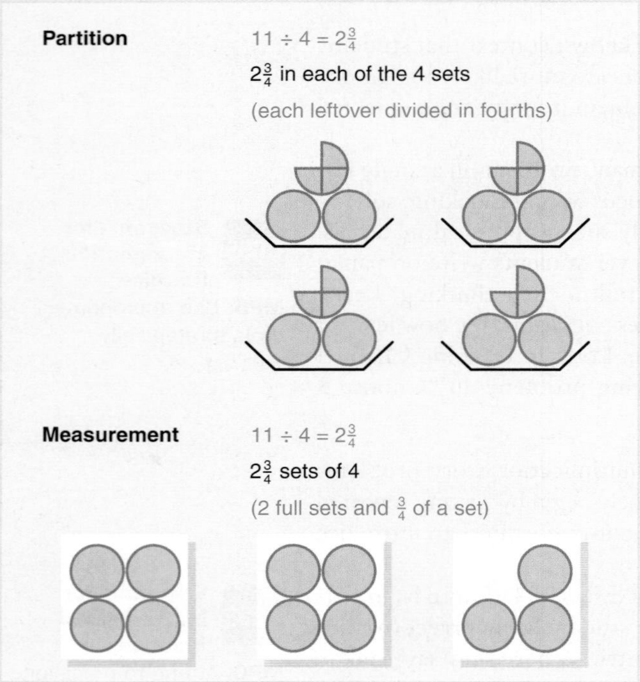

1. You have 30 strawberries to give in fair shares to 7 friends. How many strawberries will each child receive?
   Answer: 4 strawberries and 2 left over (left over)

2. Each jar holds 8 ounces of liquid. If there are 46 ounces in the pitcher, how many jars will be filled?
   Answer: 5 and $\frac{6}{8}$ jars (partitioned as a fraction)

3. The rope is 25 feet long. How many 7-foot jump ropes can be made?
   Answer: 3 jump ropes (discarded)

4. The ferry can hold 8 cars. How many trips will it have to make to carry 25 cars across the river?
   Answer: 4 trips (forced to next whole number)

5. Six children are planning to share a bowl of 50 grapes. About how many grapes will each child get?
   Answer: About 8 grapes for each child (rounded, approximate result)

Partition $11 \div 4 = 2\frac{3}{4}$

$2\frac{3}{4}$ in each of the 4 sets

(each leftover divided in fourths)

Measurement $11 \div 4 = 2\frac{3}{4}$

$2\frac{3}{4}$ sets of 4

(2 full sets and $\frac{3}{4}$ of a set)

FIGURE 8.11   Remainders expressed as fractions.

Students should not just think of remainders as "R 3" or "left over." Addressing what to do with remainders must be central to teaching about division. In fact, one of the most common errors students make on high-stakes assessments is to divide and then not pay attention to the context when selecting their answer. For example, in problem 4 above, answering with $3\frac{1}{8}$ trips doesn't make any sense.

⏸ Pause & Reflect

It is useful for you to make up problems using different contexts. See if you can come up with division problems whose contexts would result in remainders dealt with as fractions, "forced" or rounded up, and rounded down. ●

Model-Based Problems. In the beginning, students will be able to use the same models—sets, bar diagrams, and number lines—for all four operations. A model not often used for addition but extremely important and widely used for multiplication and division is the array. An *array* is any arrangement of things in rows and columns, such as a rectangle of square tiles or blocks (see the 10×10 Array).

MyLab Education   **Blackline Master: 10 $\times$ 10 Array**

To make clear the connection to addition, very early multiplication activities can also include writing an addition sentence for the same model. A variety of models are shown in Figure 8.12.

As with additive problems, students benefit from activities with models to focus on the meaning of the operation and the associated symbolism, such as Activity 8.5.

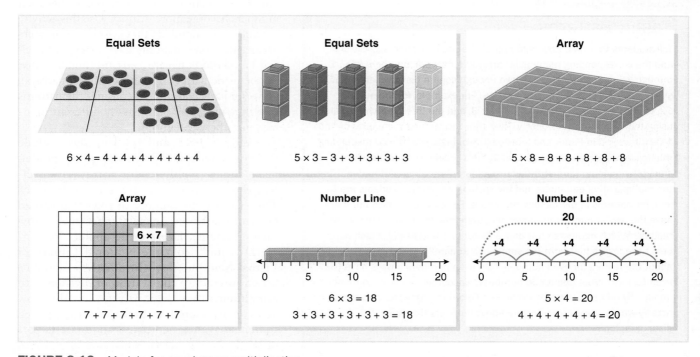

Equal Sets	Equal Sets	Array
$6 \times 4 = 4 + 4 + 4 + 4 + 4 + 4$	$5 \times 3 = 3 + 3 + 3 + 3 + 3$	$5 \times 8 = 8 + 8 + 8 + 8 + 8$

Array	Number Line	Number Line
6 × 7		20
$7 + 7 + 7 + 7 + 7 + 7$	$6 \times 3 = 18$ $3 + 3 + 3 + 3 + 3 + 3 = 18$	$5 \times 4 = 20$ $4 + 4 + 4 + 4 + 4 = 20$

FIGURE 8.12   Models for equal-group multiplication.

Activity 8.5

CCSS-M: 4.OA.B.4

Factor Quest

STUDENTS
with
SPECIAL
NEEDS

Start by having students think about a context that involves arrays such as parade formations (see the "Literature Connections" at the end of the chapter), seats in a classroom, or patches on a quilt. Then assign a number that has several factors—for example, 12, 18, 24, 30, or 36. Have students build as many rectangular arrays as they can (perhaps made from square tiles or cubes). Then have them record their arrays by drawing them on grid paper— see the Factor Quest Activity Page. For each, write the corresponding multiplication equations. For students with physical disabilities who may have limited motor skills to manipulate the materials, try the Factorize applet on the NCTM Illuminations website.

MyLab Education **Activity Page: Factor Quest**

CCSS Standards for Mathematical Practice

MP7. Look for and make use of structure.

Draw students' attention to the dimensions of the arrays, having them make the connection between the factors in the multiplication expression they have written to the number of rows and columns (the dimensions of the rectangle). Your class will undoubtedly want to decide whether a rectangle that is 3 by 8 should be counted differently from one that is 8 by 3. Leave the decision to the class, but take advantage of the opportunity to discuss how 3 rows of 8 are the same amount as 8 rows of 3. Note that if equal sets are made with paper plates rather than arrays are made, 3 sets of 8 look very different from 8 sets of 3. So, as students begin to think about the commutative property of multiplication, arrays provide a helpful representation.

Activity 8.6 is an extension of "Factor Quest" in that students look for patterns in the factors they find for numbers, such as the number of factors, the type of factors, the shape of the resulting array, and so on. Rather than assigning numbers that have several factors, this activity suggests including numbers that have only a few factors so that differences between numbers become more distinct. Use this activity to explore the numbers that are *prime* (numbers greater than one that only have a factor of itself and 1) and those that are *composites* (numbers that can be made with two or more different arrays). Have students continue to consider the patterns that they notice as they classify different numbers into these categories.

Activity 8.6

CCSS-M: 4.OA.B.4

Factor Patterns

Tell students that their task is to find all the multiplication expressions and the corresponding rectangular array(s) for several numbers (e.g., 1 through 16 or 10 through 25). Have enough square tiles available that students can explore all possible arrays. For example, for the number 12, they can build 12×1, 6×2, 4×3, and the three matching pairs using the commutative property. Then they record their rectangles on the 1-Centimeter Grid Paper and label each rectangle with the corresponding multiplication expression (e.g., 6×2). This organization helps when students are comparing arrays across different numbers. After identifying the multiplication equations and the rectangular arrays, students are to look for patterns in the factors and arrays. For example, which numbers have the fewest number of arrays and, therefore, the fewest number of factors? Which numbers have only a factor of 1 and itself? Which numbers have arrays that form the shape of a square? What can you say about the factors for even numbers? Do even numbers always have two even factors? What about odd numbers? Encourage students to think about why different patterns occur. See Feldman (2014) for another activity where students conjecture about numbers that have 2, 3, 4 or 5 distinct factors.

MyLab Education **Blackline Master: 1-Centimeter Grid Paper**

Activities 8.5 and 8.6 can also include division concepts by changing the model. Have children build or draw arrays by specifying how many squares are to be in the array. Then specify the number of rows that should be made (partition) or the number in each row (measurement). Explore the applet "Rectangle Division" from the National Library of Virtual Manipulatives (http://nlvm.usu.edu/) for an interactive illustration of division with remainders that demonstrates vividly how division is related to multiplication. When students have learned that 3 and 6 are factors of 18, they can write the equations $18 \div 3 = 6$ and $18 \div 6 = 3$ along with $3 \times 6 = 18$ and $6 + 6 + 6 = 18$ (assuming that three sets of six were modeled).

Activity 8.7   CCSS-M: 3.OA.A.2

Divide and Conquer

STUDENTS with SPECIAL NEEDS

Using the context of a story about sharing, such as *Bean Thirteen* (McElligott, 2007), provide children with a supply of counters (beans) and a way to place them into small groups (small paper cups). Have children count out a number of counters to be the whole or total amount and record this number. Next, specify either the number of equal groups to be made or the size of the groups: "Separate your counters into four equal-sized groups," or "Make as many groups of four as is possible." Have children write the corresponding multiplication equation for what their materials show; under that, have them write the division equation. For ELs, be sure they know what *groups, equal-sized groups,* and *groups of four* mean. For students with disabilities, start with a partition approach (i.e., separate your counters into three groups), in which they distribute the counters by placing one at a time into each cup.

Explore the Expanded Lesson: Divide and Conquer for additional details about this activity.

ENGLISH LEARNERS

MyLab Education   Expanded Lesson: Divide and Conquer

An excellent elaboration of this activity is having students create word problems to fit what they did with the tiles, cubes, or counters. By connecting the situation, materials and equation students can demonstrate their depth of understanding.

MyLab Education   Video Example 8.7

Watch this video for additional ways to students to model division problems.

When students consider both situations—the number of equal groups unknown and group size unknown you can discuss how the two situations are different, how each is related to multiplication, and how each is written as a division equation. You can show the different ways to write division equations at this time, such as $13 \div 4$, $4\overline{)13}$, and $\frac{13}{4}$. Do Activity 8.7 several times including whole quantities that are multiples of the divisor (no remainders) and situations with remainders. Note that it is technically incorrect to write the answer to a problem like $31 \div 4$ as 7 R 3 because this notation is not a number (a quotient should be a number). As written, the 3 is not well defined because it is really $\frac{3}{4}$. However, in the beginning, the form 7 R 3 may be the most appropriate. When modeling multiplicative comparison problems, consider exploring them with a bar diagram. See Figure 8.13 for a bar diagram related to the following situation:

Zane has five small toy cars. Madeline has four times as many cars. How many does Madeline have?

Activity 8.8   CCSS-M: 4.NBT.B.6

The Broken Division Key

Have students find methods of using a calculator to solve division exercises without using the divide key. "Find at least two ways to figure out $135 \div 5$ or $61 \div 14$ without pressing the divide key." If the problem is put in a story context, one method may actually match the problem better than another. Good discussions may follow different solutions with the same answers. Are they both correct? Why or why not?

Consider ways to explore a broken multiplication key as well.

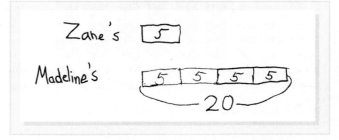

FIGURE 8.13 A student's work shows a model for multiplicative comparisons.

⏸ Pause & Reflect

Can *you* find three ways to solve 61 ÷ 14 on a calculator without using the divide key? For a hint, see the footnote.*•

MyLab Education **Self-Check 8.3**

MyLab Education **Application Exercise 8.2: Strategies for Teaching Operation Through Contextual Problems** Click the link to access this exercise, then watch the video and answer the accompanying questions.

Properties of Multiplication and Division

There are some multiplicative properties that are useful and thus worthy of attention. The emphasis should be on the ideas and applications rather than the terminology or definitions.

Commutative and Associative Properties of Multiplication. It is not obvious that 3 × 8 is the same as 8 × 3 or that, in general, the order of the numbers makes no difference (the *commutative property*). A picture of 3 sets of 8 objects cannot immediately be seen as 8 piles of 3 objects, nor on a number line are 8 hops of 3 noticeably the same as 3 hops of 8. The array, by contrast, is quite powerful in illustrating the commutative property, as shown in Figure 8.14(a). Students should build or draw arrays and use them to demonstrate why each array represents two equivalent multiplication expressions.

As in addition, there is an *associative property* of multiplication that is fundamental in flexibly solving problems (Ding, Li, Caprano, & Caprano, 2012). This property allows that when you multiply three numbers in an expression you can multiply either the first pair of numbers and then multiply that answer by the third number or multiply the last pair of numbers and then multiply that answer by the first number. Either way the product remains the same. A context is helpful, so here is an example that could be shared with students. Each tennis ball costs $2. Each can has 3 tennis balls. How much will it cost if we need to buy 6 cans? After analyzing the problem by showing actual cans of tennis balls or illustrations, students should try to consider the problem from two ways: (1) find out the cost for each can and then the total cost, 6 × (3 × 2); and (2) find out how many balls in total and then the total cost, (6 × 3) × 2 (Ding, 2010). See Figure 8.14(b).

Zero and Identity Properties. Factors of 0 and, to a lesser extent, 1 often cause conceptual challenges for students. In textbooks, you may find that a lesson on factors of 0 and 1 has students use a calculator to examine a wide range of products involving 0 or 1 (423 × 0, 0 × 28, 1536 × 1, etc.) and look for patterns. The pattern suggests rules for factors of 0 and 1, but not a reason. In another lesson, a word problem asks how many grams of fat there are in 7 servings of celery with 0 grams of fat in each serving. This contextual approach is far preferable to an arbitrary rule, because it asks students to reason. Make up interesting word problems involving 0 or 1, and discuss the results. Problems with 0 as a first factor are challenging. Note that on a number line, 5 hops of 0 lands at 0 (5 × 0). What would 0 hops of 5 be? Another fun activity is to try to model 6 × 0 or 0 × 8 with an array. (Try it!) Arrays for factors of 1 are also worth investigating.

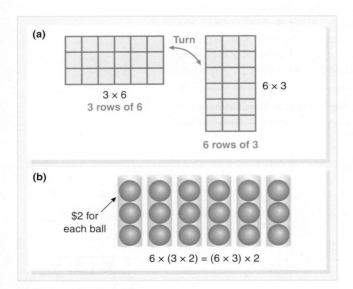

(a)

3 × 6
3 rows of 6

Turn

6 × 3

6 rows of 3

(b)

$2 for each ball

6 × (3 × 2) = (6 × 3) × 2

FIGURE 8.14 A model for the commutative property for multiplication (a), and an illustration of a problem showing the associative property of multiplication (b).

---

*There are two measurement approaches to find out how many 14's are in 61 (by repeatedly adding or subtracting). A third way is related to partitioning by finding 14 times what number is close to 61.

Distributive Property. The *distributive property of multiplication over addition* refers to the powerful idea that you can split (*decompose*) either of the two factors in a multiplication problem into two or more parts and then multiply each of the parts by the other factor and add the results. The final product is the same as when the original factors are multiplied. The concept involved is very useful in relating one basic fact to another, and it is also involved in the development of two-digit computation. But concrete representations and the use of real contexts are essential for students to make sense of this critically important property (Ding & Li, 2014). For example, to find the number of yogurts in 9 six-packs, use the logic that 9×6 is the same as $(5 \times 6) + (4 \times 6)$. The 9 packs have been split into 5 six-packs and 4 six-packs. Figure 8.15 illustrates how the array model (with square tiles or grid paper) can be used to demonstrate that a product can be broken up into two parts. Students should also can consider the distributive property in the opposite direction as in $70 + 40 = (7 + 4) \times 10$ (Ding & Li, 2010) to enhance their algebraic development. The next activity is designed to help students discover how to partition factors or, in other words, learn about the distributive property of multiplication over addition.

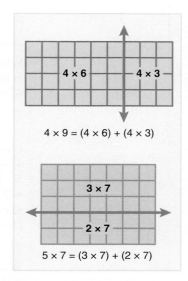

FIGURE 8.15 Models for the distributive property of multiplication over addition.

Activity 8.9   CCSS-M: 3.OA.B.5; 5.OA.A.1

Divide It Up

STUDENTS with SPECIAL NEEDS

Supply students with several sheets of 1-Centimeter Grid Paper or color tiles to represent a small garden that will be planted with two different kinds of vegetables. Assign each pair of students a garden plot size, such as 6×8. Garden sizes (products) can vary across the class to differentiate for students with disabilities or students who need a challenge. Ask students to find all of the different ways to make a single slice or cut through the garden to divide the plot for the two different vegetables. For each slice, students write an equation. For a slice that results in one row of 8, students would write $6 \times 8 = (5 \times 8) + (1 \times 8)$. Record student's suggestions using these conventions, even though students learn about the use of grouping symbols such as parentheses in fifth grade, and the full discussion of the order of operations is in the sixth grade. The individual expressions can be written inside the arrays as is shown in Figure 8.15.

MyLab Education Blackline Master: 1-Centimeter Grid Paper

Why Not Division by Zero? Sometimes students are simply told, "Division by zero is not allowed," often because teachers do not fully know how to explain this concept (Ojose, 2014; Quinn, Lamberg, & Perrin, 2008). Some children harbor misconceptions that the answer should be either zero or the number itself. To avoid merely sharing an arbitrary rule, pose problems to be modeled that involve zero: "Take 30 counters. How many sets of 0 can be made?" or "Put 12 blocks in 0 equal groups. How many are in each group?" or "Can you show me how to share 5 oranges with 0 children?" Then move students toward reasoned explanations (Crespo & Nicol, 2006) that consider the inverse relationship of multiplication and division and take the answer and put it back into a multiplication problem as a check. Then, with the orange problem you would ask, "What when multiplied by 0 produces an answer of 5?" Right, there is no answer. Therefore, division by 0 is undefined; it just doesn't make sense when we use our definition of division and its inverse relationship to multiplication.

MyLab Education Self-Check 8.4

Strategies for Teaching Operations through Contextual Problems

We have suggested the use of contextual problems or story problems to help children develop meanings for multiplication and division. But often students are at a loss for what to do when given a word problem. In this section, you will learn some techniques for helping them.

Analyzing Context Problems. Consider the following problem:

In building a road through a neighborhood, workers filled in large holes in the ground with dirt brought in by trucks. 638 truckloads of dirt were required to completely fill the holes. The average truck carried $6\frac{1}{4}$ cubic yards of dirt, which weighed 7.3 tons. How many tons of dirt were used to fill the holes?

Typically, in fifth-grade, problems of this type are found as part of a series of problems revolving around a single context or theme. Data may be found in a graph or chart, or perhaps a short news item or story. Students may have difficulty deciding on the correct operation and are often challenged to identify the appropriate data for solving the problem. Sometimes they will find two numbers in the problem and guess at the correct operation. Instead, students need tools for analyzing problems. At least two strategies can be taught that are very helpful: (1) thinking about the answer before solving the problem, or (2) working a simpler problem.

FORMATIVE ASSESSMENT Notes. What do you do if a student is having difficulty solving word problems? Use the Multiplicative Word Problem Activity Page and give each child a collection of these problems. Provide appropriate physical materials (e.g., counters, square tiles, grid paper), for testing ideas. Have students select two or three of the problems that they think are similar. Then they use a glue stick to paste the problems they choose onto the top of the Word Problem Sort Activity Page. Direct students to use the bottom of the page to write an explanation of their thinking and tell how they decided the problems are alike. This sorting process (based on Caldwell, Kobett, & Karp, 2014) helps students analyze the meaning of the story problem sentence by sentence and look for structure. ■

| MyLab Education | Activity Page: Multiplicative Word Problem |
| MyLab Education | Activity Page: Word Problem Sort |

Think about the Answer before Solving the Problem. Students who struggle with solving word problems need to spend adequate time thinking about the problem and imagining the situation. In addition, ELs need to comprehend both the contextual words (like *dirt*, *filled*, and *road*) and the mathematical terminology (*cubic yards*, *weighed*, *tons*, and *how many*). Instead of rushing in and beginning to do calculations believing that "number crunching" is what solves problems, students should spend time talking about (and, later, thinking about) what the answer might look like. In fact, one great strategy for differentiation is to pose the problem with the numbers missing or covered up (Holbert & Barlow, 2012/2013). This approach eliminates the tendency to number crunch. For our sample problem above, it might look like this:

What is happening in this problem? Some trucks were bringing dirt to fill up holes.

Is there any extra information we don't need? We don't need to know about the cubic yards in each truck.

What will the answer tell us? It will give us how many tons of dirt were needed to fill the holes. The answer will be some number of tons.

Will that be a small number of tons or a large number of tons? There were 7.3 tons on each truck, but there were a lot of trucks, not just one. The answer is probably going to be a lot of tons.

About how many tons do you estimate it will be? If there were 1000 trucks, it would be 7300 tons. So, it will be less than that. But it will be more than half of 7300, so the answer is more than 3650 tons.

In this type of discussion, three things are happening. First, children are focusing on the problem and the meaning of the answer instead of on numbers. The numbers are not important

CCSS Standards for Mathematical Practice

MP1. Make sense of problems and persevere in solving them.

in thinking about the structure of the problem. Second, with a focus on the structure of the problem, children identify the numbers that are important as well as numbers that are not important. Third, the thinking leads to a rough estimate of the answer and the unit of the answer (tons in this case). In any event, thinking about what the answer tells and about how large it might be is a useful starting point.

Work a Simpler Problem. The reason that models are rarely used with problems such as the dirt problem is that the large numbers are very challenging to model. Distances in thousands of miles and time in minutes and seconds—data likely to be found in the upper grades—are sometimes difficult to model. The general problem-solving strategy of "try a simpler problem" can almost always be applied to problems with unwieldy numbers.

A simpler-problem strategy has the following steps:

1. Substitute small whole numbers for all relevant numbers in the problem.
2. Model the problem (with counters, drawings, number lines, bar diagrams, or arrays) using the new numbers.
3. Write an equation that solves the simpler version of the problem.
4. Write the corresponding equation, substituting back the original numbers.
5. Calculate!
6. Write the answer in a complete sentence, and decide whether it makes sense.

Figure 8.16 shows how students simplified the numbers in the dirt problem. It also shows an alternative in which only one of the numbers is made smaller and the other number is illustrated symbolically. Both methods are effective.

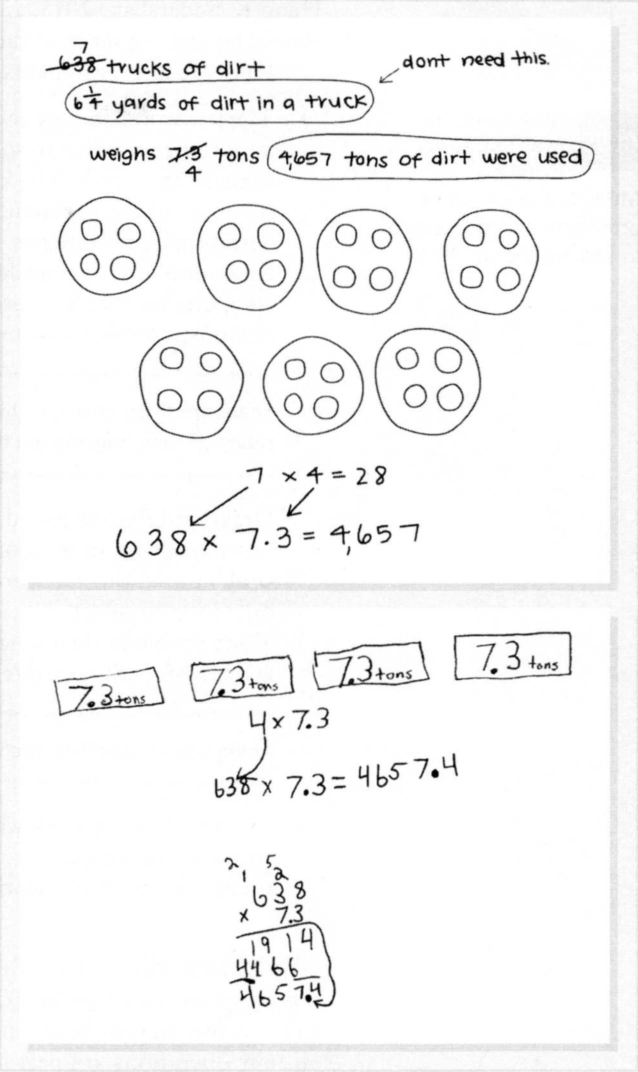

Students need strategies they can consistently use to analyze a problem instead of using the "word problem game" (De Corte & Verschaffel, 1985) where they are basically circumventing the process of making sense of the situation and instead guessing which operation to use. It is much more useful to have students do a few problems in which they must use a model or a drawing to justify their solution than to give them a lot of problems in which they guess at a solution but don't use reasoning and sense making.

Caution: Avoid the Key Word Strategy! In the past, it was often suggested that students should be taught to find *key words* in story problems to use to decide whether to add, subtract, multiply, or divide. Some students are still encouraged to use lists of key words with the corresponding operation linked to the word. For example, this strategy suggests that is you see the words *altogether* and *in all* in a story problem that means you should add, and *left* and *fewer* indicate you should subtract. The word *each* they would say suggests multiplication. This approach is unfortunately reported in the research as the most commonly identified method teachers say they use to help students solve word problems (Pearce, Bruun, Skinner, & Lopez-Mohler, 2013). To some extent, the overly simple and formulaic story problems sometimes found in textbooks reinforce this ill-advised approach (Sulentic-Dowell, Beal, & Capraro, 2006). When problems are written in this prescribed way, it may appear that the key word strategy is effective.

In contrast with the belief that this approach is useful, researchers and mathematics educators have long cautioned against the key word strategy (e.g., Clement & Bernhard, 2005;

FIGURE 8.16   Two ways students created a simpler problem.

Heng & Sudarshan, 2013, Karp, Bush & Dougherty, 2014; Sowder, 1988). Instead students should be making sense of the operations (Dixon, Nolan, Adams, Tobias, & Barmoha, 2016). Here are four arguments against presenting the key word approach:

CCSS **Standards for Mathematical Practice**
MP1. Make sense of problems and persevere in solving them.

1. The key word strategy sends a terribly wrong message about doing mathematics. The most important approach to solving any contextual problem is to analyze it and make sense of it using all the words. The key word approach encourages children to ignore the meaning and structure of the problem. Mathematics is about reasoning and making sense of situations. Sense-making strategies always work!

2. Key words are often misleading. Many times, the key word or phrase in a problem suggests an operation that is incorrect. The following problem shared by Drake and Barlow (2007) demonstrates this possibility:

There are three boxes of chicken nuggets on the table. Each box contains six chicken nuggets. How many chicken nuggets are there in all? (p. 272)

Drake and Barlow found that a student generated the answer of 9, using the words *how many in all* as a suggestion to add 3 + 6. Instead of making sense of the situation, the student used the key word approach as a shortcut in making a decision about which operation to select.

3. Many problems do not have key words. A student who has been taught to rely on key words is then left with no strategy. Here's an example:

Aidan has 28 goldfish. Twelve are orange and the rest are yellow. How many goldfish are yellow?

---

4. Key words don't work with two-step problems or more advanced problems, so using this approach on simpler problems sets students up for failure with more complex problems because they are not learning how to read for meaning.

Multistep Word Problems. Two-step word problems appear for the first time in the *Common Core State Standards* (NGA Center & CCSSO, 2010) when second-graders are expected to solve two-step addition and subtraction word problems. Then two-step word problems in all four operations are part of the third-grade standards and multistep problems in all four operations with whole numbers are expected starting in fourth grade, including problems with remainders that must be interpreted. Fifth-graders use multistep problems with measurement scenarios, and logically, multistep problems continue with a variety of numbers and contexts in middle school and beyond. Yet, students often have difficulty with the multistep problems particularly students with learning disabilities (Hord & Marita, 2014). To start, be sure children can analyze the structure of one-step problems in the way that we have discussed. The following ideas, adapted from Huinker (1994), are designed to help students see how two problems can be linked together to help think about multistep problems.

1. Give students a one-step problem and have them solve it. Before discussing the answer, have the students use the answer to the first problem to create a second problem. The rest of the class can then be asked to solve the second problem. Here is an example:

Given problem: It took 3 hours for the Morgan family to drive the 195 miles to Washington, D.C. What was their average speed?
Second problem: The Morgan children remember crossing the river at about 10:30 a.m., or 2 hours after they left home. About how many miles from home is the river?

---

2. Make a *hidden question*. Repeat the approach above by giving groups different one-step problems. Have them solve the first problem and write a second problem. Then they

should write a single combined problem that leaves out the question from the first problem. That question from the first problem is the *hidden question*, as in this example:

Given problem: **Toby bought three dozen eggs for 89 cents a dozen. How much was the total cost?**
Second problem: **How much change did Toby get back from $5?**
Hidden-question problem: **Toby bought three dozen eggs for 89 cents a dozen. How much change did Toby get back from $5?**

Have other groups identify the hidden question. Because all students are working on a similar task (be sure to mix the operations), they will be more likely to understand what is meant by a *hidden question*.

3. Pose standard two-step problems, and have the students identify and answer the hidden question. Consider this problem:

The Marsal Company bought 275 widgets wholesale for $3.69 each. In the first month, the company sold 205 widgets at $4.99 each. How much did the company make or lose on the widgets? Do you think the Marsal Company should continue to sell widgets?

MyLab Education **Application Exercise 8.3: Observing and Responding to Student Thinking** Click the link to access this exercise, then watch the video and answer the accompanying questions.

VIDEO EXAMPLE

Begin by considering the questions that were suggested earlier: "What's happening in this problem?" (something is being bought and sold at two different prices). "What will the answer tell us?" (how much profit or loss there was). These questions will get you started. If students are stuck, you can ask, "Is there a hidden question in this problem?" Although the examples given here provide a range of contexts, for ELs, using the *same* (relevant and familiar) context across this three-step process would reduce the linguistic demands and therefore make the stories more comprehensible—and the mathematics more accessible.

Another approach is to use a table to support students' working memory (Hord & Marita, 2014). By having students organize information into categories such as "What is the question? What is the important information? and What is the first thing you should do?," students can start to make sense of the problem. Then they repeat this process until all of the problem's multiple steps are addressed.

FORMATIVE ASSESSMENT Notes. One of the best ways to assess knowledge of the meaning of the operations is to have students generate story problems for a given equation or result (Drake & Barlow, 2007; Whitin & Whitin, 2008). Use the Translation Task Activity Page based on the work of Shield and Swinson (1996) as an assessment. Give students an expression such as 5×7; ask that they record and answer it in the upper left-hand quarter, write a story problem representing the expression in the upper right quarter, draw a picture (or model) in the lower left section, and describe how they would tell a younger child how to solve this problem in the last section. (Students with disabilities could dictate the story problem and the description of the solving process while the teacher transcribes.) Students who can ably complete all sections will demonstrate their depth of understanding, whereas students who struggle may reveal areas of strength and weakness. Adapt the assessment by providing the result (e.g., "24 cents") and asking students to write a division problem (or other operation) that will generate that answer, along with models and word problems written in the remaining quarters. ■

MyLab Education   Activity Page: Translation Task

MyLab Education   Self-Check 8.5

MyLab Education   Math Practice: Need to practice or refresh your math content knowledge? Click to access practice exercises associated with the content from this chapter.

Knowing common student challenges and misconceptions is a critical part of planning and can greatly influence how a lesson is structured and what problems you use. See Table 8.1, for possible ways to help students.

TABLE 8.1   COMMON CHALLENGES AND MISCONCEPTIONS RELATED TO THE MEANING OF THE OPERATIONS

Common Challenge or Misconception	What It Looks Like	How to Help
1. Student treats the equal sign as an operation symbol or as a signal to compute	For 5 + 4 = ___ + 3, says the ___ should be 9 because 5 + 4 = 9. When asked if 6 = 6, says no, because there is no computation to do. When asked if 7 = 3 + 4, says no, because "you can't write it that way because there is no computation to do. Its backwards."	• Use a number balance to illustrate the relational meaning of the equal sign. • Read the equal sign as "is the same as" and "equals." • Avoid reading 5 + 3 "makes" 8 because the word "makes" sounds like an operation or that you have to carry out an action. • Pose true/false number sentences in a variety of equation formats.
2. Student overgeneralizes the commutative property of addition to subtraction	In solving 24 − 7, subtracts 4 − 7 as 7 − 4 for an answer of 23.	• Have students first model problems with single digit numbers and show how you cannot subtract 7 cubes from 4 cubes.
3. Student thinks that adding zero makes a number bigger and subtracting zero makes a number smaller	6 + 0 = 7 or 12 − 0 = 11	• Use story problems that introduce adding and subtracting zero in a meaningful context that students can act out.
4. Student when using a number line counts tick marks or numbers on the instead of the units (or intervals) between the numbers	When the student counts using a number line the count is consistently off by 1. Points to tick marks or numbers as they count.	• Use the sequence of number line models in Figure 8.6 to emphasize that the unit is what is counted on a number line. • Use physical hops and steps as well as arrow and arcs to show what is being counted.
5. There is no relationship between addition and subtraction and/or multiplication and division (they do not see the inverse relationship)	Students don't use addition to solve subtraction situations. Students don't use multiplication to solve division problems.	• Avoid the rote use of fact families to teach the inverse relationship as that emphasizes procedures without having students see the inverse relationship. • Use concrete materials and have students act out a series of problems with the same three numbers—showing how the part-part-whole or the number in each group, the number of groups and the product relate to each other.
6. Addition or multiplication make numbers bigger (and the corollary that the factors in multiplication problems are always smaller than the product)	Students believe that they should always get a larger answer in an addition or multiplication problem.	• When students point out these patterns say that these ideas are only true for some numbers (Karp, Bush, & Dougherty, 2014). • Point out counterexamples that are within their reach such as that 54 + 0 = 54 or that 15 × 0 = 0.

Common Challenge or Misconception	What It Looks Like	How to Help
7. Subtraction and division make numbers smaller. The divisor must be less than the dividend.	Students believe that they should always get a smaller answer in a subtraction or division problem. Students use this idea to check for a reasonable answer or to justify their thinking.	• Provide examples as well as counterexamples such as $8 \div 1 = 8$. • Have students discuss when this "rule" works and when it does not. • Have students find ways to equally share 3 cookies with 5 friends. This approach will help them act out the division and see that the divisor can be greater than the dividend. • Avoid using generalizations that may appear to be "rules" unless the students are clear of the circumstances in which the rule always works.
8. Student relies solely on a key word strategy to determine which operation to use in a word problem.	When solving a word problem, the student scans the problem for the numbers and a key word to help determine which operation to use. *Sarah ate 34 marshmallows. Sarah ate 6 more marshmallows than Rich. How many marshmallows did Rich eat?* The student solves the problem by adding 34 and 6 because s/he interprets the word "more" to mean "add." The student is stumped when faced with story problems that have no key words, such as: *Laurie has 83 pennies. 16 of them are shiny. The others are dull. How many are dull?*	• Cover up the number "6" in the word problem, ask the student to read the problem. Then ask the student who ate more marshmallows. • Have the student use bar diagrams to represent the amounts for Sarah and the amounts for Rich to help make more explicit the relationship between the quantities. • Do not teach key words to solve word problems. • Make sure to pose story problems and contextual problems that include all four problem types (join, separate, part-part-whole, compare) with the unknown quantity in different locations so children gain experience thinking about and solving a variety of situations. • Have available and encourage the use of physical materials for students to model story/contextual problems. Discuss what they have done to determine the answer. • Suggest to the student some of the recommendations for analyzing contextual problems (e.g., think about the answer before solving the problem; solve a simpler problem).
9. Students choose the wrong operation in word problems	Students guess, just add or use the operation you've been studying all week to answer all word problems.	• Focus on the structure of the problems using graphic organizers or the story problem sorting activities discussed in this chapter.
10. Students think the remainder is left over and not part of the answer	Students write 9 R 2 and do not use the remainder in deciding how to answer the question. Students forget about the remainder and do not include it in their answer.	• Give students the multiple problems shared in this chapter that show the various ways remainders need to be interpreted and how that interpretation affects the answer. • Give students problems from anonymous students that have the remainder interpreted improperly. Have students "grade" the problems and share the findings in a class discussion.
11. Students are unsure about division by zero	Students write: $5 \div 0 = 0$	• Students must focus on division as having an inverse relationship with multiplication. What number when you multiply it by zero will equal 5? • Ask students to take out 5 counters. How many sets of 0 can be made? Or put 5 blocks in 0 equal groups. How many blocks are in each group?

RESOURCES FOR CHAPTER 8

LITERATURE CONNECTIONS

Books with stories or pictures concerning collections, the purchase of items, measurements, and so on can be used to pose problems or, better, to stimulate students to invent their own problems. A favorite for this purpose is *The Doorbell Rang* by Pat Hutchins (1986). Here are others:

Bedtime Math
Overdeck (2013)

This book (and accompanying website) helps parent incorporate math problems into the nighttime (or daytime) routine. There are three levels of problem difficulty: "wee ones" (preK), "little kids" (K–2), and "big kids" (grade 2 and up). Each set of problems revolves around a high-interest topic such as roller coasters, foods, and animals. Teachers can use these problems in class for engaging students in all four operations.

One Hundred Hungry Ants
Pinczes (1999)

A Remainder of One
Pinczes (2002)

These books, written by a grandmother for her grandchild, help students explore multiplication and division. The first tells of 100 ants on a trip to a picnic. To speed their travel, the ants move from a single-file of 100 to two rows of 50, then four rows of 25, and so forth. This story uses visual representation of arrays and students can be given different sizes of ant groups to explore factors and products. The second book describes the trials and tribulations of a parade formation of 25 bugs. As the queen views the rectangular outline of the parading bugs, she notices that 1 bug is trailing behind. The group tries to create different numbers of rows and columns (arrays), but again 1 bug is always a "leftover" (remainder). Students can be given different parade groups and can generate formations that will leave 1, 2, or none out of the group.

RECOMMENDED READINGS

Articles

Champagne, Z., Schoen, R., & Riddell, C. (2014). Variations in both-addends-unknown problems. *Teaching Children Mathematics, 21*(2), 114–121.

The focus of the article is on the problem type of both addends unknown. The authors share examples of problems, students' thinking about their solution methods and student work samples.

Clement, L., & Bernhard, J. (2005). A problem-solving alternative to using key words. *Mathematics Teaching in the Middle School, 10*(7), 360–365.

This article explores the use of sense making in solving word problems as a replacement for using a key word strategy. The emphasis is on the meanings of the operations as common student misconceptions are analyzed.

Books

Carpenter, T. P., Fennema, E., Franke, M. L., Levi, L., & Empson, S. (2014). *Children's mathematics: Cognitively guided instruction.* (2nd Edition) Portsmouth, NH: Heinemann.

This is the classic book for understanding word-problem structures for all operations. The structures are explained in detail along with methods for using these problems with students. Videos of classrooms and children modeling strategies are included.

Caldwell, J., Kobett, B., & Karp, K. (2014). *Putting essential understanding of addition and subtraction into practice in grades prekindergarten–2.* Reston, VA: NCTM.

Lannin, J., Chval, K., & Jones, D. (2013). *Putting essential understanding of multiplication and division into practice in grades 3–5.* Reston, VA: NCTM.

These two books offer the big ideas about how to teach the four operations, including the mathematical content teachers need to know and connections to topics that come before and after these critical ideas.

CHAPTER 9

Developing Basic Fact Fluency

LEARNER OUTCOMES

After reading this chapter and engaging in the embedded activities, you should be able to:

9.1 Describe approaches to developing fact fluency, especially the three-phase strategy-based process.

9.2 Illustrate strategies for helping students derive addition, subtraction, multiplication, and division facts.

9.3 Justify an effective approach for reinforcing and remediating basic fact fluency.

Basic facts for addition and multiplication are the number combinations where both addends or both factors are less than 10. Basic facts for subtraction and division are the corresponding combinations. Thus, $15 - 8 = 7$ is a subtraction fact because the corresponding addition parts are less than 10. When a student is able to give an accurate response within 3 seconds, they have automaticity or mastery. But, the goal for basic facts is to develop fluency. Fluency is not only about speed, it includes being able to flexibly, accurately, efficiently, and appropriately solve problems (NRC, 2001, NGA Center & CCSSO, 2010). Therefore teaching and assessing basic facts must focus on all four of these components. Spoiler alert: To do this we must eliminate practices such as timed-tests and use strategies that build student number sense and confidence!

BIG IDEAS

◆ Students move through three phases in developing fluency with basic facts: counting, reasoning strategies, and mastery. Instruction and assessment must help students through these phases without rushing them.

◆ Number relationships provide the basis for strategies that help students remember basic facts or figure out unknown facts. For example, when solving $8 + 6$ students can decompose 6 into $2 + 4$, and add the 2 to the 8 to make a 10, and then solve $10 + 4 = 14$.

◆ When students struggle with the basic facts, they may need to return to the use of strategies; more drill is not the answer.

Teaching and Assessing the Basic Facts

Developing fact fluency begins in kindergarten and continues through middle school, with improvements in basic facts leading to gains in mathematics achievement (Nelson, Parker, & Zaslofsky, 2016). *Addition and subtraction* fact fluency begins in kindergarten and continues through grade 2, when students must know their addition facts from memory (i.e., have mastered the facts or have automaticity). Similarly, *multiplication and division* fact fluency begins in grade 2, with mastery or automaticity often expected by the end of grade 3.

Developmental Phases for Learning Basic Facts

Developing fluency with basic facts is a developmental process—just like every topic in this book! Flash cards and timed tests are *not* the best way to develop fluency. Instead, focus on number sense (the four components of fluency). Research indicates that early number sense predicts school success more than other measures of cognition, like verbal, spatial, or memory skills or reading ability (Jordan, Kaplan, Locuniak, & Ramineni, 2007; Locuniak & Jordan, 2008; Mazzocco & Thompson, 2005).

Students progress from counting to eventually "just knowing" that $2 + 7$ is 9 or that 5×4 is 20. This developmental progression takes time and many experiences. Baroody describes three phases of learning facts (2006, p. 22):

> *Phase 1: Counting strategies:* Using object counting (e.g., blocks or fingers) or verbal counting to determine the answer. (Example: $4 + 7 = $ _____. Student starts with 7 and counts on verbally 8, 9, 10, 11.)
>
> *Phase 2: Reasoning strategies:* Using known information to logically determine an unknown combination. (Example: $4 + 7$. Student knows that $3 + 7$ is 10, so $4 + 7$ is one more, 11.)
>
> *Phase 3: Mastery:* Producing answers efficiently (quickly and accurately). (Example: $4 + 7$. Student quickly responds, "It's 11; I just know it.")

Because phase 1 is addressed in Chapters 7 and 8, this chapter primarily focuses on phase 2 and phase 3. Phase 2 is often under-emphasized or neglected entirely, yet it is an essential bridge between inefficient counting strategies and mastery (automaticity). Phase 2 utilizes, and further develops, students' relational understanding, and students can become so quick at applying a strategy that it becomes as automatic as recall (Baroody, Purpura, Eiland, Reid, & Paliwal, 2016). Figure 9.1 outlines the developmental process for solving basic addition and subtraction problems.

FORMATIVE ASSESSMENT Notes. When are students ready to work on reasoning strategies? When they are able to (1) use counting-on strategies (start with the largest and count up) and (2) see that numbers can be decomposed (e.g., that 6 is $5 + 1$). Interview students by posing one-digit addition problems and ask how they solved it. For example, $3 + 8$ (Do they count on from the larger?) and $5 + 6$ (Do they see $5 + 5 + 1$?). For multiplication, 3×8 (Do they know this is 3 eights? Do they see it as 2 eights and one more eight?). ■

Approaches to Teaching Basic Facts

Over the last century, three main approaches have been used to teach the basic facts. The pros and cons of each approach are briefly discussed in this section.

Memorization. This approach moves from presenting concepts of addition and multiplication straight to memorization of facts, not devoting time to developing strategies (Baroody, Bajwa, & Eiland, 2009). There is strong evidence that this method simply does not work. You may be tempted to respond that you learned your facts in this manner; however, as long ago as

	Addition	**Subtraction**
Counting	Direct modeling (counting objects and fingers) • Counting all • Counting on from first • Counting on from larger Counting abstractly • Counting all • Counting on from first • Counting on from larger	Counting objects • Separating from • Separating to • Adding on Counting fingers • Counting down • Counting up Counting abstractly • Counting down • Counting up
Reasoning	Properties • $a + 0 = a$ • $a + 1 =$ next whole number • Commutative property Known-fact derivations (e.g., $5 + 6 = 5 + 5 + 1$; $7 + 6 = 7 + 7 - 1$) Redistributed derived facts (e.g., $7 + 5 = 7 + (3 + 2) = (7 + 3) + 2 = 10 + 2 = 12$)	Properties • $a - 0 = a$ • $a - 1 =$ previous whole number Inverse/complement of known addition facts (e.g., $12 - 5$ is known because $5 + 7 = 12$) Redistributed derived facts (e.g., $12 - 5 = (7 + 5) - 5 = 7 + (5 - 5) = 7$)
Retrieval	Retrieval from long-term memory	Retrieval from long-term memory

FIGURE 9.1   The developmental process for basic fact mastery for addition and subtraction.
Source: Henry, V. J., & Brown, R. S. (2008). "First-Grade Basic Facts: An Investigation into Teaching and Learning of an Accelerated, High-Demand Memorization Standard." *Journal for Research in Mathematics Education, 39*(2), p. 156. Reprinted with permission. Copyright © 2008 by the National Council of Teachers of Mathematics, Inc. All rights reserved.

1935 studies concluded that students develop a variety of strategies for learning basic facts in spite of the amount of isolated drill that they experience (Brownell & Chazal, 1935).

A memorization approach skips phase 2 of the developmental process, resulting in numerous limitations (Baroody, 2006):

• *Inefficiency.* There are too many facts to memorize. Without using strategies, students must memorize 100 addition facts (just for the addition combinations 0–9) and 100 multiplication facts (0–9), along with the 200 subtraction and division facts. Yikes!
• *Inflexibility.* Students don't learn strategies, so resort to counting strategies, never developing flexibility (a component of fluency).
• *Inappropriate applications.* Students misapply the facts and don't check their work (they don't have strategies to use to confirm if the sum or product is correct).

Importantly, low achieving students do not use strategies, they use counting techniques (Boaler, 2016), and therefore it seems that strategy instruction is needed in order to increase overall achievement in mathematics. Finally, memorization and drill causes unnecessary anxiety and undermines student interest and confidence in mathematics. Unfortunately, this memorization approach is the most widely used in the United States. We hope you will commit to be part of a movement away from this approach to the ones described next.

Explicit Strategy Instruction. For more than three decades, explicit strategy instruction has been used in many classrooms. Students learn a strategy (e.g., combinations of 10). Students then explore and practice the strategies (e.g., using a ten-frame to see which facts equal 10). Research supports the use of explicit strategy instruction as effective in helping all students learn (and remember) their basic facts (e.g., Baroody, et al., 2009; Baroody, et al., 2016; Thornton, 1978; Fuson, 1992; Rathmell, 1978; Thornton & Toohey, 1984).

MyLab Education   **Video Example 9.1**

Watch a video of John Van de Walle discussing the importance of basic facts and of using a strategy approach.

VIDEO EXAMPLE

Explicit strategy instruction is intended to *support* student thinking rather than give the students something new to remember. A heavy focus on memorizing strategies results in students with lower number sense (Henry & Brown, 2008). The key is to help students see the possible strategies and then *choose* one that helps them solve the problem without counting. Such reasoning strategies are provided in the next sections.

CCSS **Standards for Mathematical Practice**
MP2. Reason abstractly and quantitatively.

Guided Invention. Guided invention also focuses on strategies, but in a more open-ended manner. It is focused on having students select a strategy based on their knowledge of number relationships (Gravemeijer & van Galen, 2003). A teacher might post the fact $6 + 7$. One student may think of $6 + 7$ as "double 6 is 12 and one more is 13." Another student sees it as $7 + 3$ (to make 10) and then 3 more. Another student may take 5 from each addend to make 10 and then add the remaining 1 and 2. The key is that each student is using number combinations and relationships that make sense to them.

In *guided invention* the teacher may not explain a strategy, but carefully sets up tasks where students notice number relationships. For example, in the $6 + 7$ task, the teacher might show a quick image of counters in two ten-frames and ask students to think of different ways they can mentally move the counters to find the total.

Teaching Basic Facts Effectively

Teaching basic facts takes time, and subsets within the facts are approached in a developmentally appropriate order (the sequence of strategies listed in the next section reflect that order). As you are working on a subset of facts, your goal is to help students progress through the three phases. For example, ask students how they solved $7 + 4$. Some will have counted all, some will have counting on (phase 1), and others will use the Making 10 or other reasoning strategy. Help the students who are counting to count on, for those counting on to apply a reasoning strategy. Through number talks, basic fact games, and other experiences, provide engaging and diverse experiences for students to use and talk about their strategies. Students will move to more efficient strategies over the course of the year, become quicker at applying them, and eventually will develop mastery (automaticity).

Use Story Problems. Research has found that when a strong emphasis is placed on solving problems, students not only become better problem solvers but also master more basic facts than students in a drill program (National Research Council, 2001). In fact, posing a story problem each day, followed by a brief discussion of the strategies that children used, can improve student's accuracy and efficiency with basic facts (Rathmell, Leutzinger, & Gabriele, 2000). Story problems provide context that can help students understand the situation and apply flexible strategies for doing computation. For example, if you wish to elicit the Making 10 strategy, you might use this story:

CCSS **Standards for Mathematical Practice**
MP1. Make sense of problems and persevere in solving them.

Rachel had 9 ponies in one barn and 6 ponies in the pasture. How many ponies did she have altogether?

The numbers and situation in this story lend to thinking of $9 + 6$ as equivalent to $10 + 5$ (one pony could be moved to the other barn).

Multiplication stories can focus on array situations. Arrays help students see how to decompose a fact (splitting the rows) and see the commutative property (e.g., $3 \times 7 = 7 \times 3$). For example, consider that a class is working on the 7 facts. The teacher points to the calendar (an array) and poses the following question:

In 3 weeks we will be going to the zoo. How many days until we go to the zoo?

A student might solve this by starting with double 7 (14) and then adding 7 more. The teacher might then ask other students to explain if/why this strategy works. Then, the teacher might extend the idea of doubling to other facts. For example, asking, "How might doubling help us figure out how many days in 4 weeks (4 × 7)? After giving students time on this question, the teacher can help students see that single facts can be broken apart into known facts (e.g., that 4 × 7 is 2 × (2 × 7) or 7 doubled and doubled again), applying important properties of multiplication.

Some teachers are hesitant to use story problems with ELs or students with disabilities because of the additional language or reading required. However, using story problems with all students is important because language and context supports understanding. The key is that the contexts you use are relevant, support mathematical reasoning, and are understood by each student.

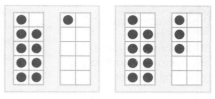

FIGURE 9.2 Sequencing quick images can help students develop reasoning strategies.

Use Quick Images. The purpose of quick images is to move students beyond counting to seeing the way numbers can be composed or decomposed. For young children, this is a high leverage routine (McCoy, Barnett, & Combs, 2013; Shumway, 2011). You can use Dot Cards, Five-Frames and Ten-Frames (see Relationships between Numbers 1 through 10 section in Chapter 7 for many ideas). The instructional process is: Flash the image for a few seconds. Hide it. Flash it again. Ask students how many they see. Then, importantly, listen as different students tell *how* they saw that quantity. Five-frames and ten-frames help students see number relations and develop strategies. Sequencing quick images can help students see relationships. For example, see the two quick images in Figure 9.2.

MyLab Education	Blackline Master: Dot Cards
MyLab Education	Blackline Master: Five-Frames
MyLab Education	Blackline Master: Ten-Frames
MyLab Education	Activity Page: Relationships between Numbers 1 through 10

❚❚ Pause & Reflect

What strategy might the sequence of quick images in Figure 9.2 help students see? What quick images might support multiplication? ●

Multiplication quick images include dot patterns, just like addition facts, but the dot patterns are in equal sized groups or in arrays. For example, if you are wanting students to notice that 3 groups of a quantity are 'a double and one more group' use a dot card like this one:

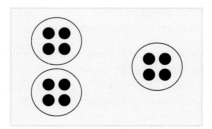

Such cards can be created with stickers and used file folders, or they are available on the internet and through various companies.

Explicitly Teach Reasoning Strategies. Specific reasoning strategies for addition, subtraction, multiplication, and division are the focus of the next section, here we outline the big idea of using reasoning strategies: students make use of *known facts* and relationships to

CCSS **Standards for Mathematical Practice**

MP3. Construct viable arguments and critique the reasoning of others.

derive unknown facts. For example, students must know their Combinations of 10 addition facts and the 10 + _____ facts before they are ready to learn the Making 10 strategy. They must know the doubles multiplication facts in order to do the "double and one more group" strategy. For example, to solve an unknown fact, like $7 + 5$, students look to take apart one number in order to make a combination of 10, noticing that $7 + 5 = 7 + 3 + 2$.

MyLab Education   **Video Example 9.2**

Watch how Connor uses known facts to solve $6 +$ _____ $= 13$.

MyLab Education   **Video Example 9.3**

Watch how Myrna uses known facts to solve $6 +$ _____ $= 13$.

MyLab Education   **Video Example 9.4**

Watch how Miguel uses known facts to solve $6 +$ _____ $= 13$.

Don't expect to have a strategy introduced and understood with just one lesson or activity. Students need lots of opportunities to make a strategy their own. Plan many quick images, games and interactive activities as part of daily work at school and home. Across these opportunities, emphasize talking about the strategies. You can display lists of reasoning strategies for students to reference, so that students have a shared language around the strategies they are using (e.g., "Strategy for $\times$ 3s: Double and add one more group. Ex: $3 \times 7 = (2 \times 7) + 7 = 14 + 7 = 21$").

Assessing Basic Facts Effectively

A glance back at Chapter 5 will illustrate many formative assessment strategies: observations, interviews, performance tasks, and writing. Why do we use formative assessment strategies? To figure out what students know and what they do not know so that we can focus instruction on what students need to know, do, or understand. Formative assessment improves student achievement (Wiliam, Lee, Harrison, & Black, 2004; Wiliam & Thompson, 2007). Why, then, is assessment of basic facts often limited to timed tests? We must do better if we are going to ensure that all students learn (and retain) their basic facts.

What Is Wrong with Timed Tests? First, timed tests do not assess the four elements of fluency. You gain no insights into which strategies students are using, nor if they are flexible in using those strategies. Tests give a little insight into how efficient students are, but you don't really learn enough, because students might use very inefficient strategies for some facts while going quickly through others. So, at best, you get a sense of which facts they are getting correct (accuracy). Second, timed tests negatively affect students' number sense and recall of facts (Boaler, 2012, 2014; Henry & Brown, 2008; Ramirez, Gunderson, Levine, & Beilock, 2013). Third, timed tests are not needed for students to master basic facts (Kling, 2011), and therefore waste time that could be used in meaningful learning and formative assessment experiences.

CCSS **Standards for Mathematical Practice**

MP2. Reason abstractly and quantitatively.

How Might I Assess Basic Fact Fluency? As you assess, remember there is no one "best" strategy for any fact. For example, $7 + 8$ could be solved using Making 10 or near-doubles. The more you emphasize choice, the more students will be able to find strategies that work for them, and that will lead to their own fact fluency.

Think about each of the aspects of fluency and ask yourself, "How can I determine if each of my students is able to do that for this set of facts?" Table 9.1 offers a few ideas for each component of fluency (based on Kling & Bay-Williams, 2014).

Activity 9.1 is good for assessing students' flexibility and ability to select an appropriate strategy for a fact, and could be used as a routine or a number talk.

Activity 9.1
CCSS-M: 1.OA.C.6; 2.OA.B.2; 3.OA.B.5; 3.OA.C.7

If You Didn't Know

Pose the following task: If you did not know the answer to 8 + 5 (or any fact that you want students to think about), how could you figure it out without counting? Encourage students to come up with more than one way (hopefully using the strategies suggested previously). ELs and reluctant learners benefit from first sharing their ideas with a partner and then with the class.

ENGLISH LEARNERS

The more students are engaged in activities and games, the more chance you have to use observations and interviews to monitor which *strategies* students know and don't know and which *facts* they know and don't know (games are discussed in the Reinforcing Basic Fact Mastery section). Then, you can adapt the games and instruction to address their needs.

MyLab Education　**Self-Check 9.1**

Reasoning Strategies for Addition Facts

Recall that basic fact mastery depends on progressing through three phases. The second phase, reasoning strategies, warrants significant attention; too often students are asked to go from counting (phase 1) to memorization (phase 3). Therefore a significant part of this chapter is devoted to what reasoning strategies are important to teach and how to teach them well.

TABLE 9.1　EFFECTIVE STRATEGIES FOR ASSESSING BASIC FACT FLUENCY

Aspects of Fluency	Observation	Interview Probes	Writing (Journals or Tests)
Appropriate strategy selection	As they play a game, are they picking a strategy that makes sense for that fact? For example, for 9 + 2 they might count on, but not for 9 + 6.	Nicolas solved 6 + 8 by changing it in his mind to 4 + 10. What did he do? Is this a good strategy? Tell why or why not.	Review the multiplication table. Write which facts are your "toughies." Next to each one, tell a strategy that you want to remember to use.
Flexibility	As for strategy selection, do they pick Making 10 for 9 + 6? Do they notice that 8 × 3 is also 3 × 8?	Solve 6 × 7 using one strategy. Now try solving it using a different strategy.	Explain how you think about these two problems: 13 − 3 = 12 − 9 =
Efficiency	How long does it take to select a strategy? Are they quick to use doubles? Does efficiency vary with certain facts, like facts over 10 (add) or the 7s facts (multiply)?	Go through this stack of cards and sort by the ones you *just know* and the ones you *use a strategy*.	Solve these (basic fact) problems (provide a set of 10). If you *just knew* the answer, circle it. If you *used a strategy,* write the strategy's name (e.g., Close Fact).
Accuracy	Which facts are they consistently getting correct?	What is the answer to 7 × 8? How do you know it is correct (how might you check it)?	Review your (3s facts) with your partner. Make a stack of the ones when you were correct and not correct. Record which facts you have "down pat" and which you are still learning.

Reasoning strategies for addition facts are directly related to one or more number relationships that were developed in Chapter 7. It takes many experiences over many months for students to move from using strategies to just knowing their facts.

MyLab Education Video Example 9.5

Watch teachers emphasize reasoning strategies and number relationships to develop fluency.

Notice that no memorization is needed—just many activities like the ones shared here (and in Chapters 7 and 8)! The first five strategies listed are foundational strategies, so they should be developed through phase 3 (mastery/automaticity) before developing the other strategies.

One More Than and Two More Than (Count On)

Each of the 36 facts highlighted in the following chart has at least one addend of 1 or 2. These facts are a direct application of the one-more-than and two-more-than relationships described in Chapter 7. Being able to count on, then, is a necessary prerequisite to being able to apply this strategy (Baroody et al., 2009).

+	0	1	2	3	4	5	6	7	8	9
0		1	2							
1	1	2	3	4	5	6	7	8	9	10
2	2	3	4	5	6	7	8	9	10	11
3		4	5							
4		5	6							
5		6	7							
6		7	8							
7		8	9							
8		9	10							
9		10	11							

Create story problems in which one of the addends is a 1 or a 2. For example, "Seven children were waiting for the slide. Then 2 more children got in line. How many children were waiting for the slide?" Ask different students to explain how they got the answer of 9. Some will count all, some will count on from 7, and some will 'just know' that 2 more than 7 is 9. Help students see the connection between counting on and adding 2, for example showing a number line.

Activity 9.2

CCSS-M: 1.OA.A.1; 1.OA.C.6; 2.OA.B.2

How Many Feet in the Bed?

Read *How Many Feet in the Bed?* by Diane Johnston Hamm. On the second time through the book, ask students how many more feet are in the bed when a new person gets in. Ask students to record the equation (e.g., 6 + 2) and tell how many. Two less can be considered as family members get out of the bed. Find opportunities to make the connection between counting on and adding using a number line. For ELs, be sure that they know what the phrases "two more" and "two less" mean (and clarify the meaning of *foot,* which is also used for measuring). Acting out with students in the classroom can be a great illustration for both ELs and students with disabilities.

ENGLISH LEARNERS

STUDENTS with **SPECIAL NEEDS**

In the context of this activity, the sum is set up with the larger number first. However, when the sum is reversed (e.g., 2 + 6) students may count on from the first number, rather than the larger number. A focus on strategies (e.g., counting on from the larger) helps students, particularly those with disabilities select the more efficient strategy (Dennis, Sorrells, & Falcomata, 2016). Activity 9.3 is a way for students to practice using efficient strategies.

Activity 9.3
CCSS-M: 1.OA.C.5; 1.OA.C.6; 2.OA.B.2

One More Than and Two More Than with Dice and Spinners

As illustrated in Figure 9.3, you need a die labeled +1, +2, +1, +2, "one more," and "two more" and a second die labeled 3, 4, 5, 6, 7, and 8 (or whatever values students need to practice). After each roll of the dice, students should say the complete fact: "Four and two more is six." Alternatively, roll one die and use a spinner with +1 on one half and +2 on the other half. For students with disabilities, you may want to start with a die that just has +1 on every side and then another day move on to a +2 die. This will help emphasize and practice one approach. Similarly, in Expanded Lesson: Two More Than/Two Less Than, students use Dot Cards to connect the idea of more and less to adding and subtracting.

STUDENTS with SPECIAL NEEDS

MyLab Education   Expanded Lesson: Two More Than/Two Less Than
MyLab Education   Activity Page: Dot Cards

Adding Zero

Though adding 0 is generally an easier fact to learn, some students overgeneralize the idea that answers to addition problems are bigger than the addends. They also may have a harder time when the 0 comes first (e.g., 0 + 8). Use story problems involving zero and use drawings that show two parts with one part empty.

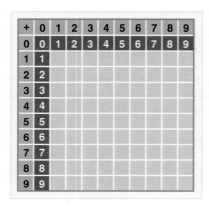

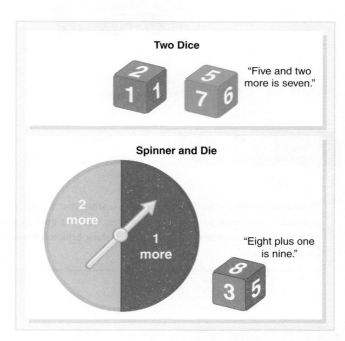

FIGURE 9.3   One-more and two-more activities.

Asking students to generalize from a set of problems is a good way to reinforce reasoning and avoid overgeneralization. Explore a set of zero facts, some with the zero first and some with the zero second, using the Zero Sums Activity Page. Ask students what they notice about the problems, and what they notice across problems. Ask them to create their own stories and/or to illustrate the problems to go with each problem.

CCSS   Standards for Mathematical Practice
MP7. Look for and make use of structure.

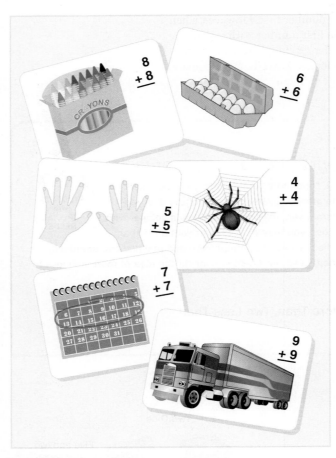

FIGURE 9.4 Situations for doubles facts.

Doubles

There are ten doubles facts from $0 + 0$ to $9 + 9$. These facts are foundational, provided the basis for near doubles strategy. Many students find doubles easier to grasp than other facts.

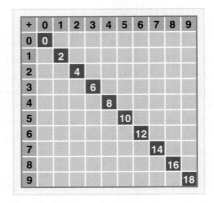

However, all students, and especially students with disabilities, can benefit from using and creating picture cards for each of the doubles as shown in Figure 9.4. Story problems can focus on pairs of like addends: "Alex and Zack each found 7 seashells at the beach. How many did they find together?"

Activity 9.4   CCSS-M: 1.OA.C.5; 1.OA.C.6; 2.OA.B.2

Double Trouble

Read Double the Ducks (Murphy, 2002), a story that begins with 5 ducks each bringing home a friend. Have students work with a partner. Give each pair a set of counters. The first partner selects some of those counters to be the ducks. Their partner tells how many ducks there will be when each duck brings a friend. To support student reasoning, ducks (counters) can be placed on a ten-frame.

Activity 9.5   CCSS-M: 1.OA.C.6; 2.OA.B.2

Calculator Doubles

Students work in pairs with a calculator. Students enter the "double maker" ($2\times$) into the calculator. One student says a double—for example, "Seven plus seven." The other student presses 7, says what the double is, and then press $=$ to see the correct double (14) on the display. The students then switch roles and reset the calculator ($2\times$). For ELs who are just learning English, invite them to say the double in their native language or in both their native language and English. (Note that the calculator is also a good way to practice $+ 1$ and $+ 2$ facts.)

ENGLISH LEARNERS

Combinations of 10

Perhaps the most important strategy for students to know is the combinations that equal 10. It is a foundational fact from which students can derive many facts (Kling, 2011). Consider story situations such as the following and ask students to tell possible answers.

There are ten boys and girls on the bus. How many girls and how many boys might be on the bus?

There are many children's books focused on the concept of 10. While they might be counting books, you can incorporate questions like, "How many more to equal 10?" Such books could be used as a context for Activity 9.6.

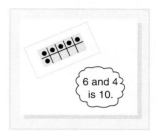

FIGURE 9.5 Combinations of 10 on a ten-frame.

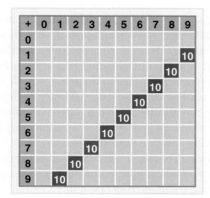

Activity 9.6   CCSS-M: 1.OA.B.4; 1.OA.C.6; 2.OA.B.2

How Many More to Equal 10?

Place counters on one Ten-Frame (see Figure 9.5) and ask, "How many more to equal 10?" This activity can be repeated using different start numbers. Eventually, display a blank ten-frame and say a number less than 10. Students start with that number and complete the "10 fact." If you say, "four," they say, "four plus six equals ten." This can be completed as whole class or with students working with a partner. Students who are still in phase 1 of learning the facts (using counting strategies) or students with disabilities may need additional experience or one-on-one time working on this process.

MyLab Education   Blackline Master: Ten-Frame

10 + _____

Adding onto 10 is not an official basic fact, but in preparation for the Making 10 strategy, students must know Combinations of 10 *and* 10 + _____ facts. Using a full ten-frame and a partial ten-frame can help students with this group of facts. Just like with one more and two more, the goal is to move from counting on to "just knowing." A number line or hundreds chart can help students notice the relationship in these sums that will help them move beyond counting.

Making 10

All of the basic facts with sums greater between 11 and 18 can be solved by using the Making 10 strategy. Students use their known facts that equal 10 and then add the rest of the number onto 10. For example, to solve 6 + 8, a student might start with the larger number (8), see that 8 is 2 away from 10; therefore, they take 2 from the 6 to make 10 and then add on the remaining 4 to get 14. Making 10 is also aptly called *Break Apart to Make Ten (BAMT)* (Sarama & Clements, 2009) and *Up over 10* (the CCSS-M uses the phrase *Making 10*).

+	0	1	2	3	4	5	6	7	8	9
0										
1										
2										11
3									11	12
4								11	12	13
5							11	12	13	14
6						11	12	13	14	15
7					11	12	13	14	15	16
8				11	12	13	14	15	16	17
9			11	12	13	14	15	16	17	18

This reasoning strategy is extremely important and is heavily emphasized in high-performing countries (Korea, China, Taiwan, and Japan) where students learn facts sooner and more accurately than U.S. students (Henry & Brown, 2008). Yet this strategy is not emphasized enough in the United States. A study of California first graders found that this strategy contributed more to developing fluency than using doubles (even though using doubles had been emphasized by teachers and textbooks in the study) (Henry & Brown, 2008).

The Making 10 strategy can also be applied to larger numbers. For example, for 28 + 7, students can make 30, seeing that 28 + 7 = 30 + 5. Thus, this reasoning strategy deserves significant attention in teaching addition (and subtraction) facts.

Quick images or manipulating Double Ten-Frames (see Blackline Master 15) can help students develop the Making 10 strategy. For example, cover two ten-frames with a problem, like 6 + 8. Ask students to visualize moving counters from one frame to fill the other ten-frames and explain their thinking. Move to doing this mentally. Activities 9.7 and 9.8 are designed for this purpose.

MyLab Education   Blackline Master: Double Ten-Frames

Activity 9.7

CCSS-M: 1.OA.B.3; 1.OA.C.6; 2.OA.B.2

Move It, Move It

Distribute the Move it, Move it Activity Page and a mat with Double Ten-Frame (Blackline Master 15). Flash cards with facts are placed next to the double ten-frame, or a fact can be given orally. The students cover each frame with counters to represent the problem (9 + 6 would mean covering nine places on one frame and six on the other). Ask students to "move it"—to decide a way to move the counters so that they can find the total without counting. Ask students to explain what they did and connect to the new equation. For example, 9 + 6 may have become 10 + 5 by moving one counter to the first ten-frame. Emphasize strategies that are working for that student (5 as an anchor and/or Combinations of 10 and/or Making 10).

> **MyLab Education   Activity Page: Move It, Move It**
> **MyLab Education   Blackline Master: Double Ten-Frame**

Activity 9.8

CCSS-M: 1.OA.B.3; 1.OA.C.6; 2.OA.B.2

Frames and Facts

STUDENTS
with
SPECIAL
NEEDS

Make Little Ten-Frame Cards and display them to the class on a projector. Show an 8 (or 9) card. Place other cards beneath it one at a time as students respond with the total. Have students say aloud what they are doing. For 8 + 4, they might say, "Take 2 from the 4 and put it with 8 to make 10. Then 10 and 2 left over is 12." Move to harder cards, like 7 + 6. After modeling with whole group, place students with partners, trading off who is placing the frame and who is figuring out the sum. Ask students to record each equation (see Figure 9.6). Especially for students with disabilities, highlight how they should explicitly think about filling in the little ten-frame starting with the higher number. Show and talk about how it is more challenging to start with the lower number as a counterexample.

MyLab Education **Activity Page: Little Ten-Frame Cards**

Use 10

Use 10 is recently researched reasoning strategy (Baroody, Purpura, Eiland, & Reid, 2014; Baroody et al., 2016). The thinking process of Use 10 is different than Making 10, and it works for the same facts as highlighted above. You start with 10 + _____ fact and adjust the answer. For example, for 9 + 6, a student thinks, 10 + 6 is 16, 9 is one less than 10, so the sum is also one less, 15. Notice this does not require decomposing or recomposing a number. Students who learned this strategy and practiced it while playing games, did substantially better than their peers on addition facts involving adding 8s or 9s (Baroody et al., 2016).

Using 5 as an Anchor

Using 5 as an anchor means looking for fives in the numbers in the problem. For example, in 7 + 6, a student may see that 7 is 5 + 2 and that 6 is 5 + 1. The student would add 5 + 5 and then the extra 2 from the 7 and the extra 1 from the 6, adding up to 13. The ten-frames can help students see numbers as 5 and some more. And because the ten-frame is a visual model, it may be a strategy that visual learners and students with disabilities find particularly valuable. Like Making 10 and Use 10, this strategy works for all the facts with sums between 11 and 18 (see graphic in Making 10 section).

Near-Doubles

Near-doubles are also called "doubles-plus-one" or "doubles-minus-one" facts and include all combinations where one addend is one more or less than the other. The strategy is to double the smaller number and add 1 or to double the larger and then subtract 1. Therefore, students must know their doubles before they can work on this strategy.

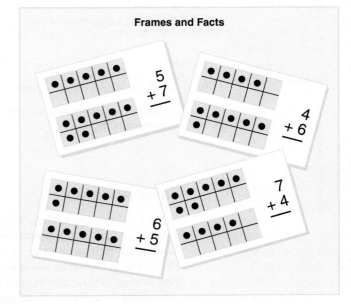

Frames and Facts

To develop this strategy, begin with a double fact quick image, such as 6 + 6, and follow it with a quick image of 6 + 7. Transition to using expressions, writing a doubles fact and a near-doubles, as the ones illustrated here:

4 + 4	5 + 5	6 + 6	8 + 8
4 + 5	5 + 6	6 + 5	7 + 8

Ask students how the first equation might help them solve the second equation. Activity 9.9 elaborates on this idea.

FIGURE 9.6 Frames and Facts Activity.

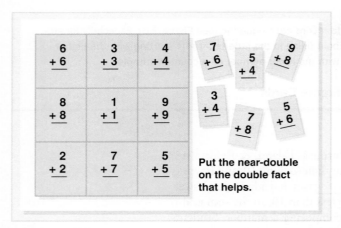

Put the near-double on the double fact that helps.

FIGURE 9.7 Near-doubles fact activity.

Activity 9.9

CCSS-M: 1.OA.B.3; 1.OA.C.6; 2.OA.B.2

On the Double!

Create a display (on the board or on paper) that illustrates the doubles (see Figure 9.7). Prepare cards with near-doubles (e.g., 4 + 5). Ask students to find the doubles fact that could help them solve the fact they have on the card and place it on that spot. Use Little Ten-Frame Cards with doubles and near doubles to help students, particularly those with disabilities, visualize the relationships. Ask students if there are other doubles that could help.

STUDENTS with SPECIAL NEEDS

MyLab Education **Activity Page: Little Ten-Frame Cards**

Near-doubles can be more difficult for students to recognize and therefore may not be a strategy that all students find useful. In that case, do not force it.

 ## Reasoning Strategies for Subtraction Facts

Subtraction facts prove to be more difficult than addition, perhaps because it receives less attention and because it requires knowing the related addition facts. Figure 9.1 at the beginning of the chapter lists the ways students might subtract, moving from counting to mastery. Without opportunities to learn and practice reasoning strategies, students continue to rely on counting strategies for subtraction, a slow and often inaccurate approach. Therefore, spend sufficient time working on the reasoning strategies for subtraction to help students move to phase 2 and eventually on to mastery/automaticity (phase 3).

MyLab Education **Video Example 9.6**

Listen to John Van de Walle describe reasoning strategies for subtraction facts.

Think-Addition

As the label implies, in this strategy students use known addition facts to produce the unknown quantity or part of the subtraction. For 13 − 8, a student thinks, "What plus 8 equals 13? Students taught this strategy do significantly better than their peers on subtraction (Baroody et al., 2016). The value of think-addition cannot be overstated; however, it requires that addition facts be mastered. If this important relationship between parts and the whole—between addition and subtraction—can be made, subtraction facts will be much easier for students to learn. One way to build this relationship is to illustrate facts on triangle or T cards as illustrated in Figure 9.8. Both cards help students see the relationship between addition and subtraction. The T is particularly useful, as it mimics the part-part-whole relationship between addition and subtraction (Baroody et al., 2016).

Activity 9.10

CCSS-M: 1.OA.B.4; 1.OA.C.6; 2.OA.B.2; 3.OA.B.5; 3.OA.B.6; 3.OA.C.7

What's under My Thumb?

Create a set of triangle or T cards with fact families for each pair of students or have students create their own based on the facts they are learning. You can begin this activity as a whole class to model and then move to partners. Hold up a card with your thumb over one number. Ask, "What is under my thumb?" Call on several students to share how they reasoned to get the answer. Place students in partners to continue play.

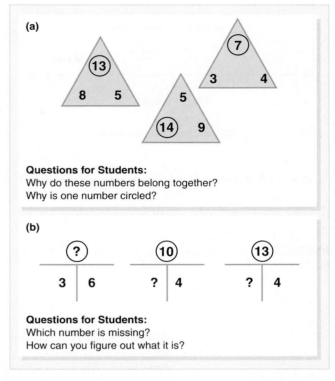

(a)

Questions for Students:
Why do these numbers belong together?
Why is one number circled?

(b)

Questions for Students:
Which number is missing?
How can you figure out what it is?

FIGURE 9.8   Facts cards that show relationship between addition and subtraction. Note: These are shown for addition/subtraction but work well for multiplication/division, too.

⏸ Pause & Reflect

Before reading further, look at the three subtraction facts shown here, and reflect on what thought process you use to get the answers. Even if you "just know them," think about what a likely process might be.

$$
\begin{array}{ccc}
11 & 12 & 15 \\
-9 & -6 & -7 \\
\end{array}
$$

What stories might you tell that will help students "think addition?" ●

Story problems that promote think-addition are those that sound like addition but have a missing addend: *join, initial part unknown*; *join, change unknown*; and *part-part-whole, part unknown* (see Chapter 8). As with addition facts, it is helpful to begin with facts that have totals of 10 or less (e.g., $8 - 3, 9 - 7$) before working on facts that have a total (minuend) higher than 10 (e.g., $13 - 4$). Here is an example:

Janice had 5 fish in her aquarium. Grandma gave her some more fish. Then she had 12 fish. How many fish did Grandma give Janice?

Notice that the action is *join*, which suggests addition. There is a high probability that students will think, "Five and how many more equals 12?" In the discussion in which you use problems such as this, your task is to connect this thought process with the subtraction fact, $12 - 5$. Students may use a 10 as a benchmark to solve this, thinking "It takes 5 to get to 10 and 2 more to 12 is . . . 7". Encourage such explanations as students practice this strategy.

 Standards for Mathematical Practice
MP3. Construct viable arguments and critique the reasoning of others.

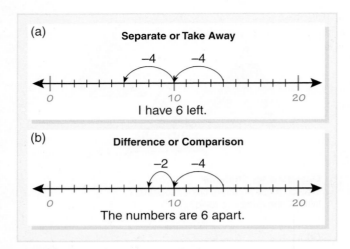

FIGURE 9.9   Down under 10 illustrated on the number line for 14 − 8.

Down under 10

The Down under 10 is the reverse of Making 10, and there are two ways to think about it—separate and comparison. Let's look at 14 − 8. For separate, you are taking away 8, so jump down 4 to get to 10, then jump down 4, and the answer is 6 (see Figure 9.9[a]). For comparison, you are finding the difference or distance. How far apart are 14 and 8? Jump down 4 to the 10 and two more to the 8—they are 6 apart (see Figure 9.9[b]). Like the Making 10 strategy discussed previously, this strategy is emphasized in high-performing countries but not emphasized enough in the United States (Fuson & Kwon, 1992).

To develop the Down under 10 strategy, write pairs of facts in which the difference for the first fact is 10 and the second fact is either 8 or 9: 16 − 6 and 16 − 7; 14 − 4 and 14 − 6, and so on. Have students solve each problem and discuss their strategies. If students do not naturally see the relationship, ask them to think about how the first fact can help solve the second. Illustrate on a number line. Use story problems such as these:

Becky walks 16 blocks to school. She has walked 7. How many more blocks does Becky have left? (Separate)

Becky walks 16 blocks to school; Corwin walks 9 blocks. How many more blocks does Becky walk? (Comparison)

Activity 9.11   CCSS-M: 1.OA.B.4; 1.OA.C.6; 2.OA.B.2

Apples in the Trees

Project a Double Ten-Frame (Blackline Master 15) as a display with chips (apples) covering the first ten-frame and some of the second (e.g., for 16 apples in the trees, place 10 in the first frame and 6 on the second frame). Tell students some apples have fallen to the ground—you will tell them how many and they will tell you how many are still in the trees. Ask them to share how they thought about it. Repeat with different values.

   MyLab Education   **Blackline Master: Double Ten-Frame**

Take from 10

This excellent strategy is not as well known or commonly used in the United States but is consistently used in high-performing countries. It takes advantage of students' knowledge of the combinations that make 10, taking the initial value apart into 10 + _____. This is how it works for 15 − 8:

(1) Think: 10 + 5   **(2) Take from the 10: 10 − 8 = 2**   **(3) Add 5 back on: 2 + 5 = 7**
             − 8

Try it on these examples:

      12 − 8 =   **17 − 9 =**   **14 − 6 =**

If you have students from other countries, they may know this strategy and can share it with others. It can be used for all subtraction facts having minuends greater than 10 (the "toughies") by just knowing how to subtract from 10 and knowing addition facts.

Activity 9.12   CCSS-M: 1.OA.B.3; 1.OA.B.4; 1.OA.C.6; 2.OA.B.2

Apples in Two Trees

Adapting Activity 9.11, explain that each ten-frame is a different tree. Tell students you will tell them how many apples fall out of the "full" tree and they will tell you how many apples are left (on both trees). Connect to the related equations, as illustrated above by recording students ideas and eventually having students record their equations.

In the discussion of addition and subtraction strategies, you have seen a lot of activities. Activities and games provide a low-stress approach to practicing strategies and working toward fluency. More games and activities for all operations can be found later in this chapter.

MyLab Education   **Self-Check 9.2A**

Reasoning Strategies for Multiplication and Division Facts

Using a problem-based approach and focusing on reasoning strategies are just as important, if not more so, for developing mastery of the multiplication and related division facts (Baroody, 2006; Wallace & Gurganus, 2005). As with addition and subtraction facts, start with story problems as you develop reasoning strategies. Understanding the commutative property cuts the basic facts to be remembered in half! For example, a 2×8 array can be described as 2 rows of 8 or 8 rows of 2. In both cases, the answer is 16. Multiplication facts should not be presented in numerical order starting with 0s, 1s, and so on up though the 9s. Instead, build on students' strengths and prior knowledge, and working on mastery of foundational facts for multiplication that can then be used for all the remaining facts.

MyLab Education   **Video Example 9.7**

Listen as John Van de Walle overviews foundational multiplication facts.

VIDEO EXAMPLE

Foundational Facts: 2, 5, 10, 0, and 1

A good place to begin multiplication facts is with 2s, 5s, and 10s. These facts connect to students' experiences with skip counting and addition doubles (Heege, 1985; Kamii & Anderson, 2003). Tens are not basic facts (because ten is two digits), but it is listed here because knowing 10s facts is an important way to derive facts (e.g., 9s and 8s). Next, 0s and 1s are foundational facts, though 0 facts do not help generate other facts. Be sure these are understood, not just memorized.

Twos. Facts that have 2 as a factor are equivalent to the addition doubles and should already be known by students. Help students realize that 2×7 is the same as $7 + 7$. Use story problems in which 2 is the number of sets. Later, use problems in which 2 is the size of the sets, helping students recognize the commutative property of multiplication.

George was making sock puppets. Each puppet needed 2 buttons for eyes. If George makes 7 puppets, how many buttons will he need for the eyes?

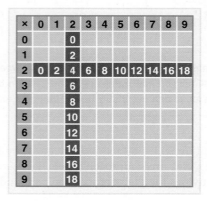

Fives. Practice skip counting by fives. Keep track of how many fives have been counted (If we jump by 5s four times on the number line, where will we land?). Use arrays that have rows with five dots. Point out that such an array with six rows is a model for 6 × 5, eight rows is 8 × 5, and so on. Time is also a good context for fives because of the way analog clocks are made.

Activity 9.13 CCSS-M: 3.OA.A.1; 3.OA.C.7

Clock Facts

Focus on the minute hand of the clock. When it points to a number, how many minutes after the hour is it? See Figure 9.10(a). Connect this idea to multiplication facts with 5. Hold up a Clock Fact Card as in Figure 9.10(b), and then point to the number on the clock corresponding to the other factor. In this way, the fives facts become the "clock facts."

MyLab Education   **Activity Page: Clock Fact Card**

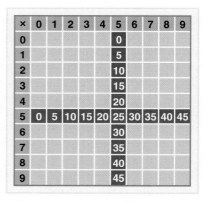

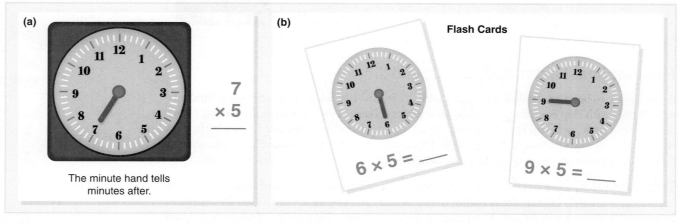

FIGURE 9.10   Using clocks to help learn fives facts.

While twos and fives are developed from skip counting, that is still phase 1. It is important that as these facts are learned students are developing more efficient ways to know 8 × 5 than by skip counting.

CCSS Standards for Mathematical Practice

MP7. Look for and make use of structure.

Zeros and Ones. These facts, though apparently easy on a procedural level, tend to get confused with "rules" that some students learned for addition—for example, the fact 6 + 0 stays the same, but 6 × 0 is always zero, or that 1 + *n* is the next counting number, but 1 × *n* stays the same. The concepts behind these facts can be developed best through story problems. For example, invite students to tell stories to match a problem.

---

6 × 0 = _____ . There are six bowls for raisins. Each bowl is empty. How many raisins?
0 × 6 = _____ . You worked 0 hours babysitting at $6 an hour. How much money did you make?

Avoid telling students rules that aren't conceptually based, such as "Any number multiplied by zero is zero."

Illustrate ones using arrays to show commutativity (8 × 1 = 1 × 8) and use stories like the ones for zero. With 0 and 1, help students notice this patterns through exploring stories and using concrete tools, and then generalize what it means to have *n* × 0, 0 × *n*, 1 × *n*, and *n* × 1.

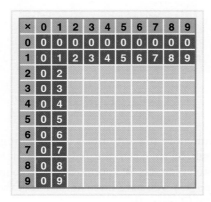

Nines

Nines are in a category by themselves. They aren't used for deriving the other facts, but there are several reasoning strategies and patterns specific to nines. Nines can actually be derived from tens. For example, 7 × 9 can be found by finding 7 × 10 and removing one set of 7, or 70 − 7. Because students often can multiply by 10 and subtract from a decade value, this strategy is effective. You might introduce this idea by showing a set of bars such as those in Figure 9.11 with only the end cube a different color. After explaining that every bar has 10 cubes, ask students if they can think of a good way to figure out how many are yellow.

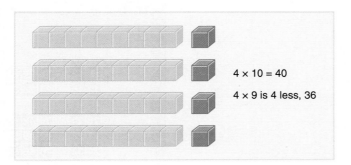

FIGURE 9.11 Using tens to think of the nines.

Nines facts have interesting patterns that can help to find the products: (1) the tens digit of the product is one less than the non-nine factor and (2) the sum of the two digits in the product equals 9. For $7 \times 9 = 63$, the tens digit is one less than 7 and $6 + 3 = 9$. Ask students to explore and discover nines patterns and write down patterns they notice. After discussing all the patterns, ask students how these patterns can be used to figure out a product to a nines fact. Challenge students to think about why this pattern works.

×	0	1	2	3	4	5	6	7	8	9
0										0
1										9
2										18
3										27
4										36
5										45
6										54
7										63
8										72
9	0	9	18	27	36	45	54	63	72	81

A tactile way to help remember the nifty nines is to use fingers—but not for counting. Here's how: Hold up both hands. Starting with the pinky on your left hand, count over for which fact you are doing. For example, for 4×9, you move to the fourth finger (see Figure 9.12). Bend it down. Look at your fingers: You have three to the left of the folded finger representing 3 tens and six to the right—36! (Barney, 1970).

Derived Multiplication Fact Strategies

CCSS **Standards for Mathematical Practice**
MP2. Reason abstractly and quantitatively.

The following chart shows the remaining 25 multiplication facts. Notice if students recognize the commutative property, there are only 15 facts to learn. These remaining facts can be learned by using foundational facts of 1, 2, 5, and 10. If students do not know these facts, they are not ready to learn their other facts. The reasoning strategies shared here are sequenced in a developmentally appropriate order.

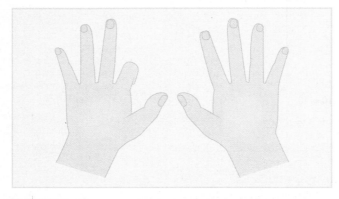

FIGURE 9.12 Nifty nines using fingers to show 4×9.

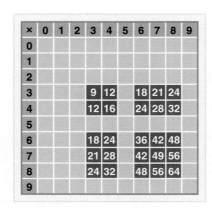

×	0	1	2	3	4	5	6	7	8	9
0										
1										
2										
3				9	12			18	21	24
4				12	16			24	28	32
5										
6				18	24			36	42	48
7				21	28			42	49	56
8				24	32			48	56	64
9										

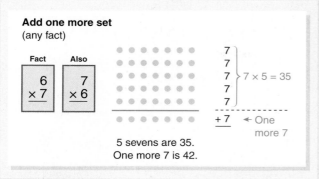

Add one more set
(any fact)

5 sevens are 35.
One more 7 is 42.

FIGURE 9.13 Adding a group reasoning strategy.

Adding or Subtracting a Group. This strategy can generate many other facts! For example, all 3s facts can be thought of as × 2 and 1 more _____. All 6 facts can be thought of × 5 and 1 more _____. As described earlier, all 9s can be generated as × 10 and 1 less _____. Figure 9.13 illustrates this strategy for 6 × 7. Using set language "5 sevens" is helpful in remembering that one more 7 is needed (not one more 5).

Doubling and Halving. Doubling applies the × 2 foundational facts, and is a very effective reasoning strategy in helping students learn the difficult facts (Flowers & Rubenstein, 2010/2011). The Double and Double Again strategy shown in Figure 9.14(a) is applicable to all facts with 4 as one of the factors. Remind students that the idea works when 4 is the second factor as well as when it is the first.

If either factor is even, a Half Then Double strategy as shown in Figure 9.14(b) can be used. Select the even factor and cut it in half. If the smaller fact is known, that product is doubled to get the new fact.

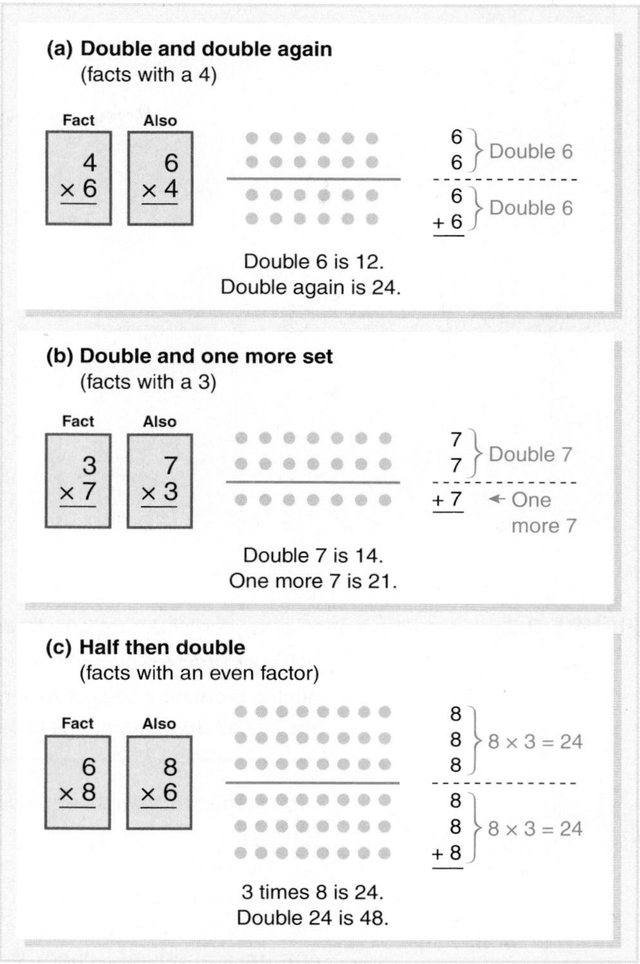

Break Apart. This strategy, also referred to as "Take Apart," involves decomposing (taking apart) one of the factors into two addends, multiplying each addend by the other factor, and adding them back together for the total. Adding a group is an example of this strategy, with 1 being one of the addends. Now, we broaden that strategy, asking students to decompose in any way that makes the problem manageable. For example, for 8 × 6 you can decompose 8 into 5 + 3. Both of these parts are multiplied by 6: 5 × 6 equals 30 and 3 × 6 equals 18. The sum of 30 and 18 equals 48. Arrays are powerful thinking tools for deriving multiplication facts. Figure 9.15(a) illustrates a Multiplication Array with lines through a 10 by 10 array to show fives (known facts). Students can use this hint to decompose one factor. For example, to see 7 × 7 as (5 × 7) + (2 × 7), or 35 + 14 (Figure 9.15[b]).

(a) Double and double again
(facts with a 4)

Double 6 is 12.
Double again is 24.

(b) Double and one more set
(facts with a 3)

Double 7 is 14.
One more 7 is 21.

(c) Half then double
(facts with an even factor)

3 times 8 is 24.
Double 24 is 48.

FIGURE 9.14 Using doubles (known facts) to derive unknown facts.

MyLab Education **Blackline Master: Multiplication Array**

Division Facts

Mastery of multiplication facts and connections between multiplication and division are key elements of division fact mastery. For example, to solve 36 ÷ 4, we tend to think, "Four times what is thirty-six?" In fact, because of this, the reasoning facts for division are to (1) think multiplication and then (2) apply a multiplication reasoning fact, as needed. Missing factor stories can assist in making this connection.

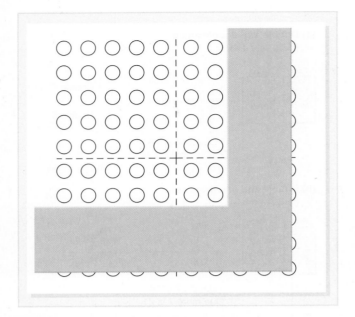
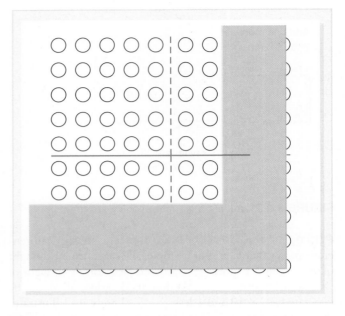

FIGURE 9.15   A multiplication array can illustrate how to decompose a factor.

Analea is creating bags of mini muffins for a bake sale. She puts four in a bag and fills up bags until she has all 36 mini muffins in bags. How many bags did she fill?

Notice this story can be represented as 4 × _____ = 36 (missing factor) or as 36 ÷ 4 = _____ (division).

Beyond division facts, students benefit from practicing near division facts (e.g., 50 ÷ 6) because near division situations are more likely to happen in real life, required for estimating, and required for solving larger division problems. To determine the answer to 50 ÷ 6, students employ a guess-and-check strategy: 6 times 7 (low), 6 times 8 (within 2, that must be it). Students should be able to do these near-fact problems mentally and efficiently.

Activity 9.14   CCSS-M: 3.OA.A.2; 3.OA.A.4; 3.OA.B.6

How Close without Going Over?

This can be a game for small groups or an activity with the full class. Begin with the whole class to model how it can be played. Begin by posting missing factor equations such as these:

   4 × □ → 23, _____ left over

   6 × □ → 27, _____ left over

   □ × 7 → 55, _____ left over

Ask students to mentally decide on the missing factor and be ready to share the missing factor. Then, ask several students to share their factor and how they figured it out. Finally, ask what the left over will be for that factor. This can be repeated with equations written as division:

   40 ÷ 9 → □, _____ left over

MyLab Education   Self-Check 9.2B

MyLab Education   Application Exercise 9.1: Reasoning Strategies for Multiplication and Division Facts Click the link to access this exercise, then watch the video and answer the accompanying questions.

VIDEO EXAMPLE

Reinforcing Basic Fact Mastery

When students "just know" a fact, or can apply a reasoning strategy so fast they almost don't realize they have done it (e.g., Making 10), they have reached phase 3: mastery. CCSS-M uses the phrase "know from memory" (NGA Center & CCSSO, 2010, pp. 19, 23). Repeated experiences with reasoning strategies are effective in committing facts to memory; memorizing is not. Therefore, games or activities that focus on reasoning strategies are more effective than drilling with flash cards (and more palatable for students). Students must be fluent with the basic facts, as students who continue to struggle with the facts often fail to understand higher mathematics concepts. Their cognitive energy gets pulled into computation when it should be focusing on the more sophisticated concepts being developed (Forbringer & Fahsl, 2010).

Games to Support Basic Fact Fluency

Games are fun to play over and over again and therefore are an excellent way to provide repeated experiences for students to learn their facts. Playing games that infuse reasoning strategies helps students be able to flexibly select strategies, decide which strategy is most appropriate for the given problem, and become more efficient and accurate in finding the answer (Bay-Williams & Kling, 2014; Godfrey & Stone, 2013; Kling & Bay-Williams, 2015). This is what it takes to become *fluent* with the basic facts! In addition, games increase student involvement, encourage student-to-student interaction, and improve communication—all of which are related to improved academic achievement (Forbringer & Fahsl, 2010; Kamii & Anderson, 2003; Lewis, 2005).

Games can help students learn and practice reasoning strategies. This game (and others like it) helps students look for known facts in an unknown fact problem. The more they play, the better students become at partitioning unknown facts into known facts. As you use games, remember to focus on related clusters of facts and on what individual students need to practice. Also, encourage students to talk about their strategies and to self-monitor, working towards using efficient strategies. Activity 9.15 is one example of such a game because the use of arrays helps students see how they can decompose and recompose to use known facts to solve unknown facts.

CCSS Standards for Mathematical Practice
MP3. Construct viable arguments and critique the reasoning of others.

Activity 9.15

CCSS-M: 3.OA.A.1; 3.OA.B.5; 3.OA.C.7

Strive to Derive

STUDENTS with SPECIAL NEEDS

You will need Multiplication Array Cards (e.g., for 3s, 4s, 6s, and 9s), a straight thin stick (like uncooked spaghetti), and two dice, one labeled with 3, 3, 6, 6, 9, and 9; one with 0, 1, 4, 6, 7, and 8. To make Multiplication Array Cards, use 1-Centimeter Grid Paper and cut out each possible size. In marker, write the product both ways (e.g., cut out a 5-by-6 array and write 5 × 6 and 6 × 5 on the array). Spread the cards on the table so they can be seen. Player 1 rolls the dice and selects the related array card. Player 1 then places the stick to partition the array into known facts. If Player 1 rolled a 3 and a 6, she would pick the 3-by-6 array. She can partition it as 2 × 6 and 1 × 6 or as 3 × 5 and 3 × 1. If Player 1 can solve the fact using a derived fact, she scores 1 point. Return array card to the collection. Player 2 repeats the process. Continue to 10 points. Initially, or to modify for students who struggle, focus on one foundation set of facts, for example, Strive to Derive from 5.

MyLab Education Activity Page: Multiplication Array Cards
MyLab Education Blackline Master: 1-Centimeter Grid Paper

Salute! Is a game that reinforces both addition and subtraction (or multiplication and division) and only requires a deck of cards.

Activity 9.16

CCSS-M: 1.OA.B.4; 1.OA.C.6; 2.OA.B.2; 3.OA.B.5; 3.OA.B.6; 3.OA.C.7

ENGLISH LEARNERS

Salute!

Place students in groups of three, and give each group a deck of cards (omitting face cards and using aces as ones). Two students draw a card without looking at it and place it on their forehead facing outward (so the others can see it). The student with no card tells the sum (or product). The first of the other two to correctly say what number is on their forehead "wins" the card set. Each student explains how they found the sum/ product or figured out the card on their forehead. After each student explains, rotate roles and continue play. For ELs, students with disabilities, and reluctant learners, speed can inhibit participation and increase anxiety, so remove those barriers. This game can be differentiated by including only certain cards (e.g., addition facts using only the numbers 1 through 5).

STUDENTS *with* **SPECIAL NEEDS**

Table 9.2 offers some ideas for how classic games can be adapted to focus on basic fact mastery (reflects ideas from Forbringer & Fahsl, 2010, and Kamii & Anderson, 2003). Also included are ideas for differentiating the games.

When all facts are learned, continued reinforcement through occasional games and activities is important. Consider the following activity that engages students in creatively applying all four operations.

Activity 9.17

CCSS-M: 2.OA.B.2; 3.OA.C.7; 5.OA.A.1

ENGLISH LEARNERS

Bowl-a-Fact

In this activity (suggested by Shoecraft, 1982), you draw circles placed in triangular fashion to look like bowling pins, with the front circle labeled 1 and the others labeled consecutively through 10. Use the Bowl-a-Fact Activity Page that includes lines for recording equations. For culturally diverse classrooms, be sure that students are familiar with bowling. (If they are not, consider showing a videoclip.)

Take three dice and roll them. Students use the numbers on the three dice to come up with equations that result in answers that are on the pins. For example, if you roll 4, 2, and 3, they can "knock down" the 5 pin with $4 \times 2 - 3$. If they can produce equations to knock down all 10 pins, they get a strike. If not, roll again and see whether they can knock the rest down for a spare. After doing this with the whole class, students can work in small groups.

MyLab Education   **Activity Page: Bowl-a-Fact**

FORMATIVE ASSESSMENT Notes. As students are engaged in games and activities, interview students to find out whether they are using counting strategies, reasoning strategies, or quick recall. Ask students to tell what strategy they just used. If you observe counting, ask the student to try a reasoning strategy. If many students are counting, more experiences (e.g., with ten-frames) are needed. ■

TABLE 9.2   CLASSIC GAMES ADAPTED TO BASIC FACT MASTERY

Classic Game	How to Use It with Basic Fact Mastery	Suggestions for Differentiation
Bingo	Each bingo card has a fact problem (e.g., 2 × 3) in each box. The same fact will be on multiple bingo cards but in different locations on each card. You will call out an answer (e.g., 6), and the students will find a matching problem (or more than one problem) on their card.	Create bingo boards that focus on different clusters of facts (e.g., doubles or doubles +1 on some boards, and Making 10 on other boards). Be sure that the answers you call out are an even mix of the clusters so that everyone has the same chance to win.
Concentration	Create cards that have a fact problem (e.g., 3 × 5) on one half and the answers (e.g., 15) on the other half. Shuffle the cards and turn them face-down in a 6 × 4 grid. (If you like, you can make the grid larger to use more cards.)	Select cards that focus on a particular cluster of facts (e.g., +1 and × 5 facts) for each round of the game. Multiple groups can play the game simultaneously—each group will use the parts of the deck that contain the facts they are working on. Also, consider making cards that show the ten-frames below the numbers to help provide a visual for students.
Dominoes	Create (or find online) dominoes that have a fact on one side and an answer (not to that fact) on the other. Each student gets the same number of dominoes (around eight). On his or her turn, they can play one of the dominoes in their hand only if they have an answer or a fact that can connect to a domino on the board.	As with other games, select the dominoes that focus on a particular clusters of facts.
Four in a Row	Create a 6 × 6 square game board with a sum (or product) written on each square. Below, list the numbers 0 through 9. Each of the two players has counters of a different color to use as their game pieces. On the first turn, Player 1 places a marker (paper clip) on two addends/factors and then gets to place his or her colored counter on the related answer. (If you have repeated the same answer on different squares of the board, the player only gets to cover one of them.) Player 2 can only move one paper clip and then gets to place his or her colored counter on the related answer. The first player to get four in a row wins.	Rather than list all the values below the chart, just list the related addends or factors. For example, use 1, 2, 6, 7, 8, 9 if you want to work on +1 and +2, or use 3, 4, 5, 6 if you are working on these multiplication facts.
Old Maid (retitled as Old Dog)	Create cards for each fact and each answer. Add one card that has a picture of an old dog (or use your school mascot). Shuffle and deal cards. On each player's turn, they draw from the person on their right, see whether that card is a match to a card in their hand (a fact and its answer), and, if so, lay down the pair. Then the person to their left draws from them. Play continues until all matches are found and someone is left with the Old Dog. Winner can be the person with (or not with) the Old Dog, or the person with the most pairs.	See Concentration (above).

Source: Based on ideas from Forbringer & Fahsl, 2010, and Kamii & Anderson, 2003.

About Drill

Drill—repetitive non-problem-based activity—in the absence of reasoning has repeatedly been demonstrated as ineffective. However, drill can strengthen memory and retrieval capabilities (Ashcraft & Christy, 1995). Drill is only appropriate after students know strategies and have moved from phase 2 to phase 3. Drill should also be low-stress and engaging. The many games and activities in this chapter can continue to be played even after students know the facts from memory. Students will smile when they see cards coming out for another game of Salute!

Too often, drill includes too many facts too quickly, and students become frustrated and overwhelmed. Also, students progress at different paces—gifted students tend to be good memorizers, whereas students with intellectual disabilities have difficulty memorizing (Forbringer & Fahsl, 2010).

A plethora of Online Resources for Basic Fact Mastery provide opportunities to drill on the basic facts. Though currently none exist that work on strategy development, these programs can support students who are near mastery or maintaining mastery. One disadvantage of most of these sites is that they focus on all the facts at one time. Two exceptions (sites that organize drill by fact family) are *Fun 4 the Brain* (www.fun4thebrain.com) and *Math Fact Café* (www.mathfactcafe.com).

Fact Remediation

Students who have not mastered their addition facts by third grade or their multiplication facts by fourth grade (or beyond) are in need of interventions that will help them master the facts. More drill is not an intervention! Students who do not know their facts may be stuck back in counting strategies (phase 1) and likely lack number sense and reasoning strategies (phase 2). Effective remediation requires first figuring out which facts a student knows and which ones he or she does not (formative assessment). Second, effective remediation requires a focus on the three phases—determining where a student is and explicitly teaching reasoning strategies (phase 2) in order to reach mastery (phase 3). Review the ideas offered in Table 9.3 and in the Assessing Basic Facts section to figure out what students do and do not know. Then, use these ideas to help students master all of their facts.

1. *Explicitly teach reasoning strategies.* Students' fact difficulties are due to a failure to develop or connect concepts and relationships such as those that have been discussed in this chapter. They need instruction focused at phase 2, not phase 3. In a remediation program, students may not have the benefit of class discussion. Share with them strategies, check that they understand it, and provide opportunities for them to think aloud as they apply the strategies.

    For example, if a student knows his addition facts within 10, but struggles with the ones that sum to 11 to 19, then you know which facts to target. Determine if he knows the Combinations of 10 strategy. Practice it until he is fluent with it. Determine if he knows the 10+ _____ facts. Then, explicitly teach the Making 10 strategy and the Use 10 strategy. Provide opportunities for him to practice and talk about the strategies.

2. *Provide hope.* As noted in the discussion of timed tests, students' confidence can be affected. Students may feel they are doomed to use finger counting forever. Let these students know that they will explore strategies that will help them with the facts. Turn off the timers. Shorten (or eliminate) the quizzes.

3. *Inventory the known and unknown facts and reasoning strategies.* Find out which facts are known quickly and comfortably and which are not (see assessment ideas discussed previously). Invite students to do this for themselves as well. Listen and watch for which reasoning strategies they know and are using. Provide sheets of mixed multiplication facts and ask students to answer the ones they "just know" and circle the facts where they have to pause to count or use a strategy. Review the results with them and discuss which strategies and facts to work on.

4. *Build in success.* Begin with easier and more useful reasoning strategies like Combinations of 10 for addition. Success builds success! Have students find all the facts that can be solved

---

TABLE 9.3   COMMON CHALLENGES AND MISCONCEPTIONS RELATED TO BASIC FACT FLUENCY

Common Challenge or Misconception	What It Looks Like	How to Help
1. Students do not recognize inverse relationship	Student is not able to think of $14 - 9$ as, "What plus 9 equals 14?" or $36 \div 4$ as "How many groups of 4 are in 36?"	Use the triangle and T cards. Explicitly practice the language used here.
2. Students do not apply the commutative property	Student is slower to add $2 + 8$ than $8 + 2$ (they may be counting on from the first number). Student can solve 3×8, but not 8×3.	For addition, Use a ten-frames for each addend and reverse them Add contexts that can be reversed (part-part-whole stories). For multiplication, use areas and arrays that can be rotated to show that $3 \times 8 = 8 \times 3$.
3. In multiplication, applying the adding (or subtracting) a group, students lose track of the group size.	For 9×8, student uses 10×8 but instead of subtracting one *group* of 8, they subtract 1 getting the answer of 79.	Provide examples of the problems using an array. Show how the known fact is used to add or subtract a row (or column) from the array. Emphasize the group/row.

with a newly learned strategy. Use fact charts to show the set of facts you are working on. It is surprising how the chart quickly fills up with mastered facts.

5. *Provide engaging activities.* Use the many games and activities in this chapter to work on phase 2 and phase 3. As students play, ask which strategies they are using. De-emphasize competition and emphasize collaboration. Prepare take-home versions of a game and assign students to play the game at home at least once. Invite parents in for a Math Night and teach them games that they can enjoy (e.g., Salute!) and teach families to focus on reasoning strategies over memorization as they play the games.

What to Do When Teaching Basic Facts. We close this chapter with some important reminders in effectively teaching the basic facts. This is such an important life skill for all learners that it is important that we, as teachers, use what research suggests are the most effective practices.

1. *Ask students to self-monitor.* The importance of this recommendation cannot be overstated. Across all learning, having a sense of what you don't know and what you need to learn is important. Students should be able to identify their "toughies" and continue to work on reasoning strategies to help them derive those facts.

2. *Focus on self-improvement.* Help students notice that they are learning new facts or strategies or getting quicker. For example, students can keep track of which strategies they use as they go through their "fact stack" and then, two days later, pull out the same stack and see whether they are quicker (or more accurate or use a new strategy) compared to the last time.

3. *Work on facts over time.* Rather than do a unit on fact memorization, work on facts over months and months, working on one reasoning strategy or set of facts until it is learned, then moving on. Be sure foundational facts come first and are down pat before teaching derived fact strategies.

4. *Involve families.* Share the big plan of how you will work on learning facts over the year. Send games home. Ask family members to help students by using reasoning strategies when they don't know a fact (provide them with these strategies and good questions to ask).

5. *Make fact practice enjoyable.* There are many games (including those in this chapter) designed to reinforce facts that are not competitive or anxiety inducing.

6. *Use technology.* When students work with technology, they get immediate feedback and reinforcement, helping them to self-monitor.

7. *Emphasize the importance of knowing their facts.* Without trying to create pressure or anxiety, emphasize to students that in real life and in the rest of mathematics, they will be recalling these facts all the time—they really must learn them and learn them well.

What Not to Do When Teaching Basic Facts. The following list describes strategies that may have been designed with good intentions but work against student recall of the basic facts.

1. *Don't use timed tests.* As we have mentioned, little insight is gained from timed tests and they can potentially negatively affect students. Turn the timers off!

2. *Don't use public comparisons of mastery.* You may have experienced the bulletin board that shows which students are on which step of a staircase to mastering their multiplication facts. Imagine how the student who is on the step 3 feels when others are on step 6. It is great to celebrate student successes, but avoid comparisons between students.

3. *Don't proceed through facts in order from 0 to 9.* Work on foundational facts first, then move to the tougher facts.

4. *Don't work on all facts all at once.* Select a strategy (starting with easier ones) and then work on automaticity for that set of facts (e.g., doubles). Be sure these are really learned before moving on.

5. *Don't expect automaticity too soon.* This has been addressed throughout the chapter but is worth repeating. Automaticity or mastery can be obtained only after significant time has been spent on reasoning strategies.

6. *Don't use facts as a barrier to good mathematics.* Mathematics is not solely about computation. Mathematics is about reasoning, using patterns, and making sense of things. Mathematics is problem solving. There is no reason that a student who has not yet mastered all basic facts should be excluded from real mathematical experiences (allow calculators so that students don't get bogged down on computation while working on more complex tasks).

7. *Don't use fact mastery as a prerequisite for calculator use.* Requiring that students master the basic facts before they can use a calculator has no foundation. Calculator use should be based on the instructional goals of the day. If your lesson goal is for students to discover the pattern (formula) for the perimeter of rectangles, then using a calculator can quicken the computation in this lesson and keep the focus on measurement.

MyLab Education   **Self-Check 9.3**

RESOURCES FOR CHAPTER 9

LITERATURE CONNECTIONS

Colomba (2013) describes literature links and activities for each of the multiplications facts. The children's books described in Chapters 7 and 8 are also good choices when working on the basic facts. In addition to those, consider these opportunities to develop and practice basic facts. Here are two additional ideas:

One Less Fish

Toft and Sheather (1998)
This beautiful book with an important environmental message starts with 12 fish and counts back to zero fish. On a page with 8 fish, ask, "How many fish are gone?" and "How did you figure it out?" Encourage students to use the Down over 10 strategy. Any counting-up or counting-back book can be used in this way!

The Twelve Days of Summer

Andrews and Jolliffe (2005)
You will quickly recognize the style of this book with five bumblebees, four garter snakes, three ruffed grouse, and so on. The engaging illustrations and motions make this a wonderful book. Students can apply multiplication facts to figure out how many of each item appear by the end of the book. (For example, three ruffed grouse appear on days 3, 4, 5, and so on.)

RECOMMENDED READINGS

Articles

Baroody, A. J. (2006). Why children have difficulties mastering the basic fact combinations and how to help them. *Teaching Children Mathematics, 13*(1), 22–31.

Baroody suggests that basic facts are developmental in nature and contrasts "conventional wisdom" with a number-sense view. Great activities are included as exemplars.

Boaler, J. (2014). Research suggests that timed tests cause math anxiety. *Teaching Children Mathematics 20*(8), 469–474.

This is a wonderful article to challenge the longstanding practice of timed-tests. Just because we have always done this, doesn't mean it's a good idea!

Buchholz, L. (2016). A license to think on the road to fact fluency. *Teaching Children Mathematics, 22*(9), 557–562.

This is a beautifully written reflection on how this second-grade teacher had departed from her daily strategy focus (due to a new curriculum), realized the error in her ways, and her return to daily strategy use. She describes pragmatic ways she ensures that every student develops strategies and fact fluency. (See also Buchholz, 2004 for great strategy ideas).

Kling, G., & Bay-Williams, J. M. (2014). Assessing basic fact fluency. *Teaching Children Mathematics, 20*(8), 489–497.

This article is a great partner with the Boaler article listed here. Boaler describes the problem with timed tests, and these authors reinforce these concerns and offer a rich collection of alternatives to better assess students' journey to fluency.

Books

Bay-Williams, J., & Kling, G. (2017). *Quick reference guide: Games and tools for teaching addition facts.* Alexandria, VA: ASCD.

As the title implies, this is a 6-page laminated foldable that offers guidance on teaching and assessing addition facts, six games, and ideas for sharing the vision with families.

O'Connell, S., & SanGiovanni, J. (2011). *Mastering the basic math facts in multiplication and division: Strategies, activities and interventions to move students beyond memorization.* Portsmouth, NH: Heinemann.

Both this book and the partner book about addition and subtraction (same authors and parallel title) are excellent resources for planning and teaching basic facts effectively!

CHAPTER 10

Developing Whole-Number Place-Value Concepts

LEARNER OUTCOMES

After reading this chapter and engaging in the embedded activities and reflections, you should be able to:

10.1 Identify the pre-base-ten understandings based on a count-by-ones approach to quantity.

10.2 Recognize the foundational ideas of place value as an integration of three components: base-ten concepts through groupings and counting, numbers written in place-value notation, and numbers that are spoken aloud.

10.3 Demonstrate how to develop students' skills in place value through the use of base-ten models.

10.4 Explain how students can use grouping activities to deepen their understanding of place-value concepts.

10.5 Explain strategies to support students' ability to write and read numbers.

10.6 Recognize that there are patterns in our number system that provide the foundation for computational strategies.

10.7 Describe how the place-value system extends to large numbers.

Number sense, a rich, relational understanding of number, is linked to a complete understanding of place value and our base-ten number system, including extensions from whole numbers to decimal numeration. In kindergarten and first grade, students count up to 100 and 120 respectively and are exposed to patterns in these numbers. But, importantly, they learn to think about groups of ten objects as a unit. By second grade, these initial ideas of patterns and groups of ten are formally connected to three-digit numbers, and fourth-grade students extend their understanding to numbers up to 1,000,000 in a variety of contexts. In fourth and fifth grades, students generalize place value understanding to see the relationship of the value of the positions of the digits in a number as ten times the value of the previous digit as they move to the left which will soon be linked to decimals as digits in a number are one-tenth the value of the position as they move to the right. This relationship is critical as students consider the powers of ten (NGA Center & CCSSO, 2010).

A significant part of place value development includes students putting numbers together (*composing*) and taking them apart (*decomposing*) in a wide variety of ways as they solve addition and subtraction problems with two- and three-digit numbers. Place value is a way for students to think about larger quantities (Mix, Prather, Smith, & Stockton, 2013) and to enhance their ability to invent their own computation strategies. Without a firm foundation and understanding of place value, students may face chronic low levels of mathematics performance (Chan & Ho, 2010; Moeller, Martignon, Wessolowski, Engel, & Nuerk, 2011). The following big ideas are the foundational concepts that will lead students to a full understanding of place value and its importance in computation.

BIG IDEAS

- ◆ Sets of 10 (and tens of tens) can be perceived as single entities or units; for example, three sets of 10 and two singles is base-ten method language to describe 32 single objects.

- ◆ The positions of digits in numbers determine what they represent and which size group they count. This is the major organizing principle of place-value numeration and is central for developing number sense.

- ◆ There are patterns to the way that numbers are formed. For example, each decade has a symbolic pattern reflective of the 0-to-9 sequence (e.g., 20, 21, 22 . . . 29).

- ◆ The groupings of ones, tens, and hundreds can be taken apart in different but equivalent ways. For example, beyond the typical way to decompose 256 of 2 hundreds, 5 tens, and 6 ones, it can be represented as 1 hundred, 14 tens, and 16 ones, or 25 tens and 6 ones. Decomposing and composing multidigit numbers in flexible ways is a necessary foundation for computational estimation and exact computation.

- ◆ "Really big" numbers are difficult to conceptualize and are best understood in terms of familiar real-world referents. The number of people who will fill the local sports arena is, for example, a meaningful referent for those who have experienced that crowd.

MyLab Education   Video Example 10.1

Watch this video of former NCTM President Francis "Skip" Fennell who is discussing the big ideas of place value.

 ## Pre-Place-Value Understandings

Children know a lot about numbers with two digits (10 to 99) as early as kindergarten. After all, kindergartners learn to count to 100 and count out sets with as many as 20 or more objects. They count students in the room, turn to specific page numbers in their books, and so on. However, initially their understanding is quite different from yours. It is based on a count-by-ones approach to quantity, so the number 18 to them means 18 ones. They are not able to separate the quantity into place-value groups—after counting 18 teddy bears, a young child might tell you that the 1 stands for 1 teddy bear and the 8 stands for 8 teddy bears. Such students have not had enough experiences to realize we are always grouping by tens.

Recall Wright and his colleagues' three levels of understanding: (1) children understand ten as ten ones; (2) children see ten as a unit; and (3) children easily work with units of ten. Let's look at a way to assess where students are in this trajectory.

FORMATIVE ASSESSMENT Notes. In a diagnostic interview, ask first or second graders to count out 53 tiles. Watch closely to note whether they count out the tiles one at a time and push them aside without any type of grouping or if they group them into tens. Have the students write the number that tells how many tiles they just counted. Some may write "35" instead of "53," a simple reversal. You may find that early on students count the tiles one by one and are not yet thinking of ten as a unit (level 1), and are therefore in a pre-place-value stage. The students just described know that there are 53 tiles "because I counted them." Writing the number and saying the number are usually done correctly, but their understanding of 53 derives from the count-by-ones approach. Without your help, students may not easily or quickly develop a meaningful use of groups of ten to represent quantities.

Even if students can tell you that in the numeral 53, the 5 "is in the tens place" or that there are "3 ones," they might just know the name of the positions without understanding that the "tens place" represents how many groups of ten. Similarly, if students use base-ten blocks, they may name a rod of ten as a "ten" and a small cube as a "one" but may not be able to tell how many ones are required to make a ten. Students may attach words to both materials and groups without realizing what the materials or symbols represent.

Students do know that 53 is "a lot" and that it's more than 47 (because you count past 47 to get to 53). But, initially they think of the "53" as a single numeral. In this stage, they do not know that the 5 represents five groups of ten things and the 3 represents three single things (Fuson, 2006). Fuson and her colleagues refer to students' pre-base-ten understanding of number as *unitary*. That is, there are no groupings of ten, even though a two-digit number is associated with the quantity. They initially rely on unitary counts to understand quantities. ■

MyLab Education   **Self-Check 10.1**

Developing Whole-Number Place-Value Concepts

Place-value understanding requires an *integration* of new and sometimes difficult-to-construct concepts of grouping by tens (the base-ten concept) with procedural knowledge of how groups are recorded in our place-value system and how numbers are written and spoken. Importantly, learners must understand the word *grouping*, especially English learners (ELs) who may become confused because the root word *group* is frequently used for instructing students to work together.

Integrating Base-Ten Groupings with Counting by Ones

Once students can count out a set of 53 by ones, help them see that making groupings of tens and leftovers is a way of counting that same quantity. Each of the sets in Figure 10.1 has 53 tiles, yet students move through three distinct grouping stages to construct the idea that all of these sets are the same.

There is a subtle yet profound difference between students at these stages: Some know that *base-ten* grouping stage is 53 because they understand the idea that 5 groups of ten and 3 more is the same amount as 53 counted by ones; others simply say, "It's 53," because they have been told that when things are grouped this way, it's called 53. The students who understand place value will see no need to count the base-ten grouping by ones. They understand the "fifty-threeness" of the *unitary* and *base-ten* grouping to be the same. The students in the pre-place-value stage may not be sure how many they will get if they count the tiles in the base-ten grouping by ones or if the groups were "ungrouped" how many there would then be.

Standards for Mathematical Practice
MP2. Construct viable arguments and critique the reasoning of others.

Your foremost objective should be helping students integrate what they already know about numbers from counting by ones with the grouping-by-tens concept. If they only count by ones, ask them, "What will happen if we count these items by groups and singles (or by tens and ones)?" If a set has been grouped into tens and singles and counted, then ask, "How can we be really certain that there are 53 things here?" or "How many do you think we will get if we count by ones?" You cannot just *tell* students that these counts will all be the same and hope that it will make sense to them—it is a relationship they must construct themselves.

Grouping Stage	Visual Representation	Counting Approach	Students Can:
UNITARY Count by ones	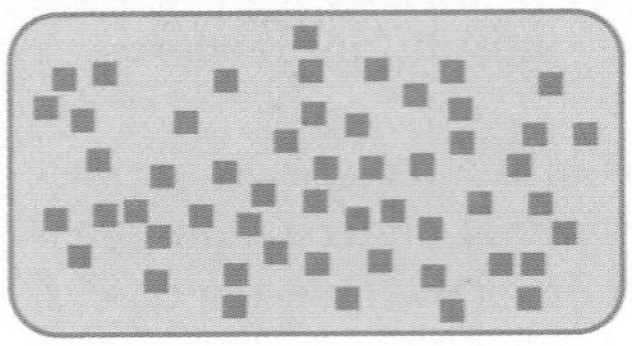	1, 2, 3, 4, 5, 6, 7, 8, 9, 10, 11, and so on	• Name a quantity or "tell how many" by counting each piece. • Are not yet able to think of 10 as a single unit. • Use counting by ones as the only way they are convinced that different sets have the same amount.
BASE-TEN Count by groups of tens and ones	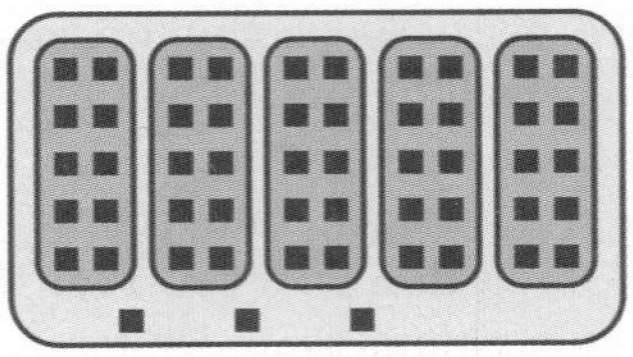	1, 2, 3, 4, 5 groups of 10 and 1, 2, 3, ones (singles) or 10, 20, 30, 40, 50, 51, 52, 53	• Count a group of 10 objects as a single item (unitizing). • Coordinate the base-ten approach with a count by ones to as a means of telling "how many."
EQUIVALENT Non-standard base-ten	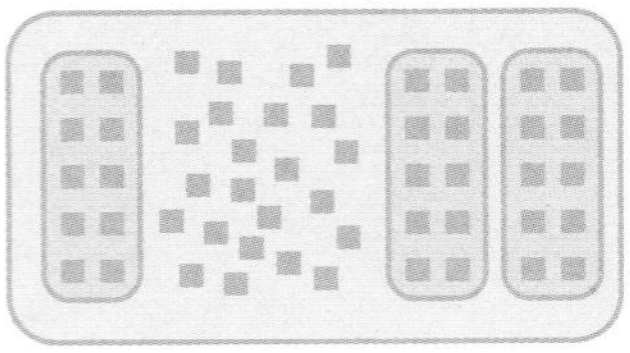	Before counting students would trade and then count 10, 20, 30, 40, 50, 51, 52, 53	• Group the pieces flexibly into versions that include tens and ones but all trades have not been carried out. • Use these alternate groupings to relate to computation by being able to trading or regroup numbers in a variety of ways.

FIGURE 10.1 Three stages of the grouping of 53 objects.

❚❚ Pause & Reflect

What are some defining characteristics of "pre-place-value" students and students who understand place value? •

Groupings with fewer than the maximum number of tens are referred to as *equivalent groupings*. Understanding the equivalence of the *base-ten grouping* and the *equivalent grouping* indicates that grouping by tens is not just a rule that is followed, but also that any grouping by tens, including all or some of the singles, can help tell how many. Many computational techniques (e.g., regrouping in addition and subtraction) are based on equivalent representations of numbers.

Integrating Base-Ten Groupings with Words

The way we say a number such as "fifty-three" must also be connected with the grouping-by-tens concept. The counting methods provide a connection. The count by tens and ones results in saying the number of groups and singles separately: "five tens and three." Saying the number of tens and singles separately in this fashion can be called *base-ten language*. Students can associate the base-ten language with the *standard language*: "five tens and three—fifty-three."

There are several variations of the base-ten language for 53: 5 tens and 3, 5 tens and 3 ones, 5 tens and 3 singles, and so on. Each may be used interchangeably with the standard name, "fifty-three." If you have ELs, it is best to select one approach (e.g., 5 tens and 3 ones) and consistently connect it to the standard language. Other languages often use the base-ten format (e.g., 17 in Spanish is *diecisiete*, literally meaning "ten and seven"), so this association can be a good cultural connection.

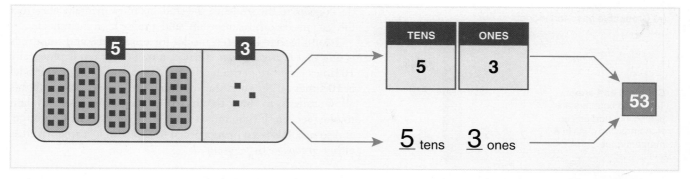

FIGURE 10.2 Groupings by 10 are matched with numerals, recorded in labeled places, and eventually written in standard form.

Be precise in your language. Whenever you refer to a number in the tens, hundreds, or thousands (or beyond), make sure you do not just say "six," but instead refer to it with its place value location, such as 6 tens (or 60). Students are often confused when numbers are discussed as digits rather than describing their actual value.

 **Standards for Mathematical Practice**
MP6. Attend to precision.

Integrating Base-Ten Groupings with Place-Value Notation

The symbolic scheme that we use for writing numbers (ones on the right, tens to the left of ones, and so on) must be coordinated with the grouping scheme. Activities can be designed so that students physically associate groupings of tens and ones with the correct recording of the individual digits, as Figure 10.2 indicates.

Language again plays a key role in making these connections. The explicit count by groups and singles matches the individual digits as the number is written in the usual left-to-right manner. A similar coordination is necessary for hundreds and other place values. Keep in mind that students will initially find it challenging to see "ten" as both 10 ones and 1 ten.

Figure 10.3 summarizes the ideas of an integrated place-value understanding that have been discussed so far. Note that all three methods of counting shown in the figure support relational understanding when students can flexibly integrate base-ten concepts, written names, and oral names.

MyLab Education   **Self-Check 10.2**

Base-Ten Models for Place Value

When students are learning base-ten concepts, they are combining multiplicative understanding (each place is ten times the value of the place to the right) with a positional system (each place has a value)—something hard to do prior to learning about multiplication! Physical models for base-ten concepts play a key role in helping students develop the idea of "a ten" as both a single entity and as a set of 10 units especially for students with lower ability (Mix, Smith, Stockton, Cheng & Barterian, 2016). Remember, though, that the models do not "show"

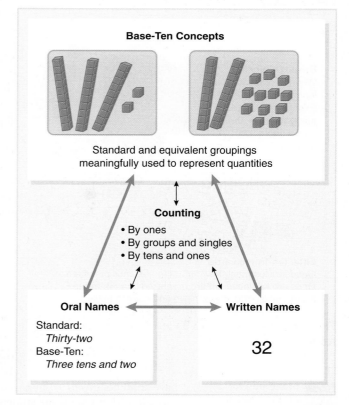

FIGURE 10.3 Relational understanding of place value integrates three components shown as the corners of the triangle.

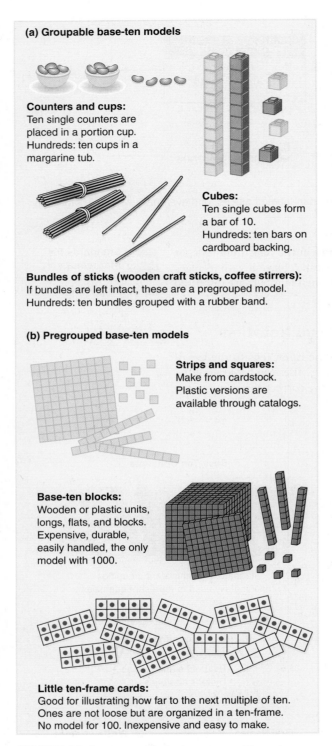

(a) Groupable base-ten models

Counters and cups:
Ten single counters are placed in a portion cup. Hundreds: ten cups in a margarine tub.

Cubes:
Ten single cubes form a bar of 10.
Hundreds: ten bars on cardboard backing.

Bundles of sticks (wooden craft sticks, coffee stirrers):
If bundles are left intact, these are a pregrouped model.
Hundreds: ten bundles grouped with a rubber band.

(b) Pregrouped base-ten models

Strips and squares:
Make from cardstock.
Plastic versions are available through catalogs.

Base-ten blocks:
Wooden or plastic units, longs, flats, and blocks. Expensive, durable, easily handled, the only model with 1000.

Little ten-frame cards:
Good for illustrating how far to the next multiple of ten. Ones are not loose but are organized in a ten-frame. No model for 100. Inexpensive and easy to make.

FIGURE 10.4 Groupable and pregrouped base-ten models.

the concept to the students; the students must mentally construct the "ten makes one relationship" and impose it on the model.

An effective base-ten model for ones, tens, and hundreds is one that is *proportional*. That is, a model for ten is physically 10 times larger than the model for a one, and a hundred model is 10 times larger than the ten model. Proportional materials allow students to check that ten of any given piece is equivalent to one piece in the column to the left (10 tens equals 1 hundred, and so on). Base-ten proportional models can be categorized as either *groupable* or *pregrouped*.

Groupable Models

Models that most clearly reflect the relationships of ones, tens, and hundreds are those for which students can build the ten from the single pieces or units and verify its value. When students put 10 beans in a cup, the cup of 10 beans literally *is the same as* the 10 single beans. Bundles of wooden craft sticks or coffee stirrers can be grouped with rubber bands. Plastic connecting cubes can be built into rods of ten and thereby provide a useful transition to pregrouped rods because they form a similar shape. Examples of these groupable models are shown in Figure 10.4(a).

As students begin to make groupings of ten, start introducing the language of "tens" by matching the objects, such as "cups of tens and ones" or "bundles of tens and singles." Then graduate to a general phrase, such as "groups of tens and ones." Eventually you can abbreviate this language simply to "tens" such as "four tens and seven."

When students become more familiar with these models, collections of tens can be made in advance by the students and kept as ready-made tens (e.g., craft sticks can be left bundled, connecting cubes left connected). This approach is a good transition to the pregrouped models described next.

Pregrouped Models

Models that are pregrouped are commonly shown in textbooks and are often used in instructional activities. Pregrouped models, such as those in Figure 10.4(b) and the Base-Ten Materials, cannot be taken apart or put together. When 10 single pieces are accumulated, they must be exchanged or traded for a ten, and likewise, tens must be traded for hundreds. The advantage of these physical models is their ease of use and the efficient way they model large numbers.

MyLab Education	**Blackline Master: Base-Ten Materials**

With pregrouped models, make an extra effort to confirm that students understand that a ten piece really is the same as 10 ones. Although there is a pregrouped cube to represent 1000, have students group 10 hundred pieces and attach them together as a cube to show how it is formed. Otherwise, some students may only count the square units they see on the surface of the six faces and may think the cube represents 600.

The Little Ten-Frames effectively link to the familiar ten-frames students used early on to think about numbers, and as such, may initially be more meaningful than base-ten materials made from paper strips and squares. Little ten-frames have the distinct advantage of always showing the distance to the next decade. For example, when 47 is shown with 4 ten cards and a seven card, a student can see that three more will make five full cards, or 50.

MyLab Education   Blackline Master: Little Ten-Frames

A significant challenge with using the pregrouped physical models occurs when students have not first had adequate experiences with groupable models. Then there is the potential for students to use them without reflecting on the ten-to-one relationships. For example, if students are just *told* to trade 10 ones for a ten, it is quite possible for them to make this trade without attending to the "ten-ness" of the piece they call a ten. Similarly, students can "make the number 42" by simply picking up 4 tens and 2 ones pieces without understanding that if all the pieces were broken apart there would be 42 ones.

 TECHNOLOGY **Note.** Using electronic versions of base-ten manipulatives, students (including those with disabilities) can place ones, tens, hundreds, or thousands on the screen with simple mouse clicks. Number Pieces (https://www.mathlearningcenter.org/resources/apps/number-pieces) help learners explore place value while helping students visualize operations with multi-digit numbers. Students use the pieces to represent multi-digit numbers, regroup, add, subtract, multiply, and divide. Two versions of the web or app-based tool are available depending on the grade level and concepts to be explored. Students can represent larger numbers and multiplication and division concepts using the regular version of Number Pieces. A simplified version, Number Pieces Basic, is available for use with primary students. Number Pieces Basic has fewer features, putting greater focus on place value, counting, addition, and subtraction.

Compared to real base-ten blocks, these digital materials are free, easily grouped and ungrouped, available in "endless" supply, and can be manipulated by students and displayed by projector or smart board. Remember though, virtual models are no more conceptual than physical models and as such are only a representation for students who understand the relationships involved. ■

> **CCSS Standards for Mathematical Practice**
> **MP5.** Use appropriate tools strategically.

Nonproportional Models

Nonproportional models, or models where the ten is not physically 10 times larger than the one, are *not* used for introducing place-value concepts. They may be used when students already have a conceptual understanding of the numeration system and need additional reinforcement, or by older students who may need to return to place-value concepts because they are struggling with content that requires place-value understanding. Examples of nonproportional models include an abacus that has same-sized beads on wires in different columns, money, or chips that are given different place values by color.

MyLab Education   Self-Check 10.3

MyLab Education   Application Exercise 10.1: Base-Ten Models for Place Value Click the link to access this exercise, then watch the video and answer the accompanying questions.

Activities to Develop Base-Ten Concepts

Now that you have a sense of the important place-value concepts, we turn to activities that assist students in developing these concepts. This section focuses on base-ten concepts or grouping by tens (see the top of Figure 10.3). Connecting this important idea with the oral and written names for numbers (the rest of Figure 10.3) is discussed separately to help you focus on how to do each. However, in the classroom, the oral and written names for numbers can and should be developed in concert with conceptual ideas.

Grouping Activities

Reflect for a moment on how strange it must sound to say, "seven ones." Certainly, students have never said they were "seven ones" years old. The use of the word *ten* as a singular group name can be even more mysterious. Consider the phrase "Ten ones makes one ten." The first *ten* carries the usual meaning of 10 things, but the other *ten* is a singular noun, a thing. How can something the student has known for years as the name for a lot of things suddenly become one thing? And if you think this idea is confusing for native speakers, imagine the potential difficulty for ELs.

Because students come to their development of base-ten concepts with a count-by-ones idea of number, you must begin there. You cannot arbitrarily impose grouping by ten on students. Students need to experiment with showing amounts in groups of like size and perhaps come to an agreement that ten is a very useful size to use. The following activity could be done toward the end of first grade as an example of a first effort at developing grouping concepts.

Activity 10.1

CCSS-M: K.NBT.A.1; 1.NBT.B.2a

Counting in Groups

Find a collection of items between 25 and 100 that students might be interested in counting—perhaps the number of shoes in the classroom, a container of cubes, a long chain of plastic links, or the number of crayons in the classroom crayon box. Then pose the question, "How could we count our shoes in some way that would be easier than counting by ones?" Whatever suggestions children suggest, try them. After testing several methods, you can have a discussion of what worked well and what did not. If no one suggests counting by tens, you might casually suggest that as an idea to try.

One teacher challenged her students to find a good way to count all the connecting cubes being held by the students after the children collected a cube for each of their pockets. The first suggestion was to count by sevens. That was tried but did not work very well because none of the students could easily count by sevens. In search of a more efficient way, the next suggestion was to count by twos. This approach did not seem to be much better than counting by ones. Finally, they settled on counting by tens and realized that this method was a good and "fast" way of counting.

This activity and similar ones provide you with the opportunity to suggest that materials actually be arranged into groups of tens before the "fast" way of counting is begun. Remember that students may count "ten, twenty, thirty, thirty-one, thirty-two" but not fully realize the "thirty-two-ness" of the quantity. To connect the count-by-tens method with their understood method of counting by ones, the students need to count both ways and discuss why they get the same result.

The idea in the next activity is for students to make groupings of ten and record or say the amounts. Number words are used so that students will not mechanically match tens and ones with individual digits. It is important that students confront the actual quantity in a manner meaningful to them.

Activity 10.2

CCSS-M: K.NBT.A.1; 1.NBT.B.2a; 1.NBT.B.2b; 1.NBT.B.2c

Groups of Ten

STUDENTS with SPECIAL NEEDS

Prepare bags of different types of objects such as toothpicks, buttons, beans, plastic chips, connecting cubes, craft sticks, or other items. Students should use the Bag of Tens Activity Page a recording sheet similar to the top left of Figure 10.5. The bags can be placed at stations around the room or given to pairs of students. Students empty the bags and count the contents. The amount is recorded as a number word. Then the objects are grouped in as many tens as possible. The groupings are recorded on the form. After returning the objects to the bags, bags are traded, or students move to another station. Note that students with disabilities may initially need to use a ten-frame to support their counting. Then the use of the ten-frame should eventually fade.

MyLab Education **Activity Page: Bag of Tens**

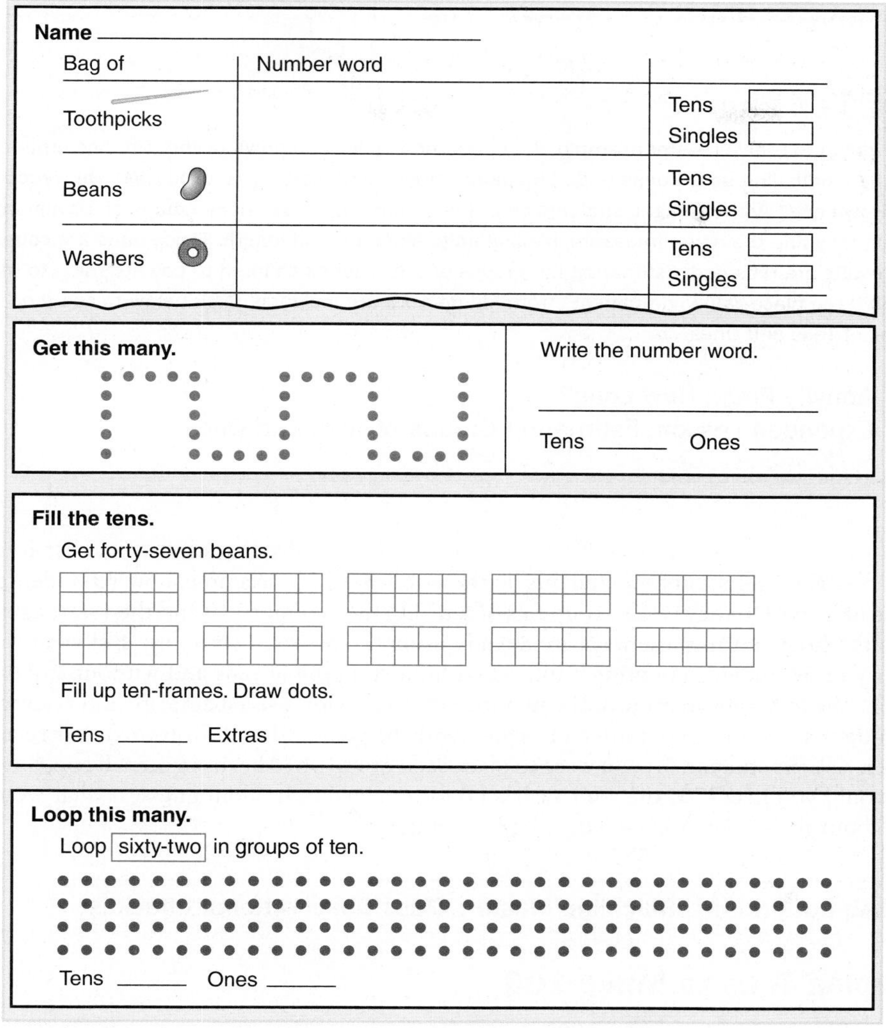

Name _____

Bag of	Number word		
Toothpicks		Tens	☐
		Singles	☐
Beans		Tens	☐
		Singles	☐
Washers		Tens	☐
		Singles	☐

Get this many.

Write the number word.

_____

Tens _____ Ones _____

Fill the tens.

Get forty-seven beans.

Fill up ten-frames. Draw dots.

Tens _____ Extras _____

Loop this many.

Loop sixty-two in groups of ten.

Tens _____ Ones _____

FIGURE 10.5 Activities involving number words and making groups of ten.

Variations of the "Groups of Ten" activity are suggested by the three other recording sheets in Figure 10.5. On Get This Many Activity Page, students count the dots and then count out the corresponding number of counters. Provide small cups to put the groups of ten in. Notice that the activity requires students to first count the set in a way they understand (e.g., count by ones), record the amount in words, and then make the place-value groupings. The Fill the Tens and Loop This Many Activity Pages begin with a verbal name (number word), and students must count the indicated amount and then make groups.

MyLab Education	Activity Page: Get This Many
MyLab Education	Activity Page: Fill the Tens
MyLab Education	Activity Page: Loop This Many

Activity 10.3

CCSS-M: K.NBT.A.1; 1.NBT.B.2a; 1.NBT.B.2b

Estimating Groups of Tens and Ones

Give students a length that they are going to measure—for example, the length of a child lying down or the distance around a sheet of newspaper. At one end of the length, line up 10 units (e.g., 10 linking cubes, toothpicks, rods, or blocks). On a recording sheet (see Figure 10.6 and the How Long? Activity Page), students record an estimate of how many groups of 10 and ones they think will match the length. Next they find the actual measure, placing units along the full length. These units are counted by ones and grouped in tens. Both results are recorded. Estimating the groups of ten requires children to pay attention to the ten as a group or unit. Notice that all three place-value components from Figure 10.3 are included. Click below to see the Expanded Lesson: Estimating Groups of Tens and Ones.

MyLab Education **Activity Page: How Long?**
MyLab Education **Expanded Lesson: Estimating Groups of Tens and Ones**

***FORMATIVE ASSESSMENT* Notes.** Use a Class Observational Checklist to record observations about how students do these activities. For example, how do students count out the objects? Do they make groupings of ten? Do they count to 10 and then start again at 1? Students who count in these ways are already using the base-ten structure. But what you may see early on is students counting a full set without stopping at tens and without any effort to organize the materials in groups. If you notice that behavior, use a diagnostic interview and ask the student to count a container of beans (with between 30 and 50 beans) and record the number. Ask the student, "If you were to place each group of 10 beans in a small cup, how many cups would you need?" If the student has no idea or makes random guesses, what would you know about the student's knowledge of place value? ■

MyLab Education **Blackline Master: Class Observational Checklist**

Grouping Tens to Make 100

In second grade, numbers up to 1000 become important. Here the issue is not just connecting a count-by-ones concept to a group of 100, but rather seeing the number in multiple ways, including as 100 single objects, as 10 tens, and as a singular thing. In textbooks, this connection is often presented on one page showing how 10 rods of ten can be put together to make 1 hundred piece. This quick demonstration may be lost on many students. Additionally, the word *hundred* is equally strange and can get even less attention. These word names are not as simple as they seem!

NAME Jessica

ITEM	ESTIMATE	ACTUAL
straws	5 TENS 6 ONES	3 TENS 2 ONES thirty-two Number Word
______	___ TENS ___ ONES	___ TENS ___ ONES ______ Number Word

FIGURE 10.6 Recording sheet for estimating groups of tens and ones.

To reinforce the idea that a hundred is a group of 10 tens and also 100 singles, consider the estimation activity Too Many Tens.

MyLab Education   Activity Page: Too Many Tens

Activity 10.4   CCSS-M: 2.NBT.A.1

Too Many to Count?

Show students any quantity with 250 to 1000 items. For example, you might use a container of lima beans, a long chain of connecting links or paper clips, a box of pennies, or a grocery bag full of straws. First, have students make and record estimates of how many beans, for example, are in the container. Discuss how students determined their estimates. Then distribute portions of the beans to pairs or triads of students to put into cups of 10 beans. Collect leftover beans and put them into groups of ten as well. Now ask, "How can we use these groups of ten to tell how many beans we have? Can we make new groups from the groups of ten? What is 10 groups of ten called?" Be prepared with some larger containers or baggies into which 10 cups (or other collections of 10 tens) can be placed. When all groups are made, count the hundreds, the tens, and the ones separately. Record the total as 4 hundreds + 7 tens + 8 ones. This activity can be extended to third graders with amounts more than 1000.

In this activity, it is important to use a groupable model so that students can see how the 10 groups are the same as the 100 individual items. At first you may think this activity will take too much time. But this activity helps cement the connection that is often lost in the rather simple display of a hundreds piece or a paper hundreds square in the pregrouped base-ten models.

MyLab Education   **Video Example 10.2**

Watch a video of a student playing a race to 100 game with a teacher. This game will also help students carry out the equal trades that reinforce the use of pregrouped base-ten models.

VIDEO EXAMPLE

Equivalent Representations

An important variation of the grouping activities is aimed at the equivalent representations of numbers. For example, pose the following task to students who have just completed the Groups of Ten Activity 10.2.

What is another way you can show 42 besides 4 groups of ten and 2 singles? Let's see how many ways you can find.

Interestingly, most students will go next to 42 singles. The following activities focus on creating other equivalent representations.

Activity 10.5   CCSS-M: 1.NBT.B.2; 1.NBT.C.5

Can You Make the Link?

Show a collection of materials that are only partly grouped in sets of ten. For example, you may have 5 chains of 10 links and 17 additional unconnected links. Be sure the students understand that each chain has 10 links. Have students count the number of chains and the number of singles in any way they wish to count. Ask, "How many in all?" Record all responses and discuss how they got their answers. Next, before their very eyes, change the groupings (make a ten from the singles, or break apart one of the tens) and repeat. Do not change the total number of links from one time to the next. Once students begin to understand that the total does not change, ask in what other ways the items could be grouped if you use tens and ones.

If you are teaching in second grade, equivalent representations for hundreds as groups of tens can help with the concept of a hundred as 10 tens. The next activity is similar to "Can You Make the Link?" but is done using pregrouped materials and includes hundreds.

Activity 10.6   CCSS-M: 2.NBT.A.1; 2.NBT.A.3; K.CC.B.5

Three Other Ways

Students work in groups or pairs. First, they show 463 on their desks with base-ten materials in the standard representation (4 hundreds pieces, 6 tens and 3 ones). Next, they find and record at least three other ways of representing this quantity. A variation is to challenge students to find a way to show an amount with a specific number of pieces. "Can you show 463 with 31 pieces?" (There is more than one way to do this.)

When students have sufficient experiences with pregrouped materials, a semi-concrete square-line-dot notation can be used for recording ones, tens, and hundreds (see Figure 10.7 and Square Line Dot Activity Page). Use the drawings to reinforce the notion of unitizing (i.e., one ten, one hundred) and as a suggestion for how students can record their thinking and their results.

MyLab Education   Activity Page: Square Line Dot

The next activity begins to incorporate oral language with equivalent representation ideas.

Activity 10.7   CCSS-M: 1.NBT.A.1; 2.NBT.A.1; 2.NBT.A.3

Base-Ten Riddles

Base-ten riddles can be presented orally or in written form (see Base-Ten Riddle Cards). In either case, students should use base-ten materials to help solve the riddles. The examples here illustrate a variety of different levels of difficulty. Have students write new riddles when they complete these.

I have 23 ones and 4 tens. Who am I?

I have 4 hundreds, 12 tens, and 6 ones. Who am I?

I have 30 ones and 3 hundreds. Who am I?

I am 45. I have 25 ones. How many tens do I have?

I am 341. I have 22 tens. How many hundreds do I have?

I have 13 tens, 2 hundreds, and 21 ones. Who am I?

If you put 3 more tens with me, I would be 115. Who am I?

I have 17 ones. I am between 40 and 50. Who am I? How many tens do I have?

MyLab Education   Activity Page: Base-Ten Riddle Cards

MyLab Education   Self-Check 10.4

Reading and Writing Numbers

In this section, we focus on helping students connect oral and written names for numbers (see bottom of Figure 10.3) with their emerging base-ten concepts of using groups of 10 or 100 as efficient methods of counting. Note that the ways we say and write numbers are conventions, not concepts. Students must learn these conventions by being told rather than through problem-based activities. Remember that for EL students, the convention or pattern in our English number words is probably not the same as it is in their native language especially for the numbers 11 to 19.

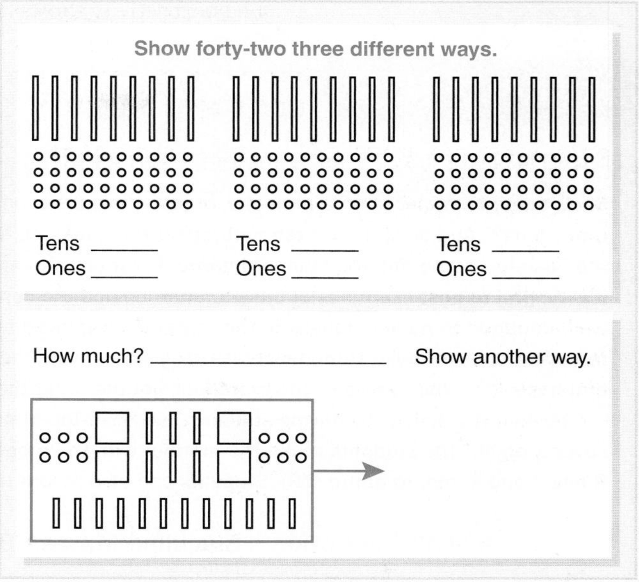

Two-Digit Number Names

In kindergarten and first grade, students need to connect the base-ten concepts with the oral number names they have repeatedly used. They know the words but have not thought of them in terms of tens and ones. In fact, early on they may want to write twenty-one as 201.

When teaching oral names, you will want to use base-ten models. Initially, rather than using standard number words, use the more explicit base-ten language (e.g., "4 tens and 7 ones" instead of "forty-seven"). Base-ten language is rarely misunderstood. When it seems appropriate, begin to pair base-ten language with standard language. Emphasize the teens as exceptions to the pattern. Acknowledge that they are formed "backward" and do not fit the patterns. The next activity helps introduce oral names for numbers.

Show forty-two three different ways.

Tens _____   Tens _____   Tens _____
Ones _____   Ones _____   Ones _____

How much? _____   Show another way.

FIGURE 10.7 Equivalent representations using square-line-dot pictures.

Activity 10.8   CCSS-M: 1.NBT.B.2c

Counting Rows of Ten

ENGLISH LEARNERS

Project the 10 × 10 Multiplication Array of dots. Cover up all but two rows, as shown in Figure 10.8(a). "How many tens? [2.] Two tens is called twenty." Have the class repeat. Show another row. "Three tens is called thirty. Four tens is forty. Five tens could have been fivety but is just fifty. How many tens does sixty have?" The names sixty, seventy, eighty, and ninety all fit the pattern. Slide the cover up and down the array, asking how many tens and the name for that many. ELs may not initially hear the difference between fifty and fifteen, sixty and sixteen, and so on, so explicitly compare these words and clearly enunciate—even overemphasize the word endings.

Use the same 10 × 10 multiplication array to work on names for tens and ones. Show, for example, four full lines: "forty." Next, expose one dot in the fifth row. "Four tens and one. Forty-one." Add more dots one at a time. "Four tens and two. Forty-two." "Four tens and three. Forty-three." This visual is shown in Figure 10.8(b). When that pattern is established, repeat with other decades from 20 through 90. Eventually connect the array to a Hundreds Chart to connect the oral name and the written numeral. For example, children can locate 43 as three rows of ten down and over to the right three ones.

MyLab Education   Blackline Master: 10 × 10 Multiplication Array
MyLab Education   Blackline Master: Hundreds Chart

The next activity shows how this basic approach might be done with other base-ten models.

Activity 10.9   CCSS-M: 1.NBT.B.2; 1.NBT.C.5

Counting with Base-Ten Models

ENGLISH LEARNERS

Show some tens pieces on a projector, or just place them on the carpet in a mixed arrangement. Ask, "How many tens?" Add or remove a ten and repeat the question. Next, add some ones. Always have students give the base-ten name and the standard name. For many students, including ELs and students with disabilities, it is helpful to post examples of base-ten names and the corresponding standard names on the math word wall. Continue to make changes in the materials displayed by adding or removing 1 or 2 tens and by adding and removing ones (or have students create problems). Avoid the standard left-to-right order for tens and ones; the emphasis is on the names of the materials, not the order they are in.

STUDENTS with SPECIAL NEEDS

Reverse the activity by having students use Base-Ten Materials at their desks. For example, say, "Make seventy-eight." The students make the number with the models and then give the base-ten name (7 tens and 8 ones) and standard name (78). Students can also record their work (see Figure 10.9).

MyLab Education   **Blackline Master: Base-Ten Materials**

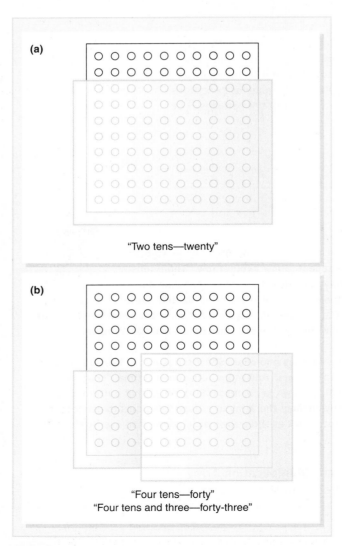

(a)

"Two tens—twenty"

(b)

"Four tens—forty"
"Four tens and three—forty-three"

FIGURE 10.8   10 × 10 dot arrays are used to model sets of tens and ones.

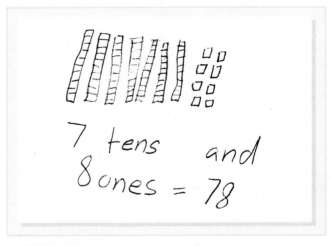

FIGURE 10.9   A student's recording of 78 with models and the base-ten name.

Activity 10.10   CCSS-M: 1.NBT.B.2a; 1.NBT.B.2b; 1.NBT.B.2c

Tens, Ones, and Fingers

Ask your class, "Can you show 6 fingers [or any amount less than 10]?" Then ask, "How can you show 37 fingers?" Some students will figure out that at least four students are required. Line up four students, and have three students hold up 10 fingers while the last student holds up 7 fingers. Have the class count the fingers by tens and ones. Ask for other students to show different numbers. Emphasize the number of sets of ten fingers and the single fingers (base-ten language), and pair this model with standard language.

Activities 10.8, 10.9, and 10.10 will be enhanced by having students explain their thinking. If you don't require students to reflect on their responses, they soon learn how to give the response you want, matching number words to models without actually thinking about the total quantities.

Three-Digit Number Names

The approach to three-digit number names starts by showing mixed arrangements of base-ten materials and have students give the base-ten name (4 hundreds, 3 tens, and 8 ones) and the standard name (438). Vary the arrangement from one example to the next by changing only one type of piece; that is, add or remove only ones or only tens or only hundreds. It is important for students with disabilities to see counterexamples, so purposely point out that some (anonymous!) students wrote 200803 for two hundred eighty-three, and ask them whether that is correct and explain their reasoning. The connection between oral and written numbers is not straightforward, with some researchers suggesting that an early milestone on the route to full understanding is this early (incorrect) expanded form of writing numbers (Byrge, Smith, & Mix, 2013). These discussions allow students to explore their initial ideas and clear up any misunderstandings.

Standards for Mathematical Practice
MP3. Construct viable arguments and critique the reasoning of others.

The major challenge with three-digit numbers is with numbers involving no tens, such as 702 (or later with numbers such as 1046). As noted earlier, the use of base-ten language is quite helpful here. The difficulty of zero-tens (or more generally the internal zero) is more pronounced when writing numerals. For example, students frequently incorrectly write 7,002 for seven hundred two. Emphasizing meaning in the oral base-ten language will be a significant help. At first, students do not see the importance of zero in place value and do not understand that zero helps us distinguish between such numbers as 203, 23, and 230 (Dougherty, Flores, Louis, & Sophian, 2010). Carefully avoid calling zero a "placeholder," because it is a number with a value. ELs may need additional time to think about how to say and write the numerals, because they are translating all the terms involved with the number.

Researchers note that there are significantly more errors with four-digit number names than three-digit numbers, so do not think that students will easily generalize to larger numbers without actually exploring additional examples and tasks (Cayton & Brizuela, 2007).

Written Symbols

Place-value mats are simple mats divided into two or three sections to hold ones and tens or ones, tens, and hundreds pieces, as shown in Figure 10.10. You can suggest to your students that the mats are a good way to organize their materials when working with base-ten blocks. Explain that the standard way to use a place-value mat is with the space for the ones on the right and the tens and hundreds places to the left.

Although it is not commonly seen in textbooks, it is strongly recommended that two ten-frames be drawn in the ones place as shown on the Place-Value Mat. That way, the amount of ones on the ten-frames is always clearly evident, eliminating the need for repeatedly counting the ones. The ten-frame also makes it very clear how many additional ones are needed to make the next set of ten. If students are modeling two numbers at the same time, one ten-frame could be used for each number.

MyLab Education	Blackline Master: Place-Value Mat

As students use their place-value mats, they can be shown how the left-to-right order of the pieces is also the way that numbers are written. To show how the numbers are "built," have a set of Place-Value Cards—one for each of the hundreds

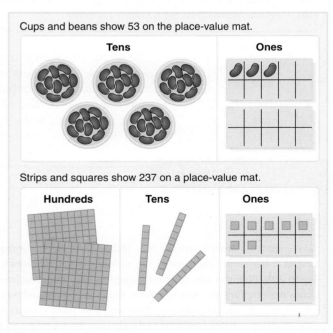

Cups and beans show 53 on the place-value mat.

Strips and squares show 237 on a place-value mat.

FIGURE 10.10 Place-value mats with two ten-frames in the ones place promote the concept of groups of ten.

FIGURE 10.11   Building numbers with a set of place-value cards.

(100–900), one for each of the tens (10–90), and ones cards for 1 through 9 (see Figure 10.11). Notice that the cards are made so that the tens card is twice as long as the ones card and the hundreds card is three times as long as the ones card.

> **MyLab Education**   **Activity Page: Place-Value Cards**

As students place the materials for a number (e.g., 457) on the mat, have them also place the matching cards (e.g., 400, 50, and 7) below the materials. Then, starting with the hundreds card, layer the others on top, right aligned. This approach will show how the number is built while allowing the students to see the individual place value parts of the number which is especially helpful if there are zero tens. The place-value mat and the matching cards demonstrate the important link between the base-ten models and the written form of the numbers.

The next two activities are designed to help students make connections between models, oral language (base-ten and standard), and written forms. The activities can be done with two- or three-digit numbers, depending on students' needs.

Activity 10.11

CCSS-M: 2.NBT.A.1a; 2.NBT.A.1b; 2.NBT.A.3

Say It/Press It

Display models of ones, tens, hundreds (and thousands, if appropriate) in a mixed arrangement. Use a projector, virtual manipulatives, or simply draw on the board using the square-line-dot method. Students say the amount shown in base-ten language ("four hundreds, one ten, and five ones") and then in standard language ("four hundred fifteen"); next, student enter it on their calculators or use paper and pencil to respond. Have someone share his or her display and defend it. Make a change in the materials and repeat. You can also do this activity as "Show It/Press It" by saying the standard name for a number and then having students use base-ten materials to show that number and enter it on their calculators (or write it). Again, pay attention to numbers with components in the teens (e.g., 317) and numbers with internal zeros (e.g., 408). ELs may need additional time to think of the words that go with the numbers, especially as the numbers get larger.

ENGLISH LEARNERS

To support students struggling with reading a number with an internal zero you may want to show (or say) 7 hundreds and 4 ones. Then the class says, "Seven hundreds, zero tens, and four ones, which is—seven hundred (*slight pause*) four." The pause and the base-ten language support the correct reading of the three-digit number.

The next activity is also a good assessment to see whether students really understand the value of digits in two-, three- or four-digit numbers.

Activity 10.12

CCSS-M: 1.NBT.B.2; 1.NBT.C.5; 1.NBT.C.6; 2.NBT.A.1; 2.NBT.A.3; 2.NBT.B.5; 2.NBT.B.8

Digit Change

Have students enter a specific two-, three-, or four-digit number on the calculator. The task is to change one of the digits in the number without simply entering the new number. For example, change 48 to 78. Change 315 to 305 or to 295. Changes can be made by adding or subtracting an appropriate amount. Students should write or discuss explanations for their solutions. Students with disabilities may at first need the visual support of having cards that say "add ten" or "add one." They may also need support with Base-Ten Materials to be able to conceptualize the number and then move to more abstract work using only the calculator.

STUDENTS with SPECIAL NEEDS

> **MyLab Education**   **Blackline Master: Base-Ten Materials**

FORMATIVE ASSESSMENT Notes. Students are often able to disguise their lack of place value understanding by following directions, using the tens and ones pieces in prescribed ways, and using the language of place value.

The diagnostic interviews presented here are designed to help you look more closely at students' understanding of the integration of the three components of place value. Designed as interviews rather than full-class activities, these tasks have been used by several researchers and are adapted primarily from Labinowicz (1985), Kamii (1985), and Ross (1986).

The first interview is referred to as the Digit Correspondence Task. Take out 36 blocks. Ask the student to count the blocks, and then have the student write the number that tells how many there are. Circle the 6 in 36 and ask, "Does this part of your 36 have anything to do with how many blocks there are?" Then circle the 3 and repeat the question. As with all diagnostic interviews, do not give clues. Based on responses to the task, Ross (1989, 2002) has identified five distinct levels of understanding of place value:

1. *Single numeral.* The student writes 36 but views it as a single numeral. The individual digits 3 and 6 have no meaning by themselves.
2. *Position names.* The student correctly identifies the tens and ones positions but still makes no connections between the individual digits and the blocks.
3. *Face value.* The student matches 6 blocks with the 6 and 3 blocks with the 3.
4. *Transition to place value.* The 6 is matched with 6 blocks and the 3 with the remaining 30 blocks but not as 3 groups of 10.
5. *Full understanding.* The 3 is correlated with 3 groups of ten blocks and the 6 with 6 single blocks.

For the second interview, write the number 342. Have the student read the number. Then have the student write the number that is 1 more. Next, ask for the number that is 10 more. You may wish to explore further with models. One less and 10 less can be checked the same way. Observe whether the student is counting on or counting back or whether the student immediately knows that ten more is 352. This interview can also be done with a two-digit number.

A third interview can also provide interesting evidence of depth of understanding. Ask the student to write the number that represents 5 tens, 2 ones, and 3 hundreds. Note that the task does not give the places in order. What do you think will be a common misunderstanding? If the student doesn't write 352, then ask the students to show you the number with base-ten materials, and to say what number they have with the materials. Compare to what they wrote previously, if different. What information can you obtain from the results of this interview? ∎

MyLab Education   Video Example 10.3

Watch Zenaida and consider what she knows about place value based on her responses to the interviewer's questions.

MyLab Education   Self-Check 10.5

Place Value Patterns and Relationships—A Foundation for Computation

In this section, the focus will be the relationships of numbers to important special numbers called *benchmark numbers* and ten-structured thinking—that is, flexibility in using the structure of tens in our number system. These ideas begin to provide a basis for computation as students simultaneously strengthen their understanding of number relationships and place value.

The Hundreds Chart

The Hundreds Chart (see Figure 10.12) deserves special attention in the development of place-value concepts. K–2 classrooms should have a hundreds chart displayed prominently and used often.

1	2	3	4	5	6	7	8	9	10
11	12	13	14	15	16	17	18	19	20
21	22	23	24	25	26	27	28	29	30
31	32	33	34	35	36	37	38	39	40
41	42	43	44	45	46	47	48	49	50
51	52	53	54	55	56	57	58	59	60
61	62	63	64	65	66	67	68	69	70
71	72	73	74	75	76	77	78	79	80
81	82	83	84	85	86	87	88	89	90
91	92	93	94	95	96	97	98	99	100

FIGURE 10.12 A hundreds chart.

MyLab Education **Blackline Master: Hundreds Chart**

A useful version of a hundreds chart can be made of transparent pockets into which each of the 100 numeral cards can be inserted. You can cover numbers, give students numbers to place on the chart or highlight patterns such as skip counting by 2 (even numbers), 5, and 10. You can also have students skip count by threes and fours and color in each number they count. Discuss the pattern shown on the chart as well as the patterns in the numbers.

In kindergarten and first grade, students can count and recognize two-digit numbers on the hundreds chart including the decade numbers from 10 to 100. Additionally, first graders can use the hundreds chart to develop a base-ten understanding of adding two-digit numbers with multiples of 10, noticing that jumps up or down are jumps of ten, while already recognizing that jumps to the right or left are jumps of one.

There are lots of patterns on the hundreds chart, and during discussions, different students will describe the same pattern in several ways. Accept all ideas. Here are some of the important place-value-related patterns students may point out:

- The numbers in a column all end with the same number, which is the same as the number at the top of the chart.
- In a row, the first number (tens digit) stays the same and the "second" number (ones digit) counts 1, 2, 3, . . . 9, 0) changes as you move across.
- In a column, the first number (tens digit) "counts" or goes up by ones as you move down.
- You can count by tens going down the far right-hand column.
- Starting at 11 and moving down on the diagonal, you can find numbers with the same digit in the tens and ones (e.g., 11, 22, 33, 44, and so on).

For students, these patterns are not obvious or trivial. For example, one student may notice the pattern in the column under the 4—every number ends in a 4. Two minutes later, another student will "discover" the parallel pattern in the column headed by 7. That this pattern is in every column may not be completely obvious.

Once you've discussed some of the patterns, try the next activity.

Activity 10.13

CCSS-M: K.CC.A.1; K.NBT.A.1; 1.NBT.A.1; 1.NBT.B.2; 1.NBT.C.5

Missing Numbers

Provide students with a hundreds chart on which some of the number cards have been removed. The students' task is to replace the missing numbers. To begin, have only a random selection of individual numbers removed. Later, remove sequences of several numbers from three or four different rows. Finally, remove all but one or two rows or columns. Eventually, challenge students to replace all of the numbers on the Blank Hundreds Chart. For students with disabilities, model the placement of a missing number using a "think-aloud" to describe how you make your decision and what key features of the number you think about as you place the number properly on the chart.

STUDENTS with SPECIAL NEEDS

MyLab Education **Blackline Master: Blank Hundreds Chart**

FORMATIVE ASSESSMENT Notes. Replacing the number cards on a blank chart is a good station activity for two students to try. By listening to how students determine the correct places for numbers, you can assess how well they have constructed an understanding of the 1-to-100 sequence and whether they recognize and purposefully use patterns in our number system to recreate the hundreds chart. ■

Activity 10.14   CCSS-M: K.CC.A.1; K.NBT.A.1; 1.NBT.A.1; 1.NBT.B.2; 1.NBT.C.5

Finding Neighbors on the Hundreds Chart

Begin with a blank or nearly Blank Hundreds Chart (projecting it on a screen or giving copies to individual students). Then, circle a particular missing number. Students should fill in the designated number and its "neighbors," the numbers to the left, right, above, and below. After students become comfortable naming the neighbors of a number, ask what they notice about the neighboring numbers. The numbers to the left and right are one less and one more than the given number. Those above and below are ten less and ten more, respectively. How do numbers differ on the diagonal? By discussing these relationships on the chart, students begin to see how the sequence of numbers is related to numerical relationships.

MyLab Education   Blackline Master: Blank Hundreds Chart

In the following activity, number relationships are made more explicit by modeling the numbers with base-ten materials and associating those models with the hundreds chart.

Activity 10.15   CCSS-M: K.CC.A.1; K.NBT.A.1; 1.NBT.A.1; 1.NBT.B.2; 1.NBT.C.5

Models with the Hundreds Chart

Use either Base-Ten Materials or the Little Ten-Frame Cards to model two-digit numbers with which the students are familiar.

- Give students one or more numbers to first make with the models and then find on the hundreds chart. Use groups of two or three numbers in either the same row or the same column. Ask students how are the numbers alike and how are they different.

- Indicate a number on the chart. What would you have to change to make each of its neighbors (the numbers to the left, to the right, above, and below)?

As a first step in moving to larger numbers, continue your hundreds charts to 200 and extend the same questions to the larger numbers. Then extend the hundreds chart to a thousands chart.

MyLab Education   Blackline Master: Base-Ten Materials
MyLab Education   Blackline Master: Little Ten-Frame Cards

TECHNOLOGY Note. Several web-based resources include hundreds charts that allow students to explore patterns. Learning about Number Relationships is an example from NCTM's Illuminations (https://illuminations.nctm.org) that has a calculator and hundreds chart and allows for a variety of explorations. (There are extensions to thousands charts, too.) Students can skip-count by any number and also begin their counts at any number. ABCya's (http://www.abcya.com) Interactive Number Chart (0–99 or 1–100) allows students to find and document patterns by coloring the squares that contain the numbers. ■

Activity 10.16

CCSS-M: 2.NBT.A.1; 2.NBT.A.2; 2.NBT.A.3; 2.NBT.B.8

The Thousands Chart

Provide students with several Blank Hundreds Charts. Assign groups of three or four students the task of creating a 1-to-1000 chart. The chart is made by taping 10 hundreds charts together in a long vertical strip. Students should decide how they will divide up the task, with different students taking different parts of the chart. The thousands chart should be discussed as a class to examine how numbers change as you count from one hundred to the next, what the patterns are, and so on. All of the earlier hundreds chart activities can be extended to thousands charts.

MyLab Education **Blackline Master: Blank Hundreds Chart**

Relative Magnitude Using Benchmark Numbers

Number sense also includes having a grasp on the size of numbers. Relative magnitude refers to the size relationship one number has with another—is it much larger, much smaller, close or about the same? How students think about these comparisons is supported by the use of models and by the development of benchmark numbers that can be used as signposts for a number's location (as on a number line).

A valuable feature of both the hundreds chart and the little ten-frame cards is how clearly they illustrate the distance to the next multiple of 10—the number of spaces to the end of the row on the chart or the blank spaces on the ten-frame card. Multiples of 10, 100, and occasionally other numbers, such as multiples of 25, are referred to as *benchmark* numbers. Students learn to use this term when they work with informal methods of computation. When finding the difference between 74 and 112, a student might say, "First, I added 6 onto 74 and that equals 80, which is a benchmark number. Then I added 2 tens onto 80 to get to 100 because that's another benchmark number." Whatever terminology is used, understanding how numbers are related to these special numbers is an important step in students' development of number sense and place value understanding.

In addition to the hundreds chart, the number line is an excellent way to explore how one number is related to another and is a predictor of future mathematics performance (Dietrick, Huber, Dackermann, Moeller & Fischer, 2016; van den Bos, et al. 2015). The next two activities are suggestions for using the Number Lines Activity Page as a student recording sheet.

MyLab Education **Activity Page: Number Lines**

Activity 10.17

CCSS-M: 1.NBT.A.1; 1.NBT.B.2; 1.NBT.B.3; 2.NBT.A.1; 2.NBT.A.2; 2.NBT.A.4

STUDENTS with SPECIAL NEEDS

Who Am I?

Draw a long line (or use cash register tape) and label 0 and 100 at opposite ends. Mark a point with a "?" (on a sticky note) that corresponds to your secret number. Have students try to guess your secret number. For each guess, place and label a mark at that number on the line until your secret number is discovered. Have students explain how they are making their estimations including highlighting any use of benchmark numbers. As a variation, use the Who Am I? Activity Page where the end points are different such as 0 and 1000, 200 and 300, or 500 and 800. For students with disabilities, mark the guesses that have occurred and where they are located. Labeling those numbers at their actual locations will support students' reasoning in the process of identifying the secret number.

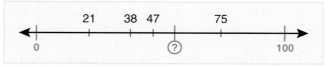

MyLab Education **Activity Page: Number Lines**
MyLab Education **Activity Page: Who Am I?**

Activity 10.18

CCSS-M: 1.NBT.A.1; 1.NBT.B.2; 1.NBT.B.3; 2.NBT.A.1; 2.NBT.A.2; 2.NBT.A.4

Who Could They Be?

Label two points on a Number Line (not necessarily the ends) with benchmark numbers. Show students different points labeled with letters and ask what numbers they might be and why they think that. In the example shown here, B and C are less than 100 but probably more than 60. E could be about 180. You can also ask where 75 might be or where 400 is located. About how far apart are A and D? Why do you think D is more than 100? For ELs, and children with disabilities say as well as write the numbers on a note card, or ask students to both write and say the numbers. Use the Who Could They Be? Activity Page for more examples.

STUDENTS
with
SPECIAL NEEDS

ENGLISH LEARNERS

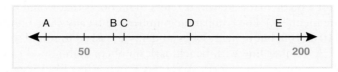

MyLab Education   **Activity Page: Number Lines**
MyLab Education   **Activity Page: Who Could They Be?**

The next activity has students apply some of the same ideas about benchmark numbers that we have been exploring.

Activity 10.19

CCSS-M: 1.NBT.A.1; 1.NBT.B.2; 1.NBT.B.3; 2.NBT.A.1; 2.NBT.A.2; 2.NBT.A.4

Close, Far, and In Between

Put any three numbers on the board that are appropriate for your students. With these three numbers as referents, ask questions such as the following, encouraging discussion of all responses:

ENGLISH LEARNERS

STUDENTS
with
SPECIAL NEEDS

Which two numbers are closest? How do you know?

Which is closest to 300? To 250?

Name a number between 457 and 364.

Name a multiple of 10 between 219 and 364.

Name an even number that is greater than all of these numbers.

About how far apart are 219 and 500? 219 and 5000?

If these are "big numbers," what are some small numbers? Numbers that are about the same? Numbers that make these seem small?

For ELs, this activity can be modified by using prompts that are similar (rather than changing the prompts each time, which increases the linguistic demand). Also, ELs and students with disabilities will benefit from using a visual, such as a number line, and from writing the numbers rather than just hearing/saying them.

Look at the corresponding Expanded Lesson: Close, Far, and In Between, where students estimate the relative size of a number between 0 and 100, and strengthen their conceptual understanding of number size and place value.

MyLab Education   **Expanded Lesson: Close, Far, and In Between**

FIGURE 10.13 An empty number line can be labeled in different ways to help students round numbers.

Approximate Numbers and Rounding

The most familiar form of computational estimation is rounding, which is a way of changing the numbers in a problem to others that are easier to compute mentally. The *Common Core State Standards* say that students in third grade are expected to use place-value understanding to round numbers to the nearest 10 or 100 and students in fourth grade should be able to round any multidigit whole number to any place value. At third and fourth grade students use rounding to assess the reasonableness of answers. Fifth graders will be using place value understanding to round decimals to any place.

To be useful in estimation, rounding should be flexible and conceptually well-understood. To round a number simply means to select a compatible number. (Note that the term *compatible* is not a mathematical term. It refers to numbers that would make the problem easier to compute mentally.) The compatible number can be any close number and need not be a multiple of 10 or 100, but in many cases students are asked to round to one of these places.

A number line with benchmark numbers highlighted can be useful in helping students select compatible numbers. An empty number line like the one shown in Figure 10.13 can be made using strips of poster board taped end to end or cash register tape. Labels are written above the line. The ends can be labeled 0 and 100, 100 and 200, . . . 900 and 1000. Indicate the location of a number above the line that you want to round. Discuss the locations of numbers that are close. Teach students the convention that if a number that is being rounded has a 5 in the place being considered, although it is halfway between two numbers, they round up. The number line is a powerful tool for these discussions.

Connections to Real-World Ideas

As students study place-value concepts, encourage them to notice numbers in the world around them. Students K–1 should be thinking of numbers to 100 and 120 respectively while students in the second grade should be thinking about numbers up to 1000 (NGA Center & CCSSO, 2010). Where are these numbers found in the school? You might use the number of children in the third grade, the number of minutes devoted to mathematics each week, or the number of days since school has started. There are measurements, numbers discovered on a field trip, numbers in books in other subject areas, and so on. What do you do with these numbers? Turn them into interesting graphs, write stories using them, and make up problems. For example, how many cartons of chocolate and plain milk are served in the cafeteria each month? Can students estimate how many cartons will be sold in a year? Collecting data and then grouping into tens and hundreds (or thousands) will help cement the value of grouping in situations when you need to count and compare quantities.

The particular way you bring number and the real world together in your class is up to you. But do not underestimate the value of connecting the real world to the classroom.

MyLab Education	Self-Check 10.6

Numbers Beyond 1000

For students to have good concepts of numbers beyond 1000, the place-value ideas that have been carefully developed must be extended. This development is sometimes difficult to do because physical models for thousands are not readily available, or you may just have one large cube to show. At the same time, number-sense ideas must also be developed. In many ways, connecting very large numbers to real amounts is just as important as connecting smaller numbers to real quantities.

Extending the Place-Value System

Two important ideas developed for three-digit numbers should be extended to larger numbers as students move to thinking about 1,000,000 in fourth grade (NGA Center & CCSSO, 2010).

First, the multiplicative structure of the number system should be generalized. That is, ten in any position makes a single thing (group) in the next position to the left, and vice versa. Second, the oral and written patterns for numbers in three digits are duplicated in a clever way for every three digits to the left. These two related ideas are not as easy for students to understand as adults seem to believe. Because models for large numbers are so difficult to demonstrate or visualize, textbooks must deal with these ideas in a predominantly symbolic manner. That is not sufficient!

Activity 10.20

CCSS-M: 2.NBT.A.1; 2.NBT.A.3

What Comes Next?

Use Base-Ten Materials where the unit or ones piece is a 1-cm square the tens piece is a 10-cm × 1-cm strip and the hundreds piece is a square, 10 cm × 10 cm. What is next? Ten hundreds is called a thousand. What shape would a thousand be? Tape together a long strip made of 10 paper hundreds squares. What comes next? (Reinforce the idea of "10 makes 1" that has progressed to this point.) Ten one-thousand strips would make a square measuring 1 meter (m) on each side, making a paper 10,000 model. Once the class has figured out the shape of each piece, the problem posed to them is, "What comes next?" Let small groups work on the dimensions of a 100,000 piece (they will likely need space in the hallway to do this!).

MyLab Education   Blackline Master: Base-Ten Materials

How far you want to extend this square-strip–square-strip sequence depends on your class. The idea that 10 in one place makes 1 in the next can be brought home dramatically and memorably. It is quite possible with older students to make the next 10-m × 10-m square using chalk lines on the playground. The next strip is 100 m × 10 m. This model can be measured out on a large playground with students marking the corners. By this point, the payoff includes an appreciation of both the increase in size of each successive amount and the 10-makes-1 progression (powers of ten). The 10-m × 10-m square models 1 million, and the 100 m × 10 m strip is the model for 10 million. The difference between 1 million and 10 million is dramatic. Even the concept of 1 million tiny centimeter squares is impressive.

Try the "What Comes Next?" discussion in the context of three-dimensional models. The first three shapes are distinct: a *cube*, a *long*, and a *flat*. What comes next? Stack 10 flats and they make a cube—the same shape as the first one, only 1000 times larger. What comes next? (See Figure 10.14.) Ten cubes make another long. What comes next? Ten big longs make a big flat. The first three shapes have now repeated! Ten big flats will make an even bigger cube, and the trio of shapes begins again. The pattern of "10 of these makes 1 of those" is "infinitely extendable" (Thomas, 2004, p. 305). Note that students with disabilities may have difficulty interpreting spatial information, which plays into their challenges with interpreting the progression of place-value materials (Geary & Hoard, 2005). Although we are using the terms *cube*, *long*, and *flat* to describe the shape of the materials, students will see the shape pattern made as each piece gets 10 times larger. In fact, it is still critical to call these representations "ones, tens, and hundreds," particularly for students with disabilities. We need to consistently name them by the number they represent rather than their shape. This language reinforces conceptual understanding and is less confusing for students who may struggle with these concepts.

Each cube has a name. The first one is the *unit* cube, the next is a *thousand*, the next a *million*, then a *billion*, and so on. Each long is 10 cubes: 10 units, 10 thousands, and 10 millions. Similarly, each flat shape is 100 cubes.

To read a number, first mark it off in triples from the right. The triples are then read, stopping at the end of each

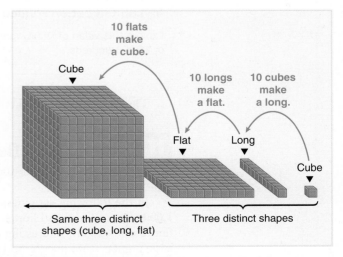

FIGURE 10.14   With every three places, the shapes repeat. Each cube represents a 1, each long represents a 10, and each flat represents a 100.

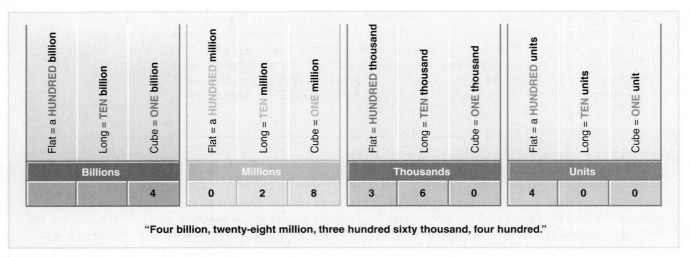

"Four billion, twenty-eight million, three hundred sixty thousand, four hundred."

FIGURE 10.15 The triples system for naming large numbers.

to name the unit for that triple (see Figure 10.15). Leading zeros in each triple are ignored. If students can learn to read numbers like 059 (fifty-nine) or 009 (nine), they should be able to read any number. To write a number, use the same scheme. If first mastered orally, the system is quite easy. Remind students *not* to use the word "and" when reading a whole number. For example, 106 should be read as "one hundred six," not "one hundred *and* six." The word "and" will be needed to signify a decimal point. Please make sure you read numbers accurately.

It is important for students to realize that the system does have a logical structure, is not totally arbitrary, and can be understood.

Conceptualizing Large Numbers

The ideas just discussed are only partially helpful in thinking about the actual quantities involved in very large numbers. For example, in extending the paper square-strip-square-strip sequence, some appreciation for the quantities of 1000 or of 100,000 is acquired. But it is hard for anyone to translate quantities of small squares into quantities of other items, distances, or time.

MyLab Education   **Video Example 10.4**

Explore this video of Donny reasoning about 192,000 as 19,200 tens or 1920 hundreds.

These ideas are important to discuss as a class as students need to explore these relationships.

⏸ Pause & Reflect

How do you think about 1000 or 100,000? Do you have any real concept of a million? ●

In the following activities, numbers like 1000, 10,000 (see 10,000 Grid Paper), or even 1,000,000 are translated literally or imaginatively into something that is more meaningful or fun to think about. Interesting quantities become lasting reference points or benchmarks for large numbers and thereby add meaning to numbers encountered in real life.

MyLab Education   **Blackline Master: 10,000 Grid Paper**

Activity 10.21
CCSS-M: 2.NBT.A.2; 2.NBT.A.3

Collecting 10,000

As a class or grade-level project, collect some type of object with the objective of reaching some specific quantity—for example, 1,000 or 10,000 bread tabs or soda can pop tops. If you begin aiming for 100,000 or 1,000,000, be sure to think it through. One teacher spent nearly 10 years with her classes before amassing a million bottle caps. It takes a small dump truck to hold that many!

Activity 10.22
CCSS-M: 2.NBT.A.2; 2.NBT.A.3

Showing 10,000

Sometimes it is easier to create large amounts than to collect them. For example, start a project in which students draw 100 or 200 or even 500 dots on a sheet of paper. Each week, different students contribute a specified number. Another idea is to cut up newspapers into pieces the same size as dollar bills to see what a large quantity would look like. Paper chain links can be constructed over time and hung down the hallways with special numbers marked. Let the school be aware of the ultimate goal.

Activity 10.23
CCSS-M: 2.NBT.A.1a; 2.NBT.A.3

How Long?/How Far?

In this activity, talk about real or imagined distances with students by posing investigations for them to consider such as, How long is a million baby steps? Other ideas that address length include a line of toothpicks, dollar bills, or energy bars end to end; students holding hands in a line; blocks or bricks stacked up; or students lying down head to toe. Standard measures—feet, centimeters, meters—can also be used with students noting that larger numbers emerge when the smallest units are used.

Activity 10.24
CCSS-M: 3.MD.A.1

A Long Time

How long is 1000 seconds? How long is a million seconds? A billion? How long would it take to count to 10,000 or 1,000,000? (To make the counts all the same, use your calculator to do the counting. Just press the ⊟.) How long would it take to do some task like buttoning a button 1000 times?

Activity 10.25
CCSS-M: 2.MD.A.3; 3.MD.A.1; 3.MD.C.5

Really Large Quantities

Ask how many:

- Energy bars would cover the floor of your classroom
- Steps an ant would take to walk around the school building
- Grains of rice would fill a cup or a gallon jug
- Quarters could be stacked in one stack from floor to ceiling
- Pennies can be laid side by side down the entire hallway
- Pieces of notebook paper would cover the gym floor
- Seconds you have lived

Big-number projects need not take up large amounts of class time. They can be explored over several weeks as take-home projects, done as group projects, or, perhaps best of all, translated into great schoolwide estimation events.

MyLab Education   Self-Check 10.7

MyLab Education   Blackline Master: Base-Ten Materials

Now that you've explored many of the main ideas in this chapter, look at Table 10.1 for some of the possible common challenges and misconceptions your students may face. Suggestions on what you might notice and how to help are included.

TABLE 10.1   COMMON CHALLENGES AND MISCONCEPTIONS IN PLACE VALUE AND HOW TO HELP

Common Challenge or Misconception	What It Looks Like	How to Help
1. Students lose track of the fact that each digit in a multidigit numeral carries a value dependent on its position in the number.	When students are asked to compare the numbers (2) bolded in the two amounts that follow they will say they are the same. **2**357 and 49,99**2**.	• Use Base-Ten Materials and have student show with materials the value of these two numbers. The reading of numbers in addition or subtraction problems as digits (saying 5 instead of 5 tens or fifty) confuses students. • Use the place value cards discussed previously to reinforce how numbers are built. • Students hear numbers like 2357 read as two, three, five, seven—when they should always be read two thousand, three hundred, fifty-seven. • Use the digit correspondence task described in this chapter to identify which of the five levels of understanding matches your student's performance. • Reinforce that the value of an individual digit in a multidigit number is the product of that digit multiplied by the value assigned to its position in the number
2. Student reverse the digits when writing two-digit numbers.	Writes "53" when should write "35."	• Have students use virtual base-ten materials that display the corresponding number to check their answer. • Have the child model both 53 and 35 with base-ten materials and describe how the numbers are similar and different.
3. Student represents a number with base-ten materials using the face value of the digits.	When asked to represent 13 with base-ten materials, the student uses one piece for the "1" and three pieces for the "3" as shown **1** **3** □ □ □ □	• Have the student use base-ten materials to count out 13 single units. Then ask them to compare that amount to what they previously showed. • Have the student build the number with the place value cards and then use base-ten materials to represent the corresponding amounts. Again, compare to the amount originally shown.
4. Students put the word "and" in a number when they read it aloud.	When reading 1016 students will say "one thousand and sixteen."	• Students must practice reading numbers without using the word "and." The only time the word "and" is used is to represent a decimal point.
5. Students use a form of "expanded number writing" (Byrge, Smith, & Mix, 2013).	Students write "three hundred eighty-five" as something like 300805, 310085 or 3085.	• Provide examples of the actual materials on a place value mat and use the place value cards to show how the matching number is built.
6. When shown a collection of base-ten materials where there is an internal zero the students ignore the zero or misunderstand the zero.	Given 5 hundreds and 8 units in base-ten materials, students will write that number as 85. The student believes that 802 and 8002 represent the same amount.	• Focus on the meaning of a zero in any number by starting with a number like 408 and asking how that would be shown with materials. Explicitly discuss the role of an internal 0 in the number. • Never refer to 0 as a "placeholder." This terminology gives the impression that it is not a numerical value and it is there just as a way to fill a space. • Never read or refer to 0 as oh or zip. Say "zero" as it is a number.
7. If students are given the place values of numbers out of order they write the number as given left to right regardless of the place value.	When students are asked to write the number that represents: 7 ones, 4 tens, 1 thousand, and 3 hundreds. They write 7413.	• Go back to the base-ten materials and use the place value mat to take out the same amount of base-ten materials as in the number. Then have the student write the number of base-ten materials. The student should then compare the two answers to consider which one is accurate
8. Students misinterpret the value of the base-ten materials.	Students think the value of the large 1000 place value block is actually 600 by just calculating the number of squares on each face of the cube.	• Particularly with the 1000 place value block, if students don't see the building of the block (grouping into a unit), they may confuse the value. So, explicitly show the building of the cube by taking ten hundreds blocks and forming a cube with them (holding them together with elastic bands.)

 **RESOURCES** FOR CHAPTER 10

LITERATURE CONNECTIONS

Books that emphasize groups of things, even simple counting books, are a good beginning to the notion of ten things in a single group. Many books have wonderful explorations of large quantities and how the numbers can be composed and decomposed.

100th Day Worries
Cuyler (2005)

The 100th Day of School from the Black Lagoon
Thaler, 2014

Both of these books focus on the 100th day of school, which is one way to recognize the benchmark number of 100. Through a variety of ways to think about 100 (such as collections of 100 items), students will be able to use these stories to think about the relative size of 100 or ways to make 100 using a variety of combinations.

How Much Is a Million?
Schwartz (2004)

If You Made a Million
Schwartz (1994)

On Beyond a Million: An Amazing Math Journey
Schwartz (2001)

The Magic of a Million Activity Book—Grades 2–5
Schwartz & Whitin (1999)

Schwartz authored a collection of entertaining and conceptually sound books about the powers of ten or what makes a million—from visual images of students standing on one another's shoulders in a formation that reaches the moon to various monetary collections. The activity book by Schwartz and Whitin provides activities to help students interpret large numbers.

If I Had a Million Bucks
Johnson (2012)

This story is about Ada, a girl who likes to plan. Ada is thinking about what she could do if she had one million dollars. This planning is a fun way to have students think about what could be purchased with large amounts of money.

RECOMMENDED READINGS

Articles

Burris, J. T. (2013). Virtual place value. *Teaching Children Mathematics, 20*(4), 228–236.

This interesting study explores teaching place value using several activities with technology. Students worked with both concrete base-ten materials and virtual versions to help reinforce conceptual structures, particularly for showing equivalent representations.

Kari, A. R., & Anderson, C. B. (2003). Opportunities to develop place value through student dialogue. *Teaching Children Mathematics, 10*(2), 78–82.

Two teachers describe a first-/second-grade classroom, where students' understanding of two-digit numbers is shown to be quite mistaken, but can be developed conceptually with the aid of discussion. At first, the student in the article is convinced that 11 + 11 + 11 is 60. This article emphasizes the wide range of student ideas and the value of classroom discourse.

Book

Richardson, K. (2003). *Assessing math concepts: Grouping tens.* Bellingham, WA: Mathematical Perspectives.

This book is one of a nine-part series on using diagnostic interviews and other assessment tools (including blackline masters) to understand students' grasp of a concept—in this case, grouping by tens. Tips are shared about conducting observations, with suggestions for instruction.

11 Developing Strategies for Addition and Subtraction Computation

LEARNER OUTCOMES

After reading this chapter and engaging in the embedded activities and reflections, you should be able to:

11.1 Identify the interplay between place value understanding and addition and subtraction computational strategies.

11.2 Identify three types of computational strategies.

11.3 Explain multiple invented strategies for addition and subtraction with multidigit numbers.

11.4 Explain the development of the standard algorithms for addition and subtraction including ways to record students' thinking.

11.5 Identify ways to teach computational estimation to develop students' flexibility and ability to recognize reasonable answers.

11.6 Describe computational estimation strategies for addition and subtraction.

M uch of the public sees computational skills as the hallmark of what it means to know mathematics at the elementary school level. Although that is far from the whole story, learning computational skills with whole numbers is, in fact, a critical component of the curriculum. Expectations for competency in today's workforce as well as in daily life mean that changes are warranted in how computation is taught.

Rather than presenting a single method of adding or subtracting, the most appropriate method can and should change flexibly as the numbers and the context change. In the spirit of the *Common Core State Standards* (NGA Center & CCSSO, 2010) and the *Principles to Actions* (NCTM, 2014), the goal is no longer just a matter of "knowing how to subtract three-digit numbers," rather, it is the development over time of an assortment of flexible skills and procedures that are meaningfully linked to conceptual understanding. *Adding It Up* (National Research Council, 2001) describes it this way:

More than just a means to produce answers, computation is increasingly seen as a window on the deep structure of the number system. Fortunately, research is demonstrating that both skilled performance and conceptual understanding are generated by the same kinds of activities. (p. 182)

According to the *Common Core State Standards*, students should solve addition and subtraction problems with numbers appropriate for their grade level (within 10 for kindergarten students, within 100 for first-grade students, and within 1000 for second-grade students). First-grade students are expected to add two-digit numbers to one-digit numbers or to a multiple of 10.

Second-grade students are expected to add two- and three-digit numbers. As students enter the intermediate grades, they continue working with addition and subtraction of large numbers as they fluently solve problems within 1000 using a variety of strategies. Importantly, the addition and subtraction standard algorithms are not required until fourth grade (NGA Center & CCSSO, 2010). The expected solution methods before that time range from using concrete models or drawings to strategies based on place value, meanings of operations, and number sense. To support the development of flexible addition and subtraction strategies, students are expected to be able to compose and decompose numbers less than 20 for kindergartners, numbers less than 100 for first-grade students, and numbers less than 1000 for second-grade students (NGA Center & CCSSO, 2010). To reach these expectations the following big ideas are essential.

BIG IDEAS

- ◆ Flexible methods of addition and subtraction computation involve taking apart (decomposing) and combining (composing) numbers in a wide variety of ways. Most of the decomposing of numbers is based on place value or *compatible numbers*—which are number pairs that work easily together, such as 25 and 75.

- ◆ Invented strategies provide flexible methods of computing that vary with the numbers and the situation. Successful use of the strategies requires that they be understood by the one who is using them—hence the term *invented*.

- ◆ Flexible methods for computation require a deep understanding of the operations and properties of the operations (the commutative property and the associative property). How addition and subtraction are related as inverse operations is also important.

- ◆ Standard algorithms are elegant strategies for computing that are based on performing the operation on one place value at a time with transitions to an adjacent position (trades or regrouping). Standard algorithms can tend to cause students to think in terms of digits rather than the composite number that the digits make up, so students often lose track of the actual place value of a digit.

- ◆ Multidigit numbers can be built up or taken apart in a variety of ways to make the numbers easier to work with. These parts can be used to estimate answers in calculations rather than using the exact numbers involved. For example, 36 is the same as 30 and 6 or 25 and 10 and 1. Also, 483 can be thought of as 500 − 20 + 3.

- ◆ Computational estimations involve using easier-to-handle parts of numbers or substituting difficult-to-handle numbers with close compatible numbers so that the resulting computations can be done mentally.

Toward Computational Fluency

Addition and subtraction strategies that build on decomposing and composing numbers in flexible ways contribute to students' overall number sense. In most everyday instances, these alternative strategies for computing are easier and faster than standard algorithms (procedures for computing) and can often be done mentally. Therefore, it is best to have students learn a variety of methods that they can select from as needed. Many classrooms are engaging in what has become commonly known as "number talks" (Humphreys & Parker, 2015; Parrish, 2014) where students have opportunities to engage in solving and discussing alternative strategies to solve computation problems.

Consider the following problem:

Mary has 114 spaces in her photo album. So far, she has placed 89 photos in the album. How many more photos can she put in before the album is full?

Pause & **Reflect**

Try solving the photo album problem using a method other than the standard algorithm you were taught in school. If you are tempted to begin with the 9 and the 4, try a different approach. Can you solve it mentally using number sense? Can you solve it in more than one way? Work on this problem before reading further. ●

Here are five of many possible methods used by students in the primary grades to solve the computation in the photo album problem:

89 + 11 equals 100. 11 + 14 equals 25.

90 + 10 equals 100 and 14 more is 24 plus 1 (because we should have started at 89, not 90) equals 25.

From 114 subtract 14 and then subtract 10 more which equals 90, and then subtract 1 more to get to 89, which is 25 in all.

89, 99, 109 (that's 20), 110, 111, 112, 113, 114 (keeping track on fingers) is 25.

89 + 11 equals 100. Adding the same amount of 11 to 114 equals 125. The difference between 125 and 100 equals 25.

 Standards for Mathematical Practice

MP2. Reason abstractly and quantitatively.

Strategies such as these can be done mentally, are generally faster than standard algorithms, and make sense to the person using them. Every day, too many students and adults resort to standard algorithms that they don't fully understand and so, are often error prone when other, more meaningful methods would be faster and more accurate (Biddlecomb & Carr, 2011; Fuson Beckmann, 2012/2013). For a closer look at several alternative algorithms that explicitly emphasize place value and number sense, go to the University of Chicago's *Everyday Mathematics* website and search "Algorithms." This site provides video examples of various computational algorithms including the research base for why we should help students learn these alternative approaches. As students learn how quantities can be *decomposed* (broken apart) and *composed* (put together) in different ways, they build a foundation for interpreting the properties of operations (NCTM, 2014).

MyLab Education   **Video Example 11.1**

To get a sense of the relationship between developing conceptual understanding and computational fluency, watch this video (https://www.youtube.com/watch?v=ZFUAVO0bTwA) about how the *Common Core State Standards* takes a balanced approach.

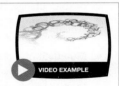

VIDEO EXAMPLE

Flexibility with a variety of computational strategies is an important tool for a mathematically literate citizen to be successful in daily life. It is time to broaden our perspective of what it means to compute. If you haven't developed these strategies on your own, you will learn them as you read this chapter and as you teach your students to use them! Let's resume where we just left off—place value.

Connecting Addition and Subtraction to Place Value

One important shift has been to blend instruction on numeration and place value with computation with two- and three-digit numbers (and beyond). Research suggests that problems involving addition and subtraction are a good context for learning place-value concepts (Carpenter, Franke, Jacobs, & Fennema, Empson, 1998; Wright, Martland, Stafford, & Stanger, 2008). If students only understand computation as a digit-by-digit exercise and not the value of the numbers involved, they make many errors and are often unable to judge the reasonableness of their answers. So here we will connect place value to addition and subtraction. The key purpose of the following activities is whether students can apply their emerging understanding of place value to computation. Remember, place value is not only a basis for computation; students also develop place-value understanding as a result of finding their own methods of computing.

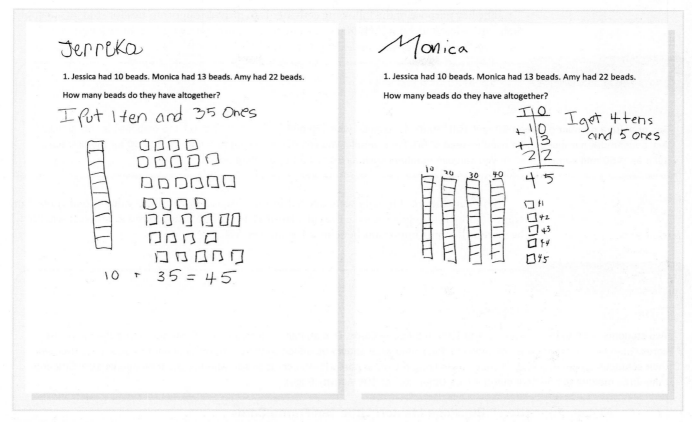

FIGURE 11.1   The work of two first-grade students in January. They both solved the problem 10 + 13 + 22.

Consider, Jerrika, in January of the first grade, who solves a story problem for 10 + 13 + 22 using connecting cubes. Her written work (Figure 11.1) shows she is still at a pre-place-value stage. We can observe that she is beginning to use the idea of "1 ten" but most likely counted on the remaining 35 cubes by ones. Her classmate, Monica, solved the same problem but has clearly utilized more base-ten ideas (Figure 11.1). Ideas such as these continue to grow with additional problem solving and sharing of ideas during class discussions.

The activities in this chapter are designed to further students' understanding of place value concepts while engaging them in addition and subtraction. The first of these bridging activities involves adding or subtracting a constant using the calculator. The flexibility of this activity allows for it to be used over and over at various skill levels, always challenging students and improving their mental math skills.

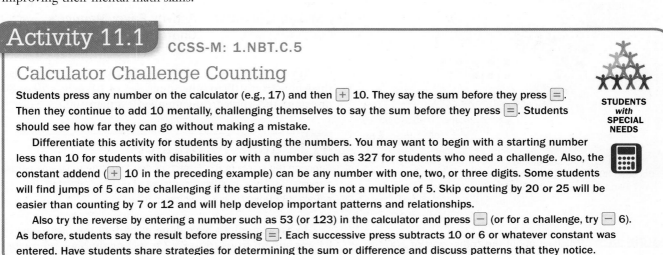

Activity 11.1   CCSS-M: 1.NBT.C.5

Calculator Challenge Counting

STUDENTS with SPECIAL NEEDS

Students press any number on the calculator (e.g., 17) and then ⊞ 10. They say the sum before they press ═. Then they continue to add 10 mentally, challenging themselves to say the sum before they press ═. Students should see how far they can go without making a mistake.

Differentiate this activity for students by adjusting the numbers. You may want to begin with a starting number less than 10 for students with disabilities or with a number such as 327 for students who need a challenge. Also, the constant addend (⊞ 10 in the preceding example) can be any number with one, two, or three digits. Some students will find jumps of 5 can be challenging if the starting number is not a multiple of 5. Skip counting by 20 or 25 will be easier than counting by 7 or 12 and will help develop important patterns and relationships.

Also try the reverse by entering a number such as 53 (or 123) in the calculator and press ⊟ (or for a challenge, try ⊟ 6). As before, students say the result before pressing ═. Each successive press subtracts 10 or 6 or whatever constant was entered. Have students share strategies for determining the sum or difference and discuss patterns that they notice.

The key purpose of the following activities is to provide opportunities for students to apply their emerging understanding of place value to computation using benchmark numbers.

Activity 11.2   CCSS-M: 1.NBT.B.4

50 and Some More

Say or write a number between 50 and 100. Students respond with "50 and _____." For 63, the response is "50 and 13." Any benchmark number can be used instead of 50. For example, you could use any number that ends in 50 for the first part, such as "450 and some more." Or you can use numbers such as 70 or 230 as starting points.

The benchmark numbers we explored in our discussions of place value are also used in computational strategies to make the calculations easier. The next activity is aimed at what may be one of the most important benchmark numbers: 100.

Activity 11.3   CCSS-M: 1.NBT.B.4; 2.NBT.B.5

The Other Part of 100M

Two students work together with a set of Little Ten-Frame Cards. One student makes a two-digit number using the ten-frame cards. Then both students work mentally to determine what should be added to the ten-frame amount to equal 100. They write their solutions on paper and then check by making the other part with the cards to see whether the total equals 100. Students take turns making the original number (see Other Part of 100 Activity Page).

MyLab Education   Blackline Master: Little Ten-Frame Cards
MyLab Education   Activity Page: Other Part of 100

Figure 11.2 shows three different thought processes that students might use.

Have students look at Maurice's Chart. Have them decide whether Maurice is right or wrong and, if needed, describe how to correct the mistake.

MyLab Education	Activity Page: Little Ten-Frame Cards
MyLab Education	Activity Page: Other Part of 100
MyLab Education	Activity Page: Maurice's Chart

If your students are adept at finding parts of 100, change the whole from 100 to other multiples of 10 such as 70 or 80 or extend the whole to any number less than 100.

❚❚ Pause & Reflect

Suppose the whole is 83. Sketch or use four little ten-frame cards showing 36. Looking at your cards, what number added to 36 equals 83? How did you think about it? ●

What you might have done in finding the other part of 83 was add up from 36 to 83. Or you might have subtracted

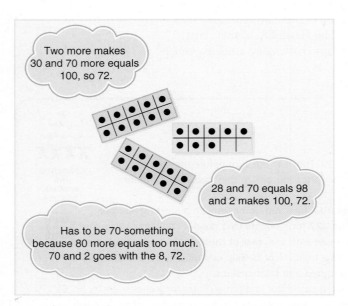

FIGURE 11.2   Thinking about the "other part of 100."

33 from 83, which equals 50 and then subtracted 3 more. Either way, notice that you did not regroup. Most likely you did it in your head, possibly using benchmark numbers and place value. With more practice, you (and students as early as second grade) can do this computation without the aid of the cards.

Compatible numbers for addition and subtraction are numbers that easily combine to equal benchmark numbers. Numbers that equal tens or hundreds are the most common examples. Compatible sums also include numbers that end in 5, 25, 50, or 75, because these numbers are easy to work with as well. Your task is to get students accustomed to looking for combinations that work together and then looking for these combinations in computational situations.

Activity 11.4   CCSS-M: 2.NBT.B.5

Compatible Pairs

Searching for compatible pairs can be done as an activity with the full class. One at a time, project the 4 suggested searches in Figure 11.3 or use the Compatible Pairs Activity Pages. The possible searches are at different difficulty levels. Have students name or connect the compatible pairs as they see them.

MyLab Education   Activity Page:
Compatible Pairs

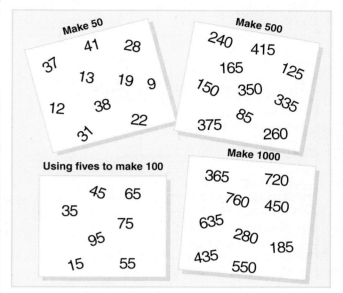

FIGURE 11.3   Compatible-pair searches.

The next activity combines base-ten representations with symbolism.

Activity 11.5   CCSS-M: 2.NBT.B.7

Numbers, Squares, Lines, and Dots

Use the Squares, Lines, and Dots Activity Page to introduce students to the use of squares (hundreds), lines (tens), and dots (ones) to represent base-ten materials with simple drawings. Then, as illustrated in Figure 11.4 (addition) or Figure 11.5 (subtraction), display problems using a number along with a quantity represented using squares, lines and dots. Students then mentally compute the totals or the differences. Note that the subtraction problems with the removed amount represented by the numeral will be easiest to start with.

MyLab Education   Activity Page Squares,
Lines, and Dots

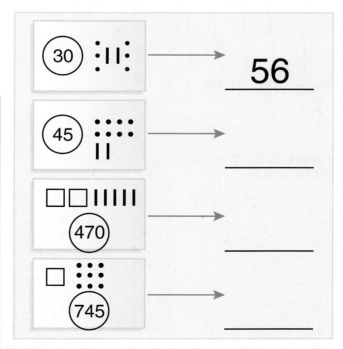

FIGURE 11.4   Flexible counting on or addition using both models and numerals.

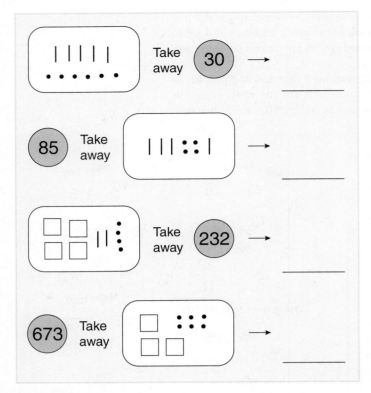

FIGURE 11.5 Take away subtraction using both models and numerals.

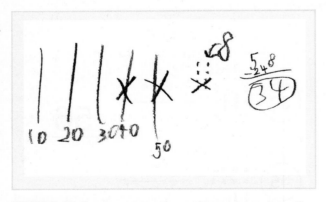

FIGURE 11.6 A student shows subtraction using a line and dot model.

If this activity is done with the whole class, discuss each task before moving to the next. If you use the activity sheet, display individual problems or cut the page into single problems and have students write how they solved each. But it is still important to have a discussion with the class. Students can also show these representations as a way to calculate or check answers, as shown in the work of a second grader in Figure 11.6.

> **MyLab Education**   Activity Page: Squares, Lines, and Dots

The next activity extends the use of the hundreds chart by using it for addition.

Activity 11.6
CCSS-M:
2.NBT.B.5

Hundreds Chart Addition

Display a hundreds chart (or a thousands chart) for the class to see or, alternatively, give students their own individual hundreds charts using the Four Small Hundreds Charts. Students use the hundreds chart to add two numbers (e.g., 38 and 14). There are many ways that students can use the hundreds chart for addition, so the value is in the class discussions. Have students work on one sum at a time and then have a discussion to compare the different methods students used.

MyLab Education   Blackline Master: Four Small Hundreds Charts

The hundreds chart can be thought of as a stacked number line—one that highlights the distance from any number to the next multiple of 10. A jump down a row is the same as adding 10, and a jump up a row is 10 less. As illustrated in Figure 11.7(a)), you will see that a student added 13 + 12 by just counting by ones. Many students will simply count on 12 individual squares from 13—an indication that they may not understand how to count by tens from any starting value (an important place-value concept). Consider how a student might use the hundreds chart to help think about the sum of 27 and 12. This next student's approach is to begin at 27, jump down one row, and count over 2 to 39. See Figure 11.7(b). Figure 11.7(c) shows a subtraction problem with a drawing of part of a hundreds chart, beginning at 39, jumping up one row, and backing off 2. Notice how the student checked her answer by using an equation.

The following activity is similar to Hundreds Chart Addition but explores the idea of "think-addition" as a method of subtraction.

Activity 11.7　CCSS-M: 2.NBT.B.5

How Much Between?

Provide students with a Blank Hundreds Chart. Give the students two numbers. Their task is to determine how much from one number to the next.

MyLab Education　**Blackline Master: Blank Hundreds Chart**

Your choice of the two numbers for this activity will have an impact on the strategies students will use. The easiest pairs are in the same column on the hundreds chart, such as 24 and 64, which is a good place to begin. When the larger number is in a different column from the smaller number (e.g., 24 and 56), students can add on tens to get to the target number's row and then add or subtract ones. Of course, this strategy is also reasonable for any two numbers. But consider 17 and 45, where the column that 45 is in on the chart is to the left of the column that 17 is in. A student might count by tens and go down 3 rows (+30) to 47 and then count back 2 (−2) to 45. The total count is now 30 − 2 or 28. There are also other possible approaches. The next activity uses little ten-frame cards instead of the hundreds chart.

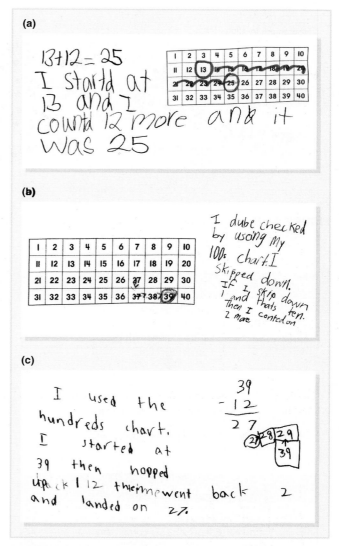

FIGURE 11.7　Three students use the hundreds chart to add or subtract.

Activity 11.8　CCSS-M: 2.NBT.B.5

Little Ten-Frame Sums

Provide pairs of students with two sets of Little Ten-Frames. Each student chooses a number. An example (47 + 36) is shown in Figure 11.8. Partners work to find the total number of dots recording the pair of numbers and the sum. The activity can also be done by showing the two ten-frames on the projector for 10–15 seconds and asking the students to give the total. Show them for a second look if students request another look.

MyLab Education　**Blackline Master: Little Ten-Frames**

FORMATIVE ASSESSMENT Notes. Students who exhibit difficulty with any of these activities may be challenged with invented computation strategies. Therefore, conduct a diagnostic interview to find how students strategize the exercises in

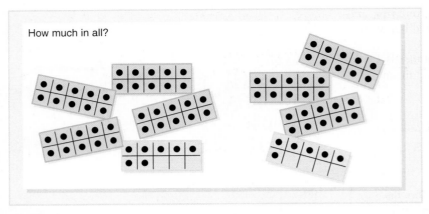

FIGURE 11.8 Using little ten-frame cards to add.

Activity 11.5, "Numbers, Squares, Lines, and Dots." That activity requires that students have sufficient understanding of base-ten concepts to use them in meaningful counts. If students are still counting by ones, then back up and consider additional counting activities in which students have opportunities to see the value of grouping by ten before moving on. ■

MyLab Education **Self-Check 11.1**

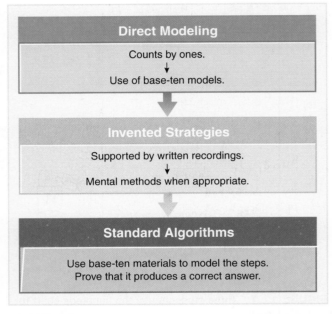

FIGURE 11.9 An instructional sequence of three types of computational strategies. The arrows show how students move from acting out situations with direct modeling to invented strategy use to the development of standard algorithms.

FIGURE 11.10 A possible direct modeling of 36 + 27 using base-ten models.

Three Types of Computational Strategies

Figure 11.9 lists a general instructional sequence that includes three types of computational strategies. The *direct modeling* methods can, with guidance, develop into an assortment of more flexible and useful *invented strategies*, many of which can be carried out mentally. The *standard algorithms* remain an important part of what students need to learn. However, reinforce that, just like the other strategies, the standard algorithm is more useful in some instances than in others. Discuss which methods seem best in which situations.

Direct Modeling

The developmental step that usually precedes invented strategies is called *direct modeling*. This strategy involves the use of manipulatives or drawings along with counting to directly represent the meaning of an operation or story problem (see Figure 11.10).

Students who consistently count by ones in additive situations most likely have not developed base-ten grouping concepts. That does not mean you should avoid giving them problems involving two-digit numbers. Rather, as you work with students who are still struggling with seeing ten as a unit, suggest that they use a tool to help them think, such as placing counters in a ten-frame or making bars of tens from connecting cubes. Some students will initially use the base-ten rod of 10 as a counting device to keep track of counts of ten, even though they are counting each 10 rod by ones. As students complete each intermediate count, have them write down the corresponding numbers for memory support.

When students have constructed the idea of ten as a unit, they begin to use this idea to move from direct modeling to invented strategies derived from number sense and the properties of operations. But direct modeling is a necessary phase for students to work through. These developmental strategies are important because they provide students who are not ready for more efficient methods with a way to explore the same problems as classmates who have progressed beyond this stage. Do not push students to prematurely abandon concrete approaches using materials, however, some students may need encouragement to move away from direct modeling. Here are some ideas to promote the fading of direct modeling:

- Record students' verbal explanations on the board in ways that they and others can follow.
- Ask students who have just solved a problem with models if they can do it mentally.
- Ask students to make a written numeric record of how they solved the problem with models. Then have them try the same written method on a new problem.

Invented Strategies

An *invented strategy* refers to any strategy other than the standard algorithm or that does not involve the use of physical materials or counting by ones as (Carpenter et al., 1998). For first- and second-grade students, the *Common Core State Standards* (NGA Center & CCSSO, 2010) describe these strategies as "based on place value, properties of operations, and/or the relationship between addition and subtraction" (pp. 16, 19). More specifically, students are expected to "develop, discuss, and use efficient, accurate, and generalizable methods to compute sums and differences of whole numbers in base-ten notation, using their understanding of place value and the properties of operations" (p. 17). At times, invented strategies become mental methods after the ideas have been explored, used, and understood. For example, after some experience, students may be able to do $75 + 19$ mentally ($75 + 20$ is 95, less 1 is 94). For $847 + 256$, students may need to write down intermediate steps (i.e., add 3 to 847) to support their memory as they work through the problem. (Try that one yourself.) In the classroom, written support is often encouraged as strategies develop because they are more easily shared and help students focus on the ideas. Distinctions among written, partially written, and mental computation are not important, especially in the development period.

A number of research studies have focused attention on how students of a variety of ages handle computational situations when they have been given options for multiple strategies (Csikos, 2016; Keiser, 2010; Lynch & Star, 2014; Rittle-Johnson, Star, & Durkin, 2010; Verschaffel, Greer, & De Corte, 2007). "There is mounting evidence that students both in and out of school can construct methods for adding and subtracting multi-digit numbers without explicit instruction" (Carpenter et al., 1998, p. 4). One of the best ways for students to grow their repertoire is to listen to the strategies invented by classmates as they are shared, explored, and tried out by others. However, students should not be permitted to use any strategy without understanding it.

Contrasts with Standard Algorithms. Consider the following significant differences between invented strategies and standard algorithms.

1. *Invented strategies are number oriented rather than digit oriented.* Using the standard algorithm for $45 + 32$, students think of $4 + 3$ instead of 40 and 30. Kamii, longtime advocate for invented strategies, claims that standard algorithms "unteach" place value (Kamii & Dominick, 1998). By contrast, an invented strategy works with the complete numbers. For example, an invented strategy for $618 - 254$ might begin with $600 - 200$ is 400. Another approach might begin with 254, and add 46 which is 300. Then 300 more to 600 and so on. In either case, the computation is number-oriented.

2. *Invented strategies are left-handed rather than right-handed.* Invented strategies often begin with the largest parts of numbers (leftmost digits) because they focus on the entire number. For $263 + 126$, many invented strategies will begin with "$200 + 100$ equals 300," providing some sense of the size of the eventual answer in just one step. In contrast, the standard algorithm begins with $3 + 6$ equals 9. By beginning on the right with a digit orientation, the solution is hidden until the end. The exception is the standard long-division algorithm.

3. *Invented strategies are a range of flexible options rather than "one right way."* Invented strategies are dependent on the numbers involved so that students can make the computation easier. Try each of these problems mentally: $465 + 230$ and $526 + 98$. Did you use the same method? The standard algorithm suggests using the same tool on all problems. The standard algorithm for $7000 - 25$ typically leads to student errors, yet a mental strategy is relatively simple.

Benefits of Invented Strategies. The development and use of invented strategies generate procedural proficiency and more. The positive benefits are:

- *Students make fewer errors.* Research reveals that students using methods they understand make many fewer errors because they understand their own methods (Gravemeijer & van Galen, 2003). If students do not understand the underlying concepts of standard algorithms not only do they make errors, but the errors are often systematic and difficult to remediate. Errors with invented strategies are less frequent and rarely systematic.

- *Less reteaching is required.* Teachers often are concerned when students' early efforts with invented strategies are slow and time consuming. But the productive struggle in these early stages builds a meaningful and well-integrated network of ideas that is robust, long lasting, and significantly decreases the time required for reteaching.

- *Students develop number sense.* Students' development and use of number-oriented, flexible algorithms offers them a rich understanding of the number system through strategies they understand. In contrast, some students who move to standard algorithms too early are unable to explain why they work.

- *Invented strategies are the basis for mental computation and estimation.* When invented strategies are the norm for computation, there is no need to talk about mental computation as if it were a separate skill. As students become more proficient with these flexible methods, they find they are able to use them mentally or sometimes only need to jot down intermediate steps.

- *Flexible methods are often faster than standard algorithms.* Consider $76 + 46$. An invented strategy might involve $70 + 40 = 110$ and $6 + 6 = 12$. The sum of 110 and 12 equals 122. This computation is done mentally, or even with some recording, in much less time than the steps of the standard algorithm.

- *Algorithm invention is itself a significantly important process of "doing mathematics."* Students who invent a computational strategy, or who adopt a meaningful strategy shared by a classmate, are involved in the processes of sense making and building confidence. This development of procedures was often hidden from learners (possibly yourself included) when algorithms were just "told" to students. By engaging in this developmental aspect of mathematics, a different and valuable view of "doing mathematics" is revealed to learners.

- *Invented strategies serve students well on standardized tests.* Evidence suggests that students using invented strategies do as well or better than students using standard algorithms in computation on standardized tests (Fleischman, Hopstock, Pelczar, & Shelley, 2010; Fuson, 2003).

Activity 11.9

CCSS-M: 2.NBT.B.5; 2.NBT.B.6; 2.NBT.B.7; 3.NBT.B.2; 4.NBT.B.2; 4.NBT.B.4

City Populations

Have students combine or compare the populations of classrooms, cities or counties in your school or region. Place the names of the cities, for example, on cards and either write the population directly on the card or have a corresponding chart for students to refer to. Then give students two cards and use the City Population Word Problem Activity Page, or have students create their own word problems. Students who are ready for larger numbers can work with densely populated locations, while students needing a gentler ramp up to the content can start with two sparsely populated areas.

STUDENTS with SPECIAL NEEDS

ENGLISH LEARNERS

MyLab Education **Activity Page: City Population Word Problem**

Mental Computation. A mental computation strategy is simply any invented strategy that is done mentally. What may be a mental strategy for one student may require written support by another. Initially, students may not be ready to do computations mentally, as they may still be at the direct modeling stage or need to notate parts of the problem as they think it through. As your students become more adept, they can and should be challenged to do appropriate computations mentally. You may be quite amazed at the ability of students (and at your own ability) to do mental mathematics.

MyLab Education   **Video Example 11.2**

Watch Connor use two different invented strategies to mentally solve a two-digit addition problem.

Try mental computation with this example:

$$342 \ + \ 153 \ + \ 481$$

 Pause & Reflect

For this task, try the following method: Begin by adding the hundreds, saying the totals as you go—"3 hundred, 4 hundred, 8 hundred." Then add on to this partial sum the tens in successive manner and finally the ones. Give it a try. ●

Standard Algorithms

There are three main components in the trajectory of learning about the standard algorithms: (1) knowing the step by step procedure and how it is performed; (2) knowing why the algorithm works and how it can be applied; and (3) knowing when an algorithm should be used and comparing the value and usefulness of different algorithms (Fan & Bokhove, 2014). The focus in teaching standard algorithms should not be as merely a memorized series of steps, but as making sense of the procedure as a process. Algorithms should have the characteristics of certainty (precise procedures), reliability (always a correct answer if carried out properly), transparency (the process is understood), efficiency (effective approach) and generalizability (solves a collection of similar problems) (Fan & Bokhove, 2014).

The *Common Core State Standards* (NGA Center & CCSSO, 2010) require that students eventually have knowledge of the standard algorithms (addition and subtraction with multidigit whole numbers in grade 4, multiplication with multidigit whole numbers in grade 5, and division of multidigit whole numbers in grade 6). Notice that the grades in which this knowledge of standard algorithms is required is long after the time when the topic is introduced. This timeline points to the need for full conceptual development to take place first. Importantly, there is the recognition that starting by teaching only the standard algorithm doesn't allow students to explore other useful approaches. Understanding how algorithms work and when they are the best choice (over an invented approach) is central to development of procedural proficiency.

Standard Algorithms Must Be Understood. Students may learn the standard algorithms from siblings and other family members while you are still trying to teach a variety of invented strategies. Some of these students may resist learning more flexible strategies thinking that they already know the "right" approach. What do you do then?

First and foremost, apply the same rule to standard algorithms as to all strategies: *If you use it, you must understand why it works and be able to explain it.* In an atmosphere that says, "Let's figure out why this procedure works," students can profit from making sense of standard algorithms just as they should be able to reason about other approaches. But the responsibility for the explanations should be theirs, not yours. Remember, "Never say anything a kid can say!" (Reinhart, 2000).

The standard algorithm, once understood, is one more strategy to put in the students' "toolbox" of methods. Algorithms are a significant part of the development of a deep understanding of mathematics (Fan & Bokhove, 2014). But reinforce the idea that just like the other strategies, it may be more useful in some instances than in others. For example, pose problems in which a mental strategy is more useful than an algorithm, such as $504 - 498$ as well as a problem such as $4568 + 12{,}813$ where the standard algorithm has distinct advantages. Discuss which strategy seems best in a variety of situations.

Standards for Mathematical Practice

MP7. Look for and make use of structure.

Standard Algorithm	When Topic Is Introduced and Developed	When Standard Algorithm Is Required
Add and Subtract Multidigit Whole Numbers	Grades 1–3	Grade 4
Multiply Multidigit Whole Numbers	Grades 3 and 4	Grade 5
Divide Multidigit Whole Number	Grades 3 and 4	Grade 6
Add, Subtract, Multiply, and Divide Decimals	Grade 5	Grade 6

FIGURE 11.11   What the CCSS document suggests regarding the delay of standard algorithms

MyLab Education   **Video Example 11.3**

Watch this video clip of third-grade student Estephania, who compares the use of a mental strategy with the standard subtraction algorithm.

Delay! Delay! Delay! Students are unlikely to invent standard algorithms. You will need to introduce and explain each algorithm to them and help them understand how and why it works. No matter how carefully you introduce these algorithms into your classroom as simply another alternative, students are likely to sense that this approach is the "one right way." So, spend a significant amount of time with invented strategies—months, not weeks. Again, note that the *Common Core State Standards* (NGA Center & CCSSO, 2010) require that students learn a variety of strategies based on place value and properties of the operations one or two years before standard algorithms are expected to be mastered (see Figure 11.11). The understandings students gain from working with invented strategies makes it easier for you to meaningfully teach standard algorithms. If you think you are wasting precious time by delaying, just be reminded of how many years the same standard algorithms are taught over and over to students who still make errors and are unable to explain them.

MyLab Education   **Application Exercise 11.1: Standard Algorithms for Addition and Subtraction** Click the link to access this exercise, then watch the video and answer the accompanying questions.

Cultural Differences in Algorithms. Some people falsely assume that mathematics is universal and is easier than other subjects for students who are not native English speakers. In fact, there are many international differences in notation, conventions, and algorithms. Knowing more about the diverse algorithms students might bring to the classroom and their ways of recording symbols for "doing mathematics" will assist you in supporting students and responding to families. What the United States calls the "standard algorithm" may not be customary in other countries, so encouraging a variety of algorithms is important in valuing the experiences of each and every student.

For example, *equal addition* is a subtraction algorithm used in many Latin and European countries. It is based on the knowledge that adding the same amount to both the minuend and the subtrahend will not change the difference (answer). Therefore, if the expression to be solved is $15 - 5$, there is no change to the answer (or the difference) if you add 10 to the minuend and subtrahend and solve $25 - 15$. There is still a difference of 10. Let's consider $62 - 27$. Using the algorithm that you may think of as "standard," you would likely regroup by crossing out the 6 tens, adding the 10 with a small "1" to the 2 in the ones column (making 12 ones), and then subtract 7 from the 12 and so forth. In the *equal addition* approach (see Figure 11.12[a]), you add 10 to the ones place (2) in 62 by just mentally adding a small "1" in the ones column (to represent the 10) resulting in 12, and then counteract that addition of 10 to the minuend by mentally adding 10 to the 27 (subtrahend), by increasing the tens column by one and subtracting 37.

Thinking about the distances between numbers, particularly on a number line is helpful (Whitacre et al., 2016/2017). A student, using a strategy based on equal additions called *same difference* (Humphreys & Parker, 2015) might add 3 to both 62 and 27, which results in 65 − 30, a much easier problem to solve (Figure 11.12[b]). The student is basically moving the same difference to a new location on the number line. This approach may sound confusing to you—but try it. Especially when there are zeros in the minuend (e.g., 302 − 178), you may find this method a productive option. More important, your possible confusion can give you the sense of how your students (and their families) may react to a completely different procedure from the one they know and find successful.

Why does the equal additions method result in the same answer? Using an open number line, mark the two numbers in the subtraction problem, 302 − 178. Note the difference or the distance between the two numbers (124). Now, using equal additions, change the numbers to create an easier problem to subtract. Note the difference or distance between the two numbers in this new problem is the same as in the original problem. Adding (or subtracting) the same amount from the minuend and the subtrahend just shifts the numbers the same distance along the number line but maintains the difference *between* the two numbers.

Another key component to understanding cultural differences in algorithms is the emphasis on mental mathematics in other countries (Perkins & Flores, 2002). In fact, some students pride themselves on their ability to do math mentally. Don't be surprised if students from other countries can produce answers without showing work.

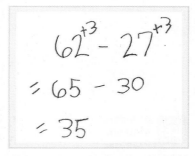

FIGURE 11.12(A) The "equal addition" algorithm.

$$62^{+3} - 27^{+3}$$
$$= 65 - 30$$
$$= 35$$

FIGURE 11.12(B) A strategy using "equal addition" or "same difference"

MyLab Education   Self-Check 11.2

Development of Invented Strategies in Addition and Subtraction

Usually, students do not spontaneously invent computational methods while you sit back and watch, instead teachers and programs have an effect on the methods students develop (Verschaffel et al., 2007). Here we discuss pedagogical methods that support students' development of invented strategies for multidigit addition and subtraction.

Creating a Supportive Environment for Invented Strategies

Invented strategies are developed out of a strong understanding of numbers. The development of place-value concepts begins to prepare students for the challenges of inventing computational strategies. For example, the NGA Center & CCSSO (2010) suggests that second-grade students should be able to use mental computation to find a number that is 10 or 100 more (or less) than a given number between 100 and 900. This standard calls for young learners to publicly share emerging ideas. Therefore, students need a classroom environment where they can act like mathematicians and explore ideas without fear. When students in your classroom attempt to investigate new ideas such as invented strategy use, they should find your classroom a safe and nurturing place for expressing naive or rudimentary thoughts.

Some of the characteristics described previously regarding the development of a problem-solving environment need to be reiterated here to establish the climate for taking risks, testing conjectures, and trying new approaches. Students also need to know that they will need to persevere and be ready for *productive struggle*; as that is when learning takes place. Hiebert and Grouws (2007) stated, "We use the word *struggle* to mean that students expend effort to make sense of mathematics, to figure something out that is not immediately apparent. . . . We do not mean the feelings of despair that some students can experience when little of the material makes sense" (p. 387). We need to encourage students to persist with material that is challenging but within their grasp and understandable.

Keep these factors in mind:

- Avoid immediately identifying the right answer when a student states it. Give other students a chance to consider whether they think the answer and approach are correct.
- Expect and encourage student-to-student interactions, questions, discussions, and conjectures. Allow plenty of time for discussions.
- Encourage students to clarify previous knowledge and make attempts to construct new ideas.
- Promote curiosity and openness to trying new things.
- Talk about both right and wrong ideas in a nonevaluative and nonthreatening way.
- Move unsophisticated ideas to more sophisticated thinking through coaching and strategic questioning.
- Use familiar contexts and story problems to build background and connect to students' experiences. Avoid using "naked numbers" as a starting point, as they do not encourage strategy development.
- Show samples of anonymous students' work and allow students to critique the reasoning of others.

Standards for Mathematical Practice

MP3. Construct viable arguments and critique the reasoning of others.

Models to Support Invented Strategies

There are four common types of invented strategies to solve addition and subtraction situations that can be extended to higher numbers: *break apart strategy* or *split strategy* (also called decomposition), *jump strategy* (similar to counting on or counting back), and *shortcut strategy* (sometimes known as compensation) (Heinze, Marschick, & Lipowsky, 2009; Torbeyns, De Smedt, Ghesquiere, & Verschaffel, 2009). The notion of "breaking" a number into parts (often by place value) is a useful strategy for all operations. When recording students' ideas, try using arrows or lines to explicitly indicate how two computations are joined together, as shown in Figure 11.13(a).

The *break apart strategy* for a problem such as 146 + 321 uses students' understanding of place value to start with the first number (146) and say 146 + 300 + 20 + 1. This strategy is also a very successful way to compute mentally.

The *break apart strategy* emphasizes decomposition through place value.

MyLab Education   Video Example 11.4

Watch this video (https://www.youtube.com/watch?v=8N4N2EE1uYg) of students explaining their thinking during a process of using the break apart strategy to add two-digit numbers.

VIDEO EXAMPLE

The *jump strategy* uses an *empty number line* (also known as an *open number line*) shown in Figure 11.13(b) which is a number line with no prewritten numbers or tick marks. Students can use it to incorporate a sequential jump strategy that is very effective for thinking about addition and subtraction situations (Caldwell, Kobett, & Karp, 2014; Gravemeijer & van Galen, 2003; Verschaffel et al., 2007). The empty number line is much more flexible than the usual number line because it can be jotted down anywhere, works with any numbers, and eliminates confusion with tick marks and the spaces between them. Also, students are less prone to making computational errors when using an empty number line (Gravemeijer & van Galen, 2003; Verschaffel et al., 2007).

Introduce the empty number line by using it to model a student's thinking for the class, especially when you link it to their early understanding of a unit. They need to be

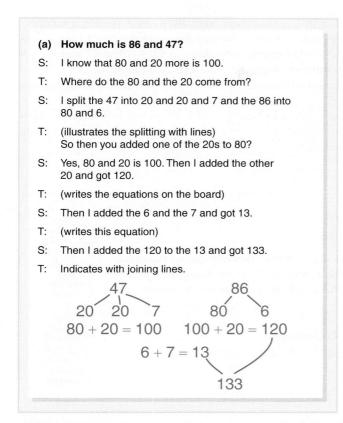

(a) How much is 86 and 47?

S: I know that 80 and 20 more is 100.

T: Where do the 80 and the 20 come from?

S: I split the 47 into 20 and 20 and 7 and the 86 into 80 and 6.

T: (illustrates the splitting with lines) So then you added one of the 20s to 80?

S: Yes, 80 and 20 is 100. Then I added the other 20 and got 120.

T: (writes the equations on the board)

S: Then I added the 6 and the 7 and got 13.

T: (writes this equation)

S: Then I added the 120 to the 13 and got 133.

T: Indicates with joining lines.

$$47 \quad\quad\quad 86$$
$$20 \quad 20 \quad 7 \quad\quad 80 \quad 6$$
$$80 + 20 = 100 \quad 100 + 20 = 120$$
$$6 + 7 = 13$$
$$133$$

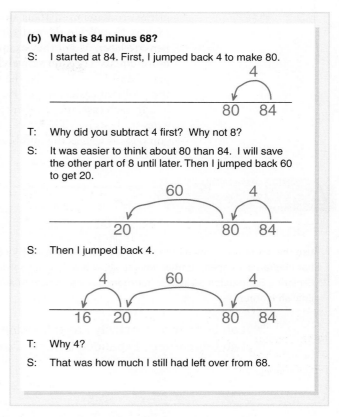

(b) What is 84 minus 68?

S: I started at 84. First, I jumped back 4 to make 80.

T: Why did you subtract 4 first? Why not 8?

S: It was easier to think about 80 than 84. I will save the other part of 8 until later. Then I jumped back 60 to get 20.

S: Then I jumped back 4.

T: Why 4?

S: That was how much I still had left over from 68.

FIGURE 11.13   Two methods of recording students' thought processes so that the class can follow the strategy.

reminded that the number line, like a ruler, is a length marked off into particular units—and in the case of the empty number line, they are creating their own units with jumps. Students determine the start and result numbers based on the problem they are solving. Then they often use "friendly numbers" to make their jumps and then calculate the total of the jumps (Barker, 2009). The jumps on the line can be recorded as the students share or explain each step of their solution counting up or down from an initial number. With time and practice, students will find the empty number line to be an effective tool to support and explain their thinking.

CCSS Standards for Mathematical Practice

MP5. Use appropriate tools strategically.

TECHNOLOGY Note: You can find interactive number lines on the internet where children can practice using a jump strategy. For example, search "ICT games number line jump." With this version, you can change where the number line starts (−100 to 200), the number of spaces on the number line (26 spaces versus 66 spaces), and the size of the jumps. ■

Bar diagrams can also be effectively used to support students' thinking and help them explain their ideas to others. Bar diagrams work particularly well for contexts that fit a comparison situation and a part-part-whole model. See Figure 11.14 for a sample of each.

The *shortcut strategy* involves the flexible adjustment of numbers. For example,

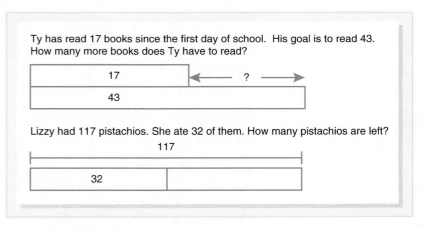

FIGURE 11.14   Using bar diagrams to help think about quantities and their relationship to each other.

just as students used 10 as an anchor in learning their facts, they can move from numbers such as 38 or 69 to the nearest 10 (in this case 40 or 70) and then take the 2 or 1 off to compensate later. As another example, 51 − 37 can be thought of as 37 + 10 = 47 and 47 + 4 more equals 51. Alternatively, the same problem 51 − 37 can be thought of as 51 + 6 to get 57 and 57 − 37 = 20; then subtract 6 (because you added 6 to the start amount to make the problem easier) to get 14. So, 51 − 37 = 14.

In each case, the numbers in the problem and the type of problem will influence the strategies students use. Therefore, it is important to think carefully about the type of story problem you pose as well as the numbers you select!

Activity 11.10   CCSS-M: 2.OA.A.1

Exploring Subtraction Strategies

Use the set of problems on the Looking at Collections Activity Page. Ask students, "How can you use strategies, bar diagrams, or open number lines to show how you are solving these problems?" See the Expanded Lesson: Exploring Subtraction Strategies for more details on how to adapt this activity for students with disabilities and English learners.

MyLab Education   **Activity Page: Looking at Collections**
MyLab Education   **Expanded Lesson: Exploring Subtraction Strategies**

STUDENTS
with
SPECIAL
NEEDS

ENGLISH
LEARNERS

The *Common Core State Standards* recommend that by the end of second grade, students should be able to "add and subtract within 1000" using strategies based on "place value, properties of operations, and/or the relationship between addition and subtraction" (NGA Center & CCSSO, 2010, p. 19). Emphasizing invented strategies before moving to standard algorithms can enhance students' number sense and place value understanding. Try your hand at doing these computations without using the standard algorithms: 487 + 235 and 623 − 587. For subtraction, a counting-up strategy is sometimes the easiest, especially when the numbers are relatively close together as in 623 − 587. Occasionally, other strategies are more advantageous. For example, "chunking off" multiples of 50 or 25 is often a useful method. For 462 + 257, pull out 450 and 250 to equal 700. That leaves 12 and 7 more, for 719. These are just a few of the many invented strategies students can use.

Students should use strategies that they understand and can use efficiently and effectively. Your goal might be that each of your students has at least one or two methods that are reasonably efficient, mathematically correct, and useful with lots of different numbers. Expect different students to settle on different strategies that play to their strengths. In other words, all students do not have to use the same strategy for the same problem. Here we explore a variety of invented strategies that students often use.

Adding and Subtracting Single-Digit Numbers

When adding or subtracting small amounts or finding the difference between two reasonably close numbers, many students will use counting to solve the problems. One goal should be to extend students' knowledge of basic facts and the ten-structure of the number system so that counting is not required. When the calculation crosses a ten (e.g., 58 + 6), using the decade number (60) and thinking 58 + 2 + 4, for example, extends students' use of the Make 10 strategy (e.g., add on to equal 10 and then add the rest). Similarly, for subtraction, students can extend the Down Under 10 strategy. For instance, for 53 − 7, subtract 3 to equal 50, then 4 more is 46.

Activity 11.11

CCSS-M: 1.NBT.C.4; 2.OA.A.2

Crossing a Decade

Quickly review the Make 10 and Down Under 10 Strategies for basic facts (from Chapter 9) using little ten-frames. Then have Little Ten-Frames, and Base-Ten Materials, a Place-Value Mat with Double Ten-Frames, or a Hundreds Chart available for students use. Pose an addition or subtraction story problem that crosses a decade number and involves a change or difference of less than 10. Here are some example problems:

- Tommy was on page 47 of his book. Then he read 8 more pages. What page did he end up on?
- How far is it from 68 to 75?
- Ruth had 52 cents. She bought a small toy for 8 cents. How much does she have left?

MyLab Education   Blackline Master: Little Ten-Frames
MyLab Education   Blackline Master: Base-Ten Materials
MyLab Education   Blackline Master: Place-Value Mat with Double Ten-Frames
MyLab Education   Blackline Master: Hundreds Chart

Listen for students who are counting on or counting back without paying attention to the ten and suggest they use either the hundreds chart or the little ten-frames as shown in Figure 11.15 to support their thinking. Also, find out how they solve fact combinations such as $8 + 6$ and $13 - 5$. The use of tens for these facts is essentially the same as for the higher-decade problems. Have students who use the strategy share their ideas with others. They might say, for $47 + 6$, "I added 3 from the 6 to the 47 to equal 50. Then I added the remaining 3 to equal 53."

As you transition students from single-digit to two-digit numbers, adding and subtracting tens and hundreds is an important intermediate step. Sums and differences involving multiples of 10 or 100 are easily computed mentally. Write a problem such as the following:

$$300 + 500 + 20$$

Challenge students to solve it mentally. Ask students to share their thinking. Listen for the use of place-value words: "3 *hundred* and 5 *hundred* is 8 *hundred*, and 20 more equals 820." Start with problems that do not require regrouping and then evolve to more difficult problems such as $70 + 80$. Continue to use base-ten models to help students think in terms of units of tens and hundreds.

 **Standards for Mathematical Practice**
MP7. Look for and make sense of structure.

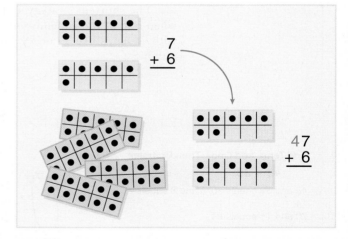

FIGURE 11.15 Students extend the Make 10 strategy to larger numbers.

Activity 11.12

CCSS-M: 1.NBT.C.4; 1.NBT.C.5; 1.NBT.C.6

I Am, but Who Is?

Have students practice their mental calculations and prepare for multidigit computation by adding or subtracting multiples of tens (or other familiar combinations) with two-digit numbers. Use the I Am/Who Is? Game Cards for a class up to 30 students. If you have fewer than 30 students, give students who need a challenge two cards. There are also some easier combinations (e.g., Who is $20 + 10$? Who is $37 + 10$?) so give those cards to students with disabilities to ensure they understand the game and are using units of ten. Start the game by calling out any number you see on a card, such as "Who is 22?" The student should respond with "I am 22, who is. . . " and then read the rest of the card. The game will loop all the way around through the thirty problems.

STUDENTS *with* **SPECIAL NEEDS**

MyLab Education   Activity Page: I Am/Who Is? Game Cards

Adding Multidigit Numbers

The development of fluency with multidigit addition and subtraction begins in grade 1 with the addition of multiples of 10 and continues through grade 4, when students are expected to "Fluently add and subtract multi-digit whole numbers using the standard algorithm" (NGA Center & CCSSO, 2010). This fluency must be built with years of explorations using concrete models or drawings and strategies based the inverse relationship between addition and subtraction, place value, and the properties of operations. Although double-digit addition is a focus in second grade, students in grades 3 and 4 may still be challenged by these computations. Problems involving the sum of 2 two-digit numbers will usually elicit a wide variety of invented strategies and it is those strategies that are the foundation for adding three-digit numbers (and beyond). Some strategies will involve starting with one or the other number and working from that point, either by adding on to get to the next ten or by adding tens from one number to the other.

Let's start by looking at the following story problem.

Two Scout troops went on a field trip. There were 46 Girl Scouts and 38 Boy Scouts. How many Scouts went on the trip?

Figure 11.16 illustrates four different invented strategies for this story problems. The ways that the solutions are recorded are suggestions, but note the frequent use of the empty number line.

The shortcut strategy and compensation strategies focusing on making ten is useful when one of the addends ends in 8 or 9. To promote these strategies, present problems with addends like 39 or 58. Note that it is often only necessary to adjust one of the two numbers.

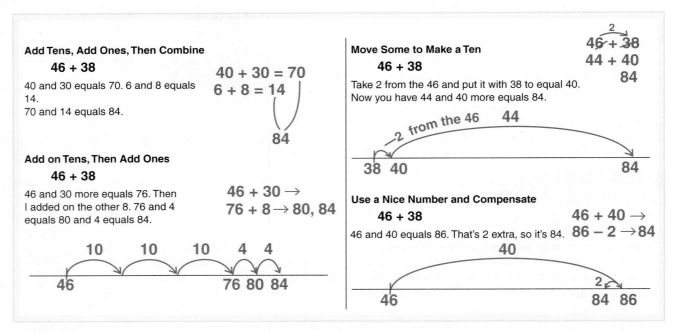

FIGURE 11.16 Four different invented strategies for addition with two-digit numbers.

⏸ Pause & Reflect

Try adding 367 + 155 in as many different ways as you can. How many of your ways are like those in Figure 11.16? ●

The following activity supports students' thinking about adjusting numbers by using 10 as an anchor.

Activity 11.13   CCSSM-M: 2.NBT.B.5; 2.NBT.B.9

STUDENTS
with
SPECIAL
NEEDS

Just Adjust It

Create a series of problems using numbers that will increase the likelihood that students will gravitate toward the idea of using 10 or use the Just Adjust It Activity Page. The point is to try to help students become more aware of different ways to adjust numbers. Consider using this series of problems:

$$50 + 30 \qquad 48 + 30 \qquad 50 + 32 \qquad 51 + 28 \qquad 53 + 29$$

Project one problem at a time and give students time to solve it before you ask for answers and then for explanations of their approaches. Record students' strategies so that you can refer back to them. If no student suggests the idea of using 50 + 30 to help solve the subsequent related problems, challenge them to determine how they could use that problem to help them solve all the others. By listening to classmates, other students, particularly students with disabilities, can become more aware of different ways to adjust numbers.

MyLab Education   **Activity Page: Just Adjust It**

There are multiple ways to add the numbers from the preceding activity by using 10 as an anchor. For example, for 51 + 28, a student may change 51 to 50 and 28 to 30, add 50 + 30 to equal 80, and then subtract 2 to adjust for adding 30 (instead of 28) and add 1 for adding 50 (instead of 51) to get 79. Other students may think that 51 is really close to 50 and they add the 1 from 51 to the 28 and add 50 + 29 to equal 79. Still other students may add the tens (50 + 20) and then the ones (1 + 8) to equal 79. Remember your goal is to help students develop strategies that are efficient and that make sense to them. By having students listen to how their classmates reasoned to find the sums, you expose students to a variety of strategies.

📋 **FORMATIVE ASSESSMENT Notes.** Periodically focus on one student to determine his or her flexible use of strategies. Pose the following problem in a diagnostic interview: 46 + 35. See if the student begins by breaking the numbers apart by place value or to make the next ten. That is, for 46 + 35, a student may add on 4 to the 46 to equal 50 and then add the remaining 31. Or, first add 30 to 46 to get to 76, then add 4 to equal 80 and then add the remaining 1. In either case, be mindful of how flexibly the student uses ten as a unit. Students may use an open number line and count up with jumps of 10 using a technique where they count by tens and ones. They would count up saying "46, 56, 66, 76." as they draw corresponding arcs marked with their jump of +10 and so on. Another approach may involve splitting the numbers into other parts of numbers such as 50 or 25 as an easier "compatible number" to work with. If a student is not consistently using ten as a unit, you may need to develop more place-value ideas. ■

The following activity provides students with experience in determining whether a sum of two numbers if odd or even.

Activity 11.14 CCSS-M: 2.OA.C.3

Odd or Even?

Start the class off with a two-digit addition problem that looks at two consecutive numbers. Have them write the problem on the top line of the Odd or Even Activity Page. Is the sum odd or even? How do you know? Try other two- or three-digit addends. Are the sums odd or even? Do you think the sum will always be that way? Why or why not?

MyLab Education Activity Page: Odd or Even

Subtraction as "Think-Addition"

CCSS Standards for Mathematical Practice

MP2. Reason abstractly and quantitatively.

Students who know the *think-addition* strategy for their basic facts can also use the same concept for solving problems with multidigit numbers. This strategy is an amazingly powerful way to subtract and is particularly successful with students with disabilities (Peltenburg, van den Heuvel-Panhuizen, & Robitzsch, 2012). For example, for 38 − 19, the idea is to think, "How much do I add to 19 to get to 38?" Notice that this strategy is probably not as efficient for 42 − 6. Using *join with change unknown* problems or *missing-part* problems (discussed in Chapter 8) will encourage the use of the think-addition strategy. Here is an example of each.

Sam had 46 baseball cards. He went to a card show and got some more cards for his collection. Now he has 73 cards. How many cards did Sam buy at the card show?

Juanita counted all of the teacher's pencils. Some were sharpened and some not. She counted 73 pencils in all; 46 pencils were not sharpened. How many were sharpened?

Figure 11.17 shows invented strategies that use "think addition" to solve subtraction story problems. As you can see, using tens is also an important part of these strategies. Simply asking for the difference between two numbers may also prompt these strategies.

Add Tens to Get Close, Then Ones

73 − 46

46 and 20 equals 66. (30 more equals too much.) Then 4 more equals 70 and 3 equals 73. That's 20 and 7 or 27.

$$46 + 20 = 66$$
$$66 + 4 = 70$$
$$70 + 3 = 73$$
$$20 + 4 + 3 = 27$$

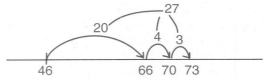

Add Tens to Overshoot, Then Come Back

73 − 46

46 and 30 equals 76. That's 3 too much, so it's 27.

$$46 + 30 \longrightarrow 76 - 3 \longrightarrow 73$$
$$30 - 3 = 27$$

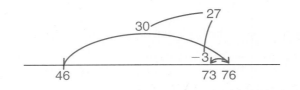

Add Ones to Make a Ten, Then Tens and Ones

73 − 46

46 and 4 equals 50. 50 and 20 equals 70 and 3 more equals 73. The 4 and 3 equals 7 and 20 equals 27.

$$46 + 4 \longrightarrow 50$$
$$50 + 20 \longrightarrow 70$$
$$70 + 3 \longrightarrow 73$$
$$4 + 20 + 3 = 27$$

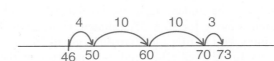

Similarly, 46 and 4 equals 50. 50 and 23 equals 73. 23 and 4 equals 27.

$$46 + 4 \longrightarrow 50$$
$$50 + 23 \longrightarrow 73$$
$$23 + 4 = 27$$

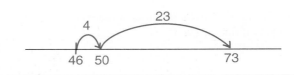

FIGURE 11.17 Three different invented strategies for subtraction by "think addition."

Activity 11.15   CCSS-M: 2.NBT.B.5; 2.NBT.B.9

How Far to My Number?

Students work in pairs with a single set of Little Ten-Frames. One student uses the cards to make a number less than 50 while the other student writes a number greater than 50 on a piece of paper, as shown in Figure 11.18. For students with a disability or students who need a challenge you may choose to suggest the size of the second number (e.g., less than 100, less than 500). The task is for the students to work together to find out how much more must be added to the number shown with the ten-frames to get to the larger number and write the corresponding equation. Once an answer is determined, they should demonstrate how their answer combined with the smaller number matches the larger number. Over time, you can fade the use of the little ten-frame cards.

STUDENTS with SPECIAL NEEDS

MyLab Education   Activity Page: Little Ten-Frame Cards

Take-Away Subtraction

Using a take-away action is considerably more difficult to do mentally. However, take-away strategies are common, probably because some textbooks emphasize "take away" as the meaning of subtraction (even though there are other meanings). Four different strategies are shown in Figure 11.19 for the following story problem.

There were 73 students on the playground. The 46 second-grade students came in first. How many students were still on the playground?

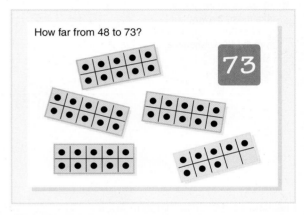

How far from 48 to 73?

FIGURE 11.18   Use think-addition to solve "How Far?" problems.

The two methods that begin by taking tens from tens are reflective of what most students do with their base-ten materials. The other two methods leave one of the numbers intact to do the subtraction. When the subtracted number is a multiple of 10 or close to a multiple of 10, take-away can be a method to do mentally. Try $83 - 29$ in your head by first taking away 30 and adding 1 back. Some students may initially become confused when they hear a classmate describe this strategy for $83 - 29$. In particular, they might not understand why you add 1 back. They think because you added 1 to 29 to equal 30, you should subtract 1 from the answer. Let them act it out with Base-Ten Materials so they can see that when they take away 30, they took 1 too many away and that is why they need to add 1 back.

TECHNOLOGY Note. Virtual Base-Ten Blocks for Addition and Subtraction (at the National Library of Virtual Manipulatives) use base-ten blocks on a place-value chart. You can form any problem you wish up to four digits. The subtraction model shows the number being subtracted (subtrahend) in red instead of blue. When the blocks representing the minuend (whole) are dragged onto the red blocks, they disappear. Although you can begin in any column, the model forces a regrouping strategy as well as a take-away model for subtraction. ■

⏸ Pause & Reflect

Try computing $82 - 57$. Use both take-away and think addition methods. Can you identify all of the strategies in Figures 11.17 and 11.19 without looking? ●

Remember the "equal additions" or "same difference" strategy (Humphreys & Parker, 2015) that was described earlier in this chapter? There are some students who use this strategy with take-away subtraction. For example, for $32 - 17$, students might think that 17 is 3 away from 20, so if they add 3 to 17 to equal 20, they need to add 3 to 32 to equal 35 (to maintain the difference between the two numbers). Now the problem is $35 - 20$ or 15. Encourage students to use an empty number line to see why $32 - 17$ and $35 - 20$ have equivalent answers.

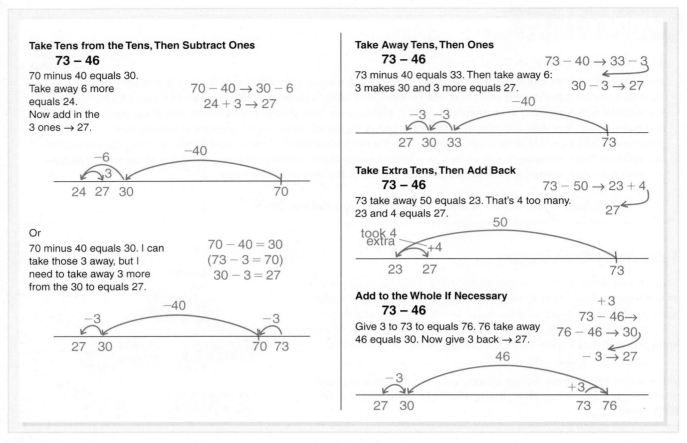

FIGURE 11.19 Four different invented strategies for take-away subtraction.

Keep in mind that for many subtraction problems, especially those with three digits, the think-addition approach is significantly easier than a take-away approach. For students who could benefit from a think-addition strategy but are not using it, you may want to revisit some simple missing-part activities to encourage that type of thinking.

Extensions and Challenges

Each of the examples in the preceding sections involved sums less than 100, and all involved *crossing a ten*; that is, if done with a standard algorithm, they required regrouping or trading. As you plan instruction you should consider whether a problem requires crossing a ten, the size of the numbers, and the potential for students doing problems mentally.

Crossing a Ten (or More). For most of the strategies, it is easier to add or subtract when crossing a ten is not required. Try each strategy with $34 + 52$ or $68 - 24$ to see how it works. Easier problems have their purpose, one of which is to build confidence. They also permit you to challenge your students by asking, "Would you like a harder one?" There is also the issue of crossing 100 or 1000. Try $58 + 67$ with different strategies. Crossing across hundreds is also an issue for subtraction. Problems such as $128 - 50$ or $128 - 45$ are more difficult than problems that do not cross a hundred as in $298 - 187$.

Larger Numbers. Second-grade students should add and subtract three-digit numbers using a variety of strategies (NGA Center & CCSSO, 2010). How would you do these problems without using the standard algorithms: $487 + 235$ and $623 - 247$? Again, for subtraction, a think-addition strategy is usually effective. Occasionally, students will use other strategies with larger numbers such as, "chunking off" multiples of 50 or 25. For $462 + 257$, pull out 450 and 250 to equal 700. That leaves 12 and 7 more, which equals 719.

MyLab Education   Self-Check 11.3

Standard Algorithms for Addition and Subtraction

Students are not likely to invent standard algorithms, so you will need to introduce and explain them, and help students understand how and why algorithms work. Given that it is critical that you teach algorithms in a conceptual manner, help students understand the units of hundreds, tens and ones as they work.

The standard algorithms require an understanding of *regrouping*, exchanging 10 in one place-value position for 1 in the position to the left—or the reverse, exchanging 1 for 10 in the position to the right. The terms *carrying* and *borrowing* are obsolete and conceptually misleading and should not be used. The word *regroup* may initially have little meaning for young students, so start with the term *trade*. Ten ones are *traded* for a ten. A hundred is *traded* for 10 tens. Notice that none of the invented strategies involves regrouping.

Standard Algorithm for Addition

Two things to remember in teaching the standard algorithm for addition: (1) Be sure students continue to view it as one possible algorithm that is a good choice in some situations (just as invented strategies are good choices in some situations), and (2) as with any procedure (algorithm), it must begin with the concrete, and then explicit connections must be made between the concept (regrouping) and the procedure. The algorithm is a record of acting out the operation with the materials.

Begin with Models Only. In the beginning, focus on regrouping without recording the numerical process. Provide students with Place-Value Mats and Base-Ten Materials. Have students use the base-ten materials to make one number at the top of the mat and a second beneath it, as shown in the top portion of Figure 11.20. Point out this procedure: *Begin in the ones column.* Then let students solve the problem on their own. Allow plenty of time and then have students explain what they did and why. Let students display their work on the projector or use interactive whiteboard models to help with their explanations. One or two problems in a lesson with lots of discussion are more productive than a lot of problems based on rules students don't understand.

MyLab Education	Blackline Master: Place-Value Mats
MyLab Education	Blackline Master: Base-Ten Materials

Develop the Written Record. Use the Addition and Subtraction Recording Pages to help students record numerals in columns as they model each step of the procedure they do with the base-ten materials. The first few times you do this, guide each step carefully through questioning, as shown in Figure 11.21. A similar approach would be used for three-digit problems. Have students work in pairs with one responsible for the models and the other recording the steps. They should reverse roles with each problem.

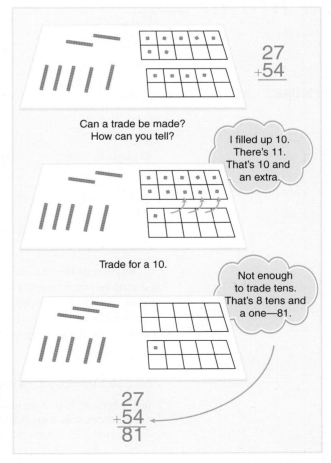

FIGURE 11.20 Working from right to left in addition.

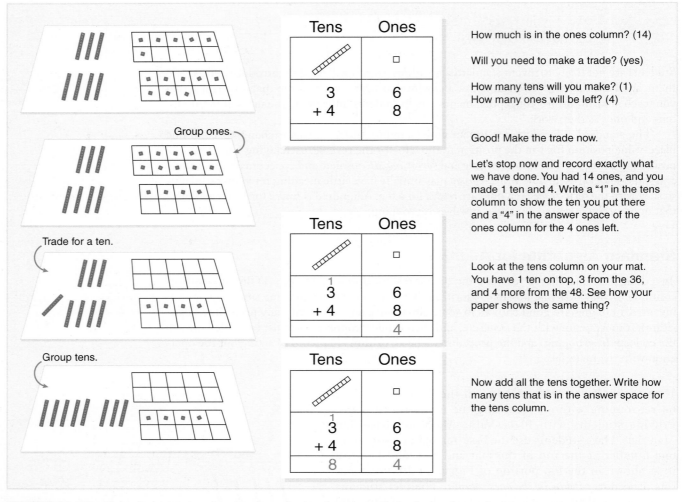

How much is in the ones column? (14)

Will you need to make a trade? (yes)

How many tens will you make? (1)
How many ones will be left? (4)

Good! Make the trade now.

Let's stop now and record exactly what we have done. You had 14 ones, and you made 1 ten and 4. Write a "1" in the tens column to show the ten you put there and a "4" in the answer space of the ones column for the 4 ones left.

Look at the tens column on your mat. You have 1 ten on top, 3 from the 36, and 4 more from the 48. See how your paper shows the same thing?

Now add all the tens together. Write how many tens that is in the answer space for the tens column.

FIGURE 11.21 Help students record on paper each step they do on their place-value mats.

MyLab Education **Activity Page: Addition and Subtraction Recording Pages**

A common error students make is to record their answers in this way:

$$\begin{array}{r} 57 \\ +69 \\ \hline 1116 \end{array}$$

As you can see, this student has lost her connection to place-value and is treating the ones and tens as two separate problems. The student should try to use another way to check her answer—in this case, suggest having her estimate a reasonable answer by asking, "Do you think your answer will be between 100 and 200 or 200 and 300?" to help the student see that an answer in the thousands is not logical. Then have her use base-ten blocks to model the problem.

MyLab Education **Video Example 11.5**

Take a look at Talecia as she too loses her connection to the value of the numbers she is recording when she adds 34 + 57.

Figure 11.22 shows a variation of the traditional recording scheme that is very effective because it highlights the actual value of the numbers and is relatively efficient, at least for up to three digits. This way of recording is known as the partial sums approach and it avoids the "carried ones" by focusing attention on the actual value of the digits. If students start adding on the left as they are inclined to do, partial sums would just be a vertical recording scheme for the invented strategy "add tens, add ones, then combine" (Figure 11.16). This adaptation is particularly effective with students with disabilities.

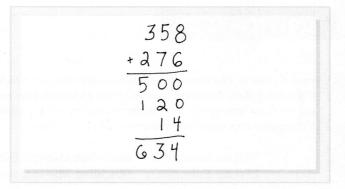

FIGURE 11.22   The partial sums approach can be used from left to right as well as from right to left.

MyLab Education
Video Example 11.6

Let's look at this video of author Jennifer Bay-Williams as she discusses partial sums as well as partial differences.

Standard Algorithm for Subtraction

The general approach to developing the subtraction algorithm is the same as for addition. When the procedure is completely understood with models, a do-and-record approach connects it with a written form.

Begin with Models Only. Start by having students treat the subtraction problem as a "take-away" situation. With this meaning of subtraction, they model only the top number (minuend) in a subtraction problem on the top half of their place-value mats using the top double ten-frame for any ones. For the amount to be subtracted, have students write each digit on a small piece of paper and place these numerals near the bottom of their mats in the respective columns, as in Figure 11.23. To avoid errors, suggest making all trades first. That way, the full amount on the paper slip can be taken off at once. Also, explain to students that they are to begin working with the ones column first, as they did with addition.

Anticipate Difficulties with Zeros. Problems in which zeros are involved tend to cause special difficulties.

MyLab Education
Video Example 11.7

Watch this video of Mike calculating 100 − 1 and notice how he can respond doing mental math but is challenged when given the written problem.

The common errors that emerge when students "regroup across zero" are best addressed at the modeling stage. For example, in 403 − 138, students must make a double trade: trading a hundreds piece for 10 tens and then a tens piece for 10 ones. After students have experience with making trades using base-ten materials, use the following activity before giving students any hints about how they might approach regrouping across a zero.

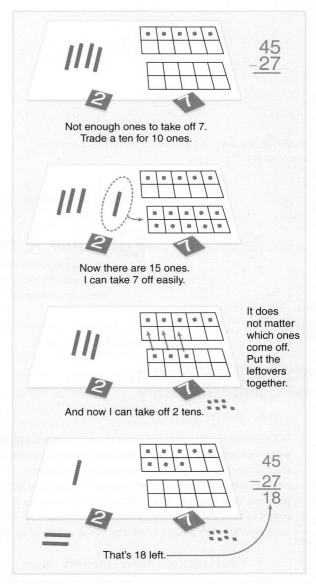

Not enough ones to take off 7. Trade a ten for 10 ones.

Now there are 15 ones. I can take 7 off easily.

It does not matter which ones come off. Put the leftovers together.

And now I can take off 2 tens.

That's 18 left.

FIGURE 11.23   Two-digit subtraction with models.

Activity 11.16   CCSS-M: 2.NBT.B.7; 2.NBT.B.9

Trading across Zero

Pose a problem that requires regrouping across zero, such as 103 − 78. Students work in pairs using Base-Ten Materials and Place-Value Mats. Once they have identified an answer, they now check their answer using an invented strategy. If they did not get the same answer with the base-ten materials and the invented strategy encourage them to determine why. Follow up with a discussion that starts with students sharing their ideas.

MyLab Education   **Blackline Master: Place-Value Mats**
MyLab Education   **Blackline Master: Base-Ten Materials**

FIGURE 11.24   A left-hand recording scheme for subtraction.

Develop the Written Record. The process of recording each step as it is done is the same as was suggested for addition using the Addition and Subtraction Recording Pages. When students can explain the use of symbols involved in the recording process, fade the use of the physical materials and move toward the complete use of symbols. Again, be attentive to problems with zeros.

If students follow their natural instincts and begin with the biggest pieces (from the left instead of the right), recording schemes similar to that shown in Figure 11.24 are possible. The trades are made from the pieces remaining *after* the subtraction in the column to the left has been done. A "regroup across zero" difficulty will still occur in problems like 462 − 168. Try it.

MyLab Education   **Activity Page: Addition and Subtraction Recording Pages**

⏸ Pause & Reflect

Contrast teaching students to regroup in subtraction, especially regrouping across zero, with think-addition. For example, try solving this: 428 and how much equals 703? Now think about teaching students to regroup across zero to solve 703 − 428. Which is easier? Why? ●

The next activity asks students to determine which strategy from a variety of strategies might be most useful.

Activity 11.17   CCSS-M: 1.NBT.C.4; 2.NBT.B.5; 2.NBT.B.6; 2.NBT.B.7; 2.NBT.B.9

Pick Your Strategy

Tell students you are going to show them a problem, but they are *not* to solve it—instead they should decide which method from their invented strategies and standard algorithms they would choose and why. Projecting a list of strategies for addition and subtraction problems will support students with disabilities and ELs. After students make their selection, call out each method and have them raise their hand to indicate which strategy they selected. Then they use their selected method to solve the problem. When finished, they raise their thumb and hold it to their chest. Have students share solutions for each different strategy used. Then ask the class which method seemed to work best for each problem and why. Use a variety of problems whose numbers lend themselves to different strategies.

ENGLISH LEARNERS

MyLab Education   **Activity Page: List of Strategies**

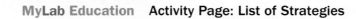

MyLab Education   **Self-Check 11.4**

Introducing Computational Estimation

Computational estimation is a higher-level thinking skill that involves students in decisions that they need opportunities to think about and discuss. So, besides knowing how to reach exact solutions to problems, everyone needs to solve numerical situations that need an "about" answer. You have likely been in a circumstance where a friend has quickly done some approximate calculations in her head and you realize how useful and important that mental math skill is. This computational estimation is the abstract thinking and reasoning that provide a foundation for future mathematical topics; because we want students to estimate either before they compute to reinforce their number sense or after they compute to assess reasonableness of their answer or both!

Whenever we are faced with a computation in real life, we have a variety of choices to make concerning how we will find a reasonable answer. A first decision is: "Do we need an exact answer, or will an approximation be okay?" If precision is called for, we can use an invented strategy, a standard algorithm, or even a calculator. How close an estimate must be to the actual computation is a matter of context, as was the original decision to use an estimate.

The goal of computational estimation is to be able to flexibly and quickly produce an approximate result that will work for the situation and be reasonable. Mathematical Practice 5 from the *Common Core State Standards* states that students should "detect possible errors by strategically using estimation and other mathematical knowledge" (p. 7). Good estimators tend to employ a variety of computational strategies they have developed over time.

Understanding Computational Estimation

The goal of computational estimation is to be able to flexibly and quickly produce a reasonable *estimate* that is a suitable approximation for an exact number given the particular context. In the K–8 mathematics curriculum, *estimation* refers to three quite different ideas:

- *Measurement estimation:* Determining an approximate measure without making a precise measurement. For example, we can estimate the length of a room or the weight of a watermelon.
- *Quantity estimation:* Approximating the number of items in a collection. For example, we might estimate the number of students in the auditorium or jelly beans in the "estimation jar."
- *Computational estimation:* Determining a number that is an approximation of a computation that we cannot or do not need to determine precisely. For example, we might want to know the approximate amount we are spending at a store and need to add the cost of several items to see whether $20.00 will cover the amount.

Students are not as good at computational estimation as they are at producing exact answers and sometimes find computational estimation uncomfortable (Siegler & Booth, 2005). Many students confuse the idea of estimation with guessing. None of the three types of estimation involves guessing. Each involves reasoning and sense making. Computational estimation, for example, involves actually computing. Therefore, it's important to (1) avoid using the words *guess* and *guessing* when working on estimation activities and (2) explicitly help students see the difference between a guess and a reasonable estimate.

Computational estimation may be underemphasized in situations where the focus is on the standard algorithm. But, if you recall the problem-solving process, the last of the four steps is to look back. If students practice estimating when they are computing and look back after completing a computation, they should be able to see whether the answer is in the ballpark. Take 403 − 138, mentioned previously. At a glance, this answer should be more than 200, so an incorrect answer of 175 (a common error) would be recognized as impossible.

Suggestions for Teaching Computational Estimation

Here are some general principles that are worth keeping in mind as you help your students develop computational estimation skills.

Use Real Examples. Discuss real-life situations in which computational estimations are used. Some common examples include comparative shopping (which store has the item for less); adding up distances in planning a trip; determining approximate monthly totals (school supplies, lawn-mowing income, time playing games on a tablet); and figuring the cost of going to a sporting event or movie, including transportation, tickets, and snacks. Look at newspaper headlines to find where numbers are the result of estimation and where they are the result of precision (e.g., "Hundreds of Students Leave School Ill" versus "Fourteen Students Injured in Bus Accident"). Students are more motivated with real examples—for example, asking older students, "Are you a million seconds old? How can you find out?"

Use Estimation Language. Words and phrases such as *about, close, just about, a little more* (or *less*) *than*, and *between* are part of the language of estimation. Students should understand that they are trying to get as close as possible using efficient methods, but there is no "one correct" or "winning" estimate. Language can help convey that idea.

Use a Context. Situations play a role in estimation. For example, it is important to know whether the cost of a car would be $950 or $9500. Could attendance at the school play be 30 or 300 or 3000? A simple computation can provide the important digits, with knowledge of the context providing the rest.

Accept a Range of Estimates, Offer a Range as an Option. Because estimates are based on computation, how can there be different answers? The answer, of course, is that any particular estimate depends on the strategy used and the kinds of adjustments made in the numbers. Estimates also vary with the need for the estimate. Estimating someone's age from an approximate year they were born is quite different from trying to decide whether your last $5 will cover three items you need at Fast Mart.

What estimate would you give for 270 + 325? If you use 200 + 300, you might say 500. Or you might use 250 for the 270 and 350 for the 325, making 600. You could also use 300 for 270 and add 325, getting 625. Is only one of these "right"? By sharing students' estimates and letting them discuss how and why different estimates resulted, they can begin to see that estimates generally fall in a range around the exact answer.

Important teacher note: Do not reward or overemphasize the estimate that is the closest. It is already very difficult for students to handle "approximate" answers; worrying about accuracy and pushing for the one closest answer exacerbates this problem. Instead, focus on whether the answers given are *reasonable* for the situation or problem at hand. Offer ranges for answers that are estimates. Ask whether the answer will be between 300 and 400, 450 and 550, or 600 and 700.

Focus on Flexible Methods, Not Answers. Remember that having students reflect on the strategies used by classmates will lead to additional strategy development. Class discussions are just as important as they were for the development of invented strategies. For any given estimation, there are often several very good but different methods of estimation. Here is an activity in which a specific number is not required to answer the questions.

Activity 11.18   CCSS-M: 3.OA.C.8

ENGLISH LEARNERS

Over or Under?

Use the Over or Under Activity Page on a document projector (as in Figure 11.25). In this case, each answer is either over or under $1.50, but the "over or under" number can be changed for each task. You can add an interesting context to make the activity accessible to more learners, but remember that using multiple contexts can be difficult for ELs, who must learn each new context. Consider playing "Over or Under?" by picking one context (e.g., the price of energy bars or fruit) and then varying the values (5 at 43 cents each, then 6 at 37 cents each, etc.).

MyLab Education   Activity Page: Over or Under

Here are some addition examples for the "Over or Under?" activity:

---

37 + 75 (over/under 100)

712 − 458 (over/under 300)

Computational Estimation Strategies

There are numerous strategies that are helpful in computing estimates in addition and subtraction. Here are a few to present to students.

Front-End Methods

A front-end approach is reasonable for addition or subtraction when all or most of the numbers have the same number of digits. Figure 11.26 illustrates this idea. Notice that when a number has fewer digits than the rest, that number may be ignored initially. Also note that only the front (leftmost) number is used and the computation is then done as if there were zeros in the other positions.

After adding or subtracting the front digits, an adjustment is made to correct for the digits or numbers that were ignored. Making an adjustment is actually a separate skill. For young students, practice first just using the front digits.

The front-end strategy can be easy to use because it does not require rounding or changing numbers. You do need to be sure that students pay close attention to place value and only consider digits in the largest place, especially when the numbers vary in the number of digits.

Rounding Methods

Students are not required to use rounding until the third grade when they are expected to "assess the reasonableness of answers using mental computation and estimation strategies including rounding" (NGA Center & CCSSO, 2010, p. 23). In grades 3 and 4 students use place-value understanding to round whole numbers. When several numbers are to be added, it is usually a good idea to round them to the same place value. Keep a running sum as you round each number. Figure 11.27 shows an example of rounding.

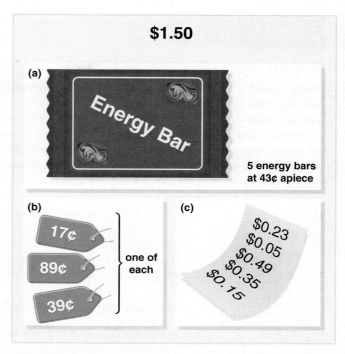

FIGURE 11.25   Over or Under? is a good beginning estimation activity.

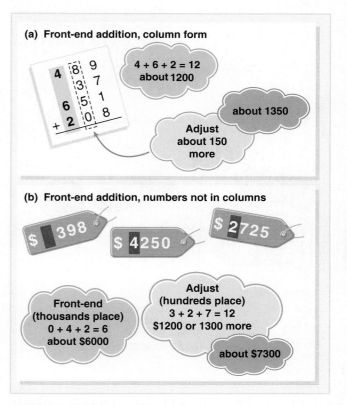

FIGURE 11.26   Front-end estimation in addition.

Activity 11.19   CCSS-M: 3.NBT.A.1

Round Up?

Create a number line on the floor with painter's tape, clothesline, or cash register tape. Use sticky notes to label the benchmark numbers of the tens (10, 20, 30, . . .), hundreds (100, 200, 300, . . .) or whatever range of numbers you are considering as a class. Have the numbers far apart so that 3 to 4 students can stand facing forward between each number. Then distribute numbers for students to round. For example, give 53. The student stands on the line where 53 should be, then rounds to the nearest ten (50). Talk about the case of a 5 in the ones position (or in other halfway positions for larger numbers) as a convention—we all agree that we round up when we are midway between numbers.

For addition and subtraction problems involving only two numbers, one strategy is to round only one of the two numbers. For example, you can round only the subtracted number such as 6724 − 1863 becomes 6724 − 2000, resulting in 4724. You can stop here, or you can adjust. Adjusting might go like this: Because you subtracted a bigger number, the result must be too small. Adjust to about 4800.

Compatible Numbers

Sometimes it is useful to look for two or three compatible numbers that can be grouped to equal benchmark values (e.g., 10, 100, 500). If numbers in the list can be adjusted slightly to equal these amounts, that will make finding an estimate easier. This approach is illustrated in Figure 11.28. In subtraction, it is often possible to adjust only one number to produce an easily observed difference, as illustrated in Figure 11.29.

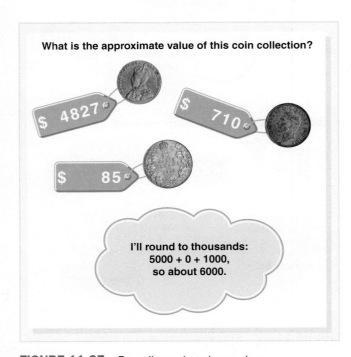

FIGURE 11.27   Rounding using place value.

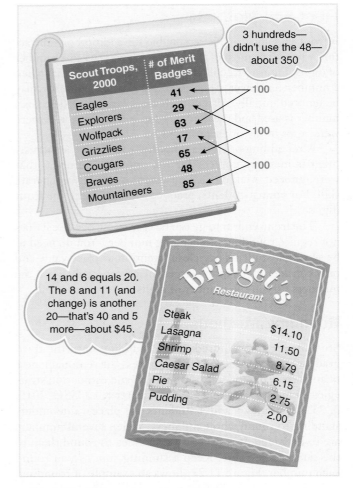

FIGURE 11.28   Compatible numbers used in addition.

FIGURE 11.29 Compatibles can help find the difference.

The following activity (adapted from Coates & Thompson, 2003) blends mental computation and estimation. Figuring out where the numbers go to create the exact solution involves estimation.

Activity 11.20   CCSS-M: 2.NBT.B.5

**STUDENTS
with
SPECIAL
NEEDS**

Box Math

Use the Number Cards and give students three digits to use (e.g., 3, 5, 7) and two Operations Cards
(+ and −), cut out from card stock so they can manipulate them easily on the Box Math Template. Show
students a set of equations with answers only and ask them to use their number cards (in the squares)
and operations (in the circle) to get to the answers shown.

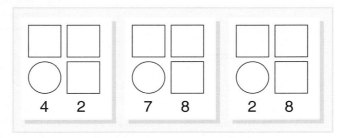

For students who have disabilities, you may want to have the operation signs built into the displays of answers (such as an
addition box and a subtraction box that generate the answer 42). These fixed problems will reduce the amount of decision
making needed and allow for a focus on the numbers.

MyLab Education   Blackline Master: Number Cards
MyLab Education   Activity Page: Operations Cards
MyLab Education   Activity Page: Box Math Template

FORMATIVE ASSESSMENT Notes. In a diagnostic interview, ask a student to solve the
following: "Charlie wants to estimate how much he needs to save to buy two video
games. One game is $99 and the other is $118. How much should he save to purchase the

two games?" Ask the student how he came up with his estimate. If the student is trying to mentally carry out the standard algorithm in the air or on the table with a finger, he likely has a limited ability with estimation strategies. Because $99 is so close to $100, it would be important for the student to use that fact in combining the two prices. If the student is unclear whether to change 99 to 100 or to 98 (as it is equally as close), that would pinpoint a lack of understanding of the purpose of estimation. Estimation cannot be easily assessed with paper-and-pencil tasks, so interviews that require explanations give more substantial evidence of student performance. ■

MyLab Education   **Self-Check 11.6**

MyLab Education   **Math Practice:** Need to practice or refresh your math content knowledge? Click to access practice exercises associated with the content from this chapter.

TABLE 11.1   COMMON CHALLENGES AND MISCONCEPTIONS RELATED TO ADDITION AND SUBTRACTION COMPUTATION

Common Challenge or Misconception	What It Looks Like	How to Help
1. Students incorrectly record the algorithm for addition by not regrouping and ignoring place value.	When students add: 56 + 97 1413 Students record the entire sum of the digits in each column.	• Have students show with base-ten materials the value of these two numbers on a place value mat. • Avoid reading numbers in addition or subtraction problems as digits (for example, just saying 5, instead of 5 tens or fifty) as this language confuses students and they may put down the individual sums rather than regrouping. • Have students estimate the answer first. Do they expect the answer will be in the hundreds? Thousands? Then ask, "Is this answer reasonable?" • Have the student use partial sums to record and find total. Have the student use another strategy to check answer.
2. Reverse regrouping.	When students add: 63 + 52 16 Students start in the tens place and add backwards, disregarding place value. So, in this case when they add 6 + 5 and get the answer of 11, they put down the one and regroup the "one" back to the ones column. 1 + 3 + 2 = 6.	• Ask students to check their answer for reasonableness—if we start with 63 items and add more can we end up with only 16 items? • Then go back to modeling the problem using base-ten materials with a place-value mat to carry out the computation. Show how the actions are recorded so that they match the standard algorithm.
3. Confusing the multiplication algorithm with the addition algorithm.	For the problem: 1 67 + 7 144 Students say, "7 + 7 equals 14, put down the 4 and regroup the 1 above the 6." Then using the 7 as would be done in multiplication says, 7 + 6 equals 13 plus one more is 14. The answer is 144."	• Again, it is back to two key pieces—estimating the answer before calculating to see what a reasonable answer might be and returning to act out the situation with the base ten materials.

Common Challenge or Misconception	What It Looks Like	How to Help
4. When subtracting two multi-digit numbers, student always subtracts the smaller number (digit) from the larger number (digit) rather than regrouping.	For the problem $$\begin{array}{r} 70 \\ -\ 23 \\ \hline 53 \end{array}$$ Students say "0 from 3 equals 3 and 2 from 7 equals 5. The answer is 53."	• Start with a reminder about subtracting from 0 or other smaller numbers. Show 3 cubes in your hand and ask, "Can you take away 5?" Reinforce the situation of asking for more than you have. • Provide the actual materials on a place value mat that correspond with the minuend. Then subtract the amount and highlight the need for regrouping when there are not enough of the units needed.
5. Student makes mistakes when regrouping across zeroes in a subtraction problem.	$$\begin{array}{r} 5\ 1\ 1 \\ \cancel{6}\cancel{0}\cancel{0}5 \\ -\ 347 \\ \hline 368 \end{array}$$ $$\begin{array}{r} 4 \\ 5 \\ \cancel{6}\cancel{0}\cancel{0}5 \\ -\ 347 \\ \hline 168 \end{array}$$	• Have the student use estimation to check for reasonableness of answer. • Have the student use base-ten materials and a place-value mat to represent the minuend and act out the subtraction of the other number. Compare to original answer and discuss the differences. • Ask the student to use another strategy to check answer.
6. Student overgeneralizes the "equal additions" or the "same difference" strategy to addition situations.	$$38^{+2} + 75^{+2}$$ $$= 40 + 77$$ $$= 117$$ For problems like 38 + 75, the student reasons that because 38 is 2 away from 40, s/he will add 2 to 38 (which is 40) and then thinks s/he needs to add 2 to 75 (which is 77) because s/he does not understand the "equal additions" strategy and why it is only applicable to subtraction situations.	• Have the student use concrete materials to represent the quantities and solve the original addition problem and the problem s/he created. Then ask the student to compare. • Have the student use a number line to represent and solve the original addition problem and the problem s/he created. Ask the student to try to determine why the answers are different. • Have the student solve a subtraction problem using "equal additions." Then show the original and the modified subtraction problems on a number line. Challenge the student to determine why the "equal additions" strategy results in equivalent answers by considering the number line representation of the problems.
7. Student thinks that s/he has to find an exact answer after finding an estimation.	When asked to estimate say, 624 − 83, the student changes 83 to 100 to find 624 − 100 or about 524. But then immediately calculates to find the exact answer.	• When students are asked to find estimates, avoid having them check their estimates by finding the exact answer. • Use real situations as examples for when estimations (and not exact answers) are useful. • Discuss why an exact answer is unnecessary when finding estimates.

RESOURCES FOR CHAPTER 11

LITERATURE CONNECTIONS

Children's literature plays a valuable role in helping you develop problems that lead to invented strategies and mental computation.

The Great Math Tattle Battle
Bowen (2006)

This entertaining book is largely about correcting errors in double-digit addition calculations. You can share a "student worksheet" that contains lots of mistakes and see whether your class can find errors and correct the paper. There's also an important message about tattling!

The Breakfast Cereal Gourmet *Hoffman (2005)*

National Geographic Kids Almanac 2018 *National Geographic (2017)*

These nonfiction books include interesting facts that can be used to create a variety of word problems. Hoffman's book provides data about breakfast eating habits; for example, the average person eats 160 bowls of cereal a year. The *National Geographic Kids Almanac* combines fascinating information with numerical data.

RECOMMENDED READINGS

Articles

O'Loughlin, T. A. (2007). Using research to develop computational fluency in young mathematicians. *Teaching Children Mathematics, 14*(3), 132–138.

This article describes a second-grade teacher's journey to improve students' computational fluency through the use of invented strategies. The interesting collection of student work and related thought-provoking debriefing by the teacher will demonstrate various methods, such as split (break apart) and jump strategies.

Wentick, M., Behrand, J. L., & Mohs, L. C. (2013) A pathway for mathematical practices, *Teaching Children Mathematics, 19*(6), 354–362.

In this article students examine the commutative property of addition, the decomposing of numbers, number relationships, and the meaning of the equal sign. Invented strategies are shared as students describe their thinking.

Books

Caldwell, J., Kobett, B., & Karp, K. (2014). *Essential understanding of addition and subtraction in practice, grades K–2.* Reston, VA: NCTM.

This book emphasizes the pedagogical content knowledge needed to teach the big ideas of addition and subtraction. There are tasks to try and samples of students' work to discuss!

12

Developing Strategies for Multiplication and Division Computation

LEARNER OUTCOMES

After reading this chapter and engaging in the embedded activities and reflections, you should be able to:

12.1 Recognize how understanding place value and the properties of operations support the learning of a variety of computational strategies in multiplication.

12.2 Identify a variety of models and recording approaches for developing the multiplication algorithm.

12.3 Explain invented strategies for division with multidigit numbers.

12.4 Explain the development of the standard algorithm for division and ways to record students' thinking.

12.5 Identify ways to teach computational estimation for multidigit multiplication and division as a way to develop students' flexibility and ability to recognize reasonable answers.

As students enter the intermediate grades, they begin to focus on computation strategies with multiplication and division. In fact, at least half of the grade 3 standards in the *Common Core State Standards* involve understanding multiplication (Kinzer & Stanford, 2013/2014). However, researchers suggest that invented strategies for multiplication and division are less well documented (Verschaffel et al., 2007) and the relationship between the operations more difficult to grasp than addition and subtraction (Robinson & LeFevre, 2012). The way to counter these challenges is to create an instructional environment that rewards flexibility so that students will successfully explore and test new ideas. As it was with addition and subtraction, students who only have knowledge of the standard multiplication and division algorithms often have difficulty following steps they do not fully understand (Biddlecomb & Carr, 2011; Burns, Ysseldyke, Nelson & Kanive, 2014; Fuson & Beckmann, 2012/2013). When students can compute multidigit multiplication and division problems in a variety of ways, complete written records of their work, explain their thinking, and discuss the merits of one strategy over another, they are developing as independent learners.

BIG IDEAS

◆ Flexible methods of computation in multiplication and division involve decomposing and composing numbers in a wide variety of ways.

◆ Flexible methods for multiplication and division require a deep understanding of the commutative property, the associative property, and the distributive property of multiplication over addition. How multiplication and division are related as inverse operations is also important.

◆ Invented strategies provide flexible methods of computing that vary with the numbers and the situation. Successful use of the strategies requires that they be understood by those who are using them—hence, they must grasp that the process and the outcome of that process are related.

◆ Standard algorithms are clever strategies for computing that have been developed over time. Each is based on performing the operation on one place value at a time with transitions to an adjacent position.

◆ Nearly all computational estimations involve using easier-to-handle parts of numbers or substituting difficult-to-handle numbers with close compatible numbers so that the resulting computations can be done mentally.

Invented Strategies for Multiplication

When students use invented strategies, they begin to understand why mathematical ideas are true as they extend their prior knowledge to new contexts. You will help students move from the basic arrays for single digit multiplication problems to larger arrays that emphasize the distributive property to recording partial products and then over time to the standard multiplication algorithm. Let's see how these ideas all fit together! For multiplication, students' ability to flexibly compose and decompose numbers is even more important than in addition or subtraction. This skill hinges on the full understanding of the distributive property of multiplication over addition. For example, to multiply 43 × 5, one might think about breaking 43 into 40 and 3, multiplying each by 5, and then adding the results. Students require ample opportunities to develop these concepts by making sense of their own ideas and those of their classmates.

MyLab Education **Video Example 12.1**

Watch Andrew as he uses the distributive property to solve 7 × 12.

Useful Representations

CCSS **Standards for Mathematical Practice**
MP5. Use appropriate tools strategically.

The problem 6 × 34 may be represented in a number of ways, as illustrated in Figure 12.1. Often the choice of a model is influenced by a story problem. To determine how many oranges 6 classes need if there are 34 students in each class, students may model 6 sets of 34. If the problem is about a rectangle's area (6 cm × 34 cm), then some form of an array is likely. But each representation is appropriate for thinking about 6 × 34 regardless of the context, and students should get to a point at which they select meaningful ways to think about multiplication and use tools strategically.

How students represent a product is directly related to their methods for determining answers. At first, the equal groups of 34 students in a class might suggest doubling 34 which equals 68 and there are three groups of those, so $68 + 68 + 68 = 204$. Remember, you want students to move away from using repeated addition and to thinking multiplicatively. Another option is to think about how the six groups of base-ten materials might be broken into tens and ones: 6 times 3 tens or 6×30 and 6 times 4 ones or 6×4 and add those two products together. Or, some students use the tens individually: 6 tens make 60. So that's 60 and 60 and 60 (180); then add on the 24 to equal 204.

All of these ideas should be part of students' repertoire of models for multidigit multiplication computation. Introduce different representations as ways to explore multiplication until you are comfortable that students' have a collection of useful ideas. Although teachers may worry that presenting multiple methods to solve problems will overwhelm and confuse students, researchers found that comparing a variety of methods from the start helped students gain flexibility and enhanced learning (Rittle-Johnson et al., 2010).

Multiplication by a Single-Digit Multiplier

As with addition and subtraction, it is helpful to place multiplication tasks in context. Let students model the problems in ways that make sense to them. The three categories described here are strategies grounded in student reasoning, as described in research on multiplicative reasoning (Baek, 2006; Confrey, 2008; Petit, 2009).

Complete-Number Strategies (Including Doubling). Students who are not yet comfortable decomposing numbers into parts will approach the numbers in the sets as single groups. Often, these early strategies will be based on repeated addition, which in the long term is neither efficient (234×78) nor useful (think about multiplication of fractions) (Devlin, 2011). Initially students may list long columns of numbers and add them up. To fade this process, encourage students to recognize that if they add two numbers, the next two will have the same sum and so on. This doubling can become the principal approach for many students (Flowers & Rubenstein, 2010/2011). Doubling capitalizes on the distributive property, whereby doubling 47 is double 40 + double 7, and the associative property, in which doubling 7 tens—or $2 \times (7 \times 10)$—is the same as doubling 7 and then multiplying by 10 or $(2 \times 7) \times 10$. Figure 12.2 illustrates two methods students may use.

Partitioning Strategies. Students decompose numbers in a variety of ways that reflect an understanding of place value, at least four of which are illustrated in Figure 12.3.

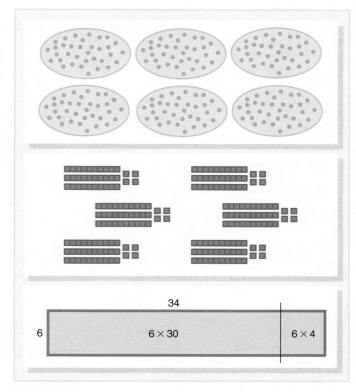

FIGURE 12.1 Different ways to model 6×34 may support different computational strategies.

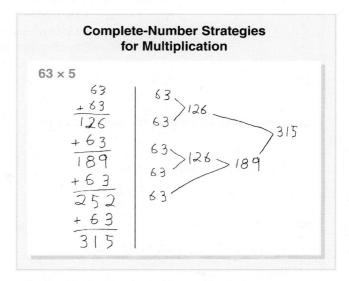

FIGURE 12.2 Students who use a complete-number strategy do not decompose numbers into decades or tens and ones.

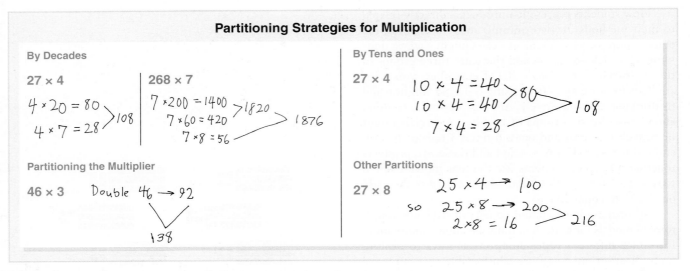

Partitioning Strategies for Multiplication

By Decades

27×4

$\left. \begin{array}{l} 4 \times 20 = 80 \\ 4 \times 7 = 28 \end{array} \right\} 108$

268×7

$\left. \begin{array}{l} 7 \times 200 = 1400 \\ 7 \times 60 = 420 \\ 7 \times 8 = 56 \end{array} \right\} \begin{array}{l} 1820 \\ \end{array} \right\} 1876$

By Tens and Ones

27×4

$\left. \begin{array}{l} 10 \times 4 = 40 \\ 10 \times 4 = 40 \end{array} \right\} 80 \\ 7 \times 4 = 28 \end{array} \right\} 108$

Partitioning the Multiplier

46×3 Double $46 \rightarrow 92$

$\searrow \swarrow$

138

Other Partitions

27×8

$25 \times 4 \rightarrow 100$
so $25 \times 8 \rightarrow 200$
$2 \times 8 = 16$ $\left. \right\} 216$

FIGURE 12.3 Four different ways to make easier partial products.

MyLab Education   **Video Example 12.2**

Watch Ally use partitioning by place value to mentally multiply.

The "by decades" partitioning strategy (which can be extended to by hundreds, by thousands, etc.) is the same as the standard algorithm except that students always begin with the largest values. This mental math strategy is very powerful. Another valuable strategy is to compute mentally with multiples of 25 and 50 and then add or subtract a small adjustment. All partitioning strategies rely on knowledge of the distributive property.

MyLab Education
Video Example 12.3

Watch Rachel as she uses partitioning to solve 45×36.

Compensation Strategies for Multiplication

$27 + 3 \rightarrow 30 \times 4 \rightarrow 120$
$3 \times 4 = 12 \rightarrow -12$
$\overline{108}$

I can split 250 in half and multiply by 10.

$125 \times 10 = 1250$

$20 \times 70 \rightarrow 1400 \overset{3 \times 70}{-210} \rightarrow 1190$

FIGURE 12.4 A compensation is made in the answer, or one factor is adjusted to compensate for a change in the other factor.

Compensation Strategies. Students and adults look for ways to manipulate numbers so that the calculations are easy. In Figure 12.4, the problem 27×4 is changed to an easier one, and then an adjustment or compensation is made. The second example shows the "half-then-double strategy," in which one factor is cut in half and the other factor doubled. This approach is often used when a 5 or a 50 is involved. Because these strategies are dependent on the numbers involved, they can't be used for all computations. However, they are valuable approaches, especially for mental math and estimation.

Multiplication of Multidigit Numbers

As you move students from single-digit to two-digit factors, there is a value in exposing them to products involving multiples of 10 and 100. This focus supports the importance of place value and an emphasis on the number rather than the separate digits. Consider the following problem:

A Scout troop wants to package 400 battery packs as a fundraising project. If each pack will have 12 batteries inside, how many batteries are the Scouts going to need?

Students can use $4 \times 12 = 48$ to figure out that 400×12 equals 4800. Make sure you discuss how to say and write "forty-eight hundred." Be alert to students who simply tack on zeros without understanding why. They may say "to multiply by 10, just add a zero on the end of the number." But very soon this rule will "expire" (Karp, Bush, & Dougherty, 2014) as students try to solve 2.5×10, a problem for which this rule will not work. Try problems in which tens are multiplied by tens, such as 30×60 or 210×40.

Then students should move to problems that involve any two-digit numbers, not just those that are multiples of 10. A problem such as the next one can be solved in many different ways.

The parade had 23 clowns. Each clown carried 18 balloons. How many balloons were there altogether?

Some students might look for smaller products such as 6×23 and then add that result three times. Another method is to find the answer to 20×23 and then subtract 2×23. Others will calculate four separate partial products: $10 \times 20 = 200$, $8 \times 20 = 160$, $10 \times 3 = 30$, and $8 \times 3 = 24$. Two-digit multiplication is both complex and challenging. But students can solve these problems in a variety of interesting ways, many of which will contribute to the development of the standard algorithm. Figure 12.5 shows three fourth-grade students' work prior to instruction on the standard algorithm. Kenneth's work shows how he is *partitioning* the factor 12 into $3 \times 2 \times 2$. Briannon is using a *complete-number strategy*. She may need to see and hear about strategies other classmates developed to move toward a more efficient approach. Nick's method is conceptually very similar to the standard algorithm. As students like Nick begin partitioning numbers by place value, their strategies are often like the standard algorithm but without the traditional recording schemes.

Cluster Problems. One approach to multidigit multiplication is called *cluster problems* or sometimes called *strings*. This approach encourages students to use a series (or string) of facts and useful combinations they already know in order to explicitly guide students in figuring out more complex computations. By using reasoning and number relationships students can use the cluster or string of problems in ways that support certain strategies. For example, to find 34×50, students might record the following cluster of known facts:

$$3 \times 50$$
$$10 \times 50$$
$$34 \times 25$$
$$30 \times 20$$

Using these problems as support, students can analyze to see which ones can be used in finding the product (there are multiple options). They can also consider adding other problems that might be helpful. In this case, have students make an estimate of the final product before doing any of the problems in the cluster. For example, in the cluster for 34×50, 3×50 and 10×50 may be helpful in thinking about 30×50. The results of 30×50 and 4×50 combine to give you 34×50. It may seem that 34×25 is harder than 34×50. However, if you know 34×25, double the answer to get the desired product. Think about how you could use 10×34 (and some other related problems) to find 34×25. At first, you may want to brainstorm clusters together as a class, but when students become familiar with the approach, they should be encouraged to make up their own cluster of problems for a given product.

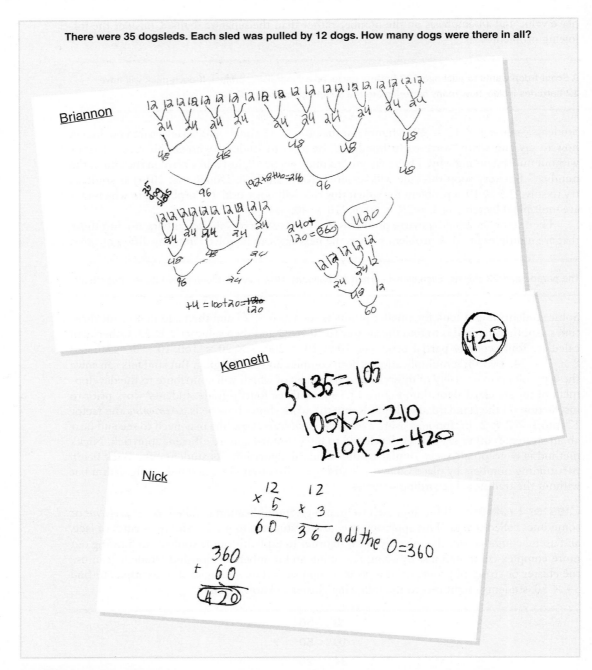

FIGURE 12.5 Three students solve a multiplication problem using invented strategies.

Cluster problems help students think about ways that they can decompose numbers into easier parts. The strategy of breaking the numbers apart and multiplying the parts—using place-value knowledge coupled with the distributive property—is an extremely valuable technique for flexible computation and prepares students for understanding the standard algorithm. The *Common Core State Standards* state that students do not have to use the formal term *distributive property*, but they expect students to understand why this property works because that knowledge is critical to understanding multiplication (and its ties to algebraic thinking).

⏸ Pause & Reflect

Try making up a cluster of problems for 86 × 42. Include all possible problems that you think might be helpful. Then use your cluster to find the product. Is there more than one way? ●

Were these problems in your cluster? Did you use others?

2 × 80	4 × 80	2 × 86	40 × 80
	6 × 40	10 × 86	40 × 86

All that is required to begin the cluster problem approach is that your cluster eventually leads to a solution.

MyLab Education   Self-Check 12.1

MyLab Education   Application Exercise 12.1: Invented **Strategies for Multiplication** Click the link to access this exercise, then watch the video and answer the accompanying questions.

Standard Algorithms for Multiplication

The standard multiplication algorithm is probably the most challenging of the four algorithms when students have not had numerous opportunities to explore their own strategies first. As with other algorithms, as much time as necessary should be devoted to the conceptual development of the multiplication algorithm using concrete or semiconcrete models with the recording of the written symbols blended in to that process.

Begin with Models

The multiplication algorithm can be developed with a variety of models but when you move to two-digit multipliers, the area model has distinct advantages.

Area Model. Start with a context and give students a drawing of a rectangular garden 6 centimeters by 47 centimeters. What is the area of the garden? Let students solve the problem in groups using base-ten materials before discussing it as a class.

As shown in Figure 12.6, the rectangle can be sliced or separated into two parts so that one part will be 6 ones by 7 ones, or 42 ones, and the other will be 6 ones by 4 tens, or 24 tens. Notice that the base-ten language "6 ones times 4 tens equals 24 tens" tells how many tens pieces are in the big section. To say "6 times 40 equals 240" is also correct and tells how many

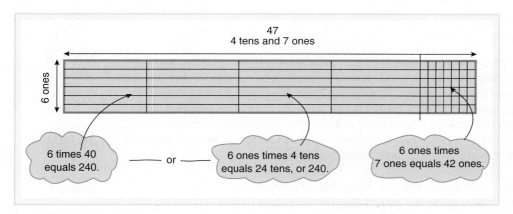

FIGURE 12.6   A rectangle covered with base-ten materials is a useful model for two-digit-by-one-digit multiplication.

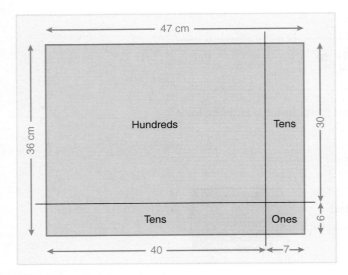

FIGURE 12.7 Ones, tens, and hundreds pieces fit exactly into the four sections of this 36 × 47 rectangle.

CCSS **Standards for Mathematical Practice**
MP5. Reasoning abstractly and quantitatively.

units or square centimeters are in the section. What you wish to avoid is saying "6 times 4" when the 4 actually represents 40. Each section is referred to as a *partial product*. By adding the two partial products, you get the total product or area of the rectangle.

The *area model*, which can be thought about as a connected array. This rectangular region is an important visual representation that can support students' multiplicative understanding and reasoning (Barmby, Harries, Higgins, & Suggate, 2009; Izsák, 2004). The area model uses a row and column structure to automatically organize equal groups and offer a visual demonstration of the commutative and distributive properties (unlike the number line). The area model can also be linked to successful representations of the standard multiplication algorithm and to future topics such as multiplication of fractions (Lannin, Chval, & Jones, 2013) and multiplication of algebraic terms (Benson, Wall & Malm, 2013).

A valuable exploration with the *area model* uses large rectangles that have been precisely prepared with dimensions between 25 centimeters and 60 centimeters and square corners. Each group of students uses one of these rectangles to determine how many small ones pieces (base-ten materials) will fit inside the rectangle. Later, students can simply be given a tracing of a rectangle on grid paper or be asked, "What is the area of a rectangle that is 36 centimeters by 47 centimeters?"

For a rectangle that is 36 centimeters by 47 centimeters, most students will cover the rectangle with as many hundreds pieces as possible. One approach is to put the 12 hundreds in one corner. This placement will leave narrow regions on two sides that can be covered with tens pieces and a final small rectangle that will hold ones. Especially if students have had earlier experiences with finding products in arrays, figuring out the size of each subrectangle and combining them to find the size of the whole rectangle is relatively straightforward. Figure 12.7 shows the four regions.

MyLab Education **Video Example 12.4**

Watch this video (https://www.youtube.com/watch?v=mjYYbwuued0) that shows the creation of an array using an interactive white board and the use of partial products.

Activity 12.1 CCSS-M: 4.NBT.B.5

Build It and Break It

Select a problem such as 23 × 18. Use Base-Ten Materials or 1-Centimeter Grid Paper to build or sketch the corresponding area model. Then, have students show and record as many ways as possible to "slice" the array into pieces. For example, they could cut the array into 23 × 10 + 23 × 8. What other vertical or horizontal slices can be made? What property does this slicing link to? Before launching this activity, provide students, particularly ELs and students with disabilities, a labeled visual of an array (or area model) that includes the terms *array, area model, slice, vertical,* and *horizontal*. In a wrap-up discussion, be sure to focus on the vocabulary of the key concepts (*distributive property, decompose, strategy,* etc.).

STUDENTS
with
SPECIAL
NEEDS

ENGLISH
LEARNERS

MyLab Education **Blackline Master: Base-Ten Materials**
MyLab Education **Blackline Master: 1-Centimeter Grid Paper**

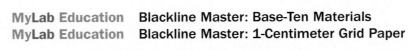

Open Array. The open array (Fosnot & Dolk, 2001; NCTM, 2014) is a semi-concrete representation of the area model and can be successfully used after students experience several constructions of area models with base-ten materials. Starting with a blank rectangle, students can mark off areas (the number of subdivisions depends on the number of digits in the factors) that align with the use of the distributive property. Students record partial products inside each subdivision. Note that the dimensions of the open array are not usually drawn to scale and therefore are often not precisely proportional. But the model can be productively used to think about the multiplication as an area of a rectangle, which aligns to the standard algorithm. The open array will also connect to future work with multiplication with fractions, two polynomials, and to the history of mathematics through explorations of Egyptian and Russian peasant multiplication (Lee, 2014). Figure 12.8 shows four steps in the process of developing an open array for the problem 72 × 36. Create an array according to the number of digits in the problem, label the sides with the factors decomposed by place value, multiply, and then add the partial products.

FIGURE 12.8 The open array is a means to record multidigit multiplication.

Activity 12.2

CCSS-M: 4.NBT.B.5

Make It Easy

Computer versions of the area model can ease some of the difficulties of physically covering rectangular grids with base-ten materials. Go to the Dreambox website (www.dreambox.com/teachertools) and find the Multiplication: Open Arrays tool.

STUDENTS
with
SPECIAL
NEEDS

Students compose arrays, use partial products, and apply the distributive property to solve multi-digit multiplication problems through the use of the area model. For students with disabilities, you may need to have a set of Base-Ten Materials nearby to show how the concrete version corresponds to the digital tools.

MyLab Education **Blackline Master: Base-Ten Materials**

Research analyzed sixth-grade students' varied strategies for solving multiplication problems on the factors of flexibility, accuracy, and efficiency. Given the problem 13 × 7, only 11 percent of the students used the standard algorithm. When multiplying 2 two-digit numbers, 20 percent used the standard algorithm, with less than half of that 20 percent reaching the correct answer (Keiser, 2010). Interestingly, this work confirmed the researcher's prior observations that the standard algorithm for multiplication was not the most popular approach for multiplying two-digit factors when students were taught other options. The array or area model was most often selected and the most accurate (the selection of the cluster problem strategy was second in accuracy and frequency).

Move from having students draw large rectangles and arrange base-ten materials using the Base-Ten Grid Paper. On the grid paper, students can draw accurate rectangles showing all of the pieces. Do not impose any recording technique on students until they understand how to use the two dimensions of a rectangle to get a product.

MyLab Education **Blackline Master: Base-Ten Grid Paper**

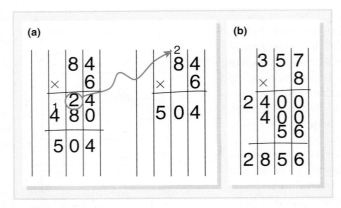

(a) **(b)**

FIGURE 12.9 In the standard algorithm, the product of ones is recorded first (a). The tens digit of this first product is written as a regrouped digit above the tens column. In (b) partial products can be recorded in any order.

Develop the Written Record

To help students develop a recording scheme, provide Multiplication Recording sheets with base-ten columns on which students can record problems. When the two partial products are written separately and added together, there is little new to learn. But, as illustrated in Figure 12.9(a), it is possible to teach students how to write the first product with a regrouped digit so that the combined product is written on one line. This recording scheme is known to be a source of errors. The little digit representing the regrouping is often the difficulty—it gets added in before the subsequent multiplication or is forgotten. Instead, to avoid errors, encourage students to record partial products. Then it makes no difference in which order the products are written. Figure 12.9(b) show how students can record partial products, which mirrors how this computation can be done mentally.

Partial Products. From the area model, the progression to record partial products with a two-digit multiplier is relatively straightforward. Rectangles can be drawn on base-ten grid paper, full-sized rectangles can be covered with base-ten materials, or an open array can be used. Now there will be four partial products, corresponding to four different sections of the rectangle.

Several variations in language might be used. Consider 36×47, as illustrated in Figure 12.10. In the partial product 30×40 if base-ten language is used—*3 tens times 4 tens equals 12 hundreds*—the result tells how many hundreds pieces are in that section. Avoid saying "three times four," which promotes thinking about digits rather than numbers. It is important to stress that a product of *tens times tens equals hundreds*.

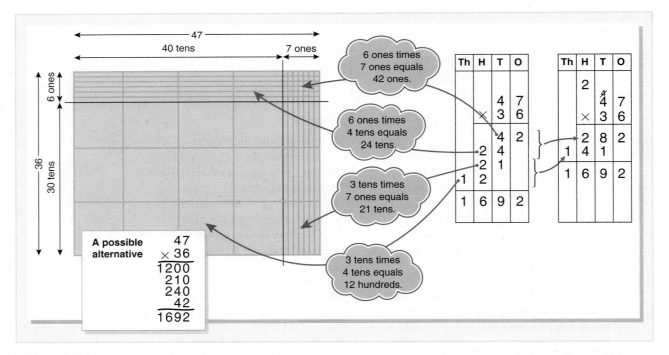

FIGURE 12.10 36×47 rectangle covered with base-ten materials. Base-ten language connects the four partial products to the written format of the standard algorithm.

Figure 12.10 also shows the recording of four partial products in the order of the standard algorithm and how these products can be collapsed to two lines if small digits representing the regrouping are used to record the trade. Here the second exchange or trade technically belongs in the hundreds column but is often written elsewhere, which is again a source of errors. The lower left of the figure shows another alterative with all four products written. Using this approach, multiplying numbers such as 538 × 29 results in six partial products, but far fewer errors!

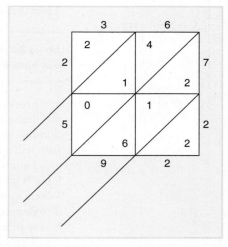

FIGURE 12.11 36 × 72 shown using a lattice multiplication technique.

MyLab Education **Video Example 12.5**

Watch this video of Jenny Bay-Williams explaining the use of partial products to fluently multiply multidigit whole numbers.

Lattice Multiplication. Another approach for recording multidigit multiplication is known as *lattice multiplication*. Historically this method has been used in a variety of cultures. Here students use a grid with squares split by diagonal lines (see Lattice Multiplication Templates) to organize their thinking along diagonally organized place-value columns. Look at Figure 12.11 to see the final recording for the problem 36 × 72.

MyLab Education **Self-Check 12.2**

MyLab Education **Activity Page: Lattice Multiplication Templates**

MyLab Education **Video Exercise 12.6**

Watch this video (https://www.khanacademy.org/math/arithmetic-home/multiply-divide/place-value-area-models/v/lattice-multiplication) on how the lattice model is set up, filled in, and calculated.

MyLab Education **Application Exercise 12.2: Invented Strategies for Multiplication** Click the link to access this exercise, then watch the video and answer the accompanying questions.

 ## Invented Strategies for Division

Even though many adults think division is the most onerous of the computational operations, students may find it easier than multiplication. Division computation strategies with whole numbers are developed in third through fifth grade with the expectation of knowing the algorithm in the fifth grade (NGA Center & CCSSO, 2010).

Recall that there are two concepts of division. First, there is the partition, or fair-sharing idea, illustrated by this story problem:

Eileen's piggy bank has 783 pennies. She wants to share them equally with her 4 friends and herself. How many pennies will Eileen and each of her friends get?

Then there is the measurement, or repeated subtraction, concept:

Jumbo the elephant loves peanuts. His trainer has 625 peanuts. If he gives Jumbo 20 peanuts each day, how many days will the peanuts last?

Students should be challenged to solve both types of problems. However, the fair-share problems are often easier to solve with base-ten materials, and they mirror the idea of partitioning that is used in the standard algorithm. Eventually, students will develop strategies that they will apply to both types of problems.

Figure 12.12 shows strategies that three fourth-grade students used to solve division problems. The first example (a) illustrates $72 \div 3$ using base-ten materials and a sharing process. When no more tens can be distributed, a ten is traded for ten ones. Then the 12 ones are distributed, resulting in 24 in each set. This direct modeling approach with base-ten materials is easy to understand and use (Boote, 2016).

The student work in Figure 12.12(b) shows that for the problem $342 \div 4$, she sets out the base-ten materials and draws a four-column recording chart to match the divisor and the image of paper plates that had been used previously as an organizational tool for sharing. After noting that there are not enough hundreds for each child, she splits 2 of the 3 hundreds in half, putting 50 in each of the four columns. That leaves her with 1 hundred, 4 tens, and 2 ones. After trading the 1 hundred for tens (now she has 14 tens), she gives 3 tens to each child, recording 30 in each column. Now she is left with 2 tens and 2 ones, or 22. She knows that 4×5 equals 20, so she gives each child 5, leaving 2. Then she splits the 2 remaining pieces into halves and writes $\frac{1}{2}$ in each column.

The student in Figure 12.12(c) solves a division problem that involves a measurement situation: How many bags with 6 stickers in each can be made if there are 164 stickers? She wants to find out how many groups of six are in 164. As a first step, she estimates and tries 6×20 by multiplying 6×10 and doubling the answer. Then, she tries adding another group of 10 and recognizes that is too high. She knows the answer is more than 20 and less than 30. She thinks about how many sixes in 44, which she knows is 7 with 2 left over. So, her answer is 27 bags with 2 stickers left over.

Missing-Factor Strategies. In Figure 12.12(c), notice that the student is using a multiplicative approach. She is trying to find out, "What number times 6 will be close to 164 with less than 6 remaining?" This approach emphasizes the inverse relationship of multiplication and division.

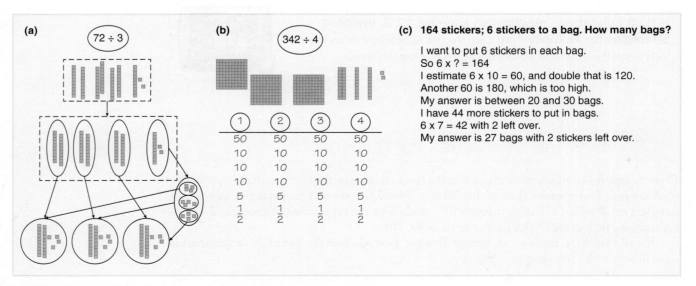

FIGURE 12.12 Students use both models and symbols to solve division tasks.

❙❙ Pause & Reflect

Before reading further, think about the quotient of 318 ÷ 7 by trying to figure out *what number times 7* (or *7 times what number*) is close to 318 without going over. Do not use the standard algorithm. ●

There are several places to begin solving this problem. For instance, because 10 × 7 equals 70 and 100 × 7 equals 700, the answer is between 10 and 100. You might start with multiples of 10. Forty sevens are 280. Fifty sevens are 350. So, 40 is not enough and 50 is too many. The answer has to be forty-something. At this point, you could test numbers between 40 and 50 or add on groups of seven. Or, you could notice that 40 sevens (280) leaves you with 20 + 18 or 38. Five sevens will be 35 of the 38 with 3 remaining. In all, that's 40 + 5 or 45 with a remainder of 3.

This missing-factor approach is likely to be invented by some students if they are solving measurement problems such as the following:

Grace can put 6 pictures on one page of her photo album. If she has 82 pictures, how many pages will she need?

Alternatively, you can simply pose a task such as 82 ÷ 6 and ask students, "What number times 6 would be close to 82?" Notice that the missing-factor strategy is equally good for one-digit divisors as two-digit divisors.

MyLab Education   Video Example 12.7

Watch this video of a teacher describing student's work with a missing factor strategy.

Let's look how an open array can support students' thinking when using the missing factor strategy. Using the problem 843 ÷ 6, look at two useful steps in Figure 12.13. First, we use the array to think about the missing factor by putting the known factor at the left of the rectangle and considering an estimate of how many hundreds, tens and ones are needed for the other factor (see the top of Figure 12.13). Then using place-value understanding, partial factors are selected to come as close as possible to the largest multiplier and the multiplication is carried out. In every case the resulting product is subtracted from the dividend so the remaining amount can be distributed. If students underestimate they can just create another section to the array to accommodate. Then they add the partial factors to get the quotient (and remainder).

Cluster Problems. Another approach to developing missing-factor strategies is to use cluster problems, as discussed for multiplication. Following are examples of two clusters for two different division problems (written in bold at the bottom of the columns):

Cluster 1	Cluster 2
100 × 4	10 × 72
500 ÷ 4	5 × 70
25 × 4	2 × 72
6 × 4	4 × 72
527 ÷ 4	5 × 72
	381 ÷ 72

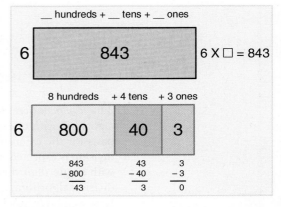

FIGURE 12.13   Using an open array to support student thinking with the missing factor strategy.

Notice that it is useful to include division problems in the cluster. In the first example, 400 ÷ 4 could easily replace 100 × 4, and 125 × 4 could replace 500 ÷ 4. The idea is to capitalize on the inverse relationship between multiplication and division.

Cluster problems provide students with a sense that problems can be solved in different ways and with different starting points. Therefore, rather than cluster problems, you can provide students with a variety of first steps for solving a problem.

 ## Pause & Reflect

Solve 514 ÷ 8 in two different ways beginning with different first steps. Do your approaches converge before you reach your solution? ●

For example, here are four possible starting points for 514 ÷ 8:

---

8 × 10   **400 ÷ 8**   **8 × 60**   **80 ÷ 8**

When you first ask students to solve problems using two different strategies, they often use an inefficient method for their second approach (or revert to a standard algorithm). For example, to solve 514 ÷ 8, a student might perform a very long string of repeated subtractions (514 − 8 = 506, 506 − 8 = 498, 498 − 8 = 490, and soon) and count how many times he or she subtracted 8. Others will actually draw 514 tally marks and loop groups of 8. These students have not developed sufficient flexibility to think of other, more efficient methods. Posing a variety of starting points can nudge students into other, more profitable alternatives, as will class discussions where flexible approaches are shared.

Break Apart or Decomposition. When considering division problems with a 3-digit dividend and a 2-digit divisor, students can manipulate the numbers to work toward their advantage. In this case, students change the numbers to a more mentally convenient form. For example, if asked to solve 157 ÷ 13, students could alter that problem by decomposing the dividend to (130 ÷ 13) + (27 ÷ 13) to get an answer of (10 + 2) with a remainder of 1. Students must be reminded again that it is the dividend that can be broken apart, not the divisor! If students need more explicit proof, use direct modeling with base-ten materials and paper plates (as described in Chapter 8) to show the base-ten materials can be grouped differently but the number of paper plates must remain stable.

MyLab Education   **Self-Check 12.3**

 ## Standard Algorithm for Division

The *Common Core State Standards* (NGA Center & CCSSO, 2010) suggest that the division algorithm with one-digit divisors is developed in the fourth grade, and it should provide the basis for the extension to two-digit divisors in the fifth grade. The algorithm for multidigit division is expected in the sixth grade. Students who are still struggling in grades 5 and beyond with single-digit divisors can also benefit from the following conceptual development. The division algorithm, out of the algorithms for the four main operations, appeared to be the one least well understood by teachers (Raveh, Koichu, Peled, & Zaslavsky, 2016).

Begin with Models

Long division is the one standard algorithm that starts with the left-hand or biggest pieces. The conceptual basis for the algorithm most often taught is the partition or fair-share method, the method we will explore in detail here.

Partition or Fair-Share Model. Traditionally, if the problem 4)583 was posed, we might hear someone say, "4 goes into 5 one time." Not surprisingly, initially this approach may be quite mysterious to students. How can you just ignore the "83" and keep changing the problem? Preferably, you want students to think of the 583 as 5 hundreds, 8 tens, and 3 ones, not as the independent digits 5, 8, and 3. One idea is to use a context such as energy bars bundled in boxes of ten with 10 boxes (100 pieces) to a carton. Then the problem becomes as follows: *We have 5 cartons, 8 boxes, and 3 energy bars to share evenly between 4 schools.* In this context, it is reasonable to share the cartons first until no more can be shared. Those remaining cartons are "unpacked," and the boxes shared, and so on.

❚❚ Pause & Reflect

Try the distributing or sharing process yourself using base-ten materials, four paper plates, and the problem 583 ÷ 4. Try to talk through the process without using "goes into" language. Think about sharing equally.

Language plays an enormous role in thinking conceptually about the standard division algorithm. Most adults are so accustomed to the "goes into" language that it is hard for them to let it go. For the problem 583 ÷ 4, here is some suggested language:

- I want to share 5 hundreds, 8 tens, and 3 ones among these four schools. There are enough hundreds for each school to get 1 hundred. That leaves 1 hundred that I can't share.
- I'll trade the remaining hundred for 10 tens. That gives me a total of 18 tens. I can give each school 4 tens and have 2 tens left over. Two tens are not enough to go around to the four schools.
- I can trade the 2 tens for 20 ones and put those with the 3 ones I already had. That makes a total of 23 ones. I can give 5 ones to each of the four schools. That leaves me with 3 ones as a remainder. In all, I gave out to each school 1 hundred, 4 tens, and 5 ones with 3 left over. ●

Activity 12.3   CCSS-M: 4.NBT.B.6

STUDENTS with SPECIAL NEEDS

Left Overs

Use the Left Over Game Board and have students work in pairs and place their game pieces at the "start" of the path. The first player uses the Left Over Spinner and spins. The amount on the spinner is used as the divisor for the number on the start square. If there are left overs after the division, the player moves the number of spaces that equals the remainder. If there is no remainder, the player stays in the same position. If they move the amount of the remainder, they get a bonus turn. The winner is the first to reach the end of the path. You can differentiate the game by using easier (or harder) divisors (see blank spinners on the Left Over Spinner Activity Page).

MyLab Education   Activity Page: Left Over Game Board
MyLab Education   Activity Page: Left Over Spinner

Partial Quotients Using a Visual Model. You can look at division with an eye to partial quotients by using a version of a bar diagram model blended with the repeated subtraction approach. Look at the problem 1506 ÷ 3. If we use multiplication facts we know as a guide,

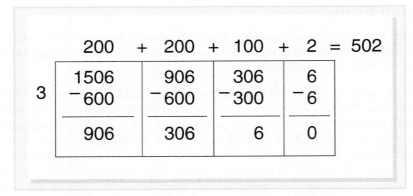

FIGURE 12.14 Using a bar diagram to show partial quotients.

then we can repeatedly subtract partial products and record them through an approach that uses measurement division (see Figure 12.14).

Develop the Written Record

The recording scheme for the standard long-division algorithm is not completely intuitive. You will need to be explicit in helping students learn to symbolically record the action of fair sharing with models. There are essentially four steps:

1. *Share* and record the number of pieces put in each group.
2. *Record* the number of pieces shared in all. Multiply to find this number.
3. *Record* the number of pieces remaining. Subtract to find this number.
4. *Trade* (if necessary) for smaller pieces, and combine with any of the same-sized pieces that are there already. Record the new total number in the next column.

When students model problems with a one-digit divisor, steps 2 and 3 seem unnecessary. Explain that these steps really help when you don't have the pieces there to count.

Explicit-Trade Method. Figure 12.15 details each step of the recording process just described. On the left, is the standard algorithm. To the right is an explicit-trade method that matches the actual action with the models by explicitly recording the trades. Instead of the "bring-down" step of the standard algorithm, traded pieces are crossed out, as is the number of existing pieces in the next column. The combined number of pieces is written in this column using, in this case, a two-digit number. In the example, 2 hundreds are traded for 20 tens, combined with the 6 that were there for a total of 26 tens. The 26 is, therefore, written in the tens column.

Students often find this *explicit-trade method* easier to follow. (The explicit-trade method is a successful approach invented by of John Van de Walle and tested with students in grades 3 to 8. You will not find it in other textbooks.) Blank Multiplication and Division Recording Charts with wide place-value columns are highly recommended for this method. By spreading out the digits in the dividend when writing down the problem, you help students avoid the common problem of leaving out a middle zero in a problem (see Figure 12.16).

MyLab Education	**Blackline Master: Multiplication and Division Recording Charts**

Repeated Subtraction. A well-known way to record an algorithm is based on repeated subtraction and the measurement model of division. This approach may be viewed as a good way to record the missing-factor approach with partial products recorded in a column to the

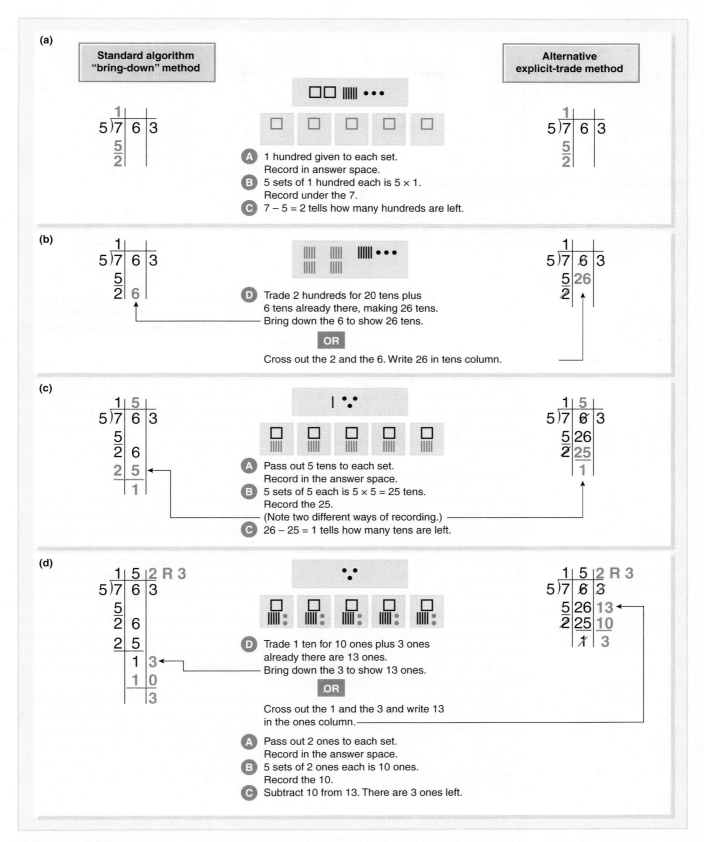

FIGURE 12.15   The standard algorithm and explicit-trade method are connected to each step of the division process.

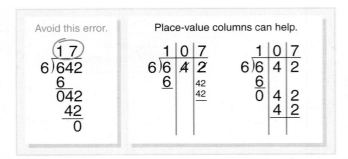

FIGURE 12.16 Using lines to mark place-value columns can help students remember to record zeros.

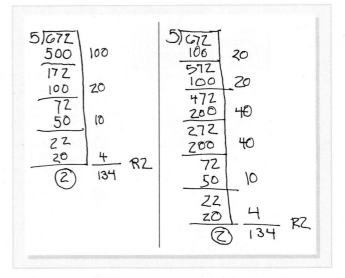

FIGURE 12.17 The numbers on the side indicate the quantity of the divisor being subtracted from the dividend. The divisor can be subtracted from the dividend in groups of any amount.

right of the division computation (see Figure 12.17). Students may prefer this strategy, especially students who bring this approach from other countries and students with learning disabilities who can select facts they already know and work from that point. This method is also useful with multidigit divisors. Explore The Quotient Café on the NCTM Illuminations website for a way to explore a repeated subtraction approach in a variety of story situations.

Two-Digit Divisors

The *Common Core State Standards* states that fifth-grade students should be able to find "whole-number quotients of whole numbers with up to four-digit dividends and two-digit divisors, using strategies based on place value, the properties of operations, and/or the relationship between multiplication and division." The CCSS-M goes on to state that students should "[i]llustrate and explain the calculation by using equations, rectangular arrays, and/or area models" (NGA Center & CCSSO, 2010, p. 35). This is particularly important as knowledge and understanding of long division is a predictor of mathematical success in high school (Siegler et al., 2012).

An Intuitive Idea. Suppose that you were sharing a large pile of shells with 36 friends. Instead of passing them out one at a time, you conservatively estimate that each person could get at least 6 shells. You give 6 to each of your friends. Now you find there are more than 36 shells left. Do you have everyone give back the 6 shells so you can then give them 7 or 8? That would be silly! You simply pass out more.

The shell example gives us two good ideas for sharing in long division. First, always underestimate how much can be shared. You can always pass out some more. To avoid overestimating, always pretend there are more sets (or people) to share with than there really are. For example, if you are dividing 312 by 43 (sharing among 43 sets or "friends"), pretend you have 50 sets instead. Round *up* to the next multiple of 10. You can easily determine that 6 pieces can be shared among 50 sets because 6 × 50 is an easy product. Therefore, because there are really only 43 sets, you can reasonably give *at least* 6 to each.

Using the Idea Symbolically. Using these ideas about reasoning with division situations, both the standard algorithm and the explicit-trade method of recording are illustrated in Figure 12.18. The rounded-up divisor, 70, is written in a little "think bubble." Rounding up has another advantage: It is easier to use the multiples of 70 (than 63) and compare them to 374. Think about sharing base-ten materials (thousands, hundreds, tens, and ones). Work through the problem one step at a time, saying exactly what each recorded step stands for.

This approach has proved successful with students who are learning division for the first time, with students in middle school in need of remediation, and with students with disabilities. It reduces the mental load of making choices and essentially eliminates the need to erase. If an estimate is too low, that's okay. And if you always round up, the estimate will never be too high. The same is true of the explicit-trade notation which is described next.

A Low-Stress Approach

With a two-digit divisor, it is harder to estimate the right amount to share at each step. First, start by thinking about place value by asking students to consider whether their answer will be in the thousands, hundreds, tens, and so on. Then create a "doubling" sidebar chart (Martin, 2009) that starts with a benchmark multiple of the divisor and then doubles each subsequent product. So, for the problem 3842 ÷ 14, decide first whether the answer is in the thousands, hundreds, or tens. Selecting hundreds in this case, the students will then develop a chart of 100, 200, 400, and 800 times 14 (see Figure 12.19). Can you see how knowing 100 times 14 can help you figure out 200 and other products? Using this doubling sidebar chart can help students with the products of the divisor multiplied by 100 through 900 by adding the products in combinations. For example, to know 300 times 14, add the products of 100 times and 200 times the divisor or subtract 100 times 14 from 400 times 14. Knowing these products will logically help the student also know what 10 through 90 times the divisor is! Then the division becomes focused on the equal groups within the dividend

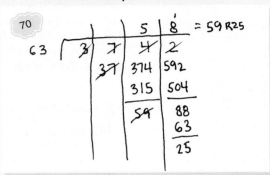

FIGURE 12.18 Round the divisor up to 70 to estimate, but multiply what you share by 63. In the ones column, share 8 with each set. Oops! 88 left over so just give 1 more to each set.

Activity 12.4

CCSS-M: 5.NBT.B.6

Double, Double—No Toil or Trouble!

Select a division problem with a two-digit divisor, such as 936 ÷ 18. Display a corresponding sidebar chart (Martin, 2009) (or give students a Sidebar Chart template) of the products of the divisor (in this case, 10, 20, 40, and 80 × 18). Then try to think about the division using a missing factor approach and repeated subtraction. See if this helps in the estimation process. When working with students with disabilities, you may need to progress in a structured way by first supplying them with the appropriate sidebar chart with the products filled in. Then, on the next day, supply them with the chart and have them fill in the products, moving toward their independent creation and completion of the chart. This fading of support moves students in an organized and systematic way to more responsibility for their learning.

STUDENTS with SPECIAL NEEDS

MyLab Education   **Blackline Master: Sidebar Chart**

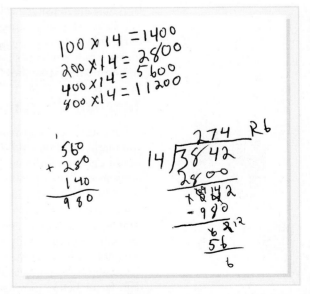

FIGURE 12.19 A student uses doubling to generate useful estimates in a sidebar chart.

and, as such, lowers stress. This scaffolding will help students estimate more successfully while allowing them to concentrate on the division process.

Research analyzed middle school students' strategies for solving division problems within a context and also as naked numbers (Keiser, 2012). Given two problems with two-digit divisors, only 4 of 91 students used the standard algorithm and of those 4 students only 2 were correct. Largely, students relied on a repeated subtraction approach or the missing-factor strategy. Errors often occurred when students misapplied mathematical properties. For example, students solving $95 \div 16$ broke it into $(95 \div 10) + (95 \div 10)$, demonstrating a common misunderstanding. Students thought that when using the distributive property you can break apart the divisor, when instead you need to split the dividend into components.

 FORMATIVE ASSESSMENT Notes. To assess understanding of division algorithms, call on different students to explain individual steps using the appropriate terminology that connects to the concept of division. Use an Observation Checklist to record students' responses, indicating how well they understand the algorithm. For students who are having difficulty, you may want to conduct a short diagnostic interview to explore their level of understanding in more detail. Begin by having the student complete $115 \div 9$ and ask them to talk about what they are thinking as they carry out specific steps in the process. If there is difficulty explaining, have the student use base-ten materials to directly model the problem and attempt to link the actions to the procedure. Then ask them to discuss verbally the connections between what was done with the models and what was written symbolically. ■

MyLab Education	Blackline Master: Observation Checklist
MyLab Education	Self-Check 12.4

Computational Estimation

Particularly in multiplicative situations, computational estimation is useful in daily events such as calculating a tip or figuring out miles per gallon of gasoline. As students move to a more technological world where calculations are frequently carried out by devices, never before has judging reasonableness been more important. Those who can estimate well will rarely be misled by a mistake in using a calculator and they can check answers to problems for reasonableness!

Computational estimation skills in multiplication and division round out a full development of flexible and fluent thinking with whole numbers. The *Common Core State Standards* state that fourth-grade students should "assess the reasonableness of answers using mental computation and estimation strategies including rounding" (NGA Center & CCSSO, 2010, p. 29).

Teaching Computational Estimation

What estimate would you give for 27×325? If you use 20×300, you might say 6000. Or, you might use 25 for the 27, noting that four 25s make 100. Because $325 \div 4$ is about 81, that would make an estimate of 8100. If you use 30×300, your estimate is 9000, and 30×320 gives an estimate of 9600. Is one of these "right"?

The more estimation strategies students experience, the better they can make a decision as to which one best suits the situation at hand. In contrast, if you just tell students to use a given strategy (e.g., round each number to one significant digit and multiply), they won't develop the skills to purposefully pick different strategies for different situations. Sometimes rounding is cumbersome and other strategies can be quicker or more accurate.

Choose the numbers in your problems wisely. First, start with problem situations with a single digit factor before moving to problems with two-digit factors multiplied by three-digit factors. Students are not surprisingly more successful with the single-digit factors (Liu, 2009). Additionally, initially choose problems where the adjustment is small rather than large. These decisions support the focus on the use of estimation strategies and thereby helps students learn the process.

Ask for Information, but No Answer. Consider the apprehension a student may perceive when you ask for an estimate of the product 7 × $89.99. As a result, students often try to quickly calculate an exact answer and then round it (Hanson & Hogan, 2000). To counter this, ask questions that focus on the result, using prompts like "Is it more than or less than 1000?" or "Will $500 be enough to pay for the tickets?" The question "About how much?" is quite different from "Is it more than $600?" Another option is to ask students to choose if they think the answer is between $100 and $400, $500 and $800, or $900 and $1200. Narrow your ranges as students become more adept.

Each activity that follows suggests a format for estimation in which a specific numeric response is not required.

Activity 12.5   CCSS-M: 4.NBT.A.3; 4.NBT.B.5

High or Low?

Display a computation and three or more possible computations that might be used to create an estimate. The students' task is to decide whether the estimation will be higher or lower than the actual computation. For example, present the computation 736 × 18. For each of the following, the students should decide whether the result will be higher or lower than the exact result and explain their thinking.

$$750 \times 10 \quad 730 \times 15$$
$$700 \times 20 \quad 750 \times 20$$

Also explore the High or Low Activity Page for additional problems and the Expanded Lesson: High or Low for an instructional plan for this activity.

MyLab Education   Activity page: High or Low
MyLab Education   Expanded Lesson: High or Low

Activity 12.6   CCSS-M: 4.OA.A.3

That's Good Enough

Present students with a computation that is reasonably difficult. For example: T-shirts with the school logo cost $6 wholesale. The Pep Club has saved $257. How many shirts can they buy for a fundraiser? The task is to describe the steps they would take to get an exact answer (but not to carry out the steps). For students with disabilities, you may give them a series of examples and counterexamples of the steps that they must choose from and put in order. Share students' ideas. Next, have students carry out one or two steps. Stop and see whether they come up with reasonable estimates.

STUDENTS
with
SPECIAL
NEEDS

Computational Estimation Strategies

Mental calculations using estimations are more complex than just the application of a procedure in that they require a deep knowledge of how numbers work (Hartnett, 2007). Mental mathematics is not doing computations "in your head" where you image the algorithm on a mental chalkboard but instead it is reasoning about numbers and making decisions about which strategy to use (Erdem, 2017; Varol & Farran, 2007). Estimation strategies help in that process (see Table 12.1).

Estimation strategies are specific approaches that produce approximate results. As you work through the strategies in this section, you may recognize many of the same approaches students developed from their invented methods. But, some of the strategies in this section may not have been developed, and then you will need to explicitly introduce these to your students.

TABLE 12.1   ESTIMATION STRATEGIES

Estimation Strategy	Description and Strategies	Examples
Front End	• This method focuses on the leading, or left-most, digits in numbers. Once the first digit it identified, then students think about the rest of the number as if there were zeros in the other positions. Adjustments are made to correct for the digits or numbers that were ignored. This method has been shown to be one of the easiest for students to learn (Star & Rittle-Johnson, 2009). • When estimating, avoid presenting division problems using the computational form 7)3482 because this format suggests a computation rather than an estimate. Present problems in context or use the algebraic form: 3482 ÷ 7.	• 480 × 7 is front-ended to 400 × 7, or 2800. • 452 × 23, consider 400 × 20, or 8000. Adjust in a second step to 9000. • 3482 ÷ 7, first decide the correct place value of the estimate (100 × 7 is too low, 1000 × 7 is too high, so the estimate will be in the hundreds). There are 34 hundreds in the dividend, so because 34 ÷ 7 is between 4 and 5, the front-end estimate is 400 or 500. In this example, because 34 ÷ 7 is almost 5, the more precise estimate is 500.
Rounding	• This method is a way of changing the numbers in the problem to others that are easier to compute mentally. In multiplication, students can either round one number or both. • Use a number line marked by a scale of 5, 10, 100, and so on. The ends can be labeled 0 and 100, 100 and 200, 100 and 1000, or a range of your choice. If given a factor such as 463 and asked to round to the nearest 100, the answer is 500; if rounding to the nearest 50 then 450 would be a possible estimate. See Figure 12.20.	• If one factor can be rounded to 10, 100, or 1000, the resulting product is easy to determine without adjusting the other factor. See Figure 12.21(a). • When one factor is a single digit, round the other factor—so for 7 × 485, round 485 to 500, and the estimate is 3500. That is too high by the amount of 7 × 15 so, if more precision is required, subtract about 100 (an estimate of 7 × 15). See Figure 12.21(b). • Another option is to round one factor up and the other down. For 86 × 28, 86 is between 80 and 90, but 28 is very close to 30. Round 86 down to 80 and 28 up to 30. The estimate of 2400 is only slightly off from the actual product of 2408. See Figure 12.21(c) for another example.
Compatible Numbers	• This method refers to changing the number to one that would make the problem easier to compute mentally. This strategy is usually used in division by adjusting the divisor or dividend (or both) to close numbers. Many percent, fraction, and rate situations involve division, and the compatible numbers strategy is quite useful.	• 413 × 24 can be thought of as 400 × 25. Because 4 × 25 equals 100, a good estimate is 10,000. • 497 ÷ 48 is approximately 500 ÷ 50, so 10 is a reasonable estimate. • See other examples in Figure 12.22.

| 400 | 463 | 500 |

FIGURE 12.20   An empty number line can be labeled in different ways to help students round numbers for estimation.

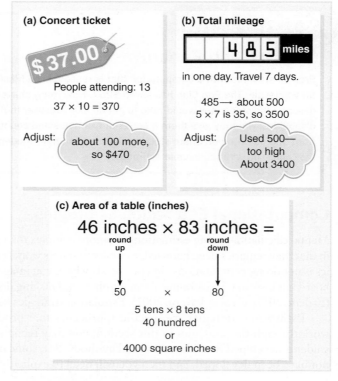

(a) Concert ticket

$37.00

People attending: 13

37 × 10 = 370

Adjust: about 100 more, so $470

(b) Total mileage

4 8 5 miles

in one day. Travel 7 days.

485 → about 500
5 × 7 is 35, so 3500

Adjust: Used 500— too high About 3400

(c) Area of a table (inches)

46 inches × 83 inches =

round up   round down

50   ×   80

5 tens × 8 tens
40 hundred
or
4000 square inches

FIGURE 12.21   Rounding in multiplication.

FORMATIVE ASSESSMENT Notes. Teachers often wonder how they can assess computational estimation so that they can identify if students are computing on paper and then just rounding the answer to make it look like an estimate. One method is to prepare performance-based tasks that include about three estimation exercises for display on a projection device. Briefly show one exercise at a time, perhaps for 20 seconds, depending on the task. Students write their estimate immediately and indicate whether they think their estimate is "low" or "high"—that is, lower or higher than the exact computation. They are not to do any written computation. Continue until you are finished. Then show all the exercises and have students write down how they did each estimate. They should indicate why they think the estimate was reasonable or not. By only doing a few estimates but having the students reflect on them in this way, you receive more information than you would with just the answers to a longer list. ■

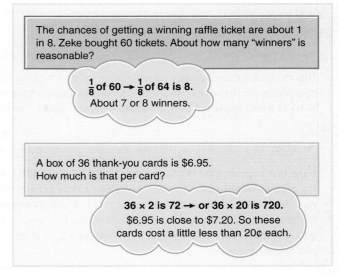

> The chances of getting a winning raffle ticket are about 1 in 8. Zeke bought 60 tickets. About how many "winners" is reasonable?

> $\frac{1}{8}$ of 60 → $\frac{1}{8}$ of 64 is 8.
> About 7 or 8 winners.

> A box of 36 thank-you cards is $6.95. How much is that per card?

> 36 × 2 is 72 → or 36 × 20 is 720.
> $6.95 is close to $7.20. So these cards cost a little less than 20¢ each.

FIGURE 12.22   Using compatible numbers in division.

Activity 12.7   CCSS-M: 4.NBT.A.3; 4.NBT.B.5

What Was Your Method?

Select a problem with an estimation given. For example, say, "Juan estimated that 139 × 43 is about 6000. How do you think he came up with 6000? Was that a good approach? Is the estimate larger or smaller than the actual answer, and how do you know? How should it be adjusted? Why might someone select 150 instead of 140 as a substitute for 139?" Almost every estimate can involve different choices and methods. Alternatives make for good discussion points, helping students see different methods and learn that there is no single correct estimate.

 **Standards for Mathematical Practice**
MP2. Reason abstractly and quantitatively.

Activity 12.8   CCSS-M: 4.NBT.B.5; 4.NBT.A.3

Jump to It

Students begin with a start number and use mental estimation to find how many times they will need to multiply that start number (estimate of jumps) to reach the goal (going over or under the amount). The numbers can be differentiated to meet the needs and experiences of your students, use the Jump to It Activity Page or use these to get you started:

STUDENTS with SPECIAL NEEDS

Jump Number	Goal	Estimate of Jumps	Was Estimate Reasonable?
5	72		
11	97		
7	150		
14	135		
47	1200		

To check estimates on the calculator, students can enter 0 ⊞ [jump number] and press ⊟ once for every estimated jump, or multiply [jump number] ⊠ [estimate of jumps]. Students with disabilities may need to have a number line close by. Then they can mark their goal number with a sticky dot and use another color dot to mark their first estimate. This strategy will support them in the process of deciding whether they need to increase or decrease their estimation of the number of jumps.

MyLab Education   Activity Page: Jump to It

Activity 12.9   CCSS-M: 4.NBT.B.5

Hit the Target

This calculator game focuses on estimation using any of the four operations. First, pick a start number and an operation. Pairs of students (or the whole class with a projection device) take turns entering the start number, ⊠ a number of choice, and ⊟ to try to make the result land in the stated target range. The following example for multiplication illustrates the activity:

Start Number: 17

Target: 800 − 830

If the first number tried is 25, pressing 17 ⊠ 25 gives 425, which is not in the target range. Then the calculator is passed to the partner, who clears the screen and picks a different number—for example, a number close to 50 because the first product was about half of numbers in the target range. A second estimate might be 17 ⊠ 45, or 765 which is closer, but still not in the target range. The calculator goes back to the first person. Continue to clear each estimate and try again until someone gets a product that hits the target range. Figure 12.23 gives examples for all four operations. Prepare a list of start numbers and target ranges.

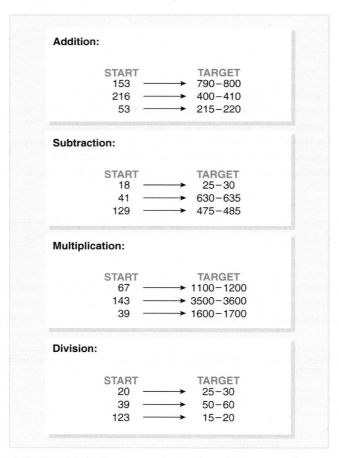

FIGURE 12.23   Possible starting numbers and targets for the Hit the Target game.

Explore common student challenges and misconceptions in Table 12.2 to support your lesson planning and help you interpret what students are thinking.

MyLab Education   Self-Check 12.5

MyLab Education   **Math Practice:** Need to practice or refresh your math content knowledge? Click to access practice exercises associated with the content from this chapter.

TABLE 12.2   COMMON CHALLENGES AND MISCONCEPTIONS RELATED TO MULTIPLICATION AND DIVISION COMPUTATION

Common Challenge or Misconception	What It Looks Like	How to Help

1. When multiplying students ignore internal zeros.	When students are given the problem:
	
	   4005
	  × 9
	  3645
	
	The student just writes the products of 9 × 5 and then 9 × 4, ignoring the multiplications of 0 tens and 0 hundreds.
		• Focus on the meaning of a zero in any number by starting with a number like 4005 and asking how that would be shown with materials. Explicitly discuss the role of a 0 in the number.
		• Never refer to 0 as a "placeholder." This terminology gives the impression that it is not a numerical value and it is there just as a way to fill a space.
		• Discuss whether this answer is reasonable by thinking about 4000 × 10.

2. Students use an approach that mimics addition by considering the tens and ones separately.	When multiplying 28 × 36, the student calculates 20 × 30 and then adds to that product 8 × 6.	• Return to direct modeling using an array. Work back to show the links between the distributive property of multiplication over addition including the listing of the partial products. Then return to their work and ask the student to show where the partial products they calculated are found in the array. What's missing?

3. Students misinterpret the regrouped number in a multiplication problem.	When students are given the problem:
	
	    3
	   37
	  × 5
	  305
	
	The student uses the regrouped 3 above the tens column by adding it before they multiply. So instead of multiplying 5 × 7 and then 5 × 30, the student is multiplying 5 × 7, adding the 3 to the "3" in the tens column and then multiplying 5 × 60, for an answer of 305.
		• Go back to the base-ten materials and use an area model to show what the partial products look like. Then consider using the open array model so the actual amounts the student should be multiplying are apparent.
		• Have the student move away from just using the algorithm until he or she can explain it.

4. Students misuse the distributive property in division.	Students solving 95 ÷ 16 broke the problem into 95 ÷ 10 + 95 ÷ 6. Students thought that when using the distributive property, you can break apart the divisor, when instead you need to decompose the dividend into components.	• Go back to using smaller numbers and show with paper plates to represent the groups—that the number of groups remains stable, it is the quantity of items that need to be "distributed equally" that can be broken up into different collections to reach the correct answer. • This misconception can be persistent so be ready for it by presenting the possible confusion early for class discussion. Don't wait for students to demonstrate this misunderstanding.
5. When dividing students ignore internal zeros.	When students given the problem: 8002 ÷ 2 they will say the answer equals 41.	• Have students estimate the answer before starting—will the answer be in the tens? Hundreds? Thousands? • Start with a smaller number such as 202 ÷ 2 and model the problem with base-ten materials and two paper plates. Then link the action to the algorithm.

RESOURCES FOR CHAPTER 12

LITERATURE CONNECTIONS

Literature often provides excellent contexts for computation and estimates, as in the following two engaging examples.

Is a Blue Whale the Biggest Thing There Is?

Wells (2005)

This intriguing book is about large objects and large distances. Blue whales look small next to Mount Everest, which in turn looks small next to the earth. The data in the book allow students to make other comparisons, such as the number of fourth-grade students who would have the same weight or volume as a blue whale or would fill the gymnasium. These comparisons are perfect opportunities for estimations and discussions about how much precision is necessary to make a meaningful comparison.

Counting on Frank

Clement (1991)

This book's narrator uses his dog, Frank, as a counting reference. For example, he explains that 24 Franks would fit in his bedroom. Because the book offers approximations, there are limitless opportunities to do computational estimation. For example, how many Franks would fit in five rooms? If there were 24 Franks, how many cans of dog food (discussed in the book) might be knocked over? The back of the book offers a helpful series of estimation questions.

RECOMMENDED READINGS

Articles

Benson, C., Wall, J., & Malm, C. (2013). The distributive property in grade 3? *Teaching Children Mathematics, 19*(8), 498–506.

Don't let the title influence you; this article is not just for those who work with third graders! The focus is on linking the numerical and geometrical interpretations of multiplication through the connection with the distributive property. Through a collection of visual representations using area of rectangular regions, the authors move students from what they know to what they don't know while building their understanding of the power of the distributive property.

Books

Fosnot, C. T., & Dolk, M. (2001). *Young mathematicians at work: Constructing multiplication and division.* Portsmouth, NH: Heinemann.

This book examines how students learn multiplication and division and how to support that learning. The authors show students' work constructing ideas about number, operations, and computation in ways not found elsewhere.

Algebraic Thinking, Equations, and Functions

LEARNER OUTCOMES

After reading this chapter and engaging in the embedded activities and reflections, you should be able to:

13.1 Describe ways to connect number and algebraic thinking, including using properties of the operations to build number sense and procedural fluency.

13.2 Illustrate and describe how to infuse teaching of patterns and functions in K–8.

13.3 Identify strategies that can builds strong understanding of equivalence, recognizing the challenges students have with symbols (e.g., equal and inequalities signs and variables).

13.4 Define mathematical modeling and describe grade-appropriate examples of it.

Algebraic thinking begins in Kindergarten as young students "represent addition and subtraction with objects, fingers, mental images, drawings, sounds (e.g., claps), acting out situations, verbal explanations, expressions, or equations" (NGA Center & CCSSO, 2010, p. 11). Elementary students are capable of understanding and applying significant algebra ideas (Blanton et al., 2015a, 2015b). This includes strong connections between arithmetic and algebra. In middle school, students begin to study algebra in more abstract and symbolic ways, focusing on understanding and using variables, expressions, and equations. CCSS-M introduces functions as a domain in grade 8, but functional thinking begins in the early grades as students consider situations that co-vary, such as the relationship between number of T-shirts purchased and the cost of those T-shirts. Algebraic thinking is present across content areas and is central to mathematical reasoning.

BIG IDEAS

♦ Algebra is a useful tool for generalizing arithmetic and representing patterns in our world. Explaining the regularities and consistencies across many problems gives students the chance to generalize.

♦ The methods we use to compute and the structures in our number system can and should be explored. For example, the generalization that $a + b = b + a$ tells us that $83 + 27 = 27 + 83$ without the need to compute the sums on each side of the equal sign.

- Functions describe relationships between two things that vary. Understanding functions is strengthened when they are explored across representations (e.g., equations, tables, and graphs).

- Symbols, especially those involving equality and variables, must be well understood conceptually for students to be successful in mathematics.

- Mathematical modeling is the process of using mathematics to analyze and provide insight into real-world issues, dilemmas, and other phenomena.

 # Strands of Algebraic Thinking

It is human to try to make sense of the world (and to see how things are related) (Fosnot & Jacob, 2010). Algebraic thinking is used to generalize arithmetic, to notice patterns that hold true in algorithms and with properties, and to reason quantitatively about such things as whether expressions are equivalent or not. Algebra must be presented in a way that students see it is a useful tool for making sense of all areas of mathematics and real-world situations.

Algebraic thinking involves forming generalizations from experiences with number and computation and formalizing these ideas with the use of a meaningful symbol system. Far from being a topic with little real-world use, algebraic thinking pervades all of mathematics and is essential for making mathematics useful in daily life.

Researchers suggest three strands of algebraic reasoning, all infusing the central notions of generalization and symbolization (Blanton, 2008; Kaput, 2008). We use these themes to organize this chapter as illustrated here (section headers in parenthesis):

1. The study of structures in the number system, including those arising in arithmetic. (Connecting Number and Algebra and Properties of the Operations)
2. The study of patterns, relations, and functions (Patterns and Functions).
3. The process of mathematical modeling (Meaningful Use of Symbols and Mathematical Modeling)

In each section we share how these strands develop across grades K–8.

 # Connecting Number and Algebra

Algebra is often referred to as generalized arithmetic. For students to generalize an operation or pattern, they must look at several examples and notice what is happening across the problems, gaining insights into the structure of the number system. Looking for structure can and should be a daily part of learning about number. Here we share several ways to connect arithmetic to algebra.

Number Combinations

Looking for generalizations in sets of problems can begin in kindergarten with decomposing numbers and continue through the early grades as students use strategies to add and subtract. The following task, based on Neagoy (2012), uses the context of birds to focus on decomposing numbers.

Seven birds have landed in your backyard, some landed on a tree, and some are at your feeder. How many birds might be in the tree and how many at the feeder?

Students can be given ten frames to illustrate each possibility, and write the corresponding equation. Seeing the visual and the equation can help students recognize the commutative property (Billings, 2017). The data can also be recorded and analyzed in a table (see Birds in the Backyard Activity Page). For a different context, use Frogs on the Pond Activity Page.

In CCSS-M variables are introduced in grade 3 and 4 as students solve for missing unknowns, and are emphasized across grades 6–8 in the Expressions and Equations Domain. For example, in the Birds in the Backyard problem, after students answer the questions in the Pause & Reflect, ask "If I have t birds in the tree, how might you describe how many birds are at the feeder?" Students might answer, "Seven minus t." Write $7 - t$. If the students answer "f" (for the variable to represent the number of birds at the feeder), then ask how t and f are related in an equation. Three equations describe this situation: $t + f = 7$, $7 - f = t$, and $7 - t = f$.

Standards for Mathematical Practice
MP4. Model with mathematics.

MyLab Education	Activity Page: Birds in the Backyard
MyLab Education	Activity Page: Frogs on the Pond

Place-Value Relationships

Fundamental to mental mathematics is applying place-value concepts – the way the number system is structured. Consider the sum $49 + 18$. How would you add it in your head? Many people will take one from the 18 and move it to the 49 to create the equivalent expression $50 + 17$ (or move two the other direction to get $47 + 20$). Many of these strategies have been addressed in the previous four chapters.

The Hundreds Chart helps students to notice the relationship between tens and ones. Ask students, "What did we add to get from 72 to 82? From 5 to 15? From 34 to 44?" Students notice across these examples (and more like them) that they are adding 10 and moving down exactly one row. Also, consider using a Bottom-Up Hundreds Chart, because it counts up, rather than down, thereby matching the language of the chart and the language of the operations (e.g., moving up 10 on the chart is an increase of 10) (Bay-Williams & Fletcher, 2017). Moves on the hundreds chart can be represented with arrows (for example, → means right one column or plus 1, and ↑ means up one row or less 10). Consider asking children to complete these problems:

14 →→←←   63 ↑↑↓↓   45 →↑←↓

Some students may count up or back using a count-by-ones approach. Others may jump 10 or 1 (up or down). Still others may recognize that a downward arrow "undoes" an upward arrow– an indication that these children are moving toward generalizations (Blanton, 2008). In other words, they recognize that $+10$ and -10 results in a zero change. Students can also write the equations for the arrow moves with numbers or with variables—for example, for the first problem, $n + 1 + 1 - 1 - 1 = n + (1 - 1) + (1 - 1) = n$. The more variables and numbers are used in looking at generalizations, the better able students become at using symbols.

MyLab Education	Blackline Master: Hundreds Chart
MyLab Education	Activity Page: Bottom-Up Hundreds Chart

FORMATIVE ASSESSMENT Notes. As students work on such tasks, observe using a checklist, noting which students are solving by counting by ones, by jumping, or by noticing the "doing" and "undoing." What you observe can help you sequence the sharing in a classroom discussion by first sharing the more basic strategies and then have students who have generalized the situation share their thinking. ■

Activity 13.1 provides an engaging context for students to explore patterns involving place value and addition.

Activity 13.1

STUDENTS
with
SPECIAL
NEEDS

CCSS-M: 1.NBT.C.4; 2.NBT.B.9; 3.OA.D.9

Diagonal Sums

Provide each student with a hard copy of a Hundreds Chart or a Bottom-Up Hundreds Chart (Counts up, rather than down so that an increase is a move up on the chart). Students select any four numbers in the hundreds chart that form a square. Ask students to add the two numbers on each diagonal as in the example shown here. For younger students or students with special needs, use calculators so that they can explore the pattern without getting bogged down in computations.

23	24
13	14

Have students share their diagonal sums with a partner. Compare what happened. Together invite students to find another square. Allow time for each pair to share why the pattern works. To extend this activity, use diagonals of rectangles; for example, the numbers 15, 19, 75, and 79.

MyLab Education **Blackline Master: Hundreds Chart**
MyLab Education **Activity Page: Bottom-Up Hundreds Chart**

  Standards for Mathematical Practice
MP7. Look for and make use of structure.

⏸ Pause & Reflect

Before reading further, stop and explore why the diagonal sums described in the previous activities are the same. What questions might you ask students to be sure they are noticing the relationship between tens and ones? ●

Here are some additional tasks you might explore on a Hundreds Chart or Bottom-Up Hundreds Chart. With each one, notice how the first aspect of the task is about number and the latter questions focus on generalizations (algebraic thinking).

- Pick a number. Move down two and over one. What is the relationship between the original number and the new number? What algebraic expression describes this move?
- Pick a number. Add it to the number to its left and to its right. Divide by 3. What answer do you get? Can you explain why this works? Can you explain using variables?
- Skip count by different values (e.g., 2, 4, 5). Which numbers make diagonal patterns? Which make column patterns? What is true about all numbers that make a column pattern?
- Find two skip-count numbers in which one number lands "on top of" the other (that is, all of the shaded values for one pattern are part of the shaded values for the other)? How are these two skip-count numbers related?

Asking questions such as "When will this be true?" and "Why does this work?" requires children to generalize and consequently, strengthen their understanding of the number concepts they are learning.

MyLab Education **Blackline Master: Hundreds Chart**
MyLab Education **Activity Page: Bottom-Up Hundreds Chart**

Algorithms

When studying the operations, students are often asked to explain how they solved a problem, for example, 504−198. As you listen to students' strategies, record their ideas using symbols. For this problem, you might record a student's mental strategy like this: 504 − 200 + 2. Ask, "Does this show how you solved it?" or "Is this equivalent to the original expression?" Such questions to the class can lead to rich discussions about the properties (Blanton et al., 2011).

Slight shifts in how arithmetic problems are presented can open up opportunities for generalizations (Blanton, 2008). For example, instead of a series of unrelated computation problems, consider a list that can lead to a discussion of a generalization:

$$3 \times 7 = ? \qquad 6 \times 7 = ?$$

In discussing the relationship, students notice that 6 is twice 3 and therefore the answer is twice as much. This strategy can be applied to any of the × 6 basic facts, helping students with what is often some of the more challenging facts to learn.

Sets of problems are good ways for students to look for and describe patterns across the problems, patterns that build an understanding for the operation and related algorithms:

$$\frac{1}{2} \times 12 = \qquad \frac{1}{4} \times 12 = \qquad \frac{1}{8} \times 12 = \qquad \frac{3}{4} \times 12 = \qquad \frac{3}{8} \times 12 =$$

Once students have solved sets of related problems, focus attention on what you want students to generalize:

What do you notice across the problems?

Why is it true?

When will this pattern be true?

In this set of problems, such a discussion can help students understand the relationship between the numerator and the denominator and what that means in multiplication situations.

CCSS Standards for Mathematical Practice

MP8. Look for and express regularity in repeated reasoning.

Properties of the Operations

The properties are essential to computation (Blanton, Levi, Crites, & Dougherty, 2011). Table 13.1 provides a list of the ones students must know, including how students might describe the property. In the CCSS-M, properties of the operations are one of the only topics mentioned in each grade 1 through 8. Importantly, the emphasis is on *using* and *applying* the properties, however, instruction and textbooks have traditionally focused *identifying* which property is reflected in an equation. That is not sufficient and should not be the focus of your instruction. Instead, focus on helping students recognize and use them to generate equivalent expressions in order to solve problems efficiently and flexibly. The properties of the operations have been discussed in several chapters in this book, as you have explored basic facts and the operations. In this chapter we highlight how to emphasize the properties, and in turn, help students notice structure in the number system.

Making Sense of Properties

Students need to notice equivalent expressions as they engage in their work with numbers. For example, consider a Number Talk with young children, where the teacher asks students to tell

TABLE 13.1 PROPERTIES OF THE NUMBER SYSTEM

Properties of the Operations		
Name of Property	Symbolic Representation	How a Student Might Describe the Pattern or Structure
Addition		
Commutative	$a + b = b + a$	"When you add two numbers in any order you will get the same answer."
Associative	$(a + b) + c = a + (b + c)$	"When you add three numbers you can add the first two and then add the third or add the last two numbers and then add the first number. Either way you will get the same answer."
Additive Identity	$a + 0 = 0 + a = a$	"When you add zero to any number you get the same number you started with."
	$a - 0 = a$	"When you subtract zero from any number you get the number you started with."
Additive Inverse	$a - a = a + (-a) = 0$	"When you subtract a number from itself you get zero."
Inverse Relationship of Addition and Subtraction	If $a + b = c$ then $c - b = a$ and $c - a = b$	"When you have a subtraction problem you can 'think addition' by using the inverse."
Multiplication		
Commutative	$a \times b = b \times a$	"When you multiply two numbers in any order you will get the same answer."
Associative	$(a \times b) \times c = a \times (b \times c)$	"When you multiply three numbers you can multiply the first two and then multiply the answer by the third or multiply the last two numbers and then multiply the answer by the first number. Either way you will get the same answer."
Multiplicative Identity	$a \times 1 = 1 \times a = a$	"When you multiply one by any number you get the same number you started with."
Multiplicative Inverse	$a \times \dfrac{1}{a} = \dfrac{1}{a} \times a = 1$	"When you multiply a number by its reciprocal, you will get one."
Inverse Relationship of Multiplication and Division	If $a \times b = c$ then $c \div b = a$ and $c \div a = b$	"When you have a division problem you can 'think multiplication' by using the inverse."
Distributive (Multiplication over Addition)	$a \times (b + c) = a \times b + a \times c$	"When you multiply two numbers, you can split one number into two parts (7 can be 2 + 5), multiply each part by the other number, and then add them together."

if $3 + 7 = 7 + 3$. A student might explain that both sides add to 10 so they are equal. Another student might say, "I just knew they were equal without adding. Its like carrots on two plates—if you switch the two plates, you still have the same number of carrots." This latter student is *applying* the commutative property of addition. To ensure the property is generalized, the teacher asks students to write it using variables (e.g., $a + b = b + a$). This makes the connection from number to algebra explicit. Using variables can be used and understood as early as first grade (Blanton et al., 2011; Carpenter, Franke, & Levi, 2003). This idea can be extended to equations such as $394 + 176 = n + 394$, which would be laborious to solve by doing the arithmetic.

Just as sets of tasks can be used to generalize an algorithm, sets of tasks can be used to focus on the properties, as illustrated in these two sets of problems:

Set 1:	35	52	23	46
	$\times 52$	$\times 35$	$\times 46$	$\times 23$

Set 2:	$\dfrac{1}{6} \times 12 =$	$12 \times \dfrac{1}{6} =$	$\dfrac{2}{3} \times 12 =$	$12 \times \dfrac{2}{3} =$

Although students may understand the commutative property of multiplication with whole numbers, they may not recognize that the property also applies to fractions (in fact, all real numbers). Ask students "Is this true for fractions?" "Is it true for other types of numbers?" "All numbers?" Activity 13.2 provides a creative way for students to understand the identity for addition and/or multiplication, as well as other properties.

Activity 13.2
CCSS-M: 1.OA.B.3; 1.OA.C.6; 1.OA.D.7; 2.OA.B.2; 3.OA.D.9

Five Ways to Zero

Place students in partners. Give each pair a number (you can use a deck of cards). If they get a 7, they are to write 5 different ways to get to 0 using number sentences. For example, they could write $7 - 5 - 2 = 0$ or it could be $7 + 3 - 10 = 0$. Be sure students are using correct notation and grouping so that their statements are true. Use counters or a number line to explore and illustrate the possibilities. Ask students to describe what they notice about their equations, looking for generalizable ideas such as inverse relationships, additive identity and commutative property of addition.

Discussing problem sets such as these, and others, helps students to make sense of the properties. In this first grade vignette, the teacher is helping students to reason about the commutative property.

> **Teacher:** [*Pointing at* $5 + 3 = 3 + 5$ *on the board.*] Is it true or false?
> **Carmen:** True, because $5 + 3$ is 8 and $3 + 5$ is 8.
> **Andy:** There is a 5 on both sides and a 3 on both sides and nothing else.
> **Teacher:** [*Writing* $6 + 9 = 9 + 6$ *on the board.*] True or false?
> **Class:** True! It's the same!
> **Teacher:** [*Writing* $25 + 48 = 48 + 25$ *on the board.*] True or false?
> **Children:** True!
> **Teacher:** Who can describe what is going on with these examples?
> **Rene:** If you have the same numbers on each side, you get the same thing.
> **Teacher:** Does it matter what numbers I use?
> **Class:** No
> **Teacher:** [*Writing* $a + 7 = 7 + a$ *on the board.*] What is a?
> **Michael:** It can be any number because it's on both sides.
> **Teacher:** [*Writing* $a + b = b + a$ *on the board.*] What are a and b?
> **Children:** Any number!

CCSS Standards for Mathematical Practice
MP7. Look for and make use of structure.

Notice how the teacher is developing the commutative property of addition in a conceptual manner—focusing on generalizing, not on memorizing.

The structure of numbers can also be illustrated geometrically. For example, 8×43 can be illustrated as a rectangular array. That rectangle can be partitioned [symbolically this is $8(40 + 3)$] and then represented as two rectangles [e.g., $(8 \times 40) + (8 \times 3)$], preserving the quantity:

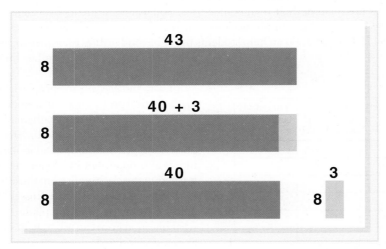

Challenge students to think about this idea *in general*. This may be described in words (at first) and then as symbols: $a \times b = (c \times b) + (d \times b)$, where $c + d = a$. Be sure students can connect the examples to general ideas and the general ideas back to examples. This is the distributive property, and it is perhaps the most important central idea in arithmetic (Goldenberg, Mark, & Cuoco, 2010).

Applying the Properties of Addition and Multiplication

Noticing generalizable properties and attempting to prove that they are true is a significant form of algebraic reasoning and is at the heart of what it means to do mathematics (Ball & Bass, 2003; Carpenter et al., 2003; Schifter, Monk, Russell, & Bastable, 2007).

Odd and even numbers provide an excellent context for exploring structure of the number system (Stephens, Blanton, Knuth, Isler, & Gardiner, 2015). Ask students to explore different numbers, finding how many pairs and how many leftovers. Students can use manipulatives such as connecting cubes (Figure 13.1[a]) and record data in a table (Figure 13.1[b]) to generalize what makes a number even or odd. Next, students can explore sums of even and odd numbers, using cubes, tables, or technology.

 Standards for Mathematical Practice

MP7. Look for and make use of structure.

Activity 13.3

CCSS-M: 1.OA.B.3; 2.OA.C.3; 2.NBT.B.5; 3.OA.D.9

Broken Calculator: Can You Fix It?

Distribute calculators to every student. In partners, have students select one of these two problems to explore. They must decide if it is possible, share an example of how to do it (if it is possible), and finally prepare a justification or illustration to describe why it does or doesn't work (in general).

1. If you cannot use any of the even keys (0, 2, 4, 6, 8), can you create an even number in the calculator display? If so, how?
2. If you cannot use any of the odd keys (1, 3, 5, 7, 9), can you create an odd number in the calculator display? If so, how?

Invite early finishers to take on the other problem or to write their justifications using variables.

❚❚ Pause & Reflect

Decide if these statements are always, sometimes, or never true:

● Adding three consecutive numbers is the same as multiplying the middle number by 3.
● One-half is greater than one-fourth. ●

 Standards for Mathematical Practice

MP3. Construct viable arguments and critique the reasoning of others.

Asking students if a statement is always, sometimes or never true, develops their skills at justification and applying properties, as well as takes on misconceptions they might have (Muir, 2015). Examples like the two here, can be an excellent Number Talk, and can establish a culture where students are making their own conjectures. Sometimes students overgeneralize, thinking something is always true simply because it is true for the cases they have tested (Yopp & Ellsworth, 2017). Conjectures can help students move beyond testing examples to proving using geometric illustrations, number lines, pictures, or variables.

Using and *applying* the properties is central to mathematical proficiency—it is emphasized in the CCSS-M content and the mathematical practices (NGA Center & CCSSO, 2010). An explicit focus on seeking generalizations and looking for structure is also important in supporting the range of learners in the classroom, from those who struggle to those who excel (Schifter, Russell, & Bastable, 2009). Doing so requires planning—deciding what questions you can ask to help students think about generalized characteristics—across the mathematical strands (not just when they are in an "algebra" unit).

Six cubes shared with two people

Nine cubes shared with two people

Extra →

(a) Sharing cubes fairly with two people

Number	Number of pairs I can Make	Number of Leftovers
4		
6		
9		
10		
11		
12		

(b) Exploring pairs of numbers and their left-overs.

FIGURE 13.1 Exploring odd and even numbers to generalize mathematical relationships.

MyLab Education   Self-Check 13.1

Activity 13.4

CCSS-M: 1.OA.B.3;
2.NBT.B.9; 3.OA.B.5;
5.OA.A.1

ENGLISH LEARNERS

Convince Me Conjectures

To begin, offer students a conjecture to explore (see Conjecture Cards Activity Page or Conjecture Cards for K–2 Activity Page). For example:

STUDENTS with SPECIAL NEEDS

Conjecture: For a multiplication problem, you can take half of one factor and double the other factor and you will get the same product.

Ask students to (1) test examples to see if they think it is always true, and (2) prove or disprove it, preparing a visual or explanation to support their argument (see Figure 13.2). Ask students how they might write the conjecture in symbols. All students, particularly ELs, benefit from "revoicing" of ideas and precise language during discussions. Students with disabilities benefit from the presentation and discussion of counterexamples.

MyLab Education   Activity Page: Conjecture Cards

MyLab Education   Activity Page: Conjecture Cards for K–2

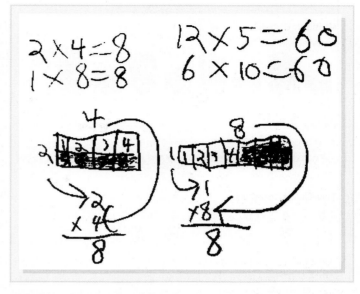

FIGURE 13.2   A student justifies a conjecture.

CCSS Standards for Mathematical Practice

MP8. Look for and express regularity in repeated reasoning.

Study of Patterns and Functions

Patterns are found in all areas of mathematics. Learning to look for patterns and how to describe, translate, and extend them is part of thinking algebraically. Two of the eight mathematical practices begin with the phrase "look for," implying that students who are mathematically proficient pay attention to patterns as they do mathematics (See Appendix A). Functional thinking begins in preK–2 when students make observations like, "Each person we add to the group we add 2 more feet" (Blanton et al., 2011). Let's look at a modified version of the Birds in the Backyard problem:

MyLab Education   Activity Page: Birds in the Backyard

Five birds have landed in your backyard, some at the feeder and some in the tree. How many ways might the birds be in the tree and at the feeder?

There are 6 ways for 5 birds to be in the tree and at the feeder, 8 ways for 7 birds, and 11 ways for 10 birds. Upper elementary and middle school students should be able to explain why this is the case: For any number of birds (n), there are $n + 1$ ways because there can be 0, 1, 2, n birds at the feeder. Using a problem that is concrete and that begins with listing numeric possibilities is

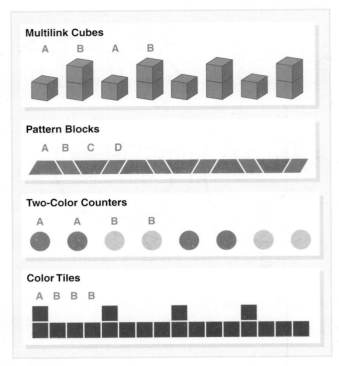

FIGURE 13.3 Examples of repeating patterns with various manipulatives.

a way to help students learn to generalize a pattern. To extend the discussion, ask students questions such as these: "What if there were 340 birds? Would the rule still hold? If there were 20 different ways in which the birds could be in the backyard, how many birds are there? Is there a rule for that?"

Repeating Patterns

Repeating patterns are those patterns that have a core that repeats. For example, red-blue could the core and a string of beads continues to repeat this pattern: red-blue-red-blue-red. . . . Repeating patterns are not mentioned specifically in the CCSS-M, but are a building block to early equations and expressions (Confrey et al., 2012). Non-number patterns can build a foundation for later noticing numeric patterns. Physical materials provide a trial-and-error approach and allow patterns to be extended beyond the few spaces provided on a page. By using a variety of materials such as colored blocks, buttons, and connecting cubes to create and extend their patterns, students begin to generalize ideas of patterns. These can be recorded symbolically, for example red-blue is an AB pattern because the core has two different elements, A and B. Figure 13.3 provides some illustrations.

An important concept in working with repeating patterns is for students to identify the *core* of the pattern (Warren & Cooper, 2008). One possible way to emphasize the core is to place shape patterns under a document camera, say aloud what is there and ask what comes next. After a few add-ons, ask students what the pattern is. Label the pattern with letters (i.e., an ABC pattern has three different shapes that repeat).

Repeating patterns are everywhere! The seasons, days of the week, and months of the year are just a beginning. Ask students to think of real-life AB patterns—for example, "to school, home from school" or "set table before eating, clear table after eating." Children's books often have patterns in repeating rhymes, words, or phrases, for example *Pattern Fish* (Harris, 2000). A very long repeating pattern can be found in *If You Give a Mouse a Cookie* (Numeroff, 1985) (or any of this series), in which each event eventually leads back to giving a mouse a cookie, with the implication that the sequence would be repeated.

> **TECHNOLOGY Note.** There are numerous web sites for exploring repeating patterns. For example, NLVM has several explorations with repeating (and growing) patterns, including Attribute Trains, Block Patterns, Color Patterns, Pattern Blocks, and Space Blocks. ∎

Oral patterns can be recited. For example, "do, mi, mi, do, mi, mi" (ABB) is a simple singing pattern. Body movements such as waving the arm up, down, and sideways can make patterns: up, side, side, down, up, side, side, down (ABBC). Repeating patterns can be used to strengthen students understanding of number, for example multiples, as in Activity 13.5.

Activity 13.5   CCSS-M: 2.OA.C.3; 4.OA.A.3, 4.OA.B.4

Predict Down the Line

Provide students with a pattern to extend (e.g., ABC pattern made with colored links). Before students begin to extend the pattern, have them predict exactly what elements (links) will be in, say, the twelfth position. (Notice that in an ABC pattern the third, sixth, ninth, and twelfth terms are the C element because they are multiples of 3.) After students predict, have them complete the pattern to check. Ask students to justify how they decided what shape goes in that position. Note that this also connects to division with remainders. To find the 100th term for ABC pattern, a student thinks that all multiples of 3 are the C shape, so a remainder of 1 would be the A shape.

A real-world context for repeating patterns is the Olympics (Bay-Williams & Martinie, 2004b). The Summer Olympics are held in 2020, 2024, and every four years after that (4*n*) and the Winter Olympics in 2022, 2024, and so on (4*n* + 2). Naming hurricanes is also a repeating pattern (Fernandez & Schoen, 2008).

Standards for Mathematical Practice
MP4. Model with mathematics.

Activity 13.6   CSSS-M: 4.OA.A.3; 4.OA.B.4; 5.OA.B.3; 6.EE.B.2a

Hurricane Names

Hurricanes are named such that the first one of the year has a name starting with A, then B, and so on. For each letter, there are six names in a six-year cycle (except those that are retired when a major hurricane has that name). The gender of the names alternate in an AB pattern. Invite students to select a letter of the alphabet and look up the list of six names. Ask students to answer questions such as these (assume the names do not get retired):

- What years will the hurricanes be the first name on the list? The last name? A girl's name?
- What will the hurricane's name be in the year 2020? 2025? 2050?
- How can you describe in words and symbols the name of a hurricane, given the year?

Growing Patterns

Beginning in the primary grades and extending through the middle school years, students can explore patterns that involve a progression from step to step. These are called sequences or growing patterns. With growing patterns, the focus is analyzing how the pattern is changing with each new element in the pattern. Figure 13.4(a) is a growing pattern in which design 1 requires three triangles, design 2 requires six triangles, and so on. Growing patterns are functions—the number of triangles needed is a function of which design it is (in this case, number of triangles = 3 × design number).

Geometric growing patterns make good exemplars because the pattern is visible in the shapes and students can manipulate the objects. Figure 13.4 shows three different growing patterns, though the possibilities for visuals and patterns are endless. The questions in Activity 13.7, mapped to the pattern in Figure 13.4(a), can be adapted to any growing pattern and help students begin to reason about functional situations.

Analyzing Growing Patterns should include the developmental progression of reasoning by looking at the visuals, then reasoning about the numerical relationships, and then extending to a larger (or *n*th) case (Friel & Markworth, 2009). Students' experiences with growing patterns should start with fairly straightforward patterns (such as in Figure 13.4) and continue with patterns that are more complicated (such as the Dot Pattern in Figure 13.5).

MyLab Education
Video Example: 13.1
This video illustrates strategies to help students figure out how the pattern is growing.

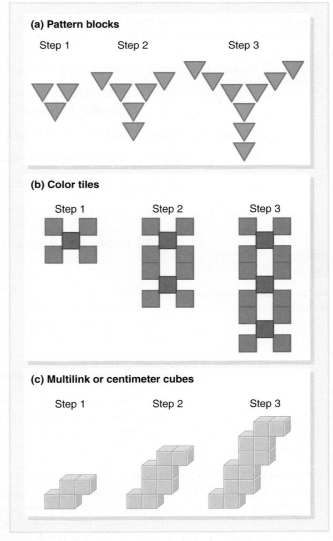

FIGURE 13.4   Geometric growing patterns using manipulatives.

Activity 13.7

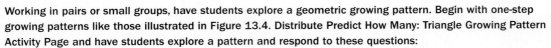

CCSS-M: 5.OA.B.3; 6.EE.C.9; 7.EE.B.4a; 8.F.A.1

Predict How Many

ENGLISH LEARNERS

Working in pairs or small groups, have students explore a geometric growing pattern. Begin with one-step growing patterns like those illustrated in Figure 13.4. Distribute Predict How Many: Triangle Growing Pattern Activity Page and have students explore a pattern and respond to these questions:

- Complete a table that shows the number of triangles for each step.

Step Number	1	2	3	4	5	10	20
Number of Triangles (Element)							

- How many triangles are needed for step 10? Step 20? Step 100? Explain your reasoning.
- Write a rule (in words) that gives the total number of pieces to build any step number.
- Write a rule in symbols using the variable *n* for step number.

Keep in mind that ELs need clarification on the specialized meanings of *step* and *table* because these words mean something else outside of mathematics. See Expanded Lesson: Exploring Functions through Geometric Growing Patterns for more details. For a two-step pattern, try Predict How Many: Windows. For a greater challenge, try Predict How Many: Dot Arrays. If you select two or more of the Predict How Many Activity Pages, students can compare these functions (the first is linear in the form $y = mx$ the second is linear in the form $y = mx + b$, and the third is quadratic).

MyLab Education   **Activity Page: Predict How Many: Triangle Growing Pattern**

MyLab Education   **Expanded Lesson: Exploring Functions through Geometric Growing Patterns**

MyLab Education   **Activity Page: Predict How Many: Windows**

MyLab Education   **Activity Page: Predict How Many: Dot Arrays**

CCSS **Standards for Mathematical Practice**

MP2. Reason abstractly and quantitatively.

TECHNOLOGY Note. There are several websites that focus on relationships in functions. Virtual function machines can be found at NLVM, Math Playground, and Shodor Project Interactive, among others. NCTM's Illuminations website has a lesson titled, "The Crow and the Pitcher: Investigating Linear Functions Using a Literature-Based Model." PBS Kids' CyberChase has a fun game called "Stop That Creature" in which students figure out the rule that runs the game to shut down the creature-cloning machine. ■

Relationships in Functions

When students are exploring a growing pattern, there are three types of patterns they might notice. These types of patterns are related, but are not dependent on each other. In other words, students can develop functional thinking without recursive thinking (Blanton et al., 2015a). Each is shared here, connected to the growing T.

Recursive Patterns. The description that tells how a pattern changes from step to step is known as a *recursive* pattern (Bezuszka & Kenney, 2008; Blanton, 2008). For most students, it is easier to see the patterns from one step to the next, seeing the increase (or decrease). For the T pattern, this is noticing that the number of tiles goes up by 3 each time.

In the Dot Pattern, the recursive pattern is adding successive even numbers (Figure 13.5[a]). This can be observed in the physical pattern in at least two ways (Figure 13.5[b] and 13.5[c]).

Covariational Thinking. *Covariational* thinking involves noticing how two quantities vary in relation to each other and being explicit in making that connection (Blanton et al., 2011). In the T pattern, a student might say, "As the step number grows by 1, the number of tiles needed goes up by 3." This is more developmentally sophisticated than noticing a skip pattern (recursive pattern), as the student is connecting how the change in one quantity affects the change in the other quantity (i.e., how they covary).

Explicit Relationship. An *explicit relationship*, also called a *correspondence relationship* is a correlation between two quantities expressed as a function rule. In other words, it is begin able to look across the table to see how to use the input (x) to generate the output (y). In the T pattern, the rule is $3x + 1$. Imagine that you needed to find the number of tiles for the hundredth step in the T pattern. If you use recursive thinking, you will need to find all of the prior 99 entries in the table. If you notice how x and y correspond (the explicit rule), you can use that rule to find how many tiles are needed for the hundredth T.

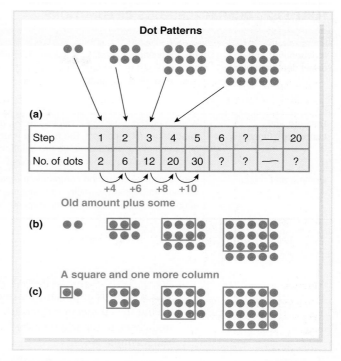

FIGURE 13.5   Analyzing relationships in the Dot Pattern.

Students in elementary grades (as early as first grade) can employ functional thinking (Blanton et al., 2015a; Tanish, 2011). Input-output activities can begin with young children and continue through middle school. The book *Two of Everything* (Hong, 1993) works well because the Haktaks put things "in the pot" and they double as they come "out of the pot." Explain that the pot changes rules on different days (see Magic Pot Mystery Rules Activity Page). Shoeboxes or large refrigerator boxes can be turned into input-output boxes. Decorate the box to look like a machine and add buttons for "easy," "medium," and "hard," and design functions that are appropriate for the grade of your students (Fisher, Roy, & Reeves, 2013). This can become a fun daily routine, trading out the explicit rule.

To support student development of functional thinking, ask questions such as these as they explore growing patterns and other covariation situations:

- What is changing? What is staying the same?
- What quantities are you comparing?
- How could you organize your information in a table?
- What relationships do you notice in the table?
- How might the quantities be represented in a graph?
- What relationships to you notice in the graph?
- How can you represent the rule in words? In symbols?

CCSS Standards for Mathematical Practice
MP2. Reason abstractly and quantitatively.

MyLab Education   Activity Page: Magic Pot Mystery Rules

Characteristics of Functions. Table 13.2 summarizes language used to describe functions, which can also become part of the discussions about functions to build meaning for students.

TABLE 13.2 CHARACTERISTICS OF FUNCTIONS

Concepts	Description	Example
Independent and dependent variables	The *independent variable* is the input, or whatever value is being used to find another value. The *dependent variable* represents the output.	In the "Pattern Blocks Perimeter" problem, the independent variable is the number of blocks in the string; the dependent variable is the perimeter. You can say that the perimeter of the block structure depends on the number of blocks used.
Discrete and continuous functions	When isolated or selected values are the only ones appropriate for a context, the function is *discrete*. If all values along a line or curve are solutions to the function, then the function is *continuous*.	Discrete: "Pattern Blocks Perimeter" problem. Only whole-number values make sense. Continuous: Walking rate, where at any given time, there is a distance walked (even if that distance is 0 meters).
Domain and range	The *domain* of a function comprises the possible values for the independent variable. The *range* is the corresponding possible values for the dependent variable.	In the "Pattern Blocks Perimeter" problem, the domain and range are all positive whole numbers.

FORMATIVE ASSESSMENT Notes. Being able to make connections across representations is important for understanding functions, and the only way to know if a student is seeing the connections is to ask. In a diagnostic interview, ask questions like the ones just listed and check to see whether students are able to link the graph to the context, to the table, and to the formula. ■

Graphs of Functions

So far, growing patterns have been represented by (1) the physical materials or drawings, (2) a table, (3) words, and (4) symbols. A graph adds a fifth representation, and one that effectively illustrates covariation. Figure 13.6 illustrates what these five representations look like with the context of selling hotdogs. Importantly, students experiences making connections and understanding these representations.

Figure 13.7 shows the graph for the T pattern and the dot pattern. Notice that the first is a straight-line (linear) relationship and the other is a curved line that would make half of a parabola if the points were joined.

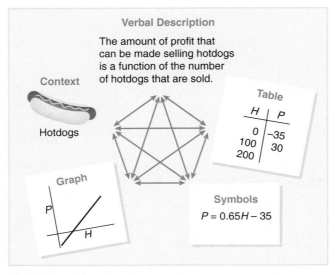

FIGURE 13.6 Five representations of a function for the situation of selling hotdogs.

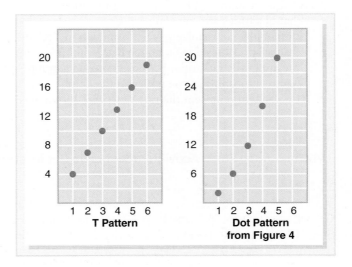

FIGURE 13.7 Graphs of two growing patterns.

Activity 13.8

CCSS-M: 6.EE.C.9; 7.EE.B.4a; 8.F.A.1; 8.F.A.2

Perimeter Patterns

Using a document camera or interactive white board, show rows of same-shape pattern blocks (see Figure 13.8). Working in pairs or small groups, have students build each pattern and explore what patterns they notice about how the perimeter grows. Ask: What is the perimeter of a row with 6 squares? 10 squares? Any number of squares? Repeat the process with trapezoids and hexagons (or have different groups of students working on different shapes). Distribute a Coordinate Grid. Ask students to create a graph to illustrate the relationship between the number of pattern blocks in the row and the perimeter. For more pattern block growing patterns, see Chan, 2015 (also described at end of chapter).

MyLab Education   **Blackline Master: Coordinate Grid—Quadrant I**

❚❚ Pause & Reflect

Which representations do you find most useful in determining the explicit rule or function? Which representation do you think students new to exploring patterns will use? ●

Having graphs of three related growing patterns provides the opportunity to compare and connect the graphs to the patterns and to the tables (see Figure 13.9). For example, ask students to discuss how to get from one coordinate to the next (e.g., up six, over one for the hexagon), where that information can be found in the table, and what it means in terms of the design itself.

 TECHNOLOGY Note. Function graphing tools permit users to create the graph of almost any function very quickly. Multiple functions can be plotted on the same axis. It is usually possible to trace along the path of a curve and view the coordinates at any point. The dimensions of the viewing area can be changed easily so that it is just as easy to look at a graph for x and y between -10 and $+10$ as it is to look at a portion of the graph thousands of units away from the origin. By zooming in on the graphs, it is possible to find points of intersection with as much precision as desired.

Digital programs, such as Desmos (https://www.desmos.com), can also be used for these purposes, and add speed, color, visual clarity, and a variety of other interesting features to help students analyze functions. Graphsketch is an online demonstration tool for making graphs of equations. ■

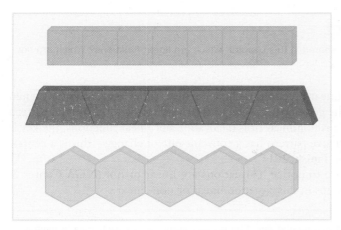

FIGURE 13.8   Same-color strings of pattern blocks. Can you determine the perimeter for n pattern blocks in a string?

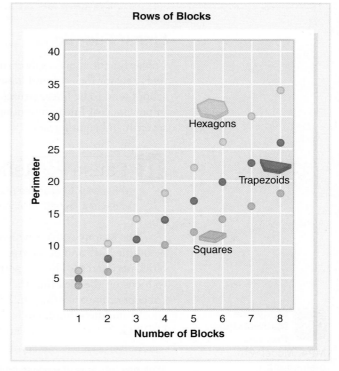

FIGURE 13.9   Graphs of the perimeters of three different pattern-block strings.

Students also need opportunities to describe graphs qualitatively. Exploring situations without exact values focuses students' attention on covariation relationships, the focus of Activity 13.9.

Activity 13.9

CCSS-M: 6.EE.D.9; 8.F.B.5

Sketch-a-Graph

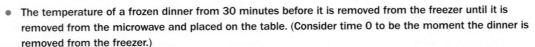
ENGLISH LEARNERS

Use the Sketch-a-Graph Activity Page, or project the stories as written here. Ask students to sketch a graph (no labels on the graphs) for one of the stories:

- The temperature of a frozen dinner from 30 minutes before it is removed from the freezer until it is removed from the microwave and placed on the table. (Consider time 0 to be the moment the dinner is removed from the freezer.)
- The value of a 1970 Volkswagen Beetle from the time it was purchased to the present. (It was kept by a loving owner and is in top condition.)
- The level of water in the bathtub from the time you begin to fill it to the time it is completely empty after your bath.
- Profit in terms of number of items sold.
- The height of a thrown baseball from when it is released to the time it hits the ground.
- The speed of the same baseball.

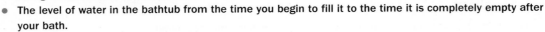
STUDENTS with SPECIAL NEEDS

After the graphs are drawn, students can pair-compare or selected graphs can be shown to the whole class. Let students examine the graph to see whether they can determine the matching situation. Be sure that the contexts you pick are familiar to students, including ELs. If they are not, change the context or provide visuals. Match a graph can be a first experience as a scaffold, or as an alternative for students with disabilities. See matching graphs in Figure 13.10. Repeat the activity in reverse—have students write a story to match a graph (see Create a Journey Story Activity Page).

MyLab Education   **Activity Page: Sketch-a-Graph**
MyLab Education   **Activity Page: Create a Journey Story**

Linear Functions

Linear functions are a subset of functions, which can be linear or nonlinear. But because linearity is a major focus of middle school mathematics, and because growing patterns in elementary school tend to be linear situations, it appears here in its own section. CCSS-M emphasizes the importance of linear functions across the middle grades, with a strong focus on linearity in seventh and eighth grade (NGA Center & CCSSO, 2010).

 Pause & Reflect

Think back to example tasks shared in this chapter. Which are linear functions? Which are not linear, but are still functions? •

The examples that involved linear functions include the birds (how many ways they could be on the bush and in the tree), the geometric growing patterns, the T pattern, and the pattern block perimeters. The dot pattern is nonlinear (it is quadratic). For linear functions, the key is to focus on the idea that the recursive pattern has a constant rate of change—this is a central concept of linearity (Smith, 2008; Tanish, 2011).

In middle school, students are to notice if situations are linear or not (NGA Center & CCSSO, 2010). Are the relationships in this situation linear or non-linear?

CCSS Standards for Mathematical Practice

MP4. Model with mathematics.

Miah has 24 yards of fence to build a rectangular pen. She is considering what dimensions to build it and wants to analyze it algebraically. (1) Write an equation to describe the relationship between the length and width. (2) Write an equation to describe the relationship between the length and the area.

An explicit formula for the width is $w = 12 - l$ (l is the length), which decreases at a constant rate, therefore looking like a line. By contrast, the explicit formula for area of the pen is $a = l(12 - l)$ —a quadratic. Students can and should determine whether a function is linear (and nonlinear) across representations (picture/objects, equation, graph, table, and situation). Figure 13.11 illustrates the rectangular pen problem using a table and graphs. You can create a card sort activity by creating an equation, graph, table, and story representation for each of a set of functions and asking students to find representations that describe the same function (see Wells, 2016/2017 for a collection of cards and ideas for connecting among representations).

Rate of Change and Slope. Rate involves two different units and how they relate to each other (see Chapter 17). Rates can be seen in a wide range of contexts, such as the geometric model of the pattern block perimeters (design number and blocks) or the rate of growth of a plant (time and height). Other rate contexts include hourly wages, gas mileage, profit, and cost of an item, such as a bus ticket.

Explorations of linear rate situations develop the concept of *slope*, which is the numeric value that describes the rate of change for a linear function. For example, one of the explicit formulas for the hexagon perimeter pattern is $y = 4x + 2$. Note that the rate of change is 4 because the perimeter increases by 4 with each new piece. All linear functions can be written in this form: $y = mx + b$ (including $y = mx$ when $b = 0$).

Conceptually, then, slope signifies how much y increases when x increases by 1. If a line contains the points (2,4) and (3, −5), you can see that as x increases by 1, y decreases by 9.

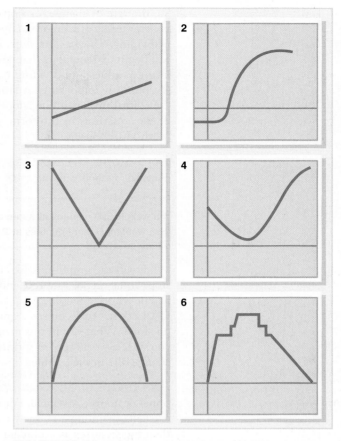

FIGURE 13.10   Match each graph with the situations described in Activity 13.9. Talk about what change is happening in each case.

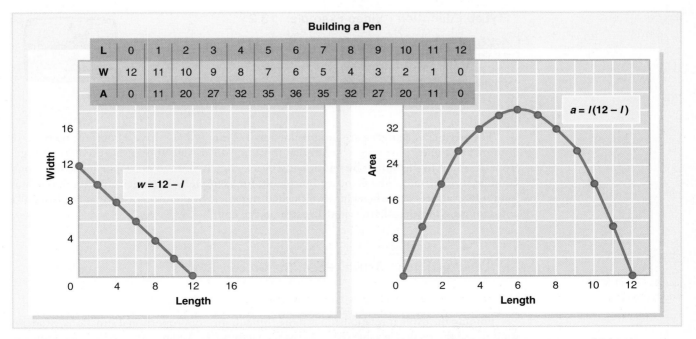

Building a Pen

L	0	1	2	3	4	5	6	7	8	9	10	11	12
W	12	11	10	9	8	7	6	5	4	3	2	1	0
A	0	11	20	27	32	35	36	35	32	27	20	11	0

$w = 12 - l$

$a = l(12 - l)$

FIGURE 13.11   The width and area graphs as functions of the length of a rectangle with a fixed perimeter of 24 units.

So, the rate of change, or slope, is -9. For the points $(4,3)$ and $(7,9)$, you can see that when x increases by 3, y increases by 6. Therefore, an increase of 1 in x results in a change of 2 in y (dividing 6 by 3). The slope is 2. After further exploration and experiences, your students will begin to generalize that you can find the rate of change or slope by finding the difference in the y values and dividing by the difference in the x values. Exploring this first through reasoning is important for students if they are to be able to make sense of and remember the algorithm for finding slope when given two points. For an interactive tool that connects linear equations in the form $y = mx + b$ to graphs, try "Interactive Linear Equation" at Math Warehouse.

Zero Slope and No Slope. Understanding these two frequently confused slopes requires contexts, such as walking rates. Consider this story:

You walk for 10 minutes at a rate of 1 mile per hour, stop for 3 minutes to watch a nest of baby birds, then walk for 5 more minutes at 2 miles per hour.

What will the graph look like for the 3 minutes when you stop? What is your rate when you stop? In fact, your rate is 0, and because you are at the same distance for 3 minutes, the graph will be a horizontal line.

Let's say that you see a graph of a walking story that includes a vertical line—a line with no slope. What would this mean? You traveled a distance with no time passing! Now, even if you were a world record sprinter, this would be impossible. Remember that rate is based on a change of 1 in the x value.

Proportional and Nonproportional Situations. Linear functions can be proportional or nonproportional. For example, the amount of money earned is proportional to hours worked (assuming an hourly rate), but if the person started with some money already saved, then the situation is no longer proportional because of the additional money (constant). All proportional situations, then, are equations in the form $y = mx$ and nonproportional linear situations are in the form $y = mx + b$. Notice that the graphs of all proportional situations are straight lines that pass through the origin. Students will find that the slope of these lines is also the rate of change between the two variables.

MyLab Education   **Video Example: 13.2**

Watch this video titled Tom's Job Problem that shows how a teacher creates a table that distinguishes money earned and money saved to help make the distinction between proportional and nonproportional situations.

The perimeter patterns are nonproportional. Although you have a constant increase of 4, there are 2 units (one on each end) that must be added. Said another way, you cannot get from the input to the output by multiplying by a factor, as you can in proportional situations. Context is important. The Grocery Store task, for example, asks students to figure out how long grocery carts are when they are pushed together. Students can see that it grows at a constant rate, but that there is a little extra on the end.

MyLab Education   **Activity Page: The Grocery Store**

Finding the explicit relationship is more difficult for nonproportional situations. Students want to use the recursive value (e.g., +4) as the factor (×4). Adding extra rows (or columns) to the table can highlight recursive and explicit relationships (Burton, 2017; Panorkou & Maloney, 2016). For the T pattern, an expanded table could look like this:

Input: Step Number [x]	Pattern	Output: Number of Tiles [y]	Shorthand
1	4	4	4 + 0(3)
2	4 + 3	7	4 + 1(3)
3	4 + 3 + 3	10	4 + 2(3)
4	4 + 3 + 3 + 3	13	4 + 3(3)
x	4 + 3 + ... •	?	4 + (x − 1)(3)
		Rule: $y = 4 + 3(x − 1)$ or $y = 3x + 1$	

Also, in proportional situations it is true that there are twice as many in the twentieth term than in the tenth term, because the relationship is multiplicative only. But when there is a constant involved, this shortcut does not work, though students commonly make this error. Having students analyze errors such as these support their learning (Lannin, Arbaugh, Barker, & Townsend, 2006).

Parallel, Same, and Perpendicular Lines. Students in eighth grade should be comparing different linear situations that result in parallel, same, or perpendicular lines (NGA Center & CCSSO, 2010). Using a context is necessary to build understanding.

Larry and Mary each earn $30 a day for the summer months. Mary starts the summer $50 dollars in debt, and Larry already has $20. In week 3, how much more money does Larry have? How much more does he have in week 7? When will Mary and Larry have the same amount of money?

The rates for Larry's and Mary's earnings are the same—and the graphs therefore go up at the same rate—that is, the slopes are the same. The graphs of Larry's earnings ($y = 30x + 20$) and Mary's earnings ($y = 30x − 50$) are parallel. We know this without even making the graphs because the rates (or slopes) are the same. Can you think of what change in Larry's and Mary's situations might result in the same line? Their initial value (and their rate) must be the same.

Slopes can also tell us when two lines are perpendicular, but it is less obvious. Analyzing perpendicular lines on a coordinate grid illustrates that slope of one line is the negative reciprocal of the other, a powerful pattern to explore using dynamic geometry software such as GeoGebra.

MyLab Education **Self-Check 13.2**

MyLab Education **Application Exercise 13.1: Study of Patterns and Functions** Click the link to access this exercise, then watch the video and answer the accompanying questions.

VIDEO EXAMPLE

Meaningful Use of Symbols

Students must have a strong understanding of symbols to be successful in mathematics. Symbols represent real situations and should be seen as useful tools for representing situations and solving real-life problems (e.g., calculating how many cookies we need to sell to make x dollars or at what rate do a given number of employees need to work to finish the project on time). Unfortunately, Algebra textbooks continue to emphasize symbolic manipulation without first developing such an understanding (Sherman, Walkington, & Howell, 2016).

Looking at equivalent expressions that describe a context is an effective way to bring meaning to numbers and symbols. The classic task in Activity 13.10 involves such reasoning.

Activity 13.10

CCSS-M: 5.OA.A.1; 5.OA.A.2; 6.EE.A.2b

Border Tiles Expressions—Part 1

Distribute the Border Tiles Expressions—Part 1 Activity Page and color tiles (optional, but recommended). Ask students to build a 8 × 8 square array representing a swimming pool with a border patio (see Figure 13.12). Challenge students to find at least two ways to determine the number of border tiles used without counting them one by one. For each idea, students record the numeric expression and connect the expression to the diagram. For example, they may see 10 squares across the top and across the bottom, and 8 squares on either side. This might be written as follows: 10 + 10 + 8 + 8 = 36 or (2 × 10) + (2 × 8) = 36

Each of the following expressions can likewise be traced to looking at the tiles in various groupings:

4 × 9

4 × 8 + 4

4 × 10 − 4

100 − 64

(More expressions are possible because students may use addition instead of multiplication.) Ask students to compare the different expressions and discuss whether they are all correct (and therefore equivalent) expressions for describing the general rule.

MyLab Education   Activity Page: Border Tiles Expressions—Part I

CCSS **Standards for Mathematical Practice**
MP2. Reason abstractly and quantitatively.

Notice that this Activity involved numeric expressions—a good place to start. This prepares students for experiences in two important areas: (1) the equal sign (=) and inequality signs ($<, \leq, >, \geq$) and (2) variables, discussed in the next two sections.

Equal and Inequality Signs

The equal sign is one of the most important symbols in elementary arithmetic, in algebra, and in all mathematics. At the same time, research dating from 1975 to the present suggests that = is a very poorly understood symbol (Kieran, 2007; RAND Mathematics Study Panel, 2003) and rarely represented in U.S. textbooks in a way to encourage students to understand the equivalence relationship—an understanding that is critical to understanding algebra (McNeil et al., 2006). CCSS-M explicitly addresses developing an understanding of the equal sign as early as the first grade.

Why is it so important that students correctly understand the equal and inequality signs? First, it is important for students to understand and symbolize relationships in our number system. These signs are how we mathematically represent quantitative relationships. Conversely, when students fail to understand the equal sign, they typically have difficulty with algebraic expressions (Knuth, Stephens, McNeil, & Alibali, 2006). Consider the equation $5x + 24 = 54$. It requires students to see both sides of the equal sign as equivalent expressions. It is not possible to "do" the left-hand side. However, if both sides are understood as being equivalent, students will see that $5x$ must be 24 less than 54 or $5x = 30$. Therefore, x must equal 6.

CCSS **Standards for Mathematical Practice**
MP2. Reason abstractly and quantitatively.

FIGURE 13.12 How many different ways can you find to count the border tiles of an 8 × 8 pool?

Relational Thinking. Students may think about equations in three ways, each developmental in nature (Stephens et al., 2013). First, as noted previously, they may have an *operational view*, meaning that the equal sign means "do something." Second, students develop a *relational—computational* view. At this phase, students understand that the equal sign symbolizes a relation between answers to two calculations, but they only see computation as the way to determine if the two sides are equal or not. Finally, students develop a *relational—structural view* of the equal sign (we will refer to this as relational). In this thinking, a student uses numeric relationships between the two sides of the equal sign rather than actually computing the amounts.

Consider two distinctly different explanations for determining that n equals 8 in the open sentence $7 + n = 6 + 9$.

- Since $6 + 9$ is 15, I need to figure out 7 plus what equals 15. It is 8, so n equals 8.
- Seven is one more than the 6 on the other side. That means that n should be one less than 9, so it must be 8.

The first student computes the result on one side and adjusts the result on the other to make the sentence true (relational–*computational* approach). The second student uses a relationship between the expressions on either side of the equal sign. This student does not need to compute the values on each side (relational–*structural* approach). When the numbers are large, a relational-structural approach is much more efficient and useful.

CCSS **Standards for Mathematical Practice**
MP7. Look for and make use of structure.

⏸ Pause & Reflect

In the following expression, what number do you think belongs in the box?

$$8 + 4 = \square + 5$$

How do you think students in the early grades or in middle school typically answer this question? ●

In a classic study, no more than 10 percent of students from grades 1 to 6 put the correct number (7) in the box. The common responses were 12 and 17. (How did students get these answers?) In grade 6, not one student out of 145 put a 7 in the box (Falkner, Levi, & Carpenter, 1999). Despite efforts to address this lack of understanding, recent research of more than 100 third graders indicates continued lack of understanding of the equal sign (See pre-test results for the two items in Figure 13.13).

Where do such misconceptions come from? A large majority of equations that students encounter in elementary school look like this: $5 + 7 = $ _____ or $8 \times 45 = $ _____ . Naturally, students come to see $=$ as signifying "and the answer is" rather than a symbol to indicate equivalence (Carpenter et al., 2003; Kieren, 1981, McNeil & Alibali, 2005). In addition to this operational view of the equal sign, other causes include: an over-focus on answers, with no focus on generalizations, not noticing properties of number and operation at play and a lack of understanding of variable notation (Carraher and Schliemann, 2007).

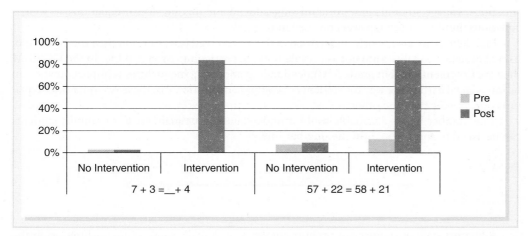

FIGURE 13.13 A third grade algebraic thinking intervention focused on the meaning of the equal sign.

Blanton, M., Stephens, S. Knuth, E., Gardiner, A. M., Isler, I., & Kim, J. (2015b). The Development of children's algebraic thinking: The impact of a comprehensive early algebra intervention in third grade. *Journal of Research in Mathematics Education, 46*(1), 39-87.

Standards for Mathematical Practice
MP8. Look for and express regularity in repeated reasoning.

As the graph in Figure 13.13 illustrates, instruction that addresses these issues does result in students who have a relational understanding of the equal sign (i.e., they understand that the two sides must balance). Shifts in the way you approach teaching computation can support such a relational understanding. For example, rather than always asking students to solve a problem (like $45 + 61$ or 4×26), ask them to instead find an equivalent expression (Blanton, 2008). For $45 + 61$, students might write $45 + 61 = 40 + 66$. For a multiplication problem, students might write $4 \times 26 = 4 \times 25 + 4$ or $4 \times 26 = 2 \times (2 \times 26)$. Activity 13.11 is a way to work on equivalent expressions, while supporting the development of Making 10 strategy for learning the basic facts (based on Fosnot & Jacob, 2010).

Activity 13.11

CCSS-M: 1.OA.C.6; 1.OA.D.7; 2.OA.B.2

Ten and Some More

Students create equivalent expressions, matching expressions in the form $10 + 1$ to $10 + 8$ with other expressions. Use the Equation Cards Activity Page as a game board, or cut them into cards, as illustrated here.

Give each pair of students a deck of cards (remove face cards, aces, and tens). Each partner draws one playing card and together they write an addition expression (e.g., $8 + 5$). If the cards drawn are less than 10, they draw a third card. They decide which note card is equivalent to their expression and record an equation: $8 + 5 = 10 + 3$. Note that the students do not need to actually add their cards; they just find an equivalent expression. Focus discussion on this idea as a way to draw attention to generalizations, properties, and meaning of the equal sign.

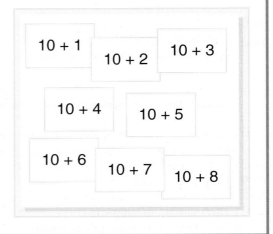

MyLab Education   **Activity Page: Equation Cards**

Another way to support a stronger understanding of symbols is to encourage students to write their mental math strategies symbolically. For example, a student might explain that they solve $0.25 \times n$ by finding one-half of the number and then one-half again. In symbols, this might be written as: $0.25 \times 26 = \frac{1}{2}(\frac{1}{2} \times 26)$. This practice increases student understanding of the equal sign *and* the relationships among numbers and forms of numbers (e.g., $\frac{1}{2} \times \frac{1}{2} = \frac{1}{4}$, so $0.5 \times 0.5 = 0.25$). Finally, as students are exploring the operations across the different situations, engage students in writing missing-addend and missing-factor equations, as well as equations with the result (answer) on the left (e.g., $50 = 5 \times 10$).

Inequalities are also poorly understood and have received less attention than the equal sign, likely because inequalities are not as prevalent in the curriculum or in real life. In the CCSS-M they are first mentioned in grade 6. Understanding and using inequalities is important and can be introduced earlier as a way for students to compare quantities: Are these two quantities equal or is one greater than the other?

The number line is a valuable tool for understanding inequalities. For example, students can be asked to show $x < 5$ on the number line:

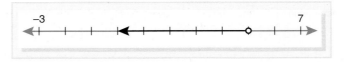

A context such as money can provide a good way to make sense of inequalities, as in the following example.

You have $100 for purchasing gift cards for your 5 friends. You want to spend the same on each, and you will also need to spend $10 to buy a package of card-holders for the gift cards. Describe this situation with symbols.

Pause & Reflect

How would you write this inequality? How might students write it? What difficulties do you anticipate? And, importantly, what questions will you pose to help students build meaning for the inequality symbols? ●

Students might record the situation in any of the following ways (using *a* for the amount of money for the gift):

$5a + 10 \leq 100$	$10 + 5a \leq 100$	$100 \geq 10 + 5a$	$100 \geq 5a + 10$

They may also make these inequalities without the equal signs: $<$ and $>$. Discuss with students what it means to say "less than" or "less than or equal to." Invite students to debate which signs make more sense given the situation. Graph the result and see if the graph makes sense given the situation.

Deciding whether to use the less than or greater than sign can be confusing for students. Invite students to say in words what the inequality means. For example, the first statement directly translates to "5 gift cards and $10 for a package of holders must be less than or equal to $100." The final example directly translates to "I have $100, which must be more than or the same as the cost of 5 cards and the holders." Ask questions that help students analyze the situation quantitatively, such as, "Which has to be more, the amount you have or the amount you spend?"

FORMATIVE ASSESSMENT **Notes.** Ask students to write a real-life story problem that involves an inequality. You can add expectations such as "It must be multi-step" and "you must illustrate the solution on a number line" (for more details see Whaley, 2012, for a full lesson, examples, rubric and discussion). Writing helps students connect representations and helps you see what they understand. ■

Conceptualizing the Equal Sign as a Balance. Helping students understand the idea of equivalence can and must be developed concretely. The next two activities illustrate how kinesthetic approaches, tactile objects, and visualizations can reinforce the "balancing" notion of the equal sign.

Activity 13.12   CCSS-M: 1.OA.D.7; 2.NBT.A.4

Seesaw Students

STUDENTS with SPECIAL NEEDS

Ask students to raise their arms to look like a seesaw. Explain that you have big juicy oranges, all weighing the same, and tiny little apples, all weighing the same. Ask students to imagine that you have placed an orange in each of their left hands (students should bend to lower left side). Then, place another orange on the right side (students level off). Next, with oranges still there, imagine an apple added to the left. Add another apple on the left (again). Then ask them to imagine the apple moving over to the right. This is a particularly important activity for students with disabilities, who may be challenged with the abstract idea of balancing values of expressions.

After acting out several seesaw examples, ask students to write seesaw equations (e.g., the ones described here are $a = a$; $a + b + b > a$; $a + b = a + b$). And, to describe their observations (e.g., "If you have a balanced seesaw and add something to one side, it will tilt to that side," or "If you take away the same object from both sides of the seesaw, it will still be balanced").

After exploring objects, explore numbers on a balance. Examples are illustrated in Figure 13.14.

Activity 13.13

CCSS-M: 2.OA.A.4; 3.OA.A.4; 5.NBT.A.3a, b; 6.EE.A.4

Tilt or Balance?

STUDENTS with SPECIAL NEEDS

Post two expressions and ask students whether they will balance or if one will be greater than the other (see Figure 13.14[a]). For whole number examples, see Tilt or Balance Equation Cards Set A; for rationale numbers, see Tilt or Balance Equation Cards Set B. These could be cut out as cards, projected for students, or just used for reference. Distribute or project two-pan balances, such as the Balance Scales Placemat, which includes one scale that is balanced and one that is tilted. Ask students to write either an equation $=$ or inequality ($>$ or $<$), using the symbols and saying verbally what they mean. Include examples for which students can make the determination by analyzing the relationships on the two sides rather than by doing the computation. Visuals and manipulatives can be a support for students with disabilities.

Also, use missing-value expressions (see Figure 13.14[b]). Ask students to find a number that will result in one side tilting downward, a number that will result in the other side tilting downward, and one that will result in the two sides being balanced. (See Expanded Lesson: Tilt or Balance for more a full lesson.)

MyLab Education   Activity Page: Tilt or Balance Equation Cards Set A
MyLab Education   Activity Page: Tilt or Balance Equation Cards Set B
MyLab Education   Activity Page: Balance Scales Placemat
MyLab Education   Expanded Lesson: Tilt or Balance

CCSS Standards for Mathematical Practice

MP5. Use appropriate tools strategically.

 TECHNOLOGY Note. There are several excellent virtual balance activities:

- PBS Cyberchase Poddle Weigh-in: Shapes are balanced with numbers between 1 and 4.
- Agame Monkey Math Balance: Students select numbers for each side of a balance to make the two sides balance (level of difficulty can be adapted).
- NCTM Illuminations Pan Balance—Numbers or Pan Balance—Expressions provide a virtual balance where students can enter what they believe to be equivalent expressions (with numbers or symbols). ■

True/False Sentences. True or false statements can help build relational understanding and address student misconceptions (Carpenter et al., 2003). Any of these could be the focus of a Number Talk. And, the concrete idea of a balance (or seesaw) can support student reasoning.

Students will generally agree on equations when there is an expression on one side and a single number on the other, although initially the less familiar form of $7 = 5 + 2$ may generate discussion. For an equation with no operation ($8 = 8$), the discussion may be lively. Reinforce

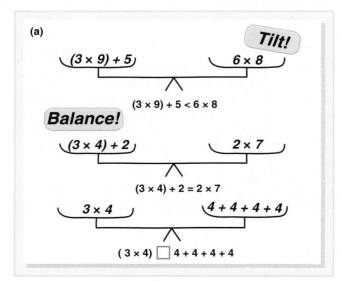

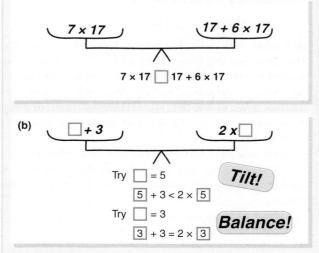

FIGURE 13.14   Using expressions and variables in equations and inequalities.

Activity 13.14

CCSS-M: 1.OA.B.3; 1.OA.D.7; 1.NBT.B.4; 2.NBT.B.5; 3.OA.B.5; 4.NBT.B.5; 5.NF.A.1

True or False?

ENGLISH LEARNERS

Introduce true/false sentences or equations with simple examples to explain what is meant by a true equation and a false equation. Then put several simple equations on the board, some true and some false. The following are appropriate for primary grades:

$$7 = 5 + 2 \qquad 4 + 1 = 6$$
$$4 + 5 = 8 + 1 \qquad 8 = 10 - 1$$

STUDENTS *with* **SPECIAL NEEDS**

Your collection might include other operations, but keep the computations simple. Ask students to talk to their partners and decide which of the equations are true equations (and why) and which are not (and why not). For older students, use fractions, decimals, and larger numbers.

$$120 = 60 \times 2 \qquad\qquad 318 = 318$$
$$\frac{1}{2} = \frac{1}{4} + \frac{1}{4} \qquad 1 = \frac{3}{4} + \frac{2}{1} \qquad 345 + 71 = 70 + 344$$
$$1210 - 35 = 1310 - 45 \qquad\qquad 0.4 \times 15 = 0.2 \times 30$$

Listen to the types of reasons that students use to justify their answers, and plan additional equations accordingly. ELs and students with disabilities will benefit from first explaining (or showing) their thinking to a partner (a low-risk practice) and then sharing with the whole group.

---

that the equal sign means "is the same as" by using that language when you read the symbol. Inequalities should be explored in a similar manner.

Solving equations. The balance is a concrete tool that can help students understand that if you add or subtract a value from one side, you must add or subtract a like value from the other side to keep the equation balanced. Figure 13.15 shows solutions for two equations, one in a balance and the other without. The notion of preserving balance also applies to inequalities—but what is preserved is imbalance. In other words, if one side is more than the other side and you subtract 5 from both, the one side is still more. Even after you have stopped using the balance, the mental

CCSS Standards for Mathematical Practice

MP3. Construct viable arguments and critique the reasoning of others.

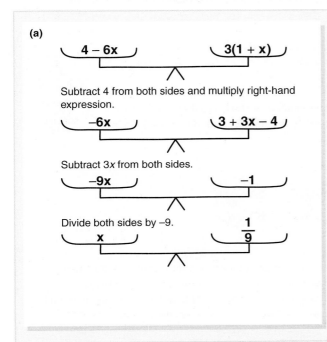

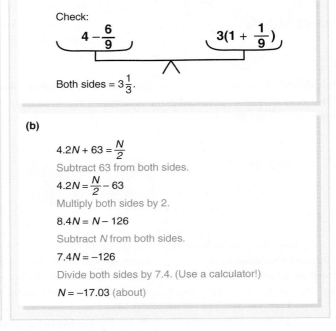

(a)

$4 - 6x$ $3(1 + x)$

Subtract 4 from both sides and multiply right-hand expression.

$-6x$ $3 + 3x - 4$

Subtract 3x from both sides.

$-9x$ -1

Divide both sides by −9.

x $\dfrac{1}{9}$

Check:

$4 - \dfrac{6}{9}$ $3(1 + \dfrac{1}{9})$

Both sides = $3\dfrac{1}{3}$.

(b)

$4.2N + 63 = \dfrac{N}{2}$

Subtract 63 from both sides.

$4.2N = \dfrac{N}{2} - 63$

Multiply both sides by 2.

$8.4N = N - 126$

Subtract N from both sides.

$7.4N = -126$

Divide both sides by 7.4. (Use a calculator!)

$N = -17.03$ (about)

FIGURE 13.15   Using a balance scale to build understanding of solving equations.

idea of balance can be used to reinforce the concept of equivalent expressions. For example, *open sentences* can be explored using reasoning strategies. As early as first grade students can understand and benefit from using variables (Blanton et al., 2011). Encourage students to look at the number sentence holistically and discuss in words what is missing (and how they reasoned to figure it out).

Activity 13.15

CCSS-M: 1.OA.D.7; 1.OA.D.8; 2.OA.A.1; 3.OA.A.4; 5.OA.A.2; 6.EE.A.3; 6.EE.B.5

What's Missing?

Prepare a set of Missing-Value Equations. Ask students to figure out what is missing and how they know. Notice that the equations are set up so that students do not always have perform the operations to figure out what is missing. Encourage them to look at the equation and see if they can figure out what is missing without solving it. Probe to see if there is more than one way to find what is missing.

Here is a sampling of ideas across the grades:

$4 + \square = 6$	$4 + 5 = \square - 1$	$\square + 5 = 5 + 8$	$3 \times 7 = 7 \times \square$
$15 + 27 = n + 28$	$12 \times n = 24 \times 5$	$6 \times n = 3 \times 8$	$15 \times 27 = n \times 27 + 5 \times 27$
$0.5 + a = 5$	$4.5 + 5.5 = a + 1$	$a \times 4 = 4.8$	$2.4 \div a = 4.8 \div 6$

Using "messy" numbers further encourages applying relational understanding to solve:

$126 - 37 = n - 40$	$37 \times 18 \div 37 = n$	$20 \times 48 = n \times 24$
$68 + 58 = 57 + 69 + n$	$7.03 + 0.056 = 7.01 + n$	$\dfrac{3}{10} + n + \dfrac{1}{10} = \dfrac{2}{5} + \dfrac{1}{5}$

MyLab Education **Activity Page: Missing-Value Equations**

Molina and Ambrose (2006), used true/false and open-ended prompts with third graders who did not have a relational understanding of the equal sign. For example, all 13 students answered $8 + 4 = \underline{\quad} + 5$ with 12. They found that asking students to *write their own* open sentences was particularly effective in helping students solidify their understanding of the equal sign.

Activity 13.16

CCSS-M: 1.OA.D.7; 1.OA.D.8; 2.OA.A.1; 3.OA.A.4; 4.NF.B.3a; 5.OA.A.2; 6.EE.B.8

STUDENTS with SPECIAL NEEDS

Make a Statement!

Ask students to write their own true/false and open sentences that they can use to challenge their classmates. This works for both equations and inequalities! To support student thinking, provide dice with numerals on them. They can turn the dice to different faces to try different possibilities.

Ask students to write three equations (or inequalities) with at least one true and at least one false sentence. For students who need additional structure, in particular students with disabilities, provide the Make a Statement Recording Page, which provides options for writing equations and inequalities. Students can trade their set of statements with other students to find the False Statement. Interesting equations/inequalities can be the focus of a follow-up whole-class discussion.

MyLab Education **Activity Page: Make a Statement Recording Page**

When students write their own true/false sentences, they often are intrigued with the idea of using large numbers and lots of numbers in their sentences. This encourages them to create sentences involving relational-structural thinking.

In middle school, students begin to manipulate equations so that they are easier to graph and/or to compare to other equations. Students need many and ongoing opportunities to explore problems that encourage relational thinking (Stephens et al., 2013). Balance activities, true/false, and open sentences help ground a student's understanding of how to preserve equivalence when "moving" numbers or variables across the equal sign (or inequality symbols).

 FORMATIVE ASSESSMENT Notes. As students work on these types of tasks, you can interview them one on one (though you may not get to everyone). Listen for whether they are using relational-structural thinking. If they are not, ask, "Can you find the answer without actually doing any computation?" This questioning helps nudge students toward relational thinking and helps you decide what instructional steps are next. ■

The Meaning of Variables

Variables can be interpreted in many ways. While the use of variables in elementary grades has been limited, researchers suggest elementary students can understand variables and such experiences are important preparation for the more complex mathematical situations they will encounter in middle school (Blanton et al., 2011). Variables can be used to represent a *unique but unknown quantity* (e.g., missing number) or *represent a quantity that varies* (e.g., output of a function). Unfortunately, students often think of the former and not the latter. Experiences in elementary and middle school must focus on both, the focus of the next two sections.

Variables Used as Unknown Values. The missing-value explorations (Activity 13.15) are examples of variables as unknowns in *equations*. Many story problems involve a situation in which the variable is a specific unknown, as in the following basic example:

> **Gary ate 9 strawberries and Jeremy ate some, too. The container of 25 was gone! How many did Jeremy eat?**

Standards for Mathematical Practice
MP1. Make sense of problems and persevere in solving them.

MyLab Education   Application Exercise 13.2: Observing and Responding to Student Thinking Click the link to access this exercise, then watch the video and answer the accompanying questions.

Although students can solve this problem without using algebra, they can begin to learn about variables by expressing it in symbols: $9 + s = 25, 25 - 9 = s$ or $25 - s = 9$. These problems can grow in difficulty over time. Illustrations can help students reason about the meaning of the story and serve as a way to help write the related equation (Gavin & Sheffield, 2015). For this task, these two illustrations might be created by students:

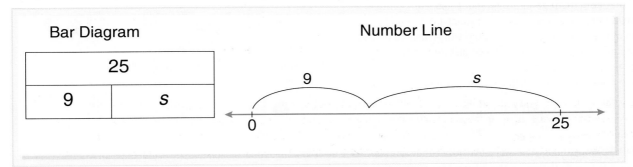

Translating stories to equations involving variables are particularly challenging for students, in particular when the word order does not match the symbol order. For example, students incorrectly write equations $6S = T$ for a problem that says, The number of students (S) was six times the number of teachers (T), (Clement, 1982). A bar diagram for this situation looks like this:

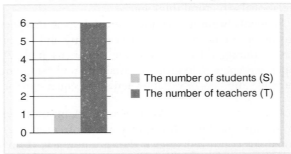

Another strategy that is helpful is to have students compare the variables (without the numbers) before the solve a problem. In this case, to reason whether there are more students or more teachers.

In Figure 13.16, a series of examples shows problems in which each different shape on the scales represents a different value. When no numbers are involved, as in the top two examples of Figure 13.16, students can find combinations of numbers for the shapes that make the balances balance. If an arbitrary value is given to one of the shapes, then values for the other shapes can be found accordingly. Problems of this type can be adjusted in difficulty for students across the grades. The last three problems in Figure 13.16 are on scales, and therefore the shapes have an unknown value that can be determined through reasoning. As noted above, several apps are available that can support solving for variables. These include NCTM's Illumination scales and NLVM Algebra Balance Scales and Algebra Balance Scales—Negative.

Activity 13.17

CCSS-M: 6.EE.A.4;
7.EE.A.2; 8.EE.C.8b

Ball Weights

Students will figure out the weight of three balls, given the following three facts:

1. baseball + football = 1.25 pounds

2. baseball + soccer ball = 1.35 pounds

3. soccer ball + football = 1.9 pounds

Ask students to look at each equation and make observations that help them generate relationships. For example, they might notice that the soccer ball weighs 0.1 pound more than the football. Write this in the same fashion as the other statements. Continue until these discoveries lead to finding the weight of each ball.

One possible approach: Add equations 1 and 2:

baseball + baseball + football + soccer ball = 2.6 pounds

Then take away the football and soccer ball, reducing the weight by 1.9 pounds (based on the information in equation 3), and you have two baseballs that weigh 0.7 pound. Divide by 2, so one baseball is 0.35 pounds.

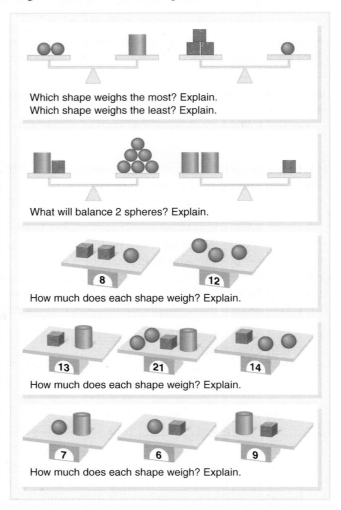

Which shape weighs the most? Explain.
Which shape weighs the least? Explain.

What will balance 2 spheres? Explain.

How much does each shape weigh? Explain.

How much does each shape weigh? Explain.

How much does each shape weigh? Explain.

FIGURE 13.16 Examples of problems with multiple variables and multiple scales.

MyLab Education **Application Exercise 13.3: Observing and Responding to Student Thinking** Click the link to access this exercise, then watch the video and answer the accompanying questions.

VIDEO EXAMPLE

As you can see in Activity 13.17, students can explore equations with three variables. The variables, or missing values, can be determined through reasoning (rather than formal strategies for solving systems of equations).

Solving systems of equations has traditionally been presented as series of procedures with little attention to meaning (e.g., solve by graphing, by substitution, and simultaneously). Mathematically proficient students should have access to multiple approaches, including these three but also to reasoning strategies. Rather than learn one way by rote each day or be tested on whether they can use each approach, students should *choose* a method that fits the situation, using appropriate tools. And, they need to understand what that point of intersection means in the context of the problem given.

Among the strategies that students must try is *observation*. Too often, students leap into solving a system algebraically without stopping to observe the values in the two equations. Look at the systems of equations here, and see which ones might be solved for *x* or *y* by observation or mentally (without employing one of the three strategies listed earlier).

CCSS Standards for Mathematical Practice
MP1. Make sense of problems and persevere in solving them.

$x + y = 25$ and $x + 2y = 25$	$3x + y = 20$ and $x + 2y = 10$
$8x + 6y = 82$ and $4x + 3y = 41$	$\frac{y}{3} = 5$ and $y + 5x = 60$

Simplifying Expressions. Simplifying expressions can be challenging for students because they are accustomed to solving equations and finding an answer, typically a number. Knowing how to simplify and recognizing equivalent expressions are essential skills for working algebraically, and are based on the properties of the operations. Students are often confused about what the instruction "simplify" means. The Activity 13.10 (Border Tiles Expressions) can be extended to variables, as described here.

Activity 13.18   CCSS-M: 6.EE.A.1; 6.EE.A.2a; b, c, 6.EE.A.3; 6.EE.A.4

Border Tiles Expressions—Part 2

Distribute the Border Tiles Expressions—Part 2 Activity Page and color tiles (optional, but recommended). Explain that Marianna's pool patio work has expanded—she is building square pools of different side-lengths. Ask students to prepare variable expressions describing efficient ways for her to determine how many patio tiles are needed for any *square-shaped* pool.

If the square had a side of length *p*, the total number of tiles could be found in similar ways:

$10 + 10 + 8 + 8$	$(2 \times 10) + (2 \times 8)$	4×9	$100 - 64$
$(p + 2) + (p + 2) + p + p$	$2 \times (p + 2) + (2 \times p)$	$4 \times (p + 1)$	$(p + 2)^2 - p^2$

Finally, challenge students to prepare a variable expression for any *rectangular-shaped* pool. Compare each expression and have students justify why any two are equivalent to each other.

MyLab Education **Activity Page: Border Tiles Expressions—Part 2**

Invite students to enter these expressions into the Table function on their graphing calculator and graph them to see whether they are equivalent (Brown & Mehilos, 2010). Looking at these options, the connection can be made for which one is stated the most simply.

One effective way to help students understand the importance of preserving equivalence is to look at *worked examples* and determine if they are correct or not, and if there are errors, explain how to fix the errors (Hawes, 2007; Renkl, 2014; Star & Verschaffel, 2016). Figure 13.17

CCSS Standards for Mathematical Practice
MP7. Look for and make use of structure.

Explain how to fix this simplification. Give reasons.
(2x + 1) − (x + 6) = 2x + 1 − x + 6

Gabrielle's solution

IF x=3 then the order of operations would take place, so the problem would look like (2·3+1) − (3+6) = 2·3+1−3+6 you would have to do 1− 3 instead of 1+6. But its actually 3+6. so that's the mistake.

Prabdheep's solution

The problem will look like this in its correct form (2x +1) − (x +6) = 2x +−1x +−6 because there is a minus sign right outside of the () on the left side it means its −1. So if you times −1 by x its −1x not 1−x. When you times −1 by 6 its −6 not 6.

Briannon's solution

Explain how to fix this problem. Give Reasons
(2x+1) − (x+6) = 2x+1−x(+)6
                    you are
                    subtracting x and 6 not
                    subtracting x and adding 6
correctly simplified the problem is
(2x+1) + (x+6) ← distribute negative
2x+1+−x+−6
⎡x+−5⎤

FIGURE 13.17 Three students provide different explanations for fixing the flawed simplification.

Source: Figure 3 from Hawes, K. (2007). "Using Error Analysis to Teach Equation Solving." *Mathematics Teaching in the Middle School, 12*(5), p. 241. Reprinted with permission. Copyright © 2007 by the National Council of Teachers of Mathematics. All rights reserved.

shows how three students have corrected the simplification of $(2x + 1) − (x + 6)$. You can create your own worked examples of simplified expressions, or post correct and incorrect examples from your students.

Activity 13.19 provides an engaging way for students to explore properties and equivalent expressions.

Activity 13.19

CCSS-M: 5.OA.A.2; 6.EE.A.2a; 7.EE.A.2

STUDENTS with SPECIAL NEEDS

Solving the Mystery

The goal of the mysteries is to figure out why they work! Begin by having students do the following sequence of operations:

Write down any number.

Add to it the number that comes after it.

Add 9.

Divide by 2.

Subtract the number you began with.

Now, you can "read their minds." Everyone ended up with 5! Ask students, "How does this trick work? And, invite them to explore it using expressions. [Start with n. Add the next number: $n + (n + 1)$. This is equivalent to $2n + 1$. Adding 9 gives $2n + 10$. Dividing by 2 leaves $n + 5$. Subtract the number you began with n, and the result is 5.] For students with disabilities or students who struggle with variables, suggest that instead of using an actual number they use an object, such as a cube, and physically build the steps of the problem, as illustrated in Figure 13.18. Next, explore a new mystery using the Solving the Mystery Activity Page. In this Mystery, the result is a two-digit number where the tens place is the first number selected and the second digit is the second number selected (ask students to explain how this happened). See also More Mysteries Activity Page. As a follow-up or for enrichment, students can generate their own number tricks.

MyLab Education Activity Page: Solving the Mystery
MyLab Education Activity Page: More Mysteries

Variables Used as Quantities That Vary. Students need experiences with variables that vary, and pairs of variables that co-vary, early in the elementary curriculum. For example, when describing the how many legs for any number of dogs, students might write L = 4 × D, meaning that the number of legs is four times the number of dogs. Importantly, you must emphasize that the variable stands for *the number of* because students can confuse the variable to be a label (Blanton et al., 2011). Let's revisit the story above, but remove the result:

Gary ate 9 strawberries and Jeremy ate some, too. How might you describe the total number of strawberries eaten?

Because the total has been removed, the goal becomes writing an expression, in this case 9 + *s*. This can also be illustrated on a number line:

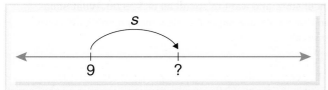

The number line is an important model in developing the concept of variable. As illustrated in Figure 13.19, finding where variables are in relation to numbers and in relation to other variables helps to build meaning (Carraher, Schliemann, & Schwartz, 2008; Darley, 2009).

When students are looking at the number line, ask questions like, "What is the value of *x*? Can it be any number? If we don't know what *x* is, how can we place $\frac{1}{3}x$ on the number line?" "Think of a value that *x* cannot be." Notice that in the two examples, *x* really can be any positive value. However, if you place *x* + 2 on the number line somewhere close to *x*, the space between these is 2, and you can use this distance as a "measure" to approximate the size of *x*. Because students use the number line with whole numbers, it is a good way to bridge to algebra. Having an algebra number line posted in your room where you can trade out what values are posted can provide many opportunities to think about the relative value of variables.

Context is important in writing equations with variables. Compare the two problems here (Blanton, 2008):

1. Annie has $10. Noah has $3 more than Annie. How much money does Noah have?
2. Annie has some money. Noah has $3 more than Annie. How much money does Noah have?

Primary grade students can list possible ways in a table and eventually represent the answer as *Annie* + 3 = *Noah* or more briefly, *A* + 3 = *N*.

The following example is appropriate for middle school students as a context for exploring variables that vary:

If you have $10 to spend on $2 granola bars and $1 fruit rolls, how many ways can you spend all your money without receiving change?

To begin exploring this problem, students record data in a table and look for patterns. They notice that when the number of granola bars changes by 1, the number of fruit rolls changes by 2. Symbolically, this representation is 2*g* + *f* = $10, where *g* is the number of granola bars and f is the number of fruit rolls.

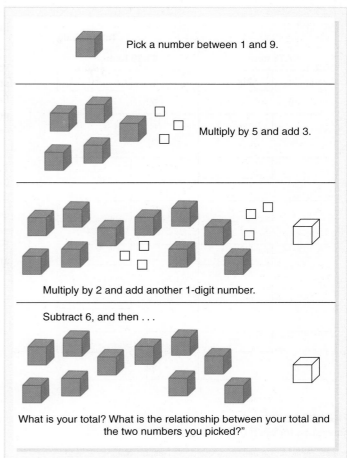

FIGURE 13.18   Cubes can illustrate the steps in "Solving the Mystery."

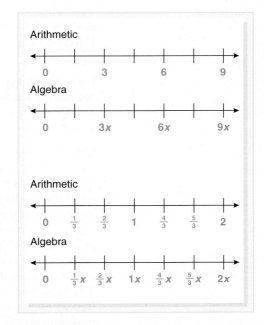

FIGURE 13.19   Using the number line to build meaning of variables.

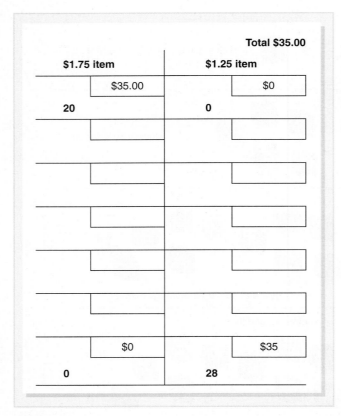

$1.75 item		$1.25 item	Total $35.00
	$35.00		$0
20		0	
	$0		$35
0		28	

FIGURE 13.20 A table adapted to include how many and how much for each row.

Source: Hyde, A., George, K., Mynard, S., Hull, C., Watson, S., and Watson, P. (2006). "Creating Multiple Representations in Algebra: All Chocolate, No Change," *Mathematics Teaching in the Middle School,* *11*(6), 262-268. Reprinted with permission. Copyright © 2006 by the National Council of Teachers of Mathematics. All rights reserved.

It is also important to include decimal and fraction values in the exploration of variables.

You are buying $1.75 pencils and $1.25 erasers from the school store and want to spend all of $35.00. What equation represents this situation? How many combinations are possible?

Once students have the equation (in this case, $1.75x + 1.25y = 35.00$), ask students to tie each number and variable back to the context. Provide time for them to find solutions, using a table or other strategy. As noted earlier, extra rows or sections on tables can help students organize and make sense of the data. For example, the adaptation in Figure 13.20 helps students keep track of how many (pencils) and how much (cost for the pencils).

MyLab Education **Self-Check 13.3**

Mathematical Modeling

The term model can mean different things in teaching mathematics and in mathematics standards documents, including manipulatives, demonstration, and conceptual models (COMAP & SIAM, 2016; Felton-Koestler, 2016/2017). Throughout this book, we have seen many examples of these ideas about models and modeling. Additionally, mathematical models can be used to describe real-world phenomena. Consider the following pumping water problem (based on Herbel-Eisenmann & Phillips, 2005):

Fall is coming and it is time to empty the swimming pool. Last year, you had created a model to describe the emptying of the pool: $W = -350(T - 4)$. (*T* is time, measured in hours and *W* is amount of water, measured in gallons).

Questions you might ask students to make sense of and use this model include: How much water is in the pool before it begins to be emptied? How many gallons are being emptied each hour? How long will it take to empty the pool? While these questions help students understand the model (equation), this task is not an example of engaging students in *mathematical modeling*. Mathematical modeling has a more precise meaning; it is, "a process that uses mathematics to represent, analyze, make predictions or otherwise provide insight into real-world phenomena." (COMAP & SIAM, 2016, p. 8). The process answers messy, authentic questions and it is something that all students, beginning in elementary school, need to learn to solve problems at home, the workplace and school (COMAP & SIAM, 2016; Usiskin, 2015). The *Guidelines for Assessment & Instruction in Mathematical Modeling Education* (GAIMME) Report (2016) provides excellent guidance for K–8 teachers to incorporate mathematical modeling into teaching.

Let's compare possible ways to engage students in multiplying (and other mathematics):

1. $14 \times 25 = 7 \times 50$ True or False? Justify your answer.
2. Eloise wants to read 25 books over the summer vacation, which is 9 weeks long. How much does she need to read each week?
3. Sydni would like to make hand-made notecards with bows on them, package them in sets to sell at fall craft shows, so she can make money. How many cards does she need to make in order to make the money she wants to have?

 ## Pause & Reflect

Which of these tasks are high quality tasks? Which ones are examples of using models? Which ones are examples of mathematical modeling? ●

All of these tasks have potential to be high quality and use models. For example, the first problem may engage students in creating rectangles so show why taking half of the first factor and doubling the second factor has the same answer. The second task can be a simple division problem, but could also open up conversation about length of books, and reading more in one week than another, if the context is taken seriously. Only the last task will engage students in mathematical modeling. If you read this problem and thought, there is not enough information here to solve it, then that is your hint that it is a mathematical modeling problem. Questions need to be asked and answered, including:

1. Design and creation of the cards (How big will the cards be? What type of paper? How much ribbon will go on each card? What other supplies might be needed?);
2. The packaging of the cards (Will she tie a set together or put them in a box? How many makes a set?);
3. Cost (How much money did it cost per box? How much is reasonable to makeper box?); and
4. Goal (How many might she like to make or how much money does she hope to earn?)

Imagine how messy this task will get, and how much multiplication and other mathematics will be used, in order to lead to a successful card-making endeavor. How will such a solution be reached? By applying the process of mathematical modeling as illustrated in Figure 13.21. And, this process is messy as well, because in practice it is not necessarily linear, you are likely to bounce back and forth among the various stages. In mathematical modeling situations,

---

MATHEMATICAL MODELING

IDENTIFY THE PROBLEM

We identify something in the real world we want to know, do, or understand. The result is a question in the real world.

MAKE ASSUMPTIONS AND IDENTIFY VARIABLES

We select 'objects' that seem important in the real world question and identify relations between them. We decide what we will keep and what we will ignore about the objects and their interrelations. The result is an idealized version of the original question.

DO THE MATH

We translate the idealized version into mathematical terms and obtain a mathematical formulation of the idealized question. This formulation is the model. We do the math to see what insights and results we get.

ANALYZE AND ASSESS THE SOLUTION

We consider: Does it address the problem? Does it make sense when translated back into the real world? Are the results practical, the answers reasonable, the consequences acceptable?

ITERATE

We iterate the process as needed to refine and extend our model.

FIGURE 13.21   The Process of Mathematical Modeling

Source: COMAP and SIAM. 2016. Guidelines for Assessment and Instruction in Mathematical Modeling Education (GAIMME). http://www.comap.com/Free/GAIMME/index.html. Accessed July 1, 2017.

students have to make genuine choices (e.g., what size the cards will be, how long the ribbon will be), and they benefit from working together as they consider options and make decisions. As a teacher, you are helping them learn the process, help them find information they are seeking, and providing feedback (via assessment) on their skills at implementing the process (not just on their product) (Cannon & Sanders, 2017; COMAP & SIAM, 2016).

Mathematical modeling is appropriate for investigating real challenges in the world. Invite students to think of a real world problem they would like to explore. More and more examples are available of such tasks. Examples include:

- Which deal will give the biggest discount (from a newspaper, or providing such options as Buy-One-Get-One half off, 30% off, Buy-Two-Get-One Free) (www.illustrativemathematics.org/practice-standards/4)
- How many students will be in our school in ten years? (Usiskin, 2015)
- Which conserves more water, taking a bath or taking a shower? (Anhalt, 2014)

Algebraic Thinking across the Curriculum

One reason the phrase "algebraic thinking" is used instead of "algebra" is that the practice of looking for patterns, regularity, and generalizations goes beyond curriculum topics that are usually categorized as algebra topics. You have already experienced some of this integration—the strong connection between number and algebra (e.g., properties and generalizations). Additionally, mathematical modeling refers to using all of mathematics, not just algebra. Here we briefly share some ways to make these connections explicit for students.

Geometry, Measurement and Algebra

Measurement formulas are functions. Each of these formulas involves at least one functional relationship. For example, the circumference of a circle is $c = 2\pi r$. We can say that the circumference is dependent on the radius. Even nonlinear formulas like volume of a cone $\left(V = \frac{1}{3}\pi r^2 h\right)$ are functions. Here the volume is a function of both the height of the cone and the radius. If the radius is held constant, the volume is a function of the height. Similarly, for a fixed height, the volume is a function of the radius.

The following activity explores how the volume of a box varies as a result of changing the dimensions.

Activity 13.20   CCSS-M: 5.MD.C.5b; 6.EE.A.2c; 6.G.A.2

Designing the Largest Box

Give each student or pair of students a piece of card stock. Explain that they are to cut out a square from each corner using an exact measurement. All four squares must be the same size. Assign different lengths for the squares that are cut out (e.g., 2 cm, 2.5 cm, 3 cm, and so on). Explain to students that after they cut out their four squares, they will fold up the four resulting flaps, and tape them together to form an open box. Have students calculate the volume of their box. Then, have students trade boxes and determine the volume of other boxes. The volume of the box will vary depending on the size of the squares (see Figure 13.22). Ask students to record their data in a table.

After students have recorded the data for several boxes, challenge them to write a formula that gives the volume of the box as a function of the size of the cutout squares. Use the function to determine what size the squares should be to create the box with the largest volume. Alternatively, make origami boxes using squares with various side lengths and see what the relationship is between the side length and the volume of the open box. (See DeYoung, 2009, for instructions for making the box and more on this idea.)

Data and Algebra

Data can be obtained from sports records, census reports, the business section of the newspaper, and many other sources. Students can gather data such as measurement examples or survey data. The Internet also has many sites where data can be found.

Experiments. There are many experiments that students can explore to see the functional relationships, if any, that exist between two variables. Gathering real data is an excellent way to engage a range of learners and to see how mathematics can be used to describe phenomena.

Data should be collected and then represented in a table or on a graph. The goal is to determine whether there is a relationship between the independent and dependent variables, and if so, whether it is linear or nonlinear, as in the following engaging experiments:

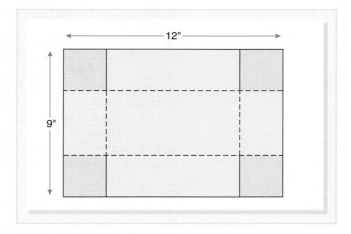

FIGURE 13.22   Cutting squares from cardstock. What size squares will result in an open box with the largest volume?

- What is the relationship between the number of [uncooked] spaghetti strands forming a 'bridge' and the amount of weight it can hold (in nickels)? (Kroon, 2016)

- How long would it take for 100 students standing in a row to complete a wave similar to those seen at football games? Experiment with different numbers of students from 5 to 25. Can the relationship predict how many students it would take for a given wave time?

- How far will a Matchbox car roll off of a ramp, based on the height the ramp is raised?

- How is the flight time of a paper airplane affected by the number of paper clips attached to the nose of the plane?

- What is the relationship between the number of dominoes in a row and the time required for them to fall over? (Use multiples of 100 dominoes.)

- Make wadded newspaper balls using different numbers of sheets of newspaper and a constant number of rubber bands to help hold the paper in a ball. What is the relationship between the number of sheets and the distance the ball can be thrown?

- What is the relationship between the number of drops of colored water dropped on a paper towel and the diameter of the spot? Is the relationship different for different brands of towels? (McCoy, 1997).

Experiments like these are fun and accessible to a wide range of learners. They also provide an opportunity for students to engage in experimental design—a perfect blend of mathematics and science.

Scatter Plots. Often in the real world, phenomena are observed that seem to suggest a functional relationship, but they are not necessarily as clean or as well defined as some of the situations we have described so far. In such cases, the data are generally plotted on a graph to produce a scatter plot of points. Two very good scatter plot generators can be found online at NLVM and NCES Kids' Zone.

A visual inspection of the scatter plot may suggest what kind of relationship, if any, exists. If a linear relationship seems to exist, for example, students can approximate a line of best fit or use graphing technology to do a linear regression to find the line of best fit (along with the equation).

Algebraic Thinking

As we began this robust chapter, we will end—algebraic thinking permeates all aspects of the curriculum. When topics are taught as rote procedures to be memorized, students miss opportunities to see patterns, recognize connections, and apply their own mathematical ideas. A lack of emphasis on algebraic thinking and connecting algebra to meaningful contexts results in the development of various challenges and misconceptions (e.g., Carpenter et al., 2003; Collins & Dacey, 2011; Kieren, 1981; Sakow & Karaman, 2015). Many were discussed within this chapter; Table 13.3 highlights some of the most prominent ones in K–8. In general, the best way to help is to emphasize understanding, algebraic thinking, and incorporate meaningful contexts.

MyLab Education **Self-Check 13.4**

MyLab Education **Math Practice:** Need to practice or refresh your math content knowledge? Click to access practice exercises associated with the content from this chapter.

TABLE 13.3 COMMON CHALLENGES AND MISCONCEPTIONS RELATED TO ALGEBRAIC THINKING AND HOW TO HELP

Common Challenge or Misconception	What It Looks Like	How to Help
1. Thinking the equal sign means "and the answer is . . . "	For the equation, $8 + 4 = \square + 5$ student puts 12 in the box (or 17). Equations such as $8 = 5 + 3$ and $6 = 6$ does not make sense it doesn't 'fit' with their interpretation of the equal sign.	• Revisit/develop the concept of balance (two-pan balances, true/false equations, open sentences, etc.). • Read the equal sign as "is the same as," or "is equal to." For example, read $4 + 5 = 9$ as "four plus five *is the same as* 9." • Revoice students' use of the word "makes" (e.g., $5 + 12$ makes 17, restate as $5 + 12$ is equal to 17). • Record children's equivalent expressions when they solve problems in different ways (e.g., $8 + 7 = 8 + 2 + 5$).
2. Thinking an equation is written "improperly" if it is not in the form of $a + b = c$ (for example).	Student is confused by equations such as: $17 = 17$ (identity statements) $5 + 7 = ? * 2$ (operations on both sides of the equation) $62 = ? - 24$ (operation on the right side of the equation).	• Use a variety of equation formats all year long. • When recording equations (e.g., that represent story problems), write more than one way (e.g., as multiplication *and* division).
3. Thinking a variable is a label rather than a quantity.	Given a problem about cans of juice in a package, a student might interpret 6c mistakenly as 6 cans when it is instead 6 times *the number of* cans in the packages. (Note: In measurement, 6 m may be a label—a unit of measure.)	• Define the variable. • Emphasize it means *the number* of. • Use different variables, so that they do not always match the context. • Ask students to select and define the variable • Have students write out labels, rather than use abbreviations. • Use boxes, blanks, and letters interchangeably in equations, emphasizing that each of these represent missing numbers.
4. Checking a few examples to decide if something always works.	Student decides that two odd numbers always add to even number because $5 + 7 = 12$ and $15 + 17 = 32$.	• Make distinction between testing and proving (see Activity 13.4). • Encourage use of visuals and manipulatives to show it is true for *any* numbers.
5. Confusing the variable x for a multiplication symbol $\times$ or vice versa.	Student does not know whether to multiply or add $4x + 5$	• Use other variables, such as n. • Point out that once variables are used the multiplication symbol becomes a dot or parenthesis in order to avoid the confusion.

Common Challenge or Misconception	What It Looks Like	How to Help
6. Simplifying expressions involving variables, ignoring the variable or the need for parenthesis	Making these errors: $5x + 9 = 14$ (or $5x + 9 = 14x$) $a + b = ab$ $l = 7$; $w = 4 + x$; Area $= 28 + x$	• Use concrete representations, such as a bag with some tiles to represent x ($5x$ is then 5 bags). • Ask students to say the meaning of the expression. • Present these as incorrectworked examples in order to discuss why they are not correct.
7. Matching words with equations in solving story problems.	For a statement like "Maria is twice as old as Alonso," the equation $2M = A$ is recorded.	• Begin by asking who is older. • Ask students to substitute in numbers to see if the equation fits the situation (and/or make a table). • Provide frequent experiences, such as warm-ups, starting basic and building to more complex statements.
8. Interpreting inequalities and their solutions.	Student doesn't know which symbols go with statements such as *less than, no more than,* or *at least.* Students don't understand how to interpret $a \leq 5$	• Use contexts and number lines (e.g., Alison has $5, show how much she might spend at the store). • Have students create contexts to go with inequalities. • Devote more time to inequalities.
9. Determining equation for linear situations, particularly when in the form $y = mx + b$	See Pattern Block patterns and Dot Patterns. Student can see what comes next (recursive relationship), but cannot determine the rule (explicit relationship)	• Use the diagram and table to see what stays the same and what changes. • Consider using a table with extra columns (as described earlier in this chapter). • Ask students what stays the same and what changes with each new step. • Find step 0 in the table and discuss its meaning and how it helps find the explicit rule.

RESOURCES FOR CHAPTER 13

LITERATURE CONNECTIONS

The following three examples of books are excellent beginnings for patterns and chart building.

Bats on Parade
Appelt and Sweet (1999)
This story includes the pattern of bats walking 1 by 1, then 2 by 2, and so on. One activity from this enjoyable book is determining the growing pattern of the number of bats given the array length (e.g., 3 for the 3 × 3 array). There is also one mouse, so this can be included in a second investigation. Activity Pages for these two ideas and two others can be found in Roy and Beckmann (2007).

Equal Shmequel
Kroll (2005)
This story is about a mouse and her friends who want to play tug-of-war. To do so, they must determine how to make both

sides equal so that the game is fair. In the end, they use a teeter-tooter to balance the weight of the friends. This focus on equal sides and balance make this a great book for focusing on the meaning of the equal sign.

Two of Everything: A Chinese Folktale
Hong (1993)
As described above, a magic pot doubles whatever goes in it. This idea of input—output is great for exploring functions; just vary the rule of the magic pot (See Magic Pot Mystery Rules Activity Page). For more details and handouts, see Suh (2007a) and Wickett and colleagues (2002).

MyLab Education   Activity Page: Magic Pot Mystery Rules

RECOMMENDED READINGS

Articles

Chan, H. H. (2015). How do they grow? *Mathematics Teaching in the Middle School, 20*(9), 548–555.

Dozens of interesting pattern block growing patterns are shared in this article. And, students are set up to compare and contrast these patterns, leading to important functional thinking!

Leavy, A., Hourigan, M., & McMahon, A. (2013). Early understanding of equality. *Teaching Children Mathematics, 20*(4), 247–252.

Nine strategies are shared for helping students strengthen their understanding of the equal sign. Each suggestion includes specific activity suggestions.

Molina, M., & Ambrose, R. C. (2006). Fostering relational thinking while negotiating the meaning of the equals sign. *Teaching Children Mathematics, 13*(2), 111–117.

This article helps us understand the conceptual considerations related to the equal sign while simultaneously illustrating the value of errors and misconceptions in creating opportunities for learning.

Mathematics Teaching in the Middle School. Focus Issue on Mathematical Modeling (February 2015).

This issue offers a strong collection of articles with mathematical modeling tasks and activities, and strategies for finding and creating more tasks.

Books

Essential Understandings Series (*Expressions, Equations, and Functions: Grades 6–8* (2011) and *Algebraic Thinking: Grades 3–5* (2011). Reston, VA: NCTM.

Each of these books provides a teacher-friendly discussion of the big ideas of algebra. Interwoven are excellent tasks to use with students.

Blanton, M. L. (2008). *Algebra and the elementary classroom.* Portsmouth, NH: Heinemann.

This is an excellent book for teachers at all levels—full of rich problems to use and helpful for expanding the reader's understanding of algebra. Great for book study.

Carpenter, T. P., Franke, M. L., & Levi, L. (2003). *Thinking mathematically: Integrating arithmetic and algebra in elementary school.* Portsmouth, NH: Heinemann.

This book is a detailed look at helping students in the primary grades develop the thinking and create the generalizations of algebra. The included CD shows classroom-based examples of the ideas discussed.

Fosnot, C. T., & Jacob, B. (2010). *Young mathematicians at work: Constructing algebra.* Portsmouth, NH: Heinemann.

Like the other books in the series, this is a gem. Full of classroom vignettes and examples that will enrich your understanding of how algebra can support arithmetic (and vice versa).

CHAPTER 14

Developing Fraction Concepts

LEARNER OUTCOMES

After reading this chapter and engaging in the embedded activities and reflections, you should be able to:

14.1 Describe and give examples for fractions constructs and fraction models.

14.2 Explain foundational concepts of fractional parts, including iteration and partitioning.

14.3 Illustrate the concept of equivalence across fraction models.

14.4 Describe strategies for comparing fractions and ways to teach this topic conceptually.

Fractions are one of the most important topics students need to understand to be successful in algebra and beyond, yet it is an area in which U.S. students, as well as students in many countries, struggle (OECD, 2014). National Assessment of Educational Progress (NAEP) results have consistently shown that students have a weak understanding of fraction concepts (Sowder & Wearne, 2006; Wearne & Kouba, 2000). This lack of understanding is then translated into difficulties with fraction computation, decimal and percent concepts, and algebra (Bailey, Hoard, Nugent, & Geary, 2012; Booth & Newton, 2012; Brown & Quinn, 2007; National Mathematics Advisory Panel, 2008; Siegler, Fazio, Bailey, & Zhou, 2013). Therefore, it is critical that you teach fractions well, present fractions as interesting and important, and commit to helping students understand the meaning of fractions.

BIG IDEAS

◆ Fractions can and should be represented across different interpretations (e.g., part-whole and division) and different models: area (e.g., $\frac{1}{3}$ of a garden), length (e.g., $\frac{3}{4}$ of an inch), and set (e.g., $\frac{1}{2}$ of the marbles).

◆ Fractions are equal shares of a whole or a unit. Therefore, equal sharing activities (e.g., 2 sandwiches shared with 4 friends) build on whole-number knowledge to introduce fractional quantities.

◆ Partitioning and iterating are ways students to understand the meaning of fractions. Partitioning can be thought of as splitting the whole equally (e.g., splitting a whole into fourths), and iterating can be thought of as making a copy of each piece and counting them (e.g., one-fourth, two-fourths, etc.).

◆ Equivalent fractions are ways of describing the same amount by using different-sized fractional parts.

◆ Fractions can be compared by reasoning about the relative size of the fractions. Estimation and reasoning are important in teaching understanding of fractions.

Meanings of Fractions

Fraction understanding is developmental in nature. Fraction experiences should begin as early as first grade. In the *Common Core State Standards* students partition shapes and refer to the fractional amounts in grades 1 and 2 as "equal shares." In grade 3, fractions are a major emphasis, with attention to using fraction symbols, exploring *unit fractions* (fractions with numerator 1), and comparing fractions. Grade 4 focuses on fraction equivalence and begins work on fraction operations (Chapter 15). This emphasis over years of time is an indication of both the complexity and the importance of fraction concepts. Students need significant time and experiences to develop a deep conceptual understanding of this important topic.

Understanding a fraction is much more than recognizing that $\frac{3}{5}$ is three shaded parts of a shape partitioned into five sections. Fractions have numerous constructs and can be represented as areas, quantities, or on a number line. This section describes these big ideas. The next sections describe how to teach fraction concepts.

Fraction Constructs

Understanding fractions means understanding all the possible concepts that fractions can represent. One of the commonly used meanings of fraction is part-whole. But many who research fraction understanding believe students would understand fractions better with more emphasis across other meanings of fractions (Clarke, Roche, & Mitchell, 2008; Lamon, 2012; Siebert & Gaskin, 2006).

 Standards for Mathematical Practice
MP7. Look for and make use of structure.

 # Pause & Reflect

Beyond shading a region of a shape, how else are fractions represented? Try to name three ideas. ●

Part-Whole. Using the part-whole construct is an effective starting point for building meaning of fractions (Cramer & Whitney, 2010). Part-whole can be shading a region, part of a group of people ($\frac{3}{5}$ of the class went on the field trip), or part of a length (we walked $3\frac{1}{2}$ miles).

Division. As with whole numbers, division means sharing into equal-sized groups. Because of the meaningful connections that can be made to equal sharing, something young students understand, fraction instruction should build from experiences of sharing and partitioning (Empson & Levi, 2011; Lamon, 2012; Siegler et al., 2010). Division is often not connected to fractions, which is unfortunate. Consider posing these two tasks to build a connection between division and fractions:

Four friends are sharing 8 cheese sticks, making sure each friend gets the same amount. How many cheese sticks will each friend get?

Four friends are sharing 10 cheese sticks, making sure each friend gets the same amount. How many cheese sticks will each friend get?

Students can determine how many cheese sticks each friend will get, and must feel comfortable being able to represent that quantity as division and as fractions: $\frac{10}{4}$, $4\overline{)10}$, $10 \div 4$, $2\frac{2}{4}$, and $2\frac{1}{2}$ (Flores, Samson, & Yanik, 2006).

Measurement. Measurement involves identifying a length and then using that length as a measurement unit to determine the length of an object. For example, in the fraction $\frac{5}{8}$, use the unit fraction $\frac{1}{8}$ as the unit and then count or measure to show that it takes five of those units to reach $\frac{5}{8}$. In other words, $\frac{5}{8}$ is thought of as 5 times $\frac{1}{8}$. Students then see fractions as *multiples* of unit fractions (Steffe & Olive, 2010).

Operator. Fraction as operator builds on the concept of seeing a fraction as a multiple of a unit fraction. Fractions can be used to indicate an operation, as in $\frac{4}{5}$ of 20 square feet, or $\frac{2}{3}$ of the audience. These situations indicate a fraction of a whole number, and students may be able to use mental math to determine the answer. This construct is not emphasized enough in school curricula (Usiskin, 2007).

Ratio. Discussed at length in Chapter 17, the concept of ratio is yet another context in which fractions are used. For example, the fraction $\frac{1}{4}$ can mean that the probability of an event is one in four. Ratios can be part-part or part-whole. For example, the ratio $\frac{3}{4}$ could be the ratio of those wearing jackets (part) to those not wearing jackets (part), or it could be part-whole, meaning those wearing jackets (part) to those in the class (whole).

Fraction Language and Notation

The way that we write fractions with a top and a bottom number and a bar between is a convention, one that is complex and difficult for young students to understand. That is why fraction instruction should begin with use of the words (e.g., one-fourth) rather than the symbols (e.g., $\frac{1}{4}$). This allows students to first focus on making sense of fractions as *part*, without the complication of also trying to make sense of the symbols. In the CCSS-M, students explore fractional parts (with words) in grades 1 and 2, being introduced to the fractions notation in grade 3. A good time to introduce the vocabulary of fractional parts is *during* the discussions of students' solutions to story problems and not before. When a brownie or other whole has been partitioned into equal shares, say, "We call these *fourths*. The whole is cut into four equal-sized parts—fourths."

Students may understand the idea of halves and fourths, yet not understand the meaning of the symbols $\frac{1}{2}$ and $\frac{1}{4}$. Building meaning for the symbols can be done through counting by fractional parts (iterating) and representing fractions across models, especially on the number line. Fractions should include examples that are less than 1, equal to one (e.g., $\frac{4}{4}$), and greater than 1 (e.g., $\frac{4}{8}$ and $\frac{4}{3}$). Engage students in counting fractional parts, then pose questions to make sense of the symbols, such as:

> What does the numerator in a fraction tell us?
>
> What does the denominator in a fraction tell us?
>
> What might a fraction equal to 1 look like?
>
> How do you know if a fraction is greater than or less than 1? Greater than or less than 2?

Here are some likely explanations for the top and bottom numbers from third graders:

- The numerator is the counting number. It tells how many shares or parts we have. It tells how many have been counted.
- The denominator tells what size piece is being counted. For example, if there are four parts in a whole, then we are counting *fourths*.

Making sense of symbols requires connections to visuals. Illustrating what $\frac{5}{4}$ looks like in terms of pizzas (area), on a number line (length), or connected to filling bags with objects (set) will help students make sense of this value.

⏸ Pause & Reflect

What fraction notation might you use for the visual here (the large square represents one unit)? ●

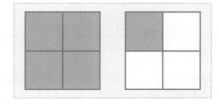

There are (at least) four ways to notate this quantity:

$$\frac{5}{4} \qquad 1\frac{1}{4} \qquad \frac{1}{4} + \frac{1}{4} + \frac{1}{4} + \frac{1}{4} + \frac{1}{4} \qquad 1 + \frac{1}{4}$$

Do you think that students would be able to describe this quantity in all these ways?

Notice that this example focuses on a fraction greater than 1. It is important to move among fractions greater than, equal to, and less than one. This helps students develop understanding of fractions as values that come between whole numbers (or can be equivalent to whole numbers). Too often, students are *not* exposed to numbers equal to or greater than 1 (e.g., $\frac{6}{6}$, $\frac{5}{2}$, or $4\frac{1}{4}$), and it interferes with students understanding the relative size of the fraction.

CCSS **Standards for Mathematical Practice**

MP1. Make sense of problems and persevere in solving them.

MyLab Education   Video Example 14.1

Watch this video of Melissa demonstrating her level of understanding of the relative size of a fraction.

MyLab Education   Video Example 14.2

Watch this video of Jacky demonstrating her level of understanding of the relative size of a fraction.

The term *improper fraction* is used to describe fractions that are greater than one, such as $\frac{5}{2}$. This term can be a source of confusion as the word *improper* implies that this representation is not acceptable, which is not the case at all—in fact, it is often the preferred representation in algebra. Instead, try not to use this phrase and instead use "fraction" or "fraction greater than 1." Note that the word *improper* is not used in the CCSS-M standards.

Fraction Size Is Relative

A fraction by itself does not describe the *size* of the whole. A fraction tells us only about the *relationship between* the part and the whole. Consider the following situation:

Pizza Fallacy: Mark is offered the choice of a third of a pizza or a half of a pizza. Because he is hungry and likes pizza, he chooses the half. His friend Jane gets a third of a pizza but ends up with more than Mark. How can that be?

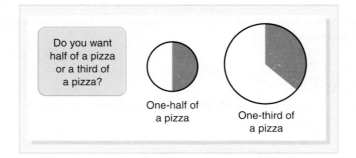

The visual illustrates how Mark got misdirected in his choice. The point of the "pizza fallacy" is that whenever two or more fractions are discussed in the same context, one cannot assume (as Mark did) that the fractions are all parts of the same size whole. Teachers help students understand fractional parts when they regularly ask, "What is the whole?" or "What is the unit?" Comparing, combining, or otherwise computing with fractions can only be done if the fractions are parts of the same-sized whole.

Models for Fractions

Substantial evidence suggests that the effective use of visuals in fraction tasks is important (Cramer & Henry, 2002; Empson & Levi, 2011; Petit, Laird, Marsden, & Ebby, 2016; Siebert & Gaskin, 2006). Using visuals are critical in learning because the use of physical tools leads to the use of mental models, which builds students' understanding of fractions (Cramer & Whitney, 2010; Petit, Laird, & Marsden, 2010). Unfortunately, when textbooks incorporate manipulatives, they tend to be only use area models (Hodges, Cady, & Collins, 2008). This means that students often do not get to explore fractions with a variety of models and/or do not have sufficient time to connect the visuals to the related concepts.

Manipulatives can help students clarify ideas that are often confused in a purely symbolic model. The same task can be represented by different visuals and students can make connections among them. Importantly, students need to experience fractions in real-world contexts that are meaningful to them (Cramer & Whitney, 2010). These contexts may align well with one representation and not as well with another. For example, if students are being asked who walked the farthest, a number line is more appropriate than fraction circles.

Table 14.1 provides an at-a-glance explanation of three types of models—area, length, and set—defining the wholes and their related parts for each model.

> **CCSS Standards for Mathematical Practice**
> **MP5.** Use appropriate tools strategically.

Area Models

Area is a good place to begin fraction explorations because it lends itself to equal sharing and partitioning. Circular Fraction Pieces are the most commonly used area model. The circular model reflects the part-whole concept of fractions and helps students see the relative size of a part to the whole (Cramer, Wyberg, & Leavitt, 2008). Other area models in Figure 14.1 demonstrate how different shapes can be the whole. Grid Paper or Dot Paper provides flexibility in selecting the size of the whole and the size of the parts (see Blackline Masters 5–11 for a selection). Many

TABLE 14.1 MODELS FOR FRACTION CONCEPTS AND HOW THEY COMPARE

Model Type	Description	Sample Contexts	Sample Manipulatives and Visuals
Area	Fractions are determined based on how a part of a region or area relates to the whole area or region.	Quesadillas (circular food) Pan of brownies Garden plot or playground	Fraction Circles/Rectangles Pattern Blocks Tangrams Geoboards Grid paper regions
Length	Fractions are represented as a subdivision of a length of a paper strip (representing a whole), or as a length/distance between 0 and a point on a number line, subdivided in relation to a given whole unit. (The number line can represent positive and negative fractions.)	Walking/distance travelled String lengths Music measures Measuring with inches or yards	Cuisenaire Rods Paper strips Number lines
Set	Fractions are determined based on how many discrete items are in the whole set, and how many items are in the part.	Students in the class, school, stadium Type of item in a bag of items	Objects (e.g., pencils, toys) Counters (e.g., two color counters, colored cubes, teddy bear, sea shells)

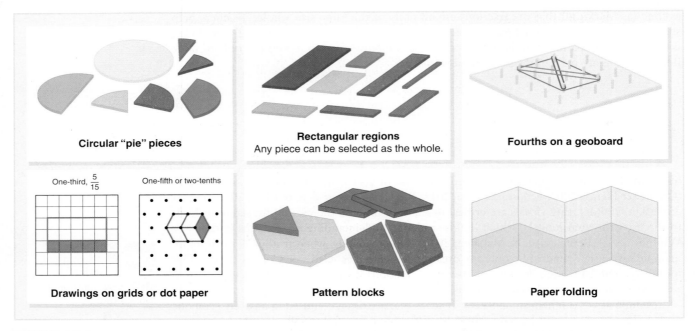

FIGURE 14.1 Area models for fractions.

commercial versions of area manipulatives are available, including circular and rectangular pieces, pattern blocks, geoboards, and tangrams. Activity 14.1 (adapted from Roddick & Silvas-Centeno, 2007) uses pattern blocks to help students develop concepts of partitioning and iterating.

MyLab Education	Activity Page: Circular Fraction Pieces
MyLab Education	Blackline Master: 1-Centimeter Grid Paper
MyLab Education	Blackline Master: 1-Centimeter Dot Paper

Activity 14.1
CCSS-M: 1.G.A.3; 2.G.A.3; 3.NF.A.1

Playground Fractions

Create this "playground" with your pattern blocks (see Playground Fractions Activity Page).

It is the whole. For each fraction below, find the pieces of the playground and draw it on your paper. For grades 1 and 2 use words, not fraction symbols (e.g., half of, one-half, or four-thirds).

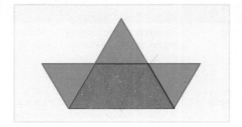

$\frac{1}{2}$ playground $\frac{1}{3}$ playground

$1\frac{1}{2}$ playgrounds $\frac{2}{3}$ playground

2 playgrounds $\frac{4}{3}$ playground

Extensions of this activity can combine different shapes of pattern blocks and address eighths, thirds, and sixths.

MyLab Education   Activity Page: Playground Fractions

Length Models

With length models, lengths or measurements are compared instead of areas. Either physical materials are compared on the basis of length or number lines are subdivided, as shown in Figure 14.2. Length models are very important in developing student understanding of fractions, yet they are not widely used in U.S. classrooms. Reviews of research on fractions (Petit et al., 2010; Siegler et al., 2010) report that the number line helps students understand a fraction as a number (rather than one number over another number) and helps develop other fraction concepts. As a result of these findings, the researchers recommend that teachers:

> Help students recognize that fractions are numbers and that they expand the number system beyond whole numbers. Use number lines as a central representational tool in teaching this and other fraction concepts from the early grades on. (Siegler et al., 2010, p. 1)

Number line experiences begin with whole numbers. In fact, students' ability to place whole numbers on a number line has been connected with success in developing fraction concepts and procedures (Jordan et al., 2013). Linear representations may help students understand fraction size because lines are one dimension. For example, students can see that a unit that fits into a paper strip two times is larger than a unit that fits into a paper strip four times (Saxe, Diakow, & Gearhart, 2012; Siegler et al., 2011).

Linear models are closely connected to the real-world contexts in which fractions are commonly used, such as measuring. Music, for example, is an excellent opportunity to explore $\frac{1}{2}, \frac{1}{4}, \frac{1}{8}$, and $\frac{1}{16}$ in the context of notes and strengthen student understanding (Courey, Balogh, Siker, & Paik, 2012; Goral & Wiest, 2007).

TECHNOLOGY Note. Virtual Cuisenaire rods and accompanying activities can be found online at various websites such as the University of Cambridge's NRICH Project. ■

Cuisenaire rods consist of the following colors and lengths:

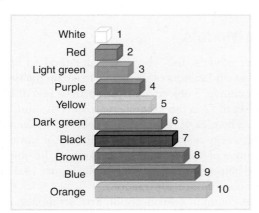

Cuisenaire rods provide flexibility because any length can represent the whole. For example, if you wanted students to work with $\frac{1}{4}$ and $\frac{1}{8}$, select the brown Cuisenaire rod, which is 8 units long, to be the unit (i.e., the brown rod is 1 whole unit of length). The four rod (purple), then, has a length of $\frac{1}{2}$, the two rod (red) has a length of $\frac{1}{4}$, and the one rod (white) has a length of $\frac{1}{8}$. For exploring twelfths, put the orange rod and red rod together to make a whole.

The number line is a significantly more sophisticated length model than the physical tools described previously (Bright, Behr, Post, & Wachsmuth, 1988), but it is an essential

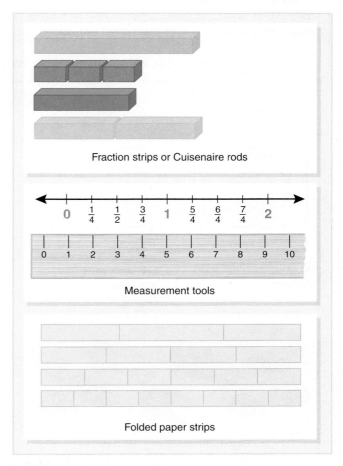

FIGURE 14.2 Length or measurement models for fractions.

Standards for Mathematical Practice

MP1. Make sense of problems and persevere in solving them.

model that needs be emphasized more in the teaching of fractions (Clarke et al., 2008; Flores et al., 2006; Siegler et al., 2010; Usiskin, 2007; Watanabe, 2006). Like with whole numbers, the number line is useful in determining the relative size of numbers. The following activity (based on Bay-Williams & Martinie, 2003) engages students in thinking about fractions through a linear model using a popular game as a context.

Activity 14.2   CCSS-M: 3.NF.A.2a, b; 3.NF.A.3a, b, d

Who Is Winning?

Use Who Is Winning? Activity Page and give students paper strips or ask them to draw a number line. This activity can be done two ways (depending on your lesson goals). First, ask students to use reasoning to answer the question "Who is winning?" Students can use reasoning strategies to compare and decide. Second, students can locate each person's position on a number line. Explain that the friends below are playing "Red Light, Green Light." The fractions tell how much of the distance they have already moved. Can you place these friends on a line to show where they are between the start and finish? Second, rather than place them, ask students to use reasoning to answer the question "Who is winning?"

ENGLISH LEARNERS

STUDENTS with SPECIAL NEEDS

Mary: $\frac{3}{4}$ Larry: $\frac{1}{2}$ Carrie: $\frac{5}{6}$ Han: $\frac{5}{8}$ Shawn: $\frac{5}{9}$ Juan: $\frac{2}{3}$

This game can be differentiated by changing the value of the fractions or the number of friends (fractions). The game of "Red Light, Green Light" may not be familiar to ELs. Modeling the game with people in the class and using estimation are good ways to build background and support students with disabilities.

MyLab Education   Activity Page: Who Is Winning?

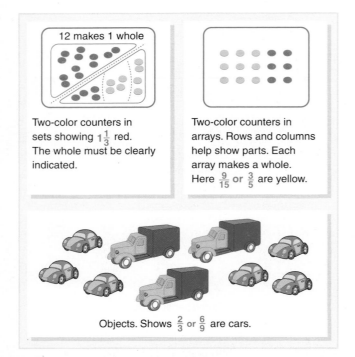

12 makes 1 whole

Two-color counters in sets showing $1\frac{1}{3}$ red. The whole must be clearly indicated.

Two-color counters in arrays. Rows and columns help show parts. Each array makes a whole. Here $\frac{9}{15}$ or $\frac{3}{5}$ are yellow.

Objects. Shows $\frac{2}{3}$ or $\frac{6}{9}$ are cars.

FIGURE 14.3 Set models for fractions.

Set Models

In set models, the whole is understood to be a set of objects, and subsets of the whole make up fractional parts. For example, 3 objects are one-fourth of a set of 12 objects. The set of 12 in this example represents the unit, the whole or 1. The idea of referring to a collection of counters as a single entity makes set models difficult for some students. Putting a piece of yarn in a loop around the objects in the set to help students "see" the whole. Figure 14.3 illustrates several set models for fractions.

A common misconception with set models is to focus on the size of a subset rather than the number of equal sets in the whole. For example, if 12 counters make a whole, then a subset of 4 counters is one-*third*, not one-fourth, because *3* equal sets make the whole. However, the set model helps establish important connections with many real-world uses of fractions and with ratio concepts.

Two color counters are an effective set manipulative. Counters can be flipped to change their color to model various fractional parts of a whole set. Any countable objects (e.g., a box of crayons) can be a set model. The following activity uses your students as the whole set. It can be done as an energizer, routine, warm-up, or full lesson.

Activity 14.3

CCSS-M: 3.NF.A.1; 3.NF.A.3b

Class Fractions

Use a group of students as the whole—for example, six students if you want to work on halves, thirds, and sixths. Invite them to come to the front of the room. Say to the group, "If you [are wearing tennis shoes, have brown hair, etc.], move to the right. If not, move to the left." Ask questions such as, "What fraction of our friends [are wearing tennis shoes]?" "How many students are in one-half of this group?" Have students record the fraction symbols and share their answers. If students offer equivalencies (e.g., one says "three-sixths" and another says "one-half"), show how sixths refers to people and halves refer to two groups of equal size. Change the number of selected students in the whole (e.g., 8 students or 12 students).

FORMATIVE ASSESSMENT Notes. As a teacher, you will not know whether they really understand the meaning of a fraction such as $\frac{1}{4}$ unless you have seen a student represent one-fourth using all three models. A straightforward way to assess students' knowledge of a fractional amount is to give them a Fraction Assessment Activity Page (or fold a piece of paper into three parts labeled *area*, *length*, and *set* at the top of each section). Give students a fractional value (e.g., $\frac{3}{4}$) and ask them to draw a representation and describing a context or example that fits with their representation. ■

MyLab Education Activity Page: Fraction Assessment

TECHNOLOGY Note. Virtual manipulatives are available for all three models. Virtual manipulatives have been found to positively affect student achievement, especially when they are paired with using the actual manipulatives (Moyer-Packenham, Ulmer, & Anderson, 2012). Recommended sites include:

Standards for Mathematical Practice
MP5. Use appropriate tools strategically.

Conceptua Fractions: This is an excellent free source that offers area, set, and length models (including the number line).

Cyberchase (PBS): *Cyberchase* is a popular television series. Their website offers videos that model fractions with real-world connections and activities such as "Thirteen Ways of Looking at a Half" (fractions of geometric shapes) and "Make a Match" (concept of equivalent fractions).

Illuminations (NCTM) Fractions Model: Explore length, area, region, and set models of fractions, including fractions greater than one, mixed numbers, decimals, and percentages.

Math Playground Fraction Bars: On this site you can explore fractional parts, the concepts of numerator and denominator, and equivalence.

National Library of Virtual Manipulatives: This site offers numerous models for exploring fractions, including fraction bars and fraction pieces. There is also an applet for comparing and visualizing fractions. ■

MyLab Education Self-Check 14.1

MyLab Education Application Exercise 14.1: Models for Fractions

Click the link to access this exercise, then read the scenario and answer the accompanying questions.

Fractions as Numbers

The first goal in the development of fractions should be to help students construct the idea of *fractional parts of the whole*—the parts that result when the whole or unit has been partitioned into *equal-sized portions or fair shares*. (Recall that Table 14.1 describes the meanings of parts and wholes across each type of model.)

One of the most significant ideas for students to develop about fractions is the sense that fractions are numbers—quantities that have values. You may not be familiar with the terms *partitioning* (splitting equally) and *iterating* (counting a repeated amount) but, as you will see, they connect to whole-number concepts you will recognize. Researchers have acknowledged for some time how important these two actions are to meaningfully working with fractions (e.g., Olive, 2002; Pothier & Sawada, 1990). These actions emphasize the numerical nature of fractions. Contexts also build meaning of fractional parts. Effective teaching of fractions begins with selecting tasks with relevant contexts that explicitly require students to engage in partitioning and iterating.

Partitioning

Sectioning a shape into equal-sized parts is called *partitioning*. When a brownie (or other area) has been partitioned into four equal shares, the parts are called *fourths*. Too often, students see illustrations of fractions (across models) where they are already partitioned into equal shares. For area models, those groups tend to also be the same shape (though they do not need to be). This results in students not noticing the critical feature of fractional parts (Watanabe, 2007).

MyLab Education   **Video Example 14.3**

Watch this video of teacher Zak Champagne describing important ideas about equal shares and partitioning.

Given students' experiences with fairly sharing items among family and friends, sharing tasks are a good place to begin the development of fractions (Siegler et al., 2010). Sharing tasks allow students to develop concepts of fractions from an activity that makes sense to them, rather than having the structure imposed on them. In this approach students do not begin with traditional part–whole tasks of identifying halves, thirds, fourths, and so on. These fractional parts and students' understanding of fractions emerge as a result of their fair sharing in meaningful contexts (Lewis, Gibbons, Kazemi, & Lind, 2015).

Sharing Tasks. Sharing tasks are generally posed in the form of a simple story problem.

Four friends are sharing two cookies. How many cookies will each friend get?

Then problems become slightly more difficult:

Suppose there are four cookies to be shared fairly among three children. How much will each child get?

See the video below about how Eduardo reasons about this sharing situation. Like Eduardo, students initially perform sharing tasks by distributing items one at a time. When this process leaves leftover pieces, they must figure out how to subdivide so that every group (or person) gets a fair share. Researchers recommend following a progression of sharing tasks that

TABLE 14.2   PROGRESSION FOR TEACHING WITH EQUAL SHARES STORY PROBLEMS

Progression	Example Problems
1. Problems whose solutions are whole numbers.	Three children want to fairly share 15 grapes. How many grapes will each child get?
2. Problems with 2, 4, or 8 sharers and whose solutions are mixed numbers (greater than 1).	Two children want to share 5 quesadillas so that everyone gets the same amount. How much will each child get?
3. Problems with 2, 4, or 8 sharers and whose solutions are less than 1.	Four children want to share 3 cookies so that everyone gets the same amount. How much will each child get?
4. Problems with 3 sharers and whose solutions are mixed numbers (greater than 1).	Three children want to share 10 sticks of clay to make clay animals. If everyone gets the same amount, how much does each child get?
5. Problems with 3 sharers and whose solutions are less than 1.	Three children want to equally share 2 pizzas. How much does each child get?

builds on children's understanding of whole-number quantities and informal partitioning strategies (e.g., Empson & Levi, 2011; Lewis, et al., 2015; Siegler et al., 2010). Table 14.2 provides such a progression with examples of corresponding story problems.

MyLab Education   Video Example 14.4

Watch this video of Eduardo solving a sharing problem.

Sharing stories have these three features:

1. The objects in the story are easy for students to draw and partition (e.g., crackers, brownies, bagels, cookies, pancakes, stick pretzels, etc.).
2. There are no fractions in the story (the fraction emerges from the partitioning).
3. They can be solved with no formal instruction on fractions or use of fraction symbols.

Sharing brownies is a classic activity that focuses on partitioning to make equal shares (see, for example, Empson, 2002). Using concrete tools such as dough can make sharing accessible even to kindergartners (Cwikla, 2014).

Activity 14.4   CCSS-M: 1.G.A.3; 2.G.A.3

Cookie Dough: Cut Me a Fair Share!

STUDENTS
with
SPECIAL
NEEDS

Give students a ball of dough and a plastic knife. Explain that they are going to be finding a way to share each group of cookies fairly with a group of students. Start with an example that is not too difficult. For example:

Four friends want to share ten brownies so that each friend gets the same amount of brownies. How much will each friend get?

To ensure 'brownies' are the same size, use square cookie cutters. Invite students to make their squares for brownies and then show how to share them fairly with four friends, using a paper knife if necessary. The Cut Me a Fair Share Activity Page provides a visual of the number of brownies and number of children, providing helpful support to many students, in particular, students with disabilities. Encourage students to share their ways of thinking. A strategy many students will use for this problem is to deal out two brownies to each child and then halve each of the remaining brownies (see Figure 14.4).

Then, offer a selection of other sharing tasks with different numbers of brownies and different number of sharers (see additional examples below).

MyLab Education   Activity Page: Cut Me a Fair Share

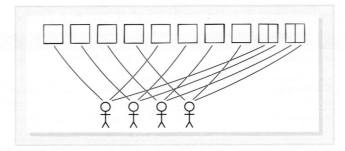

FIGURE 14.4 Ten brownies shared with four children.

You can differentiate by changing the numbers involved. Consider these variations (see Brownie Sharing Cards):

5 brownies shared with 2 children

2 brownies shared with 4 children

5 brownies shared with 4 children

4 brownies shared with 8 children

4 brownies shared with 10 children

3 brownies shared with 4 children

When the numbers allow for some items to be distributed whole (five shared with two), some children will first share whole items and then cut up the leftovers. Others will slice every piece in half and then distribute the halves. Using a halving strategy try to share five things among four children, will lead to two halves to give to four children. Some children will see they that each child gets "a half of a half" (and some may recognize that this is one-fourth). Felisha tries to find the fractional amount each of five children get when sharing two cookies, but loses track of what the whole is in determining each person's share.

MyLab Education   **Activity Page: Brownie Sharing Cards**

MyLab Education   **Video Example 14.5**

Watch this video of Felisha solving a challenging sharing task.

The last example, three brownies shared with four children, is more challenging because there are more sharers than items, and it involves more than just finding halves. One strategy is to partition each brownie into four parts and give each child one-fourth from each brownie—a total of three-fourths. Students (even adults) are surprised at the relationship between the problem and the answer.

Partitioning into three or six equal parts is challenging because students cannot rely on halving to get to the answer. Here are some examples:

4 pizzas shared with 6 children

4 pizzas shared with 3 children

5 pizzas shared with 3 children

CCSS **Standards for Mathematical Practice**
MP8. Look for and express regularity in repeated reasoning.

MyLab Education   **Application Exercise 14.2: Observing and Responding to Student Thinking** Click the link to access this exercise, then watch the video and answer the accompanying questions.

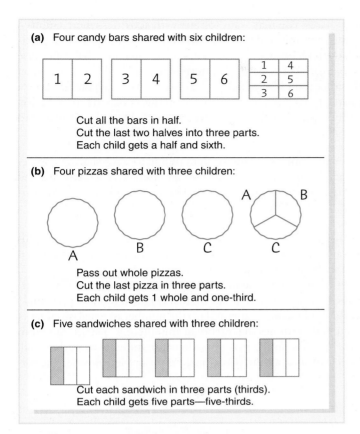

(a) Four candy bars shared with six children:

| 1 | 2 | 3 | 4 | 5 | 6 |

1	4
2	5
3	6

Cut all the bars in half.
Cut the last two halves into three parts.
Each child gets a half and sixth.

(b) Four pizzas shared with three children:

Pass out whole pizzas.
Cut the last pizza in three parts.
Each child gets 1 whole and one-third.

(c) Five sandwiches shared with three children:

Cut each sandwich in three parts (thirds).
Each child gets five parts—five-thirds.

FIGURE 14.5 Three different sharing processes for thirds and sixths.

Each of the children gets 1 and 2/3 of a pizza.

I think that however many children there are, that is how many peices you have to split the item into.

Each child gets 1 and 1/4 of a pizza.

FIGURE 14.6 Elizabeth explains a pattern for finding equal shares of a pizza.

Figure 14.5 shows some different sharing contexts and partitioning strategies students might use for these examples. Figure 14.6 shows how a student partitioned to solve "5 pizzas shared with 3 children." This took much guess and check, at which point the teacher asked, "Can you see a pattern in how you have divided the pizza and how many people are sharing?" At this point, the student noticed a pattern: If there are three people, the remaining pizzas need to be partitioned into thirds. See Expanded Lesson: Equal Sharing Stories for a lesson designed for grades 1 or 2.

MyLab Education   **Expanded Lesson: Equal Sharing Stories**

Because the level of difficulty of these sharing tasks varies, it is useful for creating a tiered lesson. In a tiered lesson, the goal (sharing) is the same, but the specific tasks vary in their challenge. Figure 14.7 shows how one teacher offers these three tiers for her lesson on sharing brownies (Williams, 2008).

Tier 1 task: For students who still need experience with halving	Tier 2 task: For students comfortable with halving and ready to try other strategies	Tier 3 task: For students ready to solve tasks in which students combine halving with new strategies
How can 2 people share 3 brownies?	How can 4 people share 3 brownies?	How can 3 people share 5 brownies?
How can 2 people share 5 brownies?	How can 3 people share 4 brownies?	How can 3 people share 2 brownies?
How can 4 people share 3 brownies?	How can 3 people share 5 brownies?	How can 6 people share 4 brownies?
How can 3 people share 4 brownies?	How can 6 people share 4 brownies?	How can 5 people share 4 brownies?

FIGURE 14.7 Example of a tiered lesson for the brownie-sharing problem.

To reinforce the idea of equal shares, you may want to start with activities where children create designated equal shares using physical models before asking children to draw and partition their own representations. Pattern blocks are a good tool to focus on equal shares because each piece is *not* an equal share, so creating shapes with pattern blocks and asking about equal shares helps students focus on the important idea of fair (equal) shares. Ask students to create a "cookie" using the six different pattern block shapes and ask, "Can this cookie be shared fairly with 6 people?" (Ellington & Whitenack, 2010). The answer is "no." Then, ask students to build a cookie that can be shared fairly.

> **TECHNOLOGY Note.** "Kids and Cookies" is an excellent online tool for sharing cookies (both round and rectangular). Display the situations on an interactive whiteboard and ask for different ways to share fairly (you can begin with whole numbers and increase in difficulty) (Center for Technology and Teacher Education, n.d.). ∎

Partitioning Across Fraction Models. As shared earlier, using different models builds a stronger understanding for students. Here we share partitioning ideas across area, length and set models. Figure 14.8 illustrates sixths across area, length, and set models.

Area models are the first types of models to use in teaching fractional parts. When partitioning an area into fractional parts, students need to be aware that (1) the fractional parts must be the same size, though not necessarily the same shape; and (2) the number of equal-sized parts that can be partitioned within the unit determines the fractional amount (e.g., partitioning into 4 parts means each part is *one-fourth* of the unit). It is important for students to understand, however, that sometimes visuals do not *show* all the partitions. For example, consider the following picture:

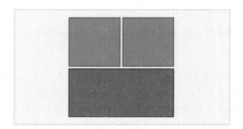

A student might think, "If I partitioned this so that all pieces were the same size, then there will be four parts; therefore, the smaller partitioned region represents one-fourth"—not one-third, as many students without a conceptual understanding of fractional parts might suggest.

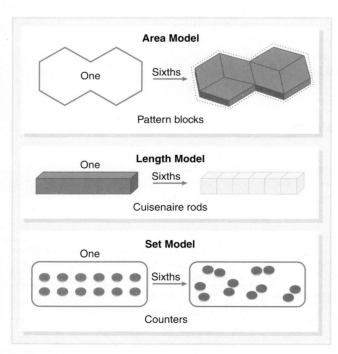

FIGURE 14.8 Which of these shapes are partitioned into sixths? Explain why or why not for each.

> **MyLab Education**
> **Video Example 14.6**
>
> Watch this video of a small group reasoning about the size of the parts when the whole is not fully partitioned.

Some manipulatives, like fraction bars or fraction circles, can mislead students to believe that fractional parts must be the same *shape* as well as the same size. Color tiles can be used to create rectangles that address this misconception, such as the one illustrated here:

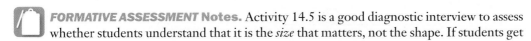

Students who recognize that each color represents thirds understand that fractional parts must be the same size, and that the shape may be different. Activity 14.1 (Playground Fractions) offers an example of using pattern blocks to focus on equal-sized parts, which can be repeated by building other shapes that use different pattern block pieces. Activity 14.5 offers a similar experience with partitioning various shapes.

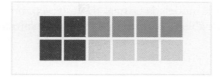

Activity 14.5   CCSS-M: 1.G.A.3; 2.G.A.3; 3.NF.A.1

Partitioning: Fourths or Not Fourths?

STUDENTS
with
SPECIAL
NEEDS

Use Fourths or Not Fourths Activity Page showing examples and nonexamples (which are very important to use with students with disabilities) of fourths (see Figure 14.9).

 Ask students to identify the wholes that are correctly divided into fourths (equal shares) and those that are not. For each response, have students explain their reasoning. Repeat with other fractional parts, such as thirds or eighths. To challenge students, ask them to draw shapes that fit each of the four categories listed on the next page for other fractional parts, such as sixths. (See Sixths or Not Sixths Activity Page.)

> MyLab Education   Activity Page: Fourths or Not Fourths
> MyLab Education   Activity Page: Sixths or Not Sixths

In the preceding activity, the shapes fall in each of the following categories:

1. Same shape, same size [equivalent]: (a) and (f)
2. Different shape, same size [equivalent]: (e) and (g)
3. Different shape, different size [not equivalent]: (b) and (c)
4. Same shape, different size [not equivalent]: (d)

FORMATIVE ASSESSMENT Notes. Activity 14.5 is a good diagnostic interview to assess whether students understand that it is the *size* that matters, not the shape. If students get

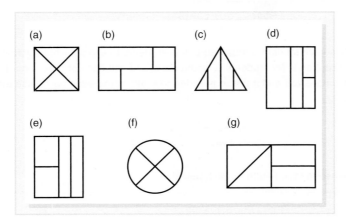

FIGURE 14.9 Which of these partitioned regions show fourths?

all correct except (e) and (g), they hold the misconception that parts should be the same shape. Future tasks are needed that focus on equivalence. For example, you can ask students to take a square and partition it themselves in as many ways as they can. ■

Partitioning with length models is critical to understanding fractions as numbers. For example, students need to be able to partition a number line into fourths and realize that each section is one-fourth:

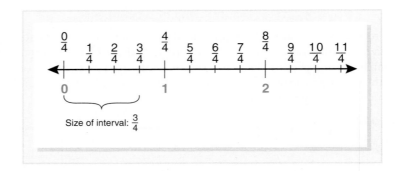

With number lines, students may ignore the size of the interval (McNamara & Shaughnessy, 2010; Petit et al., 2010). A good way to help students understand the number line is to create and use paper strips. Provide examples where the shaded sections are in different positions and where partitioning isn't already shown to strengthen students' understanding of equal parts. Activity 14.6 and Activity 14.7 provide such opportunities, one with paper strips and one with number lines.

Activity 14.6 CCSS-M: 3.NF.A.1; 3.NF.A.2a, b

What Fraction Is Colored?

Prepare a set of paper strips prior to doing this activity (you can cut 1-inch wide pieces of 8.5" by 11" paper and shade, or cut pieces of adding machine tape). Color the strips so that they have a fractional amount shaded in various positions (not just left justified!) (Sarazen, 2012). Here are a few examples:

Explain that the strip represents one whole. Give each student a paper strip. Ask students to explain what fraction is colored and explain how they know. A common misconception is for students to count parts and call each of these one-third. If a student makes this error, ask if the parts are the same-sized and if not to partition to make same-sized parts. Use toothpicks or uncooked spaghetti to illustrate the partitions:

Students can also justify their reasoning by measuring the length of each partition.

Using paper strips can help students better understand the number line, the focus of the next activity.

Activity 14.7

CCSS-M: 3.NF.A.1; 3.NF.A.2a, b

How Far Did Nicole Go?

Give students number lines partitioned such that only some of the partitions are showing. Use a context such as walking to school. For each number line, ask, "How far has Nicole gone? How do you know?"

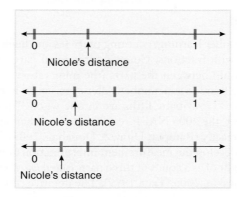

Students can justify their reasoning by measuring the length of each partition.

Locating a fractional value on a number line is particularly challenging but very important. Shaughnessy (2011) found four common errors students make in working with the number line: They (1) use incorrect notation, (2) change the unit (whole), (3) count the tick marks rather than the space between the marks, and (4) count the ticks marks that appear without noticing any missing ones. This is evidence that we must use number lines more extensively in exploring fractions, along with formative assessment tools to monitor students developing conceptions.

Partitioning using a length diagram is a strategy commonly used in Singapore (a high-performing country on international mathematics assessments) as a way to solve story problems. Consider the following story problem (Englard, 2010):

A nurse has 54 bandages. Of those, $\frac{2}{9}$ are green and the rest are blue. How many of them are blue?

To solve, a student first partitions a strip into nine parts and then figures out the equal shares of bandages for each partition:

Did you notice that this is an example of fraction as operator? These types of partitioning tasks are good building blocks for multiplying with fractions.

Students can partition with set models such as coins, counters, or baseball cards. In the example in Figure 14.8, the 12 counters are partitioned into 6 sets—*sixths*. Each share or part has two counters, but it is the number of shares that makes the partition show *sixths*. As with the other models, when the equal parts are not already figured out, then students may not see how to partition. Students seeing a picture of two cats and four dogs might think $\frac{2}{4}$ are cats (Bamberger, Oberdorf, & Schultz-Ferrell, 2010). Consider the following problem:

Eloise has 6 trading cards, Andre has 4 trading cards, and Lu has 2 trading cards. What fraction of the trading cards does Lu have?

CCSS Standards for Mathematical Practice
MP4. Model with Mathematics.

CCSS Standards for
Mathematical
Practice
MP7. Look for and make
use of structure.

A student who answers "one-third" is not thinking about equal shares but about the number of people with trading cards.

Understanding that parts of a whole must be partitioned into equal-sized parts across different models is an important step in conceptualizing fractions and provides a foundation for exploring sharing and equivalence tasks, all of which are prerequisites to performing fraction operations (Cramer & Whitney, 2010).

Iterating

In whole-number learning, counting precedes and helps students to add and later subtract. This is also true with fractions. Counting fractional parts, or *iterating*, helps students understand the relationship between the parts (the numerator) and the whole (the denominator) and to understand a fraction as a number. After experiences iterating, students should be able to answer the question, "How many fifths are in one whole?" just as they know how many ones are in ten. However, the 2008 NAEP results indicated that only 44 percent of students answered this question correctly (Rampey, Dion, & Donahue, 2009). The purpose of iterating activities is for students to develop the measurement interpretation of fractions, specifically that $\frac{3}{4}$, for example, can be thought of as a count of three parts called *fourths* (Post, Wachsmuth, Lesh, & Behr, 1985; Siebert & Gaskin, 2006; Tzur, 1999). The iterative concept builds meaning of fraction symbols:

*   The numerator *counts*.
*   The denominator tells *what is being counted*.

Iterating can be done concretely by using a single piece, representing one unit or one share, and repeating it a number of times to "measure" how many are in the whole. While equal shares can be found by partitioning, estimating one share and seeing if it is accurate builds understanding of the relative size of unit fractions (Tzur & Hunt, 2015).

Activity 14.8

CCSS-M: 3.NF.A.1; 3.NF.A.2a, b

Estimating and Counting Fair Shares

**ENGLISH
LEARNERS**

Select a length context such as pretzel sticks, licorice, or ribbon. Distribute several paper strips to each pair of students, one of which in a different color to represent one whole (pretzel). Ask students to estimate how long they think a fair share is for each of the following situations, test their estimates, and try again. Special rule: no paper folding!

Shares for 2 friends	Shares for 3 friends	Shares for 4 friends
Shares for 6 friends	Shares for 8 friends	Shares for 12 friends

For example, for shares with 3 friends, students will cut a piece from one of their additional strips that they think represents one-third and iterate it (lay it down three times or cut it out three times and lay each piece next to each other) to see if it reaches one whole. If it is too short or too long, they try again until they find a piece that is approximately accurate. Label it as "one-third" and/or $\frac{1}{3}$. As you observe, ask students to count the shares to show you the fair shares (one-third, two-thirds, three-thirds). Ask questions such as, "What strategies are you using to see if your piece is a fair share?" "Will your next try to a longer piece or a shorter piece? (Why?)" "What strategies are you using to estimate the fair share/unit length?" As you and the students describe the shares as fractional parts (e.g., fourths) emphasize the 'th' sound to distinguish from counting numbers (e.g., fours). This is particularly important for ELs.

Iterating makes sense with length models because iterating is like measuring. And, the number line is a good model for iterating with mixed number.

MyLab Education   **Video Example 14.7**

Watch this classroom video of a teacher building on students' understanding of fractions to iterate with mixed numbers.

VIDEO EXAMPLE

Emily has $2\frac{1}{2}$ yards of ribbon and needs pieces that are one-fourth yards for making bows. How many pieces can she cut?

To begin, students draw a strip (or line) representing $2\frac{1}{2}$ yards:

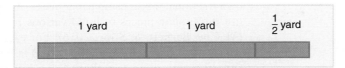

Next, the strip is partitioned into fourths (the unit) and counted—10 fourths:

Activity 14.9   CCSS-M: 3.NF.A.1; 3.NF.A.2a, b

More, Less, or Equal to One Whole

Give students A Collection of Fractional Parts Activity Page and Cuisenaire rods. Indicate the kind of fractional part they have. For example, a collection might have seven light green rods/strips with a caption or note indicating "Each light green rod is $\frac{1}{8}$." The task is to decide if the collection is less than one whole, equal to one whole, or more than one whole. Ask students to draw pictures or use symbols to explain their answer. Adding a context, such as people sharing candy bars, pizzas, or sticks of clay, can help children understand and reason through the problem. Ask, "Why does it take more fourths to make a whole than thirds?" "Why did we get two wholes with four halves but just a little more than one whole with four thirds?" Take this opportunity to connect this language to mixed numbers. "What is another way we could say ten-fourths?" (Possible responses are two wholes and two-fourths, or two wholes and one-half, or one whole and six-fourths.)

MyLab Education   Activity Page: A Collection of Fractional Parts

Students can participate in many tasks that involve iterating lengths, including ones where they are asked to find what the whole or unit is.

Activity 14.10   CCSS-M: 3.NF.A.1; 3.NF.A.2a, b

A Whole Lot of Fun

Use A Whole Lot of Fun Activity Page and the Cutouts for Fraction Strips Activity Page like the one here:

Tell students that this strip is three-fourths of one whole (unit). Ask students to sketch strips of the other lengths on their paper (e.g., $\frac{5}{2}$). You can repeat this activity by selecting other values for the starting amount and selecting different fractional values to sketch. A context, such as walking, is effective in helping students make sense of the situation. Be sure to use fractions less than and greater than 1 and mixed numbers.

MyLab Education   Activity Page: A Whole Lot of Fun
MyLab Education   Activity Page: Cutouts for Fraction Strips

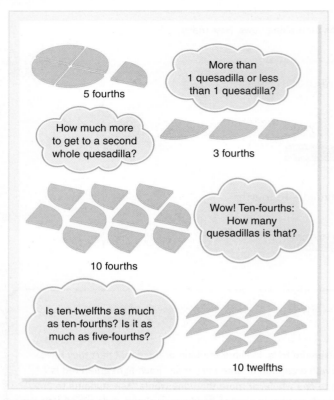

FIGURE 14.10 Iterating fractional parts in an area model.

Notice that to solve the task in Activity 14.10, students first partition the piece into three sections to find $\frac{1}{4}$ and then iterate the $\frac{1}{4}$ to find the other lengths.

Iterating can also be done with area models, for example the Circular Fractional Pieces in Figure 14.10 using the context of quesadillas. Or, engage students in creating their own fractional pieces using paper plates of various colors and use those plate pieces to build various fractional amounts (McCoy, Barnett, & Stine, 2016)! For each collection, tell students what type of piece (portion) is being shown and simply count them together: "One-fourth, two-fourths, three-fourths, four-fourths, five-fourths." Ask, "If we have five-fourths, is that more than one whole, less than one whole, or the same as one whole?" To reinforce the piece size even more, you can slightly alter your language to say, "One one-fourth, two one-fourths, three one-fourths," and so on. See Figure 14.10 for some great questions to ask as your students are counting each collection of parts. Make comparisons between different collections: "Why did we get more than two wholes with ten-fourths, and yet we don't even have one whole with ten-twelfths?"

> **MyLab Education**   **Activity Page: Circular Fractional Pieces**

Activity 14.11 returns to using pattern blocks (See Activity 14.1) to help students focus on the size of the parts, not the number of pieces or partitions (Champion & Wheeler, 2014; Ellington & Whitenack, 2010). In building creatures, students are partitioning and iterating.

Activity 14.11

CCSS-M: 3.NF.A.1; 3.NF.A.2a, b

Pattern Block Creatures

Ask students to build a Pattern Block Creature that fits with a set of rules (a creature represents one-whole). These rules can begin with just stating a fractional quantity for a color, such as "The red trapezoid is one-fourth of the creature." But, more constraints can be added to the rules. For example:

- The blue parallelogram is one-sixth of the creature. Use at least two colors to build your creature.
- The yellow hexagon is one-half of the creature. Use three colors to build your creature.
- Green triangles are one-third of your creature. Use four different colors to build your creature.

After a student creates their creature based on these rules, have them count the fractional parts to make sure they have a whole creature.

Then have students write their own rules for their own pattern block creature. Instruct them to trace the outline of their creature on a piece of paper and write a rule, such as "The red trapezoid is ____ of my creature." Students can trade with other students to see if they can figure out the fractional amounts for each other's creatures.

Iteration can also be done with set models, but it is more challenging. For example, show a collection of two-color counters and ask questions such as, "If 5 counters is one-fourth of the whole, how much of the whole is 15 counters?" These problems can be framed as engaging puzzles for students. For example: "Three counters represent $\frac{1}{8}$ of my set; how big is my set?" If the fraction is not a unit fraction, then students first partition and then iterate. For example, "Twenty counters represents $\frac{2}{3}$ of my set; how big is my set?" first requires finding find $\frac{1}{3}$

(10 counters), then iterating that three times to get 30 counters in three-thirds (one whole). Counting Counters: Find the Part Activity Page and Counting Counters: Find the Whole Activity Page provides such problems for students to solve.

| MyLab Education | Activity Page: Counting Counters: Find the Part |
| MyLab Education | Activity Page: Counting Counters: Find the Whole |

Finally, iterating can be done on a calculator, transitioning students to mentally visualizing fractional parts.

Activity 14.12   CCSS-M: 3.NF.A.1; 3.NF.A.3a, c

Calculator Fraction Counting

STUDENTS with SPECIAL NEEDS

Many calculators display fractions in correct fraction format and offer a choice of showing results as mixed numbers or simple fractions. Ask students to type in a fraction (e.g., $\frac{1}{4}$) and then + and the fraction again. To count, press 0 `Op1`, `Op1`, `Op1`, repeating to get the number of fourths wanted. The display will show the counts by fourths and also the number of times that the `Op1` key has been pressed. Ask students questions such as the following: "How many fourths to get to 3?" "How many fifths to get to 2?" These can get increasingly more challenging: "How many fourths to get to $4\frac{1}{2}$?" "How many two-thirds to get to 6? Estimate and then count by two-thirds on the calculator." Students, particularly students with disabilities, can coordinate their counts with a concrete fraction model (e.g., Cuisenaire Rods).

FORMATIVE ASSESSMENT Notes. The tasks in Figures 14.11 and 14.12 can be used as performance assessments. If students are able to solve these types of tasks, they can partition and iterate. That means they are ready to do equivalence and comparison tasks. If they are not able to solve problems such as these, provide a range of similar tasks, using real-life contexts and involving area, length, and set models. ■

Magnitude of Fractions

Number sense with fractions requires that students have some intuitive feel of the size (or magnitude) of fractions. This requires that students see a fraction as a number, which helps them develop "fraction sense" (Fennell, Kobett, & Wray, 2014). The use of contexts, models, and mental imagery can help students build a strong understanding of the relative size of fractions (Bray & Abreu-Sanchez, 2010; Petit et al., 2010; Tobias, 2014).

As with whole numbers, students are less confident and less capable of estimating than they are at computing exact answers, yet a focus on estimation can strengthen their understanding of fractions (Clarke & Roche, 2009). Therefore, you need to provide many opportunities for students

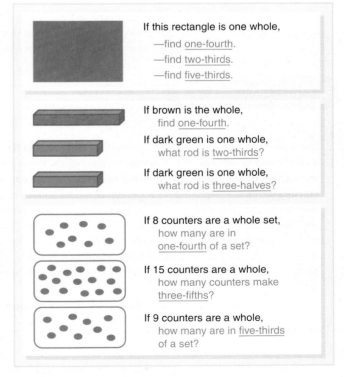

FIGURE 14.11   Given the whole and the fraction, find the part.

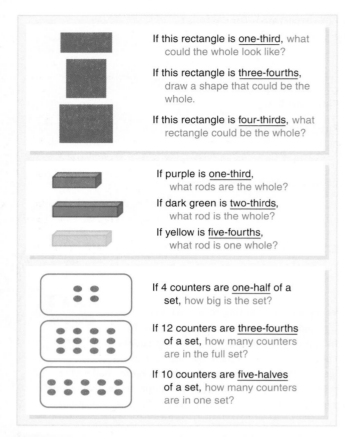

FIGURE 14.12 Given the part and the fraction, find the whole.

to reason about the relative size of a fraction. Ask questions like "About what fraction of your classmates are wearing sweaters?" Or after tallying survey data about a topic like favorite dinner, ask, "About what fraction of our class picked spaghetti?" Additionally, have students approximate fractions for shaded regions and points on the number line (See Figure 14.13).

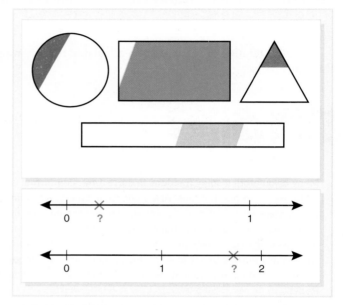

FIGURE 14.13 About how much? Name a fraction for each drawing and explain why you chose that fraction.

The number line is a good model for helping students develop a better understanding for the relative size of a fraction (Petit, Laird, & Marsden, 2010) and is therefore effective for estimating about the relative size of fractions.

Activity 14.13   CCSS-M: 3.NF.A.2a; 3.NF.A.2b

Fractions *on* the Number Line

STUDENTS with SPECIAL NEEDS

Use a piece of rope as long as the room (this works well in the hall or gym, too!) Have two students stand and hold the end of the rope and also hold number cards. For example, the student on the left end can hold 0 and the student on the right end can hold 1 (these end points can change to other values). Give out a variety of Fraction Cards (appropriate for your group of students) with clips or clothespins. Ask a volunteer to place their fraction *on* the number line. Ask, "Is this fraction in the approximate correct location?" "How do you know?" Students can fold the rope to determine benchmark fractions such as $\frac{1}{4}$, $\frac{1}{2}$, or $\frac{3}{4}$) and use other strategies to determine approximate locations on the number line. Continue to have students place their fractions on the number line. This activity can be played repeatedly with cards that include equivalent fractions (placed at the exact same point), cards with fractions greater than one (use larger pieces of rope and more holding points), and eventually decimals and variables (see Bay, 2001).

MyLab Education   Activity Page: Fraction Cards

After experiences with number lines and other models, students need opportunities to reason about the relative size of fractions using mental strategies considering what benchmark they are near. For example, if students think about where $\frac{3}{20}$ might be by partitioning a number line between 0 and 1, they will see that $\frac{3}{20}$ is close to 0, whereas $\frac{9}{10}$ is quite close to 1. And this applies to fractions greater than one—for example, $3\frac{3}{7}$ is close to the benchmark $3\frac{1}{2}$.

Activity 14.14

CCSS-M: 3.NF.A.3d; 4.NF.A.2

Zero, One-Half, or One

Create sets of Fraction Cards for each small group of students. A few should be greater than $1\frac{9}{8}$ or $\frac{11}{10}$, with the others ranging from 0 to 1. Let students sort the fractions into three groups: those close to 0, close to $\frac{1}{2}$, and close to 1. For those close to $\frac{1}{2}$, have them decide whether the fraction is more or less than half. The difficulty of this task largely depends on the fractions you select. The first time you try this, use fractions that are very close to the three benchmarks, such as $\frac{1}{20}$, $\frac{53}{100}$, or $\frac{9}{10}$. On subsequent days, mostly use fractions with denominators less than 20. You might include a few fractions that are exactly in between the benchmarks, such as $\frac{2}{8}$ or $\frac{3}{4}$. Ask students to explain how they are using the numerator and denominator to decide. For ELs, be sure the term *benchmark* is understood and encourage illustrations as well as explanations.

As an extension or alternative to differentiate this activity, ask students to create their own fractions close to each benchmark fraction.

MyLab Education   Activity Page: Fraction Cards

MyLab Education   Self-Check 14.2

Equivalent Fractions

As discussed in Chapter 13, equivalence is a critical but often poorly understood concept. This is particularly true with fraction equivalence. In the CCSS-M, fraction equivalence and comparisons are emphasized in grade 3 and applied in grade 4 (and beyond) as students engage in computation with fractions. Students cannot be successful in fraction computation without a strong understanding of fraction equivalence.

MyLab Education   Video Example 14.8

Watch this video wherein John Van de Walle describes important ideas, which are also illustrated in a whole class lesson.

Conceptual Focus on Equivalence

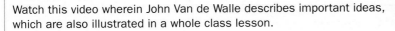

 Pause & Reflect

How do you know that $\frac{4}{6} = \frac{2}{3}$? Before reading further, think of at least two different explanations. ●

Here are some possible answers to the preceding question:

1. They are the same because you can simplify $\frac{4}{6}$ and get $\frac{2}{3}$.
2. If you have a set of 6 items and you take 4 of them, that would be $\frac{4}{6}$. But you can make the 6 into 3 groups, and the 4 would be 2 groups out of the 3 groups. That means it's $\frac{2}{3}$.

3. If you start with $\frac{2}{3}$, you can multiply the top and the bottom numbers by 2, and that will give you $\frac{4}{6}$, so they are equal.

4. If you had a square cut into 3 parts and you shaded 2, that would be $\frac{2}{3}$ shaded. If you cut all 3 of these parts in half, that would be 4 parts shaded and 6 parts in all. That's $\frac{4}{6}$, and it would be the same amount.

Standards for Mathematical Practice

MP2. Reason abstractly and quantitatively.

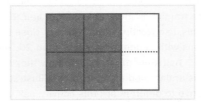

All of these answers are correct. But let's think about what they tell us. Responses 2 and 4 are conceptual, although not as efficient. The procedural responses, 1 and 3, are efficient but do not indicate conceptual understanding. Consider how different the procedure and the concept appear to be:

Concept: Two fractions are equivalent if they are representations for the same amount or quantity—if they are the same number.

Procedure: To get an equivalent fraction, multiply (or divide) the top and bottom numbers by the same nonzero number.

Rushing too quickly to the algorithm can impede students' conceptual understanding of fractions and fraction equivalence. Students need to see the connections between the concept and the procedure, and this requires multiple experiences (and time). Be patient!

Equivalent Fraction Models

To help students build a strong and flexible understanding of equivalent fractions requires the use many contexts and models in which the goal is to rename a fractional amount. This is the first time in students' experience that they are seeing that a fixed quantity can have more than one name (actually an infinite number of names). Area models are a good place to begin understanding equivalence (see Figure 14.14).

Activity 14.15   CCSS-M: 3.NF.A.1; 3.NF.3a, b, c

Making Stacks

Select a manipulative that lends to exploring fractions (e.g., pattern blocks, tangrams, fraction strips, or fraction circles). Prepare Fraction Cards with different fractional amounts, such as $\frac{2}{3}$, $\frac{1}{2}$, $\frac{3}{4}$, 1, $\frac{3}{2}$, $\frac{4}{3}$, and 2. (Note: you may want to begin with fractions less than 1, then move to fractions equal to and greater than 1.) Select a context that fits the manipulative (e.g., pancakes, quesadillas, pizza, or cookies for a circle model). Students use their manipulative to (1) determine a whole, (2) build the fraction on their card with pieces, stacking it on top of the whole, and (3) find as many equivalent fractions as possible, stacking each new equivalency on top. For example, with fraction circles, and a card of $\frac{3}{4}$, a student picks the whole circle as the whole, places 3 of the fourths pieces on top of the whole, and then looks for other fractional pieces (same size) to stack. In this case, 6 eighths can stack on top. Ask students to record all the possibilities they find, drawing a sketch and writing the equation. Ask for students to use the context to explain the equivalency. For example, if they ate 3-fourths of a pizza, it is the same as 6-eighths, just cut in different sized pieces. Repeat with different fraction cards, including fractions that are not in simplest form.

MyLab Education   Activity Page: Fraction Cards

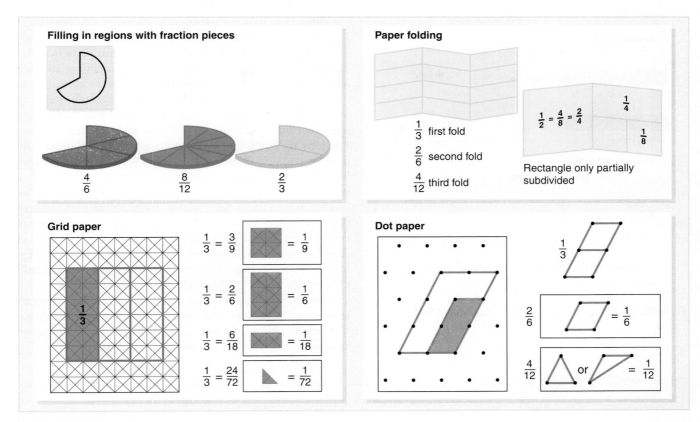

FIGURE 14.14 Area models for equivalent fractions.

In a follow-up classroom discussion, ask students to consider what other equivalencies are possible (and justify their thinking) beyond what they could build with their manipulative. For example, ask, "What equivalent fractions could you find for $\frac{3}{4}$ if we had sixteenths in our fraction kit? If you could have a piece of any size at all, what other fraction names are possible?" or "If the pizza was cut into 16 equal-sized pieces, what would your equivalent portion be?"

The next activity moves from using manipulatives to sketches on paper, opening up more fraction equivalencies for each illustration.

Activity 14.16   CCSS-M: 3.NF.A.1; 3.NF.3a, b, c

Dot Paper Equivalencies

Use Fraction Names Activity Page, which includes three different grids with a fraction shaded (each enclosed area represents one whole). Ask students how many fraction names they think the first problem has. Then ask them to see how many they can find (working individually or in partners). Invite students to share and explain the fraction names they found for problem 1. Repeat for the next two problems. Alternatively, cut this page into three task cards, laminate the cards, and place each at a station along with an overhead pen. Have students rotate in partners to a station and see how many fraction names they can find for that shape (using the pen as needed to show their ways). Rotate to the next station. See Expanded Lesson: Dot Paper Equivalencies for details.

To make additional pictures, create your own using your choice of Grid Paper or Dot Paper (see Blackline Masters 5–11). (Figure 14.14 includes an example drawn on an isometric grid).

MyLab Education   Activity Page: Fraction Names
MyLab Education   Expanded Lesson: Dot Paper Equivalencies
MyLab Education   Blackline Master: 1-Centimeter Square/Diagonal Grid Paper
MyLab Education   Blackline Master: 1-Centimeter Isometric Dot Paper

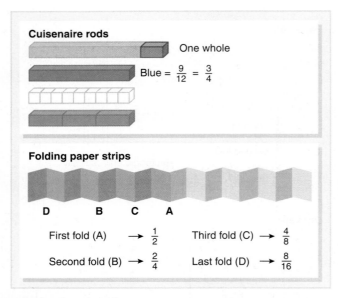

Cuisenaire rods

One whole

Blue = $\frac{9}{12}$ = $\frac{3}{4}$

Folding paper strips

D   B   C   A

First fold (A) → $\frac{1}{2}$ Third fold (C) → $\frac{4}{8}$

Second fold (B) → $\frac{2}{4}$ Last fold (D) → $\frac{8}{16}$

FIGURE 14.15 Length models for equivalent fractions.

The Dot Paper Equivalencies activity involves what Lamon (2012) calls *unitizing*—that is, given a quantity, finding different ways to chunk the quantity into parts in order to name it. She points out that this is a key ability related not only to equivalent fractions but also to proportional reasoning.

Length models must be used to develop understanding of equivalent fractions. Asking students to locate $\frac{2}{5}$ and $\frac{4}{10}$ on a number line, for example, can help them see that the two fractions are equivalent but the line is partitioned differently (Siegler et al., 2010) (see Activity 14.13 for a life-sized number line activity). Cuiseniare rods can be used to designate both a whole and a part, as illustrated in Figure 14.15. Students use smaller rods to find fraction names for the given part. To have larger wholes or values greater than one whole, use a train of two or three rods. Folding paper strips is another method of showing equivalent fractions. In the example shown in Figure 14.15, one-half is subdivided by successive folding in half. Other folds would produce other equivalent fractions.

Legos, a highly motivating manipulative, can help students learn to write fraction equivalencies (for an excellent elaboration on this idea, see Gould, 2011). Lego bricks can be viewed as an area (array) or as a set (students can count the studs).

Activity 14.17

CCSS-M: 2.G.A.3; 3.NF.A.1; 3.NF.3a, b, c; 4.NF.B.3a, b

LEGO® Land: Building Options

Hand out one 2-by-6 LEGO to each student. Ask them to describe it (there are 12 studs, two rows of 6). For second grade or as a warm-up, ask students what same-colored pieces could cover their land (e.g., 6 of the 2-by-1 pieces). Ask students to imagine that 12 pieces of LEGO blocks represents one plot of land. It can be covered with various smaller pieces as shown here:

Ask students to build the plot of land using different Lego pieces (1-by-2, 1-by-3, 2-by-2, 1-by-1, 2-by-6, etc.). After they have completed their plot of land, ask students to tell the fraction of their land that is represented by a particular piece (e.g., the 2-by-6 is $\frac{6}{12}$ as well as $\frac{1}{2}$ and $\frac{2}{4}$).

To focus on iteration and to build connections to addition (grade 4), students can write equations to describe their LEGO Land. In the one pictured here, that would be

$$\frac{6}{12} + \frac{3}{12} + \frac{2}{12} + \frac{1}{12} \quad \text{OR} \quad \frac{1}{2} + \frac{1}{4} + \frac{1}{6} + \frac{1}{12}.$$

Note that students have misconceptions about how to name fractions parts, naming the blue part as $\frac{1}{3}$ rather than $\frac{1}{4}$ because they see three pieces (Wilkerson, Bryan, & Curry, 2012). This becomes a good topic for a classroom discussion: What is the fractional value of the blue pieces (simplified)?

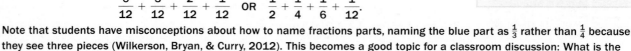

Two color counters (set model) are an effective tool for fraction equivalencies.

Activity 14.18

CCSS-M: 3.NF.A.1; 3.NF.3a, b, c

Apples and Bananas

ENGLISH LEARNERS

Use Apples and Bananas Activity Page or just have students set out a specific number of counters in two colors—for example, 24 counters, with 16 of them red (apples) and 8 of them yellow (bananas). The 24 counters make up the whole. Ask students to group the apples and bananas into equal-sized groups, such that a group has to have only apples or only bananas. Challenge them to find as many ways as they can. For each that they find, record the fraction names for apples and for bananas. They can record each option they find in a table, which helps notice patterns. Ask questions such as, "Is it possible to have the fruit in groups of 4?" to encourage students to think of different ways to form equal-sized groups. Counters can be arranged in different groups or in arrays (see illustrations in Figures 14.16 and 14.17 on the next page). ELs may not know what the term *group* means because when used in classrooms, the word usually refers to arranging students. Spend time before the activity modeling what it means to group objects.

MyLab Education   Activity Page: Apples and Bananas

In the activities so far, there has only been a hint of a rule for finding equivalent fractions. Activity 14.19 begins to build the connection between the concept and the procedure by using manipulatives.

Activity 14.19

CCSS-M: 3.NF.3a, b, c; 4.NF.A.1

Missing-Number Equivalencies

Use Missing-Number Equivalencies Activity Page or give students an equation expressing an equivalence between two fractions, but with an unknown value. Ask students to use counters or rectangles to illustrate and find the equivalent fraction. Example equations:

$$\frac{5}{3} = \frac{\ }{6} \qquad \frac{2}{3} = \frac{6}{\ } \qquad \frac{8}{12} = \frac{\ }{3} \qquad \frac{9}{12} = \frac{3}{\ }$$

The missing value can be in a numerator or a denominator; the missing number can be either larger or smaller than the corresponding part of the equivalent fraction. (All four possibilities are represented in the examples.) Figure 14.18 illustrates how Zachary represented the equivalencies with equations and partitioning rectangles. The examples shown above involve simple whole-number multiples between equivalent fractions. Next, consider pairs such as $\frac{6}{8} = \frac{\ }{12}$ or $\frac{9}{12} = \frac{6}{\ }$. In these equivalencies, one denominator or numerator is not a whole-number multiple of the other. Include equivalencies for whole numbers and fractions greater than one: $\frac{8}{x} = \frac{6}{6} \qquad \frac{10}{3} = \frac{x}{9}$

MyLab Education   Activity Page: Missing-Number Equivalencies

When doing "Missing-Number Equivalencies" you may want to specify a particular model, such as grid paper (area), paper strips/number line (length) or two-color counters (set). Students who have learning disabilities and other students who struggle with mathematics may benefit from using clocks to do equivalence; for example, to find equivalent fractions for $\frac{10}{12}, \frac{3}{4}, \frac{4}{6}$, and so on (Chick, Tierney, & Storeygard, 2007). NCTM's Illuminations website offers an excellent set of three units called "Fun with Fractions." Each unit uses one of the model types (area, length, or set) and focuses on comparing and ordering fractions and equivalencies. The five to six lessons in each unit incorporate a range of manipulatives and engaging activities to support student learning.

Fractions Greater than 1

Students must be able to move flexibly between fractions greater than 1 (e.g., $\frac{13}{6}$) and mixed numbers (e.g., $2\frac{1}{6}$). If students have counted fractional parts beyond one whole, they know how to write $\frac{13}{6}$. And, if you have encouraged them to also tell how many wholes they have counted, they will also know this is equivalent to $2\frac{1}{6}$, without having to apply an algorithm, but by knowing the meaning of the numerator and denominator. If they have not had these experiences with iterating, then you must provide such experiences. It is not appropriate to just tell students to "divide the numerator by the denominator and write the remainder as a fraction." As illustrated in Figure 14.19, connecting cubes are very effective in showing how fractions greater than one can be written as whole numbers or mixed numbers (Neumer, 2007). Students identify one cube as the unit fraction $\left(\frac{1}{5}\right)$ for the problem $\left(\frac{12}{5}\right)$. They count out 12 fifths and build wholes. Conversely,

Apples and Bananas

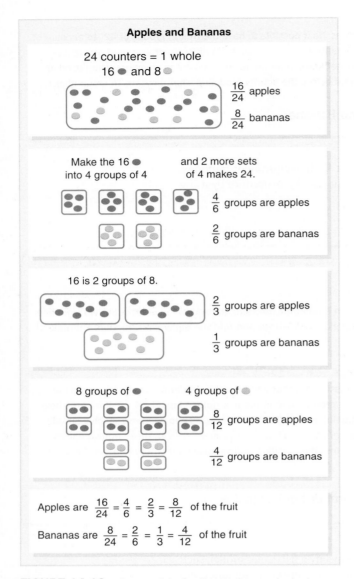

24 counters = 1 whole
16 ● and 8 ◐

$\frac{16}{24}$ apples

$\frac{8}{24}$ bananas

Make the 16 ● into 4 groups of 4 and 2 more sets of 4 makes 24.

$\frac{4}{6}$ groups are apples

$\frac{2}{6}$ groups are bananas

16 is 2 groups of 8.

$\frac{2}{3}$ groups are apples

$\frac{1}{3}$ groups are bananas

8 groups of ●   4 groups of ◐

$\frac{8}{12}$ groups are apples

$\frac{4}{12}$ groups are bananas

Apples are $\frac{16}{24} = \frac{4}{6} = \frac{2}{3} = \frac{8}{12}$ of the fruit

Bananas are $\frac{8}{24} = \frac{2}{6} = \frac{1}{3} = \frac{4}{12}$ of the fruit

FIGURE 14.16 Set models for illustrating equivalent fractions.

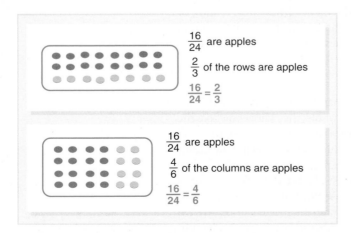

$\frac{16}{24}$ are apples

$\frac{2}{3}$ of the rows are apples

$\frac{16}{24} = \frac{2}{3}$

$\frac{16}{24}$ are apples

$\frac{4}{6}$ of the columns are apples

$\frac{16}{24} = \frac{4}{6}$

FIGURE 14.17 Arrays for illustrating equivalent fractions.

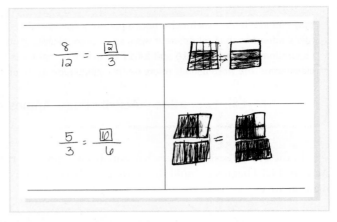

$\frac{8}{12} = \frac{\boxed{2}}{3}$

$\frac{5}{3} = \frac{\boxed{10}}{6}$

FIGURE 14.18 A student illustrates equivalence fractions by partitioning rectangles.

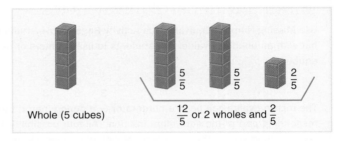

Whole (5 cubes) $\frac{5}{5}$ $\frac{5}{5}$ $\frac{2}{5}$ $\frac{12}{5}$ or 2 wholes and $\frac{2}{5}$

FIGURE 14.19 Connecting cubes are used to represent the equivalence of $\frac{12}{5}$ and $2\frac{2}{5}$.

they could start with the mixed number, build it, and find out how many total cubes (or fifths) were used. Repeated experiences in building and solving these tasks will help students to notice a pattern that actually explains the algorithm for moving between mixed numbers and fractions greater than 1.

MyLab Education
Video Example 14.9

Watch this video of a teacher moving from concrete experiences to mental images to help students see relationships between mixed numbers and fractions.

Help students move from physical models to mental images. Challenge students to figure out the two equivalent forms by just picturing the stacks in their heads. A good explanation for $3\frac{1}{4}$ might be that there are 4 fourths in one whole, so there are 8 fourths in two wholes and 12 fourths in three wholes. The extra fourth makes 13 fourths in all, or $\frac{13}{4}$. (Note the iteration concept playing a role.) Do not push the standard algorithm, as it can interfere with students making sense of the relationship between the two representations. Allow students to make this generalization through their experiences.

Developing an Equivalent-Fraction Algorithm

When students understand that fractions can have different (but equivalent) names, they are ready to develop a method for finding equivalent names for a particular value. An area model is a good visual for connecting the concept of equivalence to the standard algorithm for finding equivalent fractions (multiply both the top and bottom numbers by the same number to get an equivalent fraction). Ask students to look for a pattern in the way that the fractional parts in both the part and the whole are counted.

Standards for Mathematical Practice

MP8. Look for and express regularity in repeated reasoning.

Activity 14.20   CCSS-M: 3.NF.3b; 4.NF.A.1

Garden Plots

Have students draw a square "garden" on blank paper, or give each student a square of paper (like origami paper). Begin by explaining that the garden is divided into rows of various vegetables. In the first example, you might illustrate four rows (fourths) and designate $\frac{3}{4}$ as corn. Ask students to partition their square into four rows and shade three-fourths as in Figure 14.20. Then explain that the garden is going to be shared with family and friends in a way that each person gets a harvest that is $\frac{3}{4}$ corn. Show how the garden can be partitioned horizontally to represent two people sharing (eighths). Ask what fraction of the newly divided garden is corn $\left(\frac{6}{8}\right)$. Next, tell students to illustrate ways that more friends can share the garden (they can choose how many friends, or you can). For each newly divided garden, ask students to record what fraction of the garden is corn, using a table, equations, or both:

People sharing garden	1	2	3	4	. . .	
Sections of corn	3	6				
Sections of garden	4	8				

After students have prepared their own examples, provide time for them to look at their fractions and gardens and notice patterns about the fractions and the diagrams. Once they have time to do this individually, ask students to share. Figure 14.21 provides student explanations that illustrate the range of "noticing."

As you can see, for some of these students more experiences are needed. You can also assist in helping students

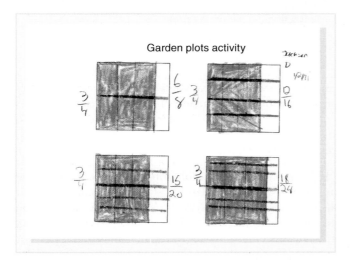

Garden plots activity

FIGURE 14.20   A third grader partitions a garden to model fraction equivalencies.

(a)

I noticed that on number 3 on both numbers you can multiply by 2 to get the new fraction,

(b)

You can multiply the numerater and the denominator wich will create an equivollnt fraction.

(c)

What do you notice? I notice if you multiply the top you also multiply it to the bottom by the same number.

FIGURE 14.21   Students explain what they notice about fraction equivalencies based on partitioning "gardens" in different ways.

make the connection from the partitioned square to the procedure by displaying a square (for example, partitioned to show $\frac{4}{5}$) (see Figure 14.22). Then, partition the square vertically into six parts, covering most of the square as shown in the figure. Ask, "What is the new name for my $\frac{4}{5}$?"

The reason for this exercise is that it helps students see the connection to multiplication. With the covered square, students can see that there are four columns and six rows to the shaded part, so there must be 4×6 parts shaded. Similarly, there must be 5×6 parts in the whole. Therefore, the new name for $\frac{4}{5}$ is $\frac{4 \times 6}{5 \times 6}$, or $\frac{24}{30}$.

Writing Fractions in Simplest Terms. The multiplication scheme for equivalent fractions produces fractions with larger denominators. But creating equivalent forms for $\frac{6}{8}$ might involve multiplication to get $\frac{12}{16}$ or division to get $\frac{3}{4}$. To write a fraction in *simplest terms* means to write it so that numerator and denominator have no common whole-number factors. One meaningful approach to this task of finding simplest terms is to reverse the earlier process, as illustrated in Figure 14.23. The search for a common factor or a simplified fraction should be connected to grouping.

Two additional things should be noted regarding fraction simplification:

1. Notice that the phrase *reducing fractions* was not used. Because this would imply that the fraction is being made smaller, this terminology should be avoided. Fractions are simplified, *not* reduced.
2. Do not tell students that fraction answers are incorrect if not in simplest or lowest terms. This also works against understanding equivalence: for $\frac{1}{6} + \frac{1}{2}$, *both* $\frac{2}{3}$ and $\frac{4}{6}$ are correct.

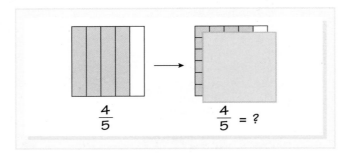

FIGURE 14.22 How can you count the fractional parts if you cannot see them all?

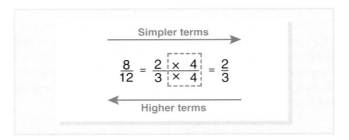

FIGURE 14.23 Using the equivalent-fraction algorithm to write fractions in simplest terms.

Multiplying by One. Mathematically, equivalence is based on the multiplicative identity (any number multiplied by 1 remains unchanged). Any fraction of the form $\frac{n}{n}$ can be used as the identity element. Therefore, $\frac{3}{4} = \frac{3}{4} \times 1 = \frac{3}{4} \times \frac{2}{2} = \frac{6}{8}$. Furthermore, the numerator and denominator of the identity element can also be fractions. In this way, $\frac{6}{12} = \frac{6}{12} \times \left(\frac{1/6}{1/6} \right) = \frac{1}{2}$. Understanding this idea is an expectation in the CCSS-M in grade 4.

TECHNOLOGY Note. The Equivalent Fractions tool from NCTM's *Illuminations* (http://illuminations.nctm.org/Activity.aspx?id=3510) has students create equivalent fractions by dividing and shading square or circular regions and then matching each fraction to its location on a number line. Students can use the computer-generated fraction or select their own. Once the rectangular or circular shape is divided, the student fills in the parts or fractional region and then builds two models equivalent to the original fraction. The three equivalent fractions are displayed in a table and on a number line. ■

MyLab Education   Self-Check 14.3

MyLab Education   Application Exercise 14.3: Equivalent Fractions Click the link to access this exercise, then watch the video and answer the accompanying questions.

 ## Comparing Fractions

When students are looking to see whether two or more fractions are equivalent, they are comparing them. If they are not equivalent, then students can determine which ones are smaller and which ones are larger. Smith (2002) suggests that the comparison question to ask is, "Which of the following two (or more) fractions is greater, or are they equal?" (p. 9). He points out that this question leaves open the possibility that two fractions that may look different can, in fact, be equal, as illustrated by Sean's thinking. Therefore, the activities for equivalence can (and should) be adapted and used for comparing fractions. For example, in Garden Plots, you might ask if these friends have the same share of the garden (if not, who has more?): Ghia has $\frac{5}{6}$ and Nita has $\frac{5}{8}$.

MyLab Education   Video Example 14.10

Watch this video of a student deciding whether two fractions are equivalent or not.

Comparing Fractions Using Number Sense

As illustrated in Ally's interview, limited understandings of fractions can make it difficult or impossible to compare the relative size of fractions. NAEP results found that only 21 percent of fourth-grade students could explain why one unit fraction was larger or smaller than another—for example, $\frac{1}{5}$ and $\frac{1}{4}$ (Kloosterman et al., 2004). For eighth graders, only 41 percent were able to correctly put in order three fractions given in simplified form (Sowder, Wearne, Martin, & Strutchens, 2004). This builds a strong case for the need to teach students *number sense* strategies to compare fractions! That is the focus of the rest of this section.

MyLab Education   Video Example 14.11

Watch this video of a student who struggles with the meaning of fractions, which makes it difficult for her to compare fractions.

Using Contexts. As stated numerous times in this chapter, contexts and visuals are essential to building an understanding (Bray & Abreu-Sanchez, 2010; Petit et al., 2010; Tobias, 2014). Using elastic strips to measure length has been effective in helping students understand equivalence of fractions and compare fractions (Harvey, 2012). Because circles are popular fraction tools, and because sharing brings to mind food, many contexts end up being about brownies, cookies and pizza. Using a more expansive collection of contexts helps students see fractions in their world. Additionally, because a number line is one-dimensional, it can make comparisons more visible. Therefore, more examples of linear situations are needed (e.g., how far people have walked/run; length of hair/banner; height of plants growing).

Activity 14.21
CCSS-M: 3.NF.A.3a, b, d; 4.NF.A.2

Stretching Number Lines

Cut strips of elastic (about 1 meter or yard in length). Hold the elastic taut and mark off ten partitions on each. Hand one out to each pair of students. Ask students to use their stretching number line to find the place on a table that represents the fraction of the distance across the table. For each pair, ask: Ask "Which distance is greater, or are they equal?"

1a. $\frac{5}{10}$ of the distance across.

1b. $\frac{1}{2}$ of the distance across.

2a. $\frac{3}{10}$ of the distance across.

2b. $\frac{3}{8}$ of the distance across. (Note: they have to rethink the whole as 8 sections.)

3a. $\frac{3}{4}$ of the distance across. (Note: they have to rethink the whole as 8 sections.)

3b. $\frac{6}{8}$ of the distance across. (Note: they have to rethink the whole as 8 sections.)

For early finishers, invite them to find their own sets (that are and are not equivalent) using their elastic, then trade with someone to determine which fraction is greater (or are they equivalent).

Comparing Unit Fractions. As noted earlier, whole-number knowledge can interfere with comparing fractions. Students think, "Seven is more than four, so sevenths should be bigger than fourths" (Mack, 1995). The inverse relationship between number of parts and size of parts cannot be "told" but must be developed in each student through many experiences, including the ones described earlier related to partitioning, iterating, magnitude of fractions, and equivalence.

Activity 14.22
CCSS-M: 3.NF.A.3d; 4.NF.A.2

Ordering Unit Fractions

List a set of unit fractions such as $\frac{1}{3}$, $\frac{1}{8}$, $\frac{1}{5}$, and $\frac{1}{10}$ (assume same size whole for each fraction). Ask students to use reasoning to put the fractions in order from least to greatest. Challenge students to explain their reasoning with an area model (e.g., circles) *and* on a number line. Ask students to connect the two representations. ("What do you notice about $\frac{1}{3}$ of the circle and $\frac{1}{3}$ on the number line?")

  Repeat with all numerators equal to some number other than 1.

  Repeat with fractions that have different numerators and different denominators. You can vary how many fractions are being compared to differentiate the task. See also, Activity 14.2 (Who Is Winning?) and Activity 14.13 (Fractions *on* the Number Line), both of which can include an area model as a strategy to locate the fractions on a number line.

Students may notice that larger denominators mean smaller fractions (this is an important pattern to notice), but it only holds true when the numerators are the same and students can overgeneralize this idea. Therefore, it makes a good conjecture to explore as a class.

Comparing Any Fractions. You have probably learned specific algorithms for comparing two fractions, such as finding a common denominators or using cross-multiplication. Too often these procedures are done with no thought about the size of the fractions, and often they are *not* the most efficient strategy. If students are taught these rules before they have had the opportunity to think about the relative sizes of various fractions, they are less likely to develop number sense (conceptual knowledge) or fluency (procedural knowledge) to effectively compare fractions.

⏸ Pause & Reflect

Examine the pairs of fractions in Figure 14.24 and select the largest of each pair using a reasoning approach that a fourth grader might use. ●

Activity 14.23 · CCSS-M: 4.a.NF.2

Which Fraction Is Greater?

Use the "Which Is Greater?" Activity Page (see Figure 14.24). Ask students to use a reasoning strategy to determine which fraction is greater. For selected problems, ask students to explain how they determined their answer. Discuss the different reasoning strategies, asking students "For what types of fractions does that strategy work?"

Here we share four different ways to compare. Students fluent in comparing fractions choose the best method, based on the fractional values being compared.

Standards for Mathematical Practice

MP2. Reason abstractly and quantitatively.

1. *Same-size denominators.* To compare $\frac{3}{8}$ and $\frac{5}{8}$, think about having 3 parts of something and also 5 parts of the same thing. (This method can be used for problems B and G.)
2. *Same numerators.* Consider the case of $\frac{3}{4}$ and $\frac{3}{7}$. If a whole is partitioned into 7 parts, the parts will certainly be smaller than if partitioned into only 4 parts. (This strategy can be used with problems A, D, and H.)
3. *More than/less than a benchmark.* The fraction pairs $\frac{3}{7}$ versus $\frac{5}{8}$ and $\frac{5}{4}$ versus $\frac{7}{8}$ do not lend themselves to either of the previous thought processes. In the first pair, $\frac{3}{7}$ is less than $\frac{1}{2}$ and $\frac{5}{8}$ is more than $\frac{1}{2}$. Therefore, $\frac{5}{8}$ is the larger fraction. In the second pair, one fraction is greater than 1 and the other is less than 1. (This method could be used on problems A, D, F, G, and H.)
4. *Closeness to a benchmark.* Why is $\frac{9}{10}$ greater than $\frac{3}{4}$? Each is one fractional part away from one whole. So, $\frac{9}{10}$ is only $\frac{1}{10}$ away from 1, so it is closer to 1 than $\frac{3}{4}$. Similarly, notice that $\frac{5}{8}$ is smaller than $\frac{4}{6}$ because it is only one-eighth more than a half, while $\frac{4}{6}$ is a sixth more than a half. (This is a good strategy for problems C, E, I, J, K, and L.)

MyLab Education   **Activity Page: Which Is Greater?**

How did your strategies for comparing the fractions in Figure 14.24 reflect these strategies? Hopefully you employed all or most of these strategies for at least one of the comparisons. Many comparisons, such as problems D and H, can be solved using several of the strategies listed, providing an excellent opportunity for students to share their thinking and to evaluate which reasoning strategies work well for which types of fractions. Figure 14.25 illustrates two students' reasoning for A-F.

These strategies should emerge from your students' reasoning; to teach "the four ways to compare fractions" defeats the purpose of learning to choose efficient strategies. Instead, select pairs of fractions that will likely elicit desired comparison strategies. Use contexts such as racing distances and installing carpet (Freeman & Jorgensen, 2015). Use number lines and other visuals to help students reason mentally. For example, you might pose two pairs of fractions with the same numerators. Ask students to tell which is greater and why they think so. Ask them to convince their partner using a visual or explanation. Have some students share their justifications. Discuss *when* this strategy works for comparing fractions.

Which Is Greater?

Use an efficient strategy to compare.
Tell how you know which fraction is greater.

A.	$\frac{4}{5}$ or $\frac{4}{9}$	G.	$\frac{7}{12}$ or $\frac{5}{12}$
B.	$\frac{4}{7}$ or $\frac{5}{7}$	H.	$\frac{3}{5}$ or $\frac{3}{7}$
C.	$\frac{3}{8}$ or $\frac{4}{10}$	I.	$\frac{5}{8}$ or $\frac{6}{10}$
D.	$\frac{5}{3}$ or $\frac{5}{8}$	J.	$\frac{9}{8}$ or $\frac{4}{3}$
E.	$\frac{3}{4}$ or $\frac{9}{10}$	K.	$\frac{4}{6}$ or $\frac{7}{12}$
F.	$\frac{3}{8}$ or $\frac{4}{7}$	L.	$\frac{8}{9}$ or $\frac{7}{8}$

FIGURE 14.24   Comparing fractions using reasoning strategies.

(a)

A. 4/5 is larger because it is 1/5 from a whole + 4/9 is close to being 1/2.
B. The denominator is the same but the NUMERATOR of 5/7 is greater, making it a bigger fraction.
C. 4/10 is greater because they are both 1 away from half, but tenths are smaller, therefore 4/10 is closer + bigger.
D. Because 5/3 is greater than whole but 5/8 is an eighth bigger than only half.
E. 9/10 is bigger because they are both 1 away from whole but tenths are smaller, making it closer to that whole but tenths are smaller, making it closer to that whole.
F. 4/7 is greater because it's denominator is smaller, + it's numerator is bigger.

(b)

a. $\frac{4}{5}$ is only one away from being a whole. $\frac{4}{9}$ is closer to $\frac{1}{2}$.

B. $\frac{5}{7}$ is greater than $\frac{4}{7}$ because $\frac{5}{7}$ is closer to a whole.

C. $\frac{4}{10}$ is greater than $\frac{3}{8}$ because $\frac{4}{10}$ would have smaller slices.

D. $\frac{5}{3}$ is greater than $\frac{5}{8}$ because $\frac{5}{3}$ is greater than one whole.

E. $\frac{9}{10}$ is greater than $\frac{3}{4}$ because $\frac{9}{10}$ would have smaller slices.

F. $\frac{4}{7}$ is greater than $\frac{3}{8}$ because $\frac{4}{7}$ is closer to a whole.

FIGURE 14.25 Two students explain how they compared the fractions in problems A through F from Figure 14.24.

Using Equivalent Fractions to Compare

Equivalent-fraction concepts can be used in making comparisons when the fractions don't lend to the strategies described above. This, too, can be a reasoning activity by asking students how they might change one or both of the fractions so they can compare them. Consider how you might compare $\frac{6}{8}$ to $\frac{4}{5}$. Beyond changing both fractions to find a common denominator (and use strategy 1 above), they can change only the $\frac{4}{5}$ to $\frac{8}{10}$ so that both fractions are two parts away from the whole (and use strategy 4 above), or change both fractions to a common *numerator* of 12 (and use strategy 2 above). Imagine the fraction number sense students will develop when this is how fraction comparisons are approached. As you will read in the next chapter this solid understanding and flexibility with fractions is essential to developing fluency with fraction operations.

Teaching Considerations for Fraction Concepts

Because the teaching of fractions is so important, and because fractions are often not well understood even by adults, a recap of the big ideas, as well as challenges with fractions, is needed. Hopefully you have recognized that one reason fractions are not well understood is that there is a lot to know about them, from part-whole relationships to division constructs, and understanding includes representing across area, length, and set models and includes contexts that fit these models. Many of these strategies may not have been part of your own learning experience, but they must be part of your teaching experience so that your students can fully understand fractions and be successful in algebra and beyond.

Iterating and partitioning must be a significant aspect of fraction instruction. Equivalence, including comparisons, is a central idea for which students must have sound understanding and skill. Connecting visuals with the procedure and not rushing the algorithm too soon are important aspects of the process.

Clarke and colleagues (2008) and Cramer and Whitney (2010), researchers of fraction teaching and learning, offer research-based recommendations that provide an effective summary of this chapter:

1. Give a greater emphasis to number sense and the meaning of fractions, rather than rote procedures for manipulating them.
2. Provide a variety of models and contexts to represent fractions.
3. Emphasize that fractions are numbers, making extensive use of number lines in representing fractions.
4. Spend whatever time is needed for students to understand equivalencies (concretely and symbolically), including flexible naming of fractions.
5. Link fractions to key benchmarks and encourage estimation.

Fraction Challenges and Misconceptions

Students build on their prior knowledge. When they encounter situations with fractions, they naturally use what they know about whole numbers to solve the problems (Cramer & Whitney, 2010; Lewis & Perry, 2017; Siegler, Carpenter, Fennell, Geary, Lewis, Okamoto, & Wray, 2010). The most effective way to help students reach higher levels of understanding is to use multiple representations, multiple approaches, and explanation and justification (Harvey, 2012; Pantziara & Philippou, 2012). Common challenges and misconceptions and how to help are presented in Table 14.3. Anticipating student challenges and misconceptions is a critical part of planning—it can greatly influence task selection and how the lesson is structured.

> **MyLab Education** **Self-Check 14.4**
>
> **MyLab Education** **Math Practice:** Need to practice or refresh your math content knowledge? Click to access practice exercises associated with the content from this chapter.

TABLE 14.3 COMMON CHALLENGES AND MISCONCEPTIONS RELATED TO FRACTION CONCEPTS

Common Challenge or Misconception	What It Looks Like	How to Help
1. Numerator and denominator are separate numbers (not seeing a fraction as a number)	$\frac{3}{4}$ is seen as a 3 over a 4. Student cannot locate a fraction such as $\frac{3}{4}$ on a number line because they don't think it is a number.	• Find fraction values on a number line (e.g., a warm-up activity each day where students place values on a classroom number line). • Measure with inches to various levels of precision (e.g., to the nearest fourth, eighth, or sixteenth). • Avoid the phrase "three out of four" (unless you are talking about ratios or probability) or "three over four"; instead, say "three-fourths" (Siebert & Gaskin, 2006).
2. Fractional parts do not need to be equal-sized	Student says $\frac{3}{4}$ (three-fourths) of the figure below is green.	• Have students create their own representations of fractions across various types of models. • Provide problems like the one illustrated here, in which all the partitions are not already drawn and have students draw or show the equal-sized parts.
3. Fractional parts must be same shape	Student says this square is not showing fourths:	• Provide examples and non-examples with partitioned shapes (see Activity 14.5, for example). • Ask students to generate as many ways as they can to show fourths (or eighths).
4. Fractions with larger denominators are bigger	Student thinks $\frac{1}{5}$ is smaller than $\frac{1}{10}$ because 5 is less than 10.	*For misconceptions 4 and 5:* • Use contexts, For example, ask students whether they would rather go outside for $\frac{1}{2}$ of an hour, $\frac{1}{4}$ of an hour, or $\frac{1}{10}$ of an hour and to explain why. • Use visuals, such as paper strips or circles to visualize the approximate size of each fraction. • Teach estimation and benchmark strategies for comparing fractions.
5. Fractions with larger denominators are smaller	Student thinks $\frac{1}{5}$ is more than $\frac{7}{10}$ because fifths are bigger than tenths.	
6. Representing fractions greater than 1	Student cannot represent a fraction such as $\frac{11}{8}$ because it is more than one whole.	• Infuse fractions of various magnitudes (less than, equal to, and greater than 1) from the beginning. • Use iterating on a number line and count beyond 1.
7. Determining a whole when given a part	Student is given an illustration and told this represents $\frac{3}{4}$ and they cannot build onto it to create one whole.	• Do more tasks involving this skill (see Figure 14.12 and Activity 14.11). • Encourage students to draw a number line or use another tool. • Focus on unit fractions (what does *one-fourth* looks like?), and then figure out the whole.

RESOURCES FOR CHAPTER 14

LITERATURE CONNECTIONS

The Doorbell Rang
Hutchins (1986)

Often used to investigate whole-number operations of multiplication and division, this book is also an excellent early introduction to fractions. The story is a simple tale of two children preparing to share a plate of 12 cookies. Just as they have figured out how to share the cookies, the doorbell rings and more children arrive. You can change the number of children to create a sharing situation that requires fractions (e.g., 8 children).

The Man Who Counted: A Collection of Mathematical Adventures
Tahan (1993)

This book contains a story, "Beasts of Burden," about a wise mathematician, Beremiz, and the narrator, who are traveling together on one camel. They are asked by three brothers to solve an argument: *Their father has left them 35 camels to divide among them: half to one brother, one-third to another, and one-ninth to the third brother.* The story is an excellent context for fractional parts of sets (and adding fractions). Changing the number of camels to 36 or 34, does not solve the challenge because the sum of $\frac{1}{2}$, $\frac{1}{3}$, and $\frac{1}{9}$ will never be one whole, no matter how many camels are involved. See Bresser (1995) for three days of activities with this book.

Apple Fractions
Pallotta (2002)

This book offers interesting facts about apples while introducing fractions as fair shares (of apples, a healthier option than books that focus on chocolate and cookies!). In addition, the words for fractions are used and connected to fraction symbols, making it a good connection for fractions in grades 1–3.

RECOMMENDED READINGS

Articles

Clarke, D. M., Roche, A., & Mitchell, A. (2008). Ten practical tips for making fractions come alive and make sense. *Mathematics Teaching in the Middle School, 13*(7), 373–380.

Ten excellent tips for teaching fractions are discussed and favorite activities are shared. An excellent overview of teaching fractions.

Lewis, R. M., Gibbons, L. K., Kazemi, E., & Lind T. (2015). Unwrapping students ideas about fractions. *Teaching Children Mathematics, 22*(3), 158–168.

This excellent read provides a how-to for implementing sharing tasks, including sequencing of tasks, questions to pose, and formatives assessment tool to monitor student understanding.

Freeman, D. W., & Jorgensen, T. A. (2015). Moving beyond brownies and pizzas. *Teaching Children Mathematics, 21*(7), 412–420.

This article describes student thinking as they compare fractions. In the more4U pages, they offer excellent sets of tasks with a range of contexts, each set focusing on a different reasoning strategy for comparing fractions.

Books

Lamon, S. (2012). *Teaching fractions and ratios for understanding: Essential content knowledge and instructional strategies.* New York, NY: Taylor & Francis Group.

As the title implies, this book has a wealth of information to help with better understanding fractions and teaching fractions well. Many rich tasks and student work are provided throughout.

McNamara, J., & Shaughnessy, M. M. (2010). *Beyond pizzas and pies: 10 essential strategies for supporting fraction sense (grades 3–5).* Sausalito, CA: Math Solutions Publications.

This book has it all—classroom vignettes, discussion of research on teaching fractions, and many activities, including student work.

Websites

Rational Number Project (http://www.cehd.umn.edu/ci/rationalnumberproject/rnp1-09.html).

This project offers excellent lessons and other materials for teaching fraction concepts effectively.

CHAPTER

15

Developing Fraction Operations

LEARNER OUTCOMES

After reading this chapter and engaging in the embedded activities and reflections, you should be able to:

15.1 Describe a process for teaching fraction operations with understanding.

15.2 Illustrate and explain how to add and subtract fractions with different fraction models.

15.3 Connect whole-number multiplication to fraction multiplication, including connecting fraction multiplication to meaningful contexts.

15.4 Connect whole-number division to fraction division using both measurement and partitive real-life examples.

A fifth-grade student asks, "Why is it when we times 29 times two-ninths that the answer goes down?" (Taber, 2002, p. 67). Although generalizations to fraction computation from whole-number computation can confuse students, they can also help students make sense of operations involving fractions. We must build on students' prior understanding of the whole-number operations to give meaning to fraction computation. This, combined with a firm understanding of fractions (including relative size and equivalence), provides the foundation for understanding fraction computation (Petit et al., 2010; Siegler et al., 2010). Fraction computation is too often taught without any meaning. Instead, fraction operations instruction must help students be able to answer questions like, "When might we need to multiply by fractions?" and "Why do we invert and multiply when dividing fractions?" Students will be able to answer these questions when these big ideas are the focus of teaching operations involving fractions.

BIG IDEAS

◆ The meanings of each operation with fractions are the same as the meanings for the operations with whole numbers. Operations with fractions should begin by applying these same meanings to fractional parts.

◆ For addition and subtraction, the numerator tells the number of parts and the denominator the unit. The parts are added or subtracted.

◆ Repeated addition and area models support development of concepts and algorithms for multiplication of fractions.

◆ Partition and measurement models lead to two different thought processes for division of fractions.

◆ Estimation should be an integral part of computation development to keep students' attention on the meanings of the operations and the expected sizes of the results.

Understanding Fraction Operations

Success with fractions, in particular computation, is closely related to success in Algebra I. If students enter formal algebra with a weak understanding of fraction computation (in other words, they have only memorized the four procedures but do not understand them), they are at risk of struggling in algebra, which in turn can limit college and career opportunities. Building such understanding takes time! The Common Core State Standards (NGA Center & CCSSO, 2010) recognize the importance and time commitment required to teach fraction operations well and suggest the following developmental process:

> Grade 4: Adding and subtracting of fractions with like denominators, and multiplication of fractions by whole numbers (p. 27).

> Grade 5: Developing fluency with addition and subtraction of fractions, and developing understanding of the multiplication of fractions and of division of fractions in limited cases (unit fractions divided by whole numbers and whole numbers divided by unit fractions) (p. 33).

> Grade 6: Completing understanding of division of fractions (p. 39).

> Grade 7: Solve real-world and mathematical problems involving the four operations with rational numbers (p. 48).

Teaching fraction operations with understanding may be a significant point of departure from what you may have experienced as a student—learning only one designated (standard) algorithm While teaching one algorithm for each operation seems quicker, it is not effective! First, none of the algorithms helps students think conceptually about the operations and what they mean. When students follow a procedure they do not understand, they have no means for knowing when to use it and no way of assessing whether their answers make sense. Second, mastery of poorly understood algorithms in the short term is quickly lost, particularly with students who struggle in mathematics. All too soon the different algorithms become a meaningless jumble. Students ask, "Do I need a common denominator, or do I just add or multiply the bottom numbers?" "Which one do you invert, the first or the second number?" Third, students can't adapt to slight changes in the fractions, such as decimals or mixed numbers. Commit to teaching fraction operations with understanding and avoid these ineffective practices.

MyLab Education   **Video Example 15.1**

Watch this video about teaching fraction operations with understanding.

Effective Teaching Process

Students must *understand* and have access to a *variety of ways* to solve fraction computation problems. In many cases, a mental or invented strategy can be applied, and a standard algorithm is not needed. Procedural fluency includes being *flexible* in how students approach fraction operations.

A report summarizing what works for teaching fraction operations suggests teachers "help students understand why procedures for computations with fractions make sense" (Siegler et al., 2010). The report suggests four steps to effective fraction computation instruction. Each is briefly described here (and then used as headers within each section of this chapter):

1. *Use contextual tasks.* This should seem like déjà vu, as this recommendation applies to nearly every topic in this book. Contextual problems for fractions help students develop their own methods and build understanding (Cramer & Whitney, 2010; Lewis, Gibbons, Kazemi, & Lind, 2015). Problem contexts need not be elaborate, but need to be familiar to students and fit the type of fractions in the problem (e.g., using halves, fourths and eighths for measuring in inches or cups, not thirds or fifths).

2. *Explore each operation with a variety of models.* Area, length, and set models give different insights into fractions, and a stronger conceptual understanding (Zhang, Clements, & Ellerton, 2015). Importantly, the models must be connected to the context (e.g., use a length model with a story about walking). Additionally, the models must be connected to the symbolic operations. The visuals will help students make sense of the symbols and related operations, but only when they are explicitly connected through repeated experiences.

3. *Let estimation and invented methods play a big role in the development of strategies.* "Should $2\frac{1}{2} \times \frac{1}{4}$ be more or less than 1? More or less than 2?" Estimation keeps the focus on the meanings of the numbers and the operations, encourages reflective thinking, and helps build number sense with fractions. Can you reason to get an exact answer without using the standard algorithm? One way is to apply the distributive property, splitting the mixed number and multiplying both parts by $\frac{1}{4}$: $\left(2 \times \frac{1}{4}\right) + \left(\frac{1}{2} \times \frac{1}{4}\right)$. Two $\frac{1}{4}$s are $\frac{2}{4}$ or $\frac{1}{2}$ and a half of a fourth is $\frac{1}{8}$. So, add an eighth to a half and you have $\frac{5}{8}$.

4. *Address challenges, common errors, and misconceptions regarding computational procedures.* Students apply their prior knowledge—in this case whole-number computation—to new knowledge. Using whole-number knowledge can be a support to learning. For example, ask, "What does 2×3 mean?" Follow this with "What might $2 \times 3\frac{1}{2}$ mean?" The concepts of each operation are the same, but the procedures are different. This means that whole-number knowledge also leads to errors (e.g., adding denominators when adding fractions). Teachers should present common misconceptions and discuss why some approaches lead to right answers and why others do not (Siegler et al., 2010).

Ongoing connections must be made between the contexts, models, and processes. It takes multiple experiences and time for these relationships to be well understood. While this chapter addresses operations in separate sections, students need opportunities to solve story problems to determine *which* operation fits the story. Too often students are given subtraction story problems on a day they are learning how to subtract, which removes the central question of "Which operation is a match to this story situation?"

Standards for Mathematical Practice
MP1. Make sense of problems and persevere in solving them.

Standards for Mathematical Practice
MP2. Reason abstractly and quantitatively.

▐▐ Pause & Reflect

Which operation can be used to solve the story situations in Figure 15.1? ●

Let's look at Jeremy's situations in Figure 15.1 (area situation). In (a) the answer is in the problem—Jeremy ate $\frac{1}{8}$ of the cake. In the second case, you must figure out $\frac{1}{8}$ of $\frac{1}{4}$, which is $\frac{1}{32}$ of the cake. In the third case, it is not clear if the cakes are the same-sized whole, so there is no way to solve this problem. If it is adapted to clarify that the cakes are the same-size, then it could be solved using addition. In Jessica's first situation (linear), the difference is needed, comparing how far she has walked to how much she needs to walk. In the latter case, the question is "How many trips?" or "How many eighths are in three-fourths?" This can be solved by counting eighths or by division: $\frac{3}{4} \div \frac{1}{8}$. A story problem like any one of these can be posted as a warm-up problem throughout year with the focus on what is happening in the story and then discussing which operation makes sense (and why).

MyLab Education   **Self-Check 15.1**

a. Jeremy's friends eat $\frac{3}{4}$ of his birthday cake. Jeremy eats $\frac{1}{8}$ of the cake. How much did Jeremy eat?

b. Jeremy's friends eat $\frac{3}{4}$ of his birthday cake. Jeremy ate $\frac{1}{8}$ of the leftover cake. How much of the cake did Jeremy eat?

c. Jeremy's friends ate $\frac{3}{4}$ of one birthday cake and $\frac{1}{8}$ of another cake. How much cake was eaten?

d. Jessica walked $\frac{1}{8}$ of a mile. Her goal is $\frac{3}{4}$ of a mile. How much further to reach her goal?

e. Jessica walks $\frac{1}{8}$ of a mile to school. How many trips to and from school are needed for her to reach her goal of walking $\frac{3}{4}$ of a mile?

FIGURE 15.1   Mixed story problems involving fractions.

Addition and Subtraction

Here we describe how the four steps described earlier are used to develop a strong understanding of addition and subtraction (usually both are taught together). Students need to find a *variety of ways* to solve problems with fractions, and their invented approaches will contribute to the development of standard algorithms (Clarke et al., 2008).

Contextual Examples

There are many contexts that can be used for adding and subtracting fractions. Recall that the CCSS-M outline addition situations, which are referenced for whole-number operations, but that also need to be applied to fraction addition and subtraction. Those situations are join, separate, part-part-whole, and compare (NGA Center & CCSSO, 2010; Chval, Lannin, & Jones, 2013). For fraction subtraction, this means including take-away situations (separate), as well as difference situations (compare). See Chapter 8 for more on whole-number addition and subtraction situations.

Consider the real-life context of measuring something in inches (sewing, cutting molding for a doorway, hanging a picture, etc.). One inch is one unit or one whole. Measurements include halves, fourths, eighths, and/or sixteenths—fractions that can be added mentally by considering the relationship between the sizes of the parts $\left(\text{e.g., } \frac{1}{2} = \frac{2}{4} = \frac{4}{8} = \frac{8}{16}\right)$. If you can easily find the equivalent fraction (e.g., that one-fourth of an inch is also two-eighths), then you can add like-sized parts mentally.

Contexts should vary and be interesting to students. Here are several good examples. As you read, think about how they differ from each other (beyond the story context):

Jacob ordered 3 pizzas. But before his guests arrived he got hungry and ate $\frac{3}{8}$ of one pizza. How much was left for the party?

On Friday, Lydia ran $1\frac{1}{2}$ miles, on Saturday she ran $2\frac{1}{8}$ miles and on Sunday she ran $2\frac{3}{4}$ miles. How many miles did she run over 3 days?

Sammy gathered $\frac{3}{4}$ pounds of walnuts and Chala gathered $\frac{7}{8}$ pounds. Who gathered the most? How much more?

In measuring the wood needed for a picture frame, Elizabeth figured that she needed two pieces that were $5\frac{1}{4}$ inches and two pieces that were $7\frac{3}{4}$ inches. What length of wood does she need to buy to build her picture frame?

Notice that these story problems (1) incorporate different addition situations (join, compare, etc.); (2) use a mix of area and linear contexts; (3) use a mix of whole numbers, mixed numbers, and fractions; (4) include both addition and subtraction situations; and (5) sometimes involve more than two addends. With each story you use, it is very important to ask students to select a picture or tool to illustrate it and write the symbols that accurately model the situation. Meaningful contexts are embedded throughout the next sections, connected to models and symbols.

FORMATIVE ASSESSMENT Notes. Any of the problems above can be used as a formative assessment with an observation checklist. On the checklist would be such concepts as: (1) can determine a reasonable estimate; (2) selects and accurately uses a manipulative or picture; (3) recognizes equivalences between fourths and eighths; and (4) can connect symbols and visuals. Students may be able to illustrate but then not find equivalences, or students may select a circle to illustrate and find it does not help them think about the situation. The next steps in instruction could include explicit attention to connecting the picture to the symbols, or to use other manipulatives or pictures to represent the situation. ■

Models

Recall that there are area, length, and set models for illustrating fractions (see Chapter 14). Set models can be confusing in adding fractions, as they can reinforce the adding of the denominator. Therefore, instruction should initially focus on area and linear models.

Area Models. Circles are an effective visual for adding and subtracting fractions because they allow students to develop mental images of the sizes of different pieces (fractions) of the circle (Cramer, Wyberg, & Leavitt, 2008). Figure 15.2 shows how students estimate first (including marking a number line) and then explain how they added the fraction using fraction circles.

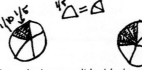

Estimate first by putting an X on the number line.

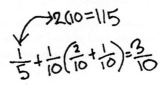

Solve with Fraction Circles. Draw pictures of what you did with the circles below.

Record what you did with the circles with symbols.

FIGURE 15.2   A student estimates and then adds fractions using a fraction circle.

CCSS Standards for Mathematical Practice
MP5. Use appropriate tools strategically.

MyLab Education   Video Example 15.2

Watch this video as Felicia uses circles to add.

MyLab Education   Video Example 15.3

Watch this video as Felicia uses circles to subtract.

Consider this problem, in which the context is circular:

Jack and Jill ordered two medium pizzas, one cheese and one pepperoni. Jack ate $\frac{5}{6}$ of a pizza, and Jill ate $\frac{1}{2}$ of a pizza. How much pizza did they eat together?

Pause & Reflect

Think of two ways that students might solve this problem without using a common-denominator symbolic approach. ●

If students draw circles as in the earlier example, some will try to fill in the $\frac{1}{6}$ gap in the pizza. Then they will need to figure out how to get $\frac{1}{6}$ from $\frac{1}{2}$. If they can think of $\frac{1}{2}$ as $\frac{3}{6}$, they can use one of the sixths to fill in the gap. Another approach, after drawing the two pizzas, is to notice that there is a half plus two more sixths in the $\frac{5}{6}$ pizza. Put the two halves together to equal one whole, and there are $\frac{2}{6}$ more—$1\frac{2}{6}$. These are certainly good solutions that represent the type of reasoning you want to encourage.

There are many other area models that can be used, such as rectangles and pattern blocks. Rectangles, like circles, can be partitioned in whatever way is useful for the problem being solved. Activity 15.1 uses a rectangular context and illustration.

Activity 15.1

CCSS-M: 4.NF.B.3a, d; 5.NF.A.1; 5.NF.A.2

Gardening Together

Distribute the Empty Garden Activity Page (or give each student a blank piece of paper to represent the rectangular garden). Explain the situation and ask each student to design the garden to illustrate these quantities:

Al, Bill, Carrie, Danielle, Enrique, and Fabio are each given a portion of the school garden for spring planting. Here are the portions:

Al $= \frac{1}{4}$	Bill $= \frac{1}{8}$	Carrie $= \frac{3}{16}$
Danielle $= \frac{1}{16}$	Enrique $= \frac{1}{4}$	Fabio $= \frac{1}{8}$

They decide to pair up to share the work. What fraction of the garden will each of the following pairs or groups have if they combine their portions of the garden? Show your work.

Bill and Danielle   Al and Carrie

Fabio and Enrique   Carrie, Fabio, and Al

To challenge students, ask them to solve puzzle-type questions like: "Which two people could work together and have the least amount of the garden? The most? Which combinations of friends could combine to work on one-half of the garden?"

MyLab Education   Activity Page: Empty Garden

Linear Models. Cuisenaire rods are linear models. Suppose that you had asked the students to solve the Jack and Jill pizza problem but changed the context to submarine sandwiches (linear context), suggesting students use Cuisenaire rods or fraction strips to model the problem. The first decision that must be made is what strip to use as the whole. That decision is not required with a circular model, where the whole is already established as the circle. The whole must be the same for both fractions. In this case, the smallest rod that will work is the 6-rod or the dark green strip, because it can be partitioned into sixths (1 rod/ white) and into halves (3 rod/light green). Figure 15.3(a) illustrates a solution.

What if you instead asked students to compare the quantity that Jack and Jill ate? Figure 15.3(b) illustrates lining up the "sandwiches" to compare their lengths. Recall that subtraction can be thought of as "separate" where the total is known and a part is removed, "comparison" as two amounts being compared to find the difference, and "how many more are needed" as starting with a smaller value and asking how much more to get to the higher value (think-addition). This sandwich example is a comparison situation—be sure to include more than "take away" examples in the stories and examples you create.

Standards for Mathematical Practice

MP4. Model with mathematics.

An important model for adding or subtracting fractions is the number line (Siegler et al., 2010). One advantage of the number line is that it can be connected to the ruler, which is a familiar context and perhaps the most common real context for adding or subtracting fractions. The number line is also a more challenging model than an area model, because it requires that the student understand $\frac{3}{4}$ as 3 parts of 4, and as a value between 0 and 1 (Izsák, Tillema, & Tunc-Pekkam, 2008). Using the number line in addition to area representations can strengthen student understanding (Clarke et al., 2008; Cramer et al., 2008; Petit et al., 2010).

(a) $\dfrac{5}{6} + \dfrac{1}{2}$

Find a strip for a whole that allows both fractions to be modeled.

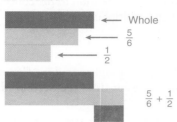

← Whole
$\dfrac{5}{6}$
$\dfrac{1}{2}$

$\dfrac{5}{6} + \dfrac{1}{2}$

The sum is 1 whole and a red rod more than a whole.
A red is $\dfrac{1}{3}$ of a dark green. So $\dfrac{5}{6} + \dfrac{1}{2} = 1\dfrac{1}{3}$.

(b) $\dfrac{5}{6} - \dfrac{1}{2}$

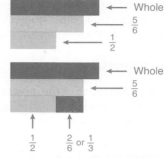

← Whole
$\dfrac{5}{6}$
$\dfrac{1}{2}$

← Whole
$\dfrac{5}{6}$

$\dfrac{1}{2}$ $\dfrac{2}{6}$ or $\dfrac{1}{3}$

Compare the lengths of the two fractions.
$\dfrac{5}{6}$ is $\dfrac{2}{6}$ longer than $\dfrac{1}{2}$, so the difference is $\dfrac{2}{6}$ or $\dfrac{1}{3}$.

FIGURE 15.3   Using Cuisenaire rods to add and subtract fractions.

Activity 15.2

CCSS-M: 4.NF.B.3a, d; 5.NF.A.1; 5.NF.A.2

Jumps on the Ruler

ENGLISH LEARNERS

Use Jumps on the Ruler Activity Page (or provide a ruler). Have students use jumps on the ruler to add or subtract (which does not require a common denominator, though students may naturally trade equivalent fractions to help them reason). Examples include:

$$\dfrac{3}{4} + \dfrac{1}{2} \qquad 4\dfrac{1}{2} - 3\dfrac{3}{4} \qquad 4\dfrac{1}{8} - \dfrac{1}{2}$$

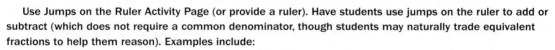

Either add a linear context (length of grass in the yard, hair growing/getting cut), or ask students to create their own stories for each. These jumps encourage students to invent strategies without having to find a common denominator (Taber, 2009). When sharing strategies, listen for students iterating (counting) and using fraction equivalencies. In the first problem, students might use 1 as a benchmark. They count up $\dfrac{1}{4}$ to get to a whole, then have $\dfrac{1}{4}$ more to add on to $1\dfrac{1}{4}$. Or, they could use $\dfrac{1}{2}$ from the $\dfrac{3}{4}$ to equal a whole with the $\dfrac{1}{2}$, then add on the $\dfrac{1}{4}$. ELs may not be as familiar with inches, because most countries measure in metric. In this case, be sure to spend time prior to the activity discussing how the inch is partitioned and add labels for fourths as a reminder that the inch is different from metric system units.

MyLab Education   Activity Page: Jumps on the Ruler

MyLab Education   Application Exercise 15.1: Observing and Responding to Student Thinking Click the link to access this exercise, then watch the video and answer the accompanying questions.

VIDEO EXAMPLE

The selected context and quantities can be adapted to steer students toward specific strategies (difference or take-away). For example, consider two ways to pose the subtraction problem:

1. Desmond runs $2\dfrac{1}{2}$ miles a day. If he has just passed the $1\dfrac{1}{4}$ mile marker, how far does he still need to go?
2. Desmond is at mile marker $2\dfrac{1}{2}$, and James is at mile marker $1\dfrac{1}{4}$. How much farther has Desmond gone?

With many experiences with area and linear models, students are ready to connect those visuals to algorithms.

TECHNOLOGY Note. Conceptua Math has free tools that help students explore various fraction concepts using area, set, and length models (including the number line). These interactive tools allow students to explore all the operations with attention to the concepts and the commutative and distributive properties of addition and multiplication. ■

Estimation

Estimation is one of the most effective ways to build understanding and procedural fluency with fraction operations (Johanning, 2011). A frequently quoted result from the Second National Assessment (Post, 1981) concerns the following item:

Estimate the answer to $\frac{12}{13} + \frac{7}{8}$. You will not have time to solve the problem using paper and pencil.

Nearly two-thirds of middle school students could find the exact answer to this problem, but only one-fourth could correctly estimate (Reys, 1998). Notice that computing this answer requires finding the common denominator of thirteenths and eighths, but to estimate requires no computation whatsoever—only a realization that each fraction is close to 1, so the answer is close to 2.

There are different ways to estimate fraction sums and differences (Siegler et al., 2010):

1. *Benchmarks.* Decide whether the fractions are closest to 0, $\frac{1}{2}$, or 1 (or to 3, $3\frac{1}{2}$, or 4—the closest whole numbers and the half in between them for mixed numbers). After making the determination for each fraction, mentally add or subtract.

Example: $\frac{7}{8} + \frac{1}{10}$. Think, "$\frac{7}{8}$ is close to 1, $\frac{1}{10}$ is close to 0, the sum is about $1 + 0$ or close to 1."

---

2. *Relative size of unit fractions.* Decide how big the fraction is, based on its unit (denominator), and apply this information to the computation.

Example: $\frac{7}{8} + \frac{1}{10}$. Think, "$\frac{7}{8}$ is just $\frac{1}{8}$ away from a whole (one) and $\frac{1}{8}$ is close to (but bigger than) $\frac{1}{10}$, so the sum will be close to, but less than, 1."

The following activity can be done frequently as a routine, warm-up or be a focus activity for a full lesson.

Activity 15.3

CCSS-M: 4.NF.B.3a; 5.NF.A.2

Over or Under 1

Tell students that they are going to estimate sums or differences of fractions. They are to decide only whether the answer is more than 1 or less than 1. Using Estimating Addition and Subtraction of Fractions Problems Activity Page, project a problem for no more than 10 seconds, then hide or remove it. Use Less Than One, More Than One cards, mini whiteboards to write "over" or "under," clickers, or thumbs up/down to see each students estimate. Then discuss how students decided on their estimates (including connecting to mental models of number lines or other models to reason). Students with disabilities might use a number line to think about the relative size of the fractions. They may also need more than 10 seconds to think about the amounts. Repeat with other examples (Figure 15.4 offers several possible problems.)

STUDENTS with SPECIAL NEEDS

MyLab Education   **Activity Page: Estimating Addition and Subtraction of Fractions Problems**
MyLab Education   **Activity Page: Less Than One, More Than One**

Over time, Activity 15.3 can include tasks that are more challenging, or it can be differentiated with different groups of students working on different over/under values. Consider the following variations:

• Use a target other than 1. For example, estimate more or less than $\frac{1}{2}$, $1\frac{1}{2}$, 2, or 3.

- Choose fraction pairs in which the fractions are both less than 1 or both greater than 1. Estimate sums or differences to the nearest half.
- Ask students to *create* equations that are slightly less than or slightly more than 1 (or other values). They can trade equations with other students, who in turn decide if the answer is over 1 or under 1 (or other values).

MyLab Education   Activity Page: Estimate, Write, Explain

‖ Pause & Reflect

Test your own estimation skills with the sample problems in Figure 15.4. Look at each computation for only about 10 seconds and write down an estimate. After writing down all six of your estimates, look at the problems and decide whether your estimate is higher or lower than the actual computation. ●

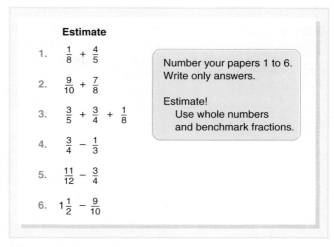

Estimate

1. $\frac{1}{8} + \frac{4}{5}$

2. $\frac{9}{10} + \frac{7}{8}$

3. $\frac{3}{5} + \frac{3}{4} + \frac{1}{8}$

4. $\frac{3}{4} - \frac{1}{3}$

5. $\frac{11}{12} - \frac{3}{4}$

6. $1\frac{1}{2} - \frac{9}{10}$

> Number your papers 1 to 6.
> Write only answers.
>
> Estimate!
>   Use whole numbers
>   and benchmark fractions.

FIGURE 15.4   Example of fraction estimation expressions.

A relevant and familiar context for fractions is cups, such as cups of water or milk (Fung and Latulippe, 2010; Zhang, et al., 2015). Activity 15.4 uses cups to engage students in estimating sums and differences.

Activity 15.4   CCSS-M: 4.NF.B.3a; 5.NF.A.2

Cups of Milk

Ask students to fill in the missing numerator and denominator with a whole number that makes the equation approximately true. They cannot use any of the numbers already in the problem. The context of milk (or water) can help students reason about the quantities. Four examples are provided here:

$$\frac{\Box}{4} + \frac{3}{\Box} \approx \frac{1}{2} \qquad\qquad \frac{3}{\Box} + \frac{\Box}{4} \leq \frac{1}{2}$$

$$\frac{\Box}{2} - \frac{2}{\Box} > 2 \qquad\qquad \frac{1}{\Box} - \frac{\Box}{2} \approx 1$$

Keep in mind that these are estimates, so many values are possible. Except in some cases, where there are no solutions (can you spot the impossible one in the list here?).

Developing the Algorithms

The algorithms develop side by side with the visuals and situations. The way fractions are notated can lead to errors when students compute fractions using symbols, even if they are able to add using models. The way to prevent this is to ensure students are connecting fraction symbols with contexts and visuals.

MyLab Education   Application Exercise 15.2: Developing the Algorithm Click the link to access this exercise, then watch the video and answer the accompanying questions.

▶ VIDEO EXAMPLE

Like Denominators. Fraction addition and subtraction begin with situations using like denominators. In the Common Core State Standards (NGA Center & CCSSO, 2010), this is

Standards for Mathematical Practice

MP7. Look for and make use of structure.

suggested for grade 4. When working on adding with like denominators, however, it is important to be sure that students are focusing on the key idea—the units are the same, so they can be combined (Mack, 2004). This is the iteration idea discussed in Chapter 14. In other words, the problem $\frac{3}{4} + \frac{2}{4}$ is asking, "How many fourths altogether?" The equation $3\frac{7}{8} - 1\frac{3}{8}$ is counting back (taking away) eighths or finding the number of eighths between the two quantities (comparing). Iteration connects fraction operations to whole-number operations and explains why the denominator stays the same.

FORMATIVE ASSESSMENT Notes. The ease with which students can or cannot add like-denominator fractions should be viewed as an important concept assessment before moving students to an algorithm. A diagnostic interview can ask students to (1) explain the meaning of the numerators and denominators, (2) connect the addition problems to a situation, and (3) illustrate with a model, which can help you determine whether they have a deep understanding of the numerator and denominator. If student responses are rule oriented and not grounded in understanding parts and wholes, then encourage students to focus on the meaning of the fractions by emphasizing the unit: "Three *fifths* plus one *fifth* is how many *fifths*?" This must be well understood before moving to adding with unlike denominators. Otherwise, any further symbolic development will almost certainly be without understanding. ■

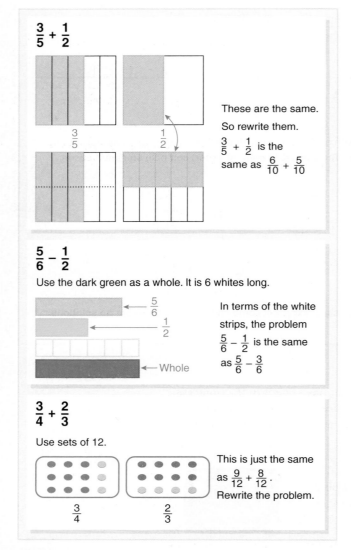

FIGURE 15.5 Illustrating common denominators with different tools.

Unlike Denominators. As discussed in Chapter 14, having a strong conceptual foundation of equivalence is critical to operations of fractions. Students who have a level of fluency in moving between $\frac{1}{2}, \frac{2}{4}, \frac{4}{8}$, and $\frac{8}{16}$ or $\frac{3}{4}, \frac{6}{8}$, and $\frac{12}{16}$ can adjust the fractions as needed to add or subtract fractions. For example, ask students to think about how far a person has walked, if the following equation represents their walking: $\frac{3}{8} + \frac{1}{2}$. Given sufficient concrete experiences, a student should be able to readily trade out one-half for four-eighths to solve:

$$\frac{3}{8} + \frac{1}{2} = \frac{3}{8} + \frac{4}{8} = \frac{7}{8}$$

Begin adding and subtracting fractions with unlike denominators with tasks where only one fraction needs to be changed, such as $\frac{5}{8} + \frac{1}{4}$. A situation might be amount of pizza eaten. Ask students to estimate whether they think one or more pizzas were eaten altogether. Then, invite students to draw or select a tool to illustrate a solution, recording fractions to go with their drawings or manipulatives. As students explain how they solved it, write equivalent expressions on the board and ask if they are equal:

$$\frac{5}{8} + \frac{1}{4} = \frac{5}{8} + \frac{2}{8}$$

Continue with examples in which both fractions need to be changed—for example, $\frac{2}{3} + \frac{1}{4}$ (or $\frac{2}{3} - \frac{1}{4}$), still using contexts, visuals, and student explanations. In the discussion of student solutions, focus attention on the idea of *rewriting an equivalent problem* to make it possible to add or subtract *equal-sized parts*. If students express doubt about the equivalence of the two problems ("Is $\frac{8}{12} + \frac{3}{12}$ really the answer to $\frac{2}{3} + \frac{1}{4}$?"), that should be a cue that the concept of equivalent fractions is not well understood, and more experience using examples, visuals, or concrete tools is needed (see Figure 15.5).

The three examples in Figure 15.5 show how tools might be used. Note that each tool requires students to think about the size of a whole that can be partitioned into the units of both fractions (e.g., fifths and halves require tenths).

Over time, the equations may be given without situations or visuals, but students should be able to create stories or visuals for any problem. As you may recall in the discussion of whole numbers and in algebra, it is important to not always have "result unknown." The parts can also be unknown. This helps students relate addition to subtraction. Any of the stories provided earlier can be adapted to have a part unknown. For example:

Sammy gathered some walnuts and Chala gathered $\frac{7}{8}$ pounds. Together they gathered $1\frac{1}{2}$ pounds. How much did Sammy gather?

Activity 15.5 provides an engaging opportunity to reason about fractions when the result is known.

Activity 15.5   CCSS-M: 4.NF.B.3a; 5.NF.A.2

Can You Make It True?

Use the Can You Make It True? Activity Page, which includes list of equations with missing values, such as the ones here:

$$\frac{\square}{6} + \frac{\square}{3} = 1 \text{ and } \frac{4}{\square} - \frac{\square}{2} = \frac{1}{2}$$

To begin, post one example and invite students to share possible whole number solutions. If they have found one way, ask "Is there more than one way to make that equation true?" Include examples that are impossible for whole number missing values, such as:

$$\frac{1}{\square} - \frac{1}{\square} = 1$$

As students work, ask them to explain the reasoning they are using. Encourage students to use visuals (e.g., number line or fraction pieces) to support their thinking.

MyLab Education   Activity Page: Can You Make It True?

Equations such as the ones in Activity 15.5 require reasoning and thinking about the role of the numerator and denominator, as well as reinforcement of why the numerators are added and the denominators are not.

Are Common Denominators "Required"? No. Teachers and websites often explain, "To add or subtract fractions, find common denominators." This is one strategy, but not the only strategy.

MyLab Education   Video Example 15.4

Watch Javier illustrate his more straightforward mental strategy.

Using reasoning strategies, students will see that many correct solutions are found without ever finding a common denominator (Taber, 2009). As described earlier, number lines can be used to solve addition and subtraction situations without finding a common denominators (see Activity 15.2 Jumps on the Ruler). Importantly, fluency requires *choosing* a strategy, so encourage students to decide on a strategy and continue to encourage reasoning strategies even after students learn to find common denominators to add/subtract.

CCSS Standards for
Mathematical
Practice
MP1. Make sense of
problems and persevere
in solving them.

Fractions Greater Than One

A separate algorithm for mixed numbers in addition and subtraction is not necessary even though mixed numbers are often treated as separate topics in traditional textbooks and in some lists of objectives (note that mixed numbers have been integrated throughout the previous discussion). Include mixed numbers in all of your stories and examples and encourage students to solve them in ways that make sense to them.

When adding mixed numbers, it makes sense to focus on whole numbers first. Consider this problem: You had $5\frac{1}{8}$ yards of fabric and used $3\frac{5}{8}$ yards. How much do you have left? What equation describes this situation? $5\frac{1}{8} - 3\frac{5}{8}$. It is a linear situation, so a number line is a good way to think about this problem. Given the context students are likely to subtract 3, leaving $2\frac{1}{8}$, and then need to subtract $\frac{5}{8}$. Students may count down (iterate), stopping at $1\frac{1}{2}$. Another approach is to take $\frac{5}{8}$ from the whole part, 2, leaving $1\frac{3}{8}$, and then add the $\frac{1}{8}$ back on to get $1\frac{4}{8}$ or $1\frac{1}{2}$. The *standard* algorithm, which is not as intuitive, is to trade one of the wholes for $\frac{8}{8}$ add it to the $\frac{1}{8}$ to get $1\frac{9}{8}$ and then take away $\frac{5}{8}$.

Students tend to make many errors when regrouping mixed numbers. An excellent alternative is to change the mixed numbers to fractions greater than 1. You may connect this strategy with multiplying fractions, but it works for addition and subtraction too. Let's revisit $5\frac{1}{8} - 3\frac{5}{8}$. This can be rewritten as $\frac{41}{8} - \frac{29}{8}$. (See Chapter 14 for conceptual ways for helping students do this.) Because 41 − 29 is 12, the solution is $\frac{12}{8}$ or $1\frac{1}{2}$. This is certainly efficient and will always work. Provide both options to students and encourage them to decide which strategy works the best in different situations.

TECHNOLOGY Note. The National Library of Virtual Manipulatives (NLVM) has three different activities that can help reinforce fraction addition and subtraction across different models:

Fractions—Adding: Two fractions and an area model for each are given. The user must find a common denominator to rename and add the fractions.

Fraction Bars: This applet places bars over a number line on which the step size can be adjusted, providing a flexible model that can be used to illustrate addition and subtraction.

Diffy: This puzzle asks you to find the differences between the numbers on the corners of a square, working to a desired difference in the center. This activity encourages students to consider equivalent forms of fractions to solve the puzzle. ∎

Challenges and Misconceptions

It is important to explicitly talk about common misconceptions with fraction operations because students naturally overgeneralize what they know about whole-number operations. Table 15.1 offers some common challenges and misconceptions, with suggestions for helping students overcome them.

TABLE 15.1 COMMON CHALLENGES AND MISCONCEPTIONS FOR ADDING AND SUBTRACTING FRACTIONS

Common Challenge or Misconception	What It Looks Like	How to Help
1. Apply whole number operation rules.	$\frac{1}{2} + \frac{1}{2} = \frac{2}{4}$	• Ask students to tell what the numerator and denominator mean. • Tell stories with familiar contexts. • Ask students to create a story using a familiar context to make sense of the operation. • Use area and linear manipulatives and be sure students connect the visual to the steps in the algorithms. • See Video Example 15.5 for more ideas.

Common Challenge or Misconception	What It Looks Like	How to Help
2. Get different answer with models than with symbols (and aren't bothered that the two answers are different (Bamberger et al., 2010).	For a task such as: **Ms. Rodriguez baked a pan of brownies for the bake sale and cut the brownies into 8 equal-sized parts. In the morning, three of the brownies were sold; in the afternoon, two more were sold. What fractional part of the brownies had been sold? What fractional part is still for sale?** Student correctly illustrates: But then writes $\frac{3}{8} + \frac{2}{8} = \frac{5}{16}$.	• Ask students to decide whether both answers could be right. • Ask students to defend which is right and why the other answer is not right. • Ask students to use the same model to show the solution. • Encourage students to do the problem on a number line.
3. Do not find a common denominator, but apply standard algorithm (Siegler et al., 2010).	$\frac{4}{5} + \frac{4}{10} = \frac{8}{10}$	• Ask students to model the problem on a number line or with fraction strips. • Go to NCTM's Illuminations "Making and Using Fraction Strips" (or other online fraction tool) to explore problems.
4. Struggle to find common denominator (lack of fluency with basic facts and with common multiples).	Student is given $\frac{5}{6} - \frac{1}{4} = $ ___ and is unsure what to use for a denominator.	• Offer games and activities to reinforce multiplication facts. • Do common multiple activities, such as Activity 15.6. • Discuss that while finding a smaller common denominator (e.g., 12) has advantages, any denominator (e.g., 24) will work. • Ask students to discuss strategies they use to find common denominators. • Explore Interference Task, which uses common multiples to determine how often two orbiting satellites will cross paths (adapt to tasks with single-digit values).
5. Mixed numbers: Subtract the smaller fraction from the larger (Petit et al., 2010; Siegler et al., 2010; Spangler, 2011).	When given a problem like $3\frac{1}{4} - 1\frac{3}{8}$, student subtracts the smaller fraction from the larger $\left(\frac{3}{8} - \frac{1}{4}\right)$.	*For all of these mixed number challenges, strategies to help include:* • Include more mixed numbers throughout addition of fraction units (rather than saving them for end of unit). • Use models and contexts, in particular the number line—think about how straight forward $4 - \frac{7}{8}$ is on the number line or ruler. • Make these errors part of public discussions, for example using worked examples with such errors.
6. Mixed numbers: Don't know what to do when one number is a whole number.	For a problem like $4 - \frac{7}{8}$, student places an 8 under the 4 to get $\frac{4}{8} - \frac{7}{8}$. See Video Example 15.6 of Jacky's thinking.	
7. Mixed numbers: Focus only on the whole-numbers in the problem.	When given a problem like $14\frac{1}{2} - 3\frac{1}{8}$, student writes $11\frac{1}{2}$ or $11\frac{1}{8}$.	

MyLab Education   **Activity Page: Interference Task**

MyLab Education   **Video Example 15.5**

Listen and watch how to address common errors in adding fractions.

MyLab Education   **Video Example 15.6**

Listen to Jacky's thinking as she tries to subtract a fraction from a whole number.

Activity 15.6

CCSS-M: 4.OA.B.4;
5.NF.A.1

Common Multiple Cards

STUDENTS with SPECIAL NEEDS

**Use Common Multiple Cards with pairs of
numbers that are potential denominators. Most
should be less than 12 (see Figure 15.6). Or,
give students a deck of cards. Place students in
pairs. On a student's turn, he or she turns over a
Common Multiple Card, or two cards from a deck of cards,
and states a common multiple (e.g., for 6 and 8, a student
might suggest 48). The partner gets a chance to suggest a
smaller common multiple (e.g., 24). The student suggesting
the least common multiple (LCM) gets to keep the card. Be
sure to include pairs that are prime, such as 9 and 5; pairs
in which one is a multiple of the other, such as 2 and 8; and
pairs that have a common divisor, such as 8 and 12. For
students with disabilities, start with the pairs wherein one
number is a multiple of the other.**

MyLab Education **Activity Page:
Common Multiple Cards**

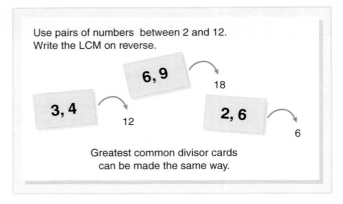

Use pairs of numbers between 2 and 12.
Write the LCM on reverse.

6, 9 → 18

3, 4 → 12

2, 6 → 6

Greatest common divisor cards
can be made the same way.

FIGURE 15.6 Least common multiple (LCM) flash cards.

MyLab Education **Self-Check 15.2**

Multiplication

Can you think of a situation that requires using multiplication of fractions? Have you used this a multiplication of
fraction algorithm outside of mathematics classes? Often the answer to these questions is no.
It is not that there are no situations involving multiplication of fractions, but that because the
meaning is not understood, the algorithm is never put into use. As you will see in the sections
that follow, the foundational ideas of iterating (counting) fractional parts and partitioning are at
the heart of understanding multiplication of fractions. If students have not had sufficient experiences with these two ideas, you must find ways to engage them in iterating and partitioning
so that they are ready to apply these ideas to multiplication.

Multiplication of fractions is really about scaling. If you scale something by a factor of
2, you multiply it by 2. When you scale by 1 (1 times the size), the amount is unchanged
(identity property of multiplication). Similarly, multiplying by $\frac{1}{2}$ means taking half of the
original size, while multiplying by $1\frac{1}{2}$ means the original size plus half the original size.
This scaling concept can enhance students' ability to decide whether their answers are
reasonable. A possible progression of problem difficulty is developed in the sections that
follow.

CCSS **Standards for
Mathematical
Practice**
MP1. Make sense of
problems and persevere
in solving them.

Contextual Examples and Models

When working with whole numbers, we would say that 3 × 5 means "3 sets of 5" (equal sets)
or "3 rows of 5" (area or array) or "5 three times" (number line). Notice the set, area, and
linear models fitting with the multiplication structures. Different models must be used and
aligned with contexts so that students get a comprehensive understanding of multiplication
of fractions. The story problems that you use to pose multiplication tasks to students need
not be elaborate, but it is important to think about the numbers and contexts that you use
in the problems. A possible progression of problem difficulty is developed in the sections
that follow.

Multiply a Fraction by a Whole Number. These problems look like this: $5 \times \frac{1}{2}$,
$6 \times \frac{1}{8}$, $10 \times \frac{3}{4}$, and $3 \times 2\frac{1}{3}$ and in the CCSS-M are introduced in grade 4. Look again at the
wording of this subsection—because the word *fraction* preceded *whole number*, there is some-
times confusion over what this means, but to multiply a fraction by a whole number means
examples such as the ones provided here. Students' first experiences should be of this type

because conceptually it is a close fit to multiplication of whole numbers using the idea of equal sets. Consider the following two situations:

 Standards for Mathematical Practice
MP8. Look for and express regularity in repeated reasoning.

Marvin ate 3 pounds of meat every day. How much meat did Marvin eat in one week?

Murphy ate $\frac{1}{3}$ pounds of meat every day. How much meat did Murphy eat in one week?

▌▌ Pause *&* Reflect

What expressions represent each situation? What reasoning strategies would you use to solve each? ●

For Marvin the expression is 7 (groups of) 3 pounds, or 7 × 3. You can solve this by skip counting 3 + 3 + 3 + 3 + 3 + 3 + 3 to get the answer of 21 pounds (but if you know your facts, you just *multiplied*). Murphy similarly ate 7 × $\frac{1}{3}$ pounds, and it can similarly be solved by skip counting, this time by his portion size of thirds: $\frac{1}{3} + \frac{1}{3} + \frac{1}{3} + \frac{1}{3} + \frac{1}{3} + \frac{1}{3} + \frac{1}{3}$, which in total is seven-thirds $\left(\frac{7}{3}\right)$. Notice the skip counting, called *iterating*, is the meaning behind a whole number times a fraction.

Activity 15.7   CCSS-M: 4.NF.B.4a, b

Hexagon Wholes

Distribute a set of hexagons to students. To start, designate the yellow hexagon as the whole. Ask students the fractional value of the green, blue, and red pieces. Ask students to find how many wholes for different quantities:

ENGLISH LEARNERS

5 blue pieces?   10 green pieces?

Ask students to write a fraction equation to represent their problem. For the two examples here:

$$5 \times \tfrac{1}{3} = 1\tfrac{2}{3} \text{ or } \tfrac{5}{3} \qquad 10 \times \tfrac{1}{6} = \tfrac{10}{6} \text{ or } 1\tfrac{4}{6} \text{ or } 1\tfrac{2}{3}$$

Create a variety of tasks. Other wholes can be used—for example, using two hexagons as one whole to vary the types of fractions that can be used. ELs may benefit from having the shapes labeled with their names and the fraction symbols written with fraction words (e.g., $\frac{1}{6}$ is "one-sixth")

Circular Fraction Pieces can be used in addition to or instead of pattern blocks to do Activity 15.7. Notice that in the answers given, the fraction (improper fraction) shows a pattern that can be generalized as $a \times \frac{1}{b} = \frac{a}{b}$, an important pattern for students to discover from having explored many examples that follow this pattern. Linear examples are also important to include. Use Jumps on the Ruler—Multiplication Activity Page to explore jumps of equal length (see Activity 15.2 for the addition/subtraction version).

MyLab Education   Activity Page: Circular Fraction Pieces

MyLab Education   Activity Page: Jumps on the Ruler—Multiplication

---

Multiply a Whole Number by a Fraction. Students' second experiences with multiplication should involve finding fractions of whole numbers, such as $\frac{2}{3} \times 12$

MyLab Education   Video Example 15.7

Watch this video of a student solving $\dfrac{2}{3} \times 12$.

VIDEO EXAMPLE

While multiplication is commutative, the thinking involved in this type of multiplication involves partitioning (not iterating). The fraction construct is fraction as operator (Lamon, 2012). Examples look like this: $\frac{1}{2} \times 8, \frac{1}{2} \times 5, \frac{1}{5} \times 8, \frac{3}{4} \times 24$, and $2\frac{1}{2} \times 3$. Notice this is a compare or *scaling* situation (think of creating a scale drawing that is $\frac{1}{5}$ of the actual size). In the CCSS-M, this type of fraction multiplication is introduced in grade 5.

These stories can be paired with manipulatives to help students understand this type of fraction operation:

1. The walk from school to the public library takes 25 minutes. When Anna asked her mom how far they had gone, her mom said that they had gone $\frac{1}{2}$ of the way. How many minutes have they walked? (Assume a constant walking rate.)
2. There are 15 cars in Michael's Matchbox car collection. Two-thirds of the cars are red. How many red cars does Michael have?

For a full lesson using multiplication stories, use Expanded Lesson: Multiplication-of-Fractions Stories.

MyLab Education   **Expanded Lesson: Multiplication-of-Fractions Stories**

CCSS Standards for Mathematical Practice

MP2. Reason abstractly and quantitatively.

Notice that the thinking in these situations is partitioning (finding a parts of the whole). How might students think through each problem? For problem 2, students might partition 15 into three groups (or partition a line into three parts) and then see how many are in two parts. Recording this in symbols ($\frac{2}{3}$ of 15) gives the following result: $15 \div 3 \times 2$.

Counters (a set model) is an effective tool for finding parts of a whole. Recall that in Chapter 14 two-color counters were used to develop the concept of partitioning and iterating with prompts such as, "If the whole is 45, how much is $\frac{1}{5}$ of the whole?" and "If the whole is 24, what is $\frac{3}{8}$ of the whole?" These can be slightly adapted to make the connection to multiplication more explicit by having students write the equations that match the question. Counting Counters: Fraction of a Whole Activity Page is designed to do this.

An area model, such a rectangle, provides an excellent visual tool for illustrating and making generalizations (Witherspoon, 2014), as can be seen in Activity 15.8.

MyLab Education   **Activity Page: Counting Counters: Fraction of a Whole**

Activity 15.8

CCSS-M: 5.NF.B.4a, b

STUDENTS with SPECIAL NEEDS

How Big Is the Banner?

Show or explain that you have a roll of paper you will be using to make banners. The roll is one-foot wide (you can also use one-yard or one-meter) and you are going to roll out several feet. The first banner you cut is **1 ft. by 6 ft.**:

Ask students, "What is the area of this banner?" ($1 \times 6 = 6$ square feet). You can ask additional questions of banners of other lengths (with a width of 1 foot). Then, explain that you want to cut the banners length-wise to make thinner banners. Ask students to use this rectangle to show banners that are $\frac{1}{2}$ ft. $\times$ 6 ft. Then ask them to tell you the square feet of the new banner:

Students fill in the strips to show that there are 3 feet in each half-strip:

	6 feet	
$\frac{1}{2}$ ft.	3 feet	
$\frac{1}{2}$ ft.	3 feet	

Repeat the process by asking the area of banners that are 6 feet long and one-third of the width.. Repeat with fourths. After exploring this 6-foot banner, use a variety of lengths (e.g., 12 feet, 15 feet) and various widths (e.g., halves, fourths, thirds). Encourage students to notice patterns that help them determine the area of the banners, considering how the banner is scaled based on the values involved in the problem. For students with disabilities or students who benefit from using physical materials, you can cut out paper strips or One-Inch Grid Paper in advance and have them fold or draw on the paper to show the partitions.

MyLab Education   Blackline Master: One-Inch Grid Paper

Multiply a Fraction by a Fraction—No Subdividing. Once students have had experiences with wholes of fractions (15 groups of $\frac{2}{3}$) and fractions of a whole ($\frac{2}{3}$ of 15), a next step is to introduce finding a fraction of a fraction, but to carefully select tasks in which no additional partitioning is required. Tasks can begin by verbally asking students to find a fraction of a fraction, for example, to find one-half of two-fifths.

MyLab Education   Video Example 15.8

Watch as a student is introduced to finding a fraction of a fraction.

See if you can mentally answer the next three problems:

You have $\frac{3}{4}$ of a pizza left. If you give $\frac{1}{3}$ of the leftover pizza to your brother, how much of a whole pizza will your brother get?

Someone ate $\frac{1}{10}$ of the loaf of bread, leaving $\frac{9}{10}$. If you use $\frac{2}{3}$ of what is left of the loaf to make French toast, how much of the whole loaf will have been used?

Gloria used $2\frac{1}{2}$ tubes of blue paint to paint the sky in her picture. Each tube holds $\frac{4}{5}$ ounce of paint. How many ounces of blue paint did Gloria use?

Figure 15.7 shows how problems of this type might be modeled. However, there are other ways to partition these problems and it is important for students to model and solve these problems in their own way. In $\frac{3}{4} \times \frac{1}{3}$, for example, you can find one-third of the three-fourths (as in Figure 15.7), or you could find $\frac{1}{3}$ of *each* fourth and then combine the pieces (Izsák, 2008).

Multiply a Fraction by a Fraction—with Subdividing. When the pieces must be subdivided into smaller unit parts, the problems become more challenging.

Zack had $\frac{2}{3}$ of the field left to mow. After lunch, he mowed $\frac{3}{4}$ of the field he had left to mow. How much of the whole field did Zack mow after lunch?

Task	Finding the starting amount	Showing the fraction of the starting amount	Solution
Pizza Find $\frac{1}{3}$ of $\frac{3}{4}$ (of a pizza) or $\frac{1}{3} \times \frac{3}{4}$			$\frac{1}{3}$ of the $\frac{3}{4}$ is $\frac{1}{4}$ of the original pizza. $\frac{1}{3} \times \frac{3}{4} = \frac{1}{4}$
Bread Find $\frac{2}{3}$ of $\frac{9}{10}$ (of a loaf of bread) or $\frac{2}{3} \times \frac{9}{10}$			$\frac{2}{3}$ of the $\frac{9}{10}$ is 6 slices of the loaf or $\frac{6}{10}$ of the whole. $\frac{2}{3} \times \frac{9}{10} = \frac{6}{10}$
Paint Find $2\frac{1}{2}$ of $\frac{4}{5}$ (ounces of paint) or $2\frac{1}{2} \times \frac{4}{5}$			$2\frac{1}{2}$ of the $\frac{4}{5}$ is $\frac{4}{5} + \frac{4}{5} + \frac{2}{5} = \frac{10}{5}$

FIGURE 15.7 Connecting representation to the procedure for three problems involving multiplication.

MyLab Education   Application Exercise 15.3: Observing and Responding to Student Thinking Click the link to access this exercise, then watch the video and answer the accompanying questions.

VIDEO EXAMPLE

The zookeeper had a huge bottle of the animals' favorite liquid treat, Zoo Cola. The monkey drank $\frac{1}{5}$ of the bottle. The zebra drank $\frac{2}{3}$ of what was left. How much of the bottle of Zoo Cola did the zebra drink?

⏸ Pause & Reflect

Pause for a moment and figure out how you would solve each of these problems. Draw pictures to help you, but do not use a computational algorithm. ●

In Zack's mowing problem, it is necessary to find fourths of two things, the two-*thirds* of the grass left to cut. In the Zoo Cola problem, you need thirds of four things, the four-*fifths* of the Zoo Cola that remain. Again, the concepts of the top number counting and the bottom number naming what is counted play an important role. Figure 15.8 shows a possible solution for Zack's lawn problem. Using a paper strip and partitioning is an effective way to solve multiplication problems, especially when they require additional partitioning (Siebert & Gaskin, 2006). As illustrated in Figure 15.8, paper is folded or partitioned to show thirds first, then shaded to show two-thirds. Next, the two-thirds must be partitioned (subdivided) to show fourths, then three-fourths is re-shaded. Finally the re-shaded part is compared back to the whole. What fraction of the whole is three-fourths of $\frac{2}{3}$? One-half. A similar approach can be used for the Zoo Cola problem.

TECHNOLOGY Note. The NLVM website has a nice collection of fraction applets. *Number Line Bars—Fractions* allows the user to place bars of any fractional length along a number line. The number line can be adjusted to have increments from $\frac{1}{2}$ to $\frac{1}{15}$, but the user

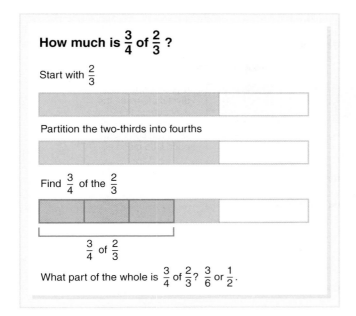

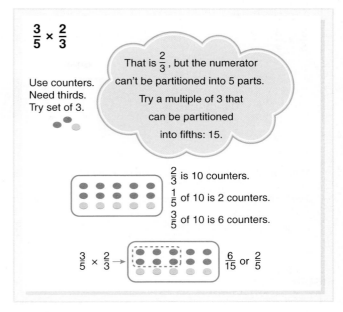

FIGURE 15.8   Solutions to a multiplication problem when the parts must be subdivided.

FIGURE 15.9   Modeling multiplication of fractions with counters.

must decide. For example, if bars of $\frac{1}{4}$ and $\frac{1}{3}$ are placed end to end, the result cannot be read from the applet until the increments are in twelfths. ■

Multiplication of fractions can also be modeled with counters (see Figure 15.9). Consider using a context that fits the illustration, for example rows of chairs. Set models, however, are challenging in terms of interpreting the whole and the answer. Do not discourage students from using counters, but be prepared to help them keep track of the whole and interpret the answer.

Using Rectangles to Illustrate Multiplication. A rectangle is a powerful visual to show that a result can be quite a bit smaller than either of the fractions used or that if the fractions are both close to 1, then the result is also close to one. And, it is a good visual for connecting to the standard algorithm for multiplying fractions.

Provide students with a square, and ask them to partition and shade to illustrate the fraction that is the initial value (see Figure 15.10). For example, in $\frac{3}{5} \times \frac{3}{4}$, you are finding $\frac{3}{5}$ of $\frac{3}{4}$, so you start with $\frac{3}{4}$ (step a in Figure 15.10). To find fifths of the $\frac{3}{4}$, draw five horizontal lines through the $\frac{3}{4}$ (step b) or all the way across the square so that the whole is in same-size partitions, and shade three of the five (step c). The overlap of the shading illustrates what is $\frac{3}{5}$ of $\frac{3}{4}$ of the original whole.

Quilting is a good context, because quilts are rectangles and the individual rectangles (or squares) within the quilt are a fraction of the whole quilt.

CCSS Standards for Mathematical Practice

MP7. Look for and make use of structure.

Activity 15.9   CCSS-M: 5.NF.B4b; 5.NF.B.5b

Quilting Pieces

Have students use grid paper to sketch a drawing of a quilt that will be 8 feet by 6 feet—or create a full-sized one for your class! Explain that each group will prepare a picture that is 3 feet by 2 feet for the quilt. Ask students to tell you what fraction of the quilt a each group will provide.

Second, rephrase the task. Explain that in the quilt, each group is to prepare a section of the quilt that is $\frac{1}{4}$ of the length and $\frac{1}{2}$ of the width. Ask students to sketch the quilt and the portion that their group will prepare. Help students make the connection that $\frac{1}{4}$ the length $\times \frac{1}{2}$ the width $= \frac{1}{8}$ of the area $\left(\frac{1}{4} \times \frac{1}{2} = \frac{1}{8}\right)$.

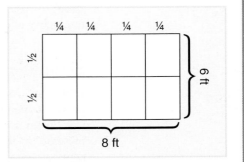

Source: Adapted from Tsankova, J. K., & Pjanic, K. (2009/2010). The area model of multiplication of fractions. *Mathematics Teaching in the Middle School, 15*(5), 281–285.

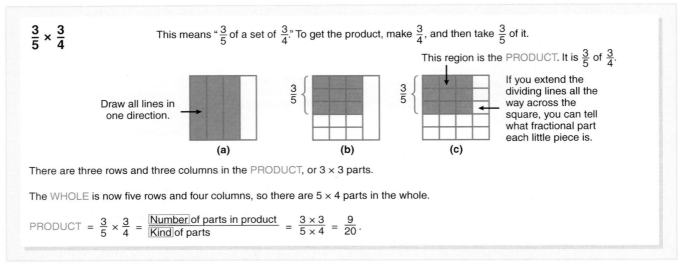

$\frac{3}{5} \times \frac{3}{4}$ This means "$\frac{3}{5}$ of a set of $\frac{3}{4}$." To get the product, make $\frac{3}{4}$, and then take $\frac{3}{5}$ of it.

This region is the PRODUCT. It is $\frac{3}{5}$ of $\frac{3}{4}$.

Draw all lines in one direction.

$\frac{3}{5}$

$\frac{3}{5}$

If you extend the dividing lines all the way across the square, you can tell what fractional part each little piece is.

(a)   (b)   (c)

There are three rows and three columns in the PRODUCT, or 3 × 3 parts.

The WHOLE is now five rows and four columns, so there are 5 × 4 parts in the whole.

PRODUCT $= \frac{3}{5} \times \frac{3}{4} = \frac{\boxed{\text{Number}}\text{ of parts in product}}{\boxed{\text{Kind}}\text{ of parts}} = \frac{3 \times 3}{5 \times 4} = \frac{9}{20}$.

FIGURE 15.10 Development of the standard algorithm for multiplication of fractions.

The following activity engages students in exploring multiplication of fractions and the commutative property.

Activity 15.10   CCSS-M: 5.NF.B.4b; 5.NF.B.6

Playground Problem

Show students the following problem.

Two communities, A and B, are building playgrounds in grassy lots that are 50 yards by 100 yards. In community A, they have been asked to convert $\frac{3}{4}$ of their lot to a playground, and $\frac{2}{5}$ of that playground should be covered with blacktop. In community B, they are building their playground on $\frac{2}{5}$ of the lot, and $\frac{3}{4}$ of the playground should be blacktop. In which park is the grassy playground bigger? In which lot is the blacktop bigger? Illustrate and explain. (Imm, Stylianou, & Chae, 2008, p. 459)

Ask students to predict which community will have the bigger playground. Record predictions. Place students in partners and ask one to solve the problem for community A and the other to solve for community B. Once they have completed their illustrations and solutions, ask students to compare their responses and to be ready to report to the class what they decided.

> **TECHNOLOGY Note.** Area models can also be found at the PBS Learning Media website (https://www.pbslearningmedia.org). The Area Models for Multiplication of Fractions interactive allows you to explore a visual model of the product of two fractions. ∎

Estimation

In the real world, there are many instances when whole numbers and fractions must be multiplied and mental estimates or even exact answers are quite useful.

For example, sale items are frequently listed as "half off," or we read of a "one-third increase" in the number of registered voters. Also, fractions are excellent substitutes for percents, as you will see in the next chapter. To get an estimate of 75 percent of $36.69, it is useful to think of 75 percent as $\frac{3}{4}$, finding one-fourth (about $9) and then three-fourths ($27).

When numbers are more complex, encourage students to use estimation strategies such as compatible numbers, benchmarks, and relative size of unit fractions.

- *Compatible numbers:* To estimate $\frac{3}{5}$ of \$36.69, for example, a useful compatible number is \$35. One-fifth of 35 is 7, so three-fifths is 3×7, or 21.

The two estimation strategies discussed in addition and subtraction also apply to multiplication:

- *Benchmarks:* $\frac{7}{8} \times \frac{5}{12} =$. Think, "This is about one times one half, but a little less, so the answer will be less than the benchmark one-half."
- *Relative size of unit fractions:* $\frac{1}{3} \times 3\frac{4}{5}$. Think "I need a third of this value. A third of 3 is 1, and $\frac{1}{3}$ of $\frac{4}{5}$ is going to be just over $\frac{1}{5}$ (since there are four parts), so about $1\frac{1}{5}$."

Which strategy students select will depend on the size of the fractions given. Invite students to share their strategies, and be sure they are not computing the exact answer and rounding in order to determine an estimate.

CCSS Standards for Mathematical Practice
MP3. Construct viable arguments and critique the reasoning of others.

Developing the Algorithms

With enough experiences using the area model (or the linear model), students will start to notice a pattern. Remember that "enough" is probably a lot more than is usually provided—in other words, this does not mean two or three examples, but several weeks working with different examples and representations. These exercises will lead students to focus on how the denominators relate to how the grid (or line) is partitioned and how the numerator affects the solution to the problem.

When students are ready to start using the standard algorithm, ask them to solve three examples such as the following:

$$\frac{5}{6} \times \frac{1}{2} \qquad \frac{3}{4} \times \frac{1}{5} \qquad \frac{1}{3} \times \frac{9}{10}$$

For each one, use a square and partition it vertically and horizontally to model the problems. Ask, "How did you figure out what the unit of the fraction [the denominator] was?" Or more specifically, on the first problem, you can ask, "How did you figure out that the denominator would be twelfths? Is this a pattern that is true for the other examples?" Then ask students to see whether they can find a similar pattern for how the number of parts (the numerator) is determined.

Continue to ask students to estimate how big they think the answer will be and why, and then to check the reasonableness of their answers. In the first example here, a student might note that the answer will be slightly less than $\frac{1}{2}$ because $\frac{5}{6}$ is close to, but less than, 1.

Factors Greater Than One

Multiplying fractions in which at least one of the factors is a mixed number—for example, $\frac{3}{4} \times 2\frac{1}{2}$ should be integrated into multiplication with fractions less than one. When mixed numbers are mixed in, students can see the the impact of multiplying by a number less than one and a number more than one. Activity 15.11 is a way to focus on this reasoning (Thompson, 1995).

CCSS Standards for Mathematical Practice
MP2. Reason abstractly and quantitatively.

Activity 15.11

CCSS-M: 5.NF.B.3; 5.NF.B.5a, b

Can You See It?

Post a partially shaded illustration like the one shown here.

Ask students the following questions, and have them explain how they see it.

Can you see $\frac{3}{5}$ of something?   Can you see $\frac{5}{3}$ of $\frac{3}{5}$?
Can you see $\frac{5}{3}$ of something?   Can you see $\frac{2}{3}$ of $\frac{3}{5}$?

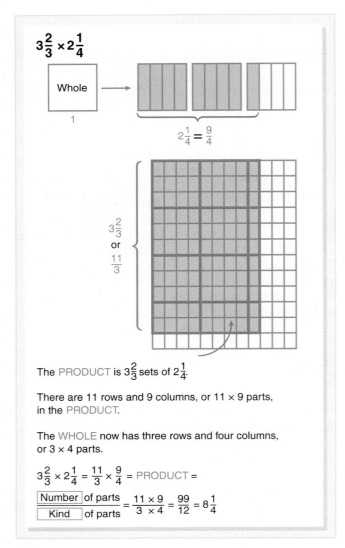

$3\frac{2}{3} \times 2\frac{1}{4}$

Whole
1

$2\frac{1}{4} = \frac{9}{4}$

$3\frac{2}{3}$
or
$\frac{11}{3}$

The PRODUCT is $3\frac{2}{3}$ sets of $2\frac{1}{4}$.

There are 11 rows and 9 columns, or 11 × 9 parts, in the PRODUCT.

The WHOLE now has three rows and four columns, or 3 × 4 parts.

$3\frac{2}{3} \times 2\frac{1}{4} = \frac{11}{3} \times \frac{9}{4} = \text{PRODUCT} =$

$\frac{\boxed{\text{Number}} \text{ of parts}}{\boxed{\text{Kind}} \text{ of parts}} = \frac{11 \times 9}{3 \times 4} = \frac{99}{12} = 8\frac{1}{4}$

FIGURE 15.11 The approach used to develop the algorithm for fractions less than 1 can be expanded to mixed numbers.

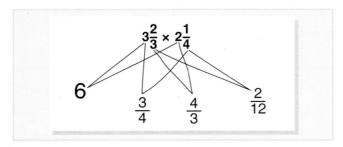

FIGURE 15.12 When multiplying two mixed numbers, there will be four partial products. These can then be added to get the total product, or an estimate may be enough.

CCSS **Standards for Mathematical Practice**

MP2. Reason abstractly and quantitatively.

Rectangles are also a good way to illustrate multiplication of fractions greater than one, as illustrated in Figure 15.11. Many textbooks have students change mixed numbers to fractions (often referred to as *improper fractions*) in order to multiply them. Changing to improper fractions is an efficient way to solve these types of problems, but it is not the only way. In fact, students can multiply either way. Students who understand that $2\frac{1}{2}$ means $2 + \frac{1}{2}$ might multiply $\frac{3}{4} \times 2$ and $\frac{3}{4} \times \frac{1}{2}$ and add the results—the distributive property. When both factors are mixed numbers, there are four partial products, just as there are when multiplying 2 two-digit numbers.

 Pause & Reflect

Find the four partial products in this multiplication:
$3\frac{2}{3} \times 2\frac{1}{4}$. ●

Figure 15.12 shows how this product might be worked out by multiplying the individual parts. The partial products process is more conceptual and lends itself to estimation. Notice that the same four partial products of Figure 15.12 can be found in the rectangle in Figure 15.11. As stated many times in this book, it is important for students to understand both ways and then be able to choose the one that they understand and that works best for them.

Challenges and Misconceptions

When students begin working with fraction multiplication, they already have internalized concepts of whole-number multiplication and fraction addition and subtraction that can lead to confusion. This is exacerbated when students are not given adequate time to explore multiplication of fractions conceptually and when they are too quickly pressed to memorize rules, such as "multiply both the bottom and the top." The result of memorizing rules that don't make sense are errors and confusion, as described in Table 15.2. These challenges become a significant barrier for solving proportions and algebraic expressions.

MyLab Education **Self-Check 15.3**

 Division

Can you think of a real-life example for dividing by a fraction? Few people can, even though we conceptually use division involving fractions in many real-life situations. Do you know the "invert and multiply" algorithm? Have you used it in real situations? Division of fractions remains one of the most mysterious algorithms in K–8 mathematics. We want to avoid this mystery at all costs and help students really understand when and how to divide with situations involving fractions.

TABLE 15.2   COMMON CHALLENGES AND MISCONCEPTIONS FOR MULTIPLYING FRACTIONS

Common Challenge or Misconception	What It Looks Like	How to Help
1. Treat the denominator the same as in addition/subtraction problems.	$\frac{1}{4} \times \frac{3}{8} = \frac{2}{8} \times \frac{3}{8} = \frac{6}{8}$	• Engage students in comparing addition and multiplication and *why* they are different procedures, for example comparing rectangle illustrations for both operations and comparing on a number line. • Be sure that visuals are connected to procedures. • Reinforce estimation before solving, and comparing answer to the estimate after solving.
2. Inability to estimate approximate size of the answer.	For a problem such as $\frac{8}{9} \times \frac{3}{5}$, the student think of $\frac{8}{9}$ as close to 1 and use that to estimate; student multiplies and then rounds to find the answer. Estimate Approximate Size of the Answer.	• Explicitly teach and practice each of the estimation strategies suggested above. • Encourage and discuss estimation for all computations, using estimates to make sure answers are reasonable.
3. Think answer is wrong because it is smaller than the factors.	Student multiplies $\frac{1}{4} \times 4\frac{1}{2}$ and gets the product $1\frac{1}{16}$, but thinks it must be wrong.	• Use visuals to illustrate. • Add contexts or ask students to create a context to fit the problem.
4. Confuse whether to multiply or divide by the given fraction.	For "What is $\frac{1}{3}$ of $24?" rather than divide by 3 or multiply by $\frac{1}{3}$ (both of which are correct), student divides by $\frac{1}{3}$.	• Estimate. • Ask, "Should the result be more or less than the initial amount?" • Ask students to interpret the situation and the answer and see if they make sense.
5. Misinterpret words like "of" in story situations.	In Zach's mowing problem above ($\frac{3}{4}$ of $\frac{2}{3}$,) a student may think the problem is: $\frac{3}{4} - \frac{2}{3}$ or $\frac{3}{4} \div \frac{2}{3}$, among other options.	• Avoid key word approach with story problems—it not only doesn't work, it makes things harder on students as problems get more complex! • Focus students' attention on the situation qualitatively (without a focus on actual numbers). • Encourage students to rewrite the situation more simply and then translate to symbols.

Partitioning and iterating, both discussed in Chapter 14, are absolutely essential prior knowledge to begin exploring division involving fractions. Division should follow a developmental progression through four types of problems:

a. A whole number divided by a whole number: $14 \div 5$ or $22 \div 7$
b. A fraction divided by a whole number: $\frac{1}{2} \div 4$ or $\frac{7}{8} \div 2$
c. A whole number divided by a fraction: $4 \div \frac{1}{3}$ or $4 \div \frac{2}{3}$
d. A fraction divided by a fraction: $\frac{7}{8} \div \frac{1}{8}$ or $2\frac{1}{4} \div \frac{1}{2}$

These types of problems are each described in the following section. In the CCSS-M, division involving fractions begins in fifth grade but is limited to the first three types, and only with unit fractions. In sixth grade, all types are explored, and in seventh grade, all types are explored using both positive and negative fractions.

MyLab Education   Video Example 15.9

In this video, author Jennifer Bay-Williams provides an explanation and overview of division of fractions.

MyLab Education   Video Example 15.10

Watch this illustration of division using tools.

Contextual Examples and Models

Begin by building on students' prior knowledge of division with whole numbers. As with whole numbers, there are two meanings of division: partitive (sharing) and measurement (equal subtraction) (Gregg & Gregg, 2007; Kribs-Zaleta, 2008; Tirosh, 2000). These meanings are both needed to develop the different types of fraction problems, as you will see in these examples.

Divide a Whole Number by a Whole Number. A partitive or sharing context is helpful in interpreting division of a whole number by a whole number (Lamon, 2012). Very young children can understand sharing (e.g., 3 cookies shared with 2 people). Because it is a foundational concept closely tied to partitioning, sharing tasks are a major topic in Chapter 14. Here we limit the discussion to developing a progression for division involving fractions.

Sharing tasks can result in each person receiving a fractional part: 5 sandwiches shared with 4 friends (5 ÷ 4). If you partition each sandwich into fourths, you see that each friend will have five-fourths (friend 1 takes the gold section from each sandwich, friend 2 takes the second (red) section, etc.):

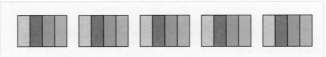

Notice that $5 \div 4 = \frac{1}{4} \times 5 = \frac{5}{4}$. The first expression means five sandwiches shared with 4 friends; the second expression means find one-fourth of 5 sandwiches (that is one person's fair share); and the final expression means five-fourths is one person's share—a fourth from each of 5 sandwiches. Students must be able to see the connections and meanings of each of these equivalent expressions.

This concept applies, no matter how messy the numbers. Think of 92 sandwiches shared with 11 people (92 ÷ 11). Still, each person would receive $\frac{1}{11}$ of each of 92 sandwiches, and so have $\frac{92}{11}$ of the sandwiches.

Having seen that division of a whole number by a whole number is the same as multiplying the number by a unit fraction, students are ready to extend the same reasoning to division of a unit fraction by a whole number.

Divide a Fraction by a Whole Number. These problem types are introduced in the CCSS-M in grade 5 as unit fractions $\left(\frac{1}{4} \div 3\right)$ and in sixth grade for non-unit fractions $\left(\frac{9}{10} \div 3 \text{ or } 2\frac{1}{2} \div 6\right)$. Notice that in partitive (sharing) problems, you are asking, "How much is the share for *one* friend?" Questions could also be "How many miles are walked in *one* hour?" or "How much ribbon for *one* bow?"

CCSS Standards for Mathematical Practice

MP8. Look for and express regularity in repeated reasoning.

⏸ Pause & Reflect

What situation might fit $\frac{1}{4} \div 3$? ●

Activity 15.12   CCSS-M: 5.NF.B.7a, c

Fractions Divided by Whole-Number Stories

Provide students with different situations to explore the same problem. Here are three stories (one area, one linear, and one set):

- *Garden Plots.* Three gardeners are equally sharing $\frac{1}{4}$ of an acre for their plots. What part of an acre is each gardener's plot? (The Garden Plots Activity Page provides four 'plots' that students can use to illustrate garden sharing problems)
- *Water Bottles.* There is $\frac{1}{4}$ of a gallon of water that is poured equally into three water bottles. How much is poured into each?
- *Cheese Sticks.* Arlo buys a bag of cheese sticks. He takes $\frac{1}{4}$ of the cheese sticks to a picnic. At the picnic he decides to share the cheese sticks equally with 2 friends (and himself). What fraction of the bag does each person get?

MyLab Education   **Activity Page: Garden Plots**

After they finish, compare their different visuals and connect the meaning of the operation to the visuals. Ask students to write an expression for each (they should be the same!). Emphasize the notion of "How much for *one*?" After exploring this initial task, students can be challenged to create their own stories to match problems like $\frac{1}{4} \div 3$.

There are many situations that can fit this equation. Notice the situations in Activity 15.12 are area, length, and set models, respectively. As you seek interesting contexts, include ideas from across these models.

Once students have explored a unit fraction divided by a whole number, they need experiences dividing any fraction (or mixed number) by a whole number, using contexts. Ribbon provides a good linear model:

CCSS **Standards for Mathematical Practice**
MP8. Look for and express regularity in repeated reasoning.

Cassie has $5\frac{1}{3}$ yards of ribbon to make four bows for birthday packages. How much ribbon should she use for each bow if she wants to use the same length of ribbon for each?

When the $5\frac{1}{3}$ is thought of as fractional parts, there are 16 thirds to share, or 4 thirds for each bow. Alternatively, one might think of allotting 1 yard per bow, leaving $1\frac{1}{3}$ yards. These 4 thirds are then shared, one per bow, for a total of $1\frac{1}{3}$ yards for each bow. The unit parts (thirds) required no further partitioning in order to do the division. Students need numerous experiences with sharing tasks that come out evenly before exploring tasks that do not.

In the following problem, the parts must be split into smaller parts:

Mark has $1\frac{1}{4}$ hours to finish his three chores. If he divides his time evenly, how many hours can he give to each chore?

Note that the question is, "How many hours for one chore?" The 5 fourths of an hour that Mark has do not split neatly into three parts. So some or all of the parts must be partitioned. Figure 15.13 shows how to model these with each type of model (area, linear, and set). In each case, all of the fourths are subdivided into three equal parts, producing twelfths. There are a total of 15 twelfths, or $\frac{5}{12}$ hour for each chore. (Test this answer against the solution in minutes: $1\frac{1}{4}$ hours is 75 minutes, which divided among 3 chores is 25 minutes per chore. $\frac{25}{60} = \frac{5}{12}$.) See Expanded Lesson: Division-of-Fraction Stories for a complete lesson using Cassie and Mark's stories.

MyLab Education	Expanded Lesson: Division-of-Fraction Stories

Divide a Whole Number by a Fraction. This problem type lends to a measurement interpretation (also called *repeated subtraction* or *equal groups*). In these situations, an equal group is taken away from the total repeatedly. For example, "If you have 13 quarts of lemonade, how many canteens holding 3 quarts each can you fill?" Notice that this is not a sharing situation but rather an equal subtraction situation. In this case, the question we ask is "How many 3s are in 13?"

The measurement interpretation is a good way to explore division by a fraction because students can draw illustrations to show the measures (Cramer et al., 2010). There are numerous ways to illustrate how to divide whole numbers by fractions. And measurement interpretation will be used to develop an algorithm for dividing fractions, so it is important for students to explore this idea in contextual situations. A good context for a measurement interpretation is counting servings of a particular size.

Activity 15.13 uses a context of serving sandwiches to build a foundation for division by unit fractions.

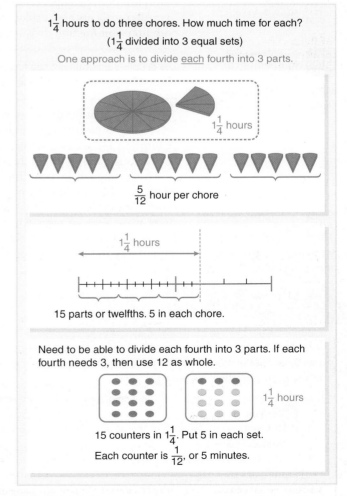

FIGURE 15.13 Three models of partitive division with a whole-number divisor.

Activity 15.13

CCSS-M: 5.NF.B.7b, c

Sandwich Servings

Super Sub Sandwiches is starting a catering business. A child's serving is $\frac{1}{6}$ of a Super Sub and an adult serving can be either $\frac{1}{3}$ or $\frac{1}{2}$ of a Super Sub, depending on whether the catering customer requests small or medium. The employees must be quick at deciding the number of subs for an event based on serving size.

1. Which portion size serves the most people—child-size $\frac{1}{6}$, small $\frac{1}{3}$, or medium $\frac{1}{2}$? Why?

$$6 \div \frac{1}{6} \qquad 6 \div \frac{1}{3} \qquad 6 \div \frac{1}{2}$$

2. Describe what is happening in each sandwich situation below (how many sandwiches and which kind of serving size). Estimate: Which situation serves the most people? Explain your reasoning.

$$8 \div \frac{1}{3} \qquad 5 \div \frac{1}{2} \qquad 6 \div \frac{1}{6}$$

Notice that question 1 (above) provides the opportunity to compare the impact of unit divisors and discuss *why* you get more servings when you have smaller fractions as divisors. This helps to build the relationship between multiplication and division and students may notice the general case: $1 \div \frac{1}{n} = n$ and therefore, $a \div \frac{1}{n} = a \times n$ (Cavey & Kinzel, 2014). The second prompt provides the opportunity for students to test their conjectures from question 1 on new examples. Both prompts can be illustrated using various visuals.

After students have explored unit divisors, they are ready to explore measurement situations with non-unit fraction divisors, such as this task:

Standards for Mathematical Practice

MP5. Use appropriate tools strategically.

Les & Colin's Smoothies Shop has just bought a machine that blends 6 pints of smoothies for one batch. Their Smoothie Cups hold $\frac{3}{4}$ of a pint. How many smoothies can be served from one batch?

A visual that fits this context might be a vertical number line or bar diagram, or it could be six rectangles partitioned into fourths. Students may be able to readily count the total number of fourths (24), but not be sure on how to count servings of *three*-fourths. Encourage students to use visuals and to group three of the fourths together as one serving.

A sharing or partitioning interpretation can (and should) be used in working with whole numbers divided by fractions. Remember that the focus question in sharing is "How much for one (e.g., person)?" or "How many for one?" You may recall that in Chapter 14 there were a set of tasks where students are asked to find the whole, given the part (see Figure 15.11). Essentially, these tasks are saying, "How much for one?" and are therefore a good way to build meaning for division by a fraction. Activity 15.14 provides a sampling of such tasks revisited to be more explicit about the connection to division.

Standards for Mathematical Practice

MP2. Reason abstractly and quantitatively.

Activity 15.14

CCSS-M: 5.NF.B.7a, c

How Much in One Whole Set?

Use Counting Counters: How Much for One? Activity Page or give students a collection of two-color counters. Ask them to sets of tasks, such as the ones provided here:

1. If 8 counters represents $\frac{1}{4}$ of the whole, how much is one whole set?
   Expression: $8 \div \frac{1}{4}$
2. If 15 counters represents $\frac{3}{5}$ of the whole, how much is one whole set?
   Expression: $15 \div \frac{3}{5}$
3. If 18 counters represents $2\frac{1}{4}$ sets, how much is one whole set?
   Expression: $18 \div 2\frac{1}{4}$

As students are working, ask them to describe their reasoning strategies. Help them to notice that they are finding how many in *one part* (e.g., one-fourth or one-fifth), and then iterating (multiplying) to find out how many in *one whole* (e.g. four-fourths or five-fifths).

MyLab Education   Activity Page: Counting Counters: How Much for One?

Sharing tasks such as this are very closely connected to the meaning of the division by a fraction algorithm, as described in the next section.

Divide a Fraction by a Fraction. Over time, using various contexts and numbers that vary in difficulty, students will be able to take on problems that are more complex both in the context and in the numbers involved. Using the measurement concept of serving size, Gregg and Gregg (2007) use cookie serving size of $\frac{1}{2}$ to bridge from a whole number divided by a fraction to a fraction divided by a fraction.

MyLab Education
Video Example 15.11
In this video we see Felisha reason about servings of jelly beans.

▶ VIDEO EXAMPLE

Examples are illustrated in Figure 15.14, but many more examples can be inserted along this progression from whole number divided by a fraction, to fraction divided by a fraction (that has a remainder). As the examples in this figure illustrate, moving slowly to more complex examples will enable students to use their whole-number concepts to build an understanding of division with fractions.

Though you may think that mixed numbers are more difficult, using mixed numbers early can help students make sense of division of a fraction by a fraction:

Farmer Brown found that he had $2\frac{1}{4}$ gallons of liquid fertilizer concentrate. It takes $\frac{3}{4}$ gallon to make a tank of mixed fertilizer. How many tankfuls can he mix?

Try solving this problem yourself. Use any model or drawing you wish to help explain what you are doing. Notice that you are trying to find out how many sets of 3 fourths are in a set of 9 fourths. Your answer should be 3 tankfuls (not 3 fourths). It is important to emphasize units with students as it is easy to forget what whole (unit) the fraction describes.

Fractions divided by fractions can also be explained using partitioning and sharing. That is the focus of this next activity.

1. A serving is $\frac{1}{2}$ cookie. How many servings can I make from 2 cookies?

2. A serving is $\frac{1}{2}$ cookie. How many servings can I make from 1 cookie?

3. A serving is $\frac{1}{2}$ cookie. How many servings can I make from $\frac{3}{4}$ cookie?

4. A serving is $\frac{1}{2}$ cookie. How many servings can I make from $\frac{3}{8}$ cookie?

5. A serving is $\frac{1}{2}$ cookie. How many servings can I make from $\frac{5}{8}$ cookie?

FIGURE 15.14   Tasks that use the measurement interpretation of "How many servings?" to develop the concept of division.

Source: Gregg, J., & Gregg, D. W. (2007). "Measurement and Fair-Sharing Models for Dividing Fractions." *Mathematics Teaching in the Middle School, 12*(9), p. 491. Reprinted with permission. Copyright © 2007 by the National Council of Teachers of Mathematics. All rights reserved.

Activity 15.15   CCSS-M: 5.NF.B.7a, c; 6.NS.A.1

How Much for 1?

Pose contextual problems where the focus question is, "How much for one ___?" Ask students to create bar diagrams or other visuals to illustrate how much for one:

Dan paid $3\frac{3}{4}$ for a $\frac{3}{4}$ pound box of cereal. How much is that per pound?

Andrea found that if she walks quickly during her morning exercise, she can cover $2\frac{1}{2}$ miles in $\frac{3}{4}$ of an hour. She wonders how fast she is walking in miles per hour.

With both problems, first find the amount of one-fourth (partitioning) and then the value of one whole (iterating). Andrea's walking problem is a bit harder because the $2\frac{1}{2}$ miles, or 5 half-miles, do not neatly divide into three parts. Hint: divide each half-mile into three parts.

Answers That Are Not Whole Numbers

Many problems are not going to come out evenly and it becomes very important to make sense of the left over. If Cassie has 5 yards of ribbon to make bows, and each bow needs $1\frac{1}{6}$ yards each, she can make only four bows because a part of a bow does not make sense. But if Farmer Brown begins with 4 gallons of concentrate, after making five tanks of mix, he will have used $\frac{15}{4}$, or $3\frac{3}{4}$ gallons, of the concentrate. With the $\frac{1}{4}$ gallon of remaining concentrate, he can make a *partial* tank of mix. He can make $\frac{1}{3}$ of a tank of mix, because it takes *3* fourths to equal a whole, and he has *1* fourth of a gallon (he has one of the three parts he needs for a tank).

Here is another problem to try:

John is building a patio. Each patio section requires $\frac{1}{3}$ of a cubic yard of concrete. The concrete truck holds $2\frac{1}{2}$ cubic yards of concrete. If there is not enough for a full section at the end, John can put in a divider and make a partial section. How many patio sections can John make with the concrete in the truck?

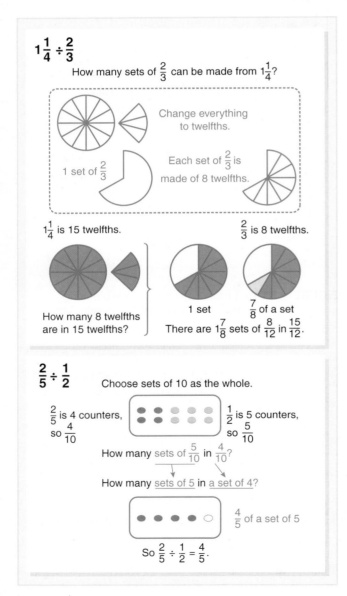

$1\frac{1}{4} \div \frac{2}{3}$

How many sets of $\frac{2}{3}$ can be made from $1\frac{1}{4}$?

Change everything to twelfths.

1 set of $\frac{2}{3}$

Each set of $\frac{2}{3}$ is made of 8 twelfths.

$1\frac{1}{4}$ is 15 twelfths.

$\frac{2}{3}$ is 8 twelfths.

How many 8 twelfths are in 15 twelfths?

1 set

$\frac{7}{8}$ of a set

There are $1\frac{7}{8}$ sets of $\frac{8}{12}$ in $\frac{15}{12}$.

$\frac{2}{5} \div \frac{1}{2}$

Choose sets of 10 as the whole.

$\frac{2}{5}$ is 4 counters, so $\frac{4}{10}$

$\frac{1}{2}$ is 5 counters, so $\frac{5}{10}$

How many sets of $\frac{5}{10}$ in $\frac{4}{10}$?

How many sets of 5 in a set of 4?

$\frac{4}{5}$ of a set of 5

So $\frac{2}{5} \div \frac{1}{2} = \frac{4}{5}$.

FIGURE 15.15 Common denominators can be used to solve division of fraction problems.

 Pause & Reflect

Try to solve this problem in some way that makes sense to you. ●

One way to do this is by counting how many thirds there are in $2\frac{1}{2}$.

Here you can see that you get 3 patio sections from the yellow whole and 3 more from the orange whole, and then you get 1 more full section and $\frac{1}{2}$ of what you need for another patio section. The answer is $7\frac{1}{2}$. Students will want to write the remainder as $\frac{1}{3}$ because they were measuring in thirds, but the question is how many sections can be made—$7\frac{1}{2}$.

Will common denominators work for division? Let's see. The problem you just solved, $2\frac{1}{2} \div \frac{1}{3}$ would become $2\frac{3}{6} \div \frac{2}{6}$, or it could be $\frac{15}{6} \div \frac{2}{6}$. The question becomes, "How many sets of 2 sixths are in a set of 15 sixths?" Or, "How many 2s in 15?" This produces the correct answer of $7\frac{1}{2}$. This is as efficient as the standard algorithm, and it may make more sense to students. Figure 15.15 shows two division problems solved this way, each with a different representation.

 FORMATIVE ASSESSMENT Notes. For all operations with fractions, using a mathematical adaptation of the Frayer Model, such as the Procedure—Illustration—Concept—Situation Activity Page can be used as a pre- or postassessment or as a performance assessment to see if students can represent the operation using visuals and symbols and explain connections between procedures and concepts. ■

MyLab Education   **Activity Page: Procedure—Illustration—Concept—Situation**

Estimation

Understanding division can be greatly supported by using estimation. What does $\frac{1}{6} \div 4$ mean? Will the answer be greater than 1? Greater than $\frac{1}{2}$? Greater than $\frac{1}{6}$? The answer to each of these questions is "no." The answer should be obvious to someone who understands the meaning of this operation (that one-sixth is being shared four ways, resulting in even smaller parts). Conversely, consider what $12 \div \frac{1}{4}$ means. Will the answer be greater than 1? Greater than 12? The answer to these questions is "yes" and again it should be obvious, because you are actually answering the question, "How many fourths in 12?" (there are 48 fourths in 12 wholes). Finding compatible numbers is effective for division of fractions. For example, for $5\frac{1}{3} \div \frac{3}{5}$ think, "$5\frac{1}{3}$ is close to five, and $\frac{3}{5}$ is close to $\frac{1}{2}$. How many halves in 5? 10."

Activity 15.16 encourages estimation with division (and can also be adapted to the other operations).

Activity 15.16

CCSS-M: 5.NF.B.7a, b, c; 6.NS.A.1

ENGLISH LEARNERS

The Size Is Right: Division

Start with either fractions divided by whole numbers or whole numbers divided by fractions, but then mix up the tasks. Use the Size is Right Activity Page or each of these problems ready to flash and cover on a document camera or Smartboard projection. Show for a few seconds, then remove. Ask students to pick one of the options from the dashboard (illustrated below). Then invite students to pair-compare their selections and decide if they are reasonable.

STUDENTS *with* **SPECIAL NEEDS**

Fractions divided by whole numbers

Dashboard:

| Less than $\frac{1}{8}$ | Less than $\frac{1}{4}$ | Less than $\frac{1}{2}$ | Less than 1 | More than 1 | More than 2 |

Examples:

$\frac{1}{2} \div 3$ $\frac{5}{6} \div 2$ $\frac{7}{9} \div 3$ $\frac{9}{2} \div 3$ $\frac{15}{4} \div 3$

Whole numbers divided by fractions

Dashboard:

| Less than 1 | More than 1 | More than 2 | More than 4 | More than 8 |

Examples:

$3 \div \frac{1}{3}$ $1 \div \frac{2}{3}$ $2 \div \frac{1}{3}$ $4 \div \frac{7}{8}$ $4 \div \frac{3}{8}$

For English learners, provide sentence starters to support the speaking opportunities: "I think the answer is [dashboard choice] because. . . ." For students with disabilities or students who benefit from visuals, have tools available such as Cuisenaire Rods or fraction circles so that they can more readily see the relative size of each fraction.

MyLab Education   **Activity Page: Size is Right**
MyLab Education   **Activity Page: Dashboard**

Activity 15.16 can also be used for fractions divided by fractions, with dashboards such as Quotient < 1, Quotient = 1 and Quotient > 1 (Johanning & Mamer, 2014). Students can write division expressions that fit in each of these categories. The more estimation students do, the more they begin to develop a much-needed number sense for fraction division.

Developing the Algorithms

There are two different algorithms for division of fractions. Methods of teaching both algorithms are discussed here.

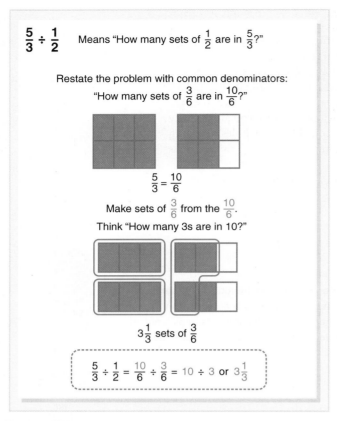

$\frac{5}{3} \div \frac{1}{2}$ Means "How many sets of $\frac{1}{2}$ are in $\frac{5}{3}$?"

Restate the problem with common denominators:
"How many sets of $\frac{3}{6}$ are in $\frac{10}{6}$?"

$\frac{5}{3} = \frac{10}{6}$

Make sets of $\frac{3}{6}$ from the $\frac{10}{6}$.
Think "How many 3s are in 10?"

$3\frac{1}{3}$ sets of $\frac{3}{6}$

$\frac{5}{3} \div \frac{1}{2} = \frac{10}{6} \div \frac{3}{6} = 10 \div 3$ or $3\frac{1}{3}$

FIGURE 15.16 Models for the common-denominator method for fraction division.

Common-Denominator Algorithm. Common denominators are a great strategy for dividing, although not widely known or used in the United States. Let's revisit $2\frac{1}{2} \div \frac{1}{3}$. The problem would become $2\frac{3}{6} \div \frac{2}{6}$ or $\frac{15}{6} \div \frac{2}{6}$. The question becomes, "How many sets of 2 sixths are in a set of 15 sixths?" Or, "How many 2s in 15?" $7\frac{1}{2}$. Figure 15.16 shows how to illustrate this idea with an area model using the problem $\frac{5}{3} \div \frac{1}{2}$. Notice that once a common denominator is found, the thought process is the same as in the whole-number problem $10 \div 3$. The resulting algorithm, therefore, is as follows: *To divide fractions, first get common denominators, and then divide the numerators.* For example, $\frac{5}{3} \div \frac{1}{4} = \frac{20}{12} \div \frac{3}{12} = 20 \div 3 = \frac{20}{3} = 6\frac{2}{3}$.

Try using circular fraction pieces, fraction strips, and then sets of counters to model $1\frac{2}{3} \div \frac{3}{4}$ using a common-denominator approach.

Invert-and-Multiply Algorithm. Providing a series of tasks and having students look for patterns in how they are finding the answers can help them discover this poorly understood and commonly taught algorithm. For example, consider this first set, in which the divisor is a unit fraction. Remember to pose the related question that goes with each equation. Servings of food can be the context.

$3 \div \frac{1}{2} =$ (How many servings of $\frac{1}{2}$ in 3 containers?)

$5 \div \frac{1}{4} =$ (How many servings of $\frac{1}{4}$ in 5 containers?)

$8 \div \frac{1}{5} =$ (How many servings of $\frac{1}{5}$ in 8 containers?)

$3\frac{3}{4} \div \frac{1}{8} =$ (How many servings of $\frac{1}{8}$ in $3\frac{3}{4}$ containers?)

Ask students to look across these problems (and others) for a pattern. They will notice they are multiplying by the denominator of the second fraction. For example, in the third example, a student might say, "You get five for every whole container, so 5×8 is 40." You can also consider these equations as partitive situations, which answers the question "How much in one?" For example, Mary paid \$3 for half a pound of coffee. How much would she pay for one pound? The computation is $3 \div \frac{1}{2}$. To find a whole pound, you would double what you have to get to one pound for \$6.

Then move to similar problems, but with a second fraction that is not a unit fraction:

$5 \div \frac{3}{4} =$

$8 \div \frac{2}{5} =$

$3\frac{3}{4} \div \frac{3}{8} =$

Have students solve these problems and compare their responses with those for the problems in the first set. For example, notice that if there are 40 one-fifths in 8, then when you group the fifths in pairs (two-fifths), you will have half as many—20. Stated in servings, if the serving is twice as big, you will have half the number of servings. Similarly, if the divisor is $\frac{3}{4}$, after finding how many fourths, you will group in threes, which means you will get $\frac{1}{3}$ the number of servings. You can see that this means you must divide by 3.

The examples given were measurements because the size of the group (serving) was known, but not the number of groups. Partitioning or sharing examples nicely illustrate the standard algorithm. Consider this example which focuses on one trip (group):

Andy rode his bike $1\frac{1}{2}$ miles and is $\frac{3}{8}$ of way to the park. What is the distance of *one* trip to the park?

If you have traveled *three* of the eighths. You may be thinking that you first need to find what one-eighth would be—which means dividing $1\frac{1}{2}$ by 3 to get $\frac{1}{2}$. Now you know that $\frac{1}{2}$ mile is one-eighth of the distance to the park. So, the full distance to the park requires multiplying by 8. And, $8 \times \frac{1}{2} = 4$. One trip to the park is 4 miles.

In either the measurement or the partitive interpretation, the denominator leads you to find out how many fourths, fifths, or eighths you have. So, the process is *multiply by the denominator*. The numerator tells the size of the serving or grouping, so the process is *divide by the numerator*. At some point, someone thought, if they just flip the divisor (fraction), it would be more straightforward—and that is why we have learned to "invert and multiply."

Challenges and Misconceptions

The biggest misunderstanding with division of fractions is just not knowing what the algorithm means. Once students realize the meaning of division involving fractions, they are able to begin thinking of different ways to approach problems and decide whether their answers make sense. A critical aspect of understanding division of fractions is understanding that the divisor is the unit (Cramer et al., 2010; Dixon & Tobias, 2013; Philipp & Hawthorne, 2015), and this must be understood in order to interpret the remainder (Coughlin, 2010/2011; Lamon, 2012; Sharp & Welder, 2014). Table 15.3 provides illustrations of this challenge, and others, along with ways to help.

> **MyLab Education**   **Self-Check 15.4: Division**
>
> **MyLab Education**   **Math Practice:** Need to practice or refresh your math content knowledge? Click to access practice exercises associated with the content from this chapter.

TABLE 15.3   COMMON CHALLENGES AND MISCONCEPTIONS FOR DIVIDING FRACTIONS

Common Challenge or Misconception	What It Looks Like	How to Help
1. Think the answer should be smaller.	Students solve a problem like $\frac{4}{5} \div \frac{1}{10} = 8$ and do not think the answer can be 8 because it is bigger than the fractions in the problem.	• Devote time to estimating. Estimation can be the goal, as in Activity 15.16, or it can be a beginning to doing a computation to later check for reasonableness. • Use visuals to illustrate. • Add contexts or ask students to create a context to fit the problem.
2. Do not connect the illustration with the correct numeric answer.	Student understands that $1\frac{1}{2} \div \frac{1}{4}$ means "How many fourths are in $1\frac{1}{2}$?" They count and get 6, but think the answer is $\frac{6}{4}$ (rather than 6) (Cramer et al., 2010).	• Emphasize the unit. Ask, "How many fourths?" • Use visuals and contexts. • Discuss why it is not $\frac{6}{4}$ (use a worked example to launch a discussion).
3. Do not know what the unit is.	A student gets an answer of $\frac{3}{8}$, but when you say "$\frac{3}{8}$ of what?" he doesn't know.	*Challenges 3 and 4 are inter-related. To support students:* • Emphasize what the unit is (the divisor). • Ask, "What is the unit?" "What is the whole?" • Use contexts for units (e.g., servings of quesadillas, feet, etc.). • For the remainder, ask, "What fraction of the next serving/piece do you have?"
4. Write remainders based on the whole, rather than the share/serving.	In the problem $3\frac{3}{8} \div \frac{1}{4}$, a student counts 4 fourths for each whole (12 fourths) and one more for $\frac{2}{8}$ and then puts the extra $\frac{1}{8}$ on the answer: $13\frac{1}{8}$ (rather than realize that $\frac{1}{8}$ is half of the unit $\frac{1}{4}$, resulting in the correct answer $13\frac{1}{28}$.	

RESOURCES FOR CHAPTER 15

LITERATURE CONNECTIONS

Alice's Adventures in Wonderland
Carroll and Gray (1865/1992)

This well-known children's story needs no introduction. Because Alice shrinks in the story, there is an opportunity to explore multiplication by fractions. Taber (2007) describes in detail how she used this story to engage students in understanding the meaning of multiplication of fractions. She begins by asking how tall Alice would be if she were originally 54″ tall but was shrunk to $\frac{1}{9}$ of her height. What height will Alice be if she is later restored to only $\frac{5}{6}$ her original height? The students write their own Alice multiplication-of-fractions equations.

The Man Who Made Parks
Wishinsky and Zhang (1999)

This nonfiction book explains the remarkable story of Frederick Olmsted, who designed Central Park in New York City. Creating a park design, students can be given fractional amounts for what needs to be included in the park—for example, $\frac{2}{5}$ gardens, $\frac{1}{10}$ playgrounds, $\frac{1}{2}$ natural habitat (streams and forest), and the rest special features (like a zoo or outdoor theater). Students can build the plan for their park on a rectangular grid. To include multiplication of fractions, include guidelines such as that $\frac{3}{4}$ of the park is natural habitat, with $\frac{1}{3}$ of that to be wooded and $\frac{1}{6}$ to be water features, and so on.

RECOMMENDED READINGS

Articles

Cavey, L. O., & Kinzel, M. T. (2014). From whole numbers to invert and multiply. *Teaching Children Mathematics, 20*(6), 375–383.

An excellent progression of teaching division of whole numbers to division of fractions in a way that makes strong connections between multiplication and division. CCSS-M included, this article helps with content knowledge and teaching ideas.

Cramer, K., Wyberg, T., & Leavitt, S. (2008). The role of representations in fraction addition and subtraction. *Mathematics Teaching in the Middle School, 13*(8), 490–496.

Illustrations and student work are used to show how to teach addition and subtraction using the fraction circle. Essential considerations of effective instruction are emphasized.

Gregg, J., & Gregg, D. U. (2007). Measurement and fair-sharing models for dividing fractions. *Mathematics Teaching in the Middle School, 12*(9), 490–496.

These authors provide a series of tasks to develop the concept of division of fractions—a must-read for a teacher needing more experiences exploring division or trying to plan a good instructional sequence.

Imm, K. L., Stylianou, D. A., & Chae, N. (2008). Student representations at the center: Promoting classroom equity. *Mathematics Teaching in the Middle School, 13*(8), 458–463.

Using a park context, these authors explain how to model multiplication of fractions. Equity and a culture for learning are emphasized.

16 Developing Decimal and Percent Concepts and Decimal Computation

LEARNER OUTCOMES

After reading this chapter and engaging in the embedded activities and reflections, you should be able to:

16.1 Describe how the place-value system is central to the understanding of decimal fractions.

16.2 Identify physical models that connect fractions to decimals.

16.3 Demonstrate how to compare and order decimal fractions.

16.4 Explain multiple strategies for computing with decimals.

16.5 Explain how percents are related to fractions and decimals.

People need to be able to interpret decimals for such varied needs as reading precise metric measures, calculating loans and mortgages, interpreting output on a calculator, and understanding sports statistics such as those at the Olympics, where winners and losers are separated by hundredths of a second. Decimals are critically important in many occupations: For nurses, pharmacists, and workers building airplanes, for example, precision affects the safety of the general public. Because students and teachers have been shown to have greater difficulty understanding decimals than fractions (Martinie, 2007; Lortie-Forgues, Tian, & Siegler, 2015; Stacey et al., 2001; Vamvakoussi, Van Dooren, & Verschaffel, 2012), conceptual understanding of decimals and their connections to fractions must be carefully developed. Research shows there is a strong relationship between teachers' content knowledge of decimals, including computation with decimals, and their pedagogical knowledge of the ways to teach these ideas to students (Depaepe et al., 2015).

In the *Common Core State Standards*, the progression for understanding decimals is:

Grade 4: Develop an understanding of decimal notation (to hundredths) for fractions and compare decimal fractions

Grade 5: Perform operations with decimals (to hundredths), expanding comparisons of decimals to thousandths, and rounding decimals.

Grade 6: Extend decimal operations beyond tenths and hundredths to all decimals, develop standard algorithms for all four decimal operations and explore percent of a quantity as a rate.

Grade 7: Develop a "unified understanding of number" to be able to move fluently between decimals, fractions, and percents.

Fractions with denominators of 10, 100, 1,000 and so on—for example, $\frac{7}{10}$ or $\frac{63}{100}$, which can also be written as 0.7 and 0.63—will be referred to as *decimal fractions*. The phrase *decimal fractions* is often shortened to *decimals*. In this chapter, we will use these terms interchangeably to express rational numbers expressed in base-ten notation. Explicitly linking the ideas of fractions to decimals can be extremely useful, both from a pedagogical view as well as a practical view. Many of these big ideas focus on that connection.

BIG IDEAS

- The base-ten place-value system extends infinitely in two directions: to very small values and to very large values. Between any two place values, the 10-to-1 ratio remains the same.

- Decimals (also called *decimal fractions*) are a way of writing fractions within the base-ten system (denominators of 10, 100, etc.).

- The decimal point is a convention that has been developed to indicate the unit's position. The position to the left of the decimal point marks the location of the units place.

- Addition and subtraction with decimals are based on the fundamental concept of adding and subtracting numbers in like position values—an extension from whole numbers.

- Multiplication and division of two numbers will produce the same digits, regardless of the positions of the decimal point. As a result, multiplicative computations with decimal fractions can be performed as whole numbers with the decimal placed by way of estimation, as well as by identifying patterns.

- Percents are simply hundredths and as such are a third way of writing both fractions and decimals.

Extending the Place-Value System

Review ideas of whole-number place value before exploring decimals with students. One of the most basic ideas is the 10-to-1 multiplicative relationship between the values of any two adjacent positions. In terms of a base-ten model such as paper strips and squares, 10 of any one piece will make 1 of the next larger (to the immediate left), and movement of a piece to the immediate right involves division by 10 (1 divided by 10 is one-tenth).

The 10-to-1 Relationship—Now in Two Directions!

As you learned when studying place value, the 10-makes-1 relationship continues indefinitely to larger and larger pieces or positional values. If you are using paper Base-Ten Materials, for example, the strip and square shapes alternate in an infinite progression as they get larger. Like-wise, each piece to the right in this continuum is divided by 10 (1 divided by 10 is one-tenth). The critical question becomes "Is there ever a smallest piece?" In the students' prior experience, the smallest piece is the centimeter square or unit piece. But couldn't that piece be divided into 10 small strips? And couldn't those small strips be divided into 10 very small squares, and so on?

MyLab Education   **Blackline Master: Base-Ten Materials**

The goal of this discussion is to help students see that a 10-to-1 relationship extends infinitely in two directions with no smallest piece and no largest piece. The symmetry of the system is around the ones place (tens to the left of the ones place, tenths to the right,

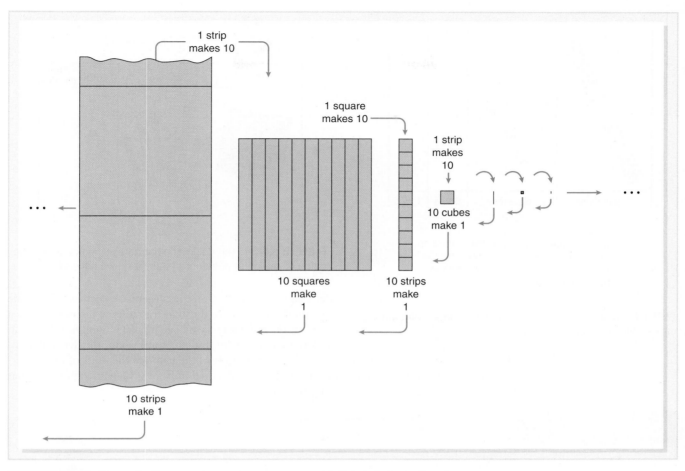

FIGURE 16.1   Theoretically, the strips and squares extend infinitely in both directions.

and so on)—not the common misconception of symmetry around the decimal point. The relationship between adjacent pieces is the same regardless of which two adjacent pieces are being considered. Figure 16.1 illustrates this idea.

Even at this stage, remind students of the powerful concept of regrouping by having students not only make 1 ten from 10 units (transforming a smaller unit to a larger unit), but flexibly think about regrouping 2451 into 24 hundreds, 5 tens and 1 unit; or 245 tens and 1 unit; or 2451 ones. As you can see, this process is essential in thinking about 0.6 as 6 tenths, as well as 60 hundredths and so on.

The Role of the Decimal Point

The decimal point marks the location of the ones (or units) place. That is why on a calculator, when there is a whole-number answer, no decimal point appears. Only when the ones place needs to be identified will the decimal point show in the display. Students also need to recognize that adding zeros to the left of a whole number or to the right of a decimal fraction does not change the value of the number.

An important idea to be realized in this discussion is that there is no built-in reason why any one position (or base-ten piece) should be chosen to be the unit or ones position. In terms of strips and squares, for example, which piece is the ones piece? The small centimeter square? Why? Why not a larger or a smaller square? Why not a strip? Any piece could effectively be chosen as the ones piece. As shown in Figure 16.2, a quantity can be written in different ways, depending on the choice of the unit or what piece is used to count the entire collection.

The decimal point is placed between two positions with the convention that the position to the left of the decimal is the units or ones position. Thus, the role of the decimal point is to designate the units position, and it does so by sitting just to the right of that position. The

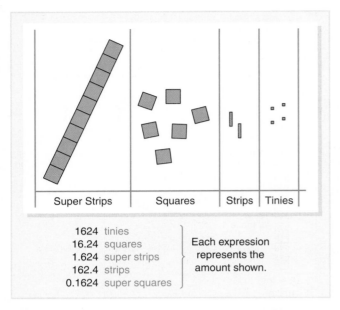

1624	tinies
16.24	squares
1.624	super strips
162.4	strips
0.1624	super squares

Each expression represents the amount shown.

FIGURE 16.2   The placement of the decimal point indicates which position is the unit.

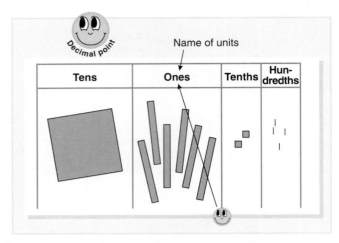

FIGURE 16.3   The decimal point always "looks up at" the name of the units position. In this case, we have 16.24.

decimal notation of a 0 in the ones place, such as 0.60, is the accepted way to write decimal fractions. This notation is a convention and a way to indicate that the number is less than 1. A reminder to help students think about the decimal point is shown in Figure 16.3, with the "eyes" focusing up toward the name of the units or ones.

Activity 16.1 illustrates the convention that the decimal indicates the named unit and that the unit can change without changing the quantity.

Activity 16.1

CCSS-M: 4.NF.C.6; 5.NBT.A.3a

The Decimal Point Names the Unit

Have students display a number of base-ten pieces on their desks. For example, put out six squares, two strips, and four tinies as in part of Figure 16.2. For this activity, refer to the pieces as *squares, strips,* and *tinies,* and reach an agreement on names for the pieces both smaller and larger as the activity requires the values of the materials to shift. To the right of tinies can be *tiny strips* and *tiny squares.* To the left of squares can be *super strips* and *super squares.* For ELs and students with disabilities it is important that you write these labels with the corresponding visuals in a prominent place in the classroom so that they can refer to this terminology. Each student should also have a "smiling" decimal point. Now ask students to write and say how many squares they have, how many super strips, and so on. The students position their decimal point accordingly and then write and say the amounts.

ENGLISH LEARNERS

STUDENTS with SPECIAL NEEDS

MyLab Education   Blackline Master: Smiling Decimal

Measurement and Monetary Units

The notion that the decimal point identifies the units place is useful in a variety of contexts as the unit must be stated in order to understand the number. For example, in the metric system, several place values have names. As shown in Figure 16.4, the decimal point can designate any of these places as the unit without changing the actual measure.

Our monetary system is also a decimal system. In $172.95, the decimal point designates the dollars position as the unit. There are 1 hundred (dollars), 7 tens, 2 singles, 9 dimes (one-tenth of a dollar), and 5 pennies (one-hundredth of a dollar) in this amount of money, regardless of how it is written. If pennies were the designated unit, the same amount would be written as 17,295 cents or 17,295.0 cents. It could also correctly be 0.17295 thousands of dollars or 1729.5 dimes.

In the case of measures such as metric lengths or weights or the U.S. monetary system, the name of the unit is written after the number rather than above the digit as on a place-value chart. In the news, we may hear about Congress spending $7.3 billion. Here the units are billions of dollars, not dollars. A city's population may be 2.4 million people which is equal to 2,400,000 individuals.

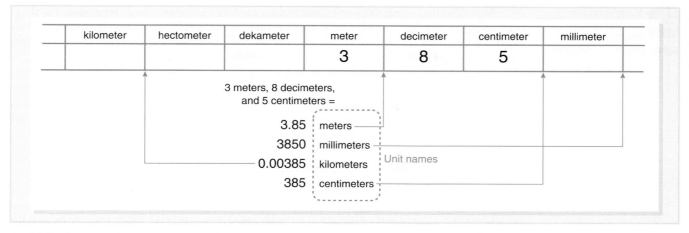

FIGURE 16.4   In the metric system, each place-value position has a name. The decimal point can be placed to designate which length is the unit length. Any of the metric positions can be the unit length.

Precision and Equivalence

The CCSS-Mathematical Practice 6 states, "[Mathematically proficient students] express numerical answers with a degree of precision appropriate for the problem context" (2010, p. 7). Consider the two measurements 0.06 and 0.060. They are equivalent in terms of numerical value, but the latter communicates a greater level of precision. By adding the additional zero, it signals that the measurement was completed to the nearest thousandth and that there were 60 thousandths. In the first case, the measurement was completed only to the nearest hundredth, so it might have been 0.058 or 0.063, not precisely 0.060. For example, baseball players' batting averages are measured in thousandths: Willie has a batting average of .345 for the season. Also, if engineers are building a bridge although 0.04500 may be equivalent to 0.045, the precision communicated by the two expressions is different and important.

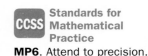

Standards for Mathematical Practice
MP6. Attend to precision.

MyLab Education   **Self-Check 16.1**

Connecting Fractions and Decimals

The symbols 3.75 and $3\frac{3}{4}$ represent the same quantity, yet for students, the world of fractions and the world of decimals are very distinct. Even adults tend to think of fractions as sets or areas (e.g., three-fourths of something), but decimals as values or numbers (e.g., weight). When we tell students that 0.75 is the same as $\frac{3}{4}$, this equivalence can be initially confusing because when decimals are written the denominators are hidden. A significant goal of instruction in decimal and fraction numeration should be to help students see that both systems represent the same concepts. Here we share ways to ensure that connections between fractions and decimals are understood. Students will later find that not all fractions can be explicitly represented as a terminating decimal.

Say Decimal Fractions Correctly

Make sure you are reading and saying decimals in ways that support students' understanding and links to fraction numeration. Always say "five and two-tenths" instead of "five point two." Using the point terminology results in a disconnect to the fractional part that exists in every decimal. This practice of attending to precision in language provides your students with opportunities to hear connections between decimals and fractions, so that when they hear "two-tenths," they think of both 0.2 and $\frac{2}{10}$. Research shows that labeling decimals by place value is particularly useful with supporting students' understanding of decimal comparisons when the role of a zero had to be considered (Loehr & Rittle-Johnson, 2016).

Standards for Mathematical Practice

MP6. Attend to precision.

Note also that using the word "and," when reading a decimal ("and" represents the decimal point) is appropriate. So, 1.16 is read as "one and sixteen hundredths." In contrast, when saying a number such as 116, you should *not* say "one-hundred and sixteen." As in that case, the "and" is not appropriate.

Highlight the "ths" at the end of decimal units as both you and the students talk about decimal fractions. Exaggerate the "ths" in your pronunciations as initially students are not accustomed to small differences in word such as tens and tenths. Stressing this sound is important for everyone, but especially for ELs and students with disabilities, who may not notice the distinction if it is not clearly emphasized.

Use Visual Models for Decimal Fractions

Many fraction manipulatives do not lend themselves to depicting decimals because they cannot show hundredths or thousandths. Additionally, research suggests that the connection of decimal numbers to pictorial representations can be challenging (Cramer et al., 2009). Provide models for decimal fractions using the same conceptual approaches that were used previously for fractions—that using multiple representations will help address misunderstandings (Cramer, 2003).

Standards for Mathematical Practice

MP5. Use appropriate tools strategically.

Area Models. Three area models that can be used to represent decimal fractions are base-ten materials, a rational number wheel and a 10×10 grid. Let's look at each one.

Base-ten materials have been mentioned previously, but explicitly link them to decimal numbers using Building Decimal-Number Cards. Place the correct card under each amount of base-ten materials, for example, tenths, hundredths, and so on, so that students can see how the decimal number is built through their place value parts (left justify the cards).

> **MyLab Education** **Activity Page: Building Decimal-Number Cards**

 TECHNOLOGY Note. A digital version of "Base Blocks—Decimals" is at the National Library of Virtual Manipulatives (http://nlvm.usu.edu/en/nav/vlibrary.html). These blocks can be placed on a place-value chart to represent decimals so students can designate any of the four blocks as the unit. Later, when students work on addition and subtraction with decimals, problems can be created or generated randomly. ∎

Students benefit from activities where the unit changes such as Activity 16.2.

Activity 16.2

CCSS-M: 4.NF.C.6; 5.NBT.A.1; 5.NBT.A.2; 5.NBT.A.3a

Shifting Units

Give students a collection of Base-Ten Materials, or base-ten blocks. Ask them to select a particular mix—for example, three squares, seven strips, and four tinies. Tell students that you have a unit hidden behind your back; when you show it to them, they are to figure out how much they have and record the value. Hold up one of the units, like the strip. Observe what students record as their value. Ask students to say their quantity aloud. For ELs and students with disabilities, write labels with the visuals as a reference. Repeat with different collections and units. Include examples in which a piece is not represented so that students will better understand decimal values like 3.07. Continue playing in partners with one student selecting the mix of base-ten pieces and the other student deciding on the unit and both writing and saying the number.

ENGLISH LEARNERS

STUDENTS with SPECIAL NEEDS

> **MyLab Education** **Blackline Master: Base-Ten Materials**

A Rational Number Wheel (see Figure 16.5), is marked with 100 equal intervals on the circumference and is cut along one radius. Two disks of different colors, slipped together as shown, can model any fraction less than one. Fractions modeled on this rational number wheel can be read as decimal fractions by noting the units marked around the circumference but can also be stated as fractions (e.g., $\frac{3}{4}$), helping students further make the connection between fractions and decimals.

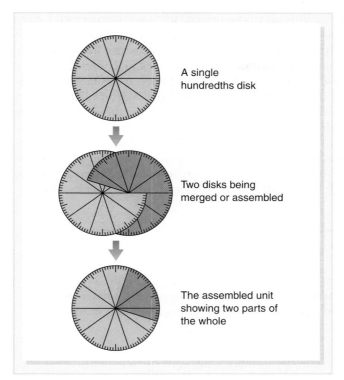

FIGURE 16.5 Rational number wheel. For example, rotate the disks to show $\frac{25}{100}$ of the blue plate (also $\frac{1}{4}$ or 25% of the circle).

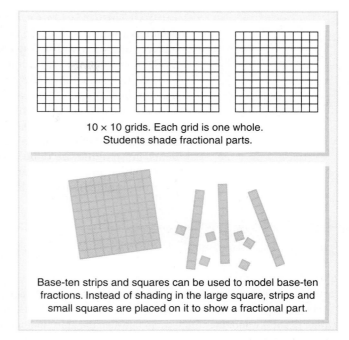

FIGURE 16.6 10 × 10 grids model decimals.

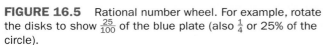

> **MyLab Education** **Blackline Master: Rational Number Wheel**

The most common area model and the one that research shows provides strong visual images for decimal fractions is a 10 × 10 Grid (see Figure 16.6) (Cramer et al., 2015; Wyberg, Whitney, Cramer, Monson, & Leavitt, 2011). Paper base-ten materials of the 10-cm square that was used as the "hundreds" now represents the whole, or 1. Each strip is then 1 tenth, and each small square ("tiny") is 1 hundredth. The 10,000 Grid Paper provides a large square that is subdivided into 10,000 tiny squares. Students can identify how many squares are needed for 0.1, 0.01, 0.001, and 0.0001, using appropriate names for the values.

> **MyLab Education** **Blackline Master: 10 × 10 Grids**
>
> **MyLab Education** **Blackline Master: 10,000 Grid Paper**

Activity 16.3   CCSS-M: 4.NF.C.5; 4.NF.C.6; 5.NBT.A.1; 5.NBT.A.3a

Decimal Roll and Cover

Give pairs of students a 10 × 10 Grid and a die with faces marked with $\frac{1}{10}$, $\frac{1}{100}$, $\frac{5}{100}$, $\frac{1}{1000}$, $\frac{5}{1000}$, $\frac{10}{1000}$ or 0.1, 0.01, 0.05, 0.001, 0.005, and 0.010 (or a combination of fractions and decimals). One student rolls the die and uses a marker to shade the amount rolled on the 10 × 10 grid. For example, if one tenth is rolled, the student shades a whole column of ten small squares on the grid. Each hundredth rolled results in one small square getting shaded and each thousandth rolled requires that a small square be first divided into half and then five more divisions made in the other direction to create ten small equal-sized pieces. Students will eventually note that the $\frac{10}{1000}$ is equivalent to $\frac{1}{100}$. If your students are only working on tenths and hundredths, adjust the die faces to reflect appropriate amounts. The team should try to cover the whole or 1. This activity will give them a very dramatic experience with the differences in size of each of these decimal fractions.

> **MyLab Education** **Blackline Master: 10 × 10 Grids**

Length Models. One of the best length models for decimal fractions is a meter stick. Each decimeter is one-tenth of the meter's length, each centimeter is one-hundredth, and each millimeter is one-thousandth. Any number-line model broken into 100 subparts is likewise a useful model for hundredths including a large number line stretched across a wall or on the floor.

Empty number lines like those used in whole-number computation are also useful in helping students compare decimals and think about scale and place value (Martinie, 2014). Given two or more decimals, students can use an empty number line to position the values, revealing what they know about the magnitude of these decimals using zero, one-half, one, other whole numbers, or other decimal values as benchmarks. The number line can effectively uncover students' grasp of the size of decimal values—which summarizes an important unifying principle across whole and rational numbers—that they can be put into order from least to greatest by their magnitude (Durkin & Rittle-Johnson, 2015; Siegler, Thompson, & Schneider, 2011).

Activity 16.4

CCSS-M: 4.NF.C.6; 4.NF.C.7; 5.NBT.A.3b

The Amazing Race

Use the Amazing Race Activity Page or give students cash register tape. The friends below are running and the decimals next to their names represent how far they are from the start line. Who do you think is winning? Can you place these friends on a line to show where they are located between the start and finish?

Aimee—0.34	Hissa—0.124	Leo—0.56
Layla—0.85	Marco—0.45	Gerard—0.732

Differentiate this activity by changing the values of the decimals or including more friends.

MyLab Education **Activity Page: Amazing Race**

Set Models. Many teachers use money as a model for decimals, and to some extent this approach is helpful. However, money is almost exclusively a two-place system and is nonproportional (e.g., one-tenth, a dime, does not physically compare to a dollar in that proportion.). Numbers like 3.2 or 12.1389 do not relate to money and can cause students confusion (Martinie, 2007). Students' initial contact with decimals should be more flexible, and so money is not recommended as an initial model, although it is certainly an important *application* of decimal numeration.

Multiple Names and Formats

Acquaint students with the various visual models to help them flexibly think of quantities in terms of tenths and hundredths, and to learn to read and write decimal fractions in different ways. Have students model a decimal fraction, say $\frac{65}{100}$, and then explore the following ideas:

- Is this fraction more or less than $\frac{1}{2}$? Than $\frac{2}{3}$? Than $\frac{3}{4}$?
- What are some different ways to say this fraction using tenths and hundredths? ("6 tenths and 5 hundredths," "65 hundredths") Include thousandths when appropriate.
- Show different ways to write this fraction ($\frac{65}{100}$ or $\frac{6}{10} + \frac{5}{100}$ or $\frac{60}{100} + \frac{5}{100}$).

Notice that decimals are usually read as a single value. That is, 0.65 is read "sixty-five hundredths." But to understand the decimal in terms of place value, the same number must be thought of as 6 tenths and 5 hundredths. A mixed number such as $5\frac{13}{100}$ is usually read the same way as a decimal: 5.13 is "five and thirteen-hundredths." For purposes of considering place value parts, it should also be understood as $5 + \frac{1}{10} + \frac{3}{100}$.

FORMATIVE ASSESSMENT Notes. Ask students to write the number that has 3 tenths, 6 hundredths, 7 ones. This task will assess students' grasp of decimal place value parts or whether they become confused and assume the common left-to-right order in which numbers are written incorrectly writing 36.7 or 0.367 instead of 7.36.

Making these expanded forms with base-ten materials will be helpful in translating fractions to decimals, which is the focus of Activity 16.5. ■

Activity 16.5

CCSS-M: 4.NF.C.6; 5.NBT.A.1

Build It, Name It

For this activity, have students use paper Base-Ten Materials. Agree that the large square represents one. Have students cover a decimal fractional amount of the square using their strips and tinies (call these pieces "tenths" and "hundredths"). For example, have them cover $2\frac{35}{100}$ of the square. Whole numbers will require additional squares. The task is to decide how to write and say this fraction as a decimal and demonstrate connections using their physical models. For students with disabilities, you may want to have amounts shaded rather than have the students try to cover exact amounts; then ask them to name and write the decimal fraction.

STUDENTS with SPECIAL NEEDS

MyLab Education   **Blackline Master: Base-Ten Materials**

In Activity 16.5, a reason why $2\frac{35}{100}$ is the same as 2.35 is because there are 2 wholes, 3 tenths, and 5 hundredths. It is important to see this relationship physically. The same materials that are used to represent $2\frac{35}{100}$ of the square can be rearranged or placed on a place-value chart with a paper decimal point used to designate the units position, as shown in Figure 16.7.

The calculator can play a significant role in developing decimal concepts.

Activity 16.6

CCSS-M: 4.NF.C.6; 5.NBT.A.1

Calculator Decimal Counting

Have students practice making a calculator "count" by pressing ⊞ 1 ⊟ ⊟. and so on. Now have them instead press ⊞ 0.1 ⊟ ⊟ and so on. When the display shows 0.9, stop and discuss what this value means and what the display will be with the next count. Students may reveal a common misconception by predicting 0.10 (thinking that 10 comes after 9). This forecast is even more interesting if, with each press, students have been accumulating base-ten materials as models for tenths. One more press would mean one more tenth, or 10 tenths. Why doesn't the calculator show 0.10? When the tenth press produces a display of 1 (calculators are not usually set to display trailing zeros to the right of the decimal), revolve your discussion around trading 10 tenths for one whole. Continue to count to 4 or 5 by tenths. How many presses to get from one whole number to the next? For students with disabilities and ELs, counting out loud along with the calculator "one tenth, two tenths, . . . " supports the concept (e.g., 10 tenths is equal to 1 whole) while reinforcing appropriate mathematical language. Remind students that a place is "full" when it has 9 of any unit and the addition of another unit will push the number to the position that is one unit to the left (like the mileage in a car). Once students work well with tenths, try counting by 0.01 or by 0.001, which dramatically illustrates how small one-hundredth and one-thousandth really are! It requires 10 counts by 0.001 to get to 0.01 and 1000 counts to reach 1.

ENGLISH LEARNERS

STUDENTS with SPECIAL NEEDS

Calculators that permit entry of fractions also have a fraction-decimal conversion key, making them valuable tools for connecting fraction and decimal symbolism. Some calculators will convert a decimal such as 0.25 to the fraction $\frac{25}{100}$ and allow for either manual or automatic simplification. Challenge students to explain why 0.25 and $\frac{25}{100}$ are equivalent rather than relying on calculators to do the conversion.

MyLab Education   **Self-Check 16.2**

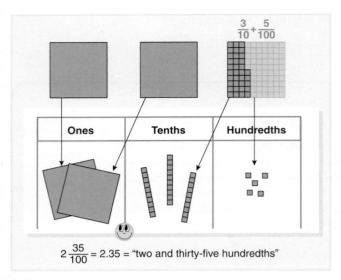

$\frac{3}{10} + \frac{5}{100}$

Ones	Tenths	Hundredths

$2\frac{35}{100} = 2.35 =$ "two and thirty-five hundredths"

FIGURE 16.7 Translation of a fraction to a decimal using physical models.

Developing Decimal Number Sense

So far, the discussion has largely focused on connecting decimals to fractions with denominators of 10 and 100. Number sense with decimals implies more—having intuition about, or a flexible understanding of, decimal numbers. To this end, it is useful to connect decimals to fractions with which students are familiar, to be able to compare and order decimals, and to approximate decimals using useful benchmarks.

Results of NAEP exams reveal that students have difficulties with the fraction-decimal relationship. In 2004, fewer than 30 percent of high school students were able to successfully translate 0.029 to $\frac{29}{1000}$ (Kloosterman, 2010). In 2009, Shaughnessy found that more than 46 percent of sixth graders she studied could not write $\frac{3}{5}$ as a decimal. Instead many wrote $\frac{3}{5}$ as 3.5, 0.35, or 0.3. She also found that more than 25 percent could not write $\frac{3}{10}$ as a decimal. This misconception was also reversed when students wrote the decimal 4.5 as $\frac{4}{5}$. Division of the numerator by the denominator may be a means of converting fractions to decimals, but it contributes little to understanding the resulting equivalence.

MyLab Education **Video Example 16.1**

Watch this video of former NCTM president Skip Fennell as he highlights the relationship between fractions and decimals.

VIDEO EXAMPLE

Familiar Fractions Connected to Decimals

Students should extend their conceptual familiarity with common fractions such as halves, thirds, fourths, and eighths to the same concepts expressed as decimal fractions. One way to gain this knowledge is to have them translate familiar fractions to decimals in a conceptual manner, which is the focus of the next two activities.

Activity 16.7

CCSS-M: 4.NF.C.7

Familiar Fractions to Decimals

Students are given a familiar or commonly used fraction (e.g., $\frac{3}{5}$) to convert to a decimal. Ask students to shade 10 × 10 Grids to illustrate that value (or build it with Base-Ten Materials). Referring to their shaded grid or base-ten pieces, ask students to write the decimal equivalent. A logical sequence is to start with halves and fifths, then fourths, and possibly eighths. Thirds work well as a challenge, as they will result in a repeating decimal. For ELs, make sure you connect the word decimal to the fact that *deci-* means tens. For students with disabilities, have some 10 × 10 grids preshaded with different fractions and ask students to find the grid that shows $\frac{1}{2}$. Have students skip count the squares that are shaded to identify the equivalent of $\frac{50}{100}$. Explore an Expanded Lesson: Familiar Fractions to Decimals for this activity.

ENGLISH LEARNERS

STUDENTS with SPECIAL NEEDS

MyLab Education Blackline Master: 10 × 10 Grids
MyLab Education Blackline Master: Base-Ten Materials
MyLab Education Expanded Lesson: Familiar Fractions to Decimals

Figure 16.8 shows how translations in the last activity might work with a 10 × 10 grid. For fourths, students often shade a 5 × 5 section (half of a half). The question then becomes how to translate this fraction to a decimal. Ask these students how they could think about each half strip as 0.05 and then use models to reason that 2 of the half strips (0.05 + 0.05) equal 0.1. Then you would have 0.1 + 0.1 + 0.05, or 0.25, and if they counted shaded squares they would find $\frac{25}{100}$. This approach starts where students' prior knowledge is and works from there toward a solution. The fraction $\frac{3}{8}$ represents a wonderful challenge. A hint might be to find $\frac{1}{4}$ first and then notice that $\frac{1}{8}$ is half of a fourth. Remember that the next smaller pieces are tenths of the "tinies" (or thousands). Therefore, a half of a "tiny" is $\frac{5}{1000}$. Note how the student found that $\frac{2}{8} + \frac{1}{8} = \frac{37}{100} + \frac{5}{1000} = 0.375$.

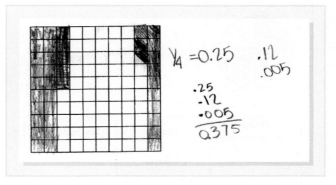

FIGURE 16.8   A student uses a 10 × 10 grid to convert $\frac{3}{8}$ to a decimal.

Because the circular model carries such a strong mental link to fractions, it is worth the time to do some fraction-to-decimal conversions using the rational number wheel shown in Figure 16.5 and used in the next activity.

Activity 16.8   CCSS-M: 4.NF.C.7

Estimate, Then Verify

With the blank side of the Rational Number Wheel facing them, direct students to adjust the wheel to show a given fraction, for example $\frac{3}{4}$ (see Figure 16.9). Next, ask students to estimate how many hundredths they think are equivalent. Then, students justify how they decided their estimate and the corresponding decimal equivalent. Repeat with other fractions. For students with disabilities, cut up some rational number wheels into tenths and even hundredths so that these parts can be used as a comparison tool (see Figure 16.9).

STUDENTS
with
SPECIAL
NEEDS

MyLab Education   Blackline Master: Rational Number Wheel

The number line is a useful model to connect decimals and fractions. The following activity continues the development of fraction-decimal equivalences.

Activity 16.9   CCSS-M: 4.NF.C.6

Decimals and Fractions on a Double Number Line

Use the Number Lines Activity Page and give students five decimal numbers that have familiar fraction equivalents. At first, keep numbers between two consecutive whole numbers such as 3.5, 3.125, 3.4, 3.75, and 3.66. Have students mark the first two number lines on the Activity Page identically with endpoints, as in this example, starting at 3.0 and ending at 4.0. Then keep the two lines either an empty number line or with subdivisions of only fourths, thirds, or tenths (no labels). The students' task is to locate each of the five given decimal numbers on the first number line and to provide the fraction equivalent for each on the parallel number line below it. Use the other number lines on the Activity Page to try another set of endpoints and five decimal amounts.

MyLab Education   Activity Page: Number Lines

The exploration of modeling $\frac{1}{3}$ as a decimal is a good introduction to the concept of an infinitely repeating decimal, which is a standard for seventh grade (NGA Center & CCSSO, 2010). Try to partition the whole 10 × 10 Grid into 3 parts using strips and tinies. Each part receives 3 strips with 1 strip left over. To divide the leftover strip, each part gets 3 tinies

CCSS Standards for
Mathematical
Practice
MP8. Look for and
express regularity in
repeated reasoning.

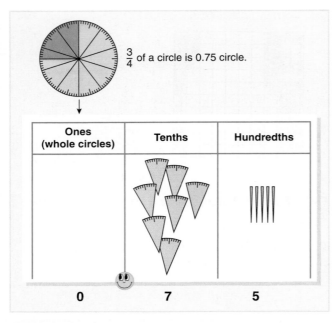

FIGURE 16.9 Fraction models could be decimal models.

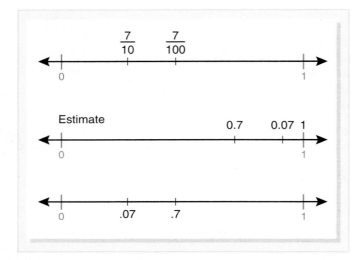

FIGURE 16.10 Three different students' attempts to draw a number line and show the numbers 0.7 and 0.07.

with 1 left over. To divide the tiny, each part gets 3 tiny strips with 1 left over. (Recall that with base-ten pieces, each smaller piece must be $\frac{1}{10}$ of the preceding piece.) It becomes apparent that this process is never-ending. As a result, $\frac{1}{3}$ is the same as 0.333333 . . . or 0.3. For practical purposes, $\frac{1}{3}$ is about 0.333. Similarly, $\frac{2}{3}$ is a repeating string of sixes, or about 0.667. Students will eventually discover that many fractions cannot be represented by a finite decimal.

MyLab Education   **Blackline Master: 10 × 10 Grids**

FORMATIVE ASSESSMENT Notes. A simple yet powerful assessment to evaluate decimal understanding has students represent two related decimal numbers, such as 0.5 and 0.05, using multiple representations: an empty number line, a 10 × 10 Grid, and Base-Ten Materials (Martinie, 2014). Ask students to describe their representations. If students have significantly more difficulty with one model over another, this challenge may mean that they have not developed full conceptual understanding of decimal fractions. Placement of decimals on an empty number line is perhaps the most interesting task—and provides the most revealing information (see Figure 16.10). ■

MyLab Education   **Blackline Master: 10 × 10 Grids**

MyLab Education   **Blackline Master: Base-Ten Materials**

Approximation with a Compatible Fraction. In the real world, decimal fractions are rarely those with exact equivalents to common fractions. What fraction would you say is close to the decimal 0.52? In the sixth NAEP exam, only 51 percent of eighth graders selected $\frac{1}{2}$. The other choices were $\frac{1}{50}$ (29 percent), $\frac{1}{5}$ (11 percent), $\frac{1}{4}$ (6 percent), and $\frac{1}{3}$ (4 percent) (Kouba, Zawojewski, & Strutchens, 1997). Again, students need to wrestle with the magnitude of decimal fractions and begin to develop a sense of familiarity with them.

As with fractions, the first decimal benchmarks to develop are 0, $\frac{1}{2}$, and 1. For example, is 7.396 closer to 7, $7\frac{1}{2}$, or 8? Why? How would you respond to these answers from students: "Closer to 7 because 3 is less than 5"? or "It is closer to $7\frac{1}{2}$ than 7?" Often the 0, $\frac{1}{2}$, or 1 benchmarks can help students make sense of a situation. If more precision is required, encourage students to consider other common fractions (thirds, fourths, fifths, and eighths). In this example, 7.396 is close to 7.4, which is $7\frac{2}{5}$. A good number sense with decimals entails the ability to think of a fraction that is a close equivalent, a skill needed in the next activity.

Activity 16.10   CCSS-M: 4.NF.C.6

Best Match

Give students a deck of Fraction-Decimal Cards with familiar fractions on half of the cards and decimals that are close to the fractions (but not exact) on the other half. In this memory-like game students pair each fraction with the decimal that best matches it. The difficulty is determined by how close various fractions are to one another. Some students might select one pairing and then realize there is a better match. For students with disabilities you may need to have them reflect each time on whether what they've turned over is close to 0, close to $\frac{1}{2}$, or close to 1 to help support their matchmaking. Have students share their thinking as their rationales provide strategies that the others will find useful. As a follow-up have students try the Close to a Familiar Fraction Activity Page to find out more about the reasoning strategies they are using.

**STUDENTS
with
SPECIAL
NEEDS**

MyLab Education   **Activity Page: Fraction-Decimal Cards**
MyLab Education   **Activity Page: Close to a Familiar Fraction**

FORMATIVE ASSESSMENT Notes. You can find out if your students have a flexible understanding of the connections between models and the two symbol systems for rational numbers—fractions and decimals—with a diagnostic interview. Provide students with a number represented as a fraction, a decimal, or a physical model, and then have them provide the other two representations along with an explanation. Here are a few examples:

- Write the fraction $\frac{5}{8}$ as a decimal. Use a drawing or a physical model (meter stick or 10×10 Grid) and explain why your decimal equivalent is correct.
- What fraction is represented by the decimal 2.6? Use a physical model and words to explain your answer.
- Use both a fraction and a decimal to tell what this point (marked with an arrow) on the number line represents. Explain your reasoning.

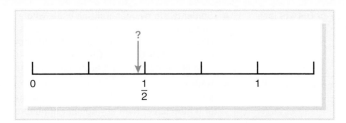

In the last example, it is especially interesting to see which representation students select first—fraction or decimal. Furthermore, do they then translate this number to the other representation or make a second independent estimate? ■

MyLab Education   **Blackline Master: 10 × 10 Grid**

Other Fraction-Decimal Equivalents. Recall that the denominator is a divisor and the numerator is a multiplier. For example, $\frac{3}{4}$ means the same as $3 \times (1 \div 4)$ or $3 \div 4$. So how would you express $\frac{3}{4}$ on a simple four-function calculator? Simply enter $3 \div 4$. The display will read 0.75.

Too often, students think that dividing the denominator into the numerator is simply an algorithm for converting fractions to decimals, and they have no understanding of why this procedure might work. Use the opportunity to help students develop the idea that in general $\frac{a}{b} = a \div b$, where b is not 0.

The calculator is an important tool when developing familiarity with decimal concepts. Finding decimal equivalents with a calculator can produce interesting patterns. Here are some questions to explore:

- Which fractions have decimal equivalents that terminate? Can you discover a pattern? Is the answer based on the numerator, the denominator, or both?
- For a given fraction, how can you tell the maximum length of the repeating part of the decimal? Try dividing by denominators of 7 and 11 and 13 and then make a conjecture.
- Explore all of the ninths: $\frac{1}{9}, \frac{2}{9}, \frac{3}{9}, \ldots \frac{8}{9}$. Remember that $\frac{1}{3}$ is $\frac{3}{9}$ and $\frac{2}{3}$ is $\frac{6}{9}$. Use only the pattern you discover to predict what $\frac{9}{9}$ should be. But doesn't $\frac{9}{9} = 1$?
- How can you find what fraction produces this repeating decimal: 3.454545 . . . ?

The last question can be generalized for any repeating decimal, illustrating that every repeating decimal is a rational number.

Comparing and Ordering Decimal Fractions

Comparing decimal fractions and putting them in order from least to greatest is a skill closely related to comparing fractions and decimals. But comparing decimal fractions (particularly "ragged" decimals with unequal length) has important distinctions from comparing whole numbers. These differences can be initially confusing and cause student errors.

FORMATIVE ASSESSMENT Notes. Consider the following list: 0.36, 0.058, 0.375, 0.97, 0, 2.0, and 0.4. Ask students to order these decimals from least to greatest. Use Table 16.1 to identify if students are exhibiting any of the common challenges and misconceptions that students often demonstrate when comparing and ordering decimals (Desmet, Gregoire, & Mussolin, 2010; Muir & Livy, 2012; Steinle & Stacey, 2004a, 2004b). Knowing these confusions in advance will help you pinpoint ways to improve students' conceptual understanding. ■

TABLE 16.1 COMMON CHALLENGES AND MISCONCEPTIONS WITH COMPARING AND ORDERING DECIMALS

Common Challenge or Misconception	What It Looks Like	How to Help
1. Longer is larger	0.375 is greater than 0.97 or 0.44 is less than 0.440.	• Students are overgeneralizing using whole number reasoning and selecting the number with more digits as being larger. Have students use decimal models to show each number and compare. Two 10 × 10 Grids with each number shaded will help students make the accurate comparison.
2. Shorter is larger	0.4 is greater than 0.97 because "a tenth is larger than a hundredth."	• Have students create representations of these two decimals focusing on the quantities. For example, ask "Is any number of tenths larger than any number of hundredths?"
3. Internal zero	0.58 is less than 0.078 thinking that "zero has no impact." Also, suggesting that 34.08 and 34.8 have the same value.	• When students are confused by a zero in the tenths position for example, have them build the number using Decimal Number Cards. Match this numerical value to a physical model if needed or match it to a number line.
4. Less than zero	0.36 is less than 0, because zero is a whole number positioned in the ones column (to the left of the decimal point), and therefore is greater than a decimal fraction (to the right of the decimal point).	• Use contexts, for example, ask students whether they would rather have 0 or 0.50 of a dollar. • Use decimal representations on grid paper to visualize the size of each decimal as compared to zero.
5. Reciprocal thinking	When students compare 0.4 and 0.6, they select 0.4 as larger because they connect 0.4 to $\frac{1}{4}$ and 0.6 to $\frac{1}{6}$ and erroneously decide 0.4 is greater.	• Use decimal materials such as shading 10 × 10 Grids to visualize the size of each decimal.
6. Equality	Students think that 0.4 is not close to 0.375 and/or that 0.3 is smaller than 0.30.	• Show the connections between these values through area models or placing these values on the number line to help students see if the amounts are close in size or as in the case of 0.3 and 0.30 are equal.

MyLab Education **Activity Page: Decimal Number Cards**

MyLab Education **Blackline Master: 10 × 10 Grids**

All of these common challenges reflect a need for students to have a conceptual understanding of how decimal numbers are constructed.

MyLab Education   Video Example 16.2

Watch this video of Vanessa comparing decimals. Which of the common challenges or misconceptions do you think she is exhibiting?

MyLab Education   Video Example 16.3

Watch this video of Madison comparing decimals. Which of the common challenges or misconceptions do you think she is exhibiting?

MyLab Education   Video Example 16.4

Watch this video of how Megan and Donna think about 4.7 and 4.70. What would have happened if the teacher didn't make it "You can't add a zero day"?

MyLab Education   **Application Exercise 16.1: Developing Decimal Number Sense** Click the link to access this exercise, then watch the video and answer the accompanying questions.

Relative Size of Decimals. Because these misconceptions often stem from not understanding the size of values in the tenths, hundredths, and thousandths places and beyond, it is important to have students find values on the number line or use other models to represent the amounts. The following activity promotes discussion about the relative sizes of decimal numbers.

Activity 16.11

CCSS-M: 4.NF.C.6; 4.NF.C.7; 5.NBT.A.1; 5.NBT.A.3a; 5.NBT.A.3b

STUDENTS *with* **SPECIAL NEEDS**

Line 'Em Up

Prepare a list of four or five decimal numbers that students might be challenged to put in order between the same two consecutive whole numbers or use the Line 'Em Up Activity Page that uses a context of the height of plants. First, have students predict the order of the numbers, from least to greatest. Then, require students to use a model of their choice—for example, an empty number line (see Figure 16.11) or 10,000 Grid Paper—to defend their ordering. As students reason about which plant (value) is taller, they will develop a deeper understanding of which digits contribute the most to the size of a decimal. For students who are struggling, some explicit instruction might be helpful. Write one of decimals on the board—3.091, for example. Start with the whole numbers: "Is it closer to 3 or 4?" Then go to the tenths: "Is it closer to 3.0 or 3.1?" Repeat with hundredths and thousandths. At each place value position, challenge students to defend their choices with the use of a model or other conceptual explanation.

> **MyLab Education**   Activity Page: Line 'Em Up
> **MyLab Education**   Blackline Master: 10,000 Grid Paper

Density of Decimals. An important concept is that there is always another number between any two numbers. When students only have examples of decimals rounded to two places, this limited view may reinforce the notion that there are no numbers between 2.37 and 2.38 (Steinle & Stacey, 2004b). Finding a decimal located between any two other decimals requires that students understand the density of decimals. Using a linear model helps to show that there is always another decimal to be found between any two decimals—a concept emphasized in the following activities.

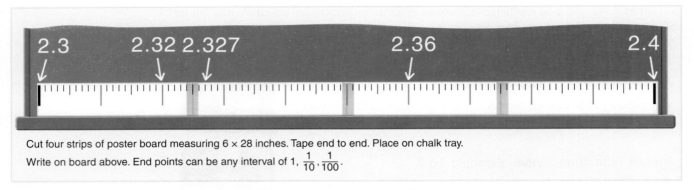

Cut four strips of poster board measuring 6 × 28 inches. Tape end to end. Place on chalk tray.

Write on board above. End points can be any interval of 1, $\frac{1}{10}$, $\frac{1}{100}$.

FIGURE 16.11 Decimals on a number line.

Activity 16.12   CCSS-M: 5.NBT.A.3b

Close Decimals

Have students name a decimal between 0 and 1.0. Next, have them name another decimal that is even closer to 1.0 than the first. Continue for several more decimals in the same manner, each decimal being closer to 1.0 than the previous. Similarly, try other benchmarks such as close to 0 or close to 0.5. Let students with disabilities use models or a number line to help them with their decision making. Later, confirm if they can explain their thinking without representations. Another option is to provide them with two decimals to choose between. Then after time fade the support and transition back to original tasks.

STUDENTS
with
SPECIAL NEEDS

Activity 16.13   CCSS-M: 5.NBT.C3b; 6.NS.C.6

Zoom

Stretch a number line (e.g., clothesline or cash register tape) across the front of the room. Ask students to mark where 0.75 and 1.0 are on the line. Then ask students to "zoom in" to find and record three more values between those two values. Ask students to share their thinking strategies. Make sure ELs are clear of the meaning of the word *between*, even demonstrating this relationship with students in the front of the room. For students with disabilities, you may need to give them a set of choices and ask them to select three decimals that are between 0.75 and 1.0. See the Expanded Lesson: Zoom: Finding Rational Numbers on the Number Line for procedures, assessment ideas, and questions to pose.

ENGLISH LEARNERS

STUDENTS
with
SPECIAL NEEDS

MyLab Education   Expanded Lesson: Zoom: Finding Rational Numbers on the Number Line

Confusion over the density of decimals also plays out when students try to find the nearest decimal (Ubuz & Yayan, 2010). Many times when having students find which decimal is closer to a given decimal, students revert to thinking that tenths are comparable to tenths and that there are no hundredths between. When asked which decimal is closer to 0.19—0.2 or 0.21—they select 0.21 (ignoring that 0.2 is equal to 0.20). They also are unsure if 0.513 is near 0.51. They may also think that 0.3 is near 0.4 but far away from 0.317. These examples provide evidence that students are in need of additional experiences focused on the density of decimals and are probably not yet ready for operations with decimals.

MyLab Education   Self-Check 16.3

MyLab Education   Application Exercise 16.2: Developing Decimal Number Sense Click the link to access this exercise, then read the scenario and answer the accompanying questions.

Computation with Decimals

Students can have a solid knowledge of the magnitude of decimals without fully understanding the results of computational operations with them (Siegler & Lortie-Forgues, 2015). In the past, decimal computation was dominated by the following rules: Line up the decimal points (addition and subtraction), count the decimal places (multiplication), and shift (or use the unfortunate phrase "get rid of") the decimal point in the divisor and dividend so that the divisor is a whole number (division). Some textbooks continue to emphasize these rules, but specific rules are not always necessary if computation is built on a firm understanding of place value and a connection between decimals and fractions. The *Common Core State Standards* expects that students understand and be able to explain why procedures make sense (NGA Center & CCSSO, 2010, p. 33). When students who were having difficulty with decimal computation were only taught strictly procedural approaches, initial levels of understanding declined rapidly. In only ten days, students' average daily performance levels of approximately 80 percent dropped to 34 percent (Woodward, Baxter, & Robinson, 1999).

Addition and Subtraction

There is much more to adding and subtracting decimals than knowing to "line up the decimal points." The *Common Core State Standards* (NGA Center & CCSSO, 2010, p. 33) say that fifth graders should "apply their understandings of models for decimals, decimal notation, and properties of operations to add and subtract decimals to hundredths. They develop fluency in these computations, and make reasonable estimates of their results."

MyLab Education   **Video Example: 16.5**

Watch this video of one of this book's authors, Karen Karp, as she gives an overview of addition and subtraction of decimals.

As always with computation, start with problems in a context and provide meaning and relevance with situations that can be easily visualized (or use models). But, there is an order in which you should consider starting presenting the decimals used in your problems by first, starting with decimals that have an equal number of digits to the right of the decimal (i.e., 2.5 + 1.4 or 0.45 − 0.33) and then moving to "ragged" decimals where the number of digits differ (i.e., 0.836 + 0.7). Subtraction with regrouping such as 0.5 − 0.321 may require more sophisticated thinking and therefore come later. Having learners keep the ideas in their minds that are needed for decimal computation, which differ in some ways from what they've been practicing with whole numbers is a challenge. And as you might expect, students sometimes inappropriately use whole number thinking such as when they add 0.26 + 0.3 and get the answer 0.29. Let's look at ways to strengthen students' strategies and avoid that result.

MyLab Education   **Video Example 16.6**

Watch this video to see Brooke sketch models to solve 4.0 − 0.7.

Estimating Decimal Sums and Differences. Estimation is important, as often an estimate is all that is needed. Students should become adept at estimating decimal computations before they learn to compute with the standard algorithm. This thinking is aligned with the CCSS (2010), where fifth graders focus on decimal computation but not until sixth grade is the standard algorithm for decimal computation required. Until students have a sound understanding of place value, equivalence, and relative size of decimals, they are not ready to develop an understanding of the operations (Cramer & Whitney, 2010). An emphasis on estimation is particularly important for students who have learned the rules for decimal computation yet cannot decide whether their answers are reasonable. An initial minimum goal for a reasonable estimate is that it contains the correct number of digits to the left of the decimal—the whole-number part.

 Pause & Reflect

Before continuing, try making whole-number estimates of the following computations. ●

1. **4.907 + 123.01 + 56.123**
2. **459.8 − 12.345**
3. **0.607 + 0.18**
4. **89.1 − 0.998**

Your estimates might be:

1. Between 175 and 200
2. A little less than 450
3. Close to 0.8
4. About 88

In these examples, an understanding of decimal numeration and basic whole-number estimation skills (e.g., front-end, rounding, and compatible numbers) can produce reasonable estimates. When encouraging students to estimate, focus on the size of the numbers, the meaning of the operations and the use of a variety of strategies. Also notice that when teaching addition and subtraction with decimals present problems to students horizontally, to emphasize the need to align the numbers according to place value.

MyLab Education   **Video Example 16.7**

Watch this Teaching Channel video (https://www.teachingchannel.org) of a fourth-grade class playing a decimal game, called Fill Two, that capitalizes on students use of an area model (10 × 10 grid) to represent and add decimal fractions. By understanding the size of the decimals, students are better able to estimate how much more they need to fill two wholes.

VIDEO EXAMPLE

Developing Addition and Subtraction Algorithms. Invented strategies receive significant attention when developing whole-number computation skills, but sometimes there is unfortunately less focus on them with fraction and decimal computation. Invented strategies are grounded in place value, are efficient, and are often more conceptual for students than standard algorithms and therefore should still be used. Research shows that intermingling lessons on decimal place value and decimal addition and subtraction results in stronger student performance (Rittle-Johnson & Koedinger, 2009). So, even after the standard algorithm is learned and understood, students should be encouraged to have a collection of strategies so they can pick the best method given the situation. This decision making is what mathematically proficient students do.

Consider this problem:

Jessica and Sumiko each timed their own quarter-mile run with a stopwatch. Jessica says she ran the quarter mile in 74.5 seconds. Sumiko was more precise in her timing, reporting she ran the quarter mile in 81.34 seconds. Who ran it the fastest and how much faster was she?

Students who understand decimal numeration should be able to tell the approximate difference—close to 7 seconds. Then they should be challenged to figure out the exact answer using a variety of strategies. The estimate will help them avoid the common error of lining up the 5 under the 4. Instead, students might note that 74.5 and 7 equals 81.5, then figure out how much extra that is (0.16) and subtract the extra to get the difference of 6.34. Other students may count on from 74.5 by adding 0.5, which equals 75, and then add 6 more seconds to reach 81, and finally add on the remaining 0.34 seconds. This strategy can be effectively represented on an empty number line, which aligns with the problem's context. Another strategy is for students to change 74.5 to 74.50 and subtract using their prior knowledge regarding whole number regrouping. Similar story problems for addition and subtraction, some involving different numbers of decimal places, will help develop students' understanding.

Standards for Mathematical Practice

MP2. Make sense of problems and persevere in solving them.

After students have had several opportunities to solve addition and subtraction story problems, it is important to see if they can flexibly think about a problem through multiple representations, as in the next activity.

Activity 16.14   CCSS-M: 5.NBT.B.7

Representing Sums and Differences

Give students a copy of the Translation Task Activity Page with a problem such as 73.46 + 6.2 + 0.582 = in the upper left-hand quadrant. Students should first estimate and then calculate the answer. The second task is to write a word problem that matches the equation. In the third quadrant, they can illustrate the operation using, for example, an empty number line or base-ten pieces. Finally, students explain their thinking by describing how they estimated and what strategies they used to add. The same approach can be used with subtraction.

MyLab Education   **Activity Page: Translation Task**

FORMATIVE ASSESSMENT Notes. As students complete Activity 16.14, use an Observation Checklist to record whether they are showing evidence of having an understanding of decimal concepts and the role of the decimal point in computation. Note whether students get a correct sum by using an algorithm they learned, but are challenged to give an explanation of their thinking, or if they are unable to describe a situation in a word problem that matches the computation or create a corresponding model and illustration. If there are difficulties in several areas of the task, shift attention back to foundational decimal concepts until those are understood. ■

MyLab Education   **Blackline Master: Observation Checklist**

As students become more proficient in adding and subtracting with the standard algorithm, continue to provide opportunities for them to estimate, illustrate by using models discussed here, use invented strategies, and explain a context to fit the situation. For example, the NLVM (http://nlvm .usu.edu/en/nav/vlibrary.html) game "Circle 3" is a challenging reasoning experience where students use logic to combine decimals to add to 3 (it is not as easy as it sounds!). Continued experiences such as this will ensure that students develop procedural proficiency for decimal addition and subtraction.

Multiplication

Multiplication of decimals tends to be poorly understood for many reasons. For example, students are initially confused when a multiplication problem with two decimal factors of 2 digits to the right of the decimal point can result in an answer with four digits to the right of the decimal point (Lortie-Forgues, Tian, & Siegler, 2015). This answer is also misaligned with students' overgeneralized whole number thinking of "multiplication makes bigger" as the answer is smaller than either factor. In the past, students were blindly told to count how many decimal places they have in the problem to decide where the decimal point would be placed in the answer. Often little attempt was made to assess if the answer was reasonable. But being mathematically proficient means having a much deeper understanding of multiplication of decimals. Students need to be able to use concrete models or drawings, invented strategies based on place value and properties of operations, and explain the reasoning used (NGA Center & CCSSO, 2010). Estimation is essential in building that understanding.

MyLab Education **Video Example 16.8**

Watch this video of author, Karen Karp, as she provides an overview of the process of supporting students' understanding of multiplication of decimals using estimation and place value knowledge.

Estimating Products. It might be argued that much of the estimation in the real world involves fractions, decimals, and percents. A key consideration in estimating is using whole numbers to estimate rational numbers.

MyLab Education **Video Example 16.9**

Watch this video of author, Jennifer Bay-Williams, to see the role of estimation in computation with decimals.

Decide what numbers you would use in each case as you estimate the problems listed below. Which ones were easy to estimate? Difficult?

1. 5.91×6.1
2. 145.33×0.109
3. 0.54×9.871

A student's reasoning might be similar to the following:

1. This problem is about 6 times 6, so the answer is about 36.
2. This is like 145 dimes, so divide by 10 and it is about 14.50. *Or,* this is about one tenth of 145, so 14.5.
3. The first value is about one-half, so half of about 10 is about 5.

When problems involve two very small decimals, estimation is difficult, but it is still possible to look at the answer to see if it is relatively smaller than the initial factor (taking a small part of a small part results in an even smaller part).

Activity 16.15 CCSS-M: 5.NBT.B.7; 6.NS.B.3

Hit the Target: Continuous Input

Select a target range. Next, enter the starting number in the calculator and hand it to the first player. For multiplication or division, only one operation is used through the whole game. After the first or second turn, decimal factors are usually required. This variation provides excellent understanding of multiplication or division by decimals. A sequence for a target of 262 to 265 might be like this:

Start with 63.

Player 1   ☒ 5 ☐ 315 (too high)

Player 2   ☒ 0.7 ☐ 220.5 (too low)

Player 1   ☒ 1.3 ☐ 286.65 (too high)

Player 2   ☒ 0.9 ☐ 257.985 (too low)

Player 1   ☒ 1.03 ☐ 265.72455 (very close!)

(What would you press next?)

This game can be played using division. Adapt the game for addition and subtraction; the first player then presses either ☐+ or ☐− followed by a number and then ☐=.

Developing the Algorithm. Explore multiplication of decimals by using problems in a context and by returning to physical models that were useful in thinking about whole-number multiplication. Estimation should play a significant role in developing a multiplication algorithm. As a beginning, consider this problem:

The farmer fills each jug with 3.7 liters of cider. If you buy 4 jugs, how many liters of cider is that?

Ask students, "Is the answer more than 12 liters? What is the most it could be?" Once an estimate of the result is decided, students use their own methods for determining a precise answer (based on place value and properties). One strategy might be to double 3.7 (which equals 7.4), double it again, and total. Another is to multiply 3×4, then add on 0.7 four times. Eventually, students will agree on 14.8 liters. Connect these strategies to the number line, showing how jumps on the decimal number line match the invented strategies.

The area model is particularly useful in illustrating decimal multiplication (Rathouz, 2011). Use a scenario such as this one that aligns with the rectangular array:

A gardener has 1.5 m² of her garden where she can plant flowers. She decides to plant bluebells on an area that is 0.6 of the garden. On how many total square meters can she plant bluebells?

See a student's solution (Figure 16.12) using a grid diagram to model the problem 0.6×1.5. Each large square represents 1 m² with each row of 10 small squares as 0.1 m² and each small square as 0.01 m² The shaded section shows 0.6 m² + 0.3 m² = 0.9 m². Notice that this model is proportional, allowing students to visualize the factors' values.

Also use problems that can be illustrated with an empty number line such as:

A frog hops 4.2 inches at every hop. How far away is she from her starting point after 5 hops?

Figure 16.13 provides illustrations of a line to illustrate the frog hops. This illustration of decimal multiplication should remind students of strategies they used to learn whole number multiplication; this connection can be used in developing meaning for the standard algorithm for decimal multiplication.

Ask students to compare a decimal product with one involving the same digits but no decimal. For example, how are 23.4×6.5 and 234×65 alike? Interestingly, both products have exactly the same digits: 15210. (The zero may be missing from the decimal product.) Have students use a calculator to explore other products that are alike except for the location of the decimals points involved. Let them notice the pattern that the digits in the answer are always alike. After students confirm this regularity, do the following activity.

CCSS Standards for Mathematical Practice
MP8. Look for and express regularity in repeated reasoning.

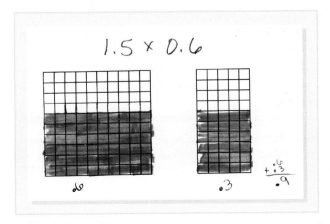

FIGURE 16.12 A student's use of 10 × 10 grids to reason about 1.5 × 0.6.

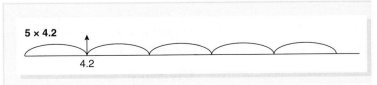

FIGURE 16.13 A number line is used to illustrate multiplication of decimals.

Activity 16.16

CCSS-M: 5.NBT.B.7; 6.NS.B.3

Where Does the Decimal Go? Multiplication

ENGLISH LEARNERS

Have students compute the following product: 24 × 63. Using only the result of this computation (1512) and estimation, have them give the exact answer to each of the following:

0.24 × 6.3   24 × 0.63   2.4 × 63   0.24 × 0.63

For each computation, they should write a rationale for how they placed the decimal point. For example, on the first one a student might explain that 0.24 is close to one-fourth and one-fourth of 6 is less than two, so the answer must be 1.512. They can check their results with a calculator. ELs may apply a different mental strategy that is common in their country of origin. Even if they have trouble articulating their reasoning, it is important to consider alternative ways to reason through the problem.

⏸ Pause & Reflect

What is the value in having students explain how they placed the decimal point rather than just having students count over the number of places? ●

Another way to support full understanding of the algorithm is to rewrite the decimals in their fraction equivalents. So, if you are multiplying 3.4 × 1.7, that is the same as $\frac{34}{10} \times \frac{17}{10}$. When multiplied, you would get $\frac{578}{100}$, which rewritten as a decimal fraction is 5.78, which corresponds to moving the decimal two places to the left (Rathouz, 2011).

The method of placing the decimal point in a product by way of estimation is more difficult as the product gets smaller. For example, knowing that 37 × 83 is 3071 does not make it easy to place the decimal in the product 0.037 × 0.83. But the standard algorithm can be developed from this problem, all the while helping students understand the properties of multiplication. Here is the process:

$$0.037 \times 0.83 = (37 \times \tfrac{1}{1000}) \times (83 \times \tfrac{1}{100})$$
$$(37 \times \tfrac{1}{1000}) \times (83 \times \tfrac{1}{100}) = 37 \times 83 \times \tfrac{1}{1000} \times \tfrac{1}{100}$$
$$37 \times 83 \times \tfrac{1}{1000} \times \tfrac{1}{100} = (37 \times 83) \times (\tfrac{1}{1000} \times \tfrac{1}{100})$$
$$(37 \times 83) \times (\tfrac{1}{1000} \times \tfrac{1}{100}) = 3071 \times \tfrac{1}{100,000} = 0.03071$$

These calculations may look complicated, but if you follow what is happening with the decimal fractions, you can grasp why you count the number of values to the right of each factor, and then place the decimal in the product so that it has the same number of decimal places. The standard algorithm for decimal multiplication is: Do the computation as if all numbers were whole numbers. When finished, place the decimal by reasoning or estimation if possible. If not possible to estimate, count the decimal places, as illustrated. Even if students have already learned the standard algorithm, they need to know the conceptual rationale centered on place value and the powers of ten for "counting" and shifting the decimal places. By focusing on rote applications of rules, students miss opportunities to understand the meaning and effects of operations and are more prone to misapply procedures (Martinie & Bay-Williams, 2003).

Questions such as the following keep the focus on number sense and provide useful information about your students' understanding.

Standards for Mathematical Practice

MP2. Reason abstractly and quantitatively.

1. Consider these two computations: $3\frac{1}{2} \times 2\frac{1}{4}$ and 2.27 × 3.18. Without doing the calculations, which product do you think is larger? Provide a reason for your answer that can be understood by someone else in this class.
2. How much larger is 0.26 × 8 than 0.25 × 8? How can you tell without doing the computation?

Student discussions and explanations as they work on these or similar questions can provide insights into their decimal and fraction number sense and the connections between the two representations.

Division

Like multiplication of decimals, division of decimals is often carried out rotely, and not well understood. Returning to whole-number understanding of the meaning of the operation of division can help students make sense of decimal division.

Estimating Quotients. Estimation and the use of concrete materials are both needed to build a strong understanding of division of decimals. In fact, the best approach to a division estimate generally comes from thinking about multiplication rather than division.

Consider the following problem:

The trip to Washington was 282 miles. It took 4.5 hours to drive. What was the average miles per hour?

To make an estimate of this quotient, think about what times 4 or 5 is close to 280. You might think $60 \times 4.5 = 240 + 30 = 270$. So maybe about 61 or 62 miles per hour.

Here is a second example without a context.

Make an estimate of 45.7 ÷ 1.83. Think only of what times $1\frac{8}{10}$ is close to 46.

 Pause & Reflect

Will the answer be more or less than 46? Why? Will it be more or less than 20? Now think about 1.8 being close to 2. What times 2 is close to 46? Use this approach to produce an estimate. •

Because 1.83 is close to 2, the estimate is near 23. And because 1.83 is less than 2, the answer must be greater than 23—say, 25 or 26. (The actual answer is 24.972677.)

Developing the Algorithm. Although estimation can produce a reasonable result, you may still require a standard algorithm in the same way it was needed for multiplication. Figure 16.14 shows division by a whole number and how that can be carried out to as many places as you wish. (The explicit-trade method described in Chapter 12 is shown on the right.) Through reasoning you are placing the decimal point—that is, trade 2 tens for 20 ones, then put 2 ones in each group—so you know the 2 in the quotient is in the ones place.

An algorithm for division is parallel to that for multiplication: Ignore the decimal points and do the computation as if all numbers were whole numbers. When finished, place the decimal using estimation. This approach is reasonable for divisors greater than 1 or close to a familiar value (e.g., 0.1, 0.5, 0.01).

23.5 ÷ 8

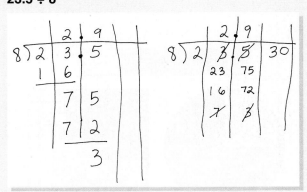

Trade 2 tens for 20 ones, making 23 ones.
Put 2 ones in each group, or 16 in all.
That leaves 7 ones.

Trade 7 ones for 70 tenths, making 75 tenths.
Put 9 tenths in each group, or 72 tenths in all.
That leaves 3 tenths.

Trade the 3 tenths for 30 hundredths.

(Continue trading for smaller pieces as long as you wish.)

FIGURE 16.14   Extension of the division algorithm.

If students have a method for dividing by 45, they can divide by 0.45 and 4.5, thinking they will get ten times as many (as 4.5 is one-tenth of 45) and therefore multiply the answer by ten.

Activity 16.17   CCSS-M: 5.NBT.B.7; 6.NS.B.3

ENGLISH LEARNERS

Where Does the Decimal Go? Division

Provide a quotient such as 146 ÷ 7 = 20857—correct to five digits but without the decimal point. The task is to use only this information and estimation to give a fairly precise answer to each of the following:

$$146 \div 0.7 \quad 1.46 \div 7 \quad 14.6 \div 0.7 \quad 1460 \div 70$$

For each computation, students should write a rationale for their answers and then check their results with a calculator. As noted in multiplication, ELs may apply a different mental strategy, and it is important to value alternative approaches. Again, engage students in explicit discussions of common challenges or misconceptions and how to fix them.

MyLab Education   Self-Check 16.4

Introducing Percents

The term *percent* is simply another name for *hundredths* and as such is a standardized ratio with a denominator of 100. If students can express fractions and decimals as hundredths, the term *percent* can be substituted for the term *hundredth*. Consider the fraction $\frac{3}{4}$. As a fraction expressed in hundredths, it is $\frac{75}{100}$. When $\frac{3}{4}$ is written in decimal form, it is 0.75. Both 0.75 and $\frac{75}{100}$ are read in exactly the same way, "seventy-five hundredths." When used as operators, $\frac{3}{4}$ of something is the same as 0.75 or 75 percent of that same thing. Thus, percent is merely a new notation and terminology, not a new concept.

Physical Models and Terminology

Physical models provide the main link between fractions, decimals, and percents, as shown in Figure 16.15, the Rational Number Wheel, and 10 × 10 Grid. Base-ten models are suitable for fractions, decimals, and percents, because they all represent the same idea. The rational number wheel with 100 markings around the circumference is a model for percents as well as a fraction model for hundredths. The same is true of a 10 × 10 grid where each little square inside is 1 percent of the grid and each row or strip of 10 squares is not only a tenth but also 10 percent of the grid.

MyLab Education   Blackline Master: Rational Number Wheel

MyLab Education   Blackline Master: 10 × 10 Grids

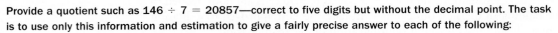

Each model shows
$\frac{3}{4}$ of a region
0.75 of a region
75% of a region

FIGURE 16.15   Models connect three different notations.

Zambo (2008) recommends linking fractions to percent using a 10 × 10 grid. By marking one out of every four squares on the chart or shading a 5 × 5 region in the corner of the grid, students can discover the link between $\frac{1}{4}$ and $\frac{25}{100}$ or 25 percent. Zambo goes on to suggest that even more complex representations, such as $\frac{1}{8}$, can lead to interesting discussions about the remaining squares left at the end resulting in $12\frac{1}{2}$ out of 100 squares or $12\frac{1}{2}$ percent (or 12.5 percent).

Similarly, common fractions (halves, thirds, fourths, fifths, and eighths) should become familiar in terms of percents as well as decimals. Three-fifths, for example, is 60 percent as well as 0.6. One-third of an amount is frequently expressed as $33\frac{1}{3}$ percent instead of 33.3333 . . . percent. These ideas should be explored with base-ten models and with contexts.

Let's look at an area model that is not 10 × 10 based on the work of Smith, Silver & Stein (2005).

Activity 16.18   CCSS-M: 6.RP.A.3c

Different Regions

Use the Different Regions Activity Page to explore students' thinking about fractions, decimals and percents without the ease of the 10 × 10 grid.

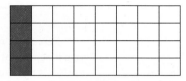

What percent of this region is shaded? What is the decimal that shows how much of the area is shaded? Explain your thinking. Students might note that in this example 2 columns is one-fourth or 25% or the area of the rectangle, so one column is 12.5%. The activity page provides other regions to consider.

MyLab Education   Activity Page: Different Regions

Data representation with circle graphs provides another opportunity for percent explorations (Whitin & Whitin, 2012). Besides using the rational number wheel another tool that can be used to represent percentages is a percent necklace as described in the next activity.

Activity 16.19   CCSS-M: 6.RP.A.3c

Percent Necklaces

Using fishing cord or sturdy string, link 100 same-sized beads and knot them tightly in a circular "necklace." Anytime a circle graph is displayed in class, this percent necklace can provide an estimation tool. Given any circle graph, even a human circle graph as shown in Figure 20.10 on page 560, place the necklace in a circle so that its center coincides with the center of the circle graph (don't try to align the necklace with the outside edge of the circle graph). If the necklace makes a wider concentric circle, students use a straight edge to extend the lines, that distinguish different categories on the graph, out to meet the necklace. If the circle graph is larger than the necklace, as it would be in Figure 20.10, use the lines that denote the categories. Have students count the number of beads between any two lines that represent a category. For example, they might count 24 beads in the section of the circle graph that shows how many students selected the Grand Canyon as where they want to go on a vacation. That count is an estimate suggesting that approximately 24 percent of the students favor the Grand Canyon. Counting the beads in a given category provides an informal approach to estimating percent while investigating a meaningful model for thinking about the per-one-hundred concept.

TECHNOLOGY Note. The activity "Fraction Models" on the NCTM Illuminations website (http://illuminations.nctm.org) explores equivalence of fractions, mixed numbers, decimals, and percents. Select the fraction and pick the type of model (length, area [rectangle or circle], or set), and it shows the corresponding visual and all the equivalences. ■

Here's another activity that focuses just on representations of percent:

Activity 16.20   CCSS-M: 6.RP.A.3c

STUDENTS
with
SPECIAL
NEEDS

Percent Memory Match

Use the Percent Cards that include circle graphs with a percentage shaded in (card with $\frac{1}{2}$ shaded) and matching percents (card with 50% written on it). Students pair each circle graph with the percent that best matches it in a memory-like game in which they flip over cards to find a matching pair. To support students with disabilities, provide rational number wheels (Figure 16.5) as a movable representation. For a virtual game with the same goal, go to the NCTM Illuminations website (http://illuminations.nctm.org) and find "Concentration," which uses representations of percents and fractions.

MyLab Education   **Activity Page: Percent Cards**
MyLab Education   **Blackline Master: Rational Number Wheel**

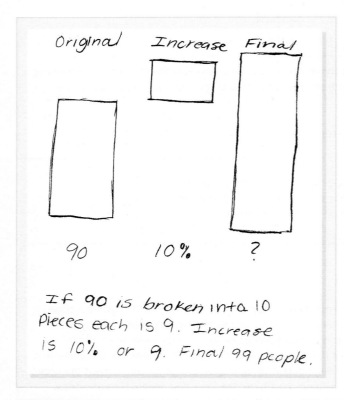

FIGURE 16.16 A student uses a proportional model for reasoning about percent.

Ones	Tenths	Percent Hundredths	Thousandths
	3	6	5

0.365 (of 1 whole) = 36.5 percent (of 1 whole)

FIGURE 16.17 Hundredths are also known as percents.

Percent concepts can be developed through other powerful visual representations that link to proportional thinking. One option is the use of a three-part model to represent the original amount, the decrease/increase, and the final amount (Lo & Ko, 2013; Parker, 2004). Using three rectangles as representations that can be positioned and divided, students can analyze aspects of a situation and then consider the relationships between each component of the model. The rectangles can be a particularly useful for the often confusing problems that include a percentage increase to find an amount greater than the original. In a 2005 NAEP item, students were asked to calculate how many employees there were at a company whose workforce increased by 10 percent over the previous level of 90 workers. Using Parker's approach of representing the components of the problem (2004), Figure 16.16 shows how a student used this representation to come up with a correct solution.

Another helpful approach to the terminology involved with percentages is through considering the role of the decimal point. Recall that the decimal point identifies the units position. When the unit is ones, a number such as 0.659 means more than 6 tenths of 1. The word *ones* is understood (6 tenths of 1 one or one whole). But 0.659 is also 6.59 tenths and 65.9 hundredths and 659 thousandths. The name of the unit must be explicitly identified. Because *percent* is another name for hundredths, when the decimal point identifies the hundredths position as the units, the word *percent* can be specified as a synonym for hundredths. Thus, 0.659 (of some whole or 1) is 65.9 hundredths or 65.9 percent of that same whole. As illustrated in Figure 16.17, the notion of placing the decimal point to identify the percent position (e.g., hundredths) is conceptually more meaningful than the rule: "To change a decimal to a percent, move the decimal two places to the right." A more conceptually focused idea is to equate hundredths with percent both orally and in notation.

Percent Problems in Context

Percents must be considered in light of the context (Bu & Marjanovich, 2017). Yet, some teachers may refer to the three percent problems because the sentence

"_____ is _____ percent of _____" (20 is 25 percent of 80) has three spaces for numbers. Then when two of the numbers are given the students are asked to produce the third (unknown). But, without a context, students tend to set up proportions but are not quite sure which numbers to put where. In other words, they are neither connecting understanding with the problem nor the procedure. Furthermore, commonly encountered percent situations, such as sales figures, taxes, food composition (% of fat), sports reporting and economic trends are rarely in the "_____ is _____ percent of _____" format.

Though students must have some experience with situations without contexts such as those in Figure 16.18, it is important to have them explore percent relationships in realistic contexts including the incorporation of models (Shahbari & Peled, 2016). Find or create percent problems, and present them in the same way that they appear in the news, on television, and in other real world settings. In addition, follow these guidelines for your instruction on percents:

- Initially limit the percents to familiar fractions (halves, thirds, fourths, fifths, and eighths) or simple percents ($\frac{1}{10}$, $\frac{1}{100}$), and use numbers compatible with these fractions. The focus of these exercises is the relationships involved, not complex computations.
- Require students to use models, drawings, and contexts to explain their solutions. It is wiser to assign three problems requiring a drawing and an explanation than to give 15 problems requiring only computation and answers. Remember that the purpose is the exploration of relationships, not just computational skill.
- Do not rush to developing rules or algorithms for different types of problems—encourage students to notice patterns.
- Use the terms *part*, *whole*, and *percent* (or *fraction*). Help students see these percent exercises as the same types of exercises they did with fractions.
- Encourage mental computation.

The following problems meet these criteria for familiar fractions and compatible numbers. Try working each problem, identifying each number as a part, a whole, or a fraction. Draw bar diagrams to explain or describe your thought process. Examples of student reasoning using bar diagrams are illustrated in Figure 16.19.

1. The PTA reported that 75 percent of the total number of families were represented at the meeting. If students from 320 families go to the school, how many were represented at the meeting?
2. The baseball team won 80 percent of the 25 games it played this year. How many games were lost?
3. In Mrs. Carter's class, 20 students, or $66\frac{2}{3}$ percent, were on the honor roll. How many students are in her class?
4. Zane bought his new computer at a $12\frac{1}{2}$ percent discount. He paid $700. How many dollars did he save by buying it at a discount?
5. If Nicolas has read 60 of the 180 pages in his library book, what percent of the book has he read so far?
6. The hardware store bought widgets at 80 cents each and sold them for $1 each. What percent did the store mark up the price of each widget?

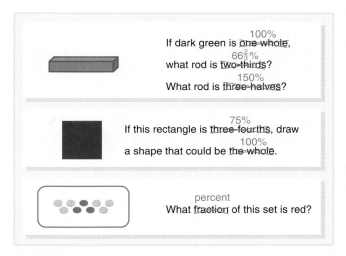

FIGURE 16.18 Part-whole fraction exercises can be translated into percent exercises.

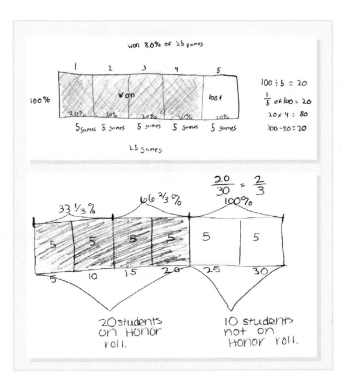

FIGURE 16.19 Students use bar diagrams to solve percent problems.

FORMATIVE ASSESSMENT Notes. These context-based percent problems are an effective performance assessment to evaluate students' understanding. Assign one or two, and have students explain why they think their answer makes sense. You might take a percent problem and substitute fractions for percents (e.g., use $\frac{1}{8}$ instead of $12\frac{1}{2}$ percent) to see how students handle these problems with fractions compared to percents.

If your focus is on reasoning and justification rather than number of problems correct, you will be able to collect all the assessment information you need to plan next instructional steps. ■

Estimation

Many percent problems do not have simple (familiar) numbers. Frequently, in real life an approximation or estimate in percent situations is enough to help one think through the situation. An estimate based on an understanding of the relationship confirms that a correct operation was performed or that the decimal point was positioned correctly.

To help students with estimation in percent situations, two ideas that have already been discussed can be applied. First, when the percent is not a simple one, substitute a close percent that is easy to work with. Second, select numbers that are compatible with the percent involved to make the calculation easy to do mentally. In essence, convert the complex percent problem into one that is more familiar. Here are some examples.

1. The 83,000-seat stadium was 73 percent full. How many people were at the game?
2. The treasurer reported that 68.3 percent of the dues had been collected, for a total of $385. How much more money could the club expect to collect if all dues are paid?
3. Max McStrike had 217 hits in 842 at bats. What was his batting average?

❚❚ Pause & Reflect

Use familiar percents, fractions, and compatible numbers to estimate solutions to each of these last three problems. •

Here are some possible estimates:

1. Use $\frac{3}{4}$ and 80,000, so about 60,000 people
2. Use $\frac{2}{3}$ and $380; the club will collect $\frac{1}{3}$ more, so about $190 more
3. The number of hits (217) is about $\frac{1}{4}$ the number of at-bats (842); $\frac{1}{4}$ is 25 percent so Max is getting a hit a little more than 25% of the time

There are several common uses for estimating percentages in real-world situations. As students gain full conceptual understanding and flexibility, there are a variety of ways to think about percents that are useful:

Tips. To figure a tip, you can find 10 percent of the amount and then half of that again to make 15 percent or double 10% for a 20% tip.

Taxes. Depending on the sales tax rate, you can find 10 percent, take half of that, and then find 1 percent and add or subtract that amount as needed. Students should also realize that finding percents is a process of multiplication; therefore, finding 8 percent (tax) of $50 will generate the same result as finding 50 percent (half) of 8, or $4.

Discounts. A 30 percent decrease is the same as 70 percent of the original amount, and depending on the original amount, using one of those percents may be easier to use in mental calculations than the other. If a $48 outfit is 30 percent off, for example, you are paying 70 percent. Round $48 to $50 and you can calculate 0.70×50 (think 7×5), so your cost is less than $35.

These are not rules to memorize, but reasoning activities to explore. Such discussions develop a full understanding of percent concepts and the commutative property.

MyLab Education   **Self-Check 16.5**

MyLab Education   **Math Practice:** Need to practice or refresh your math content knowledge? Click to access practice exercises associated with the content from this chapter.

Although we've mentioned some common challenges about comparing decimals earlier in this chapter, we include others in Table 16.2. Because incomplete understandings and naïve conceptions provide powerful learning opportunities we share ways to help students add to their every expanding knowledge of these ideas.

TABLE 16.2   COMMON CHALLENGES AND MISCONCEPTIONS IN DECIMALS AND PERCENTS AND HOW TO HELP

Common Challenge or Misconception	What It Looks Like	How to Help
1. Confusion about when zero is important in interpreting the decimal quantity and when it can be omitted from the decimal.	Students think that 0.80 is ten times larger than 0.8 (Irwin, 2016) Students are not sure that 0.6 and 0.60 are equal	• This confusion links to the inaccurate rule that to multiply by 10 just put a zero at the end of a number. • Students should continue to model what these values look like, using shading of 10×10 grids and then compare.
2. Students confuse whole numbers notation with decimal fraction notation.	Students write one hundredth as 0.100 (Irwin, 2016)	• Present two "anonymous" students' answers to this question and have students talk about why the reasoning for one is correct and why the other is not.
3. When fractions are represented as decimals student thinking is incompatible with the magnitude of the fraction and/or place value understanding.	Students write: $\frac{4}{5}$ as 4.5 $\frac{1}{4}$ as 1.4 or 0.4	• Discuss what $\frac{4}{5}$ of a pizza and 4.5 pizzas look like using models. • Shade in 10×10 grids to show $\frac{1}{4}$, 1.4 and 0.4.
4. Multiplication makes "bigger" and division makes "smaller"	Students would incorrectly choose the answer "a" for: $8 \div 0.4 =$ a. less than 10 b. greater than 10 (Fagan & Tobey, 2015)	• Students use whole number reasoning and overgeneralize. Use Base-Ten Materials to represent and act out the division problems. • Arrays can be used to act out the multiplication problems (see Figure 16.12)
5. Students confuse fractional percents with fractions or decimals.	$\frac{1}{10}$ or 0.1 are equal to $\frac{1}{10}\%$	• Students should use 10×10 grids to shade in each amount and compare if they are equivalent quantities.
6. Aligning addition or subtraction problems as right justified rather than by lining up the decimal points to align place value parts.	$5.17 + 0.2 = 5.19$ $0.25 - 0.1 = 0.24$	• This response is a sign that students are using whole number thinking and they need more time using models and explicitly translating actions and representations to symbols. Work problems with the base-ten materials and show how partial sums (or differences) should be recorded. • Whenever possible use a context as these numbers are best interpreted within a situation.
7. Students confuse the decimal addition algorithm with the procedure for multiplication of decimals.	$0.5 \times 0.2 = 0.7$	• Use easily understood numbers and either with models, estimation or reasoning show how, in the case of the example given, half of two tenths is one tenth (not 7 tenths).
8. Students confuse the whole number multiplication algorithm with decimal multiplication.	Students multiply the numbers on both sides of the decimal point by the second factor: $2.3 \times 10 = 20.30$	• Have students act this problem out using a 10×10 grid or base-ten materials. Then link the action to the recording of the procedure. • Direct students to estimate the product and justify the estimation using a real-world story. Then model or act out the problem.
9. Students think that percents cannot be greater than 100	1.45 is written as 0.145%	• Use base-ten models to investigate both values. This problem must be set in a context such as a plant growing more than 100% in a single year for students to understand the problem

(continued)

Common Challenge or Misconception	What It Looks Like	How to Help
10. Students lose track of the place value of percents and think single digit percents are tenths.	Write 9% as 0.9	• Use the rational number wheel or base-ten materials to explore these values.
11. Students add the percent change on as an increase.	Given the problem, "There are 50 people in the restaurant, then the group increased by 10%, now how many people are in the restaurant?" Students would answer 55.	• Walk through this problem slowly with models and discussion. Help students understand the nature of a percent increase. Use Figure 16.16 to show the model.
12. Student find the % increase or decrease rather than the final amount.	Given the problem, "What is the price of a magic trick set that normally costs $25.00 when the store offers a 10% discount?" Students would answer $2.50.	• Model the problem using an array with 5 columns and 2 rows in this case. The full array would represent $25.00. Color in 2.5. Discuss the differences in the discount and the discounted price.
13. Students think an increase of *n*% followed by a decrease of *n*% restores the amount to its original value.	Given the problem, Mary had her salary of $15,000 decrease by 20% last year due to budget cuts. This year she got a raise of 20%, what is her salary now? Students will say $15,000.	• Students do not recognize the "whole" the percent refers to, and that the second percent change refers to a different "whole" than the first. Have students act this situation out using a proportional model as shown above in Figure 16.16. Talk about the intermediate referent and label each "whole."

> **MyLab Education** **Blackline Master: 10 × 10 Grids**
>
> **MyLab Education** **Blackline Master: Base-Ten Materials**

RESOURCES FOR CHAPTER 16

LITERATURE CONNECTIONS

There are endless real-world connections for decimal and percent situations. Money-related increases and decreases are interesting to project over several years. If the consumer price index rises approximately 3 percent a year, how much will a $100 shopping cart of groceries cost by the time your students are 21 years old?

The Phantom Tollbooth

Juster (1961)

Mathematical ideas abound in this story about Milo's adventures in Digitopolis, where everything is number-oriented. There he meets a half of a boy, appearing in the illustration as a boy cut from top to bottom. But, the boy is actually 0.58 because he is a member of the average family: mother, father, and 2.58 children. One advantage, he explains, is that he is the only one who can drive 0.3 of a car, as the average family owns 1.3 cars. An extension is to explore averages that are interesting to students (average number of siblings, etc.) and see where these odd decimals come from. Illustrating an average number of pets can be very humorous!

Piece = Part = Portion: Fraction = Decimal = Percent

Gifford & Thaler (2008)

Illustrated with vivid photos, this book relates fractions to decimals and percents. Through common representations, such as one sneaker representing $\frac{1}{2}$ or 0.50 or 50 percent of a pair of shoes. Real-world links such as one-seventh of a week and one-eleventh of a soccer team will connect with students.

RECOMMENDED READINGS

Articles

Cramer, K., Monson, D., Wyberg, T., Leavitt, S., & Whitney, S. B. (2009). Models for initial decimal ideas. *Teaching Children Mathematics, 16*(2), 106–116.

This article describes ways of using 10 × 10 grids and decimal addition and subtraction boards to enhance students' understanding. Several diagnostic interviews are included.

Martinie, S. (2014). Decimal fractions: An important point. *Mathematics Teaching in the Middle School, 19*(7), 420–429.

By offering assessment tasks that include using multiple representations, the author taps into common misconceptions and confusions faced by students learning about decimals. A summary of student responses and samples of work help pinpoint common problems and next instructional steps.

CHAPTER
17

Ratios, Proportions, and Proportional Reasoning

LEARNER OUTCOMES

After reading this chapter and engaging in the embedded activities and reflections, you should be able to:

17.1 Describe the essential features of a ratio, including how it relates to fractions, and articulate ways to help students understand and be able to use ratios.

17.2 Contrast proportional and nonproportional situations using additive and multiplicative examples.

17.3 Illustrate the different ways to solve proportional problems and describe a developmental progression for these ways.

17.4 Compare traditional methods of teaching proportional reasoning to research-based methods.

Proportional reasoning goes well beyond the notion of setting up a proportion to solve a problem—it is a way of reasoning about multiplicative situations. Proportional reasoning, like equivalence, is considered a unifying theme in mathematics. It is estimated that more than half the population of adults are not proportional thinkers (Lamon, 2012). This is a direct result of mathematics experiences that exclusively focused on solving missing-value proportions. Such rote practice is particularly troubling in the area of proportional reasoning because it is at the core of so many important concepts, including "similarity, relative growth and size, dilations, scaling, pi, constant rate of change, slope, speed, rates, percent, trigonometric ratios, probability, relative frequency, density, and direct and inverse variations" (Heinz & Sterba-Boatwright, 2008 , p. 528). Wow!

MyLab Education   Video Example 17.1

Author Jennifer Bay-Williams provides an overview of ratios and proportions, including strategies for solving proportional situations.

Learning about ratios and proportional relationships begins in elementary school with work in measurement and in multiplication and division. In the CCSS-M, the progression looks like this:

Grade 4: Solve multiplication problems involving a multiplicative comparison.

Grade 5: Identify relationships between two varying quantities.

Grade 6: A critical area focuses on connecting ratio and rate to multiplication and division; students solve problems involving ratios and rates.

Grade 7: A critical area focuses on proportionality, solving multistep problems; students write proportions as equations and graph them, as well solve problems involving interest, tax, gratuities and so on.

BIG IDEAS

♦ A ratio is a multiplicative comparison of two quantities or measures. A key developmental milestone is the ability of a student to think of a ratio as a distinct entity, different from the two measures that made it up.

♦ Ratios and proportions involve multiplicative rather than additive comparisons. This means that equal ratios result from multiplication or division, not from addition or subtraction.

♦ Rate is a way to represent a ratio, and in fact represents an infinite number of equivalent ratios.

♦ Proportional thinking is developed through activities and experiences involving comparing and determining the equivalence of ratios. This means solving proportions in a wide variety of problem-based contexts and situations through reasoning, not rigid use of formulas.

 ## Ratios

A *ratio* is a number that relates two quantities or measures within a given situation in a multiplicative relationship (in contrast to a difference or additive relationship). Reasoning with ratios involves paying attention to two quantities that covary. Ratios and rates are described as one of the four critical areas in grade 6 (NGA Center & CCSSO, 2010). These concepts grow out of students' prior understanding of multiplicative reasoning, in particular multiplicative comparisons.

Types of Ratios

Part-to-Part Ratios. A ratio can relate one part of a whole (9 girls) to another part of the same whole (7 boys). This can be represented as $\frac{9}{7}$, meaning "a ratio of nine to seven," not nine-sevenths (the fraction). In other words, a part-to-part ratio is not a fraction, although it can be written with the fraction bar; the context is what tells you it is a part-to-part ratio.

Part-to-part ratios occur across the curriculum. In geometry, corresponding parts of similar geometric figures are part-to-part ratios. The ratio of the diagonal of a square to its side is $\sqrt{2}$. The relationship of the diameter of a circle to the circumference is in the well known ratio of π.

MyLab Education   **Video Example 17.2**

See how this teacher poses questions to focus on ratio of diameter to circumference.

In algebra, the slope of a line is a ratio of rise for each unit of horizontal distance (called the *run*). The probability of an event is a part-to-whole ratio, but the *odds* of an event occurring are a part-to-part ratio.

Part-to-Whole Ratios. Ratios can express comparisons of a part to a whole—for example, the ratio of the number of girls in a class (9) to the number of students in the class (16). This can be written as the ratio $\frac{9}{16}$, or can be thought of as nine-sixteenths of the class (a fraction). Percentages and probabilities are examples of part-whole ratios.

Ratios as Quotients. Ratios can be thought of as quotients. For example, if you can buy 4 kiwis for $1.00, the ratio of money for kiwis is $1.00 to 4 kiwis, or $\frac{1}{4}$, and is a quotient. Dividing the values results in $0.25 for one kiwi, the unit rate.

Ratios as Rates. Miles per gallon, square yards of wall coverage per gallon of paint, passengers per busload, and roses per bouquet are all rates. Rates involve two different units and how they relate to each other. Relationships between two units of measure are also rates—for example, inches per foot, milliliters per liter, and centimeters per inch. A rate represents an infinite set of equivalent ratios (Lobato, Ellis, Charles, & Zbiek, 2010), for example if a person's rate of exercise is 10 miles in 3 days, it could mean they walk 20 miles in 6 days, 30 miles in 9 days, and so on.

Ratios Compared to Fractions

Ratios are closely related to fractions, but ratios and fractions should be thought of as overlapping concepts with important distinctions (Lobato et al., 2010). Because they are represented symbolically with a fraction bar, it is important to help students see that fractions and ratios are related, but not the same thing. In the three examples below, ask, "Is this a fraction, ratio, or both?":

1. The ratio of cats to dogs at the pet store is $\frac{3}{5}$.
2. The ratio of cats to pets at the pet store is $\frac{3}{8}$.
3. Mario walked three-eighths of a mile ($\frac{3}{8}$ miles).

In the first example, the ratio is not a fraction, as fractions are not part-to-part. Notice in the second example, the ratio is part-to-whole, and it can be adapted to say three-eighths of the pets are cats. It is both a ratio and a fraction. In the third example, this fraction is a length and not a ratio, as there is not a multiplicative comparison.

Two Ways to Think about Ratio

As Lobato and colleagues (2010) state, "forming a ratio is a *cognitive task*—not a *writing task*" (p. 22, emphasis added). What they mean is that ratio is a relationship, and that relationship can be thought of in different ways, regardless of whether it is notated as $\frac{2}{5}$ or 2:5 or 2 ÷ 5. Unfortunately, ratios are often taught in a superficial manner, with students recording the symbols (3:5) to tell the ratio of girls to boys. Instead, ratios should be taught as relations that involve multiplicative reasoning—multiplicative comparisons and as composed units.

 Standards for Mathematical Practice
MP1. Make sense of problems and persevere in solving them.

Multiplicative Comparison. Multiplicative comparisons serve as an important foundation to understanding ratios (see Chapter 8). Consider the following relationship: Wand A is 10 inches long, and Wand B is 15 inches long. The ratio of the two wands is 10 to 15 or 2 to 3. But this statement does not necessarily communicate the *relationship* between the measures. There are two ways to compare the relationship multiplicatively:

The short wand is two-thirds as long as the long wand.
The long wand is three-halves as long as the short wand.

The questions related to multiplicative comparisons can be worded in two ways: "How many times greater is one thing than another?" Or "What fractional part is one thing of another?" (Lobato et al., 2010 , p. 18). When two *different* units are compared (e.g., 6 wands per 2 magicians), the ratio is a rate. Students need to solve real-world problems involving multiplicative comparisons, and those problems should increase in difficulty with experience (Cohen, 2013).

Activity 17.1

CCSS-M: 6.RP.A.1; 6.RP.A.2; 6.RP.A.3

**ENGLISH
LEARNERS**

Stocking the Pond

Use Stocking the Pond Activity Page or simply pose each of the three problems, one at a time, for students to solve. Ask students to use tape diagrams (also referred to as *strip diagrams*) as a tool to represent each problem. The first task is included here:

For every 3 bass that are put in a pond, Environmental Edwin puts 8 blue gill in the pond. If Edwin puts 24 blue gill in the pond, how many bass does he need to put in the pond?

After students have solved the problem, ask questions such as, "What fractional part is the bass compared to the blue gill?" (three-eighths) and "What fractional part is the blue gill compared to the bass?" (eight-thirds). Continue to more questions that vary what information is unknown in the story. For ELs, it is helpful to keep the same context to reduce the linguistic load and to point out the four types of fish names. Also, be sure that the word "if" is understood in the situation to mean "assume."

MyLab Education   Activity Page: Stocking the Pond

Composed Unit. The term *composed unit* refers to thinking of the ratio as one unit. For example, if kiwis are 4 for $1.00, you can think of this as a unit and then think about other multiples that would also be true, like 8 for $2.00, 16 for $4.00, and so on. (Each of these would be a unit composed of the original ratio.) This is *iterating* (also discussed in Chapter 14). There can also be other *partitioning* of the composed unit: 2 for $0.50 and 1 for $0.25. Any number of kiwis can be priced by using these composed units.

It is important that students be able to apply both types of ratios. Activity 17.2 provides a context for thinking of a composed unit and then a multiplicative comparison.

Activity 17.2

CCSS-M: 6.RP.A.1; 6.RP.A.2; 6.RP.A.3

**STUDENTS
with
SPECIAL
NEEDS**

Birthday Cupcakes

Explain to students that they are going to be icing cupcakes and selling them at school. In a recipe for icing, the instructions say that to ice 1 batch of cupcakes with aqua-colored icing, you will need 2 green drops of food coloring and 5 blue drops of food coloring. Ask students to figure out how many drops of food coloring will be needed for 1 batch of cupcakes, 2 batches, 5 batches, and so on (composed unit thinking). Students may want to record their data in a table.

Next, ask students to figure out how many blue drops for 1 drop of green, and how much green for 1 drop of blue (multiplicative comparison). Ask students to think about how this information helps them in determining the number of color drops for various numbers of batches. Students—particularly students with disabilities—may benefit from visualizing this comparison, which can be done by lining up green and blue tiles or counters (or use drawings).

MyLab Education   Self-Check 17.1

Proportional Reasoning

Contexts such as interest, taxes, and tips, as well as geometric context such as similar figures, graphing, and slope, involve comparing ratios—which requires proportional reasoning.

Reasoning proportionally begins in kindergarten with one-to-one correspondence, and continues through the grades with place value, fraction concepts, and multiplicative reasoning (Seeley & Schielack, 2007). And, in middle school it is perhaps the most significant topic, providing the foundation for algebra and geometry.

Proportional reasoning is difficult to define in a simple sentence or two. It is not something that you either can or cannot do. According to Lamon (2012), proportional thinkers do the following:

- Understand a *ratio as distinct entity* representing a relationship different from the quantities it compares. (See earlier discussion about the composed units.)
- Recognize *proportional relationships as distinct from nonproportional relationships* in real-world contexts
- Have a sense of *covariation*. They understand relationships in which two quantities vary together and are able to see how the variation in one coincides with the variation in another.
- Develop *a wide variety of strategies* for solving proportions or comparing ratios, most of which are based on informal strategies rather than prescribed algorithms.

In other words, this list describes what fluency looks like related to ratios and proportions. These last three areas are addressed in the sections that follow.

Standards for Mathematical Practice
MP2. Reason abstractly and quantitatively.

Types of Comparing Situations

Students need opportunities to compare situations and discuss whether the comparison is due to an *additive*, *multiplicative*, or *constant* relationship (Van Dooren, De Bock, Vleugels, & Verschaffel, 2010). Importantly, a ratio is a number that expresses a multiplicative relationship (part-to-part or part-to-whole) that can be applied to a second situation in which the relative quantities or measures are the same as in the first situation. For example, the kiwi problem (4 for $1.00) is a multiplicative relationship—its relative measure can be applied to other situations (8 for $2.00, 40 for $10.00, etc.).

 Pause *&* Reflect

Solve each of the following problems.

1. Janet and Jeanette were walking to school, each walking at the same rate. Jeanette started first. When Jeanette has walked 6 blocks, Janet has walked 2 blocks. How far will Janet be when Jeanette is at 12 blocks?
2. Lisa and Linda are planting corn on the same farm. Linda plants 4 rows and Lisa plants 6 rows. If Linda's corn is ready to pick in 8 weeks, how many weeks will it take for Lisa's corn to be ready?
3. Kendra and Kevin are baking cookies using the same recipe. Kendra makes 6 dozen and Kevin makes 3 dozen. If Kevin is using 6 ounces of chocolate chips, how many ounces will Kendra need?

Can you figure out which of the three problems above is an *additive*, *multiplicative*, or *constant* relationship? What are the differences in the wording of these situations that make each one an *additive*, *multiplicative*, or *constant* relationship? How can you help students distinguish between these types? ●

Standards for Mathematical Practice
MP2. Reason abstractly and quantitatively.

MyLab Education   **Application Exercise 17.1: Observing and Responding to Student Thinking** Click the link to access this exercise, then watch the video and answer the accompanying questions.

VIDEO EXAMPLE

Think about the way quantities compare in each situation. The first situation is *additive*. Janet will still be 4 blocks behind because they are walking at the same rate, so 8 blocks. The situation describes the distance (difference) between the girls, an additive situation. If the problem is solved incorrectly through multiplicative reasoning, however, you will get 4 blocks. The second situation is *constant*. It will take 8 weeks for the corn to grow, regardless of how many rows were planted. If the problem is solved using multiplicative reasoning, the incorrect answer is 12 weeks. The final situation is multiplicative, and the answer is 12 ounces. How did you do?

Analyzing Situations Additively and Multiplicatively. The way to get students to distinguish between these types of reasoning is to provide opportunities for them to make both additive and multiplicative observations about a situation and compare the responses. Consider the following example task, one that is common used by teachers in China to introduce the concept of ratio (Cai & Sun, 2002 , p. 196):

Mr. Miller's 25 students are asked if they are basketball fans (yes or no). Of these students, 20 say "yes" and 5 say "no." Describe as many relationships as you can about those who are basketball fans and those who are not.

Students might generate these relationships (among others):

- There are 15 more fans than nonfans.
- There are 15 fewer nonfans than fans.
- There are 4 times as many fans as nonfans.
- There are $\frac{1}{4}$ as many nonfans as fans.
- For every 4 students who like basketball, there is 1 who does not.

The first two focus on the difference between the two numbers—the additive relationship. The other three describe a multiplicative relationship, each expressing the 4-to-1 ratio of fans to nonfans in a slightly different way. A student may also incorrectly say "is four times more than," perhaps because they have confusion as to whether the situation is additive or multiplicative (Rathouz, Cengiz, Krebs, & Rubenstein, 2014). Explicitly ask students to compare these statements and identify which are additive and which are multiplicative, and what the appropriate phrases are that go with each type of reasoning.

The following task, adapted from the book *Adding It Up* (National Research Council, 2001), engages students in considering both additive and multiplicative interpretations.

Standards for Mathematical Practice

MP3. Construct viable arguments and critique the reasoning of others.

Two weeks ago, two flowers were measured at 8 inches and 12 inches, respectively. Today they are 11 inches and 15 inches tall. Did the 8-inch or 12-inch flower grow more?

Additive reasoning leads to the response that they both grew the same amount—3 inches. Multiplicative reasoning leads to the first flower growing more: The first flower grew $\frac{3}{8}$ of its height whereas the second grew $\frac{3}{12}$ of its height. Both additive and multiplicative reasoning produce valid answers for this context. As students critique these different approaches, they are able to better understand the difference between additive and multiplicative comparisons.

Activity 17.3

CCSS-M: 6.RP.A.1

Which Has More?

Provide students with situations similar to those in Figure 17.1. Ask students to decide which has more and share a rationale for their thinking. As students share their reasoning, help students see the difference between looking at the difference (additive reasoning) and looking at the ratio (multiplicative reasoning). For ELs, take time to build meaning for what these terms mean—connect *additive* with the word *add*, and *multiplicative* with *multiple* and *multiply*. Reasoning can be modeled through illustrations or explanations. If no one suggests one of the options, introduce it. For example, say, "Amy says it is the second group. Can you explain why she made that choice?" or "Which class team has a larger proportion of girls?"

ENGLISH LEARNERS

Students benefit from critiquing authentic issues, in particular as they relate to *social justice*, such as population growth, crime rates, racial representation in congress or immigration rates, provide valuable information about the world we live in (Simic-Muller, 2015). The following tasks provide more opportunities for students to make the distinction between additive reasoning and multiplicative reasoning as they consider real-life situations (See Simic-Muller for full discussion of these ideas and others).

1. Share the population change in two cities, towns, or communities near you (that are different in size), in which the additive difference is similar (e.g., they both increased by 2000), but the multiplicative change is quite different. Ask, "What was the change?" and "Do you think this change had the same impact on both places?"
2. Share the population and number of crimes in two different cities/counties in your area and ask, "Which community is safer and how did you decide?"

For each, discuss when each type of reasoning might make sense when interpreting that particular context. Be sure it is not just the mathematics that is discussed, but the actual situation in the problem. Tasks such as this can lead into the students selecting their own real-life situations to explore (Beigie, 2016; Simic-Muller, 2015; Turner & Strawhun, 2007).

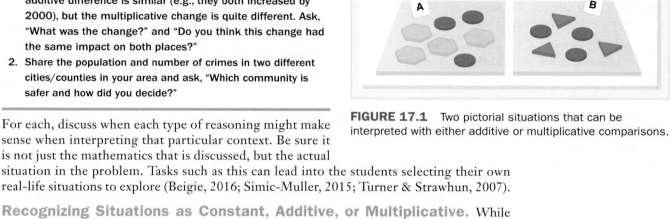

(a) Which team has more girls?

The Stars   The Comets

(b) Which set has more circles?

A   B

FIGURE 17.1 Two pictorial situations that can be interpreted with either additive or multiplicative comparisons.

Recognizing Situations as Constant, Additive, or Multiplicative. While the tasks above are effective in helping students understand the differences between constant, additive and multiplicative relationship, most tasks they will encounter cannot be solved either way—students have to recognize which relationship is described in the story (see the three tasks we shared at the beginning of this section). Using additive reasoning in a situation that calls for multiplicative, or vice versa, leads to incorrect answers. Solve the five-item assessment shown in Figure 17.2, devised to examine students' appropriate use of additive or multiplicative reasoning (Bright, Joyner, & Wallis, 2003). Which ones are multiplicative situations? Additive?

Notice that the items involving rectangular representations (1, 2, and 5) are multiplicative, looking at the ratios of the sides of the rectangles (part-to-part). The basketball task (3) can be reasoned either way and the walking comparison (2) is additive, not multiplicative.

Because textbooks and teachers use a similar style for proportion stories, and almost never mix in additive or constant situations, students recognize this pattern and automatically arrange four quantities (three known and one unknown) into a proportion without paying attention to what type of comparison is described in the story. They are focused on the structure of the proportion, not the concept of the proportion (Heinz & Sterba-Boatwright, 2008; Watson and Shaughnessy, 2004). The key is to vary problem types and focus discussion on determining which type of situation is represented.

Contrasting two very similar problems can help students distinguish between additive and multiplicative reasoning:

 Standards for Mathematical Practice

MP7. Look for and make use of structure.

1. A red car and a silver car are traveling at the same constant rate. When the red car has traveled 20 miles, the silver car has traveled 12 miles. How far will the red car be when the silver car has traveled 32 miles?
2. A red and a silver car are traveling at different but constant rates. They pass Exit 95 at the same time. When the red car has traveled 20 miles past exit 95, the silver car has traveled 16 miles. How far will the red car be when the silver car has traveled 32 miles?

Writing the relationships in variables can further help students see the differences between additive and multiplicative situations (Lim, 2009). In the first case, the relationship is red = silver + 8 because the red car is 8 miles in front of the silver car. In the latter case, the relationships is red = $\frac{5}{4}$ silver because for every five miles the red car travels, the silver car travels four.

For each problem, circle the correct answer.

1. Mrs. Allen took a 3-inch by 5-inch photo of the Cape Hatteras Lighthouse and made an enlargement on a photocopier using the 200% option. Which is "more square," the original photo or the enlargement?

   a. The original photo is "more square."
   b. The enlargement is "more square."
   c. The photo and the enlargement are equally square.
   a. There is not enough information to determine which is "more square."

2. The Science Club has four separate rectangular plots for experiments with plants:

1 foot by 4 feet	7 feet by 10 feet
17 feet by 20 feet	27 feet by 30 feet

   Which rectangular plot is most square?

   a. 1 foot by 4 feet
   b. 7 feet by 10 feet
   c. 17 feet by 20 feet
   b. 27 feet by 30 feet

3. Sue and Julie were running equally fast around a track. Sue started first. When Sue had run 9 laps. Julie had run 3 laps. When Julie completed 15 laps, how many laps had Sue run?

   a. 45 laps
   b. 24 laps
   c. 21 laps
   c. 6 laps

4. At the midway point of the basketball season, you must recommend the best free-throw shooter for the all-star game. Here are the statistics for four players:

Novak: 8 of 11 shots	Peterson: 22 of 29 shots
Williams: 15 of 19 shots	Reynolds: 33 of 41 shots

   Which player is the best free-throw shooter?

   a. Novak
   b. Peterson
   c. Williams
   d. Reynolds

5. Write your answer to this problem.
   A farmer has three fields. One is 185 feet by 245 feet, one is 75 feet by 114 feet, and one is 455 feet by 508 feet. If you were flying over these fields, which one would seem most square? Which one would seem least square? Explain your answers.

FIGURE 17.2 Five items to assess proportional reasoning. For each problem, circle the correct answer.

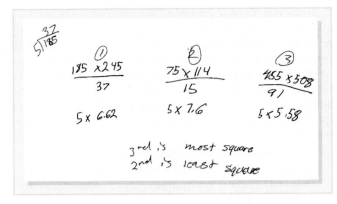

FIGURE 17.3 Jacob noticed that each length was divisible by 5; therefore, he simplified each ratio to have a side of 5 and then compared the widths.

 FORMATIVE ASSESSMENT Notes. The items in Figure 17.2 or the two tasks above could be used as a performance assessment, or select one or two to use as a diagnostic interview. For example, item 5 was given to an eighth grader, who first solved it incorrectly using an additive strategy (subtracting the sides). When asked if a very large rectangle 1,000,000 feet by 1,000,050 feet would look less square, he replied, "No—*oh*, this is a proportional situation." He then solved it using a novel strategy (see Figure 17.3). ■

Activity 17.4 describes an activity (based on Che, 2009) that can help students move from additive to multiplicative reasoning.

Activity 17.4

CCSS-M: 6.RP.A.3a; 7.RP.2b

Pencil-to-Pencil

ENGLISH LEARNERS

If possible, read a book or poem about giants (see Table 17.1). Hold up a cutout of a very large pencil (e.g., 30 inches in length). Explain to students that this is the exact size of a pencil used by a giant. Ask, "If this is her pencil, how tall is the giant?" "How long would her hand be?" Place students in partners and have them determine at least one measurement for the giant, based on knowing her pencil length (and their own pencil length).

Students who use additive reasoning will find that the giant is only about 24 inches taller than they are, which would make a 30-inch pencil still too big to manage. They might then start thinking of *how many* of their pencils would equal the extra large pencil, and see it takes about 5 of their pencils. Have students post one of their findings on posters, and illustrate or explain how they found the measures. Students from other countries are likely more familiar with centimeters, so allow students to choose which unit to use (inches or centimeters). In debriefing this activity, discuss their thought processes and why the situation is a multiplicative comparison and not an additive comparison.

TABLE 17.1   EXCELLENT CHILDREN'S AND ADOLESCENT LITERATURE FOR RATIO AND PROPORTIONS

Literature with Proportional Situations

Many books include multiplicative comparisons and therefore can be used for proportional reasoning. See *Exploring Math through Literature* (Thiessen, 2017) for lessons and activity pages for many of these books (select Ratios and Proportions tab).

If You Hopped Like a Frog Schwartz, 1999	David Schwartz compares features of various creatures with those of humans. For example, in the title comparison, Schwartz deduces that if a person had a frog's jumping ability, he or she could jump from home plate to first base in one hop. This short picture book contains 12 more fascinating comparisons. Schwartz also provides the factual data on which the proportions are based. Students can figure out how strong or tall they would be if they were one of the featured animals.
Animal Farm Orwell, *1946*	This classic novel can be an interdisciplinary opportunity with a Language Arts class. The animals chase off the human running the farm to run the farm themselves. Over time, the pigs take on a dictatorial role, for example telling the animals their "foodstuff" had increased by 200%, 300%, or 500% though the animals feel they are getting less food. This provides an opportunity to use bar diagrams to explore percent increase, connected to proportions (Martinie & Bay-Williams, 2003).
Holes Sachar, 2000	A popular book and movie, this novel tells the story of boys in a "camp" who are digging holes every day, which provides an opportunity to look at daily rates of dirt removal. Pugalee, Arbaugh, Bay-Williams, Farrell, Mathews, and Royster (2008) describe an excellent activity with this book that involves not only proportional reasoning but also measurement and algebra.
Wilma Unlimited: How Wilma Became the World's Fastest Woman. Krull, 2000	Wilma Rudolph survived polio, paralyzing her left leg. Determined to overcome her disability, she goes from hopping to walking to running, eventually winning 3 gold medals in the 1960 summer Olympics. This phenomenal true story can launch a lesson where students to measure their hopping, walking, and running rates, and use proportional reasoning to determine how quickly they would travel various distances (Martinie & Bay-Williams, 2003).

Literature with Large and/or Small People

There is a plethora of literature involving very little or very big people (or animals). With any of these books, lengths of arms, legs, or noses can be compared as a way to explore within and between ratios.

Alice's Adventures in Wonderland Carroll, 1865/1982	In this classic, Alice becomes very small and very tall, opening doors to many ratio and proportion investigations. See Taber (2005) for ideas on using this book to teach proportions.
The Borrowers Norton, 1953	A classic tale of little folk living in the walls of a house. Furnishings are created from odds and ends of the full-size human world.
Gulliver's Travels Swift, 1726; amended 1735/1999	Yet another classic story. In this case, Gulliver first visits Lilliput, where he is 12 times the size of the inhabitants, and then goes to Brobdingnag, where he is one-tenth the size of the inhabitants.
Harry Potter and the Sorcerer's Stone Rowling, 1997	In the book, Hagrid is described as twice as tall and nearly five times as wide as the usual man. Students can measure their own shoulder width and height and create a scatter plot. Placing Hagrid's measurements on the graph illustrates that he is not made in proportion to the usual person.
Jim and the Beanstalk Briggs, 1970	What happened to the giant after Jack? Jim comes along. Jim wants to help the poor, pessimistic giant. This heartwarming story is great for multiplicative or proportional reasoning.
Kate and the Beanstalk Osborne & Potter, 2000	This version of the traditional *Jack and the Beanstalk* tale includes a giantess. The giantess falls to earth, and Kate finds out that the castle belongs to her family.
The Lord of the Rings Tolkien, 1965	Hobbits are described as approximately 3 feet tall (which can be estimated at 100 cm). This height can be used to set up a ratio with the height of the typical sixth grader and the ratio then used to determine the size of various objects. To connect to the movie, ask students to be in the role of producer and figure out the size of objects used in the movie. (Beckman, Thompson, & Austin, 2004).
"One Inch Tall" in Where the Sidewalk Ends Silverstein, 1973	Shel Silverstein is a hit with all ages. This poem asks what it would be like if you were one inch tall.
Swamp Angel Isaacs & Zelinsky, 1994	A swamp angel named Angelica grows into a giant. Students can compare birth height with current height or compare Angelica's measurements with their own.

Covariation

Covariation can sound like a high school or college concept, but it simply means that two different quantities vary together. For example, five mangos cost $2.00 (two quantities in a multiplicative relationship); as the number of mangos varies (for example, to 10 mangos), so does the cost. And as the cost changes, so does the number of mangos you will get. Once you know either a new price or a new number of mangoes, you can determine the missing variable.

Within and Between Ratios. A ratio of two measures in the same setting is a *within* ratio. For example, in the case of the mangos, the ratio of mangos to money is a within ratio; that is, it is "within" the context of that example.

A *between* ratio is a ratio of two corresponding measures in different situations. In the case of the mangos, the ratio of the original number of mangos (5) to the number of mangos in a second situation (10) is a between ratio; that is, it is "between" the two situations.

The drawing in Figure 17.4 is an effective way of looking at two ratios and determining whether a ratio is between or within. A drawing similar to this will be very helpful to students in setting up proportions, especially students who struggle with abstract representations.

Standards for Mathematical Practice
MP4. Model with mathematics.

Different Objects, Same Ratios

Download Ratio Cards Activity Page and cut out the cards (see Figure 17.5) (or create your own using clipart of objects that are relevant to your students). Given one card, students are to select a card on which the ratio of the two types of objects is the same. This task moves students toward a numeric approach rather than a visual one and introduces the notion of ratios as rates. In this context, it makes the most sense to find the boxes per truck as the rate (rather than trucks per box). Finding the rate (amount for 1 unit) for pairs of quantities facilitates comparisons (just as the unit prices provided in grocery stores allow you to compare different brands).

MyLab Education   Activity Page: Ratio Cards

FORMATIVE ASSESSMENT Notes.

An observation tool can capture whether are students are using within ratios, between ratios, or both. Use a class list and check off which they are using. This same process can be used for the various ways to solve proportional situations (described later in this chapter). ■

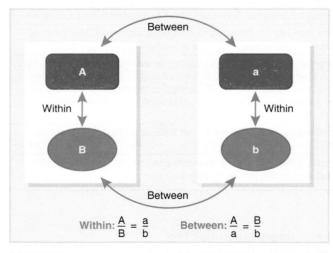

FIGURE 17.4 In a proportional situation, the two between ratios will be equivalent, as will the two within ratios.

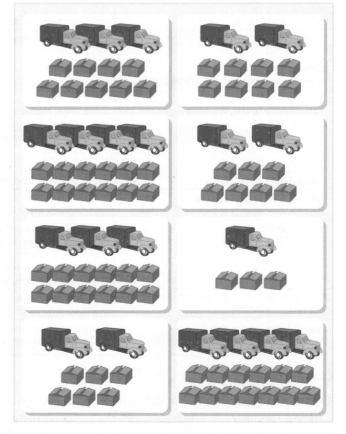

FIGURE 17.5 Ratio cards for exploring ratios and rates.

Covariation in Measurement and Geometry. Within and between ratios apply to measurement conversions. Consider that the capital A and B in Figure 17.4 is the conversion of inches to feet. How might you use within and between ratios to determine the number of feet in 60 inches?

$$\frac{12 \text{ inches}}{1 \text{ foot}} = \frac{60 \text{ inches}}{? \text{ feet}}$$

You might notice that the between ratio is × 5 (left to right), or you might notice that the within ratio is ÷ 12 (inches to feet). Measurement conversions are difficult even for adults, and are a goal in grade 6 in the CCSS-M. Setting up a between and within equation such as this one and analyzing the relationships can help students see the options they have for finding the conversion.

Within and between ratios are particularly relevant in exploring similarity with geometric shapes, a topic in grade 8 in the CCSS-M. Students often struggle to determine which features to compare to which features. Activity 17.6 can help students begin to analyze which features to compare.

Standards for Mathematical Practice

MP3. Construct viable arguments and critique the reasoning of others.

Activity 17.6   CCSS-M: 6.RP.A.1; 6.RP.A.3a; 7.RP.A.2a

Look-Alike Rectangles

Provide students with cut outs of the rectangles provided in Look-Alike Rectangles Activity Page (or have students cut out a set for themselves). Rectangles A, I, and D have sides in the ratio of 3 to 4. Rectangles C, F, and H have sides in the ratio of 5 to 8. Rectangles J, E, and G have sides in the ratio of 1 to 3. Rectangle B is a square, so its sides are in the ratio of 1 to 1.

STUDENTS *with* **SPECIAL NEEDS**

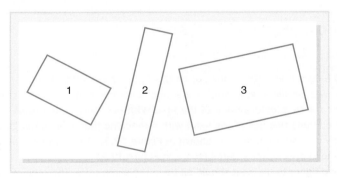

Ask students to group the rectangles into three sets that "look alike." If your students know the word *similar* from geometry, use that term instead of "look alike." To explain what "look alike" means, draw three rectangles on the board with two that are similar and one that is clearly dissimilar, as in the following example. Have students use ratio language to explain why rectangles 1 and 3 are alike.

When students have decided on their groupings, stop and discuss the reasons why they classified the rectangles as they did. Be prepared for some students to try to match sides or look for rectangles that have the same amount of difference between the sides. Encourage students to critique the explanations given. Next, have the students measure and record the sides of each rectangle to the nearest half centimeter. Use the Look-Alike Rectangles Recording Sheet. Discuss the results and ask students to offer explanations of how the ratios and groupings are related. If the groups are formed of proportional (similar) rectangles, the ratios within each group will be equivalent. Students with disabilities may need to have examples of one rectangle from each grouping as a starting point.

MyLab Education   Activity Page: Look-Alike Rectangles
MyLab Education   Activity Page: Look-Alike Rectangles Recording Sheet

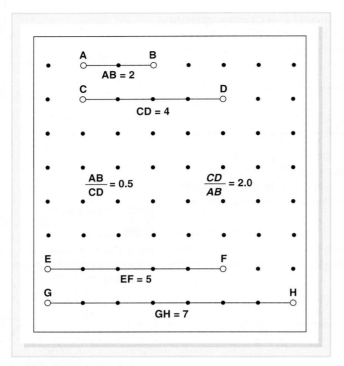

FIGURE 17.6 Dynamic software can be used to draw line segments or geometric shapes to see if a proportional relationship exists.

The connection between proportional reasoning and the geometric concept of similarity is very important. Similar figures provide a visual representation of proportions, and proportional thinking enhances the understanding of similarity. Discussion of the similar figures should focus on the ratios between and within the figures.

 TECHNOLOGY Note. Dynamic geometry software such as *GeoGebra* (a free download) offers a very effective method of exploring the idea of ratio. In Figure 17.6, two lengths are drawn on a grid with a "snap-to-grid" option. The lengths are measured, and two ratios are computed. As the length of either line is changed, the measures and ratios are updated instantly. You can also use dynamic software to explore dilations (i.e., similar figures) and corresponding measures. Figures can be drawn and then dilated (reduced or enlarged proportionally) according to any scale factor. The ratios of beginning and ending measures (lengths and areas) can then be compared to the scale factor. ■

Creating *scale drawings* is an application of similarity. Multiplication *is* scaling (making something three times bigger or one-half the size, for example). Scale drawings, then, are an important way for students to see the connection between multiplicative reasoning and proportional reasoning. Scaling activities ask students to resize a sketch that is similar to one they are given.

Activity 17.7

CCSS-M: 6.RP.A.1; 7.RP.A.3a

ENGLISH LEARNERS

Scale Drawings

On 1-Centimeter Grid Paper, 0.5-Centimeter Grid Paper, or on Dot Paper, have students use straight lines with vertices on the dots to draw a simple shape. After one shape is complete, have them draw a "scaled" drawing—a larger or smaller shape that looks similar to the first. With ELs, be sure the term *scale* is understood, so that they don't confuse this use of the word with a machine that weighs things or what fish have. This can be done on a grid of the same size or a different size, as shown in Figure 17.7. First compare ratios within the figure (see 1 in Figure 17.7), then compare ratios between the figures (see 2 in Figure 17.7).

Corresponding sides from one figure to the next should all be in the same ratio. The ratio of two sides within one figure should be the same as the ratio of the corresponding two sides in another figure.

MyLab Education   Blackline Masters: 1-Centimeter Grid Paper
MyLab Education   Blackline Masters: 0.5-Centimeter Grid Paper
MyLab Education   Blackline Masters: Dot Paper

 Standards for Mathematical Practice

MP8. Look for and express regularity in repeated reasoning.

Comparisons of corresponding lengths, areas, and volumes in proportional figures lead to some interesting patterns. If we know the length of the side of a figure, we can create the ratio of 1 to k, for example, to represent the relationship to a proportional figure. (The variable k is often used with proportions, whereas m is used with equations to describe slope—both refer to the rate or ratio between two values, which is called the *scale factor*.) If two figures are proportional (similar), then any corresponding linear dimensions will have the same scale factor.

Imagine you have a square that is 3 by 3 and you create a new square that is 6 by 6. The ratio between the side lengths is 1:2. What is the ratio between the two areas? Why is it 1:4? Try the same idea with the volume of a cube—what is the relationship of the original volume to the new volume when you double the length of the edges? Why? Returning to the sailboat in Figure 17.7, what would you conjecture is the ratio between the areas of the two sailboats? Measure and test your hypothesis.

Here are some interesting situations to consider for scale drawings:

- If you want to make a scale model of the solar system and use a ping-pong ball for the earth, how far away should the sun be? How large a ball would you need to represent the sun?
- What scale should be used to draw a scale map of your city (or some region of interest) so that it will nicely fit onto a standard piece of posterboard?
- Use the scale on a map to estimate the distance and travel time between two points of interest.
- Roll a toy car down a ramp, timing the trip with a stopwatch. How fast was the car traveling in miles per hour? If the speed is proportional to the size of the car, how fast would this have been for a real car?
- Your little sister wants a table and chair for her doll. Her doll is 14 inches tall. How tall should you make the table? The chair?
- Determine the various distances that a 10-speed bike travels in one turn of the pedals. You will need to count the sprocket teeth on the front and back gears.

TECHNOLOGY Note. Google Earth (available in online and App formats) is a great resource for doing authentic scaling activities (Roberge & Cooper, 2010). Find a Google Earth diagram that includes something for which the measure is known, and ask students to figure out other measures. For example, you know that a standard football field is 100 yards from end zone to end zone (120 yards including end zones), so zoom in on your school football field. By zooming to different levels, students can build an understanding of scale factor in an interesting context. Scale City, available for free through Kentucky Education Television features fun and engaging videos and interactive simulations for exploring scale drawings. ■

Covariation in Algebra. Covariation in algebra can also connect to measurement and geometry. As covariation focuses on graphs and equations, the connection to algebra is made. For the look-alike rectangles, ask students to stack them with the largest on the bottom so that they are aligned at one corner, as in Figure 17.8. Place a straight edge across the diagonals, and you will see that opposite corners also line up. If the rectangles are placed on a coordinate axis with the common corner at the origin, the slope of the line joining the corners is the ratio of the sides. A great connection to algebra!

Proportional situations are linear situations. Graphing equivalent ratios is a powerful way to illustrate this concept. The CCSS-M emphasizes the need to represent ratios and proportions graphically (NGA Center & CCSSO, 2010).

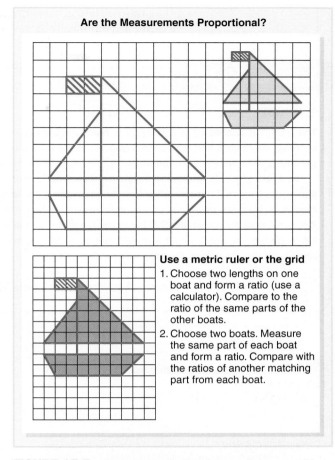

FIGURE 17.7   Comparing similar figures drawn on grids.

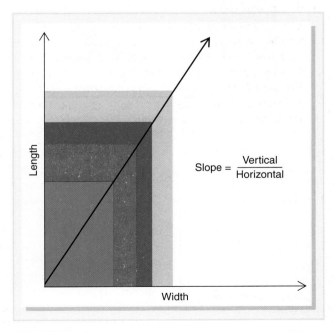

FIGURE 17.8   The slope of a line through a stack of proportional rectangles is equal to the ratio of the two sides.

The ratio or rate is the slope of the graph, and the line goes through the origin, so it is represented symbolically as $y = mx$, or sometimes as $y = kx$, where k takes on the specialized meaning of the scale factor.

Activity 17.8   CCSS-M: 7.RP.A.2a, b, c, d

Rectangle Ratios: Graph It!

This activity is connected to Activity 17.6. Using the Look-Alike Rectangles: Graph It! Activity Page, have students select one set of "alike" rectangles and record the measures in the ratio table, then create their three of their own examples of "alike" rectangles using their knowledge of equivalent ratios. Also, see if students can find a rectangle that has a noninteger side (e.g., $4\frac{1}{2}$ cm).

Next, ask students to graph the data for their 6 rectangles. The graph in Figure 17.9 is based on the ratios of two sides of similar rectangles. After the ratios have been graphed, challenge students to use their graph to determine a seventh look-alike rectangle. Also, ask questions to help students understand the graph, such as: What does a point on the graph mean (even if it is not one of the rectangles)? What is the length for a look-alike rectangle with a width of 1 cm? (This is the unit rate.) Challenge students to find the unit rate each way (also finding the width if the length is 1). The, ask students how, if they know the short side, they could find the long side (and vice versa).

MyLab Education   Activity Page: Look-Alike Rectangles: Graph It!

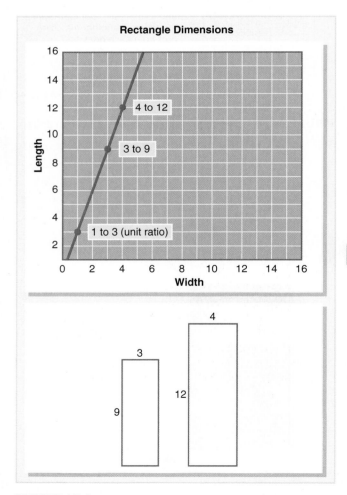

FIGURE 17.9   Graph shows ratios of sides in similar rectangles.

Students can struggle to decide what points to graph, deciding which axes to use for the two measures, and making sense of what the graph means (Kastberg, D'Ambrosio, Lynch-Davis, Mintos, & Krawczyk, 2014). With ratios, the choice of which variable is on the x-axis and which variable goes on the y-axis is arbitrary. All graphs of equivalent ratios fall along straight lines that pass through the origin. If the equation of one of these lines is written in the form $y = mx$, the slope m is always one of the equivalent ratios.

In addition to using geometric illustrations, it is important to use relevant contexts in which students analyze data and represent them in a various ways (tables, graphs, equations). For example, a situation like dripping faucets, can help students make sense of unit rates and proportional reasoning (Williams, Forrest, & Schnabel, 2006).

Activity 17.9   CCSS-M: 6.RP.A.1; 6.RP.A.3a, b; 7.RP.A.2b, c

Dripping Faucet

Pose the following problem to students: "If you brush your teeth twice a day and leave the water running when you brush, how many gallons of water will you waste in one day? In two days? In a week? A month? Any number of days?"

Invite students to gather real data, if possible. Or, use the recommended time to brush teeth (e.g., 2 minutes). Ask students to explore the ratio of number of days to water wasted, and to illustrate their data using tables, graphs and equations. Challenge students to consider other such environmental issues, determining two variables to consider, determining what ratio might exist between them, and representing that ratio in multiple ways.

This environmental investigation involves real measurement and authentic data. Stemn (2008) implemented this investigation with students and found that it aided their understanding of the difference between multiplicative and additive situations. Students in her class were challenged to figure out how many of the paper cups that they used for measuring would fill a gallon. The class figured out that 2 paper cups were equal to one-quarter gallon. Each student reasoned how many gallons he or she wasted in a day. For example, a student who wasted 5 paper cups of water reasoned that this would be two-fourths, plus a half of another fourth (or one-eighth). So, in total, five-eighths of a gallon of water is wasted per day. The class recorded what they knew in a table:

Paper cups of water wasted	1	2	3	4	5
Gallons of water wasted	$\frac{1}{8}$	$\frac{1}{4}$	$\frac{3}{8}$	$\frac{2}{4}$	$\frac{5}{8}$

The teacher encouraged students to rewrite the table with common denominators. Students recognized that the ratio of paper cups to gallons was $1:\frac{1}{8}$. Notice the connection to algebraic reasoning and to measurement. The formula $y = \frac{1}{8}x$ describes the number of paper cups (x) to gallons (y). This investigation also showed the students how to reason through measurement conversions with a nonstandard measure (the paper cup), which is a very challenging concept for students.

 TECHNOLOGY Note. For a good selection of challenging ratio and proportion problems using work and everyday life tasks, see NCTM's Figure This! Math Index: Ratios and Proportions. ■

MyLab Education **Self-Check 17.2**

MyLab Education **Application Exercise 17.2: Proportional Reasoning** Click the link to access this exercise, then watch the video and answer the accompanying questions.

VIDEO EXAMPLE

Strategies for Solving Proportional Situations

Procedural fluency includes *flexibility*, *efficiency*, *accuracy*, and *selecting appropriate strategies*. Certainly, that should be the goal in teaching students to solve proportional situations. Sometimes the numbers in the situation lend themselves to simple reasoning strategies, and sometimes they require a more sophisticated strategy. The most commonly known strategy is cross products, but as the most abstract and least intuitive strategy, it should only be introduced after students have solved proportional problems through reasoning and by using drawings such as a tape diagram or double number line and using ratio tables. Posing problems that have multiple solution strategies can help students to reason proportionally (Berk, Taber, Gorowara, & Poetzl, 2009; Ercole, Frantz, & Ashline, 2011). Strategies for solving missing value proportion problems include:

- Rate
- Scaling up or down
- Scale factors (within or between measures)
- Ratio tables
- Double line comparison
- Graphs
- Cross products

It is worth repeating that all of these strategies are useful in particular situations, and all should be taught such that as students add on new strategies they are encouraged to select from the strategies they know (rather than just use the one that they just learned). The first three are the most intuitive; therefore, they are the ones students might invent, and a good place to begin.

Rates and Scaling Strategies

Unit rate and scale factor can be used to solve many proportional situations mentally. The key is to know both strategies and pick the one that best fits the particular numbers in the problem, as the next examples illustrate.

Tammy bought 3 widgets for $2.40. At the same price, how much would 10 widgets cost?
Tammy bought 4 widgets for $3.75. How much would a dozen widgets cost?

 Pause & Reflect

Consider how students might use an approach other than the cross-product algorithm to solve these two problems. If they know the cross product, how might you encourage them to use a mental strategy? ●

In the first situation, it is perhaps easiest to determine the cost of one widget—the unit rate or unit price. This can be found by dividing the price of 3 widgets by 3. Multiplying this unit rate of $0.80 per widget by 10 will produce the answer. This approach is referred to as a *unit-rate* method of solving proportions. Notice that the unit rate is a within ratio.

In the second problem, a unit-rate approach could be used, but the division does not appear to be easy. But, because 12 is a multiple of 4, it is easier to notice that the cost of a dozen is 3 times the cost of 4, or that the scale factor between the ratios is 4. This is called a *buildup strategy*. Notice that the buildup approach applies the ratio as a composed unit. Although using scale factors (the buildup strategy) is a useful way to think about proportions, it is most frequently used when the numbers are compatible (i.e., the scale factor is a whole number). Be sure to give students problems in which the numbers work easily with both approaches so that they will explore (and compare) both methods.

Try using the unit-rate method or scale factors to solve the next two problems.

At the office superstore, you can buy 4 pencils for $0.59, or you can buy the same pencils in a large box of 5 dozen for $7.79. How much will you save per pencil if you buy the large box?

The price of a box of 2 dozen gumballs is $4.80. Bridget wants to buy 5 gumballs. What will she have to pay?

To solve the pencil problem, you might notice that the between ratio of pencils to pencils is 4 to 60 (5 dozen), or 1 to 15. If you multiply the 0.59 cents by 15, the factor of change, you will get the price of the box of 60 if the pencils are sold at the same price. In the gumball problem, the within ratio of 24 to $4.80 lends to finding the unit rate of $0.20 per gumball, which can then be multiplied by 5. See Expanded Lesson: It's a Matter of Rates and It's a Matter of Rates Activity Page for a full lesson using stories to develop strategies for reasoning about ratios and rates.

MyLab Education	**Expanded Lesson: It's a Matter of Rates**
MyLab Education	**Activity Page: It's a Matter of Rates**

Follow these tasks with problems that have more difficult numbers, asking students to apply the same strategies to reason to an answer. For example, try to apply both strategies to the next problem.

Brian can run 5 km in 17.4 minutes. If he keeps running at the same speed, how far can he run in 23 minutes?

Selecting problems that can be solved many ways is important. The following activity has been used in various studies and curricula because it can be approached in so many ways.

Activity 17.10   CCSS-M: 6.RP.A.1; 6.RP.A.3a, b; 7.RP.1; 7.RP.A.2a

Comparing Lemonade Recipes

Show students a picture of two lemonade pitchers, as in Figure 17.10. The little squares indicate the recipes used in each pitcher. In this case the recipes are:

3 cups water	4 cups water
2 cups concentrate	3 cups concentrate

A yellow square is a cup of lemonade concentrate and a blue square is a cup of water. Ask whether the lemonade in one of the pitchers will have the stronger lemon flavor or will they taste the same. Recipes can be adapted to include fractional values. For example, ask students to reason about which of these has a stronger lemon flavor:

$\frac{3}{4}$ cup water	$\frac{3}{2}$ cup water
$\frac{1}{8}$ cup of concentrate	$\frac{1}{4}$ cup of concentrate

Look at the between and within ratios in this second example. What do you notice? The within ratio for both recipes is $\times$ 6 (or $\div$ 6). The between ratio for both water and concentrate is $\times$ 2 or $\div$ 2. These recipes will taste the same!

⏸ Pause & Reflect

Solve the lemonade problem and write down your reasoning. Is there more than one way to justify the answer? ●

Comparing Lemonade Recipes is a high quality task because of the number of ways in which the comparison can be made. Here are a few ideas:

1. Figure out how much water goes with each cup of concentrate. As we will see later, this approach uses a unit rate: cups of water per cup of lemonade concentrate ($1\frac{1}{2}$ versus $1\frac{1}{3}$).
2. Use part-part fractions (concentrate to water) and compare the fractions ($\frac{2}{3}$ versus $\frac{3}{4}$ or the reverse)
3. Use part-whole fractions (lemonade concentrate to whole mixture) ($\frac{2}{5}$ versus $\frac{3}{7}$).
4. Converting to percentages.
5. Use multiples of one or both of the pitchers until either the amounts of water or the amounts of lemonade concentrate are equal.

The lemonade task can be differentiated to different levels of challenge or to encourage specific strategies. As given, there are no simple relationships between the two pitchers. If the solutions are 3 to 6 and 4 to 8 (equal flavors), the task is much simpler. For a 2-to-5 recipe versus a 4-to-9 recipe, it is easy to double the first and compare it to the second. When a 3-to-6 recipe is compared to a 2-to-5 recipe, the unit rates are perhaps more obvious (1 to 2 versus 1 to $2\frac{1}{2}$).

An excellent addition or alternative to mixing juice is to mix paint shades, creating a paint swatch.

FIGURE 17.10   A comparing ratios problem: Which pitcher will have the stronger lemon flavor, or will they be the same?

Activity 17.11 CCSS-M: 6.RP.A.1; 6.RP.A.3a, b; 7.RP.1; 7.RP.A.2a

Creating Paint Swatches

Ask students to write 5 different shades using two primary colors (e.g., use red and yellow and make recipes for shades of orange) or you can create a set of recipes. Ask students to order them (e.g., from the reddest to the yellowest), and try to include some that are equivalent ratios. Use real paint drops and have students test their ratios and create their own paint chart! (see Beswick, 2011, for details).

The last two activities were mixture type problems. The next activity is not a mixture but compares food portions, and it also can be approached in a variety of ways.

Activity 17.12 CCSS-M: 6.RP.A.1; 6.RP.A.3a, b; 7.RP.1; 7.RP.A.2a

Which Camp Gets More Pizza?

Pose the following story (or adapt it to be about your own students). Before solving it ask students to select the camp they think gets more pizza. Record the information for later. Ask students to use a rate or scaling strategy (reasoning strategy) to prepare a convincing argument for which camp gets more pizza.

Two camps of Scouts are having pizza parties. The leader of the Bear Camp ordered enough so that every 3 campers will have 2 pizzas. The leader of the Raccoon Camp ordered enough so that there will be 3 pizzas for every 5 campers. Did the Bear campers or the Raccoon campers have more pizza?

After students have each found their own way to decide, pair them with another student to compare strategies and see if they agree on which camp gets more pizza.

Figure 17.11 shows two different reasoning strategies. When the pizzas are sliced up into fractional parts as in Figure 17.11(a), the approach is to look for a unit rate—pizzas per camper. A partitioning approach has been used for each ratio (as in division). But notice that this problem does not say that the camps have only 3 and 5 campers, respectively. Any multiples of 2 to 3 and 3 to 5 can be used to make the appropriate comparisons. This scaling approach is illustrated in Figure 17.11(b). Three "clones" of the 2-to-3 ratio and two clones of the 3-to-5 ratio are made so that the number of campers getting a like number of pizzas can be compared. From the vantage of fractions, this is like getting common numerators. Because there are more campers in the Raccoon Camp ratio (larger denominator), there is less pizza for each camper.

As noted earlier, using real-life situations helps students better understand their world. Unit rates are everywhere, and can be explored through authentic comparisons. For example, comparing the pricing of products. Ideas include: comparing unit prices of different sized packaging of the same item (e.g., bags of potatoes, paper towels, etc.); comparing two different products (e.g., gallon of milk to gallon of water); or price per square unit of area (e.g., pizza) (Beigie, 2016; de la Cruz & Garney, 2016). Beyond pricing, students can explore the ethnicity of congressional representatives (e.g., Latinx per 100 people in the population and Latinx in the U.S. Senate)

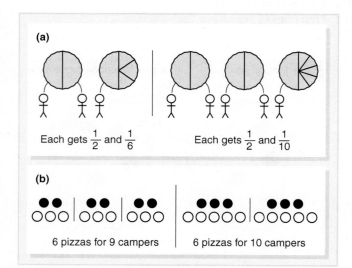

FIGURE 17.11 Rate and scaling methods for comparing pizzas per camper.

or the national debt (e.g., amount owed per person). Such real-life investigations can lead to students identifying their own topic for which they can explore, applying unit rates (Beigie, 2016).

Perhaps you have noticed that some of the problems shared in this section include all the values and ask students to compare, whereas others ask for a missing value. Some lend themselves to a unit-rate method, some to a buildup strategy, and some to other strategies. The more experiences students have in comparing and solving situations that are proportional in nature, the better they will be able to reason proportionally.

Ratio Tables

Ratio tables or charts that show how two variable quantities are related are good ways to organize information. They serve as tools for applying the buildup strategy but can be used to determine unit rate. Consider the following table:

Acres	5	10	20	60
Pine trees	75	150	300	?

In this situation, the problem posed might have asked, "How many trees for 60 acres of land?" Or it might be, "How many acres are needed for 750 pine trees?" Students can generate more columns in the table in an additive way (e.g., adding 10 to the top row and 150 to the bottom row). Or, they could look at the relationship between acres and pine trees ($\times 15$). This is the rate (15 pine trees per acre). The equation for this situation is $y = 15x$, where x is number of acres and y is the number of pine trees. Once this is discovered, students can figure out that 15×65 acres $= 975$ pine trees. But, an advantage of the ratio table is that neither variables nor equations are needed, so it is less abstract than using proportions.

Ratio tables can be used to find a specific equivalent ratio. For example, Factory Ratios Activity Page provides an interesting factory context and connects ratio tables to graphs to explore production ratios. Because different ratios are represented in the ratio table, those ratios can be compared, or a missing value found. Activity 17.13 provides examples, and Figure 17.12 gives illustrations of this use of a ratio table (ideas based on Dole, 2008, and Lamon, 2012).

MyLab Education   Activity Page: Factory Ratios

Activity 17.13   CCSS-M: 6.RP.A.3a, b; 7.RP.A.1; 7.RP.A.2b, c; 7.RP.A.3

Solving Problems Using Ratio Tables

Use the Proportional Problems Task Cards Activity Page to create task cards. The activity page includes tasks such as:

ENGLISH LEARNERS

If you run at the constant rate of $\frac{1}{2}$ mile in $\frac{1}{10}$ of an hour, how long will it take you to run a mini marathon (13 miles)?

You can give a set of cards to each pair of students, or select different cards for different groups to differentiate the activity. For each task card, ask students to (1) make a ratio table, (2) solve the problem and (3) represent the proportional relationship as an equation ($y = kx$). Note: These contexts may have language that needs reinforced with ELs. Posting visuals or translations can support their reading comprehension.

MyLab Education   Activity Page: Proportional Problems Task Cards

---

You may recognize these tasks as typical "solve the proportion" tasks. One ratio and part of a second are given, with the task being to find the fourth number. Figure 17.12 shows three different ways to use ratio tables to solve the Jupiter weight task. As this example illustrates, the ratio table has several advantages over the missing-value proportion. Students label each

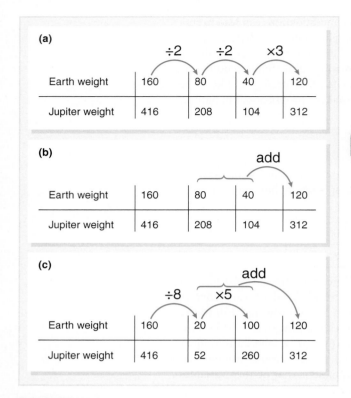

FIGURE 17.12 Something weighing 160 pounds on Earth is 416 pounds on Jupiter. If something weighs 120 pounds on Earth, how many pounds would it weigh on Jupiter? Three solutions using ratio tables.

row and are more successful at placing the values appropriately, and therefore they are able to compare. Also, a ratio table makes equivalent ratios more visible than does a missing value proportion, and illustrates that there are infinitely many equivalent ratios. Ratio tables also can be readily connected to graphs, as in the next activity (see Swanson, 2015 for details).

Activity 17.14

CCSS-M: 6.RP.A.3a, 7.RP.A.1, 7.RP.A.2b, d

Rates of Wind-Up Toys

This activity requires bringing in (or having parents donate) small wind-up toys (that travel at a constant rate). Distribute one such toy and a ruler or yardstick/meterstick to each group of students. Explain that students are going to use a ratio table and record the distance (e.g., inches or centimeters) and time for their toy, noting how far it travels in 2 seconds, 4 seconds, 6 seconds, and so on. Have students create a graph that shows the relationship (note the graph can have either time or distance on the x-axis, though it is more common to have time). Ask students to use their data to determine the unit rate for their toy. As groups are working, ask individuals to explain to you the meaning of different quantities in the ratio tables and on their graphs. Have groups prepare a poster including their toy, ratio table, graph, and unit rate. As students explore each group's findings, ask them to compare the rates of the different toys.

Tape or Strip Diagram

Tape or strip diagrams are a nice visual that helps students notice multiplicative relationships. CCSS-M defines a tape diagram as "drawings that look like a segment of tape, used to illustrate number relationships. Also known as strip diagrams, bar models or graphs, fraction strips, or length models" (NGA Center & CCSSO, 2010). Consider this statement: "The ratio of boys to girls in the class is 3 to 4." This can be set up in strips as shown here, or a similar diagram that looks more like a partitioned line segment. These can be drawn on 1-Centimeter Grid Paper, 0.5-Centimeter Grid Paper, or Dot Paper, or created by folding and cutting paper strips:

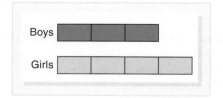

MyLab Education	Blackline Masters: 1-Centimeter Grid Paper
MyLab Education	Blackline Masters: 0.5-Centimeter Grid Paper
MyLab Education	Blackline Masters: Dot Paper

Once this basic ratio is provided, students use this sketch to solve problems. Let's look at three different ways these might be asked and sketched.

1. If there are 12 girls, how many boys? (One part is given, the other part requested)

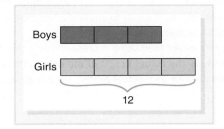

In observing the girls tape, students "see" the need to divide 12 by 4, placing 3 in each partition. Therefore, there will be 9 boys.

2. If there are 21 children, how many are boys? (The whole is given, a part is requested)

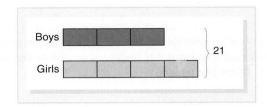

This second situation is harder for students to solve (Cohen, 2013). In particular it can be difficult for students to set up proportions to represent these situations.

3. There are 5 more girls than boys. How many girls are there? (The difference between the parts is given, a part is requested)

We can see that the five represents one-fourth of the girls, so there are 20 girls.

Notice how the tape diagram makes this situation much more accessible. The tape diagrams provide a more concrete strategy that can be done first and later connected to other strategies such as cross product.

TECHNOLOGY Note. For a nice virtual model of a tape or strip diagram, go to Math Playground and scroll down to "Thinking Blocks—Model and Solve Ratio and Proportion Word Problems." This site has instructions and practice that connects the two strips to different types of proportional situations. ■

Double Number Line Diagrams

Double number lines are similar to tape diagrams, but may not show partitions. Importantly, like with tape diagrams, labeling the two lines must be emphasized.

Standards for Mathematical Practice

MP4. Model with mathematics.

Activity 17.15

CCSS-M: 6.RP.A.3a, d; 7.RP.A.2b; 7.RP.A.3

You and the Zoo

Bring in plastic animals that are several inches long (approximate) and are in scale with each other. This activity works well with play dough but can also be done with construction paper cutouts. Explain to students that they will use double number lines to prepare a zoo scene—starting with preparing a replica of themselves!

Each pair or group of students is given a plastic animal and asked to make a representation of themselves that are in proportion to the animals. The first task is for them to determine the actual height of the animal (they may look it up online, or you may prepare this data in advance and post it), as well as their own actual height. Here is an example:

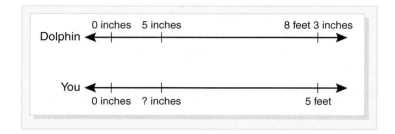

Once the "You" number line is known, students can identify other animals they would like to create for their zoo. Challenge students to select two favorite animals, or assign animals that vary in size and might not be hard to sketch or mold. Examples include: bald eagles, tree frogs, boa constrictors, pandas, tigers, and lemurs.

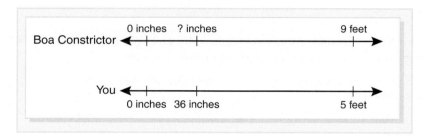

Note: Consider which measurement conversions your students need to practice; this activity can be done with metric or U.S. units.

Equations (Cross Products)

Setting up proportions (equations), and using cross products to find the missing value, is sometimes considered *the* standard algorithm for solving proportional situations. This strategy is described last in this chapter because developmentally it should be the last one taught. It is the most abstract and least intuitive, yet students are often introduced to this strategy soon after proportional reasoning is introduced or, worse, they only learn this strategy. "The central challenge of developing students' capacity to think with ratios (to reason proportionally) is to teach ideas and restrain the quick path to computation" (Smith, 2002, p. 15). When using cross products, students should understand why they work, and still be encouraged to reason in order to find the missing value, rather than just applying the cross-product algorithm. To build understanding of using proportions, connect to students understanding of equivalent ratios.

CCSS **Standards for Mathematical Practice**
MP1. Make sense of problems and persevere in solving them.

MyLab Education **Video Example 17.3**

Watch this lesson introducing proportions and the cross product strategy.

VIDEO EXAMPLE

Create a Visual Model. Rather than start with telling students to set up their proportion, ask them to illustrate the problem in a way that shows what is covarying. Figure 17.13(a) shows a simple sketch, which then leads to proportions. Figure 17.13(b) shows a sketch that reflects the context. Both examples include two equations, one that focuses on *within* ratios and one that focuses on *between* ratios. Providing visual cues to set up proportions is a very effective way to support a wide range of learners.

Solve the Proportion. Look at the situations in Figure 17.13. As students (and adults) often do naturally, you can determine the *unit rate* to solve these problems. For example, you can find the price for 1 pound of apples by dividing the $0.80 by 4 and then multiplying this result by 6 to determine the price of 6 pounds. The equation is $(0.80 \div 4) \times 6 = 1.20$. Or you can examine the *scale factor* from 4 to 6 pounds (within ratio), which is 1.5. Multiply 0.80 by the same scale factor to get $1.20. The equation is $([6 \div 4] \times .80) = 1.20$. One equation uses $0.80 in a multiplication and the other equation uses $0.80 in division. These are exactly the two devices we employed in the line segment and picture approaches: (1) *scale factor* and (2) *unit rate*. If you cross-multiply the *between* ratios, you get exactly the same result. Furthermore, you get the same result if you had written the two ratios inverted—that is, with the reciprocals of each fraction. Try it!

The cross product strategy, when understood, is useful because it is efficient when numbers are more challenging and one of the other reasoning strategies is cannot be done mentally.

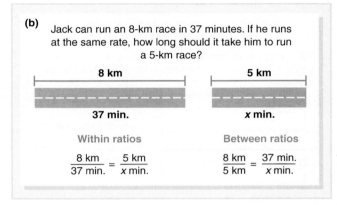

FIGURE 17.13 Drawings can help in setting up proportion equations.

FORMATIVE ASSESSMENT Notes. Because there are many ways to reason about proportional situations, it is important to capture *how* students are reasoning. Writing is an effective way to do this. You can simply ask students to explain how they solved a problem, or you can provide more structure by using specific writing prompts or sentence starters or asking students to describe two different ways they could arrive at the solution. ■

Percent Problems

Percent problems can be solved using any of the strategies in this section (e.g., a ratio table). The double number line just described above is an excellent tool for solving percent situations. It is particularly helpful in helping students to figure out which part is unknown. Once the double number line is created, students can use this diagram to set up as a proportion. The values of one number line correspond to the numbers or measures in the problem. On the second number line, the values indicate the corresponding values in terms of percents (with a whole of 100).

Activity 17.16   CCSS-M: 6.RP.3c; 7.RP.A.2c; 7.RP.A.3

Making Sense of Percent Stories

This activity can be done with any set of traditional missing value percent problems. You can post a story or create a set of cards, each with its own problem on it. Three such stories are provided in Figure 17.14, along with how they can be illustrated on a double number line. In order to make the activity interactive and to connect representations, follow these steps: (1) hand out different problems to each group; (2) have each group set up their double number line on a note card (don't solve it); (3) trade the double number line sketch with another pair of students; (4) write a proportion that matches the double number line and solve it; (5) return the cards to the original pair to check to see if the answer makes sense.

In 1960, U.S. railroads carried 327 million passengers. Over the next 20 years, there was a 14 percent decrease in passengers. How many passengers rode the railroads in 1980?

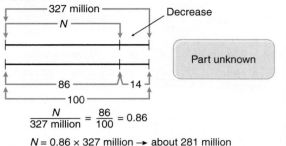

Part unknown

$$\frac{N}{327 \text{ million}} = \frac{86}{100} = 0.86$$

$N = 0.86 \times 327$ million → about 281 million

Sylvia's new boat cost \$8950. She made a down payment of \$2000. What percent of the sales price was Sylvia's down payment?

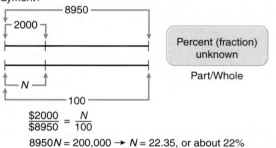

Percent (fraction) unknown

Part/Whole

$$\frac{\$2000}{\$8950} = \frac{N}{100}$$

$8950N = 200,000$ → $N = 22.35$, or about 22%

The seventh- and eighth-grade classes at Robious Middle School had a contest to see which class would sell more raffle tickets at the school festival. The eighth grade sold 592 tickets. However, this turned out to be only 62.5 percent of the number of tickets sold by the seventh grade. How many tickets did the seventh grade sell?

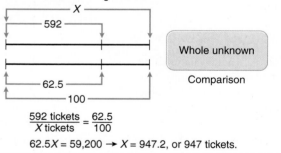

Whole unknown

Comparison

$$\frac{592 \text{ tickets}}{X \text{ tickets}} = \frac{62.5}{100}$$

$62.5X = 59,200$ → $X = 947.2$, or 947 tickets.

FIGURE 17.14 Percentage problems represented as double number lines and equations.

CCSS Standards for Mathematical Practice

MP2. Reason abstractly and quantitatively.

Notice how flexible this double number line representation is for different types of percent problems. It allows modeling of not only part-to-whole scenarios but also increase–decrease situations and those in which there is a comparison between two distinct quantities. Another advantage of a linear model is that it does not restrict students from thinking about percents greater than 100 since the line can represent percents over 100 percent (Parker, 2004).

> **MyLab Education**   **Self-Check 17.3**

Teaching Proportional Reasoning

Hopefully one take away you have from this chapter is that proportional reasoning (and multiplicative reasoning) is one of the biggest ideas in mathematics; it must be well understood for myriad of real life situations, as well as being foundational for further mathematics. Proportional reasoning can be challenging. This chapter has focused on these challenges, and they are summarized briefly in Table 17.2.

Considerable research has been conducted to determine how students reason in various proportionality tasks and to determine whether developmental or instructional factors are related to proportional reasoning (for example, see Bright et al., 2003; Lamon, 2007, 2012; Lobato et al., 2010; Siegler et al., 2010). The findings related to effective teaching of ratios and proportions are shared here as a way to summarize the chapter.

1. Use composed unit and multiplicative comparison ideas in building understanding of ratio. Learning more about multiplicative comparisons should lead to an understanding of rate, which is a strategy to be applied to proportions.
2. Help students distinguish constant, additive, and multiplicative comparisons by providing examples of each and discussing the differences.
3. Provide ratio and proportion tasks in a wide range of contexts, including situations involving measurements, prices, geometric, and other visual contexts, and rates of all sorts.
4. Engage students in a variety of strategies for solving proportions, sequencing the instruction from most intuitive to more abstract. In particular, use ratio tables, visuals (e.g., tape diagrams and double number lines), and equations to solve problems—always expecting students to apply reasoning strategies and understand the strategy they are using.
5. Recognize that the cross-product algorithm, while important to understand and use, is not the goal for teaching proportions—the goal is that students are able to recognize proportional situations and to solve them efficiently (i.e., using any of the strategies described in this chapter).

MyLab Education   Self-Check 17.4

MyLab Education   **Math Practice:** Need to practice or refresh your math content knowledge? Click to access practice exercises associated with the content from this chapter.

TABLE 17.2   COMMON CHALLENGES AND MISCONCEPTIONS RELATED TO RATIOS AND PROPORTIONS

Common Challenge or Misconception	What It Looks Like	How to Help
1. Use additive reasoning when the situation requires multiplicative reasoning.	Student thinks that because a giant's pencil is 15 inches longer than the giant is 15 inches taller than a normal person (see Activity 17.4).	• See the discussion and tasks in Types of Comparing Situations section. • Use Activities 17.3 and 17.4.
2. Use phrases that imply confusion between additive and multiplicative reasoning (Rathouz, Cengiz, Krebs, & Rubenstein, 2014).	Student says "is four times *more than*" rather than "is four times *as long as*" for a multiplicative comparison.	• Compare the two statements and their meanings. • Use precise language. • Use revoicing to help students use the correct language.
3. Experience difficulty determining how to graph ratios (Kastberg, D'Ambrosio, Lynch-Davis, Mintos, & Krawczyk, 2014).	Students cannot decide which axes to use for the two measures; students have difficulty interpreting a completed graph.	• Discuss that with ratios, the choice of which variable is on the *x*-axis and which variable goes on the *y*-axis is arbitrary. • Compare graphs that are done both ways. • Point at values and ask what they mean related to the context.

 **RESOURCES** FOR CHAPTER 17

LITERATURE CONNECTIONS

Literature brings an exciting dimension to the exploration of proportional reasoning. Many books and stories discuss comparative sizes, concepts of scale as in maps, giants and miniature people who are proportional to regular people, comparative rates (especially rates of speed), and so on. We have listed some excellent options in Table 17.1 (See p. 443).

RECOMMENDED READINGS

Articles

Ercole, L. K., Frantz, M., & Ashline, G. (2011). Multiple ways to solve proportions. *Mathematics Teaching in the Middle School, 16*(8), 482–490.

This article shares the many ways of reasoning to solve proportions: unit rate, factor of change, building up, ratio tables, and cross-multiplication. Student work is shared throughout.

Rathouz, M., Cengiz, N., Krebs, A., & Rubenstein, R. N. (2014). Tasks to develop language for ratio relationships.

Mathematics Teaching in the Middle School, 20(1), 38–44.

These authors describe how to help students use appropriate language in multiplicative reasoning as they solve a well-designed progression of a high quality tasks, using a variety of reasoning strategies.

Books

Lobato, J., Ellis, A. B., Charles, R. I., & Zbiek, R. M. (2010). *Developing essential understanding of ratios, proportions, and proportional reasoning: Grades 6–8.* Reston, VA: NCTM.

If you want to really understand the important nuances of ratios and proportions, this is a phenomenal resource. Ten essential understandings are explained, along with excellent activities for students and teaching suggestions.

Olson, T. A., Olson, M., & Slovin, H. (2015). *Putting essential understanding of ratios and proportions into practice in grades 6–8.* Reston, VA: NCTM.

An excellent sequel to the book above, this book provides a wealth of tasks, instruction and assessment strategies that will support students developing deep understanding of this topic.

CHAPTER 18

Developing Measurement Concepts

LEARNER OUTCOMES

After reading this chapter and engaging in the embedded activities and reflections, you should be able to:

18.1 Describe the measurement process, including the identification and use of nonstandard and standard units, and demonstrate how to estimate measurements.

18.2 Demonstrate how to measure the length of objects.

18.3 Explain the development of area formulas.

18.4 Explain how volume is measured.

18.5 Demonstrate strategies for comparing weights of objects.

18.6 Explain how angles are measured.

18.7 Describe the best model for teaching elapsed time.

18.8 Explain strategies for counting a collection of coins.

Measurement is the process of describing a continuous quantity with a numerical value. It is one of the most useful mathematics content strands, as it is a component in everything from occupational tasks to life skills for the mathematically literate citizen. From gigabytes that measure amounts of information to font size on computers, to miles per gallon, to recipes for a meal, people are surrounded with measurement concepts that apply to many real-world contexts. However, measurement isn't an easy topic for students to understand. Data from international studies consistently indicate that U.S. students are weaker in measurement than any other topic in the mathematics curriculum (Mullis et al., 2004; Provasnik et al., 2009; Thompson & Preston, 2004).

In the *Common Core State Standards*, the measurement domain appears in every grade from K–8, so the listing of the trajectory of ideas is massive. Instead of an overview in the chapter introduction, for each of the sections (e.g., length, area, volume, etc.) the CCSS grade level expectations will be described.

BIG IDEAS

♦ Measurement involves comparing an attribute of an item or situation with a unit that has the same attribute. Lengths are compared to units of length, areas to units of area, time to units of time, and so on.

- Estimation of measures and the development of benchmarks or referents for frequently used units of measure help students increase their familiarity with units, preventing errors and aiding in the meaningful use of measurement.

- Measurement instruments (e.g., rulers, protractors) group multiple units so that you do not have to iterate a single unit multiple times.

- Area and volume formulas provide a method of measuring these attributes by using only measures of length.

- Area, perimeter, and volume are related. For example, as the shapes of regions or three-dimensional objects change while maintaining the same areas or volumes, there is an effect on the perimeters or surface areas.

The Meaning and Process of Measuring

Suppose you asked your students to measure a bucket as in Figure 18.1. The first thing they would need to know is *what* about the bucket is to be measured. They might measure the height, depth, diameter, or circumference. All of these are length measures. The surface area of the outside of the bucket could be determined. A bucket also has volume (or capacity) and weight. Each aspect that can be measured is an *attribute* of the bucket.

Once students determine the attribute to be measured, they then choose a unit that has that attribute. Length is measured with units that have length, volume with units that have volume, and so on.

MyLab Education
Video Example 18.1

Watch this video of Zach Champagne as he discusses the importance of identifying measurable attributes.

Technically, a *measurement* is a number that indicates a comparison between the attribute of the object (or situation, or event) being measured and the same attribute of a given unit of measure. For example, to measure a length, the comparison can be done by lining up copies of the unit directly against the length being measured. For most attributes measured in schools, we can say that *to measure* means that the attribute being measured is "filled" or "covered" or "matched" with a unit of measure with the same attribute.

In summary, to measure something, one must perform three steps:

1. Decide on the attribute to be measured.
2. Select a unit that has that attribute.
3. Compare the units—by filling, covering, matching, or using some other method—with the attribute of the object being measured. The number of units required to match the object is the measure.

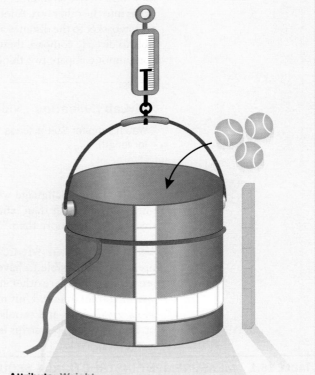

Attribute: Weight
  Units: objects that <u>stretch</u> the spring in the scale
  How many units will pull the spring as far as the bucket will?

Attribute: Volume/Capacity
  Units: cubes, balls, cups of water
  How many units will <u>fill</u> the bucket?

Attribute: Length
  Units: rods, toothpicks, straws, string
  How many units are <u>as tall as</u> the bucket?
  How much string is needed to <u>go around</u> the bucket?

Attribute: Area
  Units: index cards, squares of paper, tiles
  How many cards will <u>cover</u> the surface of the bucket?

FIGURE 18.1 Measuring different attributes of a bucket.

Measuring instruments, such as ruler, scales, and protractors are tools that make the filling, covering and matching process easier. For example, a ruler lines up the units of length and numbers them, and a protractor lines up the unit angles and numbers them.

Concepts and Skills

If students attempt to measure the length of their classroom by laying 1-meter long strips end to end, the strips sometimes overlap and the line can weave in a snakelike fashion. Do they understand the concept of length as an attribute of the classroom? Do they understand that each 1-meter strip has the attribute of length? They may understand that they are counting a line of strips stretching from wall to wall but they may not know that they are comparing the same attribute of the measuring unit (meter strip) to the object being measured (length of the classroom). The skill of measuring with a unit must be explicitly linked to the concept of measuring as a process of comparing attributes, as outlined in Table 18.1.

Making Comparisons. Sometimes with a measure such as length, a direct comparison can be made where one object can be lined up and matched to another. But often an indirect method using a third object must be used. For example, if students compare the volume of one box to another, they must devise an indirect way to compare. They may fill one box with beans and then pour the beans into the other box. Another example using length would use a string to compare the height of a wastebasket to the distance around the top. The string is the intermediary referent, as it is impossible to directly compare these two lengths. This use of a third object to make a comparison when you cannot compare two things directly is called the *transitivity principle for indirect measurement.*

MyLab Education   **Video Example 18.2**

Watch Jennifer Suh discuss transitivity using indirect measurement for length.

Use precise language when helping students make comparisons. Avoid using ambiguous phrases like "bigger than" and "smaller than"; instead use more precise language such as "longer than" or "holds more than."

Using Physical Models of Measuring Units. For most attributes measured in preK–8, it is possible to have physical models of the units of measure. Time and temperature are exceptions (as are other attributes not commonly measured in schools such as light intensity, speed, and loudness). Unit models can be found for both nonstandard (sometimes referred to as *informal*) units and standard units. For length, for example, drinking straws (nonstandard) or 1-foot-long paper strips (standard) might be used as units.

TABLE 18.1   MEASUREMENT INSTRUCTION: A SEQUENCE OF EXPERIENCES

Step	Goal	Type of Activity	Notes
1. Make comparisons	Students will understand the *attribute* to be measured.	Make comparisons based on the attribute (for example, longer/shorter, heavier/lighter). Use direct comparisons whenever possible.	When the attribute is understood, there is no further need for comparison activities.
2. Use models of measuring units	Students will understand how filling, covering, matching, or making other comparisons of an attribute with measuring units produces a number called a *measure.*	Use physical models of measuring units to fill, cover, match, or make the desired comparison of the attribute with the unit.	Begin with nonstandard units, then progress to the use of standard units. Measuring tools and formulas follow.
3. Use measuring tools	Students will use common measuring tools with understanding and flexibility.	Make measuring tools (grouped units) and compare them with the individual unit models to see how the measurement tool performs the same function.	Without a careful comparison of the nonstandard (or informal) tools with the standard tools, the connection can be lost.

To help make the notion of the unit explicit, use as many copies of the unit as are needed to fill or match the attribute measured (this action is called *tiling* and it involves equal partitioning). Giant footprints (nonstandard) could be used to measure the length of the hallway by placing multiple copies of the footprint end to end. To measure the area of the desktop with an index card (nonstandard) as your unit, you can literally tile (cover) the entire desk with index cards. Somewhat more difficult is to use a single copy of the unit (this action is called *iteration*). You may recall that counting same-size fractional parts is also iteration. That means measuring the same desktop with a single index card by repeatedly moving the card from position to position and keeping track of which areas the card has covered. Not only is this approach more difficult it can obscure the meaning of the measurement—how many units will cover the desk.

FIGURE 18.2   "How long is this crayon?"

It is useful to measure the same object with units of different size to help students understand that the unit used is important (an expectation for second graders in the CCSS-M). For each different-sized unit, estimate the measure in advance and discuss the estimate afterward. Students also must start to observe that smaller units produce larger numeric measures, and vice versa. This concept is related to converting units and it is hard for some students to understand. Students mentally construct this inverse relationship by estimating, then experimenting, and finally reflecting on the measurements.

CCSS CCSS Standards for Mathematical Practice
MP2. Reason abstractly and quantitatively.

Using Measuring Instruments. On the 2003 NAEP exam (Blume, Galindo, & Walcott, 2007), only 20 percent of fourth graders and only 56 percent of eighth graders could give the correct measure of an object not aligned with the end of a ruler, as in Figure 18.2 (Kloosterman, Rutledge, & Kenney, 2009). Students on the same exam also experienced difficulty when the increments on a measuring device were not one unit. These results point to the difference between using a measuring device and understanding how it works.

When students use unit models with which they are familiar to construct simple measuring instruments, they are more likely to understand how a tool measures. A ruler is a good example. If students line up individual physical units along a strip of card stock and mark them off, they can see that it is the *spaces* on rulers and not the tick marks or numbers that are important. It is essential that students discuss how measurement with iterating individual units compares with measurement using an instrument. Without this comparison and discussion, students may not understand that these two methods are essentially the same.

Introducing Nonstandard Units

A common approach in primary grades is to begin measurement with nonstandard units. Unfortunately, measurement activities in the upper grades, where other attributes are measured, often do not begin with this important first step. The use of nonstandard units for beginning measurement activities is beneficial at all grade levels because they:

- *Focus on the attribute being measured.* For example, when discussing how to measure the area of an irregular shape, units such as square tiles or circular counters may be suggested. Each unit covers area, and each will give a different result. The discussion can focus on what it means to measure area.
- *Avoid conflicting objectives in introductory lessons.* Is your lesson about what it means to measure area or about understanding square centimeters?
- *Provide a good rationale for using standard units.* The need for a standard unit has more meaning when your students have measured the same objects with their own collections of nonstandard units and arrived at different and sometimes confusing answers.

MyLab Education   Video Example 18.3

Watch this video of a class using nonstandard units to measure a footprint. How does the teacher link those units to standard units?

VIDEO EXAMPLE

The amount of time that should be spent using nonstandard units varies with students' age and level of understanding and with the attributes being measured. Some students need many experiences with a variety of nonstandard units of length, weight, and capacity. Conversely, fourth graders may only need to work with nonstandard units for a day or two when they learn to measure angles. When nonstandard units have served their purpose, move on.

Introducing Standard Units

Measurement sense demands that students be familiar with standard measurement units, able to make estimates in terms of these units (i.e., mentally dividing a total length into units and then count those units), and able to meaningfully interpret measures given in standard units. Perhaps the biggest challenge in teaching measurement is the difficulty in recognizing and separating two objectives: (1) understanding the meaning and technique of measuring a particular attribute, and (2) learning about the standard units commonly used to measure that attribute.

Teaching standard units of measure can be organized around three broad goals:

1. *Familiarity with the unit.* Students should have a basic idea of the size of commonly used units and what they measure. Knowing approximately how much 1 liter of water is or being able to estimate a shelf as 5 feet long is as important as measuring either accurately.
2. *Ability to select an appropriate unit.* Students should know both what is a reasonable measurement unit in a given situation and the level of precision required. Would you measure your lawn to purchase grass seed with the same precision as you would use in measuring a window to buy a pane of glass? Students need practice in selecting appropriate standard units and judging the level of precision.
3. *Knowledge of relationships between units.* Students should know the relationships that are commonly used, such as those between inches, feet, and yards or milliliters and liters.

Developing Unit Familiarity

Two types of activities can develop familiarity with standard units: (1) comparisons that focus on a single unit and (2) activities that develop personal referents or benchmarks for single units or easy multiples of units.

Activity 18.1

CCSS-M: 1.MD.A.2; 2.MD.A.1; 2.MD.A.3

About One Unit

Give students a physical model of a standard unit and have them search for objects that have about the same measure as that one unit. For example, give students a piece of rope 1-meter long and challenge them to find objects in the classroom, on the playground, around the school, or at home that are about 1 meter in length (see About a Meter Activity Page). Have them make lists of things that are about the same as, things that are a little shorter (or a little longer), or things that are twice as long (or half as long) as one meter. Be sure to include curved or circular lengths. Later, students can try to predict whether a given object is longer, shorter, or close to 1 meter.

MyLab Education Activity Page: About a Meter

MyLab Education Video Example 18.4

Watch this video (http://www.youtube.com/watch?v=6iK5b2uA2Ac) of a class estimating while using a trundle wheel to measure the length of the school hallway.

VIDEO EXAMPLE

Send home a newsletter that suggests families check distances around the neighborhood, to the school or shopping center, or along other frequently traveled paths. If possible, send home (or use in class) a 1-meter or 1-yard trundle wheel to measure distances. For other interesting looks at measuring places, go online to Google Earth's Measuring Tools, where students can measure distances in centimeters, inches, feet, yards, kilometers, and miles. The same activity can be done with other unit lengths. Families can also be enlisted to help students find local distances that are about 1 mile or about 1 kilometer.

Activity 18.2

CCSS-M: 1.MD.A.2; 2.MD.A.1; 3.MD.B.4

Familiar Measures

ENGLISH LEARNERS

Read *Measuring Penny* (Leedy, 2000) to get students interested in the variety of ways familiar items can be measured. In this book, the author bridges between nonstandard units (e.g., dog biscuits, swabs, etc.) and standard units (inches, centimeters, etc.) to measure Penny, the pet dog. Have students use this idea to find something at home (or in class) to measure in as many ways as they can think of using standard units. For a challenge or depending on the grade level, measures can be rounded to whole numbers or can include fractional units. Discuss in class the familiar items chosen and their measures so that different ideas and benchmarks are shared.

Of special interest for length are benchmarks found on our bodies. These become quite familiar over time and can be used in many situations as approximate rulers.

Activity 18.3

CCSS-M: 2.MD.A.1; 3.MD.B.4; 4.MD.B.4

Personal Benchmarks

Measure your body. About how long are your foot, your stride, your hand span (stretched or with fingers together), the width of your finger, your arm span (finger to finger and finger to nose)? Data can be graphed in a line plot. (There are wonderful proportional relationships to be found between these measures too!) Compare the distance around your neck and around your waist. Compare your height to the height of your head. Some may prove to be useful benchmarks for standard units, and some may be excellent models for single or multiples of standard units. (The average child's fingernail width is about 1 cm, and most people can find a 10-cm length somewhere on their hands.)

Choosing Appropriate Units. Should the room be measured in feet or inches? Should the concrete blocks be weighed in grams or kilograms? The answers to questions such as these involve more than simply knowing how big units are, although that is certainly required. Another consideration involves the need for precision. If you were measuring your wall in order to cut a piece of molding to fit, you would need to measure it very precisely. The smallest unit would be an inch or a centimeter, and you would also use small fractional parts. But if you were determining how many 8-foot molding strips to buy, the nearest foot would probably be sufficient.

CCSS Standards for Mathematical Practice
MP6. Attend to precision.

Activity 18.4

CCSS-M: 3.MD.A.2; 3.MD.C.5; 4.MD.A.1; 5.MD.C.3

Guess the Unit

STUDENTS with SPECIAL NEEDS

Find examples of a variety of measurements in the news, on signs, online, or in other everyday situations. Present the context and measures, but without units. For example, you may consider ads for carpeting, articles about gas prices, and so forth. You can also use the Measurement Cards. The task is to predict what units of measure were used. Have students discuss their choices. For students with disabilities, you may want to provide possible units so they can sort the real-world measures into groups (i.e., area, capacity, weight, time, length). For ELs having a list of measurement names with illustrations will support their participation.

MyLab Education Activity Page: Measurement Cards

ENGLISH LEARNERS

Measurement Systems and Units

The United States is one of three nations (Myanmar and Liberia) that have not adopted the International System of Units (SI) a synonym for the Metric System. Because of its international importance, U.S. students must know SI (metric system) for such things as product design, manufacturing, marketing, and labeling in order to participate in the global marketplace (as a consumer or an employee) (National Institute of Standards and Technology [NIST], 2015; NCTM, 2015). Yet, results of the 2004 NAEP revealed that only 37 percent of eighth-grade students knew how many milliliters were in a liter (Perie, Moran, & Lutkus, 2005). Customary units continue to be important in the United States for various careers (e.g., carpentry) and contexts, so students need to develop familiarity with multiple systems of measure (NCTM, 2015). Interestingly, U.S. students do better with metric units than with customary units (Preston & Thompson, 2004). Familiarity with the units in both systems helps students consider reasonableness of their measurements. Having everyday objects as points of reference can help: A doorway is a bit more than 2 m high, and a doorknob is about 1 m from the floor. A paper clip weighs about a gram and is about 1 cm wide. A pineapple or liter of water weigh about 1 kilogram.

The relationships between standard units within either the metric or customary systems are conventions. As such, students must simply be told what the relationships are, and instructional experiences must be devised to reinforce them. However, in the intermediate grades, knowing basic relationships between the standard units becomes more important in making conversions between units in the same system (customary or metric).

 ## The Role of Estimation and Approximation

Measurement estimation is the process of using mental and visual information to measure or make comparisons without using measuring tools. People use this practical skill almost every day. Do I have enough sugar to make cookies? Can you throw the ball 15 meters? Is this suitcase over the weight or size limit? Will my car fit into that parking space? Here are several reasons for including estimation in measurement activities:

- *Helps students focus on the attribute being measured and the measuring process.* Think how you would estimate the area of the cover of this book using playing cards as the unit. To do so, you have to think about what area is and how the units might be placed on the book cover.
- *Provides an intrinsic motivation for measurement activities.* It is interesting to see how close you can come in your estimate to the actual measure.
- *Develops familiarity with standard units.* If you estimate the height of the door in meters before measuring, you must think about the size of a meter.
- *Promotes multiplicative reasoning through using a benchmark.* The width of the building is about one-fourth of the length of a football field—perhaps 25 yards.

In all measuring activities, emphasize the use of approximate language as measurements are not exact. The desk is *about* 15 orange rods long. The front of the math book is covered by *a little less than* 8 index cards. Approximate language is very useful for students because many measurements do not result in whole numbers. As they become more sophisticated, students will search for smaller units or use fractional units to measure with for more precision, which is an opportunity to develop the idea that all measurements include some error. Acknowledge that each smaller unit or subdivision produces a greater degree of *precision*. For example, a length measure can never be more than one-half unit in error.

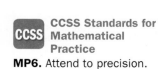

For example, suppose you are measuring a length of ribbon with a ruler that only shows quarter inches—so the unit is a quarter of an inch. If the length of ribbon falls between $3\frac{3}{4}$ and 4 inches, we would usually round to whichever number is closer. If the ribbon is more than halfway towards the 4-inch mark, we would say it's 4 inches long. However, if the ribbon is less than halfway from $3\frac{3}{4}$, we say it is closer to $3\frac{3}{4}$-inches long. In either case, we are within $\frac{1}{8}$ of an inch or one-half of the unit and are essentially ignoring the difference which constitutes our "error." If we need more precision, we use smaller units to ensure that our measurement rounding or error is within an acceptable range.

Because mathematically there is no "smallest unit," there is always some error so avoid saying a measurement is "exact." The Standards for Mathematical Practice (NGA Center & CCSSO, 2010) include, "Attend to precision" which means they expect students to be "careful about specifying units of measure" and to "express numerical answers with a degree of precision appropriate for the problem context" (p. 7).

Strategies for Estimating Measurements

Begin measurement activities with students making an estimate. Just as for computational estimation, students need specific strategies to estimate measures. Here are four strategies:

1. *Develop benchmarks or referents.* Students who have acquired mental benchmarks or reference points for measurements (for single units and also for useful multiples of standard units) *and* practice using them in class activities are much better estimators than students who have not learned to use benchmarks (Joram & Gabriele, 2016). Students must pay attention to the size of the unit to estimate well (Towers & Hunter, 2010). Referents should be things that students can easily visualize. One example is the height of a child (see Figure 18.3).

2. *Use "chunking."* Chunking involves subdividing a measurement into components to better estimate the amount. Figure 18.3 shows an example of chunking using windows, bulletin boards, and spaces between as chunks making the estimation easier. The weight of a stack of books is easier to estimate if some referent is given for the weight of an "average" book. But, if the wall length to be estimated has no useful chunks, it can be mentally subdivided in half and then in fourths or even eighths by repeated subdivisions until a manageable length is found. Length, volume, area, and surface area measurements all lend themselves to the estimation strategy of chunking.

3. *Iterate units.* For length, area, and volume, it is sometimes easy to mark off single units mentally (visualizing) or physically. You might use your hands or make marks to keep track as you go. If you know, for example, that your stride is about $\frac{3}{4}$ meter, you can walk off a length and then multiply to get an estimate. Hand and finger widths are also useful.

CCSS **CCSS Standards for Mathematical Practice**
MP7. Look for and make sense of structure.

The best approach to improving estimation skills is to have students do a lot of estimating. Keep the following tips in mind:

1. *Explicitly teach each strategy.* After learning and practicing each strategy, students can choose from the options the one that works best in a particular situation.

2. *Discuss how different students made their estimates.* These conversations will confirm that there is no single right way to estimate while reminding students of other useful approaches.

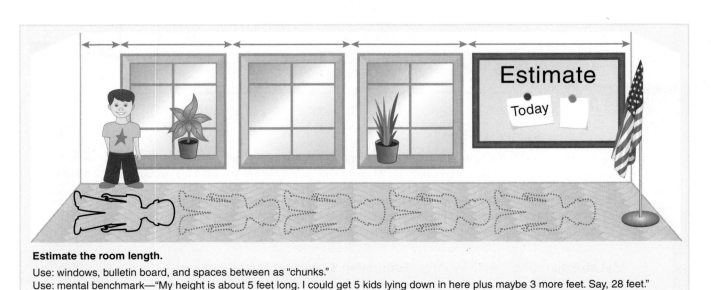

Estimate the room length.

Use: windows, bulletin board, and spaces between as "chunks."

Use: mental benchmark—"My height is about 5 feet long. I could get 5 kids lying down in here plus maybe 3 more feet. Say, 28 feet."

FIGURE 18.3   Estimating measures using benchmarks and chunking.

3. *Create a list of benchmarks.* Record and post on a class chart suggested benchmarks for common measures.

4. *Accept a range of estimates.* Think in relative terms about what is a good estimate. Within 10 percent for length is reasonable. Even 30 percent "off" may be reasonable for weights or volumes.

5. *Do not promote a "winning" estimate.* This emphasis on a contest discourages estimation and promotes only seeking the "exact" answer.

6. *Encourage students to give a range of estimates that they believe includes the actual measure.* For example, the door is between 7 and 8 feet tall. This focus on reasonable minimum and maximum values, not only is a practical real-life approach but also helps focus on the approximate nature of estimation.

7. *Make measurement estimation an ongoing activity.* Post a daily/weekly measurement to be estimated. Students can record their estimates and discuss them for five-minutes. Invite a student or a team of student to select measurements to estimate.

8. *Be precise with your language.* Do not use the word *measure* interchangeably with the word *estimate* (Towers & Hunter, 2010). Randomly substituting one word for the other will cause uncertainty and possibly confusion in students.

Measurement Estimation Activities

Any measurement activity can have an "estimate first" component. For more emphasis on the process of estimation itself, simply think of measures that can be estimated, and have students estimate. Here are two suggestions.

Activity 18.5

CCSS-M: K.MD.A.1; K.MD.A.2; 1.MD.A.1; 1.MD.A.2; 2.MD.A.3; 3.MD.A.2; 5.MD.C.4; 6.G.A.1; 6.G.A.2; 7.G.B.4; 8.G.C.9

ENGLISH LEARNERS

Estimation Exploration

Select a single object such as a box, a pumpkin, a painting on the wall of the school, or even the principal. Each day, select a different attribute or dimension to estimate. For a pumpkin, for example, students can estimate its height, circumference, weight, volume, and surface area. If you have ELs, then be sure to include metric measures or help students connect the centimeter to the inch.

MyLab Education   Video Example 18.5

Watch this video (https://youtu.be/hzsyMQ_aDFM) of a farmer demonstrating three different ways to measure a pumpkin, including circumference, to determine approximate weight.

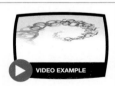

VIDEO EXAMPLE

Activity 18.6

CCSS-M: 1.MD.A.2; 2.MD.A.1; 2.MD.A.3; 4.MD.A.1

Estimation Scavenger Hunt

Conduct estimation scavenger hunts by giving teams a list of either nonstandard or standard measurements, and having them find things that are close to those measurements. At first, do not permit the use of measuring instruments. Look at the Estimation Scavenger Hunt Activity Page for possible ideas and add your own. Let students suggest how to judge results in terms of accuracy. Students with special needs may benefit from having a reference, for example, an example of 1 square inch or example of 1 milliliter. ELs are likely to have a stronger metric measurement sense, and native U.S. students of customary measures so group heterogeneously to build on the strengths of both.

STUDENTS with SPECIAL NEEDS

ENGLISH LEARNERS

MyLab Education   Activity Page: Estimation Scavenger Hunt

FORMATIVE ASSESSMENT Notes. Use an Observation Checklist to take notes about students' estimates and measures of a variety of real objects using, weight, area, volume, length and so on. Prompt students to explain how they arrived at their estimates. Asking only for a numeric estimate can mask a lack of understanding and will not give you the information you need to provide next instructional steps. ■

| MyLab Education | Blackline Master: Observation Checklist |
| MyLab Education | Self-Check 18.1 |

Length

Length is usually the first attribute students learn to measure. Length is an attribute of an object that is found by locating two endpoints and examining how far it is between those points. We measure lengths by selecting a unit (that has length) and repeatedly matching that unit to the object. Understanding length is a gateway to understanding perimeter, area and volume (Sisman & Aksu, 2016).

Comparison Activities

At the preK and kindergarten level, students begin with direct comparisons of two or more lengths and then move to indirect comparisons by the first grade (NGA Center & CCSSO, 2010; NCTM, 2006). Seek opportunities for students to compare lengths directly, as in the next two activities.

Activity 18.7 CCSS-M: K.MD.A.2; 1.MD.A.1; 2.MD.A.3

Longer, Shorter, Same

Create learning stations where students can explore which objects in a group are longer, shorter, or about the same as a specified "target" object. Change the target object and students will find the shorter item is now longer than the target. A similar task can involve putting a set of objects in order from shortest to longest.

Activity 18.8 CCSS-M: K.MD.A.2; 1.MD.A.1; 1.MD.A.2; 2.MD.A.3

Length (or Unit) Hunt

Give pairs of students a strip of card stock, a popsicle stick, a length of rope, or some other object with an obvious length dimension that will serve as a "target" unit. The task is for students to find five things in the room that are shorter than, longer than, or about the same length as their target unit. They can record what they find in pictures or words. Allow students with disabilities to have a copy of the "target" unit to make actual comparisons. By making the target length a standard unit (e.g., a meter stick or a 1-meter length of rope), the activity can be repeated to provide familiarity with important standard units.

STUDENTS with SPECIAL NEEDS

Also compare lengths that are not in straight lines. One way is to use indirect comparisons, which means using another object to make the measure, as in the next activity.

Activity 18.9

CCSS-M: 1.MD.A.1; 2.MD.A.3; 2.MD.A.4

Crooked Paths

Make some crooked or curvy paths on the floor (or outside) with masking tape or chalk. Ask students to determine which path is longest, next longest, and so on. (Some students may think about the straight line distance ("as the crow flies") from the beginning of the curved path to its end (Battista, 2012). Students should suggest ways to measure the crooked paths so that they can be compared. For a hint, provide pairs of students with a long piece of string (at first make it longer than the path). For students with disabilities, you may need to tape the end of the string to the beginning of the path and help them mark the final measurement on the string with a marker. Use another string for the other path in the same way. Then compare the string lengths. Students who argue that the straight path "looks longer" than the more compact crooked path may need to explore an example of these two paths on the floor by walking on each to see which takes longer to walk. See Expanded Lesson: Crooked Paths for an enhanced version of this activity.

MyLab Education   **Expanded Lesson: Crooked Paths**

Using Physical Models of Length Units

There are four important principles of iterating units of length, whether they are nonstandard or standard (Dietiker, Gonulates, Figueras, & Smith, 2010). Units must be:

- Equal in length or you cannot iterate them by counting.
- Aligned with the length being measured or a different quantity is measured.
- Placed without gaps or a part of the length is not measured.
- Placed without overlaps or the length has portions that are measured more than one time.

Students can begin to measure length using a variety of nonstandard units, including these:

- *Giant footprints:* Cut out about 20 copies of a large footprint about $1\frac{1}{2}$- to 2-feet long from poster board.
- *Measuring ropes:* Cut rope into 1-meter lengths. These ropes can measure the perimeter and the circumference of objects such as the teacher's desk, a tree trunk, or a pumpkin.
- *Drinking straws:* Straws can easily be cut into smaller units and can be linked together with a long string. The string of straws can be a bridge to a ruler or measuring tape.
- *Short units:* Connecting cubes, toothpicks, and paper clips are useful nonstandard units for measuring shorter lengths. Cuisenaire rods are also useful, as they are easy to place end to end and are also metric (centimeters).

The following activity encourages students to develop their own approach to measuring lengths.

Activity 18.10

CCSS-M: 1.MD.A.2; 2.MD.A.1; 2.MD.A.2; 2.MD.A.3

How Long Is the Teacher?

Explain that you have received an important request from the principal. She needs to know exactly how tall each teacher in the building is. The students are to decide how to measure the teachers and write a note to the principal explaining how tall their teacher is and detailing the process that they used. If you wish to give hints, ask, "Would it help if I lie down?" and have students make marks at your feet and head and draw a straight line between these marks.

Put students in pairs and allow them to select one nonstandard or standard unit with which to measure. For each option, supply enough units to more than cover the length. Ask students to estimate first and then use their unit to measure.

After students measure, follow up with "How did you get your measurement?" "Did students who measured with the same unit get the same answers? If not, why not?" "How could the principal make a line that was as long as the teacher?" Focus on the value of carefully lining units up end to end. Discuss what happens if you overlap units, have a gap in the units, or don't follow in a straight line. For a challenge, have students measure twice with two different units.

The following activity adds an estimation component.

Activity 18.11
CCSS-M: 1.MD.A.2; 2.MD.A.1; 2.MD.A.3

Estimate and Measure

Make lists of items in the room to measure (see Figure 18.4) or use the Estimating and Measuring with Nonstandard Units Recording Sheet. Run a piece of masking tape along the dimension of objects to be measured. Include curves or other distances that are not straight lines. Have students estimate before they measure. Students with disabilities may find it difficult to come up with a reasonable estimate, so provide possible strategies. For example, make a row or chain of exactly 10 of the units to help them visualize. They first lay 10 units against the object and then make their estimate. You can also do this activity with standard units.

MyLab Education   **Activity Page: Estimating and Measuring with Nonstandard Units Recording Sheet**

FORMATIVE ASSESSMENT Notes. Observation and discussion during these activities provide evidence of how well your students understand length measurement. Tasks that can also be used as diagnostic interviews are:

- Ask students to draw a line or mark off a distance of a prescribed number of units. Observe whether they know to align the units in a straight line without overlaps or gaps.
- Demonstrate in the classroom how a fictitious student used a ruler to measure the length of an object. Display many errors such as making gaps, overlaps, using units of different sizes in the same measure, and making a wavy line of alignment in the placement of the ruler. The students' task is to explain why these measurements may be inaccurate.
- Have students measure two different objects. Ask, "How much longer is the longer object?" Observe whether students use the two measurements they have to answer or whether they need to make a third measurement to find the difference.
- Have students measure a length with small paper clips and then again with large paper clips. Can they identify the inverse relationship between the measures they find and the size of the units?

If your assessment indicates some confusion about how length is measured exists, use the class discussion of these results to help students self-assess and come to a deeper understanding. ■

Making and Using Rulers

The jump from measuring with actual units to using standard rulers is challenging. One method to help students understand rulers is to have them make their own rulers.

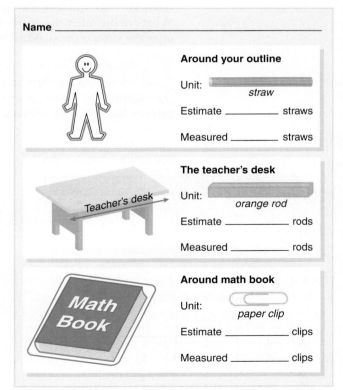

FIGURE 18.4   A recording sheet for measuring with nonstandard length units.

Activity 18.12   CCSS-M: 1.MD.A.2; 2.MD.A.1; 2.MD.A.3

Make Your Own Ruler

Use two colors of cardstock to print Ruler Strips (5-cm long and 2-cm wide). Discuss how the units could be used to measure by laying them end to end. Then provide long card stock strips and have students make their own ruler by gluing the units in alternating colors onto the card stock as shown on the top of Figure 18.5.

Have students use their new rulers to measure items on a list that you provide. Discuss the results. There might be discrepancies due to rulers that were not made properly or to a failure to understand how a ruler works.

Also consider using larger nonstandard units, such as tracings of students' footprints glued onto strips of cash register tape (without gaps or overlaps). Older students can use standard units by using inch or centimeter grid paper and coloring every other square on a row to create their own ruler. Students should use their rulers to measure lengths that are longer than their rulers and discuss how that can be done.

MyLab Education   Activity Page: Ruler Strips

Challenge students to find more than one way to measure a length with a ruler. Do you have to begin at the end? What if you begin at another unit in the center? Students can eventually put numbers on their handmade rulers, as shown in Figure 18.5. In the beginning, numbers can be written in the center of each unit to show that the numbers are a way of precounting the units. When numbers are written in the standard way, at the ends of the units, the ruler becomes a number line.

Make an explicit connection from the handmade rulers to standard rulers. Give students a standard ruler and have them identify and discuss how the self-made ruler and the standard rulers are alike and how they are different. What are the units? What do the numbers mean? What are the other tick marks for? Where do the units begin? Could you make a ruler with units the same as the standard ruler?

FORMATIVE ASSESSMENT Notes. Research indicates that when students see standard rulers with numbers on the tick marks, they often incorrectly believe that the numbers are counting the marks rather than the units or spaces between the marks—a misconception that can lead to wrong answers. As an assessment, provide students a ruler with tick marks but no numbers. Have students use the ruler to measure an item that is shorter than the ruler. Use an Observation Checklist to record whether students count spaces between the tick marks or count the tick marks.

Another excellent assessment of ruler understanding is to have students measure with a "broken" ruler, one with the first two units broken off. Use this Broken Ruler Activity Page that is divided into fractional units. Use your checklist to note whether students say that it is impossible to measure with such a ruler because there is no starting point. Also note those who match and count the units meaningfully.

Observing how students use a ruler to measure an object that is longer than the ruler is also informative. Students who simply read the last tick mark on the ruler may not understand how a ruler is a representation of a continuous row of units. ■

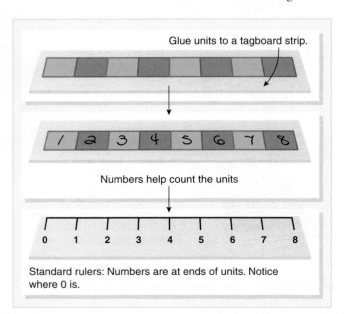

Glue units to a tagboard strip.

Numbers help count the units

Standard rulers: Numbers are at ends of units. Notice where 0 is.

FIGURE 18.5   Give meaning to numbers on rulers.

MyLab Education   Blackline Master: Observation Checklist

MyLab Education   Activity Page: Broken Ruler

TECHNOLOGY Note. GeoGebra (www.geogebra.org) offers a couple of interactive applets in which students can measure different lengths using a broken ruler (search "broken rulers" under materials). ■

Conversion

The customary system has few patterns or generalizable rules to guide students in converting units. In contrast, the metric system was systematically created around powers of ten. Understanding of the role of the decimal point as indicating the units position is a powerful concept for making metric conversions (see Figure 16.1). As students grasp the structure of decimal notation, develop the metric system with all seven places: three prefixes for smaller units (*deci-, centi-, milli-*) and three for larger units (*deka-, hecto-, kilo-*). Avoid mechanical rules such as "To convert centimeters to meters, move the decimal point two places to the left." Instead create conceptual, meaningful methods for conversions rather than rules that are often misused, misunderstood, and forgotten.

MyLab Education   **Video Example 18.6**

Watch Janet Caldwell discuss the idea of converting units.

Students in the second grade begin to consider the relationship between the size of a unit and the resulting measure (NGA Center & CCSSO, 2010). And fourth and fifth graders must be able to convert measures in the same system to larger or smaller units. However, students can find it a challenge to understand that larger units will produce a smaller measure and vice versa. Engage students in activities that emphasize this relationship like the following:

CCSS CCSS Standards for Mathematical Practice
MP2. Reason abstractly and quantitatively.

Activity 18.13   CCSS-M: 2.MD.A.2; 2.MD.A.3; 4.MD.A.1; 5.MD.A.1

Changing Units

Have students measure a length with a specified unit (e.g., Cuisenaire rods) and use the Changing Units Recording Sheet. Then provide them with a different unit that is either twice as long or half as long as the original unit. Their task is to predict the measure of the same length using the new unit. Students should write down and discuss how they made their estimates, then determine the actual measurement. Challenge students with units that are more difficult multiples of the original unit.

   MyLab Education   Activity Page: Changing Units Recording Sheet

In this activity, you reinforce the basic idea that when the unit is longer, the measure is smaller and when the unit is smaller, the measure is larger which is useful for introducing unit conversion with standard units (grades 4 and 5), and an excellent proportional reasoning task for middle school students.

After completing activities like the one that follows, encourage students to notice patterns that help them conclude that you multiply to convert a larger unit to a smaller unit. What do you predict is the process to go from a smaller unit to a larger unit?

Activity 18.14   CCSS-M: 4.MD.A.1; 5.MD.A.1

Conversion Please

Give students the Two-Column Conversion Table. Select several items around the classroom and have them measure the items in feet and then again in inches. Only have them complete half of the table. Ask them to describe the relationship between the two measurements. They are likely to notice that the longer the unit chosen, the fewer units needed and vice versa. For the second half of the table, give them the item to measure only with feet and have them convert to find how many inches. When complete, students should confirm their answers by measuring with inches. Try other units.

   MyLab Education   Activity Page: Two-Column Conversion Table

Other measures of length, such as perimeter and circumference, will be discussed in subsequent sections.

MyLab Education Self-Check 18.2

 Area

Area is the measure of two-dimensional space inside a region. As with other attributes, students must first understand the attribute of area before measuring. Data from the 2011 NAEP suggest that only 24 percent of fourth-graders were able to find the area of a square given a perimeter of 12 units and including a drawing of the square with tick marks around the sides. Instead, 44 percent merely counted the eight tick marks around the edge for their answer (National Center for Educational Statistics, 2014). Estimating and measuring area begins in third grade, as students connect to multiplication using arrays, and continues in grade 4 with finding the area of rectangles using formulas. In fifth-grade students explore area problems with fractional measures and use area to find volumes of three-dimensional shapes. By grade 6, students explore area of a wide range of polygons and learn surface area. In grade 7, students explore area of circles.

Comparison Activities

Comparing area measures is more of a conceptual challenge than comparing length measures because areas come in different shapes. Comparison activities with areas should help students distinguish between size (i.e., area) and shape, length, and other dimensions. A long, skinny rectangle may have less area than a triangle with shorter sides. Many students do not understand that rearranging areas into different shapes does not affect the amount of area (although the perimeter can change).

Direct comparison of two areas is possible only when the shapes involved have some common dimension or property. For example, two rectangles with the same width can be compared directly as in this Rectangle Comparison Activity Page, as can any two circles. Comparison of these special shapes, however, does not challenge students to think about the attribute of area. Instead, activities in which one area is rearranged (conservation of area) are suggested.

| MyLab Education
Activity Page:
Rectangle Comparison |
| --- |

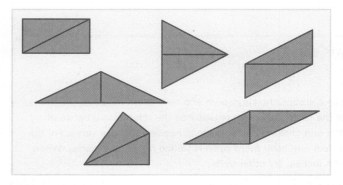

FIGURE 18.6 Different shapes, same area.

Activity 18.15 CCSS-M: 3.MD.C.5

Two-Piece Shapes

Cut a large number of rectangles from the Rectangles of the Same Area Activity Page. Each pair of students needs six rectangles. Have them fold and cut the rectangles on the diagonal, making two identical triangles. Next, have them rearrange the triangles into different shapes, including back into the original rectangle. The rule is that only sides of the same length can be matched and they must be matched precisely. Have students work in pairs to find all the shapes that can be made this way, gluing the triangles on paper as a record (see Figure 18.6). Discuss the area of each. Does one shape have a greater area than the rest? How do you know? Help students conclude that although each figure is a different shape, all the figures have the same *area*.

MyLab Education **Activity Page:**
Rectangles of the
Same Area

Students may find this cutout and reposition approach helps them appreciate the connections between area and space, particularly ELs (Fernandes, Kahn, & Civil, 2017).

Tangrams, an ancient puzzle, can be used for the same purpose. The standard set of seven Tangram Pieces is cut from a square, as shown in Figure 18.7 or in the online GeoGebra version (www.geogebra.org—search "tangram"). The two small triangles can be used to make the parallelogram, the square, and the medium triangle. This composing permits a similar discussion about the pieces having the same area but different shapes.

MyLab Education	Activity Page: Tangram Pieces

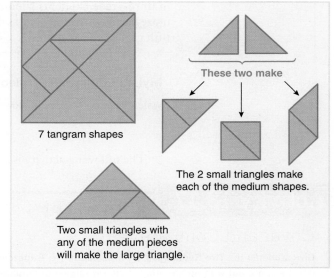

FIGURE 18.7 Tangrams provide an opportunity to investigate area concepts.

Activity 18.16

CCSS-M: 3.MD.C.5; 3.MD.C.6

Tangram Areas

Give students Outlines of Tangram Shapes and a set of Tangram Pieces, as in Figure 18.8. Ask groups to estimate which shape has the largest (or smallest) area. Then let students use tangrams to decide which shapes are the same size, which are larger, and which are smaller. Ask students to justify their conclusions. Use the animal shapes from *Grandfather Tang's Story* (Tompert, 1997) to see if they have the same or different areas. Try the tangram game at PBS Kid's Cyberchase (http://pbskids.org/cyberchase) where players use different pieces to form such things as a rabbit, duck, space ship, sailboat, etc.).

MyLab Education   Activity Page: Outlines of Tangram Shapes
MyLab Education   Activity Page: Tangram Pieces

Using Physical Models of Area Units

Students need multiple opportunities to "cover the surface" of two-dimensional shapes to develop understanding of the attribute of area.

Tiles. Although square tiles are the most commonly used tools for exploring area, anything (does not need to be a square) that easily fills up a plane region can be used, such as sticky notes, sheets of newspaper, floor tiles or playing cards. Students can choose units to measure surfaces in the room such as desktops, bulletin boards, or book covers. Large regions can be outlined with tape on the floor. Small regions can be duplicated on geoboards or grid paper so that students can work at stations. Maps of real world locations can be explored using models for finding the area (Wickstrom, Carr, & Lackey, 2017).

In area measurements, there may be units that only partially fit or spaces too small for the placement of another unit. Consider beginning with shapes in which the units fit by building a shape with units and tracing the outline. But,

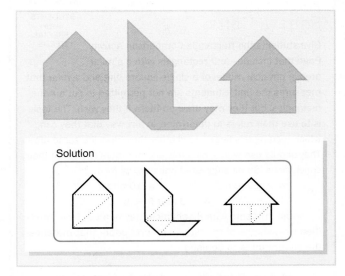

FIGURE 18.8 Compare the area of shapes made of tangram pieces.

in third grade, students should wrestle with partial units and mentally put together two or more partial units to count as one unit which prepares them for the use of fractional units in fifth grade (NGA Center & CCSSO, 2010) (see Figure 18.9).

MyLab Education   Video Example 18.7

Watch this video of Janet Caldwell as she describes how area is measured.

The following activity is a good starting point.

Activity 18.17

CCSS-M: 3.MD.C.5; 3.MD.C.6; 4.MD.A.3

Cover and Compare

STUDENTS
with
SPECIAL NEEDS

Give students the Two Rectangles, a Parallelogram, a Trapezoid and a Blob Activity Page where the areas are not the same but with no area that is clearly largest or smallest. Ask students to predict which shape has the smallest and the largest area and then use a strategy to compare the areas. Brainstorm strategies and create a list of options to support students with special needs. Students may trace or glue the same two-dimensional unit on the shapes, place tiles on them, or cut the shapes out and place them on grid paper.

     MyLab Education   **Activity Page: Two Rectangles, a Parallelogram, a Trapezoid, and a Blob**

Your objective in the beginning is to develop the idea that area is measured by covering or tiling. Do not introduce formulas yet. Groups are likely to come up with different measures for the same region. Discuss these differences with the students, and point to the difficulties involved in making estimates around the edges. Avoid the idea that there is "one right approach."

Students should begin to apply the concept of multiplication using arrays to the area of rectangles. This connection requires that students develop the ability to see a rectangular region as rows and columns. The following comparison activity is a useful step in that direction.

The goal of this activity is to apply students' developing concept of multiplication to the area of rectangles

Activity 18.18

CCSS-M: 3.MD.C.5; 3.MD.C.6; 3.MD.C.7; 5.NF.B.4b

Rectangle Comparison: Square Units

STUDENTS
with
SPECIAL NEEDS

Give students the Rectangle Comparison Activity Page that includes four rectangles with a similar area, a physical model of a single square unit and a ruler that measures the unit. Students are not permitted to cut out the rectangles, but they may draw on them if they wish. The task is to use their rulers to determine, in any way that they can, which rectangle is larger or whether they have the same area. They should use words, pictures, and numbers to explain their conclusions. Some suggested pairs are as follows:

     4 × 10 and 5 × 8   5 × 10 and 7 × 7

         4 × 6 and 5 × 5

Some students with disabilities may need to have modified worksheets of the figures on grid paper that matches the square units to be used.

     MyLab Education   **Activity Page: Rectangle Comparison**

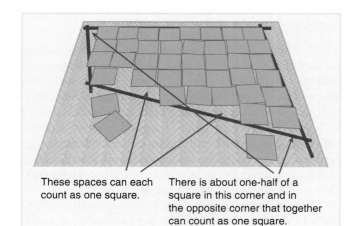

These spaces can each count as one square.

There is about one-half of a square in this corner and in the opposite corner that together can count as one square.

FIGURE 18.9 Measuring the area of a large shape with card stock squares.

without introducing a formula. In order to count a single row of squares along one edge and then multiply by the length of the other edge, the first row must be thought of as a single unit that is then replicated to fill in the rectangle (Outhred & Mitchelmore, 2004). Students may attempt to draw in all the squares. However, some may use rulers to determine the number of squares that will fit along each side and, from that, use multiplication to determine the total area (see Figure 18.10). By

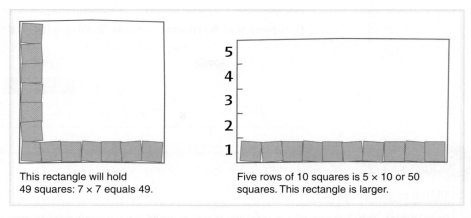

This rectangle will hold 49 squares: 7 × 7 equals 49.

Five rows of 10 squares is 5 × 10 or 50 squares. This rectangle is larger.

FIGURE 18.10   Students use multiplication to tell the total number of square units.

having students share strategies, more students move toward learning the formula through the use of multiplicative reasoning in this context.

Grids. Grids of various types can be thought of as "area rulers." A square grid does for area what a ruler does for length: It lays out the units for you. Grids of various units (2-Centimeter Grid Paper, 1-Centimeter Grid Paper, and 0.5-Centimeter Grid Paper) can be copied on clear transparency sheets and placed over a region to count the square units inside. An alternative method is to trace around a region on grid paper.

MyLab Education	**Blackline Master: 2-Centimeter Grid Paper**
MyLab Education	**Blackline Master: 1-Centimeter Grid Paper**
MyLab Education	**Blackline Master: 0.5-Centimeter Grid Paper**

The Relationship between Area and Perimeter

Student often confuse the concepts of area and perimeter. Although perimeter is a standard at grade 3 (NGA Center & CCSSO, 2010), of the eighth graders given an illustration of a rectangle with only the two side lengths on the NAEP exam, only 71 percent could accurately identify the perimeter. Perhaps confusion emerges because both area and perimeter initially often involve rectangular regions to be measured or because students are taught formulas (possibly too soon). Teaching these two concepts within a close timeframe is particularly challenging for students with disabilities (Parmar, Garrison, Clements, & Sarama, 2011).

Perimeter is a length measure of the distance around a region and, as such, it is additive. Students should be able to calculate perimeter given side measures as well as identify missing side lengths. A hint for helping students remember the concept of perimeter is that the word "rim" is in the word pe*rim*eter.

MyLab Education   Video Example 18.8

Watch this video of Janet Caldwell as she discusses the components of solving perimeter problems.

What is the perimeter of this figure?

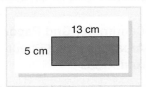

The perimeter of the rectangle below is 32. What is the length of the side marked A?

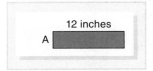

12 inches

A

Activity 18.19

CCSS-M: 3.MD.D.8

What's the Rim?

Have students select objects with a perimeter that they would like the whole class to measure (like the cover of a book) or more challenging (the top edge of a wastebasket). First, students estimate the perimeter on the What's the Rim? Activity Page. They also need to choose tools strategically (rulers, cash register tape, or nonstretching string) and measure the perimeter, noting the unit. The discussion should include class comparisons of at least one common item that will provide a basis for exploring any measurement differences or errors. Students should describe how they measured objects that were larger than the tool they were using and how they knew when to use a flexible measuring tool (i.e., string or cash register tape). For students with disabilities, have them trace the perimeter with their finger prior to measuring.

STUDENTS
with
SPECIAL NEEDS

MyLab Education   Activity Page: What's the Rim?

Even preservice teachers were confused as to whether the area of a rectangle increases with increases in the perimeter (Livy, Muir, & Maher, 2012). An interesting approach to alleviating this confusion is to contrast area and perimeter using the next two activities.

Activity 18.20

CCSS-M: 3.MD.D.8; 4.MD.A.3

Fixed Perimeters

Give students a loop of nonstretching string that is 24 centimeters in circumference and 1-Centimeter Grid Paper, or just use the grid paper alone. The task is to decide what different-sized rectangular gardens can be made so they can be fenced using a perimeter of 24 feet (1 ft = 1 cm). Each different rectangular garden can be recorded on the grid paper with the area noted inside the sketch of the garden ($A = 20$ cm^2). Then record all of the results on the Fixed Perimeter Recording Sheet.

MyLab Education   Blackline Master: 1-Centimeter Grid Paper
MyLab Education   Activity Page: Fixed Perimeter Recording Sheet

Activity 18.21

CCSS-M: 3.MD.C.6; 3.MD.C.7; 4.MD.A.3

Fixed Areas

Provide students with 1-Centimeter Grid Paper. The task is to see how many different rectangular gardens can be made with an area of 36 square feet—that is, to make filled-in rectangles, not just borders. Sketch each new garden on the grid paper (including the dimensions) and record the perimeter inside the figure ($P = 24$ cm). Then record all the results on the Fixed Area Recording Sheet. You might also use the Expanded Lesson: Fixed Areas for this activity.

MyLab Education   Blackline Master: 1-Centimeter Grid Paper
MyLab Education   Activity Page: Fixed Area Recording Sheet
MyLab Education   Expanded Lesson: Fixed Areas

❙❙ Pause & Reflect

How are area and perimeter related? For "Fixed Areas," will all of the perimeters be the same? If not, what can you say about the shapes with longer or shorter perimeters? For "Fixed Perimeters," will the areas be the same? Why or why not? Which rectangle creates the largest area? The smallest area? ●

Activity 18.22   CCSS-M: 3.MD.C.6; 3.MD.C.7; 4.MD.A.3

Sorting Areas and Perimeters

Students must first complete Activities 18.20 and 18.21 and then cut out all the figures. Have two charts labeled with "Fixed Perimeter" and "Fixed Area." Teams should place their figures (left to right) from smallest perimeter (or area) to largest perimeter (or area) on the appropriate chart. Ask students to write down observations, make conjectures, and draw conclusions.

Students will notice interesting relationships and may be surprised to find out that rectangles having the same areas do not necessarily have the same perimeters and vice versa. And, of course, this fact is not restricted to rectangles.

Also, when the area is fixed, the shape with the smallest perimeter is "square-like," as is the rectangle with the largest area when the perimeter is fixed. If you allowed for any shape whatsoever, the shape with the smallest perimeter for a fixed area is a circle. Also, they will notice that the "fatter" a shape, the shorter its perimeter; the skinnier a shape, the longer its perimeter. (These relationships are also true in three dimensions—replace perimeter with surface area and area with volume.)

CCSS **CCSS Standards for Mathematical Practice**
MP2. Reason abstractly and quantitatively.

Developing Formulas for Perimeter and Area

When students *develop* formulas, rather than just being told the formula, they gain conceptual understanding of the ideas and relationships involved, and they engage in "doing mathematics." Students form general relationships when they notice how all area formulas are related to one idea: length of the base times the height. And students who have a conceptual understanding of where formulas come from tend to remember them or can derive them, which reinforces the idea that mathematics makes sense. There is also less likelihood that students will confuse area and perimeter, and less of a chance they will confuse these formulas on an assessment.

Formulas for Perimeter. As students move to thinking about formulas, they can consider exploring how the perimeter of rectangles can be put into a general form. Begin by having students generate ways that perimeter problems can be solved. As in the rectangle shown previously, it is common for students to be given a perimeter problem in which only one length and one width are included. So if students only consider adding these two numbers, discussing the formula $P = l + w + l + w$ for a rectangle will clarify the four length dimensions that should be added. Explicitly connecting to the equation helps avoid the common error of only adding the two given dimensions. An alternative perimeter formula for rectangles that might emerge from the conversations would be $P = 2(l + w)$, which reinforces the multiplication of the pair of sides, or $P = 2l + 2w$, which emphasizes that the perimeter involves combining lengths. When you have triangles or more complex shapes, the perimeter formula is adjusted to reflect the number of sides.

 TECHNOLOGY Note. Math Playground (https://www.mathplayground.com) has a game called "Area Blocks" where students create closed polygon shapes that must match given perimeters and areas. The goal is to cover more area than your opponent before the game ends. Students can play against the computer or challenge a classmate. ∎

Formulas for Area. The results of NAEP testing indicate clearly that students do not have a very good understanding of area formulas. For example, in the 2007 NAEP, only 39 percent of

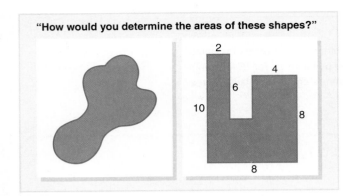

"How would you determine the areas of these shapes?"

FIGURE 18.11 Understanding the attribute of area.

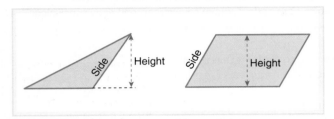

FIGURE 18.12 Heights of two-dimensional figures are not always measured along an edge.

fourth-grade students were able to calculate the area of a carpet 15 feet long and 12 feet wide. Such results may be due to an overemphasis on teaching formulas early with little or no conceptual background. Two major misconceptions related to area are:

1. *Confusing linear and square units.* The shift in third grade to multiplicative thinking may result in students having difficulty as they move from length measurement to the more abstract measurement of area. Putrawangsa, Lukito, Amin, and Wijers (2013) suggest that one of the major issues with area measurement is thinking about area as the length of two lines (length × width), rather than the measure of a surface. It's challenging for students to think about multiplying two lengths and getting an area (Kamii & Kysh, 2006). A focus on the formula and the use of a ruler to measure the *sides* confuses the unit as well as the tool for measuring area (as the use of the ruler is indirect). This confusion can cause some students to believe that if there are no sides to measure (no length and width), the shape doesn't have an area (Zacharos, 2006).

   The tasks in Figure 18.11 cannot be solved with simple formulas; they require an understanding of concepts and how formulas work. "Length times width" is not a definition of area; instead, area is a measure of a two-dimensional surface enclosed by a boundary.

2. *Difficulty in conceptualizing the meaning of height and base.* The shapes in Figure 18.12 each have a slanted side and a height given. Students tend to confuse these two. Any side of a figure can be called a *base*. For each base that a figure has, there is a corresponding height. If the figure were to slide into a room on a selected base, the *height* would be the height of the shortest door it could pass through without tipping—that is, the perpendicular distance to the base. The confusion may be because students have a lot of early experiences with the $L \times W$ formula for rectangles, in which the height is exactly the same as the length of a side.

The formula for the area of a rectangle is one of the first that is developed and is usually given as $A = L \times W$, or "area equals length times width." Thinking ahead, an equivalent but more unifying idea is $A = B \times H$, or "area equals *base* times *height*." The base-times-height formulation can be generalized to all parallelograms (not just rectangles) and is useful in developing the area formulas for triangles and trapezoids. Furthermore, the same approach can be extended to three dimensions—volumes of cylinders are given in terms of the *area of the base* times the height. Therefore, base times height connects a large family of formulas that otherwise must be mastered independently.

Area of Rectangles. Research suggests that it is a significant leap for students to move from counting squares inside of a rectangle to a conceptual development of a formula. Battista (2003) found that students often inefficiently try to fill in rectangles with drawings of squares (often unequal units) and then count the result one square at a time.

An important concept to review is the meaning of multiplication as seen in arrays with an emphasis on the structure of rows and columns of square units. When we multiply a length times a width, we are not multiplying "squares times squares." Rather, the *length* of one side indicates how many squares will fit on that side. If this set of squares is taken as a unit, then the *length* of the other side (not a number of squares) will determine how many of these *rows of squares* can fit in the rectangle. Then the number of square units covering the rectangle is the product of the length of a row and the number of rows: Column × Row = Area. If students attempt to draw in all of the squares and count them, they have not yet thought about a row of squares as a single unit that can be iterated.

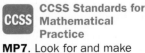

CCSS Standards for Mathematical Practice

MP7. Look for and make sense of structure.

Now, explain to students that measuring one side to tell how many squares will fit in a row along that side is considering the side as the *base* of the rectangle even though some people call it the *length* or the *width*. Then the other side can be called the *height*. Be sure that students conclude that either side could be the base and that the formula $A = B \times H$, generates the same area through the commutative property regardless of which side is the base (see Figure 18.13).

From Rectangles to the Area of Other Parallelograms. Once students understand the base-times-height formula for rectangles, the next challenge is to determine the areas of parallelograms. Rather than providing a formula, use the following activity, where students devise their own formula, building on what they know about rectangles.

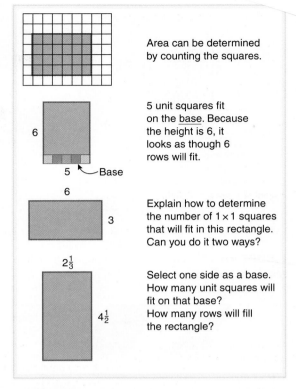

FIGURE 18.13 Developing the formula for the area of a rectangle.

Activity 18.23   CCSS-M: 6.G.A.1

Area of a Parallelogram

Give students the Grid of Parallelograms Activity Page or, for a slightly harder challenge, drawn on plain paper with all dimensions—the lengths of all four sides and the height. Ask students to use what they have learned about the area of rectangles to determine the areas of these parallelograms. Students should find a method that will work for any parallelogram, even if not drawn on a grid.

MyLab Education   Activity Page: Grid of Parallelograms

If students need support, ask them to examine ways that the parallelogram is like a rectangle or how it can be changed into a rectangle by decomposing and recomposing the shape. As shown in Figure 18.14, a parallelogram can always be transformed into a rectangle with the same base, the same height, and the same area. Therefore, the formula for the area of a parallelogram is exactly the same as for a rectangle: *base* times *height*.

From Area Parallelograms to Area Triangles. Knowing the relationship between a rectangle and parallelogram, how can the area of a triangle logically follow? Engage students in a problem-based approach, as in the next activity.

Activity 18.24   CCSS-M: 6.G.A.1

Area of a Triangle

Provide students with the Grid of Triangles Activity Page. Challenge students to use what they know about the area of parallelograms to find the area of each of the triangles and to develop a method that will work for any triangle. They should confirm that their method works for the triangles given to them as well as at least one more that they draw. For students with disabilities or those who need more structure, ask, "Can you find a parallelogram that is related to your triangle?" Then suggest that they fold a piece of paper in half, draw a triangle, and cut it out, making two identical copies. Use the triangles together to make a parallelogram. This composing of shapes provides a nice visual of how a triangle is related to a parallelogram.

STUDENTS with SPECIAL NEEDS

MyLab Education   Activity Page: Grid of Triangles

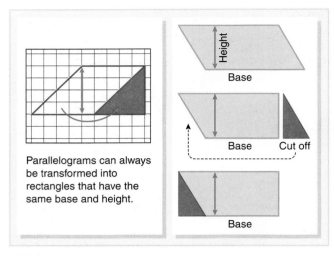

Parallelograms can always be transformed into rectangles that have the same base and height.

FIGURE 18.14 Transforming a parallelogram into a rectangle.

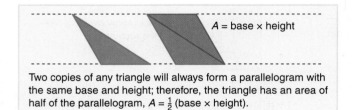

A = base × height

Two copies of any triangle will always form a parallelogram with the same base and height; therefore, the triangle has an area of half of the parallelogram, $A = \frac{1}{2}$ (base × height).

FIGURE 18.15 Two congruent triangles always form a parallelogram.

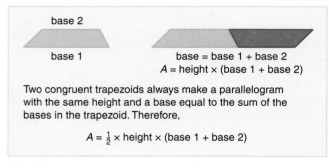

base 2

base 1

base = base 1 + base 2
A = height × (base 1 + base 2)

Two congruent trapezoids always make a parallelogram with the same height and a base equal to the sum of the bases in the trapezoid. Therefore,

$$A = \frac{1}{2} \times \text{height} \times (\text{base 1} + \text{base 2})$$

FIGURE 18.16 Two congruent trapezoids always form a parallelogram.

As shown in Figure 18.15, two congruent triangles can always be arranged to form a parallelogram with the same base and the same height as the triangle. The area of the triangle will, therefore, be one-half that of the parallelogram or $\frac{1}{2}$ Base × Height. Sound familiar?

⏸ Pause & Reflect

There are three possible parallelograms, one for each triangle side that serves as a base. Will the computed areas always be the same? How might you engage students in this exploration? ●

From Area of Parallelograms to Area of Trapezoids.
After developing formulas for parallelograms and triangles, students are ready to develop the formula for the area of a trapezoid. There are many methods of arriving at an area formula for trapezoids, each related to decomposing the trapezoid into a simpler shape or combining shapes where ways to find these areas are already known and can be summed. One method uses the same approach that was used for triangles, except students work with two identical trapezoids. Figure 18.16 shows how this method results in the formula.

Here are suggestions, each leading to a different approach to finding the area of a trapezoid and a Grid of Trapezoids Activity Sheet:

• Make a parallelogram inside the given trapezoid using three of the sides.
• Make a parallelogram using three sides that surround the trapezoid.
• Draw a diagonal forming two triangles.
• Draw a line through the midpoints of the nonparallel sides. The length of that line is the average of the lengths of the two parallel sides.
• Draw a rectangle inside the trapezoid, leaving two triangles, then put those two triangles together.
• Use transformational geometry.
• Enclose the trapezoid in a larger shape (Manizade & Mason, 2014).

MyLab Education Activity Page: Grid of Trapezoids

🔺 **TECHNOLOGY Note.** The relationship between the areas of rectangles, parallelograms, and triangles can be dramatically illustrated using dynamic geometry software such GeoGebra (www.geogebra.org). Draw two congruent segments on two parallel lines, as shown in Figure 18.17. Connect the segment end points to form a parallelogram and two triangles. The height is indicated by a segment perpendicular to the parallel lines. Either of the two line segments can be dragged left or right to change the slant of the parallelogram and triangle without changing the base or height. All area measures remain fixed! Also, explore the area of parallelograms and trapezoids applets at NCTM Illuminations to test how changes in the base and height of these shapes affect the area. ■

Surface Area. After learning to find area of two-dimensional shapes, students are ready to explore the surface area of three-dimensional shapes. Sixth-grade students begin a study of surface area by exploring shapes with rectangular faces, which extends to shapes with faces of a variety of shapes in seventh grade (NGA Center & CCSSO, 2010). Yet, on a NAEP item only about 25 percent of eighth graders could find the surface area of a rectangular prism (Blume et al., 2007).

Build on the knowledge students have of the areas of two-dimensional figures use *nets* as effective visualization tool. If students think of each solid as its two-dimensional components (nets), they can find the area of each face and then add the areas. One of the best approaches is to create several rectangular prisms, cubes, or cylinders with card stock with the sides held together by small pieces of Velcro. In this way, students can pull apart the components or the net of the figure and consider the individual faces as they calculate the surface area.

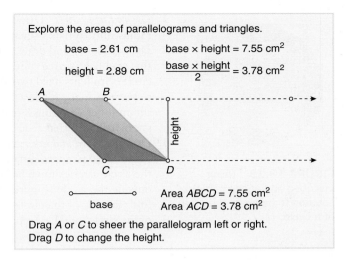

Explore the areas of parallelograms and triangles.

base = 2.61 cm   base × height = 7.55 cm^2

height = 2.89 cm $\dfrac{\text{base} \times \text{height}}{2}$ = 3.78 cm^2

Area ABCD = 7.55 cm^2
Area ACD = 3.78 cm^2

Drag *A* or *C* to sheer the parallelogram left or right.
Drag *D* to change the height.

FIGURE 18.17   Dynamic geometry software demonstrates that figures with the same base and height maintain the same area.

Activity 18.25   CCSS-M: 6.G.A.4; 7.G.B.6

Making Boxes

ENGLISH LEARNERS

Joan's Dine & Dessert Shop orders take-out boxes in three sizes (dinner, pie, and cake) and Joan wants an estimate of how much cardboard is used for each so that she can decide whether she should make her own boxes. Find how much cardboard is used for these boxes (assume they are taped and there is no overlap of cardboard).

- Dinner box: 7 in. × 7 in. × 3 in.
- Pie box: 5 in. × 4 in. × 3 in.
- Cake box: 8 in. × 8 in. × 5 in.

Use 2-Centimeter Grid Paper for students to create their net for each box. Students should compare their diagrams and surface areas. They may have picked different bases, and the illustrations may look different, but this opportunity can spur a discussion about why these different nets have equal surface areas. For ELs (and others) the term net may be confused with the internet or a net used in fishing so have visual supports available.

MyLab Education   Blackline Master: 2-Centimeter Grid Paper

Circumference and Area of Circles. The relationship between the *circumference* of a circle (the distance around or the perimeter) and the length of the *diameter* (a line through the center joining two points on the circle) is one of the most interesting that students can discover and is an expectation for seventh grade (NGA Center & CCSSO, 2010). The circumference of every circle is about 3.14 times as long as the diameter. The ratio is an irrational number close to 3.14 and is represented by the Greek letter π. So $\pi = \frac{C}{D}$, the circumference divided by the diameter. In equivalent forms, $C = \pi D$ or $C = 2\pi r$. (Activity 19.14 in Chapter 19 will discuss the concept of π and how students can discover this universal ratio.)

Area of Circles. As with polygons, students should investigate the area formula for circles, rather than just be given the formula. Here are ways to explore area of circles that build conceptual understanding for the formula:

1. *Cover a circle with tiles.* Place 1-inch square tiles on the circle or cut out squares that can be glued on. The advantage of cutouts is that students can cut squares that are only partially inside the circle and place the extra pieces somewhere else. Then students need to get a measure of the radius from the sides of the tiles.

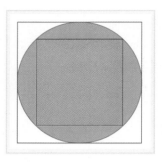

FIGURE 18.18 Using inscribed and superscribed squares to estimate the area of a circle.

2. *Use radius squares.* Draw a circle and draw a radius. Set the radius as the unit. Use the radius unit to make squares—we will call them *radius squares.* Form a grid that is 2×2 radius squares, and draw a circle inside. By observation, you see that the circle inscribed in this grid has an area of less than 4 radius squares (because much of the grid is outside the circle). Students need two identical copies of this picture—one to cut out the radius squares to see how many it takes to cover the circle in the other picture. Students can estimate that the number of radius squares needed is about 3.1 or 3.2. This technique reinforces the geometric idea that r^2 is a square with a side of r.

3. *Draw inscribed and superscribed squares.* This approach is similar to the method that Archimedes used to approximate π. Students draw a circle on grid paper with a given radius (or the circle can be drawn beforehand on a handout). They draw a square inside the circle and outside the circle (Figure 18.18). Find the areas of the two squares, and average them to find the area of the circle. Archimedes started using polygons that got closer to the shape of the circle (see the Archimedes Circles Activity Page for students to see how the estimates become closer). See NCTM Illuminations for full lessons in which this approach is used.

4. *Cut to make a parallelogram.* Cut a circle apart into sectors and rearrange them to look like a parallelogram. For example, students can cut from 3 to 12 sectors from a circle and build them into what looks like parallelogram. Recall that in the angle investigation, students made a wax paper circle. This same circle can be remade and cut to form the pieces to explore area of a circle. You may need to help them notice that the smaller the size of the sectors used, the closer the arrangement gets to a rectangle. Figure 18.19 presents a common development of the area formula $A = \pi r^2$.

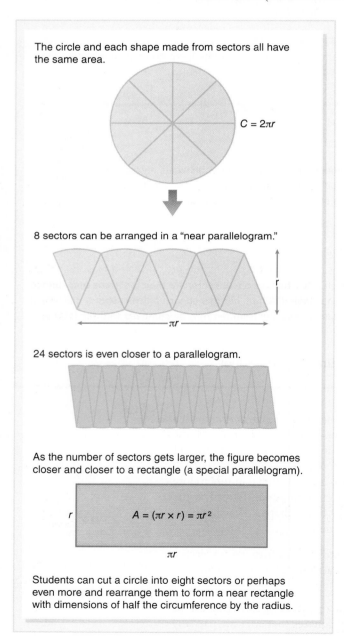

The circle and each shape made from sectors all have the same area.

$C = 2\pi r$

8 sectors can be arranged in a "near parallelogram."

πr

24 sectors is even closer to a parallelogram.

As the number of sectors gets larger, the figure becomes closer and closer to a rectangle (a special parallelogram).

$A = (\pi r \times r) = \pi r^2$

πr

Students can cut a circle into eight sectors or perhaps even more and rearrange them to form a near rectangle with dimensions of half the circumference by the radius.

FIGURE 18.19 Development of the circle area formula.

MyLab Education **Activity Page: Archimedes Circles**

MyLab Education **Self-Check 18.3**

MyLab Education
Application Exercise 18.1:
Perimeter Click the link to access this exercise, then watch the video and answer the accompanying questions.

VIDEO EXAMPLE

Volume and Capacity

Volume and *capacity* are terms for measures of the "size" of three-dimensional regions—a topic beginning in the fifth grade with rectangular prisms, with continuing emphasis in grades 6 and 8 with cylinders, cones and spheres (NGA Center & CCSSO, 2010). The term *liquid volume* or *capacity* is generally used to refer to the amount that a container will hold. Standard units of capacity include quarts, gallons, liters, and milliliters. The term *volume* can be used to refer to the capacity of a container but is also used for the amount of space occupied by three-dimensional objects. Standard units of volume of solid figures are expressed in terms of cubic units such as cubic inches or cubic centimeters.

MyLab Education   Video Example 18.9

Watch this video by Janet Caldwell that that explores the appropriate units and tools for measuring volume.

Comparison Activities

A method of comparing capacity is to fill one container with something and then pour that amount into the comparison container. By primary grades, most students understand the concept of "holds more" with reference to containers. The concept of volume of solid objects is sometimes challenging, and a method of comparison is also difficult. To compare volumes of solids such as a ball and an apple, a displacement method must be used. Have students predict which object has the smaller or greater volume and then place it in a measuring cup or beaker filled with water to see how much the water rises.

Young children should compare the capacities of different containers as in the following activity.

Activity 18.26   CCSS-M: K.MD.A.2; 3.MD.A.2; 5.MD.C.3

Capacity Sort

Provide a variety of containers, with one marked the "target." Ask students to sort the collection into those that hold more than, less than, or about the same amount as the target container. Then use the Capacity Sort Activity Page to circle the estimate of "holds more," "holds less," or "holds about the same." Provide a filler (such as beans, rice, water, or popcorn), scoops, and funnels. Working in pairs, have students measure and record results under Actual Measure on the recording sheet. Discuss what students noticed (e.g., that fatter/rounder shapes hold more).

MyLab Education   Activity Page: Capacity Sort

Activity 18.27   CCSS-M: 5.MD.C.3; 5.MD.C.4; 5.MD.C.5; 6.C.A.2

Fixed Volume: Comparing Prisms

Give each pair of students a supply of centimeter or inch cubes and a Comparing Prisms Recording Sheet. If you have ELs, provide a visual of a rectangular prism, labeling key words such as *length, width, height, surface area, cube, volume,* and *side*. Ask students to use 36 (or 64) cubes to build different rectangular prisms with that volume and record in a table the surface area for each. Ask students to describe any patterns that they notice as they compare the dimensions of each prism to its surface area. What happens as the prism becomes less like a tall, skinny box and more like a cube? Also explore the Expanded Lesson: Fixed Volume.

ENGLISH LEARNERS

MyLab Education   Activity Page: Comparing Prisms Recording Sheet
MyLab Education   Expanded Lesson: Fixed Volume

Try the following activity yourself as well as with students.

Activity 18.28

CCSS-M: 5.MD.C.3; 6.G.A.4; 7.G.B.7

Which Silo Holds More?

Give pairs of students two sheets of equal-sized paper. With one sheet they make a tube shape (cylinder) by taping the two long edges together. They make a shorter, fatter cylinder from the other sheet by taping the short edges together. Then ask, "If these were two silos, would they hold the same amount, or would one hold more than the other?" To test the conjectures, use a filler such as beans, popcorn, or pasta. Place the skinny cylinder inside the fat one. Fill the inside tube and then lift it up, allowing the filler to empty into the fat cylinder.

The eventual goal is for students to realize that surface area does not dictate volume and to recognize that there is a pattern between surface area and volume, just as there is between area and perimeter. Namely, prisms that are more cube-like have less surface area than prisms with the same volume that are long and narrow.

Using Physical Models of Volume and Capacity Units

Two types of units can be used to measure volume and capacity (liquid volume): solid units and containers. Solid units are objects like wooden cubes that can be used to fill the container being measured. The other unit model is a small container that is filled with liquid for example and poured repeatedly into the container being measured (eventually using containers with scales). The following examples are of units that you might want to collect:

- Liquid medicine cups
- Plastic jars and containers of almost any size
- Wooden cubes or same-sized blocks of any shape
- Styrofoam packing peanuts (produces conceptual measures of volume despite not packing perfectly—but harder to find than popcorn)

The following activity explores volume of two boxes.

Activity 18.29

CCSS-M: 5.MD.C.3, 5.MD.C.4, 5.MD.C.5; 6.G.A.2; 7.G.B.6

Box Comparison: Cubic Units

Provide students with a pair of small boxes that you have made from card stock (see Figure 18.20). Use unit dimensions that match the cubes that you have for units. Students are given two boxes, one cube, and a corresponding ruler (If you use 2-centimeter cubes, make a ruler with 2-centimeter units). Ask students to decide which box has the greater volume or if they have the same volume.

Here are some suggested box dimensions ($L \times W \times H$):

$$6 \times 3 \times 4 \quad\quad 5 \times 4 \times 4 \quad\quad 3 \times 9 \times 3 \quad\quad 6 \times 6 \times 2 \quad\quad 5 \times 5 \times 3$$

Students should use words, drawings, and numbers to explain their conclusions. Repeat with boxes with fractional values. For example, ask students to estimate and then determine which of the following shipping boxes has the greatest and least volume:

$$\tfrac{1}{4} \text{ ft} \times 3 \text{ ft} \times 2\tfrac{1}{2} \text{ ft} \quad\quad 4 \text{ ft} \times \tfrac{3}{4} \text{ ft} \times \tfrac{1}{2} \text{ ft} \quad\quad \tfrac{5}{12} \text{ ft} \times 2 \text{ ft} \times \tfrac{3}{4} \text{ ft} \quad\quad 2 \text{ ft} \times \tfrac{1}{4} \text{ ft} \times 3 \text{ ft}$$

A useful hint in the last activity is to first figure out how many cubes will fit on the bottom of the box. Some students will discover a multiplicative rule for the volume. The boxes can be completely filled with cubes to confirm conclusions.

Instruments for measuring capacity are generally used for small amounts of liquids or pourable materials such as rice or water. These tools are commonly found in kitchens and laboratories. Students should use measuring cups to explore recipes such those in the *Better Homes and Gardens New Junior Cookbook* (2012), which provide student-friendly opportunities to use units of capacity.

The following two activities focus on liquid volume.

Activity 18.30

CCSS-M: 3.MD.A.2

That's Cool

Give student teams beakers marked in milliliters. Tell the students they will receive three ice cubes. First, they must estimate how many milliliters of water will be in the beaker when the ice melts. Then the ice is placed in each team's container, and students wait until the ice warms and turns to water. What was the difference between their estimates and their actual answers? Students can use a line plot to record and discuss the different measures.

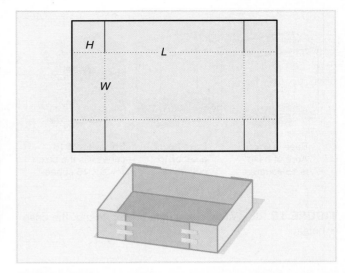

FIGURE 18.20 Make boxes by taking a rectangle and drawing a square on each corner. Cut on the solid lines, fold the box up, wrap the corner squares to the outside, and tape them to the sides.

Activity 18.31

CCSS-M: 3.MD.A.2

Squeeze Play

Students work in teams, with each team having access to a beaker marked in milliliters. Have several stations set up with buckets and different-sized sponges. Have students first estimate how much water they can squeeze from each sponge using the hand they do not write with. Does a sponge that is two times larger than another sponge provide two times the water? What do the students notice?

Developing Formulas for Volumes of Common Solid Shapes

The relationships between the formulas for volume are completely analogous to those for area. A common error that repeats from two- to three-dimensional shapes is that students confuse the meaning of height and base in their use of formulas. Note that the shapes in Figure 18.21 each have a slanted side and a height given. As mentioned before, the base of the figure can be any flat surface of a figure and to visualize the height, have students think of the figure sliding under a doorway. The *height* would be the height of the shortest door it could pass through. Keep this visual in mind as you use precise language to develop formulas for volume.

Notice similarities between rectangles and prisms, between parallelograms and slanted (oblique) prisms, and between triangles and pyramids as you read the next sections. Not only are the formulas related, but the processes for developing the formulas are similar.

Volumes of Cylinders. A *cylinder* is a solid with two congruent parallel bases and sides with parallel elements that join corresponding points on the bases. There are several special classes of cylinders, including *prisms* (with polygons for bases), *right prisms*, *rectangular prisms*, and *cubes* (Zwillinger, 2011). Interestingly, all of these solids have the same volume formula, and that one formula is analogous to the area formula for rectangles and other parallelograms.

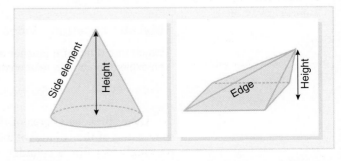

FIGURE 18.21 Heights are not always measured along an edge or surface.

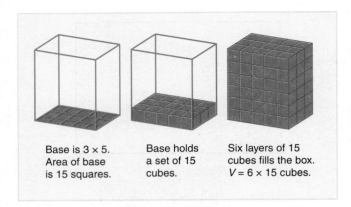

Base is 3 × 5.
Area of base
is 15 squares.

Base holds
a set of 15
cubes.

Six layers of 15
cubes fills the box.
V = 6 × 15 cubes.

FIGURE 18.22 Volume of a right prism: *Area* of the base × height.

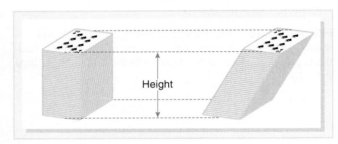

Height

FIGURE 18.23 Two prisms with the same base and height have the same volume.

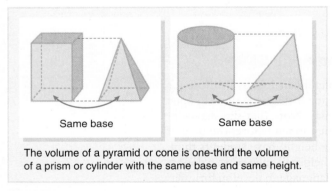

Same base

Same base

The volume of a pyramid or cone is one-third the volume of a prism or cylinder with the same base and same height.

FIGURE 18.24 Comparing volumes of pyramids to prisms and cones to cylinders.

Review Activity 18.29 comparing how the development of the volume formula is parallel to the development of the area of a rectangle as shown in Figure 18.22. The *area* of the base (instead of *length* of the base for rectangles) determines how many *cubes* can cover the base, forming a single unit—a layer of cubes. The *height* of the box then determines how many of these *layers* will fit in the box, just as the height of the rectangle determined how many *rows* of square units would fill the rectangle.

Recall that a parallelogram can be thought of as a slanted rectangle. Show students a stack of three or four decks of cards (or a stack of books). When stacked straight, they form a rectangular solid. The volume, as just discussed, is $V = A \times h$, with A equal to the area of one playing card (the base). Now, if the stack is slanted to one side, as shown in Figure 18.23, what will the volume be? Students should be able to argue that this figure has the same volume (and same volume formula) as the original stack.

What if the playing cards were another shape? If they were circular, the volume would still be the area of the base times the height; if they were triangular, still the same. The conclusion is that the volume of *any* cylinder is equal to *Area of the base* × *Height.*

Volumes of Cones, Pyramids, and Spheres. Understanding the formula for volumes of these shapes is expected in eighth grade (NGA Center & CCSSO, 2010). Recall that when parallelograms and triangles have the same base and height, the areas are in a 2-to-1 relationship. Interestingly, the relationship between the volumes of cylinders and cones with the same base and height is 3 to 1. That is, *area* is to *two*-dimensional figures what *volume* is to *three*-dimensional figures. Furthermore, triangles are to parallelograms as cones are to cylinders.

To investigate this relationship, use translucent plastic models and have students estimate the number of times the volume of the pyramid will fit into the prism. Have students test their predictions by filling the pyramid with water and emptying it into the prism. They will discover that the volume of three pyramids will precisely fill a prism with the same base and height (see Figure 18.24), making the volume of a pyramid (or cone) one-third the volume of the corresponding cylinder.

MyLab Education   **Video Example 18.10**

Watch this video of a teacher demonstrating the displacement method in an exploration of this relationship.

VIDEO EXAMPLE

Using the idea of area of the base times height, it is possible to explore the volume of a sphere as $\frac{2}{3}$ of the volume of a cylinder with the same height and base as identified through pouring water into a cylinder with the same height and base. The height of the matching cylinder is the sphere's radius doubled ($2r$). The volume of the cylinder is the area of the base (πr^2) × height ($2r$). So we find that the volume of the corresponding sphere is $\frac{2}{3}(2\pi^3)$ or $\frac{4}{3}\pi r^3$.

The connectedness of mathematical ideas can hardly be better illustrated than with the connections of all of these volume formulas to the single concept of *base times height*. A conceptual approach to the development of formulas helps students understand that they are meaningful and efficient ways to measure different attributes of the objects around us. After developing formulas conceptually, students can derive formulas from what they already know. Mathematics makes sense!

MyLab Education   **Self-Check 18.4**

Weight and Mass

Weight is a measure of the pull or force of gravity on an object. *Mass* is the amount of matter in an object and a measure of the force needed to accelerate it. On the moon, where gravity is much less than on Earth, an object has a smaller weight than on Earth but the identical mass. For practical purposes, on Earth, the measures of mass and weight will be about the same. In this discussion, the terms *weight* and *mass* will be used interchangeably.

Although the concept of heavier and lighter begins to be explored in kindergarten, the notion of units of weight or mass appears in third grade (NGA Center & CCSSO, 2010). At any grade level, experiences with informal unit weights are good preparation for standard units and scales.

Comparison Activities

The most conceptual way to compare weights of two objects is to hold one in each hand, extend your arms, and experience the relative downward pull on each which effectively communicates to a preK–1 student what "heavier" or "weighs more" means. This personal experience can then be transferred to one of two basic types of scales—balances and spring scales.

MyLab Education   **Video Example 18.11**

Watch this brief video (https://youtu.be/fqG4EDClyRM) that shows a child acting as a human balance scale.

▶ VIDEO EXAMPLE

When students place two objects in the two pans of a balance, the pan that goes down can be understood to hold the heavier object. Even a relatively simple balance will detect small differences. If two objects are placed one at a time in a spring scale, the heavier object pulls the pan down farther. Both balances and spring scales have real value in the classroom. (Technically, spring scales measure weight and balance scales measure mass. Why?)

Using Physical Models of Weight or Mass Units

Any collection of uniform objects with the same mass can serve as nonstandard weight units—that is, for light objects, large paper clips, wooden blocks, or plastic cubes, or coins (U.S. nickels weigh 5 grams and pennies weigh 2.5 grams). Large metal washers from home improvement stores can weigh slightly heavier objects. Standard weights are needed to weigh things as heavy as a kilogram or more.

Weight cannot be measured directly. With a balance scale, place an object in one pan and weights in the other pan until they balance. In a spring scale, first place the object in and mark the position of the pan on a piece of paper taped behind the pan. Remove the object and place just enough weights in the pan to pull it down to the same level. Discuss how equal weights will pull the spring with the same force.

Angles

Understanding the concept (or attribute) of angle and measuring angles begins at fourth grade, and develops in seventh grade as students consider supplementary, complementary vertical and adjacent angles (NGA Center & CCSSO, 2010). Angle measurement can be a challenge for two reasons: The attribute of angle size is often misunderstood, and protractors are commonly introduced and used without students understanding the concept behind how they work. Angle units are based on an angle formed by rays extending from the center of a circle.

Comparison Activities

The attribute of angle size might be called the "spread of the angle's rays" or the measure of rotation between two lines that meet at a point (Bustang, Zulkardi, Darmawijoyo, Dolk, & van Eerde, 2013). Angles are composed of two rays that are infinite in length with a common vertex. Angles differ in size by how widely or narrowly the two rays are spread apart or rotated around the vertex. An angle with n turns of $\frac{1}{360}$ is an angle of n degrees.

To help students conceptualize the attribute of the spread of the rays, two angles can be directly compared by tracing one and placing it over the other (see Figure 18.25). Be sure to have students compare angles with rays of different lengths. A student may think a wide angle with short rays is smaller than a narrow angle with long rays—a common misconception among students (Munier, Devichi, & Merle, 2008). As soon as students can differentiate between a large angle and a small one, regardless of the length of the rays, you can move on to measuring angles.

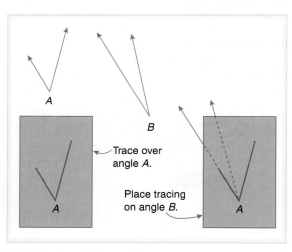

FIGURE 18.25   Which angle is larger?

Using Physical Models of Angular Measure Units

A unit for measuring an angle must be an angle. Nothing else has the same attribute of spread that we want to measure. Contrary to what many people think, you do not need to use degrees to measure angles.

Activity 18.32   CCSS-M: 4.MD.C.5; 7.G.B.5

A Unit Angle

ENGLISH LEARNERS

Give each student an index card. Have students draw a narrow angle on the card using a straightedge and cut it out or use Wedges Activity Page. The resulting wedge can then be used as a unit of angular measure by counting the number of wedges that will fit in a given angle (see Figure 18.26). Distribute the Angles Activity Page and have students use their angle unit to measure the angles. Because students made different unit angles, the results will differ and can be discussed in terms of unit size. ELs will need to know the meaning of the word degree in this context.

MyLab Education   **Activity Page: Wedges**
MyLab Education   **Activity Page: Angles**

Activity 18.32 illustrates that measuring an angle is the same as measuring length or area; unit angles are used to cover the spread of an angle just as square units cover an area. Once this concept is understood, move on to the use of measuring instruments.

Using Protractors

The tool commonly used for measuring angles is the protractor (Figure 18.27) which is introduced in the fourth grade (NGA Center & CCSSO, 2010). Yet, the protractor is poorly understood and is often used improperly (AMTE, 2017). Part of the difficulty arises because the units (degrees) are so small. It would be physically impossible for students to cut out and use a single degree to measure an angle accurately. In addition, the numbers on protractors run clockwise and counterclockwise along the edge, making the scale hard to interpret without a strong conceptual foundation. Notice that the units of degrees are based on an angle where the vertex of the rays is located at the midpoint of a circle, creating an arc. A "one-degree angle" is where the arc is $\frac{1}{360}$ of a circle as illustrated in the Degrees and Wedges Activity Page.

MyLab Education	Activity Page: Degrees and Wedges

Students can make nonstandard waxed-paper protractors (see Figure 18.28) but should soon move to standard instruments. To understand measures on a protractor, students need approximate mental images of angle sizes. Then false readings of the protractor scale will be eliminated. One approach is to use an angle maker.

Activity 18.33

CCSS-M: 4.MD.C.5; 7.G.B.5

Angle Maker

You can cut and merge two different colored paper plates in the same way as the Rational Number Wheel in Figure 16.5. Have students rotate the plates to match angles observed or to estimate benchmark angles such as 30, 45, 60, 90, 135, 180, and 270 degrees and hold up their plate. If students have a strong grasp of the approximate sizes of angles, this "angle sense" will give them the background needed to move to standard measuring tools.

MyLab Education   Blackline Master: Rational Number Wheel

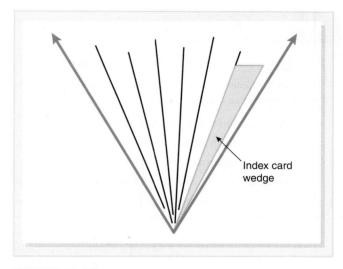

FIGURE 18.26 Using a wedge as a unit angle, this angle measures about $7\frac{1}{2}$ wedges.

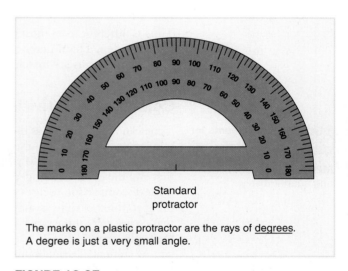

The marks on a plastic protractor are the rays of <u>degrees</u>. A degree is just a very small angle.

FIGURE 18.27 A protractor measures angles.

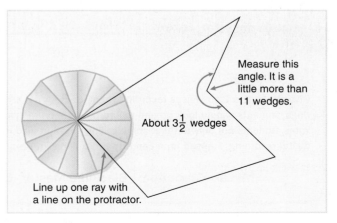

FIGURE 18.28 Measuring angles in a polygon using a waxed-paper protractor.

Activity 18.34 CCSS-M: 4.MD.C.5; 7.G.B.5

Angle Relationships

To explore supplementary, complementary, vertical, and adjacent angles, invite students to discover these relationships, by measuring angles and looking for patterns. Have students:

- Draw two intersecting lines (not perpendicular) on paper.
- Measure the four angles created and record the angles in degrees.
- Notice and record any relationships.
- Discuss as a whole class if these relationships are always true.
- Link the findings to the vocabulary of supplementary, vertical, and adjacent angles.

MyLab Education Self-Check 18.6

Time

Time is different from most other attributes commonly measured in school because it cannot be seen or felt. This difference makes it more difficult for students to comprehend units of time or how those units are matched against a given time period or duration.

Comparison Activities

CCSS Standards for Mathematical Practice

MP2. Reason abstractly and quantitatively.

Time can be thought of as the duration of an event from its beginning to its end. For students to adequately understand the attribute of time, they should make comparisons of events that have different durations. If two events begin at the same time, the shorter duration will end first and the other last longer—for example, which fidget spinner spins longer? However, this form of comparison focuses on the ending of the duration rather than the duration itself. In order to think of time as something that can be measured, it is helpful to compare two events that do not start at the same time which requires some form of time measurement be used from the beginning.

As students learn about seconds, minutes, and hours they develop some concept of how long these units are. Have students time familiar events in their daily lives: brushing teeth, eating dinner, riding to school, doing homework. Point out the duration of short and long events during the school day. Timing events of $\frac{1}{2}$ minute to 2 minutes can be fun and can be adapted from the following activity.

Activity 18.35 CCSS-M: 1.MD.B.3

Ready for the Bell

Give students a Clock Faces recording sheet. Secretly set a timer to go off at the hour, half hour, or minute. When the timer rings, students should look up and record the time on the clock face and in numerals on the recording sheet. This activity motivates students not only to think about telling time but also to consider the relationship between the analog clock reading and digital recording. Elapsed time can also be explored by discussing the time between timer rings.

MyLab Education Blackline Master: Clock Faces

Reading Clocks

The common instrument for measuring time is the clock. However, learning to tell time has little to do with time measurement and more to do with the skills of learning to read an instrument. Clock reading can be a difficult skill to teach. Starting in first grade, students are usually taught to read clocks to the hour, then the half hour, and in second and third grades to 5- and 1-minute intervals (NGA Center & CCSSO, 2010). In the early stages of this sequence, students are shown clocks set precisely to the hour or half hour. Thus, many students who can read a clock at 7:00 or 2:30 are initially challenged by 6:58 or 2:33.

MyLab Education   Video Example 18.13

Watch this video of Jennifer Suh as she highlights the key components in teaching the telling of time.

Digital clocks permit students to read times easily, but they do not relate very well to benchmark times. To know that a digital reading of 7:58 is nearly 8:00, the student must know that there are 60 minutes in an hour, that 58 is close to 60, and that 2 minutes is not a very long time. On the other hand, the analog clock shows "close to" times visually without the need for understanding large numbers or how many minutes in an hour.

The following suggestions can help students focus on the actions and functions of the minute and hour hands.

1. Begin with a one-handed clock by breaking off the minute hand from a regular clock. Use lots of approximate language: "It's about 7 o'clock." "It's a little past 9 o'clock." "It's halfway between 2 o'clock and 3 o'clock" (see Figure 18.29).
2. Discuss what happens to the big hand as the little hand goes from one hour to the next. When the minute hand is at 12, the hour hand is pointing precisely to a number. If the hour hand is about halfway between numbers, about where would the minute hand be? If the hour hand is a little past or before an hour (10 to 15 minutes), where would the minute hand be?
3. Use two clocks, one with only an hour hand and one with two hands. Cover the two-handed clock. Periodically during the day, direct attention to the one-handed clock. Have students predict where the minute hand should be. Uncover the other clock and discuss.
4. After step 3 has begun, teach 5 minute intervals by counting by fives going around the clock (grade 2 CCSS). Instead of saying the minute hand is "pointing at the 4," transition to the language "it is about 20 minutes after the hour." As skills develop, suggest that students look first at the hour hand to learn approximately what time it is and then focus on the minute hand for precision.
5. Predict the reading on a digital clock when shown an analog clock and set an analog clock when shown a digital clock. See the interactive teaching clock at Visnos Mathematics (http://www.visnos.com/demos/clock).
6. Relate the time after the hour to the time before the next hour. This approach is helpful for telling time and number sense.
7. Finally, discuss the issue of a.m. and p.m.

CCSS Standards for Mathematical Practice

MP7. Look for and make sense of structure.

"About 7 o'clock"   "A little bit past 9 o'clock"   "Halfway between 2 o'clock and 3 o'clock"

FIGURE 18.29 Approximate time with one-handed clocks.

The following activity assesses students' ability to read an analog clock.

Activity 18.36   CCSS-M: 1.MD.B.3; 2.MD.C.7

One-Handed Clocks

Prepare a page of Clock Faces by drawing an hour hand on each. Include placements that are approximately a quarter past the hour, a quarter until the hour, half past the hour, and some that are close to but not on the hour. For each clock face, ask students to write the digital time and draw the corresponding minute hand. If you have ELs, note that telling time is done differently in different cultures. For example, in Spanish any time past 30 minutes is stated as the next hour minus the time until that hour. For example, 10:45 is thought of as 15 minutes before 11, or eleven minus a quarter. Be explicit that in English it can be said either way: "10:45" or "a quarter until 11."

ENGLISH LEARNERS

MyLab Education   **Blackline Master: Clock Faces**

Elapsed Time

Determining combinations and comparisons of time intervals in minutes is a skill required starting in grade 3 (NGA Center & CCSSO, 2010). If given the digital time or the time after the hour, students must be able to tell how many minutes to the next hour. The mental process used for completing the task is counting on in multiples of 5 minutes. Avoid having students use pencil and paper to subtract 25 from 60; possibly using an analog clock face to support the skip counting at the beginning will help. This counting on approach provides a foundation for problems involving elapsed time, which is a challenge, especially when the period of time spans noon or midnight.

Figuring the time from, say, 8:15 a.m. to 11:45 a.m. is a multistep task that requires deciding what to do first and keeping track of the intermediate steps. In this case you could count on hours from 8:15 to 11:15 and add on 30 minutes. But then what do students do if they endpoints are 8:45 and 11:15?

There is also the task of finding the end time given the start time and elapsed time, or finding the start time given the end time and the elapsed time. In keeping with the spirit of problem solving and the use of models, consider having students sketch an empty timeline (similar to the empty number line, discussed for computation). The number line is also the model suggested in the CCSS-M. It is important not to be overly prescriptive in telling students how to use the timeline because there are various alternatives (Dixon, 2008). For example, in Figure 18.30, a student might count by full hours from 10:45 (11:45, 12:45, 1:45, 2:45, 3:45) and then subtract 15 minutes. Another student might count 15 minutes to 11:00 and then count by full hours to 3:00 and then add on 30 minutes.

(a) School began late today at 10:45 a.m. If you get out at 3:30, how much time will you be in school today?

10:45   3:30

   11 12 noon   3

Four hours from 11 to 3. Then 15 minutes in front and 30 minutes at the end—45 minutes. Three hours 45 minutes in all.

(b) The game begins at 11:30 a.m. If it lasts 2 hours and 15 minutes, when will it be over?

   11:30   12:30   1:45

      12 noon   1:30

One hour after 11:30 is 12:30 and a second hour gets you to 1:30 and then 15 minutes more is 1:45. It's p.m. because it is after noon.

FIGURE 18.30   A sketch of an empty timeline is useful in solving elapsed time problems.

MyLab Education
Video Example 18.14

Watch this video (https://www.youtube.com/watch?v=WPvy4knZ_YY) that uses the Iditarod Sled Dog Race in Alaska as the context for a lesson on elapsed time.

VIDEO EXAMPLE

Also explore What Time will It Be? at NLVM (http://nlvm.usu.edu/en/nav/vlibrary.html).

Money

Here is a list of the money ideas and skills typically required in the primary grades:

- Recognizing coins and identifying their value
- Counting and comparing sets of coins
- Creating equivalent coin collections (same amounts, different coins)
- Selecting coins for a given amount
- Making change
- Solving word problems involving money (starting in second grade [NGA Center & CCSSO, 2010])

The following sections support the learning of these ideas and skills.

Recognizing Coins and Identifying Their Values

The names of our coins are conventions of our social system. Students learn these names the same way that they learn the names of physical objects in their daily environment—through exposure and repetition.

The value of each coin is also a convention that students must simply be told. For these values to make sense, students must understand 5, 10, and 25 and think of these quantities without seeing countable objects. They need to interpret, "this is 5," as a coin value while we are pointing to a single nickel—a challenge for students who are still counting objects by ones. Coin value lessons should focus on purchase power—a dime can *buy the same thing* that 10 pennies can buy.

Counting Sets of Coins. Naming the total value of a group of coins is the same as mentally adding their values. Second-grade students can be asked to do the mental math required in counting a collection of different coins.

Students often sort their coins and start counting from the highest values. They can also make compatible combinations putting a nickel with a quarter to make 30 cents. Pennies aside, coins are fortunately multiples of 5 and 10 which lends itself to skip counting. The next activity is a preparation for counting money.

Activity 18.37   CCSS-M: 2.MD.C.8

Money Skip Counting

ENGLISH LEARNERS

Explain to students that they will start skip counting by one number, and at your signal they will shift to a count by a different number. Use any two of these amounts: 100, 50, 25, 10, 5, and 1—for example, 25 and 10—and write them on the board. Always start with the larger number (25) and have students skip count by 25s from that number. After three or more counts, raise your hand to indicate a pause in the counting.Then point to 10. Students continue the skip count from where they left off but now skip count by tens. If you have ELs who are recent immigrants, invite them to share the coins from their country and see how they compare to our coins.

Activity 18.38   CCSS-M: 2.MD.C.8

Hundreds Chart Money Count

Give students a Hundreds Chart and a collection of play money. Begin with two different coins—for example, a quarter and a dime. Use place value to represent the 25 cents in the same way students have previously used the chart (count two rows down and over five spaces to the right). Place the quarter on the 25 space and then count 10 more (down one row) and place the dime on 35. The total of the two coins is 35 cents. Use other coin collections and what students already know about patterns on the hundreds chart to calculate the total value.

MyLab Education   Blackline Master: Hundreds Chart

Because adding on to find a difference is such a valuable skill, it makes sense to give students experiences with "think-addition" to make change. As students become more skillful at adding on, they can see the process of making change as an extension of a skill already acquired.

MyLab Education   Self-Check 18.8

MyLab Education   Math Practice: Need to practice or refresh your math content knowledge? Click to access practice exercises associated with the content from this chapter.

See Table 18.2 for examples of common challenges and misconceptions about measurement and how to help students.

TABLE 18.2   COMMON CHALLENGES OR MISCONCEPTIONS IN MEASUREMENT AND HOW TO HELP

Common Challenge or Misconception	What It Looks Like	How to Help
1. Focus on the ending point of a ruler rather than the length.	Without attending to where an object is aligned on the left side of a ruler, students read the number on the ruler that aligns with the object's right edge. 0 1 2 3 4 5 6 7 8 9 10 11 12	• Move items along a ruler and ask students if they believe the item has changed size. • Iterate units to show how long the item is and then show how those units match the units on the ruler. • Give students experiences with the Broken Ruler.
2. Place multiple individual units with gaps between the units or with some of the units overlapping; or students use unequal units.	Students have gaps between units or use unequal units when measuring length: Students overlap units when measuring area:	• Ask students to estimate the measure before measuring the object and explain why it is a reasonable estimate. • If students use unequal units, ask what the number refers to (e.g., the number of white rods or brown rods). • If students overlap length units, have them use linking cubes to measure length. • If students overlap area units use a unit with some thickness making it difficult to overlap the pieces (e.g., plastic square tiles or pattern blocks).

Common Challenge or Misconception	What It Looks Like	How to Help
3. Count tick marks rather than units.	It's four units. 0 1 2 3 4 5	• Have students iterate units—for example, to see how a ruler is made. Then emphasize that units are what we are counting and how the number or tick mark indicates the end of the unit. • Have students make their own ruler (see Activity 18.12).
4. Bigger units result in a larger measure.	Student measures an object's length using small paperclips as the unit. When measuring the same object using paperclips twice the size, the student estimates that the measure will be a larger number.	• Provide many experiences where the students measure the same object's attribute with two different sized units (where one of the larger units is equal to several of the smaller units). Have the student predict how the measures will relate to the size of the units.
5. Measure perimeter by counting two sides.	The perimeter is 10. 7 3	• This is an artifact of the problem having only two sides labeled with numbers. Have students draw a line around the rim or highlight the sides to show what is being measured. Then suggest each side is labeled before adding the lengths.
6. Measure perimeter by counting square units rather than side lengths.	Students count the number of squares around the border of the figure rather than the length of the sides of the squares. This results in a measure that is 4 units less than the actual perimeter.	• Focus on perimeter being a length rather than an area to cover. Show with gestures how the corner needs two units (of fence for example).
7. If you know the area of a figure you know the perimeter and vice versa (Amore and Pinilla, 2006).	Students will say as the area increases so does the perimeter. Students use the formula for area to find the perimeter	• Avoid teaching the topics of area and perimeter at the same time. • Focus on the similarities, differences and relationships between the two measurements. • Review Activities 18.20, 18.21, and 18.22.
8. Cutting a shape into parts and rearranging the pieces changes its area.	The first shape has more area than the second shape.	• Have students use the same set of pattern blocks to create 3 to 4 different designs tracing around each design on paper. Discuss how they can compare each area. They may need to iterate one pattern block (i.e., green triangle), recording how many are used for each shape.
9. Area formula can be stated but they cannot describe what area is in words.	When given a blob shape, students will say it has no area as it doesn't have a length and width.	• Go back to the use of nonstandard units to focus on area as a process of covering two-dimensional space. • Use Activity 18.17.
10. As the side length of the figure doubles the area doubles.	When asked what happens to the area of a two by two inch square if the sides double to four by four inch, students say the area doubles.	• Act this problem out. Because the figure has two dimensions, this is a change in square units, not a change in lengths alone. Students should place tiles down on the new figure to prove that the area is four times as large—not doubled.

(continued)

Common Challenge or Misconception	What It Looks Like	How to Help
11. Uses $L \times W$ for the area of other figures.	Students say the area for this figure is 15 square inches 3 inches / 5 inches	• Make a parallelogram scaled to precisely 3 inches by 5 inches. Have students use one inch squares to cover the area. What do students notice?
12. Estimates of measures must be "exact" and will be graded on how close you are to the "right" answer (Muir, 2005).	Students constantly try to change their estimate to reach the "correct" answer.	• Rather than give prizes or promote "winning" estimates, give a range of estimates that are reasonable. • Avoid using the terms measure and estimate interchangeably. • Measurements always have some error so using the word "exact" should be avoided.
13. The larger the rays of the angle, the larger the angle.	Given these two angles, students will say B is the larger angle. Which angle is bigger? A B	• Use the classroom door to act angle sizes. Show how the angle is not affected by the size of the door—is it only about the spread of the space between the door and the wall of the classroom. • See Figure 18.25.
14. The height of the solid figure or container indicates its volume.	Students select the tallest container as having the greatest volume or capacity.	• Use a collection of containers (where the tallest is not the largest) and have students estimate the order from smallest to largest. Test to show the actual order.
15. The length or size of an object is an indication of its weight.	Students select the largest object as the heaviest object.	• Use a collection of items (where the longest or largest are not the heaviest) and have students estimate the order from lightest to heaviest. Test to show the actual weights.
16. Confusion about the minute and hour hands on an analog clock, or student reads the number closest to the hour hand as the hour.	When shown 6:45 on an analog clock, the student states one of the following times: 6:09 9:06 9:30 7:45	• This is due to the clock having two main scales (hours and minutes) (there are also seconds if reading a clock to greater precision) around the same circle. Start with only one scale using Activity 18.36. • Pair an analog clock with a digital clock so the student can compare the time on each.
17. The size of a coin equates to its value.	The student thinks the dime is worth less than the penny or nickel because it is smaller in size.	• Glue coins to linking cubes that represent their values or to a ten-frame that shows each coin's value (i.e., glue a penny to a ten-frame with only one space filled; glue a nickel to a ten-frame with five spaces filled; and so on).

MyLab Education   **Activity Page: Broken Ruler**

RESOURCES ON CHAPTER 18

LITERATURE CONNECTIONS
How Big Is a Foot?
Myller (1991)

This story is a fun situation for students to ponder. The king measures the queen using his feet and orders a bed 6 feet long and 3 feet wide. The carpenter's apprentice, who is very small, makes the bed according to his own feet, demonstrating the need for standard units. (Another tale of nonstandard units is *Twelve Snails to One Lizard* [Hightower, 1997].)

Just a Second
Jenkins (2011)

This beautifully illustrated book provides fascinating facts about what can happen in a second, a minute, an hour, a day, a month, and a year. Did you know a bumblebee beats its wings 200 times a second? Students can use the facts provided to explore and discuss many mathematical problems.

RECOMMENDED READINGS
Articles

Austin, R., Thompson, D., & Beckmann, C. (2005). Exploring measurement concepts through literature: Natural links across disciplines. *Mathematics Teaching in the Middle School, 10*(5), 218–224.

This article discusses almost 30 children's books that emphasize length, weight, capacity, speed, area, perimeter, and volume. Three books are described in detail as how to integrate measurement to other subject areas.

Wickstrom, M., & Jurczak, L. (2016). Inch by inch, we measure. *Teaching Children Mathematics, 22*(8), 468–475.

Using the book Inch by Inch (Lionni, 1960), the authors link inchworms to building the idea of a length unit. Through estimation and the use of multiple strategies, young students began to make sense of how rulers work.

19

Developing Geometric Thinking and Geometric Concepts

LEARNER OUTCOMES

After reading this chapter and engaging in the embedded activities and reflections, you should be able to:

19.1 Summarize the four major geometry goals for students.

19.2 Describe the van Hiele levels of geometric thinking.

19.3 Analyze strategies for teaching about shapes and properties.

19.4 Identify approaches to teaching geometric transformations.

19.5 Explore ways to engage students in thinking about location.

19.6 Illustrate approaches that develop students' imagery and visualization skills.

Geometry is a "network of concepts, ways of reasoning and representation systems" used to explore and analyze shape and space (Battista, 2007, p. 843). This critical area of mathematics appears in everything from global positioning systems to computer animation. Geometry is at the core of early mathematics, alongside the strand of number (NCTM, 2000). In many state standards documents, like measurement, geometry spans grades from K–8. As such we will describe the standards by grades in different sections of this chapter.

BIG IDEAS

- What makes shapes alike and different can be determined by geometric properties (i.e., defining characteristics). Shapes can be classified into a hierarchy of categories according to the properties they share.

- Transformations help students think about the ways properties change or do not change when a shape is moved in a plane or in space. These changes can be described in terms of translations, reflections, rotations, dilations, the study of symmetries, and the concept of similarity.

- Shapes can be described in terms of their location in a plane or in space. Young children use language such as *above*, *below*, and *next to* while later students use coordinate systems used to describe these locations more precisely. The coordinate view also offers ways to understand certain properties of shapes and can be used to measure distance, an important application of the Pythagorean theorem.

♦ Visualization includes the recognition of shapes in the environment, developing relationships between two-and three-dimensional objects, the ability to draw and recognize objects from different viewpoints, and to mentally change the orientation and size of shapes.

Geometry Goals for Students

Geometry is a way to explore and analyze shape and space. This critical area of mathematics appears in everything from global positioning systems to computer animation. But, for too long, the geometry curriculum merely emphasized learning terminology and low-level tasks such as naming shapes or angle categories such as acute or obtuse. Geometry is much more.

First, geometry involves developing and applying spatial sense. *Spatial sense* is an intuition about shapes and the relationships between them and is considered a core area of mathematical study, like number (Sarama & Clements, 2009). Spatial sense includes the ability to mentally visualize objects and spatial relationships—to turn things around in one's mind. It also includes a familiarity with geometric descriptions of objects and position. People with well-developed spatial sense appreciate geometric form in art, nature, and architecture and they use geometric ideas to describe and analyze their world.

Spatial sense also includes how students use diagrams and sketches as they develop concepts, the composing and decomposing of shapes, maps and orientation, and visualizing mathematical ideas using mental imagery (Mulligan, 2015). Students who have exceptional ability with mentally manipulating two-dimensional and three-dimensional objects have been shown to have greater creative achievements and academic success more than thirty years later, especially in STEM fields, than students who showed ability with more familiar measures of mathematics and verbal performance (Kell, Lubinski, Benbow, & Steiger, 2013; Wai, Lubinski, & Benbow, 2009).

Second, geometry has significant content strands that apply to all grade levels. This chapter is organized around these four major geometry strands: Shapes and Properties, Transformation, Location and Visualization. Each strand will begin with foundational experiences and move through more challenging experiences using van Hiele's levels of geometric thought as a guide. You will notice that more attention is devoted to the shapes and properties strand to align with the emphasis identified in the *Common Core State Standards* for grades K–8. However, notice that experiences targeted toward each of the strands have potential to enhance students' understanding of other strands.

MyLab Education   Self-Check 19.1

Developing Geometric Thinking

All learners are capable of growing and developing the ability to think and reason in geometric contexts, but this ability requires ongoing and significant experiences across a developmental progression. The research of two Dutch educators, Pierre van Hiele and Dina van Hiele-Geldof, provides insights into students' development of geometric thinking through the descriptions of different levels of thought. The van Hiele theory (1984) significantly influences geometry curricula worldwide and can help all teachers understand next steps for their students' geometry instruction.

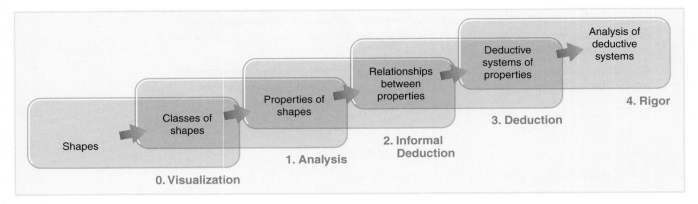

FIGURE 19.1 The van Hiele theory of geometric thought.

The van Hiele Levels of Geometric Thought

The van Hiele model is a five-level hierarchy of understanding spatial ideas (see Figure 19.1). Each level describes the thinking processes used in geometric contexts. Specifically, the levels describe how we think and what types of geometric ideas we think about (called *objects of thought*) and what students can do (*products of thought*). These levels are important for you to know because as you work with students at one level, you have an understanding of where they need to move to on the next level and the connections that should be developed.

The levels are developmental—learners of any age begin at level 0 and progress to the next level through experiences with geometrical ideas. Characteristics of the van Hiele levels are provided in Table 19.1.

Level 0: Visualization.

Students move from considering shapes and what they "look like" to developing classes or groupings of shapes that seem to be "alike."

Students at level 0 recognize and name shapes based on global visual characteristics. For example, a square is defined by a level 0 student as a square "because it looks like a square." Appearance is dominant at level 0 and can therefore overpower students' thinking about the properties of a shape. A level 0 thinker, for example, may see a square with sides that are not horizontal or vertical (it appears tilted) and believe it is a "diamond" (not a mathematical term for a shape) and no longer a square. Students at this level will sort and classify shapes based on their appearance—"I put these shapes together because they are all pointy."

The emphasis at level 0 is on shapes that students can observe, feel, build (compose), take apart (decompose), or work with in some manner. The goal is to explore how shapes are alike and different and use these ideas to create classes of shapes (both physically and mentally). Some of these classes of shapes have names—rectangles, triangles, prisms, cylinders, and so on. Properties of shapes, (i.e., parallel sides, symmetry, right angles) are included at this level but only in an informal, observational manner.

TABLE 19.1 CHARACTERISTICS OF THE VAN HIELE LEVELS

Characteristic	Implication
1. Sequential	To arrive at a level above 0, students must move through all prior levels. The products of thought at each level are the same as the objects of thought at the next level (see Figure 19.1).
2. Developmental	When instruction or language is at a level higher than that of the students, students will be challenged to understand the concept being developed. A student can, for example, memorize a fact (such as all squares are rectangles) but not mentally construct the actual relationship of how the properties of a square and rectangle are related.
3. Age independent	A third-grade student or a high school student could be at level 0.
4. Experience dependent	Advancement through the levels requires geometric *experiences*. Students should explore, talk about, and interact with content at the next level while increasing experiences at their current level.

Clements and Battista (1992) proposed a level prior to level 0 called Pre-Recognition. Clements and Sarama (2014) recommend activities in which examples and nonexamples that look alike are paired so students focus attention on a shape's critical attributes. An attribute applies to only particular shapes (two sides the same length) but a property would apply to all shapes in a category—like triangles have three sides. The next activity provides a pre-recognition experience.

Activity 19.1

CCSS-M: K.G.A.2; K.G.B.4; 1.G.A.1

Tricky Shapes

Provide pairs with Tricky Shapes for Triangles or Tricky Shapes for Rectangles that has several examples and nonexamples of a target shape (see Figure 19.2). Students should identify examples that are like the target shape and nonexamples that are not like the target shape—and state why in each case. Facilitate a whole class discussion and summarize by reviewing the shape's relevant features.

MyLab Education   Activity Page: Tricky Shapes for Triangles
MyLab Education   Activity Page: Tricky Shapes for Rectangles

FIGURE 19.2 Examples and nonexamples help students attend to critical properties.

The following activity is an example of an experience for level 0 learners as it focuses on how shapes are alike or different.

Activity 19.2

CCSS-M: K.G.B.4; 1.G.A.1; 2.G.A.1; 3.G.A.1

Shape Sorts

Group students with a set of two-dimensional shapes (see Figure 19.3) to do the following related activities in order:

- Randomly select two shapes and try to find something that is alike about the two shapes and something that is different.

- Choose one target shape at random and place it in the center of the workspace. Find all other shapes that are like the target shape according to the same property. For example, say "This shape is like the target shape because it has a curved side and a straight side," then all other shapes put in the collection must have that property. Do a second sort with the same target shape but using a different property as a challenge.

- Do a "secret sort." Create a group of about three to four shapes that fit a secret rule. Leave others that belong in that set in the larger pile. Have others find additional pieces that belong to the set and guess the secret rule.

Also explore the Expanded Lesson: Shape Sorts for more details.

MyLab Education   Activity Page: Two-Dimensional Shapes
MyLab Education   Expanded Lesson: Shape Sorts

FIGURE 19.3 A collection of shapes for sorting.

These "find-a-rule" activities elicit a wide variety of ideas. Students may initially describe shapes with ideas such as "curvy" or "looks like a rocket" rather than typical geometric properties. But as they notice more sophisticated properties, you can attach appropriate terminology to them. For example, students may notice some shapes have corners "like a square" (explain that those are called *right angles*) or that "these shapes are the same on both sides" (explain that that is called *line symmetry*). For young learners, consider using Venn diagrams as an organizational tool for the sorting (Howse & Howse, 2014/2015).

What clearly makes this activity level 0 is that students are operating on the shapes that they see in front of them and are beginning to see ways they are alike and different. By forming groups of shapes, they begin to imagine shapes belonging to classes that are not present in their current collection.

Level 1: Analysis.

> *Students move from considering classes of shapes rather than individual shapes by focusing on the properties of shapes.*

Students at the analysis level consider all shapes within a class rather than just the single shape on their desk. Instead of talking about *this* particular rectangle, they can talk about properties of *all* rectangles. By focusing on a class of shapes, students are able to think about what makes a rectangle a rectangle (four sides, opposite sides parallel, opposite sides same length, four right angles, congruent diagonals, etc.). Irrelevant features (e.g., size or orientation) fade into the background, and students begin to understand that if a shape belongs to a particular class such as cubes, it has the corresponding properties of that class: "All cubes have six congruent faces, and each of those faces is a square." These defining properties were unspoken at level 0. Students at level 1 may be able to list all the properties of squares, rectangles, and parallelograms but may not see that these shapes are subclasses of one another—that all squares are rectangles and all rectangles are parallelograms.

Although level 1 students continue to use physical models and drawings of shapes, they begin to see these individual shapes as examples of members in classes of shapes. Their understanding of properties of shapes, continues to be refined and this identification of properties is an important cognitive activity (Yu, Barrett, & Presmeg, 2009).

In the following activity, students use the properties of shapes such as symmetry, angle classification (right, obtuse, acute), parallel and perpendicular, and the concept of congruent line segments and angles.

Activity 19.3

CCSS-M: 2.G.A.1; 3.G.A.1; 4.G.A.2; 4.G.A.3

Property Lists for Quadrilaterals

ENGLISH LEARNERS

Prepare handouts for Parallelograms, Rhombuses, Rectangles, and Squares (see Figure 19.4). Assign groups of three or four students to work with one type of quadrilateral (for ELs and students with disabilities, post labeled shapes as a reference). Ask students to list as many properties as they can that apply to all of the shapes on their sheet. They will need tools such as index cards (to check right angles, compare side lengths, and draw straight lines), mirrors (to check line symmetry), and tracing paper (for identifying angle congruence). Encourage students to use the words "exactly," "at least," and "at most" when describing how many of something: for example, "rectangles have at least two lines of symmetry," because squares—included in the rectangles category—have four.

STUDENTS with SPECIAL NEEDS

   Have students prepare their Property Lists under these headings: Sides, Angles, Diagonals, and Symmetries. Groups then share their lists with the class, and eventually develop a class list for each category of shape. For ELs, having students say the words aloud, and point to the word as you say it are ways to reinforce meaning and support participation in discussions.

MyLab Education   Activity Page: Property List for Parallelograms
MyLab Education   Activity Page: Property List for Rhombuses
MyLab Education   Activity Page: Property List for Rectangles
MyLab Education   Activity Page: Property List for Squares
MyLab Education   Activity Page: Property List for Sides, Angles, Diagonals, Symmetries

Notice that students must assess whether the properties apply to all shapes in the category. If they are working on the squares, for example, their observations apply to a square mile as well as a square centimeter.

Level 2: Informal Deduction.

Students move from considering the properties of shapes to exploring the relationships between properties of geometric objects.

As students begin to think about properties of geometric objects without focusing on one particular object (shape), they develop relationships between these properties. "If all four angles are right angles, the shape must be a rectangle. If it is a square, all angles are right angles. If it is a square, it must be a rectangle." Once students can engage in *if–then* reasoning, they can classify shapes using only a minimum set of defining characteristics. For example, four congruent sides and at least one right angle are sufficient to define a square. Rectangles are parallelograms with a right angle. Observations go beyond properties themselves and begin to focus on logical arguments about the properties. Students at level 2 will be able to follow informal deductive arguments about shapes and their properties. "Proofs" may be more intuitive than deductive; however, there is the ability to follow a logical argument. An understanding of a formal deductive system (an agreed-on set of rules) may remain undiscovered until students have more experiences.

The signature characteristic of a level 2 activity is the inclusion of informal logical reasoning. Because students have developed an understanding of various properties of shapes, it is now time to encourage conjecture and to ask "Why?" or "What if?"

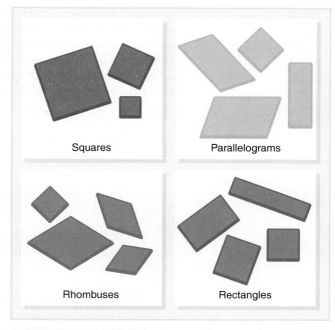

FIGURE 19.4 Shapes for the "Property Lists for Quadrilaterals" activity.

Activity 19.4 CCSS-M: 4.G.A.2; 5.G.B.3

Minimal Defining Lists

This activity is a sequel to Activity 19.3, "Property List for Quadrilaterals." Once the class has agreed upon property lists for the parallelogram, rhombus, rectangle, and square (and possibly the kite and trapezoid) post the lists. Have students work in groups to find "minimal defining lists," or MDLs, for each shape. An MDL is a subset of the properties for a shape that is defining and minimal. The term "defining" here means that any shape with all the properties on the MDL must be that shape. The term "minimal" means that if any single property is removed from the list, it is no longer defining. For example, one MDL for a square is a quadrilateral with (1) four congruent sides and (2) four right angles (two items on the list). If a shape has these two properties it must be a square. Another minimal defining list for a square is (1) is has four sides of the same length and (2) perpendicular diagonals. Challenge students to find more than one MDL for their shape. A proposed list is not defining if a counterexample—a shape other than one being described—can be produced by using only the properties on the list.

Students can also make guessing puzzles using the clues from their list and basic computer coding such as *Scratch* a free platform developed at MIT (Bolognese, 2016).

The hallmark of this activity and other level 2 tasks is the emphasis on logical reasoning: "*If* a quadrilateral has these properties, *then* it must be a square." Logic is also involved in proving that a proposed list is faulty—either not minimal or not defining. Here students begin to learn the nature of a definition and the value of counterexamples. In fact, any minimal defining list (MDL) is a potential definition. The other aspect of this activity that clearly involves level 2 thinking is that students focus on analyzing the relationships between properties (e.g., if a quadrilateral has four right angles, it also has diagonals of the same length).

Level 3: Deduction. (Note: Levels 3 and 4 are beyond the scope of this book)

Students move from considering the relationships between properties of geometric objects to developing deductive axiomatic systems for geometry.

At level 3, students analyze informal arguments; the structure of a system complete with axioms, definitions, theorems, corollaries, and postulates begins to develop and can be appreciated as the necessary means of establishing geometric truth. The student at this level is usually in high school and is able to work with abstract statements about geometric properties and make conclusions based on logic. A student operating at level 3 has an appreciation of the need to develop a proof from a series of deductive arguments.

Level 4: Rigor.

Students move from considering deductive axiomatic systems for geometry to comparing and contrasting different axiomatic systems of geometry.

At the highest level of the van Hiele hierarchy, the objects of attention are axiomatic systems themselves, not just the deductions within a system. This level is generally that of a college mathematics major studying geometry as a branch of mathematical science.

FORMATIVE ASSESSMENT Notes. How do you discover students' van Hiele level so you can select the right activities? Listen to the types of observations that students make and record them on an Observation Checklist noting if they:

- Talk about shapes as classes—referring to "rectangles," or do they base their discussion on a particular rectangle?
- Do they understand that shapes do not change when the orientation changes?
- Describe all features of the group of quadrilaterals? Triangles?
- Compare groups of shapes (e.g., rectangles) to other groups of shapes (e.g., squares)?

With simple observations such as these, you will be able to distinguish between levels 0, 1, and 2. If students are not able to understand logical arguments, are not comfortable with conjectures, and are unsure of if—then reasoning, they are likely still at level 1 or below and will need more experiences to reach level 2. The geometry in high school is primarily at level 3, so a priority in middle school is that students are moving to at least strong level 2 thinkers. ∎

MyLab Education   **Blackline Master: Observation Checklist**

Implications for Instruction

The collection of geometric experiences you provide are the single most important factor in moving students up this developmental ladder to higher levels of geometric thought! Many activities can be modified to span two levels of thinking, helping students move from one level to the next.

Consider Clements and Sarama's (2014) four features of effective early geometry instruction:

1. Show a variety of shapes and have students compare both examples and nonexamples with a focus on critical characteristics.
2. Facilitate student discussions about the properties of shapes, having them develop essential language along the way.
3. Encourage the examination classes of shapes that goes beyond the traditional, allowing students to explore relationships and recognize different categories, orientations, and sizes.
4. Provide students with a range of geometric experiences at every level, having them use physical materials, drawings, and technology.

MyLab Education   **Video Example 19.1**

Watch this video of John Van de Walle talking about activities that correspond with several early levels of geometric thinking.

Moving from Level 0 to Level 1. Instructional considerations that support students moving from level 0 to level 1 are as follows:

- *Focus on the properties of shapes rather than on simple identification.* As new geometric concepts are learned, students should be challenged to use these attributes to classify shapes.
- *Challenge students to test ideas about shapes using a variety of examples from a particular category.* Say, "Let's see if that is true for other rectangles," or "Can you draw a triangle that does not have a right angle?" Question students to see whether observations made about a particular shape apply to other shapes of the same kind.
- *Provide ample opportunities to draw, build, make, put together (compose), and take apart (decompose) shapes in both two and three dimensions.* Build these activities around understanding and using specific attributes or properties.
- *Apply ideas to entire classes of figures (such as* all *rectangles or* all *prisms) rather than to individual models.* For example, find ways to sort all possible triangles into groups. From these groups, define types of triangles.

Moving from Level 1 to Level 2. Level 2 thinking is expected to begin in grade 5, when students classify shapes based on their properties in categories and subcategories (NGA Center & CCSSO, 2010). Instructional considerations supporting students' movement from level 1 to level 2 are:

- *Challenge students to explore and test examples.* Ask questions that involve reasoning, such as "If the sides of a four-sided shape are all congruent, will you always have a square?" and "Can you find a counterexample?"
- *Encourage the making and testing of hypotheses or conjectures.* "Do you think that will work all the time?" "Is that true for all triangles or just equilateral ones?"
- *Examine properties of shapes to determine necessary and sufficient conditions for a shape to be a particular shape.* "What properties must diagonals have to guarantee that a quadrilateral with these diagonals will be a square?"
- *Use the language of informal deduction.* Say: *all, some, none, if . . . then, what if,* and so on.
- *Encourage students to attempt informal proofs.* As an alternative, require them to make sense of informal proofs that you or other students have suggested.

 Standards for Mathematical Practice
MP3. Construct viable arguments and critique the reasoning of others.

The remainder of this chapter offers activities organized around the four content goals of shapes and properties, location, transformations, and visualization. Understand that these subdivisions overlap and build on each other as activities in one section may help develop geometric thinking in another.

MyLab Education   **Self-Check 19.2**

MyLab Education   **Application Exercise 19.1: Identifying Properties of Shapes** Click the link to access this exercise, then watch the video and answer the accompanying questions.

 ## Shapes and Properties

Shapes and properties is the content area most often associated with geometry in preK–8 classrooms; when young students begin to "perceive, say, describe/discuss and construct objects in 2-D space" (National Research Council Committee, 2009, p. 177). Students need experience with a wide variety of two- and three-dimensional shapes. Triangles should be shown in more than just equilateral forms and not always with the vertex at the top or the base horizontal to the bottom of the paper on which it appears. Shapes should have curved sides, straight sides, and combinations of these. As students describe the shape or property, the terminology can be introduced, as in the next activity.

Activity 19.5

CCSS-M: K.G.A.1; K.G.A.2; K.G.B.4

Shape Show and Hunt

Use masking tape to create a large target shape that students can walk around on the community rug or floor. Ask students if they can name the shape or any attributes (e.g., straight or curved sides, number of sides, right angles, etc.). Confirm that students, especially ELs, understand the terms you use. You can also have students draw the shape in the air or on paper. Then, ask "Can you find one or two items in the classroom, on the playground, or somewhere else at school that have this shape?" Take photos of the examples students find so they can be used later for discussion. Ask, "How do you know the example is like the target shape?" For students with disabilities, provide a cutout of the target shape that they can take with them as they search for an example.

ENGLISH LEARNERS

STUDENTS *with* **SPECIAL NEEDS**

Sorting and Classifying

As young students work at classification of shapes, be prepared for them to notice features that you do not consider to be "real" geometric attributes, such as "dented" or "looks like a tree." Students at this level will also attribute to shapes ideas that are not part of the shape, such as "points up" or "has a side that is the same as the edge of the board."

For variety in two-dimensional shapes, use materials like a set of Assorted Shapes. Make multiple copies so that groups of students can all work with the same shapes. Once you have your sets constructed, try Activity 19.2, "Shape Sorts."

> **MyLab Education**   Activity Page: Assorted Shapes

In any sorting and classifying activity, the students—not the teacher—should decide how to group the shapes. By listening to the kinds of attributes that they use in their sorting, you will be able to tell what properties they know and use and how they think about shapes. Figure 19.5 illustrates a few of the possible ways a set might be sorted.

The secret sort in Activity 19.2 is one option for introducing a new property. For example, sort the shapes so that all have at least one right angle or "square corner." When students discover your rule, you have an opportunity to name the property "right angle."

The following activity also uses the two-dimensional shapes.

Activity 19.6

CCSS-M: 1.G.A.1; 2.G.A.1; 3.G.A.1; 4.G.A.2; 7.G.A.2

What's My Shape?

Cut out a double set of two-dimensional Assorted Shapes on card stock. Glue each shape from one set inside a file folder to make "secret-shape" folders. Glue the other set of shapes on cards and place them in view for reference. Designate one student as the leader who holds the secret-shape folder. The other students are to identify the shape in the folder by asking the leader "yes" or "no" questions. The group eliminates shapes (turning over the cards) as they get answers about the properties that narrow the choices to one shape. Students cannot point to a piece and ask, "Is it this shape?" Instead, they ask "Does it have all straight sides? Is it concave?" Check the final shape card against the one in the folder. Provide students with disabilities a list of possible properties and characteristics (such as number of sides) to help support their question asking. Also, adapt this activity for three-dimensional shapes. For older students cover the mystery shape with a paper curtain and slowly reveal portions. At each "reveal" let students speculate on what the shape could be and what it couldn't be until it is uncovered (Ronau, Meyer, & Crites, 2015).

STUDENTS *with* **SPECIAL NEEDS**

> **MyLab Education**   Activity Page: Assorted Shapes

The difficulty of Activity 19.6 largely depends on the shape in the folder. The more shapes in the collection that share properties with the secret shape, the more difficult the task.

FORMATIVE ASSESSMENT Notes. Adapt "Shape Sorts" (Activity 19.2) for a diagnostic interview. Make sure you have a collection that has a lot of variation (curved surfaces, etc.) such as commercially available collections of three-dimensional shapes or real objects such as cans, boxes, containers, and balls. Figure 19.6 illustrates some classifications of solids. ■

The ways students describe these three-dimensional shapes provides evidence of their level of thinking. The classifications made by level 0 thinkers are generally limited to the shapes that they have in front of them. Level 1 thinkers will begin to create categories based on properties, and their language will indicate that they know there are more shapes in the group than those present. Students may say things like "These shapes have square corners sort of like rectangles," or "These shapes look like boxes. All the boxes have square [rectangular] sides."

Activity 19.7

CCSS-M: 1.G.A.1; 2.G.A.1; 3.G.A.1; 4.G.A.2

Can You Make It?

Print out the Can You Make It? Activity Page for each student or project one item at a time for the whole class. Students take the descriptions and then create a corresponding shape on the geoboard (two of these tasks are impossible). Encourage students to create challenges for others to try. If the class keeps track of solutions to the challenges in the last activity, there is an added possibility of creating classes of shapes possessing certain properties that may result in definitions of new classes of shapes.

MyLab Education Activity Page: Can You Make It?

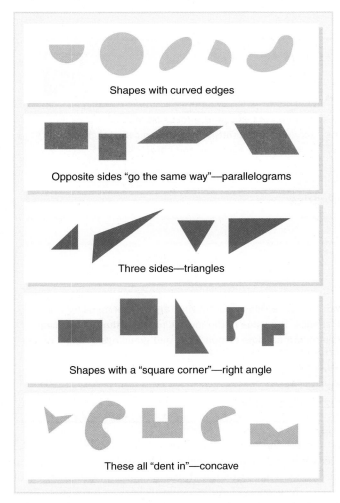

Shapes with curved edges

Opposite sides "go the same way"—parallelograms

Three sides—triangles

Shapes with a "square corner"—right angle

These all "dent in"—concave

FIGURE 19.5 By sorting shapes, students begin to recognize properties.

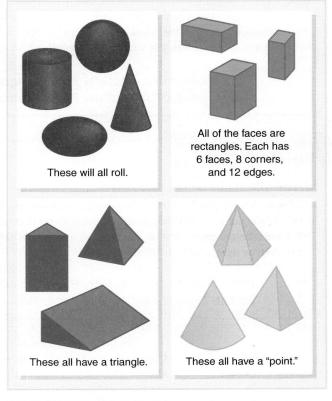

These will all roll.

All of the faces are rectangles. Each has 6 faces, 8 corners, and 12 edges.

These all have a triangle.

These all have a "point."

FIGURE 19.6 Early classifications of three-dimensional shapes.

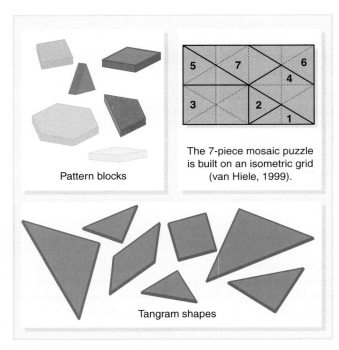

The 7-piece mosaic puzzle is built on an isometric grid (van Hiele, 1999).

Pattern blocks

Tangram shapes

FIGURE 19.7 Materials for composing and decomposing shapes.

Composing and Decomposing Shapes

Students need to freely explore how shapes fit together to form larger shapes (compose) and how larger shapes can be made of smaller shapes (decompose). In addition, in grade 7, students compose (draw) shapes in order to study the properties of the shape: "Draw (freehand, with ruler and protractor, and with technology) geometric shapes with given conditions" (NGA Center & CCSSO, 2010, p. 50). This ability to compose and decompose shapes starts in prekindergarten (Copley, 2017) and eventually supports geometric measurement such as finding area of irregular shapes, surface area, and volume.

Among two-dimensional shapes for these activities, pattern blocks and Tangram Pieces are the best known. Pierre van Hiele (1999) also describes an interesting set of tiles he calls the Mosaic Puzzle (see Figure 19.7).

MyLab Education	Activity Page: Tangram Pieces
MyLab Education	Activity Page: Mosaic Puzzle

Activity 19.8

CCSS-M: K.G.B.6; 1.G.A.2; 2.G.A.1

TECHNOLOGY

Tangram Puzzles

Using a set of Tangram Pieces, have students explore the Tangram Puzzles Activity Page where they compose shapes to create a larger figure. Also notice how the creation of these picture puzzles can also focus on area (if all seven pieces are used, the areas are the same!) ABCYa! also has a tangram game (http://www.abcya.com/tangrams.htm) with different puzzle figures that students can unlock within each of the levels: easy, medium, and hard.

MyLab Education   Activity Page: Tangram Pieces
MyLab Education   Activity Page: Tangram Puzzles

Activity 19.9

CCSS-M: K.G.B.6; 1.G.A.2; 2.G.A.1; 3.G.A.1; 4.G.A.2; 7.G.A.2

Mosaic Puzzle

Give pairs of students the Mosaic Puzzle and have them use the Mosaic Puzzle Questions Activity Page to explore using what they know about a shape's properties to compose and decompose shapes. The value of the mosaic puzzle is that the set contains five different angles (which could lead to discussions of types of informal angle comparisons and groupings of angle measures such as right, acute, and obtuse).

MyLab Education   Activity Page: Mosaic Puzzle
MyLab Education   Activity Page: Mosaic Puzzle Questions

The geoboard is one of the best devices for "constructing" two-dimensional shapes. In the beginning, teach students how to record their designs on Geoboard Recording Sheets. To help students who struggle with this transfer, suggest that they first mark the dots for the corners of their shape ("second row, end peg"). With the corners identified, it is much easier for them to draw lines between the corners to make the shape on paper. These drawings can be placed in groups for classification and discussion or sent home to families to showcase what students are learning.

Activity 19.10

CCSS-M: 1.G.A.2; 2.G.A.1; 4.G.A.1; 4.G.A.2; 4.G.A.3

Geoboard Copy

STUDENTS with SPECIAL NEEDS

Prepare Geoboard Design Cards (see Figure 19.8). Project the shapes onto a screen and have students copy them on geoboards (or Geoboard Patterns or Geoboard Recording Sheets). Begin with designs using one band, then create more complex designs, including those that show a shape composed of other smaller shapes. Discuss properties such as number of sides, parallel lines, or line symmetry, depending on the grade level. Students with disabilities may need to have a copy of the design card at their desk for closer reference.

MyLab Education   Activity Page: Geoboard Design Cards

MyLab Education   Blackline Master: Geoboard Patterns (10 by 10)

MyLab Education   Blackline Master: Geoboard Recording Sheets (10 by 10)

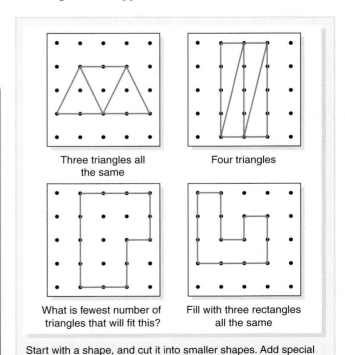

Have students copy shapes from pattern cards onto a geoboard.

Besides pattern cards with and without dots, have students copy <u>real</u> shapes—tables, houses, letters of the alphabet, and so on.

FIGURE 19.8   Shapes on geoboards.

Here are several activities appropriate for thinking about composing and decomposing shapes using a geoboard.

"Geoboard Copy" has an element of proportional thinking in it, just as any puzzles in which students work from small designs. This concept of scaling (or resizing) is particularly important for fifth graders (NGA Center & CCSSO, 2010). In addition, the use of the geoboard supports the study of area, particularly of compound shapes. Students also begin to understand that rectangles can be decomposed into equal rows or columns, which connects area to multiplication.

Activity 19.11

CCSS-M: 1.G.A.2; 1.G.A.3; 2.G.A.1; 2.G.A.3; 3.G.A.2; 3.NF.A.1

Decomposing Shapes

Show students a shape from the Decomposing Shapes Activity Page and ask them to copy it on their geoboards or Geoboard Recording Sheet. Then specify the number of smaller shapes they should decompose each large shape into, as in Figure 19.9. Specify whether the smaller shapes are all to be congruent or simply of the same type. You can connect geometry to fractions by discussing the equal parts. Then they can write the fraction of the whole for each part within the composed whole.

MyLab Education   Activity Page: Decomposing Shapes

MyLab Education   Blackline Master: Geoboard Recording Sheet (10 by 10)

Three triangles all the same   Four triangles

What is fewest number of triangles that will fit this?   Fill with three rectangles all the same

Start with a shape, and cut it into smaller shapes. Add special decompose conditions to make the activity challenging.

FIGURE 19.9   Decomposing shapes.

For any of the activities suggested for geoboards, allow students to choose the tool (geoboard, grid paper, or dot paper) that best supports their thinking on a given problem. There are also excellent digital versions of the geoboard. One is found at the Math Learning Center (https://www.mathlearningcenter.org/resources/apps) and allows students to make discoveries about angles, area, congruence, perimeter, and more.

MyLab Education	**Blackline Master: Geoboard Pattern (10 by 10)**
MyLab Education	**Blackline Master: Grid Paper (10 by 10)**
MyLab Education	**Blackline Master: Dot Paper**

Categories of Two- and Three-Dimensional Shapes

As students' attention shifts to properties of shapes (moving to level 1 thinking), the important definitions of two and three-dimensional shapes support the relationships between shapes.

Two-Dimensional Shapes. Table 19.2 lists some important categories of two-dimensional shapes. Examples of these shapes can be found in Figure 19.10.

By third grade, students must think about subcategories of quadrilaterals, and by fifth grade, they must "understand that attributes belonging to a category of two dimensional figures also belong to all subcategories of that category" (NGA Center & CCSSO, 2010, p. 38). For example, a square is a rectangle and a rhombus. All parallelograms are trapezoids,

TABLE 19.2 CATEGORIES OF TWO-DIMENSIONAL SHAPES

Shape	Description
Simple Closed Curves	
Concave, convex	An intuitive definition of concave might be "having a dent in it." If a simple closed curve is not concave, it is convex.
Symmetrical, nonsymmetrical	Shapes may have one or more lines of symmetry.
Regular	All sides and all angles are congruent.
Polygons	Simple closed curves with all straight sides.
Triangles	
Triangles	Polygons with exactly three sides.
Classified by sides	
Equilateral	All sides are congruent.
Isosceles	At least two sides are congruent.
Scalene	No two sides are congruent.
Classified by angles	
Right	One angle is a right angle.
Acute	All angles are smaller than a right angle.
Obtuse	One angle is larger than a right angle.
Convex Quadrilaterals	
Convex quadrilaterals	Convex polygons with exactly four sides.
Kite	Two opposing pairs of congruent adjacent sides.
Trapezoid	At least one pair of parallel sides.
Isosceles	A pair of opposite sides is congruent.
Parallelogram	Two pairs of parallel sides.
Rectangle	Parallelogram with a right angle.
Rhombus	Parallelogram with all sides congruent.
Square	Parallelogram with a right angle and all sides congruent.

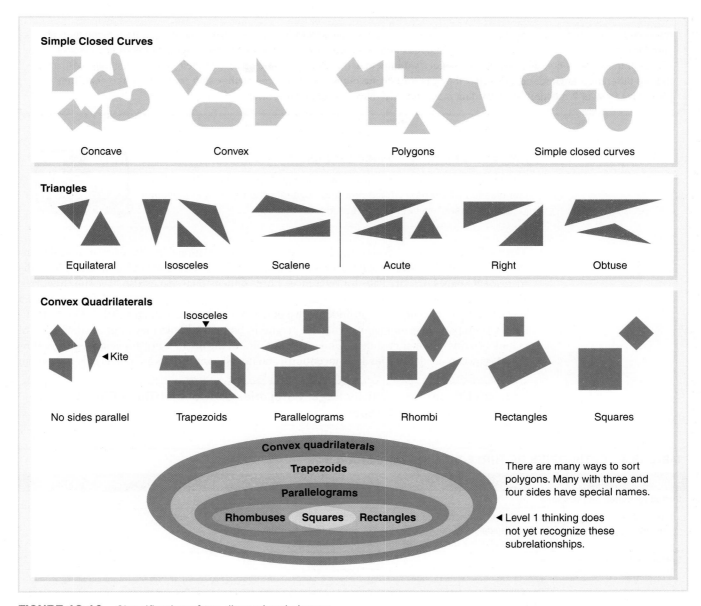

FIGURE 19.10 Classification of two-dimensional shapes.

but not all trapezoids are parallelograms.* Students often have difficulty seeing this type of subcategory. They may quite correctly list all the properties of a square, a rhombus, and a rectangle and still might classify a square as a "nonrhombus" or a "nonrectangle." To help learners think about this, suggest that a student can be on two different sports teams. A square is an example of a quadrilateral that belongs to two other "teams."

Activity 19.12

CCSS-M: K.G.A.1; K.G.B.4; 1.G.A.1; 1.G.A.2; 2.G.A.1; 3.G.A.1; 4.G.A.2

Shifting Shapes

The *Greedy Triangle* (Burns, 1995) is a delightful book about a triangle that is very busy being a sail or a roof. Soon he becomes bored and travels to a shape-shifter to get one more side and one more angle. Now a quadrilateral, he fits into

---

*Some definitions of trapezoid specify *only one* pair of parallel sides, in which case parallelograms would not be trapezoids. The University of Chicago School Mathematics Project (UCSMP) uses the "at least one pair" definition, meaning that parallelograms and rectangles are trapezoids. Some regions mandate one definition over another, so consult your local curriculum (Manizade & Mason, 2014).

four-sided figures in the environment. There are several other shape-shifts with interesting results. Using a meter-long loop of yarn for every pair of students (or three ace bandages tied in a loop for a demonstration), have students follow and discuss events in the book by creating appropriate shapes with the loop (holding it in the air between their hands). First, they can explore different triangles, and eventually they can investigate properties of shapes as they shift from one to the next. They can also move to level 2 thinking—by providing proof that they have a square, for example.

MyLab Education **Video Example 19.2**

Watch this video of Janet Caldwell as she talks about students' thinking of classes of shapes. Notice how she suggests the use of the language "special cases" to help support students' thinking.

Three-Dimensional Shapes. Important shapes and relationships also exist in three dimensions. Table 19.3 describes classifications of solids. See also the Categories of Two- and Three-dimensional Shapes Activity Page for reference. Three dimensional shapes also have subcategories. Figure 19.11 shows examples of cylinders and prisms. Notice that prisms are defined here as a special category of cylinder—a cylinder with a polygon for a base (Zwillinger, 2011). Figure 19.12 shows a comparable grouping of cones and pyramids. Some textbooks may limit the definition of cylinders to just circular cylinders. Under that definition, the prism is not a special case of a cylinder. As you can see definitions are conventions, and not all conventions are universally agreed on.

MyLab Education **Activity Page: Categories of Two- and Three-Dimensional Shapes**

TABLE 19.3 CATEGORIES OF THREE-DIMENSIONAL SHAPES

Shape	Description
Sorted by Edges and Vertices	
Spheres and "egglike" shapes	Shapes with no *edges* and no *vertices* (corners). Shapes with *edges* but no *vertices* (for example, a flying saucer). Shapes with *vertices* but no *edges* (for example, a football).
Sorted by Faces and Surfaces	
Polyhedron	Shapes made of all faces (a face is a flat surface of a solid). If all surfaces are faces, all the edges will be straight lines. Some combination of faces and rounded surfaces (circular cylinders are examples, but that is not a definition of a cylinder). Shapes with all curved surfaces. Shapes with and without edges and with and without vertices. Faces can be parallel. Parallel faces lie in planes that never intersect.
Cylinders	
Cylinder	Two congruent, parallel faces called *bases*. Lines joining corresponding points on the two bases are always parallel. These parallel lines are called *elements* of the cylinder.
Right cylinder	A cylinder with elements perpendicular to the bases. A cylinder that is not a right cylinder is an oblique cylinder.
Prism	A cylinder with polygons for bases. All prisms are special cases of cylinders.
Rectangular prism	A cylinder with rectangles for bases.
Cube	A square prism with square sides.
Cones	
Cone	A solid with exactly one face and a vertex that is not on the face. Straight lines (elements) can be drawn from any point on the edge of the base to the vertex. The base may be any shape at all. The vertex need not be directly over the base.
Circular cone	Cone with a circular base.
Pyramid	Cone with a polygon for a base. All faces joining the vertex are triangles. Pyramids are named by the shape of the base: *triangular* pyramid, *square* pyramid, *octagonal* pyramid, and so on. All pyramids are special cases of cones.

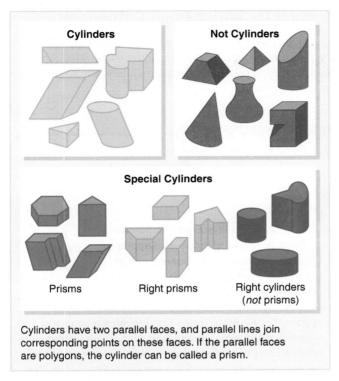

FIGURE 19.11 Cylinders and prisms.

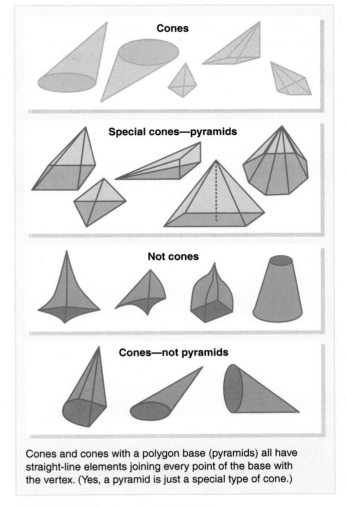

FIGURE 19.12 Cones and pyramids.

Construction Activities

Building or drawing two- and three-dimensional shapes is an important activity to help students think about properties and defining attributes of shapes (NGA Center & CCSSO, 2010). To help young learners explore solids and focus on learning about volume in the fifth grade and beyond, there is good reason to explore the construction of three-dimensional shapes. Building three-dimensional shapes is more difficult than building two-dimensional shapes, so consider the following activity for ideas.

Activity 19.13   CCSS-M: K.G.A.3; K.G.B.5; 1.G.A.2; 2.G.A.1; 6.G.A.4

Constructing Three-Dimensional Shapes

Collect one of the following sets of materials for students to use for construction:

1. Plastic coffee stirrers cut into a variety of lengths with twist ties inserted in the ends to use for attaching or modeling clay to connect corners
2. Plastic drinking straws cut lengthwise from the top down to the flexible joint—insert the slit ends into the uncut bottom ends of other straws, making strong but flexible joints
3. Rolled newspaper rods connected with masking or duct tape to create skeletons (see Figure 19.13)

With these handmade models, discuss the strength and rigidity of triangular components in the structures. Point out that triangles are used in many bridges, in the long booms of construction cranes, and in the structural parts of buildings. These models can also be used to explore volume and surface area.

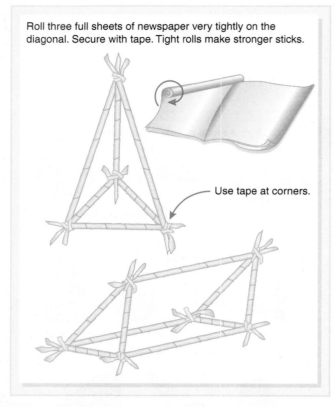

Roll three full sheets of newspaper very tightly on the diagonal. Secure with tape. Tight rolls make stronger sticks.

Use tape at corners.

FIGURE 19.13 Large skeletal structures can be built with tightly rolled newspaper.

Applying Definitions and Categories

Using definitions and categories helps students focus more deeply on the properties that make the shape what it is (and what it is not). The next activity provides a way to introduce a category of shapes.

Activity 19.14

CCSS-M: 1.G.A.1; 2.G.A.1; 3.G.A.2; 4.G.A.2

Mystery Definition

STUDENTS *with* **SPECIAL NEEDS**

Give students the Mystery Definition Activity Page, or project a grade-level-appropriate logic problem on the board (such as the example in Figure 19.14). At the top of your sheet, for your first collection, be certain that you have allowed for all possible correct options. For example, in the first grouping a square is included in the set of rhombuses. Also, choose nonexamples to be as close to the positive examples as is necessary to help develop a more precise definition. The third or mixed set should also include nonexamples that will challenge students or have confused them. Use the class discussion to hear students' justifications. The use of nonexamples is particularly important for students with disabilities.

MyLab Education Activity Page: Mystery Definition

Standards for Mathematical Practice
MP6. Attend to precision.

The value of the "Mystery Definition" activity is that students develop ideas and informal definitions based on their own concept development. After their definitions have been discussed, compared, and refined, you can contrast their ideas to the conventional definition for that shape.

MyLab Education Video Example 19.3

In this video Janet Caldwell discusses the importance of discussing the properties of shapes in figuring out how properties identify a particular shape. After students' definitions have been discussed, compared, and refined, you can contrast their ideas to the conventional definition for that shape.

VIDEO EXAMPLE

Exploring Properties of Triangles

Determining types of triangles is introduced in fourth grade with the concept of right triangles and extended in fifth grade as students focus on categories and subcategories of shapes. Then in seventh grade, students focus on the properties based on the measures of the sides and angles (NGA Center & CCSSO, 2010). For defining types or categories of triangles, the next activity is a good starting place.

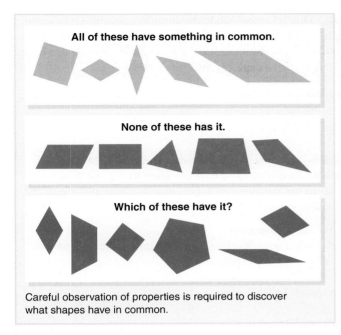

All of these have something in common.

None of these has it.

Which of these have it?

Careful observation of properties is required to discover what shapes have in common.

FIGURE 19.14   A mystery definition.

⏸ Pause & Reflect

Of the nine cells in the Triangle Sort Chart, two of them are impossible to fill. Can you tell which ones and why? ●

An important aspect of looking at types of triangles in seventh grade is to consider when given conditions result in a unique triangle, more than one triangle, or no triangle. Explore the following activity:

Activity 19.15

CCSS-M: 2.G.A.1; 3.G.A.2; 4.G.A.2; 5.G.B.3; 5.G.B.4; 7.G.A.2

Triangle Sort

STUDENTS
with
SPECIAL NEEDS

ENGLISH LEARNERS

Have teams cut out the triangles from the Assorted Triangles Activity Page, which includes examples of right, acute, and obtuse triangles; examples of equilateral, isosceles, and scalene triangles; and triangles that represent every possible combination of these categories. Ask, "Can you sort the entire collection into three discrete groups so that no triangle belongs to two groups?" When this sort is done and descriptions of the groupings have been written, students should find a second criterion for creating three different groupings. Students with disabilities may need a suggestion to look only at angle sizes or only at the issue of congruent sides, but delay giving these hints if you can. Once the groups have been determined, provide appropriate terminology. For ELs and other students who may struggle with the vocabulary, focus on the specialized meaning of these terms (such as contrasting "acute pain" and "acute angle"), and root words (*equi-* meaning *equal* and *lateral* meaning *side*). As a follow-up, challenge students to sketch a triangle in each of the nine cells of the Triangle Sort Chart. Extend the activity by repeating the process using kites and trapezoids or introduce three-dimensional shape definitions.

MyLab Education   Activity Page: Assorted Triangles
MyLab Education   Activity Page: Triangle Sort Chart

Activity 19.16

CCSS-M: 4.G.A.2; 4.G.A.3; 5.G.B.3; 5.G.B.4; 7.G.A.2

Can You Build It?

Provide questions about unique shapes and ask students if they can build or draw the shapes according to specifications. Always add the question—How many ways?

Can you make:

A. A shape with exactly one square corner and exactly four sides?
B. A shape with exactly one line of symmetry (or two lines of symmetry)?
C. A triangle with one 90-degree angle and two sides of 5 cm and 8 cm?
D. A triangle with two angles of 45 degrees?
E. A triangle with sides of 4 cm, 8 cm, and 13 cm?
F. A right triangle with legs (once right triangles are introduced; use the term legs for the two sides and hypotenuse to name the third side) of 3 units and 4 units?
G. An isosceles triangle with an 80-degree angle and a side of 5 units?

Interior Angles of a Triangle. Middle-school students should explore the relationship of angles within a triangle (adding to 180 degrees). They should also use facts about supplementary, complementary, vertical, and adjacent angles to solve for an unknown angle in a figure (NGA Center & CCSSO, 2010). Activity 19.17 explores interior angles.

Activity 19.17   CCSS-M: 5.G.B.3; 7.G.A.2; 8.G.A.5

Angle Sum in a Triangle

Distribute three copies of the Three Congruent Triangles Activity Page to pairs of students and have them label each triangle with angles A, B, and C making sure the corresponding angles on the equivalent triangles have the same letters and then cut out each set of triangles. Ask students to explore what they notice about the angles in one set of congruent triangles. If they do not discover that together they sum to 180 degrees, offer the following steps:

1. Place one triangle on a line and the second directly next to it in the same orientation.
2. Place the third triangle in the space between the triangles as shown in Figure 19.15(a). Ask, "Will this relationship be true for any kind of triangle?"
3. Test other sets of different equivalent triangles.
4. What conjecture can you make about the sum of the angles in a triangle?

MyLab Education   Activity Page: Three Congruent Triangles

Technology can be an important tool in exploring these relationships. For example, have students use a dynamic geometry program to draw a triangle, measure all the angles, and add them up. As the triangle vertices are dragged around, the sum of the angles remains at 180 degrees. Students can conjecture that the sum of the interior angles of a triangle is always 180 degrees (they can be led to the same conjecture by tearing off the angles of paper triangles and combining them to create a straight line). To know why this is true requires examining exterior angles as illustrated in Figure 19.15(a). There are lines parallel to each side of the original triangle. By using facts about supplementary, complementary, vertical, and adjacent angles formed by cutting parallel lines with a transversal, it is straightforward to argue that the sum of the angles will always be a straight line. See Figure 19.15(b) to explore a proof involving exterior angles.

Midsegments of a Triangle

The following activity illustrates a way to help students move from observation of geometric relationships to making and testing conjectures that explore why relationships hold.

Activity 19.18   CCSS-M: 7.G.A.2; 8.G.A.5

Triangle Midsegments

TECHNOLOGY

Using a dynamic geometry program, draw a triangle and label the vertices A, B, and C. Draw the segment joining the midpoints of AB and AC, and label this segment DE, as in Figure 19.16. Measure the lengths of DE and BC. Also, measure angles ADE and ABC. Drag points A, B, and C. What conjectures can you make about the relationships between segment DE (the *midsegment* of triangle ABC) and BC (the base of ABC)? Explore the Expanded Lesson: Triangle Midsegments for this activity.

MyLab Education   Expanded Lesson: Triangle Midsegments

The midsegment is half the length of the base and parallel to it. Students can explore why this is so by drawing a line through *A* parallel to *BC*. List all pairs of angles that they know are congruent. Why are they congruent? Notice that triangle *ABC* is similar to triangle *ADE*. Why

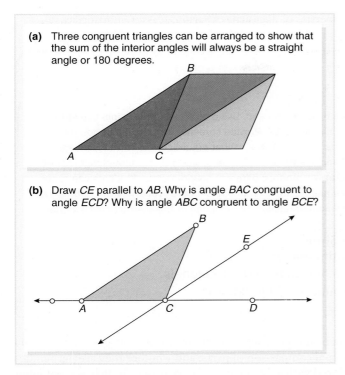

(a) Three congruent triangles can be arranged to show that the sum of the interior angles will always be a straight angle or 180 degrees.

(b) Draw *CE* parallel to *AB*. Why is angle *BAC* congruent to angle *ECD*? Why is angle *ABC* congruent to angle *BCE*?

FIGURE 19.15   Deductive, logical reasoning is necessary to prove relationships that appear true from observations.

m ∠ *FAB* = 60°   m ∠ *GAC* = 35°

m ∠ *ABC* = 60°   m ∠ *ACB* = 35°
m ∠ *ADE* = 60°   m ∠ *AED* = 35°

DE = 5.22
BC = 10.44

FIGURE 19.16   The midsegment of a triangle is always parallel to the base and half as long.

is it similar? With hints such as these, many students can begin to make logical arguments for why the things they observe to be true are in fact true for any triangle.

Exploring Properties of Quadrilaterals

Quadrilaterals (polygons with four sides) are a rich source of investigations. Once students are familiar with the concepts of right, obtuse, and acute angles, congruence of line segments and angles, and line symmetry, Activity 19.3, "Property Lists for Quadrilaterals," is a good way to bring these ideas together. This activity addresses important geometry content for grade 5 and is worth the time invested. Share property lists beginning with parallelograms, then rhombuses, then rectangles, and finally squares. Have one group present its list. Then others who worked on the same shape should add to or subtract from it. The class must agree with everything placed on the list. Generating definitions and comparing them to the common definition for that shape is an important experience for students. In addition, students can explore which of these shapes are subcategories of other shapes (e.g., squares are a subset of rectangles).

As new relationships come up introduce proper terminology such as if two diagonals intersect in a square corner, then they are perpendicular. Other terms such as *parallel, congruent, bisect, midpoint,* can be clarified. Also, introduce symbols such as ≅ for *congruent* or ∥ for *parallel.*

To understand the difference between level 1 and level 2 of the van Hiele theory, let's compare "Property Lists for Quadrilaterals (Activity 19.3)," and "Minimal Defining Lists" (Activity 19.4). The parallelogram, rhombus, rectangle, and square each have at least four MDLs with one of the most interesting consisting only of the properties of its diagonals. For example, a quadrilateral with diagonals that bisect each other and are perpendicular is a rhombus.

CCSS **Standards for Mathematical Practice**
MP3. Construct viable arguments and critique the reasoning of others.

MyLab Education   Video Example 19.4

Watch this video of Janet Caldwell as she discusses lines, sides, and angles as ways to identify shapes.

VIDEO EXAMPLE

Activity 19.19 explores the properties of diagonals of various classes of quadrilaterals.

Activity 19.19   CCSS-M: 4.G.A.2; 5.G.B.3; 5.G.B.4; 6.RP.A.1; 7.G.A.2

Diagonals of Quadrilaterals

Give each student three card stock Diagonal Strips. Punch the nine holes as marked. Use a brass fastener to join two strips. A quadrilateral is formed by joining the four end holes as shown in Figure 19.17. Provide students with the list of possible relationships for angles, lengths, and proportional comparisons of parts (ratios). Ask, "What quadrilaterals can these diagonals form when diagonals are the same length? Perpendicular? Bisect each other? Perpendicular and the same length? Have students use the strips to determine the properties of diagonals that will produce different quadrilaterals. Students can make drawings on 1-Centimeter Dot Paper to test the various hypotheses and record their findings on the Properties of Quadrilateral Diagonals Activity Page. See the Expanded Lesson: Diagonals of Quadrilaterals for a description of this instructional experience.

MyLab Education   **Activity Page: Diagonal Strips**
MyLab Education   **Blackline Master: 1-Centimeter Dot Paper**
MyLab Education   **Activity Page: Properties of Quadrilateral Diagonals**
MyLab Education   **Expanded Lesson: Diagonals of Quadrilaterals**

Every type of quadrilateral can be uniquely described in terms of its diagonals using only the conditions of length, proportional comparison of parts, and whether they are perpendicular. This activity can also be explored with a dynamic geometry program such as GeoGebra (https://www.geogebra.org), where points, lines, and geometric figures are easily constructed and objects can be moved about and manipulated in endless ways. One of the most significant ideas is that when a geometric object is created with dynamic geometry with a particular relationship to another object, that relationship is maintained no matter how either object is dragged, inverted or changed. For example, in Figure 19.18, the midpoints of a freely drawn quadrilateral *ABCD* have been joined. The diagonals of the resulting quadrilateral (*EFGH*) are also drawn and measured.

Without technology if a quadrilateral is drawn, only one shape is observed, but now because the quadrilateral can be stretched and altered in endless ways, and students can

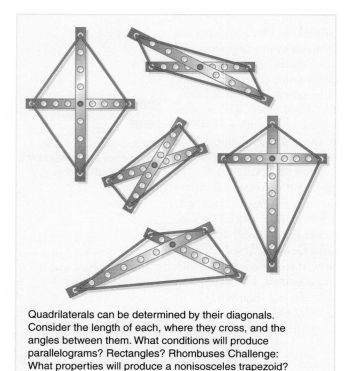

Quadrilaterals can be determined by their diagonals. Consider the length of each, where they cross, and the angles between them. What conditions will produce parallelograms? Rectangles? Rhombuses Challenge: What properties will produce a nonisosceles trapezoid?

FIGURE 19.17   Diagonals of quadrilaterals.

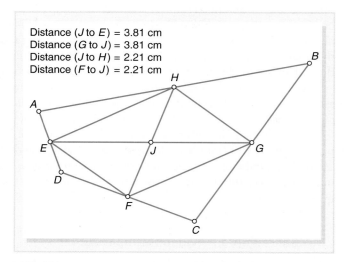

Distance (*J* to *E*) = 3.81 cm
Distance (*G* to *J*) = 3.81 cm
Distance (*J* to *H*) = 2.21 cm
Distance (*F* to *J*) = 2.21 cm

FIGURE 19.18   A construction made with dynamic geometry software illustrating an interesting property of quadrilaterals.

explore an enormous number of examples from that *class* of shapes they can test hypotheses on their own. If a property does not change when the figure changes on the dynamic geometry program, the property is attributable to the class of shapes rather than any particular shape.

Exploring Polygons

As students develop an understanding of various geometric properties and attach these properties to categories of shapes, it is essential to encourage conjecture and to explore informal deductive arguments to develop logical reasoning. This includes exploring polygons, and examining the properties and conditions that make shapes unique or possible Students should begin to attempt—or at least follow—simple proofs and explore ideas that connect directly to algebra.

The next activity supports logical reasoning is not restricted to quadrilaterals and can include three-dimensional shapes as well.

Activity 19.20

CCSS-M: 4.G.A.2; 5.G.B.3; 5.G.B.4; 7.G.A.2

True or False?

Prepare a set of true/false statements of the following forms: "If it is a _____, then it is also a _____." "All _____ are _____." "Some _____ are _____." or use the True/False Statements Activity Page. Ask students to determine whether the statements are true or false and present an argument to support the decision (see Figure 19.19). Four or five true/false statements will make a good lesson. Once this format is understood, let students challenge their classmates by making their own lists of a mixture of true/false statements.

MyLab Education   Activity Page: True/False Statements

FORMATIVE ASSESSMENT Notes. The "True or False?" activity is also a good diagnostic assessment. Notice how the student's work (Figure 19.19) gives insights into her ideas, representations, and emerging arguments for her choices. ■

Circles

Many interesting relationships can be observed among measures of different parts of the circle. One of the most astounding and important is the ratio between measures of the circumference and the diameter; pi.

Activity 19.21

CCSS-M: 7.G.B.4

Discovering Pi

Have groups of students carefully measure both the circumference and diameter of a collection of circular items such as jar lids, cans, and wastebaskets. To measure circumference, wrap string once around the object and then measure that length of string. Also measure the circumference of large circles marked on gym floors and playgrounds with a trundle wheel or rope.

Students gather the circumference and diameter from a variety of circular items and enter the measures in a Circle Table Activity Page. Have them divide to find the ratio of the circumference to the diameter for each circle. The exact ratio is an irrational number, about 3.14159, represented by the Greek letter π (pi).

MyLab Education   Activity Page: Circle Table

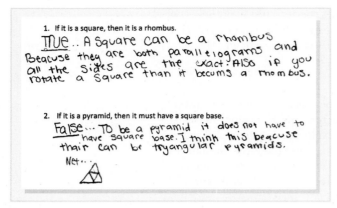

1. If it is a square, then it is a rhombus.

TRUE.. A square can be a rhombus Beacuse they are both paralleiograms and all the sides are the exact. Also if you rotate a square than it becums a rhombus.

2. If it is a pyramid, then it must have a square base.

False... To be a pyramid it does not have to have square base. I think this beacuse thair can be tryangular pyramids.
Net..

FIGURE 19.19 True or false? A fifth-grade student presents an argument to support her decision.

What is most important in Activity 19.21 is that students develop a clear understanding of π as the ratio of circumference to diameter in any circle regardless of size. The quantity π is not some mystical number that appears in mathematics formulas; it is a naturally occurring and universal ratio.

Investigations, Conjectures, and the Development of Proof

Remember, if you write a theorem on the board and ask students to prove it, you have already "told" them that it is true. If, by contrast, a student makes a statement about a geometric situation the class is exploring, it can be written with a question mark as a conjecture—a statement whose truth has not yet been determined. You can ask, "Is it true? Always? Can we prove it? Can we find a counterexample?"

On the path to more formal deduction, students should construct diagrams and consider pertinent definitions (Sinclair, Pimm, & Skelin, 2012). Students should begin to notice evidence of a pattern and then check it with multiple approaches based on mathematical properties and structure.

The Pythagorean Theorem. The *Pythagorean theorem*, explored in eighth grade, is one of the most important mathematical relationships and warrants in-depth conceptual investigation. In geometric terms, this relationship states that if a square is constructed on each side of a right triangle, the areas of the two smaller squares will together equal the area of the square on the longest side, the hypotenuse.

Activity 19.22
CCSS-M: 8.G.B.6; 8.G.B.7

The Pythagorean Relationship

Have students draw a right triangle on 0.5-Centimeter Grid Paper. Assign each student a different triangle by specifying the lengths of the two legs. Students should draw a square on each leg and the hypotenuse and find the areas of all three squares. For the square on the hypotenuse, the area can be found by making each of the sides the diagonal of a rectangle (see Figure 19.20). Have students record their own data on the Table of the Areas Activity Page and then them collect and record data from two teams with different triangles. Ask students to look for a relationship between the three squares of a particular triangle.

MyLab Education Blackline Master: 0.5-Centimeter Grid Paper
MyLab Education Activity Page: Tables of the Areas

The two large congruent squares in Figure 19.21 together show a visual proof of the Pythagorean theorem (Nelson, 2001). Notice that both large squares are decomposed into squares and triangles—and that the four triangles in each large square are the same but arranged differently. By adding up the areas of the squares and the triangles in each large square and setting them equal to each other, the Pythagorean relationship can be found by subtracting out the common areas in both squares. An algebraic recording of the thinking process is shown below the drawings. Share with students the applet at Illuminations entitled "Proof without Words: Pythagorean Theorem" or the video below.

MyLab Education **Video Example 19.5**

Watch the video (https://www.youtube.com/watch?v=gjSAE8_FahM) titled, "Pythagorean Theorem—Proof without Words" that explores this concept using paper cutouts of triangles and a square.

VIDEO EXAMPLE

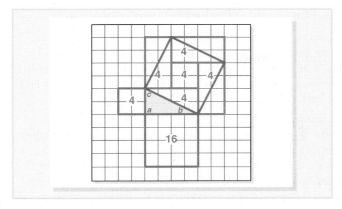

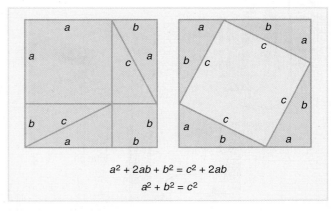

$$a^2 + 2ab + b^2 = c^2 + 2ab$$
$$a^2 + b^2 = c^2$$

FIGURE 19.20   The Pythagorean relationship. Here 4 + 16 = 20, the area in square units of the square on the hypotenuse.

FIGURE 19.21   The two large squares together are a "proof without words." Can you supply the words?

❚❚ Pause & Reflect

Use the two drawings in Figure 19.21 to create a proof of the Pythagorean relationship. ●

Eighth-grade students should be familiar with Pythagorean triples. Any set of three whole numbers that satisfy the Pythagorean theorem is called a *Pythagorean triple*. Pythagorean triples occur often in geometry tasks and are often "disguised" as multiples of commonly recognized triples.

Activity 19.23   CCSS-M: 8.G.B.6; 8.G.B.7

Finding Pythagorean Triples

Begin with the most common Pythagorean triple, 3-4-5. Ask, "Will triangles that are similar to the 3-4-5 triangle also be Pythagorean triples?" Give students a ruler, grid paper, and a calculator (or have them explore with dynamic geometric software). Ask, "Can you find at least three triples that form triangles similar to the 3-4-5 triangle?" (There are infinitely many, so once students notice a pattern, stop the exploration and discuss strategies for how to recognize the 3-4-5 in disguise.)

MyLab Education   **Self-Check 19.3**

MyLab Education   **Application Exercise 19.2: Building Triangles with Polystrips** Click the link to access this exercise, then watch the video and answer the accompanying questions.

 Transformations

Transformations are changes in position or size of a shape and are a major focus of eighth grade in the *Common Core State Standards*. Interestingly, the study of line symmetry (introduced in fourth grade in CCSS) is also included under the study of transformations. Movements that do not change the size or shape of the object moved are called "rigid motions." *Translations*, *reflections*, and *rotations* are rigid transformations that result in congruent shapes (Figure 19.22).

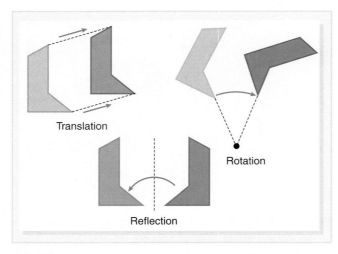

FIGURE 19.22 Translation (slide), reflection (flip), and rotation (turn).

Here are the definitions of the rigid motions:

Translation: A translation (slide) requires a *direction* and a *distance*. In a translation, every point on the preimage moves in the same direction for the same distance to form the image. On a coordinate grid, you would be moving "up 2 and over 3" for each of the points in the figure.

Reflection: A reflection (flip) requires a *line of reflection*. A reflection is a transformation in which an object is flipped across a line of reflection. The line of symmetry can be the x-axis, the y-axis, or any other line. If a shape is reflected over the x-axis, for example, the x-values of the preimage are the opposite of the x-values of the image, and the y-values in both images are the same.

Rotation: A rotation (turn) requires a *center of rotation* (point) and a *degree of rotation*. The point can be any point on the coordinate axis, although in middle school, rotation around the origin is most common. A figure can be rotated up to 360 degrees.

The Motion Man activity described next can also be used to introduce students to the terms *slide*, *flip*, and *turn*.

Activity 19.24

CCSS-M: 8.G.A.1a, b, c

ENGLISH LEARNERS

Motion Man

Make a copy for each student of the Motion Man Activity Page and the Mirror Image Motion Man Activity Page, back to back, so that they match when held to the light, as in Figure 19.23. First, have students demonstrate each of the rigid motions. A slide is simply that—Motion Man moves over a particular distance. Say, "Translate Motion Man 4 inches right and 2 inches down." A reflection requires a line, say "Draw a vertical or horizontal line and reflect Motion Man over that line." Have them demonstrate a horizontal flip (top goes to bottom) and a vertical flip (left goes to right). A rotation requires a center and a clockwise degree measure. Say, "Rotate Motion Man 90 degrees." For all students, ELs in particular, ensure that these demonstrations include explicit practice with the vocabulary and matching visuals.

MyLab Education   Activity Page: Motion Man
MyLab Education   Activity Page: Mirror Image Motion Man

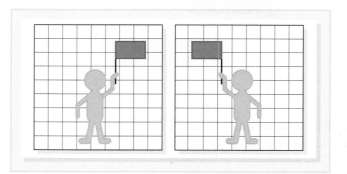

FIGURE 19.23 Motion Man is used to show slides, flips, and turns.

Begin with the Motion Man in the left position shown in Figure 19.23 (preimage). Now place a second Motion Man next to the first (image). How did he get there? Will it take one move or more than one move (transformation) to get from the first to the second Motion Man? The task is to decide and test what motion or combination of motions will get the man on the left to match the man on the right. If both men are in the same position, call that a slide. There are often numerous ways to get him to the new position.

Notice that although the center of the rotation will be the center of the figure and reflections will be flips over vertical or horizontal lines—these restrictions are for initial instruction. In fact, the center of rotation can be anywhere on or off the figure and lines of reflection can be anywhere.

MyLab Education   Video Example 19.6

Watch this video to see how a teacher debriefs two students' incorrect reflection of a pattern block figure, including a way to clear up the students' misunderstanding.

Symmetries

The bridge between transformations at the elementary level and the middle school is the area of reflection and symmetry. At first students may think line symmetry is only vertical and rotation symmetry is only around a central point, but by offering many experiences students will be challenged to expand their definitions.

Line Symmetry. If a shape can be folded on a line so that the two halves match precisely, then it is said to have *line symmetry* (sometimes called *reflectional* or *mirror symmetry*). Notice that the fold line is actually a line of *reflection*—the portion of the shape on one side of the line is reflected onto the other side. Again, that is the connection between line symmetry and transformations.

One way to introduce line symmetry to students is to show examples and nonexamples using an all-of-these/none-of-these approach, as in Figure 19.14. Here's another possibility:

Fold a sheet of paper in half and cut out a shape of your choosing on the side with the fold. When you open the paper, what do you notice?

Another approach is to use mirrors. When you place a mirror on a picture or design so that the mirror is perpendicular to the table, you see a shape with symmetry when you look in the mirror. Explore the "Shape Tool" interactive on the NCTM Illuminations website where students can investigate symmetry with a virtual mirror.

Activity 19.25   CCSS-M: 4.G.A.3

Pattern Block Mirror Symmetry

Give students a plain sheet of paper with a straight line drawn through the middle. Ask students to use about six to eight pattern blocks to make a design completely on one side of the line that touches the line in some way. When the one side is finished, students try to make the mirror image of their design on the other side of the line. After the design is complete, have students use a mirror to check their work. They place the mirror on the line and look into it from the side of the original design. With the mirror in place they should see the same image as they see when they raise the mirror. For students with disabilities, at first make the line of reflection vertical with a left and right side. Then move to a line oriented horizontally or diagonally. Challenge students to make designs with more than one line of symmetry.

STUDENTS with SPECIAL NEEDS

The same task can be done with tangram pieces or created on a geoboard. If students wish to try the geoboard, first they stretch a band to represent the line of symmetry. Then they make a design on one side of the line and its mirror image on the other. Students can also investigate quilt patterns to identify how many lines of symmetry in traditional block patterns (Roscoe & Zephyrs, 2016). You can use dynamic geometry software or on either isometric or rectangular dot grids, as described in the following activity.

Activity 19.26   CCSS-M: 4.G.A.3

Dot Grid Line Symmetry

Give students a piece of either 1-Centimeter Isometric Dot Paper or 1-Centimeter Dot Paper. Students should draw a line through several dots. This line can be horizontal, vertical, or diagonal. Students make a design completely on one side of the drawn line that touches the line, as in the figures shown on the left in Figure 19.24. Have students make the mirror image of their design on the other side of the line or have them exchange their partial design with a peer who must finish it. When finished they can check by placing a mirror on the line and looking into the mirror to see the same image as when they lift the mirror.

MyLab Education   **Blackline Master: 1-Centimeter Isometric Dot Paper**
MyLab Education   **Blackline Master: 1-Centimeter Dot Paper**

Have students try these two problems:

A shape with one line of symmetry has exactly 6 sides and two 90-degree angles. Can you draw the shape?

A quadrilateral has diagonals that do not form lines of symmetry, but the quadrilateral is symmetrical (one line). Can you draw the quadrilateral?

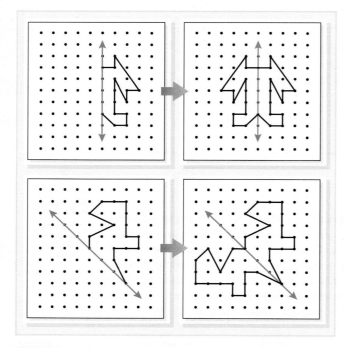

FIGURE 19.24   Exploring symmetry on dot grids.

FIGURE 19.25   A parallelogram is rotated 180 degrees.

These exercises combine several key areas of geometry such as line symmetry, properties of shapes, and visualization with reasoning. Try to have students come up with other problems for their classmates to draw.

Rotational Symmetry. A shape has *rotational symmetry* (also referred to as *point symmetry*) if it can be *rotated* about a point and land in a position exactly matching the one in which it began. A square has rotational symmetry, as does an equilateral triangle.

A good way to understand rotational symmetry is to take a shape with rotational symmetry, such as a square, and trace around it on a piece of paper. Call this tracing the shape's "footprint." The degrees refer to the smallest angle of rotation required before the shape matches itself or fits into its footprint. The parallelogram in Figure 19.25 has *180-degree rotational symmetry*. A square has *90-degree rotational symmetry*.

Composition of Transformations

One transformation can be followed by another. For example, a figure can be reflected over a line, and then that figure can be rotated about a point. A combination of two or more transformations is called a *composition*.

Have students experiment with compositions of two or even three transformations using a simple shape on 1-Centimeter Dot Paper as a step toward using coordinates on the coordinate axis. For example, have students draw an L shape on a dot grid and label it L_1 (Figure 19.26). Reflect it over a line, then rotate the image $\frac{1}{4}$ turn clockwise about a point not on the shape. Call this image L_2, the image of a composition of a reflection followed by a rotation. Notice that if L_1 is rotated $\frac{1}{4}$ turn clockwise about the same point used before (the result of which we will call L_3), there is a relationship between L_2 and L_3. Continue to explore different combinations of transformations. Don't forget to include translations (slides) in the compositions.

MyLab Education	**Blackline Master:**
	1-Centimeter Dot Paper

Compositions do not have to involve different types of transformations. For example, a reflection can be followed by another reflection. Take advantage of engaging technology for compositions of transformations such as found at NCTM Illuminations.

Tessellations. Tessellations are a motivating and artistic application of transformations. A *tessellation* is a tiling of the plane using one or more shapes in a repeating pattern with no gaps or overlaps (see Figure 19.27). Tessellations are based on a circle—if the angle measures add up to 360 degrees, the shapes will fit together at a vertex with no overlaps or gaps. A *regular tessellation* is made of a single polygon (all sides and angles congruent). Therefore, only certain polygons can be used for regular tessellations.

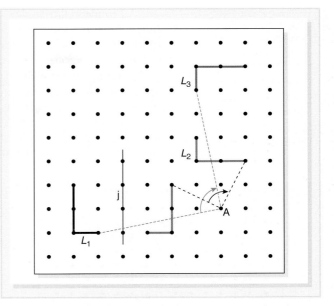

FIGURE 19.26   How are L_2 and L_3 related? Will this approach always work?

Pause & Reflect

Which regular polygons can be used to form regular tessellations? •

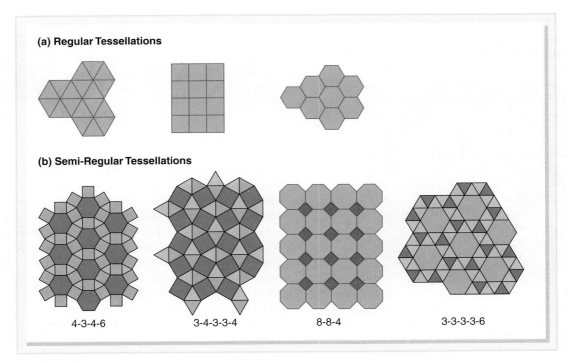

(a) Regular Tessellations

(b) Semi-Regular Tessellations

4-3-4-6   3-4-3-3-4   8-8-4   3-3-3-3-6

FIGURE 19.27   Tessellations.

An equilateral triangle has angles of 60 degrees, so six triangles can form a regular tessellation. Likewise, a square can form a regular tessellation and a checkerboard is a simple example of what that looks like. So too can regular hexagons, as in a bee hive.

A *semiregular tessellation* is made of two or more different regular polygons. At each vertex of a semiregular tessellation, the same collection of regular polygons comes together in the same order. Students can figure out which polygons are possible at a vertex and design their own semiregular tessellations. Have them use either transformations or combining compatible polygons on 1-Centimeter Grid Paper to create tessellations that are artistic and quite complex (see Figure 19.27). NCTM's Illuminations website also has a tool called "Tessellation Creator" that allows shapes to be combined to make patterns that repeat and cover the plane.

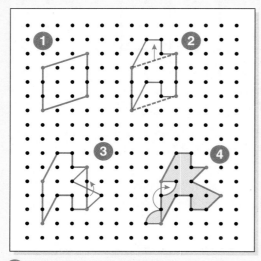

1. Start with a simple shape.

2. Draw the same curve on two opposite sides. This tile will stack up in columns.

3. Rotate a curve on the midpoint of one side.

4. Rotate a curve on the midpoint of the other side. Use this tile for tessellation (below).

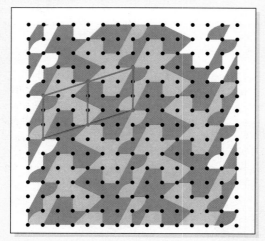

A column of the resulting tile will now match a like column that is rotated one complete turn. Find these rotated columns in the tessellation shown here.

FIGURE 19.28 Creating an Escher-type tessellation.

> **MyLab Education** **Blackline Master: 1-Centimeter Grid Paper**

The Dutch artist M. C. Escher is famous for his tessellations, in which the tiles are very intricate and are often shaped like birds, horses, or lizards. Escher took a simple shape such as a triangle, parallelogram, or hexagon and altered the sides applying transformations. For example, draw a shape on 1-Centimeter Dot Paper. Then a curve drawn along one side might be translated (slid) to the opposite side. Another idea is to draw a curve from the midpoint of a side to the adjoining vertex. This curve is then rotated about the midpoint to form a totally new side of the tile (see Figure 19.28). Once a tile has been designed, it can be traced over and over again.

> **MyLab Education** **Blackline Master: 1-Centimeter Dot Paper**
>
> **MyLab Education** **Video Example 19.7**
>
> In this video, watch how students use a dynamic geometry program to create an original tessellation through transformations. Try NCTM Illuminations "Tessellation Creator" for a similar program.
>
>

Congruence

Congruent shapes are defined in terms of transformations. Two shapes are considered congruent if you can apply rigid transformations from one shape to the other. The *Common Core State Standards* for eighth grade state that students should "understand that a two-dimensional figure is congruent to another if the second can be obtained from the first by a sequence of rotations, reflections, and translations; given two congruent figures, describe a sequence that exhibits the congruence between them" (NGA Center & CCSSO, 2010, p. 55).

Having explored foundational experiences like Motion Man and transformations on dot paper, students are ready to explore transformations and compositions of transformations on the coordinate axis. A focus on congruence helps connect these two related ideas, as in Activity 19.27.

Activity 19.27

CCSS-M: 8.G.A.1; 8.G.A.2

Are They Congruent?

Draw various triangles on the coordinate grid, some congruent and some not. Ask students to find a match of two congruent triangles and prove they are congruent by stating the transformations that they applied in order to get one shape to precisely cover the one they selected as a match.

The coordinate axis is addressed in detail in a later section, "Location," in which transformations will continue to be explored.

Similarity

Two figures are *similar* if all of their corresponding angles are congruent and the corresponding sides are proportional. This can be proved if one triangle can be superimposed on the other triangle through a series of transformations—translations, reflections, rotations, or dilations. The connection between proportional reasoning and the geometric concept of similarity is very important. Similar figures provide a visual representation of proportions, and proportional thinking enhances the understanding of similarity (as in scale drawings).

Dilation

A *dilation* is a nonrigid (can change size) transformation that produces similar two-dimensional figures (think of pinching or spreading an image on a phone or computer screen). A dilation requires a *scale factor*. Scale factors less than 1 produce smaller figures and scale factors greater than 1 produce larger figures (see Figure 19.29).

If different groups of students use the same scale factor to dilate the same figure, they will find that the resulting figures are all congruent, even with each group using different dilation points. Dynamic geometry software makes the results of this exercise quite dramatic. The software allows for the scale factors to be set at any value. Once a dilation is made, the dilation point can be dragged around the screen and the size and shape of the image clearly stay unchanged.

To understand what is required to have a rigid motion means understanding what types of transformations distort a shape. In the next activity, students see that multiplying a constant times the coordinates is a transformation that is *not* a rigid motion.

Activity 19.28

CCSS-M: 6.G.A.3; 7.G.A.1; 8.G.A.1; 8.G.A.3

Polygon Dilations

Distribute a Coordinate Grid and ask students to create a four-sided shape in the first quadrant. Next, ask them to record the coordinates for their quadrilateral. With their list, they are to create a new set of coordinates by multiplying each of the original coordinates by 2. Ask, "What do you think the new polygon will look like? How will its perimeter change? Its area?" Now, have students multiply each of the original coordinates by $\frac{1}{2}$ and plot that shape. Ask the same questions and have students record their predictions. Have students plot the new shapes. Discuss how their predictions compared to what they see. Finally, ask students to draw a line from the origin to a vertex of the largest shape. Repeat for one or two additional vertices, and ask for observations. (An example is shown in Figure 19.29.)

MyLab Education   Activity Page: Coordinate Grid

Your students may enjoy exploring dilations a bit further, including the connection to scale drawings. If they start with a drawing of a simple face, boat, or some other shape drawn with straight lines connecting vertices, they will create an interesting effect by multiplying just the first coordinates, just the second coordinates, or using a different factor for each. When only

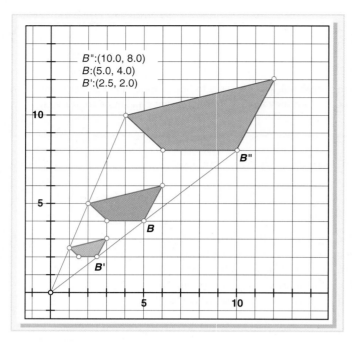

B":(10.0, 8.0)
B:(5.0, 4.0)
B':(2.5, 2.0)

B"

B

B'

FIGURE 19.29 Dilations of a trapezoid (original in red) when the scale factor is 2.0 and 0.5.

the second coordinate is multiplied, the vertical dimensions alone are dilated, so the figure is proportionately stretched (or shrunk) vertically. Students can explore this process to see how an arithmetic operation can control a figure through slides, flips, turns, and dilations, not just in the plane but also for three-dimensional figures. This process is identical to computer animation techniques.

MyLab Education   Self-Check 19.4

 Location

In preK and kindergarten, students learn about everyday positional descriptions—*above, below, beside, in front of, behind and next to* (NGA Center & CCSSO, 2010). These "place learnings" (Sarama & Clements, 2014) are useful for helping students begin to specify locations. However, helping students refine the way they think and reason about direction, distance, and location enhances spatial understandings. Geometry, measurement, and algebra are all supported by the use of a grid system with numbers or coordinates attached that can specify location.

After early development of terms for how objects are located with respect to other objects ("the ball is under the table"), location activities involve analysis of paths from point to point as on a map, and the use of coordinate systems. The first quadrant of the coordinate plane is introduced in grade 5 as students should "Graph points on the coordinate plane to solve real-world and mathematical problems" (NGA Center & CCSSO, 2010, p. 34). Then in grade 6 all quadrants are included, scale drawing and constructions are added in grade 7, and the coordinate axis is used in grade 8 for graphing lines, performing transformations and exploring distance.

The next activity can serve as a readiness task for coordinates as students refine their ways of describing location.

Activity 19.29

CCSS-M: K.G.A.1; 5.G.A.1

Hidden Positions

STUDENTS with SPECIAL NEEDS

Give each student a Hidden Positions Gameboard. Two students sit with a "screen" separating their desktop space so that neither student can see the other's grid (see Figure 19.30). Each student has four different pattern blocks. The first player places a block on four different sections of the grid. He then uses words to tell the other player where to put blocks on her grid to match his own. When all four pieces are positioned, check the two grids to see that they are alike. Then players switch roles. Model the game once by taking the part of the first student. Use words such as *top row, middle row, left, right, above, below, next to, column* and *beside*. Notice the language of rows and columns which links to second grade decomposition activities. For students with disabilities, consider starting with just one shape. then move to two, and so on. For students who need a challenge, extend the grids up to 6 × 6. As the grid size increases, notice how the need for a system of labeling positions increases.

MyLab Education   Activity Page: Hidden Positions Gameboard

The next activity explores the notion of different paths on a grid.

Activity 19.30

CCSS-M: K.G.A.1; 5.G.A.1

Paths

On a sheet of 2-Centimeter Grid Paper, mark two different points A and B as shown in Figure 19.31. Using a projection display or floor tiles, demonstrate how to describe a path from A to B. For the points in the figure, one path is "up 5 and right 6." Another path might be "right 2, up 3, right 4, up 2." Count the length of each path. As long as you always move toward the target point (in this case either right or up), the paths will always be the same length. Here they are 11 units long. Students draw three paths on their papers from A to B using different-colored crayons. For each path, they write directions that describe their paths. Ask, "What is the greatest number of turns that you can make in your path?" "What is the smallest number?" "Where would A and B have to be in order to get there with no turns?" For students who need a challenge, add a coordinate system on the grid and have students describe their paths using coordinates: For example: (1, 2), (3, 2), (3, 5), (7, 5), (7, 7).

MyLab Education   **Blackline Master: 2-Centimeter Grid Paper**

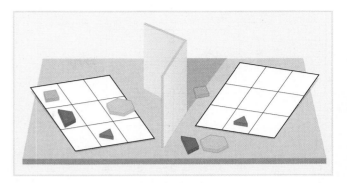

FIGURE 19.30   The "Hidden Positions" game.

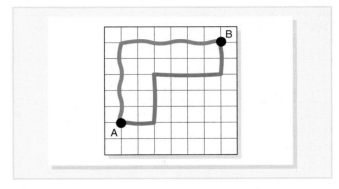

FIGURE 19.31   Different paths from A to B on a grid.

Coordinate Plane

To describe a location, students need a reference point (origin) and information about distance and direction (Goldenberg & Clements, 2014). Use a Coordinate Grid like the one shown in Figure 19.32 and explain how to use two numbers (positive whole numbers) to designate an intersection point on the grid. In Hidden Positions (Activity 19.29), objects were placed within the space and not on the grid. So, if you've used it as an early introductory activity, when transitioning to this coordinate grid emphasize the difference between the two formats. Initially use words along with the numbers: 3 right and 0 up (don't avoid 0). Select points on the grid and have students decide what two numbers name that point. If your point is at (2, 4) and students incorrectly say "four, two," then simply show where the point is that they named. Then try the next activity.

MyLab Education   **Blackline Master: Coordinate Grid—Quadrant I**

Activity 19.31

CCSS-M: 5.G.A.1

Step Right Up

Create a coordinate grid on the floor using painter's tape, or on the school playground with paint. Give each student a small whiteboard for recording. Select a student and secretly give her a set of coordinates. Then the student moves to that location. Other students write the coordinates for that location and display their answers. This can also be done with a Coordinate Grid. If you repeatedly call this activity "Step Right Up," that can act as a mnemonic for students with disabilities as they will remember to first step right, then up, to locate the position for coordinates of positive whole numbers. Make sure you tell the students that there are other directions they will be learning in the future and a "right step" will not always be the "right way to go!"

STUDENTS with SPECIAL NEEDS

MyLab Education   **Blackline Master: Coordinate Grid—Quadrant I**

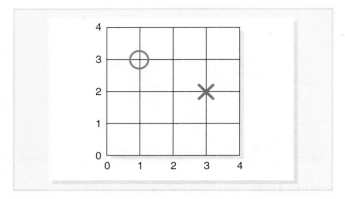

FIGURE 19.32 A simple coordinate grid. The X is at (3, 2) and the O is at (1, 3). Use the grid to play "Three in a Row" (like Tic-Tac-Toe). Put marks on intersections, not spaces.

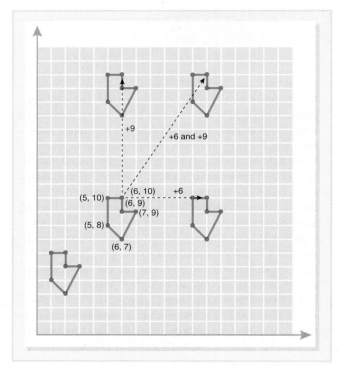

FIGURE 19.33 By adding or subtracting from the coordinates, new shapes are found that are translations (slides) of the original.

Students can also examine transformations on a coordinate plane—a standard in grade 8 (NGA Center & CCSSO, 2010)—as developed in the following activities.

Activity 19.32   CCSS-M: 6.G.A.3; 8.G.A.1; 8.G.A.3

Coordinate Slides

Ask students to plot and connect five or six points on 1-Centimeter Grid Paper to form a small shape (see Figure 19.33). Begin with all coordinates in Quadrant I with *x* and *y* values between 5 and 12. Next, students should add 6 to each of the *x*-coordinates of their shape, leaving the *y*-coordinates the same. That is, for the point (5, 10), a new point (11, 10) is plotted. This new figure should be congruent to the original and translated to the right. Then ask, "Can you create a third figure by adding 9 to each *y*-coordinate of the original coordinates?"

Ask, "What could be done to the coordinates to move the figure along a diagonal line up and to the right?" "Test your conjecture." Figure 19.33 shows a slide created by adding 6 to all of the *x* values and adding 9 to all of the *y* values, thus translating the figure and maintaining congruence. Ask, "How can you change the coordinates to make the figure slide down and to the left?" (Subtract from the coordinates instead of add.)

Ask students, "What does adding (or subtracting) a number from the first coordinates cause? What if the number is added or subtracted from the second coordinates? From both coordinates?" Have students draw lines connecting corresponding points in the original figure with one of those where both coordinates were changed. What do they notice? (The lines are parallel and the same length.)

MyLab Education   **Blackline Master: 1-Centimeter Grid Paper**

In "Coordinate Slides," the figure did not twist, turn, flip over, or change size or shape. The shape "slid" along a path that matched the lines between the corresponding points. Reflections can be explored on a coordinate grid just as successfully as translations. Begin with using the *x*- or *y*-axis as the line of reflection, as in the following activity.

Activity 19.33   CCSS-M: 8.G.A.1; 8.G.A.3

Coordinate Reflections

Ask students to draw a five-sided shape in the first quadrant on a Coordinate Grid. Label the Figure *ABCDE* and call it Figure 1 (see Figure 19.34). Use the *y*-axis as a line of symmetry and draw the reflection of the shape in the second quadrant. Label the reflected points *A'B'C'D'E'* and call it Figure 2. Now use the *x*-axis as the line of reflection and create Figure 3 (in Quadrant III) and Figure 4 (in Quadrant IV). Label the points of these figures with double and triple primes *A"* and *A'''*, and so on). Write in the coordinates for each vertex of all four figures.

- How is Figure 3 related to Figure 4? How else could you have gotten Figure 3? How else could you have found Figure 4?

- How are the coordinates of Figure 1 related to its image in the *y*-axis, Figure 2? What can you say about the coordinates of Figure 4?

- Make a conjecture about the coordinates of a shape reflected in the *y*-axis and a different conjecture about the coordinates of a shape reflected in the *x*-axis.

- Draw lines from the vertices of Figure 1 to the corresponding vertices of Figure 2. What can you say about these lines? How is the *y*-axis related to each of these lines?

MyLab Education   **Blackline Master: Coordinate Grid—4 Quadrants**

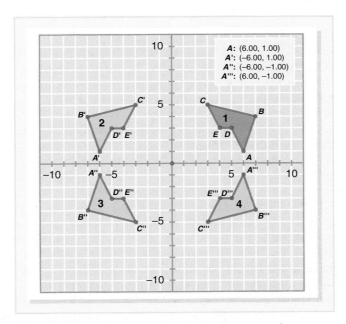

FIGURE 19.34   Exploring reflections on a coordinate grid.

While exploring the transformation activities in the last section, students might be challenged with questions that deepen their understanding of transformations, such as the following:

- How should the coordinates be changed to cause a reflection if the line of reflection is not the *y*-axis but is parallel to it?
- Can you discover a single rule for coordinates that would cause a reflection across one of the axes followed by a rotation of a quarter turn? Is that rule the same for the reverse order—a quarter turn followed by a reflection?
- If two successive slides are made with coordinates and you know what numbers were added or subtracted, what number should be added or subtracted to get the figure there in only one move?
- What do you think will happen if different factors are used for different coordinates in a dilation?

Measuring Distance on the Coordinate Plane

Measuring in the coordinate plane begins in grade 6 with students measuring vertical and horizontal lines and moves in grade 8 to student exploration of distance—eventually leading to the distance formula. The following activity has students use the coordinate grid and the Pythagorean relationship to develop a formula for the distance between points.

Activity 19.34   CCSS-M: 6.G.A.3; 8.G.B.8

Finding Distance Using the Pythagorean Theorem

Ask students to draw a line between two points in the first quadrant that are not on the same horizontal or vertical line (on Coordinate Grid paper or using dynamic geometry software). What is the length of this line? Give students time to share estimates as well as strategies. Then, ask students to draw a right triangle using the line as the hypotenuse (the vertex at the right angle will share one coordinate with each end point). Students then apply the Pythagorean theorem to find the distance. Ask students to do two to four more examples, asking them to look for patterns across their examples.

Next, have them look through all of their calculations and see how the coordinates of the two end points were used. Challenge students to use the same type of calculations to get the distance between two new points without drawing any pictures.

MyLab Education   Blackline Master: Coordinate Grid—Quadrant I

Eighth-grade students do not need to construct proofs independently but should be able to follow the rationale if shown proofs. By using the Pythagorean theorem to find the length of one line (or the distance between the end points), you provide the opportunity for students to make an important connection between two big mathematical ideas.

MyLab Education   Self-Check 19.5

 ## Visualization

Visualization might be called "geometry done with the mind's eye." It involves being able to create mental images of shapes and then turn them around mentally, thinking about how they look from different viewpoints and predicting the results of various transformations. It includes the mental coordination of two and three dimensions—in sixth grade, for example, by determining the net (a two-dimensional drawing) for a three-dimensional shape. Any activity that requires students to think about, manipulate, or transform a shape mentally or to represent a shape as it is seen visually will contribute to the development of students' visualization skills.

Two-Dimensional Imagery

At first students are thinking about shapes in terms of the way they look, so visualization activities will challenge students to think about two-dimensional shapes in different orientations.

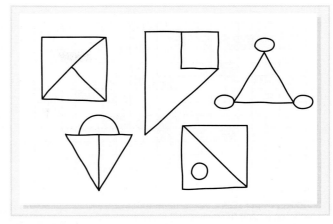

FIGURE 19.35   Examples to use in the "Can You Remember?" activity.

Activity 19.35

CCSS-M: K.G.B.4;
1.G.A.2; 2.G.A.1

Can You Remember?

Display one of these simple Sketches of Figures (see Figure 19.35) for about 5 seconds. Then have students attempt to reproduce it on their own. Show the same figure again for a few more seconds and allow students to modify their drawings. Repeat with additional figures.

**STUDENTS
with
SPECIAL
NEEDS**

MyLab Education   **Activity Page: Sketches of Figures**

Have a class discussion where students are asked to describe how they thought about the figure or give examples of attributes of the figure that helped them remember what they saw. As students learn to verbally describe what they see, their visual memory will improve. Another option is to have students with disabilities identify the displayed figure from a set of figures that look alike.

Finding out how many different shapes can be made with a given number of simple tiles demands that students mentally flip and turn shapes in their minds and find ways to decide whether they have found them all. That is the focus of the next activity.

Activity 19.36

CCSS-M: 1.G.A.2; 2.G.A.1; 3.G.A.1

Pentominoes

A pentomino is a shape formed by joining five squares as if cut from a square grid. Each square must have at least one side in common with another. Provide students with five square tiles and a sheet of 1-Centimeter Grid Paper for recording. Challenge them to see how many different pentomino shapes they can find. Shapes that are flips or turns of other shapes are not considered different. Do not tell students how many pentomino shapes there are. Good discussions will come from deciding whether some shapes are really different and if all shapes have been found. Look at the Pentominos Activity Page to see all the possible options.

MyLab Education   **Blackline Master: 1-Centimeter Grid Paper**
MyLab Education   **Activity Page: Pentominos**

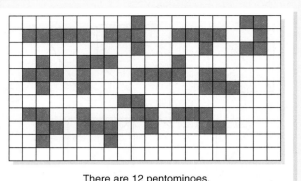

There are 12 pentominoes.

Finding all possible shapes made with five squares—or six squares (called "hexominoes") or six equilateral triangles and so on—is a good exercise in spatial problem solving.

FIGURE 19.36 There are 12 different pentomino shapes.

Once students have decided that there are just 12 pentominoes (see Figure 19.36), the 12 pieces can then be used in a variety of activities. For example, try to fit all 12 pieces into a 6 × 10 or 5 × 12 rectangle. Another task is to examine each of the 12 pentominoes and decide which will fold up to make an open box. This two-dimensional representation of a three-dimensional object is called a *net*. For those pentominoes that are "open box makers," which square is the bottom? The use of nets can be also linked to volume activities (Prummer, Amador, & Wallin, 2016).

Students can explore the number of shapes that can be made from six equilateral triangles or from four 45-degree right triangles (halves of squares). With the right triangles, sides that touch must be the same length. How many of each of these "ominoes" do you think there are? What about using 6 squares for hexominoes (there are 35). You can also use five cubes to create unique three-dimensional structures (there are 29) (Copley, 2017).

Activity 19.37   CCSS-M: 3.G.A.1; 4.G.A.1; 5.G

Geometry Necklaces

Make necklaces from Geometry Necklace Cards with two holes punched at the top and a loop of yarn long enough to easily go over all students' heads. Each card should have a two- or three-dimensional shape or any geometric figures appropriate for your students. Hang the necklace on each student's back so they cannot see it. Students should not try to look at their necklace or ask others to tell them what they are wearing. Then students walk around the room and ask only yes/no questions to help them collect information to determine their geometric figure or term. Students may only ask one question per person keeping track of questions and answers on a piece of paper. When students believe they have precisely identified what is on their necklace they should check with the teacher.

> **MyLab Education   Activity Page: Geometry Necklace Cards**

Three-Dimensional Imagery

Another aspect of visualization for young students is to be able to think about three-dimensional shapes in terms of their two-dimensional representations—focusing on faces.

Activity 19.38   CCSS-M: 1.G.A.2; 2.G.A.1; 3.G.A.1; 4.G.A.2

Face Matching

Provide students with Find a Shape Activity Page and sets of cardstock Face-Matching Cards (see Figure 19.37). There are two options: Given a Face Matching card, find the corresponding solid, or given a solid, find the matching card. For another variation, stack all of the Face Matching cards for one solid face down. Turn the cards up one at a time as clues to identifying the solid. Use the Face-Matching Card Questions Activity Page and collect student responses.

> **MyLab Education   Activity Page: Find a Shape**
> **MyLab Education   Activity Page Face-Matching Cards**
> **MyLab Education   Activity Page: Face-Matching Card Questions**

Students can use technology such as SketchUp to draw three dimensional shapes and actually develop solids through the use of three-dimensional printers (Cochran, Cochran, Laney, & Dean, 2016).

One of the main goals of the visualization strand is to be able to build three-dimensional figures from two-dimensional images as developed in the next activity.

Activity 19.39 CCSS-M: 6.G.A.4; 7.G.A.1

Building Views

For this activity, students will need 1-Centimeter Grid Paper for drawing a building plan and 1-inch blocks for constructing a building with *orthogonal* views.

- Version 1: Students begin with a building made of blocks and draw the left, right, front, and back views (these drawings are called elevations). In Figure 19.38, the building plan shows a top view of the building and the number of blocks in each position.

- Version 2: Students are given right and front elevations in drawings or photographs. Ask students to build the corresponding building. To record their solution, they draw a building plan (top elevation with numbers).

MyLab Education **Blackline Master: 1-Centimeter Grid Paper**

To make "Building Views" significantly more challenging, students can draw three-dimensional drawings with isometric views of these block buildings or match three-dimensional drawings with a building (use 2-Centimeter Isometric Dot Paper or 1-Centimeter Isometric Dot Paper). Isometric grids allow an *axonometric* drawing where the scale is preserved in all dimensions (height, depth, width). The next activity provides a glimpse at this form of visualization.

MyLab Education **Blackline Master: 2-Centimeter Isometric Dot Paper**

MyLab Education **Blackline Master: 1-Centimeter Isometric Dot Paper**

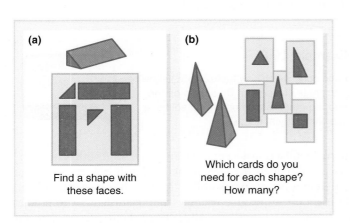

FIGURE 19.37 Matching face cards with solid shapes.

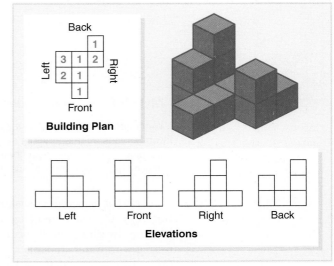

FIGURE 19.38 "Building Views" task.

Activity 19.40

CCSS-M: 6.G.A.4; 7.G.A.1

Three-Dimensional Drawings

STUDENTS with SPECIAL NEEDS

- Version 1: Students begin with an isometric three-dimensional drawing of a building created by the teacher on 2-Centimeter Isometric Grid Paper or 1-Centimeter Isometric Dot Paper. The assumption is that there are no hidden blocks. From the drawing, the students build the actual building with blocks. To record the result, they draw a building plan (top view) indicating the number of blocks in each position.

- Version 2: Students are given the four elevation views and a building plan (top view) (see Figure 19.39). They build the building accordingly and draw two or more of the elevation views. There are four possible views: the front left and right and the back left and right. For students who struggle, have them build the building on a sheet of paper labeled with the words "front," "back," "left," and "right" written on the four edges to highlight the locations of the different views.

MyLab Education Blackline Master: 2-Centimeter Isometric Grid Paper
MyLab Education Blackline Master: 1-Centimeter Isometric Dot Paper

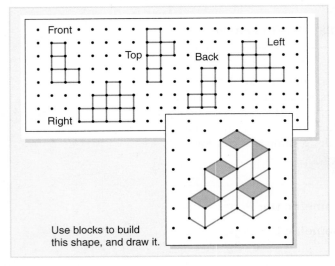

Use blocks to build this shape, and draw it.

FIGURE 19.39 Block "buildings" on isometric grids.

TECHNOLOGY Note. An amazing computer tool for drawing two-dimensional views of block buildings is the Isometric Drawing Tool, available at the NCTM Illuminations website. Using mouse clicks students can draw either whole cubes, faces, or just lines. The drawings, however, are actually "buildings" and can be viewed as three-dimensional objects that when rotated can be seen from any vantage point. Prepared investigations lead students through the features of the tool. ■

Activity 19.41

CCSS-M: 7.G.A.3

Slicing Solids

When a solid is sliced into two parts, a two-dimensional shape is formed on the slice faces. Provide groups of students with clay solids and potter's wire or plastic knife (see Figure 19.40). Pose the situation, "What shape will the remaining surface of a cube be if you slice off a corner?" Ask students, "Can you slice the solid you have to create a trapezoid face? A square face?" What will be the shape from each cut in Figure 19.40?

MyLab Education   **Video Example 19.8**

Watch this video (http://www.youtube.com/watch?v=CtmXu2yt5SE) showing two lessons on imagery in a seventh-grade classroom. One explores the building activities just described and the other lesson on slicing solids, an activity that connects two- and three-dimensional shapes.

VIDEO EXAMPLE

Another engaging task is to partially fill a translucent or clear plastic solid with water. The surface of the water simulates a slice and models the face of the solid as if it were cut at that location. By tilting the shape in different ways, every possible "slice" can be observed. Prior to testing with water students might use a list of possible triangles and quadrilaterals to predict for a given solid which can be made and which are impossible. Have them offer reasons for their hypothesis.

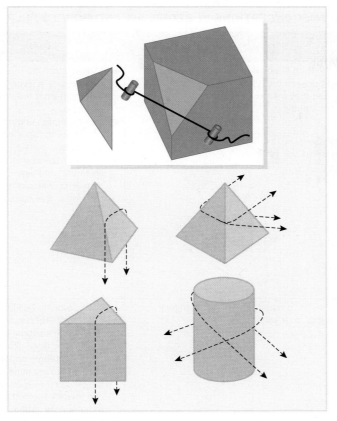

FIGURE 19.40 Predict the shape of the slice face, then cut the clay model with potter's wire.

MyLab Education **Self-Check 19.6**

MyLab Education **Math Practice:** Need to practice or refresh your math content knowledge? Click to access practice exercises associated with the content from this chapter.

Explore the following Table 19.4 to see students' common challenges and misconceptions across the four major geometry strands.

TABLE 19.4   COMMON CHALLENGES AND MISCONCEPTIONS IN GEOMETRY AND HOW TO HELP

Common Challenge or Misconception	What It Looks Like	How to Help
1. Shape is incorrectly identified due to a focus on nondefining characteristics such as orientation, size, or color.	Students call the third shape a diamond (not a mathematical shape) because it is tilted and no longer looks like a square. And they may just say the last shape is pointy but is not a triangle. 	• Expose students to a variety of examples of a given shape and ask them what the shapes have in common. • Use examples and nonexamples of shapes to focus on the defining attributes. • Carefully select posters, children's literature, and examples to avoid using/displaying inaccurate or imprecise examples of shapes.
2. Students misidentify three-dimensional shapes by focusing on the two-dimensional face.	Students call a cube "a square," a right rectangular prism "a rectangle," or a sphere "a circle."	• Have students build three-dimensional shapes by first constructing and naming the two-dimensional faces and then naming the three-dimensional shape. • Provide multiple opportunities for students to examine two- and three-dimensional shapes together so they can identify the rectangle as a face on a rectangular prism. • Avoid letting students say a box (rectangular prism) is a rectangle. Highlight that the face on one side of the box is a rectangle. • Put a three-dimensional shape into a bag, box, or sock and ask students to describe what they feel. If the student describes a face, show the two-dimensional model and ask whether that is what is in the bag.
3. Unsure of definitions that involve inclusion relations of quadrilaterals—Is a rectangle a square? Rectangle a parallelogram? Square a parallelogram?	When students are asked if this shape is a rectangle, they say "no." 	• Remind students that they could be in more than one school club or team. Shapes are able to be in more than one category in the same way. • Focus on Activities 19.2 and 19.3 where students are able to compare the properties and definitions of shapes. • Have students create the nested image in Figure 19.10.
4. When students work with the properties alone, without a visual, they think of the one shape that pops into their mental imaging rather than the whole group of shapes.	If the four sides are equal the angles must be right angles.	• Focus on the use of counterexamples which are particularly helpful way to develop students' ability to prove ideas.
5. Perpendicular lines must be horizontal and vertical.	Students will say these lines are *not* perpendicular 	• This is an artifact of having perpendicular lines shown only as a vertical and a horizontal line. Show perpendicular lines in a variety of orientations.

Common Challenge or Misconception	What It Looks Like	How to Help
6. Parallel lines must be horizontal.	Students will say these lines are *not* parallel. 	• This is an artifact of having experience only with the iconic image of parallel lines as two horizontal lines. Show parallel lines in a variety of orientations.
7. Line of symmetry must be vertical or horizontal or they must be adjacent to the side of the image (Ronau, Meyer, & Crites, 2015).	For example, given a square, students will say there are only two lines of symmetry. In this case, they miss seeing the diagonal lines of symmetry.	• Have students use many different shapes and initially tell them how many lines to look for. Then fade that support so they have to seek out the correct number of lines of symmetry in the figure.
8. Unable to identify a shape in different orientation as congruent.	When finding all the ways to rearrange three right triangles, the student thinks the following designs are different because of their orientation. 	• Provide experiences using and describing *slides*, *turns*, and *flips*, such as when putting together puzzles, making designs with pattern blocks, and using interactive applets. • Provide several copies of the shape being composed. When one design is found, have them tape it together. When another design is found, ask them to turn and flip their existing designs to see if it is new.
9. Cannot visualize a three-dimensional shape from a two-dimensional image (net).	Given a collection of nets on a grid, students are unable to mentally fold the shape to predict which can make a cube.	• After completing Activity 19.36 have students suggest which nets can be folded into a box with no top. • Consider Activity 19.38.
10. Incorrectly describes shapes they cannot see (struggles with creating a mental image) or is unable to predict what a shape looks like after it has been flipped, turned, or slid.	Student is unable to predict what Motion Man would look like if it is flipped over the indicated line segment.	• Engage students in activities where they can check their predictions by manipulating physical or virtual materials. See Activity 19.24. • Have children work puzzles (see Activities 19.8 and 19.9).
11. Incorrectly identifies the space as opposed to the intersection of the grid for location.	When asked to place a block on the location indicated by 3 right and 2 up, the student places the block in the space not on the intersection of the grid. 	• Use two pipe cleaners to help the student measure the horizontal and vertical distances. Where the two pipe cleaners intersect shows the location point. • Use a simple local map laid out on a grid to find a location. Explain that because we travel along the streets, we will indicate our location along the grid lines.
12. Reverses the ordered pair.	Students suggest that a point is located at (y, x) rather than (x, y).	Students need to know that there is a convention to the labeling of a point using ordered pairs. They need to practice the consistent pattern of the x value first then the y value (see Activity 19.31).

RESOURCES FOR CHAPTER 19

LITERATURE CONNECTIONS

I Spy Shapes in Art
Micklethwait (2007)
Museum Shapes *Metropolitan Museum of Art (2005)*
Using artwork from such masters as Matisse and Warhol, you can challenge students to look for particular shapes in paintings through an "I spy" approach. This activity can be extended to postcards of artwork from local museums or act as a catalyst for budding "mathematical" artists in the classroom.

Cubes, Cones, Cylinders and Spheres
Hoban (2000)

Shapes, Shapes, Shapes
Hoban (1996)

So Many Circles, So Many Squares
Hoban (1998)
These wordless books contain dramatic photographs of geometric shapes in the environment. Using digital cameras to create Hoban-like books invites students to seek and identify two- and three-dimensional shapes in the world around them. Send the books home for students to share with families or have students in upper grades make books for younger students.

RECOMMENDED READINGS

Articles
Edwards, M. T., & Harper, S. R. (2010). Paint bucket polygons. *Teaching Children Mathematics, 16*(7), 420–428.

> *To advance understanding of polygons, examples and nonexamples are used to help refine definitions. Using the "paint bucket" feature found in many graphics programs or Microsoft Word's "fill color" feature, students are able to define properties of polygons.*

Koester, B. A. (2003). Prisms and pyramids: Constructing three-dimensional models to build understanding. *Teaching Children Mathematics, 9*(8), 436–442.

> *Explorations with third to fifth graders include using straws and pipe cleaners to build models. The activities involve classification and definitions of shapes and seeking patterns in the number of faces, vertices, and edges.*

20

Developing Concepts of Data and Statistics

LEARNER OUTCOMES

After reading this chapter and engaging in the embedded activities and reflections, you should be able to:

20.1 Explain differences between statistics and mathematics, including what is meant by "doing statistics."

20.2 Describe techniques for collecting data, including sampling, as well as quality sources for finding data.

20.3 Determine developmentally appropriate ways for students to analyze data, including ways to help students determine which options best represent their data.

20.4 Illustrate and explain the meaning of measures of center and measures of variability.

20.5 Compose questions that help students focus on interpreting data.

Graphs and statistics bombard the public in areas such as advertising, opinion polls, population trends, health risks, and progress of children in schools. We hear that the average amount of rainfall this summer is more than it was last summer or that the average American family consists of 3.19 people. In September 2017, the *median* selling price of a home in the United States was about $314,000 and the *mean* was about $378,000 (U.S. Bureau of the Census, n.d.). Knowing these statistics should raise an array of questions: How were these data gathered? What was the purpose? Why are the median and the mean for home sales so different and which one makes more sense?

Statistical literacy is critical to understanding the world around us, essential for effective citizenship, and vital for developing the ability to question information presented in the media (Shaughnessy, 2007). Misuse of statistics occurs even in trustworthy sources like newspapers, where graphs are often designed to exaggerate a finding. Students in preK through grade 8 should have meaningful experiences with basic concepts of statistics throughout their school years. The first Mathematical Practice, for example, states, "Mathematically proficient students can explain correspondences between equations, verbal descriptions, tables, and graphs or draw diagrams of important features and relationships, graph data, and search for regularity or trends" (NGA Center & CCSSO, 2010, p. 6). The following are the big ideas that help students become statistically literate.

BIG IDEAS

- ◆ Statistics is a different field of study from mathematics; although mathematics is used in statistics, statistics is concerned with analysis of data and the resulting practical implications. With statistics, the context always matters.
- ◆ Doing statistics involves a four-step process: formulating questions, collecting data, analyzing data, and interpreting results.
- ◆ Different types of graphs and other data representations provide different information about the data and, hence, the population from which the data were taken. The choice of graphical representation can affect how well the data are understood.
- ◆ Measures that describe data with numbers are called *statistics*.
- ◆ The shape of data provides a "big picture" of the data rather than a collection of numbers. Graphs and statistics can provide a sense of the shape of the data, including how spread out or how clustered they are.

What Does It Mean to Do Statistics?

Doing statistics is, in fact, a different process from doing mathematics—a notion that has recently received much attention in standards documents and research (Burrill & Elliott, 2006; Franklin et al., 2007; Shaughnessy, 2003). As Richard Scheaffer, past president of the American Statistics Association, notes:

> Mathematics is about numbers and their operations, generalizations and abstractions; it is about spatial configurations and their measurement, transformations, and abstractions. . . . Statistics is also about numbers—but numbers in context: these are called data. Statistics is about variables and cases, distribution and variation, purposeful design or studies, and the role of randomness in the design of studies, and the interpretation of results. (2006, pp. 310–311)

Statistical literacy is needed by all students to help interpret the world. This section describes some of the big ideas and essential knowledge regarding statistics and explains a general process for doing statistics. Each of the four steps in the process is used as a major section in the organization of this chapter.

Students need to explore concepts of statistics beginning in kindergarten and continue throughout K–8. In the early grades, students learn how data can be categorized and displayed in various graphical forms (e.g., picture graph). In the upper elementary grades, students collect and organize sets of data as well as represent data in frequency tables, bar graphs, dot plots (line plots), and picture graphs. As they enter middle school, students learn new data representations such as histograms, box plots, scatter plots, and stem-and-leaf plots, as well as study measures of center and measures of variability (NGA Center & CCSSO, 2010).

MyLab Education   **Video Example 20.1**

Watch author Jennifer Bay-Williams summarize important ideas of statistics in this brief video.

Is It Statistics or Is It Mathematics?

Statistics and mathematics are two different fields; however, statistical questions are often asked in assessments with questions that are mathematical in nature rather than statistical. The harm in this is that students are not focusing on statistical reasoning, as shown by the following excellent exemplars from Scheaffer (2006).

Read the following questions and label each as "doing mathematics" or "doing statistics."

1. The average weight of 50 prize-winning tomatoes is 2.36 pounds. What is the combined weight, in pounds, of these 50 tomatoes? (NAEP sample question)

   a. 0.0472
   b. 11.8
   c. 52.36
   d. 59
   e. 118

2. Joe had three test scores of 78, 76, and 74, whereas Mary had scores of 72, 82, and 74. How did Joe's average (mean) compare to Mary's average (mean) score? (TIMSS eighth-grade released item)

   a. Joe's was one point higher.
   b. Joe's was one point lower.
   c. Both averages were the same.
   d. Joe's was 2 points higher.
   e. Joe's was 2 points lower.

3. Table 20.01 gives the times each girl has recorded for seven trials of the 100-meter dash this year. Only one girl may compete in the upcoming track meet. Which girl would you select for the meet and why?

TABLE 20.1 RACE TIMES FOR THREE RUNNERS

Runner	1	2	3	4	5	6	7
Suzie	15.2	14.8	15.0	14.7	14.3	14.5	14.5
Tanisha	15.8	15.7	15.4	15.0	14.8	14.6	14.5
Dara	15.6	15.5	14.8	15.1	14.5	14.7	14.5

Which of these involves statistical reasoning? All of them? None of them? As explained by Schaeffer, only the last is statistical in nature. The first requires knowing the formula for mean, working backwards through a formula—mathematical thinking, not statistical thinking. The second problem, the question is about a computational process. The final question is statistical in nature because the situation requires analysis—graphs or averages might be used to determine a solution. The mathematics here is basic; the focus is on statistics.

Notice the context is irrelevant in the first two problems and central to the third question, an indication that it is that last question that requires statistical reasoning. In statistics, the context is essential to analyzing and interpreting the data (Franklin et al., 2007; Lovett & Lee, 2016; Scheaffer, 2006). Looking at the spread, or shape, of data and considering the meaning of unusual data points (outliers) are determined based on the context.

CCSS Standards for Mathematical Practice

MP2. Reason abstractly and quantitatively.

The Shape of Data

A big conceptual idea in data analysis is the *shape of data*, meaning the distribution of the data. It includes how data are spread out or grouped, what characteristics the data set has as a whole. Different graphing techniques or types of graphs can provide a different snapshot

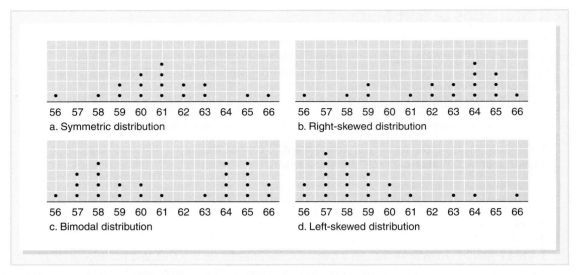

FIGURE 20.1 Dot plots showing different distributions (shape) of data.

of the data as a whole. Graphs, such as dot plots, illustrate the distributions of numerical data (Kader & Jacobbe, 2013). Figure 20.1 shows four different dot plots (line plots that use dots instead of Xs), each showing a different shape to the data. Although the dot plot in Figure 20.1(a) is not exactly symmetrical, meaning the left side of the graph looks just like the right side, we describe it as symmetrical because we are describing the shape of the data in general.

Just as line plots or dot plots provide information about the distribution of numerical data, bar graphs and circle graphs (percentage graphs) each show the distribution of categorical data. The circle graph focuses more on the relative values of this clustering, whereas the bar graph adds a dimension of quantity. The choice of which and how many categories to use in these graphs will result in different pictures of the shape of the data.

Part of understanding the shape of data is being aware of how spread out or clustered the data are. In the early grades, this can be discussed informally by looking at almost any graph. For numeric data, there are statistics that tell us how data are spread or dispersed. The simplest of these is the range. Averages (the mean and the median) tell us the "center" of the data. In high school, students will learn about the standard deviation statistic, which is also a measure of spread. At the middle school level, a simple graphical technique called the *box plot* is designed to give us visual information about the spread of data.

The Process of Doing Statistics

Just as learning addition involves much more than the procedure for combining, doing statistics is much more than being able to create a graph or a computational procedure for finding the mean. To meaningfully learn and do statistics, students should be involved in the full process, from asking and defining questions to interpreting results. This process may sound sophisticated, but with age-appropriate questions and data analysis, students in kindergarten can meaningfully participate in this process (Hourigan & Leavy, 2015/2016). This chapter is organized around this process, which is presented in Figure 20.2. Common challenges that students experience as they engage in the process of doing statistics are briefly described in Table 20.2 and discussed within the related section in this chapter.

I. Formulate Questions
- Clarify the problem at hand
- Formulate one (or more) questions that can be answered with data

II. Collect Data
- Design a plan to collect appropriate data
- Employ the plan to collect the data

III. Analyze Data
- Select appropriate graphical and numerical methods
- Use these methods to analyze the data

IV. Interpret Results
- Interpret the analysis
- Relate the interpretation to the original question

Source: Franklin, C., Kader, G., Mewborn, D., Moreno, J., Peck, R., Perry, M., & Scheaffer, R. (2007) *Guidelines for Assessment and Instruction in Statistics Education (GAISE) Report: A Pre-K–12 Curriculum Framework,* p. 11. Reprinted with permission. Copyright © 2007 by the American Statistical Association. All rights reserved.

FIGURE 20.2 Process of doing statistics.

TABLE 20.2 COMMON CHALLENGES AND MISCONCEPTIONS RELATED TO DATA AND STATISTICS

Common Challenge or Misconception	What It Looks Like	How to Help
1. Posing a question that is statistical in nature.	Student poses questions that are not statistical, such as • How old is my dog? • How much time did I spend on homework last night?	• Give examples and non-examples of statistical questions and ask students to identify the differences. • Help the student to modify his/her nonstatistical question so that it becomes a statistical question (e.g., What are the ages of our pets? Or, What is the typical time our class spent on homework?). • Emphasize that statistical questions rely on the context, can only be answered by collecting data, and involve some sense of variability (i.e., if there is only one answer, it is not a statistical question).
2. Determining categories for grouping data.	After collecting data (e.g., favorite book), a student lists each classmate's name along with the name of the favorite book, rather than sorting into categories.	• Use categorization activities (see Activities 20.4–20.6 and those listed in Table 20.3 that are based in social studies and science content). • Provide categories or brainstorm possible categories.
3. Sorting objects based on more than one rule.	A student is asked to sort attribute materials using the rule "small triangles," but sorts based only on the attribute of triangle (ignoring the size attribute).	• Initially sort materials that have visible attributes (like color). • Scaffold by first only sorting by one attribute. Increase the number of attributes as the child demonstrates successful sorts. • Have student state the sorting rules for each shape that is sorted emphasizing both attributes, for example, saying, "This shape is small *and* this shape is a triangle"

(continued)

Common Challenge or Misconception	What It Looks Like	How to Help
4. Looking at the data set within a graph as a whole (rather than at single data points).	When asked to describe something about the class graph that shows the ways their classmates travel to school, the student explains, "That's my sticky note there! I ride the bus."	• Explicitly ask questions about the shape of the data. • Draw a line or curve (e.g., connecting the tops of bar graphs) to illustrate the general shape of the data. • Compare the shapes of two different graphs (e.g., two bar graphs, or two line plots).
5. Bar graph creation: dealing with 0.	Student creates a bar graph from a survey, but leaves out the category that had zero responses. Third Grade Favorite Colors Yellow — 6 Blue — 5 Green — 0 Red — 4 Brown — 2 Purple — 5 Third Grade Favorite Colors (bar graph: Yellow 6, Blue 5, Red 4, Brown 2, Purple 5)	• Have students count the survey items and count the bars. • Include categories for which you anticipate there will be 0 responses so they encounter 0 more often. • Discuss why there still needs to be a bar for the category.
6. Pictographs: understanding the scale.	Student sees a pictograph of favorite animals, and interprets the 5 dolphins as 5 students selecting dolphins (rather than referring to the scale and seeing that each dolphin picture represents 3 students).	• Explicitly ask students why the number of pictures is not the same as the number of students surveyed. • Skip count for each category. • Ask students to discuss different results.
7. Histograms: understanding the meaning of the bars (as describing the relative frequency of data within the interval) and the meaning of the x- and y-axis.	Student reads the bar as an actual data values, rather than the frequency for the interval; student uses the y-axis to determine the center of the data; student thinks the height of bar captures the variability in the data.	• Compare histograms to bar graphs. • Compare histogram to the related numerical data. • Spend adequate time on analysis and interpretation (rather than devoting most of the instructional time on graph construction).
8. Box plots: Understanding that each quartile has 25 percent of the data points.	A student thinks a smaller box means fewer data points.	• Compare box plots to histograms. • Discuss which sections have the most data points (none) and which have the most variability.
9. Selecting appropriate graph for the data.	Student uses a line to connect categorical data. (line graph with points: Red 4, Blue 5, Green 1, Yellow 3)	• In a visible place in your classroom, post a list of options for graphing. • Before students graph, ask, "Which graphs are options for this data?" (and why?) Which graphs are not options? (and why?) • After students graph, and are sharing their displays, ask students to critique the display in terms of whether it is appropriate and whether it is a good way to communicate the data collected.

Common Challenge or Misconception	What It Looks Like	How to Help
10. Determining mean from a frequency table or dot plot (line plot).	Student cannot figure out how many of each data point there is, or does not know how many data points in all.	• Ask students to write an expression for each row and column in the table or chart. For example, if there are 6 tallies for students with 7-inch hand span, they record 6(7) next to the tally. • Ask students to revisit their answers and see if they are a reasonable measure of center.

Formulating Questions

Statistics is about more than making graphs and analyzing data. It includes both asking and answering questions about our world. Data collection should be for a purpose, to answer a question. Then the analysis of data actually adds information about some aspect of our world, just as political pollsters, advertising agencies, market researchers, census takers, wildlife managers, medical researchers, and hosts of others gather data to answer questions and make informed decisions.

Students, even young students, should have opportunities to generate their own questions, decide on appropriate data to help answer these questions, and determine methods of collecting the data (NGA Center & CCSSO, 2010; NCTM, 2006). Whether the question is teacher initiated or student initiated, students should engage in conversations about how well defined the question is. For example, if the teacher asks, "What is the typical number of siblings in our class?" there may be a need to discuss half siblings. If students want to know how many shoes each classmate owns, questions may arise as to whether they should count bedroom slippers and flip-flops.

When students formulate the questions, the data they gather become more meaningful. How they organize the data and the techniques for analyzing them have a purpose. Often questions will come naturally during the course of discussion or from questions arising in other content areas. The next two sections suggest many ideas.

 Standards for Mathematical Practice
MP1. Make sense of problems and persevere in solving them.

Classroom Questions

Students want to learn about each other, their families and pets, measures such as arm span or time to get to school, their likes and dislikes, and so on. The easiest questions are those that can be answered by each class member contributing one piece of data. Here are a few ideas:

- *Favorites:* TV shows, games, movies, ice cream, video games, sports teams, music (when there are lots of possibilities, start by restricting the number of choices)
- *Numbers:* Number of pets or siblings, hours watching TV or hours of sleep, bedtime, time spent on the computer
- *Measures:* Height, arm span, area of foot, long-jump distance, shadow length, seconds to run around the track, minutes spent traveling to school

Questions beyond Self and Classmates

The questions in the previous section are designed for students to contribute data about themselves. These questions can be expanded by asking, "How would our data compare to another class?" For example, do other second-grade students like the same movies that we like? Comparison questions are a good way to help students focus on the data they have collected and the variability within that data and between data sets (Russell, 2006). As students get older, they can begin to think about various populations and differences between them. For example, how are fifth-grade students similar to or different from middle school students? Students might examine questions where they compare responses of boys versus girls, adults or teachers versus students, or categories of full-time workers compared to college students. These situations involve issues of sampling and making generalizations and comparisons.

To further expand students' perspectives, have them compare themselves or their data to data with similar classes in other places in the state, other states, or perhaps even in a foreign country. This can open up not just a source of interesting data but also a way for your students to see beyond their own localities.

Activity 20.1

CCSS-M: 2.MD.D.10; 3.MD.B.3; 6.SP.A.1; 7.SP.B.3

Who Is in Our Village?

The picture books *If America Were a Village: A Book about the People of the United States* (Smith, 2009) and *If the World Were a Village: A Book about the World's People* (Smith, 2011) provide an excellent opportunity to compare class data or school data to the wider population in the United States and in the world, respectively. Each book explores relative wealth, culture, language, and other influences, providing the statistics in the adapted case of the country (world) being a village of 100 people. Read the books in their entirety or select several excerpts to read to the class. For selected topics, ask students if they think data from our class (or school) will be similar to the data in the book. Gather and compare class data to the U.S. and world data. Then ask students what else they think might be interesting data that could be added to the pages of the book. (See Riskowski, Olbricht, & Wilson, 2010, for a project exploring concepts of statistics using 100 students.)

The local newspaper suggests all sorts of data-related questions. For example, how many advertisements are included on different days of the week? How many sports stories are about different types of sports (e.g., basketball, football, swimming, etc.)? How many pages is the local paper each day of the week? What types of stories are on the front page? Which comics are really for kids and which are not?

Science is about inquiry and is full of measurements and data, and therefore provides excellent opportunities for interdisciplinary learning experiences. For example, consider this short list of ideas:

- How many plastic bottles or aluminum cans are placed in the school's recycling bins over a given week?
- How many times do different types of balls bounce when each is dropped from the same height?
- How many days does it take for different types of bean, squash, and pea seeds to germinate when kept in moist paper towels?
- Which brand of bubble gum will give you the largest bubble?
- Do some liquids expand more than others when frozen?
- Does a plant grow faster when watered with water, soda, or milk?

Before going on a field trip, students can develop questions for which they can gather data on the trip (Mokros & Wright, 2009). For example, when visiting the zoo, students might record data (e.g., keeping tallies in a chart) related for questions such as:

- How many animals at the zoo are bigger than me?
- How many animals have no legs, two legs, four legs, and more than four legs?
- Are their more animals with fur or without fur?
- From what continents are the animals at the zoo?

Discussions about communities provide a good way to integrate social studies and mathematics.

As noted earlier, a distinguishing feature of statistics is that the context is front and center. Therefore, it is particularly important that the context be culturally meaningful. Culturally meaningful contexts create a supportive classroom environment (McGlone, 2008). This can be as simple as asking about favorite family meal or game, or can include an exploration of family customs. The key to having such questions lead to a supportive classroom environment is sharing the results in a way that helps others in the class appreciate the unique lives of their classmates.

Activity 20.2

CCSS-M: 1.MD.C.4; 2.MD.D.10; 6.SP.A.1; 6.SP.B.4; 6.SP.B.5

What Can We Learn about Our Community?

This activity plays out over several days. First, ask students to turn in a note card with three statistical questions they would like to investigate during the year. This could be assigned as homework, with students' families helping to brainstorm ideas. Collect these ideas. When you have time to start the investigation, take one question from the set. As a class, refine the question to one that can be answered using statistics. Examples of questions include:

- How many different kinds of restaurants or stores are in our community (fast food restaurants versus "sit down" restaurants; Italian, Mexican, or American; convenience stores, grocery stores, clothing stores, variety stores)?

- How many responses are made by local firefighters each month? How many different types of responses are made by local firefighters each month (fire, medical, hazardous, public service)? (Data can usually be found on websites of local institutions.)

- How many state and local government officials do voters elect?

Discuss ways to gather the data. Set up a plan and deadline for gathering the data. When students bring in the data, encourage students to select and use data displays (e.g., circle graph, pie chart, line plot, etc.). Invite students to share. Return to the question and ask, "What does our data tell us about _____?" Consider how the different data displays communicate the answer to this question. See Expanded Lesson: Using Data to Answer a Question for a full lesson of this activity.

MyLab Education   Expanded Lesson: Using Data to Answer a Question

---

Students will need help in designing questions that can be answered using statistics. These are questions that include variability and for which data can be gathered. Providing examples and nonexamples can help students, in particular students with disabilities, focus on the elements of an appropriate statistical question. For example, consider which of the following questions can be answered using statistics and which cannot.

Standards for Mathematical Practice
MP5. Use appropriate tools strategically.

1. How much change do I have in my pocket?
2. What is the typical amount of loose change a person carries in their pocket?
3. What cereal is most healthy?
4. What reasons do people use in selecting gum (e.g., taste, cost, bubble-making quality, long lasting, good breath)?
5. How long do different kinds of gum keep their flavor?
6. Which store has the best prices?
7. Where will you buy shampoo?

▐▐ Pause & Reflect

Which of the previous questions are statistical and which ones are not statistical in nature? ●

Questions 1, 3, and 7 are *not* statistical in nature. Question 3 could be adapted to a statistical question with a more specific focus on what is meant by healthy. Similarly, question 7 is very broad and will need to be focused in order to collect the data needed to answer it. Facilitating discussions with students about examples and nonexamples as well as questions they develop improves their ability to generate appropriate statistical questions.

MyLab Education   Self-Check 20.1

Data Collection

How to collect data effectively is an important (and sometimes skipped) part of the discussion as students learn statistics. Consider the following (true) scenario in a first-grade classroom:

A teacher asks her students to gather data to find out how many of their classmates are 6. The students agree on the question, "Are you 6?" The teacher instructs students to gather data from each of their classmates and gives them a signal to begin. Eighteen eager students stand up and begin asking each other "Are you 6?" tallying yes or no, then walking up to another classmate. After about 5 minutes of exchanges, the teacher asked everyone to sit down to look at the data they had collected and count how many students were 6. Each student had different data to report.

How did this happen? The students did not pay attention to who they had surveyed. This provided an excellent entry into a discussion about how statisticians must gather data.

MyLab Education Video Example 20.2

This video shows a class exploring how to collect data on favorite jelly bean flavors.

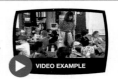

Figure 20.3 shows how a kindergarten class decided to organize their data collection on favorite ice cream flavors (Cook, 2008). Students may gather data by counting events or hand raising, then move to using a ballot with limited and then unlimited response options (Hudson, Shupe, Vasquez, & Miller, 2008).

Beyond surveys, data can be collected through experiments or observations. For example, set up a bird feeder outside the classroom window and collect data at different times during the day to count the number or type of birds. Students can also conduct observational data collection events on field trips and in evening or weekend activities with their families.

There are two types of data that can be collected—categorical and numerical. Categorical data are (as the name implies) data grouped by labels (categories) such as favorite vacations, colors of cars in the school parking lot, and the most popular suggestion for a mascot for the middle school team. Numerical data, on the other hand, counts things or measures. Numerical data are ordered and scaled, like a number line, and can include fractions and decimals. This kind of data includes how many miles to school, the temperature in your town over a one-week period, or the weight of the students' backpacks. Students need to explicitly explore the idea that statistical measures such as mean or median involve using numerical data (Leavy, Friel, & Mamer, 2009).

FIGURE 20.3 Kindergartners collect data on favorite ice cream flavors, tally the data, and create a horizontal bar graph.

Source: Cook, C. D. (2008). "I Scream, You Scream: Data Analysis with Kindergartners." *Teaching Children Mathematics, 14*(9), p. 539. Reprinted with permission.

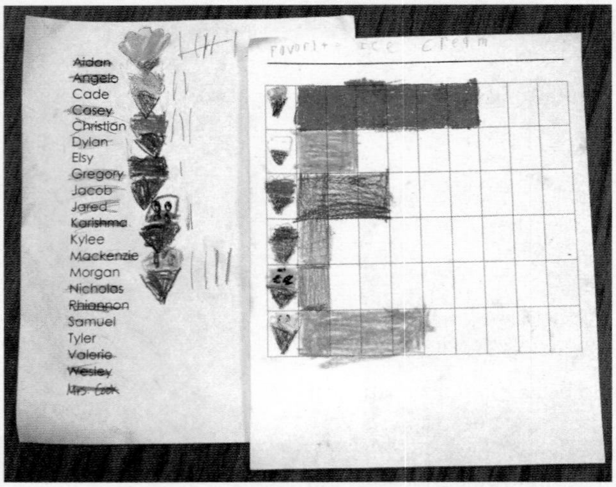

Sampling

When asking a question about a small population, like your class, data can be gathered on everyone. But statistics generally does not involve gathering data from the whole population and instead uses a representative sample. CCSS-M identifies learning about samples in order to make inferences about a population as a critical area for seventh-grade students (NGA Center & CCSSO, 2010).

Sampling must take into consideration *variability*. For example, a poll on favorite TV shows will produce different

answers from a survey of seventh-grade students than a group of teachers or third-grade students. It may also vary for girls and for boys or culturally. Answers also may vary based on the day the question is asked or whether a particular show has been recently discussed.

To help students determine if they have identified a representative sample, ask, "What is the population for your question?" or "Who or what is the subject of your question?" Then ask students to consider how they will gather data that will include representatives across that population. For example, if they are hoping to learn the movie choice for a seventh-grade movie night at your school, they need to poll girls and boys across the seventh-grade teams within the middle school. Provide opportunities for students to justify if the data are representative and to critique the explanation of others as they describe what is a representative sample.

Even when it may appear that a sample is representative, it may not be. Unintentional biases can occur, and we cannot always know what subsets might exist within a population. Therefore, *random sampling* is used in statistics. It increases the validity of the results, and therefore gives more confidence in being able to make inferences. Seventh-grade students who begin informal work with random sampling start to consider the importance of representative samples for drawing inferences (NGA Center & CCSSO, 2010). Activity 20.3 can help students develop an awareness of the importance of sampling.

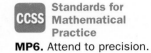

Standards for Mathematical Practice
MP6. Attend to precision.

Activity 20.3 — CCSS-M: 6.SP.A.1; 6.SP.A.2; 7.SP.A.1; 7.SP.B.3

How Do We Compare?

Using *Book of Lists: Fun Facts, Weird Trivia, and Amazing Lists on Nearly Everything You Need to Know!* by James Buckley and Robert Stremme (2006), or a similar book or online resource, find a list that includes sampling a group of people. Use the How Do We Compare? Activity Page. Read the question to the students and gather data using the class as the sample. Ask students, "Do you think our class will be a representative sample of the population targeted in this question?" Ask students to offer why the class might be or might not be a representative sample. Gather data from the class. Compare the two data sets. If appropriate, create a circle graph, pie chart, dot plot (line plot), or stem-and-leaf plot to compare the two data sets. After displaying the two sets, ask students what technique they think the authors might have used to sample the population.

MyLab Education   **Activity Page: How Do We Compare?**

Although this activity involved people, "population" in statistics is used broadly to mean "group or subject of study." The population could be a species of a plant, an insect, or a type of car. The activity above can be replicated with other data. For example, you can look up favorite car colors online and then see if cars that drive by the school form a representative sample of all cars.

Standards for Mathematical Practice
MP5. Use appropriate tools strategically.

Using Existing Data Sources

Data do not have to be collected by survey; existing data abound in various places, such as the following sources of print and Web data.

Print Resources. Newspapers, almanacs, sports record books, maps, and various government publications are possible sources of data that may be used to answer student questions.

Children's literature is another excellent and engaging resource. Young students can tally words in a repeating verse like "Hickory, Dickory, Dock" (Niezgoda & Moyer-Packenham, 2005). Similarly, books like *Goodnight Moon* (Brown, 1947) or *Green Eggs and Ham* (Seuss, 1960) have many repeated words or phrases. Nonfiction literature can be another source of data, especially for older students. For example, *Book of Lists: Fun Facts, Weird Trivia, and Amazing Lists on Nearly Everything You Need to Know!* (Buckley & Stremme, 2006), mentioned in Activity 20.3, reports on various statistics and includes surveys at the end of every section. Books on sports, such as *A Negro League Scrapbook* (Weatherform, 2005), can have very interesting statistics about historic periods that students can explore and compare.

Web Resources. The Internet provides seemingly limitless data that are often accessed by simply typing the related question into a search. Students may be interested in facts about another country as a result of a social studies unit or a country in the news. Olympic records in various events over the years or data related to environmental issues are other examples of topics around which student questions may be formulated. For these and hundreds of other questions, data can be found online. These websites provide a lot of interesting data.

- The Official Olympic Records contains all Olympic records, providing information about the games and events, such as the medalists in every Olympic event since Athens 1896.
- data.gov is the home of the U.S. governments open data and provides access to all data sets available from the U.S. government, all on one site.
- The USDA Economic Research Service Food Consumption site offers wonderful data sets on the availability and consumption of hundreds of foods. Annual per capita estimates often go back to 1909.
- Google Public Data Explorer makes large data sets available to explore, visualize, and interpret.
- Better World Flux provides data related to the progress of countries and the world over the years, highlighting interesting trends and patterns.
- NCTM Illuminations State Data Map is a source that displays state data on population, land area, political representation, gasoline use, and so on.
- The Central Intelligence Agency (CIA) World Fact Book provides demographic information for every nation in the world: population, age distributions, death and birth rates, and information on the economy, government, transportation, and geography.
- U.S. Census Bureau has copious statistical information by state, county, or voting district.

Data Analysis: Classification

Data analysis begins with organizing the data in a meaningful way, using techniques such as sorting or graphing, with the resulting visual providing a snapshot of the data. The data are then analyzed with the goal in mind of how the information answers the questions that started the statistical inquiry and provided the purpose for collecting the data.

Classification involves making decisions about how to categorize things, a basic activity that is fundamental to data analysis. To formulate questions and decide how to represent data that have been gathered, decisions must be made about how things might be categorized. This is not easy for young students who may just list the data (Clements & Sarama, 2009). For example, when asked to represent the class data about how they arrived at school (bus, car, walk), young students may just list each classmates' response, rather than group them into categories. Engage students in discussions about how they can group things. For example, students might group farm animals by number of legs; by type of product they provide; by those that work, provide food, or are pets; by size or color; by the type of food they eat; and so on. Each of these groupings is based on a different attribute of the animals. CCSS-M places classification by attributes as a kindergarten topic. Attribute activities are explicitly designed to develop flexible reasoning about the characteristics of data.

Attribute Materials

Attribute materials can be any set of objects that lend themselves to being sorted and classified in different ways—for example, seashells, leaves, the students themselves, or the students' shoes. The *attributes* are the ways that the materials can be sorted. For example, hair color, height, and gender are attributes of students. Each attribute has a number of different *values:* for example, blond, brown, black, or red (for the attribute of hair color); tall or short (for height); male or female (for gender). Commercially available attribute blocks come in sets of 60, with each piece having four attributes: color (red, yellow, blue), shape (circle, triangle, rectangle, square, hexagon), size (big, little), and thickness (thick, thin). The specific values, number of values, or number of attributes that a set may have is not important.

Initially, attribute activities are best done by sitting in a large circle on the floor where all students can see and have access to the materials to be sorted. Digital versions of attribute blocks can be found by visiting the National Library of Virtual Manipulatives or Glencoe's Virtual Manipulatives website.

Activity 20.4   CCSS-M: K.MD.3; 1.MD.C.4

What about "Both"

Give students two large loops of string and attribute blocks. Direct them to put all the red pieces inside one string and all triangles inside the other. Let the students try to resolve the difficulty of what to do with the red triangles. When the notion of overlapping the strings to create an area common to both loops is clear, more challenging activities can be explored. Students with disabilities will need to use labels on each loop of string.

In addition to attribute blocks, use Woozle Cards (see Figure 20.4). To make, copy the Woozle Cards Activity Page on different colored cardstock (or print on white and color each page a different color). Select two attributes (e.g., shape and number of dots) and follow the same steps described for the attribute blocks.

STUDENTS with SPECIAL NEEDS

MyLab Education   Activity Page: Woozle Cards

As shown in Figure 20.5, the labels need not be restricted to single attributes. If a piece does not fit in any region, it is placed outside all of the loops.

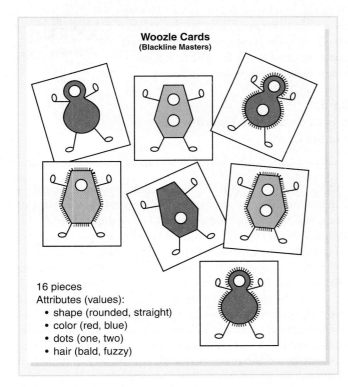

FIGURE 20.4   Sample set of Woozle Cards and list of attributes.

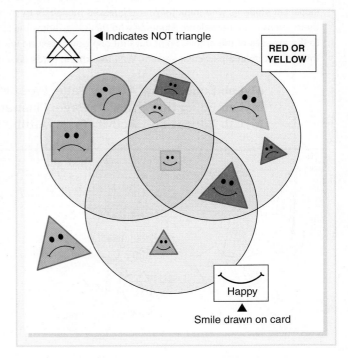

FIGURE 20.5   A Venn diagram activity with attribute pieces. A rule is written on a card for each Venn diagram circle.

Standards for Mathematical Practice

MP6. Attend to precision.

As students progress, it is important to introduce labels for negative attributes such as "not red" or "not small." Also important is the eventual use of *and* and *or* connectives, as in two-value rules such as "red and square" or "big or happy." This use of *and*, *or*, and *not* significantly widens students' classification schemes.

An engaging and challenging activity is to infer how things have been classified when the loops are not labeled. The following activities require students to make and test conjectures about how things are being classified.

Activity 20.5

CCSS-M: K.MD.3; 1.MD.C.4

Guess My Rule

For this activity, try using students instead of shapes as attribute "pieces." Decide on an attribute such as "wearing blue jeans" or "stripes on clothing," but do not tell your rule to the class. Silently look at one student at a time, and move the student to the left or right according to this secret rule. After a number of students have been sorted, have the next student come up and ask students to predict which group he or she belongs in. Before the rule is articulated, continue the activity for a while so that others in the class will have an opportunity to determine the rule. This same activity can be done with virtually any materials that can be sorted, such as students' shoes, shells, or buttons. Encourage ELs to use their native language and English to describe the rule.

ENGLISH LEARNERS

Activity 20.6

CCSS-M: K.MD.3; 1.MD.C.4

Hidden Labels

Place loops of string (one, two, or three) in the form of a Venn diagram. Use attribute blocks, Woozle Cards (see Figure 20.4) or illustrations of geometric figures. Use Attribute Label Cards or write labels on notecards for each loop of string. Place the cards facedown. Ask students to select a piece for you to place. For ELs and students with disabilities, provide a list of the labels with pictures and/or translations for each as a reference. Begin to sort pieces according to the hidden rules. As you sort, have students try to determine what the labels are for each of the loops. Let students who think they have guessed the labels try to place a piece in the proper loop, but avoid having them guess the labels aloud. Students who think they know the labels can be asked to "play teacher" and respond to the guesses of the others. Point out that one way to test an idea about the labels is to select a piece that you think might go in a particular section. Wait to turn the cards up until most students have figured out the rule.

ENGLISH LEARNERS

STUDENTS *with* **SPECIAL NEEDS**

MyLab Education   Activity Page: Woozle Cards
MyLab Education   Activity Page: Illustrations of Geometric Figures
MyLab Education   Activity Page: Attribute Label Cards

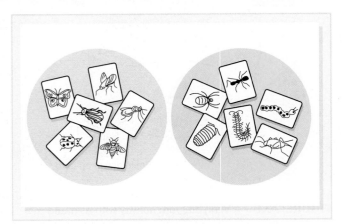

FIGURE 20.6   Can you guess the rule that was used to sort these bugs?

"Guess my Rule" and "Hidden Labels" can and should be repeated with real-world materials connected to other content areas and to students' experiences. For example, if you were doing a unit on wildlife in the backyard, you can use pictures of creatures (see Figure 20.6) to sort by relevant attributes. To connect reading and data, students can sort and analyze data within a book (e.g., types of events) or across books (e.g., kinds of books). Students can bring in things they can recycle and these objects can be sorted by type (English, 2013). Table 20.3 lists additional ideas that can be used for classification activities related to social studies and science. Using ideas related to content and the real world helps students understand that data analysis is useful as well as engaging!

MyLab Education   **Self-Check 20.2**

TABLE 20.3   TOPICS IN SOCIAL STUDIES AND SCIENCE THAT CAN BE CLASSIFIED

Social Studies	Science
• Places in the United States and outside the United States • Country or state of origin of classmates • Past, present, and future events • Goods (such as, bread, milk, apples, pants, socks, shoes) and services (such as, waiting tables at a restaurant, mowing yards, repairing cars) • Continents and oceans • U.S. presidents according to the state where they were born • Availability of items (scarce, average, abundant) • Jobs in the local community • Climates in the United States	• Sensory descriptors for items (hard/soft, rough/smooth, cold/warm, loud/quiet, sweet/sour/bitter/salty, high/low, and bright/dull) • Relative size or weight of a collection of objects (big/little, large/small, heavy/light, wide/thin, long/short) • Position of objects found in the classroom (over/under, in/out, above/below, left/right) • Speed (fast/slow) of different animals (ants, turtles, snakes, cheetahs) or types of transportation (car, bicycle, airplane, walking) • Materials or objects that float or sink in water • Weather observations (sunny, cloudy, raining, snowing) • Substances that will or will not dissolve in water • Characteristics of plants (edible/nonedible, flowering/nonflowering, evergreen/deciduous) • Physical characteristics of animals (body coverings or methods of movement) • Other characteristics of animals (wild/tame, water homes/land homes, hibernate/do not hibernate, migrate/do not migrate, camouflage/no camouflage)

Data Analysis: Graphical Representations

Graphs summarize the data that were collected. In the CCSS-M, representing and interpreting data begins in grade 1 and is included at each grade thereafter, with increasingly complex representations and analysis expected. How data are organized should be directly related to the question that caused you to collect the data in the first place. For example, suppose students want to know how many pockets they have on their clothing (Russell & Economopoulos, 2008). Data collection involves each student counting his or her pockets. Different classifications would produce different graphs. A picture or bar graph can be made with one bar per student. However, is this the best way to showcase the data in order to analyze it? If the data were instead categorized by number of pockets, then a graph showing the number of students with two pockets, three pockets, and so on will illustrate which number of pockets is most common and how the number of pockets varies across the class.

Middle school students might have questions about music, such as, "How many songs do students in our class listen to in one day?" For data collection, you might decide to have students keep track on a school day (Tuesday, for example) and come to class on Wednesday with their own totals. Each student records the number on a sticky note and places the sticky note on the board. A *dot plot* (also called a *line plot*) could be used to illustrate the spread and shape of the data. A histogram can be created to capture how many students fall within a range of songs listened to (e.g., between 0 and 10, 11 and 20, etc.). A box plot can be created, boxing in the middle 50 percent to focus attention on the center of the data as well as the range. Each of these displays gives a different snapshot of the data and provides different insights into the question posed.

Creating Graphs

Students should be involved in deciding how they want to represent their data, but they will need to be introduced to what the options are and when each display can and cannot be used. Creating graphs requires care and precision, including determining appropriate scales and labels so that an audience is able to see at a glance the summary of the data gathered on a particular question.

Instruction should not focus solely on the details of graph construction. The focus must be on what the graph tells the people who see it related to the question posed. Analyzing data that are numerical (e.g., number of pockets) versus categorical (e.g., color of socks) is an added challenge for students as they struggle to make sense of the graphs (Russell, 2006). If, for example, the graph has seven stickers above the five, students may think that five people have seven pockets or seven people have five pockets (see Figure 20.7).

CCSS **Standards for Mathematical Practice**
MP4. Model with mathematics.

CCSS **Standards for Mathematical Practice**
MP6. Attend to precision.

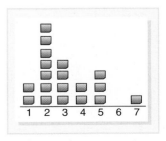

FIGURE 20.7 Looking at the "5" column, does this graph mean that five people have three pockets or three people have five pockets?

TECHNOLOGY Note. Use the time saved by technology to create graphs to instead focus on analyzing and interpreting the data! Computer programs and graphing calculators provide a variety of graphical displays. Two free and effective websites are Tuva Datasets and CODAP. Tuva has more than 350 authentic databases from primary sources, reading to be used in the classroom, or you can input your own data sets and use Tuva tools to explore, visualize, and analyze your data. Common Online Data Analysis Platform (CODAP) provides an easy-to-use data analysis tools for middle and high school students (and teachers). CODAP can also be used to help students summarize, visualize and interpret data, and it offers several data sets (e.g., mammals and data games) to help learn the system and to explore data. Graphing calculator produce data displays, such as pie charts, bar graphs, and picture graphs, and can compute and graph lines of best fit. To simply enter their own data and select a data display (e.g., bar graph, pie charts, line graph, etc.), try Create a Graph (NCES Kids Zone) or Illuminations Data Grapher. ■

Bar Graphs

Bar graphs include object graphs (real objects used in the graph), picture graphs, and regular bar graphs and are typically used to graph categorical data.

MyLab Education   **Video Example 20.3**

In this video author Karen Karp talks about teaching bar and picture graphs.

Object Graphs. An object graph uses the actual objects being graphed. Examples include types of shoes, favorite apple, energy bar wrappers, and books. Each item can be placed in a square or on a floor tile so that comparisons and counts are easily made. Notice that an object graph is a small step from sorting. If real objects are sorted into groups, those groups can be lined up for comparison—an object graph!

MyLab Education   **Video Example 20.4**

This video (https://www.youtube.com/watch?v=4SIY1-idRqY &list=PLRY-hkA4OX06NRPAADyqsG-FWoNwfU3Sq&index=3) illustrates how preschoolers are able to create object graphs (and transition to picture graphs).

Picture Graphs. Picture graphs (also called *pictographs*) move up a level of abstraction by using a drawing or picture of some sort that represents what is being graphed. The picture can represent one piece of data or it can represent a designated quantity. Students need to learn to interpret the scale for the pictograph.

MyLab Education   **Video Example 20.5**

Watch this video where the teachers use pictures of spoons for a pictograph of favorite fruits.

Students can make their own drawings, but this can often become time consuming and tedious. There are various ways to make the creation of picture graphs easier to create, and thereby keep the focus on the meaning of the graph rather than the creation of it. For example, you can use stickers, objects cut out with a die-cut, or clip art (copied repeatedly on a page that can then be cut out).

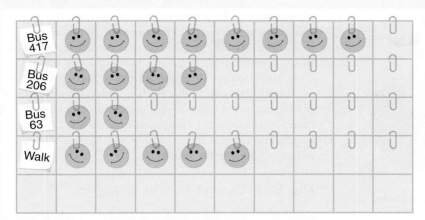

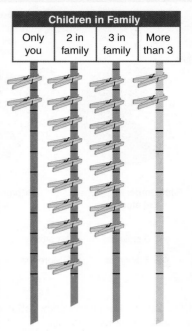

Clip paper pictures or symbols on a chart that has a paper clip prepared in each square.

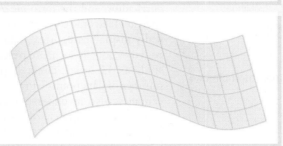

A graph mat can be made on a sheet of plastic about 8 to 10 feet long and used on the floor. Make 5 or 6 columns with 12 to 15 squares in each column. Students place real objects in the columns to show the number of each.

Hang ribbons with marks at even intervals for placing clothespins, and have students clip on pinch-style clothespins.

FIGURE 20.8   Some ideas for quick graphs that can be used again and again.

Bar Graphs. After object and picture graphs, bar graphs are among the first ways used to group and present data with students in preK–2. To help transition from picture graphs to bar graphs, have students use something to represent the pieces of data or the things being counted. Figure 20.8 illustrates a few techniques that can be used to make a graph quickly with the whole class. These can be stuck directly to the board or to a chart and rearranged if needed. Initially bar graphs should be made with each bar consisting of countable parts so that the individual pieces of data do not seem to disappear. The sticky notes in the next activity, "Picture Graphs to Bar Graphs," serve this purpose.

MyLab Education   Video Example 20.6

This lesson on size of families begins with a human bar graph that is then translated into a bar graph on chart paper.

VIDEO EXAMPLE

Activity 20.7   CCSS-M: 2.MD.D.4; 3.MD.B.3

Picture Graphs to Bar Graphs

Determine a question that lends itself to preset categories and is of interest to students (e.g., favorite pet). Give each student a sticky note and ask them to draw a picture of their favorite choice (e.g., cat), place their sticky notes in a "row" on the white board (or wall) so that there is a little space between the sticky notes. Invite students to make observations about their picture graph. Discuss with students how they might make a *bar graph* to illustrate their data. Move the sticky notes so there is no space between them to look like a bar. Discuss ways to know how long the bar is and add a scale next to the bars to show the height of each bar. This activity can be done with a scaled situation, too. For example, they might decide to use one picture of a baseball to represent 3 students. In the bar graph, the scale will skip count by 3s, which can be physically illustrated by stacking three sticky notes on top of each other. Ask students to figure out what to do when there are not three (use thirds). Have students record their scale (e.g., 1 ball = 3 students).

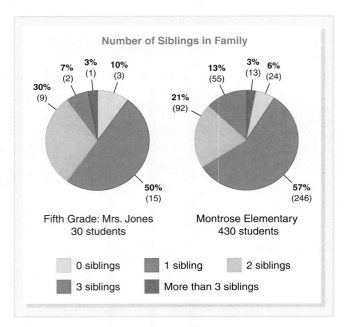

Number of Siblings in Family

Fifth Grade: Mrs. Jones
30 students

7% (2) 3% (1) 10% (3) 30% (9) 50% (15)

Montrose Elementary
430 students

13% (55) 3% (13) 6% (24) 21% (92) 57% (246)

- 0 siblings
- 1 sibling
- 2 siblings
- 3 siblings
- More than 3 siblings

FIGURE 20.9 Pie charts show ratios of part-to-whole and can be used to compare ratios.

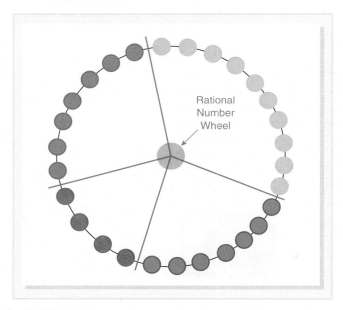

Rational Number Wheel

FIGURE 20.10 A human circle graph: Students are arranged in a circle, with string stretched from the center to show the pie pieces.

Once a graph has been constructed, engage the class in a discussion of what information the graph tells or conveys. Ask questions such as, "What can you tell about our class by looking at this shoe graph?" Graphs convey factual information (more students wear sneakers than any other kind of shoe) and also provide opportunities to make inferences that are not directly observable in the graph (kids in this class do not like to wear leather shoes). Students can examine graphs found in newspapers or magazines and discuss the facts in the graphs and the message that may have been intended by the person who made the graph.

Pie Charts and Circle Graphs

Pie charts (sometimes called *pie graphs*) and circle graphs mean the same thing; the term *circle graph* may be more common in curriculum and the term *pie chart* is used with graphing tools such as electronic spreadsheets. Pie charts, like bar graphs, typically display categorical data. They also typically show percentages and, as such, are perceived as too advanced for young students. However, circle graphs can be set up to indicate the number of data points from a total set, without calculating percentages. Also, an understanding of percentages is not required when using computer software to create the graph.

Pie charts and circle graphs are commonly found in newspapers. However, they are less used in statistics, as it can be more difficult for comparisons within a data set (angle measures are harder to compare than lengths of bars). Pie charts are, however, very useful for comparing two different-sized data sets. Figure 20.9, for example, shows a pie chart for classroom data and schoolwide data illustrating the percentages of students with different numbers of siblings.

Easily Constructed Circle Graphs. There are several engaging and simple ways to make a pie chart. For example, students can first form lines for their response to, "What is your favorite after school activity?" and then lines can be joined end-to-end to make a circle. See Expanded Lesson: Bar Graphs to Circle Graphs for a full lesson on this idea and Figure 20.10 for an illustration.

MyLab Education   **Expanded Lesson: Bar Graphs to Circle Graphs**

Alternatively, students can convert bar graphs to pie charts by cutting out the bars and taping them together. Once a bar graph is complete, cut out the bars themselves and tape them together end to end. Next, tape the two ends together to form a circle. Estimate where the center of the circle is, draw lines to the points where different bars meet, and trace around the full loop. You can estimate percentages using the rational number wheel or percent necklaces as described in Chapter 16.

Determining Percentages. The concrete circle-making helps make sense of the mathematics of a circle graph. The numbers in each category are added to form the total or whole. The percent of one section is computed by dividing each of parts by the whole (and multiplying by 100). It is an interesting proportional problem for students to convert between percents and degrees because one is out of 100 and the other out of 360. It is helpful to start with common values like

50 percent, 25 percent, and 10 percent before moving to more difficult values. A table with one row for percent and one row for degrees can serve as an important tool to help students reason.

FORMATIVE ASSESSMENT Notes. Students should write in a journal about their graphs, explaining what the graph tells and why they selected that type of graph to illustrate the data. As you evaluate students' responses, it is important not to focus undue attention on the skills of constructing a graph, but instead to focus on whether they chose an appropriate representation and have provided a good rationale for its selection that connects back to their question (step 1). ■

Continuous Data Graphs

Bar graphs or picture graphs are useful for illustrating categories of data that have no numeric ordering—for example, favorite colors or TV shows. On the other hand, when data are grouped along a continuous scale, they should be ordered along a number line. Examples of such information include temperatures that occur over time, height or weight over age, and percentages of test takers' scoring in different intervals along the scale of possible scores.

Stem-and-Leaf Plots. Stem-and-leaf plots (sometimes called *stem plots*) display numeric data as a list, grouped within ranges of data. By way of example, consider the National League baseball teams total wins for the 2016 season:

East Division Teams	Number of Wins	Central Division Teams	Number of Wins	West Division Teams	Number of Wins
Washington Nationals	95	Chicago Cubs	103	Los Angeles Dodgers	91
New York Mets	87	St. Louis Cardinals	86	San Francisco Giants	87
Miami Marlins	79	Pittsburgh Pirates	78	Colorado Rockies	75
Philadelphia Phillies	71	Milwaukee Brewers	73	Arizona Diamondbacks	69
Atlanta Braves	68	Cincinnati Reds	68	San Diego Padres	68

   If the data are to be grouped by tens, list the tens digits to form the stem, as shown in Figure 20.11(a). Next, write the ones digits next to the appropriate tens digit, as shown in Figure 20.11(b), ordered from smallest to largest, forming the "leaves." The result shows the shape of data, indicating where the data clusters and where the outliers are. Furthermore, every piece of data can be retrieved from the graph.

   Stem-and-leaf plots are not limited to two-digit data. For example, if the data ranged from 600 to 1300, the stem could be the numerals from 6 to 13 and the leaves made of two-digit numbers separated by commas.

   Figure 20.12 shows how to illustrate two sets of data (back to back stem plot) with the leaves extending in opposite directions from the same stem. In this example, notice that the data are grouped by fives instead of tens.

   Notice that stem-and-leaf plots show the shape of the data. Students can observe how the data spread and how they cluster, and students can describe the shape numerically using range, median, mean, mode, and outliers.

Line Plots and Dot Plots. Line plots (also called *dot plots*) are counts of things along a numeric scale on a number line. Both terms are used in the CCSS-M standards, with line plots introduced in grade 2 using whole-number units and progressing to displaying data in fractions of a unit in grade 5. In middle school, the term *dot plot* replaces *line plot*, but the only difference is that line plots use Xs to represent each data point and dot plots use dots (NGA Center & CCSSO, 2010).

Standards for Mathematical Practice

MP1. Make sense of problems and persevere in solving them.

3						
4						
5						
6						
7						
8						
9						
10						

3						
4						
5						
6	8	8	8	9		
7	1	3	5	8	9	
8	6	7	7			
9	1	5				
10	3					

(a)
First make the stem.

(b)
Write in the leaves directly from the data.

FIGURE 20.11 Making a stem-and-leaf plot.

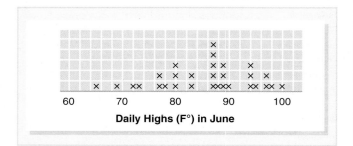

Test Scores

Mrs. Day				Mrs. Knight						
			4	5						
				•	9					
		2	3	6						
	7	7	8	•	5					
3	0	4	2	4	7	1	0			
	7	9	5	•	8	6	9	9		
	3	4	1	8	4	0	1	3	1	2
	5	8	7	•	9	5				
				9	3	1	0			
		9	6	•	7					
		0	0	10	0					

FIGURE 20.12 Stem-and-leaf plot can be used to compare two sets of data.

Line plot with x marks over a number line labeled 60, 70, 80, 90, 100 with title **Daily Highs (F°) in June**

FIGURE 20.13 Line plot of temperatures in June.

To make a line or dot plot, a number line is drawn and an X or dot is made above the corresponding value on the line for every corresponding data element. One advantage of a line plot is that every piece of data is shown on the graph. Students can therefore be a good first step to then creating a box plot or histogram, which are more difficult graphical representations because they do not illustrate each data point (Groth & Bargagliotti, 2012). An example of a line plot is shown in Figure 20.13.

To introduce line plots in a concrete manner, connect to picture graphs, but use a numeric scale rather than a categorical scale. That is the focus in Activity 20.8. Having students be "in the graph" is an important experience and will enable them to better understand the more abstract graphical representation.

Activity 20.8

CCSS-M: 1.MD.C.4; 2.MD.D.10; 3.MD.B.4

Stand by Me

ENGLISH LEARNERS

Use masking tape to create a bar graph or line plot on the floor of the classroom or gymnasium. Label it with numbers ranging from 0 minutes to 20 minutes (or whatever is appropriate for your students). Have students write on a sticky note how many minutes it takes them to travel to school. By groups, ask students to stand on the location above that number on the line. Encourage peers to confirm they are standing in the correct place. Then, ask students to leave their sticky note where they were standing and sit down. Recreate the line plot on the interactive whiteboard and have students create one on their own paper. Ask students questions about their data (e.g., how many more or less are in one category). In summary, ask students to write one observation. ELs will benefit from sentence starters like, "I notice that _____ students walk _____."

Because of the numeric scale, line and dot plots can be used to show measurements. Students might measure and plot, for example, their foot length, their cubit (length of forearm from elbow to finger tips), height of the stack of books they happen to have brought to class, and so on. Data can also be gathered from plants growing, time passing, or weather, as in the next activity.

Activity 20.9

CCSS-M: 3.MD.B.4; 4.MD.B.4; 5.MD.B.2; 6.SP.B.4; 7.SP.B.3

Storm Plotter

Create a class line plot (grades 2 and 5) or dot plot (middle school) and chart the amount of rain (or snow) that falls with each storm (install a rain gauge or access the information online). Place the data from each storm on the line/dot plot. This can be done all year and color-coded by month. As more data are gathered, you can ask, "What do we notice about rain fall in our area?" Focus on both variability and center. If you don't want to take months gathering data, instead look up the rain or snow fall in various cities and towns after a storm has passed through and use that to create a storm plot. Seventh-grade students can explore and compare two different locations.

Line and dot plots work well for comparisons. For example, if data are gathered from two different groups, separate dot plots can be created, providing a great visual to see the difference in the shape of the data.

Histograms. Though line and dot plots are widely used for small data sets, in many real data sets, there is a large amount of data and many different numbers. A dot plot would be too tedious to create and not illustrate the spread of data as effectively. In this case, a histogram is an excellent choice as data are grouped in appropriate intervals. A histogram displays numeric data in consecutive equal intervals. The number of data elements falling into that particular interval determines the height or length of each bar. Histograms differ from the other bar graphs, which are used for categorical data, and for which the order of the bars doesn't matter (Metz, 2010). Histograms effectively show the distribution of data values, especially the shape of the distribution and any outlier values.

Students struggle to understand and interpret histograms (Cooper, & Shore, 2008; Kaplan, Gabrosek, Curtiss, & Malone, 2014; Meletiou-Mavrotheris & Lee, 2010). These challenges include:

1. Understanding the distinction between bar graphs and histograms
2. Finding the center of the distribution (students focus on the heights of the bars (*y*-axis) instead of the distribution (*x*-axis).
3. Interpreting a flatter histogram to mean there is less variability in the data.

Histograms can be challenging to construct: What is the appropriate interval to use for the bar width? What is a good scale to use for the length of the bars? The need for all of the data to be grouped and counted within each interval causes further difficulty. Figure 20.14 shows a histogram for the same temperature data used in Figure 20.13. Notice how similar the two displays are in illustrating the spread and clustering of data. Histograms can and should be created with computer software or calculators so that sufficient attention can be devoted to making sense of the histogram and analyzing data.

Box Plots. Box plots (also known as *box and whisker plots*) are a method for visually displaying not only the center (median) but also the range and spread of data. Importantly, a box plot highlights the interquartile range, making visible the middle 50 percent (the box). In Figure 20.15, the ages in months for 27 sixth-grade students are given, along with stem-and-leaf plots for the full class and the boys and girls separately. The stem-and-leaf is a good way to prepare for creating a box plot. To find the two quartiles, find the medians of the upper and lower halves of the data. Mark the two extremes, the quartiles, and the median. Then create the box plot on a number line. Box plots for the same data are shown in Figure 20.16.

Each box plot has these three features:

1. A box that contains the "middle half" of the data, one-fourth to the left and right of the median. The ends of the box are at the *lower quartile*, the median of the lower half of the data, and the *upper quartile*, the median of the upper half of the data.

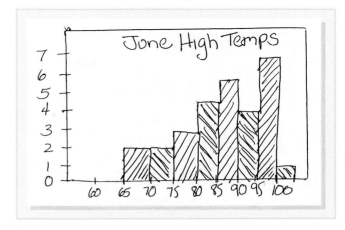

FIGURE 20.14   Histogram of June high temperatures.

The following numbers represent the ages in months of a class of sixth-grade students.

Boys		Girls	
132	122	140	131
140	130	129	128
133	134	141	131
142	125	134	132
134 Joe B.	147	124	130
(137)	131	129 Whitney	127
139	129	(125)	

All students

```
12 | 2, 4
 • | 5, 5, 7, 8, (9,) 9, 9,
13 | 0, 0, 1, 1, (1,) 2, 2, 3, 4, 4, 4
 • | (7,) 9
14 | 0, 0, 1, 2
 • | 7
```

Boys		Girls	
12	2	12	4
•	5, 9	•	5, 7,|8, 9, 9
13	(0,) 1, 2, 3, |4, 4	13	(0,) 1, 1, 2, |4
•	7, (9)	•	
14	0, 2	14	0, 1
•	7	•	

FIGURE 20.15   Stem-and-leaf plots of for sixth-grade students' ages in months. Medians and quartiles are circled or marked by a vertical bar if they fall between two elements.

   **Standards for Mathematical Practice**

MP6. Attend to precision.

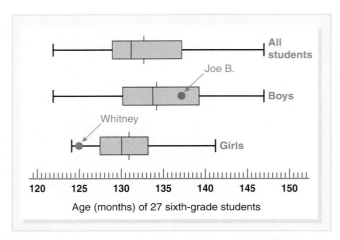

FIGURE 20.16 Box plots for the sixth-grade students' ages in months data. In addition to showing how data are distributed, data points of particular interest can be shown.

2. A line inside the box at the median of the data.
3. A line (sometimes known as the *whisker*) extending from the end of each box to the *lower extreme* and *upper extreme* of the data. Each line, therefore, covers the upper and lower fourths of the data.

Look at the information these box plots provide at a glance! The box and the lengths of the lines provide a quick indication of how the data are spread out or bunched together. Because the median is shown, this spreading or bunching can be determined for each quarter of the data. The entire class in this example is much more spread out in the upper half than the lower half. The girls are much more closely grouped in age than either the boys or the class as a whole. The range of the data (the difference between upper and lower extremes) is represented by the length of the plot, and the extreme values can be read directly. The mean is indicated by the small marks above and below each box. A box plot provides useful visual information to help understand the shape of a data set. Therefore, it is a great choice for looking at data from different disciplines. For example, consider creating a box plot for the age of each president at inauguration (Patterson & Patterson, 2014). This can teach interesting history lessons and the value of using a box plot to analyze data.

To make a box plot, put the data in order. Next, find the median. This can be done on stem-and-leaf plots. To find the two quartiles, ignore the median itself, and find the medians of the upper and lower halves of the data. Mark the two extremes, the two quartiles, and the median above an appropriate number line. Draw the box and the lines.

Because box plots have so much information and proportional thinking, students may be challenged to interpret box plots (Bakker, Biehler, & Konold, 2004). An effective strategy for transitioning students from interpreting displays of individual data, such as dot plots, to interpreting aggregate displays, such as box plots, is to display both types simultaneously. This can be done efficiently using CODAP. One reason for students' difficulties is due to the fact that each section of the box plot contains approximately the same number of points (approximately 25% of the data). As a result, the *smallest sections* of a box plot represent the greatest densities of values, whereas the *tallest sections* of a histogram represent the greatest densities of values. With box plots, a common misconception is that a long box represents more values rather than more diversity in values.

Standards for Mathematical Practice
MP5. Use appropriate tools strategically.

Remember that a box plot, like any graph, is a tool for learning about the question posed, not an end in itself (McClain, Leckman, Schmitt, & Regis, 2006). Because a box plot offers so much information on the spread and center of the data, much can be learned from careful examination, and particularly from comparing two box plots with related data.

 TECHNOLOGY Note. Beyond CODAP, graphing calculators and some computer programs draw box plots (i.e., spreadsheets), making this process even more accessible. Graphing calculators can draw box plots for up to three sets of data on the same axis. The Desmos Box Plot Generator (https://www.desmos.com) allows students to input data sets to create box plots. ▪

⏸ Pause & Reflect

Notice that in Figure 20.16 the box for the boys is actually a bit longer than the box for the whole class. How can that be when there are clearly more students in the full class than there are boys? How would you explain this apparent discrepancy to a class of seventh-grade students? ●

Bivariate Data

In eighth grade, the focus of statistics is to analyze *bivariate data* (NGA Center & CCSSO, 2010). The phrase *bivariate data* may be new to eighth-grade curriculum, but the concept is not. Stated

a. Surveyed sixth-grade and eighth-grade students report on the super power they would choose.

	Super Strength	Ability to Fly	Invisibility	Razor Vision	Total
Sixth-grade students	15	36	17	6	74
Eighth-grade students	25	17	28	11	81
Total	40	53	45	19	155

b. Relative frequency of sixth-grade and eighth-grade students super power selections.

	Super Strength	Ability to Fly	Invisibility	Razor Vision	Total
Sixth-grade students	10%	23%	11%	4%	48%
Eighth-grade students	16%	11%	18%	7%	52%
Total	26%	34%	29%	11%	100%

FIGURE 20.17   Example of bivariate categorical data, with raw data and relative frequency data.

simply, *bivariate* means that two things are varying together (e.g., number of people attending, the number of hot dogs sold). Concepts and activities related to covariation are addressed in Chapter 13 (Algebraic Thinking, Equations, and Functions) and in Chapter 17 (Ratios, Proportions, and Proportional Reasoning). In statistics, the focus of bivariate data is on the distribution and related patterns in the covariation. Graphs and tables are effective in displaying these distributions so that patterns or trends are more observable (Kader & Jacobbe, 2013).

CCSS Standards for Mathematical Practice
MP2. Reason abstractly and quantitatively.

Bivariate Categorical Data. As the name implies, these situations involve two variables that are both categorical, such as favorite superpower and grade level. Bivariate categorical data are often presented in a two-way table, as illustrated in Figure 20.17(a). The data can also be analyzed and reported in terms of relative frequency, as illustrated in Figure 20.17(b). Notice that data can be analyzed looking across one row (e.g., boys) or down one column (e.g., readers), as well as analyzed for overall totals.

Line Graphs. A coordinate axis allows for the plotting of bivariate numerical data. When data are continuous, a line connects the data points and illustrates the trend in the data. For example, a line graph might be used to show how the length of a flagpole shadow changed from one hour to the next during the day. The horizontal scale would be time, and the vertical scale would be the length of the shadow. Data can be gathered at specific points in time (e.g., every 15 minutes), and these points can be plotted. A straight line can be drawn to connect these points because time is continuous and data points do exist between the plotted points. See the example in Figure 20.18 for a line graph on temperature change.

Scatter Plots. Scatter plots are an emphasis in grade 8 (NGA Center & CCSSO, 2010). Bivariate numerical data can be plotted on a scatter plot, a graph of points on a Coordinate Grid with each axis representing one of the two numerical variables. Each pair of numbers from the data, when plotted, produces a visual image of the data as well as a hint concerning any possible relationships. One way to help students analyze a scatter plot is to look at a vertical "slice" and consider what that slice means (Cobb, McClain, & Gravemeijer, 2003). By thinking about the scatterplot as a sequence of univariate distributions along one variable, students can better explore the relationship between variables.

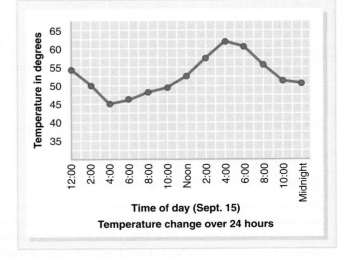

FIGURE 20.18   Line graph of one day's temperatures.

MyLab Education   **Blackline Master: Coordinate Grid**

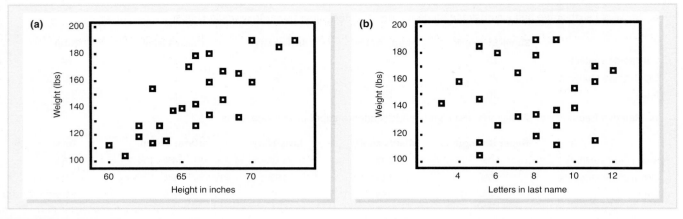

FIGURE 20.19 Scatter plots show potential relationships or lack of relationships.

For example, you might gather data from 25 eighth-grade boys on their height in inches, weight in pounds, and number of letters in their last name and create (a) a scatter plot of weight versus height, and (b) a scatter plot of weight versus name length (see Figure 20.19). Begin by asking about a slice of the graph, for example, asking what students notice about students with a height of 66 inches, or with a last name with 8 letters. Then, continue to ask questions that focus on the relationship between the variables: "Is there a relationship between their weight and height?" and "Is there a relationship between weight and name length?"

The first scatter plot indicates a positive relationship between the boys' weights and heights, though there is some variation. But there is no relationship between name length and weight. Encourage students to plot many data sets and look for relationships in the scatter plots, including data sets that suggest linear relationships and those that indicate no apparent relationship between the variables, or a non-linear relationship (such as parabolic). Activity 20.10 provides engaging ways to explore the relationship between bivariate numerical data.

Activity 20.10   CCSS-M: 8.SP.A.1

Is There a Relationship?

Prepare cards with different questions on them about bivariate situations or use Is There a Relationship Cards. For example, is there a relationship between:

ENGLISH LEARNERS

- Distance a toy car rolls and its weight?
- Distance a toy car rolls and height of ramp?
- Distance a toy car rolls and how high it starts on the ramp?
- Foot length and height?
- Shoulder width and height?
- Nose length and hand span?
- Months of age and height?
- Head circumference and wrist circumference?
- Minutes watching TV and minutes doing homework?

Distribute cards to groups of four students and a Coordinate Axis. Ask students to (1) predict if they think there is a relationship and (2) determine how they will gather data. Have students gather data and create a scatter plot on paper that they will display to the class. ELs may be more familiar with metric measures and will benefit from seeing what is being measured through gestures or demonstration. Each group reports on their findings and explains whether they think there is a relationship or not. Other groups listen and determine whether they agree that there is a relationship, and what that relationship is. As an extended experience, have students generate their own questions where they wonder, "Is there a relationship between *x* and *y*?"

MyLab Education   **Activity Page: Is There a Relationship Cards**
MyLab Education   **Blackline Master: Coordinate Axis**

Best-Fit Lines. If a scatter plot indicates a relationship, it can be simply described in words. "As boys get taller, they get heavier." This may be correct but is not particularly useful. What exactly is the relationship? If I knew the height of a boy, could I predict what his weight might be? Like much of statistical analysis, the value of a statistic is to create a model to predict what has not yet been observed. (For example, we poll a small sample of voters before an election to predict how the full population will vote.)

    The relationship in this case is a ratio between the two measures. If the scatter plot seems to indicate a steadily increasing relationship (as in the height–weight graph) or steadily decreasing relationship, you can find the ratio between the variables by drawing a straight line through the data points that "best" represent the pattern or shape of all of the dots, or a *line of best fit*.

> **CCSS** **Standards for Mathematical Practice**
> **MP3**. Construct viable arguments and critique the reasoning of others.

MyLab Education   **Application Exercise 20.1:**
Data Analysis and Graphical Representations

Click the link to access this exercise, then watch the video and answer the accompanying questions.

> **CCSS** **Standards for Mathematical Practice**
> **MP4**. Model with mathematics.

Activity 20.11

CCSS-M: 8.SP.A.1; 8.SP.A.2

Spaghetti Lines

Engage students in gathering bivariate data (see list in Activity 20.10). For example, ask students to measure foot length and height, and record the data in a class table. Give students a copy of a Coordinate Axis (Quadrant I). Ask students to plot the coordinates on their own graph, then place a piece of uncooked spaghetti until they feel it is the "best fit" for the data and tape it down. Then, ask students to write an equation to represent their line. Invite students to compare and discuss the different equations. For example, ask students to use their equation or line to tell how big Big Foot might be (e.g., if his foot is 25 inches long).

MyLab Education   **Blackline Master: Coordinate Axis (Quadrant I)**

    What determines best fit? From a strictly visual standpoint, the line you select defines the observed relationship and could be used to predict other values not in the data set. The more closely the dots in the scatter plot cluster around the line you select, the greater the confidence you would have in the predictive value of the line. Certainly, you could try to draw a straight line somewhere in the name length–weight graph, but you would not have much confidence in its predictive capability because the dots would be quite dispersed from the line.

    Encourage students to use a "mathematical" reason for why a line might be best. Because a good line is one around which most dots cluster, a good-fitting line is one where the distances from all of the dots to the line are minimal. This general notion of least distance to the line for all points is the basis for an algorithm that will always produce a unique line for a given set of points, which is introduced in high school.

TECHNOLOGY NOTE. Graphing calculators can be directed to locate the best-fit line. These techniques are programmed into graphing calculators. Students can enter their data into the table feature, plot it on the graph, and then find the line of best fit. If students have already drawn a line by hand, then the calculator provides a good opportunity to compare equations to see whether they are both reasonable. ■

MyLab Education   Self-Check 20.3

MyLab Education   Application Exercise 20.2:
Data Analysis and Graphical Representations

Click the link to access this exercise, then watch the video and answer the accompanying questions.

Data Analysis: Measures of Center and Variability

Although graphs provide visual images of data, measures of center and variability of the data are also important ways to summarize, analyze, and describe the data. Measures of center include *mean*, *median*, and *mode* and measures of variability include *range* and *mean absolute deviation*. The emphasis of mean, median, and mode should *not* be on how to find each (or which one is which), but on selecting the appropriate measure based on the context and the population. Students can get an idea of the importance of these statistics by exploring the ideas informally.

Measures of Center

The term *average* is heard quite frequently in everyday usage. Sometimes it refers to an exact arithmetic average, as in "the average daily rainfall." Sometimes it is used quite loosely, as in "She is about average height." In either situation, an average is a single number or measure that describes a set of numbers. Students' understanding of average may be any of the following: average as mode (what is there most of?), average as something reasonable, average as the standard algorithm for finding mean, and average as midpoint and average as point of balance (Konold, & Pollatsek, 2002; Mokros & Russell, 1995).

Mode. The mode is the most frequently occurring value in the data set. The mode is the least frequently used as a measure of center because data sets may not have a mode, may have more than one mode, or the mode may not be descriptive of the data set.

Median. The median is the middle value in an ordered set of data. Half of all values lie at or above the median and half at or below. The median is easier to understand and to compute and is not affected, as the mean is, by one or two extremely large or extremely small values outside the range of the rest of the data. The most common misconception using the median emerges when students neglect to order the numbers in the data set from least to greatest. The median and the mean first appear as standards in the sixth grade in the CCSS-M (NGA Center & CCSSO, 2010).

Mean. Ask an adult what the mean is, and they are likely to tell you something like, "The mean is when you add up all the numbers in the set and divide the sum by the number of numbers in the set." This is not what the mean *is*, this is how you calculate the mean. This is a reminder of the procedurally driven curriculum in our history and the need to shift to a more conceptually focused approach. Another limited conception about the mean is that it is considered *the* way to find a measure of center regardless of the context (McGatha, Cobb, & McClain, 1998). In fact, in the CCSS-M, sixth-grade students are expected to determine when the mean is appropriate and when another measure of center (e.g., the median) is more appropriate: "Students recognize that a data distribution may not have a definite center and that different ways to measure center yield different values" (NGA Center & CCSSO, 2010, p. 39). The next section focuses on developing the concept of the mean.

MyLab Education   **Video Example 20.7**

Author Karen Karp shares an overview of measures of center.

VIDEO EXAMPLE

Understanding the Mean

There are two effective ways to help students develop an understanding of the mean, a fair-share or leveling-off interpretation and a central balance point interpretation.

Fair-Share or Leveling Interpretation. Suppose that the average number of family members for the students in your class is 5. One way to interpret this is to think about distributing the entire collection of moms, dads, sisters, and brothers to each of the students so that each would have a "family" of the same size. To say that you have an average score of 93 for the four tests in your class is like spreading the total of all of your points evenly across the four tests. It is as if each student had the same family size and each test score were the same, but the totals matched the actual distributions. An added benefit of this explanation of the mean is that it connects to the algorithm for computing the mean.

Standards for Mathematical Practice
MP1. Make sense of problems and persevere in solving them.

Activity 20.12   CCSS-M: 6.SP.A.2; 6.SP.A.3; 6.SP.B.5

Mean Cost of Games

ENGLISH LEARNERS

Post a copy of Games Costs Activity Page. Have students make a bar graph of the data using connecting cubes (one cube per dollar). Choose a situation with 5 or 6 values. For example, Figure 20.20(a) shows cube stacks for the price of each game. The task for students is to use the stacks of cubes (bars) to determine what the price would be if all of the games were the same price. Encourage students to use various techniques to rearrange the cubes to "level" the prices, or make the price the same for each item. See Figure 20.20(b) . Be sure that ELs understand the meaning of "leveling" the bars.

MyLab Education   **Activity Page: Games Costs**

Explain to students that the size of the leveled bars (fair shares) is the mean of the data—the amount that each item would cost if all items cost the same amount but the total of the prices remained fixed. Follow "Mean Cost of Games" with the next activity to help students develop an algorithm for finding the mean.

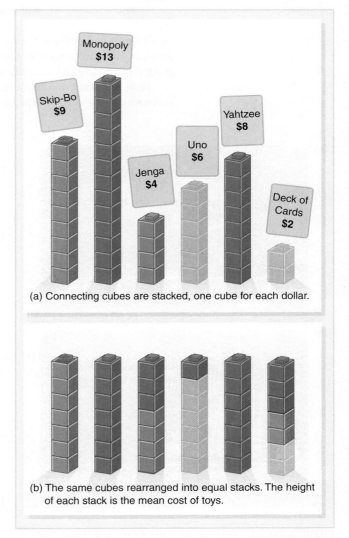

(a) Connecting cubes are stacked, one cube for each dollar.

(b) The same cubes rearranged into equal stacks. The height of each stack is the mean cost of toys.

FIGURE 20.20   Understanding the mean as a leveling of the data.

Activity 20.13

CCSS-M: 6.SP.A.2; 6.SP.A.3; 6.SP.B.5

The Mean Foot

Pose the following question: "What is the mean length of our feet in inches?" This context needs to be clear to ELs because *foot* is not being used as a measurement unit, but as an object. Also, consider measuring in centimeters rather than inches. Have each student cut a strip of cash register tape that matches the length of his or her foot. Students record their names and the length of their feet in inches on the strips. Suggest that before finding a mean for the class, you will first get means for smaller groups. Put students into groups of four, six, or eight (use even numbers). In each group, have the students tape their foot strips end to end. The task for each group is to come up with a method of finding the mean without using any of the lengths written on the strips. They can only use the combined strip. Each group will share their method with the class. From this work, they will devise a method for determining the mean for the whole class. For students with disabilities, help them fold the strip to see how to divide the cash register strip into equal lengths.

ENGLISH LEARNERS

STUDENTS with SPECIAL NEEDS

‖ Pause & Reflect

Before reading on, what is a method that the students could use in "The Mean Foot"? ●

To evenly distribute the inches for each student's foot among the members of the group, they can fold the strip into equal parts so that there are as many sections as students in the group. Then they can measure the length of any one part.

How can you find the mean for the whole class? Suppose there are 23 students in the class. Using the strips already taped together, make one very long strip for the whole class. It is not reasonable to fold this long strip into 23 equal sections. But if you wanted to know how long the resulting strip would be, how could that be done? The total length of the strip is the sum of the lengths of the 23 individual foot strips. To find the length of one section if the strip were folded in 23 parts, simply divide by 23. In fact, students can mark off "mean feet" along the strip. There should be close to 23 equal-length "feet." This dramatically illustrates the algorithm for finding the mean.

Balance Point Interpretation. Statisticians think about the mean as a point on a number line where the data on either side of the point are balanced. To help think about the mean in this way, it is useful to think about the data placed on a line plot. Notice that what is important includes how many pieces of data are on either side of the mean *and* their distances from the mean.

To illustrate, draw a number line on the board and arrange 8 sticky notes above the number 3, as shown in Figure 20.21(a). Alternatively, you can use a stack of cubes. Each sticky note represents one family. The notes are positioned on the line to indicate how many pets the family owns. Stacked like this indicates that all families have the same number of pets. The mean is 3 pets. But different families are likely to have different numbers of pets. We could think of 8 families with a range of numbers of pets. Some may have 0 pets, and some may have 10 pets or even more. How could you change the number of pets for these 8 families so that the mean remains at 3? Students will suggest moving the sticky notes in opposite directions, probably in pairs. This will result in a symmetrical arrangement. But what if one of the families has 8 pets, a move of 5 spaces from the 3? This might be balanced by moving two families to the left, one 3 spaces to the 0, and one 2 spaces to

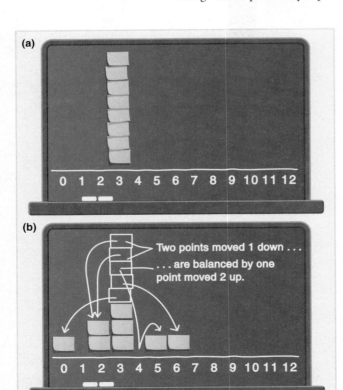

FIGURE 20.21 (a) If all data points are the same, the mean is that value. (b) By moving data points away from the mean in a balanced manner, different distributions can be found that have the same mean.

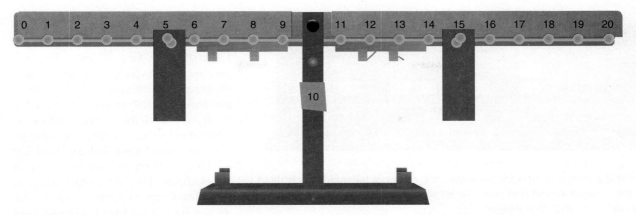

FIGURE 20.22   Adapt a number balance in order to illustrate the balance interpretation of the mean.

the 1. Figure 20.21(b) shows one way the families could be rearranged to maintain a mean of 3. To help them reason about the balancing of the mean, ask students, "Can you find at least two other distributions of the families, each having a mean of 3?"

A very concrete way to illustrate balance is on a number balance that is adapted to have values between 0 and 20 (see Figure 20.22) (Peters, Bennett, Young, & Watkins, 2016). Notice that as one plastic piece (data point) is placed on the right, one or more other data points must be placed on the left. Using this model, students instantly see if there is a balance because the balance otherwise physically tilts to one side. The next two activities also focus on finding the balance point given the data.

Activity 20.14   CCSS-M: 6.SP.A.2; 6.SP.A.3; 6.SP.B.5

Balancing Cubes

Give students a ruler, a block such as a pattern block piece, and cubes, such as Unifix cubes. Have students balance the ruler on the pattern block. Notice that the 6-inch mark of the ruler is at the center. Explain that students are going to be creating data sets with a mean of 6 (O'Dell, 2012). Ask students to place 4 cubes on the ruler so that there is a balance point (mean) of 6. Students might, for example, place a cube on 4 (2 away from the mean of 6) and then one on the 8 to balance it. You can increase the challenge by having students do the following: Use only one data point on each side, use exactly 5 cubes, add one cube that keeps the balance, move two cubes to maintain the balance, and place cubes with a wide distribution or with a narrow distribution.

Activity 20.15   CCSS-M: 6.SP.A.2; 6.SP.A.3; 6.SP.B.5

Balance Point Sticky Notes

Use the Balance Point Activity Page, or just have students draw a number line from 0 to 13 with about 2 inches between the numbers. Use six small sticky notes to represent the prices of six games, as shown in Figure 20.23. Have them place a light pencil mark on the line where they think the mean might be. Ask students to determine the mean by moving the sticky notes in toward the "center." That is, the students are to find out what price (point on the number line) balances out the six prices. For each move of a sticky one space to the left, a different sticky must be moved one space to the right. Eventually, all sticky notes should be stacked above the same number, the balance point or mean.

MyLab Education   Activity Page: Balance Point

❚❚ Pause & Reflect

Stop and try this exercise yourself. What do you notice about how you can move the values? ●

After any pair of moves that keep the distribution balanced, you actually have a new distribution of prices with the same mean. The same was true when you moved the sticky notes

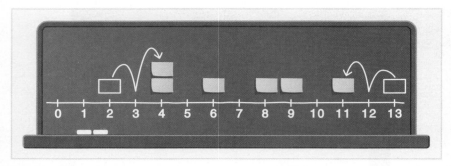

FIGURE 20.23 Move data points in toward the center or balance point without changing the balance around that point. When you have all points at the same value, that is the balance or the mean.

out from the mean when they were all stacked on the same point.

Changes in the Mean. The balance approach to finding the mean clearly illustrates that different data distributions can have the same mean. Especially for small sets of data, the mean is significantly affected by extreme values. For example, suppose another game with a price of $20 is added to the six we have been using in the examples. Therefore, while the mean provides a representative value of the data, it (or the median) is not sufficient for fully describing a distribution (because distributions with the same value for the mean can be considerably different). This provides an entry point to discuss variability with students (discussed later in this section).

 FORMATIVE ASSESSMENT Notes. Consider using a diagnostic interview to assess whether students are able to determine the best measure of center to use in a given situation, such as the average height of students in the class. You can begin with general questions such as these: What does the mean represent? What does the median represent? What is the difference between the mean and the median? What is each useful for? Then move to more analytical questions: Which should we use for this set of data? Might we use a different measure of center in another class? When you've found the average height of the students in our class, is it possible that no one is that height? Why? ■

Choosing a Measure of Center

CCSS
Standards for Mathematical Practice

MP1. Make sense of problems and persevere in solving them.

The median and the mean can be quite different for a set of data, especially when the data set is skewed left, skewed right, or has outliers (Groth, Kent, & Hitch, 2015/2016). Therefore, it is important to consider the context and data to decide how to best represent the center. For example, in reporting home prices (see first page of this chapter), the median is quite different from the mean, with the mean being higher. Which better portrays the cost of housing? The median is a better measure—the median is *resistant* to outliers. In other words, it is more likely to still represent the center of the data. Activities 20.16 and 20.17 provide strategies for engaging students in selecting a measure of center.

Activity 20.16   CCSS-M: 6.SP.A.2; 6.SP.A.3; 6.SP.B.5

Which Measure of Center Makes Sense?

STUDENTS with SPECIAL NEEDS

Prepare possible questions to investigate using available data sets like the ones listed here:

● How many pencils does a sixth grader have?

● What is the cost of used cars in our area?

● What is the height of a typical cereal box?

● What is the average monthly cost of a mobile phone?

The students' task is to decide which measure of center makes the most sense and be able to justify their decision. The first question can be explored by gathering classroom data (Johnson, 2011), and then selecting and justifying which measure of center makes sense. For the other situations, you can assign a topic to a group. Each group does the following: (a) selects which measure of center they think makes the most sense for their topic, (b) prepares a data set that illustrates their point, and (c) prepares a justification of why they picked their measure. Students with special needs may benefit from being given several sets of data for their topic as a way to consider which measure might be best. Also discuss the spread and overall shape of the data gathered (e.g., Does the height of cereal crowd the center? Is there a lot of variation in the phone bills?).

Exploring how new data affect each measure of center provides valuable insights to students in comparing the pros and cons of each. Let's revisit the cost of games activity.

Activity 20.17
CCSS-M: 6.SP.A.2; 6.SP.A.3; 6.SP.B.5

Average Cost of More Games

Distribute copies of Average Game Costs Activity Page and post the Games Costs Activity Page. Ask students to predict how the mean, median, and mode will change if a new game costing $20 is part of the game set. What if the $2 game is removed? Then, ask students to figure out the price of a game that was added that increased the mean to $9. For a full lesson, see Expanded Lesson: Playing with Measures of Central Tendency.

> MyLab Education   Activity Page: Average Game Costs
> MyLab Education   Activity Page: Games Costs
> MyLab Education   Expanded Lesson: Playing with Measures of Central Tendency

Having to make decisions using statistics is an authentic reason for choosing a measure of center, the focus of the next activity.

Activity 20.18
CCSS-M: 6.SP.A.2; 6.SP.A.3; 6.SP.B.5

You Be the Judge

Use the You Be the Judge Activity Page. The gymnastics coach can only send one person on to the all-star state competition. She wants to select the student with the best average and most consistency this season. The following table gives overall scores for the eight most recent competitions. Whom should she pick?

Meet	Jenna	Miah	Leah
1	9	9	5
2	3	9	6
3	10	7	7
4	9	8	6
5	7	7	9
6	5	9	8
7	10	9	10
8	9	8	10

Ask students questions such as the following: Which measure of center seems to be the fairest way to judge the competition? What variability do you notice for each person? Which person would you pick and why?

> MyLab Education   Activity Page: You Be the Judge

In addition to selecting the measure that makes sense, students need to understand how characteristics of a data set (e.g., distribution of data, outliers) affect the mean, median, and mode. In seventh grade and beyond, students must be able to compare the characteristics of one data set to another (NGA Center & CCSSO, 2010). For example, students can gather data on the time it takes fizz to die down for two different brands of soda (repeated trials for each brand) (Kader & Jacobbe, 2013).

Standards for Mathematical Practice
MP2. Reason abstractly and quantitatively.

 TECHNOLOGY Note. Data can be found online and used for comparison with class data. For example, CNN recently reported that the average youth owns 7 pairs of jeans.

Mooney and Bair (2011) used this data to compare to data gathered by their class, which varied from the reported average, and discussed what might cause the deviation. Also, students can efficiently investigate how the mean and median are affected by each piece of data using the Mean and Median applet on NCTM Illuminations. ■

Variability

Although measures of center are a long-standing topic, measures of variability also need explicit attention in the curriculum (Franklin et al., 2007; Kader & Jacobbe, 2013; Scheaffer, 2006). Increased attention to variability is needed, and this may not be adequately addressed in textbooks. As noted in the discussion of measures of center, data sets can have the same mean, but have very different distributions. Comparing such data sets can help students see the need to also describe the variability in the data.

Three different kinds of variability can be explored by elementary and middle school students: natural, measurement, and induced (Franklin et al., 2007; Groth, 2015). Natural variability is inherent in nature. For example, variability in students' shoulder width. Measurement variability includes measurement error or change. For example, the number of seconds to run 100 meters. Finally, induced variability, as the name implies, is when the variability is intentionally created, for example, having plants placed in different locations to see how sunlight might impact their growth. With experiences students understanding of variability can develop from basic notions to more sophisticated ideas.

Instruction on variability grows in sophistication (Franklin et al., 2007). In the elementary grades, focus on variability within a group—for example, the varying lengths of students' names, varying family sizes, and so on. When students create a bar graph of class data and compare the data collected, they are discussing the variability within a group. In middle school, variability within a group continues, but groups of data are also considered. Students might compare the variability of fifth-grade students' favorite music choices with eighth-grade students' music choices, an example of variability between groups. In addition, middle school students study how the change in one variable relates to change in another variable—yes, algebra! Students also explore sampling variability (Franklin et al., 2007). When students flip a coin 10 times as a sample, they may get 5 heads and 5 tails, but they also may get many other results (even 0 heads and 10 tails).

Variability can be analyzed by looking at data in a table—for example, looking at the frequency of occurrences of categorical data (Kader & Jacobbe, 2013). Figure 20.24 shows the frequency and relative frequency of students' favorite Saturday activity. Students first submitted their favorite activity on a sticky note and stuck them to the whiteboard. These were sorted into six categories.

One way to help students understand variability is to ask questions about variability in the discussion of data. Friel, O'Conner, and Mamer (2006), using the context of heart rates, suggest the following questions as examples of how to get students to focus on data and variability:

- If the average heart rate for 9- to 11-year-olds is 88 beats per minute, does this mean every student this age has a heart rate of 88 beats per minute? (Note: the range is actually quite large—from 60 to 110 beats per minute.)
- If we found the heart rate for everyone in the class (of 30), what might the distribution of data look like?
- If another class (of 30) was measured, would their distribution look like the one for our class? What if they just came in from recess?
- Would the distribution of data from 200 students look like the data from the two classes?

Comparing different data sets or playing a game repeatedly provides the opportunity for students to analyze the spread of data and think about variation in data (Franklin & Mewborn, 2008; Kader & Mamer, 2008).

Just like with measures of center, measures of variability can be resistant (or not) to outliers. For example, the interquartile

Activity	Frequency	Relative Frequency
Play a sport	7	$\frac{7}{28}$ = .25 = 25%
Go to the movies	3	$\frac{3}{28}$ = .107 = 11%
Read	3	$\frac{3}{28}$ = .107 = 11%
Play outside	6	$\frac{6}{28}$ = .214 = 21%
Hang out with friends	4	$\frac{4}{28}$ = .143 = 14%
Play with electronics	5	$\frac{5}{28}$ = .178 = 18%
TOTAL	28	100%

FIGURE 20.24 Frequency and relative frequency describe the variability in the data.

range is resistant to outliers, which is why it often is used in conjunction with the median to describe skewed distributions or distributions with outliers. The mean absolute deviation is not resistant, which is why it typically is used with the mean to describe symmetric, typically mound-shaped distributions.

Range. Range is a *measure* of variability. Range of a data set is the difference between the highest and lowest data points. The *interquartile range* of the data is connected to the box plot described earlier. It is the difference between the lower and upper quartiles (Q3 − Q1), or the range of the middle 50 percent of the data. Let's look at an example.

The data set below is the number of hours seventh-grade students spent playing sports or playing outside over the weekend (data has already been placed in order).

0 0 0 1 3 4 4 4 5 5 5 5 6 6 7 8 8 9 10 10

Find the interquartile range. What does the result tell you about the variation in the data set?

In this case, the median is 5 (because the tenth and eleventh values of the 20 values are both 5). This is also referred to as quartile 2. Quartile 1 (Q1) is the median of the lower half of the data. This median is the average of the fifth and sixth value in the data set, which is 3.5. Quartile 3 (Q3) is the median of the upper half of the data set, which in this case falls between 7 and 8, so it is 7.5. The interquartile range is 7.5 − 3.5, or 4. For hours spent exercising, the interquartile range is fairly small, showing there is a lot of clustering around the center of the data.

Mean Absolute Deviation. Whereas the range relates to the median, the *mean absolute deviation (MAD)* relates to the mean. It is the mean of the how far away each data point is from the mean, telling us the "average" distance from the mean for the data set. MAD, therefore, describes how spread out the data are (Kader & Jacobbe, 2013). In other words, a large MAD means that there is a lot of deviation (difference) between data points and the mean, so the data are spread out. In the CCSS-M, MAD is introduced in sixth grade, with the intent being that it is explored in an informal manner to develop a deeper understanding of variability. Let's use the previous data set to explore MAD.

Use the following data set to find the mean absolute deviation:

0 0 0 1 3 4 4 4 5 5 5 5 6 6 7 8 8 9 10 10

What does the result tell you about the variation in the data set?

Figure 20.25 places that data in a dot plot. Dot plots can be used to illustrate absolute deviations from the mean (Hudson, 2012/2013). Students draw a vertical line at the mean (in this case 5), and draw or observe how far away each data point is (absolute deviation).

The first step in finding the mean absolute deviation is to find the deviation (difference) of each data point from the mean. Figure 20.26(a) illustrates these differences in a dot plot. The *absolute* deviation is the distance from the mean, which means the positive difference. See Figure 20.26(b). Finally, the mean of the absolute deviation is the mean of all these differences. See Figure 20.26(c)— in this case, 2.4. Did you notice that you started with the end of the phrase "mean absolute deviation" by first finding the deviation, then finding absolute deviation, and finally the mean absolute deviation? Pointing this out can help students, in particular students with disabilities, focus on the meaning of what they are doing and why.

In context, this value indicates that the average distance from the mean hours of exercise is around two and a half hours,

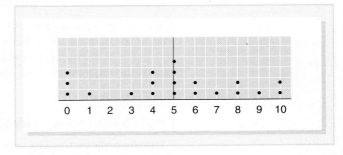

FIGURE 20.25 A dot plot illustrates the data on hours spent exercising over the weekend.

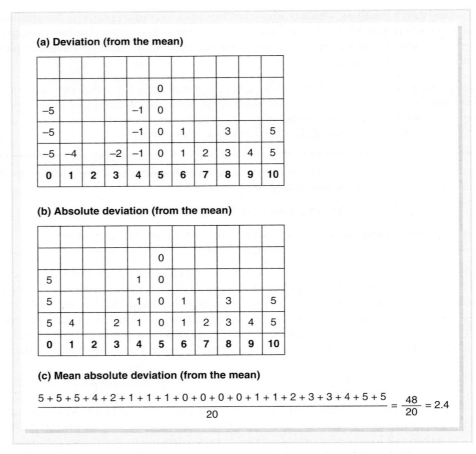

(a) Deviation (from the mean)

					0					
−5				−1	0					
−5				−1	0	1		3		5
−5	−4		−2	−1	0	1	2	3	4	5
0	**1**	**2**	**3**	**4**	**5**	**6**	**7**	**8**	**9**	**10**

(b) Absolute deviation (from the mean)

					0					
5				1	0					
5				1	0	1		3		5
5	4		2	1	0	1	2	3	4	5
0	**1**	**2**	**3**	**4**	**5**	**6**	**7**	**8**	**9**	**10**

(c) Mean absolute deviation (from the mean)

$$\frac{5+5+5+4+2+1+1+1+0+0+0+0+1+1+2+3+3+4+5+5}{20} = \frac{48}{20} = 2.4$$

FIGURE 20.26 Dot plots illustrate the differences from the mean for each data point for hours spent exercising over the weekend.

CCSS **Standards for Mathematical Practice**
MP2. Reason abstractly and quantitatively.

not much variability. A good way to have students focus on variability is to have two data sets, one that will have a very small absolute mean deviation, and one that will have a large one. Select two sets that have the same mean to emphasize the importance of having a measure of variation.

Analyzing Data

Once a graph has been constructed, engage the class in a discussion of what information the graph tells or conveys—the analysis. For analyzing graphs, consider these three levels of graph comprehension (Friel, Curcio, & Bright's, 2001):

1. Reading the data (literal),
2. Reading between the data (making comparisons, observing relationships), and
3. Reading beyond the data (making inferences).

Questioning and assessment should focus on how effectively the graph communicates the findings of the data gathered. For example, ask, "What can you tell about our class by looking at this graph of the number of songs listened to in one day?" To answer such questions requires understanding aspects of the graph, like the scale on a pictograph.

MyLab Education **Video Example 20.8**

This video shows how students can struggle to interpret scales as they analyze the data.

Graphs convey factual information (e.g., there is a wide variability in the number of songs sixth-grade students listen to in one day) and provide opportunities to make inferences that are not directly observable in the graph (e.g., most sixth-grade students listen to between 20 and 30 songs a day). Discussions about graphs the students have created help them analyze and interpret other graphs and charts that they see in newspapers and on TV. For example, you can select graphs from websites and publications and ask students "What can you learn from this graph?" "What do you not know that you wish you knew?" These questions help students focus on what different graphs can and cannot illustrate.

The difference between *actual facts* and the *inferences that go beyond the data* is an important idea in data analysis. Students can examine graphs found in newspapers or magazines and discuss the facts in the graphs and the message that may have been intended by the person who made the graph. Students' conceptual ability to analyze data and draw conclusions and interpretations is often weak (Tarr & Shaughnessy, 2007); discussing, analyzing and interpreting data are ways to support this higher-level thinking skill.

MyLab Education   Self-Check 20.4

Interpreting Results

Interpretation is the fourth step in the process of doing statistics and extends the analysis process. As seen in the sample test items shown earlier, sometimes questions focus on mathematical ideas rather than statistical ideas. In the interpreting phase, students make inferences to the classroom and acknowledge that results may be different in another class, other group, or the larger population. Older students also are able to describe differences between two or more groups with respect to center, spread, and shape.

Activity 20.19 engages students in designing their own data analysis and then interpreting their results to make an accurate estimate of how many words on the page of a book (Wilburne and Kulbacki, 2014).

Activity 20.19   CCSS-M: 6.SP.A.1; 6.SP.A.2; 6.SP.B.5

How Many Words on the Page?

Select a book that is very popular with students. Project a picture of a page where most of the page is covered up, showing only about 7 to 10 lines of text. Ask students to use their statistical reasoning skills to explore this problem and determine how many words are on this page. Ask students to model the statistical process by producing data displays, and then interpreting their results. Explain that in the end, they will have to argue for their result, explaining what methods they used to determine their answer. As they are working, and as they present their solutions, ask questions that fall across the three levels of data analysis questions.

Interpreting data questions should not just focus on the specific question under investigation, but also focus on key ideas of statistics, such as variability, center of the data, and the shape of the data. During interpretation, students might want to create a different data display to get a different look at the data or gather data from a different population to see whether their results are representative.

Different researchers have recommended questions that focus on statistical thinking (Franklin et al., 2007; Friel, O'Conner, & Mamer, 2006; Russell, 2006; Shaughnessy, 2006). Figure 20.27 offers ideas from their lists to get you started on having meaningful discussions

 Standards for Mathematical Practice
MP3. Construct viable arguments and critique the reasoning of others.

STATISTICAL QUESTIONS FOR INTERPRETING DATA

- What do the numbers (symbols) tell us about our class (or other population)?
- If we gathered the same kind of data from another class (population), how would that data look? What if we asked a larger group, how would the data look?
- How do the numbers in this graph (population) compare to this graph (population)?
- Where are the data "clustering"? How much of the data are in the cluster? How much are not in the cluster? About what percent is or is not in the cluster?
- What kinds of variability might need to be considered in interpreting these data?
- Would the results be different if . . . [change of sample/population or setting]? (Example: Would gathered data on word length in a third-grade book be different from a fifth-grade book? Would a science book give different results from a reading book?)
- How strong is the association between two variables (scatter plot)? How do you know? What does that mean if you know x? If you know y?
- What does the graph not tell us? What might we infer?
- What new questions arise from these data?
- What is the maker of the graph trying to tell us?

FIGURE 20.27 Questions that focus on interpreting data.

about interpreting data. These question prompts apply across many data displays. It certainly should be a major focus of your instruction. Consider it the *after* phase of your lesson, though some of these questions will be integrated in the *during* phase as well.

Our world is inundated with data, from descriptive statistics to varied graphs. It is essential that we prepare students to be literate about what can be interpreted from data and what cannot be interpreted from data, what is important to pay attention to and what can be discarded as misleading or poorly designed statistics. This is important for success in school, as well as for being a mathematically literate citizen.

MyLab Education **Self-Check 20.5**

MyLab Education **Math Practice:** Need to practice or refresh your math content knowledge? Click to access practice exercises associated with the content from this chapter.

RESOURCES FOR CHAPTER 20

LITERATURE CONNECTIONS

Literature is full of situations in which things must be sorted, compared, or measured. As noted earlier in this chapter, books of lists also are fruitful beginnings for data explorations. Students can use the data in the books and compare similar data collected themselves.

The Best Vacation Ever

Murphy (1997)

In this book, appropriate for first or second grade, a little girl gathers data from her family on what is important to them to decide where the family would have the best vacation. This book nicely introduces the concept of gathering data to answer a question.

Frog and Toad Are Friends

Lobel (1970)

When Frog and Toad go walking, Frog loses a button. As they search to find the button, they find many buttons. Whenever Frog's friends ask, "Is this your button?" Frog responds (with a touch of frustration), "No, that is not my button! That button is _____, but my button was _____."

This classic story is a perfect lead-in to sorting activities as described in this chapter. Young students can model the story directly with sets of buttons, shells, attribute blocks, Woozle Cards (see Woozle Cards Activity Page), or other objects with a variety of attributes.

MyLab Education **Activity Page: Woozle Cards**

200% of Nothing: An Eye-Opening Tour through the Twists and Turns of Math Abuse and Innumeracy

Dewdney (1993)
This middle school friendly book has explanations of the many ways that "statistics are turned" to mislead people. Because the examples are real, provided by readers of *Scientific American*, this book is an excellent tool for showing how important it is to be statistically literate in today's society. Reading the examples can launch a mathematics project into looking for errors in advertisements and at how overlapping groups (as in a Venn diagram) can be reported separately to mislead readers. (See Bay-Williams & Martinie, 2009, for more ways to use this book.)

If the World Were a Village: A Book about the World's People (2nd ed.)

Smith (2011) (www.youtube.com/watch?v=QrcOdLYBIw0)
This book explores global wealth, culture, language, and other influences. Each beautiful two-page spread shares the statistics for the topic (e.g., language). This book can give rise to other questions about the world, which can be researched and interpreted into the village metaphor. An article that links this idea to a project exploring concepts of statistics using 100 students is a great follow up (Riskowski, Olbricht, & Wilson, 2010).

RECOMMENDED READINGS

Articles

Peters, S. A., Bennett, V. M., Young, M., & Watkins, J. D. (2016). A fair and balanced approach to the mean. *Mathematics Teaching in the Middle School, 21*(6), 364–372.

Five engaging, high quality tasks sequenced developmentally are described to help students understand the mean as fair-shares and as a balance point. Activity pages are provided.

Franklin, C. A., & Mewborn, D. S. (2008). Statistics in the elementary grades: Exploring distribution of data. *Teaching Children Mathematics, 15*(1), 10–16.

Kader, G., & Mamer, J. (2008). Statistics in the middle grades: Understanding center and spread. *Mathematics Teaching in the Middle Grades, 14*(1), 38–43.

Both articles use the process of doing statistics as a launching point to frame effective statistics instruction. Both include excellent examples of activities, including questions and data displays.

Books

Curcio, F. (2010). *Developing data-graph comprehension in grades K–8*. Reston, VA: NCTM.

This NCTM book shares 30 graphing activities on exploring, investigating, reasoning, and communicating about data. Each activity includes procedures, discussion questions, writing and reading prompts, and ways to use technology.

Franklin, C., Kader, G., Mewborn, D., Moreno, J., Peck, R., Perry, M., & Scheaffer, R. (2007). *Guidelines for assessment and instruction in statistics education* (GAISE Report). Alexandria, VA: American Statistical Association.

This excellent framework provides examples for teaching statistics, including great tasks to use with students in preK–8.

Exploring Concepts of Probability

LEARNER OUTCOMES

After reading this chapter and engaging in the embedded activities and reflections, you should be able to:

21.1 Describe the probability continuum, including examples from impossible to certain.

21.2 Contrast theoretical probability and experiments, including how to integrate both into instruction to better develop a strong understanding of probability.

21.3 Illustrate and explain strategies for determining sample space for compound events in a developmental manner.

21.4 Explain what a simulation is and how to set up such experiences for middle school students.

References to probability are all around us: The weather forecaster predicts a 60 percent chance of snow, medical researchers predict that people with certain diets have a high chance of heart disease, investors calculate the risks of specific investments, and so on. Simulations of complex situations are frequently based on probabilities and then used in making decisions about such situations as airplane safety under different weather circumstances, highway traffic patterns after new housing has been built, and disaster plans.

Statistical literacy encompasses both statistics and probability, both of which contribute to students' ability to reason about situations involving chance (English & Watson, 2016). Realistic concepts of chance require considerable development before students are ready to construct formal ideas about the probability of an event. Optimally, this development occurs as students consider and discuss the outcomes of a wide variety of probabilistic situations. The emphasis should be on exploration rather than on rules and formal definitions. These informal experiences will provide a useful background from which more formal ideas can be developed in middle and high school.

BIG IDEAS

- Probability is based on two foundational ideas: variability (discussed in Chapter 20) and expectation (prediction of what will happen).
- Probability that an event will occur is on a continuum from impossible (0) to certain (1). A probability of $\frac{1}{2}$ indicates an even chance of the event occurring.
- For some events, the exact probability can be determined by analyzing the sample space. A probability determined in this manner is called a *theoretical probability*.
- The relative frequency of outcomes (e.g., from *experiments* or *simulations*) can be used as an estimate of the probability of an event. The larger the number of trials, the better the estimate will be.
- *Simulation* is a technique used for answering real-world questions or making decisions in complex situations in which an element of chance is involved; a model is designed that has the same probabilities as the real situation to explore how likely an event is.

 ## Introducing Probability

Probability is a ratio that compares the desired outcomes to the total possible outcomes. Probability does not appear in the Common Core State Standards expectations until seventh grade. Notions of chance, however, should be developed early in school as students play games and consider events that are likely or not likely. Although such intuition can be a positive thing, in probability it can also be a preconception that works against understanding the randomness of events (Abu-Bakare, 2008; Kustos & Zelkowski, 2013).

Likely or Not Likely

Probability is about how likely an event is. Therefore, a good place to begin is with a focus on possible and not possible (Activity 21.1) and later impossible, possible, and certain (Activity 21.2). Asking students to first predict what they think might happen and then explore through experiments (e.g., games) supports students emerging ideas about probability (English & Watson, 2016). Such questioning applies to all the activities throughout this chapter. In preparation for these activities, discuss the meaning of *impossible* and *certain*. These experiences can be woven into discussions across the curriculum, as in Activity 21.1 or connected to science and social studies, as in Activity 21.2.

Activity 21.1   CCSS-M: 7.SP.C.5

Events in Lyrics: Possible or Not Possible?

Create a table, labeling one column "Impossible" and the other "Possible," or download the Events in Lyrics Activity Page. Use literature or poems that include either possible or impossible occurrences. Nursery rhymes, such as "Hey, Diddle, Diddle" can be fun even for middle school students as they debate whether something is possible. Songs and raps are also engaging. Record each statement in the appropriate column. After sharing some examples, ask students to find more in their favorite songs or poems. Repeat the Activity with having them sort the "possible" into likely or not likely. This is also an opportunity to have ELs share a song or poem from their country or family.

ENGLISH LEARNERS

MyLab Education   **Activity Page: Events in Lyrics**

Activity 21.2

CCSS-M: 7.SP.C.5

Is It Likely?

Ask students to judge various events as *certain, impossible,* or *possible* ("might happen"). Consider these examples:

- It will rain tomorrow.
- Drop a rock in water and it will sink.
- A sunflower seed planted today will bloom tomorrow.
- The sun will rise tomorrow morning.
- A hurricane/tornado will hit our town.
- In an election, candidate A is elected.
- If you ask someone who the second U.S. president was, they will know.
- You will have two birthdays this year.
- You will be in bed by 9:00 P.M.

For each event, students should justify their choice of how likely they think it is. Notice that the last two ideas are about the students. This is an opportunity to bring in students' identities and cultures. Ask students to work with their families to write down family events that are certain, impossible, or possible. Encourage native language use, as appropriate, for ELs. For students with disabilities, use a strip of cash register tape and label the ends with the words *impossible* and *certain* to assist them in organizing their thinking. Write the events on cards so that students can place them along the strip.

Standards for Mathematical Practice

MP5. Use appropriate tools strategically.

The use of random devices (tools) that can be analyzed (e.g., spinners, number cubes, coins to toss, colored cubes drawn from a bag) can help students make predictions about how likely a particular occurrence is. Begin with the use of random devices with which students can count the outcomes, such as tossing a coin. Colored dots can be stuck on the sides of a wooden cube to create different color probabilities. Color tiles (e.g., eight red and two blue) can be placed in opaque bags. Students draw a tile from the bag and then return it after each draw.

MyLab Education   **Video Example 21.1**

Listen to this small group discussion of students' intuitions about what will happen when a coin is flipped ten times and compare their predictions to actually flipping a coin ten times.

VIDEO EXAMPLE

TECHNOLOGY Note. Science NetLinks offers an interactive tool, Marble Mania, for exploring probability of different colored marbles in a bag. You can determine how many and what color marbles to place in a virtual marble bag. An advantage of such digital resources is that you can run a large number of different trials in a short amount of time. In addition, the National Library of Virtual Manipulatives (NLVM) has a large collection of probability tools in their Data Analysis and Probability Manipulatives, organized across grade bands. There are also a number of apps for generating random numbers (e.g., Randomness for iOS and numerous dice-rolling apps for iOS/Android). Even if data is gathered by actually tossing a coin or rolling a dice, using a spreadsheet such as excel (as in this classroom video) can help to create graphs displaying the data, and to combine small data sets with larger data sets. ■

The following dice activities have unequal outcomes. However, students may not initially connect that having more of something means it is more likely. A common initial misconception is that there is a one-in-three chance of each of the values (1, 2, and 3), because each one is possible.

Activity 21.3

CCSS-M: 7.SP.C.5; 7.SP.C.6

1-2-3 How Likely?

Make number cubes with sides labeled as follows: 1, 1, 2, 3, 3, 3. Ask students to predict what number they might get when they roll the cube and record the results in a bar graph. What is likely? What is impossible? Or, more specifically, which row will fill the fastest or will the rows fill at equal rates? (See 1-2-3 How Likely? Activity Page.) Students mark an X in the column for 1, 2, or 3 each time the cube shows that value and stop when one row is full. After they stop, students reflect on how likely each number is.

MyLab Education   Activity Page: 1-2-3 How Likely?

Activity 21.4

CCSS-M: 7.SP.C.5; 7.SP.C.6; 7.SP.C.8a

1-2-3 How Likely Are Sums?

This game requires two cubes labeled as in Activity 21.3. It is a more difficult task because it considers the probability of two events (two dice rolls). Students take turns rolling the two cubes and recording the sums of the two numbers. Before the game begins, ask students to predict which row will fill the fastest or if the rows will fill at equal rates. Ask students to keep track of their data on 1-2-3 How Likely Are Sums? Activity Page. Students roll the cubes until one of the rows is full. Then discuss with their partner what happened and how likely they now think each number is.

MyLab Education   Activity Page: 1-2-3 How Likely Are Sums?

After exploring either 1-2-3 activity, ask, "Which numbers 'won' the most and the least often?" and "If you play again, which number would you pick to win and why?" In Activity 21.4, 1 is impossible and all outcomes 2 through 6 are possible. A sum of 4 is the most likely. Sums of 2 or 6 are not likely.

Area representations, such as spinners, are more challenging because students cannot count the possible outcomes as readily (Abu-Bakare, 2008). Activity 21.5 uses spinners and counting spins to build this connection.

 Standards for Mathematical Practice

MP1. Make sense of problems and persevere in solving them.

Activity 21.5

CCSS-M: 7.SP.C.6; 7.SP.C.7a, b

Race to Ten

Use the Race to Ten Activity Page. Refer to the spinner and ask: "If we count spins that land on red and ones that land on blue, which one will reach ten first?" Two players take turns spinning the spinner, each time placing an X in the matching column. The Activity Page includes a spinner that is three-fourths red and one-fourth blue (give students a paperclip to use as a pointer), but this activity can be played with different spinners (see Figure 21.1). Before playing, each student predicts which color will win, red or blue (or gold). Play continues until one color reaches ten. After the activity, discuss which color won and why. Ask students to explain how likely it is for red to win or for blue to win.

MyLab Education   Activity Page: Race to Ten

Repeat this activity with a variety of spinners, ones that have two colors with the same area, and colors covering different areas, as shown Figure 21.1. This activity provides an opportunity to explore how likely an event is with an area model, but because 10, the total goal, is a small number, students may have surprising results. This issue is addressed in the section "The Law of Large Numbers."

Students do not always see that the first spinner, third spinner, or a spinner partitioned into just two sections (50% blue, 50% red), have the same chance of getting blue (Cohen, 2006; Nicolson, 2005). Therefore, it is important to use

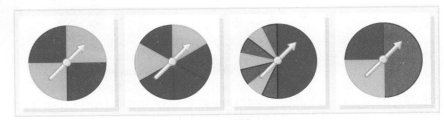

FIGURE 21.1   Possible spinners for Race to Ten.

spinners that are partitioned in different ways. Spinner faces can easily be made to adjust the chances of different outcomes. For virtual spinners, NCTM Illuminations "Adjustable Spinner" can be designed to have any number of sections of any size and can be virtually spun any number of times.

FORMATIVE ASSESSMENT **Notes.** Diagnostic interviews can uncover student misconceptions or preconceptions about the probability of an event. Ask students about the probability using color tiles or dice (countable objects). For example, ask, "If there are 3 red and 1 blue tile in this bag and I draw one out, what do you think I will get?" and "If I draw four times and put the tile back each time, what do you think I will get?" Ask about the chance of rolling selected outcomes on a die. Some students may think 5 is a more likely outcome on a die than a 2 because 5 is bigger than 2. Or students may think a 1 is not as likely as rolling a 5 on a die, perhaps because they are familiar with a game in which 1 is desirable. The 1 is not likely compared to the combined possibility of the other 5 choices, but it is as likely as any other number (Nicolson, 2005; Watson & Moritz, 2003). Finally, ask about how likely outcomes are in an area representation such as a spinner. These questions will help you know whether you need to focus on counting or area representations, and what kinds of questions or experiences to prepare in order to help students understand that probability is based on knowing all the possible outcomes and how likely each one is. ■

The Probability Continuum

The number line is an important representation across mathematical concepts, and it is emphasized across the content strands in the CCSS-M (NGA Center & CCSSO, 2010). Probability is no exception. Presenting probability on a number line from 0 (impossible) to 1 (certain) provides a visual representation of how likely an event can be. The number line can be connected to spinners, as illustrated in Figure 21.2. Post the probability continuum in the classroom, where it can be used as a reference for other opportunities to talk about how likely something is (see the questions in Activity 21.2 for a start to the many things you could ask). Some things change in their probability; for example, the chance of a snow day could be posted and moved from day to day.

In order to deepen students' understanding of the probability continuum, select a particular mark along the continuum—for example, $\frac{1}{4}$—and have students create a spinner with a color that is about that likely to occur. This can also be done with counters, as in Activity 21.6. This activity engages students in conjecturing about how likely an event is, experimenting, and comparing their predictions with experimental outcomes as they continue to explore and refine their conjectures about theoretical probability. This builds a strong foundation for the more advanced probability techniques they will develop in seventh grade and beyond.

CCSS **Standards for Mathematical Practice**

MP4. Model with mathematics.

CCSS **Standards for Mathematical Practice**

MP3. Construct viable arguments and critique the reasoning of others.

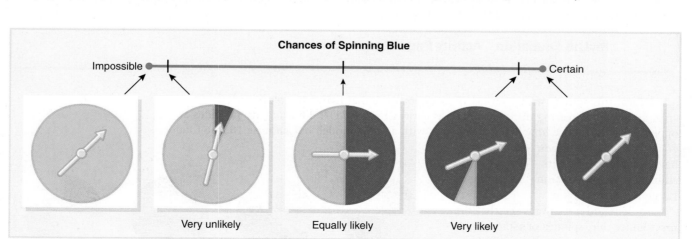

FIGURE 21.2 The probability continuum. Use these spinner faces to help students see how chance can be at different places on a continuum between impossible and certain.

Activity 21.6

CCSS-M: 7.SP.C.6

Design and Test Bags

ENGLISH LEARNERS

Provide each pair or group of students with a copy of the Design a Bag Activity Page and give each group a value on the probability continuum (e.g., $\frac{1}{3}, \frac{3}{4}, \frac{1}{6}$). Ask each group to choose a designated color for their tiles so that the probability of selecting that color is the probability they have been assigned. Once they have colored the tiles on the Activity Page to match their fraction (e.g., $\frac{1}{3}$ are red), the students trade papers. With the new Activity Page students do the following:

STUDENTS with SPECIAL NEEDS

1. Mark the probability line at the point they think matches the number of tiles colored red.
2. Place actual colored tiles into brown paper bags based on what is colored on the "Design a Bag" they received. They draw tiles from this bag (with replacement) 50 times. Remind students to shake their bag each time to ensure random sampling.
3. Determine the fraction of times they have drawn a red tile.
4. Return the papers to the group that colored the Design a Bag and find out what the original probability was. (They will have to decide if their fraction is close to the assigned fraction.) For example, is $\frac{17}{30}$ close to $\frac{1}{3}$?

At the end of the activity, have students explain (on the back of the handout or in their journals) how they decided where to place their mark on the probability line. ELs and students with disabilities can benefit from sentence starters, such as, "In the bag we received, there were _____ red and _____ blue tiles. We first thought _____. After we did our experiment, we thought _____. We picked this probability because _____."

> **MyLab Education   Activity Page: Design a Bag**

Activity 21.7

CCSS-M: 7.SP.C.6; 7.SP.C.7a,b

Mystery Bags

This activity builds from Activity 21.6. Ask each original group to select a probability (e.g., $\frac{1}{4}, \frac{1}{6}, \frac{3}{4}, \frac{3}{8}$) and design an opaque bag using 24 two different colored cubes or tiles, such that $\frac{1}{6}$ of the tiles are red if they selected the probability of $\frac{1}{6}$. Students need to give their bag a name so they can get it back! On a secret card, they record the probability they selected and tuck it away. Groups trade bags. The new group cannot look in the bag. The second group conducts 10 draws (with replacement) and on paper write the name of the bag, a prediction for how many tiles they think are red, and what they think the probability is of drawing red. Trade bags again. This time, each group conducts 30 draws (with replacement) and again records the name of their bags and their prediction for how many tiles they think are red and what they think the probability is of drawing red. Return bags to original owners. During share time, each group holds up their bag, hears the prediction from the group that drew 10 times and from the group that drew 30 times, and then reveals the answer. As a whole class, discuss the connection between probability and number of counters, and how many draws are needed to make a good prediction of what is in the bag.

You may notice that probability is closely connected to fractions. Although probability is not explicitly discussed in the grades 3–5 curriculum, fractions are heavily emphasized (NGA Center & CCSSO, 2010). Activities such as Design and Test Bags and Mystery Bags are excellent for thinking about relative size of fractions, comparing fractions, equivalence of fractions, and multiplication of a whole number by a fraction.

> **MyLab Education   Self-Check 21.1**

Theoretical Probability and Experiments

The *probability* of an event is a measure of the chance of that event occurring (Franklin et al. 2005). Students to this point have only been asked to place events on a continuum from impossible to certain or to compare the probability of one event with another. So how do you measure chance of an event? There are two ways: theoretical probability and relative frequency estimates.

Theoretical probability is used when there is a known sample space of equally likely outcomes (e.g., flipping a fair coin or rolling a dice). Theoretical probability is calculated by determining the proportion of favorable outcomes compared to the total possible. For example:

What is the probability of rolling a value less than three with a fair die?

In this case, the sample space is 1, 2, 3, 4, 5, 6. The favorable outcomes are 1, 2. The theoretical probability can be determined based on this information ($\frac{1}{3}$). Now consider these questions and how the probability might be determined.

What is the probability that Jon V. will make his free throws?
What is the chance of rain?

Notice that in both of these cases, there is not a known sample space with equally likely outcomes, therefore empirical data, such as previous free throw record or data on how often it has rained under similar conditions, must be used (Colgan, 2006; Nicolson, 2005). *Relative frequency estimates* are based on data collected through an experiment or simulation related to the topic being analyzed. These estimates are explored through experiments or simulations, and as these experiments are repeated a large number of times, the estimate shows less variability and approaches what might be considered the 'true' probability (Konold et al., 2011). Although this type of probability is less common in the school curriculum, it is the most applicable to fields that use probability and therefore important to include in your teaching (Franklin et al., 2005).

In both cases, experiments or simulations can be designed to explore the phenomena being examined. (Sometimes in the school curriculum/textbooks this is referred to as *experimental probability*, but because this terminology is not employed by statisticians, it is not used here.) Some experiments have outcomes that are equally likely, whereas other experiments do not. With coin flips, there are two possible outcomes that are equally likely, so each has a probability of $\frac{1}{2}$. Hence, the theoretical probability of obtaining a head is $\frac{1}{2}$. When all possible outcomes of a simple experiment are equally likely, the probability of an event can be expressed as follows:

$$\frac{\text{Number of outcomes in the event}}{\text{Number of possible outcomes}}$$

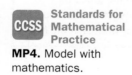

Standards for Mathematical Practice

MP4. Model with mathematics.

Consider the shift in meaning of the question, "Is this coin fair?" This is a statistics problem that can only be answered by doing an experiment and establishing the frequency of heads and tails over the long run (Franklin et al., 2005). The answer requires empirical data and the probability will be as follows:

$$\frac{\text{Number of observed occurrence of the event}}{\text{Number of trials}}$$

Because it is impossible to conduct an infinite number of trials, we can only consider a relative frequency estimate based on a very large number of trials as an approximation of the theoretical probability. This emphasizes the notion that probability is more about predictions over the long term than about predictions of individual events.

Process for Teaching Probability

Probability, like all content, can and should be taught through a problem-based approach. Probability investigations are an excellent fit to the *before, during, after* lesson plan model. In the *before* phase, students make predictions of what they think will be likely; in the *during* phase, students experiment to explore how likely the event is; and in the *after* phase, students compile and analyze the experimental results to determine more accurately how likely the event is. English and Watson (2016) describe three phases, which they found were effective in increasing elementary students' understanding of probability:

1. Concrete exploration: Students make predictions about what they think will happen and then engage in hands-on experiments.
2. Representation: Students organize and represent the data gathered in phase 1, selecting their own ways to summarize the data, which might include lists, tally charts, tables, dot plots, bar and circle graphs, or pictorial representations.
3. Construction: Students analyze their representations, and construct a model describing the probability. This is presented symbolically and diagrammatically.

Notice that this follows the concrete, semi-concrete, abstract (CSA) approach described in Chapter 6, which makes the learning comprehensible and accessible to all students, particularly students with disabilities. CSA is also called concrete-representational-abstract, or CRA, in mathematics teaching. Phase 2 brings in the representations discussed in the previous chapter on statistics. Importantly, statistics and probability are closely related and should be connected. Using data displays helps make sense of how likely an outcome is (statistical displays support understanding of probability). Conversely, analyzing data displays to notice how likely an outcome is makes the creation of data displays more relevant (probability supports understanding of statistics).

Theoretical Probability

A problem-based way to introduce theoretical probability is to engage students in an activity with an unfair game. In the following activity, the results of the game will likely be contrary to students' intuitive ideas. This in turn will provide a real reason to analyze the game in a logical manner and find out why things happened as they did—theoretical probability.

Activity 21.8

CCSS-M: 7.SP.C.6; 7.SP.C.7a

ENGLISH LEARNERS

Fair or Unfair Games

For each of these games, ask students to first predict if they believe the game is fair, then play the game, considering if the game is fair or unfair (and why). You can play these games back to back within one lesson, or on different days.

Game 1: Three students form a group and are given two like coins (e.g., two pennies). For each flip, one player gets a point, based on the following rules:

Player A: Two heads   Player B: Two tails   Player C: One of each

The game is over after 20 tosses. The player who has the most points wins. Have students play the game two or three times.

Game 2: Partners compete in this game, flipping two like coins (e.g., two pennies). For each flip, one player gets a point, based on the following rules:

Player A: Same face (e.g., both heads)   Player B: One of each

After playing the game, ask students to create data displays of their group's data. Two-coin experiments lend to many representations (e.g., tables, lists, various versions of tree diagrams) and these representations help students understand theoretical probability (English & Watson, 2016). When the full class has played the game several times, conduct a discussion on the fairness of the game. Challenge students to make an argument based on the data and game rules as to whether the game is fair or not. For ELs, discuss the meaning of *fair* prior to beginning the game and review the term when asking students to create an argument. To design their own fair game, see Expanded Lesson: Design a Fair Game.

MyLab Education   **Expanded Lesson: Design a Fair Game**

Standards for Mathematical Practice

MP2. Reason abstractly and quantitatively.

A common analysis of game 1 in Activity 21.8 might go something like this: At first students think that because there are three outcomes—two tails, one head and one tail, or two heads—that each has an equal chance, so the game should be fair. However, after playing, students find that player C (the player who gets a point for a mixed result) appears to have an unfair advantage (especially if they have played several games or the class has pooled its data). This observation counters the notion that the outcomes are equally likely. When students from fifth through eleventh grades performed a similar two-coin task and were asked for the probability of getting a head and a tail with two coins, similar misconceptions were found (Rubel, 2006, 2007). About 25 percent of the students said the probability was $\frac{1}{3}$ because one of three things could happen: two heads, one of each, or two tails. Although about half answered correctly, many of these students used faulty reasoning, explaining that they picked that answer because there is a 50 percent chance in any experiment. See, for example, Figure 21.3.

In game 2, students may think that the player B has an advantage, thinking (incorrectly) that different results are more likely than same results (referred to as the *representativeness* (Kustos & Zelkowski, 2013). Through playing the game an analyzing results using different representations (e.g., an organized list or tree diagram), students realize this is a fair game (Degner, 2015).

Standards for Mathematical Practice

MP1. Make sense of problems and persevere in solving them.

To help students connect how likely an event is to the possible outcomes, encourage students to analyze the situation and generate all the possible outcomes—for example, use a table such as the one in Figure 21.4. Getting a head and a tail happens in two out of the four possible outcomes. Figure 21.5 provides an example of a student's correct explanation for "Fair or Unfair." This theoretical probability is based on a logical analysis of the experiment, not on experimental results.

"Rock-paper-scissors" is a great context for exploring fair games and possible outcomes. It can be played in the normal way or adapted so that "same" scores 1 point for one player and "different" scores 1 point for the other player. Challenge students to determine whether this is a fair game (Ellis, Yeh, & Stump, 2007–2008).

Area has important connections to probability. In the CCSS-M, students explore both area of circles and probability in grade 7. The following activity is an excellent way to integrate these two important ideas.

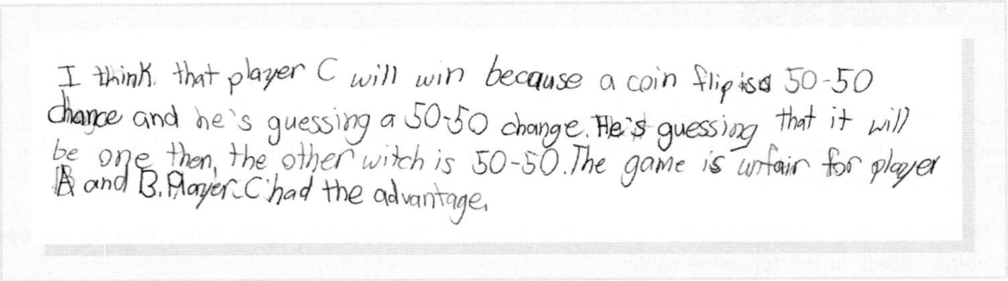

> I think that player C will win because a coin flip is a 50-50 chance and he's guessing a 50-50 change. He's guessing that it will be one then, the other witch is 50-50. The game is unfair for player B and B. Player C had the advantage.

FIGURE 21.3 Correct conclusion but incomplete reasoning on "Fair or Unfair?"

First Coin	Second Coin
Head	Head
Head	Tail
Tail	Head
Tail	Tail

FIGURE 21.4 Four possible outcomes of flipping two coins.

I think this game is unfair because it is more likley to get a mix than two of the same sides. This is true because there are more possibilitys for a mix such as heads tails, and tails heads, but the only possibility for player A is two heads, and the only possibility for player B is a tails. So for player C they have a 1/2 chance for geting a point, but for the other two they only have a 1/4 chance of geting a point.

FIGURE 21.5   Student reasoning for "Fair or Unfair?" that connects outcomes to probability.

Activity 21.9   CCSS-M: 7.G.B.4; 7.SP.C.6; 7.SP.C.7b

Chance of Hitting the Target?

Project a target such as the one illustrated here with concentric circles having radii of 2 inches, 6 inches, 8 inches, and 10 inches, each region shaded a different color. Ask students to determine the fraction and percent of each colored region in the circle.

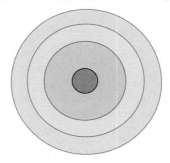

Ask students to discuss what the probability for landing on the center (assuming all throws land on the circle and are thrown randomly). Ask students to discuss why data may or may not match the percent of the area that is covered (e.g., people with good aim will be able to hit the smaller areas more often). Then, have students propose what point values they would assign to each region. Students may assign values in various ways. For example, they may think the skinny outer circle is harder to land on and give it more points than other sections, even though the area of that region may be more. Allow them time to share their reasoning and to critique others' ways of assigning points.

Dartboards can be made many different ways, not just in the traditional way (Williams & Bruels, 2011). For example, using a 10 × 10 Grid, any combination of shapes can be drawn in such a way that the area can be calculated. Students can determine the area of various regions and use the areas to determine the probability of different outcomes, an excellent connection between measurement and probability.

> **MyLab Education**   **Blackline Master: 10 × 10 Grid**

Experiments

As noted previously, some probabilities cannot be determined by the analysis of possible outcomes of an event; instead, they can be determined only through gathering empirical data. The data may be preexisting or may need to be established through an experiment, with a sufficiently large number of trials conducted to become confident that the resulting relative frequency is an approximation of the theoretical probability. For example, the probability of a hurricane is based on historical data. The United States Landfalling Hurricane Web Project provides such probabilities for hurricanes (by state and county).

The following activities are examples of situations in which the only way to establish how likely an outcome is, is to do an experiment and use the results of a large number of trials.

Activity 21.10

CCSS-M: 7.SP.C.7b

Drop It!

In this activity, students drop an object to explore the likelihood of various outcomes. The number of possible outcomes varies with the different objects. Any object can be used. Here are a few ideas to try:

1. *Cup Toss.* Provide a small plastic cup to each pair of students. Ask them to list the possible ways that the cup could land if they tossed it in the air and let it fall on the floor. Which of the possibilities (upside down, right side up, or on the side) do they think is most likely and which least likely? Why? Have students toss the cup 20 times, each time recording how it lands. Students should agree on a uniform method of tossing the cups to ensure unbiased data (e.g., dropping the cups from the same height). Record each pair's data in a class chart. Discuss the differences and generate reasons for them. Have students predict what will happen if they pool their data. Pool the data and compute the three ratios: one for each type of landing (upside down, right side up, or on the side). The relative frequency of the combined data should approximate the actual probability.

2. *Toy Animal Drop.* Bring in small plastic toys that can land in different ways. Repeat the activity above. (See Nelson & Williams, 2009, or Young, 2016, both which provide a series of engaging activities with tossing toy pigs, and include Activity Pages.)

3. *Falling Kisses.* Using Hershey's Kisses, conduct an experiment to see how often they land directly on their base (Gallego, Saldamando, Tapia-Beltran, Williams, & Hoopingarner, 2009). Alternative foods include Hershey's Rolo Caramels, or for a healthier option, consider fish crackers (the direction in which they face).

In these experiments, there is no practical way to determine the results before you start. However, once you have results for 200 tosses (empirical data), you will feel more confident in predicting the results of the next 100 tosses. After gathering data for 1000 trials, you will feel even more confident. In other words, the more tosses that are made, the more confident you become. For example, in dropping the cup, after 100 or so trials, you may have determined a probability of $\frac{4}{5}$, or 80 percent, for the cup to land on its side.

The Law of Large Numbers. The phenomenon in which the relative frequency of an event becomes a closer approximation of the actual probability or the theoretical probability as the size of the data set (sample) increases is referred to as the *law of large numbers*. The larger the size of the data set, the more representative the sample is of the population. In thinking about statistics, a survey of 1000 people provides more reliable and convincing data about the larger population than does a survey of 5 people. The larger the number of trials (people surveyed), the more confident you can be that the data reflect the larger population. The same is true when you are attempting to determine the probability of an event through data collection.

Although critical to understanding probability, this concept is difficult for students to grasp. Students commonly think that a probability should play out in the short term, a false assumption sometimes referred to as "the law of small numbers" (Flores, 2006; Tarr, Lee, & Rider, 2006). Comparing small data sets to large data sets is one way to help students think more deeply about the fact that the size of the trial matters. The next two activities are designed with this purpose in mind.

CCSS Standards for Mathematical Practice

MP8. Look for and express regularity in repeated reasoning.

Activity 21.11

CCSS-M: 7.SP.C.6

Get All 6!

Ask students to list the numbers 1 through 6 at the bottom of a frequency table. Students should roll a die and mark an X over each number until they have rolled each number at least once. Repeat five or six times. Discuss how the frequency charts compare in each case. Students will see that in some cases there were many fours, for example, or that it took 25 rolls before all numbers were rolled, whereas in other cases they got all the numbers in only 10 rolls. Now, pool all the data and discuss the relative frequencies for the numbers that emerge. Focus discussion on the fact that in the short run, data varies a lot—it is over the long run that the data "evens out." This activity can also be done on a graphing calculator (see Flores, 2006).

Truly random events often occur in unexpected groups; a fair coin may turn up heads five times in a row. A 100-year flood may hit a town twice in 10 years. Using random devices such as spinning spinners, rolling dice, or drawing cubes from a bag (physically or virtually with an app) gives students an intuitive feel for the imperfect distribution of randomness. The next activity is designed to help students with this difficult idea.

Activity 21.12

CCSS-M: 7.SP.C.6

What Are the Chances?

Use a copy of What Are the Chances? Activity Page. Provide pairs of students with a spinner face that is half red and half blue. Discuss the chances of spinning blue. Mark the halfway point on the continuum of impossible to certain and draw a vertical line down through all of the lines below this point. Then have the students in each pair spin their spinner 10 times, tallying the number of red and blue spins. Mark the number of blue spins on the second line. For example, if there are 3 blue and 7 red spins, place a mark at about 7 on the 0-to-10 number line. If the result of the 10 spins is not exactly 5 and 5, discuss possible reasons why this may be so.

   Repeat 10 more times. Add the tallies for the first 10 spins and again mark the total in the right hand box of the third line. Repeat at least two more times, continuing to add the results of new spins to the previous results. Using a graphing calculator or applet, even 1000 trials are possible in a short amount of time. Ask students to reflect on what they notice in each number line.

MyLab Education   Activity Page: What Are the Chances?

The successive number lines used in "What Are the Chances?" each have the same length and each represent the total number of trials. When the results are plotted on any one number line, the position shows the fraction of the total spins as a visual portion of the whole line. With more trials, the marks will get closer and closer to the $\frac{1}{2}$ mark. Note that 240 blue spins out of 500 is 48 percent, or very close to one-half. This is close to even, though there are 20 more red spins (260) than blue.

The What Are the Chances? Activity Page and process of accumulating data in stages can and should be used for other experiments. For example, try using this approach with the cup toss experiment in Activity 21.10. Rather than drawing a vertical line before collecting data, decide on the best guess at the actual probability after the number of trials has become large, and then draw the vertical line in the appropriate position. Observe and record on the number lines 10 additional trials, 20 additional trials, and 50 additional trials. Compare these smaller data sets with the larger data set. Write the probabilities as fractions and as percents to show the connection between these representations.

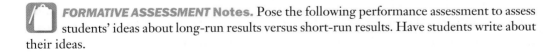

MyLab Education   Activity Page: What Are the Chances?

FORMATIVE ASSESSMENT Notes. Pose the following performance assessment to assess students' ideas about long-run results versus short-run results. Have students write about their ideas.

Margaret spins the spinner 10 times. Blue turns up on three spins. Red turns up on seven spins. Margaret says that there is a 3-in-10 chance of spinning blue. Carla then spins the same spinner 100 times. Carla records 53 spins to blue and 47 spins to red. Carla says that the chance of spinning blue on this spinner is about even.

   Who do you think is more likely to be correct: Margaret or Carla? Explain. Draw a spinner that you think they may have been using.

Look for evidence that students understand that the result of 10 spins is not very good evidence of the probability and that the result of 100 spins tells us more about how likely each color is, and therefore what percent of the spinner might be blue or red. Also, to assess whether students understand the big idea that chance has no memory, have students write in their journal about the following:

Duane has a lucky coin that he has tossed many, many times. He is sure that it is a fair coin with an even chance of heads or tails. Duane tosses his coin six times and heads come up six times in a row. Duane is sure that the next toss will be tails because he has never been able to toss heads seven times in a row. What do you think the chances are of Duane tossing heads on the next toss? Explain your answer.

In this case, you are looking for the idea that each toss of the coin is independent of prior tosses. ◼

Why Use Experiments?

Actually conducting experiments and examining outcomes in teaching probability are important in helping students address false assumptions about probability and build a deeper understanding for why certain things are more likely than others.

Specifically, experiments:

Standards for Mathematical Practice

MP1. Make sense of problems and persevere in solving them.

- Provide a connection to counting strategies (lists, tree diagrams) to increase confidence that the probability is accurate
- Provide an experiential background for examining the theoretical model (when you begin to sense that the probability of two heads is $\frac{1}{4}$ instead of $\frac{1}{3}$ through experiments, the analysis in Figure 21.4 seems more reasonable)
- Help students see how the ratio of a particular outcome to the total number of trials begins to converge to a fixed number (for an infinite number of trials, the relative frequency and theoretical probability would be the same)
- Help students learn more than students who do not engage in doing experiments (Gurbuz, Erdem, Catlioglu, & Birgin, 2010)

Try to use an experimental approach whenever possible, posing interesting problems to investigate. If a theoretical analysis is possible (e.g., as in the two-coin experiment in "Fair or Unfair?"), it should also be examined and the results compared with the expected outcomes.

Use of Technology in Experiments

Standards for Mathematical Practice

MP5. Use appropriate tools strategically.

Random outcomes can be generated by computer applications, notebook apps, and calculators. Calculators, for example, produce random numbers that can then be interpreted relative to the possible outcomes in the experiment. Random numbers can be related to the possible outcomes in an experiment. For example, if the final digit is odd, you can assign it to represent one outcome, and if it is even to represent a second outcome. If there are four outcomes, you can look at the remainder when the last two digits are divided by 4 (i.e., the remainder will be 0, 1, 2, or 3) and assign a remainder to each outcome. In addition, some calculators, like the TI-73, TI-83, and TI-84, can run the free Probability Simulation App, an interactive tool that simulates tossing coins, rolling number cubes, using spinners, and generating random numbers.

Computer interactives can be used to virtually flip coins, spin spinners, or draw numbers from a hat. NCTM's Illuminations website has a series of lessons, "Probability Explorations," in which students explore probability through virtual experiments, and can also graph the results.

As long as students accept the results generated by the technology as truly random or equivalent to those of hands-on devices, these virtual devices have the advantage of being quick, more motivating to some students, and accessible when the actual devices (e.g., spinners with various partitions) are not. Web-based tools, such as the Math Playground's probability and graphing spinner (https://www.mathplayground.com/probability.html), have the advantage of generating many more trials in much less time. Due to the speed at which an experiment can be done, these digital devices afford the opportunity for teachers to explore probability across a variety of tools (virtual dice, coins, cards, etc.), including the use of graphic displays of the trials. Also, in a virtual world, dice can be "loaded" and used to challenge students' thinking ("Are these fair dice? How can you find out?") (Beck & Huse, 2007; Phillips-Bey, 2004).

MyLab Education   **Self-Check 21.2**

Sample Spaces and the Probability of Compound Events

Understanding the concepts *sample space* and *event* is central to understanding probability. The *sample space* for an experiment or chance situation is the set of all possible outcomes for that experiment. For example, if a bag contains two red, three yellow, and five blue tiles, the sample space consists of all ten tiles. An *event* is a subset of the sample space. The event of drawing a yellow tile has three elements or outcomes in the sample space, and the event of drawing a blue tile has five elements in the sample space. For rolling a single common die, the sample space consists of the numbers 1 through 6. A two-event experiment requires two (or more) actions to determine an outcome. Examples include rolling two dice, drawing two tiles from a bag, and the combination of the occurrence of rain and forgetting your umbrella.

When two-event experiments are explored, there is another factor to consider: Does the occurrence of the event in one stage have an effect on the occurrence of the event in the other? In the following sections, we will consider two-event experiments of both types—those with independent events and those with dependent events.

MyLab Education   **Video Example 21.2**

This lesson (https://www.youtube.com/watch?v=2cIIwwhOKz0) illustrates sixth grade students conducting simulations of dependent and independent events using bags of objects.

VIDEO EXAMPLE

Independent Events

In Activity 21.8, students explored the results of tossing two coins. The toss of one coin had no effect on the toss of the other. Tossing a coin twice is an example of *independent events;* the occurrence or nonoccurrence of one event has no effect on the other.

Let's explore rolling two dice and adding the results. Suppose that your students gather data on the sums that they get for rolling two dice. The results might be recorded in a dot plot, as in Figure 21.6(a). These events (sums) do not appear to be equally likely, and in fact the sum of 7 appears to be the most likely outcome. To explain this, students might look for the combinations that equal 7: 1 and 6, 2 and 5, and 3 and 4. But there are also three combinations for 6 and for 8. It seems as though 6 and 8 should be just as likely as 7, and yet they are not.

Now suppose that the experiment is repeated. This time, for the sake of clarity, suggest that students roll two dice of different colors and that they keep the tallies in a chart like the one in Figure 21.6(b). The results of a large number of dice rolls indicate what one would expect—namely, that all 36 cells of this chart are equally likely. (However, the sums are not equally likely. Why?) Compare the sums of 6, 7, and 8, the most common sums. Notice that for 7, red 3, green 4 is different from red 4, green 3, and there are 3 such pairs for a total of 6 outcomes that result in a sum of 7 out of a total of the sample space (36), for a probability of $\frac{6}{36}$ or $\frac{1}{6}$. The sums for 6 and for 8 each include a double, and therefore each sum has five outcomes (not 6), for a probability of $\frac{5}{36}$. The color-coded dice can help students see how possibilities are counted, addressing the fact that while $3 + 4$ is the same as $4 + 3$, these are each separate outcomes in rolling dice.

To create the sample space for two independent events, use a chart or diagram that keeps the two events separate and illustrates all possible combinations. The matrix in Figure 21.6(b) is effective when there are only two events. A tree diagram (Figure 21.7) is another method of creating sample spaces that can be used with any number of events. The tree diagram is more

 Standards for Mathematical Practice
MP2. Reason abstractly and quantitatively.

Sum of Two Dice

Number of times sum appears	Sum										
	2	3	4	5	6	7	8	9	10	11	12
10											
9											
8											
7											
6											
5						•					
4						•		•			
3			•	•	•	•	•				
2			•	•	•	•	•	•			
1	•	•	•	•	•	•	•	•	•	•	

(a)

Red Die

Green Die	1	2	3	4	5	6
1	卅	卅 I	卅 III	卅 II	卅 III	(卅 II)
2	卅 III	卅 III	卅 I	卅 卅	(卅 III)	卅 II
3	卅 卅	卅 II	卅 III	(卅 III)	卅 卅 II	卅 III
4	卅 II	卅 卅 II	(卅 III)	卅 卅 II	卅 卅 II	卅 II
5	卅 III	(卅 卅 II)	卅 卅 III	卅 III	卅	卅 III
6	(卅 III)	卅 IIII	卅 III	卅 II	卅 IIII	卅 II

There are six ways to get 7.

(b)

FIGURE 21.6 Exploring the frequencies (dot plot) and possible outcomes (matrix) for the sum of two dice.

abstract, but efficient for finding probabilities. Connecting a list or chart to a tree diagram can help students make sense of a tree diagram. For example, consider the context of creating an ice cream cone. You can choose a waffle cone or a regular cone, ice cream that is dipped or not dipped, and then any of three single flavors. This can be simulated with coins and a spinner, as illustrated in Figure 21.7.

MyLab Education   **Video Example 21.3**

See this video of a lesson connecting tables to tree diagrams to determine probabilities of two events (coin toss and pick a color cube).

VIDEO EXAMPLE

⏸ Pause & Reflect

Use a chart or tree diagram to analyze the sum of two number cubes each with sides 1, 1, 2, 3, 3, and 3. (These were the cubes used in Activities 21.3 and 21.4.) What is the probability of each sum, 1 through 6? How might these tools support student understanding of sample space and the probability of independent events? •

A common process to help students connect sample space with probability is to ask them first to make a prediction of the probability of the event, second to conduct an experiment with a large number of trials, and third to compare the prediction with what happened. Then ask students to create the sample space and see how it compares with the prediction and the results of the experiment. Games provide an excellent context for such explorations, as described in Activity 21.13.

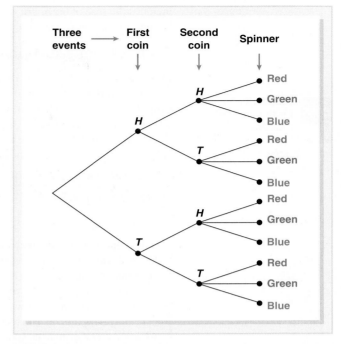

FIGURE 21.7 A tree diagram showing all possible outcomes for two coins and a spinner that is $\frac{1}{3}$ red, $\frac{1}{3}$ green, and $\frac{1}{3}$ blue.

Activity 21.13

CCSS-M: 7.SP.C.7a; 7.SP.C.8a

Lu-Lu

This Hawaiian game involves taking turns tossing four stones and calculating the resulting score. (You can create stones like the ones pictured here by getting glass stones from a craft store and marking dots on one side.)

Player 1 tosses the four stones (marked on only one side). If all 4 are face up, they score 10 and take a second turn, adding 10 to their second sum. If all 4 are not face up, Player 1 re-tosses the face-down stones and adds any face-up stones to their first toss. Repeat for each player. Play several rounds, recording scores each time. High score wins.

After the students have played, ask what they notice about the sums they are getting.

- What sums are possible?
- What sums are common?
- What are all the outcomes (possible combinations of stones)?
- What is the probability of each score?

Students from other countries may also have games to share that include probability, and these games can be explored in a similar manner. (See McCoy, Buckner, & Munley, 2007, for more on this game.)

ENGLISH LEARNERS

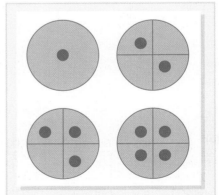

The following are additional examples of probabilities of independent events. Any one of these could be explored as part of a full lesson.

- Rolling an even sum with two dice
- Spinning blue twice on a spinner
- Having a tack *or* a cup land up when each is tossed once
- Getting at *least* two heads from tossing four coins
- Rolling two dice and getting a difference that is *no more than* 3

Words and phrases such as *and*, *or*, *at least*, and *no more than* may cause students some confusion and therefore require explicit attention. Of special note is the word *or* because its meaning in everyday usage is generally not the same as its strict logical meaning in mathematics. In mathematics, *or* includes the case of both. For example, in the tack-cup toss experiment, the event of "tack (or cup) landing up" includes tack (only) up, cup (only) up, and both tack and cup up.

Area Representation

 **Standards for Mathematical Practice**
MP4. Model with mathematics.

One way to determine the theoretical probability of a multiple events is to list all possible outcomes and count the number of outcomes that make up the event. This is effective but has some limitations. First, a list implies that all outcomes are equally likely. Second, lists can get tedious when there are many possibilities. Third, students can lose track of which possibilities they have included in the list and may leave off some of the possibilities. For all of these reasons, an area representation is a good option for determining probability, the focus of Activity 21.14.

Activity 21.14

CCSS-M: 7.SP.C.8a, b

Are You a Spring Dog?

Before doing this activity, determine which Chinese birth year animals are likely to be represented in the classroom (e.g., the dog and the rooster). Spend some time discussing the Chinese birth year animals with students. (This would be particularly timely at the Chinese New Year.) Begin by finding out what percentage of the class is represented by each animal. Ask, "If I name one of the Chinese birth year animals, what is the probability it will be *your* birth year animal?" Illustrate this percentage by partitioning a rectangle, as in Figure 21.8(a). (This particular illustration finds that 64 percent of the students in the class were born in the year of the dog, and 36 percent were born in the year of the rooster.) Ask, "If I name one of the seasons, what is the probability it will be *your* season?" Ask students to illustrate their response by partitioning and shading a rectangle. See Figure 21.8(b). Then ask, "What is the probability of being both a spring *and* a dog?"

 **Standards for Mathematical Practice**
MP8. Look for and express regularity in repeated reasoning.

In Figure 21.8(b), you can visually see that students in the year-of-the-dog and spring groups make up $\frac{1}{4}$ of 64 percent, or 16 percent of the population. This should look familiar because the same process is used for multiplying fractions (and whole numbers).

The area representation is also effective in solving *or* situations. Consider the question, "What is the probability you were born in summer or fall, *or* that you are a rooster?" The shading for this example is illustrated in Figure 21.8(c). Half of the students are born in summer or fall, and 36 percent are born in the year of the rooster. Students can add up the percentages in the boxes, or they can think about the two situations separately: 50 percent are born in summer or fall and 36 percent are born in the year of the rooster. The sum of these two separate results would be 86 percent, but some students are "both" and have therefore been double-counted (see overlap in diagram). In this example, the overlap (students falling in "both") is 18 percent. Therefore, the population that is born in summer or fall *or* born in the year of the rooster is $50 + 36 - 18 = 68$ percent of the population. Challenge students to generalize the patterns they are noticing in their, connecting the area representation to the following formula for the probability of two independent events:

$$P(A \text{ or } B) = P(A) + P(B) - P(A \text{ and } B)$$

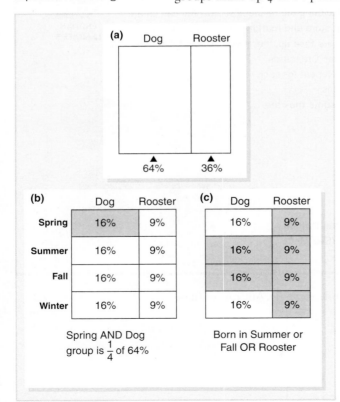

FIGURE 21.8 An area representation for determining probabilities.

The area representation is accessible to a range of learn as it is less abstract than equations or tree diagrams.

Designing a spinner is a challenging and engaging way for students to think about the probability of independent events (Ely & Cohen, 2010). The following activity is challenging and an area representation can be used to help students reason about how to design their spinner.

Activity 21.15   CCSS-M: 7.SP.C.6; 7.SP.C.7a; 7.SP.C.8a, b

Design a Winning Spinner

Explain that each student is going to create a winning spinner, which means that when it is spun twice, the sum will be on a number strip with values 2, 3, 4, 5, 6, 7, and 8. Students create their own spinner, partitioning the circle however they like and writing a number in each sector. Once students have their spinner, they pair with someone else and play the game with their own spinner: Student A spins twice and adds the two values. If the sum is 5, Student A covers 5 on his or her number strip. Student B takes a turn. The first partner to cover all numbers on his or her strip wins. Play three rounds. Next, ask students to redesign their spinner, find a new partner, and play three more rounds. If possible, repeat a third time. Afterwards, discuss how they designed a winning spinner.

In going backwards (from the desired outcome to the spinner), students can build a deeper understanding of how to determine the probability of independent events.

Dependent Events

A dependent event is a second event whose result depends on the result of a first event. For example, suppose that there are two identical boxes. One box contains one genuine dollar bill and two counterfeit bills, and the other box contains one genuine and one counterfeit bill (you do not know which box is which). You may choose one box and from that box select one bill without looking. What are your chances of getting a genuine dollar bill? Here there are two events: selecting a box and selecting a bill. The probability of getting a dollar in the second event depends on which box is chosen in the first event. The events are *dependent*.

Standards for Mathematical Practice
MP4. Model with mathematics.

Activity 21.16

CCSS-M: 7.SP.C.8a, b

Keys to a New Car

Use the Keys to a New Car Activity Page, or pose the following problem: In a game show, you can win a car—if you make it through the maze to the room where you have placed the car key. You can place the keys in either Room A or Room B (see maze in Figure 21.9). At the start and at each fork in the path, you must spin the indicated spinner and follow the path that it points to. Once you've reached Room A or Room B, the game is over—there is no going back through the maze. In which room should you place the key to have the best chance of winning the car?

MyLab Education   Activity Page: Keys to a New Car

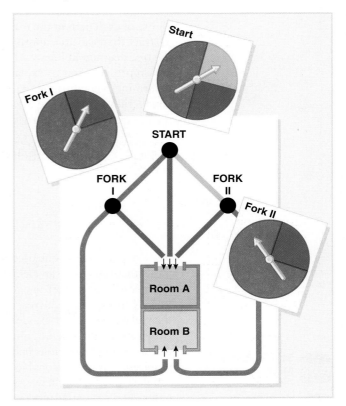

FIGURE 21.9 Should you place your key in Room A or Room B to have the best chance at winning?

You can also use the area representation to determine the probability for dependent events. Figure 21.10 illustrates the "Keys to a New Car" task.

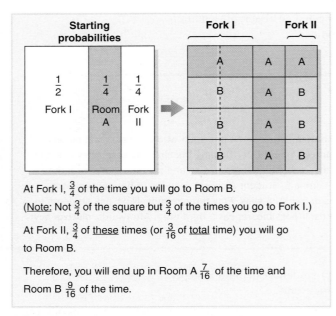

At Fork I, $\frac{3}{4}$ of the time you will go to Room B.

(Note: Not $\frac{3}{4}$ of the square but $\frac{3}{4}$ of the times you go to Fork I.)

At Fork II, $\frac{3}{4}$ of these times (or $\frac{3}{16}$ of total time) you will go to Room B.

Therefore, you will end up in Room A $\frac{7}{16}$ of the time and Room B $\frac{9}{16}$ of the time.

FIGURE 21.10 Using the area representation to solve the maze problem.

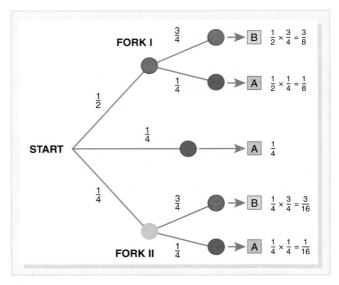

FIGURE 21.11 A tree diagram is another way to representation the outcomes of two or more dependent events.

Pause & Reflect

How would the area representation for the car problem be different if the spinner at Forks I and II were $\frac{1}{3}$ A and $\frac{2}{3}$ B spinners? What questions like this one can you ask students in order to help them think about how one event depends on the next? ●

Figure 21.11 shows a tree diagram for the "Keys to a New Car" problem, with the probability of each path in the maze written on the "branch" of the tree. The tree diagram is more abstract than the area approach, but it applies to a wider range of situations. Each branch of the tree diagram in Figure 21.11 matches with a section of the square in Figure 21.10. Use the area representation to explain why the probability for each complete branch of the tree is determined by multiplying the probabilities along the branch. Having students describe the connection between the area and the tree diagram representations can help build meaning for the tree diagram approach, which can be used in any multiple-events probability task.

MyLab Education   Self-Check 21.3

Simulations

Simulation is a technique used for answering real-world questions or making decisions in complex situations where an element of chance is involved. Many times simulations are conducted because it is too dangerous, complex, or expensive to manipulate the real situation. To see what is likely to happen in the real event, a model must be designed that has the same probabilities as the real situation. For example, in the designing of a rocket, a large number of related systems all have some chance of failure that might cause serious problems with the rocket. Knowing the probability of serious failures will help determine whether redesign or backup systems are required. It is not reasonable to make repeated tests of the actual rocket. Instead, a model that simulates all of the chance situations is designed and run repeatedly with the help of a computer. The computer model can simulate thousands of flights, and an estimate of the chance of failure can be made.

Standards for Mathematical Practice

MP5. Use appropriate tools strategically.

Activity 21.17

CCSS-M: 7.SP.C.8b, c

Probability of Getting Water

Show students an illustration of a water pump system like the one illustrated in Figure 21.12. Explain that the five pumps that connect A and B are aging, and it is estimated that at any given time, the probability of pump failure is $\frac{1}{2}$. If a pump fails, water cannot pass that station. For example, if pumps 1, 2, and 5 fail, water flows only through pumps 4 and 3. Ask students to discuss how likely they think it is that water will make it through the pump. Have students mark how likely on a probability continuum. Follow the steps for teaching a simulation (described next). After students have completed their simulation, revisit the important probability questions:

- What is the probability that water will flow at any time?
- On the average, about how many stations need repair at any time?

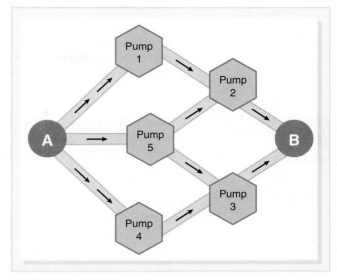

FIGURE 21.12   Each of these five pumps has a 50 percent chance of failure. What is the probability that some path from A to B is working?

Shodor's Project Interactivate offers a realistic simulation of actual forest fires. The simulation, titled "A Better Fire," uses a virtual "die" to see whether a tree should be planted for each square. Then the fire is set and allowed to burn.

For any simulation, the following steps can serve as a useful guide. Here the steps are explained for use with Activity 21.17.

1. *Identify key components and assumptions of the problem.* The key component in the water problem is the condition of a pump. Each pump is either working or not working. In this problem, the assumption is that the probability that a pump is working is $\frac{1}{2}$.
2. *Select a random device for the key components.* Any random device can be selected that has outcomes with the same probability as those of the key component—in this case, the pumps. Here a simple choice might be tossing a coin, with heads representing a working pump.
3. *Define a trial.* A *trial* consists of simulating a series of key components until the situation has been completely modeled one time. In this problem, a trial could consist of tossing a coin five times, each toss representing a different pump (heads for pump is working and tails for pump is not working).
4. *Conduct a large number of trials and record the information.* For this problem, it would be useful to record the number of heads and tails in groups of five because each set of five is one trial and represents all of the pumps.
5. *Use the data to draw conclusions.* There are four possible paths for the water, each flowing through two of the five pumps. As they are numbered in the drawing, if any one of the pairs 1-2, 5-2, 5-3, and 4-3 is open, it makes no difference whether the other pumps are working. By counting the number of trials in which at least one of these four pairs of coins both come up heads, we can estimate the probability of water flowing. To answer the second question, the number of tails (pumps not working) per trial can be averaged.

Here are a few more examples of problems for which a simulation can be used to gather empirical data.

In a true-or-false test, what is the probability of getting 7 out of 10 questions correct by guessing alone?
Key component: Answering a question.
Assumption: Chance of getting the answer correct is $\frac{1}{2}$.
Simulation option: Flip a coin 10 times for one trial.

In a group of five people, what is the chance that two were born in the same month?
Key component: Month of birth.
Assumption: All 12 months are equally likely.
Simulation option: Use 12-sided dice or 12 cards. Draw/roll one, replace, and draw/roll again.

Casey's batting average is .350. What is the chance he will go hitless in a complete nine-inning game?
Key component: Getting a hit.
Assumptions: The probability of a hit for each at-bat is .35. Casey will get to bat four times in the average game.
Simulation option: Use a spinner that is 35 percent shaded. Spin four times for one trial.

Krunch-a-Munch cereal packs one of five games in each box. About how many boxes should you expect to buy before you get a complete set?
Key component: Getting one game.
Assumption: Each game has a $\frac{1}{5}$ chance.
Simulation option: Use a spinner with five equal sections. Spin until all sections occur at least once. Record how many spins it took (this is one trial). Repeat. The average length of a trial answers the question.
Extension: What is the chance of getting a set in eight or fewer boxes?

Students often have trouble selecting an appropriate random device for simulations. Spinners are a reasonable choice because areas can be adjusted to match probabilities. A standard die can be used for probabilities that are multiples of $\frac{1}{6}$. There are also dice available online and on smartphones with 4, 8, 12, and 20 sides. Coins or two-colored counters are useful for probabilities of $\frac{1}{2}$. Many calculators include a key that will produce random numbers that can be used to simulate experiments (e.g., 1 means true and 2 means false). Usually, the random numbers generated are between 0 and 1, such as 0.8904433368. How could a list of decimals like this replace flipping a coin or spinning a spinner? Suppose each was multiplied by 2. The results would be between 0 and 2, as shown here:

$$0.8904433368 \times 2 = 1.7808866736$$

$$0.0232028877 \times 2 = 0.0464057754$$

$$0.1669322714 \times 2 = 0.3338645428$$

If you focus on the ones column, you have a series of zeros and ones that could represent heads and tails, boys and girls, true and false, or any other pair of equally likely outcomes. For three outcomes, the same as a $\frac{1}{4}/\frac{1}{4}/\frac{1}{2}$ spinner, you might decide to look at the first two digits of the number and assign values from 0 to 24 and from 25 to 49 to the two one-quarter portions and values from 50 to 99 to the one-half portion. The NCTM Illuminations "Adjustable Spinner" can be set up for such simulations. Alternatively, each randomly generated number could be multiplied by 4 and the decimal part ignored, resulting in random numbers 0, 1, 2, and 3. These could then be assigned to the desired outcomes.

In this activity, consider how you would design a simulation.

Activity 21.18

CCSS-M: 7.SP.C.8b,c

Chance of Triplet Girls

Ask students, "What is the chance that a woman having triplets will end up with all girls?" Record estimates. Ask students to create a simulation to model this problem using the five steps previously described. Encourage students to use various tools to simulate (flipping three coins, using a random number generator, spinning a two-color spinner three times, etc.). After examining the results, ask questions to relate the predictions to the results. This may lead to creating a tree diagram of the options to make sense of the results. See also, Goodwin and Ortiz (2015) for ideas and Activity Pages related to having three children.

> **MyLab Education   Application Exercise: 21.1: Simulations** Click the link to access this exercise, then read the scenario and answer the accompanying questions.

Student Assumptions Related to Probability

Tasks like "Chance of Triplet Girls" can lead to interesting follow-up questions: "Are three girls less likely or more likely than two girls and a boy?" and "If a family already has two girls, what do you think they will have for their third child?" (Tillema, 2010). These questions are focused on addressing some (incorrect) assumptions students have related to probability. These challenges, including two shared earlier, are summarized in Table 21.1.

Whether doing simulations, experiments, or theoretical probability, it is important for students to use many representations (lists, area, tree diagrams) and discuss developing probability conceptions explicitly. In addition to being more interesting, teaching probability in this way allows students to understand important concepts that have many real-world implications. This final activity is designed to apply different representations as well as simulations.

Standards for Mathematical Practice
MP3. Construct viable arguments and critique the reasoning of others.

Activity 21.19   CCSS-M: 7.SP.C.8a,b,c

Money in Two Piggy Banks

Use the Money in Two Piggy Banks Activity Page or post the following problem for students:

Use an area representation and a tree diagram to determine the probability for the following situation:

In a game at the County Fair, the game leader puts one $5 bill and three $1 bills in the Piggy Bank 1. In Piggy Bank 2, he puts one $5 bill and one $1 bill. To play the game, you get to take one bill from Piggy Bank 1 (without looking) and put it in Piggy Bank 2. After mixing Piggy Bank 2, you get to take one bill from that bank. The game costs $2 to play. Should you spend your money?

Ask students to illustrate the theoretical probability using (1) an area representation and (2) a tree diagram. This can be done by having some groups work on one and other groups work on the other, then compare and then share and compare their diagrams. Or, everyone can create both. After these illustrations are complete, ask students how they might design a simulation to test this game. Invite students to explain their simulation and present it. Ask other students to determine if the simulation accurately models the game.

MyLab Education   Activity Page: Money in Two Piggy Banks

> **MyLab Education   Self-Check 21.4**
>
> **MyLab Education   Math Practice:** Need to practice or refresh your math content knowledge? Click to access practice exercises associated with the content from this chapter.

TABLE 21.1   CHALLENGES (FALSE ASSUMPTIONS) RELATED TO PROBABILITY

False Assumptions or Intuitions	What It Looks Like	How to Help
1. *Commutativity confusion.* Knowing that 3 + 4 is the same as 4 + 3, the chance of an outcome such as one boy and two girls is considered one event, not three (BGG, GBG, GGB).	Student considers two girls and one boy is one possible outcome, and therefore think that the chance of one boy and two girls is the same as having three girls.	• Have students think of all the ways an event can occur. • Discuss this confusion explicitly. • Use different colored dice in simulations to highlight this issue. • Do experiments and discuss the variability across students' data sets.
2. *Gambler's fallacy.* The notion that what has already happened influences the event.	Student argues if there are two sisters, then a son is more likely. Similarly, if a coin has had a series of four heads, student thinks that tails are more likely for the fifth flip (Ryan & Williams, 2007).	• Point out that a coin has no memory, and the probability of heads or tails is always 50%.
3. *Law of small numbers.* Students expect small samples to be like the greater population (Flores, 2006; Tarr, Lee, & Rider, 2006).	Student thinks that having five tails in a row when flipping a coin should not happen.	• Engage in activities that challenge this expectation, such as Activities 21.11 and 21.12. • Point out that in the case of the coins, it is not so unusual—it is just a very small data set, so it is not likely to resemble the larger population.
4. *Possibility counting.* Students assume that each possibility is equally likely.	Student assumes a spinner that is 75% red and 25% blue has a 50% chance of each color.	• Do experiments to challenge their predictions. • Use Activities 21.3, 21.4, and 21.5, which are designed to help students focus on frequency rather than possible outcomes.
5. *Representativeness.* The (incorrect) idea that outcomes that seem more random are more likely to happen (Kustos & Zelkowski, 2013).	Student thinks that a Pick 3 lottery ticket such as 10, 21, 35 is more likely than 10, 11, 12.	• Use experiments and simulations. • Explicitly discuss representativeness.

RESOURCES FOR CHAPTER 21

LITERATURE CONNECTIONS

The books described here offer both fanciful and real-life data for investigating probability. These books can also be paired with activities in this chapter.

Go Figure! A Totally Cool Book about Numbers

Ball (2005)
This wonderful book could be placed in every chapter of this text. About 40 different topics are covered, one of which is called "Take a Chance." This two-page spread is full of interesting contexts for probability, including a match-dropping experiment and genetics.

Harry Potter and the Sorcerer's Stone

Rowling (1998)
The game of Quidditch can lend itself to creating a simulation to explore the probability of winning. Wagner and Lachance (2004) suggest that sums of two dice be linked to Quidditch actions. For example, a roll of 7 means a player scores a Quaffle, which is worth 10 points. Rolls of 2 or 12 mean the player catches the Snitch and the game ends, 150 points; 3, 5, 9, 11 means hit by Bludger, lose a turn; 4, 6, 8, 10 means dodge a Bludger, no points. Students play and then explore the probability of winning.

Do You Wanna Bet? Your Chance to Find Out about Probability

Cushman (2007)
The two characters in this book, Danny and Brian, become involved in everyday situations both in and out of school. Each situation involves an element of probability. For example, two invitations to birthday parties are for the same day. What is the chance that two friends would have the same birthday? In another situation, Danny flips heads several times and readers are asked about Brian's chances on the next flip. Students can create simulations to examine some of the ideas.

My Little Sister Ate One Hare

Grossman (1996)
This counting book will appeal to the middle school set as well as to young students due to the somewhat gross thought of a little girl eating one rabbit, two snakes, three ants, and so

on, including bats, mice, worms, and lizards. Upon eating ten peas, she throws up everything she ate.

Bay-Williams and Martinie (2004b) used this tale to explore probability. If one of the things the little sister "spilled" on the floor is picked up at random in the process of cleaning up, what is the probability of getting a polliwog (or other animal or category of animal)? Students can use cards representing things eaten and approach the task experimentally.

RECOMMENDED READINGS

Articles

Coffey, D. C., & Richardson, M. G. (2005). Rethinking fair games. *Mathematics Teaching in the Middle School, 10*(6), 298–303.

Students explore the fairness of a matching game both experimentally and using a theoretical model. They then set out to create a variation of the game that would be fair by assigning points to a match and to a mismatch. A TI-73 program is included that simulates the revised game.

Lim, V., Rubel, L., Shookhoff, L., Sullivan, M., & Williams, S. (2016). The lottery is a mathematics Powerball. *Mathematics Teaching in the Middle School, 21*(9), 526–532.

This article describes an innovative and high quality exploration "Color Pick" that is then used analyze the lottery. Additional excellent activities help students explore social justice issues through the lens of mathematics.

McCoy, L. P., Buckner, S., & Munley, J. (2007). Probability games from diverse cultures. *Mathematics Teaching in the Middle School, 12*(7), 394–402.

As the title suggests, this article includes games from African, Hawaiian, Jewish, Mexican, and Native American cultures. Games include probability connections, handouts, and questions to pose to students.

McMillen, S. (2008). Predictions and probability. *Teaching Children Mathematics, 14*(8), 454–463.

This article provides a series of high-quality probability lessons—various contexts and representations are used, as well as calculators. The lessons include a number of key concepts discussed in this chapter, and two handouts are provided.

Book

Shaughnessy, J. M. (2003). Research on students' understanding of probability. In J. Kilpatrick, W. G. Martin, & D. Schifter (Eds.), *A research companion to Principles and Standards for School Mathematics* (pp. 216–226). Reston, VA: NCTM.

Shaughnessy's chapter offers interesting insights from research and makes useful recommendations about successful ways to teach probability concepts.

CHAPTER
22

Developing Concepts of Exponents, Integers, and Real Numbers

LEARNER OUTCOMES

After reading this chapter and engaging in the embedded activities and reflections, you should be able to:

22.1 Describe strategies to meaningfully engage students in understanding exponents, order of operations, scientific notation, and very large and very small numbers.

22.2 Compare quantity and number line visuals for teaching integers, and contrast the different contexts for teaching about positive and negative numbers.

22.3 Illustrate and explain conceptual approaches to teaching operations with positive and negative numbers.

22.4 Construct a visual that illustrates the relationships among different types of numbers (irrational, whole, etc.) and describe conceptual ways to introduce irrational numbers.

In elementary school, students explore whole numbers and positive fractions and decimals; in middle school students explore an expanded number system and learn new ways to represent numbers, including scientific and exponential notation, negative numbers, and irrational numbers. The ideas presented in this chapter build on ideas that have been developed throughout this book. Exponents are used in algebraic expressions and add to the operations. Scientific notation expands how large and small numbers are represented, building on place-value concepts. Integers move beyond the positive counting numbers to numbers less than 0 and therefore extend the number line (as well as operations) to include negative values. As students expand their knowledge of how to represent numbers and explore new types of numbers, it is important that the following big ideas are at the center of that instruction.

BIG IDEAS

- Our number system includes whole numbers, fractions, decimals, and integers, all of which are rational numbers. Every rational number can be expressed as a fraction.

- Integers are the negative and positive counting numbers and 0. Positive and negative numbers describe quantities having both magnitude and direction (e.g., temperature above or below zero).

- Exponential notation is a way to express repeated products of the same number. Specifically, powers of 10 express very large and very small numbers in an economical manner.

- Many numbers are not rational; the irrationals can be expressed only symbolically or approximately using a close rational number. Examples include $\sqrt{2} \approx 1.41421\ldots$ and $\pi \approx 3.14159$.

Exponents

As numbers in our increasingly technological world get very small or very large, expressing them in standard form can become cumbersome. Exponential notation is more efficient for conveying numeric or quantitative information. In the CCSS-M, exponents are first introduced in fifth grade related to powers of ten and place value. In sixth grade, students learn to write and evaluate numeric expressions involving whole-number exponents. In eighth grade, students work with radicals and integer exponents.

Exponents in Expressions and Equations

The "rules" of exponents may be confusing for students. For example, with only a rule-based background they may not remember whether you add or multiply the exponents when you raise a number to a given power. This is an indication that students lack a conceptual understanding of the operations and the notation. Students need to explore exponents with whole numbers before they use exponents with variables. By looking at whole-number exponents, they are able to notice patterns in solving problems and are able to generate (and understand) the "rules" of exponents themselves. A whole-number exponent is simply shorthand for repeated multiplication of a number times itself; for example, $3^4 = 3 \times 3 \times 3 \times 3$.

At first, symbols for exponents are abstract and unfamiliar and thereby require explicit attention. First, an exponent applies to its immediate base. For example, in the expression $2 + 5^3$, the exponent 3 applies only to the 5, so the expression is equal to $2 + (5 \times 5 \times 5)$. However, in the expression $(2 + 5)^3$, the 3 is an exponent of the quantity $2 + 5$ and is evaluated as $(2 + 5) \times (2 + 5) \times (2 + 5)$, or $7 \times 7 \times 7$. Notice that the process follows the order of operations. As with any topic, start with what is familiar and concrete. With exponents, this means beginning with exploring powers of 2 and 3—operations that can be represented geometrically.

CCSS **Standards for Mathematical Practice**
MP8. Look for and express regularity in repeated reasoning.

Minia knows that square animal pens are the most economical for the amount of area they provide (assuming straight sides). Can you provide a table for Minia that shows the areas of square pens that have between 4 meters and 10 meters of fence on each side?

Students may set up a table similar to the one in Figure 22.1, showing possible areas for the square pens with different side lengths.

Another way to explore exponents is to explore algebraic growing patterns involving squares and/or cubes. The classic Painted Cube Problem prepared on the Painted Cube Activity Page and illustrated in Figure 22.2 is an excellent way to explore squares and cubes. The painted cube is made up of centimeter cubes (called blocks here for clarity); each face of the cube is painted. As the painted cube grows, so does the size of each square face (excluding the edges), as well as the number of cubes hidden inside the large painted cube. In a $2 \times 2 \times 2$ painted cube, the faces are 2×2; in a $3 \times 3 \times 3$ painted cube the faces are 3×3. Note that although each face is 3×3, the outer cubes are corners, so that more sides

Side length	pen picture	equation	area
4 meters	4	$4 \times 4 = 4^2$	$16 \, m^2$
5 meters	5	$5 \times 5 = 5^2$	$25 \, m^2$
6 meters	6	$6 \times 6 = 6^2$	$36 \, m^2$
7 meters	7	$7 \times 7 = 7^2$	$49 \, m^2$
8 meters	8	$8 \times 8 = 8^2$	$64 \, m^2$
9 meters	9	$9 \times 9 = 9^2$	$81 \, m^2$
10 meters	10	$10 \times 10 = 10^2$	$100 \, m^2$

FIGURE 22.1 A student records possibilities for making a square pen.

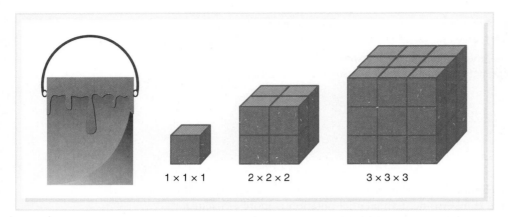

FIGURE 22.2 The Painted Cube Problem asks students to figure out how many sides of the little cubes are painted when the larger cubes are dipped in paint.

CCSS Standards for
Mathematical
Practice
MP1. Make sense of
problems and persevere
in solving them.

are painted, whereas the inner 2×2 square on each face is a centimeter cube with one side painted. Consider what is happening with the cubes in the middle of the painted cube. In a $2 \times 2 \times 2$ cube, there are no inside blocks; in the $3 \times 3 \times 3$ cube, there is a $1 \times 1 \times 1$ (1) "hidden" centimeter cube inside that will not be painted on any face. In a $4 \times 4 \times 4$, there will be $2 \times 2 \times 2$ (8) hidden cubes. As you can see the number of cubes with one side painted grows at a quadratic rate and the number of "hidden" cubes grows at a cubic rate. In exploring the pattern, students get experience with algebraic rules that are linear, squared, and cubed.

| MyLab Education   Activity Page: Painted Cube |

TECHNOLOGY Note. Exponential growth is very interesting to explore in real-world contexts. A powerful exploration of exponential growth is to look at Powers of 10 on the Florida State University Molecular Expressions website. This interactive starts way out in the Universe (10^{23}), then continues to zoom in until it reaches earth (with real screen shots, and ends with zooming in on cells to a quark at 10^{-14}. ■

Order of Operations

Working with exponents extends the *order of operations*. As early as third grade, students need to know the order of operations for addition, subtraction, multiplication, and division, and in sixth grade, exponents are added to the order of operations (NGA Center & CCSSO, 2010). An exponent indicates the number of times the base is used as a factor, so it indicates repeated multiplication and it precedes other multiplication and division, as well as addition and subtraction. In the expression $5 \times 4^2 - 6$, 4^2 is computed first. If multiplication is computed first, then the answer will be different. When we want to communicate that operations are to be computed in a different order, we have to use grouping symbols, such as parentheses.

Although the order of operations follows some convention (e.g., working from left to right, using parentheses), the order of the computations can be developed conceptually and is not as rigid as it is often portrayed (Bay-Williams & Martinie, 2015; Dupree, 2016). A context can make this point clearer, which is the focus of Activity 22.1.

Activity 22.1   CCSS-M: 3.OA.D.8; 6.EE.A.2c

Stacks of Coins

Select a story situation that includes such things as stacks of coins, bricks, or notebooks. If you have the book *Two of Everything* by Lily Hong (1993), you can show that the Haktaks' stacks of coins from their magic pot and use that as the context. Tell stories and ask students to (1) write an expression and (2) tell you how many. For example: "Mrs. Haktak had one stack with seven coins and four stacks with ten coins. How many coins did she have?" (Students should write $7 + 4 \times 10$ or $4 \times 10 + 7$ for the expression.) Ask "Could we write it either way? Why or why not?" and "Could we add the seven to the four and then multiply by 10? Why or why not?" Then write expressions with addition and multiplication and ask students to tell their own stories as they solve the problem.

⏸ Pause & Reflect

Simplify these two expressions:

(a) $12 - 2 \cdot 4 + 8 \cdot 3 - 12 + 8$

(b) $12 \cdot 15 \div 6$ ●

How did you solve the first? You may have first multiplied to get $12 - 8 + 24 - 12 + 8$. What did you do next? Dupree (2016) found that many teachers combined the opposites ($12 + {}^{-}12$ and -8 and 8) to simplifying, getting the answer of 24. This is efficient and correct, but notice it 'breaks' the order of operations. How about the second task? You might have thought of it as $\frac{12 \times 15}{6}$ and then divided first in order to have a simple computation of 2×15, which equals 30. The point is that the order of operations is not as rigid as it is sometimes interpreted and must be considered alongside of properties such as the commutative property, inverse operations, and the associate property.

Mnemonics *must not* replace an understanding of why the order of operations is what it is. The mnemonic **"P**lease **E**xcuse **M**y **D**ear **A**unt **S**ally," or more simply PEMDAS, has misled students into thinking multiplication precedes division and addition precedes subtraction (Ameis, 2011, Jeon, 2012). Rather than use this mnemonic, consider an improved version that involves writing the order in hierarchical levels (therefore avoiding the common errors students make):

CCSS Standards for Mathematical Practice
MP7. Look for and make use of structure.

P = parenthesis

E = exponents

MD = multiplication and division (whichever is first from left to right)

AS = addition and subtraction (whichever is first from left to right)

A visual can more effectively illustrate that multiplication and division are at the same level and addition and subtraction are at the same level (Ameis, 2011). Two such possible posters are pictured in Figure 22.3. Notice the pyramid has only three levels. These are the three categories of operations (parentheses are used to change the order so are referred to next to the triangle).

Another important point about the order of operation is that it is not as rigid as the list might imply. For example, consider the expression $14 \times 7 - 5 \times 7$. It doesn't matter which product is figured first, as long as multiplication precedes addition. In fact, the CCSS-M describes mathematically proficient students as students with the disposition to look closely at the structure of a problem—for example, noticing that in this example, they could apply the distributive property, factoring out a 7, so that they can first subtract $14 - 5$ and then multiply 7 by 9 (which can all be done mentally).

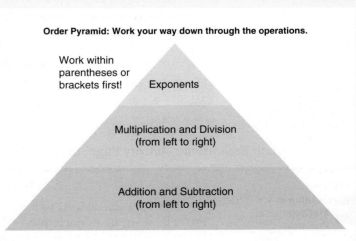

⏸ Pause & Reflect

How would you calculate: 13(5 + 10)? Would you apply the distributive property, then add 65 + 130, or would you work inside the parenthesis first, and then multiply 13 × 15? Is one way more efficient? ●

FIGURE 22.3 Two possible posters for illustrating the order of operations.

You can also strengthen students' understanding of order of operations by having them use appropriate symbols to record expressions, as in the next activity.

Activity 22.2

CCSS-M: 6.EE.A.2a, b, c; 6.EE.B.6

Guess My Number

ENGLISH LEARNERS

In this activity, you will give hints about a number and students will think backwards to find it (by using logical reasoning). For ELs and students with disabilities, provide the statements in writing and verbally. Students create equations, using parentheses appropriately to reflect the clues you give, as in the following three examples:

- I am thinking of a number; I add 5, double it, and get 22. $[(n + 5) \times 2 = 22]$
- I am thinking of a number; I subtract 2, square it, and get 36. $[(n - 2)^2 = 36]$
- I am thinking of a number; I double it, add 2, cube it, and get 1000. $[(2n + 2)^3 = 1000]$

STUDENTS with SPECIAL NEEDS

For students with disabilities, you may want to start with a known number rather than an unknown number—for example, start with 5, square it, add 11, divide by 6. They should write $(5^2 + 11) \div 6 = n$.

FORMATIVE ASSESSMENT Notes. Give students an expression that includes all the operations and the use of parentheses—for example, $(4 + 2)^2 \times 2 \div 4$ —and ask them to write a matching story, using a context of their choice, to fit the expression. Having students write these stories in journals provides an excellent assessment of their understanding of the order of operations. As you review students' stories, see if the stories show students understanding that multiplication and division (and addition and subtraction) are equal in the hierarchy of order and should therefore be solved left to right. ■

Another way to engage students or assess their understanding of exponents and order of operations is to have them determine if given equations are true or false. This is the focus of Activity 22.3.

Activity 22.3

CCSS-M: 3.OA.D.8; 6.EE.A.3; 6.EE.A.4

True or False Equations

Write an equation that addresses one or more aspects of the order of operations. For example, $24 \div (4 \times 2) = 24 \div 4 \times 2$. If students think that multiplication comes before division, or if they are not aware of the left-to-right prioritizing, they will write "true." Hand out Order of Operations: True or False Equation Activity Page or use examples (appropriate to the grade level) such as:

$17 \times 3 = 15 + 2 \times 3$

$2 + 5^3 = 7^3$

$3.2^2 + 3.2^2 = 3.2^4$

$4(2 + x) = 8 + 4x$

$4y - y = 4$

$3.2 - 1.2 + 0.04 = (3.2 - 1.2) + 0.04$

$(3.6 + 0.4)^2 = 4^2$

$6 \cdot 2^4 = 12^4$

$x + x^2 = x^3$

$3z + z = z + z + z + z$

MyLab Education **Activity Page: Order of Operations: True or False Equation**

Standards for Mathematical Practice

MP3. Construct viable arguments and critique the reasoning of others.

There are several ways to incorporate true/false equations into instruction. First, one or two of these equations can be part of a daily warm-up routine. Second, equations can be written on cards and partners can work together. Both partners think of the answer, one student says true or false, and the partner agrees or disagrees. If the partners disagree, they try to convince each other of the correct responses. They create a stack of their true equations and a stack of their false equations. When you check each group's progress, you can formatively assess by seeing if the cards in the true and false piles are correct.

True-false tasks set up an excellent opportunity for students to debate, justify, and critique the justifications of their peers. True-false statements can uncover and address commonly misunderstood aspects of the order of operation. Such tasks make explicit what misconceptions students might have (for example, that multiplication always precedes division).

Exploring Exponents on the Calculator

Calculators are a powerful tool for exploring impact of operations. For example, to evaluate 3^8, press 3 $\times$ =======. (The first press of = will result in 9, or 3 $\times$ 3.) Students will be fascinated by how quickly numbers grow. Enter any number, press $\times$, and then repeatedly press = . Try two-digit numbers. Try 0.1. Calculators designed for middle grades often use algebraic logic (follow the order of operations) and include parenthesis keys so that both $3 + 2 \times 7$ and $(3 + 2) \times 7$ result in the correct answer of 17. Basic calculators, however, will often calculate in the order the values are entered, in this case adding 3 plus 2 first and getting an answer of 35. The fact that calculators are programmed differently can be an investigation in and of itself, but is certainly something students need to know about their own calculator so that they enter expressions correctly.

Standards for
Mathematical
Practice
MP5. Use appropriate tools strategically.

Activity 22.4   CCSS-M: 6.EE.A.3; 6.EE.A.4

Entering Expressions

Provide students with Simplify Expressions Using Technology Activity Page, which includes pairs of numeric expressions like these:

1	$3 + 4 \times 8$	$4 \times 8 + 3$
2	$3 + 5^2$	$(3 + 5)^2$
3	$2^4 - 15 + 8$	$2^4 - (15 + 8)$

If students are using a basic calculator, they will find that they need to enter the numbers and operations differently than if they are using a scientific calculator. Ask, "How will you enter these expressions to preserve the order of operations?" Listen to suggestions and record them on the board. Have students work individually on the first few. Then have them pair-compare with someone else. Revisit the question of how they must enter the expressions. Have students continue to solve the rest of the problem set, and again compare results with their peers.

MyLab Education   **Activity Page: Simplify Expressions Using Technology**

A common misconception with exponents is to think of the two values as factors, so 5^3 is thought of as 5×3, rather than the correct equivalent expression of $5 \times 5 \times 5$. This is further problematic when students hear things like "It is five three times," since the word "times" indicates multiplication. Avoid confusing language and spend significant time having students state and write the equivalent expressions. Students should write equivalent expressions without exponents or include parentheses to indicate explicit groupings. For example:

$$(7 \times 2^3 - 5)^3 = (7 \times (2 \times 2 \times 2) - 5) \times (7 \times (2 \times 2 \times 2) - 5) \times (7 \times (2 \times 2 \times 2) - 5)$$

$$= ((7 \times 8) - 5) \times ((7 \times 8) - 5) \times ((7 \times 8) - 5)$$

$$= (56 - 5) \times (56 - 5) \times (56 - 5)$$

$$= 51 \times 51 \times 51$$

For many expressions, there is more than one way to proceed, and sharing different ways is important. Activity 22.3 "True or False Equations" can be adapted to focus on equivalence of simplified and expanded forms.

CCSS Standards for
Mathematical
Practice
MP7. Look for and make
use of structure.

Even though calculators with algebraic logic will automatically produce correct results (i.e., follow the order of operations), students must know the order of operations, including when they have to do one operation before another, and when it doesn't matter which goes first. This flexibility and awareness become the foundation for symbolic manipulation in algebra.

Integer Exponents

What does 2^{-4} mean? This is a good question to ask students who have been working with positive exponents. The following two related options can help students explore the possibilities of negative exponents. First, looking for patterns as the power of 10 changes directly relates to place value and helps students see the regularity in the base 10 system.

Ask students to continue the pattern of 10^n as follows:

$$10^4 = 10,000$$
$$10^3 = 1000$$
$$10^2 = 100$$
$$10^1 = 10$$
$$10^0 = ?$$
$$10^{-1} = ?$$

CCSS Standards for
Mathematical
Practice
MP8. Look for and express
regularity in repeated
reasoning.

To continue the pattern, 10^0 would be 1, which it is! (This is the definition of 10^0, in fact any number to the zero power is 1). The next value would be one-tenth of 1. And each successive number is one-tenth of the one that comes before it:

$$10^{-1} = 0.1 = \frac{1}{10}$$
$$10^{-2} = 0.01 = \frac{1}{100} = \frac{1}{10^2}$$
$$10^{-3} = 0.001 = \frac{1}{1000} = \frac{1}{10^3}$$

Students may notice that the negative exponent is the reciprocal of the value it would be without the negative sign.

 TECHNOLOGY Note. Students can explore negative exponents on a calculator. For example, ask students to figure out what 4^{-3} or 2^{-5} equal. If the calculator has the decimal-to-fraction conversion function, suggest that students use that feature to help develop the meaning of negative exponents. Figure 22.4 gives an example of how this might look on a graphing calculator. Ask students to notice patterns that they think can be generalized and to test their conjectures. ■

Students often confuse exponent rules. Identifying a mistake in someone else's work (i.e., a worked example) is another effective way to help students think about the correct (and incorrect) order in a problem, as illustrated in Activity 22.5.

Activity 22.5   CCSS-M: 8.EE.A.1

Find the Error

Distribute a copy of the Find the Error Activity Page for each student, or create your own set of worked examples that are solved incorrectly. Ask students to explain what the student did wrong and how to simplify it correctly. Two examples are provided here:

Wilma: $\dfrac{20x^8}{5x^2} = 4X^4$ *Yoli:* $3^3 \times 3^{-5} = 3^{-2} = -9$

Examples can be increasingly more challenging and can be mixed with correct solutions. For additional examples, see Johnson and Thompson (2009).

MyLab Education   Activity Page: Find the Error

Scientific Notation

The more common it becomes to find very large or very small numbers in our daily lives, the more important it is to have convenient ways to represent them. Numbers can be written in common form, but when this becomes cumbersome a better option is scientific notation. In the CCSS, scientific notation is an eighth-grade expectation within the domain of Expressions and Equations (NGA Center & CCSSO, 2010). Scientific notation means a number is changed to be the product of a number greater than or equal to 1 and less than 10 multiplied by a power of 10. For example, 3,414,000,000 can also be written as 3.414×10^9.

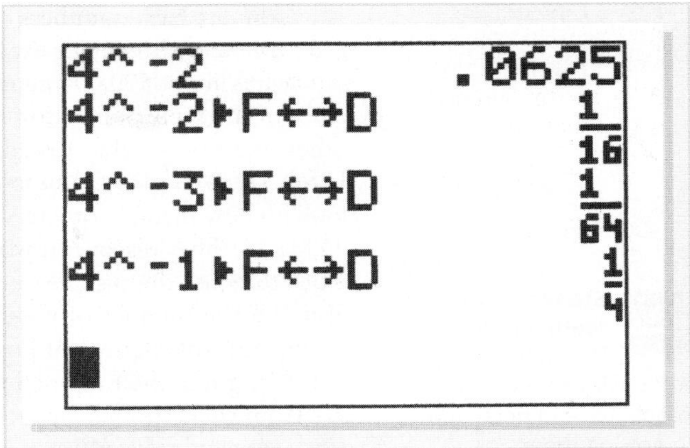

Different notations have different purposes and values. For example, the population of the world on 6/24/17 was estimated to be 7,513,768,345 (U.S. Census Bureau, n.d.) (You can go to the go to the U.S. Census Bureau Population Clock to get actual data for the day/minute you do this activity). This can be expressed in various ways:

7,513 million

7.5×10^9

About 7.5 billion

Each way of stating the number has value and purpose in different contexts. Rather than spend time with exercises converting numbers from standard form to scientific notation, consider large numbers found in newspapers, magazines, and atlases. How are they written? How are they said aloud? When are they rounded and why? What forms of the numbers seem best for the purposes? What level of precision is appropriate for the situation? And how do these numbers relate to other numbers? How does the population of the world relate to the population in your state or your continent?

FIGURE 22.4 Graphing calculators evaluate expressions as decimals. This figure shows the screen of a TI-73 calculator. The F-D key converts fractions to decimals as shown here.

TECHNOLOGY Note. U.S. Census Bureau (and other sites) makes population data readily available. The NCTM Illuminations lesson titled "The Next Billion" provides a high-quality lesson for exploring when the world population will reach 8 billion. Students discuss their predictions, past trends in population growth, and social factors—a good interdisciplinary opportunity. ■

Contexts for Very Large Numbers. The real world is full of very large quantities and measures. We see references to huge numbers in the media all the time. Unfortunately, most of us have not developed an appreciation for extremely large numbers, such as the following examples:

* Exploring lottery combinations and then probabilities can help students understand social justice issues using mathematics (Lim, Rubel, Shookhoff, Sullivan, & Williams, 2016). A state lottery with 40 numbers has $40 \times 39 \times 38 \times 37 \times 36 \times 35$ possible ways in which the balls could come out of the hopper (2,763,633,600). But the order is not important, so we divide by the different arrangements of 6 numbers ($6 \times 5 \times 4 \times 3 \times 2 \times 1 = 720$), and that equals 3,838,380 possible lottery numbers (about 4 million possibilities).
* The estimated size of the universe is 40 billion light-years. One light-year is the number of miles light travels in one year. The speed of light is 186,281.7 miles per second, or 16,094,738,880 miles in a single day.
* The human body has about 100 billion cells.
* The distance to the sun is about 150 million kilometers.
* The population of the world (various population estimates can be found by seeking out worldometers on the Internet.)

Connect large numbers to meaningful points of reference to help students get an idea of their true magnitude. For example, suppose students determine that the population in their city or town is about 500,000 people. They can then figure that it would take approximately 15,000 cities of the same population size to generate the population of the world (This raises a host of other questions—what would that list look like? Are there that many cities of that size in the U.S.? The World?). Or suppose students want to make sense of the distance to the sun. They look up how many kilometers it is from San Francisco, California, to Washington, D.C. (about 4600 km). They discover it would take more than 32,000 trips back and forth between these two cities to equal the distance between the earth and the sun. Lim et al. (2016) helped students visualize the number of possible combinations in the New York lottery (about 4 million) by having students figure out how tall a stack of pennies (1.52 mm each) would be and relate that to the height of the Empire State Building. The result was 14 Empire State Buildings tall! Building from such familiar or meaningful reference points helps students develop benchmarks to work with and make sense of large numbers, and better understand the world in which they live.

Standards for Mathematical Practice

MP1. Make sense of problems and persevere in solving them.

The following activity uses real data to develop an understanding of scientific notation and the relative size of numbers.

Activity 22.6

CCSS-M: 8.EE.A.4

How Far Away from the Sun?

ENGLISH LEARNERS

Use the How Far Away? Activity Page (or have students look online for the data).

Mercury	57,909,000	Jupiter	778,400,000
Venus	108,200,000	Saturn	1,423,600,000
Earth	149,600,000	Uranus	2,867,000,000
Mars	227,940,000	Neptune	4,488,400,000

Explain to students that they are going to compare planetary distances from the sun (in km), record the data in scientific notation, and create a scaled illustration of the distances. Encourage students to develop strategies to figure out the relative distance between two planets.

Distribute give a long strip of adding machine paper to each group and have the students mark the sun on one end and Neptune on the other, locating the other planets in their relative distance from the sun. For ELs, reinforce the names of thousands, millions, and billions. (Note: billion can mean one million millions in some countries, not one thousand millions as it does in the United States.)

MyLab Education **Activity Page: How Far Away?**

Standards for Mathematical Practice

MP8. Look for and express regularity in repeated reasoning.

A common error students make when converting between scientific notation and large numbers is to think the exponent tells the numbers of zeros to add onto the number (rather than the number of places the decimal moves). Avoid giving students short cuts that don't make sense to them, and explore enough examples that students make the distinction between adding zeros and moving the decimal place (and how this connects to multiples to 10).

Contexts for Very Small Numbers. It is also important to use real examples of very small numbers. As with large numbers, connecting very small numbers to points of reference can help students conceptualize how tiny these numbers really are, as shown by the following real-world examples:

- The chance of winning the lottery. Continuing the example above, there is a 0.00000026 or $\frac{26}{100,000,000}$ or 2.6×10^{-7} chance of winning.
- The length of a DNA strand in a cell is about 10^{-7} m. This is also measured as 1000 angstroms. (Based on this information, how long is an angstrom?) For perspective, the diameter of a human hair is about 2.54×10^{-5} m.

- Human hair grows at the rate of 10^{-8} miles per hour.
- Garden snails have been clocked at about 3×10^{-2} mph.
- The mass of one atom of hydrogen is 0.000 000 000 000 000 000 000 001 675 g. The mass of one paper clip is about 1 g.
- Sound takes 0.28 second (2.8×10^{-1}) to travel the length of a football field. In contrast, a TV signal travels a full mile in about 0.000005368 second, or 5.3×10^{-6} second. A TV viewer at home hears the football being kicked before the receiver on the field does.

Finding real data that are very, very small or very, very large can build meaning of small and large numbers *and* insights into the world.

Activity 22.7   CCSS-M: 8.EE.A.4

At a Snail's Pace

The speed of garden snails have been clocked at about 3×10^{-2} mph. Ask students to estimate how long it will take a snail to travel 1 mile. To explore, have them record the decimal equivalent of 3×10^{-2} (0.03). They can use the calculator's counting function (enter .03 + .03 =). On many calculators, when you hit = repeatedly, the calculator counts by the last value entered (.03). Each = represents 1 hour. Ask students to count or use other strategies to determine the time it will take the snail to go 1 mile. Share solutions and strategies.

Extend this investigation by repeating the problem, but for a snail moving at a rate of 3×10^{-3}. Students should conclude that it will take the snail ten times longer.

Scientific Notation on the Calculator. Students may learn how to multiply by 10, by 100, and by 1000 by simply moving the decimal point. Help students expand this idea by examining powers of 10 on a calculator that handles exponents. Students need to become familiar with the power-of-ten expressions in written forms and the calculator form. For example, on some calculators, the product of 45,000,000 × 8,000,000 is displayed as 3.6E14, meaning 3.6×10^{14}, or 360,000,000,000,000 (360 trillion).

Activity 22.8   CCSS-M: 8.EE.A.3

Exploring Powers of 10

Have students use Exploring Powers of 10 Activity Page and any calculator that permits entering exponents to explore powers of 10 using the calculator. Questions from the Activity page include:

- Explore 10^n for various values of *n*. What patterns do you notice? What does 1E15 mean? (1E15 is the typical calculator form of 1×10^{15}.) What does 1E–09 mean?
- What can you find out about adding numbers written in scientific notation, such as $(4.5 \times 10^n) + (27 \times 10^k)$? What about multiplying numbers?

MyLab Education   Activity Page: Exploring Powers of 10

Operations with Scientific Notation. The goal of doing operations with scientific notation is that students understand how to use both expanded form and scientific notations and *can select the form* that lends to efficiently solving the problem. For example, compare these two multiplication problems:

$$30,000,000 \times 900,000 \qquad 3 \times 10^7 \times 9 \times 10^5$$

The answer is 27×10^{12} or 2.7×10^{13}. In this case either form can be done mentally. If a problem is presented in scientific notation, students need to be able to understand the structure.

Standards for Mathematical Practice

MP7. Look for and make use of structure.

For example $(4.5 \times 10^7) \times (8 \times 10^6)$ can be solved mentally by multiplying 4.5×8, which equals 36 and then multiplying $10^7 + 10^6$, which equals 10^{13}. Combining these products, the total is 36×10^{13} or 3.6×10^{14}. Writing each of these out in expanded notation is not efficient.

> **MyLab Education**   **Self-Check 22.1**

Positive and Negative Numbers

Every day, students have interactions with numbers less than 0, as shown in the following list:

    Temperature

    Altitude (above and below sea level)

    Golf (above and below par)

    Money

    Timelines (including B.C.)

    Football yardage (gains/losses)

Generally, negative numbers are introduced with integers—the whole numbers and their negatives or opposites—instead of with fractions or decimals. However, it is a mistake to only focus on integer values, because students must understand where numbers like $^-4.5$ and $^-1\frac{1}{4}$ are positioned on the number line in relation to integer values. In fact, because noninteger negative numbers are not addressed adequately in middle school, many students cannot accurately locate noninteger negative numbers on the number line, for example, placing $^-1\frac{1}{4}$ between $^-1$ and 0 instead of between $^-2$ and $^-1$ because they are used to having mixed numbers located to the right of the whole number. In the CCSS-M, positive and negative numbers are introduced and developed in sixth grade, and in seventh grade students "Solve multi-step real-life and mathematical problems posed with positive and negative rational numbers in any form (whole numbers, fractions, and decimals), using tools strategically" (p. 49). But students may encounter and make sense of integers at a much younger age.

    Learning about negative numbers is developmental, just as any topic. Initially, students may ignore the negative sign (minus sign), but through experiences students formalize their understanding of negative numbers, seeing the number line as symmetric around 0 (Bofferding, 2014). Looking for and making use of underlying structures to reason about positive and negative numbers is important in supporting students' understanding of integers and integer operations (Bishop et al., 2014). For example, students need opportunities to make sense of situations new to them, such as subtracting more than are there (e.g., $5 - 8$), and recognizing that some generalizations they have constructed or been told (e.g., that addition always makes larger) are not always true (Bishop et al., 2014; Karp, Bush, & Dougherty, 2014).

Standards for Mathematical Practice

MP1. Make sense of problems and persevere in solving them.

Contexts for Exploring Positive and Negative Numbers

As with any new topic or type of number, it is important to start with familiar contexts so that students can use prior knowledge to build meaning. With integers, students are often not sure which direction they are moving when they compute, so having a context is particularly important. For many students, in particular ELs, it is important to include visuals with the contexts to support language development (Swanson, 2010). As students learn to compare and compute, they can use the contexts to ground their thinking and justify their answers. In CCSS-M, grade 6, students must "Understand that positive and negative numbers are used together to describe quantities having opposite directions or values (e.g., temperature above/below zero, elevation above/below sea level, credits/debits, positive/negative electric charge); use positive and negative numbers to represent quantities in real-world contexts, explaining the meaning of 0 in each situation" (p. 43).

Standards for Mathematical Practice

MP2. Reason abstractly and quantitatively.

Quantity Contexts. Quantity contexts provide an opportunity for students to match opposites (4 and ⁻4) to equal zero. Quantity contexts can be illustrated with two-color counters or other counting objects.

Golf Scores. In golf, scores are often written in relationship to a number considered par for the course. So, if par for the course is 70, a golfer who ends the day at 67 has a score of ⁻3, or 3 strokes under par. Consider a player in a four-day tournament with day-end scores of ⁺5, ⁻2, ⁻3, ⁺1. What would be his or her final result for the tournament? How did you think about it? You could match up the positive and the negatives (in this case, ⁺5 with ⁻2 and ⁻3 to get a net score of 0), and then see what is left (in this case, ⁺1). The notion that opposites (5 and ⁻5) equal zero is an important concept in teaching of positive and negative numbers. You can post a mixed-up leaderboard of golf scores and ask students to order the players from first through tenth place. Emphasize that first place is the *lowest* score—and therefore the *smallest* number.

Item	Payments or Deposits	Balance
Mowing lawn	+12.00	$34.00
Phone bill	−55.00	−21.00
iTunes downloads	−9.00	−30.00
Paycheck	+120.00	90.00

FIGURE 22.5 A checkbook as a context for adding and subtracting positive and negative numbers.

Money: Payments and Deposits. Suppose that you have a bank account. At any time, your records show how many dollars are in your account. The difference between the payments and deposit totals tells the amount of money in the account. If there is more money deposited than paid out, the account has a positive balance, or is "in the black." If there are more payments than deposits, the account is in debt, showing a negative cash value, or is "in the red." This is a good context for exploring addition and subtraction, as in the example illustrated in Figure 22.5. Net worth is a similar way to look at positive and negative numbers (assets and debts). Considering the net worth of famous people can engage students in making sense of positive and negative numbers (Stephan, 2009) and students can successfully draw on their experiences with assets, debts, and net worth values to create meaning for integer addition and subtraction involving positive and negative numbers (Stephan & Akyuz, 2012).

Activity 22.9   CCSS-M: 6.NS.C.5

What Is Her Net Worth?

On the Internet, look up the net worth of someone interesting to your students (e.g., a singer, athlete, or actor). Make up two to three assets and two to three debts, and ask your students to figure out her net worth. Then, with the students, look up the net worth of other people of their choice. Have them suggest possible assets and debts for that person. One clever way to do this is to have a net worth page filled out with two to three assets and two to three debts, but a smudge on the paper so that all students can see is the net worth (Stephan, 2009). This visual is particularly important for students with disabilities because they can see the missing value in a real situation.

STUDENTS with SPECIAL NEEDS

Eventually debts can be represented as negative values, and a connection is made to integer addition and subtraction.

Linear Contexts. Many of the real contexts for negative numbers are linear. The number line provides a good tool for understanding the ordering of negative numbers and can support reasoning in doing operations with positive and negative numbers (Bishop et al., 2014). CCSS-M emphasizes the need for sixth graders to be able to represent integers on a number line as well as a coordinate axis (NGA Center & CCSSO, 2010). See the Math Goodies website for a good introduction to integers on a number line.

Temperature. The "number line" measuring temperature is vertical. This context demonstrating negative numbers may be the most familiar to students, because they have either experienced temperatures below zero or know about temperatures at the North or South Pole. A good starting activity for students is finding where various temperatures belong on a thermometer. For example, Figure 22.6 displays a thermometer marked in increments of five degrees, and students

FIGURE 22.6   Thermometers provide an excellent tool for exploring positive and negative numbers.

are asked to place on the number line the following temperatures from a week in North Dakota: 8°, ⁻2°, ⁻12°, 4°, ⁻8°. Ask students to order the temperatures from the coldest to the warmest (least to greatest). Temperatures as a context have the advantage that you can also use fractional and decimal values.

Altitude. Another vertical number line model, altitude, is also a good context for positive and negative numbers. The altitudes of sites below sea level are negative, such as the town of Dead Sea, Israel (with an altitude of ⁻1371 feet), and Badwater, California, in Death Valley (which has an altitude of ⁻282 feet). Positive values for altitude include Mount McKinley (the tallest mountain in North America) at 20,322 feet. Students can order the altitudes of various places around the world (data easily found through the Internet) or find the difference between the altitudes of two different places—a good context for subtraction of integers (interpreting subtraction as *difference* rather than as take-away).

Timelines. Asking students to place historical events on a timeline is an excellent interdisciplinary opportunity. The timeline is useful for examples with larger values (e.g., 1950) as well as negative values (e.g., ⁻3000 or 3000 B.C.). Or students can explore their own personal timeline (Weidemann, Mikovch, & Hunt, 2001), in which students find out key events that happened before they were born (e.g., the birth of an older sibling) and have happened since they were born (e.g., the move to a new house). Students place these events on a number line with 0 representing the day they were born. By partitioning a year into months, students can gain experience with rational numbers (halves, fourths, or twelfths) on the number line. Continue to reinforce the connection to the size of numbers, asking students, "Which number (year) is less (earliest)?"

Football. A statistic reported on every play in a football game is yards gained and yards lost, which provides a good context for exploring integers, especially when it comes to comparing and adding integers. Students can be asked questions like these: "If the Steelers started their drive on the 20-yard line and the first three plays were recorded as ⁻4, ⁺9, ⁺3, did they get a first down?" or "On the Ravens' first play, the yardage is ⁻4. Where are they in relation to the line of scrimmage (using negatives, if behind the line of scrimmage, in this case ⁻4), and where are they in relation to the first down marker (⁻14)?"

Activity 22.10

CCSS-M: 6.NS.C.5; 6.NS.C.6a

Football Statistics

ENGLISH LEARNERS

Look up the average yards gained for some of the best running backs in the NFL or from college teams popular with your students. Ask students to use average yards gained per down to create a possible list of yardage gains and losses for each player. For example, if a player had an average of 4 yards per carry in a game, the following could have been his data:

10, ⁻3, ⁻2, 21, ⁻5, 3, ⁻1, 5, ⁻1, 13

You may want to do one like this together and then have students create their own. The football context provides an excellent way to use integers meaningfully, integrated with the important concept of averages. ELs may not be familiar with American football, because football in most countries is what is called soccer in the United States. Role playing the game with students is a fun way to be sure the game is understood by all. Also, a yard is a U.S. measurement that may not be familiar and could be confused with the other meaning of yard. Comparing a yard to a meter can provide a point of reference that will help build meaning for this activity.

Meaning of Negative Numbers

Negative numbers are defined in relation to their positive counterparts. For example, the definition of negative 3 is the solution to the equation $3 + ? = 0$. In general, the *opposite of n* is the solution to $n + ? = 0$. If n is a positive number, the *opposite of n* is a negative number. The set of integers, therefore, consists of the positive whole numbers, the opposites of the whole numbers (or negative integers), and 0, which is neither positive nor negative.

Absolute Value. Absolute value is introduced in sixth grade in the CCSS-M. The *absolute value of a number* is defined as the distance between that number and zero. Knowing the distance between two points, either on a number line or on a plane, is often needed in applications of mathematics. For example, we need to be able to determine how far a helicopter is from a hospital, regardless of its direction. The notation for absolute value consists of two vertical bars on either side of the number. Thus, the absolute value of a number n is $|n|$. Opposites, such as $^-12$ and 12, are the same distance from zero, and therefore have the same absolute value.

When students' absolute value experiences are limited to simplifying expressions like $|^-8|$ or $|6 - 10|$ they do not connect the procedure with the meaning of absolute value or see real purpose for doing this. Add in a context to make it meaningful. For example, $|6 - 10|$ can be the distance between the 10-mile marker and the 6-mile marker. In this example, you can see that both $10 - 6$ or $6 - 10$ can lead to the answer, and distance is positive (absolute value), so the answer is 4.

Minus Sign Notation. Through their early years in school, students recognize the "$-$" sign to mean "subtract." They need a deeper understanding of other meanings of this symbol in order to solve equations and to make sense of variables (Lamb et al., 2012). There are three meanings of the minus symbol (Bofferding, 2014; Lamb et al., 2012). Each is illustrated with examples here:

> **CCSS** Standards for Mathematical Practice
> **MP6.** Attend to precision.

Subtraction: $25 - 12 = $ _____ or $9 - $ _____ $= 4.5$

Negative number: $25 + {}^-12 = $ _____ or $9 - $ _____ $= {}^-4.5$

The opposite of: $^-(^-5) = 5$ or ^-x

To further the challenge of the minus sign, it can switch meanings in the middle of simplifying an equation. For example, consider the equation $3.5 - x = {}^-0.6$. A step in simplifying might be to add $^-3.5$ to both sides, leaving $^-x = {}^-4.1$. Here, the equation reads, "The opposite of x is equal to negative 4.1 (or the opposite of 4.1)." The different heights at which the negative sign may appear (e.g., -7 and $^-7$) may also be confusing. Parentheses are placed around the number so that it is separate from the operation—for example, $8 - (^-5)$. Students have not seen parentheses used in this way and may think they should multiply. It is important to connect to their prior knowledge and explicitly build meaning for the new use of the minus sign and parentheses. The following activity, based on Lamb and colleagues (2012), is designed to do this.

Activity 22.11

CCSS-M: 6.NS.C.5; 6.NS.C.6a

Greater, Less, Equal, or Don't Know?

ENGLISH LEARNERS

Use the Greater, Less, Equal or Don't Know Activity Page or write an equation on the board that addresses different meanings of the minus symbol and/or parentheses. Have students vote on whether it is equal or not equal. Encourage students to work with a partner to prepare a rationale for whether they think it is equal or not equal. Facilitate a debate, as appropriate. Examples include:

$$2-(^-3) \text{_____} 1 \qquad ^-x \text{_____} x \qquad ^-(^-8) \text{_____} 8$$

In this case, you might ask students, "When do we use parentheses in mathematics?" Students might say they are used for grouping a series of computations to show what to do first and that it can also mean multiplication. Point out that parentheses are also used to make a number sentence more readable—separating the negative number from the operation. ELs may benefit from additional vocabulary support with words such as minus, negative, and opposite. Pointing and saying the words as a class can help all students learn the appropriate terminology. Also, not all countries use the same notations; if you see different ways of notating expressions invite students to share their notations and compare them.

MyLab Education   Activity Page: Greater, Less, Equal, or Don't Know

Tools for Illustrating Positive and Negative Numbers

Two tools, one denoted by quantity and the other by linear operations, are popular for helping students understand comparisons and the four operations (+, −, ×, and ÷) with negative and positive numbers. Counters can be used for integer values (counting numbers, including 0), and number lines are needed to illustrate positive and negative non-counting numbers.

Counters. Two-color counters are a great fit for showing positive and negative integers because one side (e.g., yellow) can represent positive counts and the other side (e.g., red) can represent negative counts. One counter of each type results in zero ($^+1 + {^-1} = 0$), illustrating that they are opposites. Consider money: If yellow counters are credits and red counters are debits, having 5 yellows and 7 reds is the same as having 2 reds or 2 debits and is represented as $^-2$ (see Figure 22.7). It is important for students to understand that it is always possible to add to or remove from a collection of any number of pairs consisting of one positive and one negative counter without changing the value (i.e., it is like adding equal quantities of debits and credits). Annenberg Learner's website has a nice teacher tutorial titled, "Colored-Chip Models," which teaches how to use chip counters to help explore concepts related to integer operations.

Number Lines. The number line is the second visual tool for modeling computation with negative numbers and it has a number of advantages. A number line:

1. Is familiar to students from their computation with whole numbers, fractions, and decimals
2. Is an excellent tool for representing the operations conceptually. To add a context, consider using small cutouts of grasshoppers that jump up and down the line (Swanson, 2010). Or, use your school's mascot! Students can see that as the grasshopper moves to the left it goes to smaller numbers and as it moves to the right it goes to larger numbers.
3. Shows the distance from 0 (or the absolute value of the number).
4. Allows students to explore noninteger negative and positive values (e.g., $^-4\frac{1}{4} + 3\frac{1}{3}$ or $^-9.2 - 4.5$), which is very difficult to do with counters.
5. Connects to the coordinate axis, which involves two perpendicular number lines.

Arrows can be used in operations with negative numbers to show distance and direction. For example, 4 can be modeled with an arrow 4 units long starting at any location on the number line and pointing to the right, and $^-3$ can be modeled with an arrow 3 units long starting at any location on the number line and pointing to the left (see Figure 22.8). The arrows help students think of integer quantities as directed distances. A positive arrow never points left, and a negative arrow never points right. Furthermore, each arrow is a quantity with both length (magnitude or absolute value) and direction (sign). These properties are constant for each arrow regardless of its position on the number line.

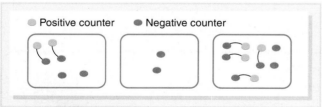

FIGURE 22.7 Each collection is a representation of $^-2$.

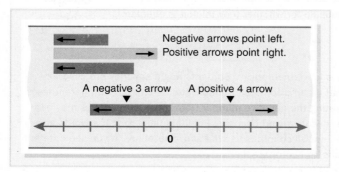

FIGURE 22.8 Number line visual for negative and positive numbers.

Which Tool to Use. Although the counters and the number line appear quite different, they are alike mathematically. Integers involve two concepts—magnitude and direction. Magnitude is modeled by the number of counters or the length of the arrows. Direction is represented as different colors or directions. Seeing how positive and negative numbers are represented across these two tools while making connections between the visuals can help students develop the intended concepts. The context should also decide the representation: if the context is height, the number line is a better fit.

MyLab Education   Self-Check 22.2

Operations with Positive and Negative Numbers

Once your students understand how integers are represented, in particular as numbers on the number line, they are ready to solve problems involving operations with negative numbers. Exploring operations with positive and negative numbers must not be about memorizing rules (e.g., when you see subtraction, change it to addition and change the sign of the second number). This approach is not effective and deprives students of the opportunity to reason quantitatively. As students extend their understanding of the operations to include negative numbers, they need opportunities to consider how underlying structures and generalizations of arithmetic might be applied with negative numbers (Bishop, Lamb, Philipp, Whitacre, & Schappelle, 2016a).

Standards for Mathematical Practice
MP7. Look for and make use of structure.

Addition and Subtraction

Introduce negative values using one of the contexts discussed earlier such as golf scores. Personalize the story by telling students that each weekend you golf a round on Saturday and on Sunday. The first weekend your results were $^+3$ and $^+5$, the next weekend you scored $^+3$ and $^-5$, and on the last weekend you scored $^-6$ and $^+2$. How successful was your game each weekend? Overall? Because this is a quantity model, counters are a good choice for modeling (though number lines can also be used). A linear context could be used with football yards gained and lost on two plays.

Conversely, ask students to create their own stories for integer operations. One way to scaffold this is to ask students three prompts (Swanson, 2010):

Where did you start?

How far did you go?

Where are you now?

So, for $^-3 - 5 = ?$, a student might write, "I was 3 feet under water, then dove down 5 feet. Where am I now?" ($^-8$)

Contexts are an important place to begin, but students also need to be able to reason about the numbers themselves, and draw on their experiences and understanding of addition and subtraction. Rather than tell students a rule for solving, pose open number sentences involving negative numbers and ask students what they think the answer might be. Examples include:

$$5 - 11 = n \qquad ^-7 + 12 = n \qquad ^-3 + n = 7$$

Standards for Mathematical Practice
MP1. Make sense of problems and persevere in solving them.

Bishop and colleagues (2016b) found that students could apply their understandings of the structure of numbers and the meaning of addition and subtraction. A student might reason about the first example thinking they are going down and therefore the answer is $^-6$ and reason that they start at $^-7$ on the number line and *go up* 12 to 5. Another student might apply the commutative property, changing the equation (mentally) to $12 + ^-7 = n$ and then reason that they *go down* 7 to 5. Students use *logical necessity*, meaning they use familiar mathematical principles and ideas (e.g., commutativity and inverses) to make logical inferences and deductions to solve integer arithmetic tasks (Bishop et al. 2016b). These researchers suggest asking questions that help students focus on the structure of numbers, such as:

Standards for Mathematical Practice
MP1. Make sense of problems and persevere in solving them.

- How do these two problems compare? (e.g., $^-4 + 5 = n$ and $^-4 - 5 = n$)
- How might you explain to a younger student why you can change that equation (e.g., $7 - ^-3 = n$ to $7 + 3 = n$).
- How does knowing $5 + 4$ help you think about $5 + ^-4$?
- I see that you counted up for this problem, why did you count up (and not back)? (e.g., $^-9 - ^-3$ (correct to count up) or $^-9 - 3$ (incorrect to count up)

Contrast this approach that builds on students' understanding of the operations and on the structures of numbers, compared to telling students, "When you see subtraction, change it to addition and change the sign of the second number . . . " While these rules take less time to teach, they rob students of the opportunity to understand negative numbers, making it impossible for them to determine if an answer is reasonable or for them to apply mental, logical strategies for arithmetic involving negative numbers.

A focus on opposites can help students understand addition and subtraction. Activity 22.12 provides an excellent way to explore integers quantitatively with a focus on using opposites as they think about integer addition (Friedmann, 2008).

MyLab Education **Video Example 22.1**

This video shows how use counters to illustrate subtraction involving integers with a focus on using opposites.

Activity 22.12

CCSS-M: 7.NS.1a, b, c

STUDENTS with SPECIAL NEEDS

Find the Zero

Before beginning the activity, ask students to tell you the sums of several opposites (e.g., 4 + ⁻4). Distribute the Find the Zero Activity Page. Then, ask students to look at a sum that is not opposites (e.g., 7 + ⁻4) and ask if they can find a zero by decomposing one of the numbers (e.g., (3 + 4) + ⁻4) and solve. Using a number line, students can find the difference between these numbers. Students, particularly students with disabilities, may benefit from creating a zero box below each problem as they solve it, as illustrated below.

$$12 + {}^-5 =$$

Zero Box: $\boxed{5 + {}^-5}$

$$(7 + 5) + {}^-5 = 7 + (5 + {}^-5) = 7 + 0 = 7$$

Students must continue to illustrate what is happening when they are adding and subtracting negative numbers. If they do not, they will get lost in the symbols and which direction to head on the number line. See Expanded Lesson: Find the Zero for details on teaching this activity.

MyLab Education **Activity Page: Find the Zero**
MyLab Education **Expanded Lesson: Find the Zero**

Addition and subtraction can be modeled with counters or number lines (see Figure 22.9). Adding with counters utilizes the idea of adding opposites. Adding on the number line can also involve this idea, but can also just move to the negative values on the number line. To add using the number line model, note that each added arrow begins at the arrowhead end of the previous arrow.

MyLab Education **Video Example 22.2**

This video shows how to add integers on the number line and by finding zero pairs.

Subtraction can be interpreted as separate (take-away) or compare (the difference or distance between the values). An advantage to the number line model is that it can be used for both separate and comparison situations. Consider the problem ⁻5 − ⁺2, the second example modeled in Figure 22.10. If using a quantity model, the context could be money, such as, "I start with a debit of $5 and then withdraw (take out) $2 more from my account. What balance will my bank account show (if no fees have been charged yet for my overdrawn account)?" To model this problem, you start with the five red counters. To remove two positive counters from a set that has none, two neutral pairs (one positive, one negative) must be added so that two positive counters can be removed. Then, 2 positive counters (yellow) can be taken away. The net effect is to have a debt of $7 or ⁻7 (less money because $2 was taken away).

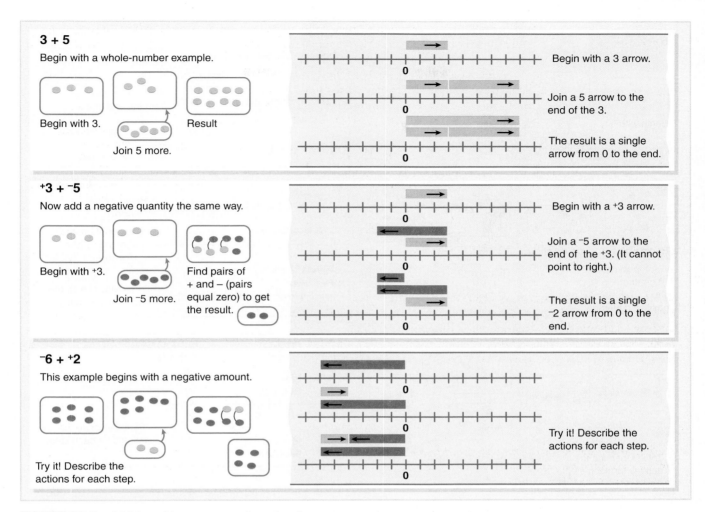

FIGURE 22.9   Addition with counters and number lines.

With the number line, subtraction can be illustrated using arrows for separate and comparison situations. Consider take-away as a way to think about the second example in Figure 22.10. Using temperature as a context, the explanation could be: "The day begins at 5° below zero. Then the temperature drops +2°, which means it just got colder and is now ⁻7°. The difficulty in the take-away thinking comes when trying to provide an authentic explanation of subtracting a negative value. Consider, for example, for ⁻4 − ⁻7 (see the third example in Figure 22.10). You start with taking away, but because it is negative temperature (or coldness) that is being taken away, you are in fact doing the opposite—warming up by 7 degrees. With the number line, you start at ⁻4, then reverse the arrow going left to one going right 7 moves.

Number lines can also be used for comparison or distance situations. For subtraction, this can make a lot more sense to students (Tillema, 2012). In this example, the comparison question is "What is the difference from ⁻7 to ⁻4?" In other words, how do you get from ⁻7 to ⁻4? You count up 3. Notice if this were written in reverse (⁻4 − ⁻7) it would be the difference from ⁻4 to ⁻7, still three, but the direction is to the left, so ⁻3.

⏸ Pause & Reflect

Try to explain the problems in Figures 22.9 and 22.10 using both a quantity and a linear context. For subtraction, explain each using a separate situation and a comparison situation. What kinds of stories or contexts might fit with these different ways to think about addition and subtraction? ●

A significant challenge for students is to connect visual representations to their symbolic computations. One way to help students is to ask them to notate basic number line illustrations

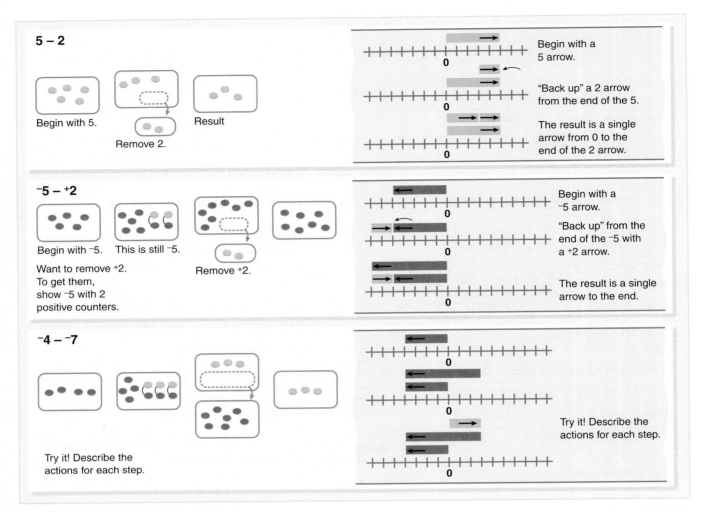

FIGURE 22.10   Subtraction illustrated with counters and a number line.

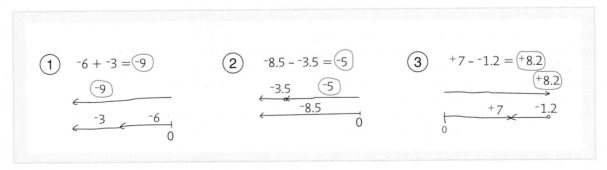

FIGURE 22.11   Students use arrow sketches to represent addition and subtraction.

CCSS   **Standards for Mathematical Practice**

MP4. Model with mathematics.

with their equations. Figure 22.11 illustrates how a student might draw arrows to represent addition and subtraction exercises. You can also have students write story situations as a third representation.

It is important for students to see that ⁺3 + ⁻5 is the same as ⁺3 − ⁺5 and that ⁺2 − ⁻6 is the same as ⁺2 + ⁺6. Illustrating addition and subtraction problems on the number line and explicitly discussing how the two expressions are related will help students see the connections between these expressions.

In seventh grade, students must learn to "Solve multi-step real-life and mathematical problems posed with positive and negative rational numbers in any form (whole numbers, fractions, and decimals), using tools strategically" (NGA Center & CCSSO, 2010, p. 49). The examples in this section have been limited to integers, but with the use of a ruler or any number line partitioned into fractional amounts, the same arrow illustrations can help students reason about rational number addition and subtraction.

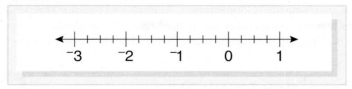

And, empty number lines can be used in the same way they were used with whole numbers, decimals, and fractions.

TECHNOLOGY Note. LearnZillion (https://learnzillion.com) has a number of quality video lessons that model the use of the number line and two-color counters/chips as representation tools for solving problems involving operations with positive and negative numbers (as well as many other topics!). ∎

Multiplication

Multiplication of integers is an extension of multiplication of whole numbers, fractions, and decimals. Just like with addition and subtraction, students need opportunities to apply their existing understanding of number and operations to consider how those structures apply to negative numbers. For example, students challenged to solve and make sense of $\frac{1}{2} \times {}^-6$, were able to use a number line model and apply their knowledge of fraction operations of positive numbers, dispelling one of the student's initial assumption that finding half should make the answer smaller (Carter, Prince, & Schwartz, 2017). These students thought of this problem as scaling. This makes sense because the first factor tells how many sets there are. This translates to integer multiplication quite readily when the first factor is positive, regardless of the sign of the second factor. The first example in Figure 22.12 illustrates a positive first factor and a negative second factor $(3 \times {}^-4)$, which translates into the question "If I have three groups of ${}^-4$, how much do I have?" With a context, options include: "If I lost four dollars three days in

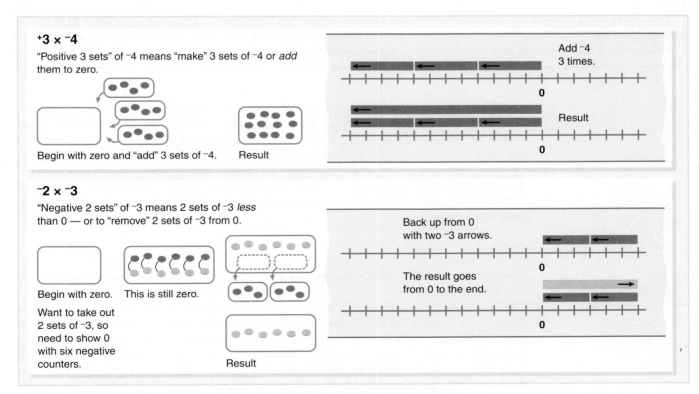

FIGURE 22.12 Multiplication by a positive first factor is repeated addition. Multiplication by a negative first factor is repeated subtraction.

Standards for Mathematical Practice

MP7. Look for and make use of structure.

a row, how much have I lost?"; "Three days in a row Hans scored ⁻4 in his golf tournament; what is his score?" or, "Three times today the temperature dropped four degrees. How much has the temperature changed?" Connecting to contexts and looking at repeated examples can lead to students creating conjectures about the "rules" for multiplying (and dividing) with negative numbers (Choppin, Clancy, & Koch, 2012). That is the focus of the next activity.

MyLab Education **Video Example 22.3**

This video illustrates how to use number lines and patterns to illustrate the meaning of multiplication involving negative numbers.

Activity 22.13 CCSS-M: 7.NS.A.2a, b

Creating Stories and Conjectures for Operations with Negative Numbers

ENGLISH LEARNERS

This activity is described here for multiplication but could be replicated for any of the operations with negative numbers. Ask students to make a conjecture about what they think the sign will be on a product of a positive factor times a negative factor. Ask students to predict what they think the sign of the answer will be. Discuss briefly or have students vote. Next, give students a set of multiplication problems with a positive times a negative (keep first factor a whole number to better see the pattern), such as:

$$3 \times {}^-10 = \qquad 5 \times -\tfrac{1}{4} = \qquad 8 \times {}^-0.5 =$$

Invite students to create the stories to match each of the equations. You can display a menu of contexts (see the list of contexts provided in the section above). After telling stories for each, ask students to make a generalization about a positive number times a negative number.

Repeat this process for a negative number times a positive number:

$$^-3 \times 4 = \qquad {}^-5 \times \tfrac{1}{2} = \qquad {}^-10 \times 0.25 =$$

Then ask students to revisit and revise (as needed) their conjectures regarding the product of a negative factor times a positive factor. Connect their conjectures to the contexts that were selected. If there are ELs in the class, you may select one context to explore, rather than several, to limit the unnecessary language demands.

What could the meaning be when the first factor is negative, as in ⁻2 × ⁻3? If a positive first factor means repeated addition (how many times added to 0), a negative first factor should mean repeated subtraction (how many times subtracted from 0). The second example in Figure 22.12 illustrates how multiplication with the first factor negative can be modeled.

TECHNOLOGY Note. The National Library of Virtual Manipulatives (NLVM) "Rectangle Multiplication of Integers" supports student understanding of multiplication with negative numbers. ■

Division

Connect division of negative numbers with what students know about multiplication. Recall that division with whole numbers has two possible meanings to two missing-factor expressions. The equation 4 × ? = 24 asks, "Four sets of what sized group equals twenty-four?," whereas the equation ? × 6 = 24 asks, "How many groups of six equal twenty-four?" The latter question (? × 6 = 24) is the one that fits well with thinking about negative values because it lends to skip counting to 24. The first example in Figure 22.13 illustrates how the two visual models (two-color counters and number line) work for whole numbers. Following that is an example in which the divisor is positive but the dividend is negative.

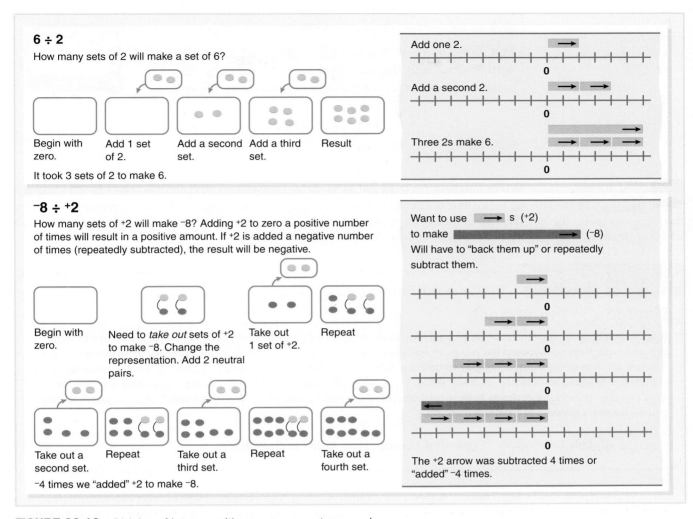

FIGURE 22.13 Division of integers with a measurement approach.

MyLab Education **Video Example 22.4**

This video illustrates how to use the meaning of multiplication involving negative numbers to understand multiplication involving negative numbers.

VIDEO EXAMPLE

⏸ Pause & Reflect

Try talking through examples and drawing pictures for $^-8 \div {}^+2$. Check your understanding with the examples in Figure 22.13. Now try $^+9 \div {}^-3$ and $^-12 \div {}^-4$. What contexts can fit these equations? ●

Understanding division with negatives numbers rests on a good conceptual understanding of multiplication problems in which the first factor is negative and knowledge of the relationship between multiplication and division. Encourage students to first think about how to visualize the whole-number situation and then connect that understanding to negative numbers. Extend these explorations to decimal and fraction values and continue to have students draw illustrations to accompany their equations.

MyLab Education **Self-Check 22.3**

MyLab Education **Application Exercise 22.1: Operations with Positive and Negative Numbers** Click the link to access this exercise, then watch the video and answer the accompanying questions.

 Real Numbers

 **Standards for Mathematical Practice**
MP7. Look for and make use of structure.

Whole numbers, fractions and decimals, and integers are all rational numbers because they can all be written as a fraction with an integer over a nonzero integer. An interesting fact is that there are infinitely many rational numbers between any two numbers. Exploring this idea can deepen students' understanding of rational numbers.

Activity 22.14   CCSS-M: 6.NS.C.5, 7.NS.A.2d

How Many in Between?

Post two fractions for students, such as $\frac{1}{2}$ and $\frac{9}{10}$. Ask students to locate those fractions on a number line, and then to insert four additional fractions *between* the two given fractions. Encourage students to use different strategies to reason about what fractions come in between. Students may convert one-half to five-tenths and readily find $\frac{6}{10}$, $\frac{7}{10}$, and $\frac{8}{10}$, but be challenged to find the fourth equivalence (there are many, e.g., $\frac{2}{3}$, $\frac{3}{4}$, $\frac{5}{6}$, $\frac{7}{8}$ and $\frac{8}{9}$). Or, they may convert to decimal equivalencies to find decimals and then convert the decimals back to fractions. See Expanded Lesson: How Many in Between? for a full lesson exploring rational numbers between two rational numbers.

MyLab Education   **Expanded Lesson: How Many in Between?**

Irrational numbers are numbers such as $\sqrt{2}$—numbers whose value cannot be written as a fraction and whose exact value can only be estimated. Eighth-grade students begin to explore irrational numbers and to find their rational approximation (NGA Center & CCSSO, 2010). All these numbers are part of the *real numbers*, which are the only types of numbers students explore until high school, where they consider the square roots of negative numbers, called *imaginary numbers*. These sets of numbers are interrelated, and some are subsets of other sets. Figure 22.14 provides an illustration of the types of numbers and how they are interrelated.

Rational Numbers

Rational numbers comprise the set of all numbers that can be represented as a fraction—or a ratio of an integer to an integer. Even when numbers are written as whole numbers or as terminating decimals, they can also be written as fractions and thus are rational numbers. In fact, in school mathematics the term *rational numbers* is often used to refer to fractions, decimals (terminating and repeating), and percents. These are rational numbers, but so are integers, including whole numbers.

Moving among Representations. In sixth grade, students should be able to recognize a rational number as a point on a number line (NGA Center & CCSSO, 2010). In seventh grade, "students develop a unified

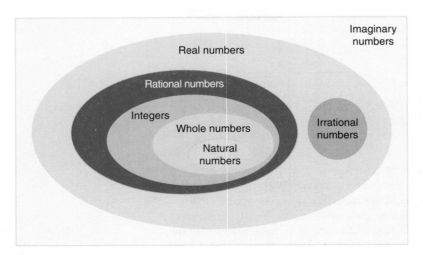

FIGURE 22.14   An illustration of the organization of the real numbers.

understanding of number, recognizing fractions, decimals (that have a finite or a repeating decimal representation), and percents as different representations of rational numbers" (p. 46). This means that given any value, students are able to think about it and operate it on it across representations, moving flexibly among different representations. For example, students should be able to explain equivalence, as noted here:

- $4\frac{3}{5}$ is equivalent to 4.6 because $\frac{3}{5}$ is six-tenths of a whole, so 4 wholes and six-tenths is 4.6.
- $4\frac{3}{5}$ is equivalent to $\frac{23}{5}$, and that is the same as $23 \div 5$, or 4.6 if I use decimals.
- 4.6 is read "four and six-tenths," so I can write that as $4\frac{6}{10} = 4\frac{3}{5}$.

Similarly, compare these three expressions:

$$\frac{1}{4} \text{ of } 24 \qquad \frac{24}{4} \qquad 24 \div 4$$

This discussion can lead to a general development of the idea that a fraction can be thought of as division of the numerator by the denominator, or that $\frac{a}{b}$ is the same as $a \div b$.

When a fraction is converted to a decimal, the decimal either terminates (e.g., 3.415) or repeats (e.g., 2.5141414 . . .). Is there a way to tell in advance whether a given fraction is a terminating decimal or a repeating decimal? The following activity can be used to discover if that prediction is correct.

 Standards for Mathematical Practice
MP7. Look for and make use of structure.

Activity 22.15   CCSS-M: 7.NS.A.2d

Repeater or Terminator?

Have students generate a table listing in one column the first 20 unit fractions $\left(\frac{1}{2}, \frac{1}{3}, \frac{1}{4}, \ldots \frac{1}{21}\right)$. The second column is for listing the prime factorization of the denominators; and the third column is for listing the decimal equivalents of the fractions (use calculators to get the precise decimal form).

After they have completed the table, ask students if they can determine a rule that will tell in advance whether the decimal will repeat or terminate. They can test the rule with fractions that have denominators beyond 21. Challenge students to confirm that their rule applies even if the numerator changes.

As students work on this task, they will notice various patterns, as can be seen in the student work provided in Figure 22.15. As this student has discovered, the only fractions with terminating decimals have denominators that factor with only combinations of twos and fives. Why is this the case?

Middle school students must understand that any rational number, positive or negative, whole or not whole, can be written as a fraction and as a decimal. So, $^{-}8$ can be written as the fraction $\frac{-8}{1}$ or $\frac{-16}{2}$, or as the decimal $^{-}8.0$. In fact, there are infinite ways to write equivalencies for $^{-}8$. Fluency with equivalent representations is critical and requires much more than teaching an algorithm for moving from one representation to another.

Irrational Numbers

Students encounter *irrational numbers* in seventh grade when they learn about π and continue exploration of irrational numbers more explicitly in eighth grade (NGA Center & CCSSO, 2010). As noted earlier, irrational numbers are not rational, meaning they cannot be written in fraction form. The irrational numbers together with the rational numbers make up the *real numbers*. The real numbers fill in all the holes on the number line, even when the holes are infinitesimally small.

TECHNOLOGY Note. YouTube has some interesting videos. First, a very old but great middle-school video, "The Weird Number." This is a scary (funny) story of a village of whole numbers in the mountains that "hear" there are other numbers beyond the hills. ■

Students' first experience with irrational numbers typically occurs when exploring square roots of whole numbers. The following activity provides a good introduction to square roots and cube roots.

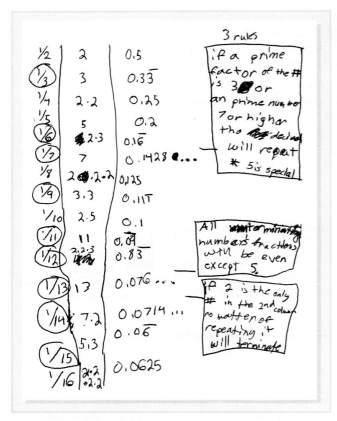

FIGURE 22.15 Jacob notes patterns as he explores the "Repeater or Terminator" activity.

Activity 22.16

CCSS-M: 8.NS.A.1; 8.EE.A.2

Edges of Squares and Cubes

Show students pictures of three squares (or three cubes) as in Figure 22.16. The sides (squares) and edges (cubes) of the first and last figure are consecutive whole numbers. The areas or volumes of all three figures are provided. Ask students to use a calculator to find the length of the sides (squares) or edges (cubes) of the figure in the center. Explain to students that they are not to use the square root or cube root key, but to estimate what they think the length of the side would be and test it by squaring or cubing it. Ask students to continue to estimate until they have found a value to the hundredths place that gets as close to 45 as possible (or 30 in the case of the cube). Solutions will satisfy these equations:

$$\square \times \square = 45, \text{ or } \square^2 = 45$$

and

$$\square \times \square \times \square = 30, \text{ or } \square^3 = 30$$

To solve the cube problem, students might start with 3.5 and find that 3.5^3 is 42.875, which is much too large. Through trial and error, they will find that the solution is between 3.1 and 3.2. Continued use of strategic trial and error will lead to a close approximation. Although a calculator can find these square or cube roots quickly, the estimation activity strengthens students' understanding of squares and square roots and the relative sizes of numbers.

⏸ Pause & Reflect

Use a calculator to continue getting a better approximation of the cube root of 30 to the hundredths place. ●

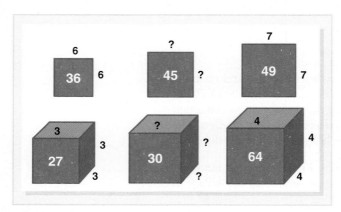

FIGURE 22.16 A geometric interpretation of square roots and cube roots.

From this introduction, students can be challenged to find solutions to equations such as $(\square^2 = 8)$. At this point students are ready to understand the general definition of the nth root of a number x as the number that when raised to the nth power equals x. The square and cube roots are simply other names for the second and third roots. It is important to point out that $\sqrt{6}$ is a *number*, not a computation (since it looks so much like a division problem). The cube root of eight is the same as $\sqrt[3]{8}$, which is equivalent to 2.

In middle school, students encounter irrational numbers primarily when working with the Pythagorean Theorem ($a^2 + b^2 = c^2$), which is used to find the distance between two points (the distance being the diagonal, or c). If $a = 3$ and $b = 4$, then $c = 5$. All sides are rational numbers. But this case is the exception to the rule. More often sides will be something like 4 and 7 units, in which case

$c = \sqrt{16 + 49} = \sqrt{65}$. Although sometimes there is a perfect square that can be simplified, in this case there is not one and the distance is $\sqrt{65}$, an irrational number.

An engaging middle school project applying the Pythagorean Theorem and irrational numbers is a Wheel of Theodorus, as described in Activity 22.16. Theodorus was one of the early believers in the existence of irrational numbers (This was quite a contentious issue for the Pythagoreans, who reportedly threw Hippasus off a boat to keep the idea of irrationals a secret (Havil, 2012)).

Activity 22.17   CCSS-M: 8.NS.A.2; 8.EE.A.2

Wheel of Theodorus

Ask students to construct a right triangle that measures 1 centimeter on each side adjacent to the right angle and then draw the hypotenuse and record its measure. They then use the hypotenuse as side *a* of a new right triangle drawing side *b* 1 cm long. Connect the endpoints of side *a* and side *b*. Draw and record the new hypotenuse ($\sqrt{3}$). Create the next triangle, which will have sides of $\sqrt{3}$ and 1 and a hypotenuse of $\sqrt{4}$ or 2, and so on. Doing this about 30 times will form a wheel. (See Bay-Williams & Martinie, 2009, for a complete lesson or search online for instructions and diagrams of a Wheel of Theodorus.)

 TECHNOLOGY Note. The Math Page has a link called *The Evolution of the Real Numbers*, which is an interesting description of many topics related to the real number system. Although mostly text, the pages are filled with interactive questions. ■

Supporting Student Reasoning about Number

Hopefully a theme that has come through this chapter is that students can reason and understand numbers. As they expand the types of numbers they encounter to negative values, very large, very small, and irrational numbers, they must have the opportunity to connect what they already know about number and operations, to the new types of numbers. This requires a strong focus on reasoning and looking at structure, which must be a part of daily instruction on these topics. Students who do not have these opportunities will struggle to make sense of and correctly solve problems involving rational numbers, which leads to struggles throughout high school and beyond. We close this chapter summarizing some common errors and misconceptions students have related to the topics in this chapter in Table 22.1 so that you can prioritize and attend to these concepts and ensure your students have a solid understanding of rational numbers.

 Standards for Mathematical Practice
MP2. Reason abstractly and quantitatively.

MyLab Education   **Self-Check 22.4**

MyLab Education   **Math Practice:** Need to practice or refresh your math content knowledge? Click to access practice exercises associated with the content from this chapter.

TABLE 22.1 COMMON CHALLENGES AND MISCONCEPTIONS RELATED TO EXPONENTS, ORDER OF OPERATIONS, NEGATIVE NUMBERS AND REAL NUMBERS

Common Challenge or Misconceptions	What It Looks Like	How to Help
1. *Order of Operations.* Thinking addition precedes subtraction.	Simplifies the expression $15 - 10 + 5$ by first adding, getting an incorrect answer of 0.	• Do not use PEMDAS as they way to remember the order of operations. • Give many examples where subtraction appears before addition in the expression. • Use worked examples with this error in it.
2. *Order of Operations.* Thinking multiplication precedes division.	Simplifies the expression $60 \div 10 \times 2$ by first multiplying, getting an incorrect answer of 3.	• See strategies in (1).
3. Not distinguishing between exponents and multiplication.	Student simplifies 2^3 thinking it is 2×3 and gets 6 instead of 9.	• Have students write exponents out in long form. • Explore worked examples, such as in Activity 22.5 to explicitly discuss this error (and others).
4. In scientific notation, thinking the exponent tells the numbers of zeros to "add on" to a number.	Student writes expanded form of 3.6×10^{14} as 3,600,000,000,000,000, with 14 zeros.	• Avoid giving short cuts that don't make sense to students or are not conceptually grounded. • Ask questions to bring attention to this challenge. For example, "Why are there 13 zeros and not 14? "Is there a relationship between the exponent and the number of zeros?" • Explore much smaller numbers (e.g., 5.9×10^3), writing the number different ways and noticing patterns that are true/not true.
5. Locating negative non-integer values on the number line.	Student places $^-1\frac{1}{4}$ between $^-1$ and 0 instead of between $^-2$ and $^-1$.	• Use more noninteger values through instruction of negative numbers. • Use the number line frequently to illustrate location of values and to do operations. • Don't forget to use negative numbers when lesson goals focus on decimal and fraction operations.
6. Multiple meanings of the minus sign.	Student does not know the meaning of $-(^-8)$ because they don't see a number to subtract from; Student thinks they should multiply an expression such as $8.6 - (^-4)$	• Explicitly teach the three meanings of the minus sign. • In simplifying expressions repeatedly ask, "What does this symbol mean here?" • Use Activity 22.11
7. Integer operations, making sense of the meaning of the operation and the answer.	Student thinks that $9 - 18$ is impossible; Student does not know if $^-5.7 - 9$ should be less than or more than $^-5.7$.	• Use many contexts in teaching integer operations • Use both counters and number lines, but particularly number lines. • When students get different answers, provide time for students to debate which is correct and why.
8. Thinking square root notation indicates an operation.	Student thinks $\sqrt{6}$ means some number is being divided into 6.	• Emphasize that $\sqrt{6}$ is actually a number in and of itself, and relatedly $\sqrt[3]{8}$ is equivalent to 2. Both are numbers.

RESOURCES FOR CHAPTER 22

LITERATURE CONNECTIONS

Why Pi? And Go Figure!

Ball (2005, 2019, 2016)

These two nonfiction books offer interesting facts on a range of mathematical topics, including very big number. *Why Pi?* uses powers of 10 to describe the galaxy and *Go Figure!* Explores exponential growth connected to historical and classic problems.

The Number Devil

Enzensberger (1997)

Full of humor and wit, *The Number Devil* presents a collection of interesting ideas about numbers. Robert, a boy who hates mathematics, meets up with a crafty number devil in each of 12 dreams (one per chapter). On the fourth night's dream, Robert learns about infinitely repeating decimals and the "rutabaga of two" (the square root of two), providing a connection to rational and irrational numbers.

Oh, Yikes! History's Grossest, Wackiest Moments

Masoff and Sirrell (2006)

In this picture-rich reference book, the authors describe important historical events and people with facts that are interesting to middle schoolers (e.g., "Aztec Antics," "Cruel Constructions," "Humongous Hoaxes"). Selecting a topic, such as brushing teeth, the author describes how this was handled across all of history—an opportunity for timelines that include dates such as 2500 B.C. Students can create a timeline that is proportionally accurate to describe the events related to their topic. This lesson involves integers, measuring, proportional reasoning, and fractions.

RECOMMENDED READINGS
Articles

Dupree, K. M. (2016). Questioning the order of operations. *Mathematics Teaching in the Middle School, 22*(3): 152–159.

Mnemonics perpetuate misconceptions. This article provides examples of student misconceptions and describes a more effective way to teach this critically important topic.

Swanson, P. E. (2010). The intersection of language and mathematics. *Mathematics Teaching in the Middle School, 15*(9), 516–523.

Weaving in many strategies to support ELs, the author shares how she engaged students in real contexts to learn integer operations. Visuals and language support are used to ensure students understand.

Standards for Mathematical Practice

The Standards for Mathematical Practice found in the *Common Core State Standards* describe varieties of expertise that mathematics educators at all levels should seek to develop in their students. These practices rest on important "processes and proficiencies" with longstanding importance in mathematics education. The first of these are the NCTM process standards of problem solving, reasoning and proof, communication, representation, and connections. The second are the strands for mathematical proficiency specified in the National Research Council's report *Adding It Up*: adaptive reasoning, strategic competence, conceptual understanding (comprehension of mathematical concepts, operations, and relations), procedural fluency (skill in carrying out procedures flexibly, accurately, efficiently, and appropriately), and productive disposition (habitual inclination to see mathematics as sensible, useful, and worthwhile, coupled with a belief in diligence and one's own efficacy).

1. Make sense of problems and persevere in solving them.

Mathematically proficient students start by explaining to themselves the meaning of a problem and looking for entry points to its solution. They analyze givens, constraints, relationships, and goals. They make conjectures about the form and meaning of the solution and plan a solution pathway rather than simply jumping into a solution attempt. They consider analogous problems and try special cases and simpler forms of the original problem in order to gain insight into its solution. They monitor and evaluate their progress and change course if necessary. Older students might, depending on the context of the problem, transform algebraic expressions or change the viewing window on their graphing calculator to get the information they need. Mathematically proficient students can explain correspondences between equations, verbal descriptions, tables, and graphs or draw diagrams of important features and relationships, graph data, and search for regularity or trends. Younger students might rely on using concrete objects or pictures to help conceptualize and solve a problem. Mathematically proficient students check their answers to problems using a different method, and they continually ask themselves, "Does this make sense?" They can understand the approaches of others to solving complex problems and identify correspondences between different approaches.

2. Reason abstractly and quantitatively.

Mathematically proficient students make sense of quantities and their relationships in problem situations. They bring two complementary abilities to bear on problems involving quantitative relationships: the ability to *decontextualize*—to abstract a given situation and represent it symbolically and manipulate the representing symbols as if they have a life of their own, without necessarily attending to their referents—and the ability to *contextualize*, to pause as needed during the manipulation process in order to probe into the referents for the symbols involved. Quantitative reasoning entails habits of creating a coherent representation of the problem at hand; considering the units involved; attending to the meaning of quantities, not just how to compute them; and knowing and flexibly using different properties of operations and objects.

3. Construct viable arguments and critique the reasoning of others.

Mathematically proficient students understand and use stated assumptions, definitions, and previously established results in constructing arguments. They make conjectures and build a logical progression of statements to explore the truth of their conjectures. They are able to analyze situations by breaking them into cases and can recognize and use counterexamples. They justify their conclusions, communicate them to others, and respond to the arguments of others. They reason inductively about data, making plausible arguments that take into account the context from which the data arose. Mathematically proficient students are also able to compare the effectiveness of two plausible arguments, distinguish correct logic or reasoning from that which is flawed, and—if there is a flaw in an argument—explain what it is. Elementary students can construct arguments using concrete referents such as objects, drawings, diagrams, and actions. Such arguments can make sense and be correct, even though they are not generalized or made formal until later grades. Later, students learn to determine domains to which an argument applies. Students at all grades can listen or read the arguments of others, decide whether they make sense, and ask useful questions to clarify or improve the arguments.

4. Model with mathematics.

Mathematically proficient students can apply the mathematics they know to solve problems arising in everyday life, society, and the workplace. In early grades, this might be as simple as writing an addition equation to describe a situation. In middle grades, a student might apply proportional reasoning to plan a school event or analyze a problem in the community. By high school, a student might use geometry to solve a design problem or use a function to describe how one quantity of interest depends on another. Mathematically proficient students who can apply what they know are comfortable making assumptions and approximations to simplify a complicated situation, realizing that these may need revision later. They are able to identify important quantities in a practical situation and map their relationships using such tools as diagrams, two-way tables, graphs, flowcharts, and formulas. They can analyze those relationships mathematically to draw conclusions. They routinely interpret their mathematical results in the context of the situation and reflect on whether the results make sense, possibly improving the model if it has not served its purpose.

5. Use appropriate tools strategically.

Mathematically proficient students consider the available tools when solving a mathematical problem. These tools might include pencil and paper, concrete models, a ruler, a protractor, a calculator, a spreadsheet, a computer algebra system, a statistical package, or dynamic geometry software. Proficient students are sufficiently familiar with tools appropriate for their grade or course to make sound decisions about when each of these tools might be helpful, recognizing both the insight to be gained and their limitations. For example, mathematically proficient high school students analyze graphs of functions and solutions generated using a graphing calculator. They detect possible errors by strategically using estimation and other mathematical knowledge. When making mathematical models, they know that technology can enable them to visualize the results of varying assumptions, explore consequences, and compare predictions with data. Mathematically proficient students at various grade levels are able to identify relevant external mathematical resources, such as digital content located on a website, and use them to pose or solve problems. They are able to use technological tools to explore and deepen their understanding of concepts.

6. Attend to precision.

Mathematically proficient students try to communicate precisely to others. They try to use clear definitions in discussion with others and in their own reasoning. They state the meaning of the symbols they choose, including using the equal sign consistently and appropriately. They are careful about specifying units of measure and labeling axes to clarify the correspondence with quantities in a problem. They calculate accurately and efficiently, express numerical answers with a degree of precision appropriate for the problem context. In the elementary grades, students give carefully formulated explanations to each other. By the time they reach high school, they have learned to examine claims and make explicit use of definitions.

7. Look for and make use of structure.

Mathematically proficient students look closely to discern a pattern or structure. Young students, for example, might notice that three and seven more is the same amount as seven and three more, or they may sort a collection of shapes according to how many sides the shapes have. Later, students will see 7×8 equals the well-remembered $7 \times 5 + 7 \times 3$, in preparation for learning about the distributive property. In the expression $x^2 + 9x + 14$, older students can see the 14 as 2×7 and the 9 as $2 + 7$. They recognize the significance of an existing line in a geometric figure and can use the strategy of drawing an auxiliary line for solving problems. They also can step back for an overview and shift perspective. They can see complicated things, such as some algebraic expressions as single objects or as being composed of several objects. For example, they can see $5 - 3(x - y)^2$ as 5 minus a positive number times a square and use that to realize that its value cannot be more than 5 for any real numbers x and y.

8. Look for and express regularity in repeated reasoning.

Mathematically proficient students notice if calculations are repeated and look both for general methods and for shortcuts. Upper elementary students might notice when dividing 25 by 11 that they are repeating the same calculations over and over again, and conclude they have a repeating decimal. By paying attention to the calculation of slope as they repeatedly check whether points are on the line through $(1, 2)$ with slope 3, middle school students might abstract the equation $(y - 2)/(x - 1) = 3$. Noticing the regularity in the way terms cancel when expanding $(x - 1)(x + 1)$, $(x - 1)(x^2 + x + 1)$, and $(x - 1)(x^3 + x^2 + x + 1)$ might lead them to the general formula for the sum of a geometric series. As they work to solve a problem, mathematically proficient students maintain oversight of the process while attending to the details. They continually evaluate the reasonableness of their intermediate results.

NCTM Mathematics Teaching Practices from *Principles to Actions*

Establish mathematics goals to focus learning.

Effective teaching of mathematics establishes clear goals for the mathematics that students are learning, situates goals within learning progressions, and uses the goals to guide instructional decisions.

Implement tasks that promote reasoning and problem solving.

Effective teaching of mathematics engages students in solving and discussing tasks that promote mathematical reasoning and problem solving and allow multiple entry points and varied solution strategies.

Use and connect mathematical representations.

Effective teaching of mathematics engages students in making connections among mathematical representations to deepen understanding of mathematics concepts and procedures and as tools for problem solving.

Facilitate meaningful mathematical discourse.

Effective teaching of mathematics facilitates discourse among students to build shared understanding of mathematical ideas by analyzing and comparing student approaches and arguments.

Pose purposeful questions.

Effective teaching of mathematics uses purposeful questions to assess and advance students' reasoning and sense making about important mathematical ideas and relationships.

Build procedural fluency from conceptual understanding.

Effective teaching of mathematics builds fluency with procedures on a foundation of conceptual understanding so that students, over time, become skillful in using procedures flexibly as they solve contextual and mathematical problems.

Support productive struggle in learning mathematics.

Effective teaching of mathematics consistently provides students, individually and collectively, with opportunities and supports to engage in productive struggle as they grapple with mathematical ideas and relationships.

Elicit and use evidence of student thinking.

Effective teaching of mathematics uses evidence of student thinking to assess progress toward mathematical understanding and to adjust instruction continually in ways that support and extend learning.

Appendix C

Guide to Blackline Masters

This Appendix has images of all 34 Blackline Masters (BLM) that you and your students will find useful to engage in many math activities. You can create full-sized masters from these images, print them from point of use pop-ups throughout the text or from the contents listing in the navigation bar of your eText.

Suggestions for Use and Construction of Materials

Card Stock Materials

A good way to have many materials made quickly and easily for students is to have them duplicated on card stock, laminated, and then cut into smaller pieces if desired. Once cut, materials are best kept in clear freezer bags with zip-type closures. Punch a hole near the top of the bag so that you do not store air.

The following list is a suggestion for materials that can be made from card stock using the masters in this section. Quantity suggestions are also given.

Five-Frames and Ten-Frames—12–14

Five-frames and ten-frames are best duplicated on light-colored card stock. Do not laminate; if you do, the mats will curl and counters will slide around.

10 × 10 Multiplication Array—16

Make one per student in any color. Lamination is suggested. Provide each student with an L-shaped piece of card stock to frame the array.

Base-Ten Materials—32

Run copies on white card stock. One sheet will make 4 hundreds and 10 tens or 4 hundreds and 100 ones. Cut into pieces with a paper cutter. It is recommended that you not laminate the base-ten pieces. A kit consisting of 10 hundreds, 30 tens, and 30 ones is adequate for each student or pair of students.

Place-Value Mat (with Ten-Frames)—17

Mats can be duplicated on any pastel card stock. It is recommended that you not laminate these because they tend to curl and counters slide around. Make one for every student.

Rational Number Wheel—24

These disks should be made on card stock. Duplicate the master on two contrasting colors. Laminate and cut the circles and also the slot on the dotted line. Make a set for each student.

Many masters lend themselves to demonstration purposes. The 10 × 10 array, the blank hundreds board, and the large geoboard are examples. The place-value mat can be used with strips and squares or with counters and cups directly on the document camera. The missing-part blank and the record blanks for the four algorithms are pages that you may wish to write on as a demonstration.

The 10,000 grid is the easiest way there is to show 10,000 or to model four-place decimal numbers.

The degrees and wedges page is the very best way to illustrate what a degree is and also to help explain protractors.

All of the line and dot grids are useful for modeling. You may find it a good idea to have several copies of each easily available.

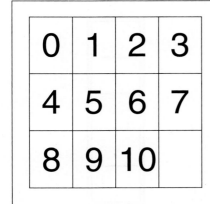

Number Cards 0–10—1

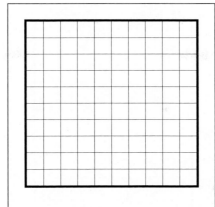

Blank Hundreds Chart—2

Hundreds Chart—3

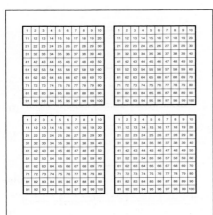

Four Small Hundreds Charts—4

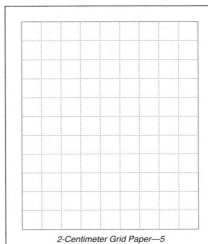

2-Centimeter Grid Paper—5

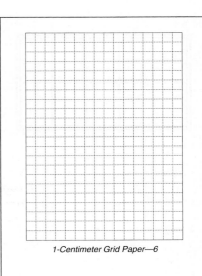

1-Centimeter Grid Paper—6

0.5-Centimeter Grid Paper—7

1-Centimeter Dot Paper—8

2-Centimeter Isometric Grid Paper—9

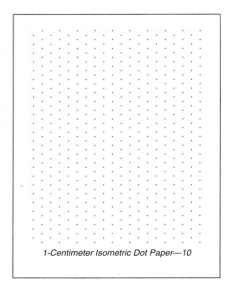

1-Centimeter Isometric Dot Paper—10

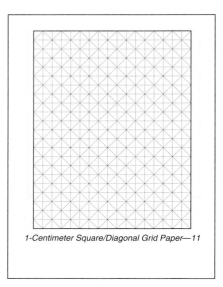

1-Centimeter Square/Diagonal Grid Paper—11

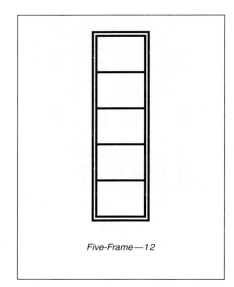

Five-Frame—12

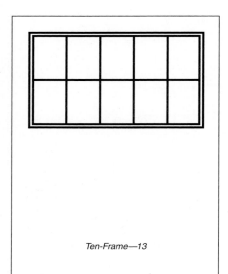

Ten-Frame—13

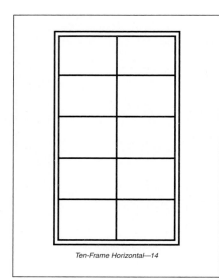

Ten-Frame Horizontal—14

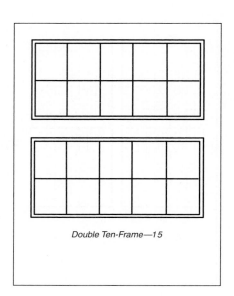

Double Ten-Frame—15

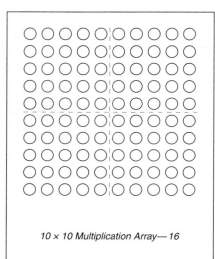

10 × 10 Multiplication Array—16

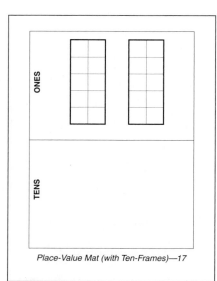

Place-Value Mat (with Ten-Frames)—17

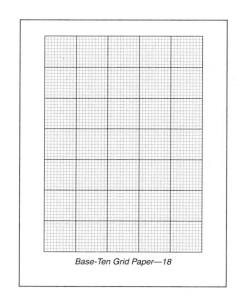

Base-Ten Grid Paper—18

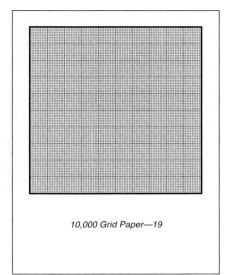

10,000 Grid Paper—19

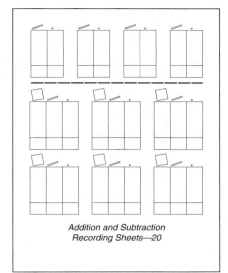

Addition and Subtraction Recording Sheets—20

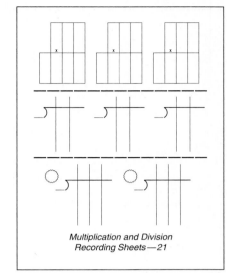

Multiplication and Division Recording Sheets—21

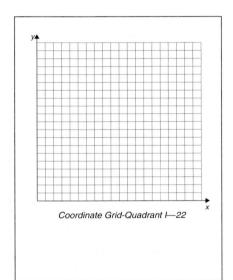

Coordinate Grid-Quadrant I—22

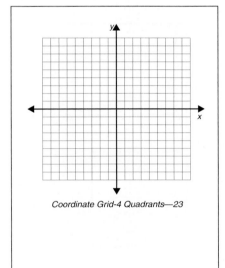

Coordinate Grid-4 Quadrants—23

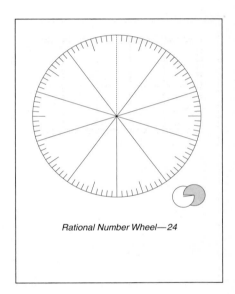

Rational Number Wheel—24

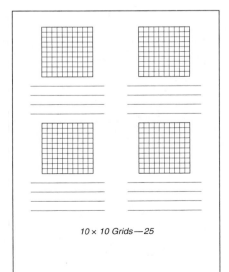

10 × 10 Grids—25

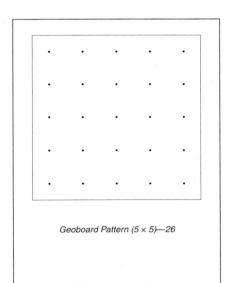

Geoboard Pattern (5 × 5)—26

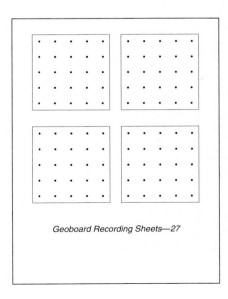

Geoboard Recording Sheets—27

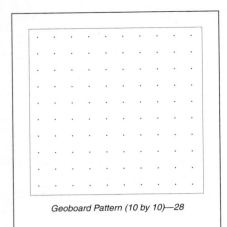

Geoboard Pattern (10 by 10)—28

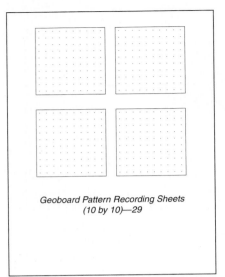

*Geoboard Pattern Recording Sheets
(10 by 10)—29*

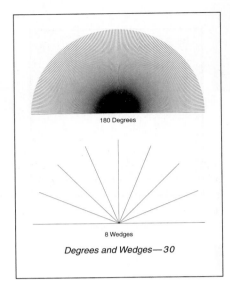

180 Degrees

8 Wedges

Degrees and Wedges—30

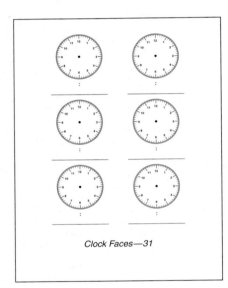

Clock Faces—31

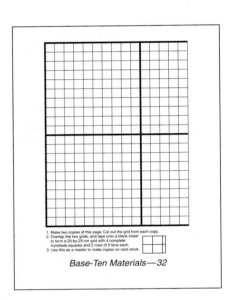

1. Make two copies of this page. Cut out the grid from each copy.
2. Overlap the two grids, and tape onto a blank sheet
   to form a 20-by-25-cm grid with 4 complete
   hundreds squares and 2 rows of 5 tens each.
3. Use this as a master to make copies on card stock.

Base-Ten Materials—32

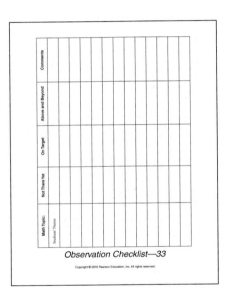

Observation Checklist—33

Sidebar Chart

10 × ___ = _____	100 × ___ = _____
20 × ___ = _____	200 × ___ = _____
40 × ___ = _____	400 × ___ = _____
80 × ___ = _____	800 × ___ = _____

10 × ___ = _____	100 × ___ = _____
20 × ___ = _____	200 × ___ = _____
40 × ___ = _____	400 × ___ = _____
80 × ___ = _____	800 × ___ = _____

10 × ___ = _____	100 × ___ = _____
20 × ___ = _____	200 × ___ = _____
40 × ___ = _____	400 × ___ = _____
80 × ___ = _____	800 × ___ = _____

This table lists the named and numbered activities in Part II of the book. In addition to providing an easy way to find an activity, the table provides the main mathematics content and the related Common Core State Standards. Remember that this is a book about teaching mathematics and not a book of activities. It is extremely important not to take any activity as a suggestion for instruction without reading the full text in which it is embedded.

Chapter 7 Developing Early Number Concepts and Number Sense

Activity		Mathematics Content	CCSS-M	Page
7.1	Learning Patterns	Develop instant recognition of an amount in a dot pattern	K.CC.B.4	128
7.2	Dot Plate Flash	Practice recognition of amounts without counting	K.CC.B.4a, b	128
7.3	Up and Back Counting	Practice skill of counting forward and counting backward	K.CC.A.1 K.CC.A.2	129
7.4	Fill the Tower	Develop one-to-one counting skills	K.CC.B.5	131
7.5	Number Necklaces	Practice number matching and develop basic addition	K.CC.A.3	132
7.6	Number Tubs	Develop counting skills and need for number names	K.CC.B.4; K.CC.B.5	132
7.7	Line Them Up!	Practice number sequence and the use of the number line	K.CC.B.4c; K.CC.A.2	132
7.8	Counting On with Counters	Practice counting on	K.CC.A.2; K.CC.B.5	133
7.9	Real Counting On	Practice counting on to tell all	K.OA.A.1; 1.OA.B.5	133
7.10	Counting Moose Tracks	Develop one-to-one correspondence and cardinality	K.CC.B.4a	134
7.11	Make Sets of More/Less/Same	Develop relational concept of more/less/same	K.CC.C.6	135
7.12	Find the Same Amount	Identify sets with more/less/same	K.CC.A.3; K.CC.C.6	135
7.13	More, Less, or the Same	Develop concept of 1-more, 2-more, 1-less, 2-less, zero	K.CC.A.3; K.CC.C.6; K.OA.A.1	135
7.14	Make a Two-More-Than Set	Develop concept of 1-more, 2-more, 1-less, 2-less	K.OA.A.2; 1.OA.C.5	137
7.15	A Two-More-Than Machine	Practice 1-more-, 2-more-, 1-less-, 2-less-than relationships	1.OA.C.5	138
7.16	Five-Frame Tell-About	Develop benchmark of 5 for numbers to 10	K.CC.C.7; K.OA.A.5	138
7.17	Number Medley	Develop the benchmark of 10 for numbers to 10	K.CC.C.6; K.CC.C.7	139
7.18	Ten-Frame Flash	Practice benchmarks of 5 and 10 for numbers to 10	K.CC.B.5	140

(Continued)

Chapter 7 (Continued)

Activity		Mathematics Content	CCSS-M	Page
7.19	Build It in Parts	Practice part-whole concepts in a symbolic form	K.OA.A.3; 1.OA.C.6	141
7.20	Covered Parts	Develop missing part concepts	K.OA.A.2	142
7.21	Missing-Part Cards	Practice missing part concepts	K.OA.A.4	142
7.22	I Wish I Had	Practice missing part concepts	K.OA.A.1; K.OA.A.2	143
7.23	Double War	Practice comparison of numbers to 20	K.CC.C.6	144
7.24	Difference War	Practice finding the difference between two sets	K.CC.C.6; K.OA.A.2	144
7.25	Number Sandwiches	Practice missing part concepts	K.OA.A.2; 1.OA.C.6	144
7.26	Ten and Some More	Develop concept of teen numbers	K.NBT.A.1	146
7.27	More and Less Extended	Extend one-more, two-more, one-less, two-less relationships to teen numbers	K.CC.C.6; K.NBT.A.1	146
7.28	Add a Unit to Your Number	Connect number to real-world measures	K.MD.A.1	148
7.29	Is It Reasonable?	Connect number to real-world measures	K.MD.A.1	149

Chapter 8 Developing Meanings for the Operations

Activity		Mathematics Content	CCSS-M	Page
8.1	Up and Down the Number Line	Practice using units on a number line	K.OA.A.2; 1.OA.A.1; 1.OA.A.2; 2.OA.A.1	162
8.2	Missing-Part Subtraction	Develop subtraction as a name for a missing part	K.OA.A.2; 1.OA.A.1; 1.OA.A.2; 2.OA.A.1	163
8.3	Guinea Pigs in Cages	Develop strategies for exploring both addends unknown problems	K.OA.A.3; 1.OA.A.1; 1.OA.B.4	163
8.4	More Than Two Addends	Practice adding more than two addends	1.OA.B.2	165
8.5	Factor Quest	Develop the connection between multiplication and division	4.OA.B.4	172
8.6	Factor Patterns	Develop patterns between arrays and factors	4.OA.B.4	172
8.7	Divide and Conquer	Develop measurement and partition concepts of division	3.OA.A.2	173
8.8	The Broken Division Key	Develop division as repeated subtraction and missing factor	4.NBT.B.6	173
8.9	Divide It Up	Develop the distributive property	3.OA.B.5; 5.OA.A.1	175

Chapter 9   Developing Basic Fact Fluency

Activity		Mathematics Content	CCSS-M	Page
9.1	If You Didn't Know	Use known facts to determine unknown facts	1.OA.C.6; 2.OA.B.2; 3.OA.B.5; 3.OA.C.7	189
9.2	How Many Feet in the Bed?	Practice facts for +2 and −2	1.OA.A.1; 1.OA.C.6; 2.OA.B.2	190
9.3	One More Than and Two More Than with Dice and Spinners	Practice addition facts for +1 and +2	1.OA.C.5; 1.OA.C.6; 2.OA.B.2	191
9.4	Double Trouble	Practice addition doubles facts	1.OA.C.5; 1.OA.C.6; 2.OA.B.2	192
9.5	Calculator Doubles	Practice addition doubles facts	1.OA.C.6; 2.OA.B.2	192
9.6	How Many More to Equal 10?	Practice combinations of 10 facts	1.OA.B.4; 1.OA.C.6; 2.OA.B.2	193
9.7	Move It, Move It	Develop Making 10 strategy	1.OA.B.3; 1.OA.C.6; 2.OA.B.2	194
9.8	Frames and Facts	Develop Making 10 strategy	1.OA.B.3; 1.OA.C.6; 2.OA.B.2	194
9.9	On the Double!	Practice near-doubles addition facts	1.OA.B.3; 1.OA.C.6; 2.OA.B.2	196
9.10	What's under my Thumb?	Connect addition and subtraction facts or multiplication and division facts	1.OA.B.4; 1.OA.C.6; 2.OA.B.2; 3.OA.B.5; 3.OA.B.6; 3.OA.C.7	197
9.11	Apples in the Trees	Practice subtraction to 20	1.OA.B.4; 1.OA.C.6; 2.OA.B.2	198
9.12	Apples in Two Trees	Develop missing-value concept, relating addition to subtraction	1.OA.B.3; 1.OA.B.4; 1.OA.C.6; 2.OA.B.2	199
9.13	Clock Facts	Develop minute intervals on the clock as a strategy for fives multiplication facts	3.OA.A.1; 3.OA.C.7	200
9.14	How Close without Going Over?	Looking for near-division facts	3.OA.A.2; 3.OA.A.4; 3.OA.B.6	204
9.15	Strive to Derive	Use known facts to determine unknown facts	3.OA.A.1; 3.OA.B.5; 3.OA.C.7	205

(Continued)

Chapter 9 (Continued)

Activity	Mathematics Content	CCSS-M	Page
9.16 Salute!	Identify the missing addend or factor	1.OA.B.4; 1.OA.C.6; 2.OA.B.2; 3.OA.B.5; 3.OA.B.6; 3.OA.C.7	206
9.17 Bowl-a-Fact	Practice creating equations in addition, subtraction, multiplication, and division	2.OA.B.2; 3.OA.C.7; 5.OA.A.1	206

Chapter 10 Developing Whole-Number Place-Value Concepts

Activity	Mathematics Content	CCSS-M	Page
10.1 Counting in Groups	Develop concept of groups of ten as an efficient method of counting	K.NBT.A.1; 1.NBT.B.2a	218
10.2 Groups of Ten	Develop concept of groups of ten as a method of counting	K.NBT.A.1; 1.NBT.B.2a, b, c	218
10.3 Estimating Groups of Tens and Ones	Developing the concepts of two-digit numbers as ten and some more	K.NBT.A.1; 1.NBT.B.2a, b	220
10.4 Too Many to Count?	Estimate and group quantities into hundreds, tens, and ones	2.NBT.A.1	221
10.5 Can You Make the Link?	Develop alternative groupings of ten to represent a number	1.NBT.B.2; 1.NBT.C.5	221
10.6 Three Other Ways	Develop alternative groupings of tens and hundreds to represent a number	K.CC.B.5 2.NBT.A.1; 2.NBT.A.3	222
10.7 Base-Ten Riddles	Develop alternative groupings of tens and hundreds to represent a number	1.NBT.A.1; 2.NBT.A.1; 2.NBT.A.3	222
10.8 Counting Rows of Ten	Develop and connect three oral counting strategies	1.NBT.B.2c	223
10.9 Counting with Base-Ten Models	Develop and connect three oral counting strategies	1.NBT.B.2; 1.NBT.C.5	224
10.10 Tens, Ones, and Fingers	Develop and connect three oral counting strategies	1.NBT.B.2a, b, c	224
10.11 Say It/Press It	Connect oral and symbolic names for numbers to physical representation	2.NBT.A.1a, b; 2.NBT.A.3	226
10.12 Digit Change	Apply place-value concepts to symbolic representations	1.NBT.B.2; 1.NBT.C.5; 1.NBT.C.6; 2.NBT.A.1; 2.NBT.A.3; 2.NBT.B.5; 2.NBT.B.8	226
10.13 Missing Numbers	Practice sequence of numbers to 100	K.CC.A.1; K.NBT.A.1; 1.NBT.A.1; 1.NBT.B.2; 1.NBT.C.5	228
10.14 Finding Neighbors on the Hundreds Chart	Explore patterns in numbers to 100	K.CC.A.1; K.NBT.A.1; 1.NBT.A.1; 1.NBT.B.2; 1.NBT.C.5	229

Activity		Mathematics Content	CCSS-M	Page
10.15	Models with the Hundreds Chart	Develop concepts of 1-more/less and 10-more/less for two-digit numbers	K.CC.A.1; K.NBT.A.1; 1.NBT.A.1; 1.NBT.B.2; 1.NBT.C.5	229
10.16	The Thousands Chart	Extend patterns for 1 to 100 to patterns to 1000	2.NBT.A.1; 2.NBT.A.2; 2.NBT.A.3; 2.NBT.B.8.	230
10.17	Who Am I?	Develop relative magnitude of numbers to 100	1.NBT.A.1; 1.NBT.B.2; 1.NBT.B.3; 2.NBT.A.1; 2.NBT.A.2; 2.NBT.A.4	230
10.18	Who Could They Be?	Develop relative magnitude of numbers to 100	1.NBT.A.1; 1.NBT.B.2; 1.NBT.B.3; 2.NBT.A.1; 2.NBT.A.2; 2.NBT.A.4	231
10.19	Close, Far, and In Between	Explore relative differences between three-digit numbers	1.NBT.A.1; 1.NBT.B.2; 1.NBT.B.3; 2.NBT.A.1; 2.NBT.A.2; 2.NBT.A.4	231
10.20	What Comes Next?	Develop the continuing pattern in the place-value system	2.NBT.A.1; 2.NBT.A.3	233
10.21	Collecting 10,000	Develop an understanding of the size of large numbers	2.NBT.A.2; 2.NBT.A.3	235
10.22	Showing 10,000	Develop an understanding of the size of large numbers	2.NBT.A.2; 2.NBT.A.3	235
10.23	How Long?/How Far?	Develop an understanding of the size of large numbers	2.NBT.A.1a; 2.MD.A.3	235
10.24	A Long Time	Connect units of time to large numbers	3.MD.A.1	235
10.25	Really Large Quantities	Develop ability to estimate large quantities	2.MD.A.3; 3.MD.A.1; 3.MD.C.5	235

Chapter 11 Developing Strategies for Addition and Subtraction Computation (note that Chapter 11 shares activities with Chapter 10)

Activity		Mathematics Content	CCSS-M	Page
11.1	Calculator Challenge Counting	Develop mental addition strategies through skip counting	1.NBT.C.5	241
11.2	50 and Some More	Develop 50 as a part of numbers between 50 and 100	1.NBT.B.4	242
11.3	The Other Part of 100M	Develop missing part strategies with a whole of 100	1.NBT.B.4; 2.NBT.B.5	242
11.4	Compatible Pairs	Explore addition combinations that make multiples of 10 or 100	2.NBT.B.5	243
11.5	Numbers, Squares, Lines, and Dots	Develop invented strategies for addition and subtraction	2.NBT.B.7	243
11.6	Hundreds Chart Addition	Practice adding two-or three-digit numbers	2.NBT.B.5	244

(Continued)

Chapter 11   (*Continued*)

Activity	Mathematics Content	CCSS-M	Page
11.7 How Much Between?	Develop strategies to find the difference	2.NBT.B.5	245
11.8 Little Ten-Frame Sums	Develop invented strategies for addition	2.NBT.B.5	245
11.9 City Populations	Develop and solve word problems using invented strategies	2.NBT.B.5 2.NBT.B.6 2.NBT.B.7 3.NBT.B.2 4.NBT.B.2 4.NBT.B.4	248
11.10 Exploring Subtraction Strategies	Practice solving word problems with two-digit numbers	2.OA.A.1	254
11.11 Crossing a Decade	Extend the Making 10 strategy to two-digit numbers	1.NBT.C.4; 2.OA.A.2	255
11.12 I Am, but Who Is?	Practice mental math with addition and subtraction of decade numbers	1.NBT.C.4; 1.NBT.C.5; 1.NBT.C.6	255
11.13 Just Adjust It	Practice using algebraic thinking to add related problems	2.NBT.B.5; 2.NBT.B.9	257
11.14 Odd or Even?	Develop patterns when adding two-digit numbers	2.OA.C.3	258
11.15 How Far to My Number?	Develop missing-part strategies for two-digit numbers	2.NBT.B.5; 2.NBT.B.9	259
11.16 Trading across Zero	Develop strategies to subtract with internal zeros in the minuend	2.NBT.B.7 2.NBT.B.9	264
11.17 Pick Your Strategy	Develop the ability to choose a strategy	1.NBT.C.4 2.NBT.B.5 2.NBT.B.6 2.NBT.B.7 2.NBT.B.9	264
11.18 Over or Under?	Develop strategies to make computational estimations	3.OA.C.8	266
11.19 Round Up?	Develop strategies to round numbers to the nearest ten or hundred	3.NBT.A.1	268
11.20 Box Math	Practice computation and estimation through problem solving	2.NBT.B.5	269

Chapter 12   Developing Strategies for Multiplication and Division Computation

Activity	Mathematics Content	CCSS-M	Page
12.1 Build It and Break It	Develop the distributive property	4.NBT.B.5	280
12.2 Make It Easy	Develop the standard algorithm for multiplication	4.NBT.B.5	281
12.3 Left Overs	Develop the concept of remainders	4.NBT.B.6	287
12.4 Double, Double—No Toil or Trouble!	Develop a division strategy through doubling	5.NBT.B.6	291
12.5 High or Low?	Develop estimates of double digit multiplication	4.NBT.A.3; 4.NBT.B.5	293
12.6 That's Good Enough	Develop estimates of multiplication situations	4.OA.A.3	293
12.7 What Was Your Method?	Develop estimation strategies	4.NBT.A.3; 4.NBT.B.5	295
12.8 Jump to It	Estimate division using a missing factor strategy	4.NBT.B.5; 4.NBT.A.3	295
12.9 Hit the Target	Estimate for any of the four operations on a calculator	4.NBT.B.5	296

Chapter 13   Algebraic Thinking, Equations, and Functions

Activity		Mathematics Content	CCSS-M	Page
13.1	Diagonal Sums	Explore place-value relationships and generalize patterns	1.NBT.C.4; 2.NBT.B.9; 3.OA.D.9	302
13.2	Five Ways to Zero	Apply properties, such as identity for addition and/or multiplication, to creating equations	1.OA.B.3; 1.OA.C.6; 1.OA.D.7; 2.OA.B.2; 3.OA.D.9	305
13.3	Broken Calculator: Can You Fix It?	Explore properties of odd and even numbers	1.OA.B.3; 2.OA.C.3; 2.NBT.B.5; 3.OA.D.9	306
13.4	Convince Me Conjectures	Make and test generalizations about whole number operations (and properties)	1.OA.B.3; 2.NBT.B.9; 3.OA.B.5; 5.OA.A.1	307
13.5	Predict Down the Line	Explore the structure of repeating patterns analytically	2.OA.C.3; 4.OA.B.4	308
13.6	Hurricane Names	Explore the structure of repeating patterns analytically	4.OA.A.3; 4.OA.B.4; 5.OA.B.3; 6.EE.B.2a	309
13.7	Predict How Many	Develop functional relationships in growing patterns	5.OA.B.3; 6.EE.C.9; 7.EE.B.4a; 8.F.A.1	310
13.8	Perimeter Patterns	Generalize and graph geometric growing patterns (functions)	6.EE.C.9; 7.EE.B.4a; 8.F.A.1; 8.F.A.2	313
13.9	Sketch-a-Graph	Explore graphical representations of functional relationships	6.EE.D.9; 8.F.B.5	314
13.10	Border Tiles Expressions—Part 1	Explore a pattern to develop a generalization	5.OA.A.1; 5.OA.A.2; 6.EE.A.2b	318
13.11	Ten and Some More	Develop idea of equivalence while supporting basic fact development	1.OA.C.6; 1.OA.D.7; 2.OA.B.2	320
13.12	Seesaw Students	Develop the concept of the equal sign as a balance	1.OA.D.7; 2.NBT.A.4	321
13.13	Tilt or Balance?	Develop understanding of the equal sign and the less-than and greater-than symbols	2.NBT.A.4; 4.NBT.A.1; 5.NBT.A.3a, b; 6.EE.A.4	322
13.14	True or False?	Explore the meaning of the equal sign	1.OA.B.3; 1.OA.D.7; 1.NBT.B.4; 2.NBT.B.5; 3.OA.B.5; 4.NBT.B.5; 5.NF.A.1	323

(Continued)

Chapter 13 (*Continued*)

Activity	Mathematics Content	CCSS-M	Page
13.15 What's Missing?	Explore the meaning of the equal sign	1.OA.D.7; 1.OA.D.8; 2.OA.A.1; 3.OA.A.4; 5.OA.A.2; 6.EE.A.3; 6.EE.B.5	324
13.16 Make a Statement!	Create equivalent expressions	1.OA.D.7; 1.OA.D.8; 2.OA.A.1; 3.OA.A.4; 4.NF.B.3a; 5.OA.A.2	324
13.17 Ball Weights	Explore variables in context	6.EE.A.4; 7.EE.A.2; 8.EE.C.8b	326
13.18 Border Tiles Expressions—Part 2	Write expressions to represent a situation; Show variable expressions are equivalent	6.EE.A.1; 6.EE.A.2a, b, c; 6.EE.A.3; 6.EE.A.4	327
13.19 Solving the Mystery	Explore properties and equivalent expressions	5.OA.A.2; 6.EE.A.2a; 7.EE.A.2	328
13.20 Designing the Largest Box	Explore volume and surface area algebraically	5.MD.C.5b; 6.EE.A.2c; 6.G.A.2	332

Chapter 14 Developing Fraction Concepts

Activity	Mathematics Content	CCSS-M	Page
14.1 Playground Fractions	Develop concepts of equal shares using an area model	1.G.A.3; 2.G.A.3; 3.NF.A.1	342
14.2 Who Is Winning?	Develop fractional concepts using a linear model	3.NF.A.2a, b; 3.NF.A.3a, b, d	344
14.3 Class Fractions	Develop concepts of fractions using a set model	3.NF.A.1; 3.NF.A.3b	345
14.4 Cookie Dough: Cut Me a Fair Share!	Explore a sharing task and connect to partitioning	1.G.A.3; 2.G.A.3	347
14.5 Partitioning: Fourths or Not Fourths?	Develop understanding of fractional parts	1.G.A.3; 2.G.A.3; 3.NF.A.1	351
14.6 What Fraction Is Colored?	Determine shaded region on number strips where not all partitions are shown	3.NF.A.1; 3.NF.A.2a, b	352
14.7 How Far Did Nicole Go?	Determine shaded region on number strips where not all partitions are shown	3.NF.A.1; 3.NF.A.2a, b	353
14.8 Estimating and Counting Fair Shares	Iterate fraction parts using length contexts	3.NF.A.1; 3.NF.A.2a, b	354
14.9 More, Less, or Equal to One Whole	Develop understanding of fractional parts	3.NF.A.1; 3.NF.A.2a, b	355

Chapter 15   Developing Fraction Operations

(Continued)

Chapter 15 (Continued)

Activity		Mathematics Content	CCSS-M	Page
15.7	Hexagon Wholes	Explore multiplication of a fraction by a whole number (e.g., $3 \times \frac{1}{4}$)	4.NF.B.4a, b	387
15.8	How Big Is the Banner?	Explore multiplication of a whole number by a fraction (e.g., $\frac{1}{2} \times 6$)	5.NF.B.4a, b; 5.NF.B.4a, b	388
15.9	Quilting Pieces	Develop multiplication of fractions with an area model	5.NF.B4b; 5.NF.B.5b	391
15.10	Playground Problem	Explore multiplication of fractions and the commutative property	5.NF.B.4b; 5.NF.B.6	392
15.11	Can You See It?	Relate parts to wholes to explore multiplication of fractions greater than 1	5.NF.B.3; 5.NF.B.5a, b	393
15.12	Fractions Divided by Whole-Number Stories	Explore different contexts for understanding division of a fraction by a whole number	5.NF.B.7a, c	396
15.13	Sandwich Servings	Develop meaning for division by a fraction	5.NF.B.7b, c	398
15.14	How Much in One Whole Set?	Explore whole number divided by a fraction	5.NF.B.7a, c	398
15.15	How Much for 1?	Explore fraction divided by a fraction	5.NF.B.7a, c; 6.NS.A.1	399
15.16	The Size Is Right: Division	Estimate division of fraction problems	5.NF.B.7a, b, c; 6.NS.A.1	401

Chapter 16 Developing Decimal and Percent Concepts and Decimal Computation

Activity		Mathematics Content	CCSS-M	Page
16.1	The Decimal Point Names the Unit	Develop an understanding of the purpose of the decimal point	4.NF.C.6; 5.NBT.A.3a	408
16.2	Shifting Units	Practice shifting the unit in place value	4.NF.C.6; 5.NBT.A.1; 5.NBT.A.2; 5.NBT.A.3a	410
16.3	Decimal Roll and Cover	Explore the size of decimals using an area model	4.NF.C.5 5.NBT.A.1 5.NBT.A.3a	411
16.4	The Amazing Race	Explore the size of decimals using a length model	4.NF.C.6 4.NF.C.7 5.NBT.A.3b	412
16.5	Build It, Name It	Practice connecting the decimal notation to a physical model	4.NF.C.6; 5.NBT.A.1	413
16.6	Calculator Decimal Counting	Develop an understanding of the patterns in decimal notation	4.NF.C.6; 5.NBT.A.1	413
16.7	Familiar Fractions to Decimals	Develop a conceptual connection between fractions and decimal notations	4.NF.C.7	414
16.8	Estimate, Then Verify	Develop a conceptual connection between fractions and decimal notations	4.NF.C.7	415
16.9	Decimals and Fractions on a Double Number Line	Develop a conceptual connection between fractions and decimal notations	4.NF.C.6	415
16.10	Best Match	Practice estimation of decimal numbers with simple fractions	4.NF.C.6	417

Chapter 17　Ratios, Proportions, and Proportional Reasoning

(Continued)

Chapter 17   (*Continued*)

Activity	Mathematics Content	CCSS-M	Page
17.10 Comparing Lemonade Recipes	Explore proportional situations and compare ratios	6.RP.A.1; 6.RP.A.3a, b; 7.RP.A.1; 7.RP.A.2a	451
17.11 Creating Paint Swatches	Create and compare ratios using the context of paint mixes.	6.RP.A.1; 6.RP.A.3a, b; 7.RP.A.1; 7.RP.A.2a	452
17.12 Which Camp Gets More Pizza?	Compare ratios using food portions.	6.RP.A.1; 6.RP.A.3a, b; 7.RP.1; 7.RP.A.2a	452
17.13 Solving Problems Using Ratio Tables	Develop proportional reasoning through scaling	6.RP.A.3a, b; 7.RP.A.1; 7.RP.A.2b, c; 7.RP.A.3	453
17.14 Rates of Wind-Up Toys	Using ratio tables to solve problems	6.RP.A.3a; 7.RP.A.1; 7.RP.A.2b, d	454
17.15 You and the Zoo	Use double number lines to solve situations involving proportions	6.RP.A.3a, d; 7.RP.A.2b; 7.RP.A.3	456
17.16 Making Sense of Percent Stories	Use double number lines to solve situations involving percents	6.RP.A.3c; 7.RP.A.3	457

Chapter 18   Developing Measurement Concepts

Activity	Mathematics Content	CCSS-M	Page
18.1 About One Unit	Develop familiarity with standard units (any attribute)	1.MD.A.2 2.MD.A.1 2.MD.A.3	464
18.2 Familiar Measures	Explore a variety of real word benchmarks or references for standard units	1.MD.A.2; 2.MD.A.1; 3.MD.B.4	465
18.3 Personal Benchmarks	Explore useful benchmarks using body lengths	2.MD.A.1; 3.MD.B.4; 4.MD.B.4	465
18.4 Guess the Unit	Develop the concept of various units of measure	3.MD.A.2; 3.MD.C.5; 4.MD.A.1; 5.MD.C.3	465
18.5 Estimation Exploration	Practice estimating different attributes	K.MD.A.1; K.MD.A.2; 1.MD.A.1; 1.MD.A.2; 2.MD.A.3 3.MD.A.2 5.MD.C.4 6.G.A.1 7.G.B.4 8.G.C.9	468
18.6 Estimation Scavenger Hunt	Practice measurement estimation in real contexts	1.MD.A.2; 2.MD.A.1; 2.MD.A.3 4.MD.A.1	468

(Continued)

Chapter 18   (*Continued*)

Activity		Mathematics Content	CCSS-M	Page
18.26	Capacity Sort	Develop the concept of capacity	K.MD.A.2; 3.MD.A.2; 5.MD.C.3	485
18.27	Fixed Volume: Comparing Prisms	Explore the relationship between volume and surface area of prisms when the volume is constant	5.MD.C.3; 5.MD.C.4; 5.MD.C.5 6.C.A.2	485
18.28	Which Silo Holds More?	Explore volume of cylinders with nonstandard units	5.MD.C.3 6.G.A.4 7.G.B.7	486
18.29	Box Comparison: Cubic Units	Develop the concept of volume; readiness for volume formula for prisms	5.MD.C.3; 5.MD.C.4; 5.MD.C.5 6.G.A.2 7.G.B.6	486
18.30	That's Cool	Develop estimation with units of liquid capacity	3.MD.A.2	487
18.31	Squeeze Play	Develop estimation with units of liquid capacity	3.MD.A.2	487
18.32	A Unit Angle	Develop an understanding of how units are used to measure angle size	4.MD.C.5 7.G.B.5	490
18.33	Angle Maker	Estimate the size of benchmark angles	4.MD.C.5 7.G.B.5	491
18.34	Angle Relationships	Explore supplementary, complementary, vertical, and adjacent angles	7.G.B.5	492
18.35	Ready for the Bell	Explore time as the duration of an event	1.MD.B.3	492
18.36	One-Handed Clocks	Develop an understanding of the hour hand in reading a clock	1.MD.B.3; 2.MD.C.7	494
18.37	Money Skip Counting	Develop skill in counting money	2.MD.C.8	495
18.38	Hundreds Chart Money Count	Explore a strategy for counting money	2.MD.C.8	496

Chapter 19   Developing Geometric Thinking and Geometric Concepts

Activity		Mathematics Content	CCSS-M	Page
19.1	Tricky Shapes	Attend to relevant properties of shapes	K.G.A.2 K.G.B.4 1.G.A.1	503
19.2	Shape Sorts	Develop ways that two-dimensional shapes are alike and different	K.G.B.4; 1.G.A.1; 2.G.A.1; 3.G.A.1	503
19.3	Property Lists for Quadrilaterals	Explore all properties attributable to special classes of quadrilaterals	2.G.A.1; 3.G.A.1; 4.G.A.2; 4.G.A.3	504
19.4	Minimal Defining Lists	Develop logic and reasoning to minimally define shapes	4.G.A.2; 5.G.B.3	505
19.5	Shape Show and Hunt	Explore attributes of two-dimensional shapes and identify their location in the environment	K.G.A.1; K.G.A.2; K.G.B.4	508

Activity		Mathematics Content	CCSS-M	Page
19.6	What's My Shape?	Develop oral descriptions of shapes	1.G.A.1; 2.G.A.1; 3.G.A.1; 4.G.A.2 7.G.A.2	508
19.7	Can You Make It?	Practice representing shapes	1.G.A.1 2.G.A.1 3.G.A.1 4.G.A.1 4.G.A.2 4.G.A.3	509
19.8	Tangram Puzzles	Practice composing shapes	K.G.B.6; 1.G.A.2; 2.G.A.1	510
19.9	Mosaic Puzzle	Explore properties of two-dimensional shapes and compose and decompose shapes	K.G.B.6; 1.G.A.2; 2.G.A.1; 3.G.A.1; 4.G.A.2	510
19.10	Geoboard Copy	Practice representation of shapes	1.G.A.2; 2.G.A.1; 4.G.A.1; 4.G.A.2; 4.G.A.3	511
19.11	Decomposing Shapes	Practice decomposing shapes	1.G.A.2; 1.G.A.3; 2.G.A.1; 2.G.A.3; 3.G.A.2 3.NF.A.1	511
19.12	Shifting Shapes	Constructing and identifying two-dimensional shapes and their properties	K.G.A.1 K.G.B.4 1.G.A.1 1.G.A.2 2.G.A.1 3.G.A.1 4.G.A.2	513
19.13	Constructing Three-Dimensional Shapes	Explore the construction of three-dimensional shapes	K.G.A.3; K.G.B.5; 1.G.A.2; 2.G.A.1; 6.G.A.4	515
19.14	Mystery Definition	Develop defining properties of special classes of shapes	1.G.A.1; 2.G.A.1; 3.G.A.2; 4.G.A.2	516
19.15	Triangle Sort	Develop defining properties of triangles	2.G.A.1; 3.G.A.2; 4.G.A.2; 5.G.B.3; 5.G.B.4 7.G.A.2	517
19.16	Can You Build It?	Draw shapes based on descriptions and properties	4.G.A.2 4.G.A.3 5.G.B.3 5.G.B.4 7.G.A.2	517

(Continued)

Chapter 19 *(Continued)*

Activity		Mathematics Content	CCSS-M	Page
19.17	Angle Sum in a Triangle	Draw conjectures for the sum of the angles in a triangle	7.G.A.2 8.G.A.5;	518
19.18	Triangle Midsegments	Explore geometric relationships and making conjectures	7.G.A.2; 8.G.A.5	518
19.19	Diagonals of Quadrilaterals	Explore the relationships between diagonals of classes of quadrilaterals	4.G.A.2; 5.G.B.3; 5.G.B.4	520
19.20	True or False?	Explore informal deductive statements concerning properties of shapes	4.G.A.2; 5.G.B.3; 5.G.B.4 7.G.A.2	521
19.21	Discovering Pi	Develop an understanding of pi as the ratio of circumference to diameter	7.G.B.4	521
19.22	The Pythagorean Relationship	Explore the meaning of the Pythagorean relationship in geometric terms	8.G.B.6; 8.G.B.7	522
19.23	Finding Pythagorean Triples	Investigate triangles that are Pythagorean triples	8.G.B.6; 8.G.B.7	523
19.24	Motion Man	Develop the concepts of slides, flips, and turns	8.G.A.1a, b, c	524
19.25	Pattern Block Mirror Symmetry	Develop the concept of line symmetry	4.G.A.3	525
19.26	Dot Grid Line Symmetry	Explore relationship between line symmetry and reflection	4.G.A.3	526
19.27	Are They Congruent?	Explore congruent triangles using translations on a grid	8.G.A.1; 8.G.A.2	529
19.28	Polygon Dilations	Explore the result of multiplying coordinates by a constant	6.G.A.3 7.G.A.1 8.G.A.1 8.G.A.3	529
19.29	Hidden Positions	Develop a readiness for coordinates	K.G.A.1; 5.G.A.1	530
19.30	Paths	Explore the concept of location using coordinates on a grid	K.G.A.1; 5.G.A.1	531
19.31	Step Right Up	Write the ordered pair for points on a coordinate grid	5.G.A.1	531
19.32	Coordinate Slides	Develop the way coordinates are used to control translations	6.G.A.3; 8.G.A.1; 8.G.A.3	532
19.33	Coordinate Reflections	Explore the effect on coordinates when shapes are reflected about an axis	8.G.A.1; 8.G.A.3	533
19.34	Finding Distance Using the Pythagorean Theorem	Develop the formula for the distance between two points	6.G.A.3; 8.G.B.8	534
19.35	Can You Remember?	Develop early spatial visualization skills and visual memory	K.G.B.4; 1.G.A.2; 2.G.A.1	535
19.36	Pentominoes	Develop spatial visualization skills	1.G.A.2; 2.G.A.1 3.G.A.1	535
19.37	Geometry Necklaces	Identifying mystery geometric shapes, etc. using deduction	3.G.A.1 4.G.A.1 5.G.B.3	536
19.38	Face Matching	Explore solids in terms of their faces or sides	1.G.A.2; 2.G.A.1; 3.G.A.1; 4.G.A.2	536

Chapter 20   Developing Concepts of Data and Statistics

Chapter 20 (*Continued*)				
Activity		**Mathematics Content**	**CCSS-M**	**Page**
20.15	Balance Point Sticky Notes	Explore a balancing point interpretation of the mean	6.SP.A.2; 6.SP.A.3; 6.SP.B.5	571
20.16	Which Measure of Center Makes Sense?	Decide which measure of center, median or mean, makes more sense given various contexts	6.SP.A.2; 6.SP.A.3; 6.SP.B.5	572
20.17	Average Cost of More Games	Explore how new data impact each measure of center	6.SP.A.2; 6.SP.A.3; 6.SP.B.5	573
20.18	You Be the Judge	Make decisions using your choice of statistical measures	6.SP.A.2; 6.SP.A.3; 6.SP.B.5	573
20.19	How Many Words on the Page?	Design strategy for gathering and analyzing data to solve a real-life problem	6.SP.A.1; 6.SP.A.2; 6.SP.B.5	577

Chapter 21 Exploring Concepts of Probability				
Activity		**Mathematics Content**	**CCSS-M**	**Page**
21.1	Events in Lyrics: Possible or Not Possible?	Introduce concept of probability	7.SP.C.5	581
21.2	Is It Likely?	Introduce concept of probability	7.SP.C.5	582
21.3	1-2-3 How Likely?	Explore how likely particular outcomes are	7.SP.C.5; 7.SP.C.6	583
21.4	1-2-3 How Likely Are Sums?	Explore how likely particular outcomes are with two events	7.SP.C.5; 7.SP.C.6; 7.SP.C.8a	583
21.5	Race to Ten	Use area context for exploring probability	7.SP.C.6; 7.SP.C.7a, b	583
21.6	Design and Test Bags	Explore probability through experiments	7.SP.C.6	585
21.7	Mystery Bags	Explore probability through experiments	7.SP.C.6; 7.SP.C.7a, b	585
21.8	Fair or Unfair Games	Explore games theoretically and through experiments	7.SP.C.6; 7.SP.C.7a	587
21.9	Chance of Hitting the Target?	Explore probability in an area model	7.G.B.4; 7.SP.C.6; 7.SP.C.7b	589
21.10	Drop It!	Determine how likely outcomes are based on empirical data	7.SP.C.7b	590
21.11	Get All 6!	Explore impact of size of the trial	7.SP.C.6	590
21.12	What Are the Chances?	Develop the concept of randomness	7.SP.C.6	591
21.13	Lu-Lu	Compare results of game (experiment) with sample space	7.SP.C.7a; 7.SP.C.8a	595
21.14	Are You a Spring Dog?	Use an area model to determine how likely independent events are	7.SP.C.8a, b	596

Chapter 22   Developing Concepts of Exponents, Integers, and Real Numbers

References

Chapter 1

Association of Mathematics Teacher Educators. (2017). *Standards for preparing teachers of mathematics*. Retrieved from amte.net/standards February 5, 2017.

Bailey, D. H., Siegler, R. S., & Geary, D. C. (2014). Early predictors of middle school fraction knowledge. *Developmental Science, 17*(5), 775–785.

Clements, D., & Sarama, J. (2014). *Learning and teaching early math: The learning trajectories approach* (2nd ed.). New York, NY: Routledge.

Cobb, P., & Jackson, K. (2011). Assessing the quality of the Common Core State Standards for mathematics. *Educational Researcher, 40*(4), 183–185.

Confrey, J., Maloney, A., & Corley, A. (2014). Learning trajectories: A framework for connecting standards to curriculum. *ZDM, 46*(5), 719–733. doi 10.1007/s11858-014-0598-7.

Corcoran, T., Mosher, F., & Rogat, A. (2009). *Learning progressions in science: An evidence-based approach to reform* (Research Report No. RR-63). Philadelphia, PA: Consortium for Policy Research in Education.

Dossey, J. A., McCrone, S. S., & Halvorsen, K. T. (2016). *Mathematics education in the United States 2016*. Reston, VA: NCTM and the U.S. National Commission on Mathematics Instruction.

Dweck, C. S. (2007). The perils and promises of praise. *Educational Leadership, 65*(2), 34–39.

Friedman, T. (2007). *The world is flat 3.0: A brief history of the twenty-first century*. New York, NY: Picador.

Green, E. (2014). (New math) – (new teaching) = failure. *New York Times Magazine*, July 27, 22–27, 40–41.

Hacker, A. (2016). The wrong way to teach math. *New York Times*, (February 28), 2.

Jong, C., & Hodges, T. (2015). Assessing attitudes toward mathematics across teacher education contexts. *Journal of Mathematics Teacher Education*. DOI: 10.1007/s10857-015-9319-6.

Karp, K., Bush, S., & Dougherty, B. (2016) Establishing a mathematics whole school agreement. *Teaching Children Mathematics, 23*(2), 69–71.

Kloosterman, P., Rutledge, Z., & Kenney, P. A. (2009). A generation of progress: Learning from NAEP. *Teaching Children Mathematics, 15*(6), 363–369.

Koestler, C., Felton, M., Bieda, K., & Otten, S. (2013). *Connecting the NCTM process standards and the CCSSM practices*. Reston, VA: NCTM.

Leinwand, S. (2007). Four teacher-friendly postulates for thriving in a sea of change. *Mathematics Teacher, 100*(9), 582–584.

Ma, L. (1999). *Knowing and teaching elementary mathematics: Teachers' understanding of fundamental mathematics in China and the United States*. Mahwah, NJ: Erlbaum.

Maloney, E., Gunderson, E. Ramirez, G., Levine, S., & Beilock, S. (2014). *Teachers' math anxiety relates to girls' and boys' math achievement*. Unpublished manuscript.

Morris, A. K., & Hiebert, J. (2017). Effects of teacher preparation courses: Do graduates use what they learned to plan mathematics lessons? *American Educational Research Journal, 54*(3), 524–567.

National Center for Education Statistics. (2014). Retrieved from www.nationsreportcard.gov/reading_math_2015/#?grade=4

NCTM (National Council of Teachers of Mathematics). (1989). *Curriculum and evaluation standards for school mathematics*. Reston, VA: NCTM.

NCTM (National Council of Teachers of Mathematics). (1995). *Assessment standards for school mathematics*. Reston, VA: NCTM.

NCTM (National Council of Teachers of Mathematics). (2000). *Principles and standards for school mathematics*. Reston, VA: NCTM.

NCTM (National Council of Teachers of Mathematics). (2006). *Curriculum focal points for prekindergarten through grade 8 mathematics: A quest for coherence*. Reston, VA: NCTM.

NCTM (National Council of Teachers of Mathematics). (2014). *Position statement on access and equity in mathematics education*. Reston, VA: NCTM.

NGA Center (National Governors Association Center for Best Practices) & CCSSO (Council of Chief State School Officers). (2010). *Common core state standards*. Retrieved from corestandards.org

OECD. (2016). *Equations and inequalities: Making mathematics accessible to all*. Paris: OECD Publishing. dx.doi.org/10.178/9789264258495-en.

Palardy, G. J., & Rumberger, R. W. (2008). Teacher effectiveness in the first grade: The importance of background qualifications, attitudes, and instructional practices for student learning. *Educational Evaluation and Policy Analysis, 30*, 111–140.

Porter, A., McMaken, J., Hwang, J., & Yang, R. (2011). Common core standards: The new U.S. intended curriculum. *Educational Researcher, 40*(3), 103–116.

Rittle-Johnson, B., Schneider, M., & Star, J. R. (2015). Not a one-way street: Bidirectional relations between procedural and conceptual knowledge of mathematics. *Educational Psychology Review, 27*(4), 587–597.

Rothwell, J. (2014). *Still searching: Job vacancies and STEM skills*. Washington, DC: Brookings Institution.

Steen, L. A. (Ed.). (1997). *Why numbers count: Quantitative literacy for tomorrow's America*. New York: The College Board.

Stigler, J., & Hiebert, J. (2009). Closing the teaching gap. *Phi Delta Kappan, 91*(3), 32–37.

Tobias, S. (1995). *Overcoming math anxiety*. New York: Norton.

Toppo, G. (2015). Johnny can't always read, but slide in math scores puzzles. *USA Today*, October 28, 1.

Walkowiak, T. A. (2015). Information is a common core dish best served first. *Phi Delta Kappan, 97*(2), 62–67.

Warshauer, H. (2015). Strategies to support productive struggle. *Mathematics Teaching in the Middle School, 20*(7), 390–393.

Watts, T. W., Duncan, G. J., Siegler, R. S., & Davis-Kean, P. E. (2014). What's past is prologue: Relations between early mathematics knowledge and high school achievement. *Educational Researcher, 43*(7), 352–360.

Wiggins, G. (2013, May 5). Letter to the Editor. *New York Times*, 2.

Chapter 2

Anderson, L. W., & Krathwohl, D. R. (Eds.) (2001). *A taxonomy for learning, teaching, and assessing: A revision of Bloom's Taxonomy of educational objectives: Complete Edition.* New York, NY: Addison Wesley, Longman.

Ball, D. L. (1992). Magical hopes: Manipulatives and the reform of math education. *American Educator, 16*(2), 14–18, 46–47.

Baroody, A. J., Feil, Y., & Johnson A. R. (2007). An alternative reconceptualization of procedural and conceptual knowledge. *Journal for Research in Mathematics Education, 38*(2), 115–131.

Boaler, J. (2016). *Mathematical mindsets: Unleashing student potential through creative math, inspiring messaging, and innovative teaching.* San Francisco, CA: Jossey Bass.

Bransford, J., Brown, A., & Cocking, R. (Eds.) (2000). *How people learn: Brain, mind, experience, and school: Expanded edition.* Washington, DC: National Academies Press.

Carter, S. (2008). Disequilibrium & questioning in the primary classroom: Establishing routines that help students learn. *Teaching Children Mathematics, 15*(3), 134–137.

Clements, D. H., & Battista, M. T. (1990). Constructivist learning and teaching. *Arithmetic Teacher, 38*(1), 34–35.

Cobb, P. (1988). The tension between theories of learning and instruction in mathematics education. *Educational Psychologist, 23*(2), 87–103.

Cobb, P. (1994). Where is the mind? Constructivist and sociocultural perspectives on mathematical development. *Educational Researcher, 23*(7), 13–20.

Davis, B., & Sumara, D. (2012). Fitting teacher education in/to/for an increasingly complex world. *Complicity: An International Journal of Complexity and Education, 9*(1), 30–40.

Fillingim, J. G., & Barlow, A. T. (2010). From the inside out. *Teaching Children Mathematics, 17*(2), 80–88.

Fosnot, C. T. (1996). Constructivism: A psychological theory of learning. In C. T. Fosnot (Ed.), *Constructivism: Theory, perspectives, and practice* (pp. 8–33). New York, NY: Teachers College Press.

Forman, E. A. (2003). A sociocultural approach to mathematics reform: Speaking, inscribing, and doing mathematics within communities of practice. In J. Kilpatrick, W. G. Martin, & D. Schifter (Eds.), *A research companion to Principles and Standards for School Mathematics* (pp. 333–352). Reston, VA: NCTM.

Goos, M. (2004). Learning mathematics in a classroom community of inquiry. *Journal for Research in Mathematics Education, 35*(4), 258–291.

Hiebert, J., & Grouws, D. A. (2007). The effects of classroom mathematics teaching on students' learning. In F. K. Lester (Ed.), *Second handbook of research on mathematics teaching and learning* (pp. 371–404). Charlotte, NC: Information Age Publishing.

Kobiela, M., & Lehrer, R. (2015). The codevelopment of mathematical concepts and the practice of defining, *Journal for Research in Mathematics Education, 46*(4), 423–454.

Lappan, G., & Even, R. (1989). *Learning to teach: Constructing meaningful understanding of mathematical content* (Craft Paper 89–3). East Lansing, MI: Michigan State University.

Lesh, R. A., Cramer, K., Doerr, H., Post, T., & Zawojewski, J. (2003). Model development sequences. In R. A. Lesh & H. Doerr (Eds.), *Beyond constructivism: A models and modeling perspective on mathematics teaching, learning, and problem solving* (pp. 35–58). Mahwah, NJ: Erlbaum.

Martinie, S. L. (2014). Decimal fractions: An important point. *Mathematics Teaching in the Middle School, 19*(7), 420–429.

NCTM (National Council of Teachers of Mathematics). (2014). *Position statement on access and equity in mathematics education.* Reston, VA: NCTM.

National Research Council. (2001). *Adding it up: Helping children learn mathematics.* J. Kilpatrick, J. Swafford, & B. Findell (Eds.). Washington, DC: National Academies Press.

NGA Center (National Governors Association Center for Best Practices) & CCSSO (Council of Chief State School Officers). (2010). *Common core state standards.* Retrieved from corestandards.org

Norton, A., & D'Ambrosio, B. S. (2008). ZPC and ZPD: Zones of teaching and learning. *Journal for Research in Mathematics Education, 39*(3), 220–246.

Rathouz, M. (2011). 3 ways that promote student reasoning. *Teaching Children Mathematics, 18*(3), 182–189.

Schifter, D., & Fosnot, C. T. (1993). *Reconstructing mathematics education.* New York: Teachers College Press.

Schneider, M., Rittle-Johnson, B., & Star, J. R. (2011). Relations among conceptual knowledge, procedural knowledge, and procedural flexibility in two samples differing in prior knowledge. *Developmental Psychology, 47*, 1525–1538.

Skemp, R. (1978). Relational understanding and instrumental understanding. *Arithmetic Teacher, 26*(3), 9–15.

Stein, M. K., & Bovalino, J. W. (2001). Manipulatives: One piece of the puzzle. *Teaching Children Mathematics, 6*(6), 356–359.

Suh, J. M. (2007). Tying it all together: Building mathematics proficiency for all students. *Teaching Children Mathematics, 14*(3), 163–169.

Thompson, P. W. (1994). Concrete materials and teaching for mathematical understanding. *Arithmetic Teacher, 41*(9), 556–558.

von Glasersfeld, E. (1996). Introduction: Aspects of constructivism. In Fosnot, C. T. (Ed.), *Constructivism: Theory, perspective, and practice* (pp. 3–7). New York: Teachers College Press.

Vygotsky, L. S. (1978). *Mind and society.* Cambridge, MA: Harvard University Press.

Whitacre, I., Schoen, R. C., Champagne, Z., & Goddard, A. (2016). Relational thinking: What's the difference? *Teaching Children Mathematics, 23*(5), 303–309.

Wilburne, J. M., Wildmann, T., Morret, M., & Stipanovic, J. (2014). Classroom strategies to make sense and persevere. *Mathematics Teaching in the Middle School, 20*(3), 144–151.

Chapter 3

Aguirre, J. M., Mayfield-Ingram, K., & Martin, D. (2013). *The impact of identity in K–8 mathematics learning and teaching: Rethinking equity-based practices.* Reston, VA: NCTM.

AIMS (2005). *Looking at Lines: Interesting objects and linear functions.* Fresno, CA: AIMS Education Foundation.

Barlow, A. T. (2010). Building word problems: What does it take? *Teaching Children Mathematics, 17*(3), 140–148.

Bay-Williams, J. M., & Martinie, S. L. (2009). *Math and non-fiction: Grades 6–8.* Sausalito, CA: Marilyn Burns Books.

Bay-Williams, J. M., & Stokes Levine, A. (2017). The role of concepts and procedures in developing fluency. In D. Spangler & J. Wanko (Eds.), *Enhancing classroom practice with research behind PtA.* Reston, VA: NCTM.

Boaler, J. (2008, April). Promoting "relational equity" and high mathematics achievement through an innovative mixed ability approach. *British Educational Research Journal, 34*, 167–194.

Boaler, J., (2016). *Mathematical mindsets*. San Francisco: Jossey-Bass.

Boaler, J., & Sengupta-Irving, T. (2016). The many colors of algebra: The impact of equity focused teaching upon student learning and engagement. *The Journal of Mathematical Behavior, 41*, 179–190.

Boaler, J., & Selling, S. K. (2017). Psychological imprisonment or intellectual freedom? A longitudinal study of contrasting school mathematics approaches and their impact on adults' lives. *Journal for Research in Mathematics Education, 48*(1), 78–105.

Bransford, J., Brown, A., & Cocking, R., Eds. (2000). *How people learn: Brain, mind, experience, and school: Expanded edition*. Washington, DC: National Academies Press.

Breyfogle, M. L., & Williams, L. E. (2008–2009). Designing and implementing worthwhile tasks. *Teaching Children Mathematics, 15*(5), 276–280.

Buckley, J., Jr., & Stremme, R. (2006). *Book of lists: Fun facts, weird trivia, and amazing lists on nearly everything you need to know!* Santa Barbara, CA: Scholastic.

Cai, J. (2010). Helping elementary school students become successful mathematical problem solvers. In D. Lambdin (Ed.), *Teaching and learning mathematics: Translating research to the classroom* (pp. 9–14). Reston, VA: NCTM.

Carpenter, T. P., Franke, M. L., Jacobs, V. R., Fennema, E., & Empson, S. B. (1998). A longitudinal study of invention and understanding in children's multidigit addition and subtraction. *Journal for Research in Mathematics Education, 29*(1), 3–20.

Chapin, S., O'Conner, C., & Anderson, N. C. (2013). *Talk Moves: A Teacher's Guide for Using Classroom Discussions in Math* (3rd ed.). Sausalito, CA: Math Solutions.

Clifford, P., & Marinucci, S. J. (2008). Voices inside schools: Testing the waters: Three elements of classroom inquiry. *Harvard Education Review, 78*(4), 675–688.

Cobb, P., Gresalfi, M. S., & Hodge, L. L. (2009). An interpretive scheme for analyzing the identities that students develop in mathematics classrooms. *Journal for Research in Mathematics Education, 40*(1), 40–68.

Diversity in Mathematics Education. (2007). Culture, race, power, and mathematics education. In F. Lester, Jr. (Ed.), *Second handbook of research on mathematics teaching and learning* (pp. 405–434). Charlotte, NC: Information Age Publishing and NCTM.

Franke, M. L., Kazemi, E., & Battey, D. (2007). Mathematics teaching and classroom practice. In F. K. Lester (Ed.), *Second handbook of research on mathematics teaching and learning* (pp. 225–256). Reston, VA: NCTM.

Fuson, K. C., Kalchman, M. & Bransford, J. D. (2005). Mathematical understanding: An introduction. In M. Suzanne Donovan & J. Bransford (Eds.), *How students learn mathematics in the classroom* (pp. 217–256). Washington DC: National Academy of Sciences.

Guerrero, S. M. (2010). The value of guess & check. *Mathematics Teaching in the Middle School, 15*(7), 392–398.

Heaton, R. M., & Lewis, W. J. (2011). A mathematician–mathematics educator partnership to teach teachers. *Notices of the American Mathematical Society, 58*(3), 394–400.

Herbel-Eisenmann, B. A., & Breyfogle, M. L. (2005). Questioning our patterns of questioning. *Mathematics Teaching in the Middle School, 10*(9), 484–489.

Hiebert, J., Carpenter, T. P., Fennema, E., Fuson, K., Human, P., Murray, H., et al. (1996). Problem solving as a basis for reform in curriculum and instruction: The case of mathematics. *Educational Researcher, 25*(4), 12–21.

Hiebert, J., Carpenter, T. P., Fennema, E., Fuson, K., Wearne, D., Murray, H., . . . Human, P. (1997). *Making sense: Teaching and learning mathematics with understanding*. Portsmouth, NH: Heinemann.

Hiebert, J., & Grouws, D. A. (2007). The effects of classroom mathematics teaching on students' learning. In F. K. Lester (Ed.), *Second handbook of research on mathematics teaching and learning* (pp. 371–404). Charlotte, NC: Information Age Publishing.

Hong, L. T. (1993). *Two of everything: A Chinese folktale*. New York, NY: Albert Whitman.

Jacobs, V. R., Martin, H. A., Ambrose, R. C., & Philipp, R. A. (2014). Warning signs! *Teaching Children Mathematics, 21*(2), 107–113.

Kazemi, E., & Hintz, A. (2014). *Intentional talk: How to structure and lead productive mathematical discussions*. Portland, ME: Stenhouse Publishers.

Kilic, H., Cross, D. I., Ersoz, F. A., Mewborn, D. S., Swanagan, D., & Kim, J. (2010). Techniques for small-group discourse. *Teaching Children Mathematics, 16*(6), 350–357.

Kline, K. (2008). Learning to think and thinking to learn. *Teaching Children Mathematics, 15*, 144–151.

Lampe, K. A., & Uselmann, L. (2008). Pen pals: Practicing problem solving. *Mathematics Teaching in the Middle School, 14*(4), 196–201.

Langer-Osuna, J. (2011). How Brianna became bossy and Kofi came out smart: Understanding the differentially mediated identity and engagement of two group leaders in a project-based mathematics classroom. *The Canadian Journal for Science, Mathematics, and Technology Education, 11*(3), 207–225.

Lannin, J., Ellis, A. B., Elliott, R. (2011). *Developing essential understanding of mathematical reasoning: PreK–Grade 8*. Reston, VA: NCTM.

Leatham K. R., & Hill, D. S. (2010). Exploring our complex math identities. *Mathematics Teaching in the Middle School, 16*(4), 224–231.

Lesh, R. A., & Zawojewski, J. S. (2007). Problem solving and modeling. In F. K. Lester, Jr. (Ed.), *The handbook of research on mathematics teaching and learning* (2nd ed., pp. 763–804). Reston, VA: NCTM; Charlotte, NC: Information Age Publishing.

Levasseur, K., & Cuoco, A. (2003). Mathematical habits of mind. In H. L. Shoen (Ed.), *Teaching mathematics through problem solving: Grade 6–12* (pp. 23–37). Reston, VA: NCTM.

Lynch, S. D., Lynch, J. M., & Bolyard, J. (2013). Informing practice: I-THINK I can problem solve. *Mathematics Teaching in the Middle School, 19*(1), 10–14.

Mark, J., Cuoco, A., Goldenberg, E. P., & Sword, S. (2010). Developing mathematical habits of mind. *Mathematics Teaching in the Middle School, 15*(9), 505–509.

Moschkovich, J. N. (1998). Supporting the participation of English language learners in mathematical discussions. *For the Learning of Mathematics, 19*(1), 11–19.

Murrey, D. L. (2008). Differentiating instruction in mathematics for the English language learner. *Mathematics Teaching in the Middle School, 14*(3), 146–153.

NCTM (National Council of Teachers of Mathematics). (2014). *Position statement on access and equity in mathematics education*. Reston, VA: NCTM.

NGA Center (National Governors Association Center for Best Practices) & CCSSO (Council of Chief State School Officers). (2010). *Common core state standards*. Retrieved from corestandards.org

Partnership for 21st Century Skills. (n.d.). *Framework for 21st century learning*. Washington, DC: Author. Retrieved from www.p21.org/storage/documents/1.__p21_framework_2-pager.pdf

Petersen, J. (2004). *Math and nonfiction: Grades K–2.* Sausalito, CA: Math Solutions Publications.

Pólya, G. (1945). *How to solve it.* Princeton, NJ: Princeton University Press.

Pugalee, D. K., Arbaugh, F., Bay-Williams, J. M., Farrell, A., Mathews, S., &. Royster, D. (2008). *Navigating through mathematical connections in grades 6–8.* Reston, VA: NCTM.

Rasmussen, C., Yackel, E., & King, K. (2003). Social and sociomathematical norms in the mathematics classroom. In H. L. Schoen & R. I. Charles (Eds.), *Teaching mathematics through problem solving: Grades 6–12* (pp. 143–154). Reston, VA: NCTM.

Rowling, J. K. (1998). *Harry Potter and the sorcerer's stone.* New York, NY: A. A. Lewine.

Schneider, M., Rittle-Johnson, B., & Star, J. R. (2011). Relations among conceptual knowledge, procedural knowledge, and procedural flexibility in two samples differing in prior knowledge. *Developmental Psychology, 47,* 1525–1538.

Schroeder, T. L., & Lester, F. K., Jr. (1989). Developing understanding in mathematics via problem solving. In P. R. Trafton (Ed.), *New directions for elementary school mathematics* (pp. 31–42). Reston, VA: NCTM.

Silver, E. A., & Stein, M. K. (1996). The QUASAR project: The "revolution of the possible" in mathematics instructional reform in urban middle schools. *Urban Education, 30*(4), 476–521.

Smith, M. S., Bill, V., & Hughes, E. K. (2008). Thinking through a lesson: Successfully implementing high-level tasks. *Mathematics Teaching in the Middle School, 14*(3), 132–138.

Smith, M. S., Hughes, E. K., Engle, R. A., & Stein, M. K. (2009). Orchestrating discussions. *Mathematics Teaching in the Middle School, 14*(9), 548–556.

Smith, M. S., & Stein, M. K. (1998). Selecting and creating mathematical tasks: From research to practice. *Mathematics Teaching in the Middle School, 3*(5), 344–350.

Smith, M. S., & Stein, M. K. (2011). *5 Practices for orchestrating productive mathematics discussions.* Thousand Oaks, CA: Corwin Press.

Steele, D. F. (2007). Understanding students' problem solving knowledge through their writing. *Mathematics Teaching in the Middle School, 13*(2), 102–109.

Suh, J. M. (2007). Developing "algebra-'rithmetic" in the elementary grades. *Teaching Children Mathematics, 14*(4), 246–253.

Thomas, D., & Brown, J. S. (2011). *A new culture of learning: Cultivating the imagination for a world of constant change* (Vol. 219). Lexington, KY: CreateSpace.

Thomas, K. R. (2006). Students THINK: A framework for improving problem solving. *Teaching Children Mathematics, 13*(2), 86–95.

Tomaz, V. S., & David, M. M. (2015). How students' everyday situations modify classroom mathematical activity: The case of water consumption. *Journal for Research in Mathematics Education, 46*(4), 455–496.

Towers, J. (2010). Learning to teach mathematics though inquiry: A focus on the relationship between describing and enacting inquiry-oriented teaching. *Journal of Mathematics Teacher Education, 13*(3), 243–263.

Wagganer, E. L. (2015). Creating math talk communities. *Teaching Children Mathematics, 22*(4), 248–254.

White, J. (2014). *Using children's literature to teach problem solving in math: Addressing the Common Core in Grade K–2.* New York, NY: Taylor & Francis.

Wickett, M., Kharas, K., & Burns, M. (2002). *Lessons for algebraic thinking.* Sausalito, CA: Math Solutions Publications.

Wood, T., Williams, G., & McNeal, B. (2006). Children's mathematical thinking in different classroom cultures. *Journal for Research in Mathematics Education, 37*(3), 222–255.

Wu, Z., An, S., King, J., Ramirez, M., & Evans, S. (2009). Second-Grade "professors." *Teaching Children Mathematics, 16*(1), 34–41.

Yackel, E., & Cobb, P. (1996). Sociomathematical norms, argumentation, and autonomy in mathematics. *Journal for Research in Mathematics Education, 27*(4), 458–477.

Zollman, A. (2009). Mathematical graphic organizers. *Teaching Children Mathematics, 16*(4), 222–229.

Chapter 4

Barlow, A., Gerstenschlager, N. E., & Harmon, S. E. (2016). Learning from the unknown student. *Teaching Children Mathematics, 23*(2), 75–81.

Barnard, W. M. (2004). Parent involvement in elementary school and educational attainment. *Children and Youth Services Review, 26*(1), 39–62.

Bay-Williams, J. M., Duffet, A., & Griffith, D. (2016). *Common core mathematics in the K–8 classroom: Results from a national teacher survey.* Thomas B. Fordham Institute, Washington, DC.

Boaler, J. (2009). *What's math got to do with it?: How parents and teachers can help children learn to love their least favorite subject.* New York, NY: Penguin Books.

Boaler, J., & Humphreys, C. (2005). *Connecting mathematical ideas: Middle school video cases to support teaching and learning.* Portsmouth, NH: Heinemann.

Booth, J. L., Cooper, L., Donovan, M. S., Huyghe, A., Kodeinger, K. R., & Paré-Blagoev, E. J. (2015). Design-based research within constraints of practice: Algebra by example. *Journal of Education for Students Placed at Risk, 20*(1–2), 79–100.

Booth, J. L., Lange, K. E., Koedinger, K. R., & Newton, K. J. (2013). Example problems that improve student learning in algebra: differentiating between correct and incorrect examples. *Learning and Instruction, 25,* 24–34.

Bray, W. S. (2009). The power of choice. *Teaching Children Mathematics, 16*(3), 178–184.

Buschman, L. (2003). *Share and compare: A teacher's story about helping children become problem solvers in mathematics.* Reston, VA: NCTM.

Cassone, J. D. (2009). Differentiating mathematics by using task difficulty. In D. Y. White & J. S. Spitzer (Eds.), *Mathematics for every student: Responding to diversity, grades Pre-K–5* (pp. 89–98). Reston, VA: NCTM.

Civil, M., & Menéndez, J. M. (2010). *NCTM research brief: Involving Latino and Latina parents in their children's mathematics education.* Retrieved from www.nctm.org/uploadedFiles/Research_News_and_Advocacy/Research/Clips_and_Briefs/Research_brief_17-civil.pdf

Civil, M., & Planas, N. (2010). Latino/a immigrant parents' voices in mathematics education. In E. L. Grigorenko & R. Takanishi (Eds.), *Immigration, diversity, and education* (pp. 130–150). New York, NY: Routledge.

Coates, G. D., & Mayfield, K. (2009). Families Ask: Cooperative learning. *Mathematics Teaching in the Middle School, 15*(4), 244–245.

Cooper, H. (2007). *The battle over homework: Common ground for administrators, teachers, and parents* (3rd ed.). Thousand Oaks, CA: Corwin Press.

Davis, B., & Simmt, E. (2006). Mathematics-for-teaching: An ongoing investigation of the mathematics that teachers (need to) know. *Educational Studies in Mathematics, 61*(3), 293–319.

Davis, B., Sumara, D., & Luce-Kapler, R. (2008). *Engaging minds: Changing teaching in complex times.* New York, NY: Routledge.

Elhert, D. (2015, October). Promoting growth mindset with 3 Act Math. *MTMS Blog: Blogarithm,* Accessed at www.nctm.org/Publications/Mathematics-Teaching-in-Middle-School/Blog/Promoting-Growth-Mindset-with-3-Act-Math/

Else-Quest, N. M., Hyde, J. S., & Hejmadi, A. (2008). Mother and child emotions during mathematics homework. *Mathematical Thinking and Learning, 10,* 5–35.

Ernst, K., & Ryan, S. (2014). Success from the start: Your first years teaching elementary school. Reston, VA: NCTM.

Ghousseini, H., Lord, S., & Cardon, A. (2017). Supporting math talk in small groups. *Teaching Children Mathematics, 23*(7), 422–428.

Gilbert, M. C., & Musu, L. E. (2008). Using TARGETTS to create learning environments that support mathematical understanding and adaptive motivation. *Teaching Children Mathematics, 15*(3), 138–143.

Goldenberg, P., & Mason, J. (2008). Shedding light on and with examples spaces. *Educational Studies in Mathematics, 69,* 183–194.

Heck, T. (2006). *Team building games on a shoestring.* Retrieved from www.teachmeteamwork.com/teachmeteamwork/files/Teambuilding_on_a_Shoestring_sml.pdf

Hiebert, J., & Grouws, D. A. (2007). The effects of classroom mathematics teaching on students' learning. In F. K. Lester (Ed.), *Second handbook of research on mathematics teaching and learning* (pp. 371–404). Charlotte, NC: Information Age Publishing.

Hildebrandt, M. E., Biglan, B., & Budd, L. (2013). Let's take a road trip. *Teaching Children Mathematics, 21*(2), 548–553.

Jacobs, V. R., & Ambrose, R. C. (2008). Making the most of story problems. *Teaching Children Mathematics, 15*(5), 260–266.

Jacobs, V. R., Lamb, L. L. C., & Philipp, R. A. (2010). Professional noticing of children's mathematical thinking. *Journal for Research in Mathematics Education, 41*(2), 169–202.

Jacobs, V. R., Martin, H. A., Ambrose, R. C., & Philipp, R. A. (2014). Warning signs! *Teaching Children Mathematics, 19*(7), 107–113.

Jones, A. (1999). *Team building activities for every group.* Richland, WA: Rec Room Publishing.

Kingore, B. (2006, Winter). Tiered instruction: Beginning the process. *Teaching for High Potential,* 5–6.

Kliman, M. (1999). Beyond helping with homework: Parents and children doing mathematics at home. *Teaching Children Mathematics, 6*(3), 140–146.

Knapp, A. K., Jefferson, V. M., & Landers, R. (2013). Learning together. *Teaching Children Mathematics, 19*(7), 432–439.

Lappan, G., & Even, R. (1989). *Learning to teach: Constructing meaningful understanding of mathematical content* (Craft Paper 89–3). East Lansing, MI: Michigan State University.

Larson, M. (2016, November). The need to make homework comprehensible. *President's Message.* Reston, VA: NCTM.

Lee, J., & Bowen, N. K. (2006). Parent involvement, cultural capital, and the achievement gap among elementary school children. *American Educational Research Journal, 43*(2), 193–218.

Legnard, D., & Austin, S. (2014). The Math Promise: Celebrating at home and school. *Teaching Children Mathematics, 21*(3), 178–184.

Matthews, M. E., Hlas, C. S., & Finken, T. M. (2009). Using lesson study and four-column lesson planning with preservice teachers. *Mathematics Teacher, 102*(7), 504–508.

McCoy, A., Barnett, J., & Combs, E. (2013). *High-yield routines: Grades K–8.* Reston, VA: NCTM.

McGinn, K. M., Lange, K. E., & Booth, J. L. (2015). A worked example for creating worked examples. *Mathematics Teaching in the Middle School, 21*(1), 27–33.

Mistretta, R. M. (2013). "We *do* care," say parents. *Teaching Children Mathematics, 19*(9), 572–580.

Muir, T. (2016). Out of the classroom into the home. *Teaching Children Mathematics, 22*(8), 497–504.

Munter, C., Stein, M. K., & Smith, M. S. (2015). Is there a common pedagogical core? Examining instructional practices of competing models of mathematics teaching. *National Council for Supervisors of Mathematics Journal, 16*(2): 3–13.

Nebesniak, A. L., & Heaton, R. M. (2010). Student confidence & student involvement. *Mathematics Teaching in the Middle School, 16*(2), 97–103.

NGA Center (National Governors Association Center for Best Practices) & CCSSO (Council of Chief State School Officers). (2010). *Common core state standards.* Retrieved from corestandards.org

Otten, S., Cirillo, M., & Herbel-Eisenmann, B. A. (2015). Making the most of going over homework. *Mathematics Teaching in the Middle School, 21*(2), 98–105.

Parrish, S. (2014). *Number talks: Helping children develop mental math and computation strategies, grades K–5.* Sausalito, CA: Math Solutions.

Parrish, S., & Dominick, A. (2016). *Number talks: Fractions, decimals, and percentages.* Sausalito, CA: Math Solutions.

Phelps, K. A. G. (2012). The power of problem choices. *Teaching Children Mathematics, 19*(3), 152–157.

Remillard, J. T., & Jackson, K. (2006). Old math, new math: Parents' experiences with standards-based reform. *Mathematical Thinking and Learning, 3*(6), 231–259.

Rodríguez-Brown, F. V. (2010). Latino families: Culture and schooling. In E. G. Murillo, Jr., S. A. Villenas, R. T. Galván, J. S. Muñoz, C. Martínez, & M. Machado-Casas (Eds.), *Handbook of Latinos and education: Theory, research, and practice* (pp. 350–360). New York, NY: Routledge.

Schwartz, S. L. (1996). Hidden messages in teacher talk: Praise and empowerment. *Teaching Children Mathematics, 2*(7), 396–401.

Seeley, C. L. (2009). *Faster isn't smarter: Messages about math, teaching, and learning in the 21st century.* Sausalito, CA: Math Solutions.

Shumway, J. F. (2011). *Number sense routines: Building numerical literacy every day in Grades K–3.* Portland, ME: Stenhouse Publishers.

Sikes, S. (1995). *Feeding the zircon gorilla and other team building activities.* Tulsa, OK: Learning Unlimited Corporation.

Small, M. (2017). *Good questions: Great ways to differentiate math instruction in the standards-based classroom.* (3rd Edition). Reston, VA: NCTM and New York, NY: Teachers College Press.

Smith, M. S., Bill, V., & Hughes, E. K. (2008). Thinking through a lesson: Successfully implementing high-level tasks. *Mathematics Teaching in the Middle School, 14*(3), 132–138.

Smith, M. S., & Stein, M. K. (2011). *5 Practices for orchestrating productive mathematics discussions.* Thousand Oaks, CA: Corwin Press.

Star, J. R., & Verschaffel, L. (2016). Providing support for student sense making: Recommendations from cognitive science for the teaching of mathematics. In Jinfa Cai (Ed.), *Compendium for Research in Mathematics Education.* Reston, VA: NCTM.

Stein, M. K., Remillard, J., & Smith, M. S. (2007). How curriculum influences student learning. In F. J. Lester, Jr. (Ed.), *Second handbook of research on mathematics teaching and learning* (pp. 319–369). Charlotte, NC: Information Age Publishing.

Tomlinson, C. A., & McTighe, J. (2006). *Integrating differentiated instruction.* Alexandria, VA: Association for Supervision and Curriculum Development.

Wallace, A. H. (2007). Anticipating student responses to improve problem solving. *Mathematics Teaching in the Middle School, 12*(9), 504–511.

Walk, L., & Lassak, M. (2017). Making homework matter to students. *Mathematics Teaching in the Middle School, 22*(9), 547–553.

Whitenack, J. W., Cavey, L. O., & Henney, C. (2015). *It's Elementary: A Parent's Guide to K–5 Mathematics.* Reston, VA: NCTM.

Wieman, R., & Arbaugh, F. (2014). Making homework more meaningful. *Mathematics Teaching in the Middle School, 20*(3), 160–165.

Chapter 5

Accardo, A. L., & Kuder, S. J. (2017). Monitoring student learning in algebra. *Mathematics Teaching in the Middle School, 22*(6), 352–359.

Association of Mathematics Teacher Educators, & National Council of Supervisors of Mathematics. (n.d.). *Improving student achievement in mathematics through formative assessment in instruction.* Joint position paper, amte.net/sites/default/files/overview_amte_ncsm_position_paper_formative_assessment.pdf.

Barlow, A. T., Gerstenschlager, N. E., & Harmon, S. E. (2016). Learning from the unknown student. *Teaching Children Mathematics, 23*(2), 74–81.

Bray, W. S. (2011). A collective case study of the influence of teachers' beliefs and knowledge on error-handling practices during class discussion of mathematics. *Journal for Research in Mathematics Education, 42*(1), 2–38.

Bray, W., & Santagata, R. (2014). Making mathematical errors: Springboards for learning. In K. Karp & A. Roth-McDuffie (Eds.), *Using research to improve instruction* (pp. 239–248). Reston, VA: NCTM.

Casa, T. M., Firmender, J. M., Cahill, J., Cardetti, F., Choppin, J. M., Cohen, J., Zawodniak, R. (2016). *Types of and purposes for elementary mathematical writing: Taskforce recommendations.* Retrieved from mathwriting.education.uconn.edu.

Danielson, C., & Luke, M. (2006). If I only had one question: Partner-quizzes in middle school mathematics. *Mathematics Teaching in the Middle School, 12*(4), 206–213.

Daro, P., Mosher, F., & Corcoran, T. (2011). *Learning trajectories in mathematics: A foundation for standards, curriculum assessment and instruction.* Philadelphia, PA: Consortium for Policy Research in Education.

Duckor, B., Holmberg, C., & Rossi Becker, J. (2017). Making moves: Formative assessment in mathematics. *Mathematics Teaching in the Middle School, 22*(6), 334–342.

Fagan, E. R., Tobey, C. R., & Brodesky, A. R. (2016). Targeting Instruction with Formative Assessment Probes. *Teaching Children Mathematics, 23*(3), 146–157.

Fennell, F., Kobett, B. M., & Wray, J. (2015). Classroom-based formative assessments: Guiding teaching and learning. In C. Suurtamm & A. Roth McDuffie (Eds.), *Annual Perspectives in Mathematics Education: Assessment to Enhance Teaching and Learning.* (pp. 51–62). Reston, VA: NCTM.

Fennell, F., Kobett, B. M., & Wray, J. (2017). *Formative five: Everyday assessment techniques for every math classroom.* Thousand Oaks, CA: Corwin.

Frayer, D. A., Fredrick, W. C., & Klausmeier, H. J., (April 1969). *A schema for testing the level of concept mastery (Working Paper No. 16),* University of Wisconsin Center for Educational Research.

Griffin, L., & Lavelle, L. (2010). *Assessing mathematical understanding: Using one-on-one mathematics interviews with K–2 students.* Presentation given at the Annual Conference of the National Council of Supervisors of Mathematics, San Diego, CA.

Hattie, J. (2009). *Visible learning: A synthesis of over 800 meta-analyses relating to achievement.* New York, NY: Routledge.

Hattie, J. (2015). The effective use of testing: What the research says. *Education Week,* October 28.

Heritage, M., Kim, J., Vendlinski, T., & Herman, J. (2009). From evidence to action: A seamless process in formative assessment? *Education Measurement: Issues and Practice, 28,* 24–31.

Jacobs, V. R., Lamb, L. L. C., & Philipp, R. A. (2010). Professional noticing of children's mathematical thinking. *Journal for Research in Mathematics Education, 41*(2), 169–202.

Kazemi, E., Gibbons, L, K., Lomax, K., & Franke, M. L. (2016). Listening to and learning from student thinking. *Teaching Children Mathematics, 23*(3), 182–190.

Kulm, G. (1994). *Mathematics and assessment: What works in the classroom.* San Francisco, CA: Jossey-Bass.

Lepak, J. (2014). Enhancing students' written mathematical arguments. *Mathematics Teaching in the Middle School, 20*(4), 212–219.

Morrow-Leong, K. (2016). Evidence-centered assessment. *Teaching Children Mathematics, 23*(2), 82–89.

National Governors Association & Council of Chief State School Officers. (2010, June). *Common Core State Standards Initiative.* Retrieved from www.corestandards.org

National Research Council. (2001). *Adding it up: Helping children learn mathematics.* J. Kilpatrick, J. Swafford, & B. Findell (Eds.). Washington, DC: National Academies Press.

NCTM (National Council of Teachers of Mathematics). (2014). *Principles to Action: Ensuring Mathematical Success of All.* Reston, VA: NCTM.

NCTM (National Council of Teachers of Mathematics). (2016). *Large-scale mathematics assessment and high-stakes decisions: A position statement of the National Council of Teachers of Mathematics.* Retrieved February 13, 2017 from www.nctm.org/Standards-and-Positions/Position-Statements/Large-Scale-Mathematics-Assessments-and-High-Stakes-Decisions/

Nyquist, J. B. (2003). *The benefits of reconstruing feedback as a larger system of formative assessment: A metaanalysis.* Unpublished master's thesis. Vanderbilt University, Nashville, TN.

Ocak, G., & Yamac, A. (2013). Examination of the relationships between fifth graders' self-regulated learning strategies, motivational beliefs, attitudes, and achievement. *Educational Sciences: Theory & Practice, 13*(1), 380–387.

Pace, M. H., & Ortiz, E. (2016). Get the goof! *Teaching Children Mathematics, 23*(3), 138–144.

Parker, R., & Breyfogle, L. (2011). Learning to write about mathematics. *Teaching Children Mathematics, 18*(2), 90–99.

Petit, M., & Zawojewski, J. (2010). Formative assessment in elementary school mathematics. In D. Lambdin & F. K. Lester, Jr. (Eds.), *Teaching and learning mathematics: Translating research for elementary school teachers* (pp. 73–79). Reston, VA: NCTM.

Pintrich, P. R. (2003). A motivational science perspective on the role of student motivation in learning and teaching contexts. *Journal of Educational Psychology, 95*(4), 667.

Popham, W. J. (2008). *Transformative assessment.* Alexandria, VA: Association for Supervision and Curriculum Development.

Rigelman, N., & Petrick, K. (2014). Student mathematicians developed through formative assessment cycles. In K. Karp &

A. Roth-McDuffie (Eds.), *Using research to improve instruction* (pp. 215–227). Reston, VA: NCTM.

Sawchuk, S. (2010, June 23). Three groups apply for race to top test grants. *Education Week*.

Simpson, A., Mokalled, S., Ellenburg, L., & Che, S. M. (2014/2015). A tool for rethinking questioning. *Mathematics Teaching in the Middle School, 20*(5), 294–302.

Smith, M. S., & Stein, M. K. (2011). *5 Practices for orchestrating productive mathematics discussions*. Thousand Oaks, CA: Corwin Press.

Stephan, M., McManus, G., & Dehlinger, R. (2014). Using research to inform formative assessment techniques. In K. Karp & A. Roth-McDuffie (Eds.), *Using research to improve instruction* (pp. 229–238). Reston, VA: NCTM.

Webb, N. L. (2002). Alignment study in language arts, mathematics, science, and social studies of state standards and assessments for four states. Washington, DC: Council of Chief State School Officers.

Wieser, E. T. (2008). Students control their own learning: A metacognitive approach. *Teaching Children Mathematics, 15*(2), 90–95.

Wiliam, D. (2007). Content *then* process: Teacher learning communities in the service of formative assessment. In D. B. Reeves (Ed.), *Ahead of the curve: The power of assessment to transform teaching and learning* (pp. 183–204). Bloomington, IN: Solution Tree.

Wiliam, D., & Leahy, S. (2015). *Embedding formative assessment: Practical techniques for K–12 classrooms*. West Palm Beach, FL: Learning Sciences International.

Wilson, L. D., & Kenney, P. A. (2003). Classroom and large-Scale assessment. In J. Kilpatrick, W. G. Martin, & D. Schifter (Eds.), *A research companion to Principles and Standards for School Mathematics* (pp. 53–67). Reston, VA: NCTM.

Yüksel, I. (2013) Impact of activity-based mathematics instruction on students with different prior knowledge and reading abilities. *International Journal of Science and Mathematics Education, 12*, 1445–1468.

Chapter 6

Aguirre, J. M., & del Rosario Zavala, M. (2013). Making culturally responsive mathematics teaching explicit: a lesson analysis tool. *Pedagogies: An International Journal, 8*(2), 163–190.

Aguirre, J., Mayfield-Ingram, K., & Martin, D. (2013). *The impact of identity in K–8 mathematics: Rethinking equity-based practices*. Reston, VA: NCTM.

Assouline, S. G., & Lupkowski-Shoplik, A. (2011). *Developing math talent: A comprehensive guide to math education for gifted students in elementary and middle school* (2nd ed.). Waco, TX: Prufrock Press.

Baker, S., Lesaux, N., Jayanthi, M., Dimino, J., Proctor, C. P., Morris, J., Gersten, R., Haymond, K., Kieffer, M. J., Linan-Thompson, S., & Newman-Gonchar, R. (2014). *Teaching academic content and literacy to English learners in elementary and middle school* (NCEE 2014–4012). Washington, DC: National Center for Education Evaluation and Regional Assistance (NCEE), Institute of Education Sciences, U.S. Department of Education. Retrieved from the NCEE website: ies.ed.gov/ncee/wwc/publications_reviews.aspx.

Banse, H. W., Palacios, N. A., Merritt, E. G., & Rimm-Kaufman, S. E. (2016). 5 strategies for scaffolding math discourse with ELLs. *Teaching Children Mathematics, 23*(2), 100–108.

Baroody, A. J. (2011). Learning: A framework. In F. Fennell (Ed.), *Achieving fluency: Special education and mathematics* (pp. 15–58). Reston, VA: NCTM.

Bartell, T., Turner, E., Aguirre, J., Drake, C., Foote, M., & Roth McDuffie, A. (2017). Connecting children's mathematical thinking with family and community knowledge in mathematics instruction. *Teaching Children Mathematics, 23*(6), 326–328.

Bay-Williams, J. M., & Livers, S. (2009). Supporting Math Vocabulary Acquisition. *Teaching Children Mathematics, 16*(4), 238–246.

Benard, B. (1991). *Fostering resiliency in kids: Protective factors in the family, school and community*. Portland, OR: Northwest Regional Educational Laboratory.

Boaler, J. (2008). Promoting "relational equity" and high mathematics achievement through an innovative mixed ability approach. *British Educational Research Journal, 34*(4), 167–194.

Boaler, J., & Staples, M. E. (2014). Creating mathematical futures through an equitable teaching approach: The case of Railside School. In N. S. Nasir, C. Cabano, B. Shreve, E. Woodbury, & N. Louie (Eds.), *Mathematics for equity: A framework for successful practice*. New York: Teachers College Press.

Bruner, J. S., & Kenney, H. J. (1965). Representation and mathematics learning. *Monographs of the Society for Research in Child Development, 30*(1), 50–59.

Bush, S., Karp, K., Lenz, T., & Nadler, J. (2017). Venn diagrams "intersect" art and math. *Teaching Children Mathematics, 23*(7), 414–421.

Bush, S., Karp, K, Nadler, J., & Gibbons, M. (2016). Exploring proportional reasoning using artwork. *Mathematics Teaching in the Middle School, 22*(4), 216–225.

Cabana, C., Shreve, B., Woodbury, E., & Louie, N. (Eds.). (2014). *Mathematics for equity: A framework for successful practice*. Teachers College Press.

Carter, P. L., & Welner, K. G. (2013). *Closing the opportunity gap: What America must do to give every child an even chance*. Oxford, UK: University Press.

Celedón-Pattichis, S. (2009). What does that mean? Drawing on Latino and Latina students' language and culture to make mathematical meaning. In M. W. Ellis (Ed.), *Responding to diversity: Grades 6–8* (pp. 59–74). Reston, VA: NCTM.

Celedón-Pattichis, S., & Ramirez, N. G. (2012). *Beyond good teaching: Advancing mathematics education for ELLs*. Reston, VA: NCTM.

Chao, T., Murray, E., & Gutiérrez, R. (2014). NCTM equity pedagogy research clip: What are classroom practices that support equity-based mathematics teaching? A research brief. Reston, VA: NCTM.

Choppin, J. (2014). Situating expansions of students' explanations in discourse contexts. In K. Karp & A. Roth-McDuffie (Eds.), *Annual perspectives in mathematics education 2014: Using research to improve instruction* (pp. 119–128) Reston, VA: NCTM.

Cirillo, M., Steele, M., Otten, S, Herbel-Eisenmann, B. A., McAneny, K., & Riser, J. Q. (2014). Teacher discourse moves: Supporting productive and powerful discourse. In K. Karp & A. Roth-McDuffie (Eds.), *Annual perspectives in mathematics education 2014: Using research to improve instruction* (pp. 141–150). Reston, VA: NCTM.

Cobb, P., Gresalfi, M. S., & Hodge, L. L. (2009). An interpretive scheme for analyzing the identities that students develop in mathematics classrooms. *Journal for Research in Mathematics Education, 40*(1), 40–68.

Cummins, J. (1994). Primary language instruction and the education of language minority students. In C. F. Leyba (Ed.), *Schooling and language minority students: A theoretical framework* (pp. 3–46). Los

Angeles, CA: California State University, National Evaluation, Dissemination and Assessment Center.

DiSalvo-Ryan, D. (1994). *City Green.* New York: Harper-Collins.

Dobbins, A., Gagnon, J. C., & Ulrich, T. (2014). Teaching geometry to students with math difficulties using graduated and peer-mediated instruction in a response-to-intervention model. *Preventing School Failure: Alternative Education for Children and Youth, 58*(1), 17–25.

Dunleavy, T. K. (2015). Delegating mathematical authority as a means to strive toward equity. *Journal of Urban Mathematics Education, 8*(1), 62–82.

Echevarria, J. J., Vogt, M. J., & Short, D. J. (2012). *Making content comprehensible for English Learners: The SIOP model* (4th ed.). New York: Pearson.

Flores, M., Hinton, V., & Strozier, S. (2014). Teaching subtraction and multiplication with regrouping using the concrete-representational-abstract sequence and strategic instruction model. *Learning Disabilities Research and Practice, 29*(2), 75–88.

Gagnon, J., & Maccini, P. (2001). Preparing students with disabilities for algebra. *Teaching Exceptional Children, 34*(1), 8–15.

Garrison, L. (1997). Making the NCTM's Standards work for emergent English speakers. *Teaching Children Mathematics, 4*(3), 132–138.

Gavin, M. K., & Sheffield, L. J. (2010). Using curriculum to develop mathematical promise in the middle grades. In M. Saul, S. Assouline, & L. J. Sheffield (Eds.), *The peak in the middle: Developing mathematically gifted students in the middle grades* (pp. 51–76). Reston, VA: NCTM, National Association of Gifted Children, & National Middle School Association.

Gómez, C. L. (2010). Teaching with cognates. *Teaching Children Mathematics, 16*(8), 470–474.

Griffin, C. C., Jossi, M. H., & van Garderen, D. (2014). Effective mathematics instruction in inclusive schools. In J. McLeskey, N. L. Waldron, F. Spooner, & B. Algozzine (Eds.), *Handbook of effective inclusive schools: Research and practice* (pp. 261–274). New York: Routledge.

Gutierrez, R. (2009). Embracing the inherent tensions in teaching mathematics from an equity stance. *Democracy and Education, 18*(3), 9–16.

Gutiérrez, R. (2015). HOLA: Hunt for opportunities–learn–act. *Mathematics Teacher, 109*(4), 270–277.

Haas, E., & Gort, M. (2009). Demanding more: Legal standards and best practices for English language learners. *Bilingual Research Journal, 32*, 115–135.

Heddens, J. (1964). *Today's mathematics: A guide to concepts and methods in elementary school mathematics.* Chicago, IL: Science Research Associates.

Hord, C., & Marita, S. (2014). Students with learning disabilities tackle multistep problems. *Mathematics Teaching in the Middle School, 19*(9), 548–555.

Hunter, A. E., Bush, S. B. & Karp, K. (2014). Systematic interventions for teaching ratios. *Mathematics Teaching in the Middle School, 19*(6), 360–367.

Janzen, J. (2008). Teaching English language learners in the content areas. *Review of Educational Research, 78*(4), 1010–1038.

Johnsen, S., & Sheffield, L. (Eds.). (2014). *Using the Common Core State Standards for mathematics with gifted and advanced learners.* Waco, TX: Prufrock Press, Inc.

Johnsen, S. K., Ryser, G. R., & Assouline, S. G. (2014). *A teacher's guide to using the Common Core State Standards with mathematically gifted and advanced learners.* Waco, TX: Prufrock Press.

Karp, K., & Howell, P. (2004). Building responsibility for learning in students with special needs. *Teaching Children Mathematics, 11*(3), 118–126.

Karp, K. & Ronau, R. (2009). *Birthdays and the binary system.* Illuminations lesson at illuminations.nctm.org/LessonDetail .aspx?id=L245

Kersaint, G., Thompson, D. R., & Petkova, M. (2009). *Teaching mathematics to English language learners.* New York, NY: Routledge.

Khisty, L. L. (1997). Making mathematics accessible to Latino students: Rethinking instructional practice. In M. Kenney & J. Trentacosta (Eds.), *Multicultural and gender equity in the mathematics classroom: The gift of diversity* (pp. 92–101). Reston, VA: NCTM.

Kisker, E. E., Lipka, J., Adams, B. L., Rickard, A., Andrew-Ihrke, D., Yanez, E. E., & Millard, A. (2012). The potential of a culturally based supplemental mathematics curriculum to improve the mathematics performance of Alaska native and other students. *Journal for Research in Mathematics Education, 43*(1), 75–113.

Lewis, K. (2014). Difference not deficit: Reconceptualizing mathematical learning disabilities. *Journal for Research in Mathematics Education, 45*(3), 351–396.

Mack, N. K. (2011). Enriching number knowledge. *Teaching Children Mathematics, 18*(2), 101–109.

Maldonado, L. A., Turner, E. E., Dominguez, H., & Empson, S. B. (2009). English language learning from, and contributing to, mathematical discussions. In D. Y. White & J. S. Spitzer (Eds.), *Responding to diversity: Grades pre-K–5* (pp. 7–22) Reston, VA: NCTM.

Mancl, D. B., Miller, S. P., & Kennedy, M. (2012). Using the concrete-representational-abstract sequence with integrated strategy instruction to teach subtraction with regrouping to students with learning disabilities. *Learning Disabilities Research and Practice, 27*(4),152–166.

Mathis, S. (1975). *The Hundred Penny Box.* New York: Houghton Mifflin.

Matthews, M. S., & Peters, S. J., (2017). Methods to increase the identification rate of students from traditionally underrepresented populations for gifted services. In S. Pfeiffer, E. Shaunessy-Detrick & M. Nicpon (Eds.) *American Psychological Association handbook on giftedness and talent.* Washington, DC: American Psychological Association.

Mazzocco, M. M. M., Devlin, K. T., & McKenney, S. J. (2008). Is it a fact? Timed arithmetic performance of children with mathematical learning disabilities (MLD) varies as a function of how MLD is defined. *Developmental Neuropsychology, 33*(3), 318–344.

McMaster, K. L., & Fuchs, D. (2016). Classwide intervention using peer-assisted learning strategies. In S. Jimerson, M. Burns, & A. VanDerHeyden (Eds.), *Handbook of response to intervention* (pp. 253–268). New York: Springer.

Midobuche, E. (2001). Building cultural bridges between home and the mathematics classroom. *Teaching Children Mathematics, 7*(9), 500–502.

Miller, S. P., & Kaffar, B. J. (2011). Developing addition with regrouping competence among second graders with mathematics difficulties. *Investigations in Mathematics Learning, 4*(1), 24–49.

Moffett, G., Malzahn, K., & Driscoll, M. (2014). Multimodal communication: Promoting and revealing students' mathematical thinking. In K. Karp & A. Roth-McDuffie (Eds.), *Annual perspectives in mathematics education 2014: Using research to improve instruction* (pp. 129–139). Reston, VA: NCTM.

Moschkovich, J. N. (1998). Supporting the participation of English language learners in mathematical discussions. *For the Learning of Mathematics, 19*(1), 11–19.

Murrey, D. L. (2008). Differentiating instruction in mathematics for the English language learner. *Mathematics Teaching in the Middle School, 14*(3), 146–153.

National Center for Education Statistics. (2011). Retrieved from nces.ed.gov/nationsreportcard/itmrlsx/search.aspx?subject=mathematics

National Research Council, Mathematics Learning Study Committee. Kilpatrick, J., Swafford, J., & Findell, B. (Eds.). (2001). *Adding it up: Helping children learn mathematics*. Washington, DC: The National Academies Press.

NCES (2017). *NAEP data explorer*. Retrieved from nces.ed.gov/nationsreportcard/naepdata/

NCTM (National Council of Teachers of Mathematics). (2007). *Research brief: Effective strategies for teaching students with difficulties in mathematics*. Retrieved from www.nctm.org/news/content.aspx?id=8452

NCTM (National Council of Teachers of Mathematics). (2011, July). *Position statement on interventions*. Reston, VA: NCTM.

NCTM (National Council of Teachers of Mathematics). (2012). *Position statement on closing the opportunity gap in mathematics education*. Reston, VA: NCTM.

NCTM (National Council of Teachers of Mathematics). (2014). *Position statement on access and equity in mathematics education*. Reston, VA: NCTM.

NCTM (National Council of Teachers of Mathematics). (2016). *Position statement on providing opportunities for students with exceptional promise*. Reston, VA: NCTM.

OECD (2016). *Equations and inequalities: Making mathematics accessible to all, PISA*. Paris, France: OECD Publishing. dx.doi.org/10.1787/9789264258495-en

Plucker, J. A., & Peters, S. J. (2016). *Excellence gaps in education: Expanding opportunities for talented students*. Cambridge, MA: Harvard Education Press.

Pugalee, D. K., Harbaugh, A., & Quach, L. H. (2009). The human graph project: Giving students mathematical power through differentiated instruction. In M. W. Ellis (Ed.), *Responding to diversity: Grades 6–8* (pp. 47–58). Reston, VA: NCTM.

Read, J. (2014). Who rises to the top? *Peabody Reflector, 83*(1), 19–22.

Reis, S., & Renzulli, J. S. (2005). *Curriculum compacting: An easy start to differentiating for high potential students*. Waco, TX: Prufrock Press.

Remillard, J. T, Ebby, C., Lim, V., Reinke, L., Hoe, N., & Magee, E. (2014). Increasing access to mathematics through locally relevant curriculum. In K. Karp & A. Roth-McDuffie (Eds.), *Annual perspectives in mathematics education 2014: Using research to improve instruction* (pp. 89–96). Reston, VA: NCTM.

Renzulli, J. S., Gubbins, E. J., McMillen, K. S., Eckert, R. D., & Little, C. A. (Eds.). (2009). *Systems & models for developing programs for the gifted & talented* (2nd ed.). Mansfield Center, CT: Creative Learning Press.

Ronau, R., & Karp, K. (2012). The power over trash: Integrating mathematics, science and children's literature. Adapted from an article in *Mathematics Teaching in the Middle School*, in H. Sherard (Ed.), *Real World Math*. Reston, VA: NCTM.

Rotigel, J., & Fello, S. (2005). Mathematically gifted students: How can we meet their needs? *Gifted Child Today, 27*(4), 46–65.

Sadler, P., & Tai, R. (2007). The two pillars supporting college science. *Science, 317*(5837), 457–458.

Saul, M., Assouline, S., & Sheffield, L. J. (Eds.). (2010). *The peak in the middle: Developing mathematically gifted students in the middle grades*. Reston, VA: NCTM, National Association of Gifted Children, & National Middle School Association.

Seidel, C., & McNamee, J. (2005). Teacher to teacher: Phenomenally exciting joint mathematics—English vocabulary project. *Mathematics Teaching in the Middle School, 10*(9), 461–463.

Sheffield, L. J. (Ed.). (1999). *Developing mathematically promising students*. Reston, VA: NCTM.

Simic-Muller, K. (2015). Social justice and proportional reasoning. *Mathematics Teaching in the Middle School, 21*(3), 162–168.

Storeygard, J. (2010). *My kids can: Making math accessible to all learners, K–5*. Portsmouth, NH: Heinemann.

Tomaz, V. S., & David, M. M. (2015). How students' everyday situations modify classroom mathematical activity: The case of water consumption. *Journal for Research in Mathematics Education, 46*(4), 455–496.

Thompson, K. D. (2017). What blocks the gate? Exploring current and former English learners' math course-taking in secondary school. *American Educational Research Journal, 54*(4), 757–798.

Torgesen, J. K. (2002). The prevention of reading difficulties. *Journal of School Psychology, 40*(1), 7–26.

Turner, E. E., Celedón-Pattichis, S., Marshall, M., & Tennison, A. (2009). Fijense amorcitos, les voy a contra una historia: The power of story to support solving and discussing mathematical problems among Latino and Latina kindergarten students. In D. Y. White & J. S. Spitzer (Eds.), *Responding to diversity: Grades Pre-K–5* (pp. 23–42). Reston, VA: NCTM.

Turner, E., Sugimoto, A. T., Stoehr, K., & Kurz, E. (2016). Creating Inequalities from Real-World Experiences. *Mathematics Teaching in the Middle School, 22*(4), 236–240.

Wager, A. (2012). Incorporating out-of-school mathematics: From cultural context to embedded practice. *Journal of Mathematics Teacher Education, 15*(1), 9–23.

Whiteford, T. (2009/2010). Is mathematics a universal language? *Teaching Children Mathematics, 16*(5), 276–283.

Wigfield, A., & Cambria, J. (2010). Expectancy-Value theory: Retrospective and prospective. In S. Karabenick & T. C. Urdan (Eds.), *The decade ahead: Theoretical perspectives on motivation and achievement (advances in motivation and achievement)* (Vol. 16, pp. 35–70). Bradford, UK: Emerald Group Publishing Limited.

Woodward, J. (2006). Developing automaticity in multiplication facts: Integrating strategy instruction with timed practice drills. *Learning Disability Quarterly, 29*(4), 269–289.

Ysseldyke, J. (2002). Response to "Learning disabilities: Historical perspectives." In R. Bradley, L. Danielson, & D. Hallahan (Eds.), *Identification of learning disabilities: Research to practice* (pp. 89–98). Mahwah, NJ: Erlbaum.

Zike, D. (2003). *Dinah Zike's teaching mathematics with foldables*. Glencoe: McGraw-Hill.

Chapter 7

Baer, E. (1990). *This is the way we go to school*. New York: Scholastic.

Baroody, A. J. (1987). *Children's mathematical thinking: A developmental framework for preschool, primary, and special education teachers*. New York: Teachers College Press.

Baroody, A. J., Li, X., & Lai, M. L. (2008). Toddlers' spontaneous attention to number. *Mathematics Thinking and Learning, 10*, 1–31.

Betts, P. (2015). Counting on using a number game. *Teaching Children Mathematics, 21*(7), 430–436.

Brown, M. W. (1947). *Goodnight moon*. New York, NY: Harper & Row.

Clements, D., Baroody, A., & Sarama, J. (2013). *Background research on early mathematics*. Background Research for the National

Governor's Association (NGA) Center Project on Early Mathematics. Washington, DC: NGA.

Clements, D., & Sarama, J. (2014). *Learning and teaching early math: The learning trajectories approach* (2nd ed.). New York, NY: Routledge.

Dean, J., & Dean, K. (2016). *Pete the cat and the missing cupcakes*. New York: HarperCollins.

Ethridge, E. A., & King, J. R. (2005). Calendar math in preschool and primary classrooms: Questioning the curriculum. *Early Childhood Education Journal, 32*(5), 291–296.

Fosnot, C. T., & Dolk, M. (2001). *Young mathematicians at work: Constructing multiplication and division*. Portsmouth, NH: Heinemann.

Frye, D., Baroody, A. J., Burchinal, M., Carver, S. M., Jordan, N. C., & McDowell, J. (2013). *Teaching math to young children: A practice guide* (NCEE 2014–4005). Washington, DC: National Center for Education Evaluation and Regional Assistance (NCEE), Institute of Education Sciences (IES), U.S. Department of Education. Retrieved from whatworks.ed.gov

Hamre, B. K., Downer, J. T., Kilday, C. R., & McGuire, P. (2008). *Effective teaching practices for early childhood mathematics*. White paper prepared for the National Research Council. Washington, DC.

Henkes, K. (2008). *Chrysanthemum*. Mulberry Books.

Himmelman, J. (2010). *Ten little hot dogs*. Tarrytown, NY: Pinwheel Books.

Kamii, C. K. (1985). *Young children reinvent arithmetic*. New York: Teachers College Press.

Levine, S. C., Suriyakham, L. W., Rowe, M. L., Huttenlocher, J., & Gunderson, E. A. (2010). What counts in the development of young children's number knowledge? *Developmental Psychology, 46*(5), 1309–1319.

Metzger, S. (2008). *We're Going on a Leaf Hunt*. New York: Cartwheel Books.

Murphy, S. (2003). *3 Little Firefighters*. New York: Harper Collins.

National Research Council Committee. (2009). *Mathematics learning in early childhood: Paths toward excellence and equity*. Washington, DC: The National Academies Press.

NGA Center (National Governors Association Center for Best Practices) & CCSSO (Council of Chief State School Officers). (2010). *Common core state standards*. Retrieved from corestandards.org

Siegler, R. S. (2010). Playing numerical board games improves number sense in children from low-income backgrounds. In *BJEP Monograph Series II, Number 7-Understanding number development and difficulties* (Vol. 15, No. 29, pp. 15–29). British Psychological Society.

Slobodkina, E. (1938). *Caps for sale*. New York, NY: Scholastic Books.

Voutsina, C. (2016). Oral counting sequences: A theoretical discussion and analysis through the lens of representational redescription. *Educational Studies in Mathematics, 93*, 175–193.

Watts, T. W., Duncan, G. J., Siegler, R. S., & Davis-Kean, P. E. (2016). What's past is prologue: Relations between early mathematics knowledge and high school achievement. *Educational Researcher, 43*(7), 352–360.

Wright, R. J., Stanger, G., Stafford, A. K., & Martland, J. (2006). *Teaching number in the classroom with 4–8 year olds*. London, UK: Paul Chapman Publications/Sage.

Chapter 8

Baroody, A. J., Wilkins, J. L., & Tiilikainen, S. H. (2003). The development of children's understanding of additive commutativity: From protoquantitive concept to general concept? In A. J. Baroody & A. Dowker (Eds.), *The development of arithmetic concepts and skills* (pp. 127–160). Mahwah, NJ: Erlbaum.

Blote, A., Lieffering, L., & Ouwehand, K. (2006). The development of many-to-one counting in 4-year-old children. *Cognitive Development, 21*(3), 332–348.

Byrd, C., McNeil, N., Chesney, D., & Matthews, P. (2015). A specific misconception of the equal sign acts as a barrier to the learning of early algebra. *Learning and Individual Differences, 38*(2), 61–67.

Caldwell, J., Kobett, B., & Karp, K. (2014). *Essential understanding of addition and subtraction in practice, grades K–2*. Reston, VA: NCTM.

Champagne, Z. M., Schoen, R., & Riddell, C. (2014). Variations in both-addends unknown problems. *Teaching Children Mathematics, 21*(2), 114–121.

Clark, F. B., & Kamii, C. (1996). Identification of multiplicative thinking in children in grades 1–5. *Journal for Research in Mathematics Education, 27*(1), 41–51.

Clement, L., & Bernhard, J. (2005). A problem-solving alternative to using key words. *Mathematics Teaching in the Middle School, 10*(7), 360–365.

Crespo, S., & Nicol, C. (2006). Challenging preservice teachers' mathematical understanding: The case of division by zero. *School Science and Mathematics, 106*(2), 84–97.

Cuyler, M. (2010). *Guinea pigs add up*. New York, NY: Walker.

De Corte, E., & Verschaffel, L. (1985). Beginning first graders' initial representation of arithmetic word problems. *Journal of Mathematical Behavior, 4*, 3–21.

Ding, M. (2010, October 7). Email interaction.

Ding, M. (2016). Opportunities to learn inverse relations in U.S. and Chinese textbooks. *Mathematical Thinking and Learning. 18*(1), 45–68.

Ding, M., & Auxter, A. (2017). Children's strategies to solving additive inverse problems: A preliminary analysis. *Mathematics Educational Research Journal, 29*, 73–92.

Ding, M., & Li, X. (2010). A comparative analysis of the distributive property in U.S. and Chinese elementary mathematics textbooks. *Cognition and Instruction, 28*(2), 146–180.

Ding, M., & Li, X. (2014). Transition from concrete to abstract representations: The distributive property in a Chinese textbook series. *Educational Studies in Mathematics, 87*, 103–121.

Ding, M., Li, X., Caprano, M. M., & Caprano, R. (2012). Supporting meaningful initial learning of the associative property: Cross-cultural differences in textbook presentations. *International Journal for Studies in Mathematics Education, 5*(1), 114–130.

Dixon, J. K., Nolan, E. C., Lott Adams, T., Tobias, J., & Barmoha, G. (2016). *Making sense of mathematics for teaching grades 3–5*. Bloomington, IN: Solution Tree Press.

Dougherty, B., Flores, A., Louis, E., & Sophian, C. (2010). *Developing essential understanding of number and numeration for teaching mathematics in prekindergarten–grade 2*. Reston, VA: NCTM.

Drake, J., & Barlow, A. (2007). Assessing students' level of understanding multiplication through problem writing. *Teaching Children Mathematics, 14*(5), 272–277.

Drescher, D. (2008). *What's hiding in there?* Edinburgh, Scotland: Floris Books.

Fagnant, A., & Vlassis, J. (2013). Schematic representations in arithmetical problem solving: Analysis of their impact on grade 4 students. *Education Studies in Mathematics, 84*, 149–168.

Feldman, Z. (2014). Rethinking factors. *Mathematics Teaching in the Middle School, 20*(4), 230–236.

Fosnot, C. T., & Dolk, M. (2001). *Young mathematicians at work: Constructing multiplication and division*. Portsmouth, NH: Heinemann.

Gerofsky, S. (2009). Genre, simulacra, impossible exchange, and the real: How postmodern theory problematises word problems. In L. Verschaffel, B. Greer, & W. V. Dooren (Eds.), *Words and worlds: Modeling verbal descriptions of situations* (pp. 21–38). Rotterdam: Sense Publishing.

Goldstone, R. L., & Son, J. Y. (2005). The transfer of scientific principles using concrete and idealized simulations. *The Journal of the Learning Sciences, 14,* 69–110.

Heng, M. A., & Sudarshan, A. (2013). "Bigger number means you plus!" Teachers learning to use clinical interviews to understand students' mathematical thinking. *Education Studies in Mathematics, 83,* 471–485.

Holbert, S. & Barlow, A. (2012/2013). Engaging reluctant problem solvers. *Teaching Children Mathematics, 19*(5), 310–315.

Hord, C. & Marita, S. (2014). Students with learning disabilities tackle multistep problems. *Mathematics Teaching in the Middle School, 19*(9), 548–555.

Huinker, D. (1994, April). *Multi-step word problems: A strategy for empowering students.* Presented at the Annual Meeting of the National Council of Teachers of Mathematics, Indianapolis, IN.

Jong, C. & Magruder, R. (2014). Beyond cookies: Understanding various division models. *Teaching Children Mathematics, 20*(6), 367–373.

Karp, K., Bush, S., & Dougherty, B. (2014). 13 rules that expire. *Teaching Children Mathematics, 21*(2), 18–25.

Kinda, S. (2013). Generating scenarios of division as sharing and grouping: A study of Japanese elementary and university students. *Mathematical Thinking and Learning, 15,* 190–200.

Knuth, E. & Stephens, A. (2016). The equal sign does matter. In E. Silver & P. Kenney (Eds.), *More lessons learned from research volume 2* (pp. 135–139). Reston, VA: NCTM.

Matney, G. T., & Daugherty, B. N. (2013). Seeing spots and developing multiplicative sense making. *Mathematics Teaching in the Middle School, 19*(3), 148–155.

McElligott, M. (2007). *Bean thirteen.* New York, NY: Putnam Juvenile.

Miller-Bennett, V. (2017). Understanding the meaning of the equal sign. *New England Journal of Mathematics, 50*(1), 18–25.

Murata, A. (2008). Mathematics teaching and learning as a mediating process: The case of tape diagrams. *Mathematical Thinking and Learning, 10,* 374–406.

National Research Council Committee. (2009). *Mathematics learning in early childhood: Paths toward excellence and equity.* Washington, DC: The National Academies Press.

NGA Center (National Governors Association Center for Best Practices) & CCSSO (Council of Chief State School Officers). (2010). *Common core state standards.* Retrieved from corestandards.org

Ojose, B. (2014). Teaching certain mathematical axioms: The role played by conceptual knowledge of algebra teachers. *National Teacher Education Journal, 7*(1), 37–44.

Pearce, D. L., Bruun, F., Skinner, K., & Lopez-Mohler, C. (2013). What teachers say about student difficulties solving mathematical word problems in grades 2–5. *International Electronic Journal of Mathematics Education, 8*(1), 3–19.

Powell, S. R., Kearns, D. M., & Driver, M. K. (2016). Exploring the commention between arithmetic and prealgebraic reasoning at first and second grade. *Journal of Educational Psychology, 108*(7), 943–959.

Quinn, R., Lamberg, T., & Perrin, J. (2008). Teacher perceptions of division by zero. *Clearing House, 81*(3), 101–104.

Schifter, D. (2001). Perspectives from a mathematics educator. In Center for Education, *Knowing and Learning Mathematics for Teaching* (pp. 69–71). Washington, DC: National Academies Press.

Schwartz, S. (2013). *Implementing the Common Core State Standards through mathematical problem solving kindergarten–grade 2.* Reston, VA: NCTM.

Shield, M., & Swinson, K. (1996). The link sheet: A communication aid for clarifying and developing mathematical ideas and processes. In P. C. Elliott and M. J. Kenney (Eds.), *Communication in mathematics, K–12 and beyond* (pp. 35–39). Reston, VA: NCTM.

Siegler, R. S., & Ramani, G. B. (2009). Playing linear number board games—but not circular ones—improves low-income preschoolers' numerical understanding. *Journal of Educational Psychology, 101,* 545–560.

Sowder, L. (1988). Children's solutions of story problems. *Journal of Mathematical Behavior, 7*(3), 227–238.

Sulentic-Dowell, M. M., Beal, G., & Capraro, R. (2006). How do literacy experiences affect the teaching propensities of elementary pre-service teachers? *Journal of Reading Psychology, 27*(2–3), 235–255.

Verschaffel, L., Greer, B., & DeCorte, E. (2007). Whole number concepts and operations. In F. K. Lester (Ed.), *Second handbook of research on mathematics teaching and learning* (pp. 557–628). Charlotte, NC: Information Age Publishing.

Whitin, P., & Whitin, D. (2008). Learning to solve problems in the primary grades. *Teaching Children Mathematics, 14*(7), 426–432.

Xin, Y. P., Jitendra, A. K., & Deatline-Buchman, A. D. (2005). Effects of mathematical word problem-solving instruction on middle school students with learning problems. *Journal of Special Education, 39*(3), 181–192.

Chapter 9

Baroody, A. J. (2006). Why children have difficulties mastering the basic number combinations and how to help them. *Teaching Children Mathematics, 13*(1), 22–31.

Baroody, A. J., Bajwa, N. P., & Eiland, M. (2009). Why can't Johnny remember the basic facts? *Developmental Disabilities Research Reviews, 15,* 69–79.

Baroody, A. J., Purpura, D. J., Eiland, M. D., & Reid, E. E. (2014). Fostering first-graders' fluency with basic subtraction and larger addition combinations via computer-assisted instruction. *Cognition and Instruction, 32,* 159–197.

Baroody, A. J., Purpura, D. J., Eiland, M. D., Reid, E. E., & Paliwal, V. (2016). Does fostering reasoning strategies for relatively difficult combinations promote transfer by K–3 students? *Journal of Educational Psychology, 108*(4), 576–591.

Bay-Williams, J. M., & Kling, G. (2014). Enriching addition and subtraction fact mastery through games. *Teaching Children Mathematics, 21*(4), 239–247.

Boaler, J. (2014). Research suggests that timed tests cause math anxiety. *Teaching Children Mathematics, 20*(8), 469–474.

Brownell, W., & Chazal, C. (1935). The effects of premature drill in third grade arithmetic. *Journal of Educational Research, 29*(1), 17–28.

Buchholz, L. (2016). A license to think on the road to fact fluency. *Teaching Children Mathematics, 22*(9), 557–562.

Columba, L. (2013). So here's the story. *Teaching Children Mathematics, 19*(6), 374–381.

Dennis, M. S., Sorrells, A. M., & Falcomata, T. S. (2016). Effects of two interventions on solving basic fact problems by second graders with mathematics learning disabilities. *Learning Disabilities Quarterly, 39*(2), 95–112.

Flowers, J. M., & Rubenstein, R. N. (2010–2011). Multiplication fact fluency using doubles. *Mathematics Teaching in the Middle School, 16*(5), 296–301.

Forbringer, L., & Fahsl, A. J. (2010). Differentiating practice to help students master basic facts. In D. Y. White & J. S. Spitzer (Eds.), *Responding to diversity: Grades pre-K–5* (pp. 7–22). Reston, VA: NCTM.

Fuson, K. C. (1992). Research on whole number addition and subtraction. In D. A. Grouws (Ed.), *Handbook of research on mathematics teaching and learning* (pp. 243–275). Old Tappan, NJ: Macmillan.

Fuson, K. C., & Kwon, Y. (1992). Korean children's single-Digit addition and subtraction: Numbers structured by ten. *Journal for Research in Mathematics Education, 23*(2), 148–165.

Godfrey, C. J., & Stone, J. (2013). Mastering fact fluency: Are they game? *Teaching Children Mathematics, 20*(2), 96–101.

Gravemeijer, K., & van Galen, F. (2003). Facts and algorithms as products of students' own mathematical activity. In J. Kilpatrick, W. G. Martin, & D. Schifter (Eds.), *A research companion to Principles and Standards for School Mathematics* (pp. 114–122). Reston, VA: NCTM.

Heege, H. T. (1985). The acquisition of basic multiplication skills. *Educational Studies in Mathematics, 16*(4), 375–388.

Henry, V. J., & Brown, R. S. (2008). First grade basic facts: An investigation into teaching and learning of an accelerated, high-demand memorization standard. *Journal for Research in Mathematics Education, 39*(2), 153–183.

Hong, L. T. (1993). *Two of everything: A Chinese folktale.* New York, NY: Albert Whitman.

Jordan, N. C., Kaplan, D., Locuniak, M. N., & Ramineni, C. (2007). Predicting first grade math achievement from developmental number sense trajectories. *Learning Disabilities Research & Practice, 22*(1), 36–46.

Kamii, C. K., & Anderson, C. (2003). Multiplication games: How we made and used them. *Teaching Children Mathematics, 10*(3), 135–141.

Kling, G. (2011). Fluency with basic addition. *Teaching Children Mathematics, 18*(2), 80–88.

Kling, G., & Bay-Williams, J. M. (2015). Three steps to mastering multiplication facts. *Teaching Children Mathematics, 21*(9), 548–559.

Lewis, T. (2005). Facts + fun = fluency. *Teaching Children Mathematics, 12*(1), 8–11.

Locuniak, M. N., & Jordan, N. C. (2008). Using kindergarten number sense to predict calculation fluency in second grade. *Journal of Learning Disabilities, 41*(5), 451–459.

Mazzocco, M. M. M., & Thompson, R. E. (2005). Kindergarten predictors of math learning disability. *Learning Disabilities Research & Practice, 20*(3), 142–155.

National Research Council. (2001). *Adding it up: Helping children learn mathematics.* J. Kilpatrick, J. Swafford, & B. Findell (Eds.). Washington, DC: National Academies Press.

Nelson, P. M. Parker, D. C., & Zaslofsky, A. F. (2016). The relative value of growth in math fact skills across late elementary and middle school. *Assessment for Effective Intervention, 41*(3), 184–192.

NGA Center (National Governors Association Center for Best Practices) & CCSSO (Council of Chief State School Officers). (2010). *Common core state standards.* Retrieved from corestandards.org

Ramirez, G., Gunderson, E. A., Levine, S. C., & Beilock, S. L. (2013). Math anxiety, working memory, and math achievement in early elementary school. *Journal of Cognition and Development, 14*(2), 187–202.

Rathmell, E. C. (1978). Using thinking strategies to teach the basic skills. In M. N. Suydam (Ed.), *Developing computational skills* (pp. 13–38). Reston, VA: NCTM.

Rathmell, E. C., Leutzinger, L. P., & Gabriele, A. (2000). *Thinking with numbers.* (Separate packets for each operation.) Cedar Falls, IA: Thinking with Numbers.

Sarama, J., & Clements, D. H. (2009). *Early childhood mathematics education research: Learning trajectories for young children.* New York, NY: Routledge.

Shoecraft, P. (1982). Bowl-A-Fact: A game for reviewing the number facts. *Arithmetic Teacher, 29*(8), 24–25.

Thornton, C. (1978). Emphasizing thinking strategies in basic fact instruction. *Journal for Research in Mathematics Education, 9*(3), 214–227.

Thornton, C. A., & Toohey, M. A. (1984). *A matter of facts: (Addition, subtraction, multiplication, division).* Palo Alto, CA: Creative Publications.

Wallace, A. H., & Gurganus, S. P. (2005). Teaching for mastery of multiplication. *Teaching Children Mathematics, 12*(1), 26–33.

Chapter 10

Byrge, L., Smith, L. B., & Mix, K. (2013). Beginnings of place value: How preschoolers write three digit numbers. *Child Development, 85*(2), 437–443.

Cayton, G. A., & Brizuela, B. M. (2007). First graders' strategies for numerical notation, number reading and the number concept. In J. H. Woo, H. C. Lew, K. S. Park, & D. Y. Seo (Eds.), *Proceedings of the 31st conference of the international group for the psychology of mathematics education* (Vol. 2, pp. 81–88). Seoul, South Korea: Psychology of Mathematics Education.

Chan, B. M. Y., & Ho, C. S. H. (2010). The cognitive profile of Chinese children with mathematics difficulties. *Journal of Experimental Child Psychology, 107*, 260–279.

Dietrick, J., Huber, S., Dackermann, T., Moeller, K., & Fischer, U. (2016). Place-value understanding in number line estimation predicts future arithmetic performance. *British Journal of Developmental Psychology, 34*(4), 502–517.

Dougherty, B., Flores, A., Louis, E., & Sophian, C. (2010). *Developing essential understanding of number and numeration for teaching mathematics in prekindergarten–grade 2.* Reston, VA: NCTM.

Fuson, K. C. (2006). Research on whole number addition and subtraction. In D. Grouws (Ed.), *Handbook of research on mathematics teaching and learning* (pp. 243–275). Charlotte, NC: Information Age Publishing.

Geary, D. C., & Hoard, M. K. (2005). Learning disabilities in arithmetic and mathematics: Theoretical and empirical perspectives. In J. Campbell (Ed.), *Handbook of mathematical cognition* (pp. 253–267). New York, NY: Psychology Press.

Kamii, C. K. (1985). *Young children reinvent arithmetic.* New York: Teachers College Press.

Labinowicz, E. (1985). *Learning from children: New beginnings for teaching numerical thinking.* Menlo Park, CA: AWL Supplemental.

Mix, K. S., Prather, R. S., Smith, L. B., & Stockton, J. D. (2014). Young children's interpretation of multidigit number names: From emerging competence to mastery. *Child Development 85*(3), 1306–1319.

Mix, K., Smith, L., Stockton, J., Cheng, Y., & Barterian, J. (2016). Grounding the symbols for place value: Evidence from training and long-term exposure to base-10 models. *Journal of Cognition and Development, 18*(1), 129–151.

Moeller, K., Martignon, L., Wessolowski, S., Engel, J., & Nuerk, H. C. (2011). Effects of finger counting on numerical development: The opposing views of neuro-cognition and mathematics education. *Frontiers in Psychology, 2*, 328.

NGA Center (National Governors Association Center for Best Practices) & CCSSO (Council of Chief State School Officers). (2010). *Common core state standards.* Retrieved from corestandards.org

Ross, S. H. (1986). *The development of children's place-value numeration concepts in grades two through five.* Presented at the Annual Meeting of the American Educational Research Association, San Francisco, CA.

Ross, S. H. (1989). Parts, wholes, and place value: A developmental perspective. *Arithmetic Teacher, 36*(6), 47–51.

Ross, S. R. (2002). Place value: Problem solving and written assessment. *Teaching Children Mathematics, 8*(7), 419–423.

Thomas, N. (2004). The development of structure in the number system. In M. J. Hoines & A. B. Fuglestad (Eds.), *28th conference of the International Group for the Psychology of Mathematics Education* (pp. 305–312). Bergen, Norway: Bergen University College Press.

van den Bos, I., Kroesbergen, E., Van Luit, J., Xenidou-Dervou, I., Jonkman, L., Van der Schoot, M. & Van Lieshout, E. (2015). Longitudinal development of number line estimation and mathematics performance in primary school children. *Journal of Experimental Child Psychology, 134,* 12–29.

Chapter 11

Barker, L. (2009). Ten is the magic number! *Teaching Children Mathematics, 15*(6), 336–345.

Biddlecomb, B., & Carr, M. (2011). A longitudinal study of the development of mathematics strategies and underlying counting schemes. *International Journal of Science and Mathematics Education, 9,* 1–24.

Caldwell, J., Kobett, B., & Karp, K. (2014). *Essential understanding of addition and subtraction in practice, grades K–2.* Reston, VA: NCTM.

Carpenter, T. P., Franke, M. L., Jacobs, V. R., Fennema, E., & Empson, S. B. (1998). A longitudinal study of invention and understanding in children's multidigit addition and subtraction. *Journal for Research in Mathematics Education, 29*(1), 3–20.

Coates, G. D., & Thompson, V. (2003). *Family Math II: Achieving success in mathematics.* Berkeley, CA: EQUALS Lawrence Hall of Science.

Csikos, F. (2016). Strategies and performance in elementary students' three-digit mental addition. *Educational Studies in Mathematics, 91,* 123–139.

Fan, L., & Bokhove, C. (2014). Rethinking the role of algorithms in school mathematics: A conceptual model with focus on cognitive development. *ZDM Mathematics Education, 46,* 481–492.

Fleischman, H. L., Hopstock, P. J., Pelczar, M. P., & Shelley, B. E. (2010). *Highlights from PISA 2009: Performance of U.S. 15-Year-Old Students in Reading, Mathematics, and Science Literacy in an International Context* (NCES 2011–004). Washington, DC: U.S. Government Printing Office.

Fuson, K. C. (2003). Developing mathematical power in whole number operations. In J. Kilpatrick, W. G. Martin, & D. Schifter (Eds.), *A research companion to Principles and Standards in School Mathematics* (pp. 68–94). Reston, VA: NCTM.

Fuson, K., & Beckmann, S. (2012/2013). Standard algorithms in the Common Core State Standards. *NCTM Journal,* fall/winter, 14–30.

Gravemeijer, K., & van Galen, F. (2003). Facts and algorithms as products of students' own mathematical activity. In J. Kilpatrick, W. G. Martin, & D. Schifter (Eds.), *A research companion to Principles and Standards for School Mathematics* (pp. 114–122). Reston, VA: NCTM.

Heinze, A., Marschick, F., & Lipowsky, W. (2009). Addition and subtraction of three-digit numbers: Adaptive strategy use and the influence of instruction in German third grade. *ZDM—The International Journal on Mathematics Education, 41,* 591–604.

Hiebert, J., & Grouws, D. A. (2007). The effects of classroom mathematics teaching on students' learning. In F. K. Lester (Ed.), *Second handbook of research on mathematics teaching and learning* (pp. 371–404). Charlotte, NC: Information Age Publishing.

Humphreys, C., & Parker, R. (2015). *Making number talks matter: Developing mathematical practices and deepening understanding, grades 4–10.* Portland, ME: Stenhouse.

Kamii, C. K., & Dominick, A. (1998). The harmful effects of algorithms in grades 1–4. In L. J. Morrow (Ed.), *The teaching and learning of algorithms in school mathematics* (pp. 130–140). Reston, VA: NCTM.

Keiser, J. M. (2010). Shifting our computational focus. *Mathematics Teaching in the Middle School, 16*(4), 216–223.

Lynch, K., & Star, J. (2014). Views of struggling students on instruction incorporating multiple strategies in algebra I: An exploratory study. *Journal for Research in Mathematics Education, 45*(1), 6–18.

NCTM (National Council of Teachers of Mathematics). (2014). *Position statement on access and equity in mathematics education.* Reston, VA: NCTM.

National Research Council. (2001). *Adding it up: Helping children learn mathematics.* J. Kilpatrick, J. Swafford, & B. Findell (Eds.). Washington, DC: National Academies Press.

NGA Center (National Governors Association Center for Best Practices) & CCSSO (Council of Chief State School Officers). (2010). *Common core state standards.* Retrieved from corestandards.org

Parrish, S. (2014). *Number talks: Whole number computation, grades K–5.* Sausalito, CA: Math Solutions.

Peltenburg, M., van den Heuvel-Panhuizen, M., & Robitzsch, A. (2012). Special education students' use of indirect addition in solving subtraction problems up to 100: A proof of the didactical potential of an ignored procedure. *Educational Studies in Mathematics, 79*(3), 351–369.

Perkins, I., & Flores, A. (2002). Mathematical notations and procedures of recent immigrant students. *Mathematics Teaching in the Middle School, 7*(6), 346–351.

Reinhart, S. (2000). Never say anything a kid can say. *Mathematics Teaching in the Middle School, 5*(8), 478–483.

Rittle-Johnson, B., Star, J. R., & Durkin, K. (2010, April). *Developing procedural flexibility: When should multiple solution methods be introduced?* Paper presented at the Annual Conference of the American Educational Research Association, Denver, CO.

Siegler, R. S., & Booth, J. L. (2005). Development of numerical estimation: A review. In J. I. D. Campbell (Ed.), *Handbook of mathematical cognition* (pp. 197–212). New York, NY: New York Psychology Press.

Torbeyns, J., De Smedt, B., Ghesquiere, P., & Verschaffel, L. (2009). Acquisition and use of shortcut strategies by traditionally schooled children. *Educational Studies in Mathematics, 71,* 1–17.

Verschaffel, L., Greer, B., & DeCorte, E. (2007). Whole number concepts and operations. In F. Lester, Jr. (Ed.), *Second handbook of research on mathematics teaching and learning* (pp. 557–628). Charlotte, NC: Information Age Publishing.

Whitacre, I., Schoen, R., Champagne, Z., & Goddard, A. (2016/2017). Relational thinking: What's the difference? *Teaching Children Mathematics, 23*(5), 302–308.

Wright, R., Martland, J., Stafford, A., & Stanger, G. (2008). *Teaching number: Advancing children's skills and strategies.* London, UK: Sage.

Chapter 12

Baek, J. M. (2006). Children's mathematical understanding and invented strategies for multidigit multiplication. *Teaching Children Mathematics, 12*(5), 242–247.

Barmby, P., Harries, T., Higgins, S., & Suggate, J. (2009). The array representation and primary children's understanding and reasoning in multiplication. *Educational Studies in Mathematics, 70,* 217–241.

Benson, C. C., Wall, J. J., & Malm, C. (2013). The distributive property in grade 3? *Teaching Children Mathematics, 19*(8), 498–506.

Biddlecomb, B., & Carr, M. (2011). A longitudinal study of the development of mathematics strategies and underlying counting schemes. *International Journal of Science and Mathematics Education, 9,* 1–24.

Boote, S. K. (2016). Choosing the right tool. *Teaching Children Mathematics, 22*(8), 476–486.

Burns, M. K., Ysseldyke, J., Nelson, P. M., & Kanive, R. (2014). Number of repetitions required to retain single-digit multiplication math facts for elementary students. *School Psychology Quarterly, 30*(3), 398–405.

Confrey, J. (2008). *Student and teacher reasoning on rational numbers, multiplicative structures, and related topics.* Presentation at ICME–11, Monterrey, Mexico.

Devlin, K. (2011). *What exactly is multiplication?* Mathematical Association of America. Retrieved from www.maa.org/devlin/devlin_01_11.html

Erdem, E. (2017). Mental computation: Evidence from fifth graders. *International Journal of Science and Mathematics Education, 15,* 1157–1174.

Flowers, J. M., & Rubenstein, R. N. (2010–2011). Multiplication fact fluency using doubles. *Mathematics Teaching in the Middle School, 16*(5), 296–301.

Fosnot, C. T., & Dolk, M. (2001). *Young mathematicians at work: Constructing multiplication and division.* Portsmouth, NH: Heinemann.

Fuson, K., & Beckmann, S. (2012–13). Standard algorithms in the common core state standards. *NCSM Journal, 14*(2), 14–30.

Hanson, S. A., & Hogan, T. P. (2000). Computational estimation skill of college students. *Journal for Research in Mathematics Education, 31*(4), 483–499.

Hartnett, J. (2007). Categorisation of mental computation strategies to support teaching and to encourage classroom dialogue. In J. Watson & K. Beswick (Eds.), *Mathematics: Essential research, essential practice: Proceedings of the 30th annual conference of the Mathematics Education Research Group of Australasia* (pp. 345–352). Hobart, Tasmania, Australia: MERGA.

Izsák, A. (2004). Teaching and learning two-digit multiplication: Coordinating analyses of classroom practices and individual student learning. *Mathematical Thinking and Learning, 6,* 37–79.

Karp, K., Bush, S., & Dougherty, B. (2014). Avoiding rules that expire. *Teaching Children Mathematics, 21*(2), 18–25.

Keiser, J. M. (2010). Shifting our computational focus. *Mathematics Teaching in the Middle School, 16*(4), 216–223.

Keiser, J. (2012). Students' strategies can take us off guard. *Mathematics Teaching in the Middle School, 17*(7), 418–425.

Kinzer, C., & Stanford, T. (2013/2014). Distributive property: The core of multiplication. *Teaching Children Mathematics, 20*(5), 303–308.

Lannin, J., Chval, K., & Jones, D. (2013). *Putting essential understanding of multiplication and division into practice in grades 3–5.* Reston, VA: NCTM.

Lee, J. (2014). Deciphering multiplication algorithms with the area model. *Mathematics Teaching in the Middle School, 19*(9), 557–556.

Liu, F. (2009). Computational estimation performance on whole number multiplication by third- and fifth-grade Chinese students. *School Science and Mathematics, 109*(6), 325–337.

Martin, J. F. (2009). The goal of long division. *Teaching Children Mathematics, 15*(8), 482–487.

NCTM (National Council of Teachers of Mathematics). (2014). *Position statement on access and equity in mathematics education.* Reston, VA: NCTM.

Petit, M. (2009). *OGAP (Vermont mathematics partnership ongoing assessment project) multiplicative reasoning framework.* Communication with the author (September 2009).

Raveh, I., Koichu, B., Peled, I., & Zaslavsky, O. (2016). Four (algorithms in one (bag): An integrative framework of knowledge for teaching the standard algorithms of the basic arithmetic operations. *Research in Mathematics Education, 18*(1), 43–60.

Rittle-Johnson, B., Star, J. R., & Durkin, K. (2010, April). *Developing procedural flexibility: When should multiple solution methods be introduced?* Paper presented at the Annual Conference of the American Educational Research Association, Denver, CO.

Robinson, K., & LeFevre, J. (2012). The inverse relationship between multiplication and division: Concepts, procedures and a cognitive framework. *Educational Studies in Mathematics, 79*(3), 409–428.

Siegler, R. S., Duncan, G. J., Davis-Kean, P. E., Duckworth, K., Claessens, A., Engel, M., Susperreguy, M. I., & Chen, M. (2012). Early predictors of high school mathematics achievement, *Psychological Science, 23,* 691–697.

Star, J. R., & Rittle-Johnson, B. (2009). The role of prior knowledge in the development of strategy flexibility: The case of computational estimation. In S. Swars, D. Stinson, & S. Lemons-Smith (Eds.), *Proceedings of the 31st annual meeting of the North American Chapter of the International Group for the Psychology of Mathematics Education* (pp. 577–584). Atlanta, GA: Georgia State University.

Varol, F., & Farran, D. (2007). Elementary school students' mental computation proficiencies. *Early Childhood Education Journal, 35*(1), 89–94.

Verschaffel, L., Greer, B., & DeCorte, E. (2007). Whole number concepts and operations. In F. Lester, Jr. (Ed.), *Second handbook of research on mathematics teaching and learning* (pp. 557–628). Charlotte, NC: Information Age Publishing.

Chapter 13

Anhalt, C. O. (2014). Scaffolding in mathematical modeling for ELLs. In M. Civil & E. Turner (Eds.) *The Common Core State Standards in Mathematics for English Language Learners: Grades K–8,* pp. 111–126. Alexandria, VA: Teachers of English to Speakers of Other Languages.

Ball, D. L., & Bass, H. (2003). Making mathematics reasonable in school. In J. Kilpatrick, W. G. Martin, & D. Schifter (Eds.), *A research companion to Principles and Standards for School Mathematics* (pp. 27–44). Reston, VA: NCTM.

Bay-Williams, J. M., & Fletcher, G. (2017). A bottom-up hundreds chart? *Teaching Children Mathematics, 24*(3), e1–e6.

Bay-Williams, J. M., & Martinie, S. L. (2004). *Math and literature: Grades 6–8.* Sausalito, CA: Math Solutions Publications.

Billings, E. M. H. (2017). SMP that help foster algebraic thinking. *Teaching Children Mathematics, 23*(8), 476–483.

Blanton, M. L. (2008). *Algebra in the elementary classroom: Transforming thinking, transforming practice.* Portsmouth, NH: Heinemann.

Blanton, M., Brizuela, B. M., Gardiner, A. M., Sawrey, K., & Newman-Owens, A. (2015a). A learning trajectory in 6-year-olds' thinking about functional relationships. *Journal of Research in Mathematics Education, 46*(5), 511–558.

Blanton, M., Levi, L., Crites, T. W., & Dougherty, B. J. (2011). *Developing essential understanding of algebraic thinking for teaching mathematics in grades 3–5.* Essential Understanding Series. Reston, VA: NCTM.

Blanton, M., Stephens, S. Knuth, E., Gardiner, A. M., Isler, I., & Kim, J. (2015b). The Development of children's algebraic thinking: The impact of a comprehensive early algebra intervention in third grade. *Journal of Research in Mathematics Education, 46*(1), 39–87.

Brown, S. A., & Mehilos, M. (2010). Using tables to bridge arithmetic and algebra. *Mathematics Teaching in the Middle School, 15*(9), 532–538.

Burton, L. (2017). Discovering linear equations in explicit tables. *Mathematics Teaching in the Middle School, 22*(7), 398–405.

Cannon, S. O., & Sanders, M. (2017). Uncertainty and complexity in mathematical modeling. *Mathematics Teaching in the Middle School, 22*(7), 420–428.

Carpenter, T. P., Franke, M. L., & Levi, L. (2003). *Thinking mathematically: Integrating arithmetic and algebra in elementary school.* Portsmouth, NH: Heinemann.

Carraher, D. W., & Schliemann, A. D. (2007). Early algebra and algebraic reasoning. In F. K. Lester, Jr. (Ed.), *Second handbook of research on mathematics teaching and learning* (Vol. 2, pp. 669–705). Charlotte, NC: Information Age.

Carraher, D. W., Schliemann, A. D., & Schwartz, J. L. (2008). Early algebra is not the same as algebra early. In J. J. Kaput, D. W. Carraher, & M. L. Blanton (Eds.), *Algebra in the early grades* (pp. 235–272). New York, NY: Lawrence Erlbaum Associates.

Clement, J. (1982). Algebra word problem solutions: Thought processes underlying a common misconception. *Journal for Research in Mathematics Education, 13*(1), 16–30.

Collins, A., & Dacey, L. (2011). *The Xs and whys of algebra: Key ideas and common misconceptions.* Portland, ME: Stenhouse Publishers.

COMAP and SIAM. 2016. *Guidelines for Assessment and Instruction in Mathematical Modeling Education (GAIMME).* www.comap.com/Free/GAIMME/index.html . Accessed July 1, 2017.

Confrey, J., Nguyen, K. H., Lee, K., Panorkou, N., Corley, A. K., & Maloney, A. P. (2012). Turn-on common core math: Learning trajectories for the Common Core State Standards for Mathematics. Accessed at www.turnonccmath.net

Darley, J. W. (2009). Traveling from arithmetic to algebra. *Mathematics Teaching in the Middle School, 14*(8), 458–464.

DeYoung, M. J. (2009). Math in the box. *Mathematics Teaching in the Middle School, 15*(3), 134–141.

Falkner, K. P., Levi, L., & Carpenter, T. P. (1999). Children's understanding of equality: A foundation for algebra. *Teaching Children Mathematics, 6*(4), 232–236.

Felton, M. D., Anhalt, C. O., & Cortez. (2015). Going with the flow: Challenging students to make assumptions. *Mathematics Teaching in the Middle School, 20*(6), 342–349.

Felton-Koestler, M. D. (2016/2017). Common core confusion about modeling. *Teaching Children Mathematics, 23*(5), 269–272.

Fernandez, M. L., & Schoen, R. C. (2008). Teaching and learning mathematics through hurricane tracking. *Mathematics Teaching in the Middle School, 13*(9), 500–512.

Fisher, E., Roy, G., & Reeves, C. (2013). The functionator 3000: Transforming numbers and children. *Teaching children mathematics 29*(4), 254–260.

Fosnot, C. T., & Jacob, B. (2010). *Young mathematicians at work: Constructing algebra.* Reston, VA: NCTM.

Friel, S. N., & Markworth, K. A. (2009). A framework for analyzing geometric pattern tasks. *Mathematics Teaching in the Middle School, 15*(1), 24–33.

Gavin, M. K., & Sheffield, L. J. (2015). A balancing act: Making sense of algebra. *Mathematics Teaching in the Middle School, 20*(8), 461–466.

Goldenberg, E. P., Mark, J., & Cuoco, A. (2010). An algebraic-habits-of-mind perspective on elementary school. *Teaching Children Mathematics, 16*(9), 548–556.

Harris, T. (2000). *100 days of school.* Minneapolis, MN: Millbrook Press.

Hawes, K. (2007). Using error analysis to teach equation solving. *Mathematics Teaching in the Middle School, 12*(5), 238–242.

Herbel-Eisenmann, B. A., & Phillips, E. D. (2005). Using student work to develop teachers' knowledge of algebra. *Mathematics Teaching in the Middle School, 11*(2), 62–66.

Hong, L. T. (1993). *Two of everything: A Chinese folktale.* New York, NY: Albert Whitman.

Kaput, J. J. (2008). What is algebra? What is algebraic reasoning? In J. J. Kaput, D. W. Carraher, & M. L. Blanton (Eds.), *Algebra in the early grades.* Reston, VA: NCTM.

Kieran, C. (2007). *What do students struggle with when first introduced to algebra symbols?* Brief. Reston, VA: NCTM.

Kroon, C. D. (2016). Spaghetii bridges: Modeling linear relationships. *Mathematics Teaching in the Middle School, 21*(9), 563–566.

Knuth, E. J., Stephens, A. C., McNeil, N. M., & Alibali, M. W. (2006). Does understanding the equal sign matter? Evidence from solving equations. *Journal for Research in Mathematics Education, 37*(4), 297–312.

Lannin, J. K., Arbaugh, F., Barker, D. D., & Townsend, B. E. (2006). Making the most of student errors. *Teaching Children Mathematics, 13*(3), 182–186.

Maida, P. (2004). Using algebra without realizing it. *Mathematics Teaching in the Middle School, 9*(9), 484–488.

McCoy, L. P. (1997). Algebra: Real-life investigations in a lab setting. *Mathematics Teaching in the Middle School, 2*(4), 220–224.

McNeil, N. M., & Alibali, M. W. (2005). Knowledge change as a function of mathematics experience: All contexts are not created equal. *Journal of Cognition and Development, 6*, 285–306.

Molina, M., & Ambrose, R. C. (2006). Fostering relational thinking while negotiating the meaning of the equals sign. *Teaching Children Mathematics, 13*(2), 111–117.

Muir, T. (2015). Always, sometimes, never true. *Teaching Children Mathematics, 21*(6), 384.

Neagoy, M. (2012). *Planting the seeds of algebra, PreK–2: Explorations for the early grades.* Thousand Oaks, CA: Corwin.

NGA Center (National Governors Association Center for Best Practices) & CCSSO (Council of Chief State School Officers). (2010). *Common core state standards.* Retrieved from corestandards.org

Numeroff, L. J. (1985). *If you give a mouse a cookie.* New York, NY: HarperCollins.

Panorkou, N., & Maloney, A. P. (2016).Early algebra: Expressing covariation and correspondence. *Teaching Children Mathematics, 23*(2), 90–99.

RAND Mathematics Study Panel. (2003). *Mathematical proficiency for all students: Toward a strategic research and development program in mathematics education* (Issue 1643). Santa Monica, CA: Rand Corporation.

Renkl, A. (2014). Learning from worked examples: How to prepare students for meaningful problem solving. In V. Benassi, C. E. Overson, & C. M. Hakala (Eds.), *Applying science of learning in education: Infusing psychological science into the curriculum* (pp. 118–130). *teachpsych.org/ebooks/asle2014/index.php.* (accessed May 28, 2017).

Sakow, M., & Karaman, R. (2015). Exploring algebraic misconceptions with technology. *Mathematics Teaching in the Middle School, 21*(4), 222–29.

Schifter, D., Monk, G. S., Russell, S. J., & Bastable, V. (2007). Early algebra: What does understanding the laws of arithmetic mean in the elementary grades? In J. Kaput, D. Carraher, & M. Blanton (Eds.), *Algebra in the early grades.* Mahwah, NJ: Erlbaum.

Schifter, D., Russell, S. J., & Bastable, V. (2009). Early algebra to reach the range of learners. *Teaching Children Mathematics, 16*(4), 230–237.

Sherman, M. F, Walkington, C., & Howell, E. (2016). A comparison of symbol-precedence view in investigative and conventional textbooks used in algebra courses. *Journal for Research in Mathematics Education, 47*(2), 134–146.

Smith, E. (2008). Representational thinking as a framework for introducing functions in the elementary curriculum. In J. J. Kaput, D. W. Carraher, & M. L. Blanton (Eds.), *Algebra in the early grades* (p. 143). Mahwah, NJ: Lawrence Erlbaum Associates/Taylor & Francis Group.

Star, J. R., & Verschaffel, L. (2016). Providing support for student sense making: Recommendations from cognitive science for the teaching of mathematics. In Jinfa Cai (Ed.), *Compendium for Research in Mathematics Education.* Reston, VA: NCTM.

Stephens, A., Blanton, M, Knuth, E., Isler, I., & Gardiner, A. M. (2015). Just say YES to early algebra. *Teaching Children Mathematics, 22*(2), 92–101.

Tanish, D. (2011). Functional thinking ways in relation to linear function tables of elementary school students. *Journal of Mathematical Behavior, 30,* 206–223.

Thornton, Carol. 1978. Emphasizing Thinking Strategies in Basic Fact Instruction. *Journal for Research in Mathematics Education. 9*(3): 214–227.

Usiskin, Z. (2015). Mathematical modeling. *Mathematics Teaching in the Middle School, 20*(8), 476–482.

Warren, E., & Cooper, T. J. (2008). Patterns that support early algebraic thinking in elementary school. In C. E. Greenes & R. Rubenstein (Eds.), *Algebra and algebraic thinking in school mathematics: 70th NCTM yearbook* (pp. 113–126). Reston, VA: NCTM.

Wells, P. J. (2015/16). Understanding linear functions and their representations. *Mathematics Teaching in the Middle School, 21*(5), 308–313.

Whaley, K. A. (2012). Using students' interests as algebraic models. *Mathematics Teaching in the Middle School, 17*(6), 372–378.

Yopp, D. A., & Ellsworth, J. L. (2016/2017). Generalizing and skepticism: Bringing research to practice. *Mathematics Teaching in the Middle School, 22*(5), 284–292.

Chapter 14

Bailey, D. H., Hoard, M. K., Nugent, L. & Geary, D. C. (2012). Competence with fractions predicts gains in mathematics achievement. *Journal of Experimental Child Psychology, 113,* 447–455.

Bamberger, H. J., Oberdorf, C., & Schultz-Ferrell, K. (2010). *Math misconceptions: From misunderstanding to deep understanding.* Portsmouth, NH: Heinemann.

Bay, J. M. (2001). Developing number sense ON the number line. *Mathematics Teaching in the Middle School, 6*(8), 448–451.

Bay-Williams, J. M., & Martinie, S. L. (2003). Thinking rationally about number in the middle school. *Mathematics Teaching in the Middle School, 8*(6), 282–287.

Booth, J. L., & Newton, K. J. (2012). Fractions: could they really be the gatekeeper's doorman? *Contemporary Educational Psychology, 37,* 247–253.

Bray, W. S., & Abreu-Sanchez, L. (2010). Using number sense to compare fractions. *Teaching Children Mathematics, 17*(2), 90–97.

Bright, G. W., Behr, M. J., Post, T. R., & Wachsmuth, I. (1988). Identifying fractions on number lines. *Journal for Research in Mathematics Education, 19*(3), 215–232.

Brown, G., & Quinn, R. J. (2007). Investigating the relationship between fraction proficiency and success in algebra. *Australian Mathematics Teacher, 63*(4), 8–15.

Center for Technology and Teacher Education (n.d.) *Kids and cookies.* Retrieved from www.teacherlink.org/content/math/interactive/flash/kidsandcookies/kidcookie.php

Champion, J., & Wheeler, A. (2014). Revisit pattern blocks to develop rational number sense. *Mathematics Teaching in the Middle School, 19*(6), 337–343.

Chick, C., Tierney, C., & Storeygard, J. (2007). Seeing students' knowledge of fractions: Candace's inclusive classroom. *Teaching Children Mathematics, 14*(1), 52–57.

Clarke, D., & Roche, A. (2009). Students' fraction comparison strategies as a window into robust understanding and possible pointers for instruction. *Educational Studies in Mathematics, 72,* 127–138.

Clarke, D., Roche, A., & Mitchell, A. (2008). 10 practical tips for making fractions come alive and make sense. *Mathematics Teaching in the Middle School, 13*(7), 373–380.

Courey, S. J., Balogh, E., Siker, J. R., & Paik, J. (2012). Academic music: Music instruction to engage third-grade students in learning basic fraction concepts. *Educational Studies in Mathematics, 81,* 251–278.

Cramer, K., & Henry, A. (2002). Using manipulative models to build number sense for addition of fractions. In B. Litwiller (Ed.), *Making sense of fractions, ratios, and proportions* (pp. 41–48). Reston, VA: NCTM.

Cramer, K., & Whitney, S. (2010). Learning rational number concepts and skills in elementary school classrooms. In D. V. Lambdin & F. K. Lester, Jr. (Eds.), *Teaching and learning mathematics: Translating research for elementary school teachers* (pp. 15–22). Reston, VA: NCTM.

Cramer, K., Wyberg, T., & Leavitt, S. (2008). The role of representations in fraction addition and subtraction. *Mathematics Teaching in the Middle School, 13*(8), 490–496.

Cwikla, J. (2014). Can kindergartners do fractions? *Teaching Children Mathematics, 20*(6), 354–364.

Ellington, A. J., & Whitenack, J. W. (2010). Fractions and the funky cookie. *Teaching Children Mathematics, 16*(9), 532–539.

Empson, S. B. (2002). Organizing diversity in early fraction thinking. In B. Litwiller (Ed.), *Making sense of fractions, ratios, and proportions* (pp. 29–40). Reston, VA: NCTM.

Empson, S. B., & Levi, L. (2011). *Extending children's mathematics—fractions and decimals.* Portsmouth, NH: Heinemann.

Englard, L. (2010). Raise the bar on problem solving. *Teaching Children Mathematics, 17*(3), 156–165.

Fennell, F., Kobett, B. M., & Wray, J. A. (2014). Fractions are numbers too! *Mathematics Teaching in the Middle School, 19*(8), 486–493.

Flores, A., Samson, J., & Yanik, H. B. (2006). Quotient and measurement interpretations of rational numbers. *Teaching Children Mathematics, 13*(1), 34–39.

Freeman, D. W., & Jorgensen, T. A. (2015). Moving beyond brownies and pizzas. *Teaching Children Mathematics, 21*(7), 412–420.

Goral, M. B., & Wiest, L. R. (2007). An arts- Based approach to teaching fractions. *Teaching Children Mathematics, 14*(2), 74–80.

Gould, H. T. (2011). Building understanding of fractions with LEGO® bricks. *Teaching Children Mathematics, 17*(8), 498–503.

Harvey, R. (2012). Stretching student teachers' understanding of fractions. *Mathematics Education Research Journal, 24,* 493–511.

Hodges, T. E., Cady, J., & Collins, R. L. (2008). Fraction representation: The not-so-common denominator among textbooks. *Mathematics Teaching in the Middle School, 14*(2), 78–84

Johanning, D. I. (2008). Learning to use fractions: Examining middle school students' emerging fraction literacy. *Journal for Research in Mathematics Education, 39*(3), 281–310.

Jordan, N. C, Hansen, N., Fuchs, L. S., Siegler, R. S., Gersten, R., & Micklos, D. (2013). Developmental predictors of fraction concepts and procedures. *Journal of Experimental Child Psychology, 116,* 45–58.

Kloosterman, P., Warfield, J., Wearne, D., Koc, Y., Martin, W. G., & Strutchens, M. (2004). Fourth-Grade students' knowledge of mathematics and perceptions of learning mathematics. In P. Kloosterman & F. K. Lester, Jr. (Eds.), *Results and interpretations of the 1990–2000 mathematics assessments of the National Assessment of Educational Progress* (pp. 71–103). Reston, VA: NCTM.

Lamon, S. J. (2012). *Teaching fractions and ratios for understanding: Essential content knowledge and instructional strategies* (3rd ed.). New York, NY: Taylor & Francis Group.

Lewis, R. M., Gibbons, L. K., Kazemi, E., & Lind T. (2015). Unwrapping students ideas about fractions. *Teaching Children Mathematics, 22*(3), 158–168.

Lewis, C. L., & Perry, R. (2017). Lesson study to scale up research-based knowledge: A randomized, controlled trial of fractions learning. *Journal for Research in Mathematics Education, 48*(3), 261–299.

Mack, N. K. (1995). Confounding whole-Number and fraction concepts when building on informal knowledge. *Journal for Research in Mathematics Education, 26*(5), 422–441.

McCoy, A., Barnett, J., & Stine, T. (2016). Paper plate fractions: The counting connection. *Teaching Children Mathematics, 23*(4), 244–251.

Moyer-Packenham, P. S., Ulmer, L. A., & Anderson, K. L. (2012). Examining pictorial models and virtual manipulatives for third-grade fraction instruction. *Journal of Interactive Online Learning, 11*(3), 103–120.

National Mathematics Advisory Panel. (2008). *Foundations for success.* Jessup, MD: U.S. Department of Education.

Olive, J. (2002). Bridging the gap: Using interactive computer tools to build fraction schemes. *Teaching Children Mathematics, 8*(6), 356–61.

Organisation for Economic Co-Operation and Development (2014). A profile of student performance in mathematics. In *PISA 2012 results: What students know and can do. Student performance in mathematics, reading and science* (Rev. ed., Vol. I, pp. 31–144). Paris, France: OECD Publishing.

Pantziara, M., & Philippou, G. (2012). Levels of students' "conception" of fractions. *Educational Studies in Mathematics, 79,* 61–83.

Petit, M., Laird, R. E., & Marsden, E. L. (2010). *A focus on fractions: Bringing research to the classroom.* New York, NY: Taylor & Francis.

Petit, M., Laird, R. E., Marsden, E. L., & Ebby, C. (2016). *A focus on fractions: Bringing research to the classroom* (2nd ed.). NewYork: Taylor & Francis.

Post, T. R., Wachsmuth, I., Lesh, R. A., & Behr, M. J. (1985). Order and equivalence of rational numbers: A cognitive analysis. *Journal for Research in Mathematics Education, 16*(1), 18–36.

Pothier, Y., & Sawada, D. (1990). Partitioning: An approach to fractions. *Arithmetic Teacher, 38*(4), 12–17.

Rampey, B. D., Dion, G. S., & Donahue, P. L. (2009). *NAEP 2008 Trends in Academic Progress* (NCES 2009–479). Washington, DC: National Center for Education Statistics, Institute of Education Sciences, U.S. Department of Education.

Roddick, C., & Silvas-Centeno, C. (2007). Developing understanding of fractions through pattern blocks and fair trade. *Teaching Children Mathematics, 14*(3), 140–145.

Sarazen, D. N. (2012). Fractions: Thinking beyond the lines. *Teaching Children Mathematics, 19*(3), 208.

Saxe, G. B., Diakow, R., & Gearhart, M. (2012). Towards curricular coherence in integers and fractions: A study of the efficacy of a lesson sequence that uses the number line as the principal representational context. *ZDM: The International Journal on Mathematics Education, 45*(3), 343–364.

Shaughnessy, M. M. (2011). Identify fractions and decimals on a number line. *Teaching Children Mathematics, 17*(7), 428–434.

Siebert, D., & Gaskin, N. (2006). Creating, naming, and justifying fractions. *Teaching Children Mathematics, 12*(8), 394–400.

Siegler, R. S., Carpenter, T., Fennell, F., Geary, D., Lewis, J., Okamoto, Y., et al. (2010). *Developing effective fractions instruction for kindergarten through 8th grade: A practice guide* (NCEE 2010-4039). Retrieved from www.whatworks.ed.gov/publications/Practiceguides.

Siegler, R. S., Fazio, L. K., Bailey, D. H., & Zhou, X. (2013). Fractions: The new frontier for theories of numerical development. *Trends in Cognitive Sciences, 17*(1), 13–19.

Smith, J. P., III. (2002). The development of students' knowledge of fractions and ratios. In B. Litwiller (Ed.), *Making sense of fractions, ratios, and proportions* (pp. 3–17). Reston, VA: NCTM.

Sowder, J. T., Wearne, D., Martin, W. G., & Strutchens, M. (2004). What do 8th-grade students know about mathematics? Changes over a decade. In P. Kloosterman & F. K. Lester, Jr. (Eds.), *Results and interpretations of the 1990–2000 mathematics assessments of the National Assessment of Educational Progress* (pp. 105–143). Reston, VA: NCTM.

Sowder, J. T., & Wearne, D. (2006). What do we know about eighth-grade student achievement? *Mathematics Teaching in the Middle School, 11*(6), 285–293.

Steffe, L. P., & Olive, J. (2010). *Children's fractional knowledge.* New York, NY: Springer.

Tobias, J. (2014). Mixing strategies to compare fractions. *Mathematics Teaching in the Middle School, 19*(6), 376–381.

Tzur, R. (1999). An integrated study of children's construction of improper fractions and the teacher's role in promoting learning. *Journal for Research in Mathematics Education, 30*(4), 390–416.

Tzur, R., & Hunt, J. (2015). Iteration: Unit fraction knowledge and the French fry. *Teaching children mathematics, 22*(3), 148–157.

Usiskin, Z. (2007). Some thoughts about fractions. *Mathematics Teaching in the Middle School, 12*(7), 370–373.

Watanabe, T. (2006). The teaching and learning of fractions: A Japanese perspective. *Teaching Children Mathematics, 12*(7), 368–374.

Watanabe, T. (2007). Initial treatment of fractions in Japanese textbooks. *Focus on Learning Problems in Mathematics, 29*(2), 41–60.

Wearne, D., & Kouba, V. L. (2000). Rational numbers. In E. A. Silver & P. A. Kenney (Eds.), *Results from the seventh mathematics assessment of the National Assessment of Educational Progress* (pp. 163–191). Reston, VA: NCTM.

Wilkerson, T. L., Bryan, T., & Curry, J. (2012). An appetite for fractions. *Teaching Children Mathematics, 19*(2), 90–99.

Williams, L. (2008). Tiering and scaffolding: Two strategies for providing access to important mathematics. *Teaching Children Mathematics, 14*(6), 324–330.

Chapter 15

Bamberger, H. J., Oberdorf, C., & Schultz-Ferrell, K. (2010). *Math misconceptions: From misunderstanding to deep understanding.* Portsmouth, NH: Heinemann.

Cavey, L. O., & Kinzel, M. T. (2014). From whole numbers to invert and multiply. *Teaching Children Mathematics, 20*(6), 375–383.

Chval, K., Lannin, J., & Jones, D. (2013). *Putting essential understanding of fractions into practice: Grades 3–5.* Reston, VA: NCTM.

Clarke, D., Roche, A., & Mitchell, A. (2008). 10 practical tips for making fractions come alive and make sense. *Mathematics Teaching in the Middle School, 13*(7), 373–380.

Coughlin, H. A. (2010/2011). Dividing fractions: What is the divisor's role? *Mathematics Teaching in the Middle School, 16*(5), 280–287.

Cramer, K., & Whitney, S. (2010). Learning rational number concepts and skills in elementary school classrooms. In D. V. Lambdin & F. K. Lester, Jr. (Eds.), *Teaching and learning mathematics: Translating research for elementary school teachers* (pp. 15–22). Reston, VA: NCTM.

Cramer, K., Wyberg, T., & Leavitt, S. (2008). The role of representations in fraction addition and subtraction. *Mathematics Teaching in the Middle School, 13*(8), 490–496.

Dixon, J. K., & Tobias, J. M. (2013). The whole story: Understanding fraction computation. *Mathematics Teaching in the Middle School, 19*(3), 156–163.

Fung, M. G., & Latulippe, C. L. (2010). Computational estimation. *Teaching Children Mathematics, 17*(3), 170–176.

Gregg, J., & Gregg, D. U. (2007). Measurement and fair-sharing models for dividing fractions. *Mathematics Teaching in the Middle School, 12*(9), 490–496.

Imm, K. L., Stylianou, D. A., & Chae, N. (2008). Student representations at the center: Promoting classroom equity. *Mathematics Teaching in the Middle School, 13*(8), 458–463.

Izsák, A., Tillema, E., & Tunc-Pekkam, Z. (2008). Teaching and learning fraction addition on number lines. *Journal for Research in Mathematics Education, 39*(1), 33–62.

Johanning, D. J. (2011). Estimation's role in calculations with fractions. *Mathematics Teaching in the Middle School, 17*(2), 96–102.

Johanning, D. I., & Mamer, J. (2014). How did the answer get bigger? *Mathematics Teaching in the Middle School, 19*(6), 344–351.

Kribs-Zaleta, C. (2008). Oranges, posters, ribbons, and lemonade: Concrete computational strategies for dividing fractions. *Mathematics Teaching in the Middle School, 13*(8), 453–457.

Lamon, S. J. (2012). *Teaching fractions and ratios for understanding: Essential content knowledge and instructional strategies* (3rd ed.). New York, NY: Taylor & Francis Group.

Lewis, R. M., Gibbons, L. K., Kazemi, E., & Lind T. (2015). Unwrapping students ideas about fractions. *Teaching Children Mathematics, 22*(3), 158–168.

Mack, N. K. (2004). Connecting to develop computational fluency with fractions. *Teaching Children Mathematics, 11*(4), 226–232.

NGA Center (National Governors Association Center for Best Practices) & CCSSO (Council of Chief State School Officers). (2010). *Common core state standards.* Retrieved from corestandards.org

Petit, M., Laird, R. E., & Marsden, E. L. (2010). *A focus on fractions: Bringing research to the classroom.* New York, NY: Taylor & Francis.

Philipp, R. A., & Hawthorne, C. (2015). Unpacking referent units in fraction operations. *Teaching Children Mathematics, 22*(4), 240–247.

Post, T. R. (1981). Fractions: Results and implications from the national assessment. *Arithmetic Teacher, 28*(9), 26–31.

Reys, R. E. (1998). Computation versus number sense. *Mathematics Teaching in the Middle School, 4*(2), 110–113.

Sharp, J., & Welder, R. M. (2014). Reveal limitations through fraction division problem posing. *Mathematics Teaching in the Middle School, 19*(9), 541–547.

Siebert, D., & Gaskin, N. (2006). Creating, naming, and justifying fractions. *Teaching Children Mathematics, 12*(8), 394–400.

Siegler, R. S., Carpenter, T., Fennell, F., Geary, D., Lewis, J., Okamoto, Y., et al. (2010). *Developing effective fractions instruction for kindergarten through 8th grade: A practice guide* (NCEE 2010–4039). Retrieved from www.whatworks.ed.gov/publications/Practiceguides

Taber, S. B. (2002). Go ask Alice about multiplication of fractions. In B. Litwiller (Ed.), *Making sense of fractions, ratios, and proportions* (pp. 61–71). Reston, VA: NCTM.

Taber, S. B. (2009). Capitalizing on the unexpected. *Mathematics Teaching in the Middle School, 15*(3), 149–155.

Thompson, P. W. (1995). Notation, convention, and quantity in elementary mathematics. In J. T. Sowder & B. P. Schappelle (Eds.), *Providing a foundation for teaching mathematics in the middle grades* (pp. 199–221). New York, NY: State University of New York Press.

Tirosh, D. (2000). Enhancing prospective teachers' knowledge of children's conceptions: The case of division of fractions. *Journal for Research in Mathematics Education, 31*(1), 1, 5–25.

Tsankova, J. K., & Pjanic, K. (2009–2010). The area model of multiplication of fractions. *Mathematics Teaching in the Middle School, 15*(5), 281–285.

Witherspoon, T. F. (2014). Using constructed knowledge to multiply fractions. *Teaching Children Mathematics, 20*(7), 444–451.

Zhang, S., Clements, M. A., & Ellerton, N. F. (2015). Engaging students with multiple models of fractions. *Teaching Children Mathematics, 22*(3), 138–147.

Chapter 16

Bu, L., & Marjanovich, A. (2017). Percentages and milk fat. *Mathematics Teaching in the Middle School, 22*(8), 472–479.

Cramer, K. (2003). Using a translation model for curriculum development and classroom instruction. In Lesh, R. and Doerr, H. (Eds.) *Beyond constructivism: Models and modeling perspectives on mathematics problem solving, learning and teaching.* (pp. 449–464). Mahwah, NJ: Lawrence Erlbaum Associates.

Cramer, K. A., Monson, D., Ahrendt, S., Colum, K., Wiley, B., & Wyberg, T. (2015). 5 indicators of decimal understandings. *Teaching Children Mathematics, 22*(3): 186–195.

Cramer, K., Monsoon, D., Wyberg, T., Leavitt, S., & Whitney, S. (2009). Models for initial decimal ideas. *Teaching Children Mathematics, 16*(2), 106–117.

Cramer, K., & Whitney, S. (2010). Learning rational number concepts and skills in elementary school classrooms. In D. V. Lambdin & F. K. Lester, Jr. (Eds.), *Teaching and learning mathematics: Translating research for elementary school teachers* (pp. 15–22). Reston, VA: NCTM.

Depaepe, T. Torbeyns, J., Vermeersch, N., Janssens, D., Janssen, R., Kelchtermans, G., et al., (2015). Teachers' content and pedagogical content knowledge on rational numbers: A comparison of prospective elementary and lower secondary school teacher. *Teaching and Teacher Education, 47*, 82–82.

Desmet, L. Gregoire, J., & Mussolin, C. (2010). Developmental changes in the comparison of decimal fractions. *Learning and Instruction, 20*, 521–532.

Durkin, K., & Rittle-Johnson, B. (2015). The effectiveness of using incorrect examples to support learning about decimal magnitude. *Learning and Instruction, 22*, 206–214.

Fagan, E., & Tobey, C. R. (2015). *PD approaches to using student work: Build teacher capacity to assess decimal understanding and target instruction.* Presentation given at NCSM (April 14) Boston, MA.

Irwin, K. (2016). Using everyday knowledge of decimals to enhance understanding. In E. Silver and P. Kenney (Eds.) *More lessons learned from research: Helping all students understand important mathematics Volume 2, 32*(4), 399–420.

Kloosterman, P. (2010). Mathematics skills of 17-year-olds in the United States: 1978 to 2004. *Journal for Research in Mathematics Education, 41*(1), 20–51.

Kouba, V. L., Zawojewski, J. S., & Strutchens, M. E. (1997). What do students know about numbers and operations? In P. A. Kenney & E. Silver (Eds.), *Results from the sixth mathematics assessment of the National Assessment of Educational Progress* (pp. 87–140). Reston, VA: NCTM.

Lo, J. J., & Ko, Y. Y. (2013). A bargain price for teaching about percentage. *Mathematics Teaching in the Middle School, 19*(2), 108–115.

Loehr, A., & Rittle-Johnson, B. (2016). Putting the "th" in tenths: Providing place-value labels helps reveal the structure of our base-10 numeral system. *Journal of Cognition and Development, 18*(2), 226–245.

Lortie-Forgues, H., Tian, J., & Siegler, R. S. (2015). Why is learning fraction and decimal arithmetic so difficult? *Developmental Review, 38*, 201–221.

Martinie, S. L. (2007). *Middle school rational number knowledge* (Unpublished doctoral dissertation). Kansas State University

Martinie, S. L. (2014). Decimal fractions: An important point. *Mathematics Teaching in the Middle School, 19*(7), 420–429.

Martinie, S. L., & Bay-Williams, J. M. (2003). Investigating students' conceptual understanding of decimal fractions using multiple representations. *Mathematics Teaching in the Middle School, 8*(5), 244–247.

Muir, T., & Livy, S. (2012, December 5). What do they know? A comparison of pre-service teachers' and inservice teachers' decimal mathematical content knowledge. *International Journal for Mathematics Teaching and Learning*, 1–15.

NGA Center (National Governors Association Center for Best Practices) & CCSSO (Council of Chief State School Officers). (2010). *Common core state standards.* Retrieved from corestandards.org

Parker, M. (2004). Reasoning and working proportionally with percent. *Mathematics Teaching in the Middle School, 9*(6), 326–330.

Rathouz, M. M. (2011). Making sense of decimal multiplication. *Mathematics Teaching in the Middle School, 16*(7), 430–437.

Rittle-Johnson, B., & Koedinger, K. (2009). Iterating between lessons on concepts and procedures can improve mathematics knowledge. *British Journal of Educational Psychology, 79*, 483–500.

Shahbari, J. A., & Peled, I. (2016). Using modeling tasks to facilitate the development of percentages. *Canadian Journal of Science, Mathematics and Technology Education, 16*(3), 259–272.

Siegler, R. & Lortie-Forgues, H. (2015). Conceptual knowledge of fraction arithmetic. *Journal of Educational Psychology, 107*(3), 909–918.

Siegler, R., Thompson, C. & Schneider, M. (2011). An integrated theory of whole number and fractions development. *Cognitive Psychology, 62*, 273–296.

Smith, M., Silver, E. & Stein, M. K. (2005). *Improving instruction in rational numbers and proportionality: Using cases to transform mathematics teaching and learning.* New York: Teachers College Press.

Stacey, K., Helme, S., Steinle, V., Baturo, A., Irwin, K., & Bana, J. (2001). Preservice teachers' knowledge of difficulties in decimal numeration. *Journal of Mathematics Teacher Education, 4*, 205–225.

Steinle, V., & Stacey, K. (2004a). Persistence of decimal misconceptions and readiness to move to expertise. *Proceedings of the 28th conference of the International Groups for the Psychology of Mathematics Education, 4*, 225–232.

Steinle, V., & Stacey, K. (2004b). A longitudinal study of students' understanding of decimal notation: An overview and refined results. In I. Putt, R. Faragher, & M. McLean (Eds.), *Mathematics Education for the Third Millennium: Towards 2010. Proceedings of the 27th Annual Conference of the Mathematics Education Research Group of Australasia, 2*, 541–548.

Ubuz, B., & Yayan, B. (2010). Primary teachers' subject matter knowledge: Decimals. *International Journal of Mathematical Education in Science and Technology, 41*(6), 787–804.

Vamvakoussi, X., Van Dooren, W., & Verschaffel, L. (2012). Naturally biased? In search for reaction time evidence for a natural number bias in adults. *The Journal of Mathematical Behavior, 31*(3), 344–355.

Whitin, D. J., & Whitin, P. (2012). Making sense of fractions and percentages. *Teaching Children Mathematics, 18*(8), 490–496.

Woodward, J., Baxter, J., & Robinson, R. (1999). Rules and reasons: Decimal instruction for academically low achieving students. *Learning Disabilities Research and Practice, 14*(1), 15–24.

Wyberg, T., Whitney, S. R., Cramer, K. A., Monson, D. S., & Leavitt, S. (2011). Unfolding fraction multiplication. *Mathematics Teaching in the Middle School, 17*, 288–294.

Zambo, R. (2008). Percents can make sense. *Mathematics Teaching in the Middle School, 13*(7), 418–422.

Chapter 17

Beckman, C. E., Thompson, D., & Austin, R. A. (2004). Exploring proportional reasoning through movies and literature. *Mathematics Teaching in the Middle School, 9*(5), 256–262.

Beigie, D. (2016). Dare to compare. *Mathematics Teaching in the Middle School, 21*(8), 460–469.

Berk, D., Taber, S., Gorowara, C. C., & Poetzl, C. (2009). Developing prospective elementary teachers' flexibility in the domain of proportional reasoning. *Mathematical Thinking and Learning, 11*(3), 113–135.

Beswick, K. (2011). Make your own paint chart. *Australian Mathematics Teacher, 67*(1), 6–11.

Briggs, R. (1970). *Jim and the beanstalk.* New York, NY: Coward-McCann.

Bright, G. W., Joyner, J. M., & Wallis, C. (2003). Assessing proportional thinking. *Mathematics Teaching in the Middle School, 9*(3), 166–172.

Bush, S. B., Karp, K. S., Nadler, J., & Gibbons, K (2016). Using artwork to explore proportional reasoning. *Mathematics Teaching in the Middle School, 22*(4), 216–223.

Cai, J., & Sun, W. (2002). Developing students' proportional reasoning: A Chinese perspective. In B. Litwiller (Ed.), *Making sense of fractions, ratios, and proportions* (pp. 195–205). Reston, VA: NCTM.

Carroll, L., & Gray, D. J. (1865/1992). *Alice in wonderland.* New York, NY: Norton.

Che, S. M. (2009). Giant pencils: Developing proportional reasoning. *Mathematics Teaching in the Middle School, 14*(7), 404–408.

Cohen, J. S. (2013). Strip diagrams: Illuminating proportions. *Mathematics Teaching in the Middle School, 18*(9), 536–542.

de la Cruz, J. A., & Garney, S. (2016). Saving money using proportional reasoning. *Mathematics Teaching in the Middle School, 21*(9), 552–561.

Ercole, L. K., Frantz, M., & Ashline, G. (2011). Multiple ways to solve proportions. *Mathematics Teaching in the Middle School, 16*(8), 482–490.

Heinz, K., & Sterba-Boatwright, B. (2008). The when and why of using proportions. *Mathematics Teacher, 101*(7), 528–533.

Isaacs, A., & Zelinsky, P. O. (1994). *Swamp angel.* New York, NY: Dutton Children's Books.

Kastberg, S. E., D'Ambrosio, B. S., Lynch-Davis, K., Mintos, A., & Krawczyk, K. (2014). CCSSM Challenge: Graphing ratio and proportion. *Mathematics Teaching in the Middle School, 19*(5), 294–300.

Krull, K. (2000). *Wilma unlimited: How Wilma became the world's fastest woman.* New York: Harcourt Brace & Co.

Lamon, S. J. (2012). *Teaching fractions and ratios for understanding: Essential content knowledge and instructional strategies* (3rd ed.). New York, NY: Taylor & Francis Group.

Lim, K. H. (2009). Burning the candle at just one end. *Mathematics Teaching in the Middle School, 14*(8), 492–500.

Lobato, J., Ellis, A. B., Charles, R. I., & Zbiek, R. M. (2010). *Developing essential understanding of ratios, proportions, and proportional reasoning: Grades 6–8.* Reston, VA: NCTM.

Martinie, S. L., & Bay-Williams, J. M. (2003). Investigating students' conceptual understanding of decimal fractions using multiple representations. *Mathematics Teaching in the Middle School, 8*(5), 244–247.

National Research Council. (2001). *Adding it up: Helping children learn mathematics.* J. Kilpatrick, J. Swafford, & B. Findell (Eds.). Washington, DC: National Academies Press.

NGA Center (National Governors Association Center for Best Practices) & CCSSO (Council of Chief State School Officers). (2010). *Common core state standards.* Retrieved from corestandards.org

Norton, M. (1953). *The borrowers.* New York, NY: Harcourt Brace.

Orwell, G. (1946). *Animal farm.* New York: Harcourt, Brace & Co.

Osborne, M. P., & Potter, G. (2000). *Kate and the beanstalk.* New York, NY: Atheneum Books for Young Readers.

Parker, M. (2004). Reasoning and working proportionally with percent. *Mathematics Teaching in the Middle School, 9*(6), 326–330.

Pugalee, D. K., Arbaugh, F., Bay-Williams, J. M., Farrell, A., Mathews, S., &. Royster, D. (2008). *Navigating through mathematical connections in grades 6–8.* Reston, VA: NCTM.

Rathouz, M., Cengiz, N., Krebs, A., & Rubenstein, R. N. (2014). Tasks to develop language for ratio relationships. *Mathematics Teaching in the Middle School, 20*(1), 38–44.

Roberge, M. C., & Cooper, L. L. (2010). Map scale, proportion, and Google™ Earth. *Mathematics Teaching in the Middle School, 15*(8), 448–457.

Rowling, J. K. (1998). *Harry Potter and the sorcerer's stone.* New York, NY: A. A. Lewine.

Sachar, L. (1998). *Holes.* New York, NY: Farrar, Straus & Giroux.

Schwartz, D. M. (1999). *If you hopped like a frog.* New York, NY: Scholastic Press.

Seeley, C., & Schielack, J. F. (2007). A look at the development of ratios, rates, and proportionality. *Mathematics Teaching in the Middle School, 13*(3), 140–142.

Siegler, R. S., Carpenter, T., Fennell, F., Geary, D., Lewis, J., Okamoto, Y., et al. (2010). *Developing effective fractions instruction for kindergarten through 8th grade: A practice guide* (NCEE 2010–4039). Retrieved from www.whatworks.ed.gov/publications/Practiceguides

Silverstein, S. (1974). One inch tall. In *Where the sidewalk ends* (p. 55). New York, NY: Harper & Row.

Simic-Muller, K. (2015). Social justice and proportional reasoning. *Mathematics Teaching in the Middle School, 21*(3), 162–168.

Smith, J. P., III. (2002). The development of students' knowledge of fractions and ratios. In B. Litwiller (Ed.), *Making sense of fractions, ratios, and proportions* (pp. 3–17). Reston, VA: NCTM.

Stemn, B. (2008). Building middle school students' understanding of proportional reasoning through mathematical investigation. *Education, 36*(4), 3–13.

Swanson, P. E. (2015). Toy stories: Modeling rates. *Teaching children mathematics, 22*(2), 76–83.

Swift, J., & Winterson, J. (1726/1999). *Gulliver's travels.* Oxford, UK: Oxford University Press.

Thiessen, D. (2017). *Exploring Math through Literature.* Reston, VA: NCTM.

Tolkien, J. R. R. (1965). *The lord of the rings.* New York, NY: Ballantine Books.

Turner, E. E., & Strawhun, B. T. (2007). Problem posing that makes a difference: Students posing and investigating mathematical problems related to overcrowding at their school. *Teaching Children Mathematics, 13*(9), 457–463.

Van Dooren, W., De Bock, D., Vleugels, K., & Verschaffel, L. (2010). Just answering . . . or thinking? Contrasting pupils' solutions and classifications of missing-value word problems. *Mathematical Thinking and Learning, 12*(1), 20–35.

Watson, J. M., & Shaughnessy, J. M. (2004). Proportional reasoning: Lessons learned from research in data and chance. *Mathematics Teaching in the Middle School, 10*(2), 104–109.

Williams, M., Forrest, K., & Schnabel, D. (2006). Water wonders (math by the month). *Teaching Children Mathematics, 12*(5), 248–249.

Chapter 18

Amore, B., & Pinilla, M. (2006). Relationships between area and perimeter: Beliefs of teachers and students. *Mediterranean Journal for Research in Mathematics Education, 5*(2), 1–29.

Association of Mathematics Teacher Educators. (2017). *Standards for preparing teachers of mathematics.* Available online at amte.net/standards.

Battista, M. T. (2003). Understanding students' thinking about area and volume measurement. In D. H. Clements (Ed.), *Learning and teaching measurement* (pp. 122–142). Reston, VA: NCTM.

Battista, M. (2012). *Cognition-based assessment and teaching of geometric measurement: Building on students' reasoning.* Portsmouth, NG: Heinemann.

Blume, G. W., Galindo, E., & Walcott, C. (2007). Performance in measurement and geometry from the viewpoint of Principles and Standards for School Mathematics. In P. Kloosterman & F. K. Lester (Eds.), 2003 *Mathematics assessment of the national assessment of educational progress* (pp. 95–138). Reston, VA: NCTM.

Bustang, B., Zulkardi, Z., Darmawijoyo, H., Dolk, M., & van Eerde, D. (2013). Developing a Local Instruction Theory for Learning the Concept of Angle through Visual Field Activities and Spatial Representations. *International Education Studies, 6*(8), 58–70.

Dietiker, L., Gonulates, F., Figueras, J., & Smith, J. P. (2010, April). *Weak attention to unit iteration in U.S. elementary curriculum materials.* Presentation at the Annual Conference of the American Educational Research Association, Denver, CO.

Dixon, J. (2008). Tracking time: Representing elapsed time on an open timeline. *Teaching Children Mathematics, 15*(1), 18–24.

Fernandes, A., Kahn, L. H., & Civil, M. (2017). A closer look at bilingual students' use of multimodality in the context of an area comparison problem from a large-scale assessment. *Educational Studies in Mathematics, 95*, 263–282.

Hightower, S. (1997). *Twelve snails to one lizard: A tale of mischief and measurement.* New York: Simon & Schuster.

Joram, E. & Gabriele, A. (2016). Measurement estimation as a vehicle for making sense of measurement. In E. Silver & P. Kenney (Eds.), *More lessons learning from research: Useful and suable research related to core mathematical practices volume 1.* (pp. 165–170).

Kamii, C., & Kysh, J. (2006). The difficulty of "length × width": Is a square the unit of measurement? *Journal of Mathematical Behavior, 25*, 105–115.

Kloosterman, P., Rutledge, Z., & Kenney, P. (2009a). Exploring the results of the NAEP: 1980s to the present. *Mathematics Teaching in the Middle School, 14*(6), 357–365.

Leedy, L. (2000). *Measuring Penny.* New York, NY: Holt.

Lionni, L. (1960). *Inch by inch.* New York: HarperCollins.

Livy, S. Muir, T. & Maher, N. (2012). How do they measure up? Primary pre-service teachers' mathematical knowledge of area and perimeter. *Mathematics Teacher Education and Development, 14*(2), 91–112.

Manizade, A., & Mason, M. (2014). Developing the area of a trapezoid. *Mathematics Teacher, 107*(7), 508–514.

Muir, T. (2005). When near enough is good enough. *Australian Primary Mathematics Classroom, 20*(2), 9–14.

Mullis, I. V. S., Martin, M. O., Gonzalez, E. J., & Chrostowski, S. J. (2004). *TIMSS 2003 international mathematics report: Findings from IEA's trends in international mathematics and science study at the fourth and eighth grades.* Chestnut Hill, MA: TIMSS & PIRLS International Study Center, Boston College.

Munier, V., Devichi, C., & Merle, H. (2008). A physical situation as a way to teach angle. *Teaching Children Mathematics, 14*(7), 402–407.

National Center for Educational Statistics. (2014). *NAEP questions tool.* Retrieved from nces.ed.gov/nationsreportcard/itmrlsx/landing.aspx

National Institute of Standards and Technology (NIST) (2015). *Trade and Commerce.* Retrieved from www.nist.gov/pml/wmd/metric/trade-comm.cfm.

NCTM (National Council of Teachers of Mathematics). (2015). *Position statement on the metric system.* Reston, VA: NCTM.

NGA Center (National Governors Association Center for Best Practices) & CCSSO (Council of Chief State School Officers). (2010). *Common core state standards.* Retrieved from corestandards.org

Outhred, L., & Mitchelmore, M. (2004). Students' structuring of rectangular arrays. In M. J. Hoines & A. B. Fuglestad (Eds.), *Proceedings of the 28th PME International Conference, 3*, 465–472.

Parmar, R., Garrison, R., Clements, D., & Sarama, J. (2011). Measurement. In F. Fennell (Ed.), *Achieving fluency in special education and mathematics* (pp. 197–216). Reston, VA: NCTM.

Perie, M., Moran, R., & Lutkus, A. (2005). *NAEP 2004 trends in academic progress: Three decades of student performance in reading and mathematics.* Washington, DC: National Center for Education Statistics.

Preston, R., & Thompson, T. (2004). Integrating measurement across the curriculum. *Mathematics Teaching in the Middle School, 9*(8), 436–441.

Provasnik, S., Gonzales, P., and Miller, D. (2009). *U.S. Performance Across International Assessments of Student Achievement: Special Supplement to The Condition of Education 2009* (NCES 2009–083). U.S. Department of Education. Washington, DC: National Center for Education Statistics.

Putrawangsa, S., Lukito, A., M Amin, S., & Wijers, M. (2013). Educational design research: Developing students' understanding of area as the number of measurement units covering a surface. In Z. Zulkardi (Ed.), *Proceedings of the First South East Asia Design/Development Research (SEA-DR) International Conference, Sriwijaya University, Palembang, April 22–23* (pp. 416–426).

Sisman, G. T., & Aksu, M. (2016). A study on sixth grade students' misconceptions and errors in spatial measurement: length, area, and volume. *International Journal of Science and Mathematics Education, 14*, 1293–1319.

Thompson, T. D., & Preston, R. V. (2004). Measurement in the middle grades: Insights from NAEP and TIMSS. *Mathematics Teaching in the Middle School, 9*(9), 514–519.

Tompert, A. (1997). *Grandfather Tang's story.* New York, NY: Dragonfly Books.

Towers, J., & Hunter, K. (2010). An ecological reading of mathematical language in a grade 3 classroom: A case of learning and teaching measurement estimation. *The Journal of Mathematical Behavior, 29*, 25–40.

Wickstrom, M. H., Carr, R., & Lackey, D. (2017). Exploring Yellowstone National Park with mathematical modeling. *Mathematics Teaching in the Middle School, 22*(8), 462–470.

Wickstrom, M. H., & Jurczak, L. M. (2016). Inch by inch, we measure. *Teaching Children Mathematics, 22*(8), 468–475.

Zacharos, K. (2006). Prevailing educational practices for area measurement and students' failure in measuring areas. *Journal of Mathematics Behavior, 25*(3), 224–239.

Zwillinger, D. (Ed.). (2011). *Standard mathematical tables and formulae* (32nd ed.). Boca Raton, FL: CRC Press.

Chapter 19

Battista, M. T. (2007). The development of geometric and spatial thinking. In F. Lester (Ed.), *Second handbook of research on mathematics teaching and learning* (pp. 843–908). Reston, VA: NCTM.

Burns, M. (1995). *The greedy triangle*. New York, NY: Houghton Mifflin.

Clements, D. H., & Battista, M. T. (1990). Constructivist learning and teaching. *Arithmetic Teacher, 38*(1), 34–35.

Clements, D., & Sarama, J. (2014). *Learning and teaching early math: The learning trajectories approach* (2nd ed.). New York, NY: Routledge.

Cochran, J. A., Cochran, Z., Laney, K., & Dean, M. (2016). Expanding geometry understanding with 3D printing. *Mathematics Teaching in the Middle School, 21*(9), 534–542.

Copley, N. (2017). *Putting essential understanding of geometry and measurement into practice: Grades preK–2*. Reston, VA: NCTM.

Goldenberg, E. P., & Clements, D. H. (2014). *Developing essential understanding of geometry and measurement for teaching mathematics in prekindergarten–grade 2*. Reston, VA: NCTM.

Howse, T. D., & Howse, M. E. (2014/2015). Linking the van Hiele theory to instruction. *Teaching Children Mathematics, 21*(5), 304–313.

Kell, H. J., Lubinski, D., Benbow, C. P., & Steiger, J. H. (2013). Creativity and technical innovation: spatial ability's unique role. *Psychological Science, 24*, 1831–1836.

Mulligan, J. (2015). Looking within and beyond the geometry curriculum: Connecting spatial reasoning to mathematics learning. *ZDM Mathematics Education, 47*(3), 511–517.

National Research Council Committee. (2009). *Mathematics learning in early childhood: Paths toward excellence and equity*. Washington, DC: The National Academies Press.

NCTM (National Council of Teachers of Mathematics). (2000). *Principles and standards for school mathematics*. Reston, VA: NCTM.

Nelson, R. (2001). *Proofs without words II: More exercises in visual thinking*. Washington, DC: Mathematical Association of America.

NGA Center (National Governors Association Center for Best Practices) & CCSSO (Council of Chief State School Officers). (2010). *Common core state standards*. Retrieved from corestandards.org

Prasad, P. V. (2016). Leveraging interactive geometry software to prompt discussion. *Mathematics Teaching in the Middle School, 22*(4), 226–232.

Prummer, K. E., Amador, J. M., & Wallin, A. J. (2016). Persevering with prisms: Producing nets. *Mathematics Teaching in the Middle School, 21*(8), 472–479.

Ronau, R. N., Meyer, D., & Crites, T. (2015). *Putting essential understanding of geometry into practice in grades 9–12*. Reston, VA: NCTM.

Roscoe, M.B., & Zephyrs, J. (2016). Quilt block symmetries, *Mathematics Teaching in the Middle School, 22*(1), 18–27.

Sarama, J., & Clements, D. H. (2009). *Early childhood mathematics education research: Learning trajectories for young children*. New York, NY: Routledge.

Sinclair, N., Pimm, D., & Skelin, M. (2012). *Developing essential understanding of geometry for teaching mathematics in grades 9–12*. NCTM.

van Hiele, P. M. (1984). A child's thought and geometry. In D. Geddes, D. Fuys, & R. Tischler (Eds.), *English Translation of Selected Writings of Dina van Hiele-Geldof and Pierre M. van Hiele*, Washington, DC: National Science Foundation.

van Hiele, P. M. (1999). Developing geometric thinking through activities that begin with play. *Teaching Children Mathematics, 5*(6), 310–316.

Wai, J., Lubinski, D., & Benbow, C. (2009). Spatial ability for STEM domains: Aligning over 50 years of cumulative psychological knowledge solidifies its importance. *Journal of Educational Psychology, 101*(4), 817–835.

Yu, P., Barrett, J., & Presmeg, N. (2009). Prototypes and categorical reasoning: A perspective to explain how children learn about interactive geometry objects. In T. Craine & R. Rubenstein (Eds.), *Understanding geometry for a changing world*. Reston, VA: NCTM.

Zwillinger, D. (Ed.). (2011). *Standard mathematical tables and formulae* (32nd ed.). Boca Raton, FL: CRC Press.

Chapter 20

Bakker, A., Biehler, R., & Konold, C. (2004). Should young students learn about box plots? In *Curricular development in statistics education* (pp. 163–173). Sweden: Curricular Development in Statistics Education.

Bay-Williams, J. M., & Martinie, S. L. (2009). *Math and non-fiction: Grades 6–8*. Sausalito, CA: Marilyn Burns Books.

Burrill, G. F., & Elliot, P. (2006). *Thinking and reasoning with data and chance: 68th NCTM yearbook*. Reston, VA: NCTM.

Brown, M. W. (1947). *Goodnight moon*. New York, NY: Harper & Row.

Buckley, J., Jr., & Stremme, R. (2006). *Book of lists: Fun facts, weird trivia, and amazing lists on nearly everything you need to know!* Santa Barbara, CA: Scholastic.

Clements, D., & Sarama, J. (2014). *Learning and teaching early math: The learning trajectories approach* (2nd ed.). New York, NY: Routledge.

Cobb, P., McClain, K., & Gravemeijer, K. (2003). Learning about statistical covariation. *Cognition and Instruction, 21*(1), 1–78.

Cook, C. D. (2008). I scream, you scream: Data analysis with kindergartners. *Teaching Children Mathematics, 14*(9), 538–540.

Cooper, L. L., & Shore, F. S. (2008). Students' misconceptions in interpreting center and variability of data represented via histograms and stem-and-leaf plots, *Journal of Statistics Education, 16*(2), http://amstat.tandfonline.com/doi/full/10.1080/10691898.2008.11889559#.WjH5c1VG2Rt

English, L. (2013). Surviving an avalanche of data. *Teaching Children Mathematics, 19*(6), 364–372.

Franke, M. L., Kazemi, E., & Battey, D. (2007). Mathematics teaching and classroom practice. In F. K. Lester (Ed.), *Second handbook of research on mathematics teaching and learning* (pp. 225–256). Reston, VA: NCTM.

Franklin, C. A., & Mewborn, D. S. (2008). Statistics in the elementary grades: Exploring distribution of data. *Teaching Children Mathematics, 15*(1), 10–16.

Friel, S. N., Curcio, F. R., & Bright, G. W. (2001). Making sense of graphs: Critical factors influencing comprehension and instructional implications. *Journal for Research in Mathematics Education, 32*(2), 124–158.

Friel, S. N., O'Conner, W., & Mamer, J. D. (2006). More than "meanmedianmode" and a bar graph: What's needed to have a statistical conversation? In G. F. Burrill & P. C. Elliott (Eds.), *Thinking and reasoning with data and chance: 68th NCTM yearbook* (pp. 117–138). Reston, VA: NCTM.

Groth, R. E. (2015). Royalty, racing, and rolling pigs. *Teaching Children Mathematics, 22*(4), 218–227.

Groth, R. E., & Bargagliotti, A. E. (2012). GAISEing into the Common Core State Standards. *Mathematics Teaching in the Middle School, 18*(1), 38–45.

Groth, R. E., Kent, K. D., & Hitch, E. D. (2015/2016). Journey to centers in the CORE. *Mathematics Teaching in the Middle School, 21*(5), 295–302

Hourigan, M., & Leavy, A. (2015/2016). Practical problems: Using literature to teach statistics. *Teaching Children Mathematics, 22*(5), 282–291.

Hudson, P. J., Shupe, M., Vasquez, E., & Miller, S. P. (2008). Teaching data analysis to elementary students with mild disabilities. *TEACHING Exceptional Children Plus, 4*(3), Article 5. Retrieved from escholarship.bc.edu/education/tecplus/vol4/iss3/art5

Hudson, R. A. (2012/2013). Finding balance at the elusive mean. *Mathematics Teaching in the Middle School, 18*(5), 301–306.

Johnson, D. T. (2011). Pencils and crayons. *Teaching Children Mathematics, 18*(2), 73–74.

Kader, G. D., & Jacobbe, T. (2013). *Developing essential understanding of statistics for teaching mathematics in grades 6–8.* Reston, VA: NCTM.

Kader, G., & Mamer, J. (2008). Statistics in the middle grades: Understanding center and spread. *Mathematics Teaching in the Middle Grades, 14*(1), 38–43.

Kaplan, J. J., Gabrosek, J. G., Curtiss, P., & Malone, C. (2014). Investigating student understanding of histograms. *Journal of Statistics Education, 22*(2). www.amstat.org/publications/jse/v22n2/kaplan.pdf

Konold, C., & Pollatsek, A. (2002). Data analysis as the search for signals in noisy processes. *Journal for Research in Mathematics Education, 33*(4), 259–289.

Leavy, A., Friel, S., & Mamer, J. (2009). It's a fird! Can you compute a median of categorical data? *Mathematics Teaching in the Middle School, 14*(6), 344–351.

Lovett, J. N., & Lee, H. S. (2016). Making sense of data: Context matters. *Mathematics Teaching in the Middle School, 21*(6), 338–346.

McClain, K., Leckman, J., Schmitt, P., & Regis, T. (2006). Changing the face of statistical data analysis in the middle grades: Learning by doing. In G. F. Burrill & P. C. Elliott (Eds.), *Thinking and reasoning with data and chance: 68th NCTM yearbook* (pp. 229–240). Reston, VA: NCTM.

McGatha, M., Cobb, P., & McClain, K. (1998). *An analysis of students' statistical understandings.* Paper presented at the Annual Meeting of the American Educational Research Association, San Diego, CA.

McGlone, C. (2008, July). *The role of culturally-based mathematics in the general mathematics curriculum.* Paper presented at the Eleventh International Congress on Mathematics Education, Monterrey, Mexico.

Meletiou-Mavrotheris, M., & Lee, C. (2010). Investigating college-level introductory statistics students' prior knowledge of graphing. *Canadian Journal of Science, Mathematics and Technology Education, 10*(4), 339–355.

Metz, M. L. (2010). Using GAISE and NCTM standards as framework for teaching probability and statistics to pre-service elementary and middle school mathematics teachers. *Journal of Statistics Education, 18*(3), 1–27.

Mokros, J., & Russell, S. J. (1995). Children's concepts of average and representativeness. *Journal for Research in Mathematics Education, 26*(1), 20–39.

Mokros, J., & Wright, T. (2009). Zoos, aquariums and expanding students' data literacy. *Teaching Children Mathematics, 15*(9), 524–530.

Mooney, E. S., & Bair, S. L. (2011). Average jeans. *Mathematics Teaching in the Middle School, 17*(4), 210–211.

Niezgoda, D. A., & Moyer-Packenham, P. S. (2005). Hickory, dickory, dock: Navigating through data analysis. *Teaching Children Mathematics, 11*(6), 292–300.

NCTM (National Council of Teachers of Mathematics). (2006). *Curriculum focal points for prekindergarten through grade 8 mathematics: A quest for coherence.* Reston, VA: NCTM.

NGA Center (National Governors Association Center for Best Practices) & CCSSO (Council of Chief State School Officers). (2010). *Common core state standards.* Retrieved from corestandards.org

O'Dell, R. S. (2012). The mean as balance point. *Mathematics Teaching in the Middle School, 18*(3), 148–155.

Patterson, L. G., & Patterson, K. L. (2014). Problem solve with presidential data. *Mathematics Teaching in the Middle School, 19*(7), 406–413.

Peters, S. A., Bennett, V. M., Young, M., & Watkins, J. D. (2016). A fair and balanced approach to the mean. *Mathematics Teaching in the Middle School, 21*(6), 364–372.

Riskowski, J. L., Olbricht, G., & Wilson, J. (2010). 100 students. *Mathematics Teaching in the Middle School, 15*(6), 320–327.

Russell, S. J. (2006). What does it mean that "5 has a lot"? From the world to data and back. In G. F. Burrill & P. C. Elliott (Eds.), *Thinking and reasoning about data and chance: 68th NCTM yearbook* (pp. 17–30). Reston VA: NCTM.

Russell, S. J., & Economopoulos, K. (2008). *Investigations in number, data, and space.* New York, NY: Pearson.

Scheaffer, R. L. (2006). Statistics and mathematics: On making a happy marriage. In G. F. Burrill & P. C. Elliott (Eds.), *Thinking and reasoning about data and chance: Sixty-eighth yearbook* (pp. 309–322). Reston, VA: NCTM.

Seuss, Dr. (1960). *Green eggs and ham.* New York, NY: Random House.

Shaughnessy, J. M. (2003). Research on students' understanding of probability. In J. Kilpatrick, W. G. Martin, & D. Schifter (Eds.), *A research companion to Principles and Standards for School Mathematics* (pp. 216–226). Reston, VA: NCTM.

Shaughnessy, J. M. (2007). Research on statistics learning and reasoning. In F. Lester, Jr. (Ed.), *Second handbook of research on mathematics teaching and learning* (pp. 957–1010). Reston, VA: NCTM.

Smith, D. (2009). *If America were a village: A book about the people of the United States.* Tonawanda, NY: Kids Can Press.

Smith, D. (2011). *If the world were a village: A book about the world's people* (2nd ed.). Tonawanda, NY: Kids Can Press.

Tarr, J. E., & Shaughnessy, J. M. (2007). *Data and chance. Results from the 2003 National Assessment of Educational Process.* Reston, VA: NCTM.

U.S. Bureau of the Census, Median Sales Price for New Houses Sold in the United States [MSPNHSUS], retrieved from FRED, Federal Reserve Bank of St. Louis; fred.stlouisfed.org/series/MSPNHSUS, September 7, 2017.

Weatherform, C. B. (2005). *A Negro league scrapbook.* Honesdale, PA: Boyds Mills Press.

Wilburne, J. M., & Kulbacki, A. (2014). Connecting the "missing words" to the Common Core. *Mathematics Teaching in the Middle School, 19*(7), 430–436.

Chapter 21

Abu-Bakare, V. (2008). *Investigating students', understandings of probability: A study of a grade 7 classroom* (Master's thesis). Retrieved from hdl.handle.net/2429/4073

Beck, S. A., & Huse, V. E. (2007). A virtual spin on probability. *Teaching Children Mathematics, 13*(9), 482–486.

Cohen, R. (2006). How do students think? *Mathematics Teaching in the Middle School, 11*(9), 434–436.

Colgan, M. D. (2006). March math madness: The mathematics of the NCAA basketball tournament. *Mathematics Teaching in the Middle School, 11*(7), 334–342.

Degner, K. (2015). Flipping out: Calculating probability with a coin game. *Mathematics Teaching in the Middle School, 21*(4), 244–245.

Ellis, M., Yeh, C., & Stump, S. (2007–2008). Rock-paper-scissors and solutions to the broken calculator problem. *Teaching Children Mathematics, 14*(5), 309–314.

Ely, R. E., & Cohen, J. S. (2010). Put the right spin on student work. *Mathematics Teaching in the Middle School, 16*(4), 208–215.

English, L. D., & Watson, J. M. (2016). Development of probabilistic understanding in fourth grade. *Journal for Research in Mathematics Education, 47*(1), 28–62.

Flores, A. (2006). Using graphing calculators to redress beliefs in the "law of small numbers." In G.F. Burrill & P. C. Elliott (Eds.), *Thinking and reasoning with data and chance: 68th NCTM yearbook* (pp. 139–149). Reston, VA: NCTM.

Franklin, C. A., Kader, G., Mewborn, D., Moreno, J., Peck, R., Perry, M., & Scheaffer, R. (2005). *Guidelines for assessment and instruction in statistics education (GAISE) report.* Alexandria, VA: American Statistical Association.

Gallego, C., Saldamando, D., Tapia-Beltran, G., Williams, K., & Hoopingarner, T. C. (2009). Math by the month: Probability. *Teaching Children Mathematics, 15*(7), 416.

Goodwin C., & Ortiz, E. (2015). It's a girl! Random numbers, Simulations, and the Law of Large Numbers. *Mathematics Teaching in the Middle School, 20*(9), 561–563.

Gurbuz, R., Erdem, H., Catlioglu, O., & Birgin, E. (2010). An investigation of fifth grade students' conceptual development of probability through activity-based instruction: A quasi-experimental design. *Educational Sciences: Theory and Practice, 10*(2), 1053–1068.

Konold, C., Madden, S., Pollatsek, A., Pfannkuch, M., Wild, C., Ziedins, I., Finzer, W., Zielins, I., Finzer, W., Horton, N. J., & Kazak, S. (2011). Conceptual challenges in coordinating theoretical and data-centered estimates of probability. *Mathematical Thinking and Learning, 13*(1–2), 68–86.

Kustos, P., & Zelkowski, J. (2013). Grade-continuum trajectories for four known probabilistic misconceptions: What are students' perceptions of self-efficacy in completing probability tasks? *Journal of Mathematical Behavior, 32*(3), 508–26.

Lim, V., Rubel, L., Shookhoff, L., Sullivan, M., & Williams, S. (2016). The lottery is a mathematics powerball. *Mathematics Teaching in the Middle School, 21*(9), 526–532.

McCoy, L. P., Buckner, S., & Munley, J. (2007). Probability games from diverse cultures. *Mathematics Teaching in the Middle School, 12*(7), 394–402.

Nelson, C. Q., & Williams, N. L. (2009). Mathematical explorations: Exploring unknown probabilities with miniature toy pigs. *Mathematics Teaching in the Middle School, 14*(9), 557.

Nicolson, C. P. (2005). Is chance fair? One student's thoughts on probability. *Teaching Children Mathematics, 12*(2), 83–89.

NGA Center (National Governors Association Center for Best Practices) & CCSSO (Council of Chief State School Officers). (2010). *Common core state standards.* Retrieved from corestandards.org

Phillips-Bey, C. K. (2004). TI–73 calculator activities. *Mathematics Teaching in the Middle School, 9*(9), 500–508.

Ryan, J., & Williams, J. (2007). *Children's mathematics 4–15: Learning from errors and misconceptions.* New York, NY: McGraw-Hill Open University Press.

Rubel, L. (2006). Students' probabilistic thinking revealed: The case of coin tosses. In G. Burrill & P. C. Elliott (Eds.), *Thinking and reasoning about data and chance: Sixty-eighth yearbook* (pp. 49–60). Reston, VA: NCTM.

Rubel, L. (2007). Middle school and high school students' probabilistic reasoning on coin tasks. *Journal for Research in Mathematics Education, 38*(5), 531–557.

Tarr, J. E., Lee, H. S., & Rider, R. L. (2006). When data and chance collide: Drawing inferences from empirical data. In G. Burrill & P. C. Elliott (Eds.), *Thinking and reasoning with data and chance: 68th NCTM yearbook* (pp. 139–149). Reston, VA: NCTM.

Tillema, E. S. (2010). Math for real: A three-girl family. *Mathematics Teaching in the Middle School, 48*(5), 304.

Watson, J. M., & Moritz, J. B. (2003). Fairness of dice: A longitudinal study of students' beliefs and strategies for making judgments. *Journal for Research in Mathematics Education, 34*(4), 270–304.

Williams, N. L., & Bruels, C. (2011). Target geometry and probability using a dartboard. *Mathematics Teaching in the Middle School, 16*(6), 375–378.

Young, L. (2016). Toy pigs teach statistics. *Mathematics Teaching in the Middle School, 22*(2), 114–117.

Chapter 22

Ameis, J. A. (2011). The truth about PEDMAS. *Mathematics Teaching in the Middle School, 16*(7), 414–420.

Ball, J. (2016). *Go figure!* New York, NY: DK Publishing.

Ball, J. (2016). *Why pi?* New York, NY: DK Publishing.

Bay-Williams, J. M., & Martinie, S. L. (2009). *Math and nonfiction: Grades 6–8.* Sausalito, CA: Marilyn Burns Books.

Bay-Williams, J. M., & Martinie, S. L. (2015). Order of operations: The myth and the math. *Mathematics Teaching in the Middle School, 20*(6), 20–27.

Bishop, J. P., Lamb, L. L., Philipp, R. A., Whitacre, I., Schappelle, M. P., Lewis, M. L. (2014). Obstacles and affordances for integer reasoning: An analysis of children's thinking and the history of mathematics. *Journal for Research in Mathematics Education, 45*(1), 19–61.

Bishop, J. P., Lamb, L. L., Philipp, R. A., Whitacre, I, & Schappelle, B. P. (2016a) Unlocking the structure of positive and negative numbers. *Mathematics Teaching in the Middle School, 22*(2), 84–91.

Bishop, J. P., Lamb, L. L., Philipp, R. A., Whitacre, I, & Schappelle, B. P. (2016b) Le-veraging structure: Logical necessity in the context of integer arithmetic. *Mathematical Thinking and Learning, 18*(3), 209–232.

Bofferding, L. (2014). Negative integer understanding: Characterizing first graders' mental models. *Journal for Research in Mathematics Education, 45*(2), 194–245.

Carter, C. J., Prince, E., & Schwartz, Z. (2017). Refining concepts: Half isn't always less. *Mathematics Teaching in the Middle School, 22*(9), 524–532.

Choppin, J. M., Clancy, C. B., & Koch, S. J. (2012). Developing formal procedures through sense making. *Mathematics Teaching in the Middle School, 17*(9), 552–557.

Dupree, K. M. (2016). Questioning the order of operations. *Mathematics Teaching in the Middle School, 22*(3), 152–159.

Enzensberger, H. M. (1997). *The number devil.* New York, NY: Metropolitan Books.

Friedmann, P. (2008). The zero box. *Mathematics Teaching in the Middle School, 14*(4), 222–223.

Havil, J. (2012). The irrationals: A story of the numbers you can't count on. Princeton, NJ: Princeton University Press.

Hong, L. T. (1993). *Two of everything: A Chinese folktale.* folktale. New York, NY: Albert Whitman.

Jeon, K. (2012). Reflecting on PEMDAS. *Teaching Children Mathematics, 18*(6), 370–377.

Johnson, G., & Thompson, D. R. (2009). Reasoning with algebraic contexts. *Mathematics Teaching in the Middle School, 14*(8), 504–513.

Karp, K., Bush, S., & Dougherty, B. (2014). Avoiding rules that expire. *Teaching Children Mathematics, 21*(2), 18–25.

Lamb, L. L., Bishop, J. P., Philipp, R. A., Schappelle, B. P., Whitacre, I., & Lewis, M. (2012). Developing symbol sense for the minus sign. *Mathematics Teaching in the Middle School, 18*(1), 5–9.

Lim, V., Rubel, L., Shookhoff, L., Sullivan, M., & Williams, S. (2016). The lottery is a mathematics Powerball. *Mathematics Teaching in the Middle School, 21*(9), 526–532.

Masoff, J., & Sirrell, T. (2006). *Oh, yikes!: History's grossest, wackiest moments.* New York, NY: Workman.

NGA Center (National Governors Association Center for Best Practices) & CCSSO (Council of Chief State School Officers). (2010). *Common core state standards.* Retrieved from corestandards.org

Stephan, M. L. (2009). What are you worth? *Mathematics Teaching in the Middle School, 15*(1), 16–24.

Stephan, M., & Akyuz, D. (2012). A proposed instructional theory for integer addition and subtraction. *Journal for Research in Mathematics Education, 43*(4), 428–464.

Swanson, P. E. (2010). The intersection of language and mathematics. *Mathematics Teaching in the Middle School, 15*(9), 516–523.

Tillema, E. S. (2012). What is the difference? Using contextualized problems. *Mathematics Teaching in the Middle School, 17*(8), 473–478.

U.S. Census Bureau. (n.d.). *Population clocks.* Retrieved from www.census.gov/population/international

Credits

Cover: Petr Vaclavek/Shutterstock; Petr Vaclavek/Shutterstock

Chapter 1: p. 6: Table 1.1, Adapted with permission from NCTM (National Council of Teachers of Mathematics). (2000). *Principles and standards for school mathematics*. Reston, VA: NCTM. Copyright 2000 by the National Council of Teachers of Mathematics. All rights reserved; p. 7: quote, Based on Council of Chief State School Officers. (2010). *Common Core State Standards*. Copyright © 2010 National Governors Association Center for Best Practices and Council of Chief State School Officers. All rights reserved.

Chapter 2: p. 14: Figure 2.1, Anderson, L.W., & Krathwohl, D. R. (Eds.). (2001). *A taxonomy for learning, teaching, and assessing: A revision of Bloom's Taxonomy of educational objectives*: Complete Edition. New York, NY: Addison Wesley, Longman; p. 15: Patricia Pozza. Used by permission; p. 16: Based on Schifter & Fosnot, 1993; p. 22: Figure 2.11, National Research Council. (2001). *Adding It Up: Helping Children Learn Mathematics*, p. 5. Reprinted with permission from the National Academy of Sciences, courtesy of the National Academies Press, Washington, DC.

Chapter 3: p. 36: Table 3.1, Based on *Principles to Actions: Ensuring Mathematical Success For All* (NCTM), © 2014. p. 38: Table 3.2, Reprinted with permission from Selecting and creating mathematical tasks: From research to practice. *Mathematics Teaching in the Middle School*, 3(5), 344–350. Copyright 1998, by the National Council for Teachers of Mathematics. All rights reserved; p. 40: Figure 3.1, Reprinted with permission from Thinking Through a Lesson: Successfully Implementing High-Level Tasks. *Mathematics Teaching in the Middle School*, 14(3), 132–138. Copyright 2008, by the National Council for Teachers of Mathematics. All rights reserved; p. 44: © Copyright 2010. National Governors Association Center for Best Practices and Council of Chief State School Officers. All rights reserved; p. 45: Erik Morra. Used by permission; p. 49: Kline, K. (2008). Learning to think and thinking to learn. *Teaching Children Mathematics*, 15, 144–151; p. 50: Table 3.3, Adapted from Chapin, S., O'Conner, C., & Anderson, N. (2013). *Classroom Discussions: Using Math Talk to Help Students Learn* (3rd ed.). Sausalito, CA: Math Solutions.

Chapter 4: p. 60: Juke Wray. Used by permission; p. 63: © Copyright 2010. National Governors Association Center for Best Practices and Council of Chief State School Officers. All rights reserved; p. 75: Table 4.1, From Bay-Williams, J. M., & Meyer, M. R. (2003). What Parents Want to Know about Standards-Based Mathematics Curricula. *Principal Leadership*, 3(7), 54–60. Copyright 2003 National Association of Secondary School Principals. www.principals.org.

Chapter 5: p. 84: quote, Wiliam, D. (2010, September). *Practical Techniques for Formative Assessment*. Presentation given in Boras, Sweden. Retrieved from www.slideshare.net/BLoPP/dylan-wiliam-bors-2010.

Chapter 6: p. 106: Figure 6.1, Based on Scott, Terence, and Lane, Holly. (2001). *Multi-Tiered Interventions in Academic and Social Contexts*. Unpublished manuscript, University of Florida, Gainesville; p. 110: quote, Reprinted with permission from Building Responsibility for Learning in Students with Special Needs, p. 119. *Teaching Children Mathematics*, 11(3), p. 118–126. Copyright 2004, by the National Council for Teachers of Mathematics. All rights reserved. p. 110: quote, Karp, K., & Howell, P. (2004). Building Responsibility for Learning in Students with Special Needs. *Teaching Children Mathematics*, 11(3), p. 118–126.

Chapter 7: p. 127: Baroody, A. J. (1987). *Children's mathematical thinking: A developmental framework for preschool, primary, and special education teachers*. New York: Teachers College Press; pp. 128, 138, 148: © Copyright 2010. National Governors Association Center for Best Practices and Council of Chief State School Officers. All rights reserved; p. 129: Figure 7.3, National Research Council. (2009). *Mathematics learning in early childhood: Paths toward excellence and equity*, p. 27. Reprinted with permission from the National Academy of Sciences, courtesy of the National Academies Press, Washington, DC; p. 129: Table 7.1, Based on Clements and Sarama (2014); p. 136: Howden, H. (1989). Teaching number sense. *Arithmetic Teacher*, 36(6), 6–11; p. 137: Figure 7.9, Based on *Principles and Standards of the National Council of Teachers of Mathematics*. Copyright 2000; pp. 147, 148: National Research Council, Division of Behavioral and Social Sciences and Education, Center for Education, Committee on Early Childhood Mathematics. *Mathematics Learning in Early Childhood: Paths Toward Excellence and Equity*. ©2009. National Academies Press.

Chapter 8: pp. 154, 155, 157, 164, 178: © Copyright 2010. National Governors Association Center for Best Practices and Council of Chief State School Officers. All rights reserved; p. 159: Fosnot, C. T., & Dolk, M. (2001). *Young mathematicians at work: Constructing multiplication and division*. Portsmouth, NH: Heinemann; p. 161: Murata, A. (2008). Mathematics teaching and learning as a mediating process: The case of tape diagrams. *Mathematical Thinking and Learning*, 10, 374–406; p. 178: Drake, J., & Barlow, A. (2007). Assessing students' level of understanding multiplication through problem writing. *Teaching Children Mathematics*, 14(5), 272–277.

Chapter 9: p. 185: Figure 9.1, Henry, V. J., & Brown, R. S. (2008). "First-Grade Basic Facts: An Investigation into Teaching and Learning of an Accelerated, High-Demand Memorization Standard." *Journal for Research in Mathematics Education*, 39(2), p. 156. Reprinted with permission. Copyright © 2008 by the National Council of Teachers of Mathematics, Inc. All rights reserved; pp. 186, 188, 191: © Copyright 2010. National Governors Association Center for Best Practices and Council of Chief State School Officers. All rights reserved; p. 207: Table 9.2, Based on ideas from Forbringer & Fahsl, 2010, and Kamii & Anderson, 2003.

Chapter 10: p. 213: © Copyright 2010. National Governors Association Center for Best Practices and Council of Chief State School Officers. All rights reserved.

Chapter 11: p. 238: National Research Council. (2001). *Adding it up: Helping children learn mathematics*. J. Kilpatrick, J. Swafford, & B. Findell (Eds.). Washington, DC: National Academies Press; pp. 251–252: Hiebert, J. & Grouws, D. A. (2007). The effects of classroom mathematics teaching on students' learning. In Frank K. Lester, Jr. *Second Handbook of Research on Mathematics Teaching and Learning* (pp. 371–404), Charlotte, NC: Information Age Publishing; p. 267: © Copyright 2010. National Governors Association Center for Best Practices and Council of Chief State School Officers. All rights reserved; pp. 240, 252–253, 255: © Copyright 2010. National Governors Association Center for Best Practices and Council of Chief State School Officers. All rights reserved.

Chapter 12: pp. 274, 280, 295: © Copyright 2010. National Governors Association Center for Best Practices and Council of Chief State School Officers. All rights reserved; p. 284: Figure 12.12, Based on *Developing Mathematical Ideas: Numbers and Operations, Part I, Casebook*, by Deborah Schifter, Virginia Bastable, and Susan Jo Russell. Copyright © 2000 by the Education Development Center, Inc. Published by Pearson Education, Inc.; p, 290: Figure 12.16, Based on *Common Core State Standards*. Copyright © 2010. National Governors Association Center for Best Practices and Council of Chief State School Officers. All rights reserved; p, 292: © Copyright 2010. National Governors Association Center for Best Practices and Council of Chief State School Officers. All rights reserved.

Chapter 13: p. 319: Figure 13.13, Blanton, M., Stephens, S. Knuth, E., Gardiner, A. M., Isler, I., & Kim, J. (2015b). The Development of children's algebraic thinking: The impact of acomprehensive early alge-brainintervention in third grade. *Journal of Research in Mathematics Education, 46*(1), 39–87; p.328: Figure 13.17, Reprinted with permission from K. Hawes, "Using Error Analysis to Teach Equation Solving," in *Mathematics Teaching in the Middle School, 12*(5), 241, copyright 2007, by the National Council of Teachers of Mathematics. All rights reserved; p. 330: Figure 13.20, Reprinted with permission from A. Hyde, K. George, S. Mynard, C. Hull, S. Watson, and P. Watson, "Creating Multiple Representations in Algebra: All Chocolate, No Change," in *Mathematics Teaching in the Middle School, 11*(6), 262–268, copyright 2006, by the National Council of Teachers of Mathematics. All rights reserved; p. 331, Figure 13.21, COMAP and SIAM. 2016. *Guidelines for Assessment and Instruction in Mathematical Modeling Education (GAIMME)*. http://www.comap.com/Free/GAIMME/index.html. Accessed July 1, 2017.

Chapter 14: p. 343: Siegler, R. S., Fazio, L. K., Bailey, D. H., & Zhou, X. (2013). Fractions: The new frontier for theories of numerical development. *Trends in Cognitive Sciences, 17*(1), 13–19; p. 347: Figure 14.2, Van de Walle, John, *Elementary and Middle School Mathematics: Teaching Developmentally*, 10e, © 2019, Pearson Education, Inc., New York, NY; p. 348: Juke Wray. Used by permission.

Chapter 15: p. 374: © Copyright 2010. National Governors Association Center for Best Practices and Council of Chief State School Officers. All rights reserved; Cramer, K., Wyberg, T., & Leavitt, S. (2008). "The Role of Representations in Fraction Addition and Subtraction." *Mathematics Teaching in the Middle School, 13*(8), p. 495. Reprinted with permission. Copyright © 2008 by the National Council of Teachers of Mathematics. All rights reserved; p. 347: Figure 14.2, Cramer, K., Wyberg, T., & Leavitt, S. (2008). "The Role of Representations in Fraction Addition and Subtraction." *Mathematics Teaching in the Middle School, 13*(8), p. 495. Reprinted with permission. Copyright © 2008 by the National Council of Teachers of Mathematics. All rights reserved; pp. 378, 388, 391, 393, 397: © Copyright 2010. National Governors Association Center for Best Practices and Council of Chief State School Officers. All rights reserved; p. 392: Imm, K. L., Stylianou, D. A., & Chae, N. (2008). Student representations at the center: Promot-ing class-room equity. *Mathematics Teaching in the Middle School, 13*(8), 458–463; p. 399: Figure 15.14, Gregg, J., & Gregg, D. W. (2007). "Measurement and Fair-Sharing Models for Dividing Fractions." *Mathematics Teaching in the Middle School, 12*(9), p. 491. Reprinted with permission. Copyright © 2007 by the National Council of Teachers of Mathematics. All rights reserved.

Chapter 16: p. 409: © Copyright 2010. National Governors Association Center for Best Practices and Council of Chief State School Officers. All rights reserved; pp. 409, 410, 415, 423, 425, 426: © Copyright 2010. National Governors Association Center for Best Practices and Council of Chief State School Officers. All rights reserved.

Chapter 17: pp. 438, 444: © Copyright 2010. National Governors Association Center for Best Practices and Council of Chief State School Officers. All rights reserved; p. 442: Figure 17.2, Republished with permission of National Council of Teachers of Mathematics, from Assessing Proportional Thinking in *Mathematics teaching in the middle school*, George W. Bright, Jeane M. Joyner and Charles Wallis, 9, 2003; permission conveyed through Copyright Clearance Center, Inc.

Chapter 18: p. 467: *The Standards for Mathematical Practice* (CCSSO, 2010).

Chapter 19: pp. 507, 522: © Copyright 2010. National Governors Association Center for Best Practices and Council of Chief State School Officers. All rights reserved; p. 512: © Copyright 2010. National Governors Association Center for Best Practices and Council of Chief State School Officers. All rights reserved; p. 528: © Copyright 2010. National Governors Association Center for Best Practices and Council of Chief State School Officers. All rights reserved.

Chapter 20: p. 543: © Copyright 2010. National Governors Association Center for Best Practices and Council of Chief State School Officers. All rights reserved; p. 544: Scheaffer, R. L. (2006). Statistics and mathematics: On making a happy marriage. In G. F. Burrill & P. C. Elliott (Eds.), *Thinking and reasoning about data and chance: Sixty-eighth yearbook* (pp. 309–322). Reston, VA: NCTM; p. 547: Table 2.2, Franklin, C., Kader, G., Mewborn, D., Moreno, J., Peck, R., Perry, M., & Scheaffer, R. (2007) *Guidelines for Assessment and Instruction in Statistics Education (GAISE) Report: A Pre-K–12 Curriculum Framework*, p. 11. Reprinted with permission. Copyright © 2007 by the American Statistical Association. All rights reserved; p. 547: Table 2.2, Franklin, C., p. 552: Figure 20.3, Cook, C. D. (2008). "I Scream, You Scream: Data Analysis with Kindergartners." *Teaching Children Mathematics, 14*(9), p. 539. Reprinted with permission. Copyright © 2008 by the National Council of Teachers of Mathematics. All rights reserved; p. 568–569: © Copyright 2010. National Governors Association Center for Best Practices and Council of Chief State School Officers. All rights reserved; pp. 569, 573: © Copyright 2010. National Governors Association Center for Best Practices and Council of Chief State School Officers. All rights reserved.

Chapter 21: pp. 583, 582, 596: © Copyright 2010. National Governors Association Center for Best Practices and Council of Chief State School Officers. All rights reserved.

Chapter 22: pp. 605, 607: © Copyright 2010. National Governors Association Center for Best Practices and Council of Chief State School Officers. All rights reserved; pp. 626–627: © Copyright 2010. National Governors Association Center for Best Practices and Council of Chief State School Officers. All rights reserved.

Pop-Ups

Select Activity Pages, Expanded Lessons, Blackline Masters, and Teacher Resources from: John A. Van de Walle, Karen S. Karp, Lou Ann H. Lovin, & Jennifer M. Bay-Williams, *Teaching Student-Centered Mathematics for Grades K–2*, vol. I. Pearson Education; John A. Van de Walle, Karen S. Karp, Lou Ann H. Lovin, & Jennifer M. Bay-Williams, *Teaching Student-Centered Mathematics for Grades 3–5*, vol. II. Pearson Education; John A. Van de Walle, Karen S. Karp, Lou Ann H. Lovin, & Jennifer M. Bay-Williams, *Teaching Student-Centered Mathematics for Grades 6–8*, vol. III. Pearson Education; Jennifer M. Bay-Williams, Maggie McGatha, With Beth M. McCord Kobett, With Jonathan A. Wray (2014) *Mathematics Coaching: Resources and Tools for Coaches and Leaders, K–12*. Pearson; Bay-Williams (2013) *Field Experience Guide, Resources for Teachers of Elementary and Middle School Mathematics*.